A Commentary on Virgil's *Eclogues*

A Commentary on Virgil's *Eclogues*

ANDREA CUCCHIARELLI

Great Clarendon Street, Oxford, OX2 6DP,
United Kingdom

Oxford University Press is a department of the University of Oxford.
It furthers the University's objective of excellence in research, scholarship,
and education by publishing worldwide. Oxford is a registered trade mark of
Oxford University Press in the UK and in certain other countries

© Andrea Cucchiarelli 2023

The moral rights of the author have been asserted

All rights reserved. No part of this publication may be reproduced, stored in
a retrieval system, or transmitted, in any form or by any means, without the
prior permission in writing of Oxford University Press, or as expressly permitted
by law, by licence or under terms agreed with the appropriate reprographics
rights organization. Enquiries concerning reproduction outside the scope of the
above should be sent to the Rights Department, Oxford University Press, at the
address above

You must not circulate this work in any other form
and you must impose this same condition on any acquirer

Published in the United States of America by Oxford University Press
198 Madison Avenue, New York, NY 10016, United States of America

British Library Cataloguing in Publication Data

Data available

Library of Congress Control Number: 2023004729

ISBN 978–0–19–882776–4

Links to third party websites are provided by Oxford in good faith and
for information only. Oxford disclaims any responsibility for the materials
contained in any third party website referenced in this work.

A Commentary on Virgil's *Eclogues*

ANDREA CUCCHIARELLI

Great Clarendon Street, Oxford, OX2 6DP,
United Kingdom

Oxford University Press is a department of the University of Oxford.
It furthers the University's objective of excellence in research, scholarship,
and education by publishing worldwide. Oxford is a registered trade mark of
Oxford University Press in the UK and in certain other countries

© Andrea Cucchiarelli 2023

The moral rights of the author have been asserted

All rights reserved. No part of this publication may be reproduced, stored in
a retrieval system, or transmitted, in any form or by any means, without the
prior permission in writing of Oxford University Press, or as expressly permitted
by law, by licence or under terms agreed with the appropriate reprographics
rights organization. Enquiries concerning reproduction outside the scope of the
above should be sent to the Rights Department, Oxford University Press, at the
address above

You must not circulate this work in any other form
and you must impose this same condition on any acquirer

Published in the United States of America by Oxford University Press
198 Madison Avenue, New York, NY 10016, United States of America

British Library Cataloguing in Publication Data

Data available

Library of Congress Control Number: 2023004729

ISBN 978–0–19–882776–4

Links to third party websites are provided by Oxford in good faith and
for information only. Oxford disclaims any responsibility for the materials
contained in any third party website referenced in this work.

Acknowledgements

I shall only say a few words to accompany this English version, updated and augmented, of my commentary on the *Eclogues* published in 2012 by Carocci. The format of the Italian edition remains in place here, particularly in terms of the annotation style and the way in which bibliographical entries are selected and presented.

I wish to express all my gratitude to Stephen Harrison, who has stimulated and supported the idea of an English edition of my commentary from the very beginning and accompanied it throughout the process. The first English version of my text, including almost all additions and changes, was made with great finesse and understanding by Marco Romani Mistretta: it was my great fortune to have such a competent and attentive translator-philologist to help me. I am also indebted to Biagio Santorelli for a very careful reading of the whole book and for many suggestions on matters of Virgilian philology. To Fiachra Mac Góráin I owe some illuminating remarks on the correct use of philological English. I also had an important source of help, especially when it came to proof-reading and double-checking the indexes, in two young scholars, Martina Farese and Luigi Maria Guerci, as well as in my Sapienza colleagues Giuseppe Lentini and Francesco Ursini.

In the Italian edition, the commentary was paired with an Italian translation by the late Alfonso Traina, whom I remember with gratitude for our many discussions on textual and exegetical issues of the *Eclogues*: the *Sibylla Cumana* of the Cathedral of Siena, which had been chosen by him for the cover of the Italian edition, appears on the cover here, too.

The volume is dedicated to my wife Simona Fortini, whose attentive and intelligent care played a fundamental role in its development, and our two children, Livia and Giulio—my three dear companions along the journey of my life.

Contents

Foreword: Tityrus and the discovery of the new gods	ix
Introduction	1
1. The *Eclogues* in their time	3
2. Biographical issue	6
3. The poet, the herdsmen, and *mimesis*	8
4. Arcadia, Epicureanism, and the 'gods'	12
5. The bucolic book	18
6. Textual transmission	30

VIRGIL'S *ECLOGUES*

Note on the text	35

COMMENTARY

Eclogue 1	59
Eclogue 2	111
Eclogue 3	147
Eclogue 4	196
Eclogue 5	242
Eclogue 6	284
Eclogue 7	344
Eclogue 8	380
Eclogue 9	428
Eclogue 10	463
Bibliography	507
Index of Proper Names	551
Index of Latin Words	554
General Index	556

Foreword

Tityrus and the discovery of the new gods

1

...resonare doces Amaryllida siluas

Virgil's *siluae* may appear to be a free and open space compared to the self-contained city. Quite the opposite is true: the woods, too, are encircled by a strong sense of belonging and protection, besides being replete with sounds.

Readers of Theocritus' pastoral idylls experienced a limited horizon of images, actions, and characters. When Virgil arrived, that world became deeper and more complicated: further repetitions were added to the repetition of names (Daphnis, Menalcas, their contest, the former's sad death). The texts of Theocritus' canon are constantly modified and re-elaborated by Virgil, and sometimes literally translated. The poet then applies that same art of variation to his own inventions.

As a result, every event and detail resounds with echoes. This is the case with Virgil's characters. It is certainly impossible to group together the various occurrences of the same names, such as Tityrus, Daphnis, or Menalcas, as if these figures were mythical heroes like Achilles, Hector, Odysseus, or Aeneas. Yet we cannot merely explain the phenomenon as (accidental?) homonymy, either. The bucolic 'mask' has its own personality: each new and different usage carves a mark, a memory on it. An essential component of the 'pastoral' effect is this musicality, this soft whispering, of suggestions and allusions. There are, however, several moments in which the suggestions are unified: note, for instance, the similarities between the exiled Meliboeus in Virgil's first eclogue and Theocritus' dying Daphnis in *id.* 1.

The evocation of songs and harmonies, freely spreading among springs, pine trees, and bushes, finds its visual counterpart in the concreteness of the book roll, in its very 'unfolding' of words and poems. Virgil often lets the reader catch glimpses of his sources, and especially his own Theocritus, namely the collection of idylls he had before his eyes (and in his mind) while composing his *liber*. The book is a treasure chest of the whole patrimony of bucolic song.

For this reason, the arrangement of the eclogues contributes to a complex network of references among the individual poems: note the special significance assigned to the opening and the closing eclogue; the middle (for which eclogues 5 and 6 compete); the symmetrical correspondences between the two parts of the book; and even the 'syntagmatic' effects caused by one eclogue succeeding another.

2

Vrbem quam dicunt Romam

When Virgil wrote his *Eclogues*, and even when he published them as a volume, nothing was yet certain of what we consider to be the cornerstones of the Augustan age. To be sure, in the period of instability immediately following the assassination of Julius Caesar, the young *diui filius* played a considerable role; and yet, it was Mark Antony who was bound to appear as the strongest heir of the deceased dictator, by virtue of his age and prestige. Sextus Pompey, meanwhile, controlled the sea, and enjoyed some popularity even at Rome. Thus, the reader ought to look at the *Eclogues* from a 'defamiliarized' perspective. The book, an 'Augustan' text *par excellence* (indeed, an inaugural text of the new Augustan culture), was conceived and composed before 'Augustus' could even be imagined. Rather, Virgil himself contributed to inventing the Augustan age.

In those of his idylls that are aptly called pastoral, Theocritus never mentioned the city of Alexandria by name, or any city, except in the famous *Thalysia*, where the wanderers on Cos are described as leaving the town, on the road leading towards the countryside (*id.* 7). To be sure, Theocritus celebrated the Ptolemies and their great city, but he did so through either a playful mime (*id.* 15) or ad hoc encomiastic poems (*id.* 16 and 17). In both cases, however, he abandoned the shepherds and their world. Now, by contrast, Virgil places Rome at the outset of his pastoral book, presenting the city's greatness through the naive eyes not of two Syracusan women but of a Mantuan herdsman who had been in danger of losing all his property as a result of the expropriations.

Thus, the first eclogue immediately sets off a mythopoetic process, centred around the city of Rome, which was to become crucial to Virgil's own work and to Augustan culture as a whole, as it played a key role in Octavian's political programme from the early 30s BCE. In a typically Virgilian way, however, this mythologizing is full of chiaroscuro. While Rome appears as a beacon of redemption, it is nevertheless part of a mechanism, which produced injustice and oppression.

3

Deus, deus ille Menalca!

Not only does Tityrus proclaim Rome's unlimited greatness, but he also reveals the city's unique privilege: it is the only place where people can 'get to know' gods who are really 'present' (1.41 *tam praesentis...diuos*). Here, Virgil lays another foundation of Augustan ideology: the charismatic and divine aspect of political power. When the *Eclogues* were published as a book, no reader would have doubted the identity of the 'young god' encountered by Tityrus in Rome (and nowhere else): Caesar Octavian, still a very young man but already close to political primacy.

The kings of Alexandria, as well as those of Pergamum, Antioch, and other important centres of the Greek East, had modelled their image as sovereigns on popularly acclaimed divine figures (thereby following in Alexander's footsteps), particularly Dionysus and Heracles, but also Hermes and Apollo, and (in the queens' case) Aphrodite. Similarly, during Rome's civil wars, most of the major political figures had cultivated an association with a corresponding god, or with whichever deity best represented his intentions and aspirations. Virgil avoided falling into the trap of excessive allegorizing: a trap the interpreter must still avoid. Yet the text of the *Eclogues* is free from eulogistic rhetoric, precisely because it keeps its pastoral fiction constantly in place and blends political praise with the herdsmen's lives, as well as with other aspects of pastoral society, recalling contemporary landscape painting, especially the so-called 'sacro-idyllic' genre.

Particularly instructive is the fifth eclogue, in which ancient readers, according to Servius, saw the shadow of the assassinated and deified Julius Caesar. Yet nothing in Mopsus' and Menalcas' songs authorizes such a precise allegory. The Virgilian text stays at the sublime level of divine models. Through Daphnis and his fellow herdsmen, the *Eclogues* convey an idea of divinization that never derogates from its status as an *exemplum*. In fact, any historical actualization of it appears merely contingent, and therefore perishable. In the figure of Daphnis, just as in the *puer* of the fourth eclogue, Virgil the Epicurean strove to reconcile gods and divine values that civil strife had alienated from one another as well as from the Roman people.

Thus, should the readers become sensitive to the rhetoric of divine models in the *Eclogues*, they would discover Virgil's search for a deep synthesis (which, if not understood or at least respected, is one of the decisive reasons for Thyrsis' defeat and Corydon's victory in the seventh eclogue). Hence comes the impression that Virgil's *Eclogues* look especially to Asinius Pollio, to the dream of peace and prosperity that his consulship had represented, rather than to the oracular responses of a young god whose redeeming power had been granted solely to him by the civil wars.

INTRODUCTION

1

The *Eclogues* in their time

The date of the *E.* is much debated. A preliminary distinction is in order: that between the composition of the individual poems (which, at least in certain cases, were doubtless read immediately[1] and circulated within a restricted group around the poet) and the publication of the final collection. There are only two obvious clues to the dating of the book: the land confiscations in the territory of Cremona and Mantua, which peaked in the aftermath of the battle of Philippi[2] (though continuing during the early 30s BCE), and the consulship of Asinius Pollio, in 40 BCE (*E.* 4).

As we shall see in greater detail, it is very likely that Virgil (hereafter, V.) kept working on his pastoral book for a few years after 40;[3] but that should not distract us from an essential fact. The poet intended to situate his work between those two events: the grievous chaos generated by the confiscations and the hopes awakened by Pollio's consulship in the central section of the book. Such a chronology, which dominates current Virgilian scholarship, is consistent with two essential pieces of ancient biographical information concerning V. (which, however, cannot easily be reconciled with each other). Firstly, V. is said to have composed and published the *E.* when he was twenty-eight (in 42 BCE); secondly, V. is said to have worked on the collection for three years.[4] Thus, the likeliest hypothesis is that the

---

Here and in the commentary, Greek authors are cited with LSJ abbreviations (adapted when appropriate); citations of Latin authors follow the *ThlL* system, with extremely rare disloyalties. V.'s works are abbreviated as follows: *E.*; *G.*; *Aen.* For more information on the citation and reference style of the book see p. 507.

[1] In this regard, the best testimony is Hor. *sat.* 1.10.44–5 (around 35 BCE). In his satirical *libellus*, Horace himself shows his great familiarity with the themes and structure of V.'s work, especially when it comes to the number of poems (i.e. ten).

[2] See Appian's account, *bell. civ.* 5.3 (11–13); Cass. Di. 48.6–12.

[3] We shall not, however, posit 35 BCE as the date of the final publication: at least not on the basis of the identification of Octavian with the addressee of *E.* 8, following Bowersock (1971); cf. Tarrant's (1978) convincing refutation; for a different view, see Clausen's commentary, esp. pp. 233–7, along with our observations at 8.6n.; on the relationship between the *E.* and their historico-political context, see the balanced, comprehensive picture offered by Tarrant (1997, esp. pp. 169–75). It cannot be ruled out that V. reworked the text of the *E.* at a later stage, even without assuming a true 'second edition' (as some scholars did in the past: cf. Michel 1990, esp. p. 58 and p. 61, n. 5). At any rate, it seems preferable to interpret V.'s text as a whole in its current, definitive form, and there is no decisive argument for dating it to 35 (or later).

[4] On Virgil's age at the time of the *E.*: Serv. *praef. E.* p. 3.26–7 (III.1 Th.-H.); Prob. *praef. E.* p. 323.13 (III.2 Th.-H.) (= *uita Verg.* p. 198.6 Brugn.-Stok); cf. also p. 329.5–7 (III.2 Th.-H.) (where Asconius Pedianus is cited as source). For the three years: Serv. *uita Verg.* p. 2.8–9 Th.-H. = p. 152.10–12 Brugn.-Stok; Don. *uita Verg.* 89–90 Brumm. = p. 29.5–6 Brugn.-Stok.

4 INTRODUCTION

composition of the earliest poems, and the first samples for a selected audience, go back to 42–41; hence the tradition according to which V. published the whole work in that year. During the three following years, until 39, the most intense phase of composition and revision continued, culminating in the definitive publication of the book for a wider audience, sometime between 38 and 37. This is consistent with the fact that, in the *E.*, Maecenas is never mentioned: V. became closer to him at a later time (probably around 38 BCE).

One question still ought to be asked: why did Virgil, despite continuing to work on the *E.* for some time, want to remain loyal to an earlier setting, which corresponds to the inception and early composition of the poems? We are, of course, talking about the difficult aftermath of Philippi, when even the individual citizen's security was threatened by constant turmoil—of which confiscations and proscriptions are but some of the countless examples.[5] By emphasizing the traditional values of farming, agriculture, and animal husbandry, the *E.* draw attention to the issue of land distribution, to which the Caesarian warlords had already devoted some of their energies. Right after the murder of Caesar, in fact, Mark Antony had to manage a land distribution project that was soon abandoned. The idea was to confiscate lands and reassign them to the veterans. Note that the Perusine War broke out (at least officially) over the way in which Octavian had managed a similar project.[6] The related phenomenon of old landowners like Meliboeus being driven into exile (along with their various workers and slaves) is documented by historical and political evidence. Meanwhile, Sextus Pompey kept stirring turmoil among both the plebs and the republican aristocracy by generating food shortages. He intercepted wheat supplies and welcomed all kinds of exiles and refugees (including slaves) into his anti-triumviral army. Sextus Pompey had his headquarters in Sicily itself, Theocritus' homeland (and a key region for Roman agriculture).[7] In 40 BCE, the *foedus Brundisinum* consolidated

---

[5] As is confirmed by the victims' complaints in Appian. *bell. civ.* 5.14 (59), confiscations were even less fair than proscriptions, since the latter were used against enemies, the former against innocents. *E.* 1 may be read against Suet. *Aug.* 15.1, where Octavian is said to have replied *moriendum esse* to those asking for mercy after the capitulation of the city at the end of the Perusine War.

[6] Significantly, according to the agreement, Octavian was responsible not only for his own veterans but also for Antony's: Appian. *bell. civ.* 5.3 (11) and 13–14 (51–9); Cass. Di. 48.6–7. Mark Antony's early land confiscations (in 44 BCE) seem to be echoed in the fragments of Varius Rufus' poem *De morte*, in which Antony is harshly criticized (cf. *E.* 1.71–2n.). During the Perusine War, Lucius and Fulvia sided with the dispossessed Italian landowners against Octavian, without succeeding in getting Mark Antony directly involved: the main historical sources are Appian. *bell. civ.* 5.14–49 (54–208); Cass. Di. 48.3–14; Liv. *per.* 125–6; Vell. 2.74.2–4; Plut. *Ant.* 28–30 (for further reading see Osgood 2006, pp. 159–67). Wimmel (1998) reads the *E.* (esp. *E.* 1) in the light of the Perusine War (41–40 BCE). That many people were interested in these issues at the time is confirmed by Horace, who reports (in Book 2 of his *Satires*) that Roman commoners wondered whether the lands that Caesar Octavian intended to assign to the veterans after Actium (30 BCE) would be in Italy or in Sicily (*sat.* 2.6.55–6).

[7] The sources unanimously agree that Sextus Pompey never hesitated to welcome exiles and refugees of any sort, including slaves. Note Hor. *epod.* 9.7–10 (written after the battle of Naulochus); cf. Vell. 2.72.5; 77.2; Appian. *bell. civ.* 4.25 (105); 36 (150–2); 85 (355–7); 5.53 (219–20); 72 (304–7); 143 (596–7); Cass. Di. 47.12; 48.19.4. Sextus succeeded in forcing the triumvirs to give (some of) the

the triumvirs' alliance (particularly between Antony and Octavian), which can be regarded as Asinius Pollio's main political achievement (celebrated by V. in *E.* 4). This further kindled the anger of Sextus Pompey, who intensified pirate attacks in Sicily as well as in the harbours of Puteoli and Ostia (see Florus, *epit.* 2.18.2).[8]

In the face of such a complex situation, which lasted from the murder of Caesar to the publication of the *E.* and beyond in a constant emergence of new dangers and challenges, the poet decided to anchor the text of the *E.* to two firm points: the expropriations and Pollio's consulate. The former is one of the most obvious negative effects of the triumvirs' action, while the latter represents the hopeful climate of *détente* that followed the *foedus Brundisinum*. This can also be explained by the particular importance of Pollio[9] both in the *E.* and in the context in which they were written. V. says explicitly that Pollio was a patron of his Muse but, beyond their personal relationship, the poet probably surmised that the circle of intellectuals around Pollio (who did not come from the aristocratic elite and owed his influence to his own merit) was in the process of outlining a new model of artistic patronage. Thanks to his well-known moderation, Pollio always avoided direct conflict whenever possible, and fostered any and all attempts to harmonize different cultural and political impulses, which inevitably ended up in conflict with each other (Antony's side vs Octavian's side) despite Pollio's efforts. Pollio was himself an intellectual: he was a poet, tragedian, and (later) historian; he loved the arts and had a very well-defined taste in literature. He was also active as a culture manager, and in a way he represented a new political elite that succeeded in navigating the competitive landscape of the civil wars. His ties with Antony ultimately put an end to Pollio's political career. His model of patronage, however, had already been established: after the *E.*, V. soon reworked it and transferred it to a

---

confiscated lands back to their original owners (Appian. *bell. civ.* 5.72 [306]; Cass. Di. 48.36.4). However, as Appian frequently points out, Sextus was unable to capitalize on his victories: Appian. *bell. civ.* 5.25 (101); 91 (382–3); 140 (583); 143 (597). For the importance of Sextus Pompey in Virgil, and in the historical and political context of V.'s work, see A. Powell 2008 (pp. 181–225 for the *E.*), which is not free from some exaggeration. See also Welch (2012) on the figure of Sextus Pompey more generally (including his ideological and cultural significance).

[8] In Rome, the general public's reaction to the *foedus* was rather negative: the peace between Antony and Octavian, albeit a source of relief, was widely regarded as benefiting the two of them alone and giving them an opportunity to crush Sextus' resistance together. As a result, both plebs and landowners had to suffer from famines and higher taxes: cf. Appian. *bell. civ.* 5.67 (281–4); Cass. Di. 48.31.1–2.

[9] On Pollio's achievements in both the political and the cultural domain, see *E.* 3.84n. For further reading, see esp. Osgood (2006, pp. 54–5; 252–5; 296–7); Dufallo (2013, esp. pp. 75–92). The reader of the *E.* must keep in mind Pollio's personal relationship with Cornelius Gallus, which Pollio seems to allude to in two of his letters to Cicero (Cic. *fam.* 10.31.6 and 32.5). Their relationship may not have been conflict-free, if it is true that Gallus wrote a speech against Pollio (Quint. *inst.* 1.5.8; but cf. Manzoni 1995, pp. 23–4). Pollio's personality is best summarized by a passage of his letter to Cicero, which deserves to be quoted in full (Cic. *fam.* 10.31.2; 5): *natura autem mea et studia trahunt me ad pacis et libertatis cupiditatem. itaque illud initium ciuilis belli saepe defleui... qua re eum me existima esse qui primum pacis cupidissimus sim (omnis enim ciuis plane studeo esse saluos), deinde qui et me et rem publicam uindicare in libertatem paratus sim.*

6   INTRODUCTION

new patron, Maecenas—another 'newcomer' from the Roman aristocracy's point of view, despite his noble Etruscan lineage. Unlike Pollio, Maecenas always sided with Octavian, and was an important political figure who decided (significantly) to remain in the equestrian class.

V.'s first work contributes to the creation of a literary language that is to become a crucial resource for the 'Augustan culture'. In V.'s central eclogues, this language is closely connected with the figure of Pollio. Yet the *E.* also testify to a political transition: Pollio remains in the background, compared to the young *deus* that almost all readers (rightly) equate with Octavian.[10] While the events make Pollio appear tied to a defunct political dream (such as the conciliation of the two triumvirs), the opening of the *E.* brings Rome's young god to the foreground: a god who is all the more present and necessary after Pollio's failure.[11] History had left its mark on the ten eclogues, but V.'s new poetry for the future was already a reality.

2

Biographical issues

Closely connected to the date of the collection is another fundamental question: to what extent was V. personally affected by the confiscations? There is no reason to doubt the kernel of the ancient biographical tradition, according to which the poet's ancestral land possessions were at least temporarily confiscated. To be sure, the young poet must have shared the anxieties of his fellow citizens, family members, and friends. The biographical tradition is, however, not persuasive in its attempt to reconstruct a detailed sequence of events on the basis of *E.* 1 and 9: the results, often incoherent, are not substantiated by genuine, extra-textual (and therefore trustworthy) records.[12]

---

[10] The very structure of V.'s work reflects this transition: the reader first encounters Pollio, an illustrious patron, in *E.* 3; Pollio is then the co-protagonist of the grandiose prophecy in *E.* 4, after which his name disappears from the *E.* The sequence of *E.* 3–4 places great emphasis on Pollio within a book that starts with the *deus*-Octavian and ends with a supporter of Octavian (i.e. Cornelius Gallus, who seems to be depicted as a military commander: cf. 10.44n.). The gradual vanishing of Pollio is particularly evident in the prologue to *E.* 8, which is most probably addressed to him—yet his name is not mentioned. The subsequent poem, *E.* 9, contains an explicit mention of Varius Rufus (9.35n.), a poet who always opposed Antony (note also the verbatim quotation at 8.88n.). The opening and the 'framing' of the book, both of which centralize Octavian, hint at the fact that the equilibrium between Antony and Octavian (Pollio's main political project) has already failed the test of history.

[11] One of the achievements of the soon-to-be Augustus, and one that contributed greatly to the stability of his regime, was his ability to safeguard individuals' property (cf. Vell. 2.89.4; Galinsky 1996, esp. pp. 7 and 55–6). This is precisely what is granted to Tityrus in *E.* 1, in spite of his humble social status.

[12] For issues of priority between the two poems, see pp. 61; 430–1. Such guesswork, very common in ancient exegetical and biographical practices, is tied to a more broadly allegorizing approach, well exemplified (with sound methodological caveats) by Servius *ad E.* 1.1 *et hoc loco Tityri sub persona Vergilium debemus accipere; non tamen ubique, sed tantum ubi exigit ratio*; cf. also *praef. E.* p. 2.17–22

BIOGRAPHICAL ISSUES   7

Nevertheless, even if V. was not subject to the same vexations as Meliboeus, Menalcas, or Moeris, he was certainly aware of how his audience would react to a pastoral book in which Mantua and Cremona were mentioned by name. Theocritus, who moved from Syracuse to Alexandria (just as V. moved to Rome), set the adventures and love stories of Daphnis and the other shepherds in his native Sicily. In a non-pastoral idyll, Theocritus clearly expressed, in the form of an encomium, his wish for protection at the court of Hieron II (probably not a successful attempt, given his later decision to move to the Ptolemies' court: *id.* 16.106–7). Moreover, ancient commentators identified Simichidas (*id.* 7) with the poet himself, who was said to have spent time in Cos.[13] Thus, the Theocritean precedent would have justified, in the eyes of contemporary readers, a biographical interpretation of the *E.*: correspondingly, Tityrus' bewildered gazing at the big city's wonders may hint at the emotion felt by the young soon-to-be poet when he first set foot in Rome. Early readers of the *E.* started detecting references to historical reality in the text: Pollio's son Asinius Gallus apparently claimed to be the *puer* of *E.* 4 (Serv. Dan. *ad E.* 4.11).[14] The *E.*'s typical combination of humble pastoral life and important topics of general interest must have stimulated a sort of unbridled allegorizing, which led interpreters to read hidden references into the plainest utterances of V.'s herdsmen.[15] To this day, excessive allegorizing continues to be a dangerous temptation for readers and scholars of V.

The poet himself made a clear statement concerning the relationship between himself and his œuvre, and that statement is contained in the only explicit mention of his first poetic work: in the *envoi* of the *G.* (4.564), he distinguishes between himself and Tityrus, the object of his song, even though it is clear that

---

(III.1 Th.-H.); *ad E.* 1.12; 6.13; 7.21; Serv. and Serv. Dan. *ad E.* 9.1; Philargyrius (as he is now commonly known; Philagrius seems to be a more correct version of his name: henceforth Philargyrius/Philagrius) *ad E.* 8.1; for Menalcas-Virgil in *E.* 9, however, cf. Quintilian's testimony, *inst.* 8.6.47. V. himself legitimated allegorical readings, albeit to a minimal extent, at e.g. *E.* 6.4–5 (cf. Calp. *ecl.* 4.62–3; Mart. 8.55). Nevertheless, that we cannot group all occurrences of a given pastoral name under one identity (in this case, the poet's) was observed by Wendel in his seminal work (1901, p. 50). On V.'s biographical tradition, see further Horsfall (1995b); *Enc. Virg.* V.1, pp. 570–88, s.v. *Vitae Vergilianae* (H. Naumann, G. Brugnoli); *Virg. Enc.* II, pp. 751–5, s.v. *Lives* (F. Stok), with references. Of particular interest is also the interplay between biographies and pseudepigraphic literature, on which see Peirano (2012, esp. pp. 61–3; 107–14).

[13] Cf. *schol.* Theocr. *id.* 7.21, pp. 84–5 Wend.; in *id.* 7.93, moreover, an allusion to Zeus-Ptolemy can be detected, whereas *id.* 4.31 mentions Glauce, the renowned flute-player from Chios and mistress of the king: Fantuzzi (2008, p. 578); concerning *id.* 15, finally, the scholia presuppose an analogy between the two Syracusan women and Theocritus, since all three were 'foreign upstarts' in Alexandria (p. 305, esp. 2–3 and 14–15 Wend.); cf. Korenjak (2003, p. 68). Servius may thus be said to exaggerate in arguing that Theocritus' poems are entirely free from cues for allegorical interpretation (*praef. E.* p. 2.19–20 Th.-H.). For further reading on allegory in pastoral poetry, the sources collected in Hamblin (1928) are still useful (cf. esp. pp. 12–19 on Theocritus).

[14] A different yet comparable claim is the grammarian Remmius Palaemon's assertion that V. had predicted his infallibility as a literary critic in *E.* 3.49 (cf. Suet. *gramm.* 23.4 Brugn.).

[15] Note esp. the allegorical interpretations transmitted by Servius *ad E.* 3.74; 93; 94; 96 (see nn. *ad locc.*): it is possible that the agonistic context of *E.* 3 proved particularly conducive to allegory.

8   INTRODUCTION

they both enjoy the benefit of a calm *otium* (cf. *E.* 1.6). In other words, while making an obvious distinction between the two, V. leaves room for an overlap between the poet and his character. In *E.* 1.28, at any rate, the mention of a white beard advises against any naive identification between the roughly 30-year-old poet and Tityrus.

3

The poet, the herdsmen, and *mimesis*

The poet of the *E.* explicitly acknowledges his literary debts: the 'game' in 'Syracusan verse' (6.1) is often revealed as imitative, with a constant echo of Theocritean names and situations.[16] Equally explicit are some occasional deviations, exemplified by the opening of *E.* 4: 'Sicilian Muses, let us sing something greater for the consul Pollio'. Perhaps Theocritus could not yet conceive of the pastoral genre as such—even though he did, in effect, lay its foundations. At any rate, he certainly realized that he was inventing a new world, whose rules and customs he was to establish. Theocritus' Cyclops in *Idyll* 11, for instance, is entirely constructed in opposition to the great Homeric text of *Odyssey* 9—or, rather, carves out a pastoral space on the margin of epic poetry (which is also a way to renew a Homeric theme without 'honking' like a pathetic goose who imitates the bard of Chios: *id.* 7.47–8).

Such a systematic dependence on Theocritus does not prevent V. from paradoxically asserting his poetic freedom: his herdsmen are Theocritean in character and bear Siculo-Greek names (and often a Siculo-Greek past), but speak Latin.[17] Far from embracing any 'rationalistic' reality principle, V. combines references to the Mantuan countryside and the city of Rome with hints to Sicilian geography and, above all, with Arcadia's imaginative and poetic dimension. The merger is sketched in *E.* 1, where the Hyblaean bees of l. 54 are featured in the context of

---

[16] The most systematic catalogue of Theocritean passages imitated by V. is still Posch's (1969), but very helpful annotations are to be found in Hosius' work (now forgotten are the numerous, and in fact still useful, contributions by Weyman [from 1917 to 1931]; cf. also Gebauer 1861); add at least Garson (1971); Lipka (2001, pp. 29–65). Certain idylls are left out of obvious imitation: 14, 19, 21, 27, 28, 29, 30. For further documentation and updated literature reviews, esp. on the relationship between the *E.* and the Theocritean pastoral tradition, see *Virg. Enc.* III, pp. 1260–1, s.v. *Theocritus* (B. W. Breed); I, pp. 395–401, s.v. *Eclogues* (B. W. Breed).

[17] If indeed Valerius Messalla wrote pastoral poetry, he must have written in Greek, as *Catal.* 9.13–20 seems to suggest. A possible pastoral forerunner of V. in Rome is Porcius Licinus, who wrote a Latin epigram in elegiac couplets, featuring erotic-pastoral themes (fr. 6 Bläns. = 7 Court.); for pre-Virgilian pastoral poetry, see Luiselli (1967, pp. 49–90). Somewhat relevant to V.'s Arcadia is the tradition whereby an Arcadian, Evander, was responsible for introducing the alphabet into Rome (cf. below, p. 14, n. 34); moreover, the development of Latin itself was said to have been influenced by the Greek language via the Arcadian presence at Rome, according to a doctrine seemingly shared by Cato and Varro: Lyd. *mag. pop. Rom.* 1.5.

the Mantuan confiscations, and will reappear even more vividly in *E*. 10 (note the ring-composition effect).[18] Even Theocritus' hierarchy of pastoral values, known to ancient interpreters (in a decreasing order of importance: cowherd, shepherd, goatherd), is generally disregarded, or at least loosely employed, by V.[19] Nevertheless, the *E*. display a certain affectionate realism at the level of detail: the reader occasionally catches glimpses of a small society of herdsmen, often engaging in agricultural work as well. Their world is full of hierarchies and power dynamics, which at times bleed into the everyday minutiae typical of a farming neighbourhood (including curious glances, jealousy, and envy).[20] On the whole, V.'s botanical terminology is accurate, and his references to various agricultural tasks appear technically appropriate, generally free from the mannerist vagueness that sometimes characterizes V.'s Greek models, from Theocritus onwards.[21]

Elsewhere, V. and his characters stay faithful to Theocritus, particularly through the use of images, thought patterns, and metaphors that can indeed be categorized as 'rustic'. Due to a widespread rhetorical principle, variously applied in ancient literary criticism, immediate correspondences were perceived between a character's nature (or the poet's, or at least the speaker's) and the imagery used by him: it was hardly surprising, for instance, that Alcaeus, born on an island, was wont to employ marine metaphors (Heracl. *all. Hom.* 5.9 ὁ νησιώτης θαλαττεύει).[22]

---

[18] In *E*. 10, which begins with a reference to Theocritus' Sicily, Arcadia is revealed to be a sort of 'parallel dimension' that poets can access through poetry itself. The phenomenon is particularly evident at 10.44, where the transmitted *me* must probably be retained in the text (see n. ad loc.). Another Sicilian reference is found at 2.21, whereas at 7.31 the singing contest of the two Arcadian shepherds Corydon and Thyrsis takes place on the banks of the Mincius, with Daphnis (= the bucolic hero from Syracuse?) listening to them. For a pre-Virgilian encounter between Italian landscapes and Theocritean elements, cf. [Mosch.] *epit. Bion.* 93–7: it is possible that the Greek pastoral tradition featured other similar phenomena. Yet V. has his own distinctive way of activating Greek geography, which is made primarily of literary and metapoetic coordinates rather than concrete references to actual places (the latter, by contrast, is the case with Italian cities like Mantua and Rome). For a useful and extensive discussion on the setting of the *E*., see Flintoff (1974); cf. also Perutelli (1976, pp. 763–80); Cucchiarelli (2021b, pp. 205–12).

[19] As is clear from *E*. 1.9; Theocritus' pastoral hierarchy is well epitomized by Don. auct. *uita Verg.* p. 122.2–6 Brugn.-Stok (cf. *schol.* Theocr. *proleg.*, p. 17.21–6 Wend.): *tria sunt pastorum genera, quae dignitatem in Bucolicis habent, quorum minimi sunt qui* αἰπόλοι *dicuntur a Graecis, id est caprarii; paulo honoratiores, qui* ποιμένες, *id est ouiliones dicuntur; honestissimi et maximi* βουκόλοι, *quos bubulcos dicimus;* see Gow (1952, II, p. 20, ad *id.* 1.86); cf. also Van Groningen (1958, pp. 313–17); but cf. E. A. Schmidt (1969); significantly, the hierarchy is disobeyed in the pseudo-Theocritean *id.* 8: see Rossi (1971, pp. 6–7).

[20] The obvious relations of preeminence and subordinations (e.g. Damoetas grazing a herd that the owner, Aegon, entrusted to him: *E*. 3.1–2) are never defined at precise social levels: this is the case with Corydon, whose alleged servile status has been refuted by Mayer (1983b); cf. 2.1n.

[21] On Virgilian flora, still useful are Sargeaunt (1920) and Abbe (1965), to which we must add Maggiulli (1995) as well as Grant (2004). On V.'s plants and their cultural, literary, and ideological implications, see the acute and methodologically accurate analysis of Armstrong (2019), to which I refer for further reading; for Theocritus' flora, see Lembach (1970); on technical aspects of farming life in the Italian countryside, see White (1970); note also Dyson's (2003) synthesis, especially valuable for its archaeological and topographical approach.

[22] The idea goes back—at least—to Aristotle's ethos doctrine, formulated in *rhet.* 1.2.1356a1–20 (cf. 3.17, esp. 1418a37–9; 1418b23–9; see also [Aristot.] *rhet. ad Alex.* 22.1434b25–30).

10   INTRODUCTION

By the same token, Theocritean shepherds revealed their ethos through rural analogies, as is exemplified by *id.* 9.31–5. An elaborate rural analogy, moreover, is employed by Tityrus at the very beginning of V.'s book (*E.* 1.19–25).[23]

Here, V. begins to experiment with a focalization technique soon to become crucial to his creation of the great protagonists of the *Aeneid*. As a result, the landscape fills up with single details or actions without displaying itself as an organic spatial whole: some scrubby bushes here, some rocks and a cliff there, a marsh invading the fields, smoking chimneys and mountain-shadows, a cave hosting the singers, the oxen coming back to the barn, an old tomb. These are all fragments of a larger, yet indefinite, world, and they only reach the reader's imagination because a single herdsman-poet has cast his eyes on them: in other words, they have been filtered through pastoral imagination. The elements of 'reality' that pile up eclogue after eclogue belong to an irretrievably atomized space, perceived as a function of the observing subject and his point of view. Such a mimetic technique is interestingly paralleled by the significant (albeit rare) testimony of contemporary Roman painting, and especially of its 'landscape' genres. Here are, for instance, some of the scenes painted by Studius (or Ludius) in the Augustan age, according to Pliny the Elder's account: *lucos, nemora, colles, piscinas, euripos, amnes, litora, qualia quis optaret, uarias ibi obambulantium species aut nauigantium terraque uillas adeuntium asellis aut uehiculis, iam piscantes, aucupantes aut uenantes aut etiam uindemiantes* (Plin. *nat.* 35.116). Although there is no need for detailed comparisons, made more difficult by the uncertain chronology and context, it is clear that, when V. provides the reader's imagination with fragments of rural landscape and fleeting sketches of country life (such as hunting or agricultural work), his poetry resonates with a taste already widespread in pictorial culture.[24] The visual arts of V.'s age made the subject matter of pastoral poetry all the more familiar and welcome, while V.'s work, in turn, must have contributed to the further success of this style of painting.

---

[23] Cf. also 2.63–5; 5.16–18; 45–7; 82–4. Lysias was deemed to be a master of ethopoeia, with special regard to simple and naive characters, such as herdsmen: Dion. Hal. *Lys.* 8.19; cf. Quint. *inst.* 3.8.51. On the modalities of Theocritean characterization, which actually mitigated the humblest aspects of pastoral life, certain observations are found in the ancient exegetical tradition: *schol.* Theocr. *proleg.*, pp. 5.2–6; 11.18–21 Wend.; on the Virgilian side of things, recall Servius' note *ad E.* 1.29 *et bene tempora, quasi rusticus, computat a barbae sectione*. The so-called 'pathetic fallacy', namely the pastoral singer's illusion that nature shares his amorous feelings (esp. his lovesickness), may be explained in terms of the poet's characterization of herdsmen as naive: Fantuzzi (2006, esp. pp. 242–4) (Nemesianus dwells on the practice, perhaps with some irony: *ecl.* 2.44–52); see also Posch (1969, pp. 92–101); Jenkyns (1998, *index*, s.v. *pathetic fallacy*); and Witek (2006, esp. pp. 73–82). A comparison employed for the sake of characterization, albeit extra-pastoral (the young, handsome, sport-loving city-dweller), is found at *id.* 2.114–16. Note also the Homeric Cyclops' address to his ram, where the animal is assumed to participate in the Cyclops' grief (Hom. *Od.* 9.447–60): this may be considered the Homeric archetype of a 'pastoral' pathetic fallacy.

[24] In Pliny's passage, note the parenthetical remark on the customers' individual tendencies: *qualia quis optaret*. On Roman landscape painting, see La Rocca (2008, esp. pp. 29–61), with a rich bibliography; for spatial perception in the *E.*, see Leach (1988, pp. 148–55); specifically on garden painting, closely connected with *ars topiaria*, see Settis (2002).

In creating his 'humble' world of herdsmen, V. blends together several different cultural components, which are unified into a primeval, archaic dimension constructed of song and direct contact with nature. Various *Realien* of Italy (and the Po area in particular) are combined with elements of biographical history as well as History with a capital H—not to mention references to Greek literature and to the visual arts. All this forms the backdrop against which V.'s characters sing their songs. And each character is sketched in detail, both as an individual and as a 'type'. Certain names recur frequently: Tityrus, Meliboeus, Menalcas, Corydon, Daphnis. This elicits in the reader a sense of familiarity that makes cross-references and connections within the text more apparent. Yet it would be fruitless to assign fully fledged individual personalities to single names that occur in different eclogues. Nothing assures us, for instance, that the Meliboeus of *E.* 7 is 'the same person' as Meliboeus in *E.* 1. What we can be assured of is that each name is associated with a 'mask', a sort of stock character that appears in different contexts within the book. Readers who keep this in mind are rewarded with a stereophonic soundscape of internal echoes.[25]

At any rate, V.'s complex treatment of masks and characters is replete with irony and fun (poetry itself is a 'game' of sorts: *E.* 1.10 *ludere quae uellem*), particularly owing to the discrepancy between the 'humble' herdsmen and the learned poet. V.'s eminently urban readers must have perceived the playful component inherent to the *E.*'s pastoral world, even though V. is rather far from certain Theocritean extremes. Through his herdsmen's vicissitudes, the poet probably expects to elicit a smile or two from his privileged, well-educated readers. Commentators have appropriately called comedy to witness. At times, the *E.* share with comedy a certain humorous levity, as well as some colloquial traits of style (cf. below, pp. 26–8). According to an ancient tradition, which I deem reliable, a few eclogues were staged by famous actors.[26] The best testimony, however, is perhaps found in Horace, who ascribes a 'soft and humorous' taste to V.'s Italic Muses: i.e. the Camenae (Hor. *sat.* 1.10.44–5 *molle atque facetum / Vergilio adnuerunt gaudentes rure Camenae*). Asinius Pollio, who was V.'s patron as well as one of his first and most significant readers, most probably remembered that, by contrast, *rus* appeared *infacetum* (or *inficetum*) to Catullus (22.14). Redeeming it from that reputation was among the poetic and worldly challenges of the young, 'audacious' poet from Mantua (*G.* 4.465 *audax... iuuenta*).[27]

---

[25] Following Flintoff (1975–6) and, more recently, Kania (2016, pp. 24–32), Kronenberg (2016, p. 25) rightly argues that the *E.* display 'some degree of character consistency for characters with the same name'.

[26] Don. *uita Verg.* 90–1 Brumm. = p. 29.6–7 Brugn.-Stok *Bucolica eo successu edidit ut in scena quoque per cantores crebro pronuntiarentur*; cf. Tac. *dial.* 13.2; Serv. *ad E.* 6.11; Highet (1974); Horsfall (1995d, pp. 249–52); cf. also p. 21 and nn. 52–4 below. A further proof of the (visual) popularity of pastoral subject matters in the Roman world comes from iconographic testimonies, albeit fragmentary: Ling (1991, p. 39 and fig. 38; p. 55 and fig. 55; p. 142 and fig. 153).

[27] The idea of 'humour', to be kept distinct from that of 'ridicule', encompasses stylized elegance: Quint. *inst.* 6.3.20 (referring to Horace's mention of the *E.*) *facetum quoque non tantum circa ridicula*

12 INTRODUCTION

A recurring theme in the *E.* is the idea that the singing herdsmen have mutual relationships full of friendship, tension, conflict, alliances, and oppositions. All this probably mirrors the dynamics at play within the learned circle of intellectuals gathered around Pollio. The two dimensions overlap as soon as the illustrious patron makes his first appearance, in *E.* 3. It then becomes clear that Pollio is the centre around which many poets and artists revolve, and a special addressee thanks to whom the herdsmen's songs can be met with appreciation and applause—though also, on occasion, with scorn and contempt (see *E.* 3.84–91). While the *E.* were originally intended to be read and appreciated within a restricted literary circle, they soon acquired the status of a classic in Rome and beyond.

4

Arcadia, Epicureanism, and the 'gods'

The humorous vein occasionally perceptible in the *E.* makes the contrast with the cruelty of history all the more vivid. Certain erudite traditions, perhaps accessible to V., had connected the origin of pastoral poetry with an unsettled civil context: 'since there was once a civil war in Syracuse ($\sigma\tau\acute{a}\sigma\epsilon\acute{\omega}s$ $\pi o\tau\epsilon$ $\gamma\epsilon\nu o\mu\acute{\epsilon}\nu\eta s$), and many citizens were killed, when the people made peace Artemis was given credit for the reconciliation. The farmers ($\mathring{a}\gamma\rhoo\mathring{\iota}\kappa o\iota$) brought offerings and sang hymns to the goddess in their happiness. Subsequently, their songs became customary' (*schol.* Theocr. *proleg.*, pp. 2.21–3.2 Wend.). It is no longer Theocritus' Syracuse but the Mantuan countryside that now suffers discord, which has led Meliboeus and his fellow-citizens to so much grief and violence (1.71 *en quo discordia ciuis...*). The redeeming divine figure, replacing Artemis as the object of veneration, is that of a new, brilliant *iuuenis*.[28] Here, too, just as in Syracuse's

---

opinor consistere: neque enim diceret Horatius, facetum carminis genus natura concessum esse Vergilio. decoris hanc magis et excultae cuiusdam elegantiae appellationem puto. The notion is also employed by Pliny the Elder to qualify the painting style of Studius himself: *plurimae praeterea tales argutiae facetissimi salis* (*nat.* 35.117). Pollio must have appeared to be the right person to appreciate the *E.'s facetum*, given that his youthful *lepores* and *facetiae* were appreciated by Catullus (12.8–9; cf. *E.* 3.84n.). Regarding the much-debated passage in Horace, *sat.* 1.10, it must be noted that it is possible to take the two adjectives *molle* and *facetum* not as substantives, but as attributes referring to *epos* (43). This interpretation, while attractive, is unnecessary, because it is evident that, by naming Varius' *epos*, Horace moved to hexametric poetry (no reader of Virgil could ignore that his *E.*, unlike Theocritus' *Idylls*, were exclusively in hexameters), and Horace has already used similar forms of adjectives as substantives at l. 14 of the same *sat.* 1.10 (*ridiculum acri*). Quintilian himself, cutting the quotation from Horace in the form *cum illo Horatiano 'molle atque facetum Vergilio'* and opening the paragraph with *facetum* (see above), probably took the two adjectives as substantives.

[28] It should be noted that, in V.'s *E.*, Artemis-Diana plays a considerable role: for instance, in a programmatic context, at 7.29–32; also at 3.67; note also the references to hunting at 2.28–30; 10.55–60. She is in effect absent from Theocritus and his imitators, as Fantuzzi (2008, p. 50) observes; the absence of discord between citizens is one of the effects of Artemis' benevolence in Callim. *hymn.* 3[*Dian.*].133.

foundation myth, the first eclogue depicts the establishment of a cult, albeit one confined to private use.[29]

The virgin huntress-goddess, who lives in the woods, and whom city-dwellers regard as personifying a free, primitive life, is part of the poetic invention that represents V.'s most significant, or at least distinctive, contribution to the ancient and modern tradition of pastoral poetry: Arcadia. In the *E.*, to be sure, references to Arcadians and Arcadia (cf. *E.* 4, 7, 8, 10) are limited to the evocation of a simple lifestyle, close to nature, full of hunts and pastures, love and songs. It is only through semantic extension that we may describe V.'s Arcadia as an idealized pastoral dimension (in this sense, for instance, we may define the scene evoked by Meliboeus at 1.46–58 as 'Arcadian'). Yet, properly speaking, the current idea of Arcadia as pastoral Utopia, a world in which melancholy, songs, and love affairs, however passionate, cannot perturb an eternal serenity (sometimes an unshaken, ecstatic one), should rather be ascribed to a modern reinvention whose birth certificate is Sannazaro's *Arcadia*.[30] In fact, while Cornelius Gallus in *E.* 10 yearns for Arcadian life, so as to let his love bloom (but cf. 10.38 *quicumque furor*), in *E.* 8 the 'Maenalian song' is that of a desperate lover who has resolved on suicide.

The question remains, however, why the poet of the *E.* assigned to Arcadia a significance that, as we shall see in greater detail, is only sporadically pioneered in Theocritus and is not allotted a comparable space even in later Latin pastoral poetry. The real extent of V.'s innovation has been thoroughly discussed.[31] It is perhaps impossible, given the absence of positive data, to reach a conclusion

---

[29] Fundamental testimonies concerning the origin of pastoral poetry are Diod. Sic. 4.84; Aelian. *uar. hist.* 10.18; an exhaustive collection of the ancient sources can be found in *schol. Theocr. proleg.*, pp. 1–22 Wend. (Latin sources at pp. 13–22); cf. Luiselli (1967, pp. 7–47); see further Effe (1977); Halperin (1983, pp. 78–84); Graf (1986); Lucarini (2007). According to a wholly different tradition, pastoral poetry originated from a love song addressed by the poetess Eryphanis to the young hunter Menalcas (Clearchus, apud Athen., 14.619c–d = fr. 32 Wehrli; cf. *PMG* 850, p. 452 P.). Note that V.'s second eclogue corresponds to this alternative 'foundation myth'.

[30] This has been proven, in an accurate revision of Snell's (1945) famous argument, by E. A. Schmidt (1975), to which I refer for the rich bibliography as well; for a much more critical view, see Jenkyns (1989). On the Edenic notion of Arcadia, as defined in Snell (but also in F. Klingner), cf. Leach (1974, p. 21 and n. 6); on modern Arcadia, esp. in the visual arts and in Italian and Spanish literature, cf. *Enc. Virg.* I, pp. 273–85, s.v. *Arcadia* (A. Quondam, G. Caravaggi, A. Rinaldi); *Virg. Enc.* I, p. 117, s.v. *Arcadia* (R. Jenkyns). Fabre-Serris (2008, pp. 13–162) offers the most recent discussion of the various 'Arcadias' of ancient Rome, with useful *comparanda* based on first-century BCE and first-century CE wall painting.

[31] According to Snell (1945), the *E.*'s Arcadia is essentially V.'s own invention; others, however, have hypothesized a Peloponnesian school of pastoral poetry predating Theocritus (Reitzenstein 1893, esp. pp. 121–36; the poet Anyte of Tegea is taken to be a major representative of the school: cf. *HE* 664–759 G.P.) or assumed, conversely, V.'s debt to a post-Theocritean pastoral tradition (Jachmann 1952b, esp. p. 171). Note, finally, Wilamowitz's (1906, p. 111) hypothesis according to which V. was influenced by erudite *prolegomena* to Theocritus' corpus, not substantially different from the extant ones; for further reading, see *Enc. Virg.* I, pp. 272–3, s.v. *Arcadia* (G. Barra). Concerning Erucius' epigram, *Anth. Pal.* 6.96 (= *GPh* 2200–5 G.-P.), which shows remarkable affinities with *E.* 7.4, many scholars believe that it was later than V. (rather than the opposite), following Cichorius' arguments (1922, pp. 304–6; cf. G. Williams 1978, pp. 125–6); see now Jolowicz (2021, p. 18 and n. 131).

14 INTRODUCTION

if the question about Arcadia is posed in literary-historical terms: after all, V. may have been influenced by literary precedents entirely unknown to us today. At any rate, it is beyond doubt that V.'s Arcadia has much in common with the ancient sources' description of the Arcadian people.

Being a mountain-dwelling population, naturally isolated and as such untouched by the great migrations (Thuc. 1.2.3), the Arcadians led an extremely simple life, raising livestock (they sometimes even resorted to acorn-eating: Herodot. 1.66.2). Thus, they gained a reputation for being the oldest inhabitants of the earth, like the oak in the woods (Plut. *quaest. Rom.* 92.286a; cf. also Callim. *hymn.* 1[*Iou.*].40–1; according to Ov. *fast.* 2.289–302 they even predated Jupiter's birth).[32] Never yielding to Spartan domination, the Arcadians even retained several archaic features in their dialect, but at the same time they managed to foster music and poetry, which they practised from a very early age, according to the extensive account provided by Polybius (4.19.13–21.6: Polybius, himself an Arcadian, crucially refers to amoebean song-exchange in a rural context). While Theocritus' most significant reference to Arcadia is *id.* 1.125–6, in which Daphnis urges Pan to abandon his usual dwelling and join him (cf., however, *id.* 22.156–7), Arcadia itself and its most representative god make many appearances in Latin literature.[33] Only in the Augustan age, however, did the Arcadians enjoy unmatched prestige as the ancestors of Italic peoples, a development to which V. himself contributed (probably following late Republican antiquarianism). Dionysius of Halicarnassus explicitly identifies the Arcadians with Latium's first inhabitants, whose descendants are the Romans themselves (Dion. Hal. 1.13; cf. Plut. *quaest. Rom.* 76.282a). Finally, V. himself, in *Aeneid* 8, evokes the Arcadian Evander's settlement on the Palatine hill, emphasizing its pastoral aspect and connecting the Trojans' race (and thus the Romans') with Arcadia (cf. esp. *Aen.* 8.131–42; Dion. Hal. 1.31; Ov. *fast.* 2.267–82; and also Liv. 1.5.1–2; Plin. *nat.* 3.56).[34]

---

[32] A significant story, somewhat popular in antiquity, concerns Aglaus of Psophis: he never left his native village in Arcadia and was called by the Delphic oracle happier than Gyges (Val. Max. 7.1.2; Plin. *nat.* 7.151; and even the sceptical Pausanias, 8.24.13). Equally significant is Lucian's question (*bis acc.* 11): 'how can a sophist or a philosopher come out of Arcadia?'. At Rome, *Arcadicus* was the name of a particular kind of donkey: Varr. *rust.* 2.1.14; 2.8.3 (cf. Iuv. 7.160).

[33] For some poetic instances, cf. Porcius Licinus, fr. 3.7 Bläns. = 3.8 Court. (Arcadia); Laevius, fr. 34 Bläns. = 31 Court. (Pan); and finally Lucretius, 4.586–9 (Pan), 5.25 *Arcadius sus*. For a significant reference to Arcadia in Theocritus (but in an urban idyll), note the mention of *hippomanes* at *id.* 2.48–9 (this Arcadian plant was said to have aphrodisiac effects on mares).

[34] In the same book (*Aen.* 8), V. establishes a connection between the Lupercal and the Arcadian mountain known as Lycaeus (8.343–4), whereas the Arcadians display a certain singing ability at 8.285–305, when they sing the praises of Hercules and his endeavours (as in Theocritus; note the line-ending resonance—a typically pastoral effect—at l. 305 *consonat omne nemus strepitu collesque resultant*). It should be recalled that Evander was credited with introducing the alphabet: thus, perhaps, in Fabius Pictor, fr. 1 P.², and Cincius Alimentus, fr. 1 P.²; cf. Liv. 1.7.8; Dion. Hal. 1.33.4; Tac. *ann.* 11.14.3; see further *Enc. Virg.* I, pp. 270–2, s.v. *Arcadi* (D. Musti). The Arcadian herdsmen of *Aen.* 8, therefore, allow V. to neutralize the negative connotations (roughness and violence) commonly associated with Latium's primitive inhabitants (cf. *Aen.* 7, esp. 505; 513 *pastorale...signum*); as a matter of fact, gangs of robbing herdsmen continued to dwell in certain areas of the Italian territory, especially in the south,

Regardless of the extent to which the idea of a pastoral Arcadia was available in pre-Virgilian literature, V.'s Arcadia in the *E.* plays a very important structural role: it allows the poet to define the geographical and cultural coordinates within which his poetic invention takes place. V. must have felt the need for a 'centre of gravity' that could ensure the coherence and consistency of his pastoral world, in which Theocritus' Sicily had been replaced by the Mantuan countryside (and, conversely, the 'big city' was Rome and no longer Alexandria). In the *E.*, V.'s relationship with the historical events of his time is mediated by the Roman and Italian setting. As a result, Theocritus' Sicily is transformed into a 'parallel dimension' constructed as a free literary creation, especially given the fact that the island of V.'s time no longer corresponded to Theocritus' description of Sicily.[35] This process of abstraction, which turns Greek references to concrete realities into imaginary, literary landscapes, is a source of strength rather than weakness in V.'s pastoral world. Thus, V. adds to Theocritus' Sicily another, perhaps more primeval (and continental) land: the mountainous region of Arcadia in the ancient heart of the Peloponnese. Significantly, V. unites these two focal points, Sicily and Arcadia, through the Muse-like figure of the nymph Arethusa (see *E.* 10.1n.; 10.5n.). Both lands are part of a broader cultural landscape, which is eminently Greek: it is against this backdrop that V.'s Latin-speaking herdsmen, who live near Mantua, outline their own identity in the historical and geographical *hic et nunc* of the poet and his audience.

Being mainly a literary and poetic dimension, freely interlinked with the Italian landscape of the *E.*,[36] V.'s Arcadia includes numerous traces of idealized primitivism, which are typical of V.'s pastoral world. The herdsmen's lives in caves or simple huts, along with their direct contact with woods and herds, may bring to mind the imagined primitive founding era of Roman culture.[37] In this connection, we

---

up to V.'s time and beyond: Giardina (1997, esp. pp. 196–206). After all, even at Alexandria the βουκόλοι could be equated with brigands: Borca (1998, pp. 195–9). On pastoral myth in the *Aeneid* cf., more recently, Suerbaum (2005, with references).

[35] Rome's well-to-do citizens had direct communication with Sicily, particularly as they often owned land and goods on the island. In V.'s time, Sextus Pompey had his headquarters there: thus, Sicily became a theatre of war (see above, pp. 4–5 and nn. 7–8). As early as 130–100 BCE, two violent slave revolts took place in Sicily, as Diodorus Siculus reports (in two Byzantine excerpts: 34/35.2.1–3; 27–31). According to Strabo, skirmishes among herdsmen of servile status occurred in the Augustan age (Strab. 6.2.6). In general, on the differences between Theocritus' Sicily and the 'historical' Sicily, see Leigh (2016, esp. pp. 420–1). E. Curtius observed that the rise of pastoral poetry as a permanent part of the Western tradition was largely due to the fact that Virgil did not merely imitate Theocritus but transformed Theocritus' literary landscape: Sicily, in particular, had long been a Roman province, and was no longer a 'dreamland' ('Sizilien...war kein Traumland mehr') (Curtius 1948, p. 195 = 1953, p. 190 = 1992, p. 214).

[36] Thus, Cornelius Gallus may well be imagined as dwelling in Arcadia (where he may never have set foot) and also declare, in his own monologue, that he actually is in a battlefield (*E.* 10.44n.).

[37] Don. auct. *uita Verg.* pp. 124.12–125.5 Brugn.-Stok; according to Dicaearchus, the livestock-rearing age followed the first and oldest one, in which humans lived on the fruits spontaneously offered by nature (fr. 48 Wehrli = Varr. *rust.* 2.1.3–4; cf. also 3.1.3); Livy, 5.53.8 (among others), insists on the 'bucolic' simplicity of Rome's origins. Suffice it to recall a figure like Silvius, son of Aeneas and

16 INTRODUCTION

can explain how the city-countryside opposition, which will be allotted ample space in the Augustan age (e.g. in Horace, *carm.* 3.29 and *epist.* 1.10, not to mention love-elegy), is so clearly outlined in the *E.*, starting from the first poem, then in the eighth (within an erotic context). Ancient interpreters did not fail to notice this, as we know from Quintilian's generalization, *inst.* 10.1.55 *musa illa rustica et pastoralis non forum modo uerum ipsam etiam urbem reformidat.* Contrast Theocritus' *id.* 7, where the three companions left the city for the countryside in order to celebrate the *Thalysia*, without any tension or conflict.[38]

According to an ancient tradition, V. attended (along with Plotius Tucca, Varius Rufus, and Quintilius Varus) the Epicurean gatherings in Campania, and particularly the group led by Siro.[39] V.'s audience could not fail to notice the Epicurean colour of a type of poetry centred upon the serene pleasure of a simple life, far away from urban sophistication. Suffice it to mention, in this respect, a fragment of Epicurus' letter to Pythocles: 'shun all education ($\pi\alpha\iota\delta\epsilon\iota\alpha\nu\ldots\pi\hat{\alpha}\sigma\alpha\nu$) and go away on your little boat' (quoted in Diog. Laert. 10.6 = fr. 163 Us.; cf. Quint. *inst.* 12.2.24). The author of *Catal.* 5, whom some identify with V. himself, appears to be well aware of this exhortation, connecting it with the image of a harbour, typical of Epicureanism: *ite hinc, inanes, ite, rhetorum ampullae…nos ad beatos uela mittimus portus / magni petentes docta dicta Sironis* (1; 8–9; cf. D. Clay 2004).

Such an Epicurean atmosphere in the *E.* is enriched in detail by prominent Lucretian reminiscences located at important points within the text.[40] Some have

Lavinia, whose name derives from the *siluae* themselves: *Aen.* 6.765; Liv. 1.3.6 (where he is Ascanius' son); Dion. Hal. 1.70.2.

[38] On the motif of the city in the *E.*, see Skoie (2006), with references. It is symptomatic of a change in political climate that Calpurnius' seventh eclogue is centred entirely on the city's delights, which attract the herdsman Corydon, keeping him from returning to his usual pastoral life. The fascination of writers and intellectuals in general with the countryside is highlighted by Horace, *epist.* 2.2.77 (but cf. Quint. *inst.* 10.3.22–4, 28–30).

[39] V.'s name, along with those of Tucca and the others, has been read in a fragment of a Herculaneum papyrus transmitting a text by the Epicurean Philodemus: *PHerc. Paris* 2; cf. Gigante, Capasso (1989); Gigante (2001 and 2004); whether the poet is mentioned in *PHerc.* 1082 is much more doubtful. For a collection of ancient sources, particularly concerning V.'s apprenticeship under Siro (cf. Serv. *ad E.* 6.13), see *Enc. Virg.* II, pp. 328–31, s.v. *epicureismo* (L. Alfonsi); *Virg. Enc.* I, pp. 439–41, s.v. *Epicureanism* (L. Kronenberg); see additionally Horsfall (1995b, pp. 7–8); Janko (2000, p. 6). In his account of the journey to Brundisium, Horace recalls that Plotius, Varius, and V. joined Maecenas' other *comites* at Sinuessa (thus coming from Campania): *sat.* 1.5.40–1.

[40] Cf. esp. *E.* 1.2, where V. shows familiarity with Lucr. 4.580–9 (cf. also *E.* 2.34; 10.25–6), whereas, at the outset of the second half of the book, he echoes Lucr. 5.1398 (cf. *E.* 6.8n.). The *E.*, finally, are concluded by a 'physical' doctrine previously taught by Lucretius: cf. 10.76n. In Lucretius, too, the Epicurean ideal life appeared as a pastoral *locus amoenus* (esp. 2.29–30 *in gramine molli / propter aquae riuum*). Furthermore, according to Lucretius, poetry originated within a specifically pastoral dimension, and there is a strong connection between the sounds of nature and human music (Lucr. 5.1379–1411, esp. 5.1383 *agrestis docuere cauas inflare cicutas*; cf. *E.* 1.5 *doces* [n.]); see notably Hardie (2006, p. 281 and n. 13); for Epicureanism as a kind of 'pastoral' philosophy, see Rosenmeyer (1969, esp. pp. 11–12). A comprehensive picture of Lucretian echoes in the *E.* is offered by Castelli (1966–7); Ramorino Martini (1986); Lipka (2001, pp. 66–80); Kronenberg (2016, pp. 26–7). It would, of course, be pointless to expect philosophical coherence from Tityrus or other characters in the *E.*: see Roskam's (2007, pp. 155–60) discussion.

objected that the conspicuous presence of the gods in the *E.* is at odds with Epicureanism. It is worth noting, however, that the gods always make their appearance without any particular religious emphasis and are always seen from the point of view of simple herdsmen (who are by no means free from a magical or superstitious mentality: cf. esp. *E.* 1.16–17; 8.95–9; 9.14–16). On the other hand, it is significant that, in a Hesiodic-didactic passage such as Silenus' cosmology, the gods do not appear at all, in line with Epicurean cosmological doctrine (Traina 1965). In his proem, Lucretius had memorably celebrated the parent goddess Venus, whereas in his eulogy of Epicurus he had gone so far as to call his master *deus* (esp. Lucr. 5.8). Finally, while Epicurus fought superstition, he nevertheless taught the importance of honouring the gods: in a letter to Polyaenus (fr. 157 Us.), he is said to have asserted that the Anthesteria must be celebrated, and in another epistle (to Phirso) he seems to have declared that he personally took part in all the city's festivals, especially in the Eleusinian mysteries (fr. 169 Us.). Even in V.'s *Georgics*, the poet's mention of *mystica uannus Iacchi* (*G.* 1.166) may not have disappointed Epicurus.

If placed against the backdrop of Epicurean doctrine, the first eclogue must be read as a narrative of how humans construct their idea of deity and ascribe precise roles to it. The Hellenistic notion of *praesens deus*, which V. puts to work at the very beginning of his poetic collection,[41] clarifies the deity's practical function and lends consistency to a world in which human beings can become gods, provided that they are capable of following and actualizing a specific divine model. From this point of view, the *E.* are a foundational text of Augustan culture, as they contribute to the definition of a new language that poets and intellectuals can use to talk about divine models. Note, for instance, the opposition between Dionysus and Apollo, which is destined to great success in literature and arts (not to mention political and ideological communication).[42]

Epicureanism and Arcadia, in the sense I have attempted to clarify, are two fundamental themes of the *E.* that tend to be intertwined, acting together in

---

[41] In the opening of his next work, V. will ask the question which god Octavian is to become (*G.* 1.24–42; cf. also, towards the end, 4.560–2 *Caesar...uiam...adfectat Olympo*). This is an even more explicit treatment of Octavian's deification than *E.* 1. At the beginning of the *Aeneid*, the poet broaches the typically epic question of what role the gods play in human affairs, and seems to allude to a philosophical issue crucial to his Epicurean background: can the gods be so emotionally invested in what happens to us down on Earth? Cf. *Aen.* 1.11 *tantaene animis caelestibus irae?*, with discussion in Davis (2012, p. 5).

[42] The various divine figures, and their corresponding socio-cultural models, are harmonized in the *E.* through a very subtle interplay of cross-references and echoes between one eclogue and the next, particularly in the central poems of the collection (*E.* 4–5–6–7). The search for a poetic language capable of interlinking different values embodied by different deities is necessary to a poetic work that aims to harmonize complex ideological systems, ready to enter into conflict with one another. In this sense, the *E.* are the poetic counterpart of Pollio's *foedus Brundisinum*. Yet a true 'rhetoric' (and a dialectic) of divine models will only be fully achieved in the Augustan age, once any political reconciliation between the two protagonists (Octavian and Antony) becomes impossible: cf. Cucchiarelli (2010 and 2011).

18   INTRODUCTION

opposition to the painful dynamics of history. It is precisely this opposition that V. intended to express in a poem which, at least in the final form of the collection, he must have conceived of as 'inaugural' (*E.* 1). Through an escape from contingency made possible by his herdsmen, the poet gave birth to an intuition that would remain crucial to his whole œuvre, up to its final point (Turnus' death at the end of the *Aeneid*): the irreconcilable contrast between the fate of the vanquished and that of the conquerors—between those who stay, protected by Epicurus and the Arcadian gods, and those who are swept away by the storm of history.[43] Through his representation of a humble but foundational *rus*, V. constructs a complex literary world in which nature, human beings, and deities are in constant communication with one another as they share values and role models. The *E.* are far from being 'escapist' poems centred around idle aesthetic contemplation, as readers might expect from poems about trees and woods—note Socrates' famous statement in Plato's *Phaedrus*: τὰ μὲν οὖν χωρία καὶ τὰ δένδρα οὐδέν μ' ἐθέλει διδάσκειν, οἱ δ' ἐν τῷ ἄστει ἄνθρωποι 'The countryside and the trees won't teach me anything, while the people in the city do' (*Phaedr.* 230d). V.'s trees can and do teach us something: there can be an equilibrium in things, a consonance between human beings, nature, and the gods, as long as the destructive forces of History and strife do not intervene.

5

The bucolic book

5.1. Title

In all likelihood, the original title of the collection is *Bucolica*, a Greek nominative plural form, just like *Georgica*: it is attested in the biographical tradition (Don. *uita Verg.* 30; 66 Brumm. = pp. 22.1; 26.10 Brugn.-Stok; Prob. *praef. E.*, p. 323.13 [III.2 Th.-H.] = *uita Verg.* p. 198.6 Brugn.-Stok) and confirmed by Numitorius' parodic *Antibucolica* (Don. *uita Verg.* 172 Brumm. = p. 38.10 Brugn.-Stok). Moreover, it appears as such in the late antique manuscripts in capital script, as well as in ancient authors' and grammarians' quotations.[44] Going back to a very early period, if not to V. himself, the term *ecloga*, which involves the idea of choice

---

[43] For this reason, *E.* 1 (which, in a way, is the 'birthplace' of Virgilian poetry) is the first and foremost touchstone used by interpreters, who can be divided between the so-called 'optimists' (e.g. Otis 1963, pp. 128–36) and the 'pessimists' (e.g. Putnam 1970, pp. 51–5); for a balanced view, see Winterbottom (1976), and, more recently, R. Tarrant, *Virgil, Aeneid, Book XII*, Cambridge 2012, pp. 16–30 (focusing on the final scene of the *Aeneid*).

[44] Cf. Quint. *inst.* 8.6.46; Macr. *Sat.* 5.17.20; note also Ov. *trist.* 2.537–8 *bucolicis...modis* and Colum. 7.10.8 *bucolicum...poema* (featuring, in both cases, an allusion to V.); see, moreover, Serv. *praef. E.* pp. 2.3, 3.27, etc. (III.1 Th.-H.). For further sources and discussion, see Horsfall (1981, pp. 108–9); Geymonat (1982); Schröder (1999, pp. 68–70).

or selection, must have proved very convenient to denote each single poem.[45] The ancient tradition, once again well epitomized by Donatus (*uita Verg.* 304–15 Brumm. = pp. 51.6–52.6 Brugn.-Stok), labels each eclogue with a specific title, usually coinciding with a character's name. Such titles do appear in the manuscript tradition (which, nevertheless, also features different or more extensive titles): 1 *Tityrus*; 2 *Alexis*; 3 *Palaemon*; 4 *Pollio*; 5 *Daphnis*; 6 *Varus* or *Silenus*; 7 *Corydon*; 8 *Damon* or *Pharmaceutria*; 9 *Moeris*; 10 *Gallus*. Only in the case of *E.* 6, however, might the title retain traces of an original *praescriptio*, meant to identify the eclogue through the addressee's name (Varus): the *praescriptio* was probably included in the copy of the poem that V. sent to him as a present, and we cannot rule out that the poet kept it in the final book roll edition (but cf. *E.* 6.12n.).

5.2. Order and structure

That Theocritus' works, like those of other pastoral poets, were re-arranged by a later editor must have been clear in V.'s time, considering the epigraph placed by the grammarian Artemidorus of Tarsus (II–I cent. BCE) at the outset of his edition of pastoral poetry: 'Bucolic Muses, once dispersed: now they are all / together in a single herd, a single fold' (*Anth. Pal.* 9.205 = *Furth. Gr. Epigr.* 113–14, pp. 32–3 P.).

It is likely that V. was influenced by the shape of the Theocritean collection in arranging his pastoral book. Accordingly, interpreters have read the testimony of Servius, *praef. E.*, p. 3.20–1 (III.1 Th.-H.) *sane sciendum VII eclogas esse meras rusticas, quas Theocritus X habet* as implying the existence of a Theocritean book including ten 'purely' pastoral poems, which would have been used by V. as a model for his ten eclogues.[46] However, the available evidence only allows us to assert that a Theocritean (pastoral?) collection, perhaps much larger than the one we have, probably included at its outset a sequence of ten Theocritean poems, consisting of the current *id.* 1–11 (except *id.* 2). As for their order, we may be sure that the current *id.* 1, *Daphnis*, occupied the initial position, whereas *id.* 8 and 9, considered authentic in antiquity, must have occupied the final positions, perhaps with the addition of *id.* 11 (*Cyclops*) at the very end.[47] The existence of a Theocritean book featuring *id.* 1 and *id.* 3–11 would explain not only the decimal

---

[45] As a result, the term suggests the existence of a broader patrimony of 'songs': precisely those *carmina* to which Meliboeus bids farewell in *E.* 1.77; the term is employed, at least since Varro, to suggest an excerpt from a work (cf. Charis. *gramm.* I, p. 120.28–9 K. = p. 154.21–2 B.) or a short poetic composition (Stat. *silv.* 3 *praef.*; 4 *praef.*; Plin. *epist.* 4.14.9): *Enc. Virg.* II, p. 165, s.v. *ecloga* (A. Traina).

[46] Servius considers only seven of V.'s ten eclogues to be purely *rusticae*: the excluded poems are *E.* 4, *E.* 6 (cf. 6.21–3n.), and, as is clear from the context, *E.* 10. Significantly, Calpurnius Siculus will publish a collection of seven eclogues, which can be regarded as properly 'rustic' despite the presence of civil and political topics (always treated within a pastoral framework).

[47] According to the ancient exegetical tradition, the position of *id.* 1 was due to its grace and refinement (*schol.* Theocr. *id.* 1, p. 23.7–8 Wend. τὸ χαριέστερον καὶ τεχνικώτερον). Among the most important papyrus witnesses is *POxy* 2064 (+ 3548), II cent. BCE, from which we may infer, in all

20 INTRODUCTION

standard used by V. in his pastoral collection but also the total number of lines in the *E.*: in fact, Theocritus' total lines would be under 900,[48] not too far from V.'s 830.

Thus, it is likely that some editorial effects à la Theocritus (i.e. tracing back to the Theocritean collection as it was read in the first century BCE) are mirrored by V.'s pastoral book. The opening farewell to Daphnis, and perhaps also the Cyclops' amorous anxieties (cf. esp. Theocr. *id.* 11 / *E.* 10), are quite relevant to Meliboeus in *E.* 1 and Cornelius Gallus in *E.* 10. Finally, if the current *id.* 7 occupied the fifth or the sixth position in the Theocritean collection known to V., we would see a noteworthy correspondence with *E.* 6: in both 'Theocritus' and V., the central part of the decimal sequence would contain a poem of obvious programmatic interest.[49] It is, at any rate, beyond doubt that V.'s familiarity with Theocritus is not limited to the 'purely rustic' idylls (according to Servius' definition).[50]

Without further positive evidence, it is better to focus on the arrangement of V.'s book as it stands. In fact, regardless of any possible (Theocritean or other) precedent, the arrangement itself appears to be very carefully crafted, essentially based on two principles: sequence and balance.

In accordance with the first of these principles, V.'s book is designed for a seamless reading experience, as is shown by the numerous internal allusions, which always refer to previous eclogues—i.e. those that V.'s readers must know, if they read sequentially as the book roll unrolled. The most obvious case is *E.* 5, which includes (in its final lines) an explicit quotation of *E.* 2 and 3; but other references may be readily detected.[51]

---

likelihood, that the sequence of ten idylls also included *id.* 11 at the end (cf. Gutzwiller 1996a). As noted, the sequence could not have included *id.* 2, whose setting is urban. The order of the current *id.* 1 and 2, well attested in the manuscript tradition, and hence inherited by modern editions, was perhaps the result of a structural analogy between the two poems, both featuring a refrain. This analogy was perhaps observed by V. himself, who contaminates *id.* 2 with *id.* 1 (cf. below, p. 381).

[48] The total is 890, to be more precise, at least based on Gow's (1952) text, with an average of 89 lines per idyll. That number must be taken with a grain of salt, since even in V.'s time the Theocritean manuscript tradition may have varied significantly, due to interpolations and lacunae (for instance, in the text known to us, there may be a lacuna after *id.* 8.52, while 6.41 and 8.77 are certainly spurious). The same caution must be applied to V.'s text: see below, pp. 22–3 and nn. 56, 57.

[49] The idea of 'revamping' the pastoral song is found in *id.* 7 (echoing *id.* 1): see esp. *id.* 7.49 βουκολικᾶς ταχέως ἀρχώμεθ' ἀοιδᾶς (cf. *id.* 1.70 etc. and, of course, the prologue to *E.* 6, esp. 6.8n.). Simichidas, whom the ancients themselves identified with Theocritus, is a not-so-remote predecessor of the Tityrus-V. advised by Apollo: *E.* 6.4n. As for *E.* 7, note that its structural similarity to *id.* 8 (esp. in the opening: cf. *E.* 7.1–5n.) would be even more obvious if *id.* 8 had actually been the seventh poem in the Theocritean edition known to V.

[50] Cf. Posch's (1969, pp. 29–30) repertoire; for instance, *E.* 2 seems to presuppose *id.* 20, almost certainly spurious but pastoral in theme (V., after all, imitates extensively the post-Theocritean *id.* 8 and 9). Recall, moreover, the considerable reworking of *id.* 2 in *E.* 8.64–100 (but also the echo of *id.* 24.93–8 in *E.* 8.101–2), and that of *id.* 13.58–60 in *E.* 6.44. A separate set of echoes and re-elaborations concerns Theocritus' encomia (esp. *id.* 16, 17, and also 24), particularly evident in *E.* 4.: V., therefore, must have had access to an edition of Theocritus that was not limited to the ten pastoral idylls (perhaps, according to Wilamowitz's famous opinion, V. used the text edited by Artemidorus' son Theon): an overview of the issue in *Enc. Virg.* V.1, pp. 111–13 (G. Serrao).

[51] Thus, at the beginning of *E.* 6, the reference to 'previous' pastoral poetry is inextricably tied to what the reader has already encountered in the first half of the book: see *E.* 6.1n. That the amomum

V.'s alternate use of different stylistic forms, aiming at pleasant variations, is also enhanced by sequential reading. In fact, V. clearly alternates between the dialogic-mimetic form, in which only the characters can speak, and the narrative form, in which only the poet-narrator talks (and occasionally cedes the floor to the characters whose vicissitudes he narrates). The former is the case with the odd-numbered eclogues (*E.* 1, 3, 5, 7, 9), whereas the latter applies to the even-numbered poems (*E.* 2, 4, 6, 8, 10), all introduced by a prologue, which the poet utters *ex sua propria persona*.[52] In antiquity, Servius observed this alternation effect in his note to *E.* 3.1, referring to the originally Platonic distinction among three *characteres dicendi*: a narrative one, in which the narrator is the only speaker; a dramatic one, in which the characters are the only speakers; a mixed one, which combines the other two.[53] In Theocritus, the mimetic element was very prominent, partly as a result of his possible reworking of Hellenistic mimes (after all, Syracuse was the mimographer Sophron's homeland). Theocritus' ancient commentators made several remarks on the three *characteres dicendi*, and their comments were often similar to Servius'.[54] These exegetical notions essentially go back to Plato and Aristotle, and V. probably took them into account. In his pastoral book, however,

---

spreads 'everywhere' (*uulgo*) at 4.25 is best understood as the miraculous generalization of a prodigy that the reader came across in 3.89, where its only beneficiary was Asinius Pollio. The exhortation to Daphnis at *E.* 9.46–50 appears much more effective to readers who know *E.* 5: the same goes for Moeris' name, occurring in both *E.* 9 and 8 (9.54n.). Finally, the echo of 1.73 at 9.50 becomes much more significant if the reader recalls Meliboeus' sad fate.

[52] The distinction between the two forms entails major differences for what concerns V.'s modes of representation: the mimetic poems are more coherently realistic, whereas greater freedom of imagination characterizes the narrative ones, in which the spatial and geographical coordinates do not abide by the same criteria of order, unity, and verisimilitude that apply to the odd-numbered eclogues. Correspondingly, any realistic geographical landscape, such as the Mantuan countryside (or the city of Rome), is only featured in the odd-numbered eclogues (e.g. 1.20 *huic nostrae* [scil. *urbi*]; 26 *Romam*; 7.13 *Mincius*; 9.27–8 *Mantua...Cremonae*). By contrast, in the narrative poems V. alternates between maritime or Sicilian landscapes (*E.* 2.21 *Siculis...in montibus*; 25–6 *in litore*; 26 *mare*; 8.59–60 *in undas deferar*) and Greek or mythological ones (e.g. 6.64 *Permessi*; 65 *Aonas in montis*; 8.30 *Oetam*; 10.1 *Arethusa*; 15 *Maenalus*; 26 *Arcadiae*).

[53] Cf. also Serv. Dan. *ad E.* 6.1; 9.1; Prob. *praef. E.* p. 329.10–16 [III.2 Th.-H.]; Diom. *gramm.* I.482.14–25 K.; *Enc. Virg.* II, pp. 63–4, s.v. *diegematico/mimetico* (G. Rosati). *E.* 7 is no exception: despite the agon being inherently mimetic and dramatic, the poem is entirely narrated and, therefore, diegetic. Yet the narrator is not the poet (or an 'authorial' voice), but a pastoral character named Meliboeus (on whose characterization see p. 348).

[54] Cf. e.g. *schol.* Theocr. *proleg.* D, pp. 4–5 Wend.: 'All poetry is divided into three types: diegetic, dramatic, and mixed. Pastoral poetry is a combination of these three, as if they were blended together. This is why pastoral poetry is so pleasant: it is because of the variation produced by blending [διὸ καὶ χαριέστερον τῇ ποικιλίᾳ τῆς κράσεως]. In fact, sometimes it seems to have a diegetic form, sometimes a dramatic one, sometimes a mixed one (i.e. diegetic and dramatic at once), depending on the cases'. See further Farrell (2016, pp. 405–6). On the mimetic component of pastoral poetry, in both Theocritus and V., see Höschele (2013, p. 42). That this component was known to ancient interpreters is demonstrated also by their use of theatrical terminology: cf., for instance, Serv. Dan. *ad E.* 9.1 *haec ecloga dramatico charactere scripta est: inducuntur enim duo pastores; scaena in agro Mantuano*. It is concretely possible that the *E.* were acted out in theatres, perhaps with a mime-like *mise en scène* (as will later be the case with Ovid's poetry, according to Ov. *trist.* 2.519–20; 5.7.25–8), cf. above, p. 11 and n. 26.

22   INTRODUCTION

V. made the distinction between the mimetic and the narrative form even more apparent by systematically alternating between the two.

From a thematic perspective, another consequence of the sequential reading of the *E.* is that the reader perceives the gradual, incremental construction of V.'s pastoral world. After the first eclogue, which surprises the reader with a historical theme (the land confiscations), *E.* 2 and 3 return to the pastoral (Theocritean) tradition, which V. abandons in the central poems (*E.* 4–5–6) and rediscovers in *E.* 7–8–9 (each of which features significant innovations), only to cast it into doubt again in the conclusion (*E.* 10). The watershed between the two halves of the book, marked by *E.* 6 and its 'proem in the middle' (cf. also *E.* 5.90n.), is somewhat hidden and dissimulated by the solid unity of the three central poems (with clearly 'extra-pastoral' traits in *E.* 4 and 6, and a highly original content in *E.* 5).

The second principle (i.e. balance) affects the pastoral collection as a whole and establishes cross-references and correspondences between the two halves of the book (respectively, *E.* 1–5 and 6–10). Thus, *E.* 1 and 9 correspond to each other via the confiscation theme; 2 and 8 have an erotic motif in common; 3 and 7 are agonistic in both form and content; both 4 and 6 are exceptions to the pastoral rule. *E.* 5 and 10 are somewhat different, but even in this case it is possible to observe some correspondences, based on the model of *id.* 1 ('continued' in *E.* 5, reworked in *E.* 10). A structuring role, moreover, is played by Cornelius Gallus, opening and closing the second half of the collection (*E.* 6.64–73; 10), as well as by Daphnis, who is indirectly evoked in *E.* 1 and, above all, in *E.* 10, but is explicitly celebrated at the end of the first half of the book (*E.* 5).[55]

The thematic balance is further underscored by rather precise correspondences in the number of lines: 1 + 9 (150); 4 + 6 (149); 2 + 8 (183); 3 + 7 (181). Once again, 5 and 10 inevitably lie outside this network of symmetries, counting respectively 90 and 77 lines.[56] The 'eccentric' nature of *E.* 10 is, on the one hand, confirmed, as though it were a supplement to the pastoral book, meant to introduce a 'guest' poet. It is worth noting, on the other hand, that the sum of *E.* 5 and *E.* 10 (167 lines) lies halfway between the other four pairs (181/183; 149/150). Another kind of balance is that between the 420 lines of the first five eclogues combined and the

---

[55] A similar role is played by the word (and the idea of) *umbra*: the book begins under the cover, and thus the shade, of a beech tree (1.1); *umbrae* is the final word of *E.* 1, and appears three times (in both the singular and the plural) in the third-to-last and the second-to-last line of the whole *liber* (1.83; 10.75–6). The beech's shade will reappear in the finale of the *Georgics*, and the *Aeneid* (12.952) will be concluded by (the underworld's) *umbrae*.

[56] As mentioned, the total number of lines in V.'s *libellus* is 830 (with an average of 83 lines per eclogue). The figures used here and below, like Theocritus' numbers, may vary more or less significantly depending on whether certain lines are deleted or not (these and other calculations are based on Mynors' text, which includes, in particular, 8.28a [see n. ad loc.]: without that line, and therefore without the corresponding 8.76n., the sum of *E.* 2 and 8 would yield a total of 181 lines, equal to the sum of *E.* 3 and 7). Textual critics may take these numerical data into account, when appropriate: for instance, when evaluating a proposed deletion. After all, the 'tally' (of sheep) is a typically pastoral activity: see *E.* 6.85n.

THE BUCOLIC BOOK   23

410 lines of the last five; similarly, the position of the longest eclogues (3 and 8) at the centre of the two halves of the book contributes to its overall balance. Note, finally, that *E.* 5 is preceded by a 330-line sequence, comparable to the 333 lines that separate *E.* 5 from *E.* 10.

These numerical correspondences may seem far from obvious; yet other, more evident instances of numerical balance can hardly escape the reader's attention, thereby proving beyond reasonable doubt that V. counted his lines.[57] Note, for example, the perfect balance between Mopsus' song and Menalcas' in *E.* 5, each of which contains 25 lines. Similarly, in *E.* 8, both Damon's and Alphesiboeus' songs include the same number of lines.[58] A less evident yet equally significant correspondence is the one between the singing contests in *E.* 3 and *E.* 7, each of which has 48 lines.

The two principles that we have discussed (sequence and balance) guide V. through his process of measuring and distributing both content and form. These principles can be regarded as manifestations of an even more general principle: i.e. rationalization (or 'regularization'), which also affects the poet's relationship with his Greek models. Note, in particular, the careful way in which V. structures the herdsmen's dialogues, moving away from the somewhat whimsical freedom of Theocritus. First of all, the end of a speech always coincides with the end of a line in the *E.*, with no exceptions (Theocritus made only one exception: *id.* 5.66, which is divided between two different characters). As a result, the *E.* establish a standard that guides the rest of Roman pastoral tradition (while it is entirely ignored by other forms of dialogic hexameter poetry, such as Horace's *Satires*). Secondly, V. pursues systematic rationalization as to how speeches are distributed among characters: thus, in the 'properly dialogic' segments of odd-numbered eclogues, one of the characters opens the dialogue while the other concludes it, so that each character is given the same number of speeches.[59] In Theocritus (esp. *id.* 1 and 3–11), the situation is very different. In *id.* 1, for instance, Thyrsis opens the dialogue and the Goatherd concludes it, so that each of them has three speeches (note that Thyrsis' third speech is, in effect, Daphnis'

---

[57] In support of this argument, recall that the practice of numbering (or at least counting) lines in books was somewhat widespread in antiquity: some papyri show traces of stichometric notations, on which the standard work is still Ohly (1928). Unconvincing are, on the other hand, numerological attempts to find evidence of arcane arithmetical wisdom in V.'s book (see Maury 1944); for a balanced synthesis, with further bibliography, cf. *Enc. Virg.* I, pp. 549–52, s.v. *Bucoliche*, II, *La struttura* (J. Van Sickle); Perutelli (1995, pp. 33–4); add at least Duckworth (1962, pp. 39–40); Otis (1963, pp. 129–30); Skutsch (1969 and 1980); Saint-Denis (1976); Rudd (1976, pp. 119–44); La Penna (1983a, pp. 61–5 = 2005, pp. 53–6); more recently, Breed (2006b); Heyworth (2007, pp. 149–50); Steenkamp (2011); Cucchiarelli (2021b, pp. 196–204).

[58] *E.* 5 and *E.* 8, two 'twin' poems, are interlinked by a complex web of internal echoes and symmetries: cf., respectively, 5.20–44n. and 8.64–109n.

[59] In *E.* 1, Meliboeus begins and Tityrus concludes. In the initial dialogue of *E.* 3 (i.e. before Palaemon appears on stage at 3.55 and 'forces' a proper agon), Menalcas begins and Damoetas concludes. In *E.* 5, Menalcas has the first words and Mopsus the last; the same is true of Lycidas and Moeris in *E.* 9.

24   INTRODUCTION

song, while the Goatherd's second speech is an ecphrasis). In *id.* 4, by contrast, Battus has both the first and the last words, thereby uttering a total of sixteen speeches (while Corydon has only fifteen).

All these are but specific aspects (and certainly not *all* aspects) of a general tendency displayed by V. in the pastoral book: a tendency to aim for definite, harmonious shapes and quantities, which recur time and again throughout the collection.[60] The result is an acute sensitivity to structural patterns, which privileges the final shape of the volume (i.e. the book as it appears before the reader's eyes) over the process of composition per se. For this reason, issues of chronological priority among single eclogues lose much of their importance—even though such questions have entranced generations of scholars and critics (at any rate, it is certain that the book was composed within a relatively limited timespan: cf. above, pp. 3–4). Without a doubt, V. strove to construct a book to be read as a 'synchronic' whole. He must have intervened at various stages of its composition (and in various *loci*) to insert references and echoes. The most obvious case of relative priority, which we already mentioned, is that of *E.* 2 and 3, which, through their detailed Theocritean emulation, introduce a Theocritean style in the initial section of the book, after the unexpected opening of *E.* 1. From this point of view, *E.* 2 and 3 may have been composed among the last, with an eye to the larger picture, and then cited in the closing lines of *E.* 5 (which may themselves have been added or reworked at a later stage).[61] In fact, there is no reason why the composition process could not itself have been a source of inspiration for V. The biographical tradition informs us that V., when coming to grips with his masterpiece (the *Aeneid*), worked simultaneously on all the books into which he had divided the poem (Don. *uita Verg.* 83–9 Brumm. = pp. 28.8–29.5 Brugn.-Stok): it is possible, or even plausible, that he was already working in a similar fashion at the time of the *E.*

At the end of the collection, the poet depicts himself as a herdsman weaving together 'a basket of thin reeds' (*E.* 10.71): the pastoral book itself is the result of a similar process of weaving, featuring countless threads constantly connected to one another. The book is a finished object, to be appreciated in its entirety by the mind and the eyes alike: like a basket, it can be held and carried in the hand or

---

[60] The number five (along with its multiples) is a recurring quantity: note, above all, the two halves into which the ten-poem book is subdivided. In *E.* 5, each song has 5×5 lines. Five is also the standard number of lines in dialogic exchanges, i.e. the average length of the herdsmen's dialogic units, considering the properly 'mimetic' segments alone. In other words, if we exclude *E.* 2, the agon in *E.* 3, the two songs in *E.* 5, and the entirety of *E.* 8 and 10 as well as *E.* 7, which strictly speaking is Meliboeus' continuous narrative, the total number of lines is 250, distributed among fifty speeches: hence, an average of 5 lines per speech. Consider also the first two speeches of the book, counting 5 lines each (*E.* 1.1–10n.).

[61] Few scholars do not consider *E.* 2 to be one of the earliest eclogues: cf. La Penna (1963a, pp. 490–2). Horace himself, in his satirical *libellus*, assigns the initial position to the three satires that best approximate the cynic-diatribical style: then comes, in *sat.* 1.4, an innovative thrust (criticism of Lucilius; Old Comedy as a model).

stored away along with its content.[62] Thus, V. brings to completion an ongoing process of development in the materiality of poetic books, which seems to have undergone a great acceleration during the neoteric age. Catullus, however, lovingly put his *libellus* on display in his very first poem as though it were a miraculous event, but went on never to mention it again in the rest of his collection (at least as far as the book's physical and editorial materiality is concerned). V., by contrast, does not draw attention to the physical book right away, but gradually constructs the material perception of his work with rapid brushstrokes and flashes of colour. The pastoral book emerges as a collection of texts and pages presented sequentially and structured in the complex way outlined above. V.'s refined craftsmanship conceals the physical support precisely in the moment in which it is presupposed: the text of the *E.* contains all the information necessary to appreciate the collection's artful architecture (or, at least, all the information that the poet was interested in offering to his readers). The collection itself is like a codified matrix, which remains unchanged even if its physical support changes radically: as long as the order of the poems stays the same, the collection will stay true to its network of echoes, framing effects, cross-references, and intersections.

A long time has passed, in the history of poetic *libelli*, since the moment when Catullus offered his splendid 'little book' to Cornelius Nepos. Like his neoteric predecessor, V. speaks to an audience capable of understanding and appreciating his *libellus* as a refined repository of songs, even in its material form.[63]

5.3. Language and style

V.'s linguistic choices in the *E.* aim at two principal effects. On the one hand, he adopts a lively, colloquial tone corresponding to the herdsmen's simple ethos and to the dialogic (often mimetic) form of pastoral poetry.[64] On the other hand, he

---

[62] Not unlike Meleager's στέφανος (garland/Garland: cf. 10.71n.). Note, however, the even closer resemblance between a woven basket and a papyrus roll. In the finale of the *E.*, the poet's planning activity may include what appears to be an 'editorial link' to his next work, the *Georgics*: see *E.* 10.75–7n. (cf. also 10.24n.); Cucchiarelli (2008). On the one hand, it would hardly be surprising if, in *E.* 10, V. wanted to prearrange the transition to a poem that he had, in all probability, already decided to compose. It is possible, on the other hand, that he modified the finale of *E.* 10 at a later stage (when the *Georgics* were already under way). Both hypotheses are consistent with V.'s allusion to *E.* 1 at the end of the *Georgics*, thus confirming his own conception of the two 'rustic' works as a single whole.

[63] V.'s friends must have included several 'bibliophiles': especially Pollio, who was soon to build a large public library at the *Atrium Libertatis*. It is likely that Cornelius Gallus took an interest in the material production of books: a certain type of papyrus was prepared under his guidance during his stint as the governor of Egypt, and was later named after him (according to Isid. *orig.* 6.10.5, probably echoing Suetonius: cf. p. 132.4–5 Reiff.): *Corneliana a Cornelio Gallo praefecto Aegypti primum confecta.*

[64] The 'modesty' of the pastoral world, expressed in terms of 'delicacy' or 'frailty', is asserted on several occasions (esp. *E.* 1.2 *tenui...auena*; 4.2 *humiles myricae*; 10.71 *gracili...hibisco*); hence the ancients' well-known literary theorizations, exemplified by Servius, *praef. E.*, pp. 1.16–2.5 (III.1 Th.-H.).

26 INTRODUCTION

employs a Hellenizing colour, typical of 'refined' poetry, making the Theocritean model more vividly relevant in the reader's eyes (the importance of Greek forms in V.'s language was known to the ancients: cf. Macr. *Sat.* 5.17.19). These two effects, artfully harmonized with one another, show the way in which V., following his own path, built upon a stylistic form that was previously Catullan and neoteric: everyday language mixed with extremely sophisticated turns (which often sound Greek, and specifically Hellenistic). Like Catullus, V. occasionally resorts to a kind of elevated vocabulary that must have belonged to traditional Roman epos: note, for instance, *amnis* (5.25); *pontus* (6.35); *ratis* (6.76).[65]

In his blending activity, which aims at a 'classicizing' type of moderation, V. constantly avoids excess. On the one hand, he eschews difficult constructions or erudite vocabulary of Alexandrian origin; the Hellenizing colour primarily affects features of inflection that were in relatively common use, and in V. are normally limited to Greek proper nouns.[66] On the other hand, the colloquial style is never lowered to the level of vulgar usage, in either morphological or lexical terms: the adjective *cuius* (3.1n.), to name the most significant instance, must most likely be interpreted as an archaism belonging to colloquial language which nonetheless has some literary affectation, given its frequency in Plautus' language (it also makes the opening of *E.* 3 more memorable: the line will, in fact, be quoted at 5.87).[67] A colloquial effect is similarly produced by the use of diminutives (cf. 1.14 *gemellos*; 9.3 *agelli*) which, however, is fairly limited, especially if compared to Catullus and the neoteric poets. The lively contest of *E.* 3 shows remarkable familiarity with the language of comedy, which also occurs elsewhere, particularly in dialogic passages. At the lexical level, the subject matter fosters the use, sparing but not negligible, of technical terms, specifically belonging to the agricultural and pastoral world. These, too, contribute to the 'modest' characterization of the herdsmen's vocabulary, while also displaying signs of a malleable poetic language, capable of exactly (perhaps even affectionately) reproducing its object.[68]

According to a widespread rhetorical principle, the style aiming at the audience's delight (such as that of the *E.*) ought to stick to a 'middle' tone, free from excess, balancing various adornments, both elevated and lowly: cf. Cic. *orat.* 95–6. Moreover, the mimetic aspect of pastoral poetry often involves the use of comic language. Note that Theocritus' close relationship with Sophron's Syracusan mime is inherent to the very origins of pastoral poetry: see above p. 21 and n. 54.

[65] Cf. *suboles* at *E.* 4.49; note also plural forms such as *otia* (1.6; 5.61) and *hordea* (5.36); archaic forms like *arbos* (3.56) or even the perfect *risere* (3.9; 4.62).

[66] Nom. sing. ending in *-os* (*Hesperos*), or *-as* (*Menalcas*), or *-e* (*Aegle*); voc. and acc. sing. according to Greek declension (*Alexi; Alexin; Nerea*); gen. sing. in *-os* (*Amaryllidos*); dat. sing. in *-i* (*Orphei*); acc. plur. in short /a/ (*Dryadas*; also found in common nouns of Greek origin: *crateras, delphinas*, etc.). The nom. plur. ending in *-es* with a short vowel is perhaps favoured by metrical considerations, since it allows the poet to avoid a cretic sequence: cf. *Arcades* (7.4, etc.); *Proetides* (6.48); yet it has a primarily stylistic value, as is confirmed by its occurrence, without particular necessities, in the common noun *grypes* (8.27).

[67] Note also Numitorius' parody: 3.1n. Similar cases include *magis = potius* (*E.* 1.11); *da = dic* (1.18); *nec uertat bene = ne uertat bene* (9.6). Quite implausible, on the other hand, are attempts to find a 'true' vulgarism in *his = hi* (3.102n.).

[68] To this category belong nouns in *-men* and *-mentum*, which usually denote concrete objects, especially in the rural world: see the standard work by Perrot (1961); cf. Lipka (2001, pp. 16–21);

THE BUCOLIC BOOK   27

As for syntax, the search for simple yet elegant constructions led V. towards linguistic forms previously employed by the neoteric poets and often matching Greek usage: note the simple infinitives (1.55 *suadebit inire*; 5.9 *certet...superare*); *certare* + dat. (5.8; 8.55); and the infinitive governed by an adjective (5.1–2).[69] A Greek construction may also highlight the recollection of the model, as in the very noteworthy case of 8.41 (which presupposes *id.* 2.82). The marked position of the vocative, between noun and adjective, must be traced back to the neoteric style (cf. 6.10 *te nostrae, Vare, myricae*): the same goes for the use of parenthetic appositions, like *raucae, tua cura, palumbes* (*E.* 1.57), for which credit has been given to Cornelius Gallus (note the sobriquet *schema Cornelianum*, which is attested in Latin at least since Ennius; see n. ad loc.).

The use of anaphora and repetition, typical of Theocritus' pastoral style, is most probably meant to achieve a 'folk song' colour. Such devices abound in the *E.*, from the first poem (1.3–4) to the epilogue (10.75–7).[70] More specific to Roman taste is the use of alliteration. Already evident in the opening, where it suggests the pipe's delicate musicality (*Tityre, tu patulae*), alliteration often emphasizes meanings, as well as logical and syntactical links, sometimes with an effect of solemnity.[71] Finally, the evocation of spoken, colloquial language accounts for V.'s frequent use of hyperbaton and parentheses in the *E.*[72]

By blending elegance with colloquial tone, V.'s pastoral language proves to be very suitable both to lively dialogues and to the plain, immediate expression of the most intense emotions, such as Meliboeus' sorrow for the expropriations or Corydon's love for Alexis. Elevated vocabulary, in the wake of Hellenistic and neoteric poetry, occurs sporadically, dotting a flexible linguistic fabric which foreshadows the later developments of V.'s style, both epic and narrative. In conclusion, it must therefore be observed that already in the *E.*, V.'s linguistic creativity is

---

particularly significant is *incrementum* at 4.49. In *E.* 1, the everyday term *caseus* (34) alternates with a rather solemn periphrasis, *pressi copia lactis* (1.81n.). Other terms pertaining to agriculture: *depellere* (1.21; 3.82; 7.15); *fiscella* (10.71); *mulctra* (3.30); *nouale* (1.70); *praesepe* (7.39); *ruminare* (6.54); *upilio* (10.19). Attaining an individual bucolic style is the rationale behind V.'s preference for the adjective *formosus* (16x) over *pulcher* (2x), the latter occurring more frequently in the *Georgics* and the *Aeneid*: see Lipka (2001, pp. 8–10).

[69] Note also the acc. of respect, i.e. the so-called 'Greek' accusative (in fact a quite variable and complex construction, whose interpretation is debated), at *E.* 1.54 *florem...depasta*; 6.15 *inflatum...uenas*; 53 *latus...fultus*; 75 *succinctam...inguina*; 7.32 *suras euincta*; also 3.106 *inscripti nomina*, as well as the neut. sing. used adverbially at 3.63 *suaue rubens*; 4.43. For a collection of illustrative Virgilian passages, cf. Courtney (2004, with references); see further *Enc. Virg.* I, pp. 14–15, s.v. *accusativo alla greca* (E. Montanari).

[70] Cf. Nisbet (1991, pp. 2–6); further, with examples, Casanova-Robin (2007); comparable cases include the redoubled use of proper nouns, as in 2.69, and the epanalepsis at 6.20–1; cf. also 5.51–2n. On figures of repetition, generally very significant in Latin poetry, see Wills (1996).

[71] Examples in Merone (1961); see further *Enc. Virg.* I, pp. 113–16, s.v. *allitterazione* (A. De Rosalia); Di Lorenzo (1988); methodological definition and discussion, with bibliography, in Traina (1999b, pp. 75–7).

[72] Cf. *E.* 3.93; 8.109; 9.2–4; 23–5; 10.77; note also the elliptical construction at 3.1–2; 9.1 (two rather different instances, but both placed in a conspicuous, opening position); the euphemistic reticence at 3.8–9; and the sudden question, interrupting the thought, at 3.40, 8.7–8.

28 INTRODUCTION

expressed not so much through neologisms or other more noticeable innovations, but rather through inconspicuous slips of meaning or, syntactically, through constructions that deviate (albeit imperceptibly) from normal usage—all the while being intuitive and straightforward.[73] Thanks to this complexity of styles and registers, V.'s characters acquire substance: they are, we might say, enlivened.

Among the main reference works on the language and style of the *E.*, note the still valuable account offered by Nisbet (1991); for further reading and bibliography, see Perutelli (1995, esp. pp. 47–51); Lipka (2001, with excellent discussion); von Albrecht (2007, pp. 47–51); Maurach (2008); see also, with further references, *Enc. Virg.* I, pp. 572–6, s.v. *Bucoliche: 14 Lingua e metrica* (F. Cupaiuolo); *Virg. Enc.* II, pp. 820–6, s.v. *meter* (R. F. Thomas); III, pp. 1220–2, s.v. *style* (T. Reinhardt). More generally, on V.'s language, the reader can still profit from Bartoli (1900) and, specifically for the *E.*, Gimm (1910), to which we must add the two appendices on V.'s Latin in Jackson Knight (1966[2]) and the more recent Leclercq (1996); note also Horsfall (1995c) and Conte (2002 and 2007). The literature on more specific aspects of the *E.*'s language is vast. Several reference tools are available (among which see esp. Hofmann 1951, on the colloquial register of the herdsmen's dialogues [to be used alongside the Italian edition by L. Ricottilli, with further references, 2003[3]]). On Hellenizing features in V. and in Latin poetry, see Mayer (1999); on colloquial language in the *E.*, see Ottaviano (2013, pp. 11–12); also, more general and richly documented, Beghini (2020). On the Roman poetic language, much useful material is to be found in Lunelli (1980) (including Italian versions of famous papers by W. Kroll, H. H. Janssen, M. Leumann); on literary style more generally, see the standard work by Marouzeau (1946) (for verbal repetitions, cf. Marouzeau 1931); note also Bömer (1957). On V.'s sound effects specifically, the old work of Roiron (1908) may be complemented by Simonetti Abbolito (1987) (on euphony-cacophony, Hanssen 1942); on the so-called 'poetic plural', Gummere (1934); on chiastic structures, Pasini (1991). On minute aspects of morphology, for which the standard work is Leumann (1977), see Bömer (1953 and 1954); further De Nigris Mores (1972) (adj. in *-ax*); Segura Ramos (1974) (adj. in *-bilis*); Ernout (1949); Knox (1986) (both on adj. in *-osus*); Ernout (1970) (compounds with privative *in-*); Langlois (1961) (adj. in *-bundus*). See also, on diminutives, Gow (1932); Hakamies (1951); on hypocorisms, Opelt (1976). On V.'s neologisms, see the seminal Ladewig (1870), along with Lohmann (1915) on Hellenisms (on the inflection of Greek nouns, cf. Cottino 1906). Besides lexica and concordances, research on various aspect of V.'s vocabulary may profit from useful tools such as Ott (1974) and Bastianini (1982), which must be

---

[73] The *E.* contain the first kernel of the *Aeneid*'s linguistic innovation: V.'s language, esp. in the *Aeneid*, is distinctive not so much in terms of lexical register or word choice, but in terms of artful estrangement (which was harshly criticized by his detractors: cf. Don. *uita Verg.* 180–3 Brumm. = pp. 39.10–40.3 Brugn.-Stok); see further Conte (2002, pp. 5–63 = 2007, pp. 58–122). Dionysius of Halicarnassus, whose doctrine sums up many elements of the literary and rhetorical theory of V.'s time, insists on the idea that stylistic value is determined by *compositio* (διὰ τὴν σύνθεσιν) rather than by word choice (διὰ τὴν ἐκλογήν). The example offered by Dionysius is Telemachus' arrival to Eumaeus' hut in *Od.* 16.1–16, where Homer achieves great poetic force by employing words of everyday use, which could readily be uttered by a simple farmer (cf. Dion. Hal. *comp.* 3.7–12 Aujac-Lebel). See further de Jonge (2019, pp. 253–7, 264–5).

complemented by Lecrompe (1970) and Najock (2004), specifically on the *E.* For a thorough analysis of pastoral vocabulary (adj. and nouns), see Rumpf (1999). Devoted to several aspects of V.'s semantics and vocabulary are Heuzé (1985); Dubrocard (1990); and Dion (1993). On syntax, the standard work is still the old Antoine (1882), but for specific issues see, among the many available contributions, Vaccaro (1966); Malosti (1967); Serbat (1989). In particular, on the role of word order in defining expressiveness in V., and the mimetic or iconic use of hyperbaton, see Dainotti (2015).

5.4. Metre

Ancient metricians and interpreters had observed that a typical feature of Theocritus' hexameter style is the so-called 'bucolic diaeresis': i.e. the phenomenon by which the end of the fourth foot coincides with a word-boundary, where a syntactical break can add further emphasis. Bucolic diaeresis, which appears at the outset of the first idyll, occurs in the *E.* starting with the beginning of the first poem (1.7) and ending with the last line of the last poem (10.77).[74]

At times, V. openly displays the Hellenistic stylization of his hexameter. One of the most obvious instances is *E.* 2.24 (*Amphion Dircaeus in Actaeo Aracyntho*), which could, if transliterated into the Greek alphabet, easily appear in a poem by Callimachus or one of his successors. Yet, following a general trend of Roman poetry, the *E.*'s hexameter frees itself from the specific 'laws' (or tendencies) that previously governed Hellenistic hexameter poetry.[75] Compared to his Latin predecessors, V. intensifies dactylic rhythm in the first four feet of the hexameter (before him, by contrast, only the first foot was usually dactylic, while spondees prevailed in the following three).[76] Note also a considerable decrease in *spondeiazontes* hexameters (= lines with a spondee in the fifth foot, of which only three instances appear in the whole book: see *E.* 5.38n.; Ott 1978, p. 62). In general, V. tends to avoid metrical shapes that hold back the flow of the hexameter, such as molossus-shaped words (i.e. three consecutive long syllables). In contrast to neoteric usage, V. often employs enjambement, with the effect of connecting one line to another into long metrico-syntactical sequences: a sense break often coincides with the main caesura (a pattern even more evident in Ovid).[77]

---

[74] On bucolic diaeresis, which V. mainly employs in its dactylic form (i.e. with a dactylic fourth foot, usually occupied by a pyrrhic-shaped word), see Ceccarelli (2008, I, pp. 113–15).

[75] Cf. *Enc. Virg.* I, esp. p. 575b, s.v. *Bucoliche* (F. Cupaiuolo); Perutelli (1995, p. 52); more generally, *Enc. Virg.* II, pp. 375–9, s.v. *esametro* (F. Cupaiuolo); Horsfall (1995c, pp. 223–4); for a general overview and analysis of the main metrical phenomena in V., *Virg. Enc.* II, pp. 820–6, s.v. *meter* (R. F. Thomas). For a statistical analysis of rhythmical patterns in the *E.*, the standard work is still Ott (1978); but cf. also Duckworth (1969, pp. 46–62).

[76] The *E.*'s hexameter, however, features certain peculiarities that distinguish it clearly from that of *G.* and *Aen.*: see Ceccarelli's conclusions (2008, I, esp. pp. 82–3; 208–9).

[77] Note that *E.* 4 has opposite features, which confirm its neoteric character: esp. several molossi and fewer enjambements, for which cf. Catull. 64; see also below, p. 201.

30 INTRODUCTION

Among the distinctive traits of metre and prosody in the *E.*, in comparison to V.'s later works, note the relatively sparing (yet remarkable) use of elision.[78] By contrast, hiatus is proportionally more frequent in the *E.* than in *G.* and *Aen.* Usually appearing in Hellenizing contexts, hiatus generally affects a syllable in arsis (in the third foot: *E.* 3.6; in the fifth: 2.24), but it can also affect a shortened vowel in thesis (occurring in monosyllables: 2.65; 8.108), whereas it very rarely affects a naturally short syllable in thesis (2.53).[79] Certain cases of lengthening in arsis are best explained as echoes of archaic prosody: cf. *E.* 1.38; 3.97; 10.69 (still uncertain, however, is the case of *puer* at 9.66; but cf. 7.23). It is likely that V. meant to define his own pastoral style through specific devices, such as the clausula *et mihi Damon* (3.23n.).

6

Textual transmission

The editions by Ribbeck, Sabbadini, Mynors, Geymonat, and Conte (*Georgics* and *Aeneid*[80]) are standard works for V.'s text, as well as for the study of the manuscript tradition. The *E.* are now well served by S. Ottaviano's recent edition (2013), which is particularly noteworthy for its assessment of the manuscript tradition (including a systematic examination of six manuscripts in Beneventan script, each of which is assigned a siglum, while their consensus is denoted as *Λ*) and its thorough review of the Virgilian philological tradition from antiquity to the modern age.[81] As for the textual transmission of the *E.* (excluding the textual section between 3.72 and 4.51), we can consistently count on the testimony of at least two late antique manuscripts, as the reader can infer from the following synoptic account:

---

[78] Also known, more correctly, as synaloepha: *Enc. Virg.* II, pp. 201–2, s.v. *elisione* (M. Bonaria); still fundamental is Soubiran (1966).

[79] At 3.79 and 6.44, hiatus contributes to a very artful effect of rhythmic-prosodic variation; see *Enc. Virg.* II, pp. 886–8, s.v. *iato* (J. Veremans).

[80] Cf., respectively, *P. Vergilius Maro, Georgica*, edidit et apparatu critico instruxit G. B. Conte, Berlin-Boston 2013 (the same volume also features Ottaviano's edition of the *E.*, cited below); *P. Vergilius Maro Aeneis*, recensuit atque apparatu critico instruxit G. B. Conte, Berlin-New York 2009 (2019²; see further Conte 2016, 2020).

[81] A useful synthesis, specifically for the *E.*, is offered by Coleman, pp. 36–7; on the transmission of V.'s text, cf. Reynolds (1983); Geymonat (1995); further *Enc. Virg.* I, pp. 831–8, s.v. *codici* (M. Geymonat); III, pp. 432–43, s.v. *Medioevo, Tradizione manoscritta* (G. C. Alessio); pp. 964–5, s.v. *papiri* (A. Petrucci); *Virg. Enc.* II, pp. 786–8, s.v. *manuscripts* (C. E. Murgia, C. Kallendorf); II, pp. 966–7, s.v. *papyri and papyrology* (F. Schironi); III, pp. 1254–7, s.v. *text and transmission* (R. Tarrant). Among the most useful and noteworthy contributions to Virgilian philology, featuring divergent viewpoints, see Zetzel (1981, esp. pp. 27–54; 81–147); Timpanaro (1986 and 2001), cf. also Courtney (1981 and 2002–3).

M Mediceus (Florent. Laur. 39.1: late V cent.), containing 6.48–10.77 (but see below on γ);

P Palatinus (Vatic. Palat. Lat. 1631: V cent.), lacking 3.72–4.51 (but see below on a);

R Romanus (Vatic. Lat. 3867: early VI cent.), lacking 7.1–10.9;

V fragmenta Veronensia (Veron. XL (38): V cent.), containing 3.27–52, 5.86–6.20, 7.12–37, 8.19–44.

To the late antique manuscripts we should add other witnesses, namely the oldest Carolingian manuscripts, dating back to the ninth century. These include:

a Bernensis 172 (*E*. 1–*Aen*. 5) cum Parisino lat. 7929 (*Aen*. 6–12): the MS, cut into two halves, lacks 1.1–47 in its first half (it probably derives from R for the text of the *E*., and is therefore useful for recovering its readings in 7.1–10.9). The complete text of the *E*. is transmitted by: b Bernensis 165; c Bernensis 184; d Bernensis 255 + 239; e Bernensis 167 (deriving probably from a, but with many corrections);

f Oxoniensis Bodl. Auct. F. 2.8, complete, with the exception of 1.1–55;

h Valentianensis 407, complete;

r Parisinus lat. 7926, complete; s Parisinus lat. 7928, very fragmentary, containing 6.75–10.77; t Parisinus lat. 13043, lacking 1.1–8.11;

v Vaticanus lat. 1570 (late IX cent.), complete;

γ Guelferbytanus Gudianus lat. 2°.70, complete though very difficult to read due to its many corrections (probably a close relative of P, and therefore of some utility for recovering its readings in 3.72–4.51).

No significant contribution to the text of the *E*. has been made by the relatively scanty evidence found on papyri: note especially Pap. Strasb. Lat. 2 (Mertens-Pack[3] n. 2935), III–IV cent., containing *E*. 5.17–34 (Π_1), and Pap. Narm. inv. 66.362 (Mertens-Pack[3] n. 2935.1), I–II cent., containing *E*. 8.53–62.

Significant testimonies come from ancient grammarians, especially Servius, also surviving in an expanded version, i.e. the so-called Servius Danielis, or Servius auctus, first published by Pierre Daniel in 1600 (it is now a widely held view that the added material actually comes from other grammarians, including Donatus).[82] Finally, an inexhaustible source of information is provided by quotations of, or allusions to, V.'s text, which frequently occur in ancient literature.[83]

---

[82] On V.'s commentators, see now the useful overview in Zetzel (2018, pp. 262–7), with references.
[83] For the textual choices made here, diverging from Mynors' edition, see the *Note on the Text*, p. 35.

VIRGIL'S *ECLOGUES*

Virgil's *Eclogues*

Note on the text

The text printed here agrees with Mynors, with a few exceptions: *E.* 2.32; 4.52; 6.34; 8.43. Note also two passages in which my interpretation differs from Mynors' in terms of *personae loquentes* and use of quotation marks: Meliboeus in *E.* 7 (pp. 347–8); 8.105–6 (n. ad *E.* 8.105–8). In general, my punctuation frequently differs from Mynors' and Ottaviano's.

Ecloga I
MELIBOEUS TITYRUS

M. Tityre, tu patulae recubans sub tegmine fagi
   siluestrem tenui Musam meditaris auena;
   nos patriae finis et dulcia linquimus arua.
   nos patriam fugimus; tu, Tityre, lentus in umbra
   formosam resonare doces Amaryllida siluas.   5
T. O Meliboee, deus nobis haec otia fecit.
   namque erit ille mihi semper deus, illius aram
   saepe tener nostris ab ouilibus imbuet agnus.
   ille meas errare boues, ut cernis, et ipsum
   ludere quae uellem calamo permisit agresti.   10
M. Non equidem inuideo, miror magis: undique totis
   usque adeo turbatur agris. en ipse capellas
   protinus aeger ago; hanc etiam uix, Tityre, duco.
   hic inter densas corylos modo namque gemellos,
   spem gregis, a! silice in nuda conixa reliquit.   15
   saepe malum hoc nobis, si mens non laeua fuisset,
   de caelo tactas memini praedicere quercus.
   sed tamen iste deus qui sit, da, Tityre, nobis.
T. Vrbem quam dicunt Romam, Meliboee, putaui
   stultus ego huic nostrae similem, quo saepe solemus   20
   pastores ouium teneros depellere fetus.
   sic canibus catulos similis, sic matribus haedos
   noram, sic paruis componere magna solebam.
   uerum haec tantum alias inter caput extulit urbes

36 VIRGIL'S ECLOGUES

quantum lenta solent inter uiburna cupressi. 25
M. Et quae tanta fuit Romam tibi causa uidendi?
T. Libertas, quae sera tamen respexit inertem,
candidior postquam tondenti barba cadebat,
respexit tamen et longo post tempore uenit,
postquam nos Amaryllis habet, Galatea reliquit. 30
namque (fatebor enim) dum me Galatea tenebat,
nec spes libertatis erat nec cura peculi.
quamuis multa meis exiret uictima saeptis,
pinguis et ingratae premeretur caseus urbi,
non umquam grauis aere domum mihi dextra redibat. 35
M. Mirabar quid maesta deos, Amarylli, uocares,
cui pendere sua patereris in arbore poma;
Tityrus hinc aberat. ipsae te, Tityre, pinus,
ipsi te fontes, ipsa haec arbusta uocabant.
T. Quid facerem? neque seruitio me exire licebat 40
nec tam praesentis alibi cognoscere diuos.
hic illum uidi iuuenem, Meliboee, quotannis
bis senos cui nostra dies altaria fumant.
hic mihi responsum primus dedit ille petenti:
'pascite ut ante boues, pueri; summittite tauros'. 45
M. Fortunate senex, ergo tua rura manebunt
et tibi magna satis, quamuis lapis omnia nudus
limosoque palus obducat pascua iunco:
non insueta grauis temptabunt pabula fetas,
nec mala uicini pecoris contagia laedent. 50
fortunate senex, hic inter flumina nota
et fontis sacros frigus captabis opacum;
hinc tibi, quae semper, uicino ab limite saepes
Hyblaeis apibus florem depasta salicti
saepe leui somnum suadebit inire susurro; 55
hinc alta sub rupe canet frondator ad auras,
nec tamen interea raucae, tua cura, palumbes
nec gemere aëria cessabit turtur ab ulmo.
T. Ante leues ergo pascentur in aethere cerui
et freta destituent nudos in litore piscis, 60
ante pererratis amborum finibus exsul
aut Ararim Parthus bibet aut Germania Tigrim,
quam nostro illius labatur pectore uultus.
M. At nos hinc alii sitientis ibimus Afros,
pars Scythiam et rapidum cretae ueniemus Oaxen 65
et penitus toto diuisos orbe Britannos.

en umquam patrios longo post tempore finis
pauperis et tuguri congestum caespite culmen,
post aliquot, mea regna, uidens mirabor aristas?
impius haec tam culta noualia miles habebit,   70
barbarus has segetes. en quo discordia ciuis
produxit miseros: his nos conseuimus agros!
insere nunc, Meliboee, piros, pone ordine uitis.
ite meae, felix quondam pecus, ite capellae.
non ego uos posthac uiridi proiectus in antro   75
dumosa pendere procul de rupe uidebo;
carmina nulla canam; non me pascente, capellae,
florentem cytisum et salices carpetis amaras.
т. Hic tamen hanc mecum poteras requiescere noctem
fronde super uiridi: sunt nobis mitia poma,   80
castaneae molles et pressi copia lactis,
et iam summa procul uillarum culmina fumant
maioresque cadunt altis de montibus umbrae.

Ecloga II

Formosum pastor Corydon ardebat Alexin,
delicias domini, nec quid speraret habebat.
tantum inter densas, umbrosa cacumina, fagos
adsidue ueniebat. ibi haec incondita solus
montibus et siluis studio iactabat inani: 5
    'O crudelis Alexi, nihil mea carmina curas?
nil nostri miserere? mori me denique cogis?
nunc etiam pecudes umbras et frigora captant,
nunc uiridis etiam occultant spineta lacertos,
Thestylis et rapido fessis messoribus aestu   10
alia serpyllumque herbas contundit olentis.
at mecum raucis, tua dum uestigia lustro,
sole sub ardenti resonant arbusta cicadis.
nonne fuit satius tristis Amaryllidis iras
atque superba pati fastidia? nonne Menalcan,   15
quamuis ille niger, quamuis tu candidus esses?
o formose puer, nimium ne crede colori:
alba ligustra cadunt, uaccinia nigra leguntur.
despectus tibi sum, nec qui sim quaeris, Alexi,
quam diues pecoris, niuei quam lactis abundans.   20
mille meae Siculis errant in montibus agnae;
lac mihi non aestate nouum, non frigore defit.

38 VIRGIL'S *ECLOGUES*

canto quae solitus, si quando armenta uocabat,
Amphion Dircaeus in Actaeo Aracyntho.
nec sum adeo informis: nuper me in litore uidi, 25
cum placidum uentis staret mare. non ego Daphnin
iudice te metuam, si numquam fallit imago.
o tantum libeat mecum tibi sordida rura
atque humilis habitare casas et figere ceruos,
haedorumque gregem uiridi compellere hibisco! 30
mecum una in siluis imitabere Pana canendo
(Pan primus calamos cera coniungere pluris
instituit, Pan curat ouis ouiumque magistros),
nec te paeniteat calamo triuisse labellum:
haec eadem ut sciret, quid non faciebat Amyntas? 35
est mihi disparibus septem compacta cicutis
fistula, Damoetas dono mihi quam dedit olim,
et dixit moriens: 'te nunc habet ista secundum';
dixit Damoetas, inuidit stultus Amyntas.
praeterea duo nec tuta mihi ualle reperti 40
capreoli, sparsis etiam nunc pellibus albo,
bina die siccant ouis ubera; quos tibi seruo.
iam pridem a me illos abducere Thestylis orat;
et faciet, quoniam sordent tibi munera nostra.
huc ades, o formose puer: tibi lilia plenis 45
ecce ferunt Nymphae calathis; tibi candida Nais,
pallentis uiolas et summa papauera carpens,
narcissum et florem iungit bene olentis anethi;
tum casia atque aliis intexens suauibus herbis
mollia luteola pingit uaccinia calta. 50
ipse ego cana legam tenera lanugine mala
castaneasque nuces, mea quas Amaryllis amabat;
addam cerea pruna (honos erit huic quoque pomo),
et uos, o lauri, carpam et te, proxima myrte,
sic positae quoniam suauis miscetis odores. 55
rusticus es, Corydon; nec munera curat Alexis,
nec, si muneribus certes, concedat Iollas.
heu heu, quid uolui misero mihi? floribus Austrum
perditus et liquidis immisi fontibus apros.
quem fugis, a! demens? habitarunt di quoque siluas 60
Dardaniusque Paris. Pallas quas condidit arces
ipsa colat; nobis placeant ante omnia siluae.
torua leaena lupum sequitur, lupus ipse capellam,
florentem cytisum sequitur lasciua capella,

te Corydon, o Alexi: trahit sua quemque uoluptas.   65
aspice, aratra iugo referunt suspensa iuuenci,
et sol crescentis decedens duplicat umbras;
me tamen urit amor: quis enim modus adsit amori?
a, Corydon, Corydon, quae te dementia cepit?
semiputata tibi frondosa uitis in ulmo est: 70
quin tu aliquid saltem potius, quorum indiget usus,
uiminibus mollique paras detexere iunco?
inuenies alium, si te hic fastidit, Alexin.'

Ecloga III
Menalcas Damoetas Palaemon

M. Dic mihi, Damoeta, cuium pecus? an Meliboei?
D. Non, uerum Aegonis; nuper mihi tradidit Aegon.
M. Infelix o semper, oues, pecus! ipse Neaeram
    dum fouet ac ne me sibi praeferat illa ueretur,
    hic alienus ouis custos bis mulget in hora,   5
    et sucus pecori et lac subducitur agnis.
D. Parcius ista uiris tamen obicienda memento.
    nouimus et qui te transuersa tuentibus hircis
    et quo (sed faciles Nymphae risere) sacello.
M. Tum, credo, cum me arbustum uidere Miconis   10
    atque mala uitis incidere falce nouellas.
D. Aut hic ad ueteres fagos cum Daphnidis arcum
    fregisti et calamos: quae tu, peruerse Menalca,
    et cum uidisti puero donata, dolebas,
    et si non aliqua nocuisses, mortuus esses.   15
M. Quid domini faciant, audent cum talia fures?
    non ego te uidi Damonis, pessime, caprum
    excipere insidiis multum latrante Lycisca?
    et cum clamarem 'quo nunc se proripit ille?
    Tityre, coge pecus', tu post carecta latebas.   20
D. An mihi cantando uictus non redderet ille,
    quem mea carminibus meruisset fistula caprum?
    si nescis, meus ille caper fuit; et mihi Damon
    ipse fatebatur, sed reddere posse negabat.
M. Cantando tu illum? aut umquam tibi fistula cera   25
    iuncta fuit? non tu in triuiis, indocte, solebas
    stridenti miserum stipula disperdere carmen?
D. Vis ergo inter nos quid possit uterque uicissim
    experiamur? ego hanc uitulam (ne forte recuses,

40 VIRGIL'S *ECLOGUES*

bis uenit ad mulctram, binos alit ubere fetus)   30
depono; tu dic mecum quo pignore certes.

M. De grege non ausim quicquam deponere tecum:
est mihi namque domi pater, est iniusta nouerca,
bisque die numerant ambo pecus, alter et haedos.
uerum, id quod multo tute ipse fatebere maius   35
(insanire libet quoniam tibi), pocula ponam
fagina, caelatum diuini opus Alcimedontis,
lenta quibus torno facili superaddita uitis
diffusos hedera uestit pallente corymbos.
in medio duo signa, Conon et — quis fuit alter,   40
descripsit radio totum qui gentibus orbem,
tempora quae messor, quae curuus arator haberet?
necdum illis labra admoui, sed condita seruo.

D. Et nobis idem Alcimedon duo pocula fecit
et molli circum est ansas amplexus acantho,   45
Orpheaque in medio posuit siluasque sequentis;
necdum illis labra admoui, sed condita seruo.
si ad uitulam spectas, nihil est quod pocula laudes.

M. Numquam hodie effugies; ueniam quocumque uocaris.
audiat haec tantum — uel qui uenit ecce Palaemon: 50
efficiam posthac ne quemquam uoce lacessas.

D. Quin age, si quid habes; in me mora non erit ulla,
nec quemquam fugio: tantum, uicine Palaemon,
sensibus haec imis (res est non parua) reponas.

P. Dicite, quandoquidem in molli consedimus herba   55
et nunc omnis ager, nunc omnis parturit arbos,
nunc frondent siluae, nunc formosissimus annus.
incipe, Damoeta; tu deinde sequere, Menalca.
alternis dicetis; amant alterna Camenae.

D. Ab Ioue principium, Musae: Iouis omnia plena;   60
ille colit terras, illi mea carmina curae.

M. Et me Phoebus amat; Phoebo sua semper apud me
munera sunt, lauri et suaue rubens hyacinthus.

D. Malo me Galatea petit, lasciua puella,
et fugit ad salices et se cupit ante uideri.   65

M. At mihi sese offert ultro, meus ignis, Amyntas,
notior ut iam sit canibus non Delia nostris.

D. Parta meae Veneri sunt munera: namque notaui
ipse locum, aëriae quo congessere palumbes.

M. Quod potui, puero siluestri ex arbore lecta   70

aurea mala decem misi; cras altera mittam.
D. O quotiens et quae nobis Galatea locuta est!
    partem aliquam, uenti, diuum referatis ad auris!
M. Quid prodest quod me ipse animo non spernis, Amynta,
    si, dum tu sectaris apros, ego retia seruo? 75
D. Phyllida mitte mihi: meus est natalis, Iolla;
    cum faciam uitula pro frugibus, ipse uenito.
M. Phyllida amo ante alias; nam me discedere fleuit
    et longum 'formose, uale, uale', inquit, 'Iolla'.
D. Triste lupus stabulis, maturis frugibus imbres, 80
    arboribus uenti, nobis Amaryllidis irae.
M. Dulce satis umor, depulsis arbutus haedis,
    lenta salix feto pecori, mihi solus Amyntas.
D. Pollio amat nostram, quamuis est rustica, Musam:
    Pierides, uitulam lectori pascite uestro. 85
M. Pollio et ipse facit noua carmina: pascite taurum,
    iam cornu petat et pedibus qui spargat harenam.
D. Qui te, Pollio, amat, ueniat quo te quoque gaudet;
    mella fluant illi, ferat et rubus asper amomum.
M. Qui Bauium non odit, amet tua carmina, Maeui, 90
    atque idem iungat uulpes et mulgeat hircos.
D. Qui legitis flores et humi nascentia fraga,
    frigidus, o pueri (fugite hinc!), latet anguis in herba.
M. Parcite, oues, nimium procedere: non bene ripae
    creditur; ipse aries etiam nunc uellera siccat. 95
D. Tityre, pascentis a flumine reice capellas:
    ipse, ubi tempus erit, omnis in fonte lauabo.
M. Cogite ouis, pueri: si lac praeceperit aestus,
    ut nuper, frustra pressabimus ubera palmis.
D. Heu heu, quam pingui macer est mihi taurus in eruo! 100
    idem amor exitium pecori pecorisque magistro.
M. His certe neque amor causa est: uix ossibus haerent!
    nescio quis teneros oculus mihi fascinat agnos.
D. Dic quibus in terris (et eris mihi magnus Apollo)
    tris pateat caeli spatium non amplius ulnas. 105
M. Dic quibus in terris inscripti nomina regum
    nascantur flores, et Phyllida solus habeto.
P. Non nostrum inter uos tantas componere lites:
    et uitula tu dignus et hic, et quisquis amores
    aut metuet dulcis aut experietur amaros. 110
    claudite iam riuos, pueri; sat prata biberunt.

42 VIRGIL'S *ECLOGUES*

ECLOGA IV

Sicelides Musae, paulo maiora canamus!
non omnis arbusta iuuant humilesque myricae;
si canimus siluas, siluae sint consule dignae.
  Vltima Cumaei uenit iam carminis aetas;
magnus ab integro saeclorum nascitur ordo.   5
iam redit et Virgo, redeunt Saturnia regna,
iam noua progenies caelo demittitur alto.
tu modo nascenti puero, quo ferrea primum
desinet ac toto surget gens aurea mundo,
casta faue Lucina: tuus iam regnat Apollo.   10
teque adeo decus hoc aeui, te consule, inibit,
Pollio, et incipient magni procedere menses;
te duce, si qua manent sceleris uestigia nostri,
inrita perpetua soluent formidine terras.
ille deum uitam accipiet diuisque uidebit   15
permixtos heroas et ipse uidebitur illis,
pacatumque reget patriis uirtutibus orbem.
  At tibi prima, puer, nullo munuscula cultu
errantis hederas passim cum baccare tellus
mixtaque ridenti colocasia fundet acantho.   20
ipsae lacte domum referent distenta capellae
ubera, nec magnos metuent armenta leones;
ipsa tibi blandos fundent cunabula flores.
occidet et serpens, et fallax herba ueneni
occidet; Assyrium uulgo nascetur amomum.   25
at simul heroum laudes et facta parentis
iam legere et quae sit poteris cognoscere uirtus,
molli paulatim flauescet campus arista
incultisque rubens pendebit sentibus uua
et durae quercus sudabunt roscida mella.   30
pauca tamen suberunt priscae uestigia fraudis,
quae temptare Thetim ratibus, quae cingere muris
oppida, quae iubeant telluri infindere sulcos.
alter erit tum Tiphys et altera quae uehat Argo
delectos heroas; erunt etiam altera bella   35
atque iterum ad Troiam magnus mittetur Achilles.
hinc, ubi iam firmata uirum te fecerit aetas,
cedet et ipse mari uector, nec nautica pinus
mutabit merces; omnis feret omnia tellus.
non rastros patietur humus, non uinea falcem;   40
robustus quoque iam tauris iuga soluet arator.

nec uarios discet mentiri lana colores,
ipse sed in pratis aries iam suaue rubenti
murice, iam croceo mutabit uellera luto;
sponte sua sandyx pascentis uestiet agnos.   45
    'Talia saecla' suis dixerunt 'currite' fusis
concordes stabili fatorum numine Parcae.
adgredere o magnos (aderit iam tempus) honores,
cara deum suboles, magnum Iouis incrementum!
aspice conuexo nutantem pondere mundum,   50
terrasque tractusque maris caelumque profundum;
aspice, uenturo laetantur ut omnia saeclo!
o mihi tum longae maneat pars ultima uitae
spiritus et quantum sat erit tua dicere facta!
non me carminibus uincet nec Thracius Orpheus   55
nec Linus, huic mater quamuis atque huic pater adsit,
Orphei Calliopea, Lino formosus Apollo.
Pan etiam, Arcadia mecum si iudice certet,
Pan etiam Arcadia dicat se iudice uictum.
    Incipe, parue puer, risu cognoscere matrem   60
(matri longa decem tulerunt fastidia menses)
incipe, parue puer: qui non risere parenti,
nec deus hunc mensa, dea nec dignata cubili est.

Ecloga V
Menalcas Mopsus

Me. Cur non, Mopse, boni quoniam conuenimus ambo,
    tu calamos inflare leuis, ego dicere uersus,
    hic corylis mixtas inter consedimus ulmos?
Mo. Tu maior; tibi me est aequum parere, Menalca,
    siue sub incertas Zephyris motantibus umbras   5
    siue antro potius succedimus. aspice, ut antrum
    siluestris raris sparsit labrusca racemis.
Me. Montibus in nostris solus tibi certat Amyntas.
Mo. Quid, si idem certet Phoebum superare canendo?
Me. Incipe, Mopse, prior, si quos aut Phyllidis ignis   10
    aut Alconis habes laudes aut iurgia Codri.
    incipe: pascentis seruabit Tityrus haedos.
Mo. Immo haec, in uiridi nuper quae cortice fagi
    carmina descripsi et modulans alterna notaui,
    experiar: tu deinde iubeto ut certet Amyntas.   15
Me. Lenta salix quantum pallenti cedit oliuae,
    puniceis humilis quantum saliunca rosetis,

44 VIRGIL'S *ECLOGUES*

iudicio nostro tantum tibi cedit Amyntas.
sed tu desine plura, puer: successimus antro.
Mo. Exstinctum Nymphae crudeli funere Daphnin 20
flebant (uos coryli testes et flumina Nymphis),
cum complexa sui corpus miserabile nati
atque deos atque astra uocat crudelia mater.
non ulli pastos illis egere diebus
frigida, Daphni, boues ad flumina; nulla neque amnem 25
libauit quadripes nec graminis attigit herbam.
Daphni, tuum Poenos etiam ingemuisse leones
interitum montesque feri siluaeque loquuntur.
Daphnis et Armenias curru subiungere tigris
instituit, Daphnis thiasos inducere Bacchi 30
et foliis lentas intexere mollibus hastas.
uitis ut arboribus decori est, ut uitibus uuae,
ut gregibus tauri, segetes ut pinguibus aruis,
tu decus omne tuis. postquam te fata tulerunt,
ipsa Pales agros atque ipse reliquit Apollo. 35
grandia saepe quibus mandauimus hordea sulcis,
infelix lolium et steriles nascuntur auenae;
pro molli uiola, pro purpureo narcisso
carduus et spinis surgit paliurus acutis.
spargite humum foliis, inducite fontibus umbras, 40
pastores (mandat fieri sibi talia Daphnis),
et tumulum facite, et tumulo superaddite carmen:
'Daphnis ego in siluis, hinc usque ad sidera notus,
formosi pecoris custos, formosior ipse'.
Me. Tale tuum carmen nobis, diuine poeta, 45
quale sopor fessis in gramine, quale per aestum
dulcis aquae saliente sitim restinguere riuo.
nec calamis solum aequiperas, sed uoce magistrum:
fortunate puer, tu nunc eris alter ab illo.
nos tamen haec quocumque modo tibi nostra uicissim 50
dicemus, Daphninque tuum tollemus ad astra;
Daphnin ad astra feremus: amauit nos quoque Daphnis.
Mo. An quicquam nobis tali sit munere maius?
et puer ipse fuit cantari dignus, et ista
iam pridem Stimichon laudauit carmina nobis. 55
Me. Candidus insuetum miratur limen Olympi
sub pedibusque uidet nubes et sidera Daphnis.
ergo alacris siluas et cetera rura uoluptas
Panaque pastoresque tenet Dryadasque puellas.

nec lupus insidias pecori, nec retia ceruis 60
ulla dolum meditantur: amat bonus otia Daphnis.
ipsi laetitia uoces ad sidera iactant
intonsi montes; ipsae iam carmina rupes,
ipsa sonant arbusta: 'deus, deus ille, Menalca!'
sis bonus o felixque tuis! en quattuor aras: 65
ecce duas tibi, Daphni, duas altaria Phoebo.
pocula bina nouo spumantia lacte quotannis
craterasque duo statuam tibi pinguis oliui,
et multo in primis hilarans conuiuia Baccho
(ante focum, si frigus erit; si messis, in umbra) 70
uina nouum fundam calathis Ariusia nectar.
cantabunt mihi Damoetas et Lyctius Aegon;
saltantis Satyros imitabitur Alphesiboeus.
haec tibi semper erunt, et cum sollemnia uota
reddemus Nymphis, et cum lustrabimus agros. 75
dum iuga montis aper, fluuios dum piscis amabit,
dumque thymo pascentur apes, dum rore cicadae,
semper honos nomenque tuum laudesque manebunt.
ut Baccho Cererique, tibi sic uota quotannis
agricolae facient: damnabis tu quoque uotis. 80
Mo. Quae tibi, quae tali reddam pro carmine dona?
nam neque me tantum uenientis sibilus Austri
nec percussa iuuant fluctu tam litora, nec quae
saxosas inter decurrunt flumina uallis.
Me. Hac te nos fragili donabimus ante cicuta; 85
haec nos 'formosum Corydon ardebat Alexin',
haec eadem docuit 'cuium pecus? an Meliboei?'
Mo. At tu sume pedum, quod, me cum saepe rogaret,
non tulit Antigenes (et erat tum dignus amari),
formosum paribus nodis atque aere, Menalca. 90

Ecloga VI

Prima Syracosio dignata est ludere uersu
nostra neque erubuit siluas habitare Thalea;
cum canerem reges et proelia, Cynthius aurem
uellit et admonuit: 'pastorem, Tityre, pinguis
pascere oportet ouis, deductum dicere carmen'. 5
nunc ego (namque super tibi erunt qui dicere laudes,
Vare, tuas cupiant et tristia condere bella)
agrestem tenui meditabor harundine Musam:

non iniussa cano. si quis tamen haec quoque, si quis
captus amore leget, te nostrae, Vare, myricae,   10
te nemus omne canet; nec Phoebo gratior ulla est
quam sibi quae Vari praescripsit pagina nomen.
     Pergite, Pierides. Chromis et Mnasyllos in antro
Silenum pueri somno uidere iacentem,
inflatum hesterno uenas, ut semper, Iaccho;   15
serta procul tantum capiti delapsa iacebant
et grauis attrita pendebat cantharus ansa.
adgressi (nam saepe senex spe carminis ambo
luserat) iniciunt ipsis ex uincula sertis.
addit se sociam timidisque superuenit Aegle,   20
Aegle Naiadum pulcherrima, iamque uidenti
sanguineis frontem moris et tempora pingit.
ille dolum ridens 'quo uincula nectitis?' inquit;
'soluite me, pueri; satis est potuisse uideri.
carmina quae uultis cognoscite; carmina uobis,   25
huic aliud mercedis erit'. simul incipit ipse.
tum uero in numerum Faunosque ferasque uideres
ludere, tum rigidas motare cacumina quercus;
nec tantum Phoebo gaudet Parnasia rupes,
nec tantum Rhodope miratur et Ismarus Orphea.   30
     Namque canebat uti magnum per inane coacta
semina terrarumque animaeque marisque fuissent
et liquidi simul ignis; ut his ex omnia primis,
omnis et ipse tener mundi concreuerit orbis;
tum durare solum et discludere Nerea ponto   35
coeperit et rerum paulatim sumere formas;
iamque nouum terrae stupeant lucescere solem,
altius atque cadant summotis nubibus imbres,
incipiant siluae cum primum surgere cumque
rara per ignaros errent animalia montis.   40
hinc lapides Pyrrhae iactos, Saturnia regna,
Caucasiasque refert uolucris furtumque Promethei.
his adiungit, Hylan nautae quo fonte relictum
clamassent, ut litus 'Hyla, Hyla' omne sonaret;
et fortunatam, si numquam armenta fuissent,   45
Pasiphaen niuei solatur amore iuuenci.
a, uirgo infelix, quae te dementia cepit?
Proetides implerunt falsis mugitibus agros,
at non tam turpis pecudum tamen ulla secuta
concubitus, quamuis collo timuisset aratrum   50

nec lupus insidias pecori, nec retia ceruis 60
ulla dolum meditantur: amat bonus otia Daphnis.
ipsi laetitia uoces ad sidera iactant
intonsi montes; ipsae iam carmina rupes,
ipsa sonant arbusta: 'deus, deus ille, Menalca!'
sis bonus o felixque tuis! en quattuor aras: 65
ecce duas tibi, Daphni, duas altaria Phoebo.
pocula bina nouo spumantia lacte quotannis
craterasque duo statuam tibi pinguis oliui,
et multo in primis hilarans conuiuia Baccho
(ante focum, si frigus erit; si messis, in umbra) 70
uina nouum fundam calathis Ariusia nectar.
cantabunt mihi Damoetas et Lyctius Aegon;
saltantis Satyros imitabitur Alphesiboeus.
haec tibi semper erunt, et cum sollemnia uota
reddemus Nymphis, et cum lustrabimus agros. 75
dum iuga montis aper, fluuios dum piscis amabit,
dumque thymo pascentur apes, dum rore cicadae,
semper honos nomenque tuum laudesque manebunt.
ut Baccho Cererique, tibi sic uota quotannis
agricolae facient: damnabis tu quoque uotis. 80
Mo. Quae tibi, quae tali reddam pro carmine dona?
nam neque me tantum uenientis sibilus Austri
nec percussa iuuant fluctu tam litora, nec quae
saxosas inter decurrunt flumina uallis.
Me. Hac te nos fragili donabimus ante cicuta; 85
haec nos 'formosum Corydon ardebat Alexin',
haec eadem docuit 'cuium pecus? an Meliboei?'
Mo. At tu sume pedum, quod, me cum saepe rogaret,
non tulit Antigenes (et erat tum dignus amari),
formosum paribus nodis atque aere, Menalca. 90

ECLOGA VI

Prima Syracosio dignata est ludere uersu
nostra neque erubuit siluas habitare Thalea;
cum canerem reges et proelia, Cynthius aurem
uellit et admonuit: 'pastorem, Tityre, pinguis
pascere oportet ouis, deductum dicere carmen'. 5
nunc ego (namque super tibi erunt qui dicere laudes,
Vare, tuas cupiant et tristia condere bella)
agrestem tenui meditabor harundine Musam:

46 VIRGIL'S *ECLOGUES*

non iniussa cano. si quis tamen haec quoque, si quis
captus amore leget, te nostrae, Vare, myricae,   10
te nemus omne canet; nec Phoebo gratior ulla est
quam sibi quae Vari praescripsit pagina nomen.
    Pergite, Pierides. Chromis et Mnasyllos in antro
Silenum pueri somno uidere iacentem,
inflatum hesterno uenas, ut semper, Iaccho;   15
serta procul tantum capiti delapsa iacebant
et grauis attrita pendebat cantharus ansa.
adgressi (nam saepe senex spe carminis ambo
luserat) iniciunt ipsis ex uincula sertis.
addit se sociam timidisque superuenit Aegle,   20
Aegle Naiadum pulcherrima, iamque uidenti
sanguineis frontem moris et tempora pingit.
ille dolum ridens 'quo uincula nectitis?' inquit;
'soluite me, pueri; satis est potuisse uideri.
carmina quae uultis cognoscite; carmina uobis,   25
huic aliud mercedis erit'. simul incipit ipse.
tum uero in numerum Faunosque ferasque uideres
ludere, tum rigidas motare cacumina quercus;
nec tantum Phoebo gaudet Parnasia rupes,
nec tantum Rhodope miratur et Ismarus Orphea.   30
    Namque canebat uti magnum per inane coacta
semina terrarumque animaeque marisque fuissent
et liquidi simul ignis; ut his ex omnia primis,
omnis et ipse tener mundi concreuerit orbis;
tum durare solum et discludere Nerea ponto   35
coeperit et rerum paulatim sumere formas;
iamque nouum terrae stupeant lucescere solem,
altius atque cadant summotis nubibus imbres,
incipiant siluae cum primum surgere cumque
rara per ignaros errent animalia montis.   40
hinc lapides Pyrrhae iactos, Saturnia regna,
Caucasiasque refert uolucris furtumque Promethei.
his adiungit, Hylan nautae quo fonte relictum
clamassent, ut litus 'Hyla, Hyla' omne sonaret;
et fortunatam, si numquam armenta fuissent,   45
Pasiphaen niuei solatur amore iuuenci.
a, uirgo infelix, quae te dementia cepit?
Proetides implerunt falsis mugitibus agros,
at non tam turpis pecudum tamen ulla secuta
concubitus, quamuis collo timuisset aratrum   50

et saepe in leui quaesisset cornua fronte.
a! uirgo infelix, tu nunc in montibus erras:
ille latus niueum molli fultus hyacintho
ilice sub nigra pallentis ruminat herbas
aut aliquam in magno sequitur grege. 'claudite, Nymphae,   55
Dictaeae Nymphae, nemorum iam claudite saltus,
si qua forte ferant oculis sese obuia nostris
errabunda bouis uestigia; forsitan illum
aut herba captum uiridi aut armenta secutum
perducant aliquae stabula ad Gortynia uaccae'.   60
tum canit Hesperidum miratam mala puellam;
tum Phaethontiadas musco circumdat amarae
corticis atque solo proceras erigit alnos.
tum canit, errantem Permessi ad flumina Gallum
Aonas in montis ut duxerit una sororum,   65
utque uiro Phoebi chorus adsurrexerit omnis;
ut Linus haec illi diuino carmine pastor
floribus atque apio crinis ornatus amaro
dixerit: 'hos tibi dant calamos (en accipe) Musae,
Ascraeo quos ante seni, quibus ille solebat   70
cantando rigidas deducere montibus ornos.
his tibi Grynei nemoris dicatur origo,
ne quis sit lucus quo se plus iactet Apollo'.
    Quid loquar aut Scyllam Nisi, quam fama secuta est
candida succinctam latrantibus inguina monstris   75
Dulichias uexasse rates et gurgite in alto
a! timidos nautas canibus lacerasse marinis;
aut ut mutatos Terei narrauerit artus,
quas illi Philomela dapes, quae dona pararit,
quo cursu deserta petiuerit et quibus ante   80
infelix sua tecta super uolitauerit alis?
omnia, quae Phoebo quondam meditante beatus
audiit Eurotas iussitque ediscere lauros,
ille canit, pulsae referunt ad sidera ualles;
cogere donec ouis stabulis numerumque referre   85
iussit et inuito processit Vesper Olympo.

ECLOGA VII

MELIBOEUS

M. Forte sub arguta consederat ilice Daphnis,
    compulerantque greges Corydon et Thyrsis in unum,

48   VIRGIL'S *ECLOGUES*

Thyrsis ouis, Corydon distentas lacte capellas,
ambo florentes aetatibus, Arcades ambo,
et cantare pares et respondere parati.   5
huc mihi, dum teneras defendo a frigore myrtos,
uir gregis ipse caper deerrauerat; atque ego Daphnin
aspicio. ille ubi me contra uidet, 'ocius' inquit
'huc ades, o Meliboee; caper tibi saluus et haedi;
et, si quid cessare potes, requiesce sub umbra.   10
huc ipsi potum uenient per prata iuuenci,
hic uiridis tenera praetexit harundine ripas
Mincius, eque sacra resonant examina quercu'.
quid facerem? neque ego Alcippen nec Phyllida habebam
depulsos a lacte domi quae clauderet agnos,   15
et certamen erat, Corydon cum Thyrside, magnum;
posthabui tamen illorum mea seria ludo.
alternis igitur contendere uersibus ambo
coepere, alternos Musae meminisse uolebant.
hos Corydon, illos referebat in ordine Thyrsis: 20
C. 'Nymphae noster amor Libethrides, aut mihi carmen,
quale meo Codro, concedite (proxima Phoebi
uersibus ille facit) aut, si non possumus omnes,
hic arguta sacra pendebit fistula pinu.
T. Pastores, hedera crescentem ornate poetam,   25
Arcades, inuidia rumpantur ut ilia Codro;
aut, si ultra placitum laudarit, baccare frontem
cingite, ne uati noceat mala lingua futuro.
C. Saetosi caput hoc apri tibi, Delia, paruus
et ramosa Micon uiuacis cornua cerui.   30
si proprium hoc fuerit, leui de marmore tota
puniceo stabis suras euincta coturno.
T. Sinum lactis et haec te liba, Priape, quotannis
exspectare sat est: custos es pauperis horti.
nunc te marmoreum pro tempore fecimus; at tu,   35
si fetura gregem suppleuerit, aureus esto.
C. Nerine Galatea, thymo mihi dulcior Hyblae,
candidior cycnis, hedera formosior alba,
cum primum pasti repetent praesepia tauri,
si qua tui Corydonis habet te cura, uenito.   40
T. Immo ego Sardoniis uidear tibi amarior herbis,
horridior rusco, proiecta uilior alga,
si mihi non haec lux toto iam longior anno est.
ite domum pasti, si quis pudor, ite iuuenci.

ECLOGA VIII 49

c. Muscosi fontes et somno mollior herba,   45
    et quae uos rara uiridis tegit arbutus umbra,
    solstitium pecori defendite: iam uenit aestas
    torrida, iam lento turgent in palmite gemmae.
t. Hic focus et taedae pingues, hic plurimus ignis
    semper, et adsidua postes fuligine nigri.   50
    hic tantum Boreae curamus frigora quantum
    aut numerum lupus aut torrentia flumina ripas.
c. Stant et iuniperi et castaneae hirsutae,
    strata iacent passim sua quaeque sub arbore poma,
    omnia nunc rident: at si formosus Alexis   55
    montibus his abeat, uideas et flumina sicca.
t. Aret ager, uitio moriens sitit aëris herba,
    Liber pampineas inuidit collibus umbras:
    Phyllidis aduentu nostrae nemus omne uirebit,
    Iuppiter et laeto descendet plurimus imbri.   60
c. Populus Alcidae gratissima, uitis Iaccho,
    formosae myrtus Veneri, sua laurea Phoebo;
    Phyllis amat corylos: illas dum Phyllis amabit,
    nec myrtus uincet corylos, nec laurea Phoebi.
t. Fraxinus in siluis pulcherrima, pinus in hortis,   65
    populus in fluuiis, abies in montibus altis:
    saepius at si me, Lycida formose, reuisas,
    fraxinus in siluis cedat tibi, pinus in hortis'.
        Haec memini, et uictum frustra contendere Thyrsin.
    ex illo Corydon Corydon est tempore nobis.   70

Ecloga VIII

Pastorum Musam Damonis et Alphesiboei,
immemor herbarum quos est mirata iuuenca
certantis, quorum stupefactae carmine lynces,
et mutata suos requierunt flumina cursus,
Damonis Musam dicemus et Alphesiboei.   5
tu mihi, seu magni superas iam saxa Timaui
siue oram Illyrici legis aequoris, — en erit umquam
ille dies, mihi cum liceat tua dicere facta?
en erit ut liceat totum mihi ferre per orbem
sola Sophocleo tua carmina digna coturno?   10
a te principium, tibi desinam: accipe iussis
carmina coepta tuis, atque hanc sine tempora circum
inter uictricis hederam tibi serpere lauros.

50 VIRGIL'S *ECLOGUES*

Frigida uix caelo noctis decesserat umbra,
cum ros in tenera pecori gratissimus herba: 15
incumbens tereti Damon sic coepit oliuae.

D. Nascere praeque diem ueniens age, Lucifer, almum,
coniugis indigno Nysae deceptus amore
dum queror et diuos, quamquam nil testibus illis
profeci, extrema moriens tamen adloquor hora. 20
  incipe Maenalios mecum, mea tibia, uersus.
Maenalus argutumque nemus pinusque loquentis
semper habet, semper pastorum ille audit amores
Panaque, qui primus calamos non passus inertis.
  incipe Maenalios mecum, mea tibia, uersus. 25
Mopso Nysa datur: quid non speremus amantes?
iungentur iam grypes equis, aeuoque sequenti
cum canibus timidi uenient ad pocula dammae.
  incipe Maenalios mecum, mea tibia, uersus. 28a
Mopse, nouas incide faces: tibi ducitur uxor.
sparge, marite, nuces: tibi deserit Hesperus Oetam. 30
  incipe Maenalios mecum, mea tibia, uersus.
o digno coniuncta uiro, dum despicis omnis,
dumque tibi est odio mea fistula dumque capellae
hirsutumque supercilium promissaque barba,
nec curare deum credis mortalia quemquam. 35
  incipe Maenalios mecum, mea tibia, uersus.
saepibus in nostris paruam te roscida mala
(dux ego uester eram) uidi cum matre legentem.
alter ab undecimo tum me iam acceperat annus,
iam fragilis poteram a terra contingere ramos: 40
ut uidi, ut perii, ut me malus abstulit error!
  incipe Maenalios mecum, mea tibia, uersus.
nunc scio quid sit Amor: duris in cautibus illum
aut Tmaros aut Rhodope aut extremi Garamantes
nec generis nostri puerum nec sanguinis edunt. 45
  incipe Maenalios mecum, mea tibia, uersus.
saeuus Amor docuit natorum sanguine matrem
commaculare manus; crudelis tu quoque, mater.
crudelis mater magis, an puer improbus ille?
improbus ille puer; crudelis tu quoque, mater. 50
  incipe Maenalios mecum, mea tibia, uersus.
nunc et ouis ultro fugiat lupus, aurea durae
mala ferant quercus, narcisso floreat alnus,
pinguia corticibus sudent electra myricae,

certent et cycnis ululae, sit Tityrus Orpheus,   55
Orpheus in siluis, inter delphinas Arion.
   incipe Maenalios mecum, mea tibia, uersus.
omnia uel medium fiat mare. uiuite siluae:
praeceps aërii specula de montis in undas
deferar; extremum hoc munus morientis habeto.   60
   desine Maenalios, iam desine, tibia, uersus.
Haec Damon; uos, quae responderit Alphesiboeus,
dicite, Pierides: non omnia possumus omnes.
A. Effer aquam et molli cinge haec altaria uitta
uerbenasque adole pinguis et mascula tura,   65
coniugis ut magicis sanos auertere sacris
experiar sensus; nihil hic nisi carmina desunt.
   ducite ab urbe domum, mea carmina, ducite Daphnin.
carmina uel caelo possunt deducere lunam,
carminibus Circe socios mutauit Vlixi,   70
frigidus in pratis cantando rumpitur anguis.
   ducite ab urbe domum, mea carmina, ducite Daphnin.
terna tibi haec primum triplici diuersa colore
licia circumdo, terque haec altaria circum
effigiem duco; numero deus impare gaudet.   75
   ducite ab urbe domum, mea carmina, ducite Daphnin.
necte tribus nodis ternos, Amarylli, colores;
necte, Amarylli, modo et 'Veneris' dic 'uincula necto'.
   ducite ab urbe domum, mea carmina, ducite Daphnin.
limus ut hic durescit, et haec ut cera liquescit   80
uno eodemque igni, sic nostro Daphnis amore.
sparge molam et fragilis incende bitumine lauros:
Daphnis me malus urit, ego hanc in Daphnide laurum.
   ducite ab urbe domum, mea carmina, ducite Daphnin.
talis amor Daphnin qualis cum fessa iuuencum   85
per nemora atque altos quaerendo bucula lucos
propter aquae riuum uiridi procumbit in ulua
perdita, nec serae meminit decedere nocti,
talis amor teneat, nec sit mihi cura mederi.
   ducite ab urbe domum, mea carmina, ducite Daphnin.   90
has olim exuuias mihi perfidus ille reliquit,
pignora cara sui, quae nunc ego limine in ipso,
Terra, tibi mando; debent haec pignora Daphnin.
   ducite ab urbe domum, mea carmina, ducite Daphnin.
has herbas atque haec Ponto mihi lecta uenena   95
ipse dedit Moeris (nascuntur plurima Ponto);

52 VIRGIL'S *ECLOGUES*

his ego saepe lupum fieri et se condere siluis
Moerim, saepe animas imis excire sepulcris,
atque satas alio uidi traducere messis.
    ducite ab urbe domum, mea carmina, ducite Daphnin.   100
fer cineres, Amarylli, foras riuoque fluenti
transque caput iace, nec respexeris. his ego Daphnin
adgrediar; nihil ille deos, nil carmina curat.
    ducite ab urbe domum, mea carmina, ducite Daphnin.
aspice: corripuit tremulis altaria flammis   105
sponte sua, dum ferre moror, cinis ipse. bonum sit!
nescio quid certe est, et Hylax in limine latrat.
credimus? an, qui amant, ipsi sibi somnia fingunt?
    parcite, ab urbe uenit, iam parcite carmina, Daphnis.

ECLOGA IX

LYCIDAS MOERIS

L. Quo te, Moeri, pedes? an, quo uia ducit, in urbem?
M. O Lycida, uiui peruenimus, aduena nostri
    (quod numquam ueriti sumus) ut possessor agelli
    diceret: 'haec mea sunt; ueteres migrate coloni'.
    nunc uicti, tristes, quoniam fors omnia uersat,   5
    hos illi (quod nec uertat bene) mittimus haedos.
L. Certe equidem audieram, qua se subducere colles
    incipiunt mollique iugum demittere cliuo,
    usque ad aquam et ueteres, iam fracta cacumina, fagos,
    omnia carminibus uestrum seruasse Menalcan.   10
M. Audieras, et fama fuit; sed carmina tantum
    nostra ualent, Lycida, tela inter Martia quantum
    Chaonias dicunt aquila ueniente columbas.
    quod nisi me quacumque nouas incidere lites
    ante sinistra caua monuisset ab ilice cornix,   15
    nec tuus hic Moeris nec uiueret ipse Menalcas.
L. Heu, cadit in quemquam tantum scelus? heu, tua nobis
    paene simul tecum solacia rapta, Menalca!
    quis caneret Nymphas? quis humum florentibus herbis
    spargeret aut uiridi fontis induceret umbra?   20
    uel quae sublegi tacitus tibi carmina nuper,
    cum te ad delicias ferres Amaryllida nostras:
    'Tityre, dum redeo (breuis est uia), pasce capellas,
    et potum pastas age, Tityre, et inter agendum
    occursare capro (cornu ferit ille) caueto'.   25

certent et cycnis ululae, sit Tityrus Orpheus, 55
Orpheus in siluis, inter delphinas Arion.
    incipe Maenalios mecum, mea tibia, uersus.
omnia uel medium fiat mare. uiuite siluae:
praeceps aërii specula de montis in undas
deferar; extremum hoc munus morientis habeto. 60
    desine Maenalios, iam desine, tibia, uersus.
Haec Damon; uos, quae responderit Alphesiboeus,
dicite, Pierides: non omnia possumus omnes.

A. Effer aquam et molli cinge haec altaria uitta
uerbenasque adole pinguis et mascula tura, 65
coniugis ut magicis sanos auertere sacris
experiar sensus; nihil hic nisi carmina desunt.
    ducite ab urbe domum, mea carmina, ducite Daphnin.
carmina uel caelo possunt deducere lunam,
carminibus Circe socios mutauit Vlixi, 70
frigidus in pratis cantando rumpitur anguis.
    ducite ab urbe domum, mea carmina, ducite Daphnin.
terna tibi haec primum triplici diuersa colore
licia circumdo, terque haec altaria circum
effigiem duco; numero deus impare gaudet. 75
    ducite ab urbe domum, mea carmina, ducite Daphnin.
necte tribus nodis ternos, Amarylli, colores;
necte, Amarylli, modo et 'Veneris' dic 'uincula necto'.
    ducite ab urbe domum, mea carmina, ducite Daphnin.
limus ut hic durescit, et haec ut cera liquescit 80
uno eodemque igni, sic nostro Daphnis amore.
sparge molam et fragilis incende bitumine lauros:
Daphnis me malus urit, ego hanc in Daphnide laurum.
    ducite ab urbe domum, mea carmina, ducite Daphnin.
talis amor Daphnin qualis cum fessa iuuencum 85
per nemora atque altos quaerendo bucula lucos
propter aquae riuum uiridi procumbit in ulua
perdita, nec serae meminit decedere nocti,
talis amor teneat, nec sit mihi cura mederi.
    ducite ab urbe domum, mea carmina, ducite Daphnin. 90
has olim exuuias mihi perfidus ille reliquit,
pignora cara sui, quae nunc ego limine in ipso,
Terra, tibi mando; debent haec pignora Daphnin.
    ducite ab urbe domum, mea carmina, ducite Daphnin.
has herbas atque haec Ponto mihi lecta uenena 95
ipse dedit Moeris (nascuntur plurima Ponto);

his ego saepe lupum fieri et se condere siluis
Moerim, saepe animas imis excire sepulcris,
atque satas alio uidi traducere messis.
    ducite ab urbe domum, mea carmina, ducite Daphnin.   100
fer cineres, Amarylli, foras riuoque fluenti
transque caput iace, nec respexeris. his ego Daphnin
adgrediar; nihil ille deos, nil carmina curat.
    ducite ab urbe domum, mea carmina, ducite Daphnin.
aspice: corripuit tremulis altaria flammis   105
sponte sua, dum ferre moror, cinis ipse. bonum sit!
nescio quid certe est, et Hylax in limine latrat.
credimus? an, qui amant, ipsi sibi somnia fingunt?
    parcite, ab urbe uenit, iam parcite carmina, Daphnis.

Ecloga IX

LYCIDAS MOERIS

L. Quo te, Moeri, pedes? an, quo uia ducit, in urbem?
M. O Lycida, uiui peruenimus, aduena nostri
    (quod numquam ueriti sumus) ut possessor agelli
    diceret: 'haec mea sunt; ueteres migrate coloni'.
    nunc uicti, tristes, quoniam fors omnia uersat,   5
    hos illi (quod nec uertat bene) mittimus haedos.
L. Certe equidem audieram, qua se subducere colles
    incipiunt mollique iugum demittere cliuo,
    usque ad aquam et ueteres, iam fracta cacumina, fagos,
    omnia carminibus uestrum seruasse Menalcan.   10
M. Audieras, et fama fuit; sed carmina tantum
    nostra ualent, Lycida, tela inter Martia quantum
    Chaonias dicunt aquila ueniente columbas.
    quod nisi me quacumque nouas incidere lites
    ante sinistra caua monuisset ab ilice cornix,   15
    nec tuus hic Moeris nec uiueret ipse Menalcas.
L. Heu, cadit in quemquam tantum scelus? heu, tua nobis
    paene simul tecum solacia rapta, Menalca!
    quis caneret Nymphas? quis humum florentibus herbis
    spargeret aut uiridi fontis induceret umbra?   20
    uel quae sublegi tacitus tibi carmina nuper,
    cum te ad delicias ferres Amaryllida nostras:
    'Tityre, dum redeo (breuis est uia), pasce capellas,
    et potum pastas age, Tityre, et inter agendum
    occursare capro (cornu ferit ille) caueto'.   25

ECLOGA IX 53

M. Immo haec, quae Varo necdum perfecta canebat:
   'Vare, tuum nomen, superet modo Mantua nobis,
   Mantua uae miserae nimium uicina Cremonae,
   cantantes sublime ferent ad sidera cycni'.
L. Sic tua Cyrneas fugiant examina taxos,   30
   sic cytiso pastae distendant ubera uaccae,
   incipe, si quid habes. et me fecere poetam
   Pierides, sunt et mihi carmina, me quoque dicunt
   uatem pastores; sed non ego credulus illis.
   nam neque adhuc Vario uideor nec dicere Cinna   35
   digna, sed argutos inter strepere anser olores.
M. Id quidem ago et tacitus, Lycida, mecum ipse uoluto,
   si ualeam meminisse; neque est ignobile carmen.
   'huc ades, o Galatea; quis est nam ludus in undis?
   hic uer purpureum, uarios hic flumina circum   40
   fundit humus flores, hic candida populus antro
   imminet et lentae texunt umbracula uites.
   huc ades; insani feriant sine litora fluctus'.
L. Quid, quae te pura solum sub nocte canentem
   audieram? numeros memini, si uerba tenerem: 45
   'Daphni, quid antiquos signorum suspicis ortus?
   ecce Dionaei processit Caesaris astrum,
   astrum quo segetes gauderent frugibus et quo
   duceret apricis in collibus uua colorem.
   insere, Daphni, piros: carpent tua poma nepotes'.   50
M. Omnia fert aetas, animum quoque. saepe ego longos
   cantando puerum memini me condere soles.
   nunc oblita mihi tot carmina, uox quoque Moerim
   iam fugit ipsa: lupi Moerim uidere priores.
   sed tamen ista satis referet tibi saepe Menalcas.   55
L. Causando nostros in longum ducis amores.
   et nunc omne tibi stratum silet aequor, et omnes,
   aspice, uentosi ceciderunt murmuris aurae.
   hinc adeo media est nobis uia; namque sepulcrum
   incipit apparere Bianoris. hic, ubi densas   60
   agricolae stringunt frondes, hic, Moeri, canamus;
   hic haedos depone: tamen ueniemus in urbem.
   aut si nox pluuiam ne colligat ante ueremur,
   cantantes licet usque (minus uia laedet) eamus;
   cantantes ut eamus, ego hoc te fasce leuabo.   65
M. Desine plura, puer, et quod nunc instat agamus;
   carmina tum melius, cum uenerit ipse, canemus.

ECLOGA X

Extremum hunc, Arethusa, mihi concede laborem:
pauca meo Gallo, sed quae legat ipsa Lycoris,
carmina sunt dicenda; neget quis carmina Gallo?
sic tibi, cum fluctus subterlabere Sicanos,
Doris amara suam non intermisceat undam,   5
incipe: sollicitos Galli dicamus amores,
dum tenera attondent simae uirgulta capellae.
non canimus surdis, respondent omnia siluae.
     Quae nemora aut qui uos saltus habuere, puellae
Naides, indigno cum Gallus amore peribat?   10
nam neque Parnasi uobis iuga, nam neque Pindi
ulla moram fecere, neque Aonie Aganippe.
illum etiam lauri, etiam fleuere myricae,
pinifer illum etiam sola sub rupe iacentem
Maenalus et gelidi fleuerunt saxa Lycaei.   15
stant et oues circum (nostri nec paenitet illas,
nec te paeniteat pecoris, diuine poeta:
et formosus ouis ad flumina pauit Adonis),
uenit et upilio, tardi uenere subulci,
uuidus hiberna uenit de glande Menalcas.   20
omnes 'unde amor iste' rogant 'tibi?' uenit Apollo:
'Galle, quid insanis?' inquit. 'tua cura Lycoris
perque niues alium perque horrida castra secuta est'.
uenit et agresti capitis Siluanus honore,
florentis ferulas et grandia lilia quassans.   25
Pan deus Arcadiae uenit, quem uidimus ipsi
sanguineis ebuli bacis minioque rubentem.
'ecquis erit modus?' inquit. 'Amor non talia curat,
nec lacrimis crudelis Amor nec gramina riuis
nec cytiso saturantur apes nec fronde capellae'.   30
tristis at ille 'tamen cantabitis, Arcades', inquit
'montibus haec uestris: soli cantare periti
Arcades. o mihi tum quam molliter ossa quiescant,
uestra meos olim si fistula dicat amores!
atque utinam ex uobis unus uestrique fuissem   35
aut custos gregis aut maturae uinitor uuae!
certe siue mihi Phyllis siue esset Amyntas
seu quicumque furor (quid tum, si fuscus Amyntas?
et nigrae uiolae sunt et uaccinia nigra),
mecum inter salices lenta sub uite iaceret;   40

serta mihi Phyllis legeret, cantaret Amyntas.
hic gelidi fontes, hic mollia prata, Lycori,
hic nemus; hic ipso tecum consumerer aeuo.
nunc insanus amor duri me Martis in armis
tela inter media atque aduersos detinet hostis.   45
tu procul a patria (nec sit mihi credere tantum)
Alpinas, a! dura niues et frigora Rheni
me sine sola uides. a, te ne frigora laedant!
a, tibi ne teneras glacies secet aspera plantas!
ibo et Chalcidico quae sunt mihi condita uersu   50
carmina pastoris Siculi modulabor auena.
certum est in siluis inter spelaea ferarum
malle pati tenerisque meos incidere amores
arboribus: crescent illae, crescetis, amores.
interea mixtis lustrabo Maenala Nymphis   55
aut acris uenabor apros. non me ulla uetabunt
frigora Parthenios canibus circumdare saltus.
iam mihi per rupes uideor lucosque sonantis
ire, libet Partho torquere Cydonia cornu
spicula — tamquam haec sit nostri medicina furoris,   60
aut deus ille malis hominum mitescere discat.
iam neque Hamadryades rursus nec carmina nobis
ipsa placent; ipsae rursus concedite siluae.
non illum nostri possunt mutare labores,
nec si frigoribus mediis Hebrumque bibamus   65
Sithoniasque niues hiemis subeamus aquosae,
nec si, cum moriens alta liber aret in ulmo,
Aethiopum uersemus ouis sub sidere Cancri.
omnia uincit Amor: et nos cedamus Amori.'
     Haec sat erit, diuae, uestrum cecinisse poetam,   70
dum sedet et gracili fiscellam texit hibisco,
Pierides: uos haec facietis maxima Gallo,
Gallo, cuius amor tantum mihi crescit in horas
quantum uere nouo uiridis se subicit alnus.
surgamus: solet esse grauis cantantibus umbra,   75
iuniperi grauis umbra; nocent et frugibus umbrae.
ite domum saturae, uenit Hesperus, ite capellae.

COMMENTARY

Eclogue 1

[Tityrus]

In the first eclogue, two destinies are painfully contrasted: that of Meliboeus, forced by the confiscations to abandon his usual pastures, and that of Tityrus, who is allowed to carry on his pastoral existence, thanks to the intervention of a young 'god' he encountered in Rome. The virtually certain identification between this 'god' and Caesar Octavian (1.42) enables the first poem to play an important proemial function: even without an explicit dedication to this illustrious addressee (which the *Georgics* will have), it is clear that the whole collection is placed under the protection of the young *diui filius*. Moreover, the divine response, expressed on two occasions (1.10n.; 1.45n.), sounds like a poetic investiture for the bucolic author.

The question of which poem should be given the first position is raised in the Theocritean exegetical tradition. The answer transmitted by the scholia to the first idyll focuses on technical and literary qualities (the poem is defined as 'the finest, owing to its grace and art': ὅμως τοῦτο προτέτακται διὰ τὸ χαριέστερον καὶ τεχνικώτερον τῶν ἄλλων μᾶλλον συντετάχθαι [p. 23.7–8 Wend.]). In his opening poem, on the other hand, V. chose to situate literary values within the traumatic context of dramatic historical events. Thus, the story of Tityrus and Meliboeus is offered to the reader as the result of an age still shaken by civil strife, and cruelly accustomed to the harshest reversals of fortune, particularly so in the case of the two herdsmen. Various clues, in fact, suggest that the now exiled Meliboeus was previously better off than Tityrus. Meliboeus now talks like a Roman citizen, in more than one instance (cf. esp. 1.3–4n.; 1.71n.; note also the literary echoes of both names: 1.1n. and 1.6n.). V.'s early readers must have been shocked by the two herdsmen's vicissitudes in the aftermath of the civil wars. Land confiscations were at the core of tensions involving all political forces, especially Antony and Octavian, but also Sextus Pompey (who was not part of the triumvirate). The confiscations were an evident consequence of civil *discordia*, in the form it took after the murder of Julius Caesar. But they were also necessary to ensure the army's satisfaction, and as such they were an extremely difficult task, which Antony happily delegated to Octavian. The general climate of collective anxiety in Italy at the time is well described by Cass. Di. 48.3, who also adds insightful remarks on Octavian's predicament in 41 BCE (Octavian was simultaneously accused of both favouritism towards civilians and partisanship towards the army: Cass. Di. 48.8). The confiscations ultimately originated the Perusine War in the winter of 41–40, when Lucius Antonius directly attacked Octavian in the heart of Italy while Sextus Pompey turned the dispossessed landowners into rebels and prompted them to join his large naval force in Sicily (see Introduction, pp. 4–5; 15, n. 35). This historical context is crucial to understanding the feeling of uncertainty that pervades

60   ECLOGUE 1

E. 1: the whole poem appears to be seized by a whirlwind (1.12 *turbatur*) which makes Italy unsafe. As a result, former landowners must go into exile to resettle in far, unknown lands.

V.'s response to these dark forces involves a mythical portrait of Rome and the young 'god' who inhabits it (a response seemingly at odds with the poet's putative Epicureanism: see Introduction, pp. 16–17). At least in poetic terms, V. certainly contributed to the rise of a reassuring, salvific figure: the young *diui filius*. Octavian himself tackled such a complex situation with a conciliatory attitude: after 41 BCE, the expropriations no longer happened on Italian soil, and Augustus later compensated provincial landowners for their lands (perhaps right after Actium, or maybe in 14 BCE; see *res gest.* 16.1). Despite all this, even after Augustus' death the expropriations continued to be criticized, along with the proscriptions of 43 (Tac. *ann.* 1.10 *proscriptionem ciuium, diuisiones agrorum*). V.'s text must have played a role in the persistence of the confiscations' memory. In spite of Tityrus' praise of the redeeming *deus*, Meliboeus lends his voice to countless dispossessed exiles, thereby touching upon a delicate dilemma in the career of a young *diui filius* whose political force resides in his defence of private property (Vell. 2.89.4).

V.'s audacious choice to open the collection with Theocritean characters in the midst of the post-42 BCE confiscations has unsettled several readers within V.'s long reception history: perhaps inevitably so. References to contemporary reality, and to the poet's own life (for all those who believed in the identification Tityrus-V.), appeared to stifle the atemporal, mythopoetic ambition which characterizes the other eclogues. However, once the meagre importance of the autobiographical element has been clarified (only rarely can the reader catch glimpses of the poet's figure behind that of Tityrus: cf. 1.28n.), it should be obvious that political issues are by no means occasional intruders into V.'s pastoral world. In V., part of the significance of the pastoral myth resides in its loss: in the paradox whereby Roman society destroys it precisely while attempting to re-actualize it. In fact, the soldiers' forced return to agriculture after long years of combat (including the civil wars) triggers a vicious circle which, through land confiscation, leads to the destruction of bucolic song. One of Rome's foundation myths (i.e. the pastoral world itself) is contradicted by history, which arbitrarily selects things and people—those to be saved, those to be lost.

Here, perhaps, V. meant to develop what he might have perceived as a Theocritean suggestion. In all likelihood, the edition of the *Idylls* used by V. also began with a loss: the farewell song of the divine singer Daphnis, soon to descend into Hades, is replaced in the first eclogue by the farewell song of Meliboeus, who is himself an important bucolic singer (1.77n.). Thus, the exile motif, in which the Theocritean reminiscence makes exile all the more similar to death, comes to the fore as the 'originary scene' of V.'s poetry (another exile, Ovid, will recall the first eclogue: *Pont.* 1.8, esp. 51–2; for the idea of exile as death cf. Cic.

Pis. 21; Ov. *trist.* 1.4.27–8; Sen. *dial.* 12[*Helu.*].2.5). The mythical world of the *E.* must be accessed through Meliboeus' farewell, just as it must be left (at the other end of the collection) through Cornelius Gallus' regret: 'Would that I had been one of you [Arcadians], would that I had been guardian of your flock, or vine-dresser of ripening grapes!' (10.35–6). Gallus' words and actions are even more explicitly modelled after Daphnis' farewell in Theocritus. Nevertheless, before Gallus' poem, the land confiscations will reappear with even greater cruelty in the ninth eclogue, in which the relationship between city and countryside, history's violence and the herdsmen's peaceful existence, will be emphasized even further.

V. thus wanted the confiscations and their annihilation of the pastoral world to frame his poetic collection, thereby giving both ancient and modern biographers enough material to attempt a coherent and unifying reconstruction of his book and life at once. In particular, the relationship between *E.* 1 and *E.* 9 (and their relative chronology) has always been a *uexata quaestio* in Virgilian studies, and it is probably an unsolvable problem (overall, it seems more plausible that the first eclogue is chronologically later than the ninth, and that it is meant to depict the 'ultimate' and current situation of the pastoral world: a situation in which Tityrus, at least, has been saved; see pp. 430–1).

It appears certain, at any rate, that V.'s subtle and nuanced treatment of such a delicate, politically loaded topic (a generally clear picture with many vague and indefinite details) set a memorable example of how to strike the right poetic note that gives a voice to the victims while ultimately pointing to a reassuring conciliation. V.'s example was soon to be followed by other poets: note Horace's dispossessed farmer Ofellus (*sat.* 2.2.112–36) and Propertius' elegiac echoes of the Perusine War (Prop. 1.21; 1.22 and 4.1), besides the pseudo-Virgilian *Dirae* and the *Panegyricus Messallae* ([Tib.] 3.7.279–89). It bears observing that V.'s friend L. Varius Rufus (9.35n.), in his Epicurean-sounding yet heavily politicized poem *De morte*, reproaches Mark Antony for dispossessing Roman citizens. It seems, in fact, that Antony embarked on an early confiscation experiment in 44 BCE, soon after Caesar's death, and promptly abandoned it (see p. 4 and n. 6; 1.71–2n.).

The first eclogue, in which the dialogue mimetically reproduces the herdsmen's action, can readily be divided into three sections: an introductory look at the characters' plight (1–45), a more emotional central section focused on Meliboeus (46–78), and a short conclusion in Tityrus' voice (79–83). As happens in all the properly dialogic sections of the volume, the same number of speeches is assigned to each speaker, in this case six each (Meliboeus begins and Tityrus ends), but the one who speaks more verses is Meliboeus (46 as against the 37 of Tityrus).

On the eclogue: Bethe (1892); Leo (1903); Weyman (1917a, 1917b); Jachmann (1922, pp. 115–19); Klingner (1927); Waltz (1927); Oppermann (1932); Liegle (1943); Büchner (1955, cols. 1180–1186); Hanslik (1955); Altevogt (1956); Wagenvoort (1956b); Pöschl

62   ECLOGUE 1

(1964, pp. 9–92); Segal (1965); Smith (1965); Coleman (1966); Fredricksmeyer (1966); G. Williams (1968, pp. 307–12); Dick (1970); Putnam (1970, pp. 20–81); Smith (1970); Fedeli (1972); Nielsen (1972); Berg (1974, pp. 142–54); Leach (1974, pp. 113–42); Putnam (1975); Van Sickle (1975); von Albrecht (1977, pp. 132–63); Cremona (1977); Picone (1978); Van Sickle (1978, pp. 41–55 and 118–25); Pasqualetti (1978–9); Alpers (1979, pp. 65–95); DuQuesnay (1981); Gigante (1981a); Roberts (1983); Wright (1983); Van Sickle (1984); Pagés (1986); Van Sickle (1986, pp. 45–74); E. A. Schmidt (1987, pp. 30–5 and 129–38); M. O. Lee (1989, pp. 70–4); Picone (1989); Alpers (1990, pp. 37–47); Tracy (1990); Batstone (1990); Della Corte (1991); Picone (1993); Giordano Rampioni, Traina (1994); Traina (1994a); T. K. Hubbard (1995a, pp. 41–6 = 1998, 48–54); E. A. Schmidt (1998); Wimmel (1998); Van Sickle (2000); Perkell (2001a, pp. 29–33); Davis (2004); Breed (2006a, pp. 95–116); Papanghelis (2006, pp. 369–78); von Albrecht (2007, pp. 14–18); A. Powell (2008, pp. 181–97); Schmitzer (2008); Davis (2012, pp. 17–39); Kania (2016, pp. 42–52 and 118–23); Fernandelli (2019, pp. 232–40).

Specific issues: Wissowa (1902) (ll. 42–43); Havet (1914a, pp. 81–5) (l. 69); Phillimore (1916, pp. 146–7) (l. 69); P. Thomas (1928) (l. 79); Funaioli (1930, p. 310) (l. 69); Wili (1930, pp. 31–6) (the god Octavian); Pease (1931) (biography and fiction); Ferrarino (1940) (l. 65); J. Martin (1946) (the expropriations); Bömer (1949–50) (Tityrus' god); Mariotti (1952, p. 61 n. = 1986, p. 44 n.) (l. 65); Aymard (1955) (l. 62); J. Michel (1955) (ll. 59–66); Deman (1956) (Tityrs' social status); Monteil (1964, pp. 23–60) (*formosus*); Pietzcker (1965, pp. 7–80) (landscape); Savage (1965) (ll. 57 and 59–63); Wellesley (1966) (V.'s country); Wilkinson (1966) (the expropriations); Heurgon (1967) (Alfenus Varus and the expropriations); Traina (1968a) (ll. 82–3); Schindel (1969) (l. 69); MacKay (1971) (ll. 61–71); Verdière (1971) (ll. 56 and 59–60); Clausen (1972) (date); C. Hardie (1975, pp. 109–22) (the god Octavian); Cova (1976) (*otium* and *libertas*); Winterbottom (1976) (the expropriations); Veyne (1980) (the expropriations); Keppie (1981) (the expropriations); Bowie (1985, pp. 80–1) (Philitas as a model); Della Corte (1985a) (l. 1); Heuzé (1985, pp. 212–43) (*formosus*); Boyle (1986, pp. 15–35) (poetry and power); Dubuisson (1987) (l. 15); Hatzikosta (1987) (ll. 64–6); Leach (1988, pp. 149–54) (descriptive realism and spatial perception); Buchheit (1990) (Octavian); Langholf (1990) (allegorical interpretation in Calp. *ecl.*); Nussbaum (1990) (l. 79); Paschalis (1990) (l. 69); Perkell (1990) (ll. 79–83); Alberte (1991) (love); Glei (1991, pp. 45–9) (war); Marchetta (1994a, pp. 91–198) (*formosus*); Binder (1995, pp. 83–5) (historical context); C. Edwards (1996, p. 16) (Rome's greatness); Esposito (1996, pp. 14–20) (l. 1 and Calp. *ecl.* 4); Gutzwiller (1996b) (Theocr. *epigr.* 1 G.; Meleager); Clauss (1997) (the acrostic at ll. 5–8); Schiesaro (1997, pp. 86–7) (Tityrus and Meliboeus' epistemology); Theodorakopoulos (1997, pp. 162–4) (ll. 79–83); Cairns (1999) (ll. 1–2); Calzolari (1999) (Andes and the expropriations); Dangel (1999) (metre); Breed (2000a) (ll. 1–10); Freund (2000, p. 219) (l. 68); J. Thomas (2000) (*otium*); Timpanaro (2001, p. 10, n. 21) (l. 12); Lipka (2002) (*fagus*); Luther (2002, pp. 35–56) (historical context); Korenjak (2003) (Virgilian biography); Rundin (2003) (Epicureanism); Van Sickle (2004) (ll. 1–2); Barchiesi (2006, pp. 412–13) (l. 79 and Ov. *met.* 1.680); Galinsky (2006) (*libertas*: l. 27); Loupiac (2006) (ll. 59–64 and 65–9); Marino (2006) (the bees); Osgood (2006, pp. 108–201) (the expropriations); H. White (2006, pp. 384–5) (ll. 65 and 69); Mayer (2007) (ll. 19–25 and the 'divine' city of Rome); Cairns (2008, pp. 70–5) (*deus* = Asinius Pollio); Degl'Innocenti Pierini (2008, pp. 68–77) (Ovid's exile and Meliboeus); Tartari

Chersoni (2008) (Meliboeus' exile and Aristophanes' *Peace*); Traina (2008) (Italian translation of ll. 1–18); Courtney (2009, p. 81) (l. 69); Breed (2012) (*E.* 1 and the *Dirae*); Quartarone (2013) (l. 1); Stok (2013) (the expropriations and the *triumuiri agris diuidendis*); Roche (2014) (ll. 53–5); Heyworth (2015, pp. 198–201) (ll. 59–63); Bing (2016) (l. 42); Eckerman (2016) (Tityrus' freedom and Theocr. *id.* 14, 52–5); Paraskeviotis (2016, pp. 46–9) (l. 5); Kraggerud (2017a) (l. 69); Keith (2018, pp. 99–101) (l. 45); Cucchiarelli (2019a, pp. 512–16) (land confiscations in Varius Rufus' *De morte*); Gagliardi (2019) (ll. 59–63); Gagliardi (2021) (l. 5 and the theme of echo in the *E.*); Jolowicz (2021, pp. 292–7) (l. 1: the φηγός and the *fagus*).

1–10. The first exchange between the two characters, each uttering five lines, is perfectly symmetrical, whereas Theocritus' *id.* 1 opens with six lines in Thyrsis' voice followed by four in the goatherd's (note that five is the average number of lines per character in dialogic eclogues: see Introduction, p. 24 and n. 60). Meliboeus breaks the ice, thus defining the situation and setting forth the literary values that are customary for an incipit. As in *E.* 5 and 9 (but cf. also 3.1–54), the exchange is symmetrical: hence Tityrus will have the last word—and yet, the impression is that the poem is really concluded by Meliboeus' disappearance. Note the ring structure between the beginning and the end of the eclogue, Tityrus' last speech being five lines long (1.79–83n.), like Meliboeus' first speech: a similar structure is to be observed in *E.* 6, the 'second beginning' of the book (see 6.1–12n.). The acrostic at ll. 5–8 (*FONS*) has sometimes been considered intentional.

1 Tityre, tu patulae recubans sub tegmine fagi. The challenge to compose a memorable line is inherent in every incipit. Here the task is accomplished through an insistent alliterative jingle. As was customary in antiquity, this first line was used as a shorthand for the whole work (a sort of title—even the simple name of Tityrus sufficed: Ov. *amor.* 1.15.25; Calp. *ecl.* 4.62; but cf. *Catal.* 9.17), and was soon adopted as a classic example of the Latin hexameter. V. himself will quote it at the end of his *Georgics*, thus confirming its 'inaugural' and distinctive nature: *Tityre, te patulae cecini sub tegmine fagi* (4.566). Parodies were also common: *Tityre, si toga calda tibi est, quo tegmine fagi?* (cf. Don. *uita Verg.* 174 Brumm. = p. 39.3 Brugn.-Stok). The alliteration, underscoring the vowel play (/*u*/ and /*i*/) as in Theocritus' incipit, suggests the sound of a shepherd's pipe (*TItYre, tU patUlae recUbans sUb tegmIne fagI* ≈ *id.* 1.1–3 Ἁδύ τι τὸ ψιθύρισμα καὶ ἁ πίτυς αἰπόλε τήνα, / ἁ ποτὶ ταῖς παγαῖσι μελίσδεται, ἁδὺ δὲ καὶ τὺ / συρίσδες 'A sweet whisper, o goatherd, is the sound of that pine tree / there by the springs, and sweetly do you yourself / play the pipe'; cf. *id.* 7.88–9). Note that, after the initial downbeat (*tu*), the sound /*u*/ only occupies the upbeats, thereby eliciting a feeling of softening. In 1.2, the /*t*/ alliteration continues, whereas the second half-line of 1.4 opens with a chiastic echo: *Tityre tu / tu Tityre*. Full of sorrow, Meliboeus takes up the iterative insistence that characterized the incipit of *id.* 9: Βουκολιάζεο Δάφνι· τὺ δ' ᾠδᾶς ἄρχεο πρᾶτος, / ᾠδᾶς ἄρχεο Δάφνι 'Sing a pastoral song, Daphnis: you start singing

64   ECLOGUE 1

first, / start singing, Daphnis' (*id*. 9.1-2). **Tityre**. The name is Theocritean, fulfilling the need for echoing the genre-model in the incipit, while individualizing the single poem (the same is true of the subsequent eclogues, whose first line often includes a shepherd's name, in keeping with Theocritus' practice). For further reading see *Enc. Virg.* VI.1, pp. 196–201, s.v. *Titiro* (F. Caviglia); *Virg. Enc.* III, pp. 1275–7, s.v. *Tityrus* (J. Van Sickle, J. M. Ziolkowski); Jolowicz (2021, pp. 305–9). After Daphnis (35 occurrences), Tityrus is the name that occurs most often in the *E*. (13x), followed by Menalcas (11x). Ancient etymological attempts invariably refer to the pastoral world: (*a*) according to Servius, *praef. E.*, p. 4.7-8 (III.1 Th.-H.), the Laconian word *tityrus* indicated the *maior* ram, suitable for leading the flock (hence a name suitable for spearheading the *E*.'s poetic 'flock'); (*b*) τίτυρος is said to be synonymous with σάτυρος/σειληνός: see e.g. Aelian *uar. hist.* 3.40; cf. also *schol.* Theocr. 3.2a, p. 117.13–14; 7.72c, p. 97.20–1 Wend.; (*c*) in southern Italy's Doric dialects, the common noun τίτυρος—connected to τιτύρινος (αὐλός) and τιτυριστής, may either mean 'reed' (*schol.* Theocr. 3.2a, p. 117.16 Wend.) or indicate the καλάμινος αὐλός itself (but cf. Athen. 4.182d). In fact, V.'s Tityrus is portrayed as playing the *calamus agrestis* at 1.10 (Doric forms were conspicuous in Theocritus' incipit). One of the two Theocritean occurrences of the name refers to a subordinate figure, whom the goatherd of *id*. 3 entrusts with his flock in order to devote himself to singing for Amaryllis (*id*. 3.2-5: cf. *E*. 9.23–5; V.'s Tityrus is linked to an Amaryllis: 1.5n.; 1.30n.). In its other occurrence, the name identifies a more important character, namely the singer who, in *id*. 7.71-3, is given the task of gladdening Lycidas' rest: 'two shepherds will play for me, one from Acharnes, / the other a Lycopian: Tityrus will sing next to them / of how Daphnis the cowherd once fell in love with Xeneas'. V. takes up the Theocritean duplicity of the name by often using it, as in *id*. 3, to denote the modest status of a pastoral labourer (cf. *E*. 3.20; 96; 5.12; 9.23–4), whereas the Tityrus of *E*. 1 and 6 is a first-rate poet (and musician, as we can infer from 1.10—contrast *id*. 7, where he just sings). To be sure, a 'humble' characterization of the figure may also be perceived in *E*. 1, considering Tityrus' servile past (1.27n.) as well as his naivety (a very appropriate trait, preventing him from looking like a privileged rascal). Similarly, Apollo's use of the name at 6.3–5 may be meant to emphasize the 'humble' nature of the literary genre chosen by V. (a rather abrupt order is given collectively to *pueri* by the *deus* at 1.45; a clear hierarchy of values, i.e. Tityrus below Orpheus, is also found at 8.55-6). The future predicted by Lycidas in *id*. 7 comes true for Tityrus at the outset of V.'s *E*.: he teaches the woods to echo Amaryllis' name (1.5n.), whereas his Theocritean namesake was summoned to sing of nature's participation in Daphnis' grief (*id*. 7.74–5). After all, in the fictional time of *E*. 1, Tityrus is a *senex* (46) and seems to talk like a rich cowherd (9). V. himself seems to have alluded to some possibility of equating Tityrus and the poet of the *Eclogues*: on the one hand, specific details set V. apart from his character (note

ECLOGUE 1   65

their age difference: 1.46n.); on the other hand, Apollo calls the poet *Tityre* in 6.4n. In the finale of the *Georgics*, V. points at the separation between him and Tityrus, the object of his song (*G.* 4.566: *Tityre, te…*) while connecting his own *otium* (provided by Naples: *G.* 4.563–4 *illo Vergilium me tempore dulcis alebat / Parthenope studiis florentem ignobilis oti*) with the sheltered world of Tityrus' *otia* (*sub tegmine fagi*), fostered by a *deus* who will reappear in the *Georgics* as the conqueror of the East (= Octavian: *G.* 4.560–2; cf. 1.6n.). Besides being prominently featured in the biographical and exegetical tradition, the Tityrus-V. equation is found in Calpurnius, *ecl.* 4.62–3 and Nemesianus, *ecl.* 2.82–5. **tu … recubans sub tegmine fagi.** Tityrus' reclining posture and the sweet sound of his music spreading under the foliage re-enact the pastoral bliss of *id.* 7.88–9 τὺ δ' ὑπὸ δρυσὶν ἢ ὑπὸ πεύκαις / ἀδὺ μελισδόμενος κατεκέκλισο 'you lie down under oaks or pine trees, / sweetly singing', where the *makarismos* is addressed by Lycidas to the 'divine' Komatas (in Theocritus, however, Lycidas can keep herding goats and listening to Komatas' voice, whereas V.'s Meliboeus is forced to leave, and the woods alone will listen to Tityrus). In *id.* 3, too, the goatherd lies down (*id.* 3.38 ἀποκλινθείς) to sing of his Amaryllis by a pine tree; typically, however, the singing or playing herdsman is seated: *E.* 3.55 *consedimus*; Theocr. *id.* 1.12; 21; [Mosch.] *epit. Bion.* 21. But recall the bronze statue depicting Philitas apud Hermes. fr. 7.75–8 Pow. = 3.75–8 Light. = Phil. T 16 Sbard. = 2 Spanoud. = 4 Light. (under a plane tree, perhaps singing of his beloved Bittis); cf. Longus, 2.5.3 (1.5n.). The image of an Epicurean *umbra* is implied here (cf. 1.83n.) and longed for again at *G.* 2.489; *recubans molliter et delicate* is what Cicero polemically says of the idle Epicurean at *de orat.* 3.63. **sub tegmine fagi.** A 'covering' or dome-shaped 'roofing' (from *tego*): Lucr. 2.663 *sub tegmine caeli*; cf. also Cic. *Arat.* 47 Soub. (and *nat. deor.* 2.112; perhaps in Ennius). More common, especially in prose, is the form *tegumentum* (but *tegimen* appears in Cic. *Tusc.* 5.90). Latin poets often coin new forms ending in *-men* so as to avoid *-mentum* nouns, which are metrically unwieldy: cf., for instance, *fragmina* in lieu of *fragmenta* at *Aen.* 10.306 (with S. J. Harrison, *Vergil, Aeneid 10*, Oxford 1991, pp. 153–4 ad loc.). The dactylic word *tegmine* occupies the fifth foot of the hexameter, as is commonly the case in Latin poetry and always in V. Here, in the opening line, the notion of *umbra* is merely hinted at, soon to be set forth by *lentus in umbra* (1.4n.). V. frequently connects the root *teg-* with *umbra*: see *E.* 7.46 *tegit arbutus umbra*; *G.* 2.489 *(me) ingenti ramorum protegat umbra*; *G.* 3.145; *Aen.* 10.541. **fagi.** The *fagus* (not just a tree, but a poetic symbol specific to the *E.*) offers shelter to the herdsmen thanks to its broad and thick shade (cf. also 2.3n.), provides timber to the divine craftsman Alcimedon (3.36–7), while its naturally rather smooth bark can be a support to texts (5.13–14). The 'old beech trees' (*ueteres fagi*) of 3.12 and 9.9 are a reference point for V.'s pastoral geography; see further *Enc. Virg.* II, pp. 456–7, s.v. *faggio* (G. Maggiulli); note that a variety of beech, known as the 'weeping beech' (*Fagus sylvatica pendula*), has a vast crown of

66   ECLOGUE 1

foliage that can readily provide 'shelter' (*tegmen*). V.'s beech tree here replaces the πίτυς (pine) of *id.* 1.1, probably by contamination with the φηγός of *id.* 9.20 and 12.8 (which is actually an oak; cf. Callimachus' bucolic epigram, l. 3 Δικταίησιν ὑπὸ δρυσίν [*Anth. Pal.* 7.518.3 = *epigr.* 22.3 Pf.]). It is under the φηγοί that Acontius wants the words 'Cydippe is fair' to resound (Aristaen. *epist.* 1.10, p. 23, l. 57 Maz.; perhaps from Callimachus?—cf. *aet.* fr. 73 Pf. with the note ad loc. = fr. 172 Mass. with G. Massimilla's commentary, Pisa-Rome 2010, p. 344 = fr. 73 Hard. with A. Harder's commentary, II, Oxford 2012, pp. 576–8). Cf. also Longus, 2.5.3 πρὸς ταῖς φηγοῖς; in *G.* 3.172 *faginus axis* reworks the Homeric φήγινος ἄξων (*Il.* 5.838: that the holm-oak, a particular kind of oak, was used to build wheel axles is confirmed by Pliny, *nat.* 16.229). The two species were at times equated with each other: Varr. apud Charis. *gramm.* 1, p. 130.5–6 K. = p. 165.17–18 B. *fagus quas Graeci* φηγούς *uocant* (from *De gente populi Romani*). *Fagus*, the last word of the *E*.'s first line, will conclude the last line of the *G.* Religious significance cannot be ruled out: cf. the cult of *Iuppiter Fagutalis*, to whom the *lucus fagutalis* and the *fagutal* were consecrated (esp. Varr. *ling.* 5.49; 152). Another suitably pastoral species, in whose shadow people can rest, could have been the plane tree, typical of *locus amoenus* (cf. Plat. *Phaedr.* 230b) and appearing in Mosch. fr. 1.11 G. (cf. also Meleag. *Anth. Pal.* 7.196.8 = *HE* 4073 G.-P. ὑπὸ σκιερῇ κεκλιμένος πλατάνῳ, where the emphasis is on peaceful countryside sleep [see further 1.2n.]) and later taken up by Calp. *ecl.* 4.2 and Nemes. *ecl.* 1.72; 2.18; but plane tree never occurs in Theocritus' bucolic idylls (cf. instead πλατάνιστος in *id.* 18.44; 46; 22.76) and Virgil mentions it only twice, not in the *E*. (*G.* 2.70; 4.146 *ministrantem platanum potantibus umbram*).

2 siluestrem…Musam. An explicit marker of the pastoral genre, expressed with a Lucretian 'formula' (cf. Lucr. 4.589 *fistula siluestrem ne cesset fundere musam*), which V. the Epicurean seems to echo in several passages—here alluding to it programmatically. Cf. 6.8n. (at the beginning of the second half of the book); 10.25n.; see also 2.34n. But recall the Theocritean model, i.e. *id.* 1.20: 'you reached the bucolic Muse's excellence' (τᾶς βουκολικᾶς…μοίσας); cf. also Meleager's two epigrams on singing insects at *Anth. Pal.* 7.196.2 = *HE* 4067 G.-P. ἀγρονόμαν μέλπεις μοῦσαν (the cicada); 7.195.2 = *HE* 4059 G.-P. ἀκρίς, ἀρουραίη Μοῦσα, λιγυπτέρυγε (ἀκρίς, properly speaking, is a locust, but Meleager seems to refer to some kind of cricket). The *siluae* identify V.'s pastoral landscape (their 'resounding' will conclude Meliboeus' speech: 1.5n.), and their *musa* is correspondingly *siluestris*: cf. *E.* 2.62; 4.3. For this reason, they appear here, whereas Theocritus' Sicilian landscape was proportionally much less 'sylvan'. **tenui…auena.** V. does not specify whether this is (as seems likelier) a pan-pipe, or syrinx (σῦριγξ, δόνακες, *fistula*, *calami*: cf. *id.* 1.3), which is the most typical pastoral instrument, or a single-reed pipe (αὐλός or *tibia*), also occasionally used by Theocritean and Virgilian herdsmen (8.21n.). Due to its thin texture (*tenui*), the *auena* (oat-stem) is here a technologically unlikely object (pipes were made of marsh reeds

[*E.* 6.8] or hollow hemlock stalks [2.36; 5.85]). The epithet, however, alludes to Callimachean values of refinement, while simultaneously expressing the poet's customary initial modesty and thereby eschewing direct comparison with Theocritus' first idyll, which opened with panpipes. At the other end of the book, Cornelius Gallus will also choose the *auena* for his pastoral 'debut': 10.51n. (the term only occurs three times in the *E.*: cf. also 5.37 *steriles nascuntur auenae*). After V., cf. Ov. *met.* 1.677 *structis cantat auenis; trist.* 5.10.25 *pastor iunctis pice cantat auenis* (panpipes in both cases); Calp. *ecl.* 4.63 (reworking V.'s incipit); also Prop. 2.34.75; Tib. 2.1.53. The literary-stylistic significance of *tenuis* is grasped by Servius, albeit in strictly rhetorical terms (the 'humble style'). The adj. will reappear, with even clearer Callimachean implications and with the same metrical emphasis (note the masculine caesura), in the *E.*'s 'second proem', i.e. 6.8 *agrestem tenui meditabor harundine Musam* (n.); cf. also, towards the end of the book, 10.71 *gracili...hibisco* (n.). Note the contrastive play between the beech tree's large size (*patulae*) and the thin dimension of the 'oat-stem', which also suggests softness of sound: cf. 5.85 *fragili cicuta*; in an unpleasant sense, 3.27 *stridenti... stipula* (Theocr. *id.* 5.7). Here Meliboeus is not so much describing an object as he is highlighting his interlocutor's serene leisure. **meditaris.** Frequentative form of *medeor* ('to think of'), commonly used in post-Virgilian poetry to denote the 'meditated' composition of poetry: *E.* 6.8; 82; Hor. *epist.* 2.2.76 *uersus tecum meditare canoros* (also *sat.* 1.9.2); *Lydia* [*Dirae*] 109; [Tib.] 3.4.71; *Enc. Virg.* III, pp. 450–1, s.v. *meditor* (A. Traina). Perhaps due to the interference of the Greek term μελετάω, the verb hints at assiduous practice and careful consideration (but also deceit: *E.* 5.61); here it specifically refers to words, and thus to the hexameter's *recitativo*-like nature. Note also the contrast with Theocritus' συρίσδες, which exclusively refers to musical, instrumental sounds (*id.* 1.3 and 20.28–9). The verb perpetuates the /t/ assonance, spanning across 1.1–2 (*siluesTrem Tenui...mediTaris*).

3–4. This is V.'s first reference to Meliboeus' plight—an intrusion of contemporary reality into the pastoral world, emphasized at the level of sou: 1.3 and the first half-line of 1.4 break the homogeneous musical sequence spanning across 1.1–5. The two shepherds' opposed fates are verbally intertwined: the chiasmus *tu* (1) *nos* (3) *nos...tu* (4) is doubled by the inversion *Tityre, tu / tu, Tityre* (1/4). Note also the repetition *nos patriae...nos patriam*, typical of the pastoral style: here it appears anaphorically in line-opening position, and is probably meant to amplify pathos. Here, as well as in his subsequent speeches, Meliboeus' language is comparable to that of 'farewell speeches' (συντακτικοὶ λόγοι) as they are codified in rhetorical doctrine (esp. Men. Rhet. pp. 430.10–434.9 Speng. = pp. 194–200 R.-W.).

3 **patriae finis.** The term *patria*, emphasized by anaphora and polyptoton at 1.3 and 1.4 (*nos patriae.../ nos patriam*), immediately introduces a Roman, non-Theocritean element, and hints at Meliboeus' characterization as a Roman citizen (1.71n.). Note also the adjective at 1.67 *patrios...finis*. The term and the notion

68   ECLOGUE 1

will occur again, in the context of exile and with a likely echo of *E.* 1, at Ov. *trist.* 4.9.11–14 *omnia, si nescis, Caesar mihi iura reliquit, / et sola est patria poena carere mea. // et patriam, modo sit sospes, speramus ab illo: / saepe Iouis telo quercus adusta uiret.* **dulcia linquimus arua.** The tilled fields, along with the native borders, will reappear at 1.67–71 (in 1.46, too, Meliboeus talks like a farmer: *tua rura manebunt*). The epithet, underscoring the sorrows of exile, suggests the sweetness of Theocritus' incipit (that very sweetness is now lost, *linquimus: id.* 1.1 ἁδύ τι τὸ ψιθύρισμα); cf. *G.* 2.511 *exsilio…domos et dulcia limina mutant; Aen.* 4.281 *dulcisque relinquere terras;* 4.342; 10.782. The verb is *simplex pro composito: linquimus* for *relinquimus* (cf. Naev. *trag.* 28 R.³; Pacuv. *trag.* 186 R.³; Enn. *trag.* 128 Joc.; Catull. 61.27, etc.); contrast 15 and 30 *reliquit* (clausula in both cases).

4 fugimus. In the sense of φεύγω, 'going into exile'; but the acc. *patriam* in lieu of the expected abl. (cf. Nep. *Att.* 4.4 *ex patria fugienti;* Ov. *trist.* 1.5.66) personifies the country. Servius compared Hor. *carm.* 1.7.21–2 *Teucer Salamina patremque / cum fugeret;* the phrasing is parodically echoed at Iuv. 11.52. Most of the time, Theocritus' herdsmen are settled people: the only exception is *id.* 4, in which Aegon goes to Olympia, bringing part of his flock with him (*id.* 4.10)—not without rather negative consequences for the animals he leaves at home (*id.* 4.12–25; cf. here 1.14–15). **lentus in umbra.** The adj. *lentus* refers to the relaxed mindset and physical posture of someone who feels safe: cf. *Aen.* 12.237. Here the *umbra* is a shelter for leisure, rest, and poetry, as in Hor. *carm.* 1.32.1–2 *si quid uacui sub umbra / lusimus* (none of this is granted to Corydon in *E.* 2, not even in the midday heat: 2.8 *nunc etiam pecudes umbras et frigora captant*). The word *umbra*, used with very different connotations, will bring the eclogue to a close (1.83n.). For the bucolic diaeresis cf. 1.7n. The phrasing, like the entire line, echoes and qualifies *E.* 1.1 (*Tityre, tu…recubans sub tegmine fagi* ≈ *tu, Tityre, lentus in umbra*): Tityrus is relaxing under the 'covering of the beech tree', which is its *umbra.*

5 formosam resonare doces Amaryllida siluas. The woods resonate with the love song that Tityrus addresses to his 'fair Amaryllis'—compare the Callimachean model of Acontius and Cydippe: ἀλλ' ἐνὶ δὴ φλοιοῖσι κεκομμένα τόσσα φέροιτε / γράμματα, Κυδίππην ὅσσ' ἐρέουσι καλήν 'cut such letters in the bark of trees, / so as to say "Cydippe is fair"' (*aet.* 3, fr. 73 Pf. = 172 Mass. = 73 Hard., reworked in Aristaenet. *epist.* 1.10, p. 23, ll. 57–61 Maz.; cf. also Callim. *epigr.* 28.5 Pf.; *E.* 10.53n.). The formula '*x* is fair', attested in Greek vase inscriptions and other epigraphic sources, amounts to saying 'I love *x*'. Contrast Prop. 1.18.31, where the name appears alone: *resonent mihi 'Cynthia' siluae;* cf. also 1.8.22 *scribitur et uestris Cynthia corticibus.* For an important parallel cf. Longus, 2.5.3 'I was by your side when you played the pipe under those beech trees [πρὸς ταῖς φηγοῖς ἐκείναις, albeit botanically distinct from V.'s *fagus;* see 1.1n.] and were in love with Amaryllis'; 2.7.6 'I thanked Echo, who repeated the name of Amaryllis after me'. The parallel is perhaps to be interpreted as common dependence on a lost

ECLOGUE 1   69

Alexandrian source (Philitas?), even though it is not impossible that Longus knew V.'s text directly or indirectly. The first comprehensive introduction to the pastoral world, with which Meliboeus is entrusted, is now completed by its fundamental feature: nature's capacity to sympathize with the herdsmen's feelings, as well as to admire and learn their songs (a 'miracle' explicitly traced back to Orpheus: *E.* 3.46; 6.30; cf. also 2.13; 5.28 and 62–4; 6.10–11 and 83; 7.53–60; 8.22–4; 10.8; 13–15). V. thus re-mythologizes that echoic phenomenon which Lucretius had explained in terms of Epicurean physics, precisely in order to forestall any irrationalist interpretation of it (Lucr. 4.572–94). Nature's ability to share in human feelings, even through sounds and songs (the so-called 'pathetic fallacy'), appears in *id.* 1; cf. [Theocr.] *id.* 27.58 'the cypress trees whisper among themselves of your wedding'. The echo effect described by *resonare* becomes perceptible in *AmarYLlida sILuas* (/y/ and /i/ tended to sound similar in ancient pronunci-ation): similarly 2.12–13n.; *G.* 1.486; 2.328; 3.338 quoted below. For the internal acc. with *resonare* cf. *G.* 3.338 *litoraque alcyonen resonant, acalanthida dumi.* The phrasing introduces a poetics of 'resonance', which permeates the world of the *Eclogues* as a whole: sounds, songs, thoughts, and feelings are freely shared among plants, animals, and poets-herdsmen (on *resonare* see 7.13; actual echo effects at 3.79 and 6.44). In [Mosch.] *epit. Bion.*, the poem begins with the (mournful) res-onance of various natural elements, including groves (3 φυτά...καὶ ἄλσεα), which are addressed by the poet. In the opening of Bion, *epit. Adon.*, the poet's lament is echoed by that of the *Erotes*, with the sound effect ἀπώλετο-ὤλετο (1–2). **for-mosam.** The adj. *formosus* (Virgilian manuscripts and grammarians also attest the spelling *formonsus*) expresses physical beauty in particular (*forma* = 'appearance'), and therefore it is originally applied to animals as well: Plaut. *Merc.* 229 *for-mosam capram*; Varr. *rust.* 2.2.4; *ThlL* VI.1.1111.25–36; cf. 5.44 *formosi pecoris* (n.). A favourite of the *E.* (16x), *formosus* yields to *pulcher* in the *Aen.*, where the former never occurs. Its only appearance in the *G.* is in the pastoral-erotic context of 3.219 *formosa iuuenca*; cf. Introduction, p. 27, n. 68. Here the adj. is subtly used to signal the 'humble' stylistic level of the incipient work and its concern with love (note the emphasis provided by the trithemimeral caesura): cf. esp. 2.1 *Formosum...Alexin*; 3.79; 4.57; 10.18; for the use of colloquial language in an erotic context, cf. Catull. 86.1 *Quintia formosa est multis.* For the comparable case of *suauis* cf. 2.49n. **doces.** Theocritus' first idyll began with the pine tree's whispers and the shepherd's music, analogically paralleled with each other (1–3 ἁδύ τι τὸ ψιθύρισμα καὶ ἁ πίτυς αἰπόλε τήνα...μελίσδεται, ἁδὺ δὲ καὶ τὺ / συρίσδες [see 1.1n.]), whereas here the two elements are intertwined as the herdsman 'teaches' the woods. Teaching, i.e. transmitting songs within a teacher-pupil relationship, is a key component of the pastoral world (cf. 5.87; note also the song of the Silenus, requested by two youths at 6.18–9). Tityrus here embodies pastoral teaching. Bion, too, 'taught' nightingales and swallows to sing, according to [Mosch.] *epit. Bion.* (esp. 47 λαλέειν ἐδίδασκε). Plato's Socrates

70   ECLOGUE 1

famously asserted that trees have nothing to teach him (*Phaedr.* 230d...τὰ δένδρα οὐδέν μ' ἐθέλει διδάσκειν): here, by contrast, the poet teaches the forest a love song, thereby evoking the Lucretian connection between nature's sounds and human song and music (cf. Lucr. 5.1382–3 *et zephyri...sibila primum / agrestis docuere cauas inflare cicutas*). **Amaryllida**. It is to her that Theocritus' goatherd dedicated his naive song in *id.* 3, where the name of Amaryllis occurs right at the beginning, Κωμάσδω ποτὶ τὰν Ἀμαρυλλίδα (though Theocritus' Tityrus, mentioned three times in *id.* 3.2–5, merely took orders from the goatherd, whereas now he is Amaryllis' happy lover); cf. also *id.* 4.36–8. Her name is connected with the simplicity of rustic love (note the assonance at 2.52 *Amaryllis amabat*, reproduced by Ov. *ars* 2.267), though not without some recalcitrance, as in *E.* 2.14 and 3.81 (the name itself hints at the polarity *amores / amaros* found at 3.109–10). She will facilitate the love spell cast at 8.77–8. Her last appearance is in 9.22, right before Tityrus is mentioned. The name may be etymologically traced back to ἀμαρύσσειν, 'to twinkle', and thus to the idea of a radiant beauty (cf. 6.20n.), but the first eclogue features Galatea as the spendthrift *puella* (1.30n.), whereas Amaryllis seems to be a good, devoted, and reassuring companion (1.37n.); *Enc. Virg.* I, pp. 122–3, s.v. *Amarillide* (G. Serrao); *Virg. Enc.* I, p. 58, s.v. *Amaryllis* (M. B. Sullivan); Jolowicz (2021, pp. 297–304).

6–10. The words of the wretched Meliboeus trigger (almost by chance) a speech in praise of the young *deus*. In this and his later speeches, Tityrus' language is comparable to the *eucharistikon*, the 'speech of gratitude', given by one of his Greek archetypes at Hom. *Od.* 8.464–8; 487–98. This kind of solemn, emphatic expression of gratitude is not widely attested (cf. Catull. 49), but is rhetorically codified within the epideictic genre, either independently (Quint. *inst.* 3.4.5; cf. 11.3.153) or not (Men. Rhet. p. 422, 27–31 Speng. = p. 178 R.-W.).

6 Meliboee. Meliboeus' name does not seem to belong to any pre-Virgilian pastoral tradition (cf. *E.* 3.1 = 5.87; 7.9; note also *Catal.* 9.18). Various myths attest the similar form *Alphesiboeus* (8.1n.), but fem.; cf. *Enc. Virg.* III, pp. 459–60, s.v. *Melibeo* (F. Michelazzo); *Virg. Enc.* II, pp. 808–9, s.v. *Meliboeus* (J. Van Sickle). The likely etymology was spotted by Servius, *praef. E.*, p. 4.6–7 (III.1 Th.-H.), i.e. 'taking care of oxen' (μέλει αὐτῷ τῶν βοῶν: cf. *cura boum* at *G.* 1.3). We might therefore be dealing with V.'s own repurposing of the name, qualifying the hapless Meliboeus as the quintessential pastoral character: according to some Theocritean commentators, the scholar Didymus derived βουκολέω from βοῦς and κομέω, in the sense of ἐπιμελοῦμαι 'to take care of' (*Anecd. Estienne* 3.4 = Wendel, p. 10; cf. Wendel, p. 4; Serv. *ad ecl.* 3.1 *bucolica...a custodia boum, id est* ἀπὸ τῶν βουκόλων). In *E.* 7, Meliboeus is characterized as a scrupulous herdsman, free from female help or distraction (7.14–15); only an extraordinary event makes him take a break from work (7.17 *posthabui...mea seria ludo*). His voice is entrusted with giving an account of the whole eclogue (i.e. of the contest between Thyrsis and Corydon): a unique occurrence in the collection, almost a kind of 'compensation'

ECLOGUE 1 71

for the poet-herdsman driven into exile and, therefore, forced to quit singing (*E.* 1.77; cf. pp. 347–8). At the outset of *E.* 3, the question is whether a flock (of *oues*) belongs to him (3.1–2), whereas in *E.* 7 Daphnis hints to his *iuuenci* along with the goat and the kids (7.11n.). Here, however, only kids are mentioned by Meliboeus (1.12; 74; 77); although Tityrus refers to a lamb to be sacrificed (1.8), he acts like a shepherd of *oues* (21) and, moreover, describes the wanderings of 'his' *boues*, drawing the interlocutor's attention to them (9 *ut cernis*). Thus, Theocritus' pastoral hierarchy (cowherd, shepherd, goatherd, in descending order) is reshuffled to Tityrus' complete advantage, since he occupies the two higher roles (on the pastoral hierarchy cf. Introduction, p. 9, n. 19). The reversal of fate is also evident in V.'s characterization of the two bucolic 'masks' in this eclogue (along with their names, since at least two of the possible etymologies for Tityrus' name hint at sheep and goats: cf. 1.1n.). The civil war chaos enables the ex-slave Tityrus (1.27), who was once ready to neglect his *cura peculi* for Galatea like a comic slave character (1.32n.), to appear now in the role of a serene singer-landowner, while Meliboeus, who speaks like a *ciuis* (71) and has the 'care of oxen' in his name, must leave and acknowledge his interlocutor's luck: *ergo tua rura manebunt* (46; contrast 67–73; a certain 'georgic' preoccupation is also shown by the Meliboeus of 7.6). The paradox inherent in a protagonist of V.'s *E.* who never appears in Theocritus despite his arch-Theocritean name could be explained by both his social status as a landowning citizen and his fate as an exile, which sets him apart from the herdsmen's community. All of this seems to be clear to Nemesianus who, in his first eclogue, subtly assigns to the late Meliboeus a prominent role among the shepherds as a homage to his Virgilian importance: Timetas praises Meliboeus while addressing Tityrus (Nemes. *ecl.* 1, esp. 49–63); in Calpurnius, Meliboeus is the name of an influential patron whose protection was highly valued among herdsmen (Calp. *ecl.* 1.94; 4.36–42; 157–9). Note that labour was considered to be among the original elements of pastoral poetry: Diomus, a Sicilian cowherd, was credited with composing the first labour song for herdsmen leading their flocks to graze—whence the name of 'pastoral' song (*boukoliasmos*); cf. Athen. 14.619a–b. **deus.** In all likelihood, Caesar Octavian: cf. 1.42n. Assimilation to a deity is an encomiastic commonplace, not necessarily implying the official status of cult; here, in fact, cult is soon redefined in the private context of rustic devotion (whose agent is the naive shepherd Tityrus): 1.7–10n.; 41n.; 43n. An important parallel is Lucretius' deification of Epicurus: Lucr. 5.8 *deus ille fuit, deus, inclute Memmi*, which V. echoes again (with a similar anaphora) at *E.* 5.64 *deus, deus ille, Menalca*; cf. Hom. *Od.* 8.467–8; Cic. *p. red. ad Quir.* 11 *parens, deus, salus nostrae uitae* (P. Lentulus); *Att.* 4.16.3 *deus ille noster* (Plato); also, perhaps 8.16.1 (Julius Caesar). V. himself hints at an identification of the *deus* as Octavian in the finale of the *Georgics* (*G.* 4.560–2): the young Caesar aspires to Olympus, and is de facto equated with thunderbolt-wielding Jupiter (see also *E.* 1.1n.). It bears mentioning that a possible etymology of *Theokritos* is 'chosen by the god' (the etymology

72   ECLOGUE 1

'judge of goddesses', in the active sense, leads to his identification as Paris in the pseudo-Theocritean *Syrinx*: see *Anth. Pal.* 15.21.12; cf. Dosiadas, *Anth. Pal.* 15.26.10): Tityrus himself, chosen by the gods, is a 'Theocritean' poet. **otia**. The term, rich in implications for Roman culture and society, temporarily takes Tityrus away from pastoral stylization, amplifying the Epicurean echoes. No wonder that a deity bestows on him the pastoral *otia dia*, as Lucretius called them at 5.1387 (the poet's figure, here hidden yet perceptible, will come to the fore at *G.* 4.564, where V. defines himself *studiis florentem ignobilis oti*). The Epicurean tone of these initial lines struck many ancient readers, as e.g. in the case of Seneca, *epist.* 73.10–11; cf. *ben.* 4.13.1, where Epicurean *uoluptas* is equated with *sub densa umbra latitare* (1.1n.). Seneca himself quotes *E.* 1.6 at *Thy.* 560–1 *otium.../ quis deus fecit?*; for the Roman notion of *otium* cf. André (1966, esp. pp. 500–7); *Enc. Virg.* III, pp. 905–7, s.v. *otium* (I. Dionigi); *Virg. Enc.* pp. 740–1. s.v. *leisure* (L. Kronenberg). Recall the rhetorical commonplace (frequent in the Hellenistic age) whereby the ruler-god is the guarantor of peace and tranquillity: e.g. Theocr. *id.* 15.46–50; 16.96–7; 17.97–105; note also the famous Athenian hymn to Demetrius Poliorcetes, transmitted by Duris of Samos (esp. l. 21 πρῶτον μὲν εἰρήνην ποίησον [apud Athen. 6.253e; cf. *FGrH* 76 F 13 Jac.]); the topos was bound to wide popularity in the imperial age: e.g. Mart. 12.4.3 *quibus otia tuta dedisti* [scil. *Caesar*] and also 1.107.3; cf. Hor. *carm.* 4.5.17–24 and *E.* 4.37–45n.; 5.61 *amat bonus otia Daphnis* (note, as in the present passage, the so-called poetic plural).

7–10. The encomiastic nuance of these lines is reinforced by an insistent use of pronouns (*ille...illius...ille*), typical of divine praise (the so-called *Er-Stil*, or 'third-person style', in E. Norden's well-known formulation [*Agnostos theos*, Leipzig-Berlin 1913, pp. 163–6]), though mitigation is perceived at l. 7 *namque erit ille mihi semper deus* (emphasizing *mihi*). The benefactor's cult is confined within the private sphere and treated as the highest expression of individual gratitude. The repetition of *ille* is intertwined with first-person pronominal forms: *mihi...nostris...meas*.

7. In the second line of his first speech, Tityrus employs the bucolic diaeresis, considered in antiquity to be typical of the *bucolicum carmen*: Ter. Maur. 2114–34; Diom. *gramm.* 1, p. 495.15–16 K.; Serv. *praef. E.* p. 2.5–14 (III.1 Th.-H.); *Enc. Virg.* II, pp. 65–6, s.v. *dieresi bucolica* (G. Pascucci); see Introduction, p. 29 and n. 74. Here the technique is used in its most obvious form, in which word-end and colon-end coincide (contrast 3 *dulcia* ⋮ *linquimus arua*; also 1 *sub* ⋮ *tegmine fagi*); the same is true of Meliboeus' words at 1.11. The phenomenon was prominent, probably for 'illustrative' purposes, in Theocritus' first idyll: Hunter (1999, ad *id.* 1, p. 60). The frequency of the bucolic diaeresis in the 'Theocritean' agons of *E.* 3 and 7 confirms its stylistic significance; note that the technique is not employed in the prophetic song of *E.* 4. **erit ille mihi semper deus**. Cf. 3.104 *eris mihi magnus Apollo*; Lucan. 1.63 (Nero) *sed mihi iam*

ECLOGUE 1   73

numen; note also Lucretius' hymn in praise of Epicurus at Lucr. 5.19 *hic merito nobis deus esse uidetur* (see further *E.* 1.6n.), which authorizes Epicurus' followers (*nobis*) to praise a man 'as if' he were a god; cf. also 5.64n. The pronoun *mihi* appears here in its most archaic form, with the second vowel long (*mihī*) before the main caesura.

7–8 illius aram / saepe...imbuet agnus. Cf. Theocr. *epigr.* 1.5 G. βωμὸν δ' αἱμάξει κεραὸς τράγος οὗτος ὁ μαλός 'this white horned goat shall stain the altar with blood' (the epigram perhaps occupied the first position in the Theocritean collection known to V.). Similar deifications and sacrifices occur as early as the comic banter of Plaut. *Asin.* 712–13 (Argyripp.) *datisne argentum?* (Liban.) *si quidem mihi statuam et aram statuis / atque ut deo mi hic immolas bouem: nam ego tibi Salus sum*; cf. also *Capt.* 860–5. Even if the victim's size is modest, as it is often the case with shepherds' sacrifices (but cf. Tib. 1.1.21–2), its importance is still far from negligible, also because offerings are frequent (1.8 *saepe*). It is clear, however, that the blood-sacrifice of the lamb is not part of those monthly offerings (probably of a more modest nature) which Tityrus refers to at 1.42–3 (note also the distinction between 1.8 *aram* and 1.43n. *altaria*). The dactylic form *illĭŭs* is common in hexameter poetry (e.g. 17x in Lucretius). Note that the lamb, here as a sacrificial victim, is the first animal mentioned in the *Eclogues*: the billy goat is instead the first animal named in the *id.* 1 (l. 4; also the lamb appears a little further on, in l. 10).

9 errare. In the sense of 'grazing freely': cf. 2.21 *mille meae Siculis errant in montibus agnae*; Hor. *epod.* 2.12 *prospectat errantis greges*; [Theocr.] *id.* 9.4 πλανῶντο. **boues.** Immediately after the lamb (8 *agnus*), the most valuable and identifying animals of the *boukoliasmos* are mentioned (in the opening scene of *id.* 1 only goats and sheep appeared). Here the cows attract the reader's attention and express the good fortune of Tityrus (note *meas*).

10 ludere quae uellem calamo permisit agresti. The verb *ludere*, like Greek παίζειν, hints at the neoteric and Callimachean principles of 'light' poetry: see *E.* 6.1n.; cf. Catull. 50.1–2 *otiosi / multum lusimus in meis tabellis*; Hor. *sat.* 1.10.37; *carm.* 1.32.2; 4.9.9. Here, too, a form of poetic modesty is implicit (cf. 1.2 *tenui...auena*), and thus the reader perceives the poet's presence again (cf. *G.* 4.565 *carmina qui lusi pastorum*, mentioned above). For now, the 'god' Octavian appears lenient towards the poet Tityrus (and the young poet Tityrus/V.), quite unlike the authoritarian Muses in the proem of Hesiod's *Theogony*, the prototype of poetic initiation (see 1.44–5n.). In *E.* 6, Apollo will set the Callimachean limits—concerning both form and content—of Tityrus/ V.'s poetry. The compound verb *permitto* hints at free movement within space (cf. *errare*, said of the *boues*); another compound form of *mitto* will appear in the god's exhortation (1.45n.).

11–45. After the two herdsmen are introduced in a perfectly symmetrical way, the equilibrium continues to unfold in three dialogic sections, with the

74   ECLOGUE 1

(significant) exception of 1.26n., where the bigger picture will become gradually more apparent. Meliboeus and the reader will, in fact, learn the reason for Tityrus' luck.

11 non equidem inuideo, miror magis. 'I do not feel envy, but rather wonder': Ital. *ma* and French *mais* derive from this (probably colloquial) usage of *magis* with adversative force (= *potius*). Initially a sporadic occurrence, it becomes ever more common: cf. Catull. 68.30 *non est turpe, magis miserum est*; note also Lucr. 1.611–12 *non...sed magis aeterna pollentia simplicitate*; 2.428; Sall. *Iug.* 96.2; *ThlL* VIII.60.22–79. Meliboeus' clarification concerning the benevolent nature of his 'gaze' (*non...in-uideo*), partly prompted by Tityrus' *ut cernis*, looks forward to the omen motif at 1.16–17. For the opening phrase, cf. Hor. *epist.* 2.1.69 *non equidem insector* (2.1.71 *sed...*); for the use of *equidem* cf. *E.* 9.7n. For the bucolic diaeresis cf. 1.7n. **undique totis.** Note the hyperbaton *totis...agris*, framing the chaos described in 1.12 and thus suggesting its vast proportions (for the abl. of extension, cf. *G.* 2.468; *Aen.* 1.29).

12 usque adeo. A typically Lucretian phrase ('to such a point'), particularly frequent at the beginning of a line (Lucr. 1.412; 497; 589; etc.): cf. *G.* 4.84; *Aen.* 12.646. **turbatur.** The impersonal form, preferable to the transmitted *turbamur*, was defended by Servius (and read by Quint. *inst.* 1.4.28). It conveys the idea of total, generalized disorder, in opposition to Tityrus' protected space: cf. Lucr. 6.377 *ancipiti...bello turbatur utrimque*; also Cic. *Sull.* 57; see *Enc. Virg.* V.1, p. 317a, s.v. *turba* (R. Strati). Note also that 'official' uses of political and military language often include the employ of descriptive verbal forms as passive or impersonal (cf. Caes. *Gall.* 5.40.3 *a nostris... resistitur...nulla pars nocturni temporis...intermittitur*; E. Fraenkel, *Eine Form römischer Kriegsbulletins* [1956], in *Kl. Beiträge*, II, Rome 1964, pp. 69–73, esp. 72). The notion reappears, in a similar form ('reversals of fortune'), at the outset of *E.* 9, the other eclogue devoted to land confiscations (9.5n. *fors omnia uersat*). The metapoetical 'disturbance' is obvious in a pastoral book whose opening mixes the old, Theocritean setting with new, Roman notions and contexts. **en ipse capellas.** The interjection *en*, typical of colloquial Latin, enhances the dialogic liveliness of the first eclogue. Meliboeus will use it again twice in the span of a few lines and in a similarly pathetic context (1.67 *en umquam* and 1.71); note also *E.* 6.69; 8.7; 9; *en* occurs three times in the *Georgics* and is relatively frequent in the *Aeneid* (17 occurrences). Meliboeus pathetically emphasizes his direct involvement in pastoral activities (*ipse*: he seems to have been a rather well-off herdsman in the past and is now by no means alone on the road to exile [1.64–6n.]). He draws attention to the animals that symbolize the pastoral world: *capellae*, an affectionate diminutive, effectively replaces *caprae* in poetry (partly owing to its metrical convenience: it almost exclusively appears in line-ending position, like *agellus* at 9.3n.; see Lucr. 6.970). In V., *capellae* is always plural (with the significant exception of 2.63–4) and appears at least once in each eclogue, except *E.* 5 and 6 (but cf. 4.21n.); *capellae* is

ECLOGUE 1   75

the last word of the *E.* (10.77) and occurs twice in the *Georgics* (*G.* 2.196; 3.287), but never in the *Aeneid*. The reader may now have the impression that Meliboeus gets to hold on to his animals or at least some of them: yet his last four lines (1.75–8) suggest that he is no longer a goatherd. Here, therefore, he is probably hastening to hand over the herd to the new owner (not without anxiety: 1.13 *aeger*), after letting the goats graze one last time (this might explain the language of abandonment and pathos at 1.14–15).

13 protinus. The grammarians' distinction between *protinus* adv. of time and *protenus* adv. of place (implying that the latter is the correct reading here) is probably arbitrary. Rather, the two variants must be purely orthographic, and the form *protinus* is transmitted in many other Virgilian passages. **aeger ago.** '*ago*' *autem proprie, nam agi dicuntur pecora* (Serv.). Assonance and alliteration highlight the sorrowful meaning of the action. Note the elision with the following *hanc*, in contrast to the logico-syntactical break: the effect is agitation in Meliboeus' utterance. **uix…duco.** As opposed to *agere*, 'to drive, to push' (the shepherd usually keeps his flock in front of him: πρόβατα). Meliboeus' is forced to 'lead', almost to 'drag' (with a rope?), the she-goat. The animal is weakened by labour pain but also (as *uix* suggests) reluctant to abandon its offspring: this introduces the typically Virgilian theme of suffering, which animals share with humans (cf. 8.85n.).

14–15. The pathetic climax is marked by an event which, under normal circumstances, would appear beneficial to any Theocritean herdsman: the birth of twin goats (cf. *id.* 1.25, with *schol.*, p. 37.12–16 Wend.; Callim. *hymn.* 2[*Ap.*].53–4; a human mother, too, would consider a double childbirth to be somewhat reassuring and encouraging: Prop. 2.22a.41–2). But the pastoral world is shaken by turmoil (1.12), and the gods' omens appear far from reassuring (1.16–17). The mother abandons her kids on hard rocks, while Tityrus reclines under the sheltering shade of the *fagus*. At 1.49n., the poet shows Meliboeus to be still worried about the future of his herd: the pathetic effect is thus coupled with dramatic coherence.

14 corylos. The hazel, of the species *corylus auellana* (from *Abella*): Cat. *agr.* 18.9; Plin. *nat.* 15.88. This shrub-like plant, frequent in the *E.* but not occurring in Theocritus, is part of V.'s description of his own individual landscape: 5.3; 21; 7.63–4; cf. also *G.* 2.65; 299; *Enc. Virg.* I, p. 904b, s.v. *corylus* (G. Maggiulli). **namque.** The strong postponement of *namque*, here preceded by five words, must be taken as a feature of neoteric style, used for pathetic effects in this case: Catull. 66.65 *Virginis et saeui contingens namque Leonis* (for the postponed *nam*, similar to the Greek enclitic γάρ, cf. Catull. 23.7; note also *G.* 4.16; *Aen.* 4.421; 10.585). In the *E.* cf. also 3.33 (third position); fourth position at *Aen.* 5.733; 7.122; 10.614 (where the particle's function is mostly assertive). For *nam* cf. 9.39n. **gemellos.** Normally used of human beings, the diminutive *gemellus* conveys a sense of affection, compared to the standard term *gemini*: see *ThlL* VI.2.1735.26–43.

76   ECLOGUE 1

15. That a mother abandons her kids is by no means an uncommon event, with which the herdsman needs to be able to cope: cf. Tib. 1.1.31–2. Here the event becomes a symbol of the misfortune of both Meliboeus and his flock (1.74 *felix quondam*). The presence of 'naked' stones, far from rare in V.'s landscape, is noted again at 1.47 *lapis...nudus*. Here, in a context featuring the birth of an animal, *nudus* is emotionally charged, particularly since adult animals, and a fortiori their younglings, would normally sleep on something quite different from bare rock: cf. *G.* 3.295–9 (contrast the flower-clad *cunabula* of the newborn *puer* at *E.* 4.23). Feelings of grief are heightened by the repeated /a/ in arsis: *spem gregis, A, silice in nudA conixa reliquit* (cf. 10.46–9n.). Exclamatory *a* is used, in pathetic contexts, by the neoteric poets (e.g. Catull. 64.135); note that all its occurrences in the *E.* are eminently pathetic in nature: cf. 2.60; 6.47; 52; 77; 10.47; 48; 49. **spem gregis**. Hope is concretely understood here as future procreation and continuity: cf. *G.* 3.73 *in spem...gentis*; 473 *spemque gregemque...cunctamque...gentem* (with Servius' note: *agnos cum matribus pariter*); 4.162; *Aen.* 2.503; *Enc. Virg.* IV, p. 995, s.v. *spes* (P. Colafrancesco). **conixa**. More dramatic than the usual *enixa*, expressing 'concentrated' effort: cf. *Aen.* 10.127 *fert ingens toto conixus corpore saxum*; normalized at Ov. *met.* 11.316 *namque est enixa gemellos* (where *namque* regains the first position: see 1.14n.).

16 **malum hoc**. i.e. expropriation and exile—not just the loss of the two kids, which certainly is an emblematic event. **si mens non laeua fuisset**. Cf. *Aen.* 2.54. The adj., if applied to parts of the body or mental faculties, can mean 'clumsy', 'foolish'. By contrast, Roman augural tradition attributed a positive or favourable significance to the left side: cf. *E.* 9.15; *G.* 4.7; *Aen.* 2.693 (but see also Enn. *ann.* 146 Sk. *de caelo laeuom dedit inclutus signum*).

17 **de caelo tactas**. The phrase is a standard formula for the impact of thunderbolts as mantic or divine signs (Cat. *agr.* 14.3; Varr. apud Censor. 17.8; Cic. *diu.* 1.92; 2.47; 149; Liv. 25.7.7, etc.). The place, or object, touched by the thunderbolt was considered sacrosanct. We cannot verify the testimony related by some commentators (and perhaps based on lost ancient sources), whereby the oak hit by the thunderbolt signifies exile. An important parallel, however, is offered by the oneirocritic tradition, e.g. Artemidorus, *onir.* 4 proem.: 'If [scil. the dreamer] is ready for a journey, he will not dream of chariots, or ships, or travel blankets, or luggage or preparations for the journey, but he will have the impression of flying, or will dream of an earthquake, or a war, or a thunderbolt, or some other thing symbolizing travel'; 2.9 'A thunderbolt hitting a spot near the dreamer (without there being a thunderstorm) expels him from the place where he is: in fact, he cannot stay in proximity to a thunderbolt'. Ovid, too, mentions an oak struck by a thunderbolt in the context of exile (Ov. *trist.* 4.9.14 [see 1.3n.]; also *trist.* 2.143–4); Antonius' dream, shortly after the death of Julius Caesar (Plut. *Ant.* 16.7), also has to be mentioned: his right hand would have been struck by a thunderbolt (a sign of Octavian's hostility). **memini praedicere**. The present infinitive replaces

ECLOGUE 1   77

the expected *praedixisse*, in order to emphasize repetition (*saepe*) and continuity: cf. 7.69; 9.52. After 1.17, some of the *recentiores* manuscripts insert a line, *saepe sinistra caua dicebat ab ilice cornix*, modelled after 9.15. Perhaps an ancient reader mistakenly intended to underscore the implicit correspondence between the two eclogues, based on the omen motif. At least in this case, however, the interpolation did not spread widely within the manuscript tradition.

18 qui sit. The interrogative pronoun, used substantively, appears in the form *qui* (rather than *quis*), also for euphonic reasons—it is followed by a sibilant: cf. 2.19; 3.8; *Aen.* 3.608; 9.146 (where the reading *quis* must be rejected); but cf. Catull. 17.22; 66.42; 78b.4; see also Prop. 1.5.18; Ov. *met.* 11.279 (a likely exception is the controversial Hor. *carm.* 4.7.17 *quis scit*, where *qui scit* is supported by a minority of manuscripts). A different case is the indefinite at *E.* 6.73. **da.** In the sense of *dic* 'show', 'point to', just as *accipe* stands for *audi* (Serv.). Pre-Virgilian attestations seem to suggest colloquial usage (Plautus, Terence, Lucilius, etc.). Perhaps V.'s exemplarity promoted it to a high stylistic level (Seneca's tragedies, Lucan, Valerius Flaccus, and also Horace's heroicomic *sat.* 2.8.4–5). See further *ThlL* V.1.1687.55–1688.7. The monosyllabic and semantically 'elementary' verb contributes to the rhythmic and rhetorical strength of this line. The line is entirely composed of (four) monosyllabic and (four) disyllabic words, with the exception of the vocative *Tityre*. All of these components are strictly necessary to the particular information being requested. The opening *sed tamen*, as in *E.* 9.55, cuts the speech short and draws the interlocutor's attention to the main focal point (cf. Hor. *sat.* 1.1.27 *sed tamen amoto quaeramus seria ludo*). It seems as though the reader is meant to share Meliboeus' curiosity, so that Tityrus' reply may stand out for its vagueness (see 1.19n.).

19 Vrbem quam dicunt Romam. The opening *urbem*, followed by the name of the City, sounds rather solemn: compare its epic occurrence at *Aen.* 1.573 *urbem quam statuo uestra est* (Dido addressing her Trojan guests). Tacitus, too, begins his *Annales* with a hexameter in which *urbem* is directly followed by *Romam* (Tac. *ann.* 1.1 *Vrbem Romam a principio reges habuere*). The solemn tone is confirmed by the phrase *quam dicunt*, qualifying the City's geographical name in accordance with the conventions of highbrow literature (Enn. *ann.* 20 Sk. *est locus Hesperiam quam mortales perhibebant*; cf. also Varr. *Men.* 415 Buech. = Astb.[2] = Cèb. *amnis, quam olim Albulam dicunt uocitatam*). Here, moreover, further emphasis is provided by the slow, spondaic rhythm and by Tityrus' temporary evading of Meliboeus' precise question (1.18, then reformulated with some variation at 1.26). Ancient commentators noticed that Tityrus, while mentioning Rome and his journey, does not actually reply to Meliboeus' specific question (concerning the *deus*). Servius' explanation is probably correct, even though he himself rejects it (Serv. *ad E.* 1.19 *simplicitate utitur rustica, ut ordinem narrationis plenum non teneat, sed per longas ambages ad interrogata descendat*): Tityrus' initial vagueness is due to his 'rustic' characterization. Being a 'simpleton', Tityrus is eager to narrate

78   ECLOGUE 1

his experience and therefore allows himself some *ambages*, until Meliboeus questions him again at 1.26 (this, of course, enhances the reader's curiosity). The consul Apronianus Asterius (in his note ad loc. transmitted by **M**) tries somewhat awkwardly to resolve the impasse or, perhaps, simply fails to understand V.'s mimetic representation of a lively dialogue and the subtle characterization of its two protagonists. Apronianus takes 1.19 to be Tityrus' direct reply to Meliboeus, thus implying that Rome is his divine saviour. Yet here, besides Tityrus' self-characterization as *stultus ego* (1.20n.), homely images and metaphors play a key role in the ethopoeia of the naive shepherd. For similar cases, see *E.* 2.63–5; 5.32–4; 7.65–8; 10.29–30 (where the speaker is Pan himself, Arcadia's god); but cf. *id.* 8.57–9; 9.31–5; 10.30–1. In the pastoral, post-Theocritean world of the *E.*, the appearance of a large non-Greek city strikes a balance between epic solemnity and rustic mimesis. In Greek pastoral poetry, Italian geography is hinted at in *epit. Bion.* 94 Αὐσονικᾶς ὀδύνας…μέλος.

20 stultus. A term belonging to everyday language and low register (in V. it only occurs here and in the words of the resentful Corydon: *E.* 2.39). The contrast with the solemnity of 1.19 becomes all the more evident. **huic nostrae.** In all likelihood, Mantua, according to the ancient biographical tradition (even though, in this poem, Mantuan geography is less clearly defined than in *E.* 9). **quo.** For the relatively common use of the locative adverb *quo* in relation to a noun or pronoun (*huic nostrae* [scil. *urbi*]), see *Aen.* 6.43; 11.524 (note also, despite the obvious differences, *E.* 9.1 *quo…quo uia ducit, in urbem?*); cf. Cic. *Manil.* 55 *insula Delus…in Aegaeo mari posita, quo omnes…commeabant.* It bears mentioning that some editors have suspected textual corruption: note Burman's conjecture *quoi* = *cui* (for the error, cf. F in *G.* 3.211), which gives *depellere* the sense of 'weaning' (not necessary here: see 1.21n.).

21 ouium teneros depellere fetus. The verb points to the harsh action of 'driving away' the lambs (still very young: note *ouium…fetus*). The lambs are pushed away from the herd (and their mothers) and towards the city (1.20 *quo* [n.]). The verb can also mean 'weaning', 'sending [the lambs] away' from breast milk: here, however, this meaning is merely implied (note *ab ubere*: contrast 3.82 *dulce… depulsis arbutus haedis*; 7.15 *depulsos a lacte…agnos*; *G.* 3.187 *depulsus ab ubere matris* [similar ambiguity in all three cases]; Varr. *rust.* 2.2.17 *depulsi…agni a matribus*). To be sure, 'weaning' the lambs would not imply 'sacrificing' them: on the contrary, it would hint at a desire to see them grow (note also that the city-dwellers' favourite type of lamb is the milk lamb: nothing is there to be gained by weaning the lambs). The point is, rather, the trauma of separation: *de-pellere* is vehemently opposed to the herdsman's typical action of 'gathering' the herd (note *compellere* at 2.30, referring to goats). It is wholly accidental and ultimately irrelevant whether or not the herdsman is physically transporting the lambs on his shoulders to the city, as Moeris transports the kids in *E.* 9 (cf. 9.1 *in urbem*; 9.62 *haedos depone*). Lamb meat was highly appreciated in ancient Rome (see Colum.

ECLOGUE 1   79

7.3.13): hence the frequent occurrence of this kind of journey (cf. 1.20 *quo saepe solemus / pastores*); note *G*. 3.402 *adit oppida pastor*, and also *G*. 1.273–5.

22 canibus catulos. The juxtaposition plays on alliteration: Varr. *ling*. 9.74 *canis catulus catellus* (*catulus* seems to be related to Umbr. *katel*: Ernout-Meillet, p. 106, s.v.). Note also the anaphora of *sic*, repeated three times at 1.22–3 (each starting a new colon). Here, too, the rhetorical effect is to draw attention to the herdsman's naivety. **matribus haedos**. The *capellae* and their kids play a crucial role in V.'s world. Here they partake in the mother-child relationship described by Meliboeus (who talked about the mother's suffering as she abandons her children: cf. 13–15). Note *matribus*, which clarifies and disambiguates *canibus* ('she-dogs') but also hints at the correct analogy between the situation at hand and Rome's relationship to Mantua (motherland and colony, respectively).

23 noram…solebam. Verbs opening and closing the line, with an effect of homeoteleuton—a stylistic feature not uncommon in V. Here, as in 1.29, V. is probably imitating colloquial language with elegant nonchalance: cf. *Aen*. 6.213; 468. **paruis componere magna**. A proverbial motto: *G*. 4.176; cf. Herodot. 2.10.1 σμικρὰ…μεγάλοισι συμβαλεῖν; Thuc. 4.36.3; Cic. *Brut*. 213; *orat*. 14; Ov. *met*. 5.416–17 *quod si componere magnis / parua mihi fas est*; *trist*. 1.6.28; Stat. *silu*. 1.5.61–2; Otto (1890, pp. 204–5, no. 1008); Tosi (2007, pp. 36–7, no. 87); but Tityrus is a humble shepherd, used to little things: αἰεὶ τοῖς μικκοῖς μικκὰ διδοῦσι θεοί as a proverbial verse by Callimachus says (*aet*. fr. *SH* 253.11 = 55.11 Mass. = 137m.11 Hard.; cf. Artemid. *onir*. 4.84). Note the construction of *componere* + dat.: Catull. 68.141; K.-S., II.1, pp. 317–18.

24 caput extulit. The verb is not wholly equivalent to a present, as it is sometimes taken to be (i.e. *elatum gerit*). The implication is that Rome's rich past has seen the city grow to its present state, in which it surpasses all other cities. An important parallel in Theocritus: πιείρᾳ μεγάλα ἅτ' <u>ἀνέδραμε</u> κόσμος ἀρούρᾳ / ἢ κάπῳ κυπάρισσος … / ὧδε καὶ ἁ ῥοδόχρως Ἑλένα Λακεδαίμονι κόσμος 'as a large cypress tree grows adorning a fertile field / or a garden…, / so does rosy Helen adorn Sparta' (*id*. 18.29–31; cf. Hesych. ἀναδρομαί· αὐξήσεις, βλαστήσεις). Compare the 'aoristic' usage at *Aen*. 10.261–2 *clipeum cum deinde sinistra / extulit ardentem*; the image is based on Hom. *Od*. 6.107 πασάων δ' ὑπὲρ ἥ γε κάρη ἔχει ἠδὲ μέτωπα (Artemis stands out among other huntresses). The phrase will reappear in Vell. 2.4.6 *super totum orbem Roma extulerat caput*; Ov. *fast*. 1.209–10; 4.255–6. The personifying *caput* is common for plants or trees: cf. *Aen*. 9.681–2. Here, however, the anthropomorphic iconography of *Dea Roma* must also be part of the background.

25 lenta…uiburna. Perhaps *Viburnum lantana*, normally known as 'wayfaring tree', a wild shrub usually not taller than two metres—a relatively common type of plant that seemingly makes its first poetic appearance here, where it gives local colour to the text: cf. *Enc. Virg*. V.1, pp. 529–30, s.v. *viburnum* (G. Maggiulli). It will not appear again in V. and its few, mostly late antique occurrences are

80   ECLOGUE 1

certainly Virgilian echoes (Nemes. *ecl.* 2.86 *inter uiburna cupressos*; Paul. Nol. *carm.* 11.37). A potential assonance with *uimen* and *uieo* ('to bind, interweave') is underscored by *lenta*: a 'flexible' and tangled plant, contrasting with the definite, slender silhouette of the cypress tree. **cupressi**. A tree rich in cultic, religious, and mythological connotations, it can reach 50 metres in height: cf. *Enc. Virg.* I, pp. 789–90, s.v. *cipresso* (G. Maggiulli). Apart from its practical function of marking property boundaries, it was considered visually pleasing (*Geopon.* 11.5.4) and must have figured (as far as we can tell) in Roman landscape and garden paintings. For its pastoral use, cf. Theocr. *id.* 18.30, quoted above [1.24n.], as well as 11.45; 22.41; *epigr.* 4.7 G. Just like Rome, the cypress tree will not be mentioned again in the *E.*, even though it will reappear in the *G.*'s incipit as a tender plant, 'gift' and attribute of the god Silvanus (1.20 *et teneram ab radice ferens, Siluane, cupressum*; again in line-ending position). The image is reworked in Nemes. *ecl.* 2.85–7.

   26 Et quae tanta...tibi causa. Meliboeus' request for specific information, to which Tityrus replied elusively after 1.18 (see 1.19n.), is here reiterated. Meliboeus will not let up and asks Tityrus what the *causa* of his journey was (cf. *Aen.* 6.458 *tibi causa fui*), while simultaneously acknowledging the vast dimensions (*tanta*) of the space experienced by Tityrus (cf. 1.24–5 *tantum...quantum*). A single line is sufficient for Meliboeus to ask his question, and this is the first 'one-liner' in the *E.* (note also 3.1, 3.2, 5.8, 5.9, 9.1; Meliboeus, however, is also the character who utters the longest dialogic replies: see 1.46–7n.). Love can be the *causa* of a journey (i.e. to run away from it), as in Theocr. *id.* 14.52–6 or in comedy (cf. Men. *Sam.* 623–32), but here V. is drawing attention to civil and social unrest, even though love itself plays an important role in Tityrus' life (unrequited by Galatea, more constructive in Amaryllis' case). Note the conjunction *et*, used to introduce a question—here it expresses curiosity about the remainder of the story, mimicking the liveliness of colloquial speech; cf. Enn. *trag. inc.* 386 Joc. = 386–7 V.² *et quis illaec est quae lugubri succincta est stola?* The same is true of Greek καί, e.g. at Eur. *Iph. Taur.* 254; cf. also Soph. *El.* 236; J. D. Denniston, *The Greek Particles*, Oxford 1954², p. 310.

   27 Libertas. The *ciuis*' freedom, including full enjoyment of civil rights, as opposed to servitude. In its political meaning, the word *libertas* played a crucial role during the civil wars, at least since Caesar claimed it when crossing the Rubicon (*civ.* 1.22.5). Note that Asinius Pollio, V.'s protector at the time of the *E.*, wrote *natura mea et studia trahunt me ad pacis et libertatis cupiditatem* in a letter to Cicero from Spain, 43 BCE (*fam.* 10.31.2; later, following his triumph, Pollio will rebuild the *Atrium Libertatis* in grand style). The term was used as a slogan by both sides fighting at Philippi. Finally, on 28 BCE coins, the *princeps* is called *libertatis populi Romani uindex*; cf. Syme (1939, pp. 154–5); *Enc. Virg.* III, pp. 203–5, s.v. *libertas* (T. P. Wiseman; G. Crifò); A. J. Clark, *Divine Qualities. Cult and Community in Republican Rome*, Oxford 2007, esp. pp. 142–53 (note also the index, s.v. *libertas*). In the *Aeneid*, V. mentions the unrelenting behaviour of L. Iunius Brutus, the first Roman consul, who did not hesitate to apply the death penalty to his own children in the name of freedom (*pulchra pro libertate: Aen.* 6.821). What kind of *libertas* is referred to here? This will only be made clear, after a long clause, by the final *peculi* at 1.32, which must point to slavery (see n. ad loc.; cf. then *seruitium* at 1.40). Persius will dwell on the various meanings of *libertas* at 5.73–4, perhaps having V. in mind: *libertate opus est: non hac, ut quisque Velina / Publius emeruit*, etc. In the *Divine Comedy*, at the beginning of the *Purgatorio*, Dante's character Virgil will once again start a line with the word 'freedom', explaining to Cato (the Republican martyr) the reason for a wholly different journey, i.e. Dante's trip to Purgatory: 'libertà va cercando, ch'è sì cara, / come sa chi per lei vita rifiuta' (*Purg.* 1.71–2; note the similar use of the relative clause: 'ch'è sì cara' ≈ *quae sera tamen*). This Virgilian reminiscence, which Dante puts in his own Virgil's mouth, is ironically construed as a self-quotation and uttered in the third person rather than the first (later, in his own *Eclogues*, Dante will play the role of Tityrus: see 1.46n.). **sera tamen respexit**. The image of 'turning to look' (*respicere*) is typically associated with kind and caring deities (Greek uses a different preverb: cf. ἐφοράω vel sim.): Plaut. *Bacch.* 638 *deus respiciet nos aliquis*; *Rud.* 1316 *di homines respiciunt*; Ter. *Phorm.* 817; Cic. *Att.* 7.1.2; [Sen.] *Herc. O.* 1991. A *Fortuna Respiciens* (scil. *ad opem ferendam*) is mentioned by Cic. *leg.* 2.28. As a goddess, *Libertas* herself is frequently attested: Cic. *nat. deor.* 2.61; Varr. *apud* Serv. Dan. *ad Aen.* 8.564 (*ant. rer. diu.* fr. 222* Card.); her cult, albeit not officially recognized, must have been widespread among lower social strata in the first century BCE (see above for further reading). For the ellipsis presupposed by *sera tamen* (= 'although late, nevertheless…'; *serus* often has a concessive force), cf. Tib. 1.9.4 *sera tamen tacitis poena uenit pedibus*; Prop. 3.15.35 *sera tamen pietas* (see also 3.4.5); Cic. *Mil.* 85.

28 candidior…tondenti barba cadebat. Tityrus, now a *senex* (1.46), was already an adult at the time of his trip to Rome, and his beard was white. Perhaps V. is hinting at a type of internal chronology, given that his shepherds are generally youthful, and in some cases even 'prepubescent'. The first eclogue would then be situated at a later dramatic date than the other poems, whose sorrowful future it would predict—conversely, the other eclogues' dramatic date would have to be inferred in regressive order. Similarly, in *E.* 9, the other poem devoted to land confiscations, Moeris' youth is gone (9.51–4). In order to overcome an evident hurdle to the Tityrus-V. identification (V. was not even thirty at the time), Servius insists on connecting *candidior* with *libertas*, thus ignoring the postponement of *postquam*. Here, however, V.'s intention is probably to limit the similarities between his own personal experience and Tityrus'. The same detail (i.e. shaving) will appear again, in a chronological and autobiographical context, at Iuv. 1.25 (where it refers to youth gone by): *quo tondente grauis iuueni mihi barba sonabat* (= 10.226). Here *tondenti* (scil. *mihi*) seems to allude to the cutting (i.e.

82   ECLOGUE 1

shortening) of the herdsman's white beard, rather than to shaving (*radere*), which would not correspond to pastoral iconography. Note the alliterative sound balance between the two line-framing words (*candidior…cadebat*), which builds upon the rhyming verbs in line-ending position at 28–31, placed in a chiastic pattern (*cadebat, uenit, reliquit, tenebat*). Note also the echo of *tamen respexit* (27) at 29 *respexit tamen*; see further 1.29n. In Tityrus' words, rhetorical structure blends together with both musical effects and evocation of the past. For the white-haired chin as a sign of impending old age, see also Theocr. *id.* 14.69–70 ἐς γένυν ἕρπει / λευκαίνων ὁ χρόνος.

29 respexit…uenit. For the 'framing' arrangement of the verbs cf. 1.23n. **respexit tamen.** Cf. 1.27 *tamen respexit*: yet another repetition (in keeping with pastoral style), here embellished by the chiastic structure (cf. 1.3–4n.).

30 Galatea reliquit. Tityrus' former partner bears an important name, contrasting with the humble status of the herdsman. The best-known Galatea (Γαλάτεια) is a sea-nymph, the beautiful Nereid (Hes. *theog.* 250 εὐειδὴς Γαλάτεια) whom the Cyclops hopelessly loves in *id.* 6 and 11. In the pastoral tradition, she is the divine archetype of such elusive girls as the Amaryllis sung by the goatherd in *id.* 3 (whereas V.'s Amaryllis is a more suitable partner for Tityrus), or the pseudo-Theocritean Eunice in *id.* 20. See also *E.* 7.37; 9.39; cf., more subtly, 3.64 (and, finally, the Nereid at *Aen.* 9.103). The effect is the same for both the Cyclops and Tityrus: the former neglected his flock (*id.* 11.10–16), the latter his *peculium* (1.32n.). Philoxenus' dithyramb *Galatea*, probably known to Theocritus (a poem in hexameters entitled *Galatea* was composed by Callimachus: cf. Athen. 7.284c; frr. 378–9 Pf.; see p. 111), seems to have prompted the spread of biographical narratives focusing on the dangers that lurk in the name itself, regardless of whether its bearer is a human or a divine figure. Philoxenus, the story goes, was inspired to compose his poem by his unrequited love for Galatea, a courtesan of the tyrant Dionysius, whose wrath against the poet prompted Philoxenus to portray him satirically as the Cyclops: cf. *schol. ad* Aristoph. *Plut.* 290; Athen. 1.6e–f (quoting the Peripatetic writer Phaenias [*FHG*, II.297]). After being introduced as an active generator of love poetry (1.1 *meditaris*; 5 *doces*), Tityrus is now depicted as the passive object of two girls' agency (*nos Amaryllis habet, Galatea reliquit*; cf. 1.31 *tenebat*). Similarly, he evokes the agency of *libertas* itself, turned towards him and his *inertia* (1.27). The irresistible and often destructive force of eros, a theme dear to V., makes its first Virgilian appearance here, where it is predicated on Tityrus' humble naivety (as a matter of fact, Tityrus seems chiefly concerned with its economic consequences). In V.'s pastoral collection, the theme reappears in *E.* 2 and 6 (cf. the vicissitudes of famous heroines at 6.45–60), and then again in *E.* 8 and 10. For the Epicurean V., Amaryllis is perhaps the embodiment of the ideal life companion, with whom a carefree existence is possible: compare Lucretius' *muliercula* (Lucr. 4.1278–82).

31 (fatebor enim). Cf. *Aen.* 4.20 *Anna (fatebor enim) miseri post fata Sychaei* (same position within the line, after the opening trochee). **Galatea tenebat.** The

ECLOGUE 1   83

verb was used of a famous daughter of Nereus, i.e. Thetis, at Catull. 64.28 *tene Thetis tenuit pulcherrima Nereine?* (where *Nereine* is M. Haupt's conjecture; cf. 7.37 *Nerine Galatea*). It is, however, a common item of erotic vocabulary: cf. Prop. 2.21.12; 4.7.93; Ov. *ars* 3.563; on Tityrus, submissive to his lovers, cf. 1.30n.

32 nec spes libertatis… nec cura peculi. Tityrus' social condition is finally clarified in legal terms: as a rural slave, he needed *peculium* in order to free himself; cf. also 1.40 *seruitio* (n.). Hence we may infer that neither Galatea nor (at least initially) Amaryllis can be considered as a legitimate *coniunx*, but rather only as a *contubernalis* (lit. 'tent-companion', from military jargon). Like a comic slave, Tityrus had dissipated his savings due to a costly love affair (cf. Plaut. *Stich.* 751). Once he had recovered his wealth with Amaryllis' help, he decided to head for Rome in order to counter a new, more fearsome threat, i.e. land confiscations. While his master (here unnamed) ran the risk of losing his property, Tityrus would consequently have lost his usufruct rights and any chance of *libertas* (although it seems that the young god ensures the continuity of Tityrus' usufruct, even if a new master replaces the old). Based on Tityrus' enthusiasm, we might be tempted to believe that he obtained his freedom during the same trip to Rome: it is more realistic, however, that he received it at a later stage (cf. *pueri* at 1.45n.). At any rate, Tityrus' reversal of fortune is made very clear, and emphasized in opposition to Meliboeus' fate (1.6n.). At 1.8, 9, 33, and 46, Tityrus is even portrayed as a landowner, while in reality rural slaves would rarely be enfranchised (K. D. White 1970, pp. 352–3); cf. Theocritus' reference to the shepherd's servile status at e.g. *id.* 5.5. Discussion and further reading in *Enc. Virg.* III, p. 204, s.v. *libertas* (G. Crifò); *Virg. Enc.* II, p. 746, s.v. *libertas* (C. S. Mackay); cf. also V.1, p. 199a, s.v. *Titiro* (F. Caviglia). The term *cura*, significantly occurring again at 10.22 (cf. also 3.61; 8.89), does not carry a legal meaning here: *Enc. Virg.* I, pp. 961–3, s.v. *cura* (P. Fedeli, O. Diliberto). In any event, it is hardly productive to attempt a detailed and coherent account of the legal situation here. Through its humble protagonist, V.'s text is effectively meant to address the entirety of Rome's population, be it wealthy or not. As such, it combines different tones and overtones, and it cannot possibly have any sort of monolithic coherence. In 1.32, note the contrast between a potentially solemn, politically charged phrase like *spes libertatis* (often used by Cicero, e.g. at *Phil.* 4.16; 5.49; 8.32; cf. *ad Brut.* 18.5; *fam.* 12.25.2), which echoes 1.27 *libertas*, and the prosaic reference to *peculium*. **peculi.** In a rural slave's case, personal property could be accumulated through usufruct rights, or through actual ownership of some livestock (1.33n.): cf. Varr. *rust.* 1.2.17; 17.5; Plaut. *Asin.* 540–1 *etiam opilio qui pascit…alienas ouis, | aliquam habet peculiarem qui spem soletur suam*; *Enc. Virg.* IV, pp. 2–4, s.v. *peculio* (A. Di Porto). The term, related to *pecunia* and *pecu* 'livestock', is at home in the *E.*; V. will not use it again (note the contracted gen. ending, common in V.). It is clear that Tityrus had not yet succeeded in accumulating the *peculium* he needed to gain his freedom. His fear, probably justified, was that the old *peculia* would be

84   ECLOGUE 1

forgotten by a new owner: note that Cass. Di. 48.6.3 suggests that land confiscations entailed a complete transfer of all goods and privileges (including slaves)
from one owner to the next. Tityrus' dream of freedom would therefore have been
shattered if his master had been a victim of expropriation (see 1.40n. *neque seruitio me exire licebat*).

33 multa meis exiret uictima saeptis. Compared to *hostia*, *uictima* may hint at
a more substantial offering (*diff. gramm.* VII, p. 532.13 K. = Char. *gramm.* [?],
p. 403.28 B.); cf. Fest. p. 508 L. *uictimam Aelius Stilo ait esse uitulum ob eius uigorem;
alii…quae uincta adducatur ad altare* (contrast V.'s *exiret*). Tityrus' sacrifices did
not yield wealth or tranquillity: only in Rome could he find a truly active and
'present' god (1.41n.), whereas the small provincial town is 'ungrateful' (34): cf.
also 20–1. The term *saepta* is commonly used of pens or folds (cf. Varr. *rust.*
2.2.8); cf. the Lucretian phrase *saepta domorum* (1.489), echoed in *G.* 4.159 (bees).
In the Roman *Saepta*, mentioned here by Servius, the Roman people would cast
their ballots (Ov. *fast.* 1.53).

34 pinguis et. To be taken with *caseus* rather than *uictima* (1.33, on which
Servius is mistaken: *pinguis melius ad uictimam quam ad caseum refertur*): *et* is
postponed to second position, in accordance with neoteric usage; cf. 1.68; 2.10;
3.89; 4.54; 7.60; 8.55. The meaning of *pinguis* may be somewhat vague, but
Columella, 7.8.1, describes a type of high-fat cheese, used as a long-life dairy
product (*pingui et opimo* [scil. *liquore*]). Cf. also Varr. *rust.* 2.11.3 *est discrimen
utrum casei molles ac recentes sint an aridi et ueteres*; cf. *G.* 3.400–3; [Theocr.] *id.*
25.106. **premeretur caseus.** The verb is a technical term for cheesemaking,
whereas cheese itself is here referred to by its common name (*caseus*): cf. however 1.81 *pressi copia lactis* (n.); see also e.g. Suet. *Aug.* 76.1 *caseum…manu
pressum*.

35 non umquam. 'Not a single time': the nearby city (cf. 1.20) was 'ungrateful'
(1.34 *ingratae…urbi*), due to both its lack of generosity and the (implied) lavish
expenses that Galatea imposed on Tityrus. This final detail completes the portrait
of Tityrus as a naive shepherd. A luckier, or perhaps more prudent, figure is the
protagonist of *Moretum*: *inde domum ceruice leuis, grauis aere, redibat* (80).

36 quid…uocares. For the use of *quid* in lieu of *cur*, cf. 10.22.

37 cui…patereris. While her partner is absent, Amaryllis neglects to pick the
fruit (cf. 2.69–73n.): perhaps she does not want to take Tityrus' place, since that
was normally his duty; or, rather, she only wants to pick the fruit for Tityrus or,
at any rate, eat it with him (apples, and fruit in general, are a common erotic
symbol: cf. the goatherd's gift to Amaryllis at *id.* 3.10–11; see also *id.* 2.120; 5.88;
6.7; *E.* 2.51; 3.64; 71). Meliboeus' words will further define the personality of
Tityrus' virtuous and faithful companion (see 1.5n.; also 1.30n.). The reader can
catch glimpses of a small rural community, full of curiosity, sideways glances,
and gossip among neighbours. **sua…in arbore.** Cf. 7.54, as well as *G.* 2.82 and
Aen. 6.206.

ECLOGUE 1   85

38 aberat. Lengthening in arsis before caesura, as in *E.* 3.97 *erit*; 7.23 *facit*; 9.66 *puer*; 10.69 *Amor* (in some cases, like this one, the archaic quantity is restored: see nn. ad locc.). For other instances of *-at* in arsis cf. *Aen.* 5.853; 7.174; 10.383; 12.772.

38–9 ipsae te…pinus, / ipsi te fontes, ipsa haec arbusta uocabant. Whereas Tityrus awakened the woods' feelings at 1.4–5, making them 'repeat' Amaryllis' name, here springs, pine trees, and *arbusta* sympathize with the girl (note the line-ending echo between *uocares* [36] and *uocabant* [39]). In both cases, the observer of the phenomenon is Meliboeus. The lover's absence is made apparent by the landscape: cf. *E.* 7.53–60, esp. 7.54 *strata iacent…sua quaeque sub arbore poma* (Corydon's words, reported by Meliboeus), and 5.62–4 (joy for Daphnis' deification: note the similarly repeated *ipse*). Emotional outbursts related to the theme of absence are particularly appropriate for Meliboeus, who is about to leave the stage. **pinus.** An echo of Theocritus' opening πίτυς (described as resonant: see 1.1n.). The tree, notable for its mythological past (cf. Pitys, the nymph beloved by Pan), will play an important role in V.'s Arcadian landscape (7.24n.; 8.22n.; 10.14–15n.). **haec arbusta.** 'Groves', or small woods, either natural or (more often) planted: see *ThlL* II.429.72–430.69. The meaning 'vineyards' (or trees planted to support the vines) would be too specific here: for this usage cf. *E.* 3.10; *G.* 2.416. The force of *arbusta* may also have been generalized because of its metrical convenience (the cretic-shaped *arbores* would not fit the hexameter): cf. *E.* 4.2; 5.64; *Aen.* 10.363. After mentioning pine trees and springs, alluding to a sylvan environment, Meliboeus closes his speech on a more 'domesticated' type of nature, to which he gestures (note the deictic adj.).

40–5. Tityrus resumes his narrative, even though Meliboeus' words seem to have influenced his train of thought: he too suffered from the separation, yet he had no alternative—*quid facerem?* (40: note the colloquial immediacy; cf. 7.14). Still a slave, he had no way of escaping land expropriation: soon, however, he would obtain the right to stay, and eventually freedom, since his master's land and goods were not confiscated, as Tityrus learned from the *deus* himself (see also 1.32n.). The exceptional, divine nature of the *deus* is shown by his ability to intervene directly in Tityrus' fate. Tityrus, it seems, did not need any intermediaries to talk to him, and promptly received an answer (1.44). By contrast, the Neronian poet Calpurnius Siculus finds it natural to conjure up a protector (Pollio? Or even, anachronistically, Maecenas?) who leads Tityrus to Rome and its 'gods': *tu mihi talis eris, qualis qui dulce sonantem / Tityron e siluis dominam deduxit in urbem / ostenditque deos* (Calp. *ecl.* 4.160–2: the speaker is Corydon, who addresses Meliboeus and hopes to receive protection from him).

40 neque seruitio me exire licebat. Tityrus' juridical status is clarified here once more (see 1.32n.): in his case, the *libertas* he aspires to is the end of *seruitium*, a term which refers to slavery in comedy and elsewhere (Plaut. *Curc.* 300; Ter. *Andr.* 675; Lucr. 1.455; Liv. 2.23.6). V. must have popularized the use of the prosaic and legal term

86   ECLOGUE 1

seruitium in poetry by employing it in all his works (four times in total: here and at *G.* 3.168; *Aen.* 1.285; 3.327; cf. also Hor. *sat.* 2.5.99). In the elegiac genre, the term later acquired the 'technical' sense of *seruitium amoris*, as in Prop. 1.5.19 and Tib. 2.4.1. It is clear that V. here aims at a typical representation of slavery and freedom rather than at historical accuracy, especially considering that rural slaves were rarely emancipated (cf. 1.32n.). Note also that, in the Augustan age, the transition from slavery to freedom was far from simple (Suet. *Aug.* 40.3). Hence, in the eyes of his contemporaries, Tityrus must have appeared particularly lucky: not only were his master's properties spared from the confiscations (or, at least, Tityrus was unaffected by the expropriations: see 1.32n.), but he eventually managed to obtain freedom (1.46n. *tua rura*). To be sure, V.'s pastoral book is a game of subtle nuances and shrouded vagueness, but the underlying social reality is unmistakable here.

41 tam praesentis...diuos. The god's 'presence', deemed necessary for the success of prayers and invocations, is typical of religious vocabulary (for its connection with *tam* cf. Cic. *Tusc.* 1.28 *Hercules...tam praesens habetur deus*; Liv. 7.26.7), soon to become part of the Augustan language: *G.* 1.10; *Aen.* 9.404; Hor. *carm.* 3.5.2–3 *praesens diuus habebitur / Augustus*; Ov. *trist.* 2.53–4; Veget. 2.5.4; Pollini (1990). The Hellenistic portraits of rulers as 'nearby gods', and therefore effective ones, unlike traditional, unapproachable deities (cf. Demetrius Poliorcetes in Hermocles of Cyzicus' hymn, quoted in Athen. 6.253d–f: esp. l. 2, p. 173 Pow. τῇ πόλει πάρεισιν; ll. 15–18, p. 174 Pow.), are here reworked in the political aftermath of Philippi, when Antony, Octavian, and (initially) Sextus Pompey compete with one another even in their choice of a charismatic, divine role-model. Thus, truly 'present' gods can only be found in Rome (not elsewhere: *alibi*), the city which the young god (Octavian) had made the centre of his political activity; cf. Hor. *carm.* 4.14.43–4 *o tutela praesens / Italiae dominaeque Romae*. This idea is well received in the panegyric tradition: thus, Diocletian can be described as a 'present, visible Jupiter' and Maximian as 'the emperor Hercules' (*Paneg.* 11.3.10.5; see also 11.3.2.4); as a naive laudatory theme it already appears in comedy: e.g. Plaut. *Pers.* 99–100 *o mihi Iuppiter terrestris*. The term *diuus* is more solemn than the standard *deus*; cf. 4.15.

42 illum uidi iuuenem. According to a widespread interpretation (already attested by Servius), this is Caesar Octavian, born in 63 BCE (and therefore seven years younger than V.), who is called *iuuenis* again at *G.* 1.500 *hunc...euerso iuuenem succurrere saeclo* (where *succurrere* might perhaps activate the Varronian [?] etymology *iuuenis a iuuando*, which at best is implicit here); cf. also Hor. *sat.* 2.5.62 *iuuenis Parthis horrendus*; *carm.* 1.2.41. Youth is a salient feature of Octavian's appearance and action (*diuinus adulescens* in Cic. *Phil.* 5.43; note also 3.3), a feature which his enemies' propaganda would use against him (e.g. through offensive usage of the term *puer*: see Cic. *Phil.* 13.24). The notion is employed again, in reference to Germanicus, at Ov. *Pont.* 4.8.23 *di tibi sunt Caesar iuuenis* (as opposed to the older Tiberius). Octavian had taken up the task of distributing

ECLOGUE 1   87

land among the veterans of Philippi, while Antony had settled things in the East: Suet. *Aug.* 13.3; Appian. *bell. civ.* 5.3 (11–13); Cass. Di. 48.6–12. To 'see' the young Octavian was the wish of thousands of suppliants, or simple onlookers, who went to Rome for that very purpose ($\theta\epsilon\omega\rho\acute{\iota}\alpha\varsigma\ \acute{\epsilon}\nu\epsilon\kappa\alpha\ \tau o\hat{v}\ \pi\alpha\iota\delta\acute{o}\varsigma$: Nic. Dam. *uit. Aug.* 5.13). Moreover, *uidi* belongs to the vocabulary of divine epiphany (10.26n.). The term *iuuenis*, crucial to identifying the addressee of the volume, is artfully placed at the centre of the poem: this may be read as a first instance of the *Caesar in medio* pattern (*G.* 3.16). Note also that 1.41 (not 42 as here!) will be referred to Maecenas in *G.* 2 and 3. **quotannis.** Appearing again in the context of cultic devotion at *E.* 5.67; 7.33 (also in line-ending position).

43 bis senos…dies. 'Twelve days a year' (42 *quotannis*), i.e. one every month (hence the distributive adj.). In the first eclogue, the theme of sacrifice combines the bucolic-pastoral element with the encomiastic one, which Theocritus kept distinct. Only in the non-bucolic encomium to Ptolemy II he can write: 'He burns many fat thighs of oxen / on the reddening altars as the months roll by' (*id.* 17.126–7: the subject, however, is the king himself, who established the cult of the 'Saviour Gods', i.e. Ptolemy I and Berenice); but cf. Hom. *Il.* 2.547–51 (Erechtheus receives an annual sacrifice of bulls and lambs from the Athenians). An appropriate parallel is the Hellenistic practice of celebrating the king's birth every month (also applied to other prominent figures, e.g. the philosopher Epicurus). As early as the mid-30s BCE, various Italian communities included Octavian among their tutelary deities (Appian. *bell. civ.* 5.132 [546]; Syme 1939, p. 233; but cf. La Penna 1963b, p. 79), and similar honours had previously been tributed to Julius Caesar (Cass. Di. 44.6; cf. Appian. *bell. civ.* 2.106 [443]). Note Cicero's comments (in March 49 BCE) on Julius Caesar's popularity in small towns outside Rome: *quibus optimatibus, di boni? qui nunc quo modo occurrunt, quo modo etiam se uenditant Caesari!* etc. (Cic. *Att.* 8.16.1–2); see further Marcone (2010, esp. pp. 208–10). Later practices led to the ancient interpretation that Octavian became part of the cult of the domestic Lares, usually worshipped at least once a month (Tib. 1.3.34; on the Kalends: Prop. 4.3.53–4; but cf. Cat. *agr.* 143.2): Hor. *carm.* 4.5.34–5 *et Laribus tuum / miscet numen* (to Augustus). In fact, the joint cult of Lares and *Genius Augusti* was only officialized in 12 BCE (even though it was common to add images of loved ones to the *lararium*: Suet. *Aug.* 7.2; *Vit.* 2.5, etc.). Tityrus' piety is a form of naive, spontaneous, and strictly private devotion. In Italy, for the most part, the young Caesar continued ostentatiously to reject divine (i.e. theocratic and Hellenistic) honours for years. Extraordinary honours are, however, attested even at Rome from a rather early age: in 43 BCE, for instance, the senate decreed that an equestrian statue be placed *in rostris* (cf. Cic. *Phil.* 9.4), with a reference to Caesar's young age (Vell. 2.61.3; note also Appian. *bell. civ.* 3.51 [209], where gold-plating is mentioned, and Cass. Di. 46.29.2). Copious evidence is found on Roman coins: cf. *RRC*, I, pp. 499–500, no. 490; II, p. 740: cf. A. J. Woodman, *Velleius Paterculus, The Caesarian and Augustan Narrative*

88   ECLOGUE 1

(2.41–93), Cambridge 1983, p. 130 ad loc.; more generally on imperial cult, also for bibliography, see the well-balanced C. Letta, *Tra umano e divino. Forme e limiti del culto degli imperatori nel mondo romano*, Sarzana-Lugano 2020; more particularly on Julius Caesar and Augustus, M. Koortbojian, *The Divinization of Caesar and Augustus. Precedents, Consequences, Implications*, Cambridge 2013. As usual, V.'s text is somewhat elusive; yet it seems clear that Tityrus' monthly offerings (perhaps bloodless, as libations to the Lares tended to be) are distinct from the more plentiful sacrifices mentioned at 1.7–8. **altaria fumant**. The term *altaria* is only used in the plural form by Republican and Augustan writers (the earliest occurrence of the singular is in Petron. 135.3). In hexameter verse, it usually occupies the fifth foot, which is always the case in V. (16x), except at *Aen.* 2.550. Tityrus' offerings seem to be distinct, in both structure and function, from the blood-sacrifice of the lamb mentioned at 1.7, where an *ara* is covered with the animal's blood (*imbuet*). The term *altaria*, which folk etymology connected with the idea of height (Paul. Fest. p. 27 L. *altaria ab altitudine dicta*), implies combustion but not necessarily sacrificial killing (*altaria* can be used to burn grains, aromatic plants, or the like: herbage and frankincense are mentioned at 8.65n.). On the distinction between *ara/arae* and *altaria*, see 5.66n.

44–5. The young god speaks as an authority, even a literary one: Hes. *theog.* 24–6 τόνδε δέ με πρώτιστα θεαὶ πρὸς μῦθον ἔειπον, / Μοῦσαι Ὀλυμπιάδες, κοῦραι Διὸς αἰγιόχοιο· / 'ποιμένες ἄγραυλοι...' 'this word, first of all, the goddesses spoke to me, / the Olympian Muses, daughter of aegis-bearing Zeus: / "Rustic shepherds..."' (note the switch from the singular με to the plural ποιμένες: cf. *mihi / pueri*); Callim. *aet.* fr. 1.21–2 Pf. = Mass. = Hard. 'and when first of all [πρώτιστον] I placed a tablet on my / knees, Lycian Apollo said to me'; cf. 6.4–5n.

44 responsum. A quasi-oracular answer, as often in the *Aeneid*: cf. *Aen.* 6.44 *responsa Sibyllae*; 7.102 *responsa...Fauni*; 9.134. Here, however, the legal meaning of the term ('reply to a query or request': see *OLD²*, p. 1802, s.v. 1b) is equally important, since the *deus* is actually a Roman magistrate. **primus.** From Tityrus' point of view, it expresses his long-standing anxiety: *Aen.* 7.117–18 *ea uox audita laborum / prima tulit finem*; cf. also *E.* 4.8. The young god's word was Tityrus first source of salvation: cf. πρώτιστα / πρώτιστον in Hesiod and Callimachus quoted above, as well as e.g. *Hymn. Hom.* 5[*Ven.*].12–13. The notion belongs to the rhetoric of *eucharistikon*: the benefactor is extolled for his incomparable helpfulness, which does not need any supplication; cf. Theocr. *id.* 14.63–4 and Quint. *inst.* 3.7.16.

45. The suppliants' group joined by Tityrus seems to include slaves: thus, the poet can more readily use a generic, patronizing *pueri*, corresponding to the Greek παῖδες (we already know that Tityrus was by no means a child). Here, however, 'boys' also hints at the venerable authority of the *deus*, emphasized by the fact that he is a *iuuenis* himself: in Hom. *Il.* 7.279, παῖδε φίλω is said of Hector and Ajax by the messenger, who calms them both down thanks to his authority (for a

ECLOGUE 1   89

different usage, cf. Theocr. *id.* 10.52, where 'boys' is used among peers as a marker of synergy); for *puer/pueri* referring to servants and accompanied by an imperative, cf. *ThlL* X.2.2518.41–9. The sentence structure, reminiscent of such pastoral exhortations as *E.* 3.98 *cogite ouis, pueri* or 3.111 *claudite iam riuos, pueri*, shows that the *deus* Octavian is perfectly at home in the role of bucolic tutelary deity. Indeed, *pascere boues* is the fundamental activity of a βουκόλος (whereas Hesiod's herdsmen were concerned with sheep: *theog.* 23). Note the different points of view at 1.44 and 45: *mihi* expresses the individual significance of the event, while *pueri* refers to objective reality. Tityrus, in other words, is not the sole recipient of the young god's beneficial answer (cf. 1.44–5n.). Similarly (and even more unexpectedly), Meliboeus suggests that his own fate is shared by many others (see 1.64–6n.). **summittite tauros.** Yet another compound of *mitto*, linked with the young god (cf. 1.10 *permisit*). The exact meaning of *summittere* is debated: perhaps V. meant to confer some sort of 'oracular' quality on his *deus*. The verb should preferably be taken as a technical term, specifically referring to the breeding of stud animals—hence, simply, 'breed': cf. *G.* 3.73; 159; Varr. *rust.* 2.2.18 *quos arietes* [cf. here *tauros*] *submittere uolunt potissimum eligunt ex matribus quae geminos parere solent*; 2.3.4; Pallad. 8.4.1. An important parallel is *id.* 9.3 μόσχως βουσὶν ὑφέντες, ὑπὸ [but note ἐπὶ in **M²Cal.**: Gow in app.] στείραισι δὲ ταύρως, which however describes mating (as in the primary meaning of *summittere*). Ancient and modern attempts to interpret the verb in the sense of 'subjecting (to the yoke)' are unpersuasive. The continuity of work, regenerating both plants and animals, is a fundamental guarantee in the pastoral world: this is precisely what Meliboeus has to give up (1.73n.; see also 1.14–15n.).

46–78. Thus far, the two herdsmen have played roles of approximately equal importance in the dialogue, which now has Meliboeus as its sole protagonist. Meliboeus talks at great length (twenty-eight lines) about his frustrations, his sorrow, and his nostalgia for the lost land, while Tityrus has but five lines. As he prepares to go into exile, Meliboeus offers his audience the most complete description of the pastoral world he is about to abandon. In the opening of his speech, he outlines the archetype of the poet-herdsman who teaches the woods to sing. He then has two clusters of lines, roughly equal to each other (1.46–58 and 1.64–78, i.e. thirteen and fifteen lines, respectively), the first devoted to praising the pastoral life (which Tityrus will be able to enjoy), the second lamenting his own fate as an exile. Significantly, Meliboeus' two speeches are the longest sections of dialogue in the entire book (i.e. excluding explicitly monological texts like *E.* 2 and the singing contests in *E.* 5. and 8: see 1.64–78n.). Meliboeus subtly wards off any suspicion of ill-will on his part, since he never exaggerates in either praising Tityrus' luck (1.47–8n.) or venting his anger towards the new landowners (his invective, only three lines long, is rather restrained: 1.70–2 *impius…miles…barbarus…his*). Through the Sicilian reference at 1.54 (*Hyblaeis apibus*), Meliboeus himself becomes a standard-bearer of the *E.'s* generic model, Theocritus. His

90   ECLOGUE 1

description of the pastoral world, permeated with nostalgia, adds not only dramatic force (recall Daphnis' farewell in Theocr. *id.* 1) but also realism and sociopolitical concreteness to V.'s text. Meliboeus is not merely a literary character, given that his fate is an exemplary document of the dangerous centrifugal forces which threatened to undermine the internal stability of the great City (*Roma*, mentioned by both characters at 1.19 and 1.26, respectively). Caught in the whirlwind of discord and expropriations, many people (free-born citizens and slaves) suffered exile like Meliboeus, until they decided to join forces with the opponents of the triumvirate—particularly Sextus Pompey, whose stronghold in Sicily allowed him to dominate the seas and to welcome all sorts of outcasts and refugees (see p. 59 and Introduction, pp. 4–5). Meliboeus bids Tityrus farewell without seeming to have a precise destination in mind: as such, he represents large masses of individuals who formed a potential threat to Rome's political stability. Despite Meliboeus' restraint, the political energy in his lines remains perceptible. In fact, it must have resonated with V.'s early readers and sparked the creation of the pseudo-Virgilian *Dirae* (part of the *Appendix Virgiliana*), an invective against a new landowner. Besides being replete with echoes, rewritings, and reworkings of *E.* 1, the text of the *Dirae* also testifies to V.'s direct engagement with history in the *E.* (see further 1.49n.; 69n.; 71n.).

46 fortunate senex. This *makarismos*, with its stereotypical formula, opens the first section of Meliboeus' speech (five lines: 1.46–50) and is repeated verbatim at the beginning of the second section (1.51–8: the second part of the speech is eight lines long and expands on the content of the first). For the adjective *fortunatus*, similar to the Greek term ὄλβιος (Hom. *Od.* 24.192; Hes. *op.* 826, etc.), cf. *E.* 5.49 *fortunate puer* (n.) and 6.45; note also *G.* 2.458–9 *o fortunatos… / agricolas*, 2.493 *fortunatus et ille deos qui nouit agrestis* (also a *makarismos* of farming); *Aen.* 1.437; 9.446; 11.252. V.'s readers might also recall the famous Cic. *carm.* fr. 12 Bläns. = 8 Court. *o fortunatam natam me consule Romam* (quoted in Iuv. 10.122); cf. Hor. *sat.* 1.1.4 *o fortunati mercatores* (in a context involving the choice of *bios*). The adjective *beatus*, practically a synonym of *fortunatus*, is used at *Aen.* 1.94 *terque quaterque beati*; see also Hor. *epod.* 2.1 (the opening of Alfius' *laus ruris*). The noun *senex*, reminiscent of the white beard at 1.28, confirms Tityrus' mature age and connotes his pastoral future as a sort of long-awaited retirement (besides setting limits to the allegorical identification of Tityrus as V.: see 1.28n.); for a similar phenomenon (almost a mirror-image of this passage), cf. 5.54 *puer* in reference to Daphnis, 'limiting' the Caesarian allegory (see n. ad loc.). On the other hand, *senex* also hints at the poet-herdsman's authority (6.70n.). Dante portrays himself as a *Tityrus annosus* towards the end of his poetic career (*Eclogues* 4.12; see 1.27n.). **ergo.** 'So', used in exclamatory contexts, but often with a sorrowful nuance: Hor. *carm.* 1.24.5; Prop. 3.23.1; cf. also *Aen.* 6.456. **tua rura manebunt.** The word-order suggests an absolute use of *maneo*, with *tua* as a necessary clarification (thus, 'your fields will remain', rather than 'the fields will still be *yours*'); cf. *E.* 5.78 *semper honos nomenque* *tuum laudesque manebunt* (= *Aen.* 1.609); note also *Aen.* 9.302; the subsequent concessive conjunction (*quamuis*) immediately emphasizes the limits and flaws of those *tua rura*. On Tityrus as 'landowner' cf. 1.32n.; by contrast, the trauma of possession takes centre stage at 9.4n. *haec mea sunt*.

47–8. The concessive clause (*quamuis...iunco*) completes the *makarismos*, clarifying the sense of *magna satis*. The description of Tityrus' estate contained in these two lines is far from eulogistic: rather, it hints at the herdsman's 'humble' character (Meliboeus calls his own place of abode *pauperis...tuguri* at 1.68). Such modesty might also have to do with the fact that V. is talking about his own native land. Yet the reader can also perceive Meliboeus' tact: the herdsman 'restrains' his praise of others' fate and possessions, so as to spare Tityrus the embarrassment of an unbridled eulogy (which might sound excessive: cf. 7.27n.). The result, at any rate, is a landscape description that certainly does not abide by the visual and auditory standards of pastoral agreeableness. Indeed, this landscape can rather be called 'anti-pastoral': bare rocks, stagnant water, marshes, and reeds are not just uncongenial to aesthetic pleasure, but also incompatible with the traditional dissemination of pastoral harmonies (contrast 1.51–8; here, instead, the landscape seems anomalously silent: cf. 9.57–8n.). Note also that, in the first section of his *makarismos*, Meliboeus focuses on the agricultural aspects of rural life (which will be dominant in the *G.*). In other words, V.'s pastoral world is by no means exempt from toil, which will keep Tityrus busy but will also bear fruit (1.47 *tibi magna satis*; see 1.48n.). In the *Dirae*, marshes and reeds (here mentioned at 1.48) are invoked as dark forces, capable of annihilating soil fertility: *emanent subito sicca tellure paludes, / et metat hic iuncos, spicas ubi legimus olim* (1.72–3). According to the biographical tradition, generally based on V.'s text, V.'s farm was particularly large and productive, sufficient for sixty veterans (Prob. *praef. E.* pp. 327.33–328.1 H. [III.2 Th-H.]). Whether or not V.'s biographers are trustworthy (their narrative seems to befit *E.* 9 rather than 1: see 9.9n.), this description of Tityrus' modest farm sets the *senex* further apart from the poet, who no doubt came from a family of wealthy landowners.

47 lapis...nudus. A 'naked' stone, ill-suited to plant life: this visual detail adds colour to the landscape. The reader is familiar with a similar phrase, *silice in nuda* (1.15), but in that context the focus was on the she-goat and her two newborn kids. For *nudus* referring to soil (unsuitable for vines), cf. Catull. 62.49 *in nudo...aruo*; see also Sen. *Phoen.* 69 *nudus...silex*. Note the variant reading *nudis* (*in cautibus*) at 8.43n., where *duris* seems preferable. **omnia.** It points to the property as a whole (*tua rura*), then specified by *pascua*, which it grammatically ought to agree with, although we can think of an ἀπὸ κοινοῦ construction. Everything is covered in bare stone, and the pastures are submerged in a muddy marsh—note that the idea of 'covering' must be supplied *ad sensum*, since *obducat* is only properly suited to *palus*. For *omnia*, concisely referring to the entire estate (and its value, whatever it may be), cf. *E.* 9.10.

48 limosoque...iunco. The placing of noun and epithet at either end of the hexameter, featured in Catull. 64 (see 2.1n.) and well attested in Lucretius (cf. Lucr. 1.9 *placatumque...caelum*, 1.202 *multaque...saecla*, etc.), evokes the extension of the whole surface: cf. 1.83n. Both rushes and sedges (for the latter cf. 3.20n.) appear in the marshy landscape of *Priap.* 86.1–2 Buech. (significantly attributed to V., though actually pseudo-Virgilian). **palus.** Another feature suited to the Mantuan landscape, whose soil was made marshy by the Mincius (7.13). Note that, according to Serv. Dan. *ad E.* 9.10, the 'swampy' nature of the Mantuan soil was a source of conflict during the expropriations (cf. 9.10n.). We might suspect, then, that Tityrus' estate was saved by its poor quality: cf. Colum. 10, ll. 11–12 *nam neque sicca placet nec quae stagnata palude / perpetitur querulae semper conuicia ranae.* That such an ungenerous soil provides a sweet and sheltered space to the *senex* who knows how to benefit from it (*fortunate senex*) is a theme dear to V.: cf. the *senex Corycius* in *G.* 4.116–48, esp. 127–9 *cui pauca relicti / iugera ruris erant, nec fertilis illa iuuencis / nec pecori opportuna seges nec commoda Baccho* (in that case, a happy exile). The landscape features referred to here seems to have belonged to the repertoire of the Augustan artist Studius (or Ludius), who painted rural villas accessed through a marsh (*palustri accessu*: Plin. *nat.* 35.117): cf. p. 10; see also 1.56n. **obducat.** This particularly expressive verb paves the way for the idea of *labor*, a theme dear to V. (and dominant in the *Georgics*, which perhaps were already in his mind at the time of *E.* 1). Humans need toil and hard work to come to terms with nature, which is sometimes indifferent or even hostile to them. Stones and marshes cover the entire surface of the terrain, making agriculture more difficult. Lucretius uses the same verb for the same idea at Lucr. 5.206–9: *quod superest arui, tamen id natura sua ui / sentibus o b d u c a t ni uis humana resistat / uitai causa ualido consueta bidenti / ingemere, et terram pressis proscindere aratris.* V. reworks the Lucretian passage at *G.* 2.410–12 *bis uitibus ingruit umbra, / bis segetem densis o b d u c u n t sentibus herbae; / durus uterque labor* (note also *G.* 1.116 *obducto late tenet omnia limo*, echoing the marsh of *E.* 1).

49–50. Echoing the language of popular wisdom, V. establishes a connection between climate conditions and diseases—a Hippocratic motif Latinized by Lucretius, 6.1098–1124, esp. 1103–5 *caeli nouitate et aquarum / temptari procul a patria quicumque domoque / adueniunt* (a location change exposes the body to new, unanticipated diseases). Note that the Noric cattle plague in *G.* 3.478–80 is described in similar terms: its outbreak, too, is ascribed to climate causes (see esp. *G.* 3.481 [scil. *tempestas*] *infecit pabula tabo*; cf. *pabula* at *E.* 1.49).

49 grauis...fetas. 'Pregnant females'. Both terms are redefined by their conjunction: whereas *fetae* could mean either 'pregnant' or 'having recently delivered', *grauis* is quite uncommon in the sense of *grauida* (cf. *Aen.* 1.273–4 and 6.515–16; *ThlL* VI.2.2276.73–2277.12, s.v. *grauis*). On the care and food necessary to female animals (specifically cows) about to give birth, cf. *G.* 3.138–56. With the pregnancy slowing them down, they can easily be 'tempted' by unhealthy yet more accessible or appetizing pastures unknown to them, and therefore rather dangerous (*insueta...pabula*, whence *Dirae* 92 *mollia non iterum carpetis pabula nota*; cf. 1.78n.). Meliboeus here expresses his point of view, i.e. a goatherd's (1.50 *pecoris*). Here, too, as in 1.14–15, the herdsman is particularly concerned about the newborn animals, *spes gregis*. **temptabunt**. Used again of disease at *G.* 3.441; but cf. Lucr. 6.1104 and 1250; Hor. *epist.* 1.6.28; Cels. 3.21.4; *OLD²*, p. 2112, s.v. 10a.

50 nec mala...contagia. Cf. *G.* 3.469 *dira...contagia* (which make drastic intervention necessary). This line is perhaps echoed at Hor. *epod.* 16.61 *nulla nocent pecori contagia* (on issues of relative chronology between the epode and the *E.*, esp. *E.* 4, cf. also pp. 200–1). For *contagium* in herds cf. also Lucr. 6.1236–7 (comparing human epidemics and diseases affecting *lanigeras...pecudes et bucera saecla*).

51–8. The repetition of *fortunate senex* (cf. 46), a stylistic marker of *makarismos*, introduces the depiction of an idealized pastoral landscape. The realistic and almost anti-pastoral description of the agricultural wasteland at 1.46–48 (see 1.46–78n.; 46n.) is now counterbalanced by the second part of Meliboeus' speech. V. is here influenced by various Theocritean models of pastoral happiness: cf. *id.* 7.131–47 (cf. 1.52n.; 58n.; also 80n.) and 5.45–9. The fair season is evoked here, just as in the 'bucolic' prototype of Hes. *op.* 582–96. This flight of fancy facilitates the reference to the non-Mantuan 'Hyblaean' bees (1.54n.). Meliboeus is entrusted with V.'s explicit reference to the originary Sicilian (i.e. Theocritean) dimension of pastoral poetry. His reference to the buzzing of the bees marks a transition from the visualization of a pastoral *locus amoenus* to auditory sensation: note the farmers' work songs, the hoarse doves, and the turtledove's moan (1.56–8). These three auditory phenomena are certainly more original and less stereotypical than the buzzing of the bees.

51 flumina nota. Presumably the Mincius and the Po; *nota* is affective ('the streams you know so well'; cf. *Aen.* 7.491 *limina nota*; already Catull. 68.97): but the plural is undetermined, and leaves the reader guessing. Note the contrast with 49 *insueta...pabula* (*G.* 4.266 *pabula nota*). For the river as marking a population's identity, cf. 1.62n.

52 fontis sacros. Springs are usually sacred and nymphs dwell in them: cf. e.g. *Hymn. Hom.* 3[*Ap.*].263; 19[*Pan.*].19–20; Theocr. *id.* 7.136; Hor. *carm.* 1.1.22 *ad aquae lene caput sacrae*; Serv. *ad Aen.* 7.84 *nullus enim fons non sacer*. **frigus captabis opacum**. Cf. 2.8 *umbras et frigora captant*. The phrase looks forward to the summer tableau in the following lines, which conclude Meliboeus' speech.

53 hinc...uicino ab limite. Adv. and locative phrases are joined together: cf. *Aen.* 2.18–19 *huc...includunt caeco lateri*; cf. Hom. *Od.* 10.511 αὐτοῦ...ἐπ᾽ Ὠκεανῷ βαθυδίνῃ. The term *limes* hints at an eminently Roman landscape with its property boundaries. **quae semper**. The phrase has the force of *ut semper* (*E.* 6.15); the verb is similarly omitted at *Aen.* 1.157 *quae proxima litora* (*sunt*).

94   ECLOGUE 1

54 Hyblaeis apibus. The epithet *Hyblaeus* derives from the town of Megara Hyblaea—or, rather, from the neighbouring Hybla Maior (just north of Syracuse), well known in antiquity for its excellent honey, whose flavour was ascribed to the superior quality of the local thyme (7.37n.). According to Strabo, 6.2.2 [267], the name of the town—already in ruins—survived due to its honey: this seems to be confirmed by Ovid, e.g. *ars* 2.517; *trist.* 5.6.38, as well as later authors; see *Enc. Virg.* II, p. 889, s.v. *Ibla* (A. Fo); II, p. 632, s.v. *Hybla* (G. C. Trimble). Bees were a celebrated symbol of poetry, and especially of poetic refinement, at least since Pind. *Pyth.* 10.54 (here cf. esp. Callim. *hymn.* 2[*Ap.*].110; cf. 1.65n.). Sophocles was dubbed a 'bee' due to his ability to select and appropriate the best poetry offered by his colleagues (*uita Soph.* 20, in *TrGF*, IV, p. 39.87–9 R.-K.). Not surprisingly, bees can alleviate anxieties and facilitate rest (1.55n.); Engels, Nicolaye (2008). V.'s bees, Sicilian by origin or name, dwell in Mantuan lands and feed on willow flowers, a typically pastoral-Virgilian plant (10.40n.), thus epitomizing the new Theocritean synthesis expounded in the *E.* (whereas other epithets are mainly ornamental, e.g. *Poenos...leones* at 5.27n.; cf. 9.30; 10.59). V.'s poetic and geographical audacity will be mitigated in Hor. *carm.* 4.2.27–32 (in Tivoli, the poet is 'like' the *apis Matina*). The Sicilian reference amounts to a declaration of poetic allegiance in the pseudo-Theocritean *id.* 8.56: *ἐσορῶν Σικελικάν τ' ἐς ἅλα*. **florem depasta salicti.** A willow-grove (*salictum*) is found in Enn. *ann.* 38 Sk.; cf. also Plaut. *Aul.* 675. Willow-trees are useful to the production of honey, and hedges made of willow-trees are often used to mark property boundaries (as here: 1.53 *uicino ab limite saepes*). The multifarious applications of willow-trees, including apiculture, are observed at *G.* 2.434–6: *salices humilesque genistae, / aut illae pecori frondem aut pastoribus umbram / sufficiunt saepemque satis et pabula melli* (on the importance of willow-trees in V.'s world cf. 1.78n.). Note the dense syntax: the dative of agent (*Hyblaeis apibus*), typical of poetry, is governed by *depasta* (cf. e.g. *Aen.* 1.440 *neque cernitur ulli*; 10.6–7 *sententia uobis uersa*), with an accusative of respect (*florem*), i.e. the so-called 'Greek accusative' (on which see Introduction, p. 27, n. 69).

55 saepe leui somnum suadebit inire susurro. Insistent alliteration on the /*s*/ sound, anticipated by *salicti* at the end of 1.54 and *semper...saepes* at 1.53 (echoed here by *saepe*, which is almost perfectly homophonous with *saepes*). For a parallel usage, expressing the coming of sleep, cf. *Aen.* 2.9 *suadentque cadentia sidera somnos*. Bees and their pleasant buzzing are featured in Theocr. *id.* 1.107 (cf. Hes. *theog.* 594). The 'companionship' offered by the buzzing of an insect (especially to a love-sick poet in need of consolation) is the main topic of an epigram by Meleager, *Anth. Pal.* 7.195 (= *HE* 4058 G.-P.; note the first line: *ἀκρὶς, ἐμὸν ἀπάτημα πόθων, παραμύθιον ὕπνου* 'locust, beguiler of my loves, persuader of sleep'). For *leuis* used of sounds, cf. Catull. 64.273 *leuiterque sonant plangore cachinni*; Prop. 1.3.43. A pastoral metamorphosis (Pan and Syrinx) will humorously elicit sleep in Ov. *met.* 1, esp. 713–14. Perhaps Apul. *met.* 1.1.1 *lepido susurro permulceam* is reminiscent of our passage.

ECLOGUE 1   95

56 alta sub rupe canet. Cf. *id.* 8.55 ἀλλ' ὑπὸ τᾷ πέτρᾳ τᾷδ' ἄσομαι; 22.37; *E.* 10.14 *sola sub rupe* (Gallus); *G.* 4.508 *rupe sub aeria* (Orpheus); *rupes* is a recurring term in V., who uses it to denote the steep sides of a mountain: cf. also 1.76n. Note here the effect of sound amplification, in terms of both sonic quality and propagation (*canet...ad auras*). Further occurrences of *rupes* in the *E.* at 5.63; 6.29; 10.14; 10.58. **frondator.** Through *frondatio*, usually taking place in midsummer, excessive foliage was pruned (particularly since it could have damaged the fruit by blocking the sun's rays: 10.76n.) and turned into fodder: cf. *E.* 2.70; 9.61; *G.* 1.157; 305–6; 2.367–70; 397–419; Colum. 4.17.3; 27.5. The *frondator* represented the normal agricultural pattern (or, rather, its denial) in Catull. 64.41 *non falx attenuat frondatorum arboris umbram* (cf. Ov. *met.* 14.649 *falce data frondator erat*). Work songs, meant to relieve fatigue, evoke folk poetry: e.g. *G.* 2.417 *canit...uinitor* as well as 1.293–4 (but cf., for instance, Theocr. *id.* 10.21–3). The image, with the backdrop of a high cliff, possesses an almost painterly vividness: recall the scenes of rural work (e.g. the grape-pickers) painted by Studius, on which see Plin. *nat.* 35.116; cf. 1.48n. **ad auras.** This is the first occurrence of a hexameter clausula very frequently used by V.: cf. *G.* 1.408; 2.291; 4.486; *Aen.* 2.259; 6.561 (note also the variant *in auras*: *G.* 3.109; *Aen.* 2.791); two occurrences in Cic. *Arat.* 86; 141 Soub.

57 raucae, tua cura, palumbes. The construction, called 'parenthetic apposition' (i.e. an apposition bracketed by epithet and noun on either side), has parallels in Hellenistic poetry, but is typical of Latin verse: cf. Prop. 3.3.31 *et Veneris dominae uolucres, mea turba, columbae*. According to O. Skutsch's argument (1956, pp. 198–9), it could be traced back to Cornelius Gallus—hence the label *schema Cornelianum*; though cf. Enn. *dub.* V.1(6) Sk. *caelicolae, mea membra, dei* (Traina 1995; for a thorough and sceptical discussion see Solodow 1986). As a matter of fact, V.'s recourse to this device decreases over his works: 5x in *E.* (see also 2.3; 3.3; 7.21; 9.9), 3x in *G.* (2.146–7; 4.168; 246), and only 1x in the whole *Aen.* (6.842–3). Potential erotic-elegiac overtones would make its use quite significant in the first eclogue, with reference to 'doves' (cf. below). The phrase *tua cura* will reappear as a non-parenthetic apposition in Apollo's address to Gallus, concerning his beloved Lycoris: 10.22n. A parodic reworking is found at Iuv. 7.120 *ueteres, Maurorum epimenia, bulbi*. **palumbes.** Doves were commonly bred in the countryside: Varr. *rust.* 3.7 (and *ling.* 9.56); Colum. 8.8; Pallad. 1.24. A subtle, almost imperceptible, distinction is that between the wild variety, *palumbes*, and the domestic one, *columbae / columbi* (the latter being more usually sacred to Venus: but cf. *E.* 3.68–9n.). In Hor. *carm.* 3.4.12–13 they will miraculously save the infant poet: *fronde noua puerum palumbes / texere*. In Longus' pastoral novel (Long. 1.27), a wild dove (φάττα) makes the woods resound with a pleasant 'pastoral' song, whose meaning Daphnis explains to Chloe: a metamorphosis myth. V.'s doves are called *raucae* in reference to their typical cry (cf. 2.12–13 *raucis...cicadas*); the epithet might also hint at their

96   ECLOGUE 1

insistent attitude (which makes them 'hoarse': Plaut. *Epid.* 200 *rogitando sum raucus factus*; Hor. *sat.* 1.4.66), which parallels the turtledove's repetitive 'moan' (*E.* 1.58). For further information, both literary and ornithological, cf. Capponi (1979, pp. 176–85, esp. the conclusion on p. 184, and pp. 375–9).

58 gemere…turtur. The verb *gemere* hints at the long, repetitive song of the turtledove, with a Theocritean echo: *id.* 7.141 ἔστενε τρυγών (142 πωτῶντο… μέλισσαι: cf. here the bees at 1.53–5); note also *id.* 15.88 τρυγόνες (the two talkative women from Syracuse). V.'s *turtur* ('turtledove') is the exact equivalent of Theocritus' τρυγών, even via onomatopoeia (*tur-tur*). Note the sound /u/ in both *turtur* and the line-ending *ab Ulmo* (cf. the onomatopoea τοροτοροτορο and the like in Aristoph. *Au.* 260; 262). This species could be bred like the *palumbus*: Colum. 8.9; Capponi (1979, pp. 499–504). **aëria…ab ulmo.** Cf. Catull. 64.291 *aeria cupressu*; *E.* 3.69 *aeriae…palumbes*; *Aen.* 3.680 *aeriae quercus*; see also *G.* 4.508 *rupe sub aeria*. Elm trees are home to Horace's doves at *carm.* 1.2.9–10. On the adj., typically poetic (embellishing the idea of 'height': elm trees can be as tall as 20–25 metres), see *Enc. Virg.* I, pp. 38–41, s.v. *aer/aerius*; *aether/aetherius*; *aethra* (A. Lunelli); cf. also *E.* 10.67 *alta…ulmo.*

59–63. Tityrus, prompted by many direct references to him (note *tua* at 1.46 and 1.57; *tibi* at 1.47–53), takes five lines to declare his personal devotion (1.63 *nostro…pectore*) towards the *deus*. The traditional zoological adynaton (cf. Archil. fr. 114.7–9 Tard. = 122.7–9 W.[2]) is coupled with a contemporary one, featuring the Parthians, the Germans, and their respective rivers; cf. *Enc. Virg.* I, pp. 31–3, s.v. *adynaton* (A. Manzo); *Virg. Enc.* I, p. 12, s.v. *adynaton* (P. E. Knox). Recall esp. Herodot. 5.92 'the sky will fall under the earth, and the earth will be high up, above the sky, and humans will graze in the sea, and fish will dwell where humans used to be, when you etc.'. Further examples of rhetorical variation on natural laws in the *E.*: 5.76–8; 7.41–3; 8.26–8; 52–6; 10.29–30; a more peculiar case is that of 3.88–91 and 4.21–5 (cf. also *Aen.* 1.607–9). The positive, reassuring order pre-supposed by the adynaton makes it frequent in oath formulas, as e.g. in Hor. *epod.* 16.25–34 (cf. here 1.63: *quam nostro illius labatur*, etc.) and in the context of elegiac love oaths (cf. Prop. 2.15.31–6; Ov. *her.* 5.29–30; *met.* 14.37–9); Theocritus makes an adynaton come true at Daphnis' 'absurd' death (*id.* 1.132–6); for a reworking of the idea featuring solely 'natural' adynata, cf. Nemes. *ecl.* 1.75–80. Here V.'s choice of particularly fearsome peoples contrasts with the divine-political order expected to be established by the young Octavian. Following the victory at Naulochus, in 36 BCE, a senatorial decree conferred on him the honour of a golden picture, for 'restoring peace, long perturbed by discord, on land and sea' (Appian. *bell. civ.* 5.130 [542]). The correspondence between natural and political order will be a recurring motif of Augustan poetry: e.g. Hor. *carm.* 1.2 (cf. esp. 1.2.7–9 for fish and marine creatures grazing on the mountains). Note the fourfold structure, here occurring for the first time but relatively frequent in the *E.* In this case, each line is dedicated to one of the four hypothetical situations

ECLOGUE 1   97

described by Tityrus (1.59–62): the goal is to strengthen the final assertion (as in an oath); cf. also *E.* 2.63–5; 5.76–8; 10.29–30; 42–3; 64–8.

59 ergo. Tityrus resumes his praise of the young god. In the low-key exchange of this finale, both characters tend towards the monologue. The dialogic form itself now expresses the divergence of their fates. **in aethere**. Cf. Lucr. 3.784–5 *denique in aethere non arbor, non aequore in alto* / *nubes esse queunt nec pisces uiuere in aruis*. Ether, the finest and highest element, emphasizes the impossibility even further, compared to *in aëre*, for which cf. *G.* 1.404 *apparet liquido…in aëre* (with **My**'s reading: *aethere* R; the phrase is common, as e.g. in Plaut. *Asin.* 99 *me piscari in aëre*; Cic. *Verr.* 2.4.87; see also Lucr. 3.508; 4.736; Prop. 2.30.3; Ov. *met.* 4.677; Lucan. 1.588, etc.). The reading *in aethere* (**PR**), commended by de la Cerda, is here rejected by Ribbeck in favour of *in aequore*, transmitted by the *recentiores* and supported by Ov. *met.* 14.37–8 *prius…in aequore frondes…et in summis nascentur montibus algae* (where the speaker is the sea-god Glaucus). But this must be a normalizing conjecture, which restores the reciprocal switch typical of adynata (sea/land: deer in the sea, fish on land; cf. Archil. fr. 114.7–8 Tard. [see 1.59–63n.]; Rufin. *Anth. Pal.* 5.19[18].5–6). On the other hand, *leues* is not decisive, since it suits 'flying' deer (cf. Daedalus at *Aen.* 6.17) and may well also refer to deer grazing on the water surface, without sinking: *G.* 2.451 *undam leuis innatat alnus*; *Aen.* 5.819; ThlL VII.2.1202.49–70. Cf. the prodigious deer at Val. Fl. 3.554 *intactas leuis ipse superfugit undas*. Note also that, without a clarifying context, *aequor* is an ambiguous term: it may denote either a sea surface or a land surface (with *Aen.* 2.780 *uastum maris aequor arandum* cf. *G.* 1.50 *ignotum ferro…scindimus aequor*).

60 freta. Properly speaking, *freta* = 'straits', but is often used in poetry with the force of 'sea' or 'sea loch'. The term is, however, constantly connected with the idea of motion and unrest, here especially appropriate: see Varr. *ling.* 7.22 *dictum fretum ab similitudine feruentis aquae, quod in fretum saepe concurrat aestus atque efferuescat*; Serv. *ad Aen.* 1.607 *proprie fretum est mare naturaliter mobile ab undarum feruore nominatum*; ThlL VI.1.1311.71–1312.6.

61 pererratis amborum finibus. This migration does not seem to entail straight motion, but rather repeated wandering, perhaps an allusion to both peoples' nomadic habits. Here, at any rate, the wording amplifies the (sorrowful) notion of exile: not without some cruel irony, Meliboeus will actually be the one to go into exile at 1.64–6n. For *pererro* cf. *Aen.* 2.295 *pererrato…ponto*; note also Ov. *amor.* 3.13.33: *pererratis profugus terraque fretoque*. To be sure, this dramatic amplification seems secondary with respect to the main structure of the adynaton, while the genitive *amborum* appears somewhat obscure and awkward (do they each wander within their own land or into each other's land?). The image of an 'exile' (*exsul*) intensifies the contrast between *Parthus* and *Germania*, where the latter normally refers to a geographical region (for *Germania* in its ethnic sense, coupled with a geographical reference to the Euphrates river, cf. *G.* 1.509 quoted

98   ECLOGUE 1

below). Thus, S. Heyworth's proposed deletion of 1.61 (along with the correction *ante Ararim* at 1.62) is far from being pointless.

62 Ararim. With some difficulty, this locates the Germans, whose 'actual' river is the Rhine. The *Araris* (or *Arar*), i.e. today's Saône, is a right-bank tributary of the Rhône: even though its source borders Germanic territory (Alsace), the river flows through Gallic lands. Roman confusion between Germans and Celts is by no means rare, and sometimes deliberate; here, however, V. was perhaps prompted by the somewhat exotic sound analogy between *Araris* and *Tigris*. See further *Enc. Virg.* I, p. 264, s.v. *Arar* (A. Manzo); *Virg. Enc.* I, pp. 115–16 s.v. *Arar* (J. D. Morgan); at any rate, 1.61–2 evoke a chaotic atmosphere that precludes wholly accurate correspondences. **Parthus.** The collective singular is frequently used of enemy populations (e.g. Hor. *carm.* 2.19.12): cf. the Greek usage of βάρβαρος for the Parthians' predecessors, i.e. the Persians. **bibet.** Ever since Homer, it is customary to identify a people by the river from which their water is drawn: *Il.* 2.825 (as well as Callim. *hymn.* 1[*Iou.*].40–1); cf. *Aen.* 7.715; Hor. *carm.* 2.20.20; 4.15.21; see also 10.65n. **Germania.** The term refers to the people, i.e. to their 'nation': cf. *G.* 1.509 *hinc mouet Euphrates, illinc Germania bellum.*

63 nostro…labatur pectore uultus. Nature will have to be thrown into utter chaos before the benefactor's face might even begin to fade away. Significantly, the verb *labatur* points to the moment when the process of decay starts (cf. *G.* 3.498; *Aen.* 3.309, 4.318), almost as if Tityrus could not dare to hint at the total disappearance of the likeness he venerates. The noun *uultus* denotes not just the appearance of the *deus's* face, but also his facial expression, which in this case is presented as benevolent and reassuring: cf. *Aen.* 1.255 *uultu, quo caelum tempestatesque serenat* (Jupiter); 327–8 *haut tibi uoltus / mortalis* (hunting Venus addressed by Aeneas). The deity's face leaves an indelible imprint on Tityrus' mind (*pectore*): echoes of it resonate in V.'s description of Dido's obsessive love for Aeneas (*Aen.* 4.4 *haerent infixi pectore uoltus*). In the ancient rhetoric of charismatic power, the ruler's face plays a key role and is often endowed with divine traits (note, for instance, Calp. *ecl.* 7.84 *et Martis uultus et Apollinis esse putaui*). Augustus himself seems to have paid great attention to the effects of his gaze and facial expression, according to Suet. *Aug.* 79.2 *oculos habuit claros ac nitidos, quibus etiam existimari uolebat inesse quiddam diuini uigoris.* At any rate, V.'s text is here creating a 'physical' myth of the future *princeps*, whose likeness starts being depicted on portraits and monuments (both official and unofficial) all over Rome and the provinces (on the equestrian statue decreed by the senate, cf. 1.43n.).

64–78. In his final speech, Meliboeus expresses his sorrow and perplexity. Destined to abandon the pastoral world, in this eclogue he has a greater number of lines than the other protagonist (46 vs Tityrus' 37) and delivers the two longest speeches in the entire book (see 1.46–78n.). In the first section of this speech (1.64–6), Meliboeus considers various exile destinations. In the second part (1.67–9), he devotes a moment to a reverie of homecoming and addresses a few last words to his modest possessions. Then, in the face of a harsh reality (the new landowner: 1.70–2), Meliboeus bids farewell to the pastoral world and to his songs in the closing section of his speech (1.70–8). Note the rhetorical structure of 1.67–78, which roughly reproduces that of Meliboeus' earlier speech (1.46–58) but in a contrary mood. Tityrus was able to hold on to his estate, albeit modest, and to the opportunity of grazing his livestock in peace (1.46–50: contrast 1.67–74); correspondingly, Tityrus was also granted the bliss of pastoral *otium* (cf. 1.51–8; contrast 1.75–8).

64–6. Ironically, it is not the Parthians or the Germans (cf. 61) who are forced to relinquish their land, but Meliboeus, a *ciuis Romanus*, who will reach Africa, or Scythia, or even the mysterious Oaxes (1.65n.), or the land of the Britons, proverbial inhabitants of the far end of the world (1.66n.). Note how the four toponyms reach out to all the cardinal points: this emphasizes a notion typical of the pastoral world, whereby a long journey to faraway lands is practically equivalent to a curse or a condemnation (cf. *id.* 7.109–14, addressing Pan; see also, at the other end of V.'s pastoral collection, *E.* 10.64–8). The passage echoes the complaints of historical victims of land confiscation, who are forced to leave their lands as if they had been defeated in battle, despite being both indigenous and innocent (Appian. *bell. civ.* 5.12 [49] quoted below [1.71–2n.]). All of a sudden, the broader social dimension of land confiscations is revealed (1.64–5n.; cf. also 1.71–2 *ciuis… miseros*). It is now clear that Meliboeus' fate is shared by large masses of people dangerously uprooted from their homes and forced to wander, and now ready to react and rebel. Many of them, in fact, joined the ranks of Sextus Pompey's army, composed of both free citizens and slaves. Sextus Pompey certainly did not have a hard time gaining the consensus of those neglected or penalized by Antony and Octavian (see Introduction, pp. 4–5). Exile is similarly described as a collective experience at *G.* 2.512 *alio patriam quaerunt sub sole iacentem*, the destination of wicked citizens.

64–5 nos… alii … / pars. The initial *nos*, which could easily be mistaken as referring to Meliboeus alone (cf. Tityrus' *nostro…pectore*; *nos* = *ego* in the rest of the eclogue), is now revealed to be the marker of a collective identity. This is revealed by the distinction between *alii* and *pars*: this kind of correlation with variation (contaminating two different formulae: *alii…alii* and *pars…pars*) is rather frequent in V.: cf. *Aen.* 1.212–13; 2.399–400; note also Prop. 2.29a.5–6; Ov. *met.* 11.486–7. It also appears in the historical prose of Sallust (cf. *Iug.* 19.1.1 *Phoenices…alii…pars*; 50.4) and Livy (cf. 35.51.3). The sudden discontinuity in Meliboeus' phrasing draws attention to the fact that Meliboeus is by no means the only landowner driven into exile (cf. 1.64–6n.). Similarly, at 1.45n., Tityrus is revealed to have been one of many who appealed to the young *deus* (note the plural form of the verb in the *deus*'s command).

64 Afros. Opens a series of acc. of motion towards without preposition, a typical marker of poetic language, also combined with the typical Greek

100 ECLOGUE 1

interferences (*Scythiam*; *Oaxen*; *Britannos*): e.g. *Aen.* 1.2–3 *Italiam fato profugus Lauiniaque* [or *Lauinaque*] *uenit / litora*; but cf. Hom. *Od.* 4.84 Αἰθίοπάς θ' ἱκόμην καὶ Σιδονίους καὶ Ἐρεμβούς. The epithet *sitientis* hints specifically at the inland desert areas.

65 rapidum cretae. The adj. *rapidus* preserves the active sense of *rapio*—almost with the force of *rapax* (Sen. *epist.* 95.36 *rapacia uirtutis ingenia*), perhaps following Lucr. 1.15–17 *rapidos...amnis...fluuios...rapacis* (whence G. 3.142); cf. Plaut. *Bacch.* 85 *rapidus fluuius*; *Men.* 64–5. The adj. can therefore govern the gen. *cretae* by analogy with adjectives in *-idus*, e.g. *auidus*, *cupidus*, etc. The reading *Cretae* (as a toponym) must be rejected, in spite of Herodot. 4.154.1, which mentions the Cretan city of *Oaxós*: Mariotti (1952, p. 61 n. = 1986, p. 44, n. 65) suggests deliberate ambiguity, in the wake of Ennius' style. This river, 'polluted' by clay, and thus hinting at unpleasant, inhospitable places, plays the same role as the 'thirsty' Africans, Scythia (notoriously freezing: e.g. Hor. *carm.* 4.5.25) and the remote Britons (1.66n.). **Oaxen.** The name evokes unknown, faraway landscapes, precisely because it is extremely hard to locate—almost a fairy-tale place, as scholars' embarrassment shows; cf. *Enc. Virg.* III, p. 803, s.v. *Oasse* (M. Malavolta); *Virg. Enc.* II, pp. 923–4, s.v. *Oaxes* (R. F. Thomas). Our starting point must be the river Oxus (Plin. *nat.* 6.48: flowing from lake *Oaxus*; Mela 3.42; uncertain text in Iust. 1.8.2), i.e. today's Amu Darya, which flows muddily and turbulently from the Hindu Kush to the Aral sea (Curt. 7.10.13; cf. Arrian. *anab.* 3.29.2). Based on this information, and perhaps creatively contaminating *Araxes* with *Oxus* (confused with each other in Herodot. 1.202; the *-es* ending is common among well-known Eastern rivers, e.g. *Euphrates*), V. puts in Meliboeus' mouth a fascinating, exotic-sounding name, even more mythical than the remote river encountered by Alexander the Great during his legendary expedition (Curt. 7.10.13). According to Callimachus' well-known dictum, a literary failure is associated with a large and muddy river (preferably an Eastern one): *hymn.* 2[*Ap.*].108–9 Ἀσσυρίου ποταμοῖο μέγας ῥόος, ἀλλὰ τὰ πολλὰ / λύματα γῆς καὶ πολλὸν ἐφ' ὕδατι συρφετὸν ἕλκει 'great is the stream of the Assyrian river, but it carries / much dirt and much silt in its water'. In such a landscape, it is clear that Meliboeus will no longer be able to sing (1.77 *carmina nulla canam*), while Tityrus is blessed with the pleasure of *flumina nota* and the 'sacred spring' surrounded by bees—a symbolically poetic environment which Callimachus contrasted with the 'Assyrian river': 'bees carry water to Deó [epithet of Demeter], not just from any source / but from that which flows, pure and undefiled, / from a sacred spring, a little trickle, the choicest offering' (Callim. *hymn.* 2[*Ap.*].110–12).

66 toto diuisos orbe Britannos. See the later Hor. *carm.* 1.35.29–30 *ultimos / orbis Britannos*; 4.14.47–8; but cf. Catull. 11.11–12 *ultimos...Britannos*; Cic. *nat. deor.* 2.88.

67–73. These lines are the climax of Meliboeus' lament. Meliboeus rages against his own fate, absurd for a herdsman: he now has to abandon his fields, to

ECLOGUE 1   101

which he devoted so much labour, and hand them over to a new landowner (necessarily perceived as an 'alien': *barbarus*). Meliboeus is here characterized as a scrupulous, meticulous worker, who loves his world of plants and animals (and songs). The figure of the exiled farmer, worried about the land he takes loving care of, is found in Aristophanes' *Peace* (esp. ll. 556–9), which, however, features a happy return.

67 en umquam. The interjection *en*, also occurring at 1.12 and 1.71, is here paired with *umquam* to express impatience, as at 8.7–8 *en erit umquam / ille dies* (note the colloquial liveliness; *en* is frequent in comedy, e.g. Plaut. *Trin.* 590 *en umquam aspiciam te?*). Here, however, the wait is full of grief. **patrios...finis.** Cf. 3 *patriae finis*; note the hyperbaton between noun and epithet, underscored by the parenthetic *longo post tempore*, which seems to contain a bitter echo of 1.29 *longo post tempore* (used by Tityrus to refer to the happy ending of his journey).

68 pauperis...tuguri. A realistic term, of likely non-Latin origin, *tugurium* was traced back to *tegere*, and therefore used in the sense of 'cover', 'shelter' (*quasi tegurium* [Isid. *orig.* 15.12.2]; Maltby 1991, p. 625, s.v. *tugurium*): a folketymological association, here hinted at by *congestum caespite culmen*. For the shepherds' huts cf. 2.29 *atque humilis habitare casas* (where *humilis*, as *pauperis* in 1.68, emphasizes the modest appearance of the shelter). The term *tugurium* readily suits the nostalgic *mos maiorum* rhetoric: e.g. Liv. 42.34.2 *pater mihi iugerum agri reliquit et paruum tugurium in quo natus educatusque sum, hodieque ibi habito* (the speaker is a model farmer, Sp. Ligustinus, of Sabine origin); cf. also Varr. *rust.* 3.1.3. For *tugurium* in Latin poetry, cf. *Copa* 23; *Priap.* 86.6 and, in later antiquity, Paul. Nol. *carm.* 21.486 (with an echo of the whole Virgilian phrase *pauperis et tuguri*). The roof (*culmen*) will reappear, along with other Virgilian reminiscences (including *E.* 9), in [Quint.] *decl. mai.* 13.2, esp. p. 266.12 Håk.; note also the hut of Philemon and Baucis at Ov. *met.* 8.630 *parua quidem stipulis et canna tecta palustri*. V.'s use of a colloquial word is surprising in the context of Meliboeus' last, pathetically loaded address to his lost possessions. The herdsman, however, is not allowed to lose touch with the humble nature of his pastoral world (the same is true of 1.47–8n.). Note that, in his Roman eclogue, Calpurnius Siculus puts *mapalia* (a term analogous to *tugurium*) in the mouth of his city-dwelling *senex*: cf. Calp. *ecl.* 7.41–2 *qui nescius auri / sordida tecta casas et sola mapalia nosti* (referring to the *rusticus* Corydon). Terms of everyday language (and even 'unpoetic' words) are not uncommon in texts dealing with the expropriations: note, for instance, the technical term *pertica* at Prop. 4.1.130.

69 post. The force of *post* influences the interpretation of the whole line, which is one of the most difficult in the *E.*, to the point that several editors have proposed corrections to the text. It is likely that *post* here functions as an adv. of time, taking up *longo post tempore* (67)—which is syntactically audacious but readily explained in terms of expressiveness: cf. *G.* 2.259–62 *his animaduersis terram multo ante memento / excoquere et magnos scrobibus concidere montis, / ante*

102 ECLOGUE 1

supinatas Aquiloni ostendere glaebas / quam laetum infodias uitis genus (here, however, *quam* makes a clear difference; cf. also *G.* 3.476). Hence the interpretation: 'after (so long a time) I shall be amazed at seeing those few (*aliquot*) ears of wheat, my kingdom' (where *mea regna* is used in apposition to *aristas*, governed by *uidens mirabor*). An alternative reading (semantically better, but syntactically even more difficult) would be: 'after (so long a time) I shall be amazed at seeing my kingdom of a few ears of wheat' (where *mea regna* is governed by *uidens*). Ancient and modern attempts at taking *post* as a temporal preposition referring to *aristas*, used in the sense of *annos*, are unpersuasive: 'after "a certain number of" years'; *quasi rusticus per aristas numerat annos*, says Philargyrius/Philagrius, p. 29.10–11 (III.2 Th.-H.); cf. Aug. *quaest. hept.* 1.95, p. 36, ll. 1218–20 Fraip.; Claud. 8.382 H. *decimas emensus aristas*; Ennod. *carm.* 2.1.15. A passage like Sen. *Tro.* 76 *decumas secuit messor aristas* (cf. Eur. *Tro.* 20 and Catull. 95.1) is not a perfect parallel, since the metaphor is differently developed. Equally unsatisfactory is Leo's proposal to take *post* as a local preposition, as in 3.20 (Leo 1903, p. 11, n. 1): 'on the other side of some ears of wheat' (but why *aliquot?*). Moreover, according to Leo, a very difficult *traiectio* is required: *post…aristas* (but it is hard to see why, after its temporal use at 1.67, *post* should here be understood in a local sense). To be sure, the position of *aliquot* after *post* inevitably makes the reader think it is governed by *post* (preposition). On the rarity of *aliquot* in poetry (this is the only occurrence in V.) cf. Axelson (1945, p. 74 and n. 57).* **mea regna**. Cf. *G.* 3.476–7 *desertaque regna / pastorum*. Hellenistic philosophical overtones (the 'true' king) may be perceived here, thus adding wisdom to Meliboeus' portrait: he is wise who is content with what he has and knows how to benefit from what nature has to offer, in a space of (moral and extra-moral) autonomy. But here an important role is also played by the Homeric archetype of the exile, Odysseus ruler of Ithaca, who longs for his homeland despite Calypso's charms in the first book of the *Odyssey*: αὐτὰρ Ὀδυσσεύς, / ἱέμενος καὶ καπνὸν ἀποθρῴσκοντα νοῆσαι / ἧς γαίης, θανέειν ἱμείρεται 'but Odysseus, longing to see even just the smoke leaping up / from his native land, wants to die' (*Od.* 1.57–9; see 1.82–3n.). And yet, upon his eventual return, Odysseus feels disoriented and fails to recognize his homeland, despite being its ruler: οὐδέ μιν ἔγνω, / ἤδη δὴν ἀπεών… / …ἀλλοειδέα φαινέσκετο πάντα ἄνακτι 'he did not recognize it, / having been long away… /

---

* The considerable difficulties encountered here may make it necessary to emend the text. As a viable option I suggest the 'economic' emendation *aliquo*, which presupposes the common phrase *aliquo tempore* (e.g. Cic. *leg.* 3.5; Ov. *Pont.* 4.4.47), where *tempore* is omitted after being mentioned at 1.67 *en umquam…longo post tempore*. The transition from *longo post tempore* (1.67) to *post aliquo* would be a combination of variation and redundancy similar to 1.29–30 *longo post tempore…postquam* (and note 1.28 *postquam*). It may be that V. echoes his own phrase *post aliquo* (*mea regna uidens*), using similarly elliptical syntax, in a later rewriting of *E.* 1, i.e. his description of the Noric plague and the devastation brought about by it: …*nunc quoque p o s t t a n t o uideat desertaque regna / pastorum* (*G.* 3.476–7; note also *G.* 2.259–61 *multo ante…ante*; cf. Ov. *Pont.* 3.4.47). For a similar phenomenon, featuring the omission of a genitive, see Calp. *ecl.* 4.38–40 *ultima nuper / litora terrarum, nisi tu, Meliboee, fuisses, / ultima uisuri* (also evidently alluding to our passage and, perhaps,

ECLOGUE 1   103

...everything looked different to the king' (*Od.* 13.189–90; 194). Meliboeus, for his part, pictures not just some faraway smoke, but his own roof, which he describes in detail (*congestum caespite culmen*). However, not unlike Odysseus, he feels wonder and estrangement (*mirabor*) in front of his own 'kingdom'. For a brilliant, comic rewriting of the famous Homeric passage (with some Virgilian echoes), cf. Apul. *apol.* 57 *fumum domus suae adgnouisse patrio culmine longe exortum.* **aristas.** Properly speaking, the *arista* is the 'awn' or 'beard', i.e. the part of the ear which contains the grains: 4.28n. Meliboeus' 'surprise' (*mirabor*) carries polemical overtones: it will be surprising if the land so scrupulously farmed by Meliboeus (70 *tam culta noualia*) will bear fruit even to the new owner. Note also 1.74n. *felix quondam pecus* (a more specifically pastoral image). This passage of *E.* 1, along with 9.6n., inspires the author of the pseudo-Virgilian *Dirae*: note esp. ll. 15–19 and 72–4 (73 *metat hic iuncos, spicas ubi legimus olim*).

70–2. The profanation of the rural world, perceived as foundational for Rome's identity, expresses the full gravity of the expropriations. The *miles* is no less *impius* than civil war itself (cf. 1.70n.); he is *barbarus*, on the other hand, because of his utter strangeness to the peaceful world of the countryside rather than because of his possible non-Roman origin (for a similar notion, albeit expressed less vehemently, cf. *E.* 9.2–3n. *aduena...possessor agelli*). To be sure, both Caesar's legions and Pompey's included provincial troops, but there is no evidence that auxiliary forces composed of non-citizen soldiers were stationed in Italy. For epigraphic (and other) documentation of the historical settlement of veterans in the Italian countryside, see E. Todisco, *I veterani in Italia in età imperiale*, Bari 1999 (with bibliography). Compare Horace's *epod.* 16, in which Rome appears wearied by civil strife and its impiety (9 *impia...aetas*), and thus abandoned to barbarian invaders (11 *barbarus...uictor*), with the result that Roman citizens are forced to move away, following the example of Phocaea's inhabitants: a new, paradoxical order sanctioned by a series of adynata (25–34). Here, by contrast, the settlement of a 'barbarian' on Italian soil actualizes the adynaton described at 1.61–3. After mentioning *arua* at 1.3 and (Tityrus') *rura* at 1.46, Meliboeus now speaks in explicitly agricultural terms. Field labour occasionally appears in Theocritus

reworking *longo post tempore...post aliquo...uidens*). With *tempore* implied, *aliquo* would be free from depending on *post* and would function as a quasi-adverb. The exclamatory emphasis provided by the ellipsis would make the text smoother in both syntactical and semantic terms. Note the emotionally charged transition from the specific *longo* to the indefinite *aliquo*, i.e. from a great to an indefinite amount of time (who knows if and when...). How did the error originate? *Aliquot* may have arisen from an interlinear *t*, i.e. an abbreviation of the implied *tempore* (occurring at 1.67), even though such a type of abbreviation is not attested in the surviving documents, whose extent is very limited anyway (note, however, that entire words are abbreviated at Lucil. fr. 42 M. = 46–7 K., which numerous scholars, esp. Housman, have attempted to reconstruct in various ways). Another possibility is the trivialization *post aliquod*, where *post* is a preposition and *tempus* is implied but not expressed (cf. Phaedr. 4.19.16 *post aliquod tempus*); *aliquod* would then be further corrupted into *aliquot* (for *quod* > *quot* cf. P's variant reading at *E.* 9.6). The success of the rather uncommon *aliquot* among grammarians might have been facilitated by the interpretation *post aliquot...aristas.*

104   ECLOGUE 1

(e.g. *id.* 7) and is by no means alien to the *E.*, but here the reader might catch a glimpse of V.'s future poem, the *G.*: cf. *E.* 10.76n. (note that the first eclogue is probably one of the latest, if not the very last, in order of composition).

70 **impius...miles.** The soldier, a figure eminently alien to the pastoral world, is 'impious' due to his close connection to the civil wars (cf. 1.71 *discordia ciuis*), which is wicked by definition: *G.* 1.468; 511; *Aen.* 1.294; 6.612–13; *Enc. Virg.* IV, p. 94, s.v. *pietas* (A. Traina); *Virg. Enc.* III, p. 1008, s.v. *pietas* (L. Fratantuono). Here, moreover, V. gives voice to the vast majority of Rome's late Republican population in the face of a progressive growth in the social and political influence of the army. The army itself had become increasingly more professionalized. As for the arrogance of Macedonian soldiers, note that Cornelius Nepos observed how little the Roman veterans' behaviour differed from theirs (*sua intemperantia nimiaque licentia*), at the cost of harming both enemies and friends (Nep. *Eum.* 8.2). Meliboeus' *impius* is the climax of the herdsman's outcry (cf. also *barbarus*), which carries very strong political overtones: thus, Servius was not wholly wrong in detecting criticism of Octavian here (*hic Virgilius Octauianum Augustum <laesit>*). Note also that the adjective *impius* is a polemical reply to the triumvirs' appeal to *pietas* (a buzzword of the time, like *libertas*: see 1.27n.); *pius* will of course be an epithet of Aeneas, but even Sextus Pompey liked to be called *Magnus Pius* in honour of his father. Thus, during the Perusine War, Lucius Antonius bore the curious sobriquet of *Pietas* in honour of his brother Mark Antony (according to Cass. Di. 48.5.4–5). **noualia.** In opposition to *segetes* (71: the sown fields, ready for harvest), the *noualia* are fallow fields (which are themselves *culta*, but 'renewed' through rest): Varr. *ling.* 5.39; Plin. *nat.* 18.176; cf. also *G.* 1.71–2. This technical, agricultural term emphasizes the realism of Meliboeus' complaint (the same is true of *inserere*, 'to graft', 1.73) while pointing to Meliboeus' competence: he is a 'real' farmer, unlike the new landowner (a *miles*). This is consistent with Meliboeus' characterization as a scrupulous country man at *E.* 7.6 *dum teneras defendo a frigore myrtos*. A Greek parallel is featured in a Theocritean wish for peace: *id.* 16.94 νειοὶ δ' ἐκπονέοιντο (≈ *tam culta*) ποτὶ σπόρον 'let the fallow fields be well tilled for sowing'. Note the coincidence of ictus and word-accent (albeit a disputed notion) in the line; the same is true of *E.* 5.52; 7.33; 8.80.

71 **barbarus has segetes.** For the rhythm, cf. Hor. *epod.* 16.11 *barbarus heu cineres.* Note also Propertius' erotic-elegiac reworking of this passage (with an emphasis on *barbarus*) at Prop. 2.16.27–8 *barbarus excussis agitat uestigia lumbis / et subito felix nunc mea regna tenet* (cf. *E.* 1.69 *mea regna*).

71-2 **en quo discordia ciuis / produxit miseros.** The pairing *discordia ciuis* (subject + direct object) reappears at the end of Propertius' *monobiblos*, in reference to the Perusine War (a kind of 'civil war' closely connected to the triumvirs' confiscations): Prop. 1.22.5 *Romana suos egit discordia ciuis.* Note also *Aen.* 12.583 *trepidos inter discordia ciuis*, in the 'seminal' context of Latinus' city; cf. the paraphrase of *E.* 1 at *Dirae* 83 *tu…inimica tui semper Discordia ciuis* (where, however, *ciuis* is genitive and *discordia* is personified). By using the term *ciuis* here and *patria* at 1.3–4, Meliboeus talks like a free citizen of Rome, while the plural forms allude to the collective misfortune that has fallen upon many beside him (see 1.64–6n.). This was, in fact, the focus of most protests: the dispossessed landowners were legitimate citizens just like the new owners. In his poem *De morte*, Varius Rufus (V.'s Epicurean friend: cf. 9.35n.) criticized an early expropriation campaign decreed by Antony soon after Julius Caesar's death to meet the veterans' demands. This, at any rate, is what can be inferred from a fragment quoted by Macrobius at *Sat.* 6.1.39 *uendidit hic Latium populis agrosque Quiritum / eripuit: fixit leges pretio atque refixit* (fr. 1 Bläns. = Court. = 147 Holl.), which V. reworks at *Aen.* 6.621–2 *uendidit hic auro patriam dominumque potentem / imposuit; fixit leges pretio atque refixit* (note here the absence of the 'Quirites' fields', which were clearly on V.'s mind at the time of *E.* 1). Antony had harmed the *Quirites* according to Varius (who seems to have been generally hostile to him); here, the *ciues* are wronged by the triumvirs. Italian landowners protest in a similar way at Appian. *bell. civ.* 5.12 (49): 'without having committed any crime, and instead being Italian, they saw their lands snatched away from them as if they had been conquered in war' (οὐδὲν μὲν ἀδικῆσαι λέγοντες, Ἰταλιῶται δὲ ὄντες ἀνίστασθαι γῆς τε καὶ ἑστίας οἷα δορίληπτοι; cf. *E.* 1.70 *miles habebit*). The same is true of senatorial landowners, who nonetheless managed to hold on to their possessions thanks to their connection and influence (Cass. Di. 48.8–9). Land confiscations are a cruel example of fortune's reversals in V. (cf. *E.* 9.5 and 1.12 *turbatur*); note also Prop. 4.1.129–30 and Hor. *sat.* 2.2.112–32. Here, however, the main cause is *discordia* (for στάσις in one of the origin myths of pastoral poetry, cf. *schol.* Theocr. *proleg.*, pp. 2.21–23.2 Wend. [see Introduction, p. 12]). *Discordia* itself, along with *concordia*, is a keyword in late Republican Latin literature: cf. Lucr. 5.1305; Cic. *Phil.* 7.25; 13.1; *ThlL* V.1.1338.71–1339.10 (but note also, in a different context, Enn. *ann.* 225–6 Sk., quoted by Hor. *sat.* 1.4.60–1). For the peaceful *agricolae* of the pastoral world, normal life should look like *G.* 2.459–60 (the beginning of a famous *makarismos*): *quibus ipsa procul discordibus armis / fundit humo facilem uictum iustissima tellus.*

72 his nos conseuimus agros. A proverbial phrase, comparable to the Greek 'reaping another's harvest' (Aristoph. *Equ.* 392 τἀλλότριον ἀμῶν θέρος; cf. Callim. *hymn.* 6[*Cer.*].137 ἵν' ὃς ἄροσε τῆνος ἀμάσῃ; Otto 1890, p. 35, no. 152; Tosi 2007, p. 121, no. 263). There is resumption and further development of the motif in the following line (73). Note homeoptoton and assonance: *miseros* (in caesura)… *nos…agros.*

73. The line is a bitter reversal of the divine response to Tityrus (45); cf. also 9.50 *insere, Daphni, piros: carpent tua poma nepotes* (n.). In Meliboeus' case, a fundamental principle of agricultural ideology is subverted: the certainty that one's labour will benefit one's descendants. For a proverbial formulation of the idea

106   ECLOGUE 1

cf. Caecilius Statius, *com*. 210 R.[3] (*Synephebi*): *serit arbores quae saeclo prosint alteri* (*alteri saeclo prosint* R.[2]), to be read in the context of Cic. *Cat. Mai.* 25 *nec uero dubitat agricola, quamuis sit senex, quaerenti cui serat respondere: 'dis immortalibus, qui me non accipere modo haec a maioribus uoluerunt, sed etiam posteris prodere'* (cf. *Tusc.* 1.31; also 1.72n.). **insere.** Used in the technical sense of 'grafting', as in *G.* 2.50 (cf. also *E.* 9.50 quoted above). The agricultural term ironically corresponds to the zoological one at 1.45, *summittite*. The irony is amplified by the complexity of the grafting technique (an exclusive patrimony of skilled farmers), which often has 'miraculous' results: cf. *G.* 2.30–4 (esp. 30 *mirabile dictu*); Hor. *epod.* 2.13–14; Calp. *ecl.* 2.40–4. This kind of competence, of which Meliboeus is particularly proud, is now utterly useless. **pone ordine uitis.** The poet of the *Georgics* will teach the reader exactly how to arrange vines: cf. *G.* 2.273–87. The technical meticulousness of this line is turned into bitter irony: Meliboeus here concludes the polemical section of his speech. Then, with an abrupt change in tone, he expresses calm resignation in a bucolic command addressed to his *capellae* (1.74n.).

74 **ite meae, felix quondam pecus, ite capellae.** At the end of his speech, Meliboeus bids farewell to his goats, urging them to continue their journey and exit the scene. The pastoral *liber* as a whole will end on a similar note: *ite domum saturae, uenit Hesperus, ite capellae* (10.77n.). Cf. Thyrsis in the agon narrated by Meliboeus in *E.* 7: *ite domum pasti, si quis pudor, ite iuuenci* (7.44n.). Note the anaphora, typical of Theocritus' pastoral style: cf. *id.* 1.64 ἄρχετε…ἄρχετε; 8.28–32; 9.1–6. **felix quondam.** This is R's reading, whereas Ribbeck favoured P's *quondam felix*. For an echo cf. Tib. 1.1.19 *felicis quondam, nunc pauperis agri*. The adj. suggests nostalgia for a prosperous past that has now disappeared, as is shown by the fate of the twin kids at 1.14–15. As in the agricultural section of his speech (see 1.69 *aristas* [n.]; 1.70 *tam culta noualia*), Meliboeus here displays a pessimistic attitude towards the future health and prosperity of his herd.

75–8. Meliboeus' farewell, featuring a pathetic repetition of negations (*non…nulla…non*: three times, a number here pointing to irrevocability), echoes the words of the dying Daphnis: 'no longer am I your cowherd, Daphnis, in the woods, / nor in the thickets, nor in the groves [οὐκέτ' ἀν' ὕλαν, / οὐκέτ' ἀνὰ δρυμώς, οὐκ ἄλσεα]' (*id.* 1.116–17).

75 **non ego uos posthac.** The adverb evokes colloquial immediacy: cf. Hor. *carm.* 4.11.33–4 *non enim posthac alia calebo / femina*; note also the emotional intensity and the emphasis on personal pronouns at Catull. 65.10–11 *numquam ego te, uita frater amabilior, / aspiciam posthac?*; see 3.51n. For the line-beginning *non ego*, which pathetically highlights the first-person pronoun, cf. *E.* 3.17 (but also 2.26 and 9.34). It now becomes clear that Meliboeus will soon have to part ways with his animals and hand them over to their new owner. A second negative expression refers to the herdsman's songs (1.77 *carmina nulla*), while the third reiterates the notion one last time, with some syntactical variation (1.77 *non me*).

ECLOGUE 1   107

uiridi proiectus in antro. The cave (in this case a grotto, not necessarily a deep cavern) is a bucolic place in Theocritus, and this is its first Latin occurrence (antro = ἄντρῳ; cf. 5.16; 19; 6.13; 9.41): see id. 3.6; 7.137; 8.72; 11.44 (the Cyclops: cf. also 6.28). Its Homeric archetype is the Cyclops' dwelling in Od. 9.298 κεῖτ' ἔντοσθ' ἄντροιο τανυσσάμενος διὰ μήλων. The term antrum is quite frequent in V.: 33 occurrences in total (for its use in the E., cf. 5.6 [x2]; 19; 6.13; 9.41). For its numerous later attestations, also as a typical place for poetry, cf. Hor. carm. 1.5.3 grato...sub antro; 3.4.40 Pierio...antro; Prop. 1.1.11; 3.1.5; ThlL II.191.42–192.22; Enc. Virg. I, pp. 208–10, s.v. antrum (R. Scarcia); Virg. Enc. I, p. 249, s.v. caves and grottoes (E. W. Leach). Further specified by the mention of green vegetation (uiridi), the image seems to belong to the picturesque landscape dear to the Hellenistic and Roman taste for scenery: cf. the speluncae at G. 2.469; the detail will be reused by V. for the primitive (and protective) cave in which Vulcan places the twins and the she-wolf on Aeneas' shield: fecerat et uiridi fetam Mauortis in antro / ...lupam (Aen. 8.630–1). Caves and grottoes were often dark, gloomy places, such as the one on the island of Salamis where Euripides was said to have composed his tragedies (Gell. 15.20.5, citing Philochorus [fr. 219 Jac.]). The participle proiectus may hint at a foreground position, towards the opening of the grotto (pro): Meliboeus is a scrupulous shepherd and, even if he rests, he has to keep his eyes on his goats (76 uidebo); cf. Theocr. id. 3.6–7 τί μ' οὐκέτι τοῦτο κατ' ἄντρον / παρκύπτοισα καλεῖς 'why do you no longer call me in, / peeping out of this cave?'; id. 8.72 κἤμ' ἐκ τῶ ἄντρω...κόρα...ἰδοῖσα 'and a girl saw me from inside the cave'. At the time of his farewell, Meliboeus strikes a typically bucolic pose, similar to the one that opened the poem: Tityrus' recubans sub tegmine fagi.

76 dumosa pendere procul de rupe uidebo. For the goats' steep pastures, cf. G. 3.314–15; but also [Theocr.] id. 8.55–6 ἀλλ' ὑπὸ τᾷ πέτρᾳ τᾷδ' ᾀσομαι... / σύννομα μᾶλ' ἐσορῶν 'but under this rock I shall sing... / looking at the grazing herds'. An exiled ciuis Romanus and poet, Ovid, will remember these lines: ipse ego pendentis, liceat modo, rupe capellas, / ipse uelim baculo pascere nixus ouis (Pont. 1.8.51–2; cf. also ll. 47–8, to be compared here with 1.72–3). This is the first occurrence (ex negatiuo) of a topic crucial to Augustan poetry: i.e. the aesthetically pleasing sight of rural landscapes: cf. the conclusion of the next eclogue (2.66–8 [n.]; cf. esp. Hor. epod. 2.11–12 mugientium / prospectat errantis greges).

77 carmina nulla canam. Cf. 9.67 carmina...canemus (in a similarly sorrowful context; cf. also 9.53 nunc oblita mihi tot carmina [n.]). For the first time, the reader encounters a keyword of the E., emphasized and negated (nulla) at once, through a figura etymologica. In fact, carmen appears in every single eclogue (49x in the whole book). Singing was crucial to the opening poem of Theocritus' collection: id. 1 has it in its incipit (1.2 μελίσδεται), then again at 1.7 and, conspicuously, in the refrain (Thyrsis or song [ᾠδή] is the title of the idyll in the

108 ECLOGUE 1

manuscripts). The formula *carmen canere* appears in Catull. 64.383; 65.12; V. will also use *carmen dicere* (*E.* 6.5). **non me pascente**. It previously seemed, up to 1.75 *non ego*, that Meliboeus could retain part of his livestock and carry on with his pastoral work. Here, by contrast, his role as a herdsman is nullified, at least in relation to his beloved, and once happy, herd (1.74).

78 florentem cytisum. A fodder plant ('clover'), perhaps identifiable with a particular species of medicinal plant characterized by small yellow inflorescences (*Medicago arborea*). Theocritus' goats feed on κύτισος at *id.* 5.128; 10.30; cf. 2.64n. (identical beginning of the verse), as well as 9.31 (cows) and 10.30 (bees); *G.* 2.431; 3.394. The plant is praised for its ability to feed sheep in Varr. *rust.* 2.2.19; cf. Colum. (?) *arb.* 28.1; Plin. *nat.* 13.130; *Enc. Virg.* I, pp. 967–8, s.v. *cytisus* (G. Maggiulli). A contrast between this plant and the 'bitter' willow-trees (see below) is suggested though not expressed by *florentem*, as if Meliboeus wanted to hint at various kinds of herbivore diet (cf. 3.110 *dulcis…amaros* [n.]). Ovid's *cytisi* are *tenues*, i.e. thin and delicate, at Ov. *ars* 3.692. **salices carpetis amaras**. The willow-tree offers shelter and pasture to goats, sheep, and cows (cf. Lucr. 2.361; Nemes. *ecl.* 1.6; for the bees cf. 1.54n.). As such, the plant is representative of V.'s pastoral landscape: it typically grows on the banks of rivers and lakes, and its shadow (*G.* 2.434–6) makes it suitable for love encounters (cf. *E.* 3.65n. and 10.40n.); *Enc. Virg.* IV, pp. 652–3, s.v. *salice* (G. Maggiulli). The tree's leaves and branches certainly have a bitter flavour—yet here *amaras*, Meliboeus' last word, sounds particularly appropriate to a sorrowful farewell. Note the use of *amarus* in contexts marked by irony and sarcasm (such as *Aen.* 10.591–4; Hor. *sat.* 1.7.7; Quint. *inst.* 8.3.89). The author of the pseudo-Virgilian *Dirae* echoes Meliboeus' speech towards the end of the poem, in a rather pessimistic context (*Dirae* 92 *mollia non iterum carpetis pabula nota*; cf. 1.49n.).

79–83. Tityrus, who almost disappeared from the scene during Meliboeus' speech (1.46–78), now utters the last five lines of the eclogue (which Meliboeus had opened): thus, the two protagonists have an equal number of speeches (i.e. six each; cf. pp. 23–4), and the first and last speeches, both five lines long, compose a circular structure (see 1.1–10n.). Sunset marks the end of the song, as in *E.* 2; 6; 10 (the evening star, *Hesperus*, closes the entire collection: 10.77n.). Nightfall signals 'editorial' conclusion, from one book to another, in the *Iliad* (cf. Books 1–2; 7–8; 8–9), but here it expresses harmony between poetry and nature's time. From Meliboeus' point of view, the pastoral world is lost, and it belongs to nostalgia: Tityrus' invitation, whose impracticability seems to be expressed by the imperfect *poteras* (79), may at best be valid for one, short night—but it is through Tityrus' invitation that the reader concludes the introductory eclogue and moves on, entering the core of the pastoral book. Up to this point, Tityrus has used a pragmatic, objective tone throughout the account of his vicissitudes, while Meliboeus has pathetically evoked the pastoral world he is about to lose; now, however, Tityrus responds with sensitivity to the emotional stimuli of his interlocutor, and finally speaks like a Virgilian pastoral herdsman. His words allude to the Epicurean values of friendship and simple fare, capable of soothing sorrows and sufferings. In fact, the form of Tityrus' invitation is paralleled in Philodemus' epigrams (see 1.81n.). Tityrus' meal is a positive, reassuring image (V. is reworking Theocritus' banquet: *id.* 7.131–47); yet his invitation seems destined to be declined (see 1.80n.). When Tityrus finally devotes himself to the pastoral Muse, he does not receive a reply from Meliboeus, who has evoked pastoral scenarios and styles only to bid them farewell.

79 hanc mecum…requiescere noctem. Cf. Theocr. *id.* 11.44–5 ἅδιον ἐν τῶντρῳ παρ' ἐμὶν τὰν νύκτα διαξεῖς. / ἐντὶ δάφναι τηνεί, ἐντὶ ῥαδιναὶ κυπάρισσοι… 'more sweetly will you spend the night with me in my cave. / There are bays there, there are slender cypress trees, etc.' (a final Theocritean echo, after the initial one, 1.1–2, and the one at 1.51–8). A reference to the Cyclops, who had (vainly) invited the nymph Galatea, is particularly appropriate here: the two shepherds now belong to two completely different worlds. The lucky Tityrus, securely settled in pastoral peace, follows the stereotypical patterns of an invitation speech (κλητικὸς λόγος). In the Homeric archetype, i.e. the final book of the *Iliad*, Achilles persuaded Priam to share his dinner with him (*Il.* 24.618–19): the old king then asked for a pallet on which to spend the night (635–42). For a verbal parallel, cf. [Tib.] 3.6.53 *longas tecum requiescere noctes* (v.l. *tecum longas*). **poteras.** The verb expresses a potentiality, whose actualization seems to be precluded by the context: all the more so if compared to Theocritus' future tense (διαξεῖς). Concerning the feasibility of the wish, neither of the passages mentioned by commentators is decisive: Hor. *sat.* 2.1.16 *attamen et iustum poteras et scribere fortem*, etc. (a possibility left hanging); Ov. *met.* 1.679 *quisquis es, hoc poteras mecum considere saxo* (obvious echo of our passage, in a significant context: in this case, Mercury accepts the invitation, but Argus is the one falling asleep); contrast Cic. *Att.* 13.26.2 *etsi poteram remanere, tamen…proficiscar.* As Tityrus certainly knows, Meliboeus' evening departure (rather uncommon in antiquity) is justified by the fact that, once herd and herdsman have parted ways, Meliboeus has no reason to remain. Another evening departure, featuring Virgilian echoes (note *poteram*), is found at Iuv. 3.315–16 (Umbricius): *his alias poteram et pluris subnectere causas, / sed iumenta uocant et sol inclinat; eundum est.*

80 fronde super uiridi. A final comparison with the important model of *id.* 7 is here possible: ἔν τε βαθείαις / ἁδείας σχοίνοιο χαμευνίσιν ἐκλίνθημες 'we reclined / on deep beds of sweet rush' (132–3; cf. 1.51–8n.). **mitia poma.** 'Ripe', and therefore 'sweet': *G.* 1.448 *mitis…uuas*; 2.522. Cf. also Hor. *epod.* 2.17 *mitibus pomis* (in an idealized picture of *rus*); Mart. 10.48.18. Apples and especially chestnuts point to an autumnal setting, well suited to the sadness of farewell, following the evocation of summer at 1.51–8: cf. Calp. *ecl.* 2.82–3.

81 pressi copia lactis. Is the milk 'pressed' (i.e. cheese) or 'squeezed' (i.e. from the cow's udders)? The two options seem to be distinguished in Philargyrius/Philagrius, p. 31 (III.2 Th.-H.). The former is surely preferable: the activity

110   ECLOGUE 1

mentioned in realistic terms at 1.34 (*premeretur caseus*) reappears here in a more nuanced, poetic light (there is no room for doubt in the other case: the verb can only point to 'milking'; contrast 2.22n.). Unlike the case of 1.34, Tityrus now uses a solemn periphrasis in his final invitation to Meliboeus; cf. Philod. *epigr.* 23 Gig. = 29 Sid. (*Anth. Pal.* 9.412 = *GPh* 3280-7 G.-P.), 3 ἀρτιπαγὴς ἁλίτυρος 'freshly coagulated salted cheese'. Abundant production of cheese, still to be pressed in wicker baskets, is featured in Theocr. *id.* 5.86-7: fresh cheese, still soft and 'sweet', seems to have been particularly appreciated in antiquity.

82-3. Sunset is a horizontal vanishing line of shadows running from the mountains to the plains: the beginning of such a process is described in Apoll. Rhod. 1.450-2 'When the sun goes beyond the meridian, / and the fields are newly covered in shadows coming from the peaks (αἱ δὲ νέον σκοπέλοισιν ὑποσκιόωνται ἄρουραι), / while the sun bends over towards evening's darkness'. Tityrus' eyes can see nothing other than a serene landscape, with chimney tops smoking at dusk, so vividly contrasting with what Meliboeus' eyes see and have seen: 1.11-12 *undique totis / usque adeo turbatur agris.* To the exile Odysseus, in Athena's words, such an image meant longing for his distant home: 'he desires to catch sight of even the smoke leaping up / from his country' (Hom. *Od.* 1.58-9; see 1.69n.).

82 uillarum culmina. Rural villas are a realistic feature of the Romanized countryside, and for this reason are dear to Roman landscape painting. This is yet another, final contrast to the modest fortune with which Meliboeus would be content.

83 maioresque cadunt altis de montibus umbrae. In a sunset description, a reference to 'mountains' may appear somewhat conventional: and yet, on a bright day, the Alps and the Alpine foothills can be seen even from Mantua. Cf. Hor. *carm.* 3.6.41-2 *sol ubi montium / mutaret umbras,* as well as Tib. 2.5.96 *arboris antiquae qua leuis umbra cadit.* Note the epithet/noun arrangement, framing the line (1.48n.): V. suggests the gradual, majestic advance of darkness through the transition from bright sounds (/a/ and /e/) to darker ones (/o/ and /u/; cf. also *Maioresque...Montibus*). The closural effect is very strong when the reader reaches the final, delayed, noun: *umbrae.* The poem began under the beech tree's shade (1.1n.; 1.4 *in umbra*): evening shades bring the poem, and the entire book (*E.* 10.75-7), to a close. The end of the day, and the duplication of shadows, will also conclude Corydon's song—in this case, however, distracting him from his obsession and bringing him back to the normality of pastoral life (*E.* 2.66-8n.). For the wide semantic range of *umbra,* in which an Epicurean nuance is often perceptible, cf. Nováková (1964); *Enc. Virg.* V.1, pp. 378-84, s.v. *umbra* (A. M. Negri Rosio). For another nocturnal finale see e.g. Hor. *carm.* 3.28.16 *dicetur merita Nox quoque nenia*; in a pastoral context, Calp. *ecl.* 5.120-1; cf. also Iuv. 3.316 (see 1.79n.). The concluding keyword *umbrae* is paired with the anastrophe *altis de montibus,* a variation of Lucretius' *de montibus altis* (cf. Lucr. 4.1020;

5.313), which will occur again at *E.* 7.66 (then once in the *Georgics*, at *G.* 4.112, and several times in the *Aeneid*: cf. *Aen.* 3.675; 7.563).

Eclogue 2

[Alexis]

In the second eclogue, the shepherd Corydon laments his hopeless love for the boy Alexis. Alone amidst mountains and woods in the midday heat, he delivers an intense monologue, full of exclamations and apostrophes, addressing the boy as though he were in his presence (2.6–68). The eclogue ends on a note of resipiscence, when towards dusk he is reawakened to the thought of his agricultural labour, which he has neglected, and starts hoping for a new love (2. 69–73).

The scene is set by the poet himself, whose voice utters an analytical introduction at 2.1–5, ruling out any possibility of success (2.2 *nec quid speraret habebat*; 2.5 *studio…inani*). A fundamental precedent is *id.* 11, where a young Polyphemus courts the sea-nymph Galatea (similarly introduced by the poet: *id.* 11.1–18). In its twin piece, *id.* 6, the shepherd Damoetas plays the part of the Cyclops as lover (a poetry teacher called Damoetas is mentioned by Corydon at 2.37n.). A Theocritean motif, namely the impossibility of a life shared between the nymph's marine home and the Cyclops' pastoral world, is here converted into an opposition between Alexis' city (2.2n.) and Corydon's *sordida rura*. Perhaps V. knew *id.* 20 (almost certainly pseudo-Theocritean), which transposed the Cyclops' idylls to a non-mythological context, namely that of a young shepherd's love for a city girl. Furthermore, an echo of *id.* 3 is heard in the background, especially via a certain naivety in the characterization of the protagonist. On the other hand, the second eclogue does not share the tragically emphatic tone permeating the pseudo-Theocritean *id.* 23, in which the beloved's callousness induces the lover, after a desperate monologue in front of the boy's door, to commit suicide (the theme of 'suicide for love' will be featured in Damon's song, *E.* 8; but cf. also 2.6n.). Theocritus' *id.* 12, whose theme is requited homosexual love (note the incipit: Ἤλυθες ὦ φίλε κοῦρε), can helpfully be read alongside *E.* 2, particularly since the erotic ideal of *id.* 12, featuring a blissful reunion of two lovers, is a model of happiness for V.'s Corydon (see esp. *id.* 12.1–11, an enthusiastic accumulation of comparisons and images that may have influenced *E.* 2; cf. 2.3n.).

We know that a 'musician'-Cyclops appeared in Philoxenus' dithyramb mentioned by Plut. *quaest. conu.* 1.5.1.622c (cf. Bion, fr. 16 G.; [Bion], *epith. Achill. et Deid.* 1–3; Callim. *epigr.* 46 Pf. and also frr. 378–9 Pf.; see 1.30n.). In Theocritus, the Cyclops must have functioned as a sort of Siculo-pastoral archetype: after all, even Euripides made forays into the rustic, bucolic world in his *Cyclops* (Eur. *Cycl.* 41–8), also set in Sicily. Certain 'pastoral' images can be found even in the Homeric episode of the Cyclops (note the address to the ram at *Od.* 9.447–60; see

112   ECLOGUE 2

Introduction, p. 10, n. 23). The Cyclops will reappear as a pastoral character, but with the dreadful features of his epic (i.e. Homeric) incarnation, at *Aen.* 3.613–83. In the second eclogue, the paradoxical traits of the 'loving monster' are bracketed, and their comic potential is thereby reduced: much later, in Ovid's *Metamorphoses*, the theme of *id.* 11 will regain its original comic force through a dismantling of V.'s construction (Ov. *met.* 13.789–869). In *id.* 11, the Cyclops' plight was explicitly connected to the demonstration of a specific thesis, i.e. that poetry is the only 'medicine' capable of curing love. Thus, in the final lines of the introduction, addressed to his friend Nicias (a doctor), the poet said: '[Polyphemus] consumed himself / singing Galatea [...], / nursing in his heart a terrible wound, / which mighty Cypris' shaft inflicted on his chest; / but he found a cure (*id.* 11.17 τὸ φάρμακον εὗρε) and, seated on a tall rock / and gazing towards the sea, thus he sang...' (*id.* 11.13–18; note also the opening lines, *id.* 11.1–6; cf. Callim. *epigr.* 46.4 Pf.). Theocritus' voice framed the idyll and brought it to a close by praising Polyphemus' wise choice: he knew how to use song as a cure, instead of resorting to expensive medical treatments (*id.* 11.80–1). Thus, Hesiod's advice to grasp the present moment (*op.* 366–7) was applied to love by Polyphemus himself (*id.* 11.72–6), in opposition to such obsessive conceptions as Sappho's eros-madness; the precept is now taken over by Corydon (2.69–73n.). It is perhaps due to Theocritus' stimulus that V. prefaces the monologue with his own remarks: unlike Theocritus, however, he leaves the conclusion to Corydon himself. The early reception history of Theocritus' idyll also plays a significant role in *E.* 2: in an epigram, Callimachus had reworked Theocritus' lovesick Cyclops along with the idea of the Muses as a φάρμακον and an explicit reference to pederastic love (Callim. *epigr.* 46.6 Pf. τὰν φιλόπαιδα νόσον).

By embracing a Hesiodic, 'anti-romantic' ideology, *E.* 2 reworks another important Theocritean model, namely *id.* 10 (*The Reapers*), which is centred precisely around the opposition between eros and agricultural labour (as well as between their respective poetic genres: love song and labour song). Theocritus' *id.* 10 inspires the summer field labour in *E.* 2.8–11n. and, above all, the idea that love—naturally opposed to work, since it jeopardizes its success—may be fought against and overcome by work itself (cf. 2.70n.). On the issue of eros, one of the *E.*' last expressions will be *omnia uincit Amor* (10.69), but here the reader may catch glimpses of a 'cure', featured in V.'s next work: *labor omnia uicit / improbus* (*G.* 1.145–6).

The two great oppositions at work in Corydon's eclogue—city vs countryside, and love vs work—evoke a poetic genre of crucial importance to the *E.*, i.e. love-elegy. Although *E.* 2 does not possess elegy's typical 'courting' features (*werbende Dichtung*), since Alexis is unable to listen to Corydon's words, the poem is obviously comparable to *E.* 10, in which the elegiac poet Cornelius Gallus will again seek a *medicina* for his erotic *furor* in the pastoral dimension (10.60n.; but cf. 10.2: Lycoris must *read* her lover's poetry). Corydon's defence of country life and

ECLOGUE 2   113

its pleasures, in contrast to the city's advantages embodied by the *diues amator* Iollas (2.2n.; 57n.), sets up an opposition which, after Propertius and Tibullus, will remain essential to Latin elegy, at least until the Ovidian epistle that the shepherd Paris addresses to an urban, yet still 'rustic', Helen (Ov. *her.* 16). Also implicated is the myth of Acontius and Cydippe as it appears in Callimachus' *Aitia* (cf. 2.3n.), a foundational model of elegiac poetry which will be featured again in *E.* 10 (see 10.53–4n). The worldly aspect of such erotic-elegiac themes may have prompted interpreters to equate Corydon with the poet, like Tityrus in *E.* 1 (correspondingly, Alexis is sometimes taken to stand for a slave-boy belonging to Asinius Pollio: 2.1n.).

While the biographical allegory equating Corydon with V. and Alexis with a slave-boy owned by Pollio seems unpersuasive (besides being unprovable), Corydon is clearly portrayed as a very significant poet in the *E.*, undergoing a process of literary enrichment (in comparison to his Theocritean namesake) which is partly similar to that experienced by Tityrus (1.1n.). To be sure, it cannot be ruled out that an attractive *puer delicatus* prompted V. to write this eclogue. In the agon of *E.* 7, emphasizing his role as the lover of *formosus Alexis* (7.55n.), Corydon prevails over the Theocritean shepherd Thyrsis in the presence of Daphnis, whereas the incipit of *E.* 2 will be quoted as a pastoral 'classic' in 5.86. Albeit different from the role that Meliboeus and the 'modest' Tityrus played in the atypical opening eclogue, the task assigned to Corydon is also a very significant one: he introduces the reader to the core of V.'s pastoral world. Hence a careful inlay of allusions and imitations of the Greek *auctor* permeating the eclogue, the evocation of a pastoral archetype (the Cyclops), and some allusive references to literary geography (21 *Siculis…in montibus* [n.]; cf. 1.54n.). In *E.* 2, the feeling of beginning (further extended to *E.* 3, whose incipit will also be quoted in 5.87) may help to explain the nuance of modesty that can be perceived in 2.4 *incondita*, as well as in the ethopoeia of the naive lover (continuing that of the equally naive Tityrus). Within the sequence of the eclogues, the poet himself—along with his shepherds—makes his first literary attempts here. This, however, does not mean that *E.* 2 is actually among V.'s first compositions, as is often stated, though not without good arguments (similarly, *id.* 11 is frequently thought to be one of Theocritus' earliest attempts, if not the very first one). At any rate, Corydon's invitation to Alexis is also an invitation to V.'s reader to enter the pastoral world of the *E.*

Theocritus' *id.* 11 had a specific addressee: Nicias the doctor, whom the poet addressed at the beginning of the idyll. Here, by contrast, V. spends only a few words on his protagonist, without addressing readers or dedicatees. The next two eclogues, however, make it clear that Asinius Pollio is one of the most prominent figures in the audience (3.84n.; 4.12n.; *E.* 8, symmetrical with *E.* 2 within the book's structure and similarly devoted to an erotic theme, is most probably addressed to Pollio: see 8.6n.). Several literary, cultural, and mythological references in *E.* 2 may

114   ECLOGUE 2

have been crafted with Pollio and his tastes in mind (cf. 2.24n.). That Alexis was Pollio's *puer* is, in all likelihood, an invention of V.'s biographers; and yet this invention may be regarded as a biographical counterpart of the poet's literary and intellectual relationship with his influential patron. According to the Theocritean exegetical tradition, the aesthetic pleasure of pastoral poetry resides in the 'flowery' nature of its images: like a flower, it delights its readers (*Anecd. Estienne* 3.6 = Wendel, pp. 11–12: συμπλέκει δὲ ὅμως αὐτῷ τὸ ἀνθηρὸν τῶν λόγων εἶδος, ὃ δὴ χάριν ὁμοῦ καὶ κάλλος ἔχον τέρπει καὶ ἥδει ὥσπερ ἄνθος τοὺς ἀκροατάς). In his demonstration of pastoral skills, with which he tries to entice Alexis, Corydon accumulates flowers, colours, and scents. Corydon is a pastoral poet and is looking not just for a young lover, but also for a pupil (the transmission of poetry from older to younger poets is a pivotal theme in the entire collection, and especially in *E.* 3, 5, and 6).

Eros played a central role at the outset of Theocritus' collection, where it caused Daphnis' death (*id.* 1, esp. 19; cf. the erotic 'hunt' at 82–5). Nothing certain can be said concerning the position of *id.* 2 and 3 (the magic love potion, or φάρμακον, and the so-called 'goatherd's serenade') within the Theocritean edition used by V. (but cf. 2.10n.; see also Introduction, pp. 19–20 and nn. 47–8; below p. 381). However, the Theocritean question of a 'cure for love' must have appeared to V. in a philosophically problematized light, partly due to discussions in Epicurean circles: the issue seems to have been treated extensively in Philodemus' treatise *On Love*, Περὶ ἔρωτος (cf. also the well-known finale of Lucr. 4, esp. 1068–78; 1141–8). After *E.* 10, erotic obsession will often recur in V.'s *Georgics*, and finally in Book 4 of the *Aeneid* (on the motif cf. Traina 1999a, with references). At the outset of *E.* 2, love appears as a powerful force, esp. if we consider the contrast between the quiet, shady closure of *E.* 1 and the sunburnt landscape in which Corydon expresses his 'ardour' (1 *ardebat*; cf. 13 *sole sub ardenti*, despite 3 *umbrosa cacumina*). Towards the end, however, the sight of oxen bringing back the ploughs and the lengthening shadows (2.66–8n.) re-establish harmony between the poet and country life.

Asinius Pollio (whose interest in erotic and neoteric poetry is well documented) and the Epicurean Varius Rufus, along with other Epicurean poets and intellectuals in V.'s circle of friends, must have been interested in the erotic theme of *E.* 2. Whereas Theocritus uses the term φάρμακον to allude to his addressee's medical competencies, V.'s Corydon employs Epicurean and Lucretian expressions that ironically stimulate the philosophical background of V.'s friends (cf. 2.27n.; 65n.; 69–73n.; note also 8.35n.; 108n.). A rustic character meets the pathos of love poetry, not without irony and humour: similarly, Hellenistic philosophy and Theocritean echoes merge with Corydon's rural wisdom. The result is a unique *Musa rustica*, which was certainly received with favour by Pollio and V.'s friends (*E.* 3.84). Note also Horace's famous dictum, *molle atque facetum*, referring to the gifts of poetry that the *Camenae* bestowed upon the poet of the *E.* on

ECLOGUE 2   115

account of the pleasures of *rus* (Hor. *sat.* 1.10.44–5). On the other hand, *E.* 2 is also a laboratory of Latin erotic language: V. here experiments with forms and styles of obsessive love which will reappear in *Aen.* 4 and elsewhere.

In the first two eclogues, the city threatens the pastoral world, first with land confiscation, now with the charm of one of its dwellers. But Corydon is protected by a sense of belonging to the rural world, to its labour and to its leisure activities (hunting). Poetry, too, offers some help (without, however, proving decisive). At any rate, in the eyes of an urban, elegiac poet like Propertius, the protagonist of *E.* 2 seems quite happy: *felix intactum Corydon qui temptat Alexin / agricolae domini carpere delicias* (Prop. 2.34.73–4). If read right after *E.* 1, as the poet certainly intended, *E.* 2 may appear strikingly disengaged and focused on aestheticizing not only pederastic love but also countryside life and rural work (which, even in Sicily, was far from idyllic). Corydon talks and behaves like a free citizen (2.21n.) and a clearly well-off landowner: he even has a vineyard of his own. The resulting discontinuity between *E.* 1 and *E.* 2 gives the reader the impression of entering a naive but happy world, which was severely threatened in the first eclogue: this world remains virtually unscathed until the end of *E.* 8. The ninth eclogue, which closes the circle opened in the first, highlights once more the violence of history, which can easily damage or destroy the pastoral world. Ancient readers must have noticed the discontinuity between *E.* 1 and *E.* 2: Horace seems to rework it in his *Epodes*, where Maecenas' departure for Actium (*epod.* 1) is followed by Alfius' praise of countryside life (*epod.* 2), not without echoes of *E.* 2 and its aestheticization of *rus* (see 2.66n.).

From a rhetorical and narratological point of view, *E.* 2 is a purely narrative poem. Even though Corydon's voice dominates the text, the whole poem is uttered in the poet's voice. After a brief prologue (1–4), the poet introduces Corydon's monologue and leaves the stage to the herdsman until the very end (6–73). The monologue has a typical tripartite structure: in the opening, Corydon addresses the boy and introduces the situation (6–13); then, in the middle section, he tries to persuade Alexis to accept his invitation (14–55); finally, in the conclusion, the hapless lover regains his senses (56–73). The final section, in turn, can be subdivided into two parts (56–68: early signs of a return to sanity; 69–73: acceptance of defeat and separation).

On the eclogue: Gebauer (1861, pp. 142–76); Cartault (1897, pp. 78–84); Weyman (1917c); Helck (1932a, 1932b); Büchner (1955, cols. 1186–90); Savage (1960); La Penna (1963a); Otis (1963, pp. 120–4); Galinsky (1965); Fantazzi (1966, pp. 178–9); Leach (1966); G. Williams (1968, pp. 303–7); Posch (1969, pp. 29–53); Putnam (1970, pp. 82–119); O. Skutsch (1970); Leach (1974, pp. 146–53); Moore-Blunt (1977); Van Sickle (1978, pp. 55–9 and 125–7); Alpers (1979, pp. 116–24); DuQuesnay (1979); Geymonat (1981a); Kenney (1983); Grimal (1987); E. A. Schmidt (1987, pp. 139–58); M. O. Lee (1989, pp. 58–60); Stroppini (1993, pp. 51–76); T. K. Hubbard (1995a, pp. 46–59 = 1998, pp. 54–68 = Volk 2008, pp. 88–101); Rudd (1996, pp. 55–8); Papanghelis (1999, pp. 44–50); Holzberg

116 ECLOGUE 2

(2006, pp. 81–5); von Albrecht (2007, pp. 18–21); Fernandelli (2008); Davis (2012, pp. 99–119); Apostol (2015); Kania (2016, pp. 120–8); Leigh (2016); Stöckinger (2016, pp. 29–59); Marchetta (2018, pp. 7–97).

Specific issues: Hubaux (1927, pp. 46–64) (Hellenistic love epigrams); Alfonsi (1961) (relationship to *E.* 10); D'Anna (1965) (l. 24); Traina (1965) (l. 27 and Epicureanism in the *E.*); Alfonsi (1966) (ll. 61–2); Maia de Carvalho (1966) (l. 30); Nethercut (1967) (l. 3); Skanland (1967) (l. 25); Bettini (1972) (l. 69); Gratwick (1973) (l. 2); E. A. Schmidt (1974) (datation and chronology); Geymonat (1978–9) (l. 24); Monteleone (1979b) (Ovid as a reader of *E.* 2); Boyd (1983) (l. 51); Mayer (1983b) (Corydon's social status); Bauzá (1984, pp. 200–2) (symbolic landscape); Morelli, Tandoi (1984) (ll. 23–7); E. A. Schmidt (1984) (date); Bowie (1985, pp. 81–3) (ll. 31–9); Cancik (1986) (Corydon's social status); D'Anna (1987a) (conception of love); Geymonat (1987, pp. 56–7) (l. 24); Van Sickle (1987) (Corydon's social status); Marchetta (1994a, pp. 9–88) (l. 1); Marchetta (1994b) (ll. 60 and 69; the interjection *a*); Döpp (1995) (l. 53); Moretti (1996) (l. 53); La Penna (1997) (l. 27); Stroppini (1997) (conception of love); Fabre-Serris (1998) (l. 27); Traina (1999a) (conception of love); Binder (2000, pp. 127–30) (conception of love); Gioseffi (2004b) (Ps. Prob. on l. 48); Perotti (2004) (l. 60); Heuzé (2006, p. 106) (ll. 45–55); Kraggerud (2007, p. 87) (l. 32); Saunders (2008, pp. 117–27) (ecphrasis and landscape); Paraskeviotis (2014b, pp. 419–20) (ll. 23–7); Gagliardi (2016) (ll. 19–27); Kraggerud (2017b, p. 13) (l. 32); Gioseffi (2020) (Corydon as a mythomaniac poet); Landolfi (2020) (ll. 31–9); Seretti (2020) (ll. 32–3); Gioseffi (2021) (l. 45).

1–5. All even-numbered eclogues, including *E.* 2, begin with a prologue. Thus, the first five lines of *E.* 2 are uttered by the poet-narrator (hence the narrative form of the poem). Yet in *E.* 2, the first eclogue of its kind encountered by the reader, the poet does not indulge in a programmatic expression of his own viewpoint, and does not use the first person. Here, the first five lines have a purely 'pragmatic' function and introduce the general situation, even though they do include some of the typical words and notions of V.'s style (cf. the adjective *formosus* at 2.1, the parenthetic apposition at 2.3, and the idea of *inconditus* at 2.4). Thus, these five lines appear to epitomize V.'s book. Note that similar stylistic markers are found in the two five-line speeches that open *E.* 1 (see 1.1–10n.), and that *E.* 2 is also concluded by a five-line speech (in Corydon's voice: 2.69–73n.).

1 Formosum pastor Corydon ardebat Alexin. The opening line owes its memorability to its syntactical and semantic autonomy, as well as to its balanced structure: adj. and noun form a 'frame' for the whole line, following a neoteric pattern (e.g. Catull. 64.5; 54, etc.). For the line-enclosing word-order cf. 1.48; 1.83n. V. potentially echoes [Theocr.] *id.* 23.1 ἀνήρ τις πολύφιλτρος ἀπηνέος ἤρατ' ἐφάβω 'a man of many loves took a fancy to a cruel boy'. The incipit of *E.* 2 is quoted verbatim (with *pastor* omitted) at 5.86. The situation evokes one of the foundational myths of pastoral poetry, extant in Clearchus' account (fr. 32 Wehrli = Athen. 14.619c–d): the poetess Eriphanis (otherwise unknown: probably a mythical figure) falls in love with Menalcas, while the latter was hunting. Her love, however, is unrequited, and she roams about through woods and mountains, lamenting her

ECLOGUE 2 117

sorrow, to the point that even the most ferocious beasts are moved to compassion. She eventually composes a so-called 'pastoral' song (νόμιον), which she goes around singing and shouting aloud in the wilderness. The only surviving words of the song are 'tall are the oaks, Menalcas' (μακραὶ δρύες, ὦ Μέναλκα; cf. *PMG* 850, p. 452 P.). **Formosum…ardebat.** Both words belong to the vocabulary ('*sermo amatorius*') of Roman love-elegy. The adj., like the Greek καλός, is specifically applied to the beloved boy, and as such it immediately reveals the subject matter of the poem; cf. 1.5n. Love's 'flame' (*ardebat*) is a common image in erotic poetry: cf. the elegiac archetype in Callim. *aet.* fr. 67.1–2 Pf. = 166.1–2 Mass. 'Love himself taught Acontius the craft, when / he was ablaze with love [ἤθετο] for the fair maiden Cydippe'; cf. also Theocr. *id.* 7.56. Corydon's 'ardour' becomes concrete at 2.8–13 (esp. 13 *sole sub ardenti*, featuring the same verb as here; see also 68 *me tamen urit amor*); cf. 7.45–8; 53–6 (Corydon, in both cases). Wordplays based on the idea of 'heat/flame/love' are found in Meleager's epigram on the boy Alexis, which V. most probably knows (see below); note also Porcius Licinus' pastoral epigram, fr. 6 Bläns. = 7 Court.: *custodes ouium teneraeque propaginis, agnum, / quaeritis ignem? ite huc: quaeritis? ignis homost. // si digito attigero, incendam siluam simul omnem, / omne pecus flammast, omnia qua uideo*. Note the contrast with *umbrae* at the end of the previous eclogue: after some rest and Epicurean quiet (for Tityrus, at least), here comes the fire of passion that burns Corydon, even though he seeks shelter among the 'dense' shadows of the beech-trees (2.3; also 2.8). This is the first of a series of editorial tricks based on proximity: we may call them 'syntagmatic' effects; cf. the transition from *E.* 3 to 4 or from *E.* 8 to 9. The transitive construction of *ardeo* will be taken up in a Virgilian quotation by Mart. 8.63.1; cf. Prisc. *gramm.* III, p. 267.19–23 K.; see also Hor. *carm.* 4.9.13–14 *comptos arsit… crinis* (though note Hor. *epod.* 14.9 and *carm.* 2.4.7–8, where the more common ablative construction is used) and Prop. 1.13.23 *caelestem flagrans…Heben.* **pastor Corydon.** The protagonist's name, vaguely qualified by *pastor*, takes centre stage in the line. In Theocritus, the name Corydon is used for the cowherd in dialogue with the goatherd Battus in *id.* 4, whereas in *id.* 5 the name is assigned to a character not particularly accomplished in musical skills: 'When did you ever, Sibyrtas' slave, / possess a pipe? Are you no longer content to make music with Corydon, / whistling on a straw flute?' (*id.* 5.5–7; cf. *schol. ad id.* 5.6–7, p. 158 Wend.). Here Corydon speaks—somewhat hyperbolically—of 'a thousand she-lambs' (21), while in *E.* 7 his herd is composed of goats (3). At any rate, unlike Alexis, he is not portrayed as a slave (see 2.21n.). Important features characterizing Corydon in *E.* 2 reappear in the Corydon of *E.* 7: hunting (7.29–36n.) and, above all, his passion for *formosus Alexis* (7.55n.). In 7.4n., he will be called 'Arcadian' (along with Thyrsis). His name may perhaps be traced back etymologically to a songbird, a species of lark (*kórydos/korydallís*) quite often appearing in Theocritus, always in sunny, summer-like landscapes: *id.* 7.23; 141 (ἄειδον κόρυδοι); 10.50. In his first eclogue, Calpurnius Siculus stages a dialogue

118   ECLOGUE 2

between a Corydon and an *Ornytus* (extra-bucolic name, drawn from *Aen.* 11.677, with a vaguely 'ornithological' connotation [but note the root ὄρνιθ-]). It bears mentioning Philargyrius/Philagrius' annotation, p. 32 (III.2 Th.-H.): *Corydona...ex genere auis quae corydalis dicitur, dulce canens*; cf. Marcell. *med.* 29.30 Helmr. *corydalis auis, id est quae alauda uocatur, quae animos hominum dulcedine uocis oblectat.* At any rate, the bird's vocal abilities are inferior to the swan's (Dioscor. *Anth. Pal.* 11.195.6 = *HE* 1696 G.-P.; cf. also 9.380.1; for the bird's uncouth appearance cf. 2.25n.). Corydon's fame is entirely Virgilian, as is asserted at 7.70n.; further reading in *Enc. Virg.* I, pp. 887–9, s.v. *Coridone* (F. Caviglia); *Virg. Enc.* I, p. 307, s.v. *Corydon* (M. B. Sullivan). Corydon's name occurs five times in this eclogue (both in the narrator's prologue and in the herdsman's own mono-logue). Significantly, it is accompanied by the beloved boy's name every time, except at the very end (2.69 *a, Corydon, Corydon*), where the repetition signals separation. **Alexin.** The name is somewhat commonly used of boys who are the object of homoerotic desires. Unlike Corydon (2.21n.), Alexis is certainly a slave: *delicias domini* (2.2). V. may have recalled one of Meleager's epigrams, probably known to pre-neoteric poets (Lutat. *epigr.* 2 Bläns. = Court.), which is echoed more than once in *E.* 2: 'I saw Alexis strolling down the road at noon: summer / had just been cropped of its fruit's tresses. // Twofold rays scorched me: those of Eros, / coming from the boy's eyes, and those of the sun. // The latter were put to sleep by Night, but the former / were rekindled by a lovely phantom in my dreams. // Sleep that brings relief from cares to others brought cares to me, / portraying beauty as breathing fire in my soul' (*Anth. Pal.* 12.127 = *HE* 4420–7 G.-P.). The name is also attested in Anacreon, fr. 113 Gent. = *PMG* 394b P. (where, however, Alexis is bald and seemingly old), as well as in the erotic epigram at *Anth. Pal.* 7.100 = *Furth. Gr. Epigr.* 596–99, pp. 164–5 P., attributed to Plato. No wonder that an ancient tradition, probably speculative, identifies Alexis with a *puer*, Alexander, belonging to Pollio (himself equated with 2.2 *dominus*) and loved by V., who then received him as a gift from Pollio: *fuit seruus Asinii Pollionis, quem Vergilius, rogatus ad prandium, cum uidisset in ministerio omnium pulcherrimum, dilexit eumque dono accepit* (Serv. *ad E.* 2.1); cf. Mart. 8.55, esp. 5–20 (where, with a typical anachronism, Alexis' generous patron is Maecenas himself); note also Mart. 5.16.11–12; 6.68.5–6; 7.29.7–8; see further Iuv. 7.69; Apul. *apol.* 10.5; Don. *uita Verg.* 28–31 Brumm. = pp. 21.7–22.3 Brugn.-Stok.; Philargyrius/Philagrius, pp. 31–2 (III.2 Th.-H.). Such a relationship between patron and client had been described as typical by Horace at *epist.* 1.18.72–5. Pseudonyms were common in love-elegy: in Philoxenus' well-known dithyramb (an important precedent for Theocritus), Galatea's name pointed to her namesake, the lover of the tyrant Dionysius I of Syracuse (Gow 1952, II, p. 118; cf. 1.30n.). In the name *Alexis*, as in its extended form *Alexandros*, the root of the verb ἀλέγειν 'to aid, succour' is clearly perceptible: in Latin, the etymology is activated for Paris/Alexander at Enn. *trag.* (*Alex.*) 64 Joc. = 53 V.[2] *quapropter Parim pastores nunc Alexandrum uocant*, following

ECLOGUE 2   119

Euripides, fr. 42d Kann.; the source of Ennius' (and Euripides') fragment is Varro, *ling.* 7.82 *Alexandrum ab eo appellatum in Graecia qui Paris fuisset, a quo Herculem quoque cognominatum alexikakon, ab eo quod defensor esset hominum* (in the context, Varro criticizes Ennius for making an etymological wordplay readily intelligible in Greek but not in Latin). Significantly, the rare term ἄλεξις may be rendered as *remedium*, synonymous with φάρμακον, and the term ἀλεξιφάρμακον is also well attested, particularly in Epicurus' philosophy (as V. and his Epicurean friends probably knew). Here, however, the boy's behaviour contradicts such a meaning, at least from Corydon's point of view (2.6 *crudelis* [n.]). *E.* 2 is obsessively focalized on Alexis: thus, his name occurs six times in the poem (three times along with Corydon's name: 2.1; 56; 65), and always in structurally significant passages. Besides 2.1, the boy's name is mentioned at 6 (at the beginning of Corydon's monologue); 19 (where Corydon gets to the point); 56, 65 (where Corydon starts regaining his senses); 73 (at the very end of the poem). The poet does not say whether Alexis is a young herdsman or a servant who happened to walk through the fields, perhaps for hunting purposes (2.12n.). What is certain is that he is attracted to the urban pleasures that Iollas (2.57n.) can offer him.

   2 delicias domini. The *dominus* must probably be identified with Iollas, mentioned at 2.57. In Propertius' interpretation, he 'dwells in the *ager*' (which, however, does not rule out the *puer*'s urban origin): *Corydon qui temptat Alexin / agricolae domini carpere delicias* (Prop. 2.34.73–4); cf. 2.16n. Nothing proves that he is also Corydon's master—Corydon himself, at any rate, poses as a landowner (2.21n.). Note the alliteration, welding the lover together with the beloved into an impregnable whole: clearly, the *dominus* will never let Alexis belong to Corydon (hence *nec quid speraret habebat*). The word *deliciae* is a technical term in erotic contexts since at least Lucil. 277 M. = 297 K. (but cf. Plaut. *Stich.* 742); Catull. 32.2.

   3 densas, umbrosa cacumina, fagos. The arboreal symbol of the *E.*, again appearing in line-ending position: cf. *E.* 1.1 and 3.12; 5.13; 9.9. Beech trees replace the oaks (φηγοί) under which Acontius is said to have declared his love for Cydippe in Callimachus' account (according to the testimony of Aristaen. *epist.* 1.10, p. 23, l. 57 Maz.). The same is true of Propertius' reworking (Prop. 1.18.20). For Callimachus' model see also 2.70n.; 10.53–4n.; cf. 5.13–14n. There is no need to assume that V. misunderstood the Greek text, but he may well have been influenced by the phonetic affinity φηγός / *fagus* (1.1n.), perhaps through Gallus' mediation: note here the so-called *schema Cornelianum* or parenthetic apposition (1.57n.; 3.3n.), verbally paralleled in *E.* 9.9 *ueteres, iam fracta cacumina, fagos.* The setting of Corydon's love song, in the shady woods, is featured in the Hellenistic prototype of homoerotic love, namely Phanocles' Ἔρωτες ἢ Καλοί (*Loves, or Beautiful Boys*), fr. 1.1–6 Pow. Note the contrast between the shady landscape of Corydon's performance, here described by the poet's voice, and the sunny landscape of 2.8–13, esp. 13 *sole sub ardenti.* Cf. Theocr. *id.* 12.8–9: 'thus I rejoiced at your sight, and as the wayfarer under a shadowy oak [σκιερὴν δ' ὑπὸ φηγόν] / when

120   ECLOGUE 2

the sun is burning [ἠελίου φρύγοντος], so did I run' (the theme, i.e. ἔρως παιδικός, is analogous, but happily reciprocated in this case); see also 2.5n. It seems, therefore, that Corydon's shadowy beech-trees activate an analogy with the opening of E. 1, where Tityrus is sheltered by a large beech-tree. Corydon's *otia*, however, are undermined by restless anxiety (2.4 *adsidue ueniebat*; contrast Tityrus at 1.1 *recubans* and 1.4 *lentus*). When he addresses natural elements like mountains and forests, Corydon does not experience the same harmonious relationship with nature that Tityrus had (cf. 2.5n.). The term *cacumen* reappears in V. at E. 6.28; 9.9; G. 2.307. It is more commonly used in the plural by Latin poets (cf. Lucr. 1.898 *cacumina summa*, referring to treetops), and it is frequent in Catullus (cf. Catull. 64.240 *montis…cacumen*).

4 haec. Much like *id.* 11.18 τοιαῦτα (taken up by the closing οὕτω at 2.80), this introduces Corydon's direct speech. Unlike Theocritus, however, V. will not reappear as poet-narrator. **incondita.** The term belongs to the vocabulary of pastoral *humilitas*, and Philargyrius/Philagrius, p. 33 (III.2 Th.-H.) glosses it as *incomposita* and *agrestia* (cf. Sen. *ben.* 4.6.5; Quint. *inst.* 6.3.107). Here, along with the verb *iactabat* (2.5n.), it denotes the uncouth, dramatic nature of Corydon's monologue, full of interruptions and sudden changes of register (2.19, 28, 45, 56, 60, 66). The adj. could also be used of the early, artless forms of Roman (para-)literary production, i.e. the so-called popular *carmina*: Varr. *Men.* 363 Buech. = Astb.[2] (= 357 Cèb.): *homines rusticos in uindemia incondita cantare*; Liv. 4.53.11 *alternis inconditi uersus militari licentia iactati* (the *carmina triumphalia*; note the frequentative *iactare*, as in our passage; see also 4.20.2); cf. G. 2.386 *uersibus incomptis*. For the common use of *condere* in the sense of 'composing', cf. E. 6.7; 10.50. The pastoral genre itself is originally marked by a rustic, popular element, as the ancient sources surmised (on the role of ἄγροικοι in pastoral cf. *schol.* Theocr. *proleg.*, p. 2, esp. 9–12 Wend.). Thus, the passage is a preview of Corydon's characterization as a 'naive' shepherd, even though his figure is less of a caricature than Theocritus' Cyclops or the goatherd of *id.* 3 (cf. also Callim. *epigr.* 46.2 Pf.). V.'s humour is transparent here: the whole passage is an understated presentation of a refined mélange of styles, learning, and Hellenistic memories. **solus.** Cf. *id.* 11.14 αὐτός (better than the transmitted αὐτῷ). In *id.* 11, Polyphemus sits on a high rock and gazes at the sea in search of his beloved (17–18), while in *id.* 6 he has frequent and lively encounters with Galatea. Unlike him, V.'s Corydon experiences complete inability to communicate: his song, unable to reach Alexis (but cf. 2.6 *nihil mea carmina curas?*), has therefore chiefly an aesthetic and soothing value—different from Cornelius Gallus' elegy in 10.2. Based on 2.5, it becomes clear that the landscape, amidst woods and mountains, is situated at the wild margins of the pastoral world: cf. 10.52–4; note also [Mosch.] *epit. Bion.* 21 οὐκέτ' ἐρημαίασιν ὑπὸ δρυσὶν ἥμενος ᾄδει. Such *loca sola* must be avoided by unhappy lovers, according to Ov. *rem.* 579–608, while regular country life is an effective cure for love, especially if experienced in its agricultural form (Ov. *rem.* 169–224).

ECLOGUE 2   121

Lovers may find themselves wandering through mountains or other solitary places, like Minos in Callim. *hymn.* 3[*Dian.*].190-1, or Ariadne in Catull. 64.184-7 (but she has been abandoned; cf. Prop. 1.18.1-4; also Petron. 83.4). Secret paths and a (myrtle) forest will give shelter to unhappy lovers in the underworld at *Aen.* 6.443-4.

5 studio iactabat inani. The term *studium* denotes both erotic passion and the song deriving from it: both are devoid of purpose, especially insofar as they are unheeded and inaudible (cf. 2.4n.). By contrast, Theocritus called Polyphemus' song a φάρμακον, thus emphasizing its effectiveness in curing love (*id.* 11.17). Without warning, Corydon will eventually find peace at 2.69-73. The verb, suggesting intense and resentful expression (as in Afran. *com.* 266 R.[3]; but cf. also Liv. 4.53.11 [see 2.4n.]), will reappear in *Aen.* 1.102. The imperfect tense vividly depicts the prolonged nature of the action (and its endless repetition); cf. Polyphemus' ἄειδε in *id.* 11.18. Corydon's monologue appears to the reader as a predefined text, which the herdsman-poet is free to repeat in order to give vent to his passion: note also the imperfect tense in *adsidue ueniebat* (2.4). To some extent, the passage looks forward to the peaceful closure at 2.66-73 (at least upon a second reading). **montibus et siluis.** The *siluae* are the defining space of V.'s bucolic programme (*E.* 1.2-5 *siluestrem...siluas*; cf. also 4.3), and appear here in their least accessible form (*montibus*). Both nouns are in the dative (place is expressed by *ibi*, taking up *inter densas...fagos*). The mountains, just like the woods, can take part in pastoral feelings and songs along with the shepherds (e.g. *E.* 5.28; 62-3; 6.84). The motif of 'talking' to natural elements, such as air and winds, is particularly common in Attic drama (e.g. Eur. *Med.* 56-8; *Andr.* 91-5; cf. also Callim. [*aet.*?], fr. 714 Pf. = 275 Mass.; Alciphr. 1.8.1; Plaut. *Merc.* 3-5), then pathetically reworked by Catullus, 64.164-6; cf. 3.73n. Yet V.'s Corydon only potentially conforms to the standard set by Tityrus in *E.* 1.5 (i.e. a poet-herdsman 'teaching' the woods to sing; cf. 10.8). In fact, there seems to be virtually no communication or resonance (and, therefore, no 'teaching and learning') in the anxious way in which Corydon 'throws' (*iactabat*) his uncouth poetry at the forests and the mountains; see further 2.12-3n.

6-13. The poet entrusts Corydon with the task of outlining the space-time coordinates in which his action is set: a hot sunny afternoon, in contrast with the shadowy location in which Corydon's songs are produced (2.3).

6 O crudelis Alexi. Using *crudelis* at the outset of his speech, Corydon reaches a degree of pathos unprecedented in pastoral poetry, even though Theocritus' Cyclops had drawn attention to Galatea's rejection of his love from the very beginning of his song (*id.* 11.19-24, esp. 19 τὸν φιλέοντ' ἀποβάλλῃ). Note also the difference between the adjective here used by V. and the one Theocritus had used at the beginning of the goatherd's serenade in *id.* 3, which V. knows well: see 2.7n.: *o crudelis Alexi* ≈ *id.* 3.6 ὦ χαρίεσσ' Ἀμαρυλλί (note the vocative in the sixth line of both poems). A closer parallel might be the opening of the suicidal lover's speech at [Theocr.] *id.* 23.19 ἄγριε παῖ καὶ στυγνέ (cf. *id.* 23.48 ἀπηνέα in the final

122   ECLOGUE 2

line of the monologue, but also 23.6 ἀτειρής in the narrator's introduction). In Latin poetry, the adj. *crudelis* is used twice of Theseus by the abandoned Ariadne in Catullus, 64.136 and 175. In the Cyclops' matching incipit, ὦ λευκὰ Γαλάτεια (*id.* 11.19; cf. also 3.6), the adj. emphasized the name's etymology: there, whiteness was the key feature of a sea-nymph whose name evokes milk, γάλα, as 2.20 immediately made clear (note also the anonymous bucolic line addressed to Galatea, apud Him. *or.* 9.19 ὦ λευκότητος καὶ γάλακτος; cf. *Anth. Lat.* 154.6 R. = 143.6 Sh. B.). Here, on the other hand, *crudelis*, along with *nihil…curas*, may be a sarcastic comment on the reassuring etymology of *Alexis* from ἀλέγειν (2.1n.): the adj. comes from *cruor*, 'blood clotted from a wound'. The παῖς/*puer*'s callousness is a recurring theme of homoerotic verse, e.g. in the *corpus Theognideum*, 1259–66 and 1299–1304, then also common in epigrammatic poetry (Strat. *Anth. Pal.* 12.186; 193). Note the trochaic (or feminine) caesura.

   6–7 nihil… / nil. At the outset of Corydon's monologue, the repetition of the emphatic negative *nihil* (with variation) amplifies the pathetic effect. The same is true of 8.103 *nihil ille deos, nil carmina curat* (albeit in a finale). The notion of 'indifference' contained in 2.6 *nihil mea carmina curas* is reworked and applied to all kinds of 'gifts' at 2.56 *nec munera curat Alexis* (n.); note the linguistic echo at 3.61 *illi mea carmina curae*.

   7 mori me denique cogis? The reading *cogis* (P and a vast number of manuscripts; cf. *Anth. Lat.* 15.58 R.), which requires a question mark after the verb, is very likely to be genuine. R's variant reading, *coges*, favoured by many editors, is supported by *id.* 3.9 'you will force me (ποιήσεις) to hang myself'; the threat becomes reality in [Theocr.] *id.* 23 (Virgilian characters generally avoid suicide by hanging, considered particularly dishonourable in Rome: cf. *Aen.* 12.603 *nodum informis leti trabe nectit ab alta* with Serv. ad loc.; also 8.59n.). By using the present tense *cogis* after *curas* and *miserere*, Corydon asks a final, intense question, with an effective *tricolon*: cf. *Aen.* 2.69–70 *quae nunc tellus…quae me aequora possunt / accipere? aut quid iam misero mihi denique restat…?* (see also *Aen.* 12.793). For the use of *denique* to conclude parallel-clause structures (including interrogative ones), see *ThlL* V.1.529, esp. 27–42. Here, as in the Virgilian passages quoted above, *denique* appears in the fifth foot, which is its most common position (along with the first) in hexameter verse. V.'s wording is echoed (including the variant readings?) at Ov. *her.* 3.140–1, where the *tricolon* is slightly different, as Ovid makes use of both the present and the future tense: *quam sine te cogis uiuere, coge mori! / utque facis coges.*

   8 nunc etiam pecudes umbras et frigora captant. Midday is the natural time for both shepherds and animals to rest, as in Plato, *Phaedr.* 259a: cf. Varr. *rust.* 1.2.5; 2.2.11; Hor. *carm.* 3.29.21–2; Pers. 3.6; Plin. *epist.* 2.17.28; explicit advice in *G.* 3.331–4. At this time, it is preferable to be silent, or at least not to play the pipes, so as not to awaken the irascible Pan: *id.* 1.15–18 (singing, however, is allowed: cf. 2.19; by contrast, Theocr. *epigr.* 5 G. includes an open provocation). In *E.* 2, on the other hand, the sound effect of Corydon's monologue is far from negligible (2.13 *resonant arbusta*), and he allows himself to name the god and his pipe three times (2.31–4). For the contrast between nature's tranquillity and a character's passion, cf. *id.* 2.38–41; the hendiadys *umbras et frigora* highlights the two aspects of pastoral shelter that Corydon lacks: shade and cool air.

9 uiridis…occultant spineta lacertos. Cf. *id.* 7.21–2 'Simichidas, where are you heading to at noon, / when even the lizard [σαῦρος] sleeps in the stone-walls?' (Lycidas' opening speech). The fem. *lacertas*, originally P's reading (then corrected into *lacertos*), is not wholly unparalleled (cf. Hor. *carm.* 1.23.7), but *G.* 4.13 *picti squalentia terga lacerti* speaks against it. The green hue (*uiridis*), which is the lizards' natural colour but is not mentioned by Theocritus, visually underscores the image of their shelter, under the sun's blazing glare; cf. 1.80 *fronde super uiridi*.

10 Thestylis. One of the two enchantresses (φαρμακεύτριαι) named in *id.* 2, whose first line mentions her as assistant to Simaetha while she performs her spell: πᾷ μοι ταὶ δάφναι; φέρε Θεστυλί 'Where are the bay-leaves? Bring them over, Thestylis'. She is also featured in Sophron's mimes (according to the *schol. id.* 2, *argum.* a, pp. 269–70 Wend.), but does not appear in the *corpus Theocriteum* outside *id.* 2. V.'s reworking is contrastive: here Thestylis, in her subordinate role as the reapers' cook, prepares a mixture of simple aromatic herbs, while the herbs of *id.* 2 were enchanted (*id.* 2.59; cf. the bay-leaves in the incipit; note also *id.* 2.18–19; 95); see 2.43n.; further reading in *Enc. Virg.* V.1, pp. 147–8, s.v. *Testilide* (F. Michelazzo). In *id.* 2, the 'medicine' for love was provided by the spell: in *E.* 2, on the other hand, the cure will come from pastoral song and consideration of agricultural labour (2.69–73; on the interplay between magic, medicine, and eros here and in *id.* 11, see Faraone 2006). V.'s Thestylis is echoed by Martial 8.55.18 (cf. 2.1n.): *Thestylis…rubras messibus usta genas* (the whole epigram is full of allusions to V.'s life and works). **rapido fessis messoribus aestu.** The 'reapers' were part of the pastoral world according to Theocritus, who devoted *id.* 10 to them. Solace for their fatigue was offered there by a female figure somewhat similar to V.'s Thestylis (*id.* 10.15–16 'Polybotas' girl, / who played the pipe to the reapers… the other day'; l. 51 specifies their need to rest at midday). For *rapidus* referring to the sun, cf. *G.* 1.92; 424; 2.321; Catull. 66.3 (and later Ov. *met.* 8.225); see also Tib. 1.9.49 *rapida…flamma*; Ov. *trist.* 1.7.20 *rapidis…rogis*; and *G.* 4.425 *rapidus…Sirius*. The phrase *rapido…aestu* will reappear in Manil. 1.869; for a likely allusion to V.'s reapers and their garlic, cf. Hor. *epod.* 3.4 (see 2.11n.). Reapers and cicadas are naturally connected (cf. Theocr. *id.* 5.110–11): the insects, in fact, will soon make an appearance (2.13).

11 alia serpyllumque herbas contundit olentis. Thestylis' 'recipe', here only sketched, is further developed in the pseudo-Virgilian *Moretum* (82–9). As a 'powerfully flavoured' φάρμακον, garlic has its own magical power, which Horace will playfully exploit in his third epode (Hor. *epod.* 3.4 *o dura messorum ilia*;

124   ECLOGUE 2

cf. here 10 *messoribus*). The *serpyllum* (also spelled as *-ul-* or *-il-*) is thyme, specifically its wild variety, known as 'Breckland thyme' or 'elfin thyme', with its typical 'creeping' growth habit (from *serpere*: cf. the Greek ἕρπυλλος from ἕρπω).

12–13 at mecum raucis… / …resonant arbusta cicadis. The cicadas' song at high noon in summer heat is featured in poetry at least since Hesiod, *op.* 582–4 (cf. also *scut.* 393–7); cf. Theocr. *id.* 7.138–9; 16.94–6. Plato, *Phaedr.* 258e–259d, linked them to the Muses (on cicadas as a symbol of poetic song see 5.77n.). According to Aelian, *nat. anim.* 1.20, they remain silent until late morning (whereas Hes. *scut.* 396 has them sing at dawn). Besides referring to their typical timbre, *raucis* alludes to their proverbially 'chatty' nature: cf. Aristophon Com. *Pythagor.* fr. 10.6–7 K.-A.; Liban. *decl.* 26.41; Novius *Atell.* 25–6 R.³ *totum diem / argutatur quasi cicada*; Ov. *ars* 1.271; *Culex* 153; Nemes. *ecl.* 1.2. After the calm at 2.8–11, an echo effect breaks out, as *at* triggers the assonant wordplay *ARdenTi resonAnT ARbusTa* (note, in *arbusta*, the phonetic-semantic suggestion of *ustus*, perfect participle of *uro*); cf. *G.* 3.327–8 *inde ubi quarta sitim caeli collegerit hora / et cantu querulae rumpent arbusta cicadae*, etc. (note also *Copa* 27 *rumpunt arbusta cicadae*). For a similar effect cf. *G.* 2.328 *AVIa tUm resonant AVIbUs*; but see 1.5n. Given their human past, cicadas are all the more suitable to sympathize with Corydon's sorrow (Tithonus, Aurora's very old husband, was said to have been turned into a cicada: Serv. *ad G.* 3.328 *querulae…cicadae*). An overly rationalistic approach guides Bentley's proposal to divide *mecum* into *me*, direct object of *resonare* (as in *E.* 1.5; *G.* 3.338; cf. differently *Aen.* 7.11–12; Prop. 1.18.31 *resonent mihi*), and *cum*, governing *raucis…cicadis*. Rather, the syntax of both lines artfully tends towards an associative interplay in which both constructions overlap. Corydon may be thinking of another epigram by Meleager (besides the one for a boy named Alexis: cf. 2.1n.), in which a cicada sings in the solitude of the fields, in order to facilitate the poet's noonday rest and help him flee Eros: *Anth. Pal.* 7.196.7 = *HE* 4072 G.-P. …ὄφρα φυγὼν τὸν Ἔρωτα, μεσημβρινὸν ὕπνον ἀγρεύσω / ἐνθάδ' ὑπὸ σκιερᾷ κεκλιμένος πλατάνῳ. Here the bucolic ideal is not realized, according to which nature responds to the shepherd's song (10.10 *non canimus surdis, respondent omnia siluae*): what resounds is only the deafening noise of summer insects: see 2.5n.

12 tua dum uestigia lustro. Obsession is expressed through a metaphor traditionally belonging to the language of homosexual eros and perfectly appropriate for the situation: Alexis is likely to have run through woods and mountains during his hunting expeditions, and Corydon now follows the foot-tracks of his 'prey' (cf. 2.28–30n.); for *lustrare* see 10.55; for the beloved's *uestigia*, which the lover must follow, cf. 6.58 *errabunda…uestigia*. The coupling of hunting and homoeroticism will reappear in 3.74–5 and, in the *Aeneid*, the passion for hunting will unite Euryalus and Nisus (*Aen.* 9.245; see also 9.176–81); but cf. the metaphor in Theocr. *epigr.* 3.3 G. 'Pan and Priapus are hunting you [scil. Daphnis, the prey] down'. Love for hunting dogs, horses, and boys constituted a lifestyle in Solon's couplet, fr. 17 G.-P. = 23 W.²; cf. Theogn. 1253–6.

ECLOGUE 2   125

13 sole sub ardenti. Cf. Catull. 64.353–4 *uelut densas praecerpens messor aristas / sole sub ardenti flauentia demetit arua* (in the context of reaping; the simile refers to Achilles' invincibility during the Trojan war). Note the echo of *E*. 2.1 *ardebat*, which connects the pastoral scenery with Corydon's state of mind. Contrast the shadowy shelter at 2.3, which is where Corydon's poetic performance takes place.

14–55. Although the poet-narrator makes it clear that Corydon stands no chance of success, the core of the herdsman's monologue (preceding the first appearance of doubt: 2.56–9) is devoted to a series of arguments and invitations aimed at enticing Alexis. Yet the opening of this passage (see 2.14–16n.) contains *in nuce* traces of rustic concreteness, which must eventually prevail (cf. 2.69–73n.): would it not be better to settle for Amaryllis or Menalcas?

14–16. A first, sudden impulse towards a change of heart, since Corydon seems to realize how far he has moved away from the normality of pastoral love affairs: but this is still not enough (contrast 2.69–73n.). Hence the choice of two names typical of the pastoral world: Amaryllis and Menalcas (for the mention of both sexes cf. *E*. 10.37, featuring Phyllis and a *fuscus* Amyntas). The advice given to the παῖς, not to place too much trust in his own, inevitably fleeting, beauty, is a traditional motif of homoerotic poetry. Here, however, it is only sketched, thereby perhaps confirming Corydon's sincere devotion to Alexis: contrast e.g. Hor. *carm*. 4.10, esp. 4–5 *nunc et qui color est puniceae flore prior rosae / mutatus*, etc. (but cf. Theogn. 1299–1310; see also *Anth. Pal*. 11.36; 12.33; 35; 36; 186, etc.; add Sen. *Phaedr*. 761–76; 820–3).

14 tristis Amaryllidis iras. For a variation cf. 3.80–1 *triste…Amaryllidis irae* (one of the numerous echoes of *E*. 2 in *E*. 3). The phrase reappears at *Aen*. 3.366 *tristis…iras*; but for the conjunction cf. Cic. *carm*. 28.1 Bläns. (quoted in *Tusc*. 3.18); see also Hor. *carm*. 1.16.9; Stat. *Theb*. 12.574; Sil. 10.225. On the name, common among pastoral girls, see 1.5n.

15 Menalcan. Called *niger* in the following line. On the name, going back to an old (possibly pre-Theocritean) tradition, cf. 3.13n.; 10.9n. The finale of *E*. 5 will reveal that Menalcas is also the name of a singer who 'learned' Corydon's song from his own *cicuta* (i.e. he is its author). Hence, behind Corydon's mask, an allusion to yet another mask, namely Menalcas 'the poet'. Note also certain hints at a possible identification between V. and Menalcas in *E*. 9, suggested also at the end of *E*. 5 itself. V. himself was said to be dark-skinned (Don. *uita Verg*. 25 Brumm. = p. 21.4 Brugn.-Stok *aquilo colore*), assuming that the information does not merely derive from this passage.

16 quamuis ille niger…tu candidus esses. Dark skin was rarely celebrated, partly due to it being a sign of manual labour, whereas the adj. *candidus*, qualifying Alexis, refers to an aesthetic value typically associated with elite female bodies (the opposition male/dark vs female/bright is common in ancient iconography). V. often uses *candidus* to describe female deities (cf. 5.56–7n.); but cf. *Aen*. 9.432 *candida* *pectora* (the *puer* Euryalus, mortally wounded). Correspondingly, tanned skin can be connected with the virtue of the peasant-farmer, for both men and women: Hor. *epod.* 2.41–2. Thus after 2.2 *delicias domini*, here is a further clue to the boy's urban origin. In Longus' novel, Daphnis scolds Dorcon for his skin colour, 'white as a city woman's' (1.16.5); in Theocritus' *epigr.* 2 G., however, Daphnis himself (the pastoral hero) is described as λευκόχρως, 'white-skinned'. The imperfect subjunctive *esses*, expected after 2.14 *fuit*, casts a shadow of unattainability on Alexis' beauty.

18 alba ligustra. A very humble shrub, the privet, which V. introduces into poetry: this is the only occurrence in V.'s works. It will reappear in relation to Ovid's Galatea at *met.* 13.789 *candidior folio niuei...ligustri*; cf. Mart. 1.115.3; 9.26.3; see also Colum. 10.300 *niueo...ligustro* (where R. H. Rodgers prints Parrhasius' *niueo* in lieu of the transmitted *nigro*). Unlike its flower, its fruit is dark; its small berries can be toxic for humans. **uaccinia nigra.** Probably a type of flower, as suggested by the parallelism with *ligustra* and because Corydon will choose the *uaccinia* for his floral garland at 2.50n., thereby demonstrating the principle here asserted (*leguntur*). This plant is perhaps a species of hyacinth (ὑάκινθος), as is suggested by both the likely etymological link and the echo of *id.* 10.26–9 'Fair Bombyca, they all call you a Syrian, / they call you skinny, sunburnt: I only call you honey-dyed. / Black is the violet, and black is the mottled hyacinth [28 καὶ τὸ ἴον μέλαν ἐστὶ καὶ ἁ γραπτὰ ὑάκινθος; note here *quamuis...quamuis*; cf. *Aen.* 11.60 *seu mollis uiolae seu languentis hyacinthi*], / and yet they are chosen the first in garlands' (cf. also Long. 1.16.4). V., who elsewhere uses the Greek form *hyacinthus* (but only in line-ending position and in Hellenizing or otherwise lofty contexts: *E.* 3.63; 6.53; *G.* 4.137; 183; *Aen.* 11.69), has Corydon employ a 'rustic' term, stylistically akin to *ligustra*. Aside from *E.* 2, the only other occurrence of *uaccinia* in V. is in the speech of Cornelius Gallus, who displays great familiarity with Corydon's song as well as with its Theocritean model here, *id.* 10 (10.39n.). V.'s *uaccinia* have sometimes been identified with bilberries (the berries themselves, because their flowers are not black, but generally white or pinkish): see André (1956, p. 325; 1985, p. 268); *Enc. Virg.* V.1, pp. 413–14, s.v. *vaccinium* (G. Maggiulli). At any rate, as Servius observed (*et rustice et amatorie ex floribus facit comparationem*), Corydon here takes refuge in his pastoral world, not without some naivety (which he shares with the cowherd of *id.* 10, 'author' of the passage quoted above).

19 nec qui sim quaeris. This use of the verb *quaero* (esp. in phrases like *si quaeris* or *quid quaeris?*), colloquial in tone, is very common. Here, the negative introducing the phrase conveys an idea of marked disinterest; cf. (in epistles) Lucil. 181 M. = 182 K. *quo me habeam pacto, tam etsi non quaeris, docebo*; Cic. *fam.* 13.1.4 *si quid ipse sentiam quaeris*; Hor. *epist.* 1.8.3 *si quaeret quid agam*; Sen. *epist.* 106.5; also, for instance, Plaut. *Amph.* 816 *quaeris quid deliqueris*; Cic. *Sull.* 27; *de orat.* 3.86. For *qui sim* cf. 1.18n.

20 diues pecoris. Alexis' 'contempt' (19) leads Corydon to use the explicit term *diues* (competing with the *diues amator* Iollas?: cf. 2.57n.). According to Varro's etymology, *pecunia a pecu: a pastoribus enim horum uocabulorum origo* (*ling.* 5.92). **niuei.** Certainly agreeing with *lactis*, rather than *pecoris* (as Servius thought): note the caesura after *pecoris* and the proverbial 'whiteness' of milk (e.g. Theocr. *id.* 5.53); cf. also Ovid's reworking at *met.* 13.829 *lac mihi semper adest niueum*, as well as *fast.* 4.780. The adj. is used of feminine beauty in Catull. 64.364.

21 mille meae Siculis errant in montibus agnae. Echoing Theocritus' Cyclops: 'I graze a thousand beasts [βοτὰ χίλια], / and from them I draw the best milk for myself to drink. / I am never without cheese, in summer or fall, / or even in mid-winter' (*id.* 11.34–7). Yet Corydon amplifies the size of the flock, since a thousand is merely the number of his *agnae*—hence Calpurnius Siculus' reworking at *ecl.* 2.68–9 *mille sub uberibus balantes pascimus agnas,* / *totque Tarentinae praestant mihi uellera matres.* Further exaggeration in Nemes. *ecl.* 2.35 *mille iuuencas.* Ovid's Cyclops, on the other hand, will be superior to any form of calculation: *nec, si forte roges, possim tibi dicere, quot sint:* / *pauperis est numerare pecus* (*met.* 13.823–4). A partial quotation of V.'s line, confirming its 'appeal' as a status symbol, appears on a Pompeian graffito: Gigante (1979, p. 166); Ferraro (1982, pp. 5–6); cf. 2.56n. Whether Corydon is a free-born citizen or a slave (like Alexis) is a matter of debate. He is, first and foremost, a literary character, who plays the role of a myth-ical creature (the Cyclops, son of a god); here, he behaves like a landowner. In particular, the adjective *meae* (here referring to *agnae*) is also used by Tityrus, an ex-slave now free, in relation to his cattle at the beginning of the book (*meas...boues* at 1.9), as V.'s reader certainly knows. Despite V.'s irony and even some malicious sarcasm, it seems that the poet of the *E.* has no interest in empha-sizing Corydon's 'lowly' social status (see below). **Siculis.** An explicit token of allegiance to the Theocritean-pastoral genre, as in the first line of *E.* 6 and the incipit of *E.* 10. The adjective form, which occurs again at 10.51 *pastoris Siculi*, is as common in Latin as *Sicanus* (10.4); both appear in the *Aeneid*, where *Sicanius* is also used. In *E.* 4.1, V. uses a rarer, Hellenizing form: *Sicelides Musae* (see n. ad loc.). Here, the detail activates the possibility of Sicilian setting for the poem (a unique case in the *E.*): cf. also 2.25 *in litore;* 26 *placidum...mare.* A similar geo-graphical hint appears at *id.* 1.125 (but cf. above all the pseudo-Theocritean *id.* 8.56). By contrast, the Corydon of *E.* 7 will be called an 'Arcadian' (see 7.4n.). Note also that, in late Republican Rome, Sicily was a symbol of wealth and pros-perity for both the Roman state and the individual landowners. Thus, Corydon's boasting words could as well have been in the mouth of several Roman senators and equestrians in the City itself. Horace addresses the wealthy Pompeius Grosphus in a similar way: *te greges centum Siculaeque circum* / *mugiunt uaccae* (Hor. *carm.* 2.16.33–4). Not without subtle irony, V. strikes close to home for many of his aristocratic readers by alluding to urban elites through the mouth of a rural herdsman. At the time of the second triumvirate, Sicily was also known as the theatre of war between the triumvirs and Sextus Pompey, who controlled the seas around the island.

128   ECLOGUE 2

22 lac mihi non aestate nouum, non frigore defit. By emphasizing the continuous production of fresh (*nouum*) milk, V.'s Corydon overcomes a problem (albeit a small one) long recognized in the Theocritean model. In fact, τυρός at *id.* 11.36 must refer to fresh cheese, otherwise Servius' objection is valid: 'cheese can be preserved, and there is nothing extraordinary in having it always available' (here, however, *lac* simply refers to milk; cf. Hom. *Od.* 4.89; contrast 1.81n.). Calpurnius Siculus is keen on avoiding ambiguity, and puts the proper term in the shepherd Idas' mouth: *per totum niueus premitur mihi caseus annum* (*ecl.* 2.70; cf. 1.34n.). Corydon's boast was undermined by an ancient critic (or *Vergiliomastix*), who changed the interpunction: *lac mihi non aestate nouum, non frigore: defit* (Serv.). Used as a synonym for 'winter', *frigus* is a poetic term: cf. *G.* 1.48; Hor. *epist.* 1.15.5; Ov. *trist.* 4.1.58 (but see also *Rhet. Her.* 4.48.61). The verb *defieri* is most probably an archaism: cf. Lucr. 2.1141; 3.220; Prop. 1.1.34.

23–4. Corydon does not refrain from comparing himself to Amphion, whereas Polyphemus could at best boast about being the most skilled pipe player among the Cyclopes (*id.* 11.38–40). Lucian's nymph Doris is dismissive of Polyphemus' singing skills: 'Shut up, Galatea: we heard him sing the other day, when he played you a serenade. By Aphrodite, he sounded like a braying donkey! [...] Echo, talkative though she may be, could not bear herself to reply to such bellowing' (*dial. mar.* 1.4).

23 armenta. The noun *armentum*, normally used in the plural, belongs to the elevated style: for the fem. plur. cf. Pacuv. *trag.* 349 R.³; Enn. *ann.* 604 Sk.; for the neuter cf. Lucr. 1.163; 2.343, etc. In the *E.*, it is always used as a marked term, removed from the humble status of the pastoral *pecus*. It appears, as here, in a mythical (and generalizing) context at 6.45; cf. also 4.22. In the *G.*, on the contrary, it will commonly be used of livestock (e.g. *G.* 1.355; 2.195; in the sing. at 3.71).

24 Amphion Dircaeus. The twins Amphion and Zethus, sons of Antiope (daughter of the Theban king Nycteus) and Zeus (who raped her in satyr-like form), were both abandoned on Mount Cithaeron and raised by a shepherd; they eventually took vengeance by killing Dirce, their mother's cruel abuser. In Euripides' *Antiope*, of which but a few fragments have survived (but which was well known to the Romans through Pacuvius' version), the two youths were famously engaged in an agon—Amphion defending the contemplative existence, Zethus arguing for the practical life. At the end of the play, Zethus was granted kingship over Thebes, whereas Hermes made Amphion capable of moving stones and trees with his lyre, a gift which he put to use in order to help his brother raise the city walls (further reading in *LIMC* I.1, pp. 718–23, s.v. *Amphion* [F. Heger]; cf. Eur. fr. 223.121-4 Kann.; Hor. *carm.* 3.11.2). Based on the sources, gathering *armenta* does not seem to be among Amphion's most frequent activities (note 2.23 *si quando*, with limiting force). The only attestation is Pausan. 9.5.8 (Eumel. fr. 12 Kink. = 13 Bern.; on the effects of song on beasts, θηρία, see further *RE*, I.2, col. 1947, ll. 16–19, s.v. *Amphion I* [K. Wernicke]), whereas the Roman mosaic held in the Museo Nazionale Romano (1241) is far from helpful (cf. *LIMC* I.1, pp. 721–2, no. 16). At any rate, it is possible that, in a lost Hellenistic source, Amphion used Hermes' lyre to help his brother, whose task was to graze a herd: Apollod. 3.5.5 (43). From Corydon's point of view, the effect is to 'pastoralize' the hero, assimilating him to Orpheus (for whom cf. 3.46n.) and anticipating what is more explicitly asserted at 2.60–1. The epithet *Dircaeus*, elsewhere roughly equivalent to 'Theban' (Hor. *carm.* 4.2.25; Prop. 3.17.33), here inevitably hints at Dirce's torture: the two brothers tied her to the horns of a raging bull, then threw the remains of her body into the spring subsequently named after her. **in Actaeo Aracyntho**. That this is the location where the vengeance took place and that Amphion celebrated the 'victory' in a paean can be inferred from Prop. 3.15.41–2 *uictorque canebat / paeana Amphion rupe, Aracynthe, tua* (the only reliable ancient source on the subject). The mountain, therefore, is not the Acarnanian Aracynthus, but its less renowned namesake situated between Attica and Boeotia, presumably not far from Mount Cithaeron: cf. *Enc. Virg.* I, p. 263, s.v. *Aracinto* (M. Geymonat); *Virg. Enc.* I, p. 115 s.v. *Aracynthus* (G. C. Lacki). Hence the learned epithet *Actaeo*, which seems to presuppose the ancient name of Attica (Ἀκτή/Ἀκταία): cf. *Ciris* 102; Ov. *met.* 2.554; Sen. *Phaedr.* 900; Val. Fl. 2.68; Colum. 10.386; Stat. *Theb.* 12.196 (Ἀκταίη τις, referring to Hecale, is the incipit of Callimachus' much-celebrated poem: fr. 230 Pf. = 1 H.; cf. Petron. 135.8, ll. 15–16 *qualis in Actaea…terra /…Hecales*; the humble old protagonist was a model of virtuous rural simplicity, mentioned as *rustica Hecale* by Plin. *nat.* 26.82). Perhaps a chorus of *Attici* (= Attic citizens) appeared in Pacuvius' *Antiopa*, according to Cic. *diu.* 2.133 (with A. S. Pease's commentary, Urbana, IL, 1923, p. 379, on *Pacuuianus Amphio*; cf. P. Schierl, *Die Tragödien des Pacuuius*, Berlin-New York 2006, p. 98). The whole line, composed of a few choice words, is Hellenistic in shape: in fact, it could have directly been drawn from a Greek line. Note also the hiatus in arsis *Actaeo Aracyntho*, which is frequent in the *E.*, especially in Hellenizing contexts (but cf. 3.6n.). For a four-syllable word in line-ending position cf. *E.* 6.53; 10.12 (Greek words are featured in both cases; but cf. 4.49). Parthenius has been suggested as potential source, as in the case of *G.* 1.437 (cf. Gell. 13.27; Macr. *Sat.* 5.17.18). Here Corydon showcases his *doctrina*: Greek forms, even in proper nouns, are ubiquitous in this eclogue, which seems to be the only one explicitly set in Sicily (cf. 1 *Alexin*; 15 *Menalcan*; 26 *Daphnin*; 31 *Pana*, etc.). Asinius Pollio seems to have had an interest in the myth of Dirce: a marble sculpture of Dirce with the two brothers and the bull, imported from Rhodes and attributed to Apollonius and Tauriscus, is said to have been part of Pollio's personal collection (Plin. *nat.* 36.34; see further below, esp. pp. 149 and 287). It is possible that the well-known Farnese Bull, discovered in the baths of Caracalla, is what remains of the original sculpture (for discussion see B. Ridgway, *Hellenistic Sculpture II: The Styles of ca 200–100 B.C.*, Madison 2000, pp. 273–7).

130   ECLOGUE 2

25–6. An accurate reworking of the Cyclops of *id.* 6.34–8: 'For certainly I am not as ugly [οὐδ' εἶδος ἔχω κακόν] as they say. / Not long ago did I look at myself into the sea, which was calm [ἦς δὲ γαλάνα], / and my beard appeared beautiful to me, and so did my one eye, / as far as I can judge, and the gleam of my teeth / seemed whiter than Parian marble'. Theocritus' mention of the still sea (γαλάνα), meant to explain how a land creature can mirror itself in the marine waters, is echoed at *E.* 2.26 *cum placidum uentis staret mare* (n.), further specified by *in litore* (2.25): *litus* is a space where sea and land overlap (e.g. *Aen.* 6.362 *nunc me fluctus habet uersantque in litore uenti*; cf. also Lucan. 8.698–9). If partially immersed, a creature can look at its own reflection, provided the water is still. Despite such clarifications, Servius did not hesitate to object: *negatur hoc per rerum naturam posse fieri* (*ad* 2.25). Ovid escapes the problem by not mentioning the sea: *certe ego me noui liquidaeque in imagine uidi / nuper aquae, placuitque mihi mea forma uidenti* (Ov. *met.* 13.840–1). Lucian has a much easier time, since he focuses on Galatea herself in *dial. mar.* 1.3 (Doris to Galatea): 'sit on a rock and edge forward towards the water—if the sea is calm, look at yourself and you will see nothing but perfectly white skin'. The refined Alexis, who certainly knew about his own white skin (2.16), must have thought of such means of visual 'self-evaluation' as being rather primitive. Right after quoting the Virgilian passage, Seneca will ask himself (though in a praising tone): *qualem fuisse cultum putas ad hoc se speculum comentium* (*nat.* 1.17.5); cf. also Calp. *ecl.* 2.88. The fresco of Polyphemus and Galatea (in the so-called House of Livia) depicts the Cyclops immersed up to the chest in a calm, secluded sheet of water which reflects his image: see the drawing in La Rocca (2008, p. 115, no. 41). The unmistakable reference to the seashore (25 *in litore*; 26 *placidum…mare*) rules out the usual Mantuan setting (cf. 8.59n.; also 2.21 *Siculis…in montibus* [n.]). The point of this poem is the opposition between the humble dimension of pastoral *rus* (replete with Sicilian and Theocritean echoes) and the urban world to which Alexis is attracted (see 2.56–62).

25 informis. The adj. is perceptibly derived from *forma*, which makes it an antonym of *formosus* (cf. Alexis in 2.1): e.g. *G.* 3.354 *iacet aggeribus niueis informis* (Scythia: *carens uarietate formarum…inlimitata* [Serv. ad loc.]). As such, it can indicate monstrous deformity, as in the case of the blinded Polyphemus at *Aen.* 3.658; cf. *forma* in Ov. *met.* 13.841 (see 2.25–6n.), and Theocritus' εἶδος. Corydon seems to have an easy time praising himself, if the term of comparison in the reader's mind is the monster of the *Odyssey* (note the irony in the emphatic *adeo*). As a matter of fact, the bird etymologically connected to his name seems to evoke anything but beauty, when a human being is compared to it: cf. *schol. R ad* Aristoph. *Thesm.* 168 (the tragic poet Philocles is the target: cf. *TrGF*, I, p. 141.8b Sn.). Cf. the echo in Calp. *ecl.* 2.84 *num, precor, informis uideor tibi?*

26 placidum uentis staret mare. The winds' effect allows the sea's surface to remain calm. The force of *uentis* oscillates between instrumental and local;

ECLOGUE 2   131

cf. *G.* 4.484 *uento rota constitit.* For the sense see also *Aen.* 5.763 *placidi strauerunt aequora uenti*; Hor. *carm.* 1.3.16 (*Notus*) *tollere seu ponere uolt freta.*

26-7 non ego... / iudice te metuam. For an important parallel see Cornelius Gallus, fr. 4.3-4 Bläns. = 2.8-9 Court. *non ego, Visce, / ...iudice te uereor* (but V. is likely to be the imitator: cf. the opening of *E.* 10). The context seems appropriate for an allusion to the important *auctor* of Roman love-elegy—though V. reworks Gallus' passage to suit an erotic scenario (not a metapoetic one, as was probably the case in Gallus). Corydon feigns greater impartiality than Polyphemus at *id.* 6.37: ὡς παρ' ἐμὶν κέκριται (see *E.* 2.25-6n.).

26 Daphnin. For the comparison, meant as self-praise, cf. *id.* 5.80-1: 'The Muses love me much more than the singer / Daphnis'. Along with Damoetas, Daphnis played a central role in the agon of *id.* 6, which ended in a draw. Focusing on the Cyclops theme, *id.* 6 is one of Corydon's fundamental models (even in the present passage); a Damoetas will be mentioned at 2.37. In the *E.*, Daphnis' name occurs here for the first time, and is again evoked at *E.* 3.12. Thus, the first two eclogues that may be called stylistically Theocritean are united by his 'illustrative' presence; on Daphnis as a character cf. 5.20n. The phrase *non ego Daphnin* is the first occurrence of a type of metrical clausula that is possibly meant to single out the more properly 'bucolic' eclogues, i.e. the second and the third: cf. 3.23n. Corydon's mention of Daphnis hints at the herdsman's poetic ambitions (cf. Theocr. *id.* 5), which will soon become explicit (2.31-9). That Daphnis was rather good-looking is obvious: note Parthen. 29.1 τὴν ἰδέαν ἐκπρεπής (cf. Ael. *uar. hist.* 10.18; Diod. Sic. 4.84.3)—in sum, the very best-looking in the whole pastoral world. However, as V. ironically implies, the 'judge' Alexis is not necessarily impressed.

27 si numquam fallit imago. Both notion and terminology are common in Epicurean thought, as V.'s Epicurean friends certainly knew (see 2.65n.): reflected images are not per se deceptive, in the sense that the *simulacra* necessarily presuppose objects from which they are detached (Lucr. 4.98-101). This, however, does not rule out mistaken judgement, which can arise from misinterpretation of sense perception (Lucr. 4.464-5 *pars horum maxima fallit / propter opinatus animi quos addimus ipsi*). Cf. Ov. *met.* 3.463; Traina (1965); see also Manil. 4.306. The study of optics was a considerable part of natural philosophy, as observed by Apuleius, *apol.* 15-16 (mentioning the use of both 'liquid and solid' mirrors: *apol.* 16.1). The formulation implies modesty, mitigating the starkly self-praising tone of the context. Clearly, however, Epicurean wisdom is here used to replace the superstitious gesture of Theocritus' Cyclops (*id.* 6.39-40 'in order that the evil eye may not catch me, I thrice spat on my lap: / thus did old Cotytaris instruct me'); cf. Hor. *sat.* 1.5.97-104. The reading *fallit* (P¹) is preferable to *fallat* (P²R), which does not capture the gnomic, generalizing sense of the phrase.

28-30. Persisting in the illusion that his behaviour may entice Galatea, Polyphemus piled up realistic details of pastoral life: 'Should you go out, Galatea,

132   ECLOGUE 2

and forget, / as I do who sit here, to go back home, / and should you want to graze the herds with me, and milk the cows, / and make cheese by adding acid rennet!' (*id.* 11.63–6). More shrewdly, Corydon mentions hunting, an activity presumably valued by the *puer* (and perhaps the cause of their encounter). Homoerotic implications are in the background (2.12n.); yet such adjectives as *sordida* and *humilis* are signs of naivety, similar to Corydon's Theocritean predecessor.

28 tibi. Governed by *libeat*, but dangerously close to *sordida* (*rura*): in fact, Corydon's advances will appear 'sordid' to Alexis at l. 44 *sordent tibi munera nostra* (where the pronoun occupies the same position in the fourth foot). For the phrase *sordida rura* in a more positive context, cf. Mart. 10.96.4 *repetam saturae sordida rura casae* (with a likely echo of V.'s passage: see 2.29n.; cf. Calp. *ecl.* 7.42 *sordida tecta, casas*). For the 'optative' subjunctive, here featuring the interjection *o*, cf. 9.45n.

29 humilis…casas. Properly speaking, a hut—whose low stylistic register is emphasized by the epithet *humilis* (cf. Hor. *ars* 229 *obscuras humili sermone tabernas*, with its context). No wonder that the term *casa* reappears in evocations of a pristine, rural simplicity: cf. Tib. 2.5.26 *stabant humiles in Iouis arce casae*; Valg. *carm.* fr. 5.1 Bläns. = Court.; Liv. 5.53.8; Ov. *met.* 8.633; [Sen.] *Herc. O.* 125; note also Calp. *ecl.* 7.42; Mart. 10.96.4; *ThlL* III.509.49–72; cf. also *Moret.* 60, with A. Perutelli's commentary, Pisa 1983, p. 111, ad loc. The *casa Romuli* was venerated on the Capitol, and even in late antiquity the Romans used myrtle branches to prepare *casae* for the rural festival in honour of Venus (*Perv. Ven.* 6). Note the usual modesty of V.'s pastoral character, who takes good care of his dwelling, albeit temporary: cf. 1.68 *pauperis…tuguri* (n.). **figere ceruos.** As a hunting trophy dedicated to Artemis, deer antlers are mentioned again by Corydon at 7.30. For the verb, poetic *simplex pro composito*, cf. G. 1.308 *figere dammas*; see also Sen. *Herc. f.* 1129. In the *E.*, hunting occurs here for the first time, and will occupy a central place, especially given its ties to Arcadia (cf. 10.55–60 as well as 3.75; 5.60–1; 7.29–30), whereas it played a more marginal role in the Theocritean corpus: cf. *id.* 5.106–7; 8.58.

30 uiridi compellere hibisco. Two interpretations are possible: either (1) 'drive the baby goats toward the green hibiscus' (dat. of motion toward [Servius]), paralleled by Hor. *carm.* 1.24.18 *nigro compulerit Mercurius gregi* (the obj. is the deceased's *imago*), or (2) 'gather the baby goats with a branch of green hibiscus' (instrumental ablative). Note that Horace's dative has a comitative (rather than a locative) function, while an instrumental phrase is also expressed (*carm.* 1.24.16 *uirga…horrida*); on the other hand, no variety of hibiscus appears to have been used as fodder, particularly to wean baby goats or lambs. If eaten by humans, the plant can prove to be rather dangerous (Plin. *nat.* 19.89: but cf. Calp. *ecl.* 4.32 quoted below); it belongs to the family of *Maluaceae*: *Enc. Virg.* II, pp. 849–50, s.v. *hibiscus* (G. Maggiulli). In *E.* 3.82, V. mentions the wild strawberry as food for kids (*depulsis arbutus haedis*), whereas Columella, 7.3.19, mentions cytisus, lucerne, bran, barley, or bitter vetch flour as food for lambs, to which he adds (in the kids' case) elm seeds, ivy, mastic, and other delicate herbs (Colum. 7.6.7). Calp.

ecl. 4.32 *uiridique famem solarer hibisco* probably presupposes the interpretation of *uiridi...hibisco* as fodder: the speaker, a shepherd named Corydon, outlines the paradoxical possibility of feeding on wild berries and plants (note, however, the syntactical use of the instrumental). Thus, interpretation (2) is to be preferred, since it is supported by V.'s mention of hibiscus as a thin plant, suitable for weaving baskets (10.71: the only other occurrence of *hibiscus* in V.) as well as for being used as a soft whip (*uiridi*)—almost as a plaything, in the hands of the boy Alexis, whom Corydon seeks to entice with it after mentioning a deer hunt: the result is that *haedorum...gregem uiridi compellere hibiscus* corresponds to *figere ceruos* in the previous verse, but in a completely harmless way; cf. *schol. Bern.* p. 90 H. '*uiridi*', *ne uim patiantur pecora...'hibisco'. hibiscum genus est uirgulti quo pastores pro flagello utuntur.* Note also that herdsmen are generally expected to gather themselves sweet herbs on which to feed, when needed, the weaned kids: Theocr. *id.* 11.73–4 (but cf. Hom. *Od.* 17.224). See also Colum. 7.3.19, where the author does not mention a separate grazing pasture for the lambs (they graze together with their mothers): *a saepto mittendi agni, ut condiscant foris pasci*; a similar method applies to kids, on which, however, more control must be exercised (note *compescenda...cohibenda*): *eodem modo quo agni educantur, nisi quod magis haedorum lasciuia compescenda et arctius cohibenda est.* For *compellere* in the sense of 'gathering' (a flock) cf. *E.* 7.2 *compulerant...greges...in unum*; Calp. *ecl.* 5.57. Part of the herdsman's job is to 'gather' the kids and bring them into the fold, even to separate them from their mothers if necessary: see 7.15 *quae clauderet agnos* (n.).

31–9. The Corydon of *id.* 4 displayed certain musical skills: 'I know some music / and sweetly can I sing the arias of Glauce and Pyrrhus' (30–1). In the erotic and pedagogical project of V.'s Corydon, pipes and song play a considerable role, adding up to nine lines. His name is linked to one of the greatest poetic successes in the *E.*, as *E.* 7 will make clear. The parallel with Longus, 2.32–7, where the myth of Syrinx is evoked in a comparable context, may perhaps be explained through a common Hellenistic source (such as, once again, Philitas). In this passage, the lovesick Corydon focuses on the gifts with which he hopes to entice Alexis and proceed to an amorous 'exchange' (2.37n.). The repeated negatives at 2.56–7 (*nec munera...nec si muneribus*) will emphasize the failure of Corydon's attempt.

31 mecum una...imitabere Pana. Corydon offers the boy the most properly 'pastoral' of all divine models (is it really appropriate for the boy, though?). The phrase *mecum una* (note the amplification) places great emphasis on Corydon himself: it now becomes clear that what Corydon has in mind is an eroticodidactic relationship such as the one that Pan has with Daphnis, whom the god teaches to play the syrinx (note the sculpture by Heliodorus of Rhodes, around 100 BCE, of which various copies are extant). Pan, however, is not always a lucky lover: cf. the myth of Syrinx (on which see 2.32–3n.). In Theocr. *epigr.* 3.3 G. Pan, accompanied by Priapus, is depicted as 'hunting down' his beloved Daphnis (ἀγρεύει δὲ τυ Πὰν καὶ ὁ...Πρίηπος).

134   ECLOGUE 2

32–3. The parenthetic clause evokes a key pastoral story, whose protagonist is no less than the god Pan: Corydon shows off his pastoral knowledge, in a hopeless attempt to attract the boy's attention (cf. 2.32n.). The god's name is repeated three times, in keeping with the iterative style of pastoral poetry—which, however, waxes solemn and hymnic here (with a decreasing echo-effect: disyllabic word in arsis, monosyllable in arsis, monosyllable in thesis). Note also the enjambement, further underscoring the alliterative wordplay at 2.32 (*p p c c c p*). According to the myth, the nymph Syrinx asked for the gods' help in her effort to flee from Pan, and was· turned into a bed of reeds (σῦριγξ 'reed'), which the wind let resonate. Pan then used the reeds to produce the multiple-unit pipe that became his typical companion, almost a replacement of the beloved's body (note the physical contact: Ov. *met.* 1.710 *hoc mihi conloquium tecum…manebit*; for the whole episode cf. Ov. *met.* 1.689–712, with A. Barchiesi's commentary, Milan 2005, pp. 224–5, ad loc.; rationalist explanation in Lucr. 5.1382–3 [see 2.36n.]); further reading in *Enc. Virg.* III, pp. 948–51, s.v. *Pan* (D. M. Cosi); *Virg. Enc.* II, pp. 962–3, s.v. *Pan* (E. Fantham); see also Colafrancesco (2001). The theme is treated in a short calligram or shaped poem, the Σῦριγξ, which ancient sources attribute to Theocritus (the attribution, however, is very doubtful: *Anth. Pal.* 15.21); cf. also Long. 2.37 (2.31–9n.). In any event, the focus is on unrequited love, and Alexis seems to imitate the fleeing nymph rather than the god (*imitabere Pana*): as for Corydon, he cannot but find solace in song, just like Pan. These two lines may appear somewhat hackneyed and manneristic compared to the rest of the monologue—though Corydon's didactic attitude is part of his attempt to portray himself as an expert singer who can 'teach' Alexis (a rather clumsy attempt: the reader can readily imagine the boy's reaction). At any rate, interpolation has been suspected by many critics, particularly since the two lines could be interpreted as a patchwork of notions and phrases used elsewhere in the *E.* (see below). Note also the 'afterthought' at 2.53–5n., where Corydon mentions a further gift to the boy (fruit and aromatic herbs) persisting in his didactic attitude.

32 primus. The well-attested reading *primus* (also found in the indirect transmission: cf. Serv. *ad E.* 3.25), is overall preferable to *primum* (**PR**) and fits the individualistic rhetoric of the *primus inuentor*. For a *locus similis* cf. *E.* 8.24 *Panaque, qui primus calamos non passus inertis* (where **M** reads *primum*) and *G.* 1.147–8 *Prima Ceres ferro mortalis uertere terram / instituit*. The adverb is used by V. with a less individualized subject, and without the idea of competition (can there really be a 'contest' if nature itself is involved?), cf. *G.* 2.20 *hos natura modos primum dedit*. Corydon's ostentatious display of knowledge can be explained by the fact that, while Pan was traditionally associated with the syrinx, a mythical tradition attributed its invention to Hermes: cf. *Hymn. Hom.* 4.511–12; Apollod. 3.115. That Pan is the 'inventor' is implied by Ovid's *aition* in the *Metamorphoses* (see above); but cf. also Plin. *nat.* 7.204 and Nonn. *Dionys.* 41.372–3 (where the context is a sort of catalogue of musical instruments and their inventors). The

ECLOGUE 2   135

topic must have been a matter of debate among Hellenistic intellectuals: cf. Bion, fr. 10 G., ascribing to Pan the invention not of the syrinx but of the πλαγίαυλος, i.e. the transverse flute (l. 7 [cf. Theocr. *id.* 20.29]; Daphnis dedicates both instruments to Pan in Long. 4.26.2); note also a fragment of Euphorion's Περὶ μελοποιῶν (fr. 33 M. = 182 v. Gron. = 203 Light.), in which Pan is not even mentioned among the possible inventors of the syrinx (quoted by Athen. 4.184a). To be sure, a pastoral character like Corydon is inclined to expect such a topic to be interesting or appealing to a young boy: cf. [Theocr.] *id.* 8.18–24, where both Menalcas and Daphnis are expert builders of syrinx (which Corydon implies at 2.35–9). But that of Corydon is mere illusion.

33 curat ouis ouiumque magistros. Paraphrase of the epithet νόμιος, typical of the god: cf. *G.* 1.17 *Pan ouium custos*; for the wording cf. *E.* 3.101 *pecori pecorisque magistro* (n.).

34 nec te paeniteat. A respectful phrase, occurring again twice at *E.* 10.16–17n., where the speaker addresses Cornelius Gallus (a non-pastoral character). **calamo triuisse labellum.** Corydon anticipates the boy's concern that the use of the instrument might damage an important part of his physical beauty (for a beautiful *labellum* as typical of prepubescent youths cf. Catull. 61.213 [220]; in an erotic context cf. Lucr. 4.1080; but note Plaut. *Asin.* 668). Wind instruments are a source of worry for the vain: Minerva, for instance, was said to have thrown away the pipes she had invented at the sight of her inflated cheeks. Cf. Prop. 2.30b.16–18; Ov. *ars* 3.505–6, with R. K. Gibson's commentary, Cambridge 2003, p. 302, ad loc.; *fast.* 6.693–710 (where the satyr Marsyas finds the pipes). The 'hooked lip' in Lucretius' portrait of Marsyas is far from encouraging: 4.588 *unco saepe labro calamos percurrit hiantis* (cf. also 5.1407).

35 quid non faciebat Amyntas? An Amyntas was featured in a subordinate role at the outset of *id.* 7, where he was described as an urban dweller rather than as a pastoral character (*id.* 7.1–2): 'One day Eucritus and I went out from the city / to the Hales, and Amyntas was the third in our company [τρίτος…Ἀμύντας]'. In the *E.*, the name only appears in line-ending position, in keeping with Theocritean usage. V.'s Amyntas is described as an affable *erōmenos* (*E.* 3.66; 74; 83; cf. *id.* 7.132 χὠ καλὸς Ἀμύντιχος 'fair little Amyntas'), or, as here, a singer capable of harsh competitiveness (*E.* 5.8; 15; 18; cf. also 2.39n.), or, finally, a reassuring erotic-bucolic alternative (*E.* 10.37; 38; 41); see further *Enc. Virg.* I, pp. 137–8, s.v. *Aminta* (G. Serrao). This is perhaps Corydon's last chance: he names Amyntas twice, maybe to make Alexis jealous (note the metrical interchangeability of the two names in line-ending position, as well as the etymological correspondence: Amyntas, connected with ἀμύνω, means 'the defender'; for Alexis cf. 2.1n.). Horace's old mistress will mention an Amyntas as a convenient and gratifying erotic alternative at *epod.* 12.18. The Amyntas of 10.38, however, is *fuscus*—quite unlike Alexis.

36 disparibus septem…cicutis. The term *cicuta* occurs in the *E.* (and in V.) only here and at 5.85 *hac te nos fragili donabimus ante cicuta*, where it denotes the

136 ECLOGUE 2

instrument that 'teaches' Corydon to play his love song for Alexis (5.86). In both cases, the instrument is a gift between pastoral singers, exchanged in a context involving rivalry (here, Amyntas' envy at 2.39; cf. 5.88–90). As in *E.* 1.2 *tenui...auena*, V.'s word choice must be explained in terms of poetic 'modesty' (cf. *fragili* at 5.85), through the mediation of Lucr. 5.1383 *cauas inflare cicutas* (the invention of the pipes: primitive countryside dwellers take inspiration from the wind blowing among the reeds). The *cicuta* ('hemlock', *Conium maculatum*) is a common and 'humble' plant, whose stems—up to two metres tall—could actually be used to build wind instruments: cf. Calp. *ecl.* 4.20–1 *leuibus...cicutis* / *ludere*; *ThlL* III.1053.2–19. The title *Cicuta* was chosen by Domitius Marsus for a collection of epigrams (or part of it): cf. 3.90n. For the difference in length among the reeds (*disparibus*), cf. for instance Tib. 2.5.31–2 *fistula cui semper decrescit harundinis ordo:* / *nam calamus cera iungitur usque minor.*

37 fistula. Underscored by the enjambement, the object's name finally appears, following a description of its composite structure. The *fistula*, usually composed of seven reeds varying in length, is the pan flute, also called panpipes or syrinx (σῦριγξ), whose mythical invention has just been evoked (2.32–3). Cf. 3.22n. (owned, once again, by Damoetas); 7.24n. (Corydon); 8.33; 10.34. In V., *fistula* is an exclusively pastoral term. **Damoetas.** A shepherd named Damoetas competed with Daphnis on the Cyclops theme in *id.* 6, a poem with which Corydon is quite familiar (see 2.25–6n.; in Theocritus, as here, he made a gift of his σῦριγξ: *id.* 6.42–4). Damoetas will soon play a central role in the agon of *E.* 3 against Menalcas, where he will mention a Galatea (3.64n.). For his final appearance (in Menalcas' speech) cf. 5.72n. Through the interplay of names and situations, the *E.* hint at circles and schools of pastoral poetry (though not necessarily in a coherent way). In this case, the old master's name amounts to an acknowledgement of V.'s debt to Theocritus, even without being fully allegorical (*Enc. Virg.* I, p. 974b, s.v. *Dameta* [F. Caviglia]; *Virg. Enc.* I, pp. 332–3, s.v. *Damoetas* [J. Van Sickle]). The diptych formed by *E.* 2 and 3 will be mentioned, along with the names of Corydon and Damoetas (pupil and teacher?), in 5.85–7: to add further complexity, *E.* 5 will point to Menalcas as the 'author' of both eclogues (2.15n.). **dono...dedit olim.** In *id.* 4, the shepherd Corydon received the gift of a σῦριγξ (*id.* 4.29–30). Note how the alliterative /d/, besides emphasizing the notion of *donum*, highlights the repetition *Damoetas dono...dedit...* / *et dixit moriens...* / *dixit Damoetas.* Note, in the phrase *dono dare*, V.'s use of the dative of purpose: cf. Sall. *hist.* 2.47.12 M. *animam dono dedisse* (but also Plaut. *Mil.* 981–2 *sibi aurum atque ornamenta...* / *dono habere*). Yet this attempt to establish some continuity (Damoetas-Corydon-Alexis) is doomed to failure, as Corydon realizes at 2.56–7.

38 dixit moriens: 'te nunc habet ista secundum'. On the brink of death, the shepherd strives to perpetuate his art (Long. 1.29.3 and 2.37.3; cf. *E.* 5.85–90; 6.69–73). Damoetas may be imagined as a fairly old poetry teacher; cf. Hom. *Od.* 21.32–3 ὁ παιδὶ / κάλλιπ' ἀποθνῄσκων (Eurytus and his bow). The idea of a

ECLOGUE 2   137

'worthy successor' reappears at 5.49 *tu nunc eris alter ab illo* (for the notion of poetic succession in pastoral poetry see T. K. Hubbard 1998). For the marked sense of *secundus* cf. Hor. *sat.* 2.3.193 *Aiax, heros ab Achille secundus*; *carm.* 1.12.18; Mart. 12.8.2. V.'s use of *ista* makes the reader imagine the *fistula* as already being in the young pupil's hands, while the verb *habeo* personifies the instrument: cf. *docuit* (*nos*) at 5.87.

39 inuidit stultus Amyntas. The relationship with Amyntas is clarified in terms of rivalry: the two vied for Damoetas' favour; for a similar situation cf. *E.* 3.14 *cum uidisti puero donata, dolebas*. For *stultus* cf. 1.20n.; according to the *schol. Bern.*, p. 91 H., the poet here alludes to Cornificius, one of his rivals and detractors (cf. 5.36n.).

40–1. A scale reduction of the Cyclops' offer in *id.* 11.40–1: 'For you I raise eleven fawns, / all having marks on their necks (μαννοφόρως), and four bear-cubs.' Ovid's Polyphemus will partially return to the Theocritean model, but with V.'s more modest number: *geminos... / uillosae catulos in summis montibus ursae* (Ov. *met.* 13.834–6). For fawn-rearing in rural villas see Colum. 9.1.1. In Theocritus, the epithet μαννοφόρως seems to refer to fur colour rather than to the presence of accessories or decorations (e.g. collars, or the like). V.'s reworking goes in the same direction, with the detail at 2.41 *sparsis etiam nunc pellibus albo*. The fawns are still very young, since they still have (*etiam nunc*) the typical light-coloured spots on their fur, bound to disappear as they grow. For a similar promise of a gift cf. *id.* 3.34–6 (see 2.43–4n.).

40 nec tuta...ualle. The reference to danger adds value to the gift, implying a kind of naive braggadocio: the same is true of Ovid's Cyclops, *met.* 13.836 *in summis montibus*; cf. also *Aen.* 7.243–4 *parua.../ munera, reliquias Troia ex ardente receptas*.

42 siccant. Used in a technical context at Plin. *nat.* 10.179. To make sure that the fawns are fed to satiety is, of course, the breeder's task: Varr. *rust.* 2.2.15.

43–4. Once again, jealousy is used as a weapon—this time more openly, and with a heterosexual subject. Thestylis, mentioned in passing at 2.10, reappears here more prominently (though yet again representing rural normality). Corydon's threat echoes that of Theocritus' naive goatherd: 'For you I keep a white goat, mother of two twins, / which Mermnon's handmaid, the swarthy one, begs of me, / and I shall give it to her, since you snub me' (*id.* 3.34–6). The mischievous implication seems to be grasped and reworked (in masculine terms) by Martial 8.63.1 *Thestylon Aulus amat sed nec minus ardet Alexin* (but cf. 7.29.1).

43 abducere Thestylis orat. The wording is possibly meant to activate the etymology of Thestylis' Theocritean name (2.10n.), a hypocoristic form of Θέστη (Gow 1952, II, p. 36, *ad id.* 2.1), echoing the verb θέσσομαι (θεστός), 'to beg, entreat'. For *oro* governing an infinitive, a poetic construction here attested for the first time in Latin (H.-Sz., p. 236), cf. *Aen.* 6.313 *orantes...transmittere cursum*; 9.231; *ThlL* IX.2.1040.76–1041.14. Corydon makes it clear that his gifts are often well received, at least within his pastoral world: cf. Amaryllis at 2.52n.

138   ECLOGUE 2

44 et faciet. The use of *facio* taking up a preceding verb (here *abducere*) is colloquial: Plaut. *Amph.* 408; Cic. *Sull.* 20; Tib. 1.8.21-2 *e curru Lunam deducere temptat, / et faceret*; but cf. also *Aen.* 2.110; *ThlL* VI.1.107.31-50 (102.45-52).

45-50. Theocritus' Cyclops problematized the image of the flower wreath, common in erotic poetry. How can he simultaneously make a gift of white lilies (κρίνα λευκά) and of the red-petalled poppy (μάκων' ἁπαλὰν ἐρυθρὰ πλαταγώνι' ἔχοισαν), given that the latter blooms in summer, the former in winter? (*id.* 11.56-9: a further reason to visit Galatea all year round). A number of flowers mentioned by Corydon appear in the garland that Meleager offers to Heliodora (probably a metaphor for the poetic garland): 'I shall plait in violets, and tender narcissus / along with myrtles, and laughing lilies I shall plait, // and sweet crocus, and scarlet hyacinths too, and roses that rejoice in love' (*Anth. Pal.* 5.147.1-4 = *HE* 4236-9 G.-P.). This insistence on flowers and wreaths points to the theme of fleeting beauty, which must be enjoyed in the present: e.g. [Theocr.] *id.* 23.28-32. Beautiful flowers, multifarious poems, pleasure, and eros are all part of a single whole, as Meleager had shown in his opening epigram (*Anth. Pal.* 4.1 = *HE* 3926-83 G.-P), where the idea of 'anthology' was introduced (i.e. a 'selection' of both flowers and poems). Note also the mention of 'gifting' in the same epigram: ταύταν...χάριν (*Anth. Pal.* 4.1.4; cf. *E.* 2.57). Ancient paintings could unrealistically depict different flower species as blooming simultaneously, in a sort of heavenly botanical catalogue: cf. the well-known *uiridarium* in Livia's villa (Settis 2002, p. 16). Corydon mentions aromatic herbs (gathered by the herdsman himself) at 2.54-5n. Corydon's word choice aims at extreme delicacy: cf. 47 *pallentis*; 49 *suauibus*; 50 *mollia*; 51 *cana*.

45 huc ades, o formose puer. Hymnic style: cf. Catull. 62.5 *Hymen ades o Hymenaee*. The construction of *adesse* with *huc* (motion toward) is justified by an implicit movement, clearly perceptible in the imperative *ad-es* (which is often used in invocations): cf. *E.* 7.9; 9.39; 43; Tib. 1.7.49; 2.1.35; 3.10.1; Ov. *amor.* 1.6.54; 3.2.46; *met.* 8.598; *ThlL* II.917.47-70. The contamination of two constructions, *huc ueni* (e.g. *G.* 2.7) and *hic ades* (Hor. *sat.* 1.9.38), emphasizes the point of arrival (a static notion) and, therefore, the contact; cf. Plaut. *Amph.* 976 *nunc tu diuine huc fac adsis Sosia*. The epithet is distinctive of the boy: cf. *formosus* in the poem's opening line.

45-6 tibi lilia plenis / ecce ferunt Nymphae calathis. The Nymphs are entrusted with the task of bringing flowers: cf. Apoll. Rhod. 4.1143-5 (Jason and Medea's wedding ceremony). The ending of l. 45 will be applied to the *puer* Marcellus, who died young, at *Aen.* 6.883 *manibus date lilia plenis*. The Greek form *calathus* (κάλαθος) occurs here for the first time in V.: cf. *E.* 5.71; *G.* 3.402; *Aen.* 7.805; for a likely allusion cf. Colum. 10.300 *fer calathis uiolam...*; but see also *Copa* 16 *lilia uimineis attulit in calathis*. The use of *ecce* belongs to colloquial speech (on which cf. Dionisotti 2007), and occurs again in the *E.* at 3.50; 5.66; 9.47.

ECLOGUE 2   139

46 candida Nais. The evocation of female deities is here specified: Nais, bearing a typical nymph-like name, is *candida*, just like the *candidus* Alexis at 2.16. Her radiant appearance anticipates the chromatic play at 2.47–50.

47 pallentis uiolas. Servius quoted Hor. *carm.* 3.10.14 *tinctus uiola pallor amantium.* Besides red and white violets, yellow ones are mentioned by Plin. *nat.* 21.27; here, however, the adj. hints at a faint hue. Dark violets are a different business: cf. *E.* 10.39. For the other Virgilian occurrences of *uiola*, see *E.* 5.38; *G.* 4.32 *uiolaria*; 275; *Aen.* 11.69.

48 bene olentis anethi. Dill is used in wreaths at Sapph. fr. 81.5 V.; cf. Theocr. *id.* 7.63 and [Mosch.] *epit. Bion.* 100. Here the emphasis is on its scent: Colum. 10.120 *bene odorati…anethi*; Plin. *nat.* 19.186; *Enc. Virg.* I, p. 169, s.v. *aneto* (G. Maggiulli). Dill is mentioned here immediately after one of the best-known flowers, the narcissus: cf., also for its human past, 5.38n. (the other Virgilian occurrences of *narcissus: E.* 8.53; *G.* 4.123; 160).

49 casia. An aromatic plant (as Corydon notes: *casia atque aliis…suauibus herbis*), especially useful in apiculture: *G.* 2.213; 4.30; 182; 304. Here it is appreciated precisely for its pleasant smell, along with dill and other fragrant herbs. It is perhaps a type of lavender, but certainly distinct from the herb mentioned at *G.* 2.466 (a variety of cinnamon): see Maggiulli (1995, pp. 255–7). **suauibus herbis.** The adj. *suauis*, common in Republican Latin, will be avoided in poetry from the Augustan age onwards (no occurrences in the *Aeneid*): cf. Axelson (1945, p. 145). Corydon will use it again at 2.55, where he will also mention bay and myrtle, both known for their scent; cf. 3.63n. For *suauis* in the context of olfactory 'sweetness' cf. Lucr. 3.222; Catull. 61.7. The same line-ending appears at *G.* 4.200, in the context of apiculture (bees are known to appreciate *casia*: see above).

50 mollia luteola pingit uaccinia calta. A golden line, composed of two nouns and the two corresponding adjectives, balanced by the verb in the middle ($a^1a^2VS^1S^2$). In its 'pure' form (i.e. without adverbs, prepositions, etc.), it occurs here for the first time in the *E.*, then again at 5.7 (and 6.8n.); cf. also 4.29n. The *uaccinia* (presumably a species of hyacinth), whose black variant has appeared previously (but cf. 2.18n.), are featured here due to their softness: but we may nevertheless picture their black hue, providing a contrastive backdrop to the yellow *calta* (probably marigold or cornflower; also spelled *caltha*). Olfactory pleasure now seems to give way to chromatic pleasure: the smell of *calta* was not particularly appreciated, according to Plin. *nat.* 21.28 (cf. also Ov. *Pont.* 2.4.28).

51–2. Corydon assigns himself the task of picking fruit (the Cyclops mentioned grapes 'bearing sweet fruit' at *id.* 11.46). After Thestylis, Amaryllis appears for the second time (cf. 2.14). For a quasi-verbatim quotation cf. Ov. *ars* 2.267–8 *adferat aut uuas aut quas Amaryllis amabat, / at nunc, castaneas, non amat illa, nuces.* This list of modest gifts, which Iollas would certainly have no trouble outdoing (2.57), hints at the values of 'humble' poetry. The same is true of Leonidas' votive offerings in *Anth. Pal.* 6.300 (= *HE* 2183–90 G.-P.).

140   ECLOGUE 2

51 cana...tenera lanugine mala. Corydon starts from the most traditionally erotic fruit (cf. 1.37n.), here particularly sensual due to the reference to soft down. Servius identifies these *mala* with the *mala Cydonea*, i.e. quinces—which, however, are not normally downy, except in a particular variety, namely the so-called *malum strutheum* (cf. Plin. *nat.* 15.48; Antiphil. *Anth. Pal.* 6.252 = *GPh* 791–6 G.-P.), a fall and late fall fruit which would seem to fit well with the chestnuts at 2.52. It is not unlikely, however, that these downy *mala* refer to *mala Persica*, i.e. peaches. Echo and variation at *Aen.* 10.324 *prima lanugine malas*, referring to young Clytius' cheeks, *malae*: the warrior who accompanies him as both lover and squire is called, significantly, *Cȳdon* (*Aen.* 10.325), where the name seems to hint at the fruit itself (κῡδωνέα/*Cȳdonea mala*). For *lanugo* (*tenera* or *prima*), cf. Zonas, *Anth. Pal.* 6.22.1 ἀρτίχνουν...μῆλον (= *GPh* 3440 G.-P.); Philipp. *Anth. Pal.* 102.3 (= *GPh* 2743 G.-P.) μῆλον...λεπτῇ πεποκωμένον ἄχνῃ. Note the chromatic detail *canus*, which points to the plant's delicate 'white' down (the adjective could not be applied to the boy Clytius). For a linguistic parallel cf. the ripe crops at Ov. *met.* 10.655 *segetis canae*; it is also possible to perceive here a faint echo of *candida Nais* (2.46n.). Ancient readers were well aware of the soft, sensual qualities of this line (and its echo in the *Aeneid*), as is confirmed by Servius, despite his attempt to 'moralize' V. in comparison to his Greek predecessor (*uerecunde rem inhonestam supprimit, quam Theocritus aperte commemorat*); Calpurnius Siculus reworks both Virgilian passages and even 'explains' their implications: *etenim sic flore iuuentae / induimur uultus, ut in arbore saepe notaui / cerea sub tenui lucere cydonia lana* (Calp. *ecl.* 2.89–91; for *cerea* cf. *E.* 2.53 *cerea pruna*).

53–5. Almost as an afterthought, Corydon adds (2.53 *addam*) another kind of fruit (plums) and two more aromatic herbs, bay and myrtle (cf. 2.49). Here, as at 2.32–3, Corydon adopts a didactic approach (this time in the botanical domain): plums are worthy of attention, while myrtle and bay 'fit well' together, one next to the other (2.55 *sic positae*). Such a shift in tone can be explained with V.'s portrayal of Corydon as a humble man of the countryside, who naively feels the need to boast about his skills, in the (vain) hope of impressing the boy. Yet Corydon's argument may seem inconsistent, since there does not seem to be a need for further plants (Corydon has already composed his garland at 2.45–52, using much more exquisite flowers and herbs, and has now switched topics). As in 2.32–3, it is possible to suspect interpolation. The notion of addition (53 *addam*) and the idea of *honos* (of being mentioned?) may be meant to hint at Corydon's solemnly metalinguistic naivety. This, however, could be part of the strategy of an imitator aiming at interpolating a pseudepigraphic expansion into the text and making sure that it is worthy of Corydon (and V.).

53 cerea pruna (honos erit huic quoque pomo). Yellow plums of a very light colour, similar to that of wax: see Plin. *nat.* 15.41; Ov. *met.* 13.817–18. Note the hiatus following a short syllable (*prună*), which is a rarity in hexameter poetry: for another, isolated case, cf. *Aen.* 1.405. Here, the hiatus is facilitated by the logical

ECLOGUE 2   141

and syntactical break (the parenthetic clause), coupled with a trochaic caesura: cf. *Enc. Virg.* II, p. 887b, s.v. *iato* (J. Veremans); Trappes-Lomax (2004, esp. p. 149).

54. Bay and myrtle are often coupled together, partly because their scents combine well with each other, as observed at 2.55 (similarly apt is the combination of the god of poetry and the goddess of eros, with whom the two plants are associated as their respective attributes): cf. 7.62n.; Theocr. *epigr.* 4.7 G. δάφναις καὶ μύρτοισι; Hor. *carm.* 3.4.18–19. Corydon here refers to a specific place, where the myrtle bush is very close (*proxima*) to the bay tree. Analogously, the Cyclops described his cave starting from the bays: *id.* 11.45 ἐντὶ δάφναι τηνεῖ. All this will not prevent Ovid from calling the plant *innuba*, alluding to Daphne (Ov. *met.* 10.92).

56–73. The final section of *E.* 2 consists in two parts, almost as if Corydon were undergoing a twofold, progressive process of liberation from his erotic obsession and return to reality. In the first part (2.56–68), his language still resembles love poetry, even though he starts to realize the truth; in the second part (2.69–73) he finally regains his senses.

56 rusticus es, Corydon. Cf. 28 *sordida rura*; *rusticitas* is a negative value in erotic poetry, particularly in Ovidian elegy: cf. Ov. *amor.* 2.4.13; *ars* 1.607; *her.* 17.186 (188); Pichon (1966, pp. 256–7, s.v. *rusticum*). As early as [Theocr.] *id.* 20.2–4 (also 20.31–2), being a βουκόλος (and ἄγροικος) is a hindrance to urban love. For a reworking cf. Calp. *ecl.* 2.61. No wonder, given the homoerotic theme, that the line is quoted in Pompeian graffiti (Gigante 1979, p. 166), where the corrupted reading *rusticus est Corydon* is probably due to third-person assimilation and adjustment to an everyday-life context (*CIL* IV, p. 97, no. 1527 = Diehl 1930, p. 45, no. 789); but *est* also appears in P¹R; cf. Ferraro (1982, p. 6). After mentioning Amaryllis with her simple tastes (chestnuts: 2.52) and boasting about his rural resources (fruit and aromatic herbs: 2.54–5), Corydon begins to realize Alexis' disinterest in him. Note the transition from *tu*-Alexis to *tu*-Corydon (here and at 2.69n.). **nec munera curat.** This is the last mention of 'gifts', closing the circle: cf. 2.6 *nihil mea carmina curas* (n.).

57 Iollas. The elegiac *diues amator*, with whom competition is impossible in terms of gifts: cf. Tib. 1.5.47–8, as well as Prop. 4.5.49–54. Iollas could perhaps be identified with Alexis' *dominus*; the name also appears in *E.* 3.76, denoting a similar case of erotic pre-eminence (in relation to Phyllis). In Mart. 11.41.7, Iollas is a rich landowner in a pastoral context, where Virgilian echoes cannot be ruled out. For another Virgilian occurrence, cf. the warrior killed at *Aen.* 11.640.

58–9. Corydon's frustration is expressed in 'rustic' terms, through a twofold proverbial phrase—as if the character were going back to the pastoral world to which he is used. *Auster* is the south wind, hot and often very rainy, hostile to flowers. The second motto is a variation on the common theme *margaritas ad porcos*.

58 heu heu. For the doubled interjection cf. 3.100n.

142 ECLOGUE 2

59 perditus. Cf. 8.88n.

60–2. Both notion and style are pastoral (note the repetition *siluas/siluae*, at the end of 2.60 and 62). A defence of extra-urban landscape (especially in its sylvan form, so typically Virgilian: cf. *E.* 1.5 *resonare…siluas* and 4.3n., featuring a similar repetition) is quite appropriate here, not far from the opening of V.'s pastoral book.

60 quem fugis, a! demens? Cf. *Aen.* 5.742; 6.466; Prop. 2.30.1; Ov. *met.* 3.641. For the pathetic interjection *a!*, cf. 1.15n. **habitarunt di quoque siluas.** In his peroration, the goatherd of *id.* 3 mentioned Aphrodite's love for the shepherd Adonis (46–8); a similarly apologetic tone will be used at 10.18. Another typical *exemplum* is the story of Apollo's love for Admetus, which prompted the god to become (temporarily) a shepherd: Callim. *hymn.* 2[*Ap.*].47–9; Tib. 2.3.11–32; Ov. *ars* 2.239–40; *met.* 2.676–82. The myth will be alluded to at *G.* 3.1–2; cf. also *id.* 8.52 ὁ Πρωτεὺς φώκας καὶ θεὸς ὢν ἔνεμεν (Proteus as a paradoxical shepherd of seals, despite his divine status); *Hymn. Hom.* 19[*Pan.*].32. The contrast is underscored by the contracted form *di*, solemn and often used in cultic contexts.

61 Dardaniusque Paris. While he was grazing his flocks on Mount Idas, Paris encountered the three goddesses, who asked him for the famous judgement. The solemn epithet evokes Paris' ancestor Dardanus, the legendary king of Troy (whereas Paris is called *Phrygius…pastor* in *Aen.* 7.163; cf. Hor. *carm.* 1.15.1). A similar effect is elicited by the epithet of Amphion at 2.24. Homer portrayed Paris as the embodiment of luxury and Eastern laxity—hence the treatment of Paris as the prototypical elegiac lover: cf. *Il.* 6.321–31; Prop. 3.8.29–32; Hor. *carm.* 1.15.13–20; Ov. *her.* 17.253–4 (255–6) (in *her.* 16, attempting to obliterate his bucolic past, Paris applies the adj. *rustica* to the Spartan Helen: 285 [287]).

61–2 Pallas…arces / ipsa colat. The goddess Pallas Athena, linked to civic cult (particularly in Athens, where she protects the Acropolis: *arces*) and, of course, Παρθένος. Her effigy, the Palladium, plays a crucial role in the legend of Aeneas' arrival in Latium and, therefore, in Rome's founding. For *colere* used of deities (inhabiting the place where they are worshipped), cf. *Aen.* 1.16; Plaut. *Poen.* 950 *deos deasque…qui hanc urbem colunt*; Liv. 5.21.3. Summoning the example of the virgin Athena/Minerva, Corydon overturns the cultural stereotype whereby the city is the *locus* of eros and the woods are that of chastity (the virgin huntress Artemis rarely visits the city: Callim. *hymn.* 3[*Dian.*].19).

62 nobis placeant ante omnia siluae. A possible echo of Moschus, fr. 1.7 G. γᾶ δέ μοι ἀσπαστά, χὰ δάσκιος εὔαδεν ὕλα 'the earth pleases me, and I like the shadowy woods', as well as 1.11–12; cf. also *G.* 2.485–6. Despite the erotic context, this sounds like a statement of pastoral rather than elegiac poetics. To be sure, however, Corydon does not really have an alternative to the *laus ruris* (for which cf. Varr. *rust.* 3.1.1–5; Hor. *epod.* 2; also Tib. 2.3).

63–5. Another precise reworking of Theocr. *id.* 10.30–1 (2.18n.): 'The she-goat pursues the cytisus, the wolf pursues the she-goat, / and the crane the plough: but

ECLOGUE 2   143

I am maddened by my love for you'. Here, the logical connection of prey and predator is extended to the entire sequence (lioness—wolf—she-goat—cytisus). The pastoral and erotic significance is obvious: there is perhaps some malice in the adj. *lasciua*, used of the she-goat (2.64n.), but the wolf and the lamb are used metaphorically in homoerotic contexts (e.g. Plat. *Phaedr.* 241c–d; cf. also, but without sexual overtones, Callim. *iamb.* 12, fr. 202.70 Pf.); for the lover-hunter it is obvious to chase the prey that flees (τὰ...φεύγοντα διώκειν [Callim. *epigr.* 31.5 Pf.]). Images and characterization follow the pattern of bucolic 'naivety'. Note the fourfold structure, fairly common in the *E.* (cf. 1.59–63n.), here meant to emphasize the irrevocability of nature's order.

64 florentem cytisum. For *cytisus* see 1.78n. (same beginning of the line). 'Eager' of the cytisus is, most likely, the female goat in Callim. *aet. SH* 257.27 = 148.27 Mass. = 54b.27 Hard. καὶ λίπτουσα δακεῖν κυτίσοιο [χίμαιρα. **lasciua.** In the sense of 'frisky, playful', typical of certain herd animals, even marine ones (Livius Andronicus, *trag.* 5 R.[3] *lasciuum Nerei simum pecus*), and particularly young ones: cf. Varr. *rust.* 2.3.9; Lucr. 1.260. Here, however, an allusion to the she-goat's sexual exuberance cannot be ruled out: cf. 10.7n. and 3.64n.

65 o Alexi. Note the hiatus in thesis, with a shortened vowel in the monosyllable. Here, the phenomenon is potentially facilitated by the Greek name: but cf. 8.108n.; see also 3.79; 6.44. **trahit sua quemque uoluptas.** Variation on Lucr. 2.258 *quo ducit quemque uoluptas* (Lambinus' emendation for the transmitted *uoluntas*; cf. also, in Lucretius' hymn to Venus, 1.16 *te sequitur cupide quo...inducere pergis*): note the semantic heightening of *trahit* vs *ducit*, which highlights the spatial and dynamic character of the action. V. alludes for the second time to an Epicurean notion (2.27n.), here rather obvious: Epicurus' pleasure was easily vulgarized and misunderstood. The irony of a philosophical motto concluding a shepherd's love lament seems to have been a source of criticism: according to Servius, certain readers found fault with the poet for attributing to Corydon a doctrine *supra bucolici carminis legem aut possibilitatem*. But this must have been a source of amusement for V.'s learned Epicurean friends: while echoing Lucretius' words, Corydon begins to escape from his erotic slavery like a good Epicurean. The idea of a fatal, quasi-magnetic attraction can be traced back to a Homeric line: Hom. *Od.* 19.13 αὐτὸς γὰρ ἐφέλκεται ἄνδρα σίδηρος (for a homoerotic parody cf. Iuv. 9.37; note also the 'impossible' Prop. 4.5.9 *poterit magnes non ducere ferrum*).

66–8. Corydon suddenly realizes how much time has elapsed: it was noon at 2.8; now it is twilight. To be sure, love's flame keeps burning in the evening stillness (cf. 2.1 *ardebat* ≈ 2.13 *sole sub ardenti*), but the shepherd manages to find a proper measure, an inner *modus* corresponding to the broader rhythm of nature. Hence, at 2.69–73, the finally restored serenity. By contrast, Cornelius Gallus' elegiac passion in *E.* 10 will know no limits, like Orpheus' in the finale of *G.* 4; cf. similarly Hor. *carm.* 2.9.10–12 *nec tibi Vespero / surgente decedunt amores / nec rapidum fugiente solem* (to Valgius Rufus); see 2.67n.

144 ECLOGUE 2

66 aspice. Corydon's recovery of reason, following the philosophical motto at 2.65, is underscored by a *uerbum uidendi* in the second-person singular: the subject, however, is no longer Alexis, but, as in a dramatic monologue, Corydon himself (along with a potential, invisible, spectator). The imperative *aspice* will reappear in contexts marked by intense contemplation or, at any rate, attention: *E.* 4.50; 52; 5.6; 8.105; 9.58. **aratra iugo referunt suspensa iuuenci.** The sight of oxen returning to their sheds after a day's work, bringing back the ploughs tied to their backs, belongs to the rhetoric of *mos maiorum*, the good old days of agrarian toil: cf. Hor. *epod.* 2.63–4 *(iuuat) uidere fessos uomerem inuersum boues / collo trahentis languido* (here, too, an evening scene, towards the end of *faenerator Alfius'* monologue), as well as *carm.* 3.6.42–3; Ov. *fast.* 5.497 (for the 'unyoking of oxen', i.e. βουλυτός, as the day's conclusion, see Callim. *aet.* fr. 177.5 Pf. = 149.5 Mass. = 54c.5 Hard.; Apoll. Rhod. 3.1340–4; but cf. Hom. *Il.* 16.779; conversely, Hes. *op.* 581). Both V.'s eclogue and Horace's epode will be echoed by Statius at *silu.* 5.1.121–6, where the sound of the 'returning' plough make it clear to the farmer's industrious wife that the workday has come to an end: *propere mensasque torosque / instruit expectatque sonum redeuntis aratri* (Stat. *silu.* 5.1.125–6). For the plough, the oxen *(iuuenci)*, and the hearth as the key elements of rural life cf. Hes. *op.* 405, praised by Aristotle at *Pol.* 1.2.1252b11–16. The image of cattle returning to the byre is used as an exhortation to hurry up, in a context of quiet 'normality', in Theocr. *id.* 16.92–3; cf. also [Theocr.] *id.* 25.85–7.

67 et sol crescentis decedens duplicat umbras. This eclogue, too, abides by the rhythm of the bucolic book, repeating the twilight finale of *E.* 1, with a similar sonic suggestion: note the alliteration on the /d/ sound and the transition from the bright tones of the /e/ to the darkness of the /u/ in arsis; the keyword *umbra* is in line-ending position (cf. 1.83n.; 10.75–6n.). By contrast, Orpheus' song in *G.* 4 knows no breaks or softening: cf. esp. *G.* 4.466 *te ueniente die, te decedente canebat*; also Cinna, *carm.* fr. 6 Bläns. = Court. *te matutinus flentem conspexit Eous, / et [te* A. Hollis] *flentem paulo uidit post Hesperus idem*; Hor. *carm.* 2.9.10–12 (see 2.66–8n.).

68 quis enim modus adsit amori? The question reappears, in a more compressed form *(ecquis erit modus?)*, at the beginning of Pan's speech in *E.* 10 (see 10.28n.). The elegiac answer is confirmed, with a likely Virgilian echo, by Propertius 2.15.30 *uerus amor nullum nouit habere modum.* Love's unrestrained nature is a commonplace motif: cf. esp. Theocr. *id.* 30.12 ἀλοσύνας τί ἔσχατον ἔσσεται; 'what limit will be set to your folly?'. Cf. also Meleag. *Anth. Pal.* 12.117.3 = *HE* 4094 G.-P. τί δ' Ἔρωτι λογισμός; for V.'s phrasing cf. Plaut. *Merc.* 652 *quis modus tibi exilio tandem eueniet?*; yet here *modus* does not exclusively mean 'measure' or 'limit', as it also hints at the idea of 'method' (cf. *Aen.* 12.157 *fratrem, si quis modus, eripe morti*), not too different from Theocritus' φάρμακον.

69–73. A final, precise reworking of *id.* 11, in which Polyphemus concluded his song by calling his own attention to his usual occupations: 'O Cyclops, Cyclops, whither have your senses flown? / Should you go weave baskets and cut young shoots / to feed your lambs, perhaps you would regain your senses to a greater degree. / Milk the ewe that you have at hand; why pursue the one that shuns you? / You will find another Galatea, maybe even fairer' (*id.* 11.72–6). Compared to his model, V. omits the last three lines uttered by the character (77–9) and the two concluding lines in which Theocritus himself summed up the argument: poetry is the best remedy for lovesickness (80–1). The traditional opposition between *otium* (particularly conducive to love's destructive passion) and *negotium* may have arguably contributed to solving Corydon's crisis. Gallus' motto, *omnia uincit Amor* (10.69n.), will be echoed in the poem of agricultural labour: *labor omnia uicit* (*G.* 1.145); in the *Aeneid*, a lovesick queen (Dido) will neglect the construction of her city (*Aen.* 4.86–9). That love often forces people to neglect their duties is evident in Sapph. 102 V. (cf. Hor. *carm.* 3.12.4–5). Here, Corydon is saved by his awareness of belonging to a world that the reader has got to know in *E.* 1: *frondatio* echoes the *frondator*'s song in 1.56, and agricultural concerns were present to Meliboeus' mind (esp. 69–73). Moreover, the weaving of wicker and rush will reappear as the poet V.'s activity, just before the book's conclusion: 10.71n. The opposition between love and labour, thematically crucial to *id.* 10 (esp. 14; for a possible reconciliation mediated by poetry, cf. 10.21–3), operates in *id.* 3.1–5 and *id.* 11.10–16 as well; love is a passion of an idle mind, according to Teophrastus (πάθος ψυχῆς σχολαζούσης [Stob. 4.20.66]): cf. e.g. Ter. *Heaut.* 109–12; Ov. *rem.* 143–4 *Venus otia amat; qui finem quaeris amoris, / (cedit amor rebus) res age, tutus eris.* A Callimachean epigram (*Anth. Pal.* 12.150) makes it clear that, besides the Muses' consolation, other 'remedies' are capable of curing pederastic love: for instance, strong bodily needs like hunger (l. 6 ἐκκόπτει [scil. λιμός] τὸν φιλόπαιδα νόσον). In the eclogue's finale, after two evident Epicurean and Lucretian echoes (cf. 2.27n.; 2.65n.), Corydon's words are attuned to Epicurus' teachings. In particular, both the diagnosis (*insania*) and the remedy (redirecting one's desires elsewhere) are found in the finale of Lucr. 4 (esp. 1058–76; see 2.69n.; 73n.). In *E.* 2 and 8, the two poems where love is most prominently featured, the erotic theme prompts V. to allude to Epicurean philosophy: such references were certainly clear to his learned readers, like Varius Rufus, perhaps not without some irony at the expense of the naive herdsmen (cf. 8.35n., 8.108n.). Note, finally, the 'framing' correspondence between this five-line epilogue and the five introductory lines uttered by the poet himself: but here the speaking voice is still Corydon's, as was the case with Theocritus' Polyphemus (Corydon has addressed himself at 2.56 and 65). *E.* 1, and thus the whole book, opened with two five-line speeches (1.1–10n.).

69 a, Corydon, Corydon, quae te dementia cepit! Cf. *id.* 11.72 ὦ Κύκλωψ Κύκλωψ, πᾶ τὰς φρένας ἐκπεπότασαι; 30.12; see also *E.* 10.22 *Galle, quid insanis?* (uttered by Apollo); *G.* 4.494–5; *Aen.* 2.42; 519–20. For a verbatim quotation, cf. 6.47n.; the name is repeated twice at the end of *E.* 7 (7.70n.; for a parodic

146 ECLOGUE 2

reworking, with the less solemn interjection *o*, cf. Iuv. 9.102). The interjection *a* (cf. 1.15n.) is coupled with *dementia* (in a very different context) at 2.60 *quem fugis, a! demens?* As Lucretius shows, erotic wounds get worse by the day, bringing with them madness (*furor*) and anxiety, unless desire is redirected elsewhere: *ulcus enim uiuescit et inueterascit alendo / inque dies gliscit furor atque aerumna grauescit, / si non prima nouis conturbes uolnera plagis / uolgiuagaque uagus Venere ante recentia cures / aut alio possis animi traducere motus* (Lucr. 4.1068–72). While the transition from *tu*-Alexis to *tu*-Corydon marks the beginning of Corydon's liberation at 2.56, here Corydon addresses himself again (after addressing Alexis at 2.65) to signal definitive freedom from obsessive love. Desperate lovers frequently address themselves to acknowledge their own folly: cf. Catull. 8.1 *miser Catulle, desinas ineptire.*

70 semiputata...uitis. A reference to *frondatio*, i.e. the operation of eliminating those vine leaves that may prevent sunlight from reaching the grapes (cf. Xen. *oec.* 19.19). It must be performed before dawn or in the evening, according to Columella, 11.2.55; cf. *E.* 1.56; *G.* 2.410 *bis uitibus ingruit umbram.* Perhaps the vineyard was neglected by Callimachus' Acontius, a possibile inference from Aristaen. *epist.* 1.10, p. 23, l. 56 Maz. οὐκ ἀμπελῶνος ἔμελεν. The reference to work left unfinished, not found in Theocritus, may prove to be unpleasant or disquieting: cf. *G.* 3.519; *Aen.* 1.37. **frondosa...in ulmo.** The Romans used elm trees to support grape vines: *G.* 1.2; Colum. 5.6.5. Hence the marriage metaphor featuring the two plants, at least since Catull. 62.54 (cf. Hor. *carm.* 2.15.4–5; note also Ov. *met.* 14.665–6). Pruning and *frondatio* must obviously concern the supporting plant as well (which might otherwise 'smother' the vines). For the leafy appearance of elm trees cf. Ov. *met.* 2.557 *densa...ab ulmo.*

71 quorum indiget usus. The notion of 'utility' generalizes the realism of Theocritus' objects (baskets and young shoots: *id.* 11.73 [see 2.69–72n.]). Yet another, significant echo in the poem of *labor*: *G.* 2.22.

72 detexere. 'To interweave', coupled with the idea of 'bringing to completion' (note the preverb *de-*), which is ironically emphasized by *paras*: cf. Titin. *com.* 24–5 R³ *unam togam detexere.* For the auxiliary construction of *paro* with the infinitive cf. Caes. *Gall.* 7.71.9 *bellum parat administrare.* V. will use it again multiple times in the *Aeneid*: note, for instance, *Aen.* 1.179 *et torrere parant...et frangere*; 2.446–7 *his se...parant defendere telis*; 3.382. For *paratus* + infinitive, cf. 7.5n.

73 alium...Alexin. A final reference to the Theocritean model: *id.* 11.76 εὑρησεῖς Γαλάτειαν ἴσως καὶ καλλίον' ἄλλαν. The object of eros, no longer an exclusive obsession, is now a generic and recursive category (note the 'framing' echo of the first line, which also ended on the *puer*'s name: but he is now *alius*, no longer *formosus*; εἴτε τις ἄλλος is a homoerotic alternative in *id.* 7.105). Corydon will be able to find 'another Alexis', i.e. 'another cure' (2.1n.). This notion resonates with some of Lucretius' Epicurean precepts: *aut a l i o possis animi traducere motus* (Lucr. 4.1072; note also 4.1064 *a l i o conuertere mentem*).

Eclogue 3

[Palaemon]

The third eclogue stages a poetry contest between the shepherds Damoetas and Menalcas. In the first part (3.1–59), after a lively dialogue in which the two characters display some competitiveness, the 'neighbour' Palaemon is chosen as a referee. He decides that Damoetas will be the first to speak. In the second part (3.60–111), the two contestants challenge each other in twelve exchanges, alternating two-line sequences, until Palaemon concludes the contest by declaring a draw.

Here V. enters a typical scenario of pastoral poetry, the agon or contest, which Theocritus (or Pseudo-Theocritus) had staged in *id.* 5 (Comatas and Lacon), 6 (Daphnis and Damoetas), 8 (Daphnis and Menalcas), and 9 (Daphnis and Menalcas, again). In *E.* 3, V.'s distinctive inlay technique combines the various Theocritean models. While the figure of the divine singer, crucial to *id.* 6, 8, and 9, is not featured in the poem (though a *puer* Daphnis is tangentially mentioned at 3.12), we do encounter the names of Daphnis' Theocritean competitors, i.e. Damoetas and Menalcas. No wonder that the two occasional contenders of *id.* 5 (Lacon and Comatas) are excluded from *E.* 3: in fact, V. presents a series of contrasts with that idyll, which he reworks with great continuity (at 3.7–9; 12–15; 25–7; then again at 3.62; 64; 68–9; 89; 97), but without replicating its sceptic, often aggressive and obscene, tone. Finally, a further Theocritean source worth considering is *id.* 4, which is not properly an agon, but whose dialogic liveliness approaches the agonistic form. V. thus brings together, in a single poem, all the Theocritean texts most representative of the pastoral contest. As a result, while Theocritus' corpus features two draws (*id.* 6 and 9, in which competitiveness and agonistic scripts do not appear) and two victories (*id.* 5 and 8), V. has one draw (*E.* 3) and one victory (*E.* 7).

E. 3, along with *E.* 2, is generally believed to be one of the oldest poems in the book. A clue is provided by V. himself, who quotes both pieces towards the end of *E.* 5, i.e. of the first half of the book (5.85–7n.). Both poems are close to the atypical introductory eclogue, and precede the equally atypical *E.* 4, thereby creating a diptych. The poet here enters the heart of his Theocritean imitation, measuring himself against two of the most distinctive bucolic forms: love song and agon. The latter, in particular, could have been considered as the origin of the pastoral genre (cf. *schol.* Theocr., p. 3.2–15 Wend.; Merkelbach 1956; Cremonesi 1958; Lucarini 2007). The first poetic form produced by Hermes on his newly invented lyre was improvization, 'as young men do at banquets, sneering at one another' (*Hymn. Hom.* 4[*Merc.*].55–6). Hesiod claimed to have taken part in the funeral agon for Amphidamas at Chalcis, winning a tripod as prize (Hes. *op.* 654–7).

The reappearance of Iollas' name (3.76n.), featured in *E.* 2, may suggest a close continuity between the two eclogues: the same is true of Damoetas' name (3.1n.). Even the draw between the two competitors is perhaps meant to hint at the still

148   ECLOGUE 3

'primitive' (and therefore non-evaluable) nature of V.'s pastoral world. The referee's name, Palaemon, contains an echo of 'antiquity' (3.50n.; on the rules of
Theocritus' agon, which V. does not seem to follow in his two *certamina*, cf.
3.58–9n.; below, p. 346). Thus, even if *E.* 3 was not among the first composed,
V. clearly intended to mark it as 'initial' (along with *E.* 2).

Theocritus may have been aware of the 'original' status (and the 'antiquity') characterizing the agonistic theme: in *id.* 5, Lacon's name alludes to the continental
motherland; the herdsman, moreover, is introduced as coming from Sybaris, long
destroyed in Theocritus' time (*id.* 5.1; cf. 5.146; Dover 1971, p. 128). In V.'s poem,
on the one hand, the names of Menalcas and Damoetas obviously hint at a great
generation of Theocritean singers; and yet, on the other hand, a Roman name,
Asinius Pollio, also appears (3.84–9n.), representing V.'s novelty. Through the figure
of this important Antonian politician, the *E.* situate themselves within the literary
circle which, after Philippi, was gathering around Pollio at Rome. The scoffing of
Bavius and Maevius, two imprudent detractors (3.90n.), is best explained in terms
of the lively dynamics of a literary group, revolving around inclusion as well as
enmity. Many aspects of *E.* 3 can be analysed in relation to Pollio's literary tastes:
this is particularly true of the numerous stylistic, linguistic, and conceptual echoes
of Catullus, an author certainly known to Pollio in person, as we can glean from
Catull. 12.6 (cf. 3.84n.; for Catullan parallels, see esp. 3.16n.; 40–1n.; 58–9n.; 84n.;
111n.). Pollio was probably the first to appreciate V.'s success in combining pastoral
topics and urban refinement while avoiding Catullus' nemesis, *rusticitas*. Especially
in such a context of sophisticated *urbanitas*, we can better appreciate V.'s ability to
mitigate Theocritus' scoptic excess and aim at a graceful, lively colloquial style
(whence the numerous echoes of Plautus and Terence's language).

The folksy theme of flyting, bound to reappear in Horace's *Satires* (which often
feature lively, quarrelling characters: cf. esp. Hor. *sat.* 1.5 and 1.7), must have
pleased V.'s readers. In Roman as in Greek culture, such naive forms of 'contest'
were perceived as strongly linked to origins and identity, according to several
Augustan authors: cf. notably *G.* 2.380–96 (as well as Hor. *epist.* 2.1.139–60, esp.
145–6 *Fescennina…licentia… / uersibus alternis obprobria rustica fudit*; Liv.
7.2.5; see also Tib. 2.1.50–8). At the end of the eclogue, a typically folkloric form
will appear, i.e. the riddle (otherwise unparalleled in pastoral literature:
3.104–7n.). V. is obviously not writing a treatise on Roman literary history, but he
certainly realized that *E.* 3 'represents' a scene from the origins of Latin literature
(and literature tout court). On the other hand, his mention of Pollio situates the
contest within contemporary social and political conflicts (particularly tense in
the years between Philippi and Actium). Ancient readers certainly responded to
such stimuli, as is shown by numerous allegorical interpretations of *E.* 3, particularly interesting from the point of view of the *E.*'s 'political' reception (for instance,
Palaemon is regarded as an allegory of Octavian: see 3.50n.; cf. also 3.74n.;
94–5n.; 96n.).

ECLOGUE 3   149

A new, 'pastoral-mimetic' experiment is thus generated, alongside the pastoral-elegiac experiment of *E.* 2. V.'s blend of sensitivity, irony, and urban finesse seem to reappear in Horace's well-known verdict, *sat.* 1.10.44–5 (cf. Introduction, pp. 11–12 and n. 27). Gellius will later write, concerning V.'s Theocritean reworking at 3.64–5: *quod substituit pro eo quod omiserat non abest quin iucundius lepidiusque sit* (Gell. 9.9.5). The thoughtful self-consciousness characterizing V.'s Theocritean synthesis and emulation hints at another contest, parallel to the one between Menalcas and Damoetas. Like Menalcas, V. himself must (by Palaemon's decision) 'respond' to the stimuli of another poet's text, 'following' his interlocutor (3.58 *tu deinde sequere, Menalca*: in *E.* 5 and 9, Menalcas himself will act as a mask for V.). The description of Alcimedon's cups is not just a (pre-agonistic) testing ground for the contestants, but also an occasion for V. to compete with the Theocritean cup in *id.* 1. Here, the Roman poet counters Theocritus' detailed realism with brief, descriptive touches and a mythico-scientific motif (astronomy, Orpheus). V.'s text, albeit in the 'humble' domain of rural craftsmanship, appeals to his readers' (and Pollio's) taste for the arts of Hellenistic Greece, including portraits (*imagines*) of illustrious writers, thinkers, and scientists. Horace, too, chooses a 'humble' statue of Priapus, made of fig-tree wood, to allude to Maecenas' artistic restoration of the Esquiline hill and the *horti* named after the patron himself (Hor. *sat.* 1.8.1 *Olim truncus eram ficulnus, inutile lignum*, etc.). Similarly, V.'s herdsmen describe the wooden cups made by the 'divine Alcimedon', and the poet knows well that his addressee (like many Roman aristocrats) is an art aficionado. This is confirmed by the fact that Pollio tied his name to the monumental restoration of Rome's *Atrium Libertatis*, where a rich library full of Greek and Roman literary masterpieces was accompanied by a varied collection of Greek artworks (Plin. *nat.* 7.115; 35.9–10; 36.23; 33–4; note also Suet. *Aug.* 29.5).

The poem's structure is rather linear. The mimetic nature of *E.* 3 is apparent in the dialogic opening, where a character (later revealed to be Menalcas: 13) addresses another character, named Damoetas (1 *Dic mihi, Damoeta*). The dialogue gradually turns into a contest. The first fifty-nine lines of the eclogue (or fifty-eigth, if 3.43 is spurious: see n. ad loc.) are a sort of pre-agon, concluded by Palaemon's speech, which opens the contest itself (55–9). The competition, which starts at 60, includes twelve dialogic exchanges of four lines each (i.e. two speeches of two lines each). These add up to forty-eight lines (60–107), followed by Palaemon's verdict in the final four lines (108–11). V.'s meticulous attention to structural details is shown by the fact that the contest has exactly the same number of lines (i.e. forty-eight) as the one in *E.* 7 (cf. 7.21–68), which is composed of six dialogic exchanges (each including two four-line speeches). Yet the narrative technique is very different: in *E.* 7, the speeches are introduced by the narrator (Meliboeus) as an *almost* complete account of the competition (see 7.69n.), whereas the contest of *E.* 3 happens 'live' in front of V.'s audience, with the judge Palaemon deciding the outcome (3.111n.). *E.* 3 is thus a laboratory of V.'s mimetic

150   ECLOGUE 3

and dramatic technique, which largely follows Theocritus' example. This explains several 'stage directions' in the poem, which is best interpreted as a kind of mime with three 'actors' whose actions and gestures complement the text (as in their choice of the stakes, i.e. the *uitula*: cf. 3.29n.; 31n.; 36n.; 109n.; note also the narrative 'break' at 3.55n.). As in every (properly) dialogic section of the *E.*, the number of speeches is evenly distributed between the two protagonists: before Palaemon's intervention, which marks the beginning of the agon itself (55–111), the two herdsmen have seven speeches each, for a total of fourteen (Menalcas has the first word and Damoetas the last). In terms of line numbers, however, the scales are slightly tilted in favour of Menalcas, due to his long ecphrasis (he has a total of thirty lines, or twenty-nine if 3.43n. is deleted, while Damoetas has only twenty-four). Together with *E.* 8, *E.* 3 is by far the longest of the book: moreover the two eclogues, in which Pollio plays a central role (also, with all likelihood, in *E.* 8), could both count 110 lines, a significant number for Pollio: 3.43n.; 8.6n.).

On the eclogue: Gebauer (1861, pp. 186–226); Weyman (1917d); Büchner (1955, cols. 1190–5); Savage (1958); Klingner (1967, pp. 50–9); Segal (1967); Veremans (1969); Putnam (1970, pp. 119–35); Braun (1971); Garson (1971, pp. 192–6); O. Skutsch (1971); E. A. Schmidt (1972b, pp. 294–6); Leach (1974, pp. 170–82); Barigazzi (1975); Currie (1976); B. P. Powell (1976); Van Sickle (1978, pp. 127–31); La Penna (1981a); Farrell (1991b, pp. 280–9; 1992); Monteleone (1994); T. K. Hubbard (1995a, pp. 59–66 = 1998, pp. 68–75 = 2008, pp. 101–8); Henderson (1998b); Schäfer (2001); MacDonald (2003); Schultz (2003); Tracy (2003); Jouteur (2007); von Albrecht (2007, pp. 21–3); Saunders (2008, pp. 9–30); Dufallo (2013, pp. 74–107); Stöckinger (2016, pp. 61–89); Moch (2017).

Specific issues: Cartault (1897, pp. 123–4) (ll. 92–9; 100–3 [p. 124, n. 2 on l. 102]); Havet (1914a, pp. 85–7) (l. 102); Havet (1914b) (l. 100); Phillimore (1916, pp. 148–9) (l. 102); Klotz (1920, pp. 150–1) (ll. 92–9); Jachmann (1922, pp. 107–8) (ll. 92–9); Schauroth (1949–50) (ll. 104–7); Savage (1953–4) (ll. 104–7); Benario (1954) (l. 60); Cova (1955) (l. 79); Krenkel (1958–9) (ll. 104–5); Wormell (1960) (ll. 104–7); Ernout (1963) (l. 77); Putnam (1965) (ll. 104–5); Gallavotti (1966) (ll. 38–9); Luiselli (1967, pp. 59–72) (Asinius Pollio as a poet); Nethercut (1970) (ll. 106–7); Burckhardt (1971, p. 412) (ll. 109–10); Grillo (1971, pp. 78–84) (ll. 84–91); Clarke (1972–3) (l. 79); Cassio (1973) (l. 41); A. E. Radke (1973) (ll. 109–10); J. S. Clay (1974) (ll. 104–7); Schoepsdau (1974) (themes of love poetry); Flintoff (1975–6, pp. 21–3) (Menalcas as a character); Petersmann (1977) (ll. 92–107); Segal (1977) (Golden Age and *E.* 4); Brown (1978) (ll. 104–5); Hudson-Williams (1980, pp. 124–5) (ll. 7–9); Coleiro (1981) (ll. 109–10); Freyer (1981) (ll. 104–7); La Penna (1981b) (l. 90); J. S. Campbell (1982) (ll. 104–7); Fisher (1982) (ll. 40–2); Néraudau (1983) (Asinius Pollio as a poet); Springer (1983) (l. 42); R. F. Thomas (1983b) (l. 40); J. K. Anderson (1984) (ll. 92–3); Buchheit (1984) (ll. 88–9); Hofmann (1985) (ll. 104–7); Buchheit (1986) (ll. 55–7); Malaspina (1986) (ll. 104–7); Timpanaro (1986, pp. 151–3) (l. 38); Geymonat (1987, pp. 51–2) (l. 26); Wills (1993) (l. 1); Citroni (1995, pp. 224–9) (Pollio); Dix (1995) (ll. 104–7); Faber (1995) (l. 37); Hendry (1995) (ll. 8–9); Callataÿ (1996, pp. 11–13) (ll. 36–47); P. Hardie (1996, pp. 110–11) (ll. 104–7); Lentini (1997) (ll. 100–3); Hinds (1998, p. 6) (l. 79);

Korzeniowski (1999) (the clausula *et mihi Damon* [l. 23]); Faber (2000) (l. 38); Hunter (2001) (ll. 60–1); Loupiac (2003) (ll. 34–47); Courtney (2004, p. 428) ('Greek' acc. in ll. 106–7); Gomez Gane (2004) (l. 26); Trappes-Lomax (2004, pp. 149–51) (l. 6); Geymonat (2005) (poetry and science); Prioux (2005) (l. 42); Dion (2006, pp. 83–6) (ll. 40–2, 106–7); Karanika (2006) (the agon); Kraggerud (2006a) (ll. 1–2 and Numitorius' parody); Kraggerud (2007, pp. 87–9) (l. 62); Katz (2008, pp. 110–11) (ll. 40–2); Maurach (2008) (language and style); Saunders (2008, pp. 9–21) (the cups and the universe); Ottaviano (2010) (l. 79); Ottaviano (2011, pp. 203–8) (l. 102); Ottaviano (2012, pp. 200–1) (ll. 92–9); Heyworth (2015, pp. 201–3) (ll. 16–20); Heyworth (2015, pp. 203–5) (ll. 55–9); Heyworth (2015, pp. 205–8) (ll. 100–3); Kayachev (2017) (Aratus' presence in *ecl.* 3, esp. ll. 40–2; 104–7); Kraggerud (2017a, pp. 93–100) (ll. 100–2); Kraggerud (2017b, pp. 14–15) (l. 62); Oksanish (2017) (contention as a popular and original form of Roman culture); Stachon (2017) (Bavius and Maevius); Marchetta (2018, pp. 393–431) (Asinius Pollio); Baraz (2019, pp. 84–6) (l. 49); Barchiesi (2019) (ecphrasis); Hejduk (2020, pp. 43–4) (l. 60); Kraggerud (2020, pp. 265–71) (ll. 100–2); Cucchiarelli (2021a, pp. 88–93) (Alcimedon's cups; l. 43); Ursini (2021, pp. 133–5) (l. 16).

1–59. The first part of the eclogue is eminently mimetic. The two protagonists, Menalcas and Damoetas, exchange jokes with each other and, as in a Theocritean pre-agon, suggest that a contest is about to start. An important point in this section is the choice of the stakes, which gives V. the opportunity for an ecphrasis (Alcimedon's cups: 3.35–48). Once the choice has been confirmed (it is only revealed in 3.109 that Damoetas' proposal of the *uitula* at 3.29 was accepted), a third character, Palaemon, steps in as a judge (3.55–9). The contest can then begin.

1–2. A precise reworking of *id.* 4.1–2, replicating its bucolic diaeresis: (Βάτ.) εἰπέ μοι ὦ Κορύδων, τίνος αἱ βόες; ἦ ῥα Φιλώνδα; / (Κορ.) οὔκ, ἀλλ᾽ Αἴγωνος· βόσκειν δέ μοι αὐτὰς ἔδωκεν '(Battus) Tell me, Corydon, whose cows are these? Maybe Philondas'? / (Corydon) No, they are Aegon's: he gave me them to graze'. The names of Damoetas and Aegon, here opening the eclogue, will reappear together in Menalcas' song (*E.* 5.72). Following Theocritus, V. uses two one-liners in a row: the 'minimum viable product' in pastoral poetry (cf. 1.26n.). As in Theocritus, this makes the dialogue's opening very lively; cf. also 5.8–9n. and 9.1n. (in V., however, the banter is limited to the first two lines, whereas in Theocr. *id.* 4 it goes on for the first fourteen lines). Particularly in the opening of *id.* 4, Theocritus seems to echo the mimetic realism of Plato's dialogues, such as the *Phaedrus*. The Platonic model, certainly active in book 2 of Horace's *Satires* (esp. *sat.* 2.4 *Unde et quo Catius?*, etc.), might also play a background role in V.'s *E.* (and esp. *E.* 3).

1 Dic mihi, Damoeta, cuium pecus? The poem's mimetic nature is immediately revealed by the colloquial opening *dic mihi*, common in comedy and exactly equivalent to εἰπέ μοι / λέγε μοι (cf. Herod. *mim.* 5.1), which in Latin may have sounded less than urbane due to its directness (Don. *ad* Ter. *Andr.* 667). The same

152 ECLOGUE 3

is true of the pronominal adj. *cuium*, used in lieu of *cuius* (= τίνος in Theocritus), similarly belonging to the language of comedy (and here also serving to avoid the homeoteleuton *cuius pecus*), yet not employed by Latin poets in V.'s time—hence the parody in Numitorius' *Antibucolica: dic mihi Damoeta: cuium pecus, anne Latinum? / non, uerum Aegonis nostri; sic rure loquuntur* (quoted in Don. *uita Verg.* 171-7 Brumm. = pp. 38–9 Brugn.-Stok). V. perhaps meant it as part of a sketched linguistic characterization, corresponding to Theocritus' Doric forms (note the Doric ψε in lieu of σφε at *id.* 4.3). The boundary line between archaism and *rusticitas* is notoriously thin, as observed (regarding pronunciation) by Cic. *de orat.* 3.42; Cicero himself uses *cuium*, as a relative, in *Verr.* 2.2.127 *cuium nomen exisset, ut is haberet id sacerdotium*, where juristic language is echoed (several manuscripts trivialize into *cuius*). The colloquial nature of *cuius -a -um* is confirmed by its survival in Romance dialects and languages (e.g. Spanish *cuyo*). The name *Damoeta*, alliterating with *dic*, is connected to the Doric variant of δῆμος 'people' (the voc. ending -*a* is long, just as in Greek; cf. 3.58; *E.* 7.67; 9.2). The dying Damoetas of *E.* 2 entrusted Corydon with his *fistula* (cf. 2.37n.). The question (a rather blunt one, which Damoetas immediately answers by naming the legitimate owner twice) displays some aggressiveness: at 3.16–20, Menalcas will accuse his interlocutor of attempting to steal a billy goat. The line is quoted in Pompeian graffiti: Gigante (1979, pp. 166–7).

2 **Aegonis...Aegon.** Note the polyptoton and the artful positioning of the name at the middle and at the end of the line. The name is clearly connected to αἴξ, 'goat': here Aegon owns sheep (*oues*), whereas in Theocritus he owned βόες; 'bovine' implications, on the other hand, can be detected in Meliboeus' name, replacing Theocritus' Philondas in 3.1 (1.6n.). As for Aegon, he retains the interest in women that characterized his Theocritean predecessor: 3.4n. (note the repetition of the name, echoing Theocritus' pastoral style). Hence Menalcas' jealousy, further exacerbating his aggressive stance toward his interlocutor (3.5–6). Note the temporal adverb (*nuper*), not found in Theocritus and here used with a cunningly defensive and disclaiming function: Damoetas has 'just now' taken custody of the herd, therefore he cannot be reproached for anything (which Menalcas immediately goes on to do).

3-6. Another precise reference to *id.* 4.13–14: '(Ba.) Wretched that they are, they found a naughty cowherd! / (Co.) Yes, the poor things, and they no longer want to eat' (cf. also 26–7). Here, however, V. actualizes what Theocritus presented as a possibility, against which Aegon wisely protected himself by leaving an 'old man' to control Corydon: '(Ba.) And you milk them all on the sly, in the evening? / (Co.) No, the old man puts the calves to suck, and keeps an eye on me' (3–4). Now, instead, Aegon is distracted by his love for Neaera and gives free rein to his dependant Damoetas, who is ready to take advantage of it—at least according to Menalcas (3.5–6). Herdsmen often milk the animals for themselves after milking them for their owners: cf. *schol.* Theocr. 4.3b, p. 135 Wend.

ECLOGUE 3   153

3 Infelix o semper, oues, pecus. Parenthetic apposition, the so-called *schema Cornelianum* (1.57n.), similarly appears at the outset of *E.* 2 (also in the third line). Cf. specifically *G.* 4.168 *ignauum fucos, pecus* (= *Aen.* 1.435) and 246. The phrasing is strictly tied to the situation at hand, but it also sounds like a proverb: the underlings pay for their bad masters (for a similar notion, cf. Hor. *epist.* 1.2.14 *quidquid delirant reges, plectuntur Achiui*; Phaedr. 1.30.1). **ipse.** Used colloquially in reference to a *dominus* (*ipsa* for a *domina*); often found in comedy (dialogues between slaves). Here the idea, of proverbial origin, is that the master had better take care of his property personally: cf. Phaedrus' formulation, 2.8.28 *dominum uidere plurimum in rebus suis*; cf. Tosi (2007, pp. 472–3, no. 1014). **Neaeram.** An extra-pastoral name, hinting at 'youth' (*véa*), well attested for female lovers: marine suggestions (Neaera is the mother of two nymphs in Hom. *Od.* 12.133; being Thetis' sister, she is herself a Nereid) make her similar to Tityrus' Galatea (*E.* 1.30n.): like the latter, Neaera seems to be rather elusive; *Enc. Virg.* III, p. 676, s.v. *Neera* (F. Della Corte); *Virg. Enc.* II, p. 888, s.v. *Neaera* (G. C. Trimble).

4 dum fouet ac. Theocritus' Aegon was distracted by his love for athletic contests, which led him to Olympia (*id.* 4.6), while an unspecified 'old man' (4), who attentively keeps guard over the herd, appears nevertheless to be quite efficient with his young lover. Here, on the other hand, Aegon is distracted by his passion for Neaera, for whom he shows a protective concern: *fouet* suggests a physical attitude, almost 'nursing'; cf. *G.* 4.56 *progeniem nidosque fouent*; *Aen.* 1.718; 4.686. Here Aegon, at least in Menalcas' boast, is afraid of losing his beloved (*ueretur*); but the verb may also have sexual connotations: e.g. Tib. 1.6.5–6 *Delia furtim / nescio quem tacita callida nocte fouet*; cf. also Prop. 2.22a.37. The phrase *fouet ac* allows V. to avoid the sequence *-et et*; cf. 9.42n. **illa.** Cf. 3.5n.

5 hic. In all probability a locative adv., underscoring the opposition between the master's concerns and what actually happens 'here', out on the pasture. As an adv., *hic* often occurs in the *E.* at the beginning of a line (*E.* 1.14; 42; 44; 79; 5.3; 7.12; 24; 49; 51; 9.40; 62; 10.42–3). We cannot, however, rule out a reading of *hic* as a pronoun, emphatically taking up 3.4 *ipse…me sibi…illa* (where R's incorrect *ille* may have been prompted by such an interpretation). **alienus…custos.** The idea of 'grazing someone else's sheep', readily used as a metaphor, is rather common: cf. Plaut. *Asin.* 539–40 *opilio qui pascit…alienas ouis*; Varr. *rust.* 1.21.1. Here, however, the epithet *alienus* refers to the *custos*, underscoring his extraneousness and, therefore, his dishonesty (he exploits the animals by milking them too often: *bis…in hora*; cf. Hor. *sat.* 1.4.9 *in hora…ducentos*). The term *custos*, previously used in pastoral poetry by Porcius Licinus (fr. 6 Bläns. = Court.; cf. also *E.* 5.44; 7.34; 10.36), is sometimes replaced by *magister* in V.'s *E.* (2.33; 3.101; 5.48). V. uses both terms in the *Georgics*, too (cf., respectively, *G.* 1.17 and 2.529).

154 ECLOGUE 3

6 pecori et. A full hiatus, here between two Latin words (contrast 2.24n.): cf. *G.* 1.4 *pecori, apibus*; 3.155 *pecori armentaque*. Interestingly, the phenomenon occurs three times, and perhaps artfully so, in the case of such a 'humble' term (however, as V. will tell Gallus in *E.* 10.17, *nec te paeniteat pecoris, diuine poeta*). Cf. also 3.63n.; 7.53; 10.13 (in all three cases, the /i/ is long before *et* or *etiam*; double hiatus at 7.53). Hiatus often occurs, as here, at the main caesura. Note, however, the correction proposed by Trappes-Lomax, who restores the older form *lact* (< *lacte*), attested by **P** both here and in *E.* 2.22: the line would therefore be *et sucus pecori lact et subducitur agnis*.

7–9. Damoetas replies to Menalcas' innuendos by questioning his rival's claims to manliness (while Damoetas himself is a 'real man': 3.7 *uiris*). He alludes to a sexual episode, clearly of homoerotic nature (3.8 *qui te*), in which Menalcas had the passive role. V. here moves from *id.* 4 to evoke the sceptic tone of *id.* 5, though keeping a certain distance from it.

8–9 et qui te… / et quo. The parallelism, marked by strong assonance, and the repeated parenthetic underscore the aposiopesis, which, as Servius observed, mitigates the Theocritean harshness of *id.* 5: '(Lac.) And when, pray, can I recall having learned or heard from you / anything good, o envious and despicable little man? (Com.) When I was shafting you, and you were in pain: and these she-goats / were bleating, and the billy goat was covering them' (*id.* 5.39–42). In fact, the omission of the verb has a precedent in the much more stylized *id.* 1, in reference to the shepherd Anchises' divine love affair: οὐ λέγεται τὰν Κύπριν ὁ βουκόλος; 'don't they say that the herdsman with Cypris…?' (105); cf. Callim. *aet.* fr. 75.4–7 Pf. = 174.4–7 Mass. = 75.4–7 Hard. Further examples are offered by Terence's evasive humour: *Eun.* 479 *ego illum eunuchum, si opu' siet, uel sobrius…*; *Heaut.* 913 *qui se uidente amicam patiatur suam…?* (the 'discovery' of illicit sexual activity is featured in Men. *Dysc.* 461–3). Aposiopesis, a rhetorical device typical of everyday speech (and comedy), is also found in oratory and epic speeches: for its use in V., cf. *Aen.* 1.135; 2.100–1; 9.51–2; *Enc. Virg.* I, pp. 227–8, s.v. *aposiopesi* (L. Ricottilli); *Virg. Enc.* I, p. 103, s.v. *aposiopesis* (P. E. Knox). For the form *qui* (in lieu of *quis*), cf. 1.18n.

8 transuersa tuentibus hircis. The she-goats and billy goat featured in Theocritus (*id.* 5.41–2) are here replaced by the lewd, oblique (and envious?) gaze of the male animals: cf. esp. *Priap.* 73.1 Buech. *obliquis quid me…spectatis ocellis?* (Quint. *inst.* 11.3.76 [scil. *oculi*] *lasciui…aut limi et, ut sic dicam, uenerii*); see also *Anth. Pal.* 9.317.3–4 = *HE* 3892–3 G.-P. (for the opposite case, in which sexual desire is transferred from the animals to the herdsman, cf. *id.* 1.87–8). For the billy goat as a libidinous animal, cf. Hor. *epod.* 10.23. The phrase *transuersa tuentibus* is best explained as a Hellenizing construction (cf. λοξὰ βλέπειν), with a Latin precedent in Lucr. 5.33 *acerba tuens*, repeated at *Aen.* 9.794; cf. also *Aen.* 6.467 *torua tuentem* (Hom. *Il.* 3.342; cf. *Hymn. Hom.* 19[*Pan.*].14; maybe in Ennius?): its epic connotation makes the phrase humorously out of place here. Note that Servius

ECLOGUE 3   155

quotes a passage from Suetonius' *De uitiis corporalibus*, from which he infers that *hirqui autem sunt oculorum anguli* (fr. 171, p. 272 Reiff.); cf. *Gloss*. III, p. 247.22; V, p. 570.12 Goetz; *ThlL* VI.3.2822.34–40.

9 sed faciles Nymphae risere. The Nymphs are here called *faciles*, 'easy-going', since the desecration of a shrine could have harsh consequences—as in the case of Atalanta and Hippomenes, whom Cybele turned into lions: Ov. *met*. 10.686–704. This time, it seems, the goddesses took no notice. Cf. also *G*. 4.535 *facilis uenerare Napaeas* (with what follows: 536 *namque dabunt ueniam uotis, irasque remittent*). **risere**. The perfect in *-ēre*, common in Ennius, occurs almost twice as often as the *-ērunt* form in the *E*. (respectively, 13x vs 7x total occurrences; note also *tulĕrunt* at 4.61n.; for V.'s use of the two forms overall see Harrison's commentary [quoted above 1.1n.], p. 67, *ad Aen*. 10.32, with references). The form *risere* reappears at 4.62 and *Aen*. 5.181 (cf. the emulator Calp. *ecl*. 6.84); *riserunt* does not occur in V. (contrast Enn. *ann*. 447 Sk.). V.'s choice is partly dictated by metrical convenience; however, whenever prosody is not an issue (i.e. in line-ending position), V. uses *bibērunt* (3.111) and *tulērunt* (5.34). Note that Menalcas replies (l. 10) with the similar form *uidere*, occupying the same position in the hexameter. For a deity's smile, cf. *E*. 6.23 (note also 4.60n.).

10–11. In connection with what Damoetas has just said, Menalcas imagines that the Nymphs also witnessed another misdeed, this time committed by his rival (*me* is ironic). Besides depriving the lambs of their milk, Damoetas also damaged plants belonging to others (a serious crime, already penalized by the *XII Tables*: see Plin. *nat*. 17.7).

10 arbustum. A tree-line (cf. 1.39) used, in this case, to support the vines, as was customary in Roman culture: Varr. *rust*. 1.8.3; *ThlL* II.430.34–63; cf. also 5.32n. **Miconis**. This character similarly suffered damage in the Theocritean model: '(Com.) I hate those bushy-tailed foxes, which always visit Micon's fields / towards evening, nibbling at his grapes' (*id*. 5.112–13). Here, however, the entire vineyard—rather than a few bunches of grapes—is ruined.

11 mala uitis incidere falce nouellas. The young vines, particularly delicate and in need of loving care: *G*. 2.362–70. The adj. *nouellae* is a technical term in arboricultural contexts: Cat. *agr*. 33.4; OLD^2, p. 1314, s.v. 1b. For the *mala falx* cf. [Tib.] 3.5.20 *et modo nata mala uellere poma manu*, as well as the seemingly proverbial expression in Hor. *epist*. 2.1.220 *ut uineta egomet caedam mea*.

12–15. The misdeed is analogous to that described in *id*. 5.11–13: '(Com.) It is the dappled hide that Crocylus gave me / when he sacrificed the she-goat to the Nymphs. But you, rascal, even then you wasted away out of envy, / and now at last you stripped me of it'. Using a mimetic technique, V. prevents the reader from gaining a full understanding of facts and details: the only source of help is Theocritean-pastoral competence. The relationship between Daphnis (see 5.20n.) and Menalcas will appear much more relaxed in *E*. 5.52 *amauit nos quoque Daphnis* (where the speaker is a mature Menalcas: n. ad loc.), but the competitiveness of

156   ECLOGUE 3

id. 8 can still be perceived. The contest there was concluded by Daphnis' victory and
Menalcas' despair: 'his soul shaken and devoured by grief' (l. 90). Significantly, the
accusation is uttered by a Damoetas, whose Theocritean namesake showed an
affectionate attitude towards Daphnis: 'Thus sang Damoetas, and kissed Daphnis, /
and that to this gave a pipe, and this to that a good *aulos*. / Damoetas played the
aulos, Daphnis the cowherd played the pipe' (*id.* 6.42–4); cf. 3.12–13n. *E.* 3 is, in
many ways, still an 'introductory' poem: this is why V. now summons all the big
names (the 'founders') of pastoral poetry.

12 ad ueteres fagos. Seemingly a specific place, referred to again at *E.* 9.9 *et
ueteres, iam fracta cacumina, fagos* (n.), whereas 2.3 *densas, umbrosa cacumina,
fagos* (n.) is more generic: a group of old beech trees, perhaps with a sacred
connotation (e.g. *E.* 7.24 *sacra pendebit fistula pinu*). A grove of plane trees and
oleasters, sacred to Apollo, functioned as a reference point in the landscape of *id.*
25.20–2 (cf. the precinct sacred to Priapus in *epigr.* 4 G.). A sacred reference point
is also found at e.g. *id.* 5.14 (a sculpture of Pan by the sea). It is possible that, as in
Theocritus' epigram (on which see below), these venerable beech trees are used to
hang the objects mentioned immediately thereafter (*arcum…et calamos*), which
Menalcas perhaps tried to desecrate. Yet the beech trees could also be mere spec-
tators of Menalcas' misdeeds: maybe he attempted to deprive the owner of those
objects while they were still in use (by stealing them?). Here, V.'s artistry resides
precisely in this kind of ambiguity: a vague allusion is enough for the characters
to remember events they know perfectly well, while the reader does not have
access to the information they possess.

12–13 Daphnidis arcum / fregisti et calamos. The likeliest meaning of *calamos*
here is 'panpipes', as is normally the case in the *E.* (for the plural form, cf. 2.32; 3.13;
5.2; 48; 6.69; 8.24; the singular is used at 1.10; 2.34) and in later pastoral poetry
(Calpurnius Siculus and Nemesianus, with no exceptions; note also, before V., Lucr.
4.588; 5.1407). Thus, besides breaking the bow, Menalcas did the same to the panpipes (*et calamos*: note the emphatic hyperbaton and the enjambement). Due to the
close association with *arcum*, however, *calamos* might be taken to mean 'arrows' (in
which case, the emphasis would be equally comprehensible: 'not just the bow, but
even the arrows'). Yet the use of *calamus* in the sense of 'arrows' is more specialized
and only occurs once in V. (*Aen.* 10.140, with Harrison's note [quoted above, 1.1n.],
pp. 98–9 *ad loc.*; cf. also Ov. *met.* 7.778; Sil. 2.131). Bow and panpipes fit well
together, as they both represent rural (and pastoral) activities, particularly in the
context of homoerotic relationships (cf. 3.14 *puero*). In *E.* 2, Corydon invites Alexis
to join him for both hunting and music/poetry (cf. 2.28–39: note the mention of
gifts and envy, as here). Similarly, in *E.* 7, hunting and music are virtually coupled
together (7.24; 29–30). Note that, in Theocritus' *epigr.* 2 G., the shepherds' musical
instrument (τρητοὺς δόνακας) and hunting tools are mentioned in the same breath,
as Daphnis dedicates them to Pan (in addition to a leather pouch for carrying
apples: ll. 3–4). The case for *calamos* 'panpipes' is strengthened by the phrase

quae...donata, which seems to suggest that there were two separate gifts: bow and arrows, by contrast, are but two sides of the same coin, and the arrows are mere (and perishable: cf. e.g. Callim. *epigr.* 37.5–6 Pf.) accessories to the bow. The σῦριγξ is Daphnis' prize in *id.* 8.84, whereas in *id.* 6.43–4 it is Damoetas' gift to him (see 3.12–15n.): now another Damoetas denounces the crime. Here, too, V. is talking about a musical instrument, not a hunting one.

13–15. Envy and the resulting damage appear in *id.* 5.11–13, esp. 12–13 τὺ δ' ὦ κακὲ καὶ τόκ' ἐτάκευ / βασκαίνων, καὶ νῦν με τὰ λοίσθια γυμνὸν ἔθηκας (see 3.12–15n.; note the coordination καὶ...καί taken up by V.'s *et...et*). Cf. also *E.* 2.39; 7.26.

13 quae tu, peruerse Menalca. We finally learn the second protagonist's name, here associated with a scoptic epithet (Damoetas has been named at 3.1). Menalcas is among the oldest, most distinctive inhabitants of the pastoral world, and played a central role in *id.* 8 and 9 (besides being an object of love in Eriphanis' 'pastoral song': *PMG* 850, p. 452 P.; cf. Athen. 14.619c–d; 2.1n.; 10.20n.). After a brief mention in *E.* 2.15, he will again be seen playing a crucial role in *E.* 5 and 9 (where he is the absent protagonist: 9.10n.), then making his final appearance in 10.20. See further *Enc. Virg.* III, pp. 477–80, s.v. *Menalca* (F. Michelazzo); *Virg. Enc.* II, pp. 812–13, s.v. *Menalcas* (J. Van Sickle); also Hunter (1999, p. 66). Properly speaking, the adj. *peruersus* expresses a deviation from the right, natural path, causing trouble and harm: Plaut. *Men.* 899 *hic dies peruorsus atque aduorsus mi optigit*; Cic. *Cluent.* 71 *praeposterus atque peruersus* [scil. *C. Staienus*]; *ThlL* X.1.1862.7–74. Once again, Damoetas' words point to an aberration from the normal order of things, as in 3.8 *transuersa*. For the offensive parenthetic phrase cf. *id.* 5.12 'and you, rascal' (τὺ δ' ὦ κακέ [see 3.13–15n.]).

14 puero. Daphnis himself, called a 'boy' in *id.* 8 (l. 88 παῖς; cf. *id.* 6.1–3). The term refers to Daphnis again at *E.* 5.54 *puer ipse fuit cantari dignus* (whereas Daphnis' name is mentioned at 5.52, i.e. two lines earlier, as here: cf. 3.12). Menalcas, too, is still young (3.33n.). It is less likely and 'economical' to think that *puero* denotes a third individual, who receives Daphnis' gift, even though Damoetas may well be alluding to a dense network of homoerotic relationships among 'boys' vying for the older herdsman's favour.

16–20. Despite not addressing Damoetas' accusation, Menalcas' new aggression is meant to discredit his rival through the mention of another misdeed: here again, as in 3.3–6, an attempted theft (in this case, rustling). The opposition between *domini* and *fures*, along with the sharp tones of the altercation, may echo the language and situations of comedy: cf. e.g. Plaut. *Aul.* 645–54 (for the voc. *pessime* at l. 17 cf. *Men.* 488).

16 quid domini faciant, audent cum talia fures. For a similar sentence structure, cf. Catull. 66.47 (here echoed by V.): *quid facient crines, cum ferro talia cedant*, translating Callim. *aet.* fr. 110.47–8 Pf. = 213.47–8 Mass. = 110.47–8 Hard. τί πλόκαμοι ῥέξωμεν, ὅτ' οὔρεα τοῖα σιδή[ρῳ / εἴκουσιν. As in Catull. 66, the

158   ECLOGUE 3

two nouns should in principle be linked by a superior/inferior relationship (vel sim.), but the reader's expectations are deceived by *fures*: the line-ending word is not symmetrical to *domini* (the reader might expect *serui*). As a result, the logic of the entire sentence is restructured. Instead of saying, 'What might the masters do, when the slaves are so audacious?' (which could be interpreted in a positive sense: 'How could the masters not behave courageously, when the slaves are so heroic?'), Menalcas says: 'what could the masters do, when the thieves are so audacious?' (the implication being, 'Wretched that they are!', or the like). Servius focuses on the rhetorical qualities of the line but misses the point: *si dicas 'philosophus', nomen ipsum ponis, si autem uelis dicere 'sapientiae operam dans', personam exprimes per officium, sicut hoc loco fecit: nam pro seruo furem posuit; furta enim specialiter seruorum sunt.* Menalcas implies that Damoetas, rather than being merely a slave (which he certainly is), is actually a *fur* in the proper sense of the term: he appropriates a billy goat belonging to Damon, who has entrusted his herd not to him, but to Tityrus (and perhaps to Menalcas himself). In ll. 3–6, Damoetas is similarly portrayed as a serf, and a dishonest one at that. The Catullan echo, deliberately trivialized by Menalcas, might appeal to the taste of V.'s patron, Asinius Pollio, who greatly admired Catullus and the neoteric poets (see p. 148). Perhaps this is also one of V.'s earliest experiments with Catullan rewritings: a deep and simultaneously estranged intertext, such as the famously impressive *Aen.* 6.460 *inuitus, regina, tuo de litore cessi* (Aeneas addressing Dido), which echoes Catull. 66.39 *inuita, o regina, tuo de uertice cessi* (the lock addressing Berenice).

17 Damonis. The name does not occur in pre-Virgilian pastoral poetry (though Damon was a renowned music theorist, mentioned in Plato's *Republic*; cf. R. W. Wallace, *Reconstructing Damon*, Oxford 2015; at any rate, Damon is a fairly common name). Along with Alphesiboeus, he is the protagonist of the eighth eclogue (8.1n.). Here, perhaps, the assonance with *Damoetas* (and with *Daphnidis* at 3.12) is intentional. Menalcas' *pessime* replies in both invective and word-shape to Damoetas' *peruerse* (3.13).

18 excipere. A military term, specifically meaning 'to lie in ambush' vel sim. (Caes. *civ.* 3.38.4; cf. also *Aen.* 3.332); also used in hunting: Caes. *Gall.* 6.28.4; Hor. *carm.* 3.12.12; Prop. 2.19.24; Sen. *dial.* 3[de ira 1].11.2. **Lycisca.** Semantically obvious as the name of a female sheepdog: 'Little she-wolf' (perhaps of mixed race, i.e. a wolfdog, on which see Aristot. *hist. anim.* 8.28.607a1–3; Plin. *nat.* 8.148; Isid. *orig.* 12.2.28; cf. *Gloss.* V, p. 370.2 Goetz); Messalina chooses *Lycisca* as her *nom de guerre* in Iuv. 6.123, though clearly for different reasons (*lupa* = *meretrix*). The same is true of the 'yappy' dog *Hylax* at 8.107. For a Hellenizing echo cf. Ov. *met.* 3.220 *uelox…Lycisce*; here, however, it is the 'little she-wolf' herself who protects the billy goat, threatened by others.

19 ille. Referring to the *caper* mentioned at 3.17, which Damoetas has perhaps lured out of the herd with some trick: a malicious deed, which could nevertheless be made to appear accidental; cf. 7.7 *uir gregis ipse caper deerrauerat.* The animal is falling into a trap, as it leaves the rest of the herd and rushes out of the fold (or something similar: this is the sense of *se proripere*). Hence the need to exhort Tityrus (3.20) to gather the herd (into the fold?), which would otherwise run the risk of being scattered around (see n. ad loc.). The pronoun, referring to the animal (as in 1.13 *hanc*, referring to 1.12 *capellas*), points to a real situation, which is now merely evoked in a somewhat reticent manner (the scene, in other words, is well known to both Damoetas and Menalcas). If *ille* referred to a person, it would necessarily denote the thief (Damoetas), with a realistic depiction of the action in its unfolding ('where is he running away, that one?'). Yet this would contradict the fact that Damoetas is actually hiding behind the sedge thickets, lurking in ambush (18 *excipere insidiis*). Menalcas' loud cry (*clamarem*) is needed to stop the *caper* and alert Tityrus, thereby ruining Damoetas' plan; otherwise, Menalcas would effectively be Damoetas' accomplice, since he has seen everything (17 *ego te uidi*, perhaps upon hearing Lycisca's barking).

20 Tityre, coge pecus. Tityrus' name is here used of an unspecified performer of pastoral tasks: cf. 1.1n. In contrast to the Tityrus of *E.* 1 (a wholly Virgilian creation), here the Theocritean requirements are met: Tityrus has the role of a mere 'underling', as in Theocr. *id.* 3.3 Τίτυρε...βόσκε τὰς αἶγας. **post carecta latebas.** In its proper sense, *carectum* is a group of *carices*, i.e. marsh reeds (*G.* 3.231 *carice...acuta*) which, being thick and resistant, can be used to build hurdles (*crates pastorales* in Colum. 12.15.1). Ideal as a hideout: cf. Calp. *ecl.* 3.94 *acuta carice tectus*; *Priap.* 86.2 Buech. The detail points to a marshy, riverside landscape (near Mantua?), familiar to the reader from *E.* 1.48.

21–4. Damoetas here admits to his deed, but tries to justify it: according to him, he deserved the billy goat as a prize for winning an agon, whereas the defeated Damon, for some reason, did not abide by the agreement (24 *ipse fatebatur*); cf. 3.32–4n. Quite a difference from the Damoetas of *id.* 6, who is satisfied with the result of his contest with Daphnis (they did not even need a referee). Thus, V. tangentially introduces the theme of the agon, and that of the stakes in particular, on which the following exchange will focus (25–54). V. makes it clear that Damoetas likes using valuable animals as wagers (note the *uitula* [29–31], which will be a source of embarrassment for Menalcas: cf. 32–4). Yet he did not manage to obtain the goat he deserved in his agon with Damon, who had perhaps rashly agreed to wager it. For the instrumental gerund *cantando* (first occurrence in the *E.* here, at 3.21), see 3.25n.

22 mea...fistula. Theocritus' Damoetas is in the background, with his 'agonistic' skills: but the dying Damoetas of *E.* 2 has 'already' been praised for his ability as a *fistula*-player (2.37n.). All this is doubted by Menalcas (3.25).

23 si nescis. An ironic phrase, colloquial in tone: for parallels cf. Prop. 2.15.12; Ov. *amor.* 3.8.13; *fast.* 5.229; Iuv. 5.159. **et mihi Damon.** This type of hexameter ending, featuring a monosyllable followed by two disyllables, is somewhat more frequent in the two 'Theocritean' eclogues, i.e. the present one (cf. also 3.40; 52;

160 ECLOGUE 3

88; 94) and *E.* 2 (cf. 2.26; 37; 42; 53; 60). It occurs twice again in Menalcas' lines (*E.* 5.52; 80), where Menalcas himself is named as the 'author' of both poems (5.86–7). The clausula never occurs in *E.* 1, and appears more rarely in *E.* 4, 6, 7, 8; only one occurrence in *E.* 10 (l. 11). It is, however, featured conspicuously in the 'nostalgic' *E.* 9, centred around the characters' wait for Menalcas (9.17; 33; 51, with elision; 53; 60).

24 reddere posse negabat. Note the colloquial rapidity of the simple inf. (the subject, i.e. *se*, is omitted): such a construction is facilitated by the verb *negare*, often assimilated to a verb of saying. Cf. *G.* 2.234–5; *Aen.* 3.201; *Enc. Virg.* III, p. 682b, s.v. *nego* (G. Pascucci). Note the expressive repetition of the verb (cf. 3.21 *non redderet ille*), which forcefully concludes the argument. The verb *reddere* implies the notion of 'reestablishing' a certain equilibrium, e.g. by granting the prize that has been agreed upon (which seems to be the case here). Note also, in the context of *praemia*, *Aen.* 9.254–5 *tum cetera reddet Aeneas*; cf. Phaedr. 3 *epil.* 8 *praemium ut reddas peto quod es pollicitus*; *OLD²*, p. 1750, s.v. 9.

25–7. Cf. Theocr. *id.* 5.5–7: '(Com.) Which pipes? When did you ever, Sibyrtas' slave, / possess a pipe? Are you no longer content to make music with Corydon, / whistling on your straw flute?'

25 Cantando. An emphatic echo of 3.21, with the same rhythm (ictus on the first and the last syllables), expressing wonder and sarcasm; this instrumental gerund, for 'singing', is quite characteristic of the bucolic world: again in *E.* 6.71; 8.71; 9.52.

25–6 aut umquam fistula cera / iuncta fuit? Another polemic twist, this time echoing 3.22. While Damoetas appeared as a master of the *fistula* in *E.* 2, where the instrument was analytically described (2.36–7: it seems, rather, that he himself is the manufacturer), the Damoetas of *E.* 3 is deprived of any competence in the matter: 'when did you ever join together pipes with wax?'. Instead of the sweet onomatopoeia suggested by the dactyl-shaped *fistula*, Menalcas attributes to his rival the harsh sounds of a screeching *stipula*, 'stubble stalk' (a degraded version of the humble *cicuta* at 2.36n., or the *tenui…auena* at 1.2; the term, used in its proper botanical sense of plant-stalk, occurs frequently in the *G.*, but only here in the *E.*). In *id.* 8.18–19, Menalcas claimed to have assembled a shepherd's pipe himself, using white wax 'the same top and bottom'. Although the manuscript tradition supports *uincta* (**PR**), the preferable reading is *iuncta*, transmitted indirectly (and probably in Servius' lemma): wax makes it possible to 'join' pipes together, but not to 'bind' them; cf. 2.32 *calamos cera coniungere pluris*; Ov. *met.* 1.711–12 *disparibus calamis compagine cerae / inter se iunctis*; Calp. *ecl.* 4.19–20 *odorae uincula cerae / iungere* (possibly presupposing both variant readings) *CLE* 2.3 Buech. *iunctast tibi fistula cera* (a genuine quotation: the epigraphic context points to the late second century CE; Hoogma 1959, esp. p. 166); *ThlL* VII.2.661.29–30, s.v. *iungo*. Note the conversational liveliness of Menalcas' second question, introduced by *aut*: cf. Plaut. *Mil.* 425; see also *Aen.* 12.882.

ECLOGUE 3   161

26 in triuiis. The locus of social encounters, even with deities (e.g. *Triuia* is an epithet of Diana); also lending itself to forms of popular or naive poetry. The context is generally urban or suburban (e.g. Hor. *ars* 244–7). Hence the negative sense, as in Iuv. 7.55 *carmen triuiale*; cf. Calp. *ecl.* 1.28. The 'uncouth' (*indocte*), yet lively, improvization of the shepherds/farmers (ἄγροικοι) was deemed to lie at the root of pastoral song in the erudite tradition: *schol.* Theocr., pp. 2–3 Wend. (cf. the *carmina…rustica* in Prob. *praef. E.* p. 324.17 [III.2 Th.-H.] = p. 14.7 Wend.; cf. Diom. *gramm.* I, p. 487.5–8 K. = p. 17.10–13 Wend.; Serv. *praef. E.* p. 1.6 [III.1 Th.-H.] = p. 20.26 Wend.).

27. In this line, entirely built around harsh sounds (but cf. 3.6 *solebas*), phonetic artistry leads V. to employ the archaic verb *disperdere*, in the sense of 'spoiling, shredding' (the *carmen*). The Verona fragment (V) has the order *stridenti stipula miserum*, which makes the sound symbolism more obvious, but not more effective; cf. Calp. *ecl.* 3.60 *acerbae stridor auenae*.

28–31. This final provocation, concerning pastoral poetry, leads Damoetas to formulate his challenge. The lively, colloquial tone is apparent even in the somewhat free word-order. Note that the skirmish is also a phonetic one, since *uitulam* (29) counters *fistula* (25) and *stipula* (27). After wagering a billy goat in his contest with Damon, Damoetas now promptly offers to stake a much more valuable animal: a heifer (3.29–30n.).

28 inter nos. The dual notion of confrontation (*experiamur*) is underscored. Thus, the phrase does not hint, as Servius thought, at the absence of a referee: Menalcas will look for one, and immediately find him, at 3.50. **uicissim.** The adverb generically expresses the idea of the agon, in which two poets alternate verses (sometimes singing one piece each, as in *id.* 6 and 9; cf. *E.* 5.50). The specific form of the agon, a rapid cut-and-thrust debate, will be determined by Palaemon, the referee (3.59n.).

29 experiamur. A strong break after the trochee in the second foot (cf. *G.* 1.501), expressing agitation and emphasis.

29–30. The prize offered by Damoetas is the most valuable bucolic animal—in this case, a female specimen. The heifer's quality is exceptionally high, since she has given birth to twins (a rare occurrence, according to Aristot. *hist. anim.* 6.21.575a30; Plin. *nat.* 8.177; cf. Theocr. *id.* 1.25) and can be milked twice a day. The choice of a prize is featured in both *id.* 5.21–4 and *id.* 8.11–24, as well as in the model *id.* 1, in which the gift for Thyrsis is constituted of a she-goat and a cup (here, however, *pocula* and heifer are alternatives): 'if you will sing / as you sang in the contest with Chromis from Libya, / I shall give you a she-goat, mother of two twins, to be milked three times a day: / she has two kids, but she can fill two pails with milk. / And a deep cup, etc.' (*id.* 1.23–7; for the goat giving birth to twins cf. *E.* 1.14). The following lines (*id.* 1.27–60), describing the cup, will be echoed here in V.'s description of the *pocula* (3.36–48). The notion of 'twofoldness', crucial to this contest between two shepherds, is transferred from the *uitula* to Menalcas' father

162 ECLOGUE 3

and *nouerca* (3.34), then to the pairs of *pocula*. In the context of the dedication to Pollio, the *uitula*—and, even more so, the *taurus*—may hint at 'high' literary values (see 3.85n.; 86n.).

29 hanc uitulam. The term *uitula* emphasizes the young age and 'freshness' of the animal, which is nevertheless fully grown, with two calves and a generous amount of milk (cf. 3.30); bovine ages are classified in Varr. *rust.* 2.5.6. In the *E.*, V. also uses the term *iuuenca* (cf. 8.2), and the masculine form *uitulus* occurs rather frequently (2.66; 6.46; 7.11; 44; 8.85). While it is no surprise in *id.* 8.14 (where the speaker is the cowherd Daphnis), the appearance of a cow strikes the reader in this case: so far, only sheep have been associated with Damoetas (3.3 and 5; cf. the billy goat at 3.17 and 22), but now he is found to possess at least a young cow. The reader, however, may still be in doubt as to whether even the *uitula* belongs to Aegon, who is said to own *pecus* at 3.2 (in which case, Damoetas would be wagering something that does not belong to him, thereby behaving much less cautiously than Menalcas [cf. 32–4]). Damoetas is, at any rate, literally a *boukolos*: the term *uitula* occurs twice in his lines (3.77; 85n.), and he remarks the value of this 'exceptional' *uitula* once more at 3.48. The deictic *hanc* points at the physical presence of the wager that Damoetas proposes to Menalcas (note also the very concrete verb *depono*: 3.31n.). In Theocritus' singing contests, the prize is generally present and put on display, so that it can readily be retrieved by the winner: cf. Theocr. *id.* 5.23–4 ἠνίδε κεῖται ὦριφος; 24 τὸν εὔβοτον ἀμνὸν ἔρειδε; 30 ἴδ' ὁ τράγος οὗτος. In *id.* 8, echoed here by V. (cf. 3.32–4), the two σύριγγες used as a wager (*id.* 8.18–24) are clearly at hand (note *id.* 8.84 λάσδεο τᾶς σύριγγος). In Homer's narrative of the funeral games for Patroclus, the wagers are displayed in plain sight: Hom. *Il.* 23.257–70; 653–6 (666); 700–5; 740–51; 798–800; 883–4. The same is true of V.'s funeral games for Anchises: *munera principio ante oculos circoque locantur / in medio* (*Aen.* 5.109–10). Similarly, in *id.* 6.43–4 (not an agon but a friendly conversation), the final exchange of gifts takes place immediately, 'on stage'. The same need not be true of Menalcas' cups, at least if l. 43 is genuine: this is a good reason to suspect an interpolation (cf. 3.43n.). The presence on scene of the wager, clearly visible to the contestants (48 *si ad uitulam spectas*), makes it unnecessary to mention the *uitula* to Palaemon, who arrives later. Palaemon, in fact, has no doubt as to which prize must be awarded to the winner, and he himself mentions the *uitula* at 3.109n.

30 uenit ad mulctram. The phrase may hint at miraculous hyperdocility, which is made explicit in Hor. *epod.* 16.49 *illic iniussae ueniunt ad mulctra capellae.* A *mulctra* (fem.) is a milking pail, as in G. 3.309 (cf. G. 3.177 *implebunt mulctraria uaccae*).

31 depono. Tone and vocabulary are typical of Theocritean contests: cf. *id.* 5.21 'to wager a kid' (ἔριφον θέμεν), as well as *id.* 8.11 (note the repeated καταθεῖναι at 8.12), and 8.13. It now becomes clear that the *uitula* is Damoetas' personal property, not Aegon's: Menalcas' position is different, as will become clear from

ECLOGUE 3   163

3.32–4. The verb, immediately re-used by Menalcas at 3.32, does not necessarily describe the physical action of 'putting down' the wager, but it certainly has concrete connotations (cf. e.g. *E.* 9.62 *hic haedos depone*) which are consistent with the physical presence of the animal. The *uitula* is 'placed' in the middle, between the two contestants, because it is the prize for the winner: cf. 3.29n. and 36 *ponam* (n.). **tu dic.** The personal pronoun here accompanies the imperative and has a clear illocutionary force, i.e. it aims to compel the interlocutor to act and declare (*dic*) his wager, which he will then 'put down' himself. Note Damoetas' emphasis on his first-person action (3.29–31 *ego…depono*, with a significant hyperbaton); for similar cases of personal pronoun + imperative in the *E.*, cf. 4.8–10; 5.15; 19; 88; 7.35–6 (note also *G.* 1.344; 4.448; *Aen.* 3.388; 6.851; 7.41; 11.506); for the use of *dic* see 3.1n. **mecum quo pignore certes.** This is the colloquial language of betting (*pignus* = 'stake'), as Plautus confirms: cf. e.g. *Cas.* 75; also *Pers.* 188; *Bacch.* 1056 (each participant would customarily offer something as a prize: hence the comitative *mecum*). The verb *certare* is the most technical way of conveying the pastoral notion of agon / contest (not used in a specific sense at 2.57); cf. *E.* 4.58; 5.8; 9; 15; 7.16 (*certamen*); 8.3.

32–4. Menalcas expresses the same thought in *id.* 8.15–16: 'I shall not wager a lamb, since my father is strict, / and so is my mother: every night they count all the animals' (playing fairly, V.'s Menalcas wants to avoid Damon's predicament in case of defeat: 3.21–4n.). Here, however, the mother is replaced by a proverbial villain, the stepmother (*nouerca*): cf. *G.* 2.128; Hor. *epod.* 5.9; an idiomatic, and significant, expression in Plaut. *Pseud.* 314; P. A. Watson, *Ancient Stepmothers. Myth, Misogyny and Reality*, Leiden 1991; though obviously mothers can themselves be strict and harsh: Hor. *epist.* 1.1.22 *dura…custodia matrum.* The 'twofold' quality of Damoetas' *uitula* (*bis uenit…binos fetus*) is paralleled by the obsessive strictness of the two figures (*bisque die…ambo…alter et*): ideas and images keep mirroring one another in the two rivals' words, as is typical of an agon (e.g. Catull. 62). Menalcas' youth, which can be inferred from these lines, is crucial to understanding his aggressive characterization: he started the hostilities at 3.3–6.

34 numerant. Cf. 6.85 *numerum referre* (but here the counting happens twice a day). **alter.** One of the two (as opposed to *ambo*), not specifying which one; it may, where appropriate, refer to the stepmother.

36–43. Another precise reworking (in sequential order) of *id.* 1: 'And then I made a deep cup, bedewed with sweet wax, / twin-handled, newly made, still having the smack of chiselling upon it. / Its rim is hanged about with ivy, / curling ivy speckled with golden-tufts: around it / twines a spiral, rejoicing in the saffron fruit… / All around the cup the soft acanthus spreads, / a marvel to the herdsmen: a breathtaking wonder' (*id.* 1.27–31; 1.55–6; cf. *E.* 3.29–30n.). Theocritus' single cup is multiplied into the four cups of Menalcas and Damoetas (3.44–8n.), which must be taken to be two pairs of identical cups (see 3.40n. and 3.46n.): in fact,

164   ECLOGUE 3

pocula were generally used in pairs, as e.g. at Hor. *sat.* 1.6.117; note also Cic. *Verr.* 2.2.47 *scyphorum paria complura*; 'cups' with relief decorations will reappear at *Aen.* 9.263-4 *aspera signis / pocula*. The kind of object to which V. refers here is probably a rustic, wooden version of well-known decorated metal cups, often appearing in pairs, with an image or *emblema* in the middle, such as those described in D. E. Strong, *Greek and Roman Gold and Silver Plate*, London 1966, p. 151; cf. also *The Search for Alexander*, New York 1980, col. pl. 33; L. Pirzio Biroli Stefanelli, *Le argenterie nel mondo romano*, in L. Pirzio Biroli Stefanelli (ed.), *L'argento dei Romani. Vasellame da tavola e d'apparato*, Rome 1991, pp. 37-110, esp. pp. 66-7 (featuring pictures of a Boscoreale cup from the Louvre [cat. n. 37]). Despite the 'humble' stylistic level of the *E.*, V. draws attention to objects of art and craftsmanship that were particularly dear to members of the Roman aristocracy, including Asinius Pollio (above, p. 49): i.e. the most likely readers of V. The 'aristocratic', silver version of this object appears twice in the *Aeneid*: see 5.265-6 *tertia dona facit... / cymbia...argento perfecta atque aspera signis*; 9.263-4 *bina dabo argento perfecta atque aspera signis / pocula*. At the same time, Alcimedon's cups tangibly symbolize V.'s poetic values through the comparison with the Theocritean model, while perhaps foreshadowing the future didactic-georgic poem (3.47n.): Theocritus' ecphrasis, too, was replete with literary allusions and references, particularly to the Homeric archetype of Achilles' shield (Hom. *Il.* 18.478-607) and the pseudo-Hesiodic *Aspis* (cf. [Hes.] *Asp.* 139-324). An ecphrasis of precious objects (Europa's golden basket, depicting Io's story) is similarly featured in Moschus, *Eur.* 37-62. Note also shorter ecphrastic passages, such as the epigram of Antipater of Thessalonica, describing a pair of cups which, when combined, form an astronomical map (*Anth. Pal.* 9.541 = *GPh* 307-12 G.-P.; see 3.40n.); for further reading cf. esp. F. Manakidou, *Beschreibung von Kunstwerken in der hellenistischen Dichtung*, Stuttgart 1993. However, despite Menalcas' descriptive effort, Damoetas does not fail to highlight the greater (bucolic) value of the heifer (48).

36 pocula ponam. The simple verb has a strong phonetic effect in line-ending position (alliteration and assonance). It is no wonder that V. opts for the *simplex* form after two occurrences of the compound *deponere*: the first in Damoetas' challenge (3.31n.), and the second in Menalcas' speech (3.32). Similarly, in the pseudo-Theocritean *id.* 8, two occurrences of the compound verb καταθεῖναι (*id.* 8.11 and 8.12) are followed by the simple form (which occurs four times: *id.* 8.13-17). Based on the Theocritean model, one would expect the cups to be physically present (like the *uitula* at 3.29), so that they can be placed 'in the middle': cf. Theocr. *id.* 5.21 ἔριφον θέμεν (see *E.* 3.31n.). Yet 3.43 seems to indicate otherwise, i.e. that Menalcas is describing the cups *in absentia*. This is one of the numerous arguments against the authenticity of 3.43: see n. ad loc.

37 fagina. Beech wood, a modest material for an artwork, is well suited to the simple purposes of country life (Tib. 1.10.8 *faginus...scyphus*; Ov. *met.* 8.669-70

ECLOGUE 3   165

fabricataque fago / pocula; cf. Plin. *nat.* 16.35). For a similar wooden object (though made of willow wood), cf. Priapus' scythe at *G.* 4.110 *cum falce saligna.* Here, with an echo of the cup in *id.* 1, V. draws attention to beech wood as a raw material used in craftsmanship. Further emphasis is added by the relatively rare adjective *fagina*: cf. Calp. *ecl.* 2.59 (on which see 7.36n.); cf. also *ThlL* VI.1.172.47–67; *fagineus* is found in Cat. *agr.* 12.5. Beech trees, after all, are representative of the *E.* (see 1.1n.). **caelatum…opus**. The verb generally refers to engraving or embossing work, mostly on metal, as it does in all Virgilian occurrences (cf. *Aen.* 1.640; 5.307; 7.792; 8.701; 10.499; 527; cf. Quint. *inst.* 2.21.8–9). Here it probably emphasizes the effort, and hence the value, attached to the process of working the object: cf. *ThlL* III.77.58–81; Val. Fl. 5.6–7 *caelata…uelamina.* The whole description recalls similar elaborate artefacts found in epic: e.g. Hom. *Od.* 4.615–19. **diuini…Alcimedontis**. The name may be etymologized as 'strong-minded', and as such it is appropriate for an artisan capable of crafting non-obvious (and deeply Virgilian) imagery. Alcimedon was the name of an Arcadian hero whose daughter was seduced by Heracles (Pausan. 8.12.2–3; also of a Myrmidon chief in Hom. *Il.* 16.197): thus, the name might allude to the 'Arcadian' atmosphere that will become explicit in the *E.*'s second agon (*E.* 7.4 *Arcades ambo*). If the reading αἰολικὸν θέαμα is accepted, Theocritus' cup at *id.* 1.56 is an 'Aeolian marvel' (but most editors print αἰπολικόν, 'to the shepherds'). For the formulation *diuini opus Alcimedontis*, in keeping with the epic style of the passage, cf. [Hes.] *scut.* 244 ἔργα κλυτοῦ Ἡφαίστοιο. See also Theocritus himself, *id.* 5.104–5: 'I have a pail of cypress-wood, and a mixing bowl, / the work of Praxiteles [ἔργον Πραξιτέλευς]: I save them for my girl' (V. seems to have this passage in mind, along with *id.* 1: cf. 3.43n.). Note the hexameter clausula featuring a Hellenizing proper noun of five syllables (cf. 2.24n.). In the *E.*, the adj. *diuinus* is otherwise used of the poet-singer: 5.45n.; 10.17 (6.67 *diuino carmine pastor*); cf. *Aen.* 2.15 *diuina Palladis arte*; Sen. *epist.* 113.16.

38–9. While Theocritus' cup featured two decorative motifs, ivy (on the rims) and acanthus (on the sides), Menalcas' cups only have ivy, placed on the top and intertwined with vines (3.38 *superaddita uitis*). The two plants, joined together, have Dionysian connotations (ivy: 4.19n.; cf. also *Hymn. Hom.* 7[*Bacch.*].38–41); acanthus will be found on the cups belonging to Damoetas: see 3.45n. At 3.38, note the framing position of adj. and noun, suggesting the stretching out of the decoration (*lenta…uitis*); cf. again 3.45n.

38 torno facili. For lathe-working of wooden materials cf. *G.* 2.449 *torno rasile buxum*; see also Plin. *nat.* 16.205. The preferable reading is *facili*, attested by the indirect tradition (esp. Servius, here and *ad Aen.* 2.392; cf. also the *schol. Veron.*), whereas most manuscripts have *facilis*, referring to *uitis*. The latter would thus have two epithets of similar meaning not coordinated by a conjunction, while *torno* would not have any epithet at all (Donatus' text, to which Servius reluctantly

166   ECLOGUE 3

adjusts). Used in reference to *torno*, the adjective *facili* implies rapidity and agility of movement, necessary to the handling of a 'sinuous' (*lenta*) vine: cf. *Aen.* 6.146; 8.310; Tib. 1.1.8; Ov. *fast.* 3.536.

39 hedera…pallente. Here the colour is pale green: for the so-called 'white' ivy, cf. 7.38n. The epithet is all the more appropriate for this typically Dionysian plant, believed to be useful in countering drunkenness, due to its 'cold' nature: Plut. *quaest. conu.* 3.1.647a. This balanced line, featuring a verb in the middle, verbally depicts the interlocking of the two plants: it is as if the vine 'clothed' the cups in pale-green ivy clusters (*corymbus* means 'ivy cluster': cf. Prop. 4.7.79). Given this syntactical complexity, it is no wonder that the phrase (*diffusos hedera*)…*pallente corymbos* is reworked and simplified in later poetry: cf. *pallente corymbo* at *Culex* 405 (note also *Culex* 144 *pallore corymbos*; Calp. *ecl.* 7.9).

40–2. Three lively vignettes of everyday life were depicted on the cup of *id.* 1, in keeping with the mimetic-realistic nature of Theocritean poetry: a contest between two men in love with the same, gorgeous woman; an old yet vigorous fisherman, casting a net into the sea from a rock; and a wonderful vineyard, guarded by a boy sitting on a low wall and too absorbed in weaving a cricket cage to notice the two foxes sneaking up on him (*id.* 1.32–54). V.'s two 'portraits' (*signa*) allude to scientific-didactic themes, which make up a considerable part of his poetic interests. Even before the *G.*, the reader will encounter them again in Silenus' song (*E.* 6, esp. 31–40). The Dionysian connection (38–9) will be all the more apparent in the case of Silenus, the god's companion, who has just recovered from drunkenness (*E.* 6.15): Dionysus himself, however, enjoyed a connection with astronomy, as is clear from the jewelled crown that Ariadne offered to the god and that was subsequently transformed into a constellation (*G.* 1.222; Hor. *carm.* 2.19.13–14; Ov. *fast.* 3.459–60; cf. Eratosth. *catast.* pp. 66–9 Rob.). Such objects of craftsmanship, albeit in a 'humble', pastoral form, were probably attuned to the artistic taste of V.'s patron, Asinius Pollio (see above, p. 149). Pollio's library apparently housed portraits of several authors of scientific and literary writings, according to Plin. *nat.* 35.9–10 (cf. 7.115, where Pliny asserts that M. Terentius Varro was the only living intellectual whose *imago* was included into Pollio's collection; Varro himself was the author of an ambitious anthology entitled *Imagines* or *Hebdomades*). Note also that Pollio apparently had a penchant for Catullus' poetry: the astronomer Conon is mentioned in Catull. 66 (see further 3.40n.).

40 in medio. The detail has a programmatic significance, almost more at a conceptual level than in visual terms. While Theocritus' ecphrasis has its own figurative potential (albeit complex), here it is difficult to picture the exact shape of the two objects. The two figures are perhaps joined together and placed one in front of the other, on the outer rim, or at the bottom, of each cup (cf. also 3.46n.). The 'middle' is crucial to ecphrastic language, at least since [Hes.] *scut.* 144 (cf. Apoll. Rhod. 1.727), whereas for Theocritus it is a place of honour: *id.* 17.3–4 'among men, let Ptolemy be named first and last and in the middle [καὶ πύματος καὶ

$\mu\acute{\epsilon}\sigma\sigma\sigma s$]'. The book's centre will be occupied by Silenus' ambitious song (*E.* 6; Pollio will appear at the centre of the contest: 3.84–9n.). Cf. *G.* 3.16 *in medio mihi Caesar erit templumque tenebit* (in the very text of the *Georgics*, Caesar Octavian takes centre stage, since the proem of *G.* 3 is itself in the middle of the poem); *Aen.* 8.675 *in medio classis aeratas, Actia bella* (Actium and Augustus in the middle of Aeneas' shield; Augustus and Marcellus are at the centre of the *Aeneid*, appearing at the end of Book 6). **Conon.** A third-century Alexandrian astronomer from Samos, who was active in Sicily and southern Italy for a long time (and interacted with Archimedes). He is especially known for dedicating a new constellation to Berenice II: the *Coma Berenices*. The episode inspired Callimachus' well-known elegy, translated in Catull. 66 (where Conon himself is mentioned at l. 7); cf. 3.41n. This homage to Catullus in *E.* 3 must have interested Pollio, who was certainly familiar with Catull. 66. **et—quis fuit alter?** Among several names suggested by ancient and modern interpreters (the *schol. Veron.* ad loc. lists seven possible answers: Eudoxus, Aratus, Archimedes, Hipparchus, Euctemon, Hesiod, Euclid), one very likely option is Eudoxus, the great astronomer from Cnidus, who lived in the first half of the fourth century and played a crucial role in mapping the celestial sphere (3.41n.). His work was used by Aratus as the main source for his *Phaenomena*, reworked for a Roman audience by the young Cicero and reinterpreted by V. himself in *G.* 1: consequently the other most likely option is precisely Aratus. As an *auctor*, Aratus was of crucial importance to Roman intellectuals, and his fame certainly contributed to the renown of Eudoxus' scientific work, which was the astronomical basis of Aratus' poem (note the irony, for the 'Eudoxus' solution, in forgetting a name that can be etymologized as 'well known': cf. Achill. in Arati *phaen.* comm. frag. p. 77.29–30 Maass = Eudox. fr. 6, p. 40.22–3 Lass.; a similar irony in Lucr. 1.638–9 *Heraclitus... / clarus ob obscuram linguam*; in the second line of the *Phaenomena*, also Aratus himself seems to play on the 'sayability' of his own name using $\ddot{\alpha}\rho\rho\eta\tau\sigma\nu$ 'unspoken' or 'unspeakable'). An allusion to Aratus, perhaps a revealing one, seems to be contained in 3.42n. and Aratus' incipit is quoted at 3.60–1. The difficult choice between Eudoxus and Aratus is perhaps itself part of the game: the 'Aratus' solution was favoured by several ancient readers (cf. *schol. Veron.* ad loc.: *plerique Aratum*), even though Aratus' main achievement was at best considered to lie in adding poetic ornamentation to astronomical content, as noted by Cicero, *rep.* 1.22 (cf. *de orat.* 1.69); *E.* 3.41, by contrast, immediately highlights the astronomer's 'technical' competence (*radio*; cf. *Aen.* 6.849–50 [see 3.41n.]). Aratus, on the other hand, is mentioned e.g. in Petron. 40.1 as an astronomical-astrological authority, alongside Hipparchus; on his importance in the history of ancient astronomy, see E. Gee, *Aratus and the Astronomical Tradition*, New York 2013. In an epigram by Antipater of Thessalonica (cf. 3.36–43n.), Aratus himself is mentioned as an eminent scientific authority in the field of astronomy, to the point that the owner of two astronomical cups, L. Calpurnius Piso Frugi (consul in 15 BCE), can even do without

168   ECLOGUE 3

studying the *Phaenomena* since he has the sky map obtained by combining the two cups: ἀλλὰ σύ μηκέτ᾽ Ἄρητον ἐπίβλεπε κτλ. (*Anth. Pal.* 9.541.5 = *GPh* 311 G.-P.; cf. also the epigram by one of the Ptolemies, *SH* 712.4, p. 345 Ll.-J.-P.). Theocritus' *id.* 6, one of the most important models of *E.* 3, was perhaps dedicated to Aratus (cf. *id.* 6.2; cf. also *id.* 7.98–102; the identification with the poet from Soli is, however, generally doubted today, *pace* the ancient scholiasts). Menalcas' mild weakness in astronomical matters is maliciously underscored by his rival's final riddle (3.104–5). Menalcas' amnesia, and the way in which he expresses it (*quis fuit…?*), seem to presuppose that the simple rustic artefact does not include the name of the person depicted on it, unlike what was normally the case in the *imagines* tradition, or even in objects of (both rich and poor) craftsmanship. At any rate, epigraphic skills may be beyond Alcimedon's area of competence— particularly in the case of a wooden artefact (or does Menalcas simply need to look more closely?). Here, however, V.'s playful trick might deliberately confuse even a learned reader: is it Eudoxus or Aratus?

41 descripsit radio totum qui gentibus orbem. The model, a very fitting one, is in the *Lock of Berenice*: Callim. *aet.* fr. 110.1 Pf. = 213.1 Mass. = 110.1 Hard. πάντα τὸν ἐν γραμμαῖσιν ἰδὼν ὅρον 'Having seen the whole horizon in drawings', reworked in Catull. 66.1 *omnia qui magni dispexit lumina mundi*. Conon is explicitly mentioned in both Callimachus and Catullus (Catull. 66.7 *idem me ille Conon…uidit*; cf. Callim. *aet.* fr. 110.7 Pf. = 213.7 Mass. = 110.7 Hard. με Κόνων ἔβλεψεν): he is mentioned here at 3.40, which is why he cannot be the astronomer alluded to in 3.41. The rod is used, in particular, to draw geometric and astronomical figures: *Aen.* 6.849–50 *caelique meatus / describent radio et surgentia sidera dicent*. For the astronomer who represents the entire cosmos in a model, the sphere of Pythagoras in Hermesian. fr. 7.87–8 Pow. = 3.87–8 Light. is to be mentioned.

42 tempora quae messor, quae curuus arator. Cf. Arat. *phaen.* 7–9 '[Zeus] tells us when the soil is most fit / for oxen and hoes, he says when the right season has come / for planting trees and sowing any kind of seed', echoed in *G.* 1.253 (for the notion cf. Hes. *op.* 383–4). Aratus' proem, with its well-known incipit, will be quoted in 3.60–1. The name *Aratus* might even be hinted at by the noun *arator*: much like the 'stooping ploughman', the author of the *Phaenomena* must know how to interpret celestial signs, following the teachings of the great astronomical masters (Ἀρήτου σύντονος ἀγρυπνίη, i.e. 'Aratus' intense insomnia', immortalized by Callimachus, *epigr.* 27.4 Pf.; cf. Cinna, fr. 11.1–2 Bläns. = Court. *Arateis multum inuigilata lucernis / carmina*). For the ploughman's effort cf. also *E.* 4.41 *robustus…arator*, as well as Plin. *nat.* 18.179 *arator nisi incuruus praeuaricatur*. Echo and variation in Germanicus' *Arati Phaenomena: quid scitus uitet arator* (13).

43 necdum…labra admoui, sed condita seruo. The goatherd of *id.* 1 similarly concludes his description: τί πω ποτὶ χεῖλος ἐμὸν θίγεν, ἀλλ᾽ ἔτι κεῖται / ἄχραντον 'never yet has my lip touched it, but it still / lies unsullied' (*id.* 1.59–60); but cf. also *id.* 5.105 τᾷ παιδὶ δὲ ταῦτα φυλάσσω (cf. 3.37n.). The line is repeated

ECLOGUE 3   169

verbatim at 3.47: a one-of-a-kind case in the *E.*, where there are no other repeated lines (with the obvious exception of the refrains in *E.* 8). V. sometimes re-uses his own lines without any apparent reason, as e.g. at *G.* 4.222, which repeats *E.* 4.51 verbatim. If the repetition occurs within the same work, however, it can seem suspicious: note, for instance, *G.* 2.129 = 3.283 (where the first occurrence is generally considered an interpolation) and *Aen.* 1.73 = 4.126 (where the second occurrence is probably spurious). If the two identical lines are very close to each other, V. might be aiming at some expressive effect, as in the finale of *G.* 4, where *G.* 4.538 is repeated verbatim at 4.550 (note also the quasi-repetition of 4.540 at 4.551) to signal the ritual's completion. In Greek pastoral poetry, which features a fair amount of redundancy (in the style of folk song), verbatim repetitions, with some variation, often aim at realism, mimicking a competitive dialogue. Note especially the lively conversation between Menalcas and Daphnis at *id.* 8.11–12: χρῄσδεις ὦν ἐσιδεῖν; χρῄσδεις καταθεῖναι ἄεθλον; / χρῄσδω τοῦτ' ἐσιδεῖν, χρῄσδω καταθεῖναι ἄεθλον (a direct back-and-forth between the two characters). In the case of *E.* 3.43 and 3.47, the verbatim repetition does not add any particular value to the structure of the dialogue and does not seem to be justified, if not by Damoetas' contrarian attitude (which would be rather odd and ineffective at a distance of four lines). Thus, it seems reasonable to suspect interpolation in one of the two lines, more likely 3.43 (perhaps due to incorrect placement): without it, Menalcas' speech would end on a hanging question, which would make Damoetas' negative reply much more effective. There is also an important argument based on the agon's dynamics. In fact, the idea of 'hidden' cups, 'put away' (*condita seruo*) in some kind of secret place, in a hut or the like, does not suit a wager 'proposed' by Menalcas as a prize for the winner, corresponding to the *uitula* which is obviously 'on stage' (cf. 3.29 *hanc uitulam* [n.]; note also 31 *depono* [n.] and 36 *pocula ponam* [n.]; 109n.). In Theocr. *id.* 1.59–60, the cup is 'unsullied' (κεῖται ἄχραντον) because it is a gift that the goatherd promises to Thyrsis: here, the context of the agon is very different. In order to 'wager' them (note 36 *ponam*), Menalcas must carry the cups along and cannot possibly keep them 'hidden' somewhere else. By contrast, if Damoetas alone were to utter the line, his speech would be a very effective reply to Menalcas' praise of his own cups, which Menalcas brought along and probably has been using. Damoetas has new cups at home (or, at any rate, in a 'safe' place): they are hidden away and intact, unlike Menalcas'.* **illis.** The use of *ille* emphasizes the distant, hidden location of the cups: these are clearly not displayed on stage; cf. esp. 2.43 *illos* [42 *quos tibi seruo*; here cf. *condita seruo*]; note also 1.42; 9.6.

---

* The deletion would, of course, affect the total number of lines in the poem (see Introduction, p. 22, n. 56). Without l. 43, *E.* 3 would count 110 lines in total (10 × 11), i.e. the same as *E.* 8 (which has 110 lines if 8.28a is included, as most editors recommend). This correspondence might be significant: both eclogues, along with *E.* 4, have Pollio as their illustrious reader and addressee (though he is not explicitly mentioned in *E.* 8: see 8.6n.; cf. 3.85 *lectori...uestro*).

170 ECLOGUE 3

44–8. The agonistic spirit becomes apparent in the reply of Damoetas, who answers his rival's description point by point (note the line-opening sequence *et… et…Orpheaque*; with 3.46 *in medio* cf. 3.40), up to l. 47, which, if l. 43 is authentic, must be understood as a verbatim repetition *per irrisionem*, as Servius observes (but see n. ad loc.). Note the subtle irony in the way in which the cup, a Theocritean gift, is described as 'non-exclusive' (*Et nobis…*), and therefore not extremely valuable, by Theocritus' successor V. Nevertheless, the scenes depicted on both Menalcas' and Damoetas' cups will be 'preserved' (*condita seruo*) by V. for his future georgic poem (cf. 3.47n.).

45 et molli circum est ansas amplexus acantho. Damoetas' cups feature the second ornamental motif of Theocritus' cup: the acanthus leaves on the rims (their intertwining appearance is here suggested by the syntactical and phonetic wordplay, esp. the repeated /a/ sounds). The epithet *molli*, corresponding to ὑγρὸς (ἄκανθος) in *id.* 1.55, hints perhaps at a specific variety of the plant, called *Acanthus mollis*, as opposed to *Acanthus spinosus* (cf. Plin. *nat.* 22.76), while at the same time underscoring the craftsman's skill (e.g. Hor. *ars* 33 *mollis imitabitur aere capillos*); cf. G. 4.123 *flexi…uimen acanthi*. Like the ivy on Menalcas' cups, here the acanthus leaves visually convey the significance of the central depiction: the astronomical laws governing nature, and Orpheus' wondrous song (both of which are vital stimuli to plant life). Ivy and acanthus will be paired again to celebrate the *puer*'s birth (*E.* 4.19–20). For their well-known use in architecture, i.e. on Corinthian capitals, see Vitr. 4.1.9. Acanthus berries are mentioned at G. 2.119. In a decorative context, acanthus will reappear on Helen's veil in *Aen.* 1.649; 711; cf. also Prop. 3.9.14; Ov. *met.* 13.701 (ecphrasis of a mixing bowl). Acanthus-leaf decorations are featured in *terra sigillata* drinking cups from the first century BCE, despite their modest quality: cf. L. Mazzeo Saracino, *Terra sigillata norditalica*, in *Enc. Art. Ant., Atlante delle forme ceramiche*, II, 1985, pp. 175–230, esp. p. 191. Note the hyperbaton of adj. and noun (as in 3.38–9n.): *molli…acantho*, hinting at the mutual 'embrace' of the decorative plants. Compared to ivy, acanthus seems to be more sophisticated and artful (note its extensive praises at Theocr. *id.* 1.55–6). **amplexus.** The artist is here portrayed as an integral part of his own work, almost anticipating Orpheus' demiurgic miracle.

46 Orpheaque in medio posuit siluasque sequentis. The song of Orpheus (the legendary Thracian singer, capable of animating nature) will reappear in G. 4.510; cf. similarly Aesch. *Ag.* 1630 (though vaguer: πάντα); Eur. *Bacch.* 562–4; Hor. *carm.* 1.12.7–12, besides *ars* 391–3; Ov. *met.* 11.1–2; for an early pastoral attestation cf. [Mosch.] *epit. Bion.* 14–18 (and 116); in the *E.* Orpheus is mentioned again at 4.55; 57; 6.30; 8.55–6. On Orpheus and Orphism, see further *Enc. Virg.* III, pp. 882–4, s.v. *Orfeo* (J. Heurgon); *Enc. Or.* II, pp. 451–3, s.v. *Orfeo* (M. Cantilena); *Virg. Enc.* II, pp. 946–7, s.v. *Orpheus* (S. I. Johnston); among recent contributions, cf. esp. Guidorizzi, Melotti (2005); Bernabé, Casadesús (2008), Andrisano, Fabbri (2009). The second scene depicted by the 'divine' (3.37) craftsman translates into a magic-mythical language the scientific knowledge that took centre stage on the first two cups. Both elements will be featured in the song of an even more divine character, i.e. Silenus (*E*. 6, esp. 30; 70–1; cf. 3.40–2n.); see also 4.55n. Note that l. 46 is effectively 'in the middle' of Damoetas' speech (for the phrase *in medio* cf. 3.40n.). A single scene is mentioned as depicted on Damoetas' cups, which can thus be imagined as identical: the same is most probably true of Menalcas' cups. The scene, featuring Orpheus and the woods that follow him in awe, appears to be more complex and original compared to Menalcas' two images. Here, too, Damoetas probably implies that Alcimedon's work is by no means inferior to Menalcas' (quite the opposite!).

47. The exceptional repetition here of the entire l. 43 is rather surprising, and, if that line is not spurious (which is quite likely: see n. ad loc.), can be explained by Damoetas' competitiveness: he echoes his rival's words in order to mock him (in this case, however, something like 'me too' would seem to be missing: cf. 3.44 *et nobis*). This is essentially the solution chosen by Servius, who nonetheless exaggerates a bit (there is no need to assume that Damoetas 'despises' the cups): '*et nobis fecit' ac si diceret: putas te solum habere pocula? cui enim Alcimedon non fecit? tu pro reuerentia ea non tangis, ego ideo quia uilia esse existimo* (*ad* 44). Rather, what Servius stated about Menalcas (*ad E.* 3.43 *tantam in eis dicit uenerationem, ut necdum illis usus fuerit*) can also apply to Damoetas: he clearly appreciates the cups, but does not consider them to be remotely comparable to the *uitula*. At any rate, it is in Damoetas' interest to reject Menalcas' proposal and therefore assert that he already possesses perfectly new cups similar to his rival's. Why would he need another pair of cups? In conclusion 3.47 seems necessary here (after 3.44–6), as it expresses one last reason for Damoetas' negative reply. Damoetas has replied to Menalcas point by point (his own acanthus and Orpheus do not blush in comparison to Menalcas' ivy and astronomers: quite the opposite), and now he adds a further argument, i.e. the 'untouched' status of the cups. Then, in 3.48, the cups recede into the background to make room for the *uitula*. Taken as a whole, the four cups hint at themes (astronomy, along with its agricultural applicability, and the figure of Orpheus) that V. will later develop in the four books of the *Georgics*. In relation to such topics, V. himself could say: *condita seruo*.

48. Menalcas' offer, framed in terms of greater value (3.35 *tute ipse fatebere maius*), is now blatantly rejected by Damoetas.

49–50. Damoetas' last sentence prompts the boy to accept the challenge, in spite of the onerous conditions imposed by his rival (this makes it all the more obvious that he should feel the need for a referee: 3.50 *audiat haec tantum*). That the *uitula* is at stake, even though the agon ends in a draw, is confirmed by 3.109: cf. 3.85n.

49 Numquam hodie effugies. A likely echo of Naevius, *trag.* 13 R.[3] *numquam hodie effugies quin mea moriaris manu* (from his *Equos Troianus*), as noted by Macr. *Sat.* 6.1.38 (cf. *Aen.* 2.670 *numquam omnes hodie moriemur inulti*). As Menalcas agrees on the heifer, a very valuable prize (even in literary terms), V. echoes a tragic text: the irony could perhaps have been grasped by Asinius

172 ECLOGUE 3

Pollio, himself a tragic poet (cf. Hor. *carm.* 2.1.9–10); V. will soon promise him a *uitula* (cf. 3.85n.). The phrase, at any rate, is dramatic and colloquial in tone, as is confirmed by the numerous occurrences in comedy—often including, as here, an expressive pleonasm (*hodie numquam* = 'never ever'): cf. Plaut. *Asin.* 630 *hodie numquam ad uesperum uiuam*; *Amph.* 426; *Bacch.* 841; *Mil.* 214; Ter. *Ad.* 570; *Phorm.* 805 (but cf. also the epic occurrence at *Aen.* 2.670); *ThlL* VI.3.2851.13–34. **ueniam quocumque uocaris.** This agonistic phrasing contains echoes of alliterative everyday speech, also attested in Cicero's oratory: cf. Cic. *Flacc.* 97 *si quis illuc me uocat, uenio*; *Caec.* 82 *uenio iam quo uocas* (note also *Att.* 16.13.1 *itaque ueniam quo uocas*). For a pastoral reworking, cf. Calp. *ecl.* 1.13 *quo me cumque uocas sequor, Ornyte*—without, however, the implied competitiveness of the phrase. For V.'s use of the phrase in relation to Pollio, cf. 3.88n.

50. The choice of the referee appears to be entirely casual, as in *id.* 5.61–5: '(Lac.) But who, / who will be our judge? If only the cowherd Lycopas were around! / (Com.) No, I do not need him. But that man, / the woodcutter: if you want, we will call him, who is gathering / bracken over there, near you: it is Morson'. Cf. also *id.* 8.25–7: '(Men.) But who will be our judge? Who will listen to us? / (Daph.) Come on, let us call out to that goatherd over there, / who has a piebald dog that barks at the goats'. Here the rhythm, enriched by the bucolic diaeresis (after *uenit*), mimics the sequence of actions observed by the two herdsmen, who are now about to start the contest. **Palaemon.** A non-Theocritean name, otherwise unheard of in the *E.* and belonging to a marine, extra-pastoral myth: Palaemon, in fact, was the cultic name of Ino's son Melicertes, whose body (submerged by the waves along with his mother's, who threw herself into the sea to save him) was brought by a dolphin to Corinth, where king Sisyphus honoured him by establishing the Isthmian games. Cf. *Aen.* 5.823 *Inousque Palaemon*; *Enc. Virg.* III, p. 932, s.v. *Palemone* (C. Corbato); *Virg. Enc.* II, p. 957, s.v. *Palaemon (1–2)* (J. Van Sickle). The Corinthian connection, with its typical maritime implications, might facilitate Palaemon's appearance in a 'Syracusan' genre such as Theocritean pastoral poetry (Syracuse was a Corinthian colony: cf. *id.* 15.90–3), while his link to the Isthmian games seems to suit the contest's referee: παλαίμων 'wrestler' was an epithet of Heracles. Here the name suitably hints at seniority and authoritativeness (πάλαι / παλαιός) cannot be neglected. In Theocritus' *id.* 5, the judge is similarly 'atypical': a lumberjack, named Morson (*id.* 5.65: the name is not attested elsewhere in pastoral poetry). In *id.* 8, the cowherd Daphnis and the shepherd Menalcas must 'settle' for a mere passerby: an anonymous goatherd, who asserts his need to be taught the art of singing (*id.* 8.85). The renowned grammarian Remmius Palaemon, active during the principates of Tiberius and Claudius, is said to have read V.'s passage as a prophecy of his own role as infallible judge of poetry (Suet. *gramm.* 23.4 Brugn.). This kind of anecdote, somewhat unusual for a scholar/grammarian, is part of the prosopographical game played by the likes of Asinius Gallus, Pollio's son, who claimed to be the *puer* of V.'s fourth eclogue

ECLOGUE 3   173

(at least according to Servius: cf. p. 197). Some ancient scholars read historical and political allusions into *E.* 3: here, the *schol. Bern.* interpret Palaemon as Octavian (p. 99 H.); correspondingly, Damoetas is equated with V. and Menalcas with the poet Cornificius (*ad E.* 3.58, p. 100 H.; the reverse, i.e. Damoetas = Cornificius and Menalcas = V., is also attested: *schol. Bern. ad E.* 3.80, p. 101 H., and *ad E.* 3.82, p. 102 H.).

51 posthac. The adv. is typical of Plautus and Terence, but still very frequent in Cicero. It evokes a sort of colloquial stylization, and rarely appears in Augustan poetry (see *E.* 1.75; cf. Hor. *sat.* 1.1.21; also *carm.* 4.11.33). For the formula 'you will not even try again', or the like (*ne quemquam uoce lacessas*), cf. *id.* 5.44.

52 Quin age. Another colloquial phrase, paralleled in comedy: Ter. *Phorm.* 350 *quin tu hoc age* (in V., *age* is typically used as a mere interjection, without any true verbal meaning; cf., however, *E.* 8.17 and 9.24). It will reappear at *G.* 4.329 *quin age et…erue siluas* (then again at Ov. *her.* 14.57; Val. Fl. 4.471; Stat. *Theb.* 1.260). **si quid habes.** Despite the agonistic context, the phrase is semantically neutral ('whatever you may have') and may rather count as an expression of courtesy or politeness: e.g. Cic. *Att.* 7.9.4; 12.44.3; 14.3.2; Petron. 68.2; Gell. 20.10.2; cf. *E.* 9.32 as well as 7.10; also 5.10–11. **in me mora non erit ulla.** Here, too, a comparison with the colloquial language of comedy is in order: Plaut. *Stich.* 710 *non mora erit apud me*; Ter. *Andr.* 420 *neque istic neque alibi tibi erit usquam in me mora* (but cf. also *Aen.* 12.11 *nulla mora in Turno*; Ov. *met.* 11.160–1 *in iudice…/ nulla mora est*; Iuv. 12.111).

53 uicine. Note the voc., whose affectionate tone softens the request for serious judgement. References to neighbourship are common in Plautus and Terence (e.g. *Bacch.* 172 *saluto te, uicine Apollo*, as well as *Merc.* 793).

54 sensibus… imis. Mental faculties, taken in their whole extension (down to their 'bottom'); the phrase reappears, in a very different context, at Hor. *epod.* 14.1–2 *imis /…sensibus.* For an appeal to good judgement and impartiality, cf. Theocr. *id.* 5.68–71 (Morson). **res…non parua.** In the Theocritean corpus, there is no explicit mention of the 'importance' of any singing agon—which is featured in both of V.'s contests: here and at 7.16 (*certamen erat, Corydon cum Thyrside, magnum*). This kind of phrasing probably implies irony if read from the point of view of V. and his educated readers, who may smile upon such 'great' competitions in the world of *humiles myricae.*

55–9. Words and actions rapidly follow one another, as if to convey the conventional nature of the situation, recalling the initial scenario of an eclogue, appropriate for the start of the context episode. Palaemon, who seems to have just arrived (50 *qui uenit ecce*), does not need many details to establish the rules of the contest. Action appears to be suspended for a moment after 54, since 1.55 is set against a different backdrop: we find the three characters seated on the grass (*consedimus*), in keeping with the standard custom of Theocritus' bucolic singers; contrast *recubans* at 1.1n. The connection between spring, soft grass, and (pastoral) song appears in Lucr. 2.29–33; 5.1392–8. Note the iterative style, typical of

174   ECLOGUE 3

pastoral poetry (*nunc* is repeated four times; cf. 3.59 *alternis...alterna*), which is here coupled with a search for austere solemnity—at times through archaism, as in this sequence of 'end-stopped' lines (i.e. without enjambement). The Muses themselves are mentioned by their Latin name (3.59n.). Note, in 3.56–7, the fourfold structure typical of the *E*. (see also 1.1–5n. for the length of Palaemon's speech, i.e. five lines). In his carefully structured (and somewhat solemn) speech, Palaemon mentions some fundamental features of the contest and, in his last two lines (3.58–9), gives his final orders to the contestants (thereby 'setting the stage' for the agon itself and the length of the speeches: each contestant will get two lines per speech; cf. 3.59n.). In conclusion, Palaemon proves himself to be perfectly qualified to evaluate pastoral songs.

55 Dicite. For the verb in the context of song and poetry, and in the sense of 'singing' or 'reciting', cf. Catull. 62.4 *iam dicetur hymenaeus* (note also Catull. 61.39); it later appears e.g. at Hor. *carm. saec.* 8 *dicere carmen*; see *ThlL* V.1.977.65– 978.3. This usage is rather frequent in the *E*.: note *E*. 5.2 *dicere uersus* (and 5.51; cf. also 4.54); 6.5 *dicere carmen*; 8.63n.; 10.3n. **quandoquidem**. Common in the colloquial language of Plautus and Terence, but perceived as archaizing in V.'s time— hence its suitability for solemn contexts: its three other Virgilian occurrences are all in the *Aeneid*, and always, as here, in direct speech (note that a deity is the speaker in each of the three cases: *Aen*. 7.547; 10.105; 11.587; cf. also *Ciris* 323). Note the short quantity of the second syllable (due to enclitic shortening), convenient for hexameter poetry. Palaemon's first words characterize his style as old-fashioned and somewhat austere: at any rate, in a contest of great importance (3.54 *res est non parua* [n.]), the judge can allow himself a little solemnity, albeit in the context of a quiet spring day in the countryside. **in molli...herba**. 'Soft' in the sense of smooth, comfortable for sitting, lying down, or walking: cf. ἁπαλός in *id*. 5.55; Lucr. 2.29 *in gramine molli* (note also 5.1392); cf. differently *tener* (8.15n.). **consedimus**. The perfect tense gives two hints: the three characters have adopted the typical pose of Theocritus' singing herdsmen (see 3.55–9n.) and, as it seems, some time has passed between Palaemon's arrival (3.50) and Damoetas' request (3.53–4). In other words, there is no identity between narrative time and 'real' time: the reader must imagine a rather long pause between 3.54 and 3.55, so that the characters have some time to sit down. Naturally, *consedimus* responds to Palaemon's will: the judge is guiding the contestants' actions and movements, telling them where exactly to sit down (in 3.58–9 he will decide in which order they must sing) and then allowing the competition to begin. The verb has a similar narrative and mimetic function at 5.3n. (though see n. ad loc. for some textual issues).

56–7. The reference to the pleasant qualities of grass in 3.55 becomes now an extensive evocation of spring in fields and woods. The conjunction *et* holds the whole passage together, unifying a picture of peace and pleasure (the characters quietly enjoy a spring day on the grass), as in Lucretius' Epicurean poem (cf. Lucr. 2.29–33; 5.1392–8). Such a *locus amoenus*, agreeably described by Palaemon,

ECLOGUE 3   175

makes superfluous any debate on 'location choice', which was featured in *id.* 5.43–59 as a sort of pre-agon between the two contestants. This pastoral picture only lacks songs to be complete. Note, in both lines, the symmetry of the word-order, featuring isocola and the anaphora of *nunc* (similar fourfold structures are common in the *E.*: cf. 1.59–63n.).

56 et nunc omnis ager, nunc omnis parturit arbos. Cf. *G.* 2.330 *parturit almus ager*; Pentad. *Anth. Lat.* 235.3–4 R. = 227.3–4 Sh. B.; *Perv. Ven.* 78. For a possible model (note the matching repetition) cf. Bion, fr. 2.17 G. εἴαρι πάντα κύει, πάντ' εἴαρος ἁδέα βλαστεῖ 'in spring, everything is ready to give birth, everything sweetly shoots forth'.

57 formosissimus. A rare occurrence of the superlative form in -*issimus* in the *E.* (the other two feature *gratissimus* at 7.61 and 8.15). In this case, the adjective conspicuously occupies the fourth and the fifth foot, as is the norm for a pentasyllabic word like *fōrmōsǐssǐmǔs*. Note the alliteration with *frondent*, adding a further sound effect to the anaphoric *nunc*.

58–9. Palaemon establishes the order and the rules of the contest, both befitting the situation (even though Palaemon cannot be aware of the dialogue preceding his arrival). The first to sing will be Damoetas, who launched the challenge in 3.28–9 and directly addressed Palaemon in 3.52–4 (moreover, he is senior in age). The 'challenger rule' is stated in *id.* 6.5: 'Daphnis was the first to sing, since he was the first to launch the challenge' (thus, in Theocritus, Damoetas came second). In *id.* 8, Menalcas opens the hostilities (*id.* 8.5) and eventually starts the contest, albeit chosen by lot (*id.* 8.30). Note, finally, the anonymous judge's speech at the outset of *id.* 9.1–2: 'Sing a pastoral song, Daphnis: you start singing first, / start singing, Daphnis; then let Menalcas follow [ἐφείψάσθω δὲ Μενάλκας]' (cf. 3.58 *tu deinde sequere, Menalca*). These two lines are replete with echoes of Catull. 62, an experimental poem in which the erotic theme (i.e. the wedding hymn) is developed as an amoebean song by two choirs (*iuuenes* and *innuptae*), and most probably inspired by Theocritus: cf. particularly Catull. 62.18 *dicere iam incipient, iam respondere decebit.* For Asinius Pollio's interest in Catullus, see Introduction, p. 11; also above, p. 148; *E.* 3.84n.

59 alternis…alterna. The meaning of *uicissim* (28) is now specified. The challenge will be an amoebean one ('cut-and-thrust', δι' ἀμοιβαίων [*id.* 8.61]): the two contestants will exchange hexameter couplets, as in *id.* 5.80–135 (elegiac couplets in *id.* 8.33–60); cf. *E.* 7.18 *alternis…uersibus.* The 'minimum' amoebean mode, featuring exchanges of two lines each, is the most suited to the heated rivals of *E.* 3, since it conveys (as in *id.* 5) the aggressiveness of an actual competition. *E.* 7, which is less bellicose in tone, will feature exchanges of 4 + 4 lines each; in *id.* 6 and 9, where fairly long poems are pitted against one another, the agon is but a pretext for singing (the same is true of *E.* 8 and 5). The use of two-line exchanges is suggested by Palaemon himself, who concludes his speech with two lines, as if to 'set the tempo' for the contest to follow (3.58–9; note the correspondence with

176   ECLOGUE 3

polyptoton *alternis…alterna*, as well as the twofold *nunc* at 3.56–7). **amant alterna Camenae**. Palaemon's speech is concluded by a (rather vague) reminiscence of a Homeric passage that can be seen as the archetype of amoebean song: *Il.* 1.694 'the Muses, who sang alternately (αἳ ἄειδον ἀμειβόμεναι) with delightful voice' (note the repeated /a/ sound in Homer, as here). The *Camenae*, Italic goddesses (perhaps originally Etruscan), were identified with the Muses at least since Livius Andronicus; some tried to establish an etymological connection with *carmen* (Varr. *ling.* 7.26–7; Maltby 1991, p. 99, s.v.). The word only occurs here in V.'s works (but cf. *Catal.* 5.11–12). Horace may have had this passage in mind at *sat.* 1.10.45; cf. Introduction, p. 11 and n. 27; also 3.84 *quam vis est rustica* (n.).

60–107. After the preliminary stage has been completed, the agon proper begins and occupies a great portion of the poem, i.e. forty-eight lines in twelve exchanges (twenty-four lines for each contestant). The last four lines of the poem are occupied by Palaemon's verdict, which functions as a finale. Pollio's name takes centre stage and opens the second half of the contest (3.84–91n.). The two singers seem sometimes to reply to each other in a dialogic fashion (e.g. 3.64–7; 76–9; 84–7), sometimes each to express personal views on analogous subjects (esp. 3.92–9). The first of the two techniques will be lyrically and elegantly reworked by Horace in the dialogue of *carm.* 3.9. The thematic structure of the agon proper is quite clear: the first pair of speeches serves as a prologue (3.60–3), and is followed by five pairs of speeches on love and eros (3.64–83); then the contestants devote two speeches each to Pollio (3.84–91); four final pairs of speeches are devoted to rustic wisdom and riddles (3.92–107).

60–3. The first exchange abides by the conventional rule whereby a deity's name must be mentioned in the proem (cf. Palaemon's *Camenae*). Damoetas' Aratean Jupiter is countered by Menalcas' Apollo, bay, and hyacinth: such an association will reappear, with some reworking, to frame the final exchange, thereby facilitating the solution of the riddles (3.104–7n.). Similarly, in *id.* 5.80–3, the deity's name signals the start of the agon proper, after Morson has been chosen as a judge (3.62n.).

60 Ab Ioue principium, Musae: Iouis omnia plena. Cf. Arat. *phaen.* 1–4 ἐκ Διὸς ἀρχώμεσθα, τὸν οὐδέποτ' ἄνδρες ἐῶμεν / ἄρρητον. μεσταὶ δέ Διὸς πᾶσαι μὲν ἀγυιαί, / πᾶσαι δ' ἀνθρώπων ἀγοραί, μεστὴ δὲ θάλασσα / καὶ λιμένες· πάντῃ δὲ Διὸς κεχρήμεθα πάντες 'Let us begin with Zeus, whom we men never leave / unmentioned. Full of Zeus are all highways, / and every concourse of mortals, full of Zeus is the sea / and harbours: everywhere we need Zeus'. Alongside Aratus, whose poem he also read in Cicero's version (on the importance of Aratus' *Phaenomena* in Roman culture, see 3.40n.; 42n.), V. probably echoes Theocr. *id.* 17.1–2 ἐκ Διὸς ἀρχώμεσθα καὶ ἐς Δία λήγετε Μοῖσαι 'Muses, let us begin with Zeus and end with him as well' (it is uncertain whether Theocritus followed Aratus or vice versa, but it is more likely that Aratus came first). The invocation formula itself is much older than both Aratus and Theocritus: cf. Alcm. fr. 29 P. = 89 Cal. ἐγὼν δ' ἀείσομαι ἐκ Διὸς ἀρχομένα; Terp. fr. 698 P. Ζεῦ πάντων ἀρχά, πάντων

ECLOGUE 3   177

ἀγήτωρ, Ζεῦ σοὶ πέμπω ταύταν ὕμνων ἀρχάν (note also Pind. *Nem.* 2.1–3, as well as Hes. *theog.* 1 and 36, where the Muses are mentioned instead of Zeus). As for the threefold structure of beginning, continuation, and end, the epic archetype is Hom. *Il.* 9.96–9, esp. 97 ἐν σοὶ μὲν λήξω, σέο δ᾽ ἄρξομαι (where Nestor begins his speech by addressing Agamemnon, whom he is going to criticize rather harshly). Note the intratextual echo at *E.* 8.11 *a te principium, tibi desinam*, where the poet is talking to an anonymous addressee (most likely Pollio: see n. ad loc.). For a reworking of V.'s line, charged with metapoetic significance, cf. Calp. *ecl.* 4.82 *ab Ioue principium, si quis canit aethera, sumat* (on which see below). As Calpurnius implies, the incipit of Damoetas' portion of the agon is rather solemn and challenging. Despite the irony characterizing this lively contest between young herdsmen of low social status, the eclogue will soon feature the important patron Pollio, the consul of *E.* 4 (and Damoetas will be the first to mention him at 3.84). **Musae.** Probably voc., following *id.* 17 (cf. also 3.85n.), and similar to Ov. *met.* 10.148–9 *ab Ioue, Musa parens (cedunt Iouis omnia regno), / carmina nostra moue.* Servius' alternative interpretation (gen. sing.) is somewhat forced, though not impossible (*uel Musae meae ab Ioue est principium, uel, o Musae, sumamus ab Ioue principium*), and seems to be supported by Cicero's translation of Aratus' incipit, *Arat.* fr. 1 Soub. (apud Cic. *leg.* 2.7) *A Ioue Musarum primordia*; cf. also *Aen.* 7.219 *ab Ioue principium generis.* Attempts to equate *Musa* (singular) with 'poetry' are unpersuasive: no further adjective or specification is provided, while *mea carmina* (3.61) would be redundant; at any rate, the plur. *Musae* is the expected form, appearing soon after *Camenae* (3.59). The case of 3.84 is different: the poet refers to 'his own' Muse, using the more specific phrase *nostram...Musam.* The connection between (all) the Muses and Zeus is clearly established by Hes. *theog.* 1–4; 25; 36–43. Note that, without a voc., the line would amount to a sort of general 'law' or gnome, and would lack the hortatory tone ('let us begin!') which is required at the beginning of a song and plays a crucial role in the openings of both Aratus' and Theocritus' poems (both have ἀρχώμεσθα; cf. Hes. *theog.* 1). The formula is carefully emulated by other Roman authors, such as Cic. *rep.* 1.36...*magnis de rebus dicere exordiens a Ioue incipiendum putat*; Quint. *inst.* 10.1.46; note also Macr. *somn.* 1.17.14 (cf. Strat. *Anth. Pal.* 12.1.1). In V.'s reworking of the passage at *E.* 8.11, *a te principium* has a quasi-verbal meaning, i.e. 'I started from you' (or 'I had to start from you'), paralleling the more explicit *tibi desinam* ('I shall end with you'; note 8.11–12 *iussi carmina coepta tuis*). Quite significantly, this verbal function of the phrase ('it is necessary to begin') also operates in Calpurnius' version of the passage: Calp. *ecl.* 4.82–4 *ab Ioue principium, si quis canit aethera sumat... / ... / at mihi* etc. (where Corydon is the speaker; note Amyntas' reply at 4.87, echoing V.'s *E.* 3.62 *et me Phoebus amat* [n.]). The plural *Musae* also appears in another text crucial to V.'s third eclogue, i.e. Theocr. *id.* 5.80–2 (see 3.62n.); for the Nymphs, de facto equivalent to the Muses, see Theocr. *id.* 7.92 (and *E.* 3.61n.). For the Muses' role in pastoral openings, cf. 4.1n.

178 ECLOGUE 3

61 ille colit terras. Note V.'s addition to the Aratean model: that Jupiter 'frequents' (and fertilizes) the fields is bound to become a crucial georgic theme, which is foreshadowed here. Cf., for instance, *G.* 2.325–7. **illi mea carmina curae.** Cf. Theocr. *id.* 7.92–3 'the Nymphs taught me good songs, too, as I was grazing my flocks on the mountains, / and fame brought these songs all the way to Zeus' throne [τά που καὶ Ζηνὸς ἐπὶ θρόνον ἄγαγε φάμα]'. The king of the gods is apparently more benevolent towards Damoetas than Alexis is towards Corydon: cf. *E.* 2.6 *nihil mea carmina curas.*

62 Et me Phoebus amat. The competition is mirrored in the contestants' relationship with the gods, as in *id.* 5.80–2: '(Com.) The Muses love me much more than the singer / Daphnis… / (Lac.) Apollo loves me very much, too [καὶ γὰρ ἔμ' Ὠπόλλων φιλέει μέγα]'; cf. 3.104n. In the *E.*, Apollo appears here for the first time, and will play a fundamental role in the collection, as *E.* 4 will soon make clear (Apollonian connotations can also be detected in the young god of *E.* 1). For further reading see *LIMC* II.1, pp. 183–464, as well as *Enc. Or.* II, pp. 306–11, s.v. *Apollo* (I. Borzsák); Gagé (1955); Miller (2009). The way in which the god is summoned here ('Phoebus loves me, too') and Theocritus' mention of the Muses (*id.* 5.80) confirm that, in 3.60, Damoetas displays some familiarity with the Muses themselves, alongside Jupiter. The phrase *et me* underscores Menalcas' inclusion into the 'hall of fame' of poets appreciated by the gods, as in Damoetas' case (cf. 3.61). Similarly, in *E.* 9.32–3 (*et me fecere poetam / Pierides*), Lycidas implies a comparison between himself and Moeris, who sings the songs of Menalcas. For a later reworking, cf. Calp. *ecl.* 4.87–8 *me quoque facundo comitatus Apolline Caesar / respiciat* (on which see 3.60n.).

63 lauri. Bay, dear to the god because of its human past (Daphne, whose story is known from Ov. *met.* 1.452–567); cf. Theocr. *epigr.* 1.3–4 G. 'these dark-leaved bays are for you, Pythian Paean, / since the rock of Delphi lets this plant blossom'. For the hiatus *lauri et* cf. 3.6n.; *E.* 10.13 *lauri, etiam.* **suaue rubens hyacinthus.** The flower into which the young Hyacinthus was metamorphosed: he, too, was loved by the god (Ov. *met.* 10.162–219). Note the echo in *E.* 4.43 *suaue rubenti* (a further hint at the connection between *E.* 3 and 4). For the flower's 'purple' colour, see Sapph. fr. 105b V.; Meleag. *Anth. Pal.* 5.147.3–4 = *HE* 4238–9 G.-P.; Euphor. fr. 40.1 Pow. = 44.1 v. Gron. = Light. πορφυρέη ὑάκινθε, on which cf. 3.106–7n. (a further reference to the plant, in Menalcas' final riddle). The adj. *suauis*, uncommon in 'lofty' poetry (cf. 2.49n.), is here embellished, as in 4.43, by the adverbial acc., a mostly poetic and ultimately Grecizing construction: the phrase evokes an archaic compound such as *suauiloquens*, calqued on the Greek ἡδυεπής (Enn. *ann.* 304 Sk.). Cf. *G.* 3.239 *inmane sonat*; 4.270 *graue olentia*; Catull. 51.5 and Hor. *carm.* 1.22.23 *dulce ridentem* (Sapph. 31.3–5 V. ἆδυ φωνείσας…καὶ γελαίσας ἰμέροεν; cf. Hom. *Il.* 2.270 ἡδὺ γέλασσαν); 3.27.67 *perfidum ridens*; plur. at e.g. *G.* 3.149 *acerba sonans.* Here V. may have been influenced by passages like Catull. 61.7 *suaue olentis*; but Nemesianus will avoid *suauis* in his reworking, *ecl.* 2.45 *dulce rubens hyacinthus.*

ECLOGUE 3   179

64–6. The allusion to Apollo's love affairs is immediately corroborated by an explicitly erotic theme: the agonistic impulse leads to an opposition between heterosexual and homosexual eros (as in *id.* 5.88–91; for a broader discussion cf. Athen. 13.601d–605e). Pederastic love is proclaimed superior, for instance, in Eur. *Cycl.* 583–4 (the Cyclops is the speaker); Seleuc. p. 176 Pow.; Meleag. *Anth. Pal.* 12.86 = *HE* 4088–91 G.-P.; Prop. 2.4.17–18 (as a paradox); Iuv. 6.34. For the opposite view, cf. Rufin. *Anth. Pal.* 5.19; Ov. *ars* 2.682–4. The quarrel, after all, began with erotic and sexual innuendos in 3.3–11.

64 Malo me Galatea petit. A mischievous invitation to join her among the willow trees (3.65 *cupit ante uideri*). Theocritus' Damoetas, pretending to be Polyphemus in his reply to Daphnis, sang a similar song about the sea-dwelling Galatea: '(Daph.) O Polyphemus, Galatea throws apples / at your flock... (Dam.) I saw her, by Pan, as she was hitting the flock, / and she did not escape the notice of my sweet single eye' (*id.* 6.6–7; 21–2). In *E.* 1, too, Galatea retained some features of the elusive sea-goddess (1.30n.); cf. also Corydon's speech in *E.* 7.37–40, addressed to Galatea: *Nerine Galatea...uenito* (in that case, Galatea = the sea nymph, as the patronymic confirms, whereas here and in *E.* 1 Galatea is a common *puella*). Here the echo of *id.* 6 is contaminated with *id.* 5: '(Com.) Clearista throws apples at the goatherd / as he drives his goats along, and she calls out to him sweetly by smacking her lips [ποππυλιάσδει]' (*id.* 5.88–9; for the act of throwing apples cf. Gell. 9.9.4; Aristoph. *Nub.* 997). **lasciua puella.** The adj. chiefly expresses lively motions and attitudes of the girl (note, in this case, *petit*): cf. 2.64n. At the same time, it makes apparent the girl's naughty intention: cf. Hor. *carm.* 4.11.22–3 *puella / diues et lasciua.*

65 ad salices. Due to their green luxuriance, willow trees offer a perfect hideout (cf. Ov. *fast.* 2.466) to the fleeing girl, who clearly wants to be pursued (*cupit ante uideri*). At the same time, this *locus amoenus* bodes well for an amorous rendezvous: Cornelius Gallus imagines his encounter with a Phyllis or an Amyntas as taking place among willow trees (*E.* 10.40). For the pleasantness of willow groves, cf. Enn. *ann.* 38 Sk. *per amoena salicta*; note also Ov. *fast.* 3.17 *umbrosae salices.*

66 meus ignis. Used of a beloved person in Ov. *amor.* 2.16.11 *at meus ignis abest*; cf. Hor. *carm.* 3.7.10–11. **Amyntas.** In the *E.*, the name can evoke a certain propensity to eros: 2.35n.; he will be called *fuscus* in 10.38, whereas here V. immediately mentions a girl whose name evokes the white colour of milk, Galatea (68).

67 Delia. Most probably the goddess Diana-Artemis: this is Menalcas' first reference to the world of hunting. Menalcas brags about his dogs' ability to gain intimacy with the goddess, whose ancient depictions as a huntress often included dogs (the hunting dogs, which Artemis has just received from Pan, instantly follow her: Callim. *hymn.* 3[*Dian.*].98). On the other hand, the context, which is one of 'earthly' love (up to 3.83; cf. also *meae Veneri* in 3.68), might naturally lead V.'s readers to think of a girl, whose presence does not alert Menalcas' dogs, especially

180 ECLOGUE 3

in the proximity of his house (now visited by Amyntas). This interpretation must somehow be influenced by the fact that Delia would later become the protagonist of Tibullus' elegies (Delius is an epithet of Apollo at *Aen.* 3.162; 6.12). Servius testifies to both interpretations: *Deliam alii amicam priorem uolunt, alii Dianam quae est a Delo et est canibus nota, per quos uenamur*. As a matter of fact, the reader's hesitation is perfectly justified: the contestants have not really identified themselves yet. At any rate, a reference to a female figure and a domestic hearth (the dogs, in this case, would be guard dogs) does not quite suit Menalcas, who seems to prefer homosexual love and Amyntas (with the significant exception of his 'impersonation' of Iollas at 3.78–9; cf. also 3.107n.). Here, at the beginning of the contest, the two rivals take opposite sides: love for girls vs love for boys. Menalcas' appreciation for an unexpectedly introduced girl would seem odd, as the focus is now on the various girls mentioned by Damoetas (Galatea, Phyllis, Amaryllis) and Menalcas' insistence on *solus Amyntas* (3.83). It is significant that the name *Delia*, in its only other Virgilian occurrence, refers unambiguously to the goddess of hunting, in a context in which boar hunting and homosexuality link the singer Corydon to a *paruus* Micon (*E.* 7.29; note that the Corydon of *E.* 2.29 invites Alexis to hunt deer with him; of course *Delius* refers to Artemis' brother Apollo in its two Virgilian occurrences, *Aen.* 3.162 and 6.12; unambiguous is *Delia diua* in *Culex* 110). Here, at 3.74–5, Amyntas and Menalcas go boar hunting together. Hunting, love for Amyntas, and contrast with Damoetas make it unlikely that Menalcas refers to a domestic *amica* known to the dogs. If *Delia* is interpreted as a deity, Damoetas' answer becomes much clearer: Menalcas' virgin huntress is opposed to the flesh-and-blood Venus of the heterosexual herdsman (3.68 *parta meae Veneri*). By contrast, as we learn more about Amyntas, we find out that the boy is available (3.66 *mihi sese offert ultro*) but somewhat spoiled: at 3.70–1 he receives ten apples of exceptional quality for at least two days in a row, and during the boar hunt he monopolizes the fun (3.74–5: Amyntas flushes out the animals, while Menalcas takes care of the nets). Various deities can accompany pastoral singers on their hunting trips, as in Cornelius Gallus' reverie (*E.* 10.55–6), and even Daphnis was said to escort Artemis on her hunting adventures, acting as an attendant (Diod. Sic. 4.84.4). In pastoral poetry, dogs and nymphs (specifically, the Oreads) are paired together in Bion, *epit. Adon.* 18–19, where they mourn the death of Adonis. That dogs are particularly ready to recognize a deity is confirmed by the Homeric scene of Athena's arrival to the hut of Eumaeus (Hom. *Od.* 16.162–3). The connection between (female) dogs and female deities is very strong in the case of Hecate, an infernal goddess sometimes assimilated with Artemis/Diana, *diua triformis* (Hor. *carm.* 3.22.4): cf. *Aen.* 6.257–8 *uisaeque canes ululare per umbram / aduentante dea* (cf. *Aen.* 6.247; note also 4.609); see Theocr. *id.* 2.30–1 ταὶ κύνες ἄμμιν ἀνὰ πτόλιν ὠρύονται· / ἁ θεὸς [scil. Ἄρτεμις; cf. 28] ἐν τριόδοισι; Apoll. Rhod. 3.1216–17 ἀμφὶ δὲ τήν γε [scil. Ἑκάτην] / ...χθόνιοι κύνες ἐφθέγγοντο; Sen. *Oed.* 569.

ECLOGUE 3 181

68–9. To his beloved, here referred to as *meae Veneri* (cf. Plaut. *Curc.* 192; Lucr. 4.1185), Damoetas wants to give a nest of wild doves, close relatives of the bird sacred to Venus herself: cf. *Aen.* 6.190; Prop. 3.3.31 *Veneris dominae uolucres…columbae* (for the thin distinction between *palumbes* and *columbae*, see 1.57n.). V. keeps echoing Theocritus' *id.* 5: '(Com.) And I shall forthwith give my girl a ring-dove [φάσσαν], / catching it in the juniper: for there it is perching' (*id.* 5.96–7). Here the initial *parta*, in the sense of 'ready' (cf. *Aen.* 2.784), proves to be quite appropriate in the case of newborn (or unborn) birds, whereas *aeriae*, used of their parents, evokes the altitude of the nest (see 1.58n.), and therefore the boldness of Damoetas' endeavour (cf. 2.40n.). Menalcas' virgin hunting goddess (?) is countered by Damoetas' woman, who embodies the goddess of love: perhaps the *munera* (contrasting with *ultro*, 3.66) allude to Venus' potential 'venality'.

69 congessere. Absolute use of the verb, in the sense of 'nesting': Plaut. *Rud.* 889 *nidamenta congeret*; cf. also *G.* 4.243; *ThlL* IV.278.81–279.3.

70–1. Menalcas, too, has *munera* for his beloved, and his gifts (like Damoetas') are particularly dear to Venus: ten *aurea mala*, echoing the mythical apples of the Hesperides (cf. 6.61n.; also 8.52–3). Actually, they are 'golden' because of their exquisite taste (and perhaps their yellow colour?), hence their high value (*E.* 8.52–3). The model is *id.* 3.10–11: 'Here, I bring you ten apples; I picked them / where you told me to pick them: tomorrow I shall bring you more'. In keeping with what Damoetas said (3.68–9, esp. 69 *aeriae*), Menalcas mentions the refined nature of the gift: he stresses the difficulty of picking the apples (*quod potui*) and the remote position of the tree (*siluestri ex arbore*). Cf. the way in which Propertius addresses V. in his pastoral reworking: *tu canis…ut…decem possint corrumpere mala puellas* (Prop. 2.34.67–9; note that the epithet *aurea* is not used). Starting from 3.72, P ceases to transmit the text, resuming at *E.* 4.52.

73 uenti, diuum referatis ad auris. In other words, so that the gods may be witnesses to Galatea's promises (the girl herself bears the name of a deity: 1.30n.). For a similar idea, cf. 8.18–20. Notoriously, however, lovers' oaths do not reach the ears of the gods: Callim. *epigr.* 25.4 Pf. μὴ δύνειν οὖατ' ἐς ἀθανάτων (cf. 8.19–20n.). For the pathetic apostrophe to the winds (deaf or insensitive), see Callim. fr. 714.3–4 Pf. = 275.3–4 Mass., as well as Catull. 64.164; cf. also 2.5n.

74–5. The opposition is between Amyntas' favour (seemingly limited to the soul: 74 *animo*) and Menalcas' meagre satisfaction: he is confined to the secondary role of 'guardian' of the nets, symptomatic of the submission into which the *amator* is thrust (cf. Tib. 1.4.49–50; [Tib.] 3.9.12; Ov. *ars* 2.189; *met.* 10.171–3). Above all, Menalcas' task keeps him physically apart from his beloved. In antiquity, hunting was deemed to be particularly conducive to homosexual love (see 3.67n.), yet here Menalcas seems to imply that Amyntas' love is but a verbal promise. Quite surprisingly, Servius (*ad E.* 3.74) reads the contest 'politically' and argues that V. alludes here to his intention to follow 'Augustus' (i.e. Octavian) and his armies: *multi hunc locum allegoricos accipiunt, ut uideatur Augusto dicere: quid*

182   ECLOGUE 3

prodest quia me diligis, si ad capiendos hostes pergens in otio me relinquis? dicitur enim Vergilius sequi uoluisse Augustum contra Antonium ad Actiaca bella properantem; cf. also 3.96n.

76 **Phyllida.** A new female figure, Phyllis, is introduced (φυλλίς means 'small leaf' or 'foliage'); she reappears at 3.78 and 107; cf. also *E.* 5.10; 7.14; 59; 63. The names of Phyllis and Amyntas occur together again at *E.* 10.37–41, embodying the alternative between heterosexual and homosexual love. In all its Virgilian occurrences (only in the *E.*), Phyllis' name evokes an erotic impulse not impossible to fulfil, and often reassuring: Horace seems to have this in mind at *carm.* 4.11.3 (for Maecenas' birthday). The name has learned, Hellenistic echoes: it is mentioned in reference to a river at Nicand. *alex.* 149 and Euphor. *SH* fr. 431.11 (= 142c.13 v. Gron. = 110.11 Light.). Calpurnius Siculus will freely rework V.'s *Phyllis* in his own third eclogue, where Lycidas tells Iollas (a very different character compared to V.'s possessive lover) that he has been abandoned by Phyllis. **meus est natalis.** The birthday party is a private and personal form of celebration, usually enlivened by guests and erotic colour: Damoetas would like to have Phyllis as a birthday gift (*mitte*). Cf. Plaut. *Curc.* 656 *hic est quem ego tibi misi natali die*; Prop. 3.10.19–32; Ov. *amor.* 3.1.57. Such celebrations are common in comedy: e.g. Plaut. *Pers.* 768–70; *Pseud.* 165–93; cf. again Hor. *carm.* 4.11. **Iolla.** The name, which in V. only occurs here and at 2.57 *nec…concedat Iollas* (n.), evokes the figure of a possessive lover: this is his characterization in the dialogue between Damoetas and Menalcas (Menalcas, in fact, has him say that Phyllis considers him *formosus*: see 3.79n.).

77 **faciam uitula.** For the elliptical use of *facere* with an instrumental abl., in the sense of 'sacrificing', cf. Plaut. *Stich.* 251 *quot agnis fecerat* (for an extended form cf. *Aul.* 612 *rem diuinam faciam*); Cat. *agr.* 140; Colum. 2.21.4. Thus, *uitula* (clearly Servius' reading) is preferable (cf. esp. Macr. *Sat.* 3.2.15–16) to the MSS' trivialization *uitulam*. **pro frugibus.** A rather vague hint at a propitiatory sacrifice, perhaps similar (though reduced in scale) to the solemn countryside festival held in May, the *Ambarualia*. **ipse uenito.** Purification and fertility rites generally involved sexual abstinence: on such an occasion, Iollas (still accompanying Phyllis?) would be welcome. Note the emphatic use of the future imperative (for *ueni* cf. *G.* 2.7), here implying an ironic contrast with the more common use of the form for erotic invitations (cf. 7.40n.).

78–9. Menalcas replies to Damoetas, who addresses Iollas, by wittily pretending to be Iollas himself, as the reader finds out from the final voc.: similarly, in *id.* 6.21–2, Damoetas pretended to be Polyphemus in his reply to Daphnis; in the agon of *E.* 7, Corydon will play the role of the 'challenger', i.e. Micon (7.29–32). Note the artful echoes of names and ideas: *ipse uenito* (77) is countered by *discedere fleuit* (78); the 'framing' arrangement of *Phyllida-Iolla* (77) is now extended to the whole couplet. Note that, despite imagining being in Iollas' shoes (to be sure, Iollas does not seem interested in parting ways with the girl), Menalcas

ECLOGUE 3   183

does not abandon the homosexual inclination he displayed in all the preceding exchanges (even 3.4, after all, does not prove that he is genuinely attracted to the girl; contrast 3.7–9). At 3.107, he will mention the girl one last time, thereby settling the open question of 'Who will win Phyllis, Iollas or Damoetas?' Even if he can solve the riddle (which remains to be seen), Damoetas alone will win the girl (3.107 *solus*).

78 Phyllida amo ante alias. Cf. *id*. 5.132: '(Com.) I do not love Alcippa; (Lac.) But I am much in love with Eumedes' (ἀλλ' ἐγὼ Εὐμήδευς ἔραμαι μέγα). Note V.'s insistence on /a/ sounds (alliteration over three words). **nam me discedere fleuit.** The explicatory *nam* accounts for such a predilection. When Iollas departed, Phyllis cried and called out to him many times, showing her devotion to him like Amaryllis in *E*. 1.36–9.

79 longum 'formose, uale, uale', inquit, 'Iolla'. The fading farewell, resounding at length (*longum*), is phonetically represented by the sequence *uale* (long /e/), *uale* (/e/ shortened in prosodic hiatus; standard pronunciation in V.'s time). For a similar effect cf. *E*. 6.44; for a precise and apposite reworking (the nymph Echo, unrequited lover of Narcissus), see Ov. *met*. 3.501 *dictoque 'uale' 'uale' inquit et Echo*, with A. Barchiesi's commentary, Milan 2007, p. 206, ad loc. Here *longum* modifies *inquit*, suggesting the sound's duration, as in Hor. *ars* 459–60 *longum clamet*, quoted by Charisius, *gramm*. 1, p. 204.5–9 K. = p. 265.1–5 Barw. (volume, rather than duration, is hinted at in the Homeric formula μακρὸν ἀυτεῖν). Servius' interpretation, presupposing a different syntax, soon influenced the school tradition, as is shown especially by Hosidius Geta's reworking in *Med*. 460 *et longum, formose, uale* (*longum* with *uale*, along the lines of *multum ualere*; cf. the Greek πολλὰ χαίρειν). Several interpretations of this line (and of 3.78–9 as a whole) have been proposed, including some textual emendations: for instance, Pieter Burman the Elder changes *Iolla* into *Iollas*, making it the subject of *inquit*. In particular, it seems odd to certain scholars that Menalcas pretends to be Iollas. Yet it is natural to understand 3.78–9 as the reply of 'Iollas' (whom Menalcas impersonates, in keeping with a Theocritean technique: see 3.78–9n.), since Damoetas addresses Iollas at 3.76. Moreover, 3.78–9 must explain the reasons why Phyllis is the preferred girl (3.78 *Phyllida amo ante alias; n a m* etc.), which would not be the case in 3.79 if Iollas were the one who expressed admiration for a *formosus* Menalcas. Thus, the proper nouns *Phyllida ... Iolla*, which frame 3.76, are repeated verbatim at 3.78–9, so that Menalcas' reply is particularly effective. At the same time, the adjective *formose* is complemented by the vocative *Iolla* at the end of the passage; cf. also 3.78–9n.

80–3. The two contestants challenge each other in the use of a typically pastoral device: the rustic analogy (e.g. *E*. 1.19–25). Thus, in *id*. 8.57–9: 'Winter is a dreadful evil to trees, and to waters drought, / to birds the snare, and nets to wild beasts, / to man desire for a tender virgin'. No wonder that, right after this exchange, V.'s *musa* is called *rustica* at 3.84, even though the poet avoids naive comparisons

184 ECLOGUE 3

such as *id.* 4.39: 'dear as my goats to me, so dear are you, who departed' (Theocritus' Amaryllis).

80 Triste. For the substantive neuter (here and at 82 *dulce*), compare *id.* 8.57 (see 3.80–3n.): φοβερὸν κακόν 'a dreadful evil'; cf. also, with a different coordination, *E.* 5.45–6 *tale...quale...quale*. **maturis frugibus imbres.** The idea of crops damaged by rain will be developed in *G.* 1.316–27, where the poet will refer to his personal experience (*saepe ego...uidi*).

81 arboribus uenti. Yet another georgic development: *arboribusque satisque Notus pecorique sinister* (*G.* 1.444). The phenomenon must have impressed the poet, perhaps during his early youth. **nobis Amaryllidis irae.** A new girl, Amaryllis. Compared to the elusive Galatea (3.72), she seems to evoke a stable love bond, with its resulting *irae* (cf. 1.5n.). Damoetas' plurality of women will be forcefully countered by Menalcas' *mihi solus Amyntas* (83).

82 depulsis arbutus haedis. *Depulsus* is used in the technical sense of 'weaned': cf. 1.21n., as well as 2.30n. For the strawberry tree or arbutus, much appreciated by goats, cf. *G.* 3.300–1.

83 lenta salix feto pecori. Willow leaves, which the flock grazes on, similarly appeared at *E.* 1.78 *salices carpetis amaras* ('bitter' like exile). Such a soft grazing material (note *lenta*) is all the more suited to females who recently gave birth (1.49n.); for the same line-beginning phrase (*lenta salix*), cf. 5.16 and Ov. *met.* 8.336.

84–91. At the outset of the second half of the agon (and of the seventh exchange: see 3.60–107n.), Damoetas mentions an illustrious 'reader', Asinius Pollio: similarly, the *E.* as a whole feature Varus 'in the middle' (6.10n.); on the importance of the central position cf. 3.40n. Without a doubt, the intended readership of the *E.* here proves to be a close circle of friends. The attacks against Bavius and Maevius can also be explained as the expression of literary tastes shared by a circle of intellectuals around Pollio.

84 Pollio. C. Asinius Pollio (76 BCE–4 CE), consul in 40 BCE, was a first-rank politician, who sided with Julius Caesar and then Antony, but remained neutral during the final stages of the conflict between Antony and Octavian, constantly striving for reconciliation (he played a crucial role as a mediator in the Pact of Brundisium: cf. p. 197). It is likely that Pollio, who commanded the Roman legions in Transpadana after Philippi, played some role in the land confiscations and could therefore protect the poet's possessions. According to ancient Virgilian commentators, an official team of *tresuiri agris diuidendis* was composed by Alfenus Varus, Cornelius Gallus, and Pollio himself. This claim is not supported by any historical evidence and is probably an invention of V.'s ancient interpreters, meant to justify the crucial role that the three men play in the *E.* A lover of letters since his early youth (he is praised by Catullus, 12.8–9, as *leporum / differtus puer ac facetiarum*), Pollio devoted himself entirely to his various cultural interests in his mature age (after Actium), when he refused to take office in Rome. He oversaw

ECLOGUE 3   185

the radical reshaping of the *Atrium Libertatis* (official seat of the censors during the Republic, near the forum of Caesar) and established Rome's first public library there. He fostered literature and art, and protected Cornelius Gallus and Horace, along with V.; he was also said to have initiated the custom of public recitations, which, however, were only accessible through invitation: Sen. *contr.* 4 *praef.* 2 quoted below. Himself a poet, he was particularly appreciated as a tragedian: cf. 8.10n.; Hor. *sat.* 1.10.42–3; *carm.* 2.1.9–12. His orations and declamations were celebrated, along with an important *History of the Civil Wars.* He had a taste for literary criticism, which he practised sternly (Cicero and Caesar, Livy and Sallust were among his targets). Thus, his appreciation of V.'s Muse is all the more gratifying: it is alluded to here, in a somewhat modest tone (3.84 *quamuis est rustica*). For a valuable portrait of Pollio, cf. *Enc. Or.* I, pp. 862–5 (M. Pani); see also *Enc. Virg.* IV, pp. 172–7 (M. Pavan, F. Della Corte); *Virg. Enc.* III, pp. 1022–3 (J. Osgood); note, finally, the well-documented treatment of the topic (with further references) offered by E. Drummond, *C. Asinius Pollio*, in T. J. Cornell (ed.), *The Fragments of the Roman Historians*, I, Oxford 2013, pp. 430–45. The name *Pollio*, in the nom., appears four times in V., always featuring elision with the following word (it occupies the first foot here, at 3.86, and at 4.12; the second foot at 3.88). It is scanned as a dactyl, without elision, in Hor. *sat.* 1.10.42; 85; *carm.* 2.1.14. **quamuis est rustica.** The use of *quamuis* with an indicative emphasizes the objective nature of the statement and points to Pollio's simple benevolence: he loves V.'s rustic Muse, despite her being *rustica.* The effect is quite perceptible, since V. normally uses *quamuis* with a subjunctive: cf. *E.* 1.33; 47–8; 2.16; 4.56, etc. (for *quamuis* with the indicative, cf. *Aen.* 5.542; *quamuis est* is found in Lucr. 3.403; Horace uses the indicative quite frequently: cf. *sat.* 1.3.129; 2.5.15; *carm.* 3.7.25–8; *epist.* 1.14.6 and 17.1; *ars* 355). Thanks to his refined elegance, praised by Catullus (for his *lepores* and *facetiae* cf. Catull. 12.8–9 quoted above), Pollio must have appreciated the subtleness of V.'s work, which combines a humble, 'rustic' subject matter with delicate and highly crafted literary forms: in sum, the *E.* defy the cultural stereotype expressed by Catull. 22.14 *infaceto est infacetior rure* (cf. also 36.19). Horace knew this well, as he acknowledged that V. achieved this successful combination thanks to the Muses' consent: *molle atque facetum / Vergilio adnuerunt gaudentes rure Camenae* (Hor. *sat.* 1.10.44–5; see Introduction, p. 11 and n. 27). Like Horace's *Camenae*, Pollio loves the *rus*, but only because V. has been able to combine it with *facetum*, thereby avoiding the *infacetum* aspect which Catullus (and popular opinion) considered inherent to the *rus* itself. For the idea of a 'rustic Muse', see Meleag. *Anth. Pal.* 7.196.2 = *HE* 4067 G.-P. ἀγρονόμαν...μοῦσαν; 7.195.2 = *HE* 4059 G.-P. ἀρουραίη Μοῦσα (on both epigrams, cf. 1.2n.).

85 Pierides. The Muses, daughters of Zeus and Mnemosyne, were thought to dwell on Mount Helicon, in Boeotia, even though they originally came from Pieria, near Mount Olympus, where a specific cult was dedicated to them (cf. Hes.

theog. 1; 25; 50–5). Hence the epithet Πιερίδες, appearing as early as Solon, fr. 13.2 W.², and Pindar, *Ol.* 10.96; it was soon Latinized, e.g. in Lucr. 1.926 *auia Pieridum* (cf. Cic. *nat. deor.* 3.54). In a pastoral context, note esp. Theocr. *id.* 10.24; 11.3. See further *Enc. Virg.* IV, p. 93, s.v. *Pieridi* (F. Ferrari). According to a Boeotian tradition, they were the daughters of the eponymous hero Pierus: *RE*, Suppl. VIII, col. 496, s.v. *Pierides* (G. Herzog-Hanser). For the other Virgilian occurrences, all in the *E.*, see 6.14; 8.63; 9.33; 10.72. **uitulam…pascite.** The goddesses are asked to foster the animal's growth, so that it may eventually be sacrificed to them and propitiate them for continued happiness in Pollio's activity as V.'s reader: cf. [Theocr.] *id.* 8.35; 39, as well as Hor. *carm.* 3.23.9–12. The Muses are sometimes associated with ancient poets' pastoral activities: famously so in Hesiod's case (*theog.* 22–8), but cf. also the young Archilochus (to whom they appeared as he was leading a cow to the market: see D. Clay, *Archilochos Heros. The Cult of Poets in the Greek Polis*, Washington DC, 2004, esp. pp. 14–15) and the concluding line of Callimachus' *Aitia*, where their 'pedestrian pasture' is mentioned (fr. 112.9 Pf. = 215.9 Mass. = 112.9 Hard.). Here, the Muses are asked to perform tasks typical of a βουκόλος: note that the only animals mentioned are the most valuable bovines (i.e. a she-calf and a bull: 3.86). The corresponding pastoral hierarchy emphasizes Pollio's activity as a poet. The *uitula*, at any rate, is also the prize for the winner of the singing contest (3.29n.; cf. also 3.109), and Damoetas underlines its value (3.48). A young heifer, referred to as *iuuenca*, appears at the beginning of *E.* 8 (a poem most probably dedicated to Pollio: cf. 8.2n.). **lectori…uestro.** Pollio himself: the poet's relationship with the distinguished addressee presupposes the mediation of the written page; cf. *E.* 6.12; for other references to writing, see *E.* 5.13–14; 10.53–4 (note also, in the pseudo-Virgilian corpus, *Dirae* 26 *nostris…libellis*).

86 noua carmina. When it comes to praising Pollio, there is no disagreement between the two contestants. Menalcas now mentions Pollio's original work as a poet, motivating an even richer offering (*pascite taurum*). The vague *carmina* could refer to lighthearted, neoteric-style 'poems' (for which cf. Plin. *epist.* 5.3.5), but we cannot rule out an allusion to Pollio's tragedies: similarly, in Tac. *ann.* 14.52.3, *carmina* might refer to Seneca's tragic output. Note also that the bull is a Dionysian animal, sometimes identified with Dionysus himself, especially in the cult of Dionysus-Zagreus (the god is called ταυροφάγος in Soph. fr. 668 R.-K.). Bull meat was the ritual prize for the winner of dithyramb competitions: Pind. *Ol.* 13.19 (G. Ieranò, *Il ditirambo di Dioniso. Le testimonianze antiche*, Pisa-Rome 1997, pp. 26–8, TT 36–9). The adj. *noua* shows a refined nuance that echoes Catullan poetry (cf. *nouum libellum* in Catull. 1.1; *nouitas* will be a fundamental value in Ovid's poetry). This Virgilian portrait of Pollio as an illustrious aristocrat ready to both appreciate others' poetic work and produce poetry of his own is paralleled by other testimonials concerning Pollio's work as an author and cultural manager: cf. esp. Sen. *contr.* 4 *praef.* 2 *Pollio Asinius…primus…omnium*

Romanorum aduocatis hominibus scripta sua recitauit. For Pollio's art collection in the *Atrium libertatis,* cf. Plin. *nat.* 36.33 *Pollio Asinius...spectari monumenta sua uoluit.*

87. The line will be repeated verbatim at *Aen.* 9.629, where Ascanius solemnly promises the sacrifice of a *iuuencus* to Jupiter. Here Damoetas' choice of the bull as a sacrificial victim (a victim worthy of Jupiter) is mainly explained with his intention to honour Pollio to the highest degree, raising the stakes in response to Menalcas' *uitula* (85); but cf. 3.86n.

88 Qui te, Pollio, amat. Third occurrence of the name, now in the second foot of the hexameter: *amat,* taking up 3.84 *amat,* is in turn echoed with variation at 3.90 (*non odit, amet*). **ueniat quo te quoque gaudet.** Lit. 'let him arrive wherever he rejoices that you, too (have arrived)'. The very idea of 'reaching' the other singer is both pastoral and agonistic: for its negation cf. *id.* 5.45; see also 3.49 *ueniam quocumque uocaris* (though in the context of a challenge). V.'s phrasing here echoes a memorable Callimachean finale, i.e. the ending of Callim. *hymn.* 2[*Ap.*].113 (well known for its metapoetic significance): ὁ δὲ Μῶμος, ἵν' ὁ Φθόνος, ἔνθα νέοιτο.

89. The 'rivers of honey' and the rough bramble producing amomum (an Eastern perfume, named after the aromatic plant whose seeds are used to produce it: probably identical with cardamom) are two of the miracles typically characterizing the Golden Age, which is used as an agonistic theme in *id.* 5.124–7: '(Com.) Let Himera flow with milk instead of water, and you, Crathis, / grow dark with wine, and let your reeds bear fruit. / (Lac.) Let Sybaris flow with honey for me [ῥείτω ἐμὶν μέλι; cf. here *mella fluant illi*], and at dawn / let the girl draw honeycombs rather than water with her pitcher'. In *E.* 4, the poet will actualize the wish expressed in these lines, dedicating the Sibyl's song to Pollio: both amomum and honey will reappear (4.25; 30). Spontaneous honey is typical of the Golden Age at *G.* 1.131.

90 Bauium...Maeui. Menalcas replies to Damoetas' praise of Pollio's taste by censuring two poetasters (obviously despised by Pollio himself): whoever follows the patron's lead is entitled to enjoy Golden Age miracles; those who do not must settle for senseless and unpleasant tasks (3.91n.). Bavius and Maevius—whose names are phonetically akin to each other, as if in a comic duo—apparently made the mistake of criticizing V.'s use of *hordea* (cf. 5.36n.). We do not have reliable information on either of them: ancient commentators identified Maevius with the target of Horace's *epod.* 10, a certain M. (?) Maevius, whereas Bavius (along with his brother, i.e. apparently Maevius himself) is the target of an epigram by Domitius Marsus, transmitted by Philargyrius/Philagrius' commentary (1 Bläns. = Court.; cf. Mariotti 1963, pp. 601–12 = 2000, pp. 105–16). The name *Maeuius,* sometimes spelled *Meuius,* also occurs twice in Martial (for two different characters): note esp. Mart. 10.76.8, where Maevius is a penniless poet (whereas the Maevius of Mart. 11.46.1 is a degenerate old man).

188   ECLOGUE 3

91 iungat uulpes et mulgeat hircos. The two phrases describe two absurd actions: they depict a sort of pastoral retaliation, and are probably of proverbial origin (or, at least, proverbial in style). The act of milking billy goats seems to be very appropriate for Maevius (τράγον ἀμέλγειν in Lucian. *Demon.* 28; cf. Callim. *iamb.* inc. sed. fr. 217 Pf.), if he is to be identified with the *olentem Maeuium* of Hor. *epod.* 10.2 (the epode is concluded by the sacrifice of a billy goat: *epod.* 10.23–4). Note also that *hircus* not only is associated with someone's bad smell (e.g. Hor. *epod.* 12.5; *sat.* 1.2.27) but also represents a negative value in literature, i.e. ἀγροικία or 'rusticity'—a danger to which the pastoral poet is particularly exposed and which V.'s *rustica Musa* has managed to avoid (see 3.84n.). The 'yoking' of foxes (an obviously senseless action) is not paralleled by any ancient proverb: the only possible comparison is perhaps with the popular saying 'the fox drives the ox' (i.e. leads the ploughing animal), whose meaning, however, is significantly different (*pace* Otto 1890, p. 379, no. 1942; but cf. Tosi 2007, pp. 201–2, no. 436). Note, at any rate, that the fox often played the role of a taboo animal, as in the rustic ritual known as *Cerealia*, during which torches were lit and fastened to the animal's tail: Ov. *fast.* 4.679–712. The semantic strength of these phrases may aim to establish a connection with Pollio, whose harshly polemical style in literary controversies was famous in antiquity (*acris uehementiae* according to Plin. *nat.* 36.33).

92–103. These three exchanges, preceding the final riddles, feature typically pastoral warnings and exhortations, along the lines of *id.* 4.44–8; 5.100–3. Among the various teachings of this 'rustic science', the reader will doubtless notice the main theme of the first section of the contest, i.e. eros and its force (3.100–1). The following speeches (3.92–9) display something of a non-linear structure, without the clear 'back and forth' that characterizes the rest of the contest. Hence, some scholars have suspected that the transmitted order of lines here might be incorrect. Among the various solutions that have been proposed, the most attractive one is the transposition of 3.98–9 after 3.93, which would switch the speakers in 3.94–5 and 3.96–7. The resulting sequence is clear and coherent: 3.92–3 and 3.98–9 (exhortations to *pueri*), then 3.94–5 and 3.96–7 (instructions on animal husbandry). On the other hand, the transmitted text has a rather pleasant liveliness, especially if the speeches are imagined in the context of shouts and pastoral actions under a sunny sky, in keeping with the mimetic nature of the poem. The transmitted text, moreover, has a certain coherence: 3.92–3 and 3.94–5 (exhortation to *pueri* and animals to avoid danger); 3.96–7 and 3.98–9 (instructions on how to lead sheep and goats towards the water).

93 frigidus...anguis. The snake, cold as its blood and its poison: cf. *E.* 8.71; Theocr. *id.* 15.58 τὸν ψυχρὸν ὄφιν (but cf. Theogn. 602). The term *serpens*, originally a euphemistic kenning, will appear in 4.24n. That any contact with snakes must be avoided or, at least, remedied is a common idea, especially in reference to habitual frequenters of woods and fields: cf. Nicand. *ther.* 4–7. Note the parenthetic phrase *fugite hinc* (with a colloquial ring). Here, as in 3.94, the various

ECLOGUE 3   189

'dangers' are interpreted by Servius as an allegory of the land confiscations that affected the poet.

94 Parcite…procedere. A periphrastic, colloquial form of the negative imperative, common in comedy: here it is addressed to the *oues*. Cf. Plaut. *Pers.* 312; Prop. 1.15.26; Tib. 1.6.51. **ripae.** The river's banks are in danger of collapse, as tends to happen due to the erosive force of the water: cf. Lucr. 5.256; Hor. *sat.* 1.1.58. Servius here transmits an entirely gratuitous allegorical interpretation based on V.'s biography (as in 3.93).

96 reice. The goats must be 'driven back' with forceful action so that they do not fall into the river, given their propensity to stray and escape (*E.* 7.7); cf. Plaut. *Pers.* 319 *in bubile reïcere* (where the verb is used of metaphorical *boues*). Note the synizesis, similarly featuring a compound of *icio* in Lucr. 3.877 *se tollit et eicit* and 4.1272 (contrast *G.* 3.389; cf. also Bothe's emendation *reïcere in bubile* in Plautus' just quoted passage); see further *Enc. Virg.* IV, p. 879b, s.v. *sinizèsi* (S. Timpanaro). Here, as in 3.74, Servius transmits an absurd biographical (and political) allegory, which at least testifies to the ancient reception of *E.* 3: *id est, o Mantua, noli modo uelle aliquid agere de repetendis agris: nam ubi oportunum fuerit, 'ego omnes lauabo', id est purgabo omnes apud Caesarem, cum de Actiaco proelio reuersus fuerit* (cf. also Serv. *ad E.* 9.11; 67).

97. Cf. *id.* 5.145–6: 'Cheer up, my dear she-goats…for tomorrow / I shall wash you all in Sybaris' lake'. Note the lengthening in arsis affecting *tempus erit*: cf. *E.* 1.38; contrast 7.23n.

98 Cogite. The flock is 'gathered' in a (presumably) cool and shady place, perhaps a fold or stable, as Servius observes (note also *E.* 6.85 *cogere…ouis stabulis*): *G.* 3.331–8; *Culex* 108 *densas pastor pecudes cogebat in umbras.* **lac praeceperit aestus.** The idea that the heat forestalls natural processes, e.g. jeopardizing the milking operations (as here), is similarly expressed in Lucr. 6.1049–50 *aestus ubi… / praecepit* (though the context is entirely different); cf. Colum. (?) *arb.* 2.2.

100–1. Cf. Theocr. *id.* 4.15–16; 20: 'Look at that young heifer: she is nothing / but bone; does she feed on dewdrops, like the cicada? / …And that brown bull is lean, too'. In *id.* 4, Aegon's bulls lost vigour because of their master's absence: he had developed a passion (*id.* 4.27 ἠράσσαο) for the Olympic games. Here, through a sympathy mechanism frequent in V., eros torments both shepherd and flock.

100 Heu heu. Cf. *E.* 2.58. For the double interjection cf. the model of *id.* 4.26–7 φεῦ φεῦ βασεῦνται καὶ ταὶ βόες ὦ τάλαν Αἴγων / εἰς Ἀίδαν 'Alas, alas, even the cows will depart, wretched Aegon, / for Hades'; see also *id.* 5.86. Here, however, the flock is not led to the pasture, due to the shepherd's lovesickness: similarly in Nemes. *ecl.* 2.27–32. In the *E.*, the interjection *heu* is always either immediately doubled (here and at 2.58) or repeated soon after (9.17). **quam.** Usually taken with *macer*; however, caesura and normal word-order make it possible to take it with *pingui*: despite the considerable 'fatness' of the pasture, which the shepherd obviously took great care in providing (cf. *id.* 4.18–19; 24–5), the animal is still woefully emaciated.

190 ECLOGUE 3

101 idem amor exitium pecori pecorisque magistro. After *exitium*, R inserts *est*, which the Carolingian manuscripts either omit or place after *pecori* or *magistro* (the line is quoted without *est* in the *Comm. Einsidl. in Don. art. min.*, *GL* VIII, p. 205.12 K.). It is preferable to consider *est* as an annotation, probably a gloss, which has penetrated into the text, where different branches of the tradition placed it in different positions. The form *est* appears both in 3.100 and in 3.102: here it would be unpleasantly redundant and would wreck the nominal style of the sentence—which, lacking a verb, acquires a certain sententious force. For a similar phrase (and an echo of this line) cf. *G.* 3.242–4, esp. 244 *amor omnibus idem.* **pecori pecorisque magistro.** Cf. 2.33 *ouis ouiumque magistros*; cf. also *G.* 2.529, which features no polyptoton. Here the same word is reiterated, whereas in 3.100 two adjectives of opposite meaning were juxtaposed: *pingui macer*.

102 His certe neque. Syntax and sense are complicated by the expressive fore-grounding of the deictic pronoun, while the negative particle is postponed (cf. *Aen.* 3.496 *arua neque… / quaerenda*; 10.297 *frangere nec…puppim… recuso*). Yet this very foregrounding shows that the sentence is directly linked to Damoetas' speech: *neque* refers to *amor* and aims to contradict its focal point, i.e. *idem amor* (specifically, 'these' lambs). Note the emphatic chiasmus, centred around the ironic *certe*, which is placed between *his* (contradicting *pecori pecorisque magistro*) and *neque amor* (contradicting *idem amor*). This explains why Menalcas does not abide by the 'natural' word-order dictated by the normal use of *neque*, i.e. *neque certe his amor causa est: uix ossibus haerent*. The general thrust of the dialogue between Damoetas and Menalcas may even be summarized as follows: '(Dam.) The bull is skinny, despite such abundance of food, *because* the same love is the ruin of *both* the herd *and* the herdsman. (Men.) *But* love can *certainly* not be the cause of it all for *these* ones: they can barely walk! An evil spell must have been cast upon the lambs' (it is implied that, since the bull has plenty of pastures to graze, the speaker cannot be talking about lack of milk for the lambs, as in 3.6 *lac subducitur agnis*). The emphatic word-order *his certe neque* builds up a linguistic tension that is released in the final word *agnos*: the speaker is talking about lambs, not bulls, and *amor* can therefore not be the *causa* of their physical demise. Thus, the correct punctuation is *his certe neque amor causa est: uix ossibus haerent* (note that Servius considers *uix ossibus haerent* as an autonomous syntactical element: for he glosses '*uix ossibus haerent*': *uix ossa eorum cohaerent*). The absolute use of *neque* is relatively common in V. (particularly, but not exclusively, in parenthetical clauses): cf. *G.* 4.207 and *Aen.* 6.368 (see further *E.* 9.38 *neque est ignobile carmen; Aen.* 1.260). However, *neque* can also mean something like 'not even': *Aen.* 2.71 *cui neque apud Danaos usquam locus*; Hor. *sat.* 2.3.262–3 *nec nunc… / accedam?* (H.-Sz., p. 450); cf. Cic. *agr.* 2.36 *nam neque ea quae senatus uendenda censuit nominatim audet appellare*; Liv. 40.20.6 *ut neque scribi sibi uellet*; Sen. *contr.* 1.7.4 *quam nec tyrannus uiolauerat*; Mart. 6.77.1 (for further examples see *OLD²*, p. 1288, s.v. 2b). For the emphatic *certe* and the postponed

ECLOGUE 3   191

negative, cf. Sen. *contr.* 7.3.1 *certe nec secreta te fallunt.* The two forms *neque/nec* tend to be interchangeable (here, for instance, the reading *nec* is transmitted by two MSS in Beneventan scripts: **nδ** [Ottaviano *in apparatu*]), and it is therefore possible that this freer, more 'intuitive' use of the negative was facilitated by the archaic *nec*, which sometimes appears in the form *neque* (cf. *E.* 9.6 *quod nec uertat bene* [n.]). In sum, it does not seem necessary to correct the text, even though some conjectures have understandably been proposed: note esp. *hi certe (neque amor causa est) uix ossibus haerent* (Stephanus); *hisce cutes (neque amor causa est) uix ossibus haerent* (Cartault; Phillimore); *his pelles (neque amor causa est) uix ossibus haerent* (Heyworth); cf. also *hisce arte—neque amor causa est—uix ossibus haerent* (Ottaviano). Moreover, the parenthetical clause would weaken the effectiveness of Damoetas' reply: Damoetas considers a case in which love *cannot* be the cause, and *certe* (the word which some scholars wish to correct) is precisely the right word to use if Damoetas wants to emphasize his diagnosis (which pertains to 'magical' matters: cf. 8.107 *nescio quid c e r t e est*; below, 3.103 *nescio quis*). As an alternative (without changing the text, but considering *neque amor causa est* as parenthetical), some scholars have taken *his* as a nom. plur., equivalent to *hi*—but this is an archaism, and perhaps a vulgarism, which seems out of place here: cf. Don. *ad* Ter. *Eun.* 269. For the notion of 'skin and bones', besides *id.* 4.15–16 (see 3.100–1n.; also *id.* 2.89–90) cf. Plaut. *Aul.* 564 *ossa ac pellis totust* [subj. *agnus*]; note also *Capt.* 135; Lucr. 6.1270; Hor. *epod.* 17.22; Prop. 4.5.64; Ov. *trist.* 4.6.42. For a Virgilian reminiscence in a completely different context, cf. Gratt. *cyn.* 270 *teneris uix artibus haeret.*

103 nescio quis...oculus...fascinat. An envious eye, indefinite and yet specific, capable of exercising its negative ability (*fascinat*): cf. Catull. 7.12 *nec mala fascinare lingua.* On the power of the 'evil eye', see Pers. 2.34; Plin. *nat.* 7.16; Gratt. *cyn.* 406; Apul. *met.* 4.14.1. Note that the final *o* in *nescio* scans short, as is standard in V. for this verb: cf. *E.* 8.107; *G.* 1.412; 4.55; *Aen.* 2.735. The same is true of *scio*: 8.43; *Aen.* 3.602.

104–7. The two riddles, placed here to conclude the contest, are unparalleled in the Theocritean corpus (and in the pastoral tradition at large), but certainly belong to the agonistic form as it is attested in sympotic contexts or in actual poetic *certamina*, like the agon of Homer and Hesiod (featured in third-century BCE sources): see K. Hess, *Der Agon zwischen Homer und Hesiod, seine Entstehung und kulturgeschichtliche Stellung*, Winterthur 1960, esp. pp. 10–26; *OCD*[3], p. 314, s.v. *Certamen Homeri et Hesiodi* (M. L. West). A riddle contest between Calchas and Mopsus seems to have been featured in a short poem by Euphorion, alluded to by V. in *E.* 6.72–3; cf. *Enc. Virg.* II, esp. p. 949b, s.v. *indovinelli* (A. La Penna); cf. also, more generally, *Virg. Enc.* III, pp. 1086–7, s.v. *riddles* (R. F. Thomas). This form of popular wisdom, of a paraliterary nature, is very well suited to concluding the agonistic experiment of *E.* 3, which allowed V. to develop a pastoral sketch along the lines of Theocritus' mimetic technique. In the *Cena Trimalchionis*, the

192 ECLOGUE 3

freedman Hermeros will embark on a series of riddles, meant to re-establish (at Giton's expense) a hierarchy of age and authority: *'qui de nobis longe uenio, late uenio? solue me'. dicam tibi, qui de nobis currit et de loco non mouetur; qui de nobis crescit et minor fit* (Petron. 58.8–9: note the formulaic use of the phrase *qui de nobis*, with which cf. V.'s *quibus in terris*). The subtle mirroring of Damoetas' and Menalcas' speeches, along with the final position of the riddles and the ring-composition echo of the first exchange, may suggest looking for a solution within the eclogue. At any rate, riddles are here understood as a literary game, demanding and testing the reader's knowledge of the author. Despite their differences, both riddles might have the same solution (i.e. 'everywhere'): this would be part of the game.

104 et eris mihi magnus Apollo. Cf. *Aen.* 9.654–5 *primam hanc tibi magnus Apollo / concedit laudem.* In asking his question, Damoetas appeals to the deity mentioned by Menalcas in his first speech (3.62). Menalcas will now have to prove that he is, in fact, dear to the oracular god of Delphi (Apollo will soon reappear at *E.* 4.10). Menalcas' riddle, centred around the hyacinth, is eminently 'Apollonian'. The use of consequential *et* after an imperative clause is uncommon in archaic Latin, but widespread in Augustan poetry, perhaps partly due to the influence of Greek: cf. Ov. *rem.* 22 *desinat: et nulli funeris auctor eris*; H.-Sz., p. 481.

105 tris pateat caeli spatium non amplius ulnas. 'Where [lit. 'in what lands'] is the sky's space not wider than three ells [= 1.5–1.8 m.]?' This riddle is much harder to solve than the other one: the ancients attributed to the poet himself the intention to puzzle his interpreters (Philargyrius/Philagrius, p. 70 [III.2 Th.-H.]; the riddle is quoted as an example of *aenigma* in Quint. *inst.* 8.6.52). The possible solutions can be arranged into five groups (some of them also attested in antiquity). (*a*) Some kind of astronomical image, e.g. a celestial globe, such as the one designed by Archimedes (Cic. *rep.* 1.21–2) and Posidonius (Cic. *nat. deor.* 2.88), or a text or map representing the sky. (*b*) A well, or a jar, from which the sky's space appears considerably reduced: according to Servius, a well existed in Syene, Egypt, which was used for astronomical observations and experiments, though we do not have sufficiently reliable information on this. (*c*) The opening in the roof of the temple of Jupiter on the Capitoline hill, located above the sacred stone, *Terminus* (Ov. *fast.* 2.671–2)—note the pun *ter-minus* = *tris non amplius*, as in the old riddle transmitted by Gellius, 12.6.1–2, for which cf. Traina, Bini (1986, pp. 12–13); however, no reliable information is available on this matter. (*d*) The tomb of Caelius, a Mantuan spendthrift who, before dying, bequeathed a plot of land so small that it was barely enough to bury him—note the pun *Caelii / caeli* (the anecdote is very suspect, especially since ancient sources attribute it to V. himself). (*e*) Ajax's shield, on which the cosmos is said to be depicted. The reference is actually to Achilles' shield (Hom. *Il.* 18.478–608), won by Odysseus in the well-known contest. The shield was said to have eventually reached Ajax's tomb (in the Troad) by sea: cf. *Anth. Pal.* 9.115–16; Pausan. 1.35.4. Within the first group of solutions

ECLOGUE 3   193

(*a*), it would be particularly interesting to posit a reference to Eudoxus, author of the Ἔνοπτρον (i.e. the *Mirror*, in which the sky is 'reflected') and of the *Phaenomena*, which Aratus divulged in verse form (note V.'s *pateat*); cf. 3.40n. Thus, the reference to a length of three ells need not necessarily allude to a physical object, such as a mechanical sphere, but it could point either to Eudoxus-Aratus' book or to an astronomical map (vel sim.) derived therefrom. If so, Damoetas' final speech would come back to Aratus' text, with which he opened the contest (3.60n.), while also exploiting a weak spot in his rival's defence (cf. again 3.40n.); with *pateat caeli spatium* cf. 3.41 *descripsit…totum…gentibus orbem* (n.). If a book (whichever it may be) is alluded to here, then the answer to both riddles could ironically be 'everywhere'. If a physical object is meant here, something like a scientific instrument, the reader might think of the Archimedean sphere, of which two versions existed in ancient Rome (though only one of them was Archimedes' own creation: see Cic. *rep.* 1.21–2), both having been brought over from Sicily by M. Claudius Marcellus, the conqueror of Syracuse. Such a geographical connection (from Syracuse to Rome) would be particularly significant in a pastoral book like V.'s *E*. In other words, a Theocritean herdsman would answer the riddle with 'Syracuse'; a Virgilian one with 'Rome'. The fifth option (*e*) has the advantage of evoking Ajax, who will re-emerge in Menalcas' riddle: some commentators have posited an allusion to Euphorion (3.106–7n.), and thus to Cornelius Gallus.

106–7. In all likelihood, the solution concerns the hyacinth flower, known for its 'inscribed' markings: hence a reference to Menalcas' first speech (62–3). Two different myths explained the flower's peculiarity (Plin. *nat.* 21.66 *hyacinthum comitatur fabula duplex*). According to the first, the markings must be read as *AI*, two uppercase Greek letters forming an exclamation of grief, which was inscribed on the flower with the blood of the young Spartan Hyacinthus, accidentally killed by Apollo: cf. Nicand. *ther.* 902–6 (other sources attest an alternative interpretation featuring an uppercase *Y*, the initial letter of the boy's Greek name: Serv. *ad* 3.106; cf. also Philargyrius/Philagrius, *ad* 3.63, p. 60 [III.2 Th.-H.]). According to the second myth, the stains derived from the blood of Ajax, the Homeric king who committed suicide after being defeated by Odysseus in the contest over Achilles' arms: cf. Colum. 10.174–5 *male damnati maesto qui sanguine surgunt / Aeacii* (*Aeacidae* Heinsius; *Aiacis* Goodyear) *flores*—hence *AI*, the first two letters of his name. The two versions are reconciled in Ov. *met.* 10.207–8 (where Ajax's name is said to be 'added' to Hyacinthus' lament): cf. also Ov. *met.* 13.397–8 *littera communis mediis pueroque uiroque / inscripta est foliis, haec nominis, illa querellae*; but cf. Euphor. fr. 40 Pow. = 44 v. Gron. = Light. (apparently a short poem entitled *Hyakinthos*, which perhaps also featured other stories of fair youths). The title of 'king' seems to befit Ajax better, but may also be applied to the young Hyacinthus, of very noble ancestry. He is the grandson of Sparta's forefather Lacedaemon, whose son Amyclas is the boy's father: Hes. fr. 171 M.-W.; Apollod.

194   ECLOGUE 3

3.10.3 (116). According to another tradition, Hyacinthus is the son of the Muse Clio: Apollod. 1.3.3 (16–17). At any rate, the solution to the riddle ought to be 'everywhere', considering the geographical dissemination of the flower—which seems by no means limited to the banks of the river Eurotas, where Hyacinthus died, or to the plain between Troy and the Rhoetean promontory, where Ajax was said to have died (Serv.: *hyacinthus ubique nascitur flos*); though another correct solution might be *apud Menalcan* or '*apud te*' (cf. 3.62 *apud me*)*. A plant (flower?) contested between Sparta, home of Hyacinthus, and Salamin, home of Ajax, is mentioned in an anonymous Greek epigram: *Anth. Pal.* 9.121 (Salamis was said to produce a flower similar to hyacinth when Ajax died, according to Pausan. 1.35.4). Note, in the phrase *inscripti nomina...flores*, the so-called 'Greek' use of the accusative, here expressing the inscribed object: cf. Soph. *Tr.* 157–8; Philostr. *uita Apoll.* 2.20, p. 62.14–15 Kays.; Stat. *Theb.* 4.267–8.

107 **Phyllida solus habeto**. The winning prize is Phyllis herself—thus, there is no need to compete with Iollas any more (3.76–9): a final intratextual echo, as the agon approaches its end. The phrase sounds somewhat ironic and funny coming from Menalcas who, at least in this agon, has defended homoerotic love and declared his exclusive passion for Amyntas (3.83)—in the end, he cannot be too disappointed if Damoetas keeps the girl all to himself. The etymology of the name Phyllis befits a riddle centred around floral and botanical issues (see 10.41n.).

108–11. The referee eschews the burden of judgement, coyly declaring a draw, perhaps due to the excessive value of the prize, especially in relation to Menalcas (3.32–4). Perhaps Palaemon decides wisely not to shatter the dreams of either of the young contestants, or make it impossible to collect such a valuable prize (which is what apparently happened in Damon's case: 3.23–4). He finally allows himself a consolatory yet elusive generalization (3.109 *et quisquis*): is the experience of love's paradoxical upheaval really sufficient to deserve the prize? On the god's function as poetic teacher cf. Euripides' aphorism, fr. 663 Kann. ποιητὴν δ᾽ ἄρα / Ἔρως διδάσκει, κἂν ἄμουσος ᾖ τὸ πρίν. Love's sweetness and sadness appeared in the exchange at 3.80–3, but the god is γλυκύπικρον by definition (Sapph. fr. 130 V.; cf. Venus in Catull. 68.18, etc.). In the Theocritean corpus, no judge actually declares a draw: in *idd.* 6 and 9, which end without winners or losers, there is no real competition. A famous draw, declared by Achilles in an athletic contest, is the one between Odysseus and Ajax in Hom. *Il.* 23.736. In the *E.*, V. seems to avoid any scenes dealing with collecting prizes, an example of which will appear in the fifth book of the *Aeneid* (cf. *Aen.* 5.244–85). *E.* 7 makes no mention of stakes or prizes awarded to Corydon. Note that, when Palaemon utters his final verdict, his speech

---

* I am indebted to Sarah Pierozzi, a student at Sapienza - University of Rome, for this observation and the way in which it is formulated. Note the asymmetry between *quibus in terris...nascantur* and *apud me munera sunt* (which might make the reader think of branches and flowers plucked from the plant): such an internal echo is part of V.'s quasi-illusionistic technique of hiding and showing a 'mysterious object'.

is four lines long: i.e. the same length as the 2 + 2 exchange, which 'set the tempo' during the whole contest (cf. 3.55–9n.). Palaemon's verdict marks the end of the poem, which is now longer than one hundred lines.

108 tantas…lites. Perhaps not without a certain irony, echoing 3.54 *res est non parua!* (cf. 7.16 *certamen…magnum*). The following line, at any rate, makes it clear that the *uitula* has actually been wagered (3.49–50n.).

109 uitula. The animal makes one last appearance (note its two mentions in the agon: 3.77 and 3.85). In this (still) 'initial' eclogue, the *uitula* embodies the bucolic values (note βου-κόλος) of V.'s poetic form, after *capellae* and *oues* appeared in the first two poems. It might seem surprising that Palaemon knows of the she-calf, since the animal is never mentioned in the dialogue between him and the two contestants. At any rate, even the reader cannot be certain that the she-calf is, in fact, the prize: Menalcas, in his last speech (3.49–51), did not say this explicitly. Yet we need not assume that, from a narrative point of view, V. is only providing the reader with a partial selection of the dialogue that 'actually' took place between the characters. Rather, we ought to take important mimetic elements into account, as they are part of the dramatic technique typical of pastoral poetry. Palaemon has no trouble figuring out what the stakes are, because the stakes have physically been placed 'between' the contestants. With a realistic effect, V. does not give the reader every detail (e.g. there ought to be two *uitulae*, one for each contestant, but this is never mentioned explicitly). The reader, therefore, will never know everything about the situation, though the essential information directly provided by the poet can be indirectly supplemented by the mimetic and pragmatic aspects of the characters' interaction. This dramatic technique is frequently used in the Theocritean corpus: in *id.* 5.139, the judge Morson can award the she-lamb to Comatas without the awards themselves (*id.* 5.23–30) being mentioned to Morson after he is summoned and enters the stage (*id.* 5.66). Similarly, in *id.* 8.84, the goatherd awards the syrinx to Daphnis without it being mentioned after his arrival (*id.* 8.28–32) and without the stakes being clearly defined in the dialogue between the two contestants (*id.* 8.17–24). In these two idylls, too, the awards must be imagined as physically placed in the middle, between the contestants.

109–10 amores /…amaros. A 'vertical' effect of paronomasia between two line-ending words: cf. Plaut. *Cist.* 68 *an amare occipere amarum est, opsecro?*; *Trin.* 260 *Amor amara dat tamen*; note that such an expressive adjective as *amarus* occupies the last place in Palaemon's 'verdict', immediately preceding the final command (3.111). The pun (*amores /…amaros*) strengthens the echo effect: *amaras* was Meliboeus' last word in the first eclogue (1.78n.). These two lines have been suspected of textual corruption, but the transmitted text is most probably correct: the main idea is a depiction of love as a source of anxiety (or, in Epicurean terms, an enemy of *ataraxia*).

110 metuet. The fear is that love might vanish, or that the lover might be deceived (Serv. *ne umquam posset amor ille dissolui*): cf. Dido in *Aen.* 4.298 *omnia tuta timens.* The formulation leaves no room for the lover's pure happiness, since

196 ECLOGUE 4

he is torn between fear (even in the sweetest moments) and suffering (when things are not going well).

111 claudite iam riuos, pueri. This rustic metaphor, which Palaemon uses to bid farewell to the two young poets, translates into pastoral language Catullus' final exhortation at 61.224–5 (231–2) *claudite ostia, uirgines; / lusimus satis* (followed by the poem's concluding farewell and wishes to the newlyweds). The line also features a felicitous variation on the theme of poetry as a 'stream of water' (a spring or a river). In Calpurnius Siculus' second eclogue, featuring an agon between the young gardener Astacus and the shepherd Idas, the former's opening and closing speeches are both centred around irrigation (ll. 34–5; 96–7); cf. *G.* 1.106; 269. Physical closure is a characteristic sign of poetic closure: the same is true of satiety (cf. 10.77n.). **sat.** Shortened form of *satis*, used in somewhat solemn contexts: it will reappear at the end of the whole book (*E.* 10.70); cf. also 4.54; 7.34. **prata biberunt.** The image, featuring the circulation of water and the 'satiety' of the meadows, is well suited to the proper length of a poem (for poetry's 'meadow' cf. Aristoph. *Ran.* 1300; Choeril. fr. 2.2 Bern.; cf. also Prop. 3.3.18). The grassy fields of this finale starkly contrast with the opening of *E.* 4, which features an 'elevation' of tone (*paulo maiora*) and woods (*siluae*) worthy of the consul Pollio. For the perfect indicative, here in line-ending position (and at the very end of the eclogue), see 3.9n.

Eclogue 4

[Pollio]

After a brief prologue introducing the distinctiveness of the subject matter (4.1–3), the fourth eclogue prophesies that, in the consular year of Asinius Pollio (40 BCE: cf. 4.11n.), a boy will be born who will initiate a gradual return to the primeval Golden Age (4.4–63).

The figure of the Sibyl, to whom V. ascribes his prophecy, was customarily associated with crucial moments in Roman history: oracles of all sorts, carrying far from reassuring messages, certainly circulated in Rome during the difficult years that preceded and followed Philippi (4.4n.). Here, however, V. attempts a 'Sibylline song' (4.4 *Cumaei…carminis*) that may inspire long-suffering humankind with confidence and positive hope. Presenting itself as harbinger of a new era, fraught with aspirations to political and ideological harmony, the fourth eclogue freely integrates a Hesiodic-Aratean frame of thought (the myth of the ages) with the archetype of the 'divine child'. It combines Roman religious and moral principles with Eastern suggestions and blends Sibylline prophecies with Etruscan divination. Note also the poem's thematic and stylistic affinity with Catullus' epyllion (Catull. 64), in which an epithalamium is paired with a broader, prophetic vision of history. The pastoral book, whose opening note echoed the civil disorder of land confiscations, reaches here the universal dimension of the regeneration myth.

ECLOGUE 4   197

However, as soon as we try to define the details of this extremely broad picture, a number of difficulties and uncertainties arise.

The first interpretive hurdle is the *puer*'s identity—one of the best-known Virgilian questions, widely discussed in antiquity. V. himself contributed to his readers' confusion by applying the fourth eclogue's prophetic language to Augustus in *Aen.* 6.791–807 (but Octavian was of course an adult at the time of the *E.*, though the identification of the *puer* with the young *diui filius* is testified to by the *scholia Bernensia*, esp. p. 105 H.). An unpersuasive argument, at least as old as Servius, identifies the *puer* with a son of Pollio—either C. Asinius Gallus, born in 41 (i.e. too early), or Saloninus, apparently born in 39 and named after the Dalmatian city of Salona, supposedly conquered by Pollio (yet his existence is doubtful: cf. Serv. *ad E.* 4.1 *quem a capta ciuitate Saloninum uocauit*; see also 5.20–44n.). Asinius Gallus himself apparently claimed to be V.'s *puer*, according to Asconius Pedianus quoted in Serv. Dan. *ad E.* 4.11; see further *Enc. Virg.* IV, pp. 342–4, s.v. *puer* (F. Della Corte). How could such words as e.g. 4.17 be justified for the son of a consul, albeit illustrious? The poem only contains one explicit reference to historical reality, i.e. Pollio's consulship (4.3; 11), which does not seem to fit well with his role as the boy's father. Rather, Pollio is portrayed as the most qualified witness to the miracle and as guarantor of it: under his guidance (4.13 *te duce*), there is no doubt that the *magni menses* (4.12) of the new, great year will not be perturbed by traces of *scelus* (4.13). In fact, it is precisely Pollio's consular office that constitutes both the starting point of the poem and the decisive clue to the issue of the *puer*'s identity.

In the early fall of 40 (between late September and early October), Pollio had achieved an important diplomatic success, known as the Pact of Brundisium (*foedus Brundisinum*), negotiated by Pollio himself on behalf of Antony. According to the treaty, the Roman dominion would be subdivided into three areas: Antony would have the East, Octavian the West, Lepidus the African provinces. The outbreak of a new civil war was thereby avoided. Pollio's merit as a peace-maker is alluded to in 4.13–14 mentioned above (and by the context of the eclogue as a whole). Although he clearly sided with Antony, he managed to maintain his independence throughout his political career, nourishing hopes of reconciliation up to the very end. He did not choose sides during the Perusine War and remained neutral until the final stage of the conflict, culminating in Actium (cf. 3.84n.; Introduction, pp. 5–6). In his letters addressed to Cicero between March and June 43 BCE (*fam.* 10.31–3), Pollio had declared his great concern for peace, freedom, and the *res publica*. Thus, the double reference to Pollio's consulship (4.3; 11) must point to the late fall of 40, when Pollio was finally able to enter office at Rome (albeit for a short time) in the climate of détente that followed his admirable diplomatic operation. There could not be a more tangible proof that the post-Brundisium period started under his guidance. Pollio's consulship was followed by a proconsulship, held in a very strategic region: Macedonia, significantly situated at the border between Antony's East and Octavian's West (cf. 8.8n.).

198 ECLOGUE 4

In order to guarantee the agreement, the parties in Brundisium decided on the marriage between Antony and Octavian's sister Octavia, both recently widowed (Plut. *Ant.* 31). In accordance with a common pattern of dynastic power, Octavia was entrusted with the task of reconciling Octavian and Antony, not unlike Julius Caesar's daughter Julia, who had become Pompey's wife. The birth of a young heir, uniting the two family lines into which Julius Caesar's legacy had been divided, was to be the culmination of Pollio's political activity, first with Caesar and then on the Antonian side. Thus, a prophecy concerning the birth of a godlike son of Pollio would be not only exaggerated but also inappropriate and contrary to the political mission of Pollio himself. As a matter of fact, it was Antony's daughter Antonia Maior who was born in the fall of 39 (Plut. *Ant.* 33.5). But V. could hardly imagine his prophecy to be taken literally: rather, he offered it to the Roman audience mostly as a dream, if not as a wish, for peace and regeneration, based on the exemplarity of a semi-divine family. Far from discouraging the poet, the possibility of a new, disastrous imbalance stimulated him to appeal to the great cosmic and political values of *uirtus* and harmony. In fact, the charge of violating agreements with Octavian (by giving preference to Cleopatra and Egypt) was to be decisive in the later anti-Antonian propaganda. In *E.* 4, the poet's insistence on the fundamentally Roman figure of a *puer* who came into existence during a consul's term of service may also be explained by a general attempt to divert Antony from his attraction to Cleopatra and his dynastic projects in the East. Note that in 40 BCE, probably towards the end of the summer, the Egyptian queen had given birth to the pair of twins she had with Antony (who will not acknowledge them until 37–36 BCE, in Syria: see below, p. 200). Even after Naulochus, Octavian firmly presented Octavia as Antony's legitimate wife, allowing the couple to take part, with their children, in the sacred banquet held in the temple of the goddess Concordia (Cass. Di. 49.18.6; Kellum 1990, pp. 277–8). Even later, Octavia continued to occupy an influential position, especially as a patroness of letters (Plut. *Publ.* 17.8; Cichorius 1922, pp. 281–2). At the time of Pollio's consulship, Roman coins attribute great power and honours to Octavia, the first mortal woman (i.e. not a goddess) to appear on Roman coins (Osgood 2006, p. 189). Octavia's political importance explains why V. devotes so much space, at the end of *E.* 4, to the figure of the boy's *mater* (4.62n.), which V.'s early readers must have equated with Octavian's sister and Antony's wife. From Pollio's point of view, therefore, 4.13 *te duce* is not a vague compliment: thanks to his guidance, political equilibrium would be achieved and fear would be dispelled (4.14). This is, of course, an allusion to the Pact of Brundisium: the agreement, the marriage between Antony and Octavia (with the expected offspring), and the consequent equilibrium between Antony and Octavian were aspects of a single project, which are all reflected in *E.* 4. Rival and hostile forces are correspondingly excluded from it: particularly Sextus Pompey, a well-known charismatic general who had defeated Pollio himself in 44 BCE (during the war in Spain: Cass. Di. 45.10.4–6). Sextus Pompey threatened the stability of the *foedus Brundisinum*, which made him feel deceived:

hence his naval actions sabotaging supply chains in Sicily, Puteoli, and Ostia (Flor. *epit.* 2.18.2), which elicited protests among the Roman citizenry, suddenly facing new taxes and food shortage (Appian. *bell. civ.* 5.67 [280–3]; Cass. Di. 48.31). In 39 BCE the triumvirs sought reconciliation with Sextus through the Pact of Misenum, which temporarily boosted the citizens' morale in Rome and the rest of Italy (Appian. *bell. civ.* 5.74 [314–17]; cf. Vell. 2.77). Regardless of who the *puer* is, the fourth eclogue explicitly sets itself in 40 BCE and radiates a dream of peace and prosperity (including agricultural wealth: cf. 4.28n.) while displaying traces of looming threats such as war and conflict (4.14; 4.31–6). Both can be explained in the context of a fragile peace like the *foedus Brundisinum*, which was threatened (from Octavian's point of view) by Sextus Pompey and Antony simultaneously. On the other hand, *E.* 4 outlines a soteriological paradigm of general value, which later readers (especially Christian ones) will adapt to different contexts.

Yet V. sees Pollio as a source of hope for a better future: a new birth. This probably refers to the birth of Antony and Octavia's son. But Octavian himself would soon have a child with Scribonia, thus directly taking part in the renewal of Roman society. Yet his child, too, was a girl, Julia—hence the pretext for a divorce. Thus, rather than a single individual, the *puer* is a political symbol: a model to which the new generation ought to conform, under the leadership of one of Rome's most prominent citizens. It is undeniable that the idea of a regenerating youth resonated with the still youthful figure of a *diui filius*, who had made his debut on Rome's political scene, a few years earlier, as a *puer* (Cic. *fam.* 12.25.4; hence Antony's irony, censored by Cicero: *Phil.* 13.24 *puerum appellat quem non modo uirum sed etiam fortissimum uirum sensit et sentiet*). Messianic anecdotes and rumours started circulating early on, such as the story of Octavian appearing in a dream to Cicero, who supposedly identified him as the *puer* divinely chosen to lead Rome (Suet. *Aug.* 94.9; cf. [Cic.] *epist. ad Oct.* 6).

Hellenistic encomia had set the standard for how to praise sovereigns, equating them to divine figures. Theocritus himself, the *auctor* of pastoral poetry, had written encomia—thereby effectively linking the two genres together. In *E.* 4, echoes of Theocritus' encomiastic poetry are clearly recognizable, especially from *id.* 16 *Charites* or *Hiero*; 17 *Encomium for Ptolemy*; 24 *Heracliscus* (Heracles' childhood was a favourite topic at the Ptolemies' court, since they considered the hero as their divine ancestor). Even the charismatic prototype of Alexander the Great was pervaded by a network of reminiscences combining the heroic myth of invincible Achilles (4.36n.) with elements drawn from a variety of divine and semi-divine figures, especially Dionysus and Heracles (Seibert 1972, pp. 204–6). At Rome, in the final years of the Republic and especially since the age of Sulla, political struggles had reshaped that ideological language: it was customary for important leaders and their faction to adopt a divine figure as their emblem (for these notions, and the rich secondary literature, see P. Zanker 1987; cf. also Pollini 1990; Galinsky 1996, esp. pp. 215–19). Following in Alexander's footsteps, Mark Antony had modelled his own political image after Bacchus-Dionysus and

200   ECLOGUE 4

Hercules, whose descendant he claimed to be: see notably Plutarch, *Ant.* 60.5. Plutarch himself testifies to Antony's self-portrayal as Dionysus in early 41 BCE (cf. *Ant.* 24.4, with the commentaries ad loc. by C. B. R. Pelling, Cambridge 1988, pp. 179–80, and L. Santi Amantini, Milan 1995, p. 408; for the parallel between Antony/Octavia and Dionysus/Ariadne, cf. Osgood 2006, pp. 240–1).

In *E.* 4, the Antonian model, based on Hercules and Dionysus, is echoed in more than one passage (4.15–17; 18–20; 63). The context is, however, explicitly Apollonian (4.10 *tuus iam regnat Apollo*), thereby confirming the equilibrium to which the poem aspires. In fact, it is likely that Apollo, the *gens Iulia*'s tutelary deity (Weinstock 1971, pp. 12–15; Miller 2009, pp. 23–4, with references), was an attractive role-model for Octavian as early as the 40s BCE, even though such anecdotes as the well-known 'dinner of the twelve gods' must be taken with caution (Suet. *Aug.* 70; cf. the conclusions reached, despite his scepticism, by Gurval 1995, p. 115; also Miller 2009, pp. 15–18 and 30–9). Although Naulochus and, above all, Actium (along with the inauguration of the temple of Palatine Apollo) were still far to come, it is possible that V. coupled a vitalist, Dionysian blossoming with the Delphic god's prophetic and brightly rational values, perhaps in order to show the way ahead to the young Caesar. By contrast, it is obviously anachronistic (and incorrect) to identify Apollo with Augustus, as Servius does in his note *ad E.* 4.10. In the above-mentioned passage from *Aen.* 6, where the 'restorer' of *aurea saecula* will be identified with Augustus, the role-models of Hercules and Liber will themselves be surpassed by the *princeps'* achievements: *nec uero Alcides tantum telluris obiuit...nec...Liber, agens celso Nysae de uertice tigris* (*Aen.* 6.801 and 804–5; cf. Ov. *amor.* 3.8.51–2). Chapter 94 of Suetonius' biography, which collects a wealth of divine portents concerning the fate of the future Augustus, will include the dream of his mother Atia (modelled after that of Olympia, mother of Alexander the Great) to be read as proof that she conceived the child with Apollo; an omen of the god Dionysus, which also occurred in Alexander's case; and various godsent dreams revealing Zeus' favour (Suet. *Aug.* 94.4–9; upon learning the time of the future Augustus' birth, Nigidius Figulus is said to have remarked that 'the ruler of the world is born' [94.5]). As for Antony, while staying with Cleopatra in Antiochia, Siria (37–36 BCE), he acknowledged the pair of twins she had given birth to in 40 BCE, using names clearly alluding to a glorious Hellenistic past and to a rosy future at the same time: Alexander Helios and Cleopatra Selene (Plut. *Ant.* 36.5–6, with C. B. R. Pelling's commentary [quoted above], pp. 219–20, ad loc.; all this confirms that encomiastic-astronomical rhetoric circulated within the Antonian milieu).

Through the language of divine models, readily recognizable in Rome and widespread in the iconography, coins, and visual arts, the poet strove to sing a conciliatory song, harmonizing those political forces that were soon to prove irreconcilable. An echo of such disappointed expectations is perhaps to be found in Horace's epode 16, if indeed (as seems likely) it reverses the optimism of *E.* 4

and proceeds on the assumption that any reconciliation between Antony and Octavian has become impossible. At any rate, leaving aside issues of chronological priority, both Horace and V. certainly accompanied Maecenas on his way to Brundisium, when (in 38 BCE) they tried to renegotiate the *foedus* (witness Hor. *sat.* 1.5). The two poets must have shared expectations as well as disappointment. Many years later, during the *Ludi saeculares* of 17 BCE, Horace celebrated the new era of Augustus' long firmly established rule by echoing the old dream of *E.* 4 in more than one passage: however, he placed more emphasis on the figures of Apollo and Diana, by then thoroughly Augustan (see 4.4n.; 5n.; 10n.; 46–7n.; on the Virgilian echoes in Hor. *carm.* 4.2.33–40, cf. 4.6n.).

The historical topicality of *E.* 4 secures its place within the pastoral book: closely following *E.* 2 and 3, with their programmatically Theocritean status, the fourth eclogue employs the extreme language of prophecy to express a sorrowful contrast with contemporary events—the same contrast that frames the whole collection. *E.* 4 has at times been considered as a standlone encomiastic piece, almost mechanically inserted into V.'s book. Yet the recurring images and memories of the pastoral world, occasionally reshaped in fantastic terms (e.g. the wool of rams and lambs is spontaneously coloured at 4.42–5; cf. also the spontaneity of pastoral and agricultural production at 21–30), corroborates the poem's connection with the book as a whole—a connection that would otherwise be merely a cold, intellectualist project. The Golden Age proves to be a mythical archetype which the pastoral world, and the bucolic book in particular, can actualize. *E.* 1 and 9 describe the way in which land confiscations can destroy the sheltered world of the *rus*, whereas *E.* 4 rekindles hope for a palingenesis of both society and history, grounded in nature's elemental forces (earth, maternity). Servius makes a similar point: *nam licet haec ecloga discedat a bucolico carmine, tamen inserit ei aliqua apta operi* (*ad E.* 4.1).

Pollio's name reconnects the text to *E.* 3, which had given the reader a foretaste of the 'Golden' motif (3.89n.). Far from being an occasional parenthesis, *E.* 4 opens up a new literary path within the book—a path that will be furthered in *E.* 5 and 6, and eventually reconsidered through an agon in *E.* 7. The dedication to Pollio, who will reappear after the sequence of *E.* 4-5-6-7 (and thus in correspondence to *E.* 3: Pollio is more likely than Octavian to be the addressee of *E.* 8), is also key to understanding the intensely affectionate memory (alongside Aratus and Hesiod) of Catull. 64, the style of which is closely echoed here: cf. esp. 4.6n.; 8–9n.; 15–16n.; 46–59n.; 49n.; 63n. (certain Catullan traits have been regarded by many scholars as characterizing the poem as a whole). Catullus, in fact, must have been greatly admired by Pollio, who had the chance to meet him as a young boy (cf. Introduction, p. 11 and n. 27; above, p. 148; 3.84n.) and took part personally in the neoteric movement with his short poems.

It seems, in conclusion, that little room is left for the messianic readings that played such a fundamental role in the reception of *E.* 4. Had it not been for the

202   ECLOGUE 4

Christian interpretation, identifying the *puer* with the Messiah, V.'s fame as prophet and magician, as a pagan enlightened by God—an image of V. particularly widespread in the Middle Ages and crucial to Dante (but cf. 4.6n.)—would have had no *raison d'être* (witness the early Greek version of the poem in the so-called *Oratio Constantini Magni ad Sanctorum Coetum*, 19–21, pp. 181–7 Heikel). Similarly unpersuasive are other mystical-religious interpretations, such as the one that Eduard Norden proposed in his famous 1924 work. According to Norden, E. 4 could be traced back to a gnostic theosophy widespread across ancient Egypt and the Near East: a system of beliefs from which Christianity itself would have derived. Norden specifically pointed to two religious feasts celebrated in Alexandria between late December and early January, in honour of Helios and Aion, respectively. Such readings often appeal to esoteric lore hardly accessible to the poet—and, even less so, to his public. However, we cannot rule out that V. picked up signals from the East, which were spreading in Rome through a number of channels. Note the poem's affinity, perhaps mediated by Sibylline literature and its possible Jewish influences, with the prophetic books of the Bible (known to Roman readers through the Greek Septuagint translation), especially Joel, Hosea, Amos, and Isaiah (for the latter cf. 4.22n.). Pollio himself may have been somewhat acquainted with Judaism (see Feldman 1953; 4.12n.). Antony and Cleopatra were themselves in contact with Herod (later called 'the Great') as of 40 BCE: cf. D. W. Roller, *Cleopatra: A Biography*, Oxford 2010, esp. pp. 86–7; 91; 117–22. Such a mixture, in keeping with traditional conceptions (cf. the Eleusinian mysteries), would not be surprising in a poem so deeply conciliatory: the song of a Sibyl who strives to keep East and West together.

E. 4 is the second narrative poem in the book, and is uttered by the voice of the poet himself. For the first time, V. directly addresses a dedicatee (presupposed in 4.3, then explicitly mentioned at 4.10): this emphasizes the innovative, exceptional nature of the poem. A brief proem in three lines (1–3), in which the poet invokes his 'Sicilian' Muses, is followed by a prophetic song (4–59) which, if the transmitted text is genuine (for potential interpolations cf. 4.21–2n.; 23n.), can be divided into three parts. These sections are quantitatively balanced: the second is twice as long as each of the other two and, in each section, the number of lines is a multiple of seven (and the sum of the lines of the poem, 63, is equal to 7 × 9). In 4–17, the poet introduces the topic and invokes Lucina (8–10), then Pollio (12–17): fourteen lines in total, subdivided into two seven-line units (4–10; 11–17). In the long second section (twenty-eight lines: 18–45), the poet addresses the *puer* and keeps the focus on him until the end of the poem. Note the threefold structure of the central section: the boy's birth and nature's joyous reaction to it (18–25); the boy's adolescence, accompanied by traces of humankind's 'old sins' (26–36); the *puer*'s maturity and the ensuing Golden Age (37–45). The third and final section of the poem is fourteen lines long (46–59), like the first: here V. mentions the Parcae, delivers an exhortation to the *puer*, and declares that he hopes to

ECLOGUE 4   203

be able to sing the future world described in the prophecy (note a further biparti-
tion: 46–52; 53–9; seven lines each). The last four lines belong to the 'Sibylline
song' but form an autonomous epilogue, with a final exhortation to the *puer* and
a gnomic statement on heroic immortality. The sum of these lines and those of
the prologue is, again, seven. In this prophetic eclogue, ruled by the god of the
Sibyl, it has to be noted that seven is the number of Apollo: cf. Hes. *op.* 770–1;
Callim. *hymn.* 4[*Del.*].251–5 (with *schol. ad* 251); *ait.* (?), *SH* 277 = fr. 115 Mass. =
190f Hard.

On the eclogue: Marx (1898); Sudhaus (1901); Mayor, Fowler, Conway (1907); Austin
(1927); Weyman (1918a; 1918b); Boll (1923); Norden (1924); Corssen (1925); Weber
(1925); Alföldi (1930); Carcopino (1930); Herrmann (1930, pp. 58–106); Jeanmaire (1930);
Tarn (1932); Weinreich (1932); E. Pfeiffer (1933, pp. 68–115); Hubaux, Leroy (1934);
Jeanmaire (1939); Hommel (1950); Jachmann (1952a); C. Becker (1955); Büchner (1955,
cols. 1195–1213); Wagenvoort (1956a); Otis (1963, pp. 136–40); Bollack (1967); Gatz
(1967, pp. 87–103); Gotoff (1967); Klingner (1967, pp. 68–82); Grüber (1968); G. Williams
(1968, pp. 274–85); Putnam (1970, pp. 136–65); Leach (1971); E. A. Schmidt (1972b,
pp. 154–72); Mette (1973); Berg (1974, pp. 155–77); Leach (1974, pp. 216–31); G. Williams
(1974); Alföldi (1975); Cupaiuolo (1977, pp. 158–71); DuQuesnay (1977); V. Schmidt
(1977); Nisbet (1978); Van Sickle (1978, pp. 131–8); Alpers (1979, pp. 156–90); Della Corte
(1981); Kraus (1981); Naumann (1981); Pascucci (1981); Beaujeu (1982); E. A. Schmidt
(1982); Binder (1983); Thummer (1983); Uruschadse (1985); Pulbrook (1987a); M. O. Lee
(1989, pp. 77–88); Clausen (1990); Van Sickle (1992); Arnold (1995); T. K. Hubbard
(1995b, pp. 12–19; cf. 1998, pp. 77–85); Petrini (1995, pp. 112–21); Galinsky (1996,
pp. 90–121); Acuña (1998); P. Hardie (1998, pp. 20–1); Binder, Effe (2001, pp. 69–77);
Marinčič (2001); Breed (2006a, pp. 139–48); Osgood (2006, pp. 193–201); von Albrecht
(2007, pp. 23–5); Harrison (2007, pp. 36–44); Graf von Gries (2008); A. Powell (2008,
pp. 207–16); Davis (2012, pp. 63–77); Kania (2016, pp. 80–90).

Specific issues: Housman (1900) (l. 24); Slater (1912) (historical context); Frank (1916)
(l. 49); Phillimore (1916, pp. 149–51) (l. 61); Birt (1918) (l. 62); Stuart (1921) (ll. 60–3);
Fabia (1931) (l. 61); Lagrange (1931) (messianism); Lovejoy, Boas (1935, pp. 85–92) (primi-
tivism); Snell (1938) (Hor. *epod.* 16); Rose (1942, pp. 183–6) (Plato's *Statesman* and the age
of Kronos); Kalinka (1943) (l. 62); R. H. Martin (1943) (Golden Age and cyclical model);
Barwick (1944) (Hor. *epod.* 7; 16); Herescu (1946) (l. 61); Herrmann (1946) (l. 28); van der
Waerden (1952) (the *magnus annus*); Vazquez (1952) (Callim. *iamb.* 12); Feldman (1953)
(Asinius Pollio and Judaism); Wimmel (1953) (Hor. *epod.* 16); Herescu (1955) (l. 61);
Kurfess (1955) (Sibylline prophecies and Christianity); G. Radke (1956) (l. 7); Savage
(1956) (Apollo and Hercules); Courcelle (1957) (Christian interpretation); Herescu (1957)
(ll. 60–3); Duckworth (1958) (l. 23); Ryberg (1958) (the Golden Age in V.); Westendorp
Boerma (1958, pp. 54–6) (Catullus); A. Y. Campbell (1958–9) (ll. 62–3); Wimmel (1961)
(Hor. *epod.* 16); Schönbeck (1962, pp. 132–54) (nature's miracles); Wagenvoort (1962)
(edenic themes); Merlan (1963) (l. 63); Neugebauer (1963) (l. 61); Kinzler (1968) (l. 61);
Baldwin (1969) (l. 61); Duckworth (1969, pp. 50–2) (Catullan metre); Huxley (1969) (l. 61);
Ableitinger-Grünberger (1971) (Hor. *epod.* 7; 16); Castorina (1971) (Lucretius and the
Golden Age); V. Schmidt (1972) (Prop. 2.3); Wigodsky (1972, pp. 130–1) (Catullus);

204   ECLOGUE 4

Flintoff (1973) (ll. 8–10); Fantazzi (1974) (Arcadia and the Golden Age); Wlosok (1974) (l. 4); Traina (1975a) (l. 50); Traina (1975b) (l. 49); R. D. Williams (1976) (ll. 60–3); Segal (1977) (relationship to *E.* 3); Coleiro (1979) (Hor. *epod.* 16); Nethercut (1979) (l. 23); Pianezzola (1979) (the Golden Age); Benko (1980) (Christian interpretation); Brenk (1980) (the Golden Age); Wifstrand Schiebe (1981, pp. 20–6) (the Golden Age); Wigtil (1981) (Greek translation in the *Oratio Constantini*); Della Corte (1982) (epithalamia); Wallace-Hadrill (1982) (the Golden Age); Monteleone (1982–3) (textual problems); Bauzá (1983) (ll. 22–5); Wlosok (1983) (l. 4); Coronati (1984) (Greek translation in the *Oratio Constantini*); Buisel (1986) (who is the *puer*?); Ferrarino (1986a) (l. 62); Goold (1986) (l. 62); Curchin (1988) (who is the *puer*?); B. Thornton (1988) (ll. 42–5); Irwin (1989) (ll. 42–5); Kraggerud (1989, pp. 110–12) (l. 8); Lanternari (1989) (Neo-Pythagoreanism); Nicastri (1989) (Emmanuel's prophecy); Köves-Zulauf (1990, pp. 289–329) (ll. 60–3); Kraggerud (1990, pp. 63–6) (l. 4); Langholf (1990) (Neronian allegory in Calp. Sic.); Farrell (1991b, pp. 289–91) (*E.* 3 and 4); Glei (1991, pp. 54–7, 90–2, 258–63) (war); Brisson (1992) (the Golden Age); Cutolo (1992) (Callimacheanism); Morgan (1992) (Callimacheanism); Parker (1992) (ll. 43–5); Moya del Baño (1993) (l. 62); Nisbet (1993) (ll. 28–30); Stroh (1993) (prophetic poetry in V. and Horace); Ruiz de Elvira (1994) (l. 62); Perutelli (1995, pp. 60–1) (who is the *puer*?); Plowden (1995) (l. 24); Putnam (1995, pp. 307–10) (l. 7); Ruiz Arzalluz (1995) (Augustus and the *puer*; Nero = Apollo; ll. 4–7); Kraggerud (1996, pp. 103–7) (l. 62); Landolfi (1996, pp. 51–61) (*Virgo* and the myth of the ages); Meulder (1996) (date); Moya del Baño (1996) (l. 32); Pelling (1996, pp. 17–19) (date and historical context); Braund (1997, pp. 208–9) (cosmology); Dostálová (1997) (l. 62); Kropp (1998) (the 'divine child' as an archetype); Rochette (1998) (l. 49); Rodríguez Adrados (1998) (ll. 60–3); Buisel (1999) (myth and history); Bernardi Perini (1999–2000) (messianism); Lefèvre (2000) (Catullus); Gómez Pallarès (2001) (ll. 18–25); Hunter (2001) (Theocr. *id.* 17); Timpanaro (2001, p. 10, n. 21) (l. 62); Villaseñor Cuspinara (2001) (Hor. *carm. saec.*); Luther (2002, pp. 11–33) (historical context); Marinčič (2002) (ll. 58–9); Perkell (2002) (the Golden Age); M. Becker (2003) (l. 7); Sauron (2004) (the Golden Age in Pompeian art); Uden (2004) (Christian interpretation); Firpo (2005) (l. 61); Bernays (2006) (Hor. *epod.* 16); Guadagno (2007) (ll. 60–3); Whittaker (2007) (Eleusinian mysteries); Bernays (2008) (l. 45); Kraggerud (2008, pp. 53–4) (l. 62); J. S. Clay (2009) (l. 28); Miller (2009, pp. 254–60) (Apollo); Ebbeler (2010, pp. 188–94) (textuality; the singer Linus); Snijder (2010) (the *puer* is Octavian); Woodman (2010) (ll. 28–9); Kovacs (2011) (ll. 53–4); Braccesi (2012, pp. 10–18) (who is the *puer*?); De Nonno (2012) (ll. 62–3); Kovacs, Omrani (2012) (l. 28); Ottaviano (2013) (ll. 53–4); Scafoglio (2013b) (ll. 62–3); Heyworth (2015, pp. 208–13) (ll. 60–3); Ottaviano (2016) (ll. 62–3); Polt (2016) (ll.31–6); A. T. Zanker (2016) (ll. 43–4); Kraggerud (2017a, pp. 100–5) (ll. 60–2); Kraggerud (2017b, pp. 16–18; 81–2) (l. 8); Kraggerud (2017b, pp. 19–20) (ll. 28–9); Kraggerud (2017b, pp. 21–2) (ll. 62–3); Kraggerud (2020, pp. 272–7) (ll. 60–2); Harrison (2021) (Sextus Pompey).

1–3. After the introduction provided by *E.* 2, this is the poet's second direct intervention (followed by three further instances, in the remaining even poems, *E.* 6; 8; 10). V. thereby indicates, right after the Theocritean *E.* 2 and 3, a significant change in direction. V.'s *siluae*, symbolizing the Virgilian pastoral world (ever since *E.* 1.5), should become worthy of the consul, who is the first and foremost addressee, and whom 4.12 will reveal to be Asinius Pollio (for his part, Pollio

ECLOGUE 4   205

admired the poet's *rustica Musa*, as the reader already knows from 3.84). In the proem to *E.* 6, on the other hand, any ambition of 'elevated' poetry, honouring Varus, will have to yield to the *agrestis Musa* (esp. 6.6–8). On a closer look, however, the elevation of tone appears moderate even in this instance (*paulo maiora*, not *maiora*), despite being highlighted by the contrast with the meadows of 3.111n.; cf., at any rate, 6.39 *incipiant siluae cum primum surgere*. The Muses and the woods represent the binomial pair of art and matter (*silua* also means ὕλη, 'raw material': think of *antiqua silua* at *Aen.* 6.179, according to S. Hinds, *Allusion and Intertext. Dynamics of Appropriation in Roman Poetry*, Cambridge 1998, pp. 10–14). The rhetorical sophistication of these three lines appears evident, particularly due to the polyptoton *siluas, siluae* and the echo *canamus...si canimus*.

   1 Sicelides Musae. The intention to elevate the tone is expressed by the opening word, a solemn form ostensibly coined by the poet on the model of *Pierides* and *Castalides* (its only Greek attestation depends on V.: *E.* 4 is translated in *Orat. Const. ad sanct. coet.* 19.4, p. 181 Heikel Σικελίδες Μοῦσαι, μεγάλην φάτιν ὑμνήσωμεν). For similar phrases cf. 7.21 *Nymphae...Libethrides*; 10.9–10 *puellae Naides*. For the long vowel in the first syllable, see the bucolic precedent of [Mosch.] *epit. Bion.* 8 ἄρχετε, Σικελικαί, τῷ πένθεος ἄρχετε, Μοῖσαι 'begin, Sicilian Muses, being to mourn' (cf. Theocr. *id.* 7.40; the normal prosody is short, e.g. in *Siculis* at 2.21); note also, at the outset of a poem, [Bion], *epith. Achill. et Deid.* 1 Σικελὸν μέλος. For the geographical allusion to Sicily, with a programmatic value, following Theocr. *id.* 1.124–5, cf. 6.1 *Syracosio...uersu* (n.); 10.4 *fluctus...Sicanos*; there is a precise echo, even in terms of prosody, at Sil. 14.466–7 *Daphnin amarunt / Sicelides Musae* (but cf. Ov. *met.* 5.412 *Sicelidas...Nymphas*); for more common Latin forms (*Siculus/Sicanus*), see 2.21n. **paulo maiora canamus.** The Muses' direct involvement is typical of poetic beginnings (cf. 3.60n.), but here V.'s choice of the adverb *paulo* has a rather limiting effect. The elevation is relative (the poem is still a pastoral eclogue), as Servius observes: *bene 'paulo': nam licet haec ecloga discedat a bucolico carmine, tamen inserit ei aliqua apta operi*. The adverb *paulo* is common in Republican poetry (note *paulo maiora* at Lucr. 2.137), but is ultimately a colloquial term. In fact, Augustan poetry tends to avoid it: it appears only here in V., while Horace uses it multiple times but exclusively in the *sermones* (note also rare occurrences in Ovid and the frequent phrase *paulo ante* in early imperial poetry; cf. Catull. 66.51). V. uses *paulum* twice, at *Aen.* 3.597 and 4.649 (whereas *paulatim* is very frequent in his works: cf. here *E.* 4.28 and 6.36).

   2 myricae. Probably tamarisks, which grow in relatively low and very thick bushes, with typically small, pink flowers (a type of *Tamaricaceae*); their presence within Italy is attested by Plin. *nat.* 13.116. Here, on their first occurrence in the *E.*, they express the light refinement of a delicate kind of poetry, perhaps also due to the sound affinity with words denoting 'little' things, such as *mica* 'crumb' or, in Greek, μύρμηκες 'ants'. The Greek μυρίκη (with a short iota) appears in certain

206   ECLOGUE 4

Iliadic passages, among which note the riverside landscape serving as a backdrop for Achilles' actions: 'And then the goddess' son left his spear there, on the bank, / leaning on the tamarisks' (Hom. *Il*. 21.17–18; the beginning of the battle by the Xanthus river). Furthermore, a passage of Nicander provides information on the prophetic powers of the plant, involved in Apollo's cult: Nic. *ther*. 612–14 esp. 612 καὶ μυρίκης…νέον, with the scholion *ad* 613a (the god is said to have appeared to Alcaeus in a dream, holding a tamarisk branch in his hand: cf. fr. 444 V.). They belong to pastoral landscape, as is made clear by the opening of *id*. 1: 'By the Nymphs, o goatherd, do you want to sit here, / where the tamarisks [μυρῖκαι; note the long iota, as in the Latin *myricae*] grow around this sloping hill, / and play your pipe?' (*id*. 1.12–14), with the scholion to 1.13 [f], p. 35 Wend. 'this kind of plant mostly grows in the vicinity of rivers (cf. again Hom. *Il*. 21.17–18): it is customary to spend the afternoon in their shade'. The tamarisks will reappear in metapoetically significant passages of the book (and always in the even poems): cf. 6.10n.; 8.54n. (the miracles of the Golden Age); 10.13n.

3 siluas, siluae. Through polyptoton and chiasmus, this repetition echoes and modifies the one found at 2.60–2n. **consule.** As we can infer from 4.12, this is Asinius Pollio (cf. 3.84n.), eponymous consul in 40 BCE with his colleague Domitius Calvinus; on the actual duration of his appointment (which, due to the turmoil of that year, Pollio was only able to hold for a few months), cf. above, p. 197. For the construction *dignus* + abl. in poetic contexts, cf. 8.10n.

4–17. After the prologue, this section opens the poem proper with the key phrase *Cumaei…carminis* (4.4n.). Two parts of seven lines each can be distinguished (see above, p. 202): the first is devoted to the divine sphere (4.4–10), whereas the second focuses on the human world (Pollio and the *puer*, who is destined to rule the earth: 4.11–17). Here, however, the poet does not address the *puer* directly, as he does in 4.18. The *tu* at 4.8 is the goddess Lucina (4.10n.), different from the more abstract *Virgo*. Lucina makes the future birth more concrete. At 4.11, the *tu* is Pollio, while the *puer* is referred to in the third person (4.15 *ille*).

4. A line of elaborate structure, with two adjectives at the outset and the two corresponding nouns at the end, according to the chiastic scheme $a^1a^2VS^2S^1$ (with the verb and, here, the adverb in the middle): a key feature of Catullus 64; cf. *E*. 4.29; the effect, appropriate for the true beginning of the *carmen*, is one of oracular solemnity. A response to such solemnity, but opposite in tone, is the opening of Hor. *epod*. 16.1–2 *Altera iam teritur bellis ciuilibus aetas, / suis et ipsa Roma uiribus ruit* (on issues of priority cf., however, the above discussion at pp. 200–1). **Ultima…aetas.** The last age, which is now coming to an end before the great renewal, as is explained at 4.5: the deliberately obscure language of prophecy compresses concepts and images, but does not give up on precision. Servius identified the last age with the Sibyl's tenth age, which nevertheless could be deemed happy (*Orac. Sib*. 4.47). This, on the other hand, is but the prelude to the imminent Golden Age (the *Saturnia regna* of 4.6). **Cumaei…carminis.**

The 'Cumaean song', from the city of Cuma, in the Phlegraean fields in Campania (*Cumae, Κύμη*), home to the Sibyl, the prophetess inspired by Apollo. She is a figure of great relevance in Rome's history and historiography. The official collection of her oracles, in Greek hexameters, was preserved on the Capitol by specifically appointed *quindecemuiri sacris faciundis*. It was destroyed in the fire of 83 BCE, but was soon replaced and reinstated. In 12 BCE (or, more probably, somewhat earlier), Augustus had it deposited in the temple of Palatine Apollo, under the pedestal of the god's cult statue, after a process of revision and censorship. Documents and bibliography in *Enc. Virg.* IV, pp. 825–31, s.vv. *Sibilla*; *Sibillini, libri* (E. Flores; F. Piccirillo; L. Breglia Pulci Doria); Parke (1988); Potter (1990, esp. p. 123); *Virg. Enc.* III, pp. 1167–8, s.v. *Sibyl* (J. L. Lightfoot); and also Gowers (2005). As the *princeps* will later do through his authority, here V. proposes a reassuring interpretation of the Sibyl's prophecies, which at Rome were also circulating in private versions—obviously less subject to control, as can be inferred from Suet. *Aug.* 31.1 (cf. also *Aen.* 6.74–6). V. may have been familiar with phrases and formulas typical of Sibylline prophecies, such as certain uses of the anaphora (cf. 4.6n.; 24–5n.); yet we must be cautious in employing the *Sibylline Oracles* as a comparandum, particularly because the whole corpus is relatively late in its form known to us (though cf. 4.22n.). A complex re-elaboration of the Sibyl theme in a Virgilian perspective will appear in Tib. 2.5. Horace will also mention the *Sibyllini…uersus* in the opening of his *Carmen saeculare* (Hor. *carm. saec.* 5). Note that, in the last years of Julius Caesar's rule, Roman coins had begun to depict a symbolic cosmos in which earthly power is combined with Sibylline emblems and Golden Age imagery. Here, it seems, we ought to accept the Latinized spelling of the Greek adj. κυμαῖος, i.e. with a /u/, even though a minority of the manuscript tradition attests the variant reading *Cymaei* (for a similar issue, cf. *Aen.* 3.441 and 6.98; but note Prop. 2.2.16 *Cumaeae…uatis*; Ov. *met.* 14.135; the spelling *Cymaea* reappears in the manuscript tradition of the epic successors of V.: Val. Fl. 1.5; Sil. 9.57). *Cumanus* is the normal Latin form, used in Latin poetry to denote the Sibyl (Lucan. 1.564 *Cumanae…uatis*), which sounds more prosaic and trivial compared to the Hellenizing form *Cumaeus*, hardly surprising in a poem that began with *Sicelides* (in lieu of the more common *Siculae/Sicanae*). Hesiodic echoes are also possible: Hesiod originally came from the Aeolic Cuma, in Euboea, whence he moved to Ascra (*op.* 635–40). For *carmen* in the sense of 'prophetic song', 'prophecy', especially in connection with the Sibyl, cf. Cic. *diu.* 2.112; see also Ov. *fast.* 4.257; Liv. 10.8.2, etc.; *ThlL* III.464.9–23.

    5 magnus…saeclorum…ordo. The notion introduced in 4.4 is further specified; the *ultima…aetas*, which has already arrived (*uenit* is a perfect), is about to open up a new, momentous beginning: *nascitur* retains its inchoative force. According to various priestly traditions, the length of a *saeculum* (note the rhythmic emphasis, due to the contracted form, which necessarily replaces *saeculorum* in hexameter poetry and generates a solemn molossus) could vary between 100 and

208   ECLOGUE 4

110 years: the transition between one 'century' and the next was marked by the *Ludi saeculares*, proclaimed by the *quindecemuiri* after consulting the Sibylline books. Since the celebration of such *Ludi* is attested, before V., only in 249 and 146 BCE, the poet feels free to announce the imminent coming of a new *saeculum* (39 BCE); cf. *Enc. Virg.* IV, esp. p. 638b, s.v. *saeculum* (M. G. Angeli Bertinelli); cf. also the Sibylline oracle in Phleg. *macr.* 5.4 (*FGrH* 257 F 37 Jac.) = 6.3, pp. 81–91 Stram.; Zosim. 2.6 (in the context of the *Ludi saeculares* held in 17 BCE, close to V.'s own time). V.'s assertion that a whole new series of centuries (*magnus... ordo*) is about to begin shows the influence of both the astronomical notion of the *magnus annus*, defined by the recurrence of an identical aligning of the stars (e.g. Cic. *nat. deor.* 2.51) and the Etruscan mantic tradition, according to which the *nomen Etruscum*'s life cycle has a duration of ten *saecula* (Cens. 17.5–6); cf. *Orac. Sib.* 4.47; 8.199. The next *Ludi saeculares* will only be celebrated by Augustus in 17 BCE, marking the beginning of a new era (Horace will speak in favour of the 110-year official computation in *carm. saec.* 21). According to Servius Dan. *ad E.* 9.46, the Etruscan seer Vulcanius (maybe *Vulcatius?*) interpreted the 44 BCE appearance of the so-called *sidus Iulium* as a sign that Rome's tenth *saeculum* was going to begin (4.10n.). The idea that Rome's *saecula* need a rebirth is taken for granted in *G.* 1: once reconciliation becomes impossible, V. makes it clear that Octavian is the only source of hope (*G.* 1.500: *hunc saltem euerso iuuenem succurrere saeclo*; note also 1.468 *impia...saecula*; cf., later, *Aen.* 6.791–3 *hic uir, hic est... / Augustus Caesar...aurea condet / saecula*). **ab integro**. The phrase, obsolete and perhaps archaizing compared to the normal *de / ex integro* (Servius Dan. points to Cat. *orat.* fr. 14 Sbl. Cug. *omnia ab integro paranda erant*; cf. Cic. *Verr.* 2.1.147; Liv. 43.16.7), draws the reader's attention to the fact that the new era opens an entirely new series of *saecula*; the idea is that of a palingenesis (παλιγγενεσία), especially dear to Stoic philosophy. In this line and the whole passage, note the insistence on the /o/ sound, often in arsis or hexameter-ending position: *saeclorum*; *ordo*; *uirgo*; *caelo*; *alto*; *puero*; *quo*; *toto*; *mundo*; *Apollo*. The long second syllable of *integro* is justified by a solemn, 'detached' pronunciation (something like *integ-ro*; cf. *G.* 4.302, as well as Lucr. 1.197).

6–7. After ll. 4–5, focusing on Roman religious notions, these lines add a reference to the myth of the ages, defined by Hesiod, *op.* 106–201 and then reworked by Aratus, *phaen.* 96–136 (later also by Ovid, *met.* 1.89–150; cf. *Orac. Sib.* 1.283–307). With respect to Hesiod's five ages, V. only mentions the two most prominent and chronologically extreme ones, iron (4.8) and gold (4.9); heroes will appear at 4.35, but without the emphasis of a proper 'age' (*permixtos heroas* at 4.16 is irrelevant). Significant allusions to Saturn's reign, and Justice's presence on earth, are found in the finale of *G.* 2, esp. 536–40 (for Saturn as the god of primeval Latium cf. also *Aen.* 8.319–27): cf. 4.6n.; note also Tibullus' erotic-elegiac reminiscences (1.3.35–50) and Ovid, *amor.* 3.8.35–52 (besides *her.* 4.132; just a hint in Prop. 2.32.52); cf., finally, the speech given by Seneca (as a character) in *Octauia*,

ECLOGUE 4   209

385–434. The return of Saturn's reign is explicitly connected to Augustus in *Aen.* 6.792–4 (cf. Hor. *carm.* 4.2.33–40 [see *E.* 4.6n.]) and will later become an imperial encomiastic topos, especially from the Neronian age: Calp. *ecl.* 1.64; *Buc. Eins.* 2.23. The myth of the ages is well attested in Orphic literature as well: frr. 139–41 Kern = 363; 159; 181; 216 I; 320 II; 216 II Bern.; Orpheus will be mentioned here at 4.55–7.

6 redit et…redeunt. For the structure of this line, with emphatic repetition of the verb in a different form, cf. *Aen.* 7.327 *odit et ipse pater Pluton, odere sorores*; 8.91–2, as well as Theocr. *id.* 2.38; for a virtually identical anaphora, cf. 4.24–5 *occidet…* / *occidet* (n.). **redit et Virgo.** In Hesiod, *op.* 197–201, the goddesses of Modesty and (just) Vengeance, *Αἰδώς* and *Νέμεσις*, abandoned iron-age man, thus putting an end to the myth of the ages, whereas in Aratus the degeneration was marked by the gradual estrangement of Dike, goddess of Justice, who upon leaving earth turned into the constellation of Virgo (*phaen.* 100–36); in *G.* 2.473–4, V. will assert that *Iustitia* left her last earthly footprints in the country before flying away (the shadow of the goddess *Virgo* is significant in *Vergilius/Virgilius*); cf. Ov. *met.* 1.149–50 *Virgo…terras Astraea reliquit*; Iuv. 6.19–20; Traina (1975c, pp. 285–97). The Hesiodic-Aratean myth had been rationalized by Catullus, 64.397–8 *sed postquam tellus scelere est imbuta nefando* / *iustitiamque omnes cupida de mente fugarunt.* Nigidius Figulus also seems to have meditated on the flight of the virgin Justice, at least according to the scholion *ad* German. 96, esp. pp. 65.20–66 Breys. (= fr. 94, pp. 115–16 Swob.); sorrow for the goddess' absence was featured in Euphorion: *SH* fr. 415 (col. II), pp. 198–9 Ll.-J.-P. = 24c2 van Gron. = 26 col. II Light.; it bears mentioning that the Brundisium agreement dates from the autumn of 40 BCE—thus, presumably, under the Virgo constellation (Spica, its brightest star, was visible in the eastern sky, before dawn, from early October). In the exegetical tradition, Virgo's identification with the Virgin Mary is typically traced back to Philargyrius/Philagrius, pp. 77–8 (III.2 Th.-H.), even though this could be the result of later, Christian interpolation. At any rate, such an interpretation is a cornerstone of the Christian reading of V. in the Middle Ages. Note, however, that certain biblical prophecies include the figure of a 'young girl', i.e. a 'virgin': cf. particularly the Septuagint version of Isaiah 7.14 *ἰδοὺ ἡ παρθένος κτλ.*, quoted in Matthew 1.23. Despite his crucial role in presenting V. as a 'prophet' of Christ, Dante disambiguates *uirgo* in his reworking of *E.* 4 and glosses the term with 'justice', thereby avoiding any Christological interpretation; Dante's Statius tells V.: 'Facesti come quei che va di notte, / che porta il lume dietro e sé non giova / ma dopo sé fa le persone dotte, / quando dicesti: "Secol si rinnova; / torna giustizia e primo tempo umano, / e progenïe scende dal ciel nova"' (*Purg.* 22.67–72). **redeunt Saturnia regna.** The god Saturn, of potentially Etruscan origin, was an old Italian agricultural deity. Identified with Kronos, king of the Golden Age (Hes. *op.* 111; cf. Orph. frr. 139–41 Kern = 363; 159; 181; 216 I; 320 II; 216 II Bern.), he was pictured as establishing his reign in Latium after

210   ECLOGUE 4

Zeus-Jupiter banished him from Olympus: he then restored the Golden Age in Latium and Italy as a whole (cf. *G.* 2.538; *Aen.* 6.792–4; 8.319–27; Tib. 1.3.35; Ov. *fast.* 1.235–8; Dion. Hal. 1.36.1); it is possible that a version of the Sibylline Oracles known to V. featured the prophecy of a future age of happiness, in terms of the Hesiodic Golden Age: cf. *Orac. Sib.* 3.744–5; 749–51. Philosophical thought (cf. Plato, *Polit.* 271c–272c; *leg.* 4.713c–714a) had seen in Kronos' reign the mythical metaphor of ancient, prosperous times when justice ruled, whereas Aristotle relates (and shares) the traditional view comparing Peisistratus' peaceful tyranny to life in the age of Kronos (*Athen. const.* 16.7 ὁ ἐπὶ Κρόνου βίος; cf. Dicaearch. frr. 49–50 Wehrli; also Sen. *epist.* 90.5). Euhemerus of Messene (late fourth century BCE) was probably the first to read the figure of the god as that of a deified king (his doctrine is perhaps echoed in Diod. Sic. 5.66.4): a Euhemerist interpretation is also taken up by Servius, *ad Aen.* 8.319 *Saturnus rex fuit Cretae, quem Iuppiter filius bello pepulit.* The geographical phrase *Saturnia terra*, perhaps only referring to Latium, is attested in Ennius, *ann.* 21 Sk. (apud Varr. *ling.* 5.42), and the epithet usually refers to the whole peninsula: *G.* 2.173; *Aen.* 8.329; Ov. *fast.* 5.625; cf. also Dion. Hal. 1.18.2. See further *Enc. Virg.* IV, pp. 685–8, s.v. *Saturno* (E. Montanari); *Enc. Or.* II, pp. 485–6, s.v. *Saturno* (A. Seele); *Virg. Enc.* III, p. 1120, s.v. *Saturn* (T. Joseph). Concerning the god's 'golden' connotations, it probably bears mentioning that the *aerarium*'s treasury was kept in his temple, at the foot of the *cliuus Capitolinus*, in the ancient heart of Rome (Macr. *Sat.* 1.8.3). Saturn-Kronos seems to have been linked to a gradualist conception of history in Orphic thought, at least according to Nigidius Figulus, who attributes such a doctrine to Orpheus himself in *De dis* (Serv. Dan. *ad E.* 4.10 = fr. 67, p. 83 Swob. = Orph. fr. 29a Kern = 364 Bern. *primum regnum Saturni, deinde Iouis, tum Neptuni, inde Plutonis*). The idea of a return of his reign, as well as of Virgo (*redit…redeunt*), is unparalleled outside *E.* 4, although the end-of-year ritual called *Saturnalia* (Κρόνια for the Greeks) consisted in the periodic and episodic re-enactment of the privileges and 'liberties' typical of Saturn's age. Here, however, the Golden Age will turn out to be the final point of a new era (4.37–45). The formula *Saturnia regna* will make another appearance as the subject matter of Silenus' song in 6.41n. (there, too, in line-ending position: cf. *Aen.* 2.252). In Horace's ode 4.2 the return of the Golden Age will be presented as a possibility, in a context in which Iullus, son of Mark Antony and Fulvia, will be summoned to praise Augustus as the greatest gift sent by favourable gods to humans—a significant reworking of *E.* 4: *concines maiore poeta plectro / Caesarem… / quo nihil maius meliusue terris / fata donauere bonique diui / nec dabunt, quamuis redeant in aurum / tempora priscum* (Hor. *carm.* 4.2.33–40). For this particular use of *redire* cf. Prop. 2.26.23; Mart. 2.5.5.

7 iam noua progenies. The myth of the *puer*, still not explicitly formulated here, is grafted onto a Hesiodic transition between one age and the next, i.e. the arrival of a new generation of humans (γένος): *op.* 109; 127; 143; 159. The extraordinary nature of the event is highlighted by the *puer*'s celestial provenance,

ECLOGUE 4   211

by the adj. *noua*, and by the prefix *pro-* in a noun full of archaic solemnity (Catull. 66.44; Lucr. 2.617), which only occurs here in the *E*. but will gain great thematic importance in the *Aeneid* (cf. *Aen.* 1.19 *progeniem…Troiano a sanguine duci*; note *Aen.* 1.250; 5.565; 6.790; 7.97; 10.30; cf. also *G.* 1.414; 2.341). **caelo demittitur alto.** V. re-mythologizes Lucretius' rationalistic argument, 2.1153–4 *haud, ut opinor, enim mortalia saecla superne / aurea de caelo demisit funis in arua* (a polemic allusion to the well-known passage of Hom. *Il.* 8.19, especially in its Stoic reading). In the finale of his *Iter Brundisinum* (a narrative of the diplomatic trip to Brundisium), Horace reasserts the Epicurean-Lucretian principle: *deos didici securum agere aeuum, / nec, siquid miri faciat natura, deos id / tristis ex alto caeli demittere tecto* (*sat.* 1.5.101–3). Cicero was said to have dreamt of a boy descended from the sky, whom he later identified with the young Octavian: *puerum facie liberali demissum e caelo catena aurea ad fores Capitoli constitisse eique Iouem flagellum tradidisse* (Suet. *Aug.* 94.9; cf. Cass. Di. 45.2.2; Cicero himself, but talking about Pompey: *Manil.* 41 *de caelo delapsum*). While it is not a technical phrase, *caelo…alto* hints at the uppermost region of the sky, the ether, home of the Gods; cf. *Aen.* 4.574 *deus aethere missus ab alto*. The verb *demitto* may also hint at a sort of dynastic genealogy, the beginning of a divine lineage: *G.* 3.35 *demissae…ab Ioue gentis*. The *puer* will be described as 'flying' across the skies towards the earth at 4.48–52; l. 7 is taken up in the intensely encomiastic context of *Aen.* 6.789–90 *hic Caesar et omnis Iuli / progenies magnum caeli uentura sub axem* (note *progenies*): the idea that the soul of great men is bound to find its ultimate dwelling in heaven, where it must return, appears in Cicero, *rep.* 6.13; cf. Hor. *carm.* 1.2.45. The language resonates with the undertones of Eastern messianic or apocalyptic prophecies, which probably made their way into the Sibylline literature of V.'s time: cf. *Orac. Sib.* 3.286 'And the god of heavens will then send a king' (cf. also 3.652). Christian readers read this passage as announcing the advent of the Christ, son of the Virgin.

8–14. These lines provide the reader with all the fundamental features of the eclogue, which will be consistently developed. The *puer* is pictured at the moment of birth, which is now imminent (4.8); the vanishing of the iron generation (4.8–9 *primum / desinet*) is not an instantaneous event, as remaining traces of the old vices will need further intervention (under Pollio's guidance at 4.13–14; in the context of the *puer*'s maturity at 4.37). Only in 4.60–3 will the poet address the *puer* as already born.

8 tu modo nascenti puero. The reader's attention is drawn to the imminence of the *puer*'s birth, which the inchoative verb represents as unfolding rather than already accomplished (note also the line-opening personal pronoun, then framed by *Lucina*); cf. *nascitur* at 4.5 (*saeclorum…ordo*). On the verb, see *Enc. Virg.* III, pp. 664–5 s.v. *nascor* (S. Fasce). The adv. *modo*, following the pronoun, refers more probably to *faue* than to *nascenti* (the latter, an inchoative, does not need such a specification): 'you, indeed, be favourable'. Similarly, the pronoun's appearance in

212 ECLOGUE 4

line-opening position with a postponed imperative is featured at *G*. 3.73–4 *tu modo…impende laborem*; note also *Aen*. 4.50 (and *Aen*. 2.160, with a subjunctive). This usage is frequent and colloquial: cf. Plaut. *Aul*. 608 *tu modo caue quoiquam indicassis aurum meum esse istic, Fides; Mil*. 1123; Ter. *Phorm*. 670; Cic. *Att*. 1.6.1; Prop. 1.11.27, etc.; *ThlL* VIII.1300.36–41 (here, however, a prayerlike type of polite emphasis can be detected). In formulas like this one, *modo* is used to express respect towards the interlocutor; note also the more general illocutionary force of the pronoun + imperative phrase, on which see 3.31n; cf. also (though without the pronoun) *E*. 8.78 *necte…modo et…dic. Amor*'s divine favour is lavished on Propertius' Cynthia as she comes into the world at Prop. 2.3.23 (*tibi nascenti*), which is probably a reworking of the present passage: cf. 4.18n.; 61n.; 63n.

8–9 quo…primum / desinet ac…surget. For the causal force of the relative pronoun ('thanks to whom'), expressed by the simple ablative (which emphasizes the boy's instrumental role), cf. *E*. 9.48–9 *astrum quo segetes gauderent…et quo / duceret…uua colorem*. Here, however, the verb *desino* (opposed to *surgo*) hints at a linear dimension of time, i.e. a single *saeculum* / generation. Thus, the *puer* is represented as a spatio-temporal turning point in human history: cf., with likely echoes of this passage, Sil. 8.574 *Brundisium, quo desinit Itala tellus* (where *Brundisium*, part of a catalogue of populations, is personified). Note the hyperbaton *ferrea… / … gens aurea*, underscoring the idea, especially within a poem that generally proceeds by single, syntactically autonomous lines, following Catullus 64 (though cf. 4.15–16; 21–2; 32–3; 43–4). The trajectory from *primum* (perhaps here 'finally': but cf. 1.44n.) to *desinet* brings about a feeling of relief: that the process will be a long and complex one becomes clear from 4.31 onwards. For *desinet ac* cf. 9.42n.

9 gens aurea. Following the innovative *progenies* (4.7), the norm of Hesiodic terminology is re-established: *op*. 109 χρύσεον…γένος (then Arat. *Phaen*. 114); further reading in *Enc. Virg*. I, pp. 412–18, s.v. *aurea* (*aetas, gens; aurea saecula*) (M. Pavan); *Virg. Enc*. II, p. 565, s.v. *Golden Age* (L. Fratantuono); a possible Theocritean parallel at *id*. 12.16 χρύσειοι…ἄνδρες (but in a homoerotic context). The traditional expression *aurea aetas* is not found in V., who uses *aurea…saecula* (*Aen*. 6.792–3), but will be coined by Ovid at *met*. 1.89; 15.96 *uetus illa aetas, cui fecimus aurea nomen* (some irony on *aurea…saecula* at *ars* 2.277).

10 casta…Lucina. The ancient Latin deity overseeing birth; her name suggests 'light' (*lux*). Often assimilated to Juno (*Iuno Lucina*), she appears here in the less frequent identification with Diana (whose name may also be connected to a 'luminous' root, *dius/diuus*), corresponding to the Greek Artemis Εὔλοχος/Λοχεία ('assisting births'), sister of Apollo (whence the epithet *tuus*); cf. Callim. *hymn*. 3.[*Dian*.].20–5; *ait*. fr. 79 Pf. = 182 Mass. = 79–79a Hard. In Horace's *carm. saec*. the possibility of identifying the hunting goddess with birth-assisting deities (*Ilithyia, Lucina, Genitalis*) is only hinted at (while it seems beyond doubt in *carm*. 3.22, where nonetheless no divine name is explicitly mentioned: cf. only *diua triformis* at l. 4); by contrast, ambiguity is ruled out in Catull. 34.13–14 *tu* [i.e. *Diana*]

Lucina dolentibus / Iuno dicta puerperis; cf. Cic. *nat. deor.* 2.68. Note the trochaic caesura after *Lucina*. The reference to the goddess' chastity is pertinent within the sacral context of birth and in the age of Virgo's return: *castus* denotes purity (of the kind regulated by the marriage ritual), but not necessarily virginity (this is why the adjective can also denote mothers, as in *Aen.* 8.665–6 *castae...matres*). The appearance of Lucina, the feminine deity who ruled over births and pregnancies, is particularly significant here at the beginning of the poem (note that the Sibyl, too, is a divine *Virgo*). This can be explained by the poet's preoccupation with an actual future mother (Octavia): note that, with a ring-composition effect, the figure of the *puer's* mother will take centre stage at the end of the poem (4.60–3n.). **Apollo.** The prophetic god *par excellence*, who will inspire the Sibyl again in *Aen.* 6, esp. 77 (but cf. also 6.35 and 69, associating him with Trivia-Diana). According to Servius Dan. (quoted above, 4.6n.), Nigidius Figulus talked about a 'reign' of Apollo following that of Pluto (which may apparently be interpreted in terms of a final conflagration, perhaps due to Apollo's identification with Helios): *nonnulli etiam, ut magi, aiunt Apollinis fore regnum: in quo uiden-dum est, ne ardorem, siue illa ecpyrosis appellanda est, dicant* (fr. 67, p. 83 Swob. = Orph. fr. 29a Kern = 364 Bern.). In the laudatory language of the Hellenistic age, the god could directly be linked to royal destiny: in Callimachus, even before being born, Apollo prophesies the birth of Ptolemy II Philadelphus in Cos— then, having reached Delos, he comes into the world himself (*hymn.* 4[*Del.*].162–90; 249–74; cf. Theocr. *id.* 17.60–4). Consider also Callimachus' twelfth iambus, where Apollo's hymn is described as the best gift for the new-born Hebe (*dieg.* 9.28–31; cf. fr. 202, esp. 53–70 Pf.). The ritual pair Apollo-Diana will play a crucial role in Horace's *Carmen saeculare*, while Apollo (along with Jupiter, to whom he was connected through the ambivalent figure of Veiovis) had a major part in the *ludi* of 139 BCE: see further Mannsperger (1973, p. 393); on Jupiter, see 4.49n. Only much later, in *Aen.* 8.714–28, will V. be able to highlight Augustus' 'proximity' to Apollo's temple (esp. *Aen.* 8.720 *ipse sedens niueo candentis limine Phoebi*). But here Servius' interpretation is anachronistic, besides making little sense anyway: *tangit Augustum, cui simulacrum factum est cum Apollinis cunctis insignibus*. In 28 BCE, when the temple of Palatine Apollo was consecrated, the Sun's chariot appeared on its top (Prop. 2.31.11), whereas the inner space featured the cultic statues of Leto, Apollo, and Diana (Plin. *nat.* 36.24; 25; 32), and we know of an arch commissioned by Augustus on the Palatine hill to honour his father Gaius Octavius, with a niche containing the two divine siblings sculpted by Lysias (Plin. *nat.* 36.36 *quadriga currusque et Apollo ac Diana ex uno lapide*). The whole line is quoted at *Buc. Eins.* 2.38 (cf. 4.6–7n.). V. is here contrib-uting to the creation of the Roman eulogistic language, often used even in late antiquity to praise charismatic rulers: cf. *Paneg.* 6.21.4 *uidisti enim, credo, Constantine, Apollinem tuum comitante Victoria coronas tibi laureas offerentem* (probably also echoing Calp. *ecl.* 4.87 *comitatus Apolline Caesar*).

214   ECLOGUE 4

11 teque adeo...te. In contrast with 4.8–10, the hymnic anaphora focuses on a human object (cf. also 4.13; for the *puer* cf. 4.18 and 23); *adeo*, often occupying the second position, is used by V. solemnly to strengthen a pronoun (cf. 4.8 *tu modo* [n.]): e.g. *G.* 1.24 *tuque adeo* (in a similar context of hymnic anaphora). Cf. also 9.59n.; another anaphora at *G.* 2.323 *uer adeo frondi nemorum, uer utile siluis,* etc.; cf. Enn. *trag.* 234 Joc. = 284 V.² *Iuppiter tuque adeo summe Sol.* **decus hoc aeui, te consule, inibit.** The future tense has an eschatological nuance: Rome's history will remember that the palingenesis of humankind began (Servius: *exordium accipiet*) under Pollio's eponymous consulship. A certain ambivalence is perhaps well suited to the circumstances, since Pollio's actual consulship (in the autumn of 40) was only bound to last for a few months. In fact, *decus* is a rather vague term (Servius: *aureum scilicet saeculum*), which does not imply the *puer*'s birth, but could simply refer to his conception (an important event in the encomiastic rhetoric applied to divine sovereigns). Servius Dan. seems to allude to this: *et ideo 'inibit', non 'iniit', quia consul designatus erat.* Consider also that the phrase *decus hoc aeui*, presumably 'this pride of our time', is perhaps meant to evoke the language of Sibylline Oracles, e.g. εὐφροσύνην αἰῶνος (*Orac. Sib.* 3.786; cf. 3.771). Others read the appositional gen. as emphatic, and thus equivalent to 'this glorious time', as often in comedy, especially with a negative connotation: e.g. Plaut. *Poen.* 273 *monstrum mulieris* 'that monster of a woman', but also *Pers.* 204 *deliciae pueri.* Note the long syllable in *hoc* (originally from *hocc* < *hodce), which is customary in V.: cf. *E.* 7.29; *G.* 1.450; *Aen.* 2.664.

12 Pollio. Pollio (cf. 3.84n.) would have been a suitable addressee of a prophecy involving the idea of a boy saviour, given his contacts with Jewish circles. It is likely that he met Herod in 40 and later hosted his children in Rome (Flav. Ioseph. *ant. Iud.* 14.388–9; 15.343). **magni...menses.** Time itself is affected by the cosmic, universal power of the prophecy: thus, the months become 'great', according to the lexicon of the *magnus annus* (4.5n.). V. here introduces the idea of time dilation, which will soon be actualized in the *puer*'s life: each stage of his growth seems to correspond to a whole age of history. Then, however, the poet returns to describing the *puer* in the limited terms of a human life (cf. 4.46n.).

13 te duce. 'Leader', especially in a military sense, often referring to the *princeps* in the Augustan political language: Hor. *carm.* 1.2.52; 4.5.5; *epist.* 1.18.56; Prop. 2.10.4; Ov. *ars* 1.202; Augustus, referring to himself, at *res gest.* 25.2. There is no need to think of Pollio's later military operations in Dalmatia: after the consulship, he would have naturally furthered his activity as a political leader. Note Servius' gloss on *duce: id est auctore.* **sceleris.** A term frequently used in Augustan (and then imperial) literature to designate the greatest 'misdeed', i.e. the civil war: cf. *G.* 1.506; Hor. *epod.* 7.1–2; 17–18; *carm.* 1.2.29–30; 35.33; Lucan. 1.2. The persistence of evil, whose 'traces' are hard to erase (13 *sceleris uestigia nostri*), is echoed at 4.31 *priscae uestigia fraudis* (see 4.31–3n.).

ECLOGUE 4   215

15–16 deum uitam accipiet diuisque uidebit / permixtos heroas. The divine quality of Hesiod's Golden Age (Hes. *op.* 112 ὥστε θεοὶ δ' ἔζωον; note here *deum uitam*) will be fully experienced by the *puer* at the time of his final deification. The community of humans and gods (θεοξενία) is featured, in terms of 'mixture' (*permixtos*), in Hesiod's *Catalogue of Women*, where it is given a Golden-Age dimension: Hes. fr. 1.5–7 M.-W. 'mingled with the gods ... / For banquets were in common at the time, and so were the encounters / between immortal gods and mortal men'; Aratus' Dike freely met human beings during the Golden Age (Arat. *phaen.* 100–7); cf. Catull. 64.384–96. Consider also the comparison drawn by Theocritus between the gods' life and that of Ptolemy I Soter in *id.* 17.16–33: 'His father [scil. Zeus] made him equal in honour to the blessed / immortals, and for him a golden mansion in Zeus' dwelling / is built: he is dear to Alexander, / who sits beside him, god of the multicoloured mitre, harsh to the Persians. / Opposite rises the throne of Centaur-slayer Heracles, / made of sturdy adamant. / Here, together with the other heavenly ones, he takes part in feasts [22 ἔνθα σὺν ἄλλοισιν θαλίας ἔχει Οὐρανίδῃσι], / rejoicing immensely for the children of his children, / since the son of Kronos took old age away from their limbs: / those who were born his descendants are called immortals. / Ancestor of both kings is the valiant son of Heracles [Caranus, tenth descendant of Heracles, who was said to have given origin to the Macedonian royal house, and therefore to Ptolemy], and both ones go back to Heracles in the long last. / Thus, when he leaves the banquet, already full / of scented nectar, to reach his beloved wife's chamber, / the one he entrusts with his bow and the quiver he keeps under his arm, / the other with the iron mace, engraved with knots: / to the ambrosial chamber of white-ankled Hebe / they lead the weapons and him, the bush-bearded son of Zeus'. Cf. Hom. *Od.* 11.602–3: 'He [i.e. Heracles] among the immortal gods [αὐτὸς δὲ μετ' ἀθανάτοισι θεοῖσι] / rejoices in banquets, and possesses fair-ankled Hebe'. Here and in the finale (4.62–3), V. describes a deification pattern which, in relation to the *princeps*, will play a fundamental role within Augustan political language (the opening of the *Georgics* is explicit: G. 1.24–42). A prophecy of future deification is given to Pindar's Aristaeus right after his birth: *Pyth.* 9.59–65, esp. 63–4 θήσονταί τέ νιν ἀθάνατον, / Ζῆνα καὶ ἁγνὸν Ἀπόλλωνα 'they [scil. the Hours and Gaia] will make him immortal, / a Zeus and a holy Apollo'. Note also the image of Dionysus at the end of Nonnus' poem: [θεὸς ἀμπελόεις] οὐράνιον πίε νέκταρ ἀρειοτέροισι κυπέλλοις / σύνθρονος Ἀπόλλωνι, συνέστιος υἱέι Μαίης (*Dionys.* 48.977–8). The foolish claim to a life 'equal to the gods' is rebuked by Rhian. fr. 1.9–16 Pow., featuring an exhortation to reflect on human limits. The solemn form *diui* occurs at *E.* 1.41, referring to Octavian; cf. 3.73; 8.19; 10.70; *heroas* is a Hellenizing form both morphologically (acc. plur. in -*as*, with short vowel) and metrically, given the trochaic caesura not coupled with the hephthemimeral (cf. 4.34–5n.). The enjambement underscores the mixture: cf. 4.8–9n. Divine existence is the boy's ultimate fate, but the *puer* himself will have to play an active role in it, e.g. by smiling at his mother to signal his full self-awareness—this is what seems to be asserted in the poem's finale (cf. 4.60n.;

216 ECLOGUE 4

62n.). Note, in 4.16, the spondaic rhythm at the beginning of the line, owing to a molossus-shaped word at the outset (for which cf. 4.17 and 4.19; see also, with some variations, 4.35 *delectos heroas* [34–5n.]), an eminently archaic yet also Catullan feature.

16 et ipse uidebitur illis. It is preferable and more natural to interpret *illis* as a dat. of agent ('he will be seen by them': e.g. *E.* 6.72 *tibi…dicatur*). Such a reciprocal gaze implies familiarity and respect: cf. Theocr. *id.* 17.18–19 (quoted above) παρὰ δ' αὐτὸν Ἀλέξανδρος φίλα εἰδὼς / ἑδριάει (cf. 4.15–16n.).

17 pacatumque reget patriis uirtutibus orbem. A reference to the virtues of 'paternal' (and male) lineage, whereas the final ll. 60–3 will focus on the *puer*'s mother. It is hard to gauge to what extent his father is directly involved here as a specific figure: *patrius* may simply mean 'ancestral', 'of the forefathers' (as in *G.* 2.394; 3.346; *Aen.* 1.620; cf. also Caes. *Gall.* 2.15.5 *patriam…uirtutem*), in which case the first reference to the boy's father would be at 4.26 (but see n. ad loc.). The term *pacatus*, in keeping with the political aftermath of the *foedus Brundisinum*, will become standard in the Augustan political language, along with the goddess *Pax*: Hor. *carm.* 4.5.19; Augustus himself, *res gest.* 25.1 *mare pacaui a praedonibus*; note, in a more private context, the so-called *Laudatio Turiae* (*ILS* 8393.35–6): *pacato orbe terrarum, restituta re publica, quieta deinde nobis…tempora contigerunt.* Assimilation to the father's virtues is part of the heroic code in *Il.* 6.477; *Od.* 4.206; cf. also Callim. *hymn.* 4[*Del.*].170; Theocr. *id.* 17.63. This line, which includes the verb *reget*, offers a decisive argument against the idea that the *puer* is Pollio's son: the role of 'ruler' of the world would be excessive for him. For the year 40 BCE, the *Fasti* assert that both Antony and Octavian each received an honourable *ouatio* for the same reason, i.e. for making peace (*quod pacem…fecit*) with each other (*Inscriptiones Italiae*, XII.1, p. 568 Degrassi; cf. *CIL* I, p. 478).

18–45. This is the central section of the eclogue, in which the narrative rapidly covers the *puer*'s future life. His birth is welcomed by nature's spontaneous homage to him and immediately has positive effects on the world (4.18–25); then his adolescence features the boy's education and another 'automatic' response on nature's part (of a specifically agricultural kind, though human flaws persist: 4.26–36); in his adulthood, the Golden Age is finally apparent (4.37–45).

18–30. These lines credit the *puer* with the miraculous events typical of the Golden Age, all ultimately due to nature's exuberant 'automatism' (4.18 *nullo… cultu*): cf. Hes. *op.* 116–18 'They had / every good thing; fertile earth bore fruit / spontaneously, excellently and in great abundance'; Arat. *phaen.* 112–14 (where, however, the ploughs hint at some form of agricultural labour: cf. German. 114–19; more emphasis on the miraculous aspect in Avien. *Arat.* 316–17); see further Hor. *epod.* 16.41–50; Tib. 1.3.41–6; Ov. *met.* 1.101–12; *amor.* 3.8.35–42; *fast.* 2.295–6; cf. also *Orac. Sib.* 2.29–31; 3.620–3; 3.744–5; 5.281–5.

18–20. The description of *munuscula* (4.18n.), lavishly produced by the earth, is opened and closed by ivy and acanthus, which framed Alcimedon's *pocula* in

ECLOGUE 4   217

the preceding *E.* 3, featuring Pollio as protagonist and addressee (cf. 3.39: ivy on the cups owned by Menalcas; 3.45: acanthus on Damoetas cups). After the broader vista at 4.21–2, mentioning goats and herds, l. 23 will again focus on the narrower space surrounding the *puer*, describing his cradle along with a new natural flowering: *blandos…flores* (assuming that the transmitted sequence of lines is genuine: n. ad loc.). Despite the vast scope of the prophecy, these lines (like the finale: 4.60–3) display a delicate style that seems to address the child, regardless of his divine status. Compare the grandmother's and aunt's wishes for the little boy in Persius, 2.37–8 *hunc optet generum rex et regina, puellae / hunc rapiant; quidquid calcauerit hic, rosa fiat.*

18 munuscula. These are real 'little gifts' for the newborn, spontaneously offered by the earth (*nullo…cultu*: even *prima*, referring to *tellus*, emphasizes the earth's concern; cf. *G.* 1.127–8 *ipsaque tellus / omnia liberius nullo poscente ferebat*). In the context of childhood, cf. Cic. *Att.* 1.8.3 *Tulliola, deliciolae nostrae, tuum munusculum flagitat*; Hor. *epist.* 1.7.17; in Callim. *iamb.* 12, Athena offered newborn Hebe some toys (fr. 202.28 Pf. παίχνια), in the context of the gods' competition for the 'fairest gift'. Childhood objects of various types played a certain role in the Orphic-Dionysian cult of the divine boy: see Guthrie (1952, esp. pp. 121–6). An elegiac reworking for the newborn Cynthia in Prop. 2.3.25 *haec tibi contulerunt caelestia munera diui.*

19 errantis hederas. The first plant mentioned here is a Dionysian symbol: climbing ivy (cf. Catull. 61.34–5 *hedera…errans*), seen in its free luxuriance (*passim*), suitably represents the traits of the 'loosening' god (compare the epithets *Liber* and *Lyaeus*). In Euripides, *Phoen.* 649–54, ivy hailed the god's birth: Βρόμιον ἔνθα τέκετο μά-/τηρ Διὸς γάμοισι, / κισσὸς ὃν περιστεφὴς / ἕλικος εὐθὺς ἔτι βρέφος / χλοηφόροισιν ἔρνεσιν / κατασκίοισιν ὀλβίσας ἐνώτισεν. Cf. Philostr. *imag.* 1.14, pp. 315.29–316.1 Kays.; Nonn. *Dionys.* 9.12 (ivy is absent from the 'golden' birth of Apollo in Callimachus, *hymn.* 4[*Del.*].260–263, where the only plant mentioned is the olive tree; cf. Eur. *Iph. Taur.* 1099–1102; Catull. 34.7–8; only the Delian palm tree is mentioned in *Hymn. Hom.* 3[*Ap.*].117–19; Theogn. 5–10). Ivy leaves are used by the Nymphs of Nysa to hide the newborn god's cradle (the plant is *gratissima Baccho*), in order to protect him from the wrath of Hera/Juno (Ov. *fast.* 3.767–70). Ivy is again a symbol of (Dionysian?) poetry at *E.* 7.25; 8.12–13 (e.g. Hor. *carm.* 1.1.29). Through a joint reworking of *E.* 4 and 6, Nemesianus (*ecl.* 3) will have Pan sing the birth and the achievements of Bacchus/Dionysus. **cum baccare.** A plant of uncertain identity (perhaps *helichrysum*?), appearing again (along with ivy) at *E.* 7.27, where it seems to be endowed with apotropaic powers (protection from evil influences e.g. in Persius, 2, esp. 32–4). A certain sound affinity with *Bacchus* is here inevitable: consider also that γ, along with some Servian manuscripts, transmits the reading *bacchare* (corresponding to the Greek βάκχαρις), and that the early romanized forms *Baccus, bacca* ('maenad') were written without aspiration, which was only later restored (*ThlL* II.1660.3–5;

218   ECLOGUE 4

1664.73–7). Helichrysum and ivy are woven together in the memorable context of *id.* 1.30 κισσὸς ἑλιχρύσῳ κεκονιμένος (the goatherd's cup), which V. emulated in *E.* 3.

20 ridenti...acantho. The use of *rideo* in reference to things, paralleled in Greek at Hom. *Il.* 19.362 and Hes. *theog.* 40 (referring to flowers in Meleag. *Anth. Pal.* 5.147.2 = *HE* 4237 G.-P.), is attested in Latin since Ennius, *ann.* 446–7 Sk.; cf. Lucr. 2.559; 4.1125; Catull. 64.284; Hor. *carm.* 2.6.14; cf. *E.* 7.55 *omnia nunc rident* (n.); see further 4.60n. **colocasia.** This plant, too, is hard to identify. Its exotic connotation is clear, perhaps pointing to Egypt (κύαμος Αἰγύπτιος: probably a Nilotic water lily, *Nelumbo nucifera*, on which see André 1985, p. 71); cf. Plin. *nat.* 21.87 *in Aegypto nobilissima est colocasia quam cyamon aliqui uocant*; Athen. 3.72b ῥίζας δὲ λέγει Νίκανδρος τὰ ὑπ' Ἀλεξανδρέων κολοκάσια καλούμενα (= Nic. fr. 81 G.-S.; note the neuter form, as in V.). Due to its attractive appearance, the plant was successfully imported into Italy (see, again, Plin. *nat.* 21.87). Note the politicized and utterly anachronistic interpretation transmitted by Servius Dan.: *hanc herbam uideri uult in honorem Augusti creuisse, quae Romae post deuictam ab eo Aegyptum innotuit.* Exotic floral motifs will certainly take part in the visual celebration of Augustus' successes, as e.g. in the frieze of the *Ara Pacis* (but cf. the ornamental exuberance that characterized the so-called temple of Apollo Sosianus: *LTUR* I, esp. p. 53, s.v. *Apollo, Aedes in Circo* [A. Viscogliosi]). Egyptian elements, such as sphinxes or statues (of Isis), are found in many paintings of the Augustan age: Settis (2002, p. 56). For further reading on the importance of Egyptian culture in Rome and Italy, see M. Swetland-Burland, *Egypt in Italy: Visions of Egypt in Roman Imperial Culture*, Cambridge 2015 (with bibliographical references); cf. also F. Coarelli, *Initia Isidis. L'ingresso dei culti egiziani a Roma e nel Lazio*, Lugano 2019, pp. 65–82 (on the temple of Isis and Serapis built *in Campo Martio* by Antony and Octavian in 43 BCE).

21–2 ipsae lacte...distenta capellae / ubera. The first detail that strikes the poet's eye, as soon as the focus shifts away from the *puer*'s birth, is a specifically pastoral one: the goats return to the pen (*domum*) with udders full of milk (*distenta*, literally 'stretched out': *ubera* is highlighted through enjambement [above, 4.8–9n.]; see Lucr. 1.257–9 *pecudes... / corpora deponunt, et candens lacteus umor / uberibus manat distentis*). Cf. *E.* 7.3 *distentas lacte capellas*; 9.31 *distendant ubera uaccae*; Theocr. *id.* 11.12; note also Hor. *sat.* 1.1.110 *aliena capella gerat distentius uber.* Spontaneous production of milk is featured in Hor. *epod.* 16.49–50 *illic iniussae ueniunt ad mulctra capellae / refertque tenta grex amicus ubera* (cf. Tib. 1.3.45–6). See also *E.* 7.11 *huc ipsi potum uenient...iuuenci.* The presence of milk (and breastfeeding?) is not surprising in the context of a *puer*'s birth, albeit divine: e.g. Callim. *hymn.* 1[*Iou.*].48–9 (the goat Amalthea's udder); 4[*Del.*].274; Philostr. *imag.* 1.14, p. 316.5–6 Kays.; *ipse* often recurs in the context of the Golden Age: *G.* 1.127–8 (see 4.18n.); cf. Tib. 1.3.45, mentioned above. *E.* 4.21 contains the only mention of the book's 'spirit animal' (the *capellae*: cf. 1.12n.) in the whole 'atypical' sequence of *E.* 4–6: the poet is perhaps trying to

ECLOGUE 4   219

reconnect *E*. 4 to the rest of the pastoral world. Note, however, that these two lines may be suspected of interpolation, due to their somewhat conventional topic (and their Christian readability: 4.22n.) and the fact that they almost disrupt an otherwise coherent sequence; more generally, this part of the poem may be affected by transpositions and interpolations (4.23n.).

22 nec magnos metuent armenta leones. Another detail clearly important for the pastoral world, i.e. the absence of predators—this, too, is paralleled by Hor. *epod*. 16.33 *credula nec rauos timeant armenta leones* (note, however, the vaguer adjective used by V.: *magnos*). A Christological reading was obvious to Christian readers: the advent of the Messiah (the 'Good Shepherd') would free the faithful herd from the fear of lions, i.e. pagans (partly an allusion to the persecutions). The prophet Isaiah provided his support: *habitabit lupus cum agno / et pardus cum haedo accubabit; / uitulus et leo et ouis simul morabuntur, / et puer paruulus minabit eos. // uitulus et ursus pascentur, / simul requiescent catuli eorum; / et leo quasi bos comedet paleas. // et delectabitur infans ab ubere super foramine aspidis, / et in cauerna reguli qui ablactatus fuerit manum suam mittet. // non nocebunt et non occident in uniuerso monte sancto meo, / quia repleta est terra scientia Domini, sic ut aquae maris operientes. // in die illa radix Iesse qui stat in signum populorum, / ipsum gentes deprecabuntur, et erit sepulchrum eius gloriosum* (*Vulg. Is.* 11.6–10; cf. 65.25; see further Lact. *inst*. 7.24). But cf. also *Orac. Sib*. 3.788–95 and Theocr. *id*. 24.86–7 (the latter being, in all likelihood, a result of Christian interpolation). Here V. enhances an ascetic notion, i.e. the lack of violence and cruelty, by projecting it into the future—it is applied to a primitive age by e.g. Empedocles, 31 B 130 D.-K.: wars, however, will resurface at 4.35. For the term *armenta* cf. 2.23n. Taming naturally fierce or hostile creatures and bringing them together in peace is typical of Orpheus: the myth is often reworked in symbolic or allegorical contexts, as in Fronto's discussion of *amicitia* (Fronto, pp. 53.10–54.5 v. d. Hout[2]: cf. esp. 54.3–5 *hoc uel praecipue admirandum, quod omnis amicos tuos concordia copulas. nec tamen dissimulauerim multo hoc esse difficilius quam ut ferae ac leones cithara mitigentur*).

23 ipsa tibi blandos fundent cunabula flores. The text comes back full circle to the miracle's point of origin, i.e. the newborn child, who is again addressed directly (*tibi*). Now the cradle itself pampers him with flowers (*blandos*: childhood images and vocabulary reappear after 4.18 *munuscula*). This lively change of perspective, perhaps expressing a sort of enthusiastic disorder, pivots on the rhetorical structure of 20 *fundet... / 21 ipsae... / 23 ipsa...fundent*. Worth mentioning is the transposition proposed by W. Klouček, who placed l. 23 after l. 20, thereby obtaining a coherent sequence in which inanimate things (4.18–20; 23) are followed by animate beings (4.21–2). In this way, l. 23 emphasizes the idea of *tellus* and its automatism, already introduced at 4.18–19, but with details (*i p s a ... cunabula*) and with an emphasis on vegetation, echoed at 4.28–9. In light of the animal imagery at 4.21–2, this line may seem out of place and has been suspected of interpolation. However, it contains an extremely original image, which fits the

220   ECLOGUE 4

context. Perhaps ll. 21–2 are more worthy of suspicion, given that they insert pastoral/Horatian (but also 'Christian': cf. 4.22n.) material into an entirely plant-focused context (see also 4.24n.): *ipsa...cunabula* at 4.23 echoes and expands on ll. 18–20 (cf. esp. 19 *passim...tellus*), though an important novelty is the insertion of *ipse...capellae*. At any rate, ll. 21–2 can show that the text circulated rather fluidly among Christian readers, since Lact. *inst.* 7.24.11 places them after l. 45 (cf. the commentary by S. Freund, Berlin-New York 2009, pp. 559–60, ad loc.). A miraculous blossoming of flowers surrounds Semele's bed right after she conceives Dionysus with Zeus: Nonn. *Dionys.* 7.344–5 (cf. *Dionys.* 10.171–4).

24–5 occidet... / occidet. The anaphora of *occidet*, typical of cultic litanies, acquires here an almost fairy-tale tone, reminiscent of childhood lullabies. It is possible that here, as in 4.6 *redit...redeunt*, V. echoes the prophetic style of the *Sibylline Oracles*: cf., in the later corpus known to us, *Orac. Sib.* 3.378 φεύξετ' ἀπ' ἀνθρώπων πενίη καὶ φεύξετ' ἀνάγκη; 6.9; 7.9. The effect is to highlight the elimination of two of the greatest dangers of the vegetable kingdom, particularly perilous for a newborn child. Note also the vertical juxtaposition at the beginning of the line.

24 serpens. The term, originally a euphemistic kenning (the 'slithering' one, analogous to Greek δράκων, the 'staring' one), avoids mentioning the taboo creature: cf. *E.* 3.93 *latet anguis in herba*; 8.71 *frigidus...rumpitur anguis* (cf. *G.* 2.153–4, where, however, the *anguis* is one of monstrous proportions). For a loose parallel, cf. Hor. *epod.* 16.52 *neque intumescit alta uiperis humus*. The snake's disappearance, which will of course sound messianic to Christian readers (cf. Isaiah 11.8 [see above, 4.22n.]), makes the soil harmless, particularly in the context of flourishing plants, and at the same time underscores the *puer*'s civilizing power, in accordance with his great heroic model. While still in the cradle (i.e. one of Amphitryon's shields), Heracles strangled the two venomous snakes sent by Juno: a foreboding of his future fate as 'monster-slayer' (Theocr. *id.* 24.11–63; cf. Pind. *Nem.* 1.62–3; Bacchyl. 13.44–5; Eur. *Herc.* 20; 851–2). As a little boy, Horace is miraculously unharmed by 'black vipers' at *carm.* 3.4.17–18. **fallax herba ueneni.** The lack of poisonous plants which might deceive the gatherer's hand will reappear as a source of praise to Italy in *G.* 2.152 *nec miseros fallunt aconita legentis* (the immense *anguis* is mentioned immediately thereafter). Here *ueneni* must probably be taken as an objective gen. (i.e. *occultans uenenum*). For the phrase *fallax herba* cf. Cic. *Lael.* 68; Tib. 2.1.19; cf. also, for the whole passage, Hor. *epod.* 5.67–8 *nec herba, nec latens in asperis / radix fefellit me locis.*

25 Assyrium uulgo nascetur amomum. Most probably cardamom, specifically its aromatic variety, which in fact originates from India: hence it is not properly 'Assyrian', even though the geographical term often has a much broader meaning, sometimes referring to the East as a whole, as in Catull. 68.144 and Hor. *carm.* 2.11.16 (but Media is mentioned, along with India, as a place of production in Theophr. *hist plant.* 9.7.2). The epithet, later inherited by *amomum*

ECLOGUE 4   221

at Stat. *silu.* 2.4.34 and Mart. 8.77.3, evokes rich, exotic lands, and is justified by the fact that far Eastern fragrances, extracts, and spices reached Europe through Syria. The term's direct contact with *uulgo* suggests the paradox of the incipient new age, in which the rarest, most precious goods will be found 'everywhere' (contrast the praise of rustic life at *G.* 2.465 *alba neque Assyrio fucatur lana ueneno*). V. prompts the comparison with the only other occurrence of *amomum* in the *E.*, also in line-ending position (3.89 *ferat et rubus asper amomum*). The poet seems to play a subtle intellectual game with the illustrious addressee: if even brambles produce *amomum* for those who love Pollio (*E.* 3.88), the plant will become a common good in the new era spearheaded by Pollio. Cf. also 4.29 *rubens pendebit sentibus uua*. The contrast with snakes and poisons (4.24), along with the proximity of *laudes, facta, uirtus* (4.26–7), may hint at the paretymological connection with the Greek homophone ἄμωμος 'blameless', 'impeccable' (cf., for *arista*, 4.28n.).

26–36. A second *at*, after the one in 4.18, ushers in the second stage of the *puer*'s life: adolescence. His upbringing, based on the great masterpieces of epic poetry, corresponds to a general 'maturation' of nature, which abundantly pro-duces the primary agricultural gifts: cereals, grapes, and honey (with the excep-tion of animal husbandry, already touched upon at 4.21, the series foreshadows the *G.*'s thematic arrangement; note also that cereals and grapes hint at a seasonal sequence). To be sure, Servius Dan. exaggerates in reading l. 26 as the canonical series of genres typical of a liberal education: poetry (*heroum laudes*), history (*facta parentis*: but see n. ad loc.), and philosophy (*quae sit…cognoscere uir-tus*). Nevertheless, a didactic and programmatic intention is clear on V.'s part: cf. the analogy between the boy's 'culture' and the 'cultivation' (albeit spontaneous) of the land (4.28n.). The Theocritean model, *id.* 24, featured the young Heracles' education in poetry and music (esp. 103–10). Following the example of Xenophon's *Cyropaedia*, a whole literature on future kings' *paideia* flourished in the Hellenistic age, starting with Alexander himself (whose education was described in historical works by Onesicritus of Astypalaea and Marsyas of Pella). Paternal virtues and exemplarity will reappear, towards the end of the *Aeneid*, in relation to another momentous (and epic) *puer*, Ascanius Iulus: see *Aen.* 12.435 *disce, puer, uirtutem ex me* (cf. esp. *E.* 4.27 *quae sit poteris cognoscere uirtus*); 12.438 *mox cum matura adoleuerit aetas* (*E.* 4.37 *ubi iam firmata uirum te fecerit aetas*); 12.439–40 *sis memor et te animo repetentem exempla tuorum / et pater Aeneas et auunculus excitet Hector* (*E.* 4.26 *heroum laudes et facta parentis*); cf. also *Aen.* 9.641–2 *macte noua uirtute, puer, sic itur ad astra, / dis genite et geniture deos* (a prophecy uttered by Apollo himself, descended from the sky). We shall discover, at 4.34–6, that the heroes whose achievements the *puer* reads about will resurface in history. For the connection between the land's prosperity and its rul-er's virtue cf. 4.37–45n. In 4.28–30, nature is depicted as reaching maturity, while the *puer* is similarly making progress through his adolescence (at 4.37, he is a fully grown-up *uir*).

222   ECLOGUE 4

26 at. A new section is opened by *at*, as in 4.18. R's *ac* is thus a mere mechanical error. **heroum laudes et facta parentis.** The topics of epic poetry, closely inter-related with each other, may be divided into the heroic age and contemporary times (Servius is mistaken in regarding the latter as 'epexegetical' of the former: *quae erunt heroum laudes, tui parentis uirtutes*). The 'praises of heroes' hint pri-marily at Homeric poetry, in accordance with the formula κλέα ἀνδρῶν / ἡρώων of *Il.* 9.524–5 (cf. *Il.* 9.189, where Achilles himself is the singer), whereas the *facta parentis* allude to Roman encomiastic epic having the *puer*'s father as protagonist. The term *laudes* (cf. *E.* 6.6 *dicere laudes*) has a strong moral connotation, in keep-ing with the specifically Roman (rather than Homeric) notion of eulogistic *car-men*—as witnessed by Cicero citing Cato the Elder's *Origines*: *grauissimus auctor in Originibus dixit Cato morem apud maiores hunc epularum fuisse, ut deinceps qui accubarent canerent ad tibiam clarorum uirorum laudes atque uirtutes* (Cic. *Tusc.* 4.3 = Cat. *orig.* fr. 118 P.[2]; cf. Varr. apud Non. pp. 107–8 L. [*uita pop. Rom.* fr. 84 Rip.]). Recall the addressee's (= Pollio's) specific literary interests: he also cultivated historiography, even though his major work, the *History of Ciuil Wars*, was composed much later (cf. Hor. *carm.* 2.1 with S. J. Harrison, *Horace, Odes, Book II*, Cambridge 2017, pp. 44–6). Picturing a relatively remote future, the poet imagines himself as honouring the achievements of the *puer* (4.54 *tua dicere facta*), while the proem of *E.* 6 states the poet's utter inability to sing the praises of Varus, a task he leaves to others: *numque super tibi erunt qui dicere laudes*, etc. (6.6). Already in Evander's 'Rome', according to the archaeological reconstruction of *Aen.* 8, songs used to celebrate the exploits of the progenitor, Hercules: *car-mine laudes / Herculeas et facta ferunt* (287–8; note, as here, *laudes...et facta*). **parentis.** The transmitted reading *parentis* is correct (cf. again Callimachus, *hymn.* 4[*Del.*].170 ὁ δ' εἴσεται ἤθεα πατρός, along with 4.17n. and 62n.): *parentum* (R), which alludes to Roman history as a whole (but cf. 4.17n.), would sound repetitive after *heroum* (perhaps derived from e.g. *Aen.* 2.448 *ueterum decora alta parentum*). Augustus will refer to his adoptive father as *parens* at the outset of his *res gestae*, recalling the way in which he avenged him: *qui parentem meum [necauer]un[t, eo]s in exilium expuli*, etc. (2). In the historical context of *E.* 4, Antony is likely to be the father (*parens*) of the Virgilian *puer*.

27 legere. Reading written texts, an important component of the relationship between the *E.* and their audience, is also crucial to the *puer*'s education. Thanks to his ability to read, the boy will get to know great endeavours of the past that can stimulate his *uirtus*. Note that V.'s picture does not feature any teacher-like figure, whereas Linus (Heracles' teacher) played a prominent role in Theocritus, following the renowned Chiron-Achilles pattern: γράμματα...τὸν παῖδα γέρων Λίνος ἐξεδίδαξεν (Theocr. *id.* 24.105). V. isolates the *puer* into a heroic and divine dimension of his own. By contrast, Serv. Dan. will paraphrase V.'s text to portray the boy as a typical scion of the Roman learned aristocracy: *cum coeperis imbui studiis liberalibus.*

ECLOGUE 4   223

28–30. A typical 'Golden' landscape is sketched out: wheat, grapes, and honey thrive in abundance, without the need for agricultural labour—almost in an everlasting summer, as it were: cf. Hor. *epod.* 16.43–8 and Ov. *met.* 1.109–12. As a matter of fact, certain 'residues' of degeneration are still there. They will only be eliminated when the *puer* will become a man, at which time the true and definitive Golden Age will begin (4.37–45). The comparison between these lines and *Orac. Sib.* 3.619–23 goes back at least to Lactantius, *inst.* 7.24.13.

28 molli paulatim flauescet campus arista. The appearance of wheat-ears is a natural mirror-image of the boy's *cultus*. The very idea of 'turning golden' entails a delicate allusion to adolescence: *Aen.* 10.324 *flauentem prima lanugine malas*; Ov. *met.* 6.718 *pariter flauescere malae*. The connection between the two 'cultures' (the boy's and the wheat's) is emphasized by the bilingual wordplay between the two line-ending words, *uirtus* and *arista* (ἄριστος 'best'; cf. 4.25 *amomum* [n.]). The Latin word *arista*, possibly of remote local origin, was actually traced back to *arescere/aridus*: Varr. *rust.* 1.48.2; Serv. *ad Aen.* 7.720. In Aratus, the constellation of the Virgin Justice carries an 'Ear' in her hand (i.e. the brightest of its stars): Arat. *phaen.* 97 Παρθένον, ἥ ῥ' ἐν χειρὶ φέρει Στάχυν αἰγλήεντα. E. 4.28 has long been a matter of scholarly debate: where exactly is the 'miracle'? While V. mentions grapes among brambles and honey-producing oaks, 4.28 is merely about a wheatfield gradually 'turning golden'. Several transpositions, re-interpretations, and conjectural emendations have been proposed; yet, the text does not appear to need any correction, since it gradually leads the reader towards a climax (wheat, grapes, then honey: see 4.29n.) and the idea of 'wheat turning golden' is a symbol of prosperity in itself. Thus far, in fact, V. has talked about *munuscula*, which the earth produces spontaneously: ivy, lotus, acanthus, amomum, and the flowers in the boy's crib. V. has repeatedly insisted on the spontaneous character of the process; now, without any trace of human intervention, the most important product in ancient agriculture takes centre stage (note the emphasis on *arista*, which in *E.* 1 evoked agricultural prosperity: hence Meliboeus' marvel at *E.* 1.69). The chromatic detail (*flauescet*) and the adjective (*molli*), which implies quality and ripeness, underscore the noun *campus*, generally referring to arable land (cf. *G.* 1.126 *ne signare quidem aut partiri limite campum*; contrast *G.* 1.72 *segnem…campum*). Then, in 4.29, *incultis* points to the absence of agricultural labour, which is merely implied in 4.28 (agriculture and ploughing have to wait until 4.33). In the context of the earth's spontaneous *munuscula*, the appearance of a *flauescens campus* (which requires human labour) is at least surprising, if not 'miraculous'. Note also that the pairing of wheat and grapes is an agricultural symbol *par excellence*, reflected in the divine couple Ceres-Bacchus (cf. 4.29n.). In the aftermath of Philippi, wheat supplies were far from plentiful in Rome and, despite the *foedus Brundisinum*, the problem persisted due to Sextus Pompey's sabotage actions (cf. Flor. *epit.* 2.18.2; Appian. *bell. civ.* 5.67 [280]; Cass. Di. 48.31). The historical context further clarifies the reassuring force of 4.28, which does not need any emendation.

224 ECLOGUE 4

paulatim. A natural process, as expected, proceeds gradually: cf. *E.* 6.35–6 *tum…solum… / …rerum paulatim sumere formas*; *Aen.* 7.529 *paulatim sese tollit mare* (Lucr. 1.189 *paulatim crescunt…semine certo*). The adverb is common in V., unlike *paulo* (on which see 4.1n.).

29 incultisque rubens pendebit sentibus uua. A so-called golden line: the verb is in the middle, framed by adjectives and nouns arranged according to the scheme $a^1a^2VS^1S^2$; cf. 4.4n.; 2.50n. Similarly elaborate word-order is also found at 14; 17; 20; 23; 31. Grapes appear right after wheat (4.28): hence a pairing of the respective gods, Bacchus and Ceres (5.79n.). In the Golden Age imagined by V., wine itself flows in rivers, as can be inferred from G. 1.132 (though the passage is somewhat ironical). Here, however, it is grapes that suffice to encircle the young *puer*. For this type of miracle, compare again Isaiah, 55.13 *pro saliunca ascendet abies et pro urtica crescet myrtus* (Vulg.). Note that this is something of a 'minor' miracle (in contrast with the honey-making oaks at 4.30), since V. does not explicitly say that brambles produce grapes. Rather, the source of wonder is the fact that ripe (*rubens*), beautiful grapes appear in the midst of wild brambles, which contradicts the basic principles of viticulture (taught by V. himself in G. 2.410–1 *bis uitibus ingruit umbra, / bis segetem densis obducunt s e n t i b u s herbae*; cf. also G. 2.415 *i n c u l t i…exercet cura salicti*).

30 et durae quercus sudabunt roscida mella. The oak as a 'host' of honey symbolizes prosperity and abundance for virtuous humans since Hesiod, *op.* 232–3 'For them the earth produces much food, the mountain oak / bears acorns on its top, and bees inside its core'. Here, however, the image is presented as a true miracle, typical of ancient descriptions of the Golden Age, marking the climax of the threefold structure at 4.28–9. Note also Tib. 1.3.45 *ipsae mella dabant quercus*; Hor. *epod.* 16.47 *mella caua manant ex ilice*; Ov. *met.* 1.112 *flauaque de uiridi stillabant ilice mella* (the latter two texts featuring the evergreen holm-oak). The epithet *roscida*, containing an implicit comparison (the tree trunk is wetted by honey as if by dew: cf. *E.* 8.37 *roscida mala*, also in line-ending position), and the verb *sudabunt* present the phenomenon in terms of a prodigious distillation, comparable to that of amber in *E.* 8.54: in fact, neither bees nor swarms are mentioned (contrast the oak at *E.* 7.13 *eque sacra resonant examina quercu*). Honey, a divine gift, was said to pour down from the sky, just like dew, in order to be collected by bees: G. 4.1 *aerii mellis caelestia dona*, with Servius' note: *nam mel ex rore colligitur, qui utique defluit ex aere* (Aristot. *hist. anim.* 5.22.553b29, whence Plin. *nat.* 11.30 [see also 16.31]; cf. Theophr. *hist. plant.* 3.7.6; Colum. 9.14.20). Finally, the adj. *durae* emphasizes a further paradox: this oak produces honey rather than the symbolic austere food of primeval ages, i.e. acorns—cf. G. 1.148–9 (as well as Lucr. 5.965; Ov. *met.* 1.106; but note Varr. *rust.* 2.1.3–4, referring to Dicaearchus: cf. fr. 48 Wehrli). The terms *mella* and *amomum* (4.25), both closing a line as well as a syntactical-rhetorical unit, framed *E.* 3.89 in the context of V.'s praise of Pollio (cf. 4.25n.). The miracle of liquid honey springing from tough oaks will reappear at *E.* 8.52–3, i.e. in another eclogue (probably) dedicated to Pollio. Honey, along with milk and wine, is paralleled by the idyllic tableaux of *Orac. Sib.*, e.g. 3.622. **sudabunt mella**. For the internal accusative, cf. *E.* 8.54 *sudent electra myricae*; see also Ov. *met.* 10.308–9 *sudata...ligno / tura*; Colum. 10.18; OLD^2, p. 2050, s.v. *sudo* 3b (construction with abl. in Enn. *trag.* 165 Joc. = 181 V.²; Lucr. 6.943; cf. *G.* 1.117).

31–3. At 31, V. makes explicit a fundamental presupposition of the myth of the ages, whereby even the happiest generation harbours the seeds of decadence: those 'traces of ancestral fault' (*priscae uestigia fraudis*; cf. Catull. 64.295 *ueteris uestigia poenae*) that only the *puer*'s maturity can definitively dispel. Towards the centre of the poem (especially if the three introductory lines are not counted), V. expresses a crucial notion, which significantly repeats and amplifies 4.13–14 *te duce, si qua manent sceleris uestigia nostri, / inrita perpetua soluent formidine terras*. Thus, the *puer*'s heroic career intensifies the task that his illustrious protector was summoned to accomplish, and has already partially accomplished (through the *foedus Brundisinum*). From this perspective, any human invention is presented as a violation, whereas the return of those heroes that the *puer* knows well from his reading (4.26–7) might foreshadow an imminent new cycle of decline (4.34–6). In fact, however, the opposite (i.e. 'optimistic') conception, whereby humankind undergoes technological development towards the better, is by no means alien to Greek thought: thus Xenophan. 21 B 18 D.-K. In the aftermath of the *foedus Brundisinum*, the sea was increasingly regarded as a locus of danger, particularly due to Sextus Pompey's military actions.

32 temptare Thetim ratibus. Referring to Thetis, the sea goddess (here standing for the sea and the ocean, and therefore distinct from *Tethys*/ Τηθύς, wife of the god Oceanus, mentioned at *G.* 1.31), the verb *temptare* not only points to the foolish recklessness of the endeavour (cf. Hor. *carm.* 3.4.30–1 *Bosphorum / temptabo*) but further hints at the quasi-sexual violence of the sacrilege (e.g. Tib. 1.3.73 *Iunonem temptare Ixionis ausi*). For a possible Greek model, cf. Apoll. Rhod. 1.115 ὅσσαι ὑπ' εἰρεσίῃσιν ἐπειρήσαντο θαλάσσης, where the diction seems rather neutral and dispassionate, less emotionally charged than V.'s (see further 4.34–5n.). The goddess, after all, was a renowned object of desire (Zeus apparently wanted her for himself, and Peleus famously wrestled to subdue her: cf. Ov. *met.* 11.221– 65). A female personification of the sea is found as early as Hom. *Od.* 12.97 (Amphitrite; Thetis, however, is always the personified goddess, even in *Il.* 6.136); cf. Catull. 64.11 *illa rudem cursu prima imbuit Amphitriten* (the ship Argo: *E.* 4.34–5n.). Moralizing thought treats seafaring, with its otherwise avoidable dangers, as the offspring of greed, which pushes man towards trade and commerce: ll. 38–9 are explicit on this matter; cf. *G.* 2.503; Lucr. 5.1006 (a possible interpolation); Hor. *carm.* 1.3.21–4; *sat.* 1.4.25–32; Tib. 1.3.37–40; Ov. *amor.* 3.8.43–4; Sen. *Med.* 301–79. For this reason, there is no room for seafaring in the Golden Age, when all human desires are fulfilled (cf. Arat. *phaen.* 110–11, but

226   ECLOGUE 4

also Hes. *op.* 236–7 and 631–4; Solon, fr. 13.43–6 W.[2]). The sea, on the other hand, is commonly described as an element ill-suited to human presence; according to Plato, it is a potential source of corruption for the city: *leg.* 4.704a–705a (virtues and simple customs are 'mountain-dwelling': 3.677b–c); cf. Cic. *rep.* 2.5–9. V.'s mention of Thetis (wife of Peleus, mother of Achilles) may also serve to stress the allusion to a crucial model, i.e. Catull. 64. **ratibus.** The term *ratis* is poetic for 'ship', particularly 'warship': e.g. Enn. *ann.* 378; 515 Sk. But here, given the primitivist context, it may also refer to a 'raft', an 'assemblage of floating timber' (Varr. *ling.* 7.23; Cic. *Verr.* 2.5.5), thus underscoring human inadequacy: cf. *G.* 2.445; Sen. *Med.* 2–3 [scil. *Minerua*] *quae...domituram freta / Tiphyn nouam frenare docuisti ratem*, as well as *Med.* 301–2 *audax nimium qui freta primus / rate tam fragili perfida rupit.*

32–3 cingere muris / oppida. Standard phrase for the fortification of a city—but a physical act of possession is perceptible, especially after l. 32: Ov. *amor.* 3.8.47 *turritis incingere moenibus urbes*, along with *met.* 1.97 *nondum praecipites cingebant oppida fossae* (the Golden Age). The enjambement adds emphasis (4.8–9n.).

33 telluri infindere sulcos. The verb implies the violence of a wound. Ploughing is a frequent metaphor for sexual activity: e.g. Plaut. *Asin.* 874; *Truc.* 149–50; Mart. 9.21.4 and the well-known Soph. *Oed. tyr.* 1497; DuBois (1988, pp. 39–64); see further Adams (1982, pp. 24.82–25.154). The phrase *infindere sulcos*, here construed with the dat., is paralleled by *Aen.* 5.142 *infindunt pariter sulcos* (the sea is 'ploughed' by the ships); cf., in a technical context, Colum. 3.13.5 *atque ita sequentem sulcum infindunt*; the dat. construction follows the pattern of *inducite fontibus umbras* (*E.* 5.40). R's reading *tellurem infindere sulco*, with reverse construction, is probably a learned conjecture, modelled after e.g. *Aen.* 10.295–6 *inimicam findite rostris / hanc terram* (cf. Sil. 14.380 *caerula...findit spumantia sulco*: both passages, however, have the *simplex* form). Ploughing will be described as a requirement imposed by Zeus in *G.* 1.121–5, but here it appears uncalled for, since wheat grows spontaneously (28); it is thus dictated (*iubeant*) by greed for profit and superfluous innovation.

34–6. In Hesiod, the heroes' generation, which precedes the contemporary age of iron, had been slaughtered by violence and conflicts; however, rather than the Theban and Trojan wars (*op.* 161–5), V. mentions the Argonauts' endeavour, of which the Trojan expedition almost seems to be a mere technological consequence (first attempts with rafts at 4.32; Argo, the first ship, at 4.34; *mittetur* referring to Achilles at 4.36).

34–5 alter...Tiphys et altera quae uehat Argo / delectos heroas. The ship Argo was deemed to be the first ship that crossed the seas on a long-distance journey. Tiphys was its steersman: the heroes praised at 4.26 reappear now on board this ambivalent instrument of civilization. An Ennian reminiscence is likely: *trag.* (*Medea exul*) 212 Joc. = 250 V.[2] *Argo, quia Argiui in ea delecti uiri* (here *delectos heroas*: cf. Eur. *Med.* 5 ἀνδρῶν ἀρίστων; Apoll. Rhod. 4.831 λεκτοὺς ἡρώων; Catull. 64.4 *lecti iuuenes*; on V.'s Catullan echoes see above, 4.32n.); cf. also Theocr.

id. 13.16–18; Hor. *epod.* 16.57 *non huc Argoo contendit remige pinus*; Enc. *Virg.* I, pp. 309–10, s.v. *Argo* (G. G. Biondi). Besides the etymology *Argo-Argiui*, which Ennius makes explicit (cf. *schol. ad* Apoll. Rhod. 1.1–4e, pp. 7–8 Wend. = Pherecyd. *FGrH* 3 F 106 Jac.), V. may have thought of the adj. ἀργός in the sense of 'swift', 'rapid': cf. Catull. 64.6 *cita…puppi*; 9 *uolitantem…currum*. Note, however, the etymological pun at Apoll. Rhod. 1.111 αὐτὴ [scil. Ἀθηναίη] γὰρ καὶ νῆα θοὴν κάμε, σὺν δέ οἱ Ἄργος κτλ. The 'miracle' of the first ship is particularly significant in pastoral poetry, an inherently 'earthbound' genre. In a famous passage of Accius, an astonished shepherd observed the ship Argo from a mountain, without understanding what it was (*trag.* 391–402 R.[3] [*Medea* sive *Argonautae*]). As for *heroas*, note the trochaic caesura (as in 4.16), here accompanied by the hephthemimeral. As in 4.16 (see 4.15–16n.), a molossus-shaped word opens the line (*delectos*; cf. esp. 4.47).

36 iterum ad Troiam magnus mittetur Achilles. The Trojan war, and especially one of its greatest heroes, constituted a historical model that had already seemed to repeat itself several times (i.e. it had been the object of emulation). Alexander the Great, in particular, had taken inspiration from the figure of Achilles, even considering himself his descendant (e.g. Arrian. *anab.* 1.11.8; cf. also Theopomp. *FGrH* 115 F 355 Jac.; Lycophr. *Alex.* 1439–41, with the scholia ad loc.). Correspondingly, the historian Duris posited an exact thousand-year gap between the fall of Troy and Alexander's Asian campaign (Clem. Alex *Strom.* 1.139.4 = *FGrH* 76 F 41a Jac.). Pyrrhus, king of Epirus, similarly made reference to his supposed ancestor Achilles during his war against the Romans, Troy's descendants, as is testified to by his coins (*British Mus. Cat. of Gr. Coins: Thessaly to Aetolia*, p. 111, no. 7; see Enn. *ann.* 167 Sk.; Cic. *diu.* 2.116; cf. also Perseus of Macedon at *Aen.* 6.39 *Aeaciden genus armipotentis Achilli*; Prop. 4.11.39). The renewed topicality of Achilles is confirmed by Appian's anecdote at *bell. civ.* 3.13 (47), in which Octavian and his mother Atia are assimilated to Achilles and Thetis, respectively. In the *Aeneid*, the idea that Troy's vicissitudes are bound to be repeated will acquire great thematic and ideological significance: esp. *Aen.* 10.25–30 (but also 3.476; 9.598–9); for a close parallel, cf. the Sibyl's prophecy at *Aen.* 6.89 *alius Latio iam partus Achilles*; but recall the Parcae's prophecy in Catull. 64.338 *nascetur uobis expers terroris Achilles.* As a heroic epithet, *magnus* reappears at *Aen.* 6.122 (Hercules).

37–45. The degenerative process, entailing the subsequent beginning of a new cycle, is halted by the *puer*'s full maturity—he is now a man. Hence, once again, the miraculous spontaneity of nature, typical of the Golden Age. In comparison to 4.18–30, the marvellous dimension is further amplified here, culminating in a paradoxically bucolic description of multicoloured rams and lambs: the 'traces of guilt' enumerated at 4.31–3 disappear, one by one, at 4.38–41. No mention is made, however, of the absence of war: all conflicts seem to be over after the second heroic generation at 4.35–6. The Hellenistic language of praise associated a land's prosperity with the rule of a righteous, devoted king: e.g. Theocr.

228   ECLOGUE 4

id. 16.82–100; 17.77–116 (but cf. Hom. *Od.* 19.109–14; Hes. *op.* 225–37; conversely, Soph. *Oed. tyr.* esp. 22–30). The Epicurean Philodemus taught that the good king's land generates all sorts of products (*De bono rege,* cols. IV–V). The theme reappears in various forms at Cic. *p. red. in sen.* 34; *p. red. ad Quir.* 18, eventually becoming typical of Augustan ideology: e.g. Hor. *carm.* 4.5.17–18; 15.4–5. It is an age-old Indo-European motif: M. L. West, *Indo-European Poetry and Myth,* Oxford 2007, pp. 422–4.

37 ubi iam firmata uirum te fecerit aetas. Cf. *Aen.* 12.438 *mox cum matura adoleuerit aetas*; above, 4.26–36n.

38 nautica pinus. The epithet, still echoing the Argonauts' endeavour, is of crucial importance, since pine trees per se are typically to be found in bucolic areas (cf. *E.* 1.38), especially in Arcadia: *E.* 8.22; 10.14–15; cf. 7.24n. The word *nauis* does not appear in the *E.* (cf. *ratis* at 4.32; 6.76). For *pinus* cf. the opening of Catull. 64.1 *Peliaco quondam prognatae uertice pinus.*

39 mutabit merces. In ancient moralistic thought, the exchange of goods (which entails long and dangerous journeys) is a sign of people's foolish greed: cf., with the verb *mutare,* Hor. *sat.* 1.4.29 *hic mutat merces*; Ov. *trist.* 1.2.75–6; Pers. 5.54 (where the motif is then extensively developed: Pers. 5.132–53). **omnis feret omnia tellus.** V. contradicts common experience, whereby every soil and every plant bear its own specific fruit. Lucretius employed this idea to demonstrate that nothing is generated out of nothing (Lucr. 1.165–6 *nec fructus idem arboribus constare solerent,* / *sed mutarentur, ferre omnes omnia possent*), and V. reworks the argument in a didactic context at *G.* 2.109 *nec uero terrae ferre omnes omnia possunt* (even though he praises Italy for the remarkable fertility of its soil at *G.* 2.136–50). It is one of the most traditional miracles of Saturn's age, probably featured in a poem by Calvus: *terra omnia liberius ferente, quod Caluus canit* (*schol. Bern. ad G.* 1.125, p. 186 H.; cf. fr. 20 Bläns. = Court.); see also *G.* 1.127–8 and *E.* 6.41 *Saturnia regna* (n.).

40–1 rastros…falcem /…iuga. V. mentions three tools (and three 'works') crucial to agricultural labour, which will play a large role in the *G.* Here the emphasis is on their troublesome, almost painful (*patietur*), effect on the soil (*humus*) and the vineyard (*uinea*). The plough, operated by an overly *robustus* farmer (cf. *E.* 3.42 *curuus arator* [n.]; Lucr. 5.933 *robustus…moderator aratri*; 6.1253), is a torment of a sort for the oxen, which will finally be freed from it (*soluet*). Rake, sickle, and plough are variously described in 'agonistic', at times even warlike, terms at *G.* 1.45; 94; 98–9; 155; 160–70; 2.365; 421; 439; 3.534. No wonder, then, that they can also be melted down and used to make real weapons, as in *G.* 1.508; *Aen.* 7.635–6 (cf. Lucr. 5.1293–6; Ov. *fast.* 1.697–700). A similar 'miracle' in the Blessed Isles of Hor. *epod.* 16.43–4 *reddit ubi Cererem tellus inarata quotannis* / *et imputata floret usque uinea.*

42–5. The wonder of the new era must become apparent in a pastoral product, i.e. wool, which is the Roman standard means of clothing and, as such, is highly representative of Roman society. The reader, however, is surprised by a flock in which the ram is purple-red or yellow and the lambs are scarlet—indeed, it resembles a crowd of fashionable Romans, clothed in colourful, flamboyant togas. Thus, nature's action precedes those man-made dyeing processes that involve refined, Oriental pigments, which might appear as shameful counterfeiting to a moralistic eye: *E.* 4.42 *discet mentiri*; cf. *G.* 2.465; further variations at Lucr. 2.35; 5.1423; Hor. *epist.* 2.1.207; Tib. 2.4.27–8 *o pereat quicumque...niueam Tyrio murice tingit ouem.* A colourful crowd of dancers (albeit in the metaphorical context of oratorical style) is described by Fronto, p. 9.2–3 v. d. Hout[2]: *amicti cocco alii, alii luteo, et ostro et purpura alii aliique cohaerentes concursant.* Note that white, undyed wool was standard in official Roman clothing, and Augustus seems to have been quite fond of it (Suet. *Aug.* 40.5).

43 in pratis. That is, in a pasture, just like the lambs at 4.45 (*pascentis*). Here, however, the emphasis is on the chromatic contrast (*colores* at 4.42) between the green backdrop of the grass and the animals' vivid colours.

43–4 suaue rubenti / murice. The delicate red hue (*rubens* as in 4.29) of the *murex*, the purple-fish, or, more properly, the shell from which the well-known dye was extracted (distinct, however, from *purpura* in Cels. 2.24.3; Plin. *nat.* 5.12); cf. *Aen.* 4.262; Hor. *epist.* 2.2.181. At Rome, this was the colour of kingship or, at any rate, of supreme political and religious authority, whereas divinatory teratology of Etruscan origin considered the ram dyed in, or simply sprinkled with, purple (or gold) as a symbol of prosperity, according to Macrobius, *Sat.* 3.7.2 *purpureo aureoue colore ouis ariesue si aspergetur, principi ordinis et generis summa cum felicitate largitatem auget, genus progeniem propagat in claritate laetioremque efficit* (quoting the erudite Tarquitius Priscus, who probably lived in Julius Caesar's age; cf. also Serv. Dan. *ad E.* 4.43). Judging from Simonides' hymn to Poseidon (*PMG* 576), the famous 'golden fleece' (i.e. the fleece of Phrixus' winged ram) may in fact have been purple: cf. also *schol. ad* Eur. *Med.* 5, vol. II, p. 142 Schw. ἀπὸ τῶν ἐν τῇ θαλάττῃ πορφυρῶν κεχρῶσθαι; *schol. ad* Apoll. Rhod. 4.176–7, p. 271 Wend.; Tzetz. *Chil.* 1.433–4, p. 20 L. According to the poet's prophecy, such prodigies will be common in the future. The word naming the miracle, *murice*, is enjambed: 4.8–9n. For the phrase *suaue rubenti* (and the adj. *suauis*) cf. 3.63n.

44 croceo...luto. The second colour into which the ram seems to 'transform' its wool (*mutabit uellera*) is much more common than purple: it is a bright yellow pigment, extracted from a rather common plant (the *lutum*, i.e. *Reseda luteola*, also known as 'dyer's weed'). The adj., referring to the saffron crocus, adds an orange nuance, perhaps not unsuitable here given that *luteus* can also be an unpleasant colour, i.e. that of human pallor: e.g. Hor. *epod.* 10.16; Tib. 1.8.52. In V., both *croceus* and *luteus* will recur in the context of dawn (respectively *G.* 1.447; *Aen.* 7.26).

45 sandyx. A mineral dye, of vivid red hue, primarily extracted from lead and iron oxides (Plin. *nat.* 35.39–40; a mark of luxury in Prop. 2.25.45). Here V. seems

230   ECLOGUE 4

to imagine it as spontaneously 'clothing' the lambs (*sponte sua...uestiet*), seeping through the grass which the animals feed on after their weaning (*pascentis*; cf. *E.* 5.12). A similar explanation was offered for the colour of the Spanish flocks dwelling on the banks of the river Baetis, now Guadalquivir (Iuv. 12.40–2; cf. also Plin. *nat.* 8.191; Mart. 9.61.3–4; 12.98.2; 14.133). A mineral was perhaps the cause of the 'golden teeth' characterizing particular goats which, until the nineteenth century, lived on Tavolara, the small island off the north-eastern coast of Sardinia. It would thus be wrong to assert (as Pliny does, *nat.* 35.40) that V. mistakenly treats the *sandyx* as a plant; cf. also Servius: *herba, de qua sandicinus tinguitur color.*

46–59. In the section preceding the four final lines (4.60–3), the myth of the *puer* is redefined and historicized, i.e. traced back to the present age (= Pollio's consulship) from which the Sibyl's song had begun. On the one hand, the *puer*'s birth is yet again presented as imminent, rather than as having already occurred (4.48 *adgredere*; 4.50 *aspice*), and is projected onto a cosmic and divine canvas (4.48–52). On the other hand, the poet conjectures that he might someday be able to narrate the grown-up *puer*'s endeavours, should he be lucky enough to have a long life (4.53–4). The shift is signalled by *talia saecla* at the outset of 4.46, through which a vast stretch of time spanning entire 'generations' is reduced to the proportions of a single life, albeit an exceptional one. The *puer*'s fate, like that of any other man, is determined by the Parcae, and there is at least some hope that the poet will be able to see personally what he prophesied at 4.4–45. The spinning goddesses, whose appearance is so fitting after the multicolour 'wools' of 42–5, make explicit the reference to Catull. 64, where they also appear in person (see 4.46–7n.); but the idea of a 'thread of destiny', spun by the gods, is in Hom. *Od.* 11.139 τὰ μὲν ἄρ που ἐπέκλωσαν θεοὶ αὐτοί. Note the structural correspondence between the finale of the poem and its opening: they have the same number of lines (fourteen), equally subdivided into two seven-line units (cf. *E.* 4.4–17n.). They are thematically similar as well: they connect the Sibylline song to its historical context, symmetrically embodied by Pollio and the poet.

46–7 'Talia saecla' suis dixerunt 'currite' fusis / ...Parcae. The two words framing ll. 46–7 (*talia...Parcae*) allude to the Catullan model, where they occur in a similar position: *talia praefantes quondam felicia Pelei / carmina diuino cecinerunt pectore Parcae* (Catull. 64.382–3; cf. also 64.321–2). In addition to that, V. reworks Catull. 64.326–7 *sed uos, quae fata sequuntur, / currite ducentes subtegmina, currite, fusi* (64.327, a refrain, is then repeated eleven times), replacing Catullus' *cecinerunt* with *dixerunt*, which often means 'to sing' (*E.* 5.2; 6.5; 8.5) and here takes on a nuance of authoritative command. V.'s single *currite*, on the other hand, simplifies the iterative construction *currite...currite*, typical of folk poetry and particularly of 'work songs' (we know the names of some Greek spinners' and weavers' songs: Tryph. fr. 113, p. 78 Velsen, apud Athen. 14.618d). V. thus reduces the space allotted to the speech of the goddesses, who sang for a total of almost sixty lines in Catullus (64.323–81): hence an emphasis on irreversible solemnity, then reasserted by the predominantly spondaic rhythm of 4.47 *concordes stabili fatorum numine Parcae* (featuring a molossus-shaped word at the beginning of the line: cf. 4.16 and 4.35). It is precisely for knowing the goddesses' fateful prophecy concerning Thetis' son (destined to outdo his father) that Prometheus obtains freedom from Jupiter, to whom he reveals the secret: *qui, ueritus id quod ipse Saturno patri fecisset in simili causa, ne patris regno priuatus cogeretur, destitit Thetin uelle ducere uxorem* (Hyg. *astr.* 2.15.4). Here, however, the same Achilles who surpassed all other heroes according to Catullus' prophecy (64.343) is presented as a repeatable role model (4.36 *iterum...Achilles*), compared to which the *puer* stands out for his definitive uniqueness. The Parcae and their song will reappear, with clear Virgilian reminiscences, in Hor. *carm. saec.* 25–8.

46 'Talia saecla...currite'. *Talia saecla* has to be taken as acc. rather than voc.: the Parcae's song is addressed to the spindles (*dixerunt 'currite' fusis*, a variation on Catullus' *currite fusi*). It is harder to choose between *currere* with internal object, which appears more natural (cf. *Aen.* 3.191 *currimus aequor*; 5.862), and *currere* as causative, along the lines of *lucos...resonat* 'makes the woods resonate' (*Aen.* 7.11–12: here, therefore, the centuries would be the ones 'running'). The acc. construction is reworked by Symmachus: *iamdudum aureum saeculum currunt fusa Parcarum* (Symm. *or.* 3.9). The mention of divine figures such as the Parcae (or, elsewhere, the Muses) allows the poet to compress entire ages into the life of a single individual. This is a delicate transition point in the poem, as V. gradually moves from eternal prophecy to contemporary history, inserting his own individuality into the latter (4.53 *o mihi*).

47 concordes stabili fatorum numine. An intertwining of etymological meanings is implicit but perceptible: the goddess' concord (*concordia* from *cum* and *cor, cordis*) rests on the stable (*stabilis* from *stare*) will (*numen* from **nuo* 'to nod': cf. *Aen.* 2.123) of the 'fates' (*fari* 'to utter solemnly'). Cf. Hor. *carm. saec.* 26–7 *stabilisque rerum / terminus seruet*; a literal parallel in *Ciris* 125 *concordes stabili firmarunt* (*firmarant* Barth) *numine Parcae*. Note the redundant emphasis on the notion of 'stability', which can be explained, by contrast, in the context of chaotic historical events such as the land confiscations (cf. *E.* 1.11–12; 9.5). **Parcae.** The Roman goddess of destiny, *Parca*, etymologically connected to *pario* (note Varro apud Gell. 3.16.9–10 [*ant. rer. diu.* fr. 98 Card.]), and therefore responsible for childbirth, was soon multiplied by three, by analogy with the Greek Moirai. The latter were chthonic deities, daughters of the Night and closely connected with the dark underworld, but also Olympian deities, daughters of Zeus and Themis, and thus readily involved in other rites of passage, such as birth and marriage (the two genealogies appear in Hesiod, respectively *theog.* 211–22 and 904–6). For further reading see *Enc. Virg.* III, pp. 969–70, s.v. *Parcae* (C. Monteleone); *Virg. Enc.* II, p. 969, s.v. *Parcae* (R. Jenkyns); also *LIMC* VI.1, esp. pp. 636–8, s.v. *Moirai* (S. De Angeli). The goddesses play a more or less decisive role in the births of Dionysus (Eur. *Bacch.* 99), Asclepius (Isyll. 52–7, p. 134 Pow.), Heracles (Ant. Lib.

232   ECLOGUE 4

29.1–3—where, however, they oppose the hero's birth), Iamus son of Apollo (Pind. *Ol.* 6.41–4), and other divine children. In a cosmic or eschatological context, the Moirai mark the sequence of generations according to Plato, *rep.* 10.617c–e (where they add their own 'hymn' to the harmony of the heavenly spheres); cf. also [Aristot.] (?) *mund.* 7.401b14–22; Plut. *fat.* 2.568e–f; see *E.* 4.50n.

48–52. After 4.46–7 ascribed to the Parcae the sentence *talia saecla currite* (which ratifies the preceding prophecy: it is unlikely that, as some believe, the whole section 4.4–45 is in the goddesses' mouth), the poet addresses the boy directly, exhorting him to set out on his mission. Shifting the focus away from the motionless dimension of divine will (47 *stabili fatorum numine*: the εἱμαρμένη, carried out through the *Μοῖραι*), the poet's eye, along with the *puer*'s, looks at the cosmic world of the celestial sphere (50) and, finally, at the three 'earthly' elements (51). For an important parallel cf. Varr. At. *carm.* fr. 11 Bläns. = 15 Court., describing the motion and harmony of the heavenly spheres: cf. 4.50 *nutantem* [n.]; 4.52n.

48 adgredere o magnos (aderit iam tempus) honores. The line's structure and the notion will reappear, with some variation, at *G.* 1.42 *ingredere et uotis iam nunc adsuesce uocari* (addressed to Octavian).

49 cara deum suboles, magnum Iouis incrementum. The parallelism between the two half-lines places *suboles* and *incrementum* (both of which can be traced back to an agricultural context) in corresponding positions. The first term (from *sub-ales* [< *alo*], as in *proles, indoles*, and therefore what is 'nourished beneath', or 'planted') belongs to highbrow literary vocabulary (e.g. Lucr. 4.1232), while in prose Cicero, *de orat.* 3.153, considers it studied and archaic, yet palatable on occasions (Asinius Pollio uses it in a letter addressed to him: *fam.* 10.33.1; in V. it will recur several times in the *G.*; in the *Aen.* only at 4.328). The second is a lowly, technical-prosaic term (Servius calls it *uulgare*; *ThlL* VII.1.1043–7), which V. is the first to use in a solemn context, at the end of the hexameter, as if visually to suggest the growth process. It must thus be understood as a 'sprout' or 'seed' of Jupiter (*incrementum* is precisely the result of his generative power); cf. Theocr. *id.* 7.44 ἐκ Διὸς ἔρνος (Callim. *hymn.* 1 [*Iou.*]1 τὠπόλλωνος...δάφνινος ὄρπηξ), and also *Aen.* 8.301 *uera Iouis proles, decus addite diuis* (Hercules); *Enc. Virg.* II, p. 937, s.v. *incrementum* (A. Traina); also *Aen.* 7.656 *satus Hercule*, and the epic formula *Anchisa satus* (e.g. *Aen.* 5.244; solemn and probably archaic: cf. Plaut. *Epid.* 635); for a rustic term used in the context of offspring and succession (among lions), cf. *seminium* in Lucr. 3.742, on which see Varr. *rust.* 2.1.14. Through the idea of growth and greatness (*magnum*: close to the caesura, like *magnos* in the first half-line of 4.48), V. touches upon a field of meaning crucial to the later ideology of *Augustus* (from *augeo*). Zeus is called αὐξητής in *Hymn. Orph.* 15.8; a solemn formula indicating the coming of a child is *liberis / filio augeri*: Plaut. *Truc.* 384; Cic. *Att.* 1.2.1; *ThlL* II.1355.1–9. Octavian himself will be assimilated to an earthly counterpart of Jupiter by Hor. *carm.* 1.12.57–60; 3.5.1–4. In the final months of his life, Julius Caesar had been granted the epithet *Iuppiter*

ECLOGUE 4   233

Iulius: Cass. Di. 44.6.4; Weinstock (1971, pp. 12 and 287–317). The privileged connection between Zeus and the human sovereigns dates back at least to Hesiod, *theog.* esp. 96 ἐκ δὲ Διὸς βασιλῆες; but cf. notably Theocr. *id.* 17.73–6 (Zeus' favour to the newborn king: *id.* 17.74–5 ὅν κε φιλήσῃ / γεινόμενον τὰ πρῶτα). As for *incrementum*, note the effect of the line-ending quadrisyllabic word, here a Latin one (contrast 2.24n.). This is one of the extremely rare spondaic hexameters (i.e. with fifth-foot spondee) in the *E.* (5.38n.; cf. *G.* 1.221 *abscondantur*; by contrast, spondaic hexameters are particularly frequent in Catull. 64, clearly recalled here). More generally, spondaic patterns and molossus-shaped words occur quite frequently in *E.* 4.

50 aspice conuexo nutantem pondere mundum. The point of view is highly elevated, so as to enable the *puer* to turn his eyes to the whole cosmos (*mundus*), perceiving its 'convexity'. In a similar way, according to Plato's Er at *rep.* 10.616b–c, the souls about to return to the earth 'had to start down the path from there, in order to reach, on the fourth day, a place from which it was possible to see [καθορᾶν] a line of light, straight like a column, extending from above through the whole sky and earth… After a day's journey they arrived there, and saw that, in the midst of the light, the tops of the chains of heaven were connected to it coming down from above: for this light is the bond of heaven and holds together the circular motion of the universe like the hawsers of a trireme' (the column of light must probably be understood as the axis of the universe; Er goes on to describe the 'spindles' of Necessity and, finally, the three Moirai appear, along with their 'hymn' [617c]). See *Aen.* 6.789–90 *hic Caesar et omnis Iuli / progenies magnum caeli uentura sub axem* (here, however, the 'light' is the one seen at the moment of birth); but cf. the cosmic vision in the *Somnium Scipionis*, Cic. *rep.* 6.15–22, esp. 17 *nonne aspicis quae in templa ueneris?* That the overall shape of the universe is circular is a common idea in ancient cosmology (e.g. Cic. *nat. deor.* 1.18), but here *conuexo…pondere* presupposes formulations like Aristot. *cael.* 2.11.291b17 σφαιροειδῆ…τὸν ὄγκον (referring to the shape of stars); cf. also Lucr. 5.96 *moles…mundi* and Manil. 2.117 *hanc conuexi molem sine fine patentis.* **nutantem.** The oft-discussed participle must in all likelihood refer to the slight oscillatory motions of the cosmic sphere, due to the impulse of its own weight; for *nuto* in a similar sense, though by no means identical, cf. *Aen.* 2.629; 9.682 (in both cases, the term refers to the swinging of treetops, as in Enn. *ann.* 511 Sk.; cf. also Catull. 64.290 and, for single branches, Ov. *ars* 2.263 *dum rami pondere nutant*). As 4.52 (*laetantur*) makes clear, the *puer* is meant to interpret this phenomenon as a sign of the universe's approval of the new era. This is a sort of cosmic 'dance', like the primeval one mentioned by Lucian, *salt.* 7 (see *E.* 6.28n.). Cf. also *Orac. Sib.* 8.474–5, along with Varr. At. *carm.* fr. 11.1–4 Bläns. = 15.1–4 Court. *uidit et aetherio mundum torquerier axe / et septem aeternis sonitum dare uocibus orbes / nitentes aliis alios, quae maxima diuis / laetitia est* (the subject of *uidit* is probably Apollo). If V. really had Varro of Atax in mind, he clearly replaced *nitor*, frequent

234   ECLOGUE 4

in cosmological contexts (cf. Lucr. 1.1053 *in medium…omnia niti*), with *nuto*, whose strong impact on the imagination is especially evident in the case of a *puer*'s mind. Manilius seems to have known and imitated that text, as can be inferred from *astr.* 2.905–6 *curuata…primum / culmina nutantis summo de uertice mundi* (with many differences in terms of context and imagery). We may, however, suspect that V. wrote *conuexo nitentem pondere mundum*, using *nitor* in its typical astronomical sense (as in Varro of Atax), i.e. in reference to the stable equilibrium of the cosmos with its enormous convex mass (*conuexo…pondere*). For a similar idea, cf. *G.* 3.172 *ualido nitens sub pondere…axis*; note also *Aen.* 4.252 *paribus nitens Cyllenius alis.*

51 terrasque tractusque maris caelumque profundum. The ascending *tricolon* ends on the evocative depth of the sky (as if of a chasm). The line-ending is as early as Ennius, *ann.* 559 Sk. *caelu' profundus* (the adj. alone, used as a noun, ends the hexameter at Lucr. 5.370; 417), and V. employs it again at *Aen.* 1.58. Note the rhyme effect *mundum / profundum*, amplifying the resonant *incrementum* that concluded 4.49. In the alliterative phrase *terrasque tractusque*, the polysyndeton *-que…-que*, modelled after the Homeric τε…τε, is typical of Roman epic poetry; cf. 8.22n. (three *te* at 5.59; 6.32). Here, however, the first *-que* scans long, as e.g. in Hom. *Il.* 18.43 Δωτώ τε Πρωτώ τε Φέρουσά τε, etc.; compare *G.* 1.153 and 352, similarly on the second arsis and exceptionally, as here, preceding the *muta-cum-liquida* cluster; cf. also *Aen.* 4.146 (contrast 3.91). The entire line is repeated identically at *G.* 4.222.

52 laetantur. Here P's transmission resumes, though with the variant reading *laetentur.* The indicative is preferable, due to the greater immediacy of the para-tactic construction (*aspice*, a verb of seeing, is almost a mere interjection: 'lo!', 'behold!'; cf. *E.* 5.6–7 *aspice, ut…sparsit*; *Aen.* 6.855–6 *aspice, ut… / ingreditur*; cf. also 6.779 *uiden, ut…stant*) and probably to Hellenizing poetic language (cf. Theocr. *id.* 5.110; 142, etc.). Calpurnius Siculus has both constructions: with the subjunctive (Calp. *ecl.* 4.97–8; 102; 5.12–13) and with the indicative (*ecl.* 6.39–41). For the joy produced by cosmic motions and the resulting harmony, cf. Varr. At. *carm.* fr. 11.3–4 Bläns. = 15.3–4 Court. *quae maxima diuis / laetitia est* (quoted *in extenso* above, 4.50n.).

53–9. Pastoral language (the *siluae*), maybe along with some Georgic premon-ition (4.28–30), sufficed to describe the *puer*'s immediate future. His endeavours, however, will need an epic spirit (4.54 *spiritus…dicere facta*) in order to be narrated. Nevertheless, V. only mentions two mythical singers of wisdom, i.e. Orpheus and Linus (4.55–7), and the poet's boast is concluded against an Arcadian backdrop (4.58–9). These lines bring the text back to standard pastoral style: note, in particular, the repetitions at 4.58–9.

53 o mihi tum…maneat. Through his wish to witness the *puer*'s achievements as an old man, V. brings back the boy's figure to a real, historical dimension. By contrast, the prophetic voice often excludes itself from the enjoyment of future bliss: e.g. *Orac. Sib.* 3.371 'Blessed he [ὦ μακαριστός] who shall live in those times';

but even Hesiod complained about living in the last, most wretched era of all: 'Would that I had never been part of the fifth / generation of men—instead, I should have either died before then or lived afterwards' (Hes. *op.* 174–5). The image of the old poet who still keeps honouring the Muses has a long tradition: e.g. Eur. *Her.* 673–86; Callim. *aet.* fr. 1.33–5 Pf. = Mass. = Hard. A very different set of priorities in the elegiac Propertius, 2.10.7–8 *aetas prima canat Veneres, extrema tumultus: / bella canam, quando scripta puella mea est.* For a similar type of caution, cf. *G.* 3.10 *modo uita supersit.*

54 spiritus et quantum sat erit. The spirit, literally 'breath' or 'air': Hor. *carm.* 4.6.29–30 *spiritum Phoebus mihi, Phoebus artem / carminis nomenque dedit poetae.* The specification is not superfluous, considering that (as Moeris will say) *omnia fert aetas, animum quoque* (*E.* 9.51). Emphasis is added by both the postponed *et* (*spiritŭs*, nominative, is the subject) and the extreme syntactical brevity, expressing an afterthought in a quasi-anacoluthic way. Several interpreters have doubted the authenticity of the line, and many conjectures have been proposed. Yet the transmitted text seems acceptable, and even expressive. The phrase *quantum sat erit*, a variation on the common theme *quantum satis* (*est*), provides a forceful conclusion to the sequence 4.53–4, which must be read and interpreted as a whole (note that *spiritus* is governed by *maneat*). The poet wishes that life (years) and breath (energy) may be sufficient (*sat erit*) for the future enterprise. In other words, it is unclear whether the *pars ultima* of his life will be enough but, once the *puer*'s future endeavours have been narrated, the poet will be satisfied (*sat erit*) and will be ready to accept his death. The colloquial syntax fits the context and conveys the poet's awareness of his (human) limits as well as enthusiasm for the divine grandeur of his hero. **tua dicere facta.** In this case Virgil will be ready for encomiastic poetry and so again in 8.8 (same words in the end of the hexameter [see n. ad loc.]), but things are different in the case of Varus: cf. 6.6–7.

55–6 non…nec… / nec. For this series of negatives, cf. *E.* 10.64–8 (but also 10.28–30); 5.25–6 and, with some differences, the finale of this eclogue (4. 62–3).

55 non me carminibus uincet. The future tense is preferable (R's reading; P's *uincat* was corrected into *uincet*); cf. however 59 *dicat* (n.). In this imaginative picture, the now pastoral (and humble) V. will be able to surpass the mythical singers; a variation on the theme in Prop. 1.9.5 *non me Chaoniae uincant in amore columbae*…However, the same Apollo who is mentioned at 4.57 will soon intervene, at the outset of *E.* 6, to curb Tityrus-V.'s epic-encomiastic impetus. For the agonistic victory, perhaps featured in Theocr. *id.* 24, cf. 4.58n. **nec Thracius Orpheus.** The legendary singer appeared at 3.46n.; his final mention is, once again, in a probably 'Pollian' eclogue (8.55–6; note, similarly to the present passage, the repetition of Orpheus' name across two lines, along with the numerical correspondence at 4.55). The only other occurrence is at *E.* 6.30.

56 nec Linus. Another singer of wisdom, fitting well with Orpheus: a 'shepherd of divine song', as he will be defined in his other bucolic appearance (*E.* 6.67). Like

236   ECLOGUE 4

Musaeus, Linus was part of an Orphic constellation: just like Orpheus (and Musaeus), he was credited with treating theological matters (Cels. apud Origen. *c. Cels.* 1.16 = T 225a Kern = 1018 VII Bern.; Aug. *civ.* 18.14 = T 20 Kern = 885 I Bern.; cf. also Serv. Dan. *ad E.* 4.57). Little wonder that, in *E.* 6.69–71, Linus possesses the pipe once owned by Hesiod, capable of the Orphic miracle of moving nature (cf. esp. 6.71n.). Finally, Linus qualifies as a teacher of divine children, since he taught the young Heracles to read, according to Theocr. *id.* 24.105 (cf. 6.67n.); the same is true of Alexis' *Linos*, according to Athen. 4.164a–d (cf. fr. 140, esp. 1–7 K.-A.); Linus, moreover, is said to have invented the Greek alphabet by adapting the Phoenician writing system at Diod. Sic. 3.67.1. Further reading in *Enc. Virg.* III, pp. 228–9, s.v. *Lino* (G. Sfameni Gasparro); *Verg. Enc.* II, p. 750, s.v. *Linus* (M. L. Andrews); also *Der neue Pauly*, VII, pp. 251–2, s.v. *Linos* (J. N. Bremmer); a specific collection of testimonies and fragments in A. Bernabé, *Poetae Epici Graeci*, II.3, Berolini-Novi Eboraci 2007, pp. 54–104.

56 huic…huic. The syntactical-rhetorical construction, spilling over to 4.57, highlights the close affinity between the two singers (in terms of both wisdom and kinship). The two are often associated (Orph. TT 8–9; 15; 22; 27; 164 Kern = 873; 872; 875 I; 901; 913; 931 I Bern.). For V.'s colloquial repetition of *hic* in lieu of *hic…ille*, cf. *G.* 4.84–5; *Aen.* 7.473–4; 8.357; note also Plaut. *Most.* 778; Ter. *Heaut.* 276–7; H.-Sz., pp. 181–2. Here, however, the indiscriminate use of *hic* prompts the next line's clarification.

57 Calliopea. Often mentioned as Orpheus' mother: Orph. TT 24; 25a; 26 Kern = 883; 902; 906; 928 IV; 908; 909 Bern. (whereas Orpheus' mother is identified with Polyhymnia by a tradition surviving at *schol. ad* Apoll. Rhod. 1.23–5a, p. 9.3 Wend. = Orph. T 907 Bern.). To further confirm the poet's ambition, Calliope is considered as the most important of all Muses by Hes. *theog.* 79 (where she is associated with kings: 80; cf. Hor. *carm.* 3.4.2 *regina…Calliope*). Note the trochaic caesura, here too accompanied by the hephthemimeral (*E.* 4.35n.). For the form *Calliopea* cf. Prop. 1.2.28; Ov. *fast.* 5.80; more commonly *Calliope*, as in Lucr. 6.94; cf. *Aen.* 9.525; Hor. *carm.* 3.4.2 quoted above. **formosus Apollo**. Apollo is Linus' father in *Certam. Hom. et Hes.*, p. 227.46–7 All. = p. 239.47–8 Rz.[3] (= Orph. T 8 Kern = 873 Bern.). According to the Theban tradition, which saw Linus as the son of Urania and Amphimarus (Poseidon's son), he died by the will of Apollo himself, whom he equalled in the musical art (Pausan. 9.29.6–8; cf. Lin. T 65 Bern.). V.'s phrasing makes it impossible to rule out that Orpheus and Linus are brothers: they are both regarded as sons of Apollo and Calliope by Apollod. 1.3.2 (14) = Orph. TT 22; 63 Kern = 901 Bern. Note V.'s choice of the pastoral adj. *formosus* (cf. 1.5n.): contrast *Aen.* 3.119 *pulcher Apollo* (also in line-ending position). The god's physical beauty echoes the transparent etymology of Calliope's name (κάλλος: cf. Macr. *somn.* 2.3.2 'optimae uocis' Graeca interpretatio est).

58 Pan etiam, Arcadia mecum si iudice certet. At the outset of *id.* 1, Theocritus' Thyrsis started from the god's unquestionable primacy: 'after Pan, you will win the

ECLOGUE 4   237

second prize' (*id.* 1.3). In Longus, Philetas will boast about being second 'only to Pan in the art of piping' (Long. 2.32.3). By contrast, in the *Epitaph of Bion*, the eulogistic context suggests that the god would hesitate to play the late poet's instrument, fearing to be considered second to him ([Mosch.] *epit. Bion.* 56 μὴ δεύτερα σεῖο φέρηται). The mention of the Arcadian god would not appear so abrupt, if we took account of the pastoral implications of Orpheus and Linus: but V. goes as far as boasting about outdoing Pan himself, even if judged by the god's native land (cf. Pan's enthusiastic song, in the context of Dionysus' birth, at Philostr. *imag.* 1.14, p. 316.6–8 Kays.). The prospect of an agon, and the poet's victory (4.55 *non me…uincet*), seem to have appeared in the final lines of Theocr. *id.* 24, which only scanty papyrus fragments preserve. This, at least, is what we can infer from the marginal scholion *ad id.* 24.171 (Gow 1952, II, p. 436). Pan's arbitration in the contest between Daphnis and Menalcas may have appeared in a play by Sositheus: *TrGF*, I, 99, fr. 1a, p. 270 Sn. (cf. *schol.* Theocr. *id.* 8 *argum.* b, pp. 203–4 Wend.; 5.52n.). Familiarity with music and song was considered as a typical trait of the Arcadian people, according to Polybius, 4.19.13–21.6; the two contestants of *E.* 7 are 'Arcadians' (cf. 7.4n.; see further 10.31–3, esp. 32 *soli cantare periti*). For the 'technical' use of the verb *certare* cf. 3.31n.

59 Pan etiam Arcadia…se iudice. The reference to Arcadia is accompanied by the typically pastoral iterative style: of the seven words forming the line, four have already appeared identically at 4.58 (with the assonance *si iudice* / *se iudice*). Cf. what Macrobius observed at *Sat.* 5.14.6: comparing this passage to Hom. *Il.* 22.127–8, he includes it among the *amoenae repetitiones*. For an extreme case (repetition of an entire line) cf. 3.47n. Here the repetition elicits a definitive sense of closure, thereby highlighting the new, and final, address to the *puer* (which is actually a beginning rather than an end: *incipe*). **dicat.** The subjunctive should be printed, even though Macrobius (*Sat.* 5.14.6) attests the future indicative, perhaps arising from the parallelism with 4.55 *uincet* (whence the latter is further confirmed: see n. ad loc.). But now, continuing with the subjunctive (cf. 4.58 *certet*), the poet allows himself a certain obliquity, since the singer to whom he refers is no longer a human being (such as Linus or Orpheus), but the god Pan himself.

60–3. A four-line 'coda', where the *puer* comes back to the foreground, as the poet portrays him after his birth. The iterative rhythm resembles that of a lullaby: note esp. the identical openings of 4.60 and 62 *incipe, parue puer* (for the line-beginning repetition of *incipe*, cf. 5.10–12), the echo *matrem/matri* at 4.60–1; the emphasis on 'laughing' between 4.60 and 63, and the insistent *nec deus…dea nec* at 4.63. Compare Alcmene's lullaby to her two children at Theocr. *id.* 24.7–9 εὕδετ' ἐμὰ βρέφεα… / εὕδετ' ἐμὰ ψυχά… / ὄλβιοι εὐνάζοισθε καὶ ὄλβιοι ἀῶ ἵκοισθε. The whole passage, which includes two gnomic sequences (the mother's long troubles; how to obtain divine favour), conveys a sort of fairy-tale brightness contrasting with the lofty cosmologies and boasts of 4.46–59. Note V.'s series of simple,

238   ECLOGUE 4

repeated images: this is the right way to address a newborn. For a similar gnomic finale, with a different rhetorical twist, cf. [Theocr.] *id.* 9.35–6 οὓς μὲν ὀρεῦντι [scil. Μοῖσαι] / γαθεῦσιν [γαθεῦσαι Brunck] τὼς δ᾽ οὔτι ποτῷ δαλήσατο Κίρκα (note the anacoluthic construction in the transmitted text, possibly the one read by V.: see below, 4.60n.). For a similar idea, cf. Hes. *theog.* 81–4 ὅντινα τιμήσουσι Διὸς κοῦραι μεγάλοιο / γεινόμενόν τε ἴδωσι διοτρεφέων βασιλήων, / τῷ μὲν ἐπὶ γλώσσῃ κτλ. For an intra-textual echo of 4.62 *incipe parue puer*, cf. the linguistic reversal at *E.* 9.66 *desine plura, puer* (second-to-last line in both cases); note also 5.19 *sed tu desine plura, puer*. In *E.* 9, however, the exhortation to 'desist' coincides with the end of the poem, whereas *E.* 4's exhortation to 'begin' looks forward to a future that goes well beyond the eclogue itself. The finale of *E.* 4 emphasizes the figure of the boy's mother and the labour of childbirth, thereby closing the circle: the poem had begun with Lucina, the female deity who protects childbirth and pregnant women.

60 risu cognoscere matrem. The *puer* is expected to 'recognize his mother with a smile', i.e. in the only way in which newborns can show that they recognize their care-givers (Serv. *risu se indicant agnoscere*). The *puer*'s smile is a favourable sign of intelli-gence and affection, which is the main point of the whole passage. The simple ablative, denoting a faculty of the subject (i.e. *risus*, which, however, implies an outward mani-festation of awareness), is poetically intuitive. V.'s wording presupposes and originally reworks common phrases like *cognoscere alqd. ratione* (Cic. *Tusc.* 1.36) or *corde* (Lucr. 4.882) or *animo* (Manil. 3.276). The smile is stimulated by the insistent *incipe parue puer*, repeated twice, as well as by the emphasis on the *fastidia* of pregnancy and the whole finale of the poem (4.62–3): all this elicits the *puer*'s gratitude. Towards the end of his epithalamium, Catullus had expressed the desire that the little child might sweetly smile at his parent (in this case, his father): *Torquatus uolo paruulus / matris e gremio suae / porrigens teneras manus / dulce rideat ad patrem / semihiante labello* (Catull. 61.209–13 [216–20]). Precocious smiling (normally considered impossible before the fortieth day: Plin. *nat.* 7.2; cf. Lyd. *mens.* 4.21 R. = 4.27, p. 85.20–2 W. 'on the fortieth day, the child acquires the ability to smile and starts recognizing the mother') was said to characterize many divine children: Hermes, Dionysus, Perseus, Beroe daughter of Aphrodite, Zoroaster. According to the biographical tradition, V. himself, as a newborn baby, did not cry, but rather showed a serene expression: *adeo miti uultu fuisse, ut haud dubium spem prosperioris geniturae iam tum daret* (Don. *uita Verg.* 13–14 Brumm. = p. 19.7–9 Brugn.-Stok). Thus, it seems preferable to reject the erro-neous but not absurd interpretation 'recognize the mother by her smile', presupposed by *Orat. Const. ad sanct. coet.* 21.2, p. 187 Heikel ἄρχεο μειδιόωσαν ὁρῶν τὴν μητέρα κεδνὴν / γνωρίζειν, which better suits the reading *cui non risere parentes* (4.62n.: even if this were the correct reading, it would hardly be obvious why the mother should smile as early as 4.60). It bears mentioning that, in Roman folklore, an affectionate gesture towards the mother (or Mother Earth?) could signify a fate of absolute domin-ion. Thus, for instance, in the Delphic oracle to the Tarquinii, which Brutus alone was capable of interpreting: *imperium summum Romae habebit qui uestrum primus, o* *iuuenes, osculum matri tulerit* (Liv. 1.56.10). The same is true of Julius Caesar's Oedipal dream at Suet. *Iul.* 7.2. In the *E.*, the ability to smile/laugh is metaphorically attributed to plants and natural elements (4.20; 7.55) as well as to divine figures (3.9; 6.23). The idea that a smile can reveal divine status is activated by Theocritus in the *Thalysia* (Lycidas at *id.* 7.19–20).

61 decem...menses. The average pregnancy period is roughly equivalent to ten lunar months, and the Roman computation placed birth in the tenth month (ample discussion in Gell. 3.16). The long waiting time is perceptible in the affectionate repetition, between the end of a line and the beginning of the next, of *matrem* / *matri* (alliteration with the final *menses*). Cf. Prop. 2.3.28 *ista decem menses non peperere bona*. **tulerunt**. The perfect form with short /e/, common in colloquial Latin (contrast *E.* 5.34), is perhaps meant to contribute to the affectionate immediacy of an argument addressed to a newborn *puer*—albeit a divine one. See e.g. *Aen.* 2.774; but cf. Lucr. 4.974–5; cf. also Hor. *epist.* 1.4.7; for the phrase Quint. *inst.* 5.4.30 *fastidium tulerit* (note also *inst.* 11.1.15).

62 qui non risere parenti. The newborn child's precocious smile may be a sign of divine favour (more so than his parents' predictable smile: see 4.60n.). Hence the poet's insistence, meant to stimulate it, along the lines of a 'reward' mechanism (the reward being, judging from 4.63, immortality), which is typical of childhood logic (cf. the song of the *pueri ludentes* in Hor. *epist.* 1.1.59–60 *rex eris... / si recte facies*). Overall, this reading of the text seems the most plausible, featuring the audacious syntactical transition from the plural *qui* to the singular *hunc* (4.63) and the correction *qui...parenti* in lieu of the transmitted *cui...parentes* (see below). It bears mentioning, however, that the text of *E.* 4.62 is one of the most vexed questions not just in the *E.*, but in Latin literature as a whole, and it seems unlikely that interpreters will reach a stable consensus on the issue. As mentioned, the manuscripts (and the indirect tradition) unanimously transmit the text *cui non risere parentes*, i.e. 'he whose parents never smiled upon him' cannot enjoy divine life and happiness. The potential awkwardness of this reading (hinting at 'parents who look askance at their children'?) becomes apparent in Servius' note, citing the example of Vulcan (rejected by the Olympian gods): *sicut Vulcano contigit, qui cum deformis esset et Iuno ei minime arrisisset, ab Ioue est praecipitatus in insulam Lemnum*. In order to avoid the grotesque implications of 62, once it has been ruled out that the boy's mother smiles at 4.60 (see n. ad loc.), the most sensible interpretation of the transmitted text entails an implicit logical leap: i.e. one must presuppose that the poet is primarily interested in the *puer*'s smile, and that the boy is therefore exhorted to recognize his mother by smiling (4.60), since otherwise his parents will not smile back on him (4.62). A less plausible interpretation rules out the poet's interest in the boy's smile and assumes that the mother smiles in both 4.60 and 4.62 (with a generalizing transition from *matrem* to *parentes*). Regardless of its interpretations, the transmitted text is certainly very old and perhaps known to Horace: cf. *ars* 40–1 *cui lecta potenter erit res, / nec*

240   ECLOGUE 4

facundia deseret hunc nec lucidus ordo (note the syntactical structure *cui...nec...hunc...nec*). Yet Quintilian's authoritative testimony (Quint. *inst.* 9.3.8–9) casts the transmitted text into doubt, since it implies that 4.62 was read in the form *qui non risere* as early as the first century CE (with *qui* anacoluthically referred to by *hunc*); for a possible different but comparable anacoluth in the Theocritean corpus, see above, 4.60–3n. Quintilian describes such a rhetorical device as based on number (*est figura in numero*) and goes on to paraphrase *ex illis enim 'qui non risere', hic quem non dignata*. In the Renaissance, Politian (*Misc.* 1.89) realized that V.'s text needed to be corrected in accordance with Quintilian's testimony (*cui > qui*). Politian also noticed the problem discussed above (who is smiling?), and read *parentes* as a vocative. If the emendation *qui* is accepted, however, *parentes* can accordingly be replaced with *parenti* (this conjecture was first proposed by J. Schrader then also by E. Bonnell in his 1854 edition of Quintilian). The peculiar syntax *qui...hunc* (switching from plural to singular) is overall acceptable, especially thanks to Quintilian's testimony, even though there seem to be no parallels for it in Latin or Greek (though cf. e.g. Eur. *Her.* 195–7, switching from ὅσοι to ἀφείς): note, at any rate, *Aen.* 8.427–8 ...*fulmen erat, toto genitor quae plurima caelo / deicit in terras*; Plaut. *Curc.* 494–5; Liv. 22.57.3. Another difficulty lies in the construction of *rideo* with simple dat., paralleled by *Aen.* 5.358 *risit pater optimus olli*, where, however, the dat. form is a pronoun (as is usually the case): similarly, Stat. *silu.* 5.3.121–2 *protinus exorto...risere sorores / Aonides*, etc. (on a newborn *puer*) has the pronoun *tibi* at 123 (*mihi* in the *Matritensis*); cf. OLD^2, p. 1822, s.v. *rideo* at 123. Note also, in later antiquity, Avien. *orb. terr.* 1120 *nascenti Baccho risit pater* (possibly echoing V.); cf. also, albeit with a very different usage, passages like Lucr. 1.8 *tibi rident aequora ponti*; Hor. *carm.* 2.6.13–14; different still, due to the compound *ad-rideo*, is *Fortuna*'s 'smiling on' the abandoned children at Iuv. 6.606 *adridens nudis infantibus*; cf. also Nemes. *ecl.* 3.31 quoted below. In sum, the correction *qui* (supported by Quintilian's authority) appears to be naturally tied to the emendation *parenti* (not supported by the indirect tradition, and therefore entirely conjectural). If the *puer* is the one who smiles, and is thereby included in the category of 'those who smile', then it logically follows that his mother is the one who is smiled upon (note the mother's crucial importance in 4.60–1). The original text *qui non risere parenti* would soon have been trivialized (*qui > cui*), with the resulting corruption *parenti > parentes* (perhaps facilitated by the spelling *parentei* or by *menses* in the previous line). In the finale of *E.* 4, the *puer* displays his divine benevolence through his smile, which starts (*incipe*) with an acknowledgement of his mother and is eventually extended to the entire world. By smiling, the boy accepts his mission of universal peace, worthy of a god: the poet is looking for a clear 'signal' on the *puer*'s part, which can show the actualization of what has thus far been the object of his prophecy. The fundamental function of the boy's smile is undermined by a recently revived hypothesis, whereby Quintilian's *qui* should be accepted but *parentes* should not be corrected and should be considered as the direct object of *rideo*. The plural form, however, would be ambiguous right after *qui*, and its logical function would be unclear (would *parentes* agree with *qui* as an apposition, or would it be a vocative, as Politian supposed, or even an accusative?). Note also that *rideo* + acc. means 'to mock, to laugh at, to make fun of', not 'to smile upon'. To be sure, in some instances *rideo* may well denote a benevolent smile rather than derisive laughter: cf. Plaut. *Capt.* 481; Ter. *Eun.* 249–50; Tib. 3.6.49–50; Prop. 2.16.47–8; Ov. *ars* 1.633; and Virgil himself, *E.* 6.23; Hor. *epist.* 1.14.39; Stat. *silu.* 3.1.151–3; 5.5.74–5. The point, however, is that in all these passages laughter is generated by the direct object (accusative), thanks to the fundamental nominative-accusative connection. By contrast, the *puer*'s smile needs to be spontaneous in order to be divine: it must come from the subject. This is why the poet asks the *puer* to begin by recognizing his mother through his smile (4.60): this kind of spontaneous smile, not prompted by external factors, is a prelude to the boy's future immortality and the final confirmation that the *puer* is indeed the universal benefactor described in the prophecy. As in 4.60, the 'addressee' of the boy's smile can only be his mother (*parenti*: the noun's meaning is unambiguous in the context), whereas the vague *parentes* would divert the reader's attention from that smile, which is a spontaneous product of awareness (*cognoscere*), intelligence, and acceptance of fate. In conclusion, if *parenti* is indeed the correct reading (the authenticity of 4.26 *parentis*, referring to the father, has to be legitimately assumed: see n. ad loc.), the same term artfully reappears here, this time in reference to the mother (cf. *G.* 4.320), thereby hinting at an equilibrium within the married couple. This can readily be explained in the aftermath of the *foedus Brundisinum*, i.e. if the couple is to be identified with Antony and Octavia (note that Octavian's sister received extraordinary honours, which she enjoyed for the rest of her life). In both cases, the context clarifies. the term (here 4.60–1 *matrem / matri*; note l. 26 *facta parentis* close to 4.17 *patriis uirtutibus* and taken as paradigm of *uirtus*). The significance of the mother's role, even for the education of a young hero, is confirmed by Theocritus' (Hellenistic) Alcmene, *id.* 24, esp. 134 'thus Heracles was educated by his dear mother', and Catullus concludes his epithalamium by referring to the virtues of the mother and the mythical example of Penelope, mother of Telemachus (61.219–23 [226–30]). The smile of a young god (Bacchus) is described by Nemesianus, who highlights the way in which the tutor Silenus tickles the boy: cf. Nemes. *ecl.* 3.27–34, esp. 29 *euocat ... risum digito*; 31 *cui deus arridens*. But here it is the poet who stimulates the child's laughter by tickling him with words.

63 nec deus hunc mensa, dea nec dignata cubili est. As early as Homer, Heracles is the archetypal hero welcomed to the gods' table (and into a goddess' bed, i.e. Hebe's): *Od.* 11.602–4; Pind. *Nem.* 1.69–72; Theocr. *id.* 17.20–33; Hor. *carm.* 4.8.29–30 (see above, 4.15–16n.); but cf. also Prop. 2.3.31 ... *nec semper nobiscum humana cubilia uises* (the *puella* Cynthia, destined to Jupiter's love). As a

242 ECLOGUE 5

child, Heracles did not experience tears: Theocr. *id.* 24.31 αἰὲν ἄδακρυν. Even Hermes, a newborn god, was said to have a portentous smile: albeit not specifically directed at his mother, the god's smile predicted great things to come according to Hephaestus in Lucian. *dial. deor.* 11.1 (τὸ τῆς Μαίας βρέφος τὸ ἄρτι τεχθέν... προσγελᾷ πᾶσι καὶ δηλοῖ ἤδη μέγα τι ἀγαθὸν ἀποβησόμενον). As foretold by 4.15–16, the *puer* will be able to share a life with the gods, just as primeval humankind once did (cf. Hesiod and Aratus: see again 4.15–16n.). A re-enactment of that shared life (θεοξενία) was carried out, in a religious context, through the ritual known as *lectisternium*. That such a paradigm belonged to the imagination of V.'s contemporaries is testified to by the famous 'dinner of the twelve gods', in which Octavian took part as Apollo (regardless of the historical value of the anecdote: Suet. *Aug.* 70.1). Already in Pindar's *Nemean* 5, the Muses' song at Peleus' and Thetis' wedding banquet included an example of piety and respect for social and domestic bonds, i.e. Peleus himself, immune to the snares of Hippolyta (wife of the host Acastus), and therefore rewarded by Zeus.; cf. Hom. *Il.* 24.534–5. Note, however, V.'s last reference to the finale of Catull. 64: *quare nec talis dignantur* [subj. the gods] *uisere coetus / nec se contingi patiuntur lumine claro* (64.407–8). The domestic and social disorder of Catullus' ending is transformed by V. into a peaceful picture of maternity, a smile that is not an end, but the beginning (*incipe*) of a new era. Note that *cubili*, appearing right before the verb *est*, is practically the last word of the poem: V. places great emphasis on a goddess' bed, symbolizing fertility and posterity, particularly in the case of the Roman offspring of Anchises and Venus.

Eclogue 5

[Daphnis]

The fifth eclogue opens with an introductory scene, in which the older Menalcas exhorts the boy Mopsus to sing with him. Mopsus, whom Menalcas allows to choose the subject matter, starts singing a lament for the late Daphnis (5.20–44). After a brief interlude featuring mutual compliments (5.45–55), it is Menalcas' turn to sing: he describes the deification of Daphnis (5.56–80). In the final exchange of gifts, Mopsus receives a pipe, from which Menalcas took inspiration for composing *E.* 2 and *E.* 3. Menalcas, in turn, is offered a beautiful staff, which features well-shaped knots and bronze studs (5.81–90).

Here the reference model is *id.* 1, which V. most probably knew as the opening poem of Theocritus' collection. In *id.* 1, Thyrsis' song included the grievous lament of a lovesick Daphnis and his farewell to the pastoral world (also featuring Daphnis' descent into the underworld). In *E.* 1, Meliboeus' farewell was but a faint echo of *id.* 1 (cf. pp. 60–1), and in *E.* 2–3 Daphnis' name was only briefly mentioned (*E.* 2.26 and 3.12; unlike Theocritus in *id.* 6, 8, and 9, V. never makes the divine herdsman a protagonist; compare *E.* 7, where Daphnis plays a supporting, though quite important, role). Even the fifth eclogue shrinks from any direct emulation of the Theocritean model, since both Mopsus and Menalcas resume their song where Thyrsis leaves off (at Daphnis' sudden disappearance in a 'vortex': *id.* 1.140–1). While mourning and deification are crucial components of Theocritus' *id.* 1, their appearance here is innovative and eminently Virgilian, since they are closely connected with some fundamental themes of the *E.* (cf. 5.20–1n.; 28n.; 43–4n.).

The reader of V.'s book has previously encountered a character named Menalcas: the young singer who, in *E.* 3, challenged the older Damoetas. This precedent confers authority on the Menalcas of *E.* 5, who is immediately qualified as 'older' (5.4 *tu maior*). In fact, the reader may suspect that the situation could easily evolve into an agon, if only Menalcas were replaced by e.g. Amyntas (5.8: note the recurrence of the verb *certare*, also appearing at 5.9 and 15)—or at any rate a younger, more aggressive singer. In *idd.* 8 and 9, Menalcas behaved as a courteous contestant against Daphnis himself (whereas Damoetas reproached him for a certain animosity in *E.* 3.12–15; but cf. *id.* 8.90–1). Now he appears even more compliant and accommodating (5.8; 16–18; 45–9; 85). Mopsus' words, sharp and at times aggressive, are at the opposite end of the amoebean spectrum: his speeches constantly open on a note of opposition, sometimes with a question.

V. uses the contrasting characterization of the two protagonists to outline different poetic modes: while Menalcas' name is of old pastoral origin, Mopsus' is unknown in the pre-Virgilian pastoral tradition—the same is true of Stimichon, whom Mopsus himself mentions as an authoritative connoisseur of poetry (5.55n.). Although Mopsus is undoubtedly pastoral and Virgilian in nature, his role as Daphnis' favourite pupil is part of his characterization, like the choice of a cave (5.6). At a metrical and stylistic level, too, Mopsus is less respectful than Menalcas of V.'s typical bucolic diction (cf. his rare use of the bucolic diaeresis, contrasting with a frequent use of elision). In his aestheticizing reply to Menalcas' speech, Mopsus displays an acute sensitivity to nature: his words are made of wind—of harsh and sublime sounds, which stand directly opposed to the minimalist tone of Menalcas' 'fragile pipe' (5.81–4n.; contrast 5.45–7n.). Much like Thyrsis, defeated by Corydon in *E.* 7, Mopsus is portrayed as the spokesman of a strong poetics, which errs on the side of an enthusiastic, perhaps 'Dionysian', conception of poetic composition (cf. 5.29–31n.).

This metapoetic interest, along with a restrained agonistic atmosphere, links *E.* 5 with another Theocritean model, *id.* 7 or *Thalysia* (see 5.19n.; 28n.; 69n.; 72n.). However, whereas *id.* 7 featured an opposition between two corresponding songs, i.e. Lycidas' (*id.* 7.52–89) and Simichidas' (*id.* 7.96–127), similar to each other in length and subject matter (love: especially homosexual love), V. perfects the symmetry by juxtaposing two songs on the same topic (Daphnis), each consisting of 25 lines and featuring analogous internal subdivisions (5.20–44n.; 56–80n.).

244   ECLOGUE 5

Note also that in *id.* 7 considerable importance was granted to the motif of Daphnis' lovesickness (*id.* 7.72–7; cf. *E.* 5.28n.). Theocritus' poem, however, features an obvious reference to literary disputes in Ptolemaic Alexandria (*id.* 7, esp. 45–51), while Simichidas, as ancient scholiasts observed, presumably stands for Theocritus himself. In comparison, *E.* 5 is much more elusive: poetic schools, teachers and pupils, hostilities and affiliations fade into the background of V.'s pastoral scenery. Nevertheless, it is plausible that *E.* 5 (like *E.* 6 and 10) expresses an invitation, seeking contact with significant figures of contemporary poetry (particularly Cornelius Gallus: cf. esp. 5.1n.).

At any rate, the historical pertinence of *E.* 5 depends, above all, on one of its main exegetical issues. No wonder that the poem's focus on a single figure (Daphnis) stimulated the kind of allegorical exegesis that is typical of V.'s reception. Suetonius' biography testifies to a 'private' allegory according to which Daphnis is equated with V.'s deceased brother. Modern interpreters have proposed further hypotheses (e.g. the poet Q. Cornificius), but a consensus was established among ancient interpreters, including Servius, who considered V.'s Daphnis as an allegory for *Divus Iulius*, murdered and subsequently deified (5.20–44n.; 56–80n.). While the idea of a precise, 'historical' allegory inevitably fails to persuade, it is certainly true that *E.* 5, in the wake of *E.* 1 and 4, adds to the rhetoric of divine models. Following the encomiastic portrait of a divine *puer*, the figure of Daphnis embodies a pattern of death and deification which is crucial to the Hellenistic rhetoric of charismatic power. Theocritus himself had celebrated the deified Berenice in a short poem (Athen. 7.284a = fr. 3 G.) and, in his *Syracusan Women*, the celebrations for Adonis and Aphrodite are closely connected to the deified queen (and, more generally, to the ruling Ptolemaic family: Theocr. *id.* 15.106–11; cf. also 17.45–52): also Callimachus in the *Aitia*, in particular with the *Coma Berenices* (well known in Rome through Catullus' *carm.* 66), had shown how the sovereigns of Alexandria had the open road to heaven and divinization (it should also be remembered Callimachus' so-called *Divinization of Arsinoe*, in *iamb.* [?] 16, fr. 228 esp. 5–6 Pf.). In this connection, significant affinities can be detected between the miracles accompanying Daphnis' deification and those triggered by the *puer*'s birth in *E.* 4 (5.60–1n.). The theme of agricultural fertility, here tied to the figure of Daphnis, hints at a broader historical dimension, which situates *E.* 5 in the context of contemporary events and the public sphere of *res Romana* as a whole (including the political career of Julius Caesar and his problematic legacy).

In *E.* 9, V. credits a character named Menalcas with the authorship of five lines associating Daphnis' name with the *sidus Iulium*, the celestial form of the deified dictator—seemingly an ironic allusion to the Caesarian 'subtext' of *E.* 5 (see 9.46–50n.). For now, however, Menalcas' praise of the deified Daphnis mostly strives to keep a balance between different divine models, as was the case with Mopsus' song. Both pieces give Daphnis elements of Bacchus and Ceres, Apollo and Pales

ECLOGUE 5   245

(cf. *E.* 5.30n.; 35n.; 66n.; 69n.; 73n.). Moreover, Mopsus' name has some Apollonian implications (5.1n.); he mentions Apollo (5.35), while at the same time proclaiming himself a follower of Bacchus, due to his background as Daphnis' pupil (5.30). Perhaps V. could foresee the way in which some readers might identify his deified Daphnis with *Divus Iulius*. It is possible that he deliberately arranged certain traits of Mopsus' and Menalcas' songs to fit into such a picture (note, for instance, the frequent references to the celestial world: 5.23; 43; 51–2; 56–7; 62). Daphnis, a prominent character in the pastoral world, activates 'eulogistic' connections with historical figures dear to the poet: in *E.* 10, Cornelius Gallus (poet, friend of V.'s, and public figure) experiences his own identification as a suffering Daphnis (cf. Theocr. *id.* 1). Similarly, in *E.* 5, Daphnis can hint at Julius Caesar's death and deification, so heavily charged with historical and political significance at the time of the *E.* On the other hand, *E.* 1 offers an antidote to mechanical allegoresis: in the same way as Tityrus' mature age prevents him from being hastily equated with V. (*E.* 1.28n.), Daphnis is explicitly called *puer* (5.54n.). Thus, in *E.* 5, V. eschews any kind of detailed allegory: through the exemplary figure of a great pastoral 'master', he illustrates the mysterious correspondence between song and nature—between the gods' generative force and the order of things. In so doing, he outlines a model of deification that was ready to use in various contexts and particularly applied to the figure of Julius Caesar, besides having benefited, for example, the much less renowned Cretan goatherd Astacides, heroized in the bucolic context of a Callimachean epigram (*Anth. Pal.* 7.518 = 22 Pf.).

To sum up, the actual affinity between *E.* 5 and the divine honours awarded to Julius Caesar in 42 (when the triumvirs decreed that his *dies natalis* be solemnly celebrated, and gave the name *Iulius* to the month *Quintilis*, previously associated with Apollonian festivals) is the occasion, rather than the cause, of such a process of pastoral mythopoesis. V.'s reworking of the Hellenistic language of death and deification in *E.* 5 offers an important model to Ovid and his eulogy of *Divus Iulius* at the end of the *Metamorphoses*, where Caesar is welcomed among the stars as soon as he is murdered, thanks to Venus' intervention (a prelude to Augustus' own deification: see Ov. *met.* 15.745–860). The image of Dionysus conquering the East, formerly crucial to the myth of Alexander and the rhetoric of Hellenistic kingship (cf. 5.29–31), will keep exercising great influence on Rome's political language during the triumvirate and, later, the Augustan age—in fact, it had previously contributed to shaping the myth of Julius Caesar himself.

The forms and themes of *E.* 5, at any rate, cannot be constrained within the limits of political eulogy. This is shown by the numerous echoes of Lucretius' language: especially the language that Lucretius uses to glorify Epicurus in heroic and religious terms. In the Roman Epicurean circles known to V., Epicurus' successors and certain authoritative teachers commonly received quasi-divine honours. This kind of secular cult paradoxically drew upon the language and style

246   ECLOGUE 5

of religious cults (see D. Clay, *The Cults of Epicurus*, in *BCPE* [*Cron. Erc.*], 16, 1986, pp. 11–28; M. Beretta, F. Citti, A. Iannucci eds., *Il culto di Epicuro. Testi, iconografia e paesaggio*, Florence 2015). V. is here creating a great 'mythical' archetype in Latin pastoral poetry: the deceased civilizing hero. To that end, he reworks pivotal ideas of Roman culture, including Epicurean philosophy in its Lucretian (i.e. poetic) form. Lucretian echoes are clearly perceptible in *E.* 5 and were certainly perceived by V.'s Epicurean readers, among whom was Varius Rufus, a partisan of Caesar who had long been hostile to Antony. Varius had treated the question περὶ θανάτου in his poem *De morte*, which may well have touched upon Julius Caesar's death. The 'Caesarian' reading of *E.* 5 may therefore go back to one of V.'s first and most distinguished readers.

Marking the end of the first half of the pastoral volume, *E.* 5 collects some of its pivotal themes, which radiate their energy over the second half of the book. The Lucretian component of *E.* 5 lies especially in the eulogistic language and in the poet's evocation of a wild, Dionysian nature (cf. the thyrsus as a metaphor for poetic inspiration at Lucr. 1.923). All this looks forward to the Epicurean echoes in the Dionysian Silenus' doctrine (*E.* 6). Another theme generally frequent in the first half of the *E.* and particularly emphasized in *E.* 5 is the idea of poetic transmission: note the teacher-student relationship between the older Menalcas and the younger Mopsus (but cf. also the opening of *E.* 6, where the boys Chromis and Mnasyllus try to force the elderly Silenus to sing his Dionysian *carmina*). The poem's juxtaposition of songs composed by different poets, who treat the divine subject matter in a similar way, will be an important precedent for the 'true' agon of the *E.*, that between Thyrsis and Corydon in *E.* 7, taking place in front of Daphnis himself (see below, p. 347). However, this series of innovative eclogues at the centre of the book is concluded with *E.* 6, which features a tantalizing blend of Dionysus and Apollo. In the wake of *id.* 1, the first half of V.'s book comes to an end under Daphnis' auspices: the entire collection will be concluded, in *E.* 10, by another echo of *id.* 1, resonating in Cornelius Gallus' lament.

E. 5 is an odd-numbered poem and, therefore, a mimetic one. Its opening is eminently dialogic; the two pastoral characters are immediately mentioned and identified. The eclogue has a total of ninety lines and is clearly subdivided into five sections: the prologue (1–19); the first song (Mopsus': 20–44); the dialogic interlude between the two songs (45–55); the second song (Menalcas': 56–80); the finale (81–90). The individual sections are well balanced with one another: the two songs are exactly equivalent (twenty-five lines each, fifty in total), while the remaining three parts are fairly symmetrical in terms of length (specifically, the first section, with its nineteen lines, almost combines the lengths of the other two: eleven and nine lines, respectively). As is generally the case in the *E.*, the two protagonists of the dialogue get the same number of speeches each: except for the songs, *E.* 5 includes twelve speeches (i.e. six per character). Note, however, that Menalcas' speeches tend to be longer, given his

ECLOGUE 5   247

age and authority: he utters twenty-two lines in total, while Mopsus only has eighteen.

On the eclogue: Weyman (1918c); Rohde (1925); E. Pfeiffer (1933, pp. 56–68); Büchner (1955, cols. 1213–19); Otis (1963, pp. 133–5 and 140–1); Rohde (1963, pp. 117–39); Klingner (1967, pp. 84–99); Putnam (1970, pp. 166–94); E. A. Schmidt (1972b, pp. 186–238); Berg (1974, pp. 115–28); Leach (1974, pp. 182–97); DuQuesnay (1976–7); Buchheit (1977b); G. Lee (1977); Van Sickle (1978, pp. 138–42); Alpers (1979, pp. 190–200); Echave-Sustaeta (1980); Dönt (1981); Salvatore (1981); Segal (1981, pp. 25–65); Perret (1983); M. O. Lee (1989, pp. 89–95); T. K. Hubbard (1995b, pp. 19–22 = 1998, pp. 95–9); Rudd (1996, pp. 62–4); P. Hardie (1998, pp. 21–2); Levi (1998, pp. 54–7); Seng (1999, pp. 24–7); Baumbach (2001); Binder, Effe (2001, pp. 83–6); von Albrecht (2007, pp. 25–6); A. Powell (2008, pp. 202–7); Davis (2012, pp. 79–97); Kania (2012, pp. 679–83); Kania (2016, pp. 63–7, 90–7).

Specific issues: Knaack (1883, pp. 31–2) (l. 10); Frank (1920) (Daphnis as Q. Cornificius); Kumaniecki (1926) (date); Maass (1929) (l. 55); Sinko (1930) (Dionysian cult); Beringer (1932, p. 38) (ll. 65–6); E. A. Hahn (1944, pp. 197–9) (Mopsus and Menalcas); Grimal (1948) (imperial cult); Grimal (1949) (Julius Caesar as a god); Bömer (1952) (*sidus Iulium*); Nilsson (1955) (l. 15); O. Skutsch (1956, pp. 197–8) (Daphnis and Julius Caesar); Alfonsi (1960) (l. 11); Rostagni (1960) (l. 11); Geymonat (1964, pp. 345–7) (*Pap. Strasb. Lat. 2*: ll. 17–34); Berg (1965) (Daphnis and Aeschylus' *Prometheus*; Daphnis and Julius Caesar); Wieland (1966) (l. 15); Musso (1968) (l. 14); E. A. Schmidt (1968) (ll. 38–9); Guerrini (1973) (structure); Turcan (1977) (Julius Caesar and Dionysus); Thill (1979, pp. 51–2) (l. 49); Mizera (1982) (Lucretius in Menalcas' song); Perret (1982) (Golden Age); I. Hahn (1983) (*sidus Iulium*); De Cazanove (1986, p. 197) (Dionysian cult); Pulbrook (1987b) (Octavian); Domenicucci (1989) (catasterism of Julius Caesar); Langholf (1990) (allegorical interpretation in Calp. Sic.); Glei (1991, pp. 52–4) (war); G. Anderson (1993) (Eastern origins of the Daphnis myth); Baudy (1993, pp. 311–18) (Daphnis in *E*. 5 and 9); Dobbin (1995) (Julius Caesar); Kowara (1995) (elision in the songs of Mopsus and Menalcas); Dognini (1996–7) (Julius Caesar); Thome (2000, pp. 99–103) (nature's lament); Kraggerud (2006b, pp. 29–31) (l. 3); Kraggerud (2006b, pp. 31–2) (l. 8); Kraggerud (2006b, pp. 32–4) (l. 38); Kraggerud (2006b, pp. 34–8) (l. 66); Martínez Astorino (2006) (allegoresis and Daphnis' identity); Saunders (2008, pp. 21–30) (cosmology and catasterism); Fabre-Serris (2009, pp. 283–6) (Dionysian cult); P. Hardie (2009, pp. 133–5) (Lucretian sublime); Meban (2009) (cult and memory); Ottaviano (2011, pp. 208–12) (l. 30); Heyworth (2015, p. 213) (ll. 79–80); Farrell (2016, pp. 399–400) (l. 27); Kronenberg (2016, pp. 39–42) (Daphnis, Lucretius, and the sublime); Kraggerud (2017b, pp. 23–5) (l. 3); Kraggerud (2017b, pp. 26–7) (l. 8); Kraggerud (2017b, pp. 28–9) (l. 38); Kraggerud (2017b, pp. 30–3) (l. 66); Cucchiarelli (2021a, pp. 93–6) (l. 3).

1–19. The two protagonists of the dialogue are immediately identified and named: Mopsus (5.1) and Menalcas (5.4). Their respective characterization is crucial to the ensuing action: both are skilled singers, though Mopsus is younger than Menalcas. The text implies that the two are walking and must decide where to stop and begin singing. The situation could easily evolve into an agon,

248 ECLOGUE 5

particularly given the younger singer's energetic character. However, the age difference and Menalcas' conciliatory attitude forestall that development. Mopsus will be the first to sing, as Menalcas suggests, but the topic is not introduced (and it only becomes clear in Mopsus' first line). It seems obvious, at any rate, that the topic itself will not be among those mentioned by Menalcas at 5.10–12.

1 Cur non. A common dialogic phrase, attested as early as Plaut. *Amph.* 409; *Merc.* 471; cf. esp. Cic. *de orat.* 1.28 *cur non imitamur…Socratem illum qui est in Phaedro Platonis?* (explicitly echoing the Platonic archetype of *locus amoenus*: see 5.3n.); *Att.* 9.12.1; Catull. 33.5; Lucr. 3.938. It will reappear, in line-beginning position, at *Aen.* 12.39. **Mopse.** An extra-pastoral name, belonging to two figures connected with the divinatory art: the Lapith Mopsus, who took part in the Argonaut expedition ([Hes.] *scut.* 181; Apoll. Rhod. 1.65–6 and esp. 3.916–18: 'Mopsus, son of Ampyx, good at interpreting the appearances of birds, good at advising his companions'; his father is Apollo in Val. Fl. 1.383–4), and Mopsus son of Manto (Teiresias' daughter, from whom Mantua was said to take its name: *Aen.* 10.199–200), seer and founder of the temple of Apollo Clarius in Colophon, an Ionian city (cf. esp. Pausan. 7.3.2; *RE*, XVI.1, cols. 242–3, s.v. *Mopsos* 2 [B. Gross Kruse]). Mopsus (the Ionian) played the role of Calchas' opponent in Cornelius Gallus' short poem dedicated to the Grynean grove, in turn modelled after Euphorion (at least according to Servius, *ad E.* 6.72 = Euphor. fr. 97 Pow. = 101 v. Gron. = 102 Light.; cf. also fr. 98 Pow. = 102 van Gron. = 103 Light.; *SH* fr. 429.21 [?], p. 214 Ll.-J.-P., with app.). The possibility of identifying V.'s Mopsus with a contemporary poet must have been considered by ancient interpreters, as can be inferred from Philargyrius/Philagrius, pp. 89–90 (III.2 Th.-H.), and the *scholia Bernensia*, p. 114 H., which equate him (without evidence) with Aemilius Macer, a didactic poet slightly younger than V.; cf. *Enc. Virg.* III, pp. 584–5, s.v. *Mopso* (F. Michelazzo); *Virg. Enc.* II, p. 842, s.v. *Mopsus* (J. Van Sickle). Following V.'s mention of this extra-pastoral name, however, *E.* 5 quickly re-establishes the usual bucolic scenery (5.2–3). **boni quoniam conuenimus ambo.** A precise echo of *id.* 8: 'both [Daphnis and Menalcas] red-haired, both on the edge of youth, / both good at piping, both good at singing [ἄμφω συρίσδεν δεδαημένω, ἄμφω ἀείδεν]' (*id.* 8.3–4; but here Daphnis will be the object, rather than the subject, of song). A reminiscence of *id.* 8 will also open *E.* 7 (esp. 7.1–5n.), in the context of an actual agon, i.e. that between Corydon and Thyrsis. The construction of the adj. with an infinitive (*boni…inflare…dicere*) is a syntactical Hellenism (cf., in the sense of 'good at', Apoll. Rhod. 1.106 ἐσθλὸς…προδαῆναι; see again *id.* 8.4 just quoted); cf. *E.* 7.5 *cantare pares*; 10.32 *cantare periti*; *G.* 1.284–6; *Aen.* 6.164–5; Hor. *carm.* 1.3.25; see below, 5.54 *cantari dignus*. For the original sense of *bonus*, i.e. 'capable of, talented', cf. 5.61n.

2 tu calamos inflare leuis, ego dicere uersus. Perhaps in order to make his invitation more effective, Menalcas distinguishes between two different skills, i.e. music and poetic performance: *dicere* stands for *canere*, as in *E.* 3.55 and 4.54,

ECLOGUE 5   249

but inevitably puts an emphasis on words. Mopsus, in turn, will highlight his own skills, including his 'songwriting' ones (5.14n.), and Menalcas will praise him along similar lines: *nec calamis solum aequiperas, sed uoce magistrum* (5.48: both instrumental and vocal skills). A certain Mopsus will instead be portrayed as a poorly skilled 'musician' at Nemes. *ecl.* 1.16. Menalcas immediately underscores the 'levity' (*leuis*) of the pastoral Muse—he will do so again in his final lines: *fragili… cicuta* (5. 85).

3 hic corylis mixtas inter consedimus ulmos. For the exhortation to sit in the shade, associated with an acknowledgement of poetic skills, cf. *id.* 1.19–23 'But you, Thyrsis, sing Daphnis' sorrows / and have brought the pastoral Muse to perfection: / here, let us sit under the elm tree [ὑπὸ τὰν πτελέαν ἑσδώμεθα] in front of Priapus / and the Nymphs of springs, there where that shepherds' / seat is, and the oaks'. Note also one of the most important models for the *locus amoenus*: the scene in Plato's *Phaedrus* under the great plane-tree near the Ilissos river (*Phaedr.* 229b ἐκεῖ σκιά τ᾽ ἐστὶν καὶ πνεῦμα μέτριον, καὶ πόα καθίζεσθαι ἢ ἂν βουλώμεθα κατακλινῆναι, explicitly quoted in Cic. *de orat.* 1.29 *omnis in eis sedibus, quae erant sub platano, consedisse*). The reading *consedimus*, which is better attested, seems preferable to the present-tense form *considimus*, which appears in some ninth-century manuscripts (for a similar case cf. *G.* 4.436 *considit/consedit*). Taking up 5.1 *conuenimus*, which also occupies the fifth foot, the perfect tense *consedimus* politely emphasizes the need for the characters to stop (which could have happened long before) and mimetically defines their actions and behaviours in the larger context of the dialogue. In *E.* 3.55, the same verbal form points to the fact that Palaemon has chosen a specific location for the agon (which can therefore begin), while here the verb implies that the two herdsmen are still walking and moving beyond the shady place. By asking Mopsus *cur non…consedimus*, Menalcas is looking for a reason why they have not stopped yet, so as to begin singing (as in *E.* 3). He is therefore prompting Mopsus to sing with him, not to stop in a place they have already walked by. This explains Mopsus' reply: he politely admits to his inferiority (*tibi me est aequum parere*), but ultimately accepts the invitation to sing while he continues to walk (note the present form *succedimus* at 5.6). Mopsus would prefer a cave (hence *potius* at 5.6), and that is where the two herdsmen will stop (5.19). In his reworking of this scene (at the beginning of his first eclogue), Calpurnius Siculus uses the same indicative form *succedimus* for an explicit invitation, which receives a clear-cut answer (in a dialogue between two brothers): [Corydon] *cur non succedimus umbris? / torrida cur solo defendimus ora galero? /* [Ornytus] *hoc potius, frater Corydon, nemus, antra petamus / ista patris Fauni* etc. (Calp. *ecl.* 1.6–9; cf. below, 5.6n.). In questions starting with *cur non*, the present tense is normally used, particularly when the question is in effect an invitation (a type of 'question request'): cf. *Aen.* 12.39 *cur non…certamina tollo?*; Hor. *carm.* 2.11.13–17 *cur non…potamus?*; Ov. *her.* 10.57 *cur non discedimus ambo?*; Sil. 13.75–6. But this may have been the cause of the scribal error *consedimus* >

250 ECLOGUE 5

considimus (the latter being *lectio facilior*): here the ultimate goal of the question is to stimulate song. In practice, Menalcas' words can be read as remarking on a missed opportunity, and the perfect form *consedimus* is perhaps echoed by Mopsus' *sparsit*. Elm trees, generally associated with vines (cf. *E.* 2.70n.), are here coupled with hazelnut trees, which tend to grow as shrubs, low and thick: both are typically Virgilian and appear in *E.* 1 (cf. 1.14 *densas corylos*; 58 *turtur ab ulmo*). For the spatial adverb *hic* in the context of choosing the *locus* of song, cf. 9.60–2.

4 maior. Referring to age, without further connotations. No wonder that Mopsus, unknown to the pastoral reader, emphasizes the older age of a herdsman whose name is one of the most venerated in the bucolic tradition. Furthermore, Menalcas was featured as a protagonist in *E.* 3. **tibi me est aequum parere.** Old age, which is readily connected with didactic roles (even in an erotic sense) within the pastoral world, ought to fill the younger with respect and devotion: cf. *id.* 5.35–40 (where the sexual implication becomes immediately explicit: *id.* 5.41). The age difference between the two herdsmen is here acknowledged, thereby pointing to a difference in authoritativeness (and aggressiveness) between them. However, any potential conflict will be limited to a third-party character, Amyntas. **Menalcas.** A youngster, just like Daphnis, in the incipit of *id.* 8, and one of the most typical inhabitants of the pastoral world (*E.* 3.13n.; 9.10n.). In the *E.* he has appeared (as a *puer*) at 2.15; the Menalcas of *E.* 3 (esp. 3.7; 32–4) is also certainly young and displays a certain proud intemperance (see 3.1n.). However, this *maior* Menalcas will prove to be much more judicious and patient.

5 siue sub incertas…umbras. The first of the two alternatives is that suggested by Menalcas at 5.3, on which Mopsus immediately seems to offer a value judgement (note the epithet *incertas*). Mopsus, in fact, prefers the second alternative, as is clear from the emphatic repetition *antro…antrum* and the implicitly deictic use of the imperative *aspice*, responding to *hic* (5.3). The choice of a location for the singing session, which was entirely conflict-free in *id.* 1.12–14 and 21–3, was prone to elicit tension in Theocritus' pastoral contests, constituting a sort of 'pre-agonistic' debate (as in *id.* 5.31–4 and 45–59; in *E.* 3.55–7, on the other hand, the location seems to be chosen by the referee Palaemon). Here, as 5.19 will confirm, Menalcas is ready to acquiesce. Note the *sigmatismos*, especially at the beginning of this line and the following two (*siue sub… / siue…succedimus. aspice… / siluestris…sparsit labrusca*): Mopsus pays attention to the sounds he uses in comparing the two locations (and hinting at his own preference). In 5.82, Mopsus says that he loves the *sibilus* of the south wind (see n. ad loc.).

6 siue antro potius succedimus. The choice of a cave is even more explicitly formulated in Calp. *ecl.* 1.8 *hoc potius…nemus, antra petamus* (cf. *ecl.* 1.6 *uicinis cur non succedimus umbris?*). For the term *antrum*, sometimes used as a locus of poetry, cf. *E.* 1.75n., as well as 5.7n. An interesting parallel is Hor. *carm.* 3.25.3–6 *quibus / antris egregii Caesaris audiar / aeternum meditans decus / stellis inserere et consilio Iouis?* (encomium and celestial deification of Caesar-Augustus; a

ECLOGUE 5   251

declaration of Dionysian poetics appears in the opening: *carm.* 3.25.1–2 *quo me, Bacche, rapis tui / plenum* etc.?; for Daphnis-Julius Caesar see 5.20–44n.). Note that even the syntax lets the first hypothesis (*sub incertas…umbras*) recede into the background, since *succedere* is readily construed with the dat. *antro* (cf. the concluding 5.19 *successimus antro*, where the term, rich in evocative sounds, brings the whole preamble to an end): cf. *G.* 3.418 *tecto adsuetus coluber succedere*; *Aen.* 1.627; 2.478; 3.276; 8.123 etc.

6–7 aspice ut… / …sparsit. For the construction with the indicative cf. 4.52n.

7 siluestris raris sparsit labrusca racemis. This descriptive expansion, meant to entice Menalcas, is facilitated by the pleasantness of the place, i.e. the cave, resembling that featured in Hom. *Od.* 5.63–73 (Calypso's dwelling), esp. 68–9 'around the deep cave a domestic / vine was spread, in full bloom with clusters of grapes' (ἡμερίς, an uncommon term: cf. below, on *siluestri…labrusca*). The vine emphasizes the Dionysian significance of the cave, for which cf. 6.13n. (the drunken Silenus falls asleep in it); cave and vine are coupled together again at *E.* 9.41–2. The grape-clusters (*racemis*) are sparse (*raris*), and so is their shade (cf. *E.* 7.46 *rara…umbra*), perhaps because the plant, a wild variety, is scarcely productive, in terms of both quantity and quality. The verb *sparsit* implies a chromatic opposition between the dark backdrop and the clusters: cf. *Aen.* 7.191 *sparsitque coloribus alas* (*E.* 2.41 *sparsit pellibus albo*). The perfect tense at the end of Mopsus' speech could also be a reply to 5.3 *consedimus*. Note the so-called golden line, here in its purest form: 2.50n. **siluestris…labrusca.** A type of wild vine, not particularly appreciated in antiquity for grapes or wine (whereas its smell was deemed to be pleasant: Plin. *nat.* 12.132–3; for its use in medicine cf. 14.98–9). If left free to grow as a climbing vine, it could cover countryside hedges and boundary walls—hence the folk etymology (from *labrum*) appearing in Serv. *quia in terrae marginibus nascitur* (Non. p. 720 L. *quae in saepibus et in labris agrorum et in terminis nascitur*) and Serv. Dan. *uel quod sapore acerbo labra laedat* (Philargyrius/Philagrius, pp. 90–1 [III.2 Th.-H.]; cf. Hier. *in Os.* 10.8, ll. 262–4 Adr.; *ThlL* VII.2.813.32–51). The term, in the form *lambrusca* (attested in Virgilian manuscripts), will go on to denote the wine variety typical of Emilia-Romagna (known as Lambrusco), whose predecessors may have enjoyed a regional reputation (around Mantua) in the poet's time. The epithet *siluestris* highlights an intrinsic trait of the plant: *labrusca…a Graecis ampelos agria appellata* (Plin. *nat.* 23.19); perhaps the adj. contrastively echoes the domestic vine of the Homeric passage quoted above (ἡμερίς, which the scholion ad loc. distinguishes from the ἀγρία variety).

8–9. An example of V.'s 'minimum viable dialogue': the characters have one line each. This mimetic liveliness is significant as it is extremely rare in the *E.* (only twice). Mopsus' energetic personality and his animosity towards Amyntas might help explain it; though there might also be some hidden innuendos. Menalcas has no intention to discuss the choice of a location, which is typical of the pre-agon (cf. 5.5n.). Instead, Menalcas would have loved to be already sitting

252   ECLOGUE 5

among elms and hazelnut trees, but he does not mind being led by Mopsus towards the cave he prefers (5.6–7 *aspice ut*: Mopsus praises that *locus amoenus*). Menalcas' following statement is ironically striking: the only singer who can vie with Mopsus is Amyntas—i.e. Menalcas does not want to argue with him, as a local herdsman like Amyntas would have done (see 5.8n.; 16–18n.). Now Mopsus doubles down by dwelling on Amyntas' contentiousness in terms of poetic song (5.9 *canendo*). In the pastoral world, diverging opinions and poetic agons are common currency, at least since Theocritus: the herdsmen 'speak' in verse, and any dispute about any topic can readily turn into an agon (with or without a pre-agon). In 3.1–2n., the 'minimum viable dialogue' signals the beginning of the most mimetic (and 'comic') poem in the whole book. Menalcas will later remind Mopsus of the need to begin singing: *incipe* (5.10).

8 solus tibi certat Amyntas. Amyntas appears, once again, in the antagonist's role, as in *E*. 2, where he was envious of Corydon for Damoetas' gift, a shepherd's pipe (*E*. 2.35–9, esp. 39 *inuidit stultus Amyntas*). In *E*. 3, on the other hand, Amyntas was often featured as Menalcas' darling (cf. esp. 83 *mihi solus Amyntas*, echoed here). He will again embody a type of handsome (though dark-skinned) boy at *E*. 10.37–41; at any rate, his name seems to be associated with youth, which makes him likely to be Mopsus' age-mate. Note that, in lieu of *cum* + abl., the poet uses a simple Grecizing dat. (*tibi*) governed by a verb of fighting (cf. the Greek μάχομαι, πολεμῶ, etc.; the construction is called *Graeca figura* in [Iul. Ruf.], *schem. lex*. 32 = *RLM*, p. 56.9–12 Halm): cf. *Aen*. 4.38 *pugnabis amori*; but note Plaut. *Bacch*. 967 *pugnam conserui seni*; Lucr. 3.6–7; Catull. 62.64; see also Hor. *carm*. 1.3.13; Prop. 1.7.3; K.-S., I, p. 319; again with the verb *certare* at *E*. 8.55n.; *G*. 2.99 *cui non certauerit ulla* (as well as 96 *nec cellis ideo contende Falernis*); Hor. *epod*. 11.18 (with Porph. ad loc.); *sat*. 2.5.19 (Ps. Acron. ad loc.); Plin. *epist*. 8.8.4; *ThlL* III.894.50–895.20. The verb is here used in a broad sense, which includes but is not limited to the poetic contest: it can also mean 'discuss', 'have an argument', 'fight' (as in *Aen*. 10.7 *animis certatis iniquis*; 11.446). It is used in this sense, as an auxiliary, by Mopsus in his next speech: *certet Phoebum superare c a n e n d o* (5.9: the gerund would otherwise be unnecessary). The reading *certet* (P), identically repeated at 5.9 then again at 5.15, has some advantages, particularly since the potential subjunctive would underscore Menalcas' subjectivity: he certainly does not want to argue with Mopsus (as Amyntas would do; cf. what Menalcas himself asserts at 5.18: *iudicio nostro tantum tibi cedit Amyntas*). The indicative *certat*, generally favoured by V.'s editors, makes that implication less obvious, but emphasizes a matter-of-fact objectivity ('only Amyntas competes with you'—'I certainly won't...'). Note that the possibility of an agonistic outcome is suggested by the threefold repetition of *certare* within the span of a few lines (5.9; 15). But no *certamen* or poetic agon will take place here. For the 'technical' use of the verb cf. 3.31n.

9 Quid, si idem certet. An ellipsis typical of colloquial language, and widely attested in comedy (cf. Plaut. *Poen*. 728; *Rud*. 1086). A verb like *refert* is implied,

ECLOGUE 5   253

and the general sense is: 'And who cares, if he might just as well compete, etc.'. The usual sense of *quid, si* is rather: 'What would happen if...?' or 'What would you say if...?' (used ironically in Ter. *Heaut.* 718-19); for a similar question, cf. the dialogue between Juno and Jupiter at *Aen.* 10.628-9 *quid, si... / mente dares* etc.? **Phoebum superare canendo.** Rather than an acknowledgement of Amyntas' value, Mopsus' words imply a charge of *hybris.* Unmindful of the satyr Marsyas' fate, Amyntas is ready to challenge Apollo himself (such a statement is all the more significant in the mouth of someone whose name is full of prophetic and Apollonian implications: see 5.1n.); the implicit reference to Marsyas seems to have been grasped in *Anth. Lat.* 16a.4-6 R. One cannot really vie with Apollo in archery, either: Eurytus was punished with death in *Od.* 8.226-8 (cf. esp. 228 οὕνεκά μιν προκαλίζετο τοξάζεσθαι).

10-12. Among the three pieces that Menalcas attributes to Mopsus' repertoire, only the first and the third have exact parallels in V.'s pastoral world. All three, however, hint at non-pastoral myths, thereby letting the reader catch glimpses of the young poet's innovative abilities (such expectations will not be disappointed by his latest creation [5.13 *nuper*], i.e. the lament for Daphnis' death). In Theocritus' first idyll, the goatherd presented 'Daphnis' troubles' (*id.* 1.19 Δάφνιδος ἄλγεα) as a renowned piece composed by Thyrsis. Note, finally, that the thematic and rhetorical gamut of (erotic) 'flames', praise, and blame seems to have been experimented with in V.'s *E.* 2, 4, and 3, respectively.

10 Incipe. This is the signal to start, also establishing the order of performance, as in *E.* 3.58; the verb is repeated at 5.12, where the iteration may echo 4.60-2 *incipe, parue puer... / incipe, parue puer* (Mopsus himself will soon be called *puer* at 5.19, though in the context of an exhortation to 'desist'). Here, however, some further preliminaries will be needed, in order for Mopsus to consider Amyntas a closed chapter. Thus, the younger poet will be the first to sing, in keeping with the principle stated in Hom. *Il.* 21.439. **Phyllidis ignis.** The phrase, very compressed and ambivalent, is clarified by the context: while 5.11 will refer to 'praise' and 'blame', here *ignes* must be 'love songs' for Phyllis ('flames', i.e. 'erotic passions'; cf. 3.66n.), with a pun on the name's botanical meaning (φύλλα are 'leaves', ready to catch fire or to cause *ignes*; cf. somewhat differently, 7.59n.; 10.41n.; see also 3.107n.). The gen., like *Alconis* and *Codri*, is probably objective; at any rate, even if it is understood as subjective (i.e. if Phyllis is the 'lover'), the phrase still refers to erotic song. For a similar ambiguity between love and erotic poetry, cf. Prop. 2.34.44; Ov. *trist.* 4.10.45 *suos solitus recitare Propertius ignes* (as well as *trist.* 2.537-8). In the *E.*, Phyllis is a typical female figure, treated as an object of desire by Damoetas, in opposition to Menalcas' Amyntas (*E.* 3, esp. 76-7; Menalcas applied the image of 'fire' to Amyntas at 3.66): she is again paired with Amyntas at 10.37-41. Ovid regarded the figure of Phyllis as a symbol of V.'s juvenile carefreeness, as expressed in the *E.*: *Phyllidis hic idem* [scil. *Vergilius*] *teneraeque Amaryllidis ignes / bucolicis iuuenis luserat ante modis* (*trist.* 2.537-8). Note also a

254 ECLOGUE 5

distant extra-pastoral echo of the myth of Phyllis, a Thracian princess who fell in love with Demophoon (Theseus' son) and committed suicide, believing herself to have been betrayed by him. The story had been told by Callimachus, perhaps in the *Aitia*, and will later be reworked by Ovid in the second epistle of the *Heroides*; cf. also Ov. *rem.* 606 (featuring the name's etymology as well).

11 Alconis…laudes. The name is not otherwise attested in the pastoral tradition: the most famous Alcon is an Attic hero, son of Erechtheus and father of the young Phalerus, his only child, whom he nonetheless sent off on the Argonaut expedition (Apoll. Rhod. 1.95–100, with the scholia ad loc.; cf. Hyg. *fab.* 14.9; the young man gave his name to Athens' harbour: Pausan. 1.1.4). Thanks to his outstanding archery skills, Alcon saved his young son by killing a snake with an arrow: Val. Fl. 1.398–401; Manil. 5.304–10; Gaetul. *Anth. Pal.* 6.331 = *Furth. Gr. Epigr.* 191–6, pp. 54–5 P.; see also Sidon. *carm.* 5.154–60. Servius attributes the same achievement to an Alcon *Cretensis sagittarius* (but the Cretan origin is dubious, given Crete's renown in the field of archery), while Servius Dan. calls him *comes Herculis*, perhaps not unexpectedly (he is the father of an Argonaut), and adds further exploits: Alcon shoots an arrow through rings placed on men's heads; cuts a stretched hair; and severs wooden arrow-shafts by throwing them against upright blades. Alcon was also the name of a Spartan hero (Apollod. 3.10.5 [124]; Pausan. 3.14.7) and of a mythical artist, apparently from Boeotia: Ov. *met.* 13.683–4 [scil. *cratera*] *fabricauerat Alcon / Hyleus et longo caelauerat argumento* (Tychius, who made Ajax's shield, was also from Hyla, though it is unclear whether the city is located in Lydia or in Boeotia: Hom. *Il.* 7.220–1; in Tarrant's text, *Hyleus* is corrected into *Lindius*); cf. also *Culex* 67, where Alcon is the name of a skilled engraver, perhaps under the influence of V.'s Alcimedon (*E.* 3; cf. Athen. 11.469a). Finally, Calpurnius Siculus will devise a whole context motivating the praise of Alcon, so that the shepherd Astylus can say: *tu quoque laudatum posses Alcona probare* (*ecl.* 6.18). The reference to Alcon as an object of praise (though *laudes* may also mean 'endeavours': cf. *E.* 4.26n.) befits the bearer of a name evoking 'force', ἀλκή. iurgia Codri. In *E.* 7, a reference to Codrus will elicit disagreement between Corydon, who praises him (7.21–4), and Thyrsis, who considers him an envious rival and insults him (7.26–8). Here, too, the phrase seems to refer to 'invectives against Codrus' (cf. 7.22n. for the possible identification of Codrus with a contemporary poet, perhaps Q. Cornificius). Servius, on the other hand, points to Codrus, king of Athens, who provoked the enemy with his *iurgia* ('Codrus' insults') and, sacrificing himself, saved the city in accordance with the oracle's response: Hor. *carm.* 3.19.2 *Codrus pro patria non timidus mori* (Hellan. *FGrH* 4 F 125; Lycurg. *Leocr.* 84–7; Cic. *Tusc.* 1.116; *nat. deor.* 3.49); Alcon himself, after all, was perhaps an Athenian (cf. above). It cannot be ruled out that here, as in the case of *laudes*, V. seeks for a certain vagueness or ambiguity. The comparison with *E.* 7 might suggest that the young Mopsus belongs to the same poetic 'school' as Thyrsis, who seems to share his contempt for Codrus. Both

ECLOGUE 5   255

singers display a tendency to react sharply against perceived slights (see below, p. 346). Note also that Codrus' name evokes remote antiquity (cf. the Athenian king), if not obsolescence (*Paroem. Gr.*, II, p. 148.14–15 L.; *RE*, XI.1, cols. 993–4 s.v. *Kodros* [K. Scherling]).

12 seruabit Tityrus haedos. Cf. *id.* 3.1–2 'I shall go and sing a serenade to Amaryllis; my goats / are grazing on the mountain, and Tityrus leads them'. In *E.* 3, Menalcas makes it clear that Tityrus collaborates with him in grazing the herd (*E.* 3.19–20 *cum clamarem 'quo nunc se proripit ille? / Tityre, coge pecus'*); on Tityrus' often subordinate role cf. 1.1n. (in Theocr. *id.* 7.72–7, however, he was the singer of Daphnis' sorrows). The shepherd's worry about finding a replacement during the time he devotes to poetry is featured in *id.* 1.12–14 'Do you want…to play the pipe? In the meantime, I shall graze the goats'. The motif will be amplified in *E.* 7.14–17 (note, once again, the parallel with *E.* 7, the 'true' agon of the *E.*). Properly speaking, *seruare* here means 'to guard, protect', as in 3.75. In sum, Tityrus is somewhat 'marginalized' here: he is given the task of looking after the herd and will therefore be unable to listen to the two songs (on Daphnis), since the singers have already entered the cave. This seems to be a prelude to Tityrus' 'low-profile' role in the following eclogue (based on Apollo's commands: *E.* 6.4–5).

13–14 Immo haec, in uiridi nuper quae cortice fagi / carmina descripsi. For a similar introduction to a song, cf. 9.26 *immo haec, quae Varo necdum perfecta canebat* (*immo* is typical of colloquial language, and occurs frequently in Plautus: *ThlL* VII.1.473–80). In the *Thalysia*, Lycidas' song had been composed 'not long ago': κἠγὼ μέν, ὄρη, φίλος, εἴ τοι ἀρέσκει / τοῦθ᾽ ὅ τι πρᾶν ἐν ὄρει τὸ μελύδριον ἐξεπόνασα 'and for my part—listen, my friend, if you like / this little song that I composed not long ago on the mountain' (*id.* 7.50–1; note also the similar position of the relative clause and the final focalization *carmina descripsi* ≈ τὸ μελύδριον ἐξεπόνασα). The adverb *nuper* effectively provides a timeframe for Mopsus' song: note that, in 5.55, the reader will learn that Menalcas' song on Daphnis' deification (50–2) has been known to him for a long time (*iam pridem*). Therefore, this lament for Daphnis places Mopsus alongside both Theocritus' *id.* 1 (the foundational poem of the genre's *inuentor*) and the song of a Virgilian master, Menalcas. While the Theocritean model featured the loose Hellenistic concept of 'toil' (πόνος), V.'s formulation includes a description of the writing act itself, with the 'transcription' (*descripsi*) of the text and the addition of a melody (5.14 *et modulans alterna notaui*). The singer carves his song on the bark of a tree (in this case the *fagus*, occupying the last foot as in *E.* 1.1): his action is only paralleled by Cornelius Gallus' words in 10.53–4 (the only two mentions of writing in the *E.*), but is isolated within the pre-Virgilian pastoral tradition. The only comparable case is the 'shady plane tree' in the *Epithalamium of Helen, id.* 18.47–8: 'letters will be carved on its bark, so that passersby / may read, in the Dorian dialect, "Worship me, I am Helen's tree!"'. The motif seems ultimately to derive from the well-known erotic elegy *Acontius and Cydippe*, a prototype of the genre, which

256   ECLOGUE 5

formed part of Callimachus' *Aitia* (Acontius' lament took place under φηγοί and πτελέαι, according to Aristaenet. *epist.* 1.10, p. 23, l. 57 Maz.; R. Pfeiffer, *ad aet.* fr. 73, p. 76; cf. 2.3n.). Such a writing technique is particularly suited to a herdsman, as Servius observed in his note on 5.13 (*ubi enim debuit magis rusticus scribere?*). The smooth bark of beech trees, at any rate, lends itself to writing. It bears mentioning that, properly speaking, *liber* is the 'inner bark' of a tree, used in Rome to produce the material support for writing (whether carved or painted) before papyrus was introduced. In Calpurnius Siculus' first eclogue, the praise of the current Golden Age (= Nero's principate), for which the prophetic god Faunus is credited (*ecl.* 1.33–88), may be read on the bark of a sacred beech tree, as though this were the page of a book (*ecl.* 1.20 *sacra descripta...pagina fago*; V.'s image of the green bark is there reinterpreted as a sign of recent carving: *ecl.* 1.22–3; cf. also 4.130). For the production of 'books' through removal of the inner bark, cf. Calp. *ecl.* 3.43–4. See also Nemes. *ecl.* 1.28–9.

14 et modulans alterna notaui. The phrase, clear in its general sense but not immediately obvious, must mean that, in writing the words and the melody of his short poem, Mopsus alternated between the two (you cannot sing and play the pipe at the same time)—or, perhaps better, that he added the musical notation after transcribing the text (*et modulans...notaui*), by 'jumping' from one interlinear space to another (*alterna*). Given the Callimachean context (5.13–14n.), Mopsus' words may also marginally suggest an allusion to elegiac metre, known for its 'alternating' structure: Ov. *her.* 15.5–6 *alterna... / carmina; fast.* 2.121; *trist.* 3.1.11 (the elegiac form is plaintive by definition; hence its suitability for funeral lament—but Mopsus sings in hexameters!). Mopsus' song, like Menalcas', is divided into single sections (see 5.20–44n.; 56–80n.), perhaps suggesting that both pieces actually included musical interludes.

15 iubeto ut certet Amyntas. Amyntas' name, which seemed to have been forgotten, comes back to conclude Mopsus' speech almost by surprise, thus recalling the hostility between the two, which is hard to overcome. Note that the text of **P**, omitting the subordinating *ut*, adopts a freer, more colloquial, paratactic style, in which the phrase becomes almost an exclamation (contrast *Aen.* 10.53–4, archaizing and solemn, with the imperative in line-ending position: *magna dicione iubeto / Karthago premat Ausoniam*). Yet *ut* has the advantage of intensifying the resonance of /t/ sounds, and the subordinate clause seems more expressive here. Metrical arguments have been made in favour of *iubeto certet*, though none of them is convincing. In fact, the elision in the hephthemimere (*iubeto ut*), in connection with the break after the third trochee (i.e. after *deinde*), is rare in V. (never attested in the *E*.) though not forbidden, as is shown by its occurrences in V.'s later works: cf. *G.* 2.428; 3.323; *Aen.* 2.417; 9.57; 11.236; 669 (occasionally attested in Lucretius, e.g. 1.59; 3.10; 4.395, it will become frequent in Ovid: see Soubiran 1966, pp. 534–6). At any rate, even the absence of the hephthemimere, in connection with the metrical break after the third trochee and the bucolic diaeresis after spondee (if *iubeto certet* is accepted), would be quite rare in the *E.*, where it only occurs once (*E.* 5.52; but cf. also *G.* 4.175; *Aen.* 8.453). Further emphasis is added by the future imperative of *iubeo*, often found in prescriptive contexts (Cat. *agr.* 28.1) and, more specifically, in the juridical language (cf. Plaut. *Curc.* 526; Ov. *rem.* 671). Note Mopsus' use of the second-person pronoun with the imperative, emphasizing the pronoun's illocutionary force (cf. *E.* 3.31n.). Towards the end of the dialogue, Menalcas uses the same trick: 5.19 *sed tu desine*; and so does Mopsus, again, in his very last speech (5.88).

16–18. Menalcas' poetic value judgement concerning Mopsus and his rival is entirely favourable to the former, and is expressed (as usual) through rural images and analogies. Menalcas puts an end to all debate: by using the indicative *cedit* (5.18), he states a matter of fact while also asserting his own subjective opinion (*iudicio nostro*), in keeping with his affectionate attitude towards his younger friend (cf. esp. 5.8–9n.). In this case, however, the 'humble' nature of the *saliunca* is subordinated to the purple-red colour of the roses (cf. *E.* 4.2 *humiles myricae*). Note the chiastic correspondence between the two chromatic epithets in the middle (*pallenti* and *puniceis*) and the two epithets referring to 'structural' traits of the plant, *humilis* and *lenta*, situated at the extremes.

16 Lenta salix...pallenti...oliuae. The flexibility of the willow tree (the same line-opening phrase appears at *E.* 3.83n.) is implicitly opposed to the solidity, and thus the utility, of the olive tree. However, the epithet *pallens* (cf. *E.* 2.47; 3.39; 6.54), which is well suited to the light green colour of its trunk and leaves, hints especially at its fruit, and therefore at olive oil, a precious gift of Athena. A Virgilian encomium of the olive tree, considered as superior to the vine, is found at *G.* 2.420–5 (but cf. the entire sequence in *G.* 2.397–457). In the agon between the bay and the olive tree, an allegorical fable of literary-critical significance appearing in Callimachus' fourth iamb, the bay reproached the olive tree for its white (i.e. light green) colour, typical of the lower side of its leaves (Callim. fr. 194.22 Pf.).

17 puniceis humilis...saliunca rosetis. In vivid opposition to *pallenti*, the epithet *puniceis* draws the reader's attention to the colour, i.e. to the purple-red hue of the flower *par excellence*, the rose: cf. Hor. *carm.* 4.10.4 *puniceae...rosae*; Pind. *Isthm.* 4.18 (= 3–4, 36b Sn.-M.) φοινικέοισιν...ῥόδοις; the *saliunca* is a type of valerian, perhaps of the so-called 'Celtic' variety, whose flowers are sometimes pinkish and, in general, softly nuanced. The plant was widespread in alpine regions, and much appreciated for its scent, but was ill-suited to weaving wreaths, because of its short branches and leaves (Plin. *nat.* 21.40; 43; cf. Hor. *epist.* 1.19.26 *ne me foliis...breuioribus ornes*). The opposition between the two flowers is further emphasized by V.'s mention of 'rose gardens', which suggest large surfaces covered with roses (Paestum was famous for its rose gardens; cf. *G.* 4.119), whereas the *saliunca*, which is not a very tall plant, grows in carpets (*herba uerius quam flos*, as Pliny called it, *nat.* 21.43; *humilis*, in this sense, is a very accurate epithet).

258   ECLOGUE 5

19 sed tu desine plura, puer. The phrase *desine plura* must probably be considered elliptic (omitting a verb like *loqui*): but cf. 8.61 *desine tibia uersus*; ThlL V.1.729.28–48. In common usage, a verb like *parce* would be expected in place of *desine*. An identical wording (except for the pronoun *tu*) appears, at the end of an eclogue (but with the opposite function, i.e. signalling the end/postponement of poetic song), in *E.* 9.66 *desine plura, puer* (cf. Symm. *epist.* 1.46.2 *plura desino*). Perhaps the comparison with *E.* 9, where Moeris interrupts Lycidas, led ancient readers to attribute this line to Mopsus, as most manuscripts do; PR (Π₁ does not help) rightly make Menalcas' speech continue. With these words, Menalcas diverts Mopsus' attention from his rivalries, so that he may focus on singing: the *puer* between the two is certainly Mopsus (cf. 5.4n.), so he will be the one to start (5.10n.). Note the illocutionary force of the pronoun accompanying the imperative, particularly important in an eclogue characterized by lively dialogue and action (see 5.15n.). **successimus antro.** Only now does it become clear that the two shepherds were en route, and that they opted for the second of the two possibilities suggested by Mopsus (5.5–7). In keeping with Theocritus' mimetic technique (cf., once again, *id.* 7, the *Thalysia*, set on a countryside road in Cos), V. lets the reader guess gestures and movements: those extra-verbal elements which a dialogue can do no more than allude to (cf. e.g. *E.* 3.55–9n.). Note the explicit Platonic model: *Phaedrus* 230a ἀτάρ, ὦ ἑταῖρε, μεταξὺ τῶν λόγων, ἆρ᾽ οὐ τόδε ἦν τὸ δένδρον ἐφ᾽ ὅπερ ἦγες ἡμᾶς (cf. *E.* 5.3n.). *Wanderers* (Ὁδοιπόροι) is one of the ancient titles of *id.* 5, i.e. the agon between Comatas and Lacon.

20–44. The twenty-five lines that Mopsus devotes to the late Daphnis are divided into three sections: in the first (nine lines: 5.20–8), Mopsus evokes the grief which emanates from Daphnis' mother and is extended to the whole natural world (5.20–8); in the second (eleven lines: 5.29–39), he mentions the achievements of Daphnis as a Dionysian teacher (5.29–31), extols his irreplaceable role in the agricultural and pastoral world (5.32–4a), then describes how the fields were left barren by his death (5.34b–39); in the third section (only five lines), Mopsus mentions the honours awarded to the late Daphnis, as requested by the hero himself. Menalcas' song, featuring the same number of lines, is based on a similarly tripartite structure (5.56–80n.). The unsettling portents that follow Julius Caesar's death will be described in *G.* 1.466–88 (notably twenty-three lines, a number close to Mopsus' song): this may have been a further reason to prompt the identification between Daphnis and the murdered dictator. Servius comments on 5.20: *alii dicunt significari per allegoriam C. Iulium Caesarem, qui in senatu a Cassio et Bruto uiginti tribus uulneribus interemptus est: unde et 'crudeli funere' uolunt dictum* 'others argue that the text alludes allegorically to C. Julius Caesar, who was murdered in the senate by Cassius and Brutus with twenty-three stab wounds: hence they also explain the phrase *crudeli funere*'. Cf. also Servius Dan.'s note: *multi per matrem Venerem accipiunt, per leones et tigres populos quos subegit, per thiasos sacra quae pontifex instituit, per formosum pecus populum Romanum* 'many interpret his mother as Venus [5.23], regard lions and tigers as the populations subjugated by Caesar [5.27; 29], the thiasoi as the cults he established in his capacity as *pontifex maximus* [5.30], the "beautiful flock" [5.44] as the Roman people' (cf. again 5.56–80n.). Note that Calpurnius Siculus, in his Neronian reworking of *E.* 4, 'contaminates' it with several stimuli from *E.* 5 (cf. 5.6n.; 13–14n.) and evokes Julius Caesar's death (Calp. *ecl.* 1, esp. 82–3). This suggests that, towards the mid-first century CE, a Caesarian interpretation of the great divine songs in *E.* 4 and 5 may have been widespread. More 'private' allegorizations were also available: in particular, Daphnis could be taken to stand for V.'s brother, Flaccus, who died at an adult age (Don. *uita Verg.* 45–7 Brumm. = p. 24.4–6 Brugn.-Stok; this reading is variously expounded in Philargyrius/Philagrius *ad E.* 5.1; 22; *schol. Bern.* praef. *ad E.* 5 and *ad* 5.20), or for the poet Quintilius Varus, a friend of V.'s, whose death Horace mourns in *carm.* 1.24 (the latter hypothesis is also mentioned by Serv. *ad* 5.20). It also bears mentioning that some ancient interpreters equated Daphnis with Saloninus, the mysterious son of Asinius Pollio (*schol. Bern.* praef. *ad E.* 5), whose existence is doubtful. Saloninus' early death might seem useful when it comes to explaining his puzzling absence from the sources, but the ultimate result would be the grotesque juxtaposition of a birthday ode (*E.* 4) and an epitaph (*E.* 5), one right after the other.

   20–1 Exstinctum Nymphae...Daphnin / flebant. Epithet and proper noun frame the line, thus giving a 'title' to the song: the protagonist of *id.* 1 is now dead, and the water goddesses mourn him. In Theocritus' poem, Thyrsis started off by reproaching the Nymphs for their absence during Daphnis' sufferings (*id.* 1.66–9), but concluded his speech by praising their goodwill (*id.* 1.141 τὸν Μοίσαις φίλον ἄνδρα, τὸν οὐ Νύμφαισιν ἀπεχθῆ: thus, Mopsus starts exactly where Thyrsis left off). Note the spondaic rhythm in the opening: 5.24n. For the enjambed *flebant* (a spondee in the first foot), cf. *Aen.* 6.213, similarly emphasizing the mournful tone. The verbal participle *extinctus* and the general idea (i.e. mourning a semi-divine being) will be applied to Julius Caesar at *G.* 1.466–7 *ille* [scil. *sol*] *etiam exstincto miseratus Caesare Romam, / cum caput obscura nitidum ferrugine texit.* This might be taken to confirm the equation Daphnis = Caesar, though it is possible that the *Georgics* passage itself gave rise to the allegorical interpretation attested by Servius. **Daphnin.** The cowherd Daphnis, archetype of the herdsman-poet (whose name is already mentioned in the collection at *E.* 2.26 and 3.12), belonged to Eastern Sicilian folk mythology even before Theocritus, as we know from Timaeus (*FGrH* 566 F 83 Jac. = Parthen. *erot.* 29), as well as from Diod. Sic. 4.84 and Aelian, *uar. hist.* 10.18; *nat. anim.* 11.13; cf. also Servius Dan.'s note on the present passage. Daphnis, son of Hermes and a nymph, was abandoned under a bay tree (δάφνη), from which he drew his name—appropriate for a future singer and musician (note also that bay is often featured in myths associated with Julius Caesar and his cult: cf. Cass. Di. 41.39.2; 47.18.5). He was raised by Sicilian herdsmen and, while still a boy, reached excellence in pastoral poetry (which he himself invented,

260   ECLOGUE 5

according to certain traditions). The nymph Echenais punished him with the loss of sight for his (involuntary) adultery (Parthen. *erot.* 29; his wife is the nymph Nais in [Theocr.] *id.* 8.93; Ov. *ars* 1.732). He then found solace in song, until his premature death (here referred to as *crudeli funere*: cf. *G.* 3.263). The sources diverge on the exact cause of his demise (*E.* 5.21n.); *Enc. Virg.* I, pp. 972–3, s.v. *Dafni* (G. Cipolla); *Verg. Enc.* I, pp. 337–8, s.v. *Daphnis* (J. Van Sickle). On Daphnis and the Nymphs, see especially Larson (2001, pp. 79–81). The glorification of Daphnis, now immortal, is featured as a typically pastoral theme in Callimachus' epigram on the Cretan goatherd Astacides, abducted by a Nymph on the mountain (ἥρπασε Νύμφη ἐξ ὄρεος [*Anth. Pal.* 7.518.1–2 = *epigr.* 22.1–2 Pf.]). Ovid's Alcithoe presents Daphnis' love affairs as a well-known pastoral subject matter; Ovid testifies to Daphnis' transformation into stone (rather than his deification): *uulgatos taceo…pastoris amores / Daphnidis…quem nymphe paelicis ira / contulit in saxum* (Ov. *met.* 4.276–8).

21 (uos coryli testes et flumina Nymphis). Summoning inanimate beings as witnesses is a poetic commonplace in Latin literature, going back at least to Ennius, *sat.* 10–11 V.[2] (for nightingales and swallows, cf. Petron. 131.8, ll. 6–7 *dignus amore locus: testis siluestris aedon / atque urbana Procne*). Here, however, the emphasis on the Nymphs' grief is best explained by their ambivalent behaviour in *id.* 1 (cf. *E.* 5.20–1n.). It is a nymph, Echenais, who causes Daphnis' demise, and perhaps he died by water—Theocritus may allude to this in *id.* 1.140 (Gow 1952, II, pp. 30–1, ad loc.; Segal 1981, pp. 47–65; Hunter 1999, pp. 66–7). A spring named *Daphnis*, venerated by the Siculi, is mentioned in Serv. Dan. *ad E.* 5.20: thus, all the more significant is the reference to *flumina* (but will they be reliable witnesses, given that the Nymphs are 'their' goddesses?). Note, finally, the reappearance of those hazel bushes which were featured in 5.3 (Mopsus preferred the cave to them).

23 atque deos atque astra uocat crudelia mater. In describing the codified gestures of mourning, Mopsus makes use of epic phrases and style. The mother's name is not mentioned, but there does not seem to be any contradiction with the tradition describing her as a nymph (5.20–1n.): thus, she is one of the divine creatures mentioned at 5.20–1. Her outburst against the 'cruelty' (*crudelia* takes up 5.20 *crudeli*) of the gods and stars contrastively anticipates the deification, which will lead Daphnis above the *sidera* (5.57; he will be granted deification by a god, i.e. his father Hermes/Mercury). Note the postponement of *mater*, even more effective than *flebant* (5.21) in eliciting pathos (cf. also *nati* at the end of 5.22, vertically balancing *mater*). The singer Orpheus, who died prematurely, was similarly mourned by all the Muses, and especially by his mother Calliope, as is attested by the epigram of Antipater of Sidon, *Anth. Pal.* 7.8.5–6 = *HE* 232–3 G.-P., which V. may have read in Meleager's collection, the *Garland*. In *G.* 4.321–56, Aristaeus will invoke the help of his mother Cyrene, surrounded by her sisters, the Nymphs. On the term *astrum*, cf. *E.* 5.51–2n. **atque…atque.** The double

ECLOGUE 5   261

atque in the sense of 'both…and' is an audacious usage, later imitated by Silius Italicus, 1.93–4 *atque Hennaeae numina diuae / atque Acheronta uocat*; cf. *G.* 3.257 *atque hinc atque illinc* (where, however, the force of the first *atque* varies depending on which variant reading is adopted: either *umerosque* or *umeros*, which seems more plausible); cf. also Tib. 2.5.73 *atque tubas atque arma ferunt.* Here, perhaps, the young Mopsus must be credited with the audacity, which will not often be repeated in V.'s works. The adj. *crudelia* modifies both *deos* and *astra*, albeit agreeing with the latter alone (cf. *Aen.* 3.264 *numina magna uocat*), but its position between *uocat* and *mater* amplifies its subjective force, as though it were the mother's cry. Aristaeus will accuse his divine mother Cyrene of cruelty at *G.* 4.356 *te crudelem nomine dicit*; cf. also *Aen.* 2.745–6 *quem non incusaui amens hominumque deorumque, / aut quid in euersa uidi crudelius urbe?*

24–8. In *id.* 1, nature participated in the mourning of Daphnis: first wild animals in the woods, then cattle, then Hermes and the shepherds (ll. 71–81); Priapus and Aphrodite came next (ll. 81–98). Mopsus starts with the Nymphs and Daphnis' mother, but follows a reverse order, mentioning the shepherds first (they stop leading their cattle to the rivers: 5.24–5), then grazing animals in general (5.26), and finally lions, mountains, and *siluae* (5.27–8): the gods will only reappear, under a different light, at 5.35. Cf. also the scenes of pastoral mourning in Bion. *epit. Adon.* 31–9 (with J. D. Reed's commentary, Cambridge 1997, p. 215, ad loc.); [Mosch.] *epit. Bion.* 23–4. In *id.* 4.12–17, heifer and bull let themselves starve to death, suffering from the absence of their master, Aegon, who has left for Olympia. According to Aelian, *nat. anim.* 11.13, Daphnis' five dogs, after mourning the loss of their master, decide to die as well.

24. The line includes four spondees, i.e. the maximum number in the *E.* (contrast *Aen.* 12.18). Three spondees were featured in the opening of Mopsus' song, 5.20 (note also 5.21 *flebant*, an enjambed spondee).

25–2 nulla neque…/…nec. For a similar sequence of negatives, cf. 4.55–6n.

25 boues ad flumina. Watering cattle was one of the specific tasks of the *boukolos*, and Daphnis himself performed it, as he asserts in *id.* 1.120–1 (see 5.43–4n.). After his death, no cowherd takes care of it any longer, either for Daphnis' cattle or even for their own. Note the mention of *flumina*, ambiguously involved in Daphnis' fate (5.21n.). The hyperbaton (*pastos…boues*) highlights the rhythmic change, from spondees to dactyls, at 5.24–5. **amnem.** The term belongs to the language of elevated poetry (cf. Enn. *uar.* 12 V.^{2}; see *Enc. Virg.* l, pp. 140–1, s.v. *amnis* [P. Parroni]), and is coupled here with its 'competitor' *flumen*, more common in prose (but admitted in poetry since Enn. *ann.* 163 Sk.) and eventually standard in the Romance languages. For another refined term, cf. *libauit* (below).

26 libauit. The verb only occurs here in the *E.* It is used of animals again at *G.* 4.54; *Aen.* 5.92. Properly speaking, it belongs to the language of ritual: see *ThlL* VII.2.1340.28–73 for its poetic use in the sense of 'tasting' vel sim. (cf. Calp. *ecl.* 6.52); *Enc. Virg.* III, p. 207, s.v. *libo* (P. Soverini). **quadripes.** None (5.25 *nulla*) of

262   ECLOGUE 5

the 'four-footed creatures' drank or fed on grass. The word, appearing in Ennius (*ann.* 236 Sk.), must soon have become an established epic term (but cf. Acc. *trag.* 381 R.[3]) for the horse, the animal that, due to its gallop, is most resoundingly 'four-footed' (hence the frequent use of the participle *quadrupedans*): cf. *Aen.* 10.892 *tollit se arrectum quadripes*; 11.875 *quadripedumque putrem cursu quatit ungula campum* (for a similar sound effect cf. *Aen.* 8.596). In V.'s pastoral land-scape, which does not include any equine species (with the only exception of the adynaton at *E.* 8.27; contrast Calp. *ecl.* 6.49–56 esp. 49 *genus...equarum*), it seems natural to refer the term to common grazing animals, especially cattle (hence the fem. *nulla*: see Naev. *trag.* 25 R.[3]; Quint. *inst.* 2.10.6; *OLD*[2], p. 1686, s.v. *quadrupes* 4a), as a supplement to the mention of *pastos...boues* at 5.25. Mourning horses, at any rate, appear as early as Hom. *Il.* 17.426–8, reworked in *Aen.* 11.89–90. Here, both context and style are particularly solemn: note the mention of African lions and other wild creatures. This may have reminded V.'s early readers of a popular anecdote concerning Julius Caesar's death: according to Suetonius, *Iul.* 81.2, the horses that Julius Caesar dedicated to the river-god Rubicon cried and stopped feeding on the pastures in the days before his assassination. In the list of domestic animals featured in *id.* 1, bovines are the only species said to participate in Daphnis' grief (*id.* 1.74–5); note that all categories of herdsmen, including shep-herds and goatherds, are mentioned, although their respective animals do not appear (*id.* 1.80); cf. also [Mosch.] *epit. Bion.* 23–4 αἱ βόες αἱ ποτὶ ταύροις / πλαζόμεναι γοάντι καὶ οὐκ ἐθέλοντι νέμεσθαι. In *E.* 10 (another reworking of Daphnis' story), Cornelius Gallus is comforted by sheep, but the poet feels the need to justify this (10.16–18n.). Here the manuscript tradition is unanimous on *quadripes*, but elsewhere it oscillates between *quadripes* and *quadrupes*, which seems to be the preferable form from a phonetic point of view: the text of *E.* 5.26 could be corrected accordingly (*quadru-* preceding /p/; *quadri-* preceding any other consonant; cf. *Aen.* 7.500, with N. Horsfall's commentary, Leiden-Boston-Cologne 2000, p. 335, ad loc.). **graminis...herbam**. A solemnly pleonastic phrase, perhaps belonging to the language of ritual: Liv. 1.24.5 *fetialis ex arce graminis herbam puram attulit*. For later echoes cf. Ov. *met.* 10.87; Claud. 26.147 H. The coupling of the two nouns, almost synonymous with each other, is meant to rule out even a minimal quantity: 'not a single blade of grass'; the same is true of *G.* 1.134 *et sulcis frumenti quaereret herbam*.

27 **Poenos...leones**. The epithet, though mainly ornamental, must evoke Africa—a further broadening of the horizon with respect to the Theocritean model, i.e. *id.* 1.72 'even the lion in the woods mourned his death' (and perhaps an allusion to Julius Caesar's African campaigns). The presence of lions in Sicily is far from obvious, as ancient interpreters of Theocritus had observed: cf. *schol. ad id.* 1, esp. 72b, p. 58 Wend. τινὲς αἰτιῶνται τὸν Θεόκριτον καὶ φασιν ἐν Σικελίᾳ λέοντα μὴ εἶναι. Thus, V.'s *Poenos etiam...leones* might be a response to that ancient objection raised against Theocritus: the news of Daphnis' death,

ECLOGUE 5   263

according to V., reached even the lions—but in Africa. Thyrsis, at any rate, had an extra-Sicilian network, given his competition with the Libyan Chromis (*id.* 1.24). V.'s allusion to the Carthaginians, the Romans' historical archenemies, is paired with another exotic, and no less topical, epithet (the 'Armenian' tigers), as was the case with Theocritus' Syracuse (*id.* 16.76–96): cf. *E.* 5.29n. **ingemuisse.** The ingressive compound form (easily lost in elision) seems preferable to R's *gemuisse*, as it expressively evokes the 'beginning' of the lamentations (as soon as the news of Daphnis' death is heard). The perfect tense of the simple verb appears in *Aen.* 6.413 *gemuit sub pondere cumba* (not, however, a mourning groan). For the compound form cf. *Aen.* 1.92–3 *extemplo… / ingemit et*; 4.369 *num fletu ingemuit nostro?*; 692; 6.483, etc.; cf. *Pont.* 2.3.65–6 *ut tamen audita est nostrae tibi cladis origo, / diceris erratis ingemuisse meis.* The form *gemuisse* may have become popular because it more commonly governs an accusative (*tuum…interitum*). However, for the acc. construction of the compound verb (hardly surprising in V.), cf. Stat. *Theb.* 9.2 *ipsi…ingemuere iacentem*; *ThlL* VII.1.1516.41–58. The form *ingemuisse* underscores the initial sound *in*-, immediately echoed by *interitum* at *E.* 5.28 then again at 5.30–1 *instituit…inducere…intexere* (note also 37 *infelix*; 40 *inducite*).

28 montesque feri siluaeque. Cf. Lucr. 5.201 *montes siluaeque ferarum*; Catull. 63.89 *nemora fera.* The phrase echoes *id.* 1.72 ἐκ δρυμοῖο, which is contaminated with another Theocritean passage on Daphnis, from *id.* 7.72–4: 'Tityrus will sing next to me / of that time when Daphnis the cowherd fell in love with Xeneas, / and the mountain suffered with him, and the oaks bewailed him [χὡς ὅρος ἀμφ' ἐπονεῖτο, καὶ ὡς δρύες αὐτὸν ἐθρήνευν]'. The announcement of such a portentous event is ascribed to 'woods' and 'mountains' (*loquuntur*: cf. *E.* 1.5n.): in other words, to the pastoral tradition itself. The notion is reworked in a positive key by Menalcas at ll. 7–9 of his song (= 5.62–4 *ipsi laetitia uoces ad sidera iactant / intonsi montes* etc.; this is l. 9 in Mopsus' song). Note that P transmits the corrupted reading *ferunt* (for *feri*) and *siluasque* (*siluaesque* P[1])—hence Markland's conjecture *feros siluasque*, taking *loquuntur* as a synonym of *dicunt/ferunt* vel sim. ('they say', 'they narrate'), and thereby eliminating the reference to nature's 'loquacity'. Yet the impersonal use of forms like *loquuntur/dicunt* is typically signalled by the context and tends to refer to generally valid notions, as in *Aen.* 1.731 *Iuppiter—hospitibus nam te dare iura loquuntur* etc. (cf. *E.* 9.13 *dicunt*). For the correlated double -*que* cf. 8.22n.

29–31. Yoking the tigers, a task typical of Dionysus, will explicitly be connected with the god through the technical term *thiasos*, and then through the name *Bacchi* itself (at the end of 5.30; *hastas*, i.e. the thyrsoi, will conclude 5.31, and the vines, i.e. Dionysus' plant, will open the similes at 5.32–3). For a similar syntactical and rhetorical structure cf. *E.* 2.32–3, with the same verb (*instituere*) referring to Pan's 'inventions'. Here the emphatic repetition of the subject (note the anaphora, typical of hymnic style) introduces some variation into a polysyndetic sequence (in other words, the second *Daphnis* 'replaces' a conjunction

264 ECLOGUE 5

like *et*). Moreover, the insistence on verbal prefixes (*in-stituit / in-ducere / in-texere*) makes apparent the god's innovative action (cf. 5.30n.). The Dionysian interpretation of the figure of Daphnis, perhaps featured in Theocritus (*epigr.* 2 G.), can be paralleled by iconography: *LIMC* III.1, pp. 348–52, s.v. *Daphnis* (G. Berger-Doer). Another Daphnis, the protagonist of Longus' novel, is explicitly compared to Dionysus (Long. 2.2.1; but cf. also 1.16.4); see further Simon (1962); Wojaczek (1969, pp. 13–15); Merkelbach (1988, pp. 36–9 = 1991, pp. 47–9). The Dionysian reference places Daphnis within the framework of V.'s divine models, thereby moving away from an exclusively Caesarian allegory. A similar role of Dionysian archegete is assigned to Orpheus in Damag. *Anth. Pal.* 7.9.5 = *HE* 1383 G.-P.; for the tigers 'tamed' by Orpheus' song, cf. *G.* 4.510 (also *E.* 5.29n.).

29 Armenias curru subiungere tigris. The phrase *Armenias...tigris* balances *Poenos...leones* (27) in word-order, animal character and exotic location. The chariot drawn by tigers (or panthers, sometimes confused with the former) is a favourite of Dionysian iconography: the yoking of such wild animals, encountered by the god in the East (especially India or Hyrcania, in the tigers' case: Plin. *nat.* 8.66; cf. also *Aen.* 4.367), is an evident proof of his civilizing abilities; cf. Hor. *carm.* 3.3.13–15 *te..., Bacche pater, tuae / uexere tigres indocili iugum / collo trahentes* (in the context of Augustus' achievements); Sil. 17.647–8 *odoratis descendens Liber ab Indis / egit pampineos frenata tigride currus* (according to Diod. Sic. 4.3.1, Dionysus was the first to celebrate a triumph on the back of a similarly exotic animal, the Indian elephant). The god leads a paradoxical 'army' of feasting women and men to the most remote regions of the East (cf. Diod. Sic. 4.2.6): it is a peace-making force, capable of bringing serenity and freedom anywhere—one of the god's greatest achievements, which earned him a place among the Olympians (besides Hor. *carm.* 3.3, cf. Ov. *trist.* 5.3.19–20). But V. will attribute even greater achievements to Augustus, who will be credited with conquering lands even more remote than those subjugated by his divine predecessor (and a fortiori by any human predecessor, such as Alexander the Great): *nec qui pampineis uictor iuga flectit habenis / Liber, agens celso Nysae de uertice tigris* (*Aen.* 6.804–5). Note the form *curru*, an archaic dat., common in dactylic poetry: cf. *Aen.* 1.156; 7.724 *curru iungit...equos*. Orpheus tames tigers with his mournful song at *G.* 4.510 *mulcentem tigris et agentem carmine quercus*.

30 thiasos inducere Bacchi. The technical Hellenism (θίασος) emphasizes Daphnis' role as true initiator of the cult, here seen in its aggressive and orgiastic aspect, also evoked by the god's name *Bacchus*: cf. the verb *bacchari* or the noun *Bacchanalia*, made popular by the 186 BCE senatorial decree. In Rome, according to Dionysius of Halicarnassus, 6.17, the official cult of Dionysus-Liber was introduced (along with that of Demeter-Ceres and Kore-Libera) in 496 BCE, during the dictatorship of Aulus Postumius, who thereby expressed his gratitude to the three deities for their protection and help in averting a terrible famine (for the divine triad cf. Liv. 3.55.7; 33.25.3; Tac. *ann.* 2.49.1; see also Cic. *nat. deor.* 2.62;

Wissowa 1912, pp. 297–304; cf. *E.* 5.36–9n.). The *Liberalia*, held on the 17th of March, were dedicated to the Dionysian triad: such kind of festival will be a blueprint for the rustic feasts described by V. at *G.* 2.385–96. Servius (*ad E.* 5.29) draws attention to an allegorical interpretation, according to which Julius Caesar was the first to 'import' the cult of Liber into Rome, à la Hellenistic ruler: *hoc aperte ad Caesarem pertinet, quem constat primum sacra Liberi patris transtulisse Romam.* This reading, however, lacks any external validation (Servius Dan.'s note *ad* 5.20 [see above 5.20–44n.], is much vaguer; but cf. Turcan 1977; De Cazanove 1986). Here, in fact, Mopsus himself is the one who displays his penchant for Dionysian rites, from his choice of the cave (5.6n.) to his reaction to Menalcas' song (5.81–4n.). Note the multiple similar preverbs, *INstituit…INducere* (cf. 5.27 *INgemuisse* [n.]; 31 *INtexere*), coupled with the anaphoric repetition of Daphnis' name. Here *inducere*, like *subiungere* at 5.29 and *intexere* at 5.31, is a very concrete verb, describing the straight line-up of the parade: cf. Liv. 10.33.1 *manipulos…uia inducit* as well as *Aen.* 11.620 *turmas inducit Asilas*; note also, albeit in a different sense, *E.* 5.40 *inducite fontibus umbras.*

31 foliis lentas intexere mollibus hastas. After the mention of *thiasos* at 5.30, a further Greek term is here eschewed: the *thyrsus* (θύρσος) is not named but is described analytically as a 'flexible rod' interwoven with 'soft leaves'. In its oldest form, well attested iconographically, the *thyrsus* is a long branch featuring a tangle of ivy or vine-leaves on its top (Daremberg-Saglio, V, pp. 287–96, s.v. *thyrsos*); cf. Eur. *Bacch.* 557–8 θυρσοφορεῖς θιάσους. Here, as in *Aen.* 7.390 *mollis…thyrsos* (cf. also 7.396 *pampineas…hastas*), V. seems to insist on the harmless nature of the object: on occasions, however, it could be used (in its more rigid form) as an offensive weapon; note Lucretius' metaphor at Lucr. 1.922–3 *acri / percussit thyrso laudis spes magna meum cor.* Dionysus, in fact, is said to have killed the Giants with his 'peaceable rod crowned with ivy' (Eur. *Ion* 216–18; cf. Apollod. 1.6.2 [37]; see also Hor. *carm.* 2.19.8 [*Liber*] *graui metuende thyrso*). His followers, though 'physically' different from him, could behave in a very similar way: cf. Eur. *Bacch.* 733; 761–4 (and 25); Ov. *met.* 3.712; 11.27–8 (iconographic parallels are noteworthy: Daremberg-Saglio, V, esp. pp. 295–6). Indeed, there existed a type of thyrsus-spear, the so-called θυρσόλογχος; topped with a spearhead, it could be used as an actual weapon of war: Callixein. Rhod. *FGrH* 627 F 2.31 Jac. (apud Athen. 5.200d); Strab. 1.2.8 (19); Diod. Sic. 4.4.2; Polyaen. 1.1.1; cf. also, with varying similarities, *Anth. Pal.* 6.172.1–2 = *Furth. Gr. Epigr.* 1124–5, p. 327 P.; Catull. 64.256 *tecta…cuspide thyrsos*; Ov. *met.* 3.667 *pampineis agitat uelatam frondibus hastam*; Sen. *Herc. f.* 904; Macr. *Sat.* 7.1.22.

32–4. Daphnis' role as hero and 'glory' of the pastoral world (5.34 *tu decus omne tuis*) is aptly outlined with a rustic, agricultural simile (cf. esp. *E.* 1.19–25). Servius must have noticed this, since his note *ad* 5.32 states *locus Theocriti est*, even though no single Theocritean passage can be pinpointed as an intertext (but

266   ECLOGUE 5

cf. *id.* 8.79–80 'acorns an ornament [κόσμος ≈ *decus*] to the oak, apples to the apple tree, / heifers the cow, and the cows themselves to the herdsman'; see also *id.* 18.29–31). Yet V.'s choice of the terms of comparison is well suited to Daphnis' link with Dionysian vines (31); his status as a cowherd is of course part of the picture (since bulls also have Dionysian connotations: ταυροφάγος was an epithet of the god [Soph. fr. 668 Radt]; cf. also *E.* 5.73n.). Finally, the reference to harvesting is a contrastive anticipation of 5.34–9.

32 uitis ut arboribus decori est. This construction, featuring the predicative dative *decori* (cf. Plaut. *Asin.* 192; Lucr. 2.643; note also Ov. *met.* 13.849), draws attention to the word *decori* itself, which looks forward to the concluding *tu decus omne tuis* (34). Cf. the more compressed expression at *G.* 2.89 *non eadem arboribus pendet uindemia nostris* (where the vines are replaced by their product: the 'grape harvest'). In viticultural contexts, *arbores* usually refers to the trees used to support the vines; cf. *E.* 3.10n., as well as Cat. *agr.* 32.

34 postquam te fata tulerunt. The simple form, as often in poetry, replaces the compound *abstulerunt* (*simplex pro composito*; Serv. Dan.: *tulerunt pro abstulerunt*): as a result, the phrase is delicately vague, almost euphemistic. Cf. *E.* 9.51 *omnia fert aetas*; *Aen.* 2.555; 4.679 (with Serv. Dan. ad loc.); 5.356; 10.652. Note here a precise Homeric parallel: *Il.* 2.302 κῆρες...θανάτοιο φέρουσαι (cf. also, with a different meaning, *Aen.* 2.34 *seu iam Troiae sic fata ferebant*). No wonder that the expression is variously reworked in epigraphic poems of funerary subject matter: *CLE* 417.6; 420.13; 422.8; 1409.8 Buech.; *Enc. Virg.* II, p. 496b, s.v. *fero* (B. Zucchelli). The beginning of a new syntactic unit in the middle of the line underscores the logical consequentiality between 5.32–4a and 34b–39. For the verbal form (a line-ending perfect), cf. *E.* 3.9n.

35 ipsa Pales agros atque ipse reliquit Apollo. In the Theocritean model, after reproaching the Nymphs for their absence (*id.* 1.66–9), the poet mentioned three gods, namely Hermes, Priapus, and Aphrodite (although Aphrodite shows a somewhat ambivalent attitude: *id.* 1.96). Here, on the other hand, Pales and Apollo sorrowfully participate in Daphnis' fate—to the point that they abandon a world which he too has left. Thus, they re-enact the gods' flight from the mortal community, which marked the beginning of humankind's decline in the myth of the ages. It is in the agricultural world that the goddess Justice left her last traces according to *G.* 2.474 (cf. *E.* 4.6n.). Note also the final couplet of the (anonymous) *notissimi uersus* against Octavian: *omnia se a terris tunc numina declinarunt, / fugit et auratos Iuppiter ipse thronos* (quoted in Suet. *Aug.* 70.1). In an epigram by Meleager, the god Pan decided to leave the mountains for the city after Daphnis' death (*Anth. Pal.* 7.535.5 = *HE* 4704 G.-P.). The absence of Pales and Apollo, who will reappear together at the outset of *G.* 3 (on animal husbandry), is immediately paralleled by the agricultural barrenness mentioned at 5.36–9. Note the sound effect in *ipsA PALes / APOL*, further associating the two gods as in a ritual pair. Here *ipse* and *ipsa* are used in the normal way, i.e. as attributes of a noun, but it bears mentioning that, in everyday language, they were used to refer to the land-lord and the landlady, without further specification. For the divine pair cf. Calp. *ecl.* 7.22 *fecunda Pales aut pastoralis Apollo* (note, once again, the phonetic word-play: -*A PAL...PAS...AL...APOL*). **ipsa Pales.** An old Italian deity of herds and animal husbandry, always fem. in V. (3x): cf. *G.* 3.1 *te quoque magna Pales*; 294 *nunc, ueneranda Pales, magno nunc ore sonandum* (note, in both cases, the emphasis on her 'greatness' and 'venerability'). Servius, *ad G.* 3.1, attests a masc. form of *Pales* in certain authors, e.g. Varro (cf. *ant. rer. diu.* XIVd, p. 87 Card.). Archaic Roman deities, especially if connected to natural forces, were often so indefinite in gender as to justify ritual formulas like *siue deus siue dea* or *siue mas siue femina* (for the latter, in the opposite order, see Laev. *carm.* fr. 26.2 Bläns. = Court.; cf. Wissowa 1912, pp. 37–8). Divine hermaphroditism is a different phe-nomenon, as e.g. in the case of the Cyprian Aphrodite described in Macr. *Sat.* 3.8.2. Unparalleled in the Greek world, *Pales* must have been perceived as the original deity of Roman culture: her festival, the *Palilia* or *Parilia*, was celebrated on the 21st of April, i.e. on Rome's birthday (Ov. *fast.* 4.721–862). Her name appears to be connected with that of the early settlement on the Palatine hill, i.e. *Palatium* (Sol. 1.15); see further *Enc. Virg.* III, esp. p. 931, s.v. *Pale* (D. M. Cosi); also *Verg. Enc.* II, pp. 958–9, s.v. *Pales* (L. Fratantuono). **ipse...Apollo.** In his capacity as *Nomios*, Apollo protected places of pasture (νομοί), and his temporary experience as a herdsman (serving Admetus, king of Pherae in Thessaly) is men-tioned at *G.* 3.2; note that he also grazed the herds of king Laomedon (Hom. *Il.* 21.448). For the connection between Phoebus (Νόμιος) and livestock fertility cf. Callim. *hymn.* 2[*Ap.*].47–54. Here the god of poetry and music, whose prophetic abilities were emphasized in *E.* 4, is mentioned as a counterpoint to the Dionysian mystagogue (Daphnis) appearing at 5.29–31.

36–9. Daphnis' death causes turmoil in the natural world. V.'s description echoes the scenario that Daphnis himself foretold in his last Theocritean words: 'Now you brambles will bear violets, and so will you thorns [νῦν ἴα μὲν φορέοιτε βάτοι, φορέοιτε δ' ἄκανθαι], / and let the fair narcissus bloom on the juniper. / Let everything be changed, and the pine tree bear pears, / since Daphnis is dying' (*id.* 1.132–5). The idea that nature is barren when the beloved one is absent (cf. *id.* 8.41–8; *E.* 7.55–6) is also in the background. Becoming wild is to the fields what bodily negligence (*squalor, sordes*, vel sim.) is to humans in ancient ritual practice: a sign of mourning, quite the opposite of the miraculous luxuriance which accompanied the birth and growth of the *puer* in *E.* 4.18–30 and 37–45, and which will also accompany the appearance of the *sidus Iulium* at 9.46–50n.; cf. Bion, *epit. Adon.* 76 ὡς τῆνος τέθνακε καὶ ἄνθεα παντ' ἐμαράνθη. The cessation of plant life during winter was interpreted, especially in the Eleusinian cult, as nature's response to the demise of Persephone (see e.g. Eur. *Hel.* 1327–37; cf., dif-ferently, Sen. *Phaedr.* 469–74; Apul. *met.* 5.28.5). At Rome, the struggle against a famine is said to have led to the introduction of the Dionysian cult, along with

268   ECLOGUE 5

that of Demeter and Kore (see *E.* 5.30n.). In the difficult aftermath of Philippi, the city of Rome experienced multiple periods of scarcity, particularly due to the naval blockade instituted by Sextus Pompey: cf. Suet. *Aug.* 16.1; 70.2; Appian. *bell. civ.* 5.15 (60); 67–8 (280–9); 143 (596); Cass. Di. 48.18.1. In V.'s pastoral book, this may be the passage that most displays the poet's thorough competence in agricultural and botanical matters. It echoes Theocritean models like *id.* 5.128–31, and shows the potential of a theme (barrenness) which will be further developed in the first book of the *Georgics*.

36 grandia...hordea. The 'great barleys', in the sense of the largest and finest barley grains, produced in large quantities and specifically selected for sowing, in keeping with the practice described at *G.* 1.197–9. The use of the so-called poetic plural (e.g. *pectora* for *pectus*) in the case of a common agricultural term (cf. also *G.* 1.210 *serite hordea campis* and *Aen.* 4.405–6 *grandia...frumenta*) must have perplexed several ancient readers, since *hordeum* is generally used in the singular: Quintilian, *inst.* 1.5.16, considers it a solecism. Soon, it seems, V.'s line was parodied by the hexameter *hordea qui dixit superest ut tritica dicat* 'whoever said *hordea*—all he needs is to say *tritica* [i.e. the plural of *triticum*: wheat, the most valuable grain]'. Servius Dan. *ad G.* 1.210, attributes the line to Bavius and Maevius, whereas Cledonius, *gramm.* V, p. 43, 2 K., ascribes it to Cornificius Gallus (distinct from the poet and orator Q. Cornificius, Cicero's friend: *Enc. Virg.* III, p. 808b, s.v. *obtrectatores* [W. Görler]); cf. *ThlL* VI.3.2966.60–2967.8. Here the plural may further be justified by the echo of agricultural mottoes, such as the old one quoted by Macrobius, *Sat.* 5.20.18: *hiberno puluere, uerno luto, grandia farra, camille, metes.*

37 infelix lolium et steriles nascuntur auenae. Albeit producing ears, the darnel (or ryegrass) is not edible; rather, it is a type of unwanted weed. Hence the epithet *infelix*, 'barren', which probably belonged (in a specific, agricultural sense) to Cato's language, as can be inferred from Paul. Fest. p. 81 L. *felices arbores Cato dixit quae fructum ferunt, infelices quae non ferunt* (cf. *G.* 2.314 *infelix...oleaster*). It was deemed harmful to human eyes: Ov. *fast.* 1.691 *careant loliis oculos uitiantibus agri.* Here it is coupled with wild oats (*steriles...auenae*), as in *G.* 1.153–4 *inter...nitentia culta / infelix lolium et steriles dominantur auenae* (cf. Ov. *fast.* 1.691–2, just quoted). That darnel and similar plants could sprout from deteriorating wheat or barley was hypothesized by Theophrastus, *hist. plant.* 8.8.3, who nevertheless allowed the benefit of the doubt (cf. also *hist. plant.* 2.4.1, as well as Plin. *nat.* 18.149). Here, however, V. does not necessarily subscribe to such a view, and his formulation may simply hint at replacement (cf. 5.38 *pro...pro* 'in place of').

38 pro molli uiola, pro purpureo narcisso. The two flowers, filling the entire line along with their epithets, feature in the Theocritean model (*id.* 1.132–3 [see 5.36–9n.]); they appeared together in *E.* 2.47–8n., among the beautiful flowers offered by the Nymphs to Alexis, but now they must yield to troublesome thorny plants: *carduus et spinis...paliurus acutis* (39). For a partial reworking, within a

ECLOGUE 5   269

similar rhythmic and rhetorical structure, cf. *Aen.* 11.69 *seu mollis uiolae seu languentis hyacinthi.* Note the spondaic fifth foot, which only appears three times in the *E.*: here and at 4.49; 7.53 (with a Greek noun). A reading *purpurea*, presupposing a fem. *narcissus* (as in Theocr. *id.* 1.133; Meleag. *Anth. Pal.* 5.147, 1–2 = *HE* 4236–7 G.-P.) seems to be attested by Diomedes, *gramm.* I, p. 453.34–6 K. However, the masculine form transmitted by the manuscripts and the entire exegetical tradition (cf. also *Anth. Lat.* 11.26 R.) seems preferable here: the flower's name probably echoes the misfortunes of the mythical boy (note e.g. Ov. *fast.* 5.225 *tu quoque nomen habes cultos, Narcisse, per hortos;* cf. *G.* 4.160 *narcissi lacrimam*, with Serv. ad loc.). The similar term *hyacinthus* (which can be either masculine or feminine in Greek; mostly feminine in poetry, e.g. Theocr. *id.* 10.28) is masculine at *G.* 4.183. The noun *flos*, at any rate, is always masculine, and the phrase *purpureos...flores* is quite frequent in V. (*G.* 4.54; *Aen.* 6.884; 9.435 *purpureus...flos*; 12.413–14 *flore...purpureo*, referring to the 'pubescent' flower *dictamus*).

39 carduus. This plant (the thistle) is very common in the Italian countryside, and is conspicuous for its 'hairy' appearance, which makes it an unmistakable sign of neglect in the landscape; cf. *G.* 1.151–2 *segnisque horreret in aruis / carduus*, as well as Plin. *nat.* 18.153, where the plant is numbered, along with the darnel, among the 'plagues' of agriculture (though it is actually edible if cooked). **spinis surgit paliurus acutis.** The garland thorn, or Jerusalem thorn (*Paliurus australis*), is a rapidly growing plant, used in building boundary hedges (Colum. 11.3.4) but harmful to agriculture. The same name also denotes 'Christ's thorn', or *Zizyphus spina Christi* (cf. probably Plin. *nat.* 13.111 *Cyrenaica regio loton suae postponit paliuro*; see also Theophr. *hist. plant.* 4.3.3). The Greek equivalent, παλίουρος, is found in Theocr. *id.* 24.89 (where its gender is unclear, as here: usually masc., as in Theophr. *hist. plant.* 1.3.2; fem. in Gemin. *Anth. Pal.* 9.414.1–2 [= *GPh* 2354–5 G.-P.]). The name is glossed by the abl. *spinis...acutis*, suggesting the image of a menacing creature, which rises up (*surgit*) and appears ready to strike (in Greek, compound nouns featuring οὐρά, 'tail', may denote e.g. snakes, such as the μόλουρος in Nicand. *ther.* 491). For an echo cf. Colum. 10.22 *spinisque ferat paliuron acutis.*

40–4. After the picture of barrenness presented at ll. 36–9, leaves and branches suddenly appear, only to be thrown to the ground and into water springs. Mopsus thus goes on to outline the last honours paid to Daphnis (and requested by Daphnis himself: 5.41). They are imaginatively described as happening in the present moment.

40 spargite humum foliis, inducite fontibus umbras. The 'shedding of the leaves' to the ground (φυλλοβολία), symbolizing human frailty, is a codified gesture of mourning: cf. *Aen.* 6.883–4 *manibus date lilia plenis / purpureos spargam flores.* Flower garlands are used to decorate a tomb in e.g. Leon. *Anth. Pal.* 7.657.7–8 = *HE* 2068–9 G.-P. The covering of water springs with branches

270   ECLOGUE 5

(*umbras*) must also be interpreted in a funerary sense, and therefore kept distinct from such rituals as the *Fontanalia* or *Fontinalia*, held on the 13th of October, during which the Romans honoured fountains and wells by throwing flower wreaths into them (Varr. *ling.* 6.22). The two actions (*spargite...inducite*) produce an impressive visual effect: earth and water are covered with branches and leaves. Both will reappear, and both will be ascribed to Menalcas, in *E.* 9.19–20.

42 et tumulum facite, et tumulo. For the pointed polyptoton cf. *Aen.* 6.380 *et statuent tumulum et tumulo sollemnia mittent* (for Palinurus), similarly alliterating on the /t/ sound.

43–4. The two final lines of Mopsus' song include Daphnis' self-epitaph, which echoes and varies *id.* 1.120–1: Δάφνις ἐγὼν ὅδε τῆνος ὁ τὰς βόας ὧδε νομεύων, / Δάφνις ὁ τὼς ταύρως καὶ πόρτιας ὧδε ποτίσδων 'I am that Daphnis who here pastured his cattle, / that Daphnis who here watered heifers and bulls' (in Theocritus, the two lines appear as autonomous, framed as they are by the refrain, even though they do not conclude a speech). The farewell is now replaced by survival in the *siluae*, in the form of the burial mound, and in the heavens, among the stars (*hinc usque ad sidera* anticipating 5.51–2). Self-epitaphs are traditionally featured in poets' biographies, being considered as the last fruit of their ingenuity (V. himself is said to have dictated his own: *Mantua me genuit...*). They also play an important role in Roman love-elegy, as e.g. in Prop. 2.1.78 (at the end of a poem) *huic misero fatum dura puella fuit*; 13.35–6; Tib. 1.3.55–6; [Tib.] 3.2.29–30 (Lygdamus' epitaph, at the end of a poem); Ov. *her.* 2.147–8 (at the end of a poem); *trist.* 3.3.73–6. Considering that Mopsus' poem has been carved on the bark of a beech tree, we are dealing with an 'inscription within the inscription': for a similar phenomenon cf. Calp. *ecl.* 3.89–91 (as well as 3.43–4).

43 hinc usque ad sidera notus. This type of hyperbole occurs in Homer (cf. *Od.* 9.20 καί μευ κλέος οὐρανὸν ἵκει) and will reappear in *Aen.* 1.379 *fama super aethera notus*. Here, however, the precise spatial specification surpasses the Theocritean model (*hinc*: a point of departure, unlike the double ὧδε in *id.* 1.120–1 [see above, 5.43–4n.]), takes up the opening *astra* (5.23), and anticipates Menalcas' future songs. Hence there is a gradual progression from the *astra... crudelia* invoked by Daphnis' mother to Menalcas' *astra*, among which Daphnis is numbered (5.51–2), until the deified Daphnis sees *sidera* under his feet (5.57): these stars will be the recipients of the joyful cries coming from the whole pastoral world (5.62). Unlike *astrum* (5.51–2n.), the term *sidus* is used in the *E.* to denote physical objects, which are pictured as motionless and hugely distant from the Earth: cf. *E.* 5.62; 6.84; 9.29 (for the connection with *sido* cf. Varr. *ling.* 7.14 *sidera quae quasi insidunt*; see also Mart. Cap. 8.817: most probably an instance of folk etymology).

44 formosi pecoris custos, formosior ipse. The line, written in terse lapidary style, is memorable for its bipartite structure: the same adj. is used twice, first in the positive and then in the comparative degree. Note the semantic wordplay featuring this adj., so frequent in the *E.* (unlike *pulcher*); originally referring to livestock, *formosus* comes to denote human physical beauty (hence the seamless transition from the *pecus* to the *custos*: cf. 1.5n.).

45–55. The interlude between the two songs is an exchange of compliments between Menalcas and Mopsus. Menalcas expresses his appreciation for the younger singer's composition, then makes it clear that he wants to adopt its theme. Mopsus immediately understands which poem Menalcas is referring to, and praises it.

45–7. Menalcas' aesthetic judgement is expressed through images typical of pastoral poetry: song, water, and sweetness were associated with one another in the eulogistic song of *id.* 1.7–8 ἅδιον, ὦ ποιμήν, τὸ τεὸν μέλος ἢ τὸ καταχές / τῆν' ἀπὸ τᾶς πέτρας καταλείβεται ὑψόθεν ὕδωρ 'more sweetly, shepherd, does your song flow than / that water pouring down from the rock on high' (this is the goatherd's first speech, addressed to Thyrsis: thus, we can infer, Mopsus equals his Theocritean predecessor on the subject of Daphnis). See further *id.* 8.78 ἁδὺ δὲ τῶ θέρεος παρ' ὕδωρ ῥέον αἰθριοκοιτεῖν 'it is sweet, during the summer, to lie down in the open air by the flowing water' (cf. also *id.* 8.82), as well as Catull. 68.57–72; Lucr. 2.29–30 (5.1392–3). Sweetness is particularly well suited to an 'elegiac' song mourning the loss of a pastoral hero. Mopsus, in turn, will express enthusiasm for Menalcas' song, which celebrates Daphnis' deification.

45–6 Tale... / ...quale...quale. Three coordinated neuters ('such a thing'), cf. *E.* 3.80 and 82: thus, there is no need for agreement with the noun *sopor* (46) or substantivized infinitive *restinguere* (47); cf., in a context of evident Virgilian reminiscences, Prop. 2.34.79–80 *tale facis carmen docta testudine, quale / Cynthius* etc.

45 diuine poeta. The poet is ἔνθεος, i.e. animated by divine 'enthusiasm'. For the clausula cf. *E.* 10.17 (as well as 6.67 *diuino carmine pastor*); see further 3.37n., as well as *id.* 7.89 θεῖε Κομάτα; 9.41 τῶ θείω Λιτυέρσα; Cic. *diu.* 1.54; Hor. *ars* 400; cf. also *Catal.* 15.3; *ThlL* V.1.1624.24–5. In the *E.*, the Greek term *poeta* occurs here for the first time: it especially denotes technical versification skills—hence its opposition to the more solemn term *uates.* Cf. esp. 7.25 and 28; 9.32 and 34. V. will apply it to himself towards the end of the book (*E.* 10.70); cf. also *G.* 3.90 *Grai...poetae* (the only other occurrence in V. after the *E.*).

46 per aestum. In other words, during the summer's heat (*id.* 8.78 [see above, 5.45–7n.] τῶ θέρεος). Corydon's song, which in 5.86 will be revealed to be Menalcas' work, started with the description of a burning, sun-drenched landscape (cf. *E.* 2.10 *rapido...aestu*).

48 nec calamis solum... sed uoce magistrum. Excellence in the use of *calami*, with which Menalcas credited Mopsus in the incipit (5.2), is now coupled with excellence in singing (i.e. also in composing lyrics). The context seems to make it clear that the *magister* is Daphnis himself, as we may also infer from 5.51 *Daphninque tuum* (for Daphnis' 'teaching' skills cf. *id.* 8.85). Mopsus has just quoted two lines (5.43–4) which may have been composed by Daphnis. No

272   ECLOGUE 5

wonder, given the intensely metapoetic context, that Servius opts here for an allegorical interpretation: *uidetur allegoria quasi ad Theocritum et Vergilium respicere*
'the allegory seems to allude to Theocritus and Virgil'. **aequiperas.** The verb, an
old-fashioned term, lends an archaic flavour to the older Menalcas' language, as
he points out that Mopsus has equalled his teacher. Relatively frequent in
Republican Latin (Plautus, Ennius, Pacuvius, then Nepos and Livy), the verb is
avoided in Augustan poetry, with the exception of Ov. *Pont.* 2.2.92; 5.44. It
reappears in archaizing Latin, e.g. Fronto, p. 5.4 v. d. Hout[2] (cf. also Suet. *Aug.*
94.15), and occurs often in late antique authors: cf. *ThlL* I.1011–13.

49 fortunate puer. This type of *makarismos* also appears at *E.* 1.45 *fortunate senex*:
it is reworked here, featuring a polar opposition (*puer* in lieu of *senex*). **alter ab illo.**
The term *alter* frames the 'succession' almost in terms of identity (the 'second'
between two), with greater emphasis than e.g. at *E.* 2.38 or, in a different context,
Theocr. *id.* 1.3 (cf., for instance, Hor. *sat.* 2.3.193 *Aiax, heros ab Achille secundus*).

50 uicissim. 'In my turn', as in *E.* 3.28. The exchange will only include two
speeches, one for each poet (cf. *id.* 6 and 9).

51–2 tollemus ad astra; /…ad astra feremus. The repetition, embellished by the
chiastic structure (note also anaphora and *complexio*: *Daphninque…Daphnin…
Daphnis*), highlights the intentional ambiguity. Menalcas will bring Daphnis 'to
the stars' not only through his praise but also because he will sing of Daphnis'
deification (see 5.57n.; cf. 5.43n.). A truly 'physical' removal of Julius Caesar (i.e.
of his soul) from the earth is found at Ov. *met.* 15.846 (Venus) *caelestibus intulit
astris*; cf. also Callim. *aet.* fr. 110.55–6 Pf. = 213 Mass. = 110.55–56 Hard. (Catull.
66.55–6); *iamb.* 16 (?), fr. 228.5–6 Pf. Poetry is endowed with an Orphic, magical
quality that allows it to act upon things (cf. *E.* 6.62–3n.). Note the strong alliteration (5.51) of dental sounds, /d/ and /t/. For the typically pastoral repetition of
Daphnis' name cf. esp. *id.* 9.1–2. A trochaic caesura appears after *feremus*; here, as
in 4.16, it is unusually not accompanied by the hephthemimeral type. The term
astrum, of Greek origin (cf. 5.23), is first attested in Cic. *Arat.* 162; fr. 32.4 Soub.,
and then enters common usage. Here it is closely connected with the divine
theme of catasterism (εἰς τὰ ἄστρα τιθέναι vel sim.; cf. *ThlL* II.977.17–43, s.v.
astrum); cf. also *E.* 9.47–8. On the equivalent Latin term, *sidus*, see 5.43n.

52 amauit nos quoque Daphnis. This final assertion prompts the reader to
recall the Theocritean past of *id.* 8 and 9: in the former, Menalcas took part in a
fair contest against Daphnis, who defeated him to his great sorrow (the sorrow of
'a wife tamed by her husband': *E.* 8.91), whereas the latter featured a gift given to
both of them by the anonymous narrator (*E.* 9.22–7). Daphnis' love for Menalcas
must have been narrated in Hermesianax fr. 2 Pow. = 8 Light. (= *schol.* Theocr. *id.*
8.53–6d, p. 210 Wend.), perhaps alluded to by V. Their contest was featured in a
satyr play, *Daphnis* or *Lityerses*, by the Alexandrian tragic poet Sositheus: *TrGF*,
I.99, frr. 1a–3, pp. 270–2 Sn. In the present line, an almost purely dactylic hexameter, note the coincidence between ictus and word-accent (but cf. *E.* 1.70n.).

ECLOGUE 5   273

54 puer ipse. The deceased Daphnis, a champion of pastoral song, is here portrayed by Mopsus as a mythical, eternal 'boy'. Note the analogy between teacher and pupil, each referred to as *puer* (cf. *E.* 5.49): one is the 'mirror image' of the other, *alter ab illo*; for a similar structure, cf. *E.* 3.12–14 (mention of Daphnis followed by *puer*: 3.14n.). The epithet *puer* in reference to Daphnis sets limits to any allegorical interpretation: he is an ageless, divine figure, but also a juvenile *puer*, a model of immortality which is clearly distinct from the historical person of a specific ruler (i.e. Julius Caesar, who was murdered before turning sixty). Correspondingly, in *E.* 1, Tityrus' mature age prevents interpreters from directly equating him with the 30-year-old V. (see 1.28n.; 46n.). **cantari dignus.** The construction (*dignus* + inf.), which Mopsus will use again at 5.89, is paralleled by Catull. 68.131–2 *concedere digna / lux mea*. It will often reappear in poetry: cf. Hor. *sat.* 1.10.72; *carm.* 3.21.6; Tib. 2.6.43; *ThlL* V.1.1152.32–70.

55 Stimichon. Mopsus asserts that he already knows the song that Menalcas is about to sing (*ista...carmina*), but Stimichon's name is unfamiliar to the pre-Virgilian pastoral tradition (significantly, a phonetic connection with Echo is noted by the *schol. Bern.* ad loc.: *quasi stimulante Echo*; cf. also Philarg./Philagr. ad loc.). It will reappear in Calp. *ecl.* 6.83 (not far from a Mopsus, mentioned at 6.85); 7.9; 7.13. Here V. may simply aim at a realistic effect by evoking people and events that cannot all be obvious to the reader. However, Mopsus and Stimichon could stand for members of a (new?) poetic 'school', which honours its forefather Daphnis while distancing itself from the established (Theocritean) pastoral tradition. While Menalcas' song is said to have previously been composed (*iampridem*), it strikingly matches the total line number and inner subdivisions of Mopsus' song (cf. *E.* 5.56–80n.). Note the temporal opposition between the two songs: Mopsus asserts that his poem has been composed not long ago (*nuper*: cf. 5.13n.), though he is the first to sing. A song by Menalcas quoted in *E.* 9 juxtaposes Daphnis and the *sidus Iulium*, i.e. the celestial symbol of Julius Caesar's deification (9.46–50).

56–80. The twenty-five lines that Menalcas devotes to Daphnis appear to be divided into three major sections, following a structural pattern typical of hymns and appropriate for a god: the first (nine lines, 5.56–64) describes the joy spread in the pastoral world by Daphnis' deification; the second (eleven lines, 5.65–75) outlines the honours paid to him; the third (five lines, 5.76–80) establishes the cult of Daphnis for the future, featuring the propitious involvement of the 'new' god himself (5.76). Mopsus' song had an analogous structure: cf. 5.20–44n.; further particular correspondences can be detected between 5.20–3 and 56–9, 5.24–8 and 60–4, 5.29–35 and 65–71, 5.36–9 and 72–5, 5.40–4 and 76–80. The Caesarian allegory continues to play a role, as is testified to by Serv. Dan. *ad 56 et quibusdam uidetur per allegoriam Caesarem dicere, qui primus diuinos honores meruit et diuus appellatus est* 'some think that [V.] refers allegorically to Caesar, who first earned divine honours and was proclaimed *diuus*'. The new cult of Daphnis, as described

274   ECLOGUE 5

by Menalcas, contaminates two divine models, held together in a subtle equilibrium: Apollo (5.66) and Bacchus-Dionysus (5.79; but cf. also 5.69n.; 73n.). This must have been clear to some ancient readers: Servius (*ad* 5.66) mentions a syncretistic doctrine combining Phoebus (the sun god), Liber, and Apollo into a single figure.

56–7 Candidus… / …Daphnis. Mopsus' opening *exstinctum* is countered by Menalcas' *candidus*, immediately pointing to Daphnis' attainment of divine status. The epithet, in fact, is attributed by V. to (female) deities in *E.* 2.46 (the nymph Nais) and again in 7.38 (a Nereid, Galatea). Cf. also *Aen.* 8.138 (Maia) and 8.608 (Venus); Hor. *carm.* 1.18.11; Ov. *fast.* 3.772. The adj. is also used of celestial bodies, as in *G.* 1.217 (the constellation Taurus) and *Aen.* 7.8 (the moon). In Theocritus, *epigr.* 2.1 G., Daphnis is called λευκόχρως 'white-skinned', and here Mopsus has just called him *puer* (5.54); cf. 2.16 *quamuis tu candidus esses* (n.). Thus, Daphnis transfers a feature of his mortal beauty to the celestial world. The accusatives framing 5.20 are now countered in 5.56–7 by the nominatives of both epithet and noun, hinting at the hero's new, superhuman life. Daphnis' name appears at the very end of the couplet, after a long (syntactical) wait, with quasi-triumphal emphasis. While Mopsus' song started where Theocritus' Thyrsis ended, Menalcas now starts exactly where Mopsus left off.

56 limen Olympi. The 'threshold' hints at an architectural perception of Olympus' 'palace' (cf. *Aen.* 10.1 *domus Olympi*), importantly paralleled by Theocritus' *id.* 17.17–21; but cf. also Lucretius' 'sublime' vision at 3.18–22 (cf. below, 5.57n.).

57 sub pedibusque uidet nubes et sidera. The verb *uidet* echoes and varies *miratur* (56), while also highlighting Daphnis' survival in divine form, seemingly in an astronomical context analogous to Julius Caesar's deification: cf., in reference to *Divus Iulius*, Prop. 4.6.59 *at pater Idalio miratur Caesar ab astro*; Ov. *met.* 15.840–2 (esp. 842 *diuus ab excelsa prospectet Iulius aede*); 846 quoted above, 5.51–2n. In *E.* 9.46–50 Caesar's star, as Daphnis is prompted to observe, causes joy and pleasure in the natural world (9.48 *segetes gauderent frugibus*; cf. here 58 *alacris…uoluptas*). For a similar wording, though in a totally different context, cf. the hyperbole at Prop. 1.8.43 *nunc mihi summa licet contingere sidera plantis*. For the absolute use of the verb, denoting full possession of one's (vital) faculties, cf. Plaut. *Mil.* 331 *mihi ego uideo, mihi ego sapio*; Ter. *Heaut.* 244 *ego uero audio nunc demum et uideo et ualeo*; see also Caecil. *com.* fr. 175 R.[3] *quod diu uiuendo multa quae non uolt uidet* (the formulaic phrase *uiuus uidensque* appears e.g. at Lucr. 3.1046; cf. Hom. *Od.* 16.439). In Greek, the verb βλέπειν is used similarly, as e.g. in Aesch. *Ag.* 677; Men. *Sam.* 213; cf. *E.* 6.21 *iamque uidenti*. The 'sublime' gaze assimilates Daphnis to the *puer* in *E.* 4.50 (*aspice*), and partially echoes philosophical and cosmological visions, especially the Epicurean one (Lucr. 1.74; 2.9; cf. also 3.27–8 *sub pedibus… / … diuina uoluptas*). Here, however, the *uoluptas* is the joy spread among the inhabitants of the woods. Daphnis, like Lucretius' Epicurus or the kings praised in Hellenistic encomia, is a creator of joy and prosperity.

ECLOGUE 5 275

58 alacris...uoluptas. The phrase is somewhat paradoxical, since the epithet *alacris* hints at intense activity or industriousness (e.g. in warfare: after the *E.*, V. only uses the adj. in the *Aeneid*, as at *Aen.* 10.729 *alacer Mezentius*), or even joyous excitement; cf. *OLD*[2], p. 102, s.v. *alacer* 2. Here, however, it modifies *uoluptas*, a term generally belonging to the sphere of *otium* (see below, 5.61n.). As a result, this 'pleasure', due to its liveliness (a 'dynamic' pleasure, in Epicurean terms), distracts both gods and humans from their usual activities in the pastoral world. The first to be mentioned is a god, Pan (5.59), normally prone to enthusiasm and exultation: cf. *Hymn. Hom.* 19[*Pan.*].2 φιλόκροτον; 24 λιγυρῇσιν ἀγαλλόμενος φρένα μολπαῖς; 47 Πᾶνα δέ μιν καλέεσκον, ὅτι φρένα πᾶσιν ἔτερψε (where Pan's name is connected to πᾶς, παντός 'all'; he was also identified with the absolute 'Everything': *Hymn. Orph.* 11.1; Cornut. *nat. deor.* 27; Macr. *Sat.* 1.22.3). Unrestrained, universal joy was prophesied by the singer of *E.* 4.52: *uenturo laetantur ut omnia saeclo* (cf. here 62 *laetitia*); cf. 9.48 *segetes gauderent frugibus* (among the effects of Caesar's star).

59 Dryadasque puellas. Nymphs of the woods, to which they are connected etymologically (δρῦς 'oak': Serv. Dan. *ad G.* 1.11); cf. above, 5.58 *siluas*; *G.* 3.40 *Dryadum siluas saltusque*. For a similar clausula cf. *G.* 1.11 *Dryadesque puellae*. For a particular variety of Dryads, the *Hamadryades*, see *E.* 10.62n. The threefold correlation of *-que* also appears at 4.51 and 6.32 (cf. 8.22n.).

60 nec lupus...nec retia. The usual rural hostilities are suspended: the predator stops ambushing its prey, as was prophesied in *E.* 4.22 about the Golden Age inaugurated by the *puer*. Note also that hunting, an inevitably cruel human activity (for the use of nets in hunting cf. 3.75), would hardly fit into the context of Daphnis' deification, full of sacral purity; cf. *Perv. Ven.*, esp. 38–9 *cede, uirgo Delia, / ut nemus sit incruentum de ferinis stragibus*. The god Pan, though he played a subordinate role compared to Artemis-Diana, was in charge of hunting (cf. *Hymn. Hom.* 19[*Pan.*].12–16; Theocr. *id.* 7.106–8, with scholia ad loc., p. 104 Wend.); now he is overtaken and rendered inactive by *uoluptas*. Note a further similarity with Mopsus' song, in which a series of negatives (three: 5.24–6) appeared after the first four lines.

61 dolum meditantur. The phrase echoes and amplifies 5.60 *insidias*. For the idea of 'deception' cf. 4.31 *priscae uestigia fraudis*; 4.42 *nec...discet mentiri*. **amat bonus otia Daphnis.** *Otium*, a precondition of tranquillity and song in the pastoral world, was connected to a deity (and mentioned as his gift) at the outset of the pastoral book, *E.* 1.6 *deus nobis haec otia fecit* (an instance of 'poetic plural', as here). Now, however, Daphnis' 'virtue' is emphasized: *bonus* here has its full original force of 'valiant' and 'helpful', all the more obvious, by way of contrast, in its connection with *otia*. Cf. *Aen.* 9.572 *hic iaculo bonus*, as well as the renowned *bonum agricolam bonumque colonum* in Cat. *agr.* pr. 2; see further *E.* 5.65n.

62–3 ipsi...uoces ad sidera iactant / intonsi montes. The phenomenon is described in Lucretian terms: cf. Lucr. 2.327–8 *clamoreque montes / icti reiectant* *uoces ad sidera mundi.* V. is not talking about echo, which Epicurean physics could explain mechanistically: here the mountains themselves seem to be animated and to possess voices (for the use of *ipse* cf. 1.38-9n.). The epithet *intonsi* was interpreted by Servius in the sense of *siluosi, incaedui*: this sylvan landscape is akin to the *pinifer...Maenalus* (10.14-15), the mountain where Pan dwells. Note that *intonsus* clearly insists on the personification, given that the term is generally used of human beings or deities (*ThlL* VII.2.29.57-30.51): the same is true of the trees' 'heads' at *Aen.* 9.681-2 *quercus intonsa...caelo / attollunt capita* (a 'pastoral' use of the term, in reference to a sheep, at *Aen.* 12.170). For the resounding divine name (Iacchus/Bromius) and the mountain's 'agitation', cf. Eur. *Bacch.* 725-7. The idea of 'speaking nature', previously mentioned by Mopsus in a mournful context (*E.* 5.27-8), reappears in Menalcas' song with celebratory overtones. Note, in ll. 62-4, the typically pastoral polyptoton in asyndeton: *ipsi... / ...ipsae... / ipsa*; cf. 1.38-9; see also 4.21-3 (where, however, the transmitted text may be corrupt).

64 deus, deus ille, Menalca! Cf. Lucr. 5.8 *deus ille fuit, deus, inclute Memmi* (of Epicurus), as well as Hor. *epod.* 14.6; note also the opening of V.'s collection (*E.* 1.6-7, esp. 1.7n.). Calpurnius Siculus will describe Tityrus-V. in similar terms: Calp. *ecl.* 4.70 *est, fateor Meliboee, deus*. Mountains, cliffs, and woods address Menalcas to give him the exciting news of Daphnis' deification. The old singer's role in the deification itself is implicitly acknowledged. Note also the close relationship between nature and the poet-herdsman: Menalcas can 'listen' to what nature tells him.

65 sis bonus o felixque tuis! A formula typically used in prayer, as e.g. at *Aen.* 1.330 *sis felix nostrumque leues, quaecumque, laborem* (to Venus) and 12.646-7 (to the Manes). For *bonus* used of a propitious deity cf. Hor. *carm.* 4.2.38.

65-6 en quattuor aras: / ecce duas tibi, Daphni, duas...Phoebo. The establishment of Daphnis' cult, featuring a precise number of altars (and a precise attribution thereof), appears in Theocritus' Dionysian *id.* 26: 'they set up twelve altars, / three dedicated to Semele, nine to Dionysus' (5-6); cf. e.g. *Hymn. Hom.* 5[*Ven.*].100-1 σοὶ δ' ἐγώ... / βωμὸν ποιήσω. Here, however, Daphnis is honoured by his (numerical) equalization with Apollo (hence the need for a distinction, underscored by *altaria*: *E.* 5.66n.). As a matter of fact, the cult of Julius Caesar came to be placed side by side with (if not above) that of Apollo, especially during the month named after the dictator: Weinstock (1971, pp. 156-7). Note the use of *ecce* with acc., normal in Plautus, but obsolete in V.'s time—here, perhaps, it is facilitated by the preceding *en*: K.-S., I, p. 273. For the dedication of a 'pair' of altars, with similar phrasing, cf. *Aen.* 5.639-40 *en quattuor arae / Neptuno*; also 3.305 *geminas...sacrauerat aras*.

66 duas altaria Phoebo. The noun *altaria*, used as an apposition to 5.65 *aras* (understood here), points to an architectural and functional distinction: while an *ara* may simply be a space devoted to the performance of rural sacrifices

ECLOGUE 5   277

(esp. bloody ones: cf. the lamb at *E.* 1.7), *altaria* must hint at a more elevated structure, on which offerings were burned (see 1.43n.). That kind of elevation suits a god such as Apollo (on his inescapable primacy, but in the musical domain, cf. above, 5.9n.). This explains why the apposition *altaria* is placed next to the proper noun *Phoebo*: the singer thereby establishes an 'anti-hybristic' divine hierarchy. Servius, however, goes too far and posits a privileged connection between *altaria* and the Olympian gods: *altaria uero esse supernorum tantum deorum, quae ab altitudine constant esse nominata.* Note the folk etymology *altaria-altus*: cf. Paul. Fest. p. 27 L. *altaria ab altitudine dicta, quod antiqui diis superis in aedificiis a terra exaltatis sacra faciebant*; schol. Stat. *Theb.* 4.459; Isid. *orig.* 15.4.14; *ThlL* I.1725.41–63; *Enc. Virg.* I, p. 120, s.v. *altari* (E. Montanari). The literary sources, along with some artistic and archaeological testimonies, confirm that the term *altaria* denotes elevated and potentially movable structures, which could be 'added' to the horizontal surface of the *ara* (Serv. Dan. '*altaria*' *eminentia ararum*). Their function is eminently symbolic, since the burnt offerings (frankincense, wine, water, milk, honey, grains, etc.) send smoke towards the sky. Yet they also have a practical function: they ensure that smoke and fire go up rather than spreading elsewhere. The distinction between the two objects (and their functions) is especially clear in Lucan. 3.404 *structae diris altaribus arae*; [Quint.] *decl. mai.* 12.26, p. 261.6 Håk. *quod aris altaria non imposuimus*; Solin. 8.6; note also Tac. *ann.* 16.31.1 [*Seruilia*] *altaria et aram complexa*; cf. F. G. Cavallero, *Arae e altaria: una possibile differenza morfologica*, in *ArchClass* 68 (2017), pp. 589–601; *Arae sacrae. Tipi, nomi, atti, funzioni e rappresentazioni degli altari romani*, Rome 2018, esp. pp. 53–64. In the dense, compressed syntactical structure at 5.65–6, V. first mentions four *arae* (flat, horizontal surfaces) then specifies that two are for Daphnis and two, with added *altaria*, for Apollo.

    67 **pocula bina...quotannis.** A 'pair' of cups, full of milk: the distributive adj. suggests that, during every ritual performance, Daphnis will be offered two cups, considered as a single whole (for *pocula* coming in pairs cf. *E.* 3.36–43n.). V. perhaps implies that each of the two altars dedicated to Daphnis (5.66; cf. 5.68 *tibi*) will be assigned a pair of cups, but only one oil-vessel (hence *bina*, as opposed to the cardinal adj. *duo* at 5.68, describing the vessels as two distinct objects). The bloodless sacrifice is coherent with the idea expressed at 5.60–1. For the pairing of milk and oil (offered to the Nymphs) cf. *id.* 5.53–4 στασῶ [cf. here 5.68 *statuam*] δὲ κρατῆρα μέγαν λευκοῖο γάλακτος / ταῖς Νύμφαις, στασῶ δὲ καὶ ἁδέος ἄλλον ἐλαίω (note the mixing vessels, though different from V.'s). **nouo...lacte.** Fresh milk, as in *E.* 2.22. **quotannis.** In the sense of 'every year', 'always' (1.42n.; cf. below, 5.74 *semper*; 5.78; note also the summarizing *quotannis* at 5.79). The feast, however, seems to be composed of two rituals, one taking place in the summer, the other in the winter (5.70; multiple ritual occasions are also hinted at in 5.74–5). It is harder to imagine that a single annual ritual may take place in different seasons.

278 ECLOGUE 5

69 et multo...hilarans conuiuia Baccho. The focus is now on the banquets that follow the rituals in Daphnis' honour: Menalcas will enliven them with 'abundant Bacchus' (a common metonymy for wine, evoking the god himself). The idea that Dionysus must be honoured anyway, for one reason or another, in every season (to fight thirst during summers and cold during winters) is frequent in symposiastic literature: cf. the case of Alcaeus, observed by Athenaeus, 10.430a–c. Note that V. here stages an intersection between pastoral poetry and symposiastic practices, a Theocritean invention featured in *id.* 7 (esp. 63–85: cf. below, 5.72n.). This is the first occurrence of wine in the *E.*: wine is a distinctive element of lyric poetry, and is therefore significantly rare in V.'s pastoral book (note its mention at 6.15n., in a poem devoted to Silenus and his typical drunkenness). **in primis.** The phrase emphasizes Menalcas' personal enthusiasm—particularly related to the last type of 'liquid' that he is about to mention, following milk and honey (cf. also 5.71 *uina*). Wine is the lynchpin of the situation described in 5.69–73, and Menalcas could be specifically referring to the inaugural libations performed at the beginning of a banquet; cf. also *G.* 1.338 *in primis uenerare deos* (in a similarly festive context).

70 ante focum. The hearth, associated with feelings of protection, will reappear at *E.* 7.49. **si frigus erit; si messis.** The line's chiastic structure places *messis* in close proximity to *frigus*, i.e. winter's cold: *messis* stands for summer, the reaping season (*E.* 2.10). Cf. above, 5.67n. for the (potentially) biannual recurrence of the feast.

71 uina nouum...Ariusia nectar. Among Chian wines, all deemed to be excellent, those coming from Ariusia, a region in the north of the island, were particularly appreciated: according to Strabo, 14.1.35 (645), they were the best in Greece (cf. also Plin. *nat.* 14.73; Athen. 1.32f). New wine is offered in libations: cf. Hor. *carm.* 1.31.2–3 *de patera nouum / fundens liquorem*. But the drink is so delicious as to deserve the appositional epithet *nectar*, appropriate for a divine context (note the interlacing of epithets and nouns). Theocritus mentioned a specific variety of wine (Pteleatic) in *id.* 7.65. For wine and Bacchus in the *E.*, cf. 5.69n.

72 cantabunt mihi. Cf. *id.* 7.72–4 'Tityrus, next to me, will sing [ὁ δὲ Τίτυρος ἐγγύθεν ᾀσεῖ] / of how Daphnis the cowherd once fell in love with Xeneas, / and how the mountain suffered along with him' (*E.* 5.28n.). **Damoetas.** The reader is prompted to recall the Damoetas who competed against Menalcas in *E.* 3: he now returns as a singing and drinking companion. That Menalcas is familiar with the theme (and the text) of *E.* 3 will be shown in 5.87. In Theocritus' *id.* 6, a shepherd named Damoetas engaged in a friendly contest with Daphnis (thus, he conveniently replaces the Tityrus of *id.* 7, who sang the amours of Daphnis). **Lyctius Aegon.** A further echo of *E.* 3—particularly of its opening, where Damoetas' name was followed by Aegon's (the latter entrusted his flock to the former, at least occasionally: 3.2 *nuper mihi tradidit Aegon*). However, almost as a marker of distinction, Aegon is now called *Lyctius*, from *Lyctus* (Λύκτος/Λύττος), an important Dorian city in the north-eastern part of Crete. Already mentioned in Hom. *Il.* 2.647; 17.611 and Hes. *theog.* 477, the city is praised by Polybius, 4.54.6, as 'the oldest one' in Crete

ECLOGUE 5 279

(correspondingly, its inhabitants are universally acknowledged as 'the best among the Cretans'). Thus, the epithet must be considered as a learned synonym for 'Cretan' (cf. *Aen.* 3.401, where it is coupled with the *dux Meliboeus*, i.e. Philoctetes, from Melibea in Thessaly), perhaps with some Apollonian overtones: 'Lyctius' is applied to the god's bow in Callim. *hymn.* 2[*Ap.*].33 (note that the Cretans were renowned for their archery skills: see *E.* 10.59–60n.; for Lyctus cf. notably Pausan. 4.19.4), and Apollo was widely venerated in Crete; see further R. F. Willetts, *Cretan Cults and Festivals*, London 1962, pp. 256–71. Menalcas' choice of the epithet is doubtless explained by his taste for Callimachean *doctrina*; however, Theocritus broadened the horizon in *id.* 1 (where Chromis comes from Libya [24 Λιβύαθε]). Here, a more precise parallel is offered by *id.* 7.71–2 'two shepherds will play the *aulos* for me, one Acharnian, / the other Lycopean' (i.e. apparently, from Acharnae in Attica and Lycope in Aetolia: but cf. Hunter 1999, p. 173, ad loc.).

73 saltantis Satyros imitabitur Alphesiboeus. During the future banquet, a satyr-dance will be performed by a character whose name is not otherwise attested in the pre-Virgilian pastoral tradition (in *id.* 3.45, Alphesiboea is the daughter of Bias and Peiró, whose father is Neleus, king of Pylos; see further Gow 1952, II, p. 74, ad loc.). Like Meliboeus' name (*E.* 1.6n.), *Alphesiboeus* possesses great bucolic relevance, since it literally means 'one who acquires many oxen' (cf. Hom. *Il.* 18.593). As such, it suits a Dionysian singer (the prize for dithyrambic poets was the meat of sacrificed oxen: Pind. *Ol.* 13.19; Ieranò, *Il ditirambo* [see above, 3.86n.], pp. 26–8, TT 36–9). Fittingly coupled with Aegon, whose name evokes goats (3.2n.), Alphesiboeus will reappear in *E.* 8, dedicated to a renowned military commander and tragic-Dionysian poet (most probably Asinius Pollio): there, he will not challenge Damoetas, but Damon (8.5), and his song will be an urban invocation of Daphnis. For the imitation of dancing satyrs by human choruses cf. Plat. *leg.* 7.815c; Nonn. *Dionys.* 15.71 μιμηλὴν σατύροισι συνεσκίρτησε χορείην (on Dionysian dances see Philostr. *uita Apoll.* 4.21, p. 410.23–6 Kays). Note the emphatic alliteration *sal-sat-*. The proper noun occupies the last two feet of the hexameter: cf. *E.* 3.37n.; the same is true of all other occurrences of *Alphesiboeus* in the *E.* (8.1; 5; 62).

74–5. The cult of Daphnis is explicitly framed within a context of 'eternity' (5.74 *haec tibi semper erunt*; but cf. 5.67 *quotannis* [n.]). Echoing Mopsus' song, Menalcas associates the cult with the Nymphs (cf. 5.21) and rural or agricultural rituals, here referred to in terms of *lustratio* (cf. esp. 5.36–9n.). The notion will be further developed towards the end of the poem, 5.76–80 (cf. *semper* at the beginning of the 'epigraphic' 5.78). Temples and altars dedicated to the Nymphs are predictably found in a rural context (cf. *E.* 3.9); however, the cult of a female water-goddess (Iuturna) is also attested in an urban context such as the Campus Martius: Ov. *fast.* 1.463–4; Serv. Dan. *ad Aen.* 12.139; cf. more generally Cic. *nat. deor.* 3.43 *earum* [scil. *Nympharum*] *templa sunt publice uota et dedicata.*

75 et cum lustrabimus agros. The *lustratio agrorum* was a purification ritual held in the fields, and was particularly connected to the *Ambarualia*, a rural feast

280   ECLOGUE 5

celebrated in the second half of May as a prelude to the reaping season (hence a reference to it in Servius Dan's note here). A countryside *lustratio*, though smaller in scale and importance (and sometimes held in private households), was linked to the *Feriae Sementiuae*, in January. Thus, V's mention of the ritual excludes neither a winter nor a summer occasion (5.70); cf. Daremberg-Saglio, III.2, esp. pp. 1425–32, s.v. *lustratio*. The *lustrum* was, properly speaking, a collective ceremony of purification, celebrated by censors every five years, and affecting the entire city.

76–80. Menalcas' last five lines, corresponding to the last five lines of Mopsus' song, directly summon the figure of Daphnis (esp. 5.80 *damnabis tu quoque uotis*). However, while 5.40–4 added new material to what Mopsus had just said, Menalcas sounds somewhat repetitive here (5.76–8 reformulate the notion of *semper*, which has previously been expressed). The device probably aims at an effect of religious solemnity—but Menalcas' song must also equal that of his younger companion in length.

76–8. The unchangeable order of nature is invoked as a pledge of loyalty by the followers of the new cult, as in Tityrus' opening speech, although Tityrus used an adynaton: *ante leues ergo pascentur in aethere cerui*, etc. (*E.* 1.59–63n., with a similarly fourfold structure). The honours received by the deified Daphnis are not unlike those paid to the young *deus* of the first poem. Menalcas here employs the rhetorical formula 'as long as...always', for which cf. the echo of this passage at *Aen.* 1.607–9; see also, more generally, *Aen.* 9.447–9; Hor. *epod.* 15.7–10; *carm.* 3.30.8–9; Tib. 1.4.65–6; but cf., for instance, Theogn. 1.252; Callim. *iamb.* 12, fr. 202.68–70 Pf.; *eleg.* fr. inc. sed. 388.9–10 Pf.; Posidipp. apud Athen. 13.596c = *HE* 3148–9 G.-P. = 122.7–8 Ausl.-Bast. οὔνομα σὸν μακαριστόν, ὃ Ναύκρατις ὧδε φυλάξει [cf. *E.* 5.78 esp. *nomenque tuum*] / ἔστ' ἂν ἴῃ Νείλου ναῦς ἐφ' ἁλὸς πελάγη; *Anth. Pal.* 7.153, esp. 2 ἔστ' ἂν ὕδωρ τε νάῃ καὶ δένδρεα μακρὰ τεθήλῃ (king Midas' epitaph). Menalcas' anaphoric style, featuring a fourfold *dum* in two lines, corresponds to Mopsus' similar anaphora (*ut* repeated four times in 5.32–3).

76 dum...aper...dum piscis. An opposition between two different animal kingdoms, as in *E.* 1.59–60. But they both belong to the 'rural' sphere: wild boars in valleys and fish in rivers. fluuios. The term *fluuius*, perhaps slightly archaizing, is synonymous with the more common *flumen* (1.51; 3.96, etc.). Its only other occurrence in the *E.* is at 7.66 *populus in fluuiis* (in a similar context). Mopsus used both *flumen* and *amnis* (*E.* 5.21; 25). amabit. The verb is commonly used to express predilection, even in the sense of 'dwelling'. In this sense, it often applies to animals and plants, in both technical and non-technical literature: cf. Varr. *rust.* 3.10.7 *anseres amant locum purum* (for an adynaton, see Hor. *epod.* 16.34 *amet...hircus aequora*); Ov. *met.* 2.539; in V., note *G.* 4.124 *amantis litora myrtos*; ThlL I.1956.2–19.

77 dumque thymo pascentur apes. The opposition is now between different 'diets' (note the parallelism in 5.76–7, emphasized by both phonetic and rhythmic assonance: note the ictus on the second syllable of both *aper* and *apes*). In fact, bees feed on flowers (thyme is among their favourite foods: *G.* 4.112; 169; 181, etc.), whereas cicadas feed on dew. Both are typically pastoral insects: they

ECLOGUE 5   281

appeared at 1.54 and 2.13, respectively. **dum rore cicadae.** For dew as cicadas' (only) food cf. [Hes.] *scut.* 393–7; Aristot. *hist. anim.* 4.7.532b10–13; Theocr. *id.* 4.16; [Anacr.] 34.3 W. Bees, too, were said to gather condensed honey from the air, as if it were a sort of dew: a common belief to which V. seems to allude in *G.* 4.1; cf. Serv. ad loc.; Aristot. *hist. anim.* 5.22.553b29 (whence Plin. *nat.* 11.30; see also 16.31); Theophr. *hist. plant.* 3.7.6; Colum. 9.14.20; [Quint.] *decl. mai.* 13.4, p. 269.3–6; 5, p. 270.17–21 Håk. Cicadas, like bees (cf. *E.* 1.54n.), had become a widely acknowledged symbol of poetic song: cf. esp. the prologue of Callimachus' *Aitia*, fr. 1.32–6 Pf. = Mass. = Hard. (but cf. Plato's myth in *Phaedr.* 258e–259d), as well as Theocr. *id.* 1.148; Nemes. *ecl.* 4.42; see also *E.* 2.12–13n.

78 semper honos nomenque tuum laudesque manebunt. A line about glory and eternity (note the archaic, solemn form *honos*, avoiding the homeoteleuton with *semper*): V. will repeat it verbatim at *Aen.* 1.609; for the future of *maneo* in aetiological contexts, cf. Ov. *met.* 1.710; 10.725.

79 Baccho Cererique. The two main agricultural deities are often paired together, even in cult (esp. the Eleusinian Mysteries; see *E.* 5.30n.): *G.* 1.7–9; 338–50; but cf. Lucr. 5.14 (where Ceres and Bacchus' *reperta* are said to be inferior to Epicurus', who a fortiori deserves to be called *deus*). **tibi.** Note the prosody: the second syllable is long, presupposing the archaic form *tibei* (accounting for over one-sixth of all occurrences in V.). Here, the effect is to emphasize the new divine addressee, placed alongside the two traditional gods: cf. also 8.93; 9.57. **quotannis.** After multiple expressions of enthusiasm and eternity (*semper* at 5.74 and 78), the adverb used at 5.67 reappears, conveying a sense of closure: the cult is now established, featuring recurring annual ceremonies; note also *E.* 1.42, significantly in reference to the young *deus* (i.e. the *diui filius*, in all likelihood): see 5.76–8n.

80 damnabis tu quoque uotis. Now assimilated to a rural deity, Daphnis is also assigned the task of accepting and satisfying vows, thereby binding the requester (Serv.; cf. also Serv. Dan. *ad Aen.* 4.699). This is why the verb *damno* is sometimes accompanied by the so-called gen. 'of punishment', as in Nep. *Timol.* 5.3 *nunc demum se uoti esse damnatum* (cf. Liv. 5.25.4; 7.28.4; 10.37.16, etc.). In fact, the reading *uoti* is here transmitted by **R** and is accepted by some editors. Yet it is more likely that V. opts for the abl., as in Sisenna, *hist.* 100 P.[2] *quo uoto damnati fetum omnem dicuntur…consecrasse*; cf. German. 348 *uotis damnatus*; ThlL V.1.20.36–42. For the plural, cf. *uota* at 5.79: this kind of repetition is typical of V.'s pastoral style, particularly towards the end of an eclogue (note also *tu quoque*). For a significant echo of this line in a Caesarian context, cf. Jupiter's speech at the beginning of the *Aeneid*: *uocabitur hic quoque uotis* (*Aen.* 1.290 where, since antiquity, scholars have been debating whether V. is referring to Julius Caesar or— more probably—to his adoptive son Augustus).

81–90. The finale of the poem, mirroring the central interlude, contains Mopsus' appreciative reaction to Menalcas' song. The eclogue can now come to an end, featuring the traditional exchange of gifts (5.85–7n.).

282   ECLOGUE 5

81–4. Whereas Menalcas used images of pastoral serenity to express his aesthetic reaction to Mopsus' song (5.45–52), Mopsus here conveys his appreciation of Menalcas' song through emotionally intense imagery, with notable parallels in the ancient literary-critical language: impetuous waters and winds significantly appear in the treatise *On the sublime*, 9.11 (Homer is compared to the blowing wind); 10.3–5 (Homer's storms); 12.2 (following a lacuna: in all likelihood, Plato is the author here compared to the sea); and 12.4 (Demosthenes is likened to storm and thunder); cf. also 22.3; 34.4. Lucian. *hist. conscr.* 45 will refer to a 'poetic wind' ($\pi o \iota \eta \tau \iota \kappa o \hat{v} \ldots \mathring{a} \nu \acute{\epsilon} \mu o \nu$). See further Hor. *carm.* 4.2.5–8 *monte decurrens uelut amnis*, etc., where the image of an impetuous river (*E.* 5.84n.) is applied to Pindar's unmatched excellence. For a different image of a creek/river, emphasizing 'flow' rather than strength, cf. Quint. *inst.* 9.4.7. Such a 'sublime' feeling, aptly prompted by Menalcas' divine visions, is quite appropriate for a Dionysian singer (and, we may add, for a young one). The opposition between Menalcas' and Mopsus' characters is then highlighted by *fragili*, which Menalcas uses to describe his *cicuta* (5.85). It bears mentioning, however, that Menalcas' chosen topic is 'sublime' in and of itself: he sings of universal joy over Daphnis' deification (stylistic 'sublimity' and Bacchic jubilation appeared together in Cic. *Brut.* 276). These references to nature as an indomitable force are full of Lucretian echoes: cf., for the wind, Lucr. 1.271–97 *principio uenti uis uerberat incita pontum* etc.; at any rate, both Lucretius and V. are clearly familiar with similes, images, and descriptions used by Homer (see below).

82 uenientis sibilus Austri. A hiss, represented by repeated /s/ sounds, looks forward for a moment to the arrival of the Auster, the south wind, harbinger of storms and rain, and particularly feared by seafarers. Cf. *G.* 3.278–9; *Aen.* 1.51 *furentibus Austris* (the first occurrence in the *Aeneid*, anticipating the storm which sets the epic plot in motion); also 10.99 *murmura uenturos…prodentia uentos*; *Enc. Virg.* V.1, pp. 490–8, s.v. *venti* (M. Labate).

83 percussa…fluctu…litora. As an auditory phenomenon, the resounding noise of the waves hitting the waterfront (cf. Hom. *Il.* 2.209–10) does not seem particularly well suited to the pastoral world: cf. the case of Polyphemus in *id.* 11.43. The force of the waves is traditionally connected with that of the winds, mentioned at 5.82: cf. Hom. *Il.* 2.394–6; 13.795–9; 15.381–3; 618–28.

84 saxosas inter…flumina uallis. The impetuous flow of water streams amidst stony gorges reappears in V.'s epic poem to describe warriors' fury (cf. *Aen.* 12.523–5) and presents a dramatic expansion of Theocritus' delicate water drops falling on rocks (Theocr. *id.* 1.7–8; cf. Hor. *carm.* 4.2.5–8). In Homer, a herdsman hears the noisy clash of two overflowing waterstreams among the mountains (*Il.* 4.452–6).

85–7. Menalcas stays one step ahead of Mopsus (*ante*), proving to be a real 'friend of Daphnis' (*amauit nos quoque Daphnis*; cf. *E.* 5.52n.). In fact, his display of affectionate spontaneity recalls the ending of *id.* 6, when, at the end of their contest, Daphnis and Damoetas kissed each other and exchanged gifts (ll. 42–4). Now in his mature age (5.4), this Menalcas again appears quite different from the aggressive contestant of *E.* 3. The opening lines of *E.* 2 and 3, which Menalcas is said to have learned from the *cicuta* (*docuit* [5.87n.]), are quoted here: in the former, *pastor* is omitted (the quotation appears as a complete hexameter, only lacking the last foot), whereas the latter is cut in half (only the second half-line is quoted: a Damoetas, after all, appeared in 5.72, and a new occurrence of the name might generate confusion).

85 fragili...cicuta. The Corydon of *E.* 2 (or the author of that poem, i.e. Menalcas himself?) mentioned a gift he had received from Damoetas: a *fistula*, composed of seven stems (*cicutis* [2.36n.]). The adj. hints at a typically pastoral value, i.e. 'thinness': cf. *E.* 1.2 *tenui...auena* (n.).

87 docuit. The idea of poetic transmission, construed as teaching, is crucial to the pastoral tradition and appears at the very beginning of the *E.* (Tityrus teaches the *siluae*: *E.* 1.5 *doces*). Here the 'teacher' is a musical instrument, as in Horace's lyric poetry: *dic Latinum, / barbite, carmen* (Hor. *carm.* 1.32.3–4); for a pastoral parallel cf. Theocr. *id.* 7.91–2 πολλὰ μὲν ἄλλα / Νύμφαι κἠμὲ δίδαξαν; Mosch. fr. 2.7 G.; Bion, fr. 10.4 G.; [Mosch.] *epit. Bion.* 95. The transmission of poetry and the generational transition from older to younger singers plays a prominent role in the following eclogue, albeit in the curious scenario of Silenus' encounter with the *pueri* (*E.* 6).

88 At tu sume pedum. Mopsus replies one last time, in his typically direct (if not curt) manner. Note the illocutionary pronoun + imperative structure, this time urging Menalcas to accept the offer (the gift-giver's insistence is firm but respectful); cf. 5.15n. Note also, in the context of gifts given to deities, *E.* 7.35–6 *at tu /...aureus esto* (where *at tu* appears at the end of a line rather than at the beginning, as here). The *pedum* ('crook') was a long curved staff, which shepherds used to guide their flocks and, above all, to drag animals by their legs: Fest. p. 292 L. In *id.* 9, Daphnis received a similar gift (23 κορύναν), whereas Menalcas was presented with a sounding seashell (25–7). In *id.* 7, V.'s fundamental model, the goatherd Lycidas presented Simichidas, in a context marked by literary symbolism, with his 'curved staff' (18–19 ῥοικὰν...κορύναν): "my staff", he said, "I give to you, since you are / an offshoot of Zeus, created for truth. / I hate the architect who strives / to build a house as high as the peak of Mount Oromedon, / and the birds of the Muses, who waste their breath clamouring / vainly in front of Chios' bard"' (43–8); even more explicitly: 'and he gave me... / ...his staff, a host's gift coming from the Muses' (128–9). The Muses had presented Hesiod with the 'sceptre', a Homeric symbol of authority (*Il.* 2.101), along with the divine inspiration he needed to compose his poem (*theog.* 30): cf. also Pausan. 9.30.3; for the poet's staff cf. Pind. *Isthm.* 4.37–9 (= 3–4, 55–7 Sn.-M.); Callim. *aet.* fr. 26.5 Pf. = 30.5 Mass. = 26.5 Hard. A potentially relevant text is the much-debated Philitas, fr. 10 Pow. = 12 Sbard. = 25 Spanoud. = 8 Light., if it refers to a pastoral rod; but cf. L. Sbardella's commentary, Rome 2000, esp. p. 128). Towards the end of the

284   ECLOGUE 6

first half of the book, the reader witnesses a scene in which Menalcas (the 'author', like V., of *E*. 2 and 3) receives a gift that is at once pastoral and Hesiodic. This is perhaps meant to look forward to the didactic, theogonic experiment of *E*. 6 (cf. esp. 69–72). The second half of the book will be inaugurated by Tityrus-V., but Menalcas' name will reappear in *E*. 9, of which he is the absent protagonist, and (fleetingly) in *E*. 10. **cum saepe rogaret.** For wishes, requests, joys, snubs, and rebuffs cf. also *E*. 2.39; 43; 3.13–15.

89 non tulit Antigenes. Yet another cause of friction in Mopsus' life. This time, his interlocutor is a character literally 'born-against' (a possible etymology of *Antigenes*), who vainly asked him for his *pedum* several times. We know of an Attic dithyrambic poet named Antigenes (fifth century BCE; cf. *Anth. Pal*. 13.28 = *Furth. Gr. Epigr*. 33–44, pp. 11–15 P.) and of a famous musician and flute-player from Thebes, *Antigenidas* (fourth cent. BCE), renowned for his great talent and his haughty demeanour: Aristox. *mus*. fr. 77 Wehrli; Plut. *reg. et imp. apoph*. 20.193f; [Plut.]? *mus*. 21.1138a–b; Apul. *flor*. 4.1 (where he is called *tibicen*). Here, however, the name is chosen to allude one last time to Theocritus' *id*. 7, whose opening lines featured a certain Antigenes (seemingly a real person: *id*. 7.4).

90 formosum paribus nodis atque aere. For the 'knottiness' cf. *id*. 17.31 (a very different object: Heracles' iron club). Here, however, the reference must be to the appearance of wood (cf. the *hasta* at *Aen*. 9.743–4), whose knots were often regarded as adding value to the wood itself (Sen. *ben*. 7.9.2). In this case, the knots appear to be symmetric to nails, studs, or other bronze parts (*aere*). The presence of metal adds further value to the object—which, however, cannot be wholly metallic: not only because of its dimensions (it is a *pedum*: see above, 5.88n.), which would make it excessively heavy, but also because it would be out of place in the pastoral world. Note that Mopsus uses an adjective typically denoting pastoral beauty, i.e. *formosum* (1.5n.), which echoes Menalcas' self-quotation (86 *formosum...Alexin*). **Menalca.** Mopsus mentions Menalcas' name at the very end of the poem (taking up *at tu* [5.88]), whereas Menalcas' first line began with Mopsus' name (*Cur non, Mopse*, etc.?). A voc. concludes the first half of the book, which began with the voc. *Tityre* (cf. also 6.4n.). Both names allude, at least obliquely, to the poet himself.

Eclogue 6

[Varus]

sit Tityrus Orpheus (*E*. 8.55)

The sixth poem, like all the even-numbered eclogues, is introduced by a prologue (6.1–12: second in length only to the opening of *E*. 8, which adds up to thirteen lines). Here, V. describes Apollo's divine intervention to keep him from pursuing certain rash endeavours in the epic domain. The honours he pays to Varus (6.7n.), therefore, can only derive from his poetic *myricae*: the pastoral poem itself will be ennobled by Varus' name, since he is obviously dear to Apollo (6.9–12). The prologue is followed by a clear break, underscored by the apostrophe to the Pierides (6.13): the poet then focuses on the achievements of two young boys, Chromis and Mnasyllus, who catch the still drunk Silenus, tie him up, and (with the help of a nymph, Aegle) obtain from him the long-awaited song. Silenus' song immediately enlivens nature, even more so than it would if the singer were Apollo or Orpheus (6.13–30). The song touches on several themes. First of all, the origin of the world (6.31–40); then, the beginnings of humankind (6.41–2) and various mythical episodes: the disappearance of Hylas (6.43–4); Pasiphae (6.45–60), recalling the Proetides' fate by way of contrast (6.48–51); Atalanta (6.61); the Heliades (6.62–3). Here, the focus switches to Cornelius Gallus' poetic initiation (6.64–73): one of the Muses leads him in front of the whole *chorus* of Apollo, and the singer Linus gives him the 'pipe' (6.69 *calamos*) that once belonged to Hesiod. Gallus will be prompted to use it to celebrate the Grynean grove consecrated to Apollo (6.72). Towards the end of the poem, two more themes appear, featuring mythical women as protagonists: Scylla (6.74–7) and Philomela (6.78–81). Yet Silenus' song continues, though no longer summarized in detail: he sings of all the topics (6.82 *omnia*) of which Apollo sang on the banks of the river Eurotas. Silenus keeps singing until the flocks must return to their sheepfolds, since the evening star has appeared in the sky (6.85–6).

The prologue occupies a special position, since it opens the second half of the book: given its metapoetic function, it can readily be called a 'proem in the middle' (Conte 1980b). Whereas the young *deus* in *E*. 1 did not seem to set limits on Tityrus' poetic and 'ludic' activity (1.10 *ludere quae uellem calamo permisit agresti*), in *E*. 6 Tityrus is disciplined by Apollo's intervention, which is less repressive than redemptive (6.3–4n.; 4–5n.). Apollo brings Tityrus back to his bucolic roots: he is well versed in pastoral poetry and enjoys the favour of the Muse *Thalea* (note, in 6.1, a new occurrence of the verb *ludere*). Theocritus, alluded to in 6.1 (*Syracosio*), devoted his *id*. 7 (known as *Thalysia*) to a comparison of different poetic forms: *id*. 7 featured a scene of initiation and the transmission of the poetic staff, which has just been evoked in the finale of *E*. 5 (see 5.88n.) and reappears now as one of the main models for Gallus' initiation (*E*. 6.69–73). Regardless of what position *id*. 7 occupied in the Theocritean collection known to V. (it may well have been the sixth or the fifth poem: cf. p. 20 and n. 49), it is clear that V. could use it as a blueprint for his idea of reasserting, in a 'delayed' position within the book, his statement of poetics. Moreover, it is Theocritus who had previously defined his bucolic poetry in terms of assimilation to the Hesiodic model as well as in opposition to simplistic imitations of Homer (*id*. 7.43–51).

In both the introductory prologue and the summary of Silenus' song, *E*. 6 doubtless expresses a deeply original conception of 'pastoral' poetry. It might seem paradoxical that, after Apollo's exhortation to respect the boundaries of 'Syracusan verse', the reader is offered such an unusual piece, unheard-of in terms of both setting and themes, compared to the Theocritean pastoral tradition. By this point in the book, however, the reader should be familiar with the specifically

286   ECLOGUE 6

Virgilian features of *siluae* and *myricae*: the prophecy of *E*. 4, describing the new advent of *Saturnia regna* (here mentioned again, 6.41), and the twofold song for Daphnis in *E*. 5 are important precedents, which make Silenus' revelation not so surprising after all ('marginal' veins of pastoral poetry could also be alluded to by Chromis' name: see 6.13n.).

The later, epic developments of V.'s poetic output, as well as the occasional 'sublimity' experimented with in the *E*. (cf. e.g. the praise of heroes at 4.26), have inevitably influenced the interpretation of *E*. 6. The poem has been described as the first instance of a literary commonplace destined to enjoy great popularity in Augustan poetry: the so-called *recusatio* (6.1–12n.). It is possible that V. then felt attracted to 'kings and wars', and that he actually considered embarking on such a poetic adventure (6.3 *cum canerem*): it becomes immediately clear, however, that the type of song which Apollo prevents him from singing is encomiastic/eulogistic poetry (6.6–7 *laudes, / Vare, tuas*), which had proved to be insidious during the Alexandrian age. The poet expects his addressee not to be too interested in being honoured with a poem about *tristia... bella* (6.7), but rather to appreciate a poetic voice aware of its own means and limits, and therefore worthy of Apollo's favour (6.11). Thus, at the moment, V.'s ambition seems to be focused on a type of didactic poetry which echoes both Hesiod (the 'old man of Ascra', hinting at antiquity and authoritativeness: 6.70) and another great poet of the past, himself a follower of Hesiod: Callimachus, who wrote the *Aitia* (see esp. 6.4–5n.). An αἴτιον or 'origin' à la Callimachus, the story of the Grynean grove, is the subject matter of the song that Cornelius Gallus is prompted to compose (6.72–3).

Thus, the mysterious figure of Silenus evokes an archaic type of wisdom, connecting wild nature with a human and a divine dimension. As such, Silenus allows V. to distil, through affinities and differences, an extremely complex poetic programme. The reader, in fact, is presented only with the summary of a song which lasted an entire day. The didactic genre à la Hesiod and Callimachus is enriched through scientific and natural-philosophical themes, such as cosmology (note the Lucretian echoes: 6.31–6). An important role is also played by particular myths dear to Alexandrian (and then neoteric) poetry: e.g. Hylas and tragic heroines, such as Pasiphae. Homer (but not the *Iliad*) is among the models: cf. the capture of Proteus in *Od*. 4.351–569, which V. will rework again in *G*. 4.387–529.

Such a unifying force stimulates the poet's power, typical of the pastoral genre, to animate nature (cf. *E*. 1.5). V.'s prototype for such an ability is Orpheus, explicitly mentioned here (6.30), as in *E*. 4.55–7. In *E*. 3, the divine Alcimedon placed Orpheus (and the 'woods that follow him') at the centre of Damoetas' cups. Now, at the centre of the *E*., V.'s singers have the power to make alder trees grow (6.63n.) and to move ash trees (6.71), as well as to 'shake' oak trees (6.28). Note also that the opening cosmological sequence is modelled after the 'summary' of Orpheus' song in Apollonius' *Argonautica* (see 6.31–40n.). Affinities with Orphic thought may perhaps be detected in V.'s repeated references to light and sun-myths throughout the poem (for a specific parallel, cf. 6.37n.).

Such Orphic suggestions must have been obvious to late antique readers, as is confirmed by Servius' annotations (even though the interpretations he refers to are far from plausible). This contributes to making *E.* 6 an experiment in synthesis and unity. In fact, Orpheus (and the esoteric doctrines associated with him) combined two great divine models: Dionysus and Apollo. *E.* 6 is opened and concluded by Apollo (cf. also 6.29), but its protagonist is an evidently Dionysian figure, i.e. Silenus: hence the synthesis. V.'s Silenus can thus be traced back to Callimachus' Hesiodic poetics; but, at the same time, he goes beyond Callimachus by superseding the opposition between 'water-drinkers' and 'wine-drinkers', which played a crucial role in Callimachus' poetry and in many Hellenistic debates. Silenus' veins are still swollen under the effect of Iacchus (6.15n.), but his song (clearly a *deductum* one) culminates in an *aition* à la Callimachus (6.72 *origo*). In Nemesianus' reworking (*ecl.* 3, freely combining *E.* 4 and 6), the role of divine singer will be played by Pan, who will narrate the birth and achievements of Bacchus-Dionysus: the complexity of V.'s construction will be lost, but Nemesianus will develop the idea that divine song must revolve around a mystic theme, such as Dionysian frenzy. The Dionysian notion of 'harnessing' the forces of nature (such as Silenus or a wild beast: cf. 5.29 *curru subiungere tigris*) thanks to the 'taming' power of the god is interpreted by V. as enrichment of knowledge on the part of three dauntless youths, Chromis, Mnasyllus, and Aegle. Yet this type of scene must have been quite widespread in the artistic iconography of V.'s time. It is particularly significant that the very cult of Dionysus, conceived of both as a religious phenomenon and as an aesthetic or artistic one, was probably of great interest to one of V.'s most important readers, i.e. Asinius Pollio (cf. esp. 3.86n.). Pollio's art collection, as far as we can tell based on Pliny the Elder's testimony, allotted ample space to Dionysian subject matters: in particular, Pollio is said to have owned some of Praxiteles' *Sileni* (Plin. *nat.* 36.23; cf. p. 5 and n. 9; p. 149; *E.* 3.84; 6.14n.).

The revelations coming from Silenus' Dionysian cave are not religious in nature: while he refers to notions, places, and events pertaining to Dionysian mysticism, he alludes to them only by way of suggestion. An aura of mystic wisdom is further enhanced by literary art: Silenus allows the reader to catch glimpses of the intense dialogue involving V., Varus, Gallus, and other privileged readers of the *E.* (most notably, Asinius Pollio). Silenus' revelations concern the everyday life of the literary circles of V.'s time, and the immediately preceding generation: his song features thematic and stylistic echoes not just of Lucretius (and Epicurus), but also of Calvus and Catullus—it is a sort of poetic 'archaeology' of the *E.* (cf. l. 47, a 'source' for Corydon in *E.* 2.69).

It is unclear whether Cornelius Gallus actually performed, or had already performed, the task assigned to him by the divine herdsman Linus (though ancient

288 ECLOGUE 6

testimonies seem to confirm that he did). Ovid will put the programme of *E.* 6 into practice, and he will do so in his own way, though it is possible that Parthenius previously carried out a similar project (as suggested by Harrison 2007, pp. 44–59). The *Metamorphoses* will begin with primeval chaos and the origin of the world; then, after a series of myths and transformations, the poet will go on to narrate the apotheosis of Julius Caesar, which anticipates the deification of Augustus (but cf., in Ov. *met.* 10 and 11, the myth of Orpheus, clearly indebted to the generation of poets to which V. belongs). V., in turn, will proceed along the lines of Hesiod and Callimachus' didactic tradition in the *G.*, where Orpheus reappears in the finale (possibly featuring a last echo of Cornelius Gallus). Like Ovid, V. was probably familiar with a Hellenistic work on metamorphoses: perhaps Nicander's *Heteroioumena* or Parthenius' *Metamorphoses.*

Apollo exhorts V. to go back to his pastoral world: this, however, does not imply a return to Theocritus' bucolic 'purity' (cf. *E.* 2 and 3), as is obvious after reading *E.* 4 and 5. Chromis' and Mnasyllus' 'hope' for song, which spurs them to action, reflects hopes and ideas shared by V., Cornelius Gallus, and other friends belonging to the same literary circle. All of them were fascinated by (if not followers of) the Epicurean school. In Homer's *Odyssey*, Odysseus caught Proteus in order to obtain information crucial to his journey: now, however, Chromis and Mnasyllus demand nothing but poetry and wisdom. V.'s poetic and philosophical interests (especially his interest in Epicurean doctrine) are now merged into the sapiential figure of Silenus, frequently allegorized by ancient readers as a teacher of philosophy (Siro? cf. Serv. *ad E.* 6.13). Note also the recent attempt by Harrison (2007, pp. 44–59) to connect Silenus with Parthenius, who was V.'s Greek teacher according to Macr. *Sat.* 5.17.18: this also seems plausible. What is certain is that here, at the beginning of the second half of the *E.*, V.'s reader encounters a theme crucial to the whole collection: the desire for learning and knowledge, in the form of poetic transmission (cf. *E.* 5; see p. 246). The poem's resonance with Epicureanism (in its Lucretian form) was clear to ancient commentators of Neoplatonic inclination (such as Servius: cf. Serv. *ad E.* 6.31). In this regard, *E.* 6 is a natural continuation of *E.* 5, which is replete with evident Lucretian echoes.

The particular blend of literary and philosophical culture that characterizes *E.* 6 is full of expressive potential (even though the poem starts with a *recusatio*), as are the lively capture scene and the proem, prominently featuring a sylvan Muse and Apollo, a divine master of both poetry and animal husbandry. All this probably explains the origin of an ancient anecdote, transmitted by Servius (*ad E.* 6.11), whereby the poem was performed by a mime actress named Cytheris and appreciated by Cicero himself: *dicitur autem ingenti favore a Vergilio esse recitata, adeo ut, cum eam postea Cytheris meretrix cantasset in theatro, quam in fine Lycoridem uocat, stupefactus Cicero, cuius esset, requireret. et cum eum tandem aliquando uidisset, dixisse dicitur et ad suam et ad illius laudem 'magnae spes altera Romae': quod iste postea ad Ascanium transtulit* [*Aen.* 12.168], *sicut commentatores loquuntur* (note here the idea of 'passing the baton', quite frequent in ancient descriptions of encounters between great men: from the 'star' of Roman prose to the new champion of Roman poetry). In the 'biographical' mythology surrounding V., *E.* 6 plays an extraordinarily representative role, both because of its unique style and because V. here declares his interest in epic poetry (even though he does not feel ready for it yet, and Apollo diverts his attention from it).

From a narrative and structural point of view, *E.* 6 begins with a prologue in the poet's voice, like all even-numbered eclogues (1–12: the poet is here disguised as 'Tityrus'). After that, the main body of the poem can be divided into two main sections: a narrative 'frame' (13–30) and the summary of Silenus' song (31–86). The latter, in turn, is subdivided into two parts: the first (31–73) culminates in Linus' direct speech (69–73) and has three subsections (31–42; 43–60; 61–73); the second, much shorter, brings the poem to a close (74–86). Besides the prologue, the poet's voice can also be heard at 45–55 (comments on Pasiphae's sorrowful fate) and 74 (a direct question). Note also that the length of the prologue (twelve lines) is a 'quantitative basis' that V. seems to have kept in mind in disposing the structure of the poem: cf. the section 31–42 (twelve lines) and, less exactly, 61–73 and 74–86 (thirteen lines each); contrast the longer sections 13–30 and 43–60 (eighteen lines each).

On the Eclogue: F. Skutsch (1901, pp. 28–49); Leo (1902); F. Skutsch (1906, pp. 128–55); Weyman (1920–1, 1922–3); Jachmann (1923); Weyman (1924–5); R. Pfeiffer (1928, pp. 321–2); Desport (1952, pp. 181–229); Büchner (1955, cols. 1219–24); Evenhuis (1955); Stewart (1959); Elder (1961); Marchesi (1961, pp. 21–2); Otis (1963, pp. 125–7 and 136–40); Saint-Denis (1963); Paratore (1964); Klingner (1967, pp. 100–11); G. Williams (1968, pp. 243–9); O. Skutsch (1969, pp. 162–5); Putnam (1970, pp. 195–221); E. A. Schmidt (1972b, pp. 238–98); Leach (1974, pp. 231–44); Ross (1975, pp. 18–38 = Volk 2008, pp. 189–215); Cupaiuolo (1977, pp. 172–81); Van Sickle (1978, pp. 146–58); Alpers (1979, pp. 98–103 and 128–32); G. Williams (1980, pp. 220–5); Clausen (1982, pp. 317–19); Van Sickle (1986, pp. 119–35); M. O. Lee (1989, pp. 113–20); Rutherford (1989); Courtney (1990); Baldwin (1991); Farrell (1991b, pp. 291–314); Rudd (1996, pp. 68–70); P. Hardie (1998, pp. 14–16); T. K. Hubbard (1998, pp. 99–108); R. F. Thomas (1998); Gall (1999); Binder, Effe (2001, pp. 77–83); Lipka (2001, pp. 83–5 and 94–100); Baier (2003); Breed (2006a, pp. 74–94); von Albrecht (2007, pp. 27–8); Harrison (2007, pp. 44–59); Viarre (2007); Fernandelli (2009); Davis (2012, pp. 121–40); Stok (2014); Kania (2016, pp. 97–107).

Specific issues: Alfonsi (1942) (the myth of Silenus); Barigazzi (1952) (Euphorion); Cova (1955) (l. 17); C. Hardie (1956–7) (relationship to the *G.*); Cazzaniga (1960) (Nicander); Wimmel (1960, pp. 132–4) (Callimachus); Eisenhut (1961) (l. 5); Coleman (1962) (Cornelius Gallus); La Penna (1962) (Hesiod); Brown (1963, pp. 62–73) (structure of the poem; the pastoral book); Clausen (1964, pp. 193–5) (Callimachus); Herrmann (1964) (l. 8); Della Corte et al. (1965) (l. 72 and Euphorion); Boucher (1966, p. 98) (l. 61); Notopoulos

290 ECLOGUE 6

(1967) (*POxy* 1083); Leach (1968) (the poem's unity); Segal (1969) (Silenus as a combination of Dionysus and Apollo); Spoerri (1969) (cosmogony and Epicureanism); A. H. F. Thornton (1969) (cosmology); Spoerri (1970a) (cosmology); Spoerri (1970b) (cosmology and ancient exegesis); Grillo (1971, pp. 70–7) (ll. 64–73); Perret (1971) (theology and cosmology); Segal (1971) (ll. 13–26); McKay (1972) (humour in Gallus' initiation); Sutton (1974) (Silenus); M. Hubbard (1975) (the capture of Silenus); Clausen (1976) (l. 3); Segal (1976) (Theocritean epigrams); Clausen (1977) (l. 3); Lieberg (1977) (ll. 82–6); Van Sickle (1977a) (Gallus); Van Sickle (1977b) (the 'middle' style); Currie (1978) (ll. 13–26 and the legend of Numa/Egeria); R. F. Thomas (1979) (Licinius Calvus); Conte (1980b) ('proem in the middle'); Deschamps (1980a) (l. 27); Deschamps (1980b) (l. 27); Egan (1980) (l. 24); Hudson-Williams (1980, pp. 125–30) (ll. 9–11; 35–8; 78–81); D'Anna (1981) (Gallus); R. F. Thomas (1981, pp. 371–4) (ll. 46–53); Alfonsi (1982) (Licinius Calvus); Boneschanscher (1982) (l. 80); Geymonat (1982, p. 18) (l. 12); Jacobson (1982) (ll. 37–8); Lieberg (1982a, pp. 5–13; 1982b, pp. 255–60) (the poet as a demiurge); Kaster (1983) (l. 26 and Symmachus); Thill (1983) (ll. 45–60); R. F. Thomas (1983a, p. 96) (l. 3); Della Corte (1983–4) (Silenus and Proteus); D'Anna (1985) (ll. 1–4); Knox (1985) (Dionysian poetics and Callimacheanism); R. F. Thomas (1986) (*recusatio*); Bauzá (1987) (mystical and philosophical traditions); D'Anna (1987a) (love); Deremetz (1987) (l. 5); Huyck (1987) (l. 62); Florio (1989) (prologue and epilogue); La Penna (1989) (l. 10); A. Michel (1989) (Epicureanism); Bonanno (1990, pp. 181–93) (l. 69); Horsfall (1990, pp. 55–6) (ll. 74–7); Knox (1990) (l. 83); Viarre (1990) (ancient exegesis); Glei (1991, pp. 87–90) (war); Horsfall (1991, p. 36) (ll. 31–40); Timpanaro (1991) (ll. 74–7); Woodman (1991) (ll. 39–40); Paschalis (1993) (ll. 53; 82–3); Cameron (1995, pp. 454–83) (*recusatio*); Deremetz (1995, pp. 289–316) (models and metapoetics); Manzoni (1995, pp. 65–9) (Orpheus and Cornelius Gallus); Paschalis (1995) ([Mosch.] *epit. Bion.*); Cupaiuolo (1996) (Alexandrian form); Kyriakou (1996) (relationship to *E.* 10); O'Hara (1996, pp. 248–9) (ll. 55–60, 74–7); Bollók (1996–7) (cosmology); Braund (1997, pp. 208–9) (cosmology); Woodman (1997) (transposition of ll. 64–73 after l. 81); Francese (1999, pp. 69–70) (l. 72 and Parthenius); Lightfoot (1999, pp. 59–76) (Euphorion and Gallus); Seng (1999, pp. 17–20) (structure and position within the volume); Breed (2000b) (Silenus' song as ecphrasis); Citroni (2001, pp. 276–9) (l. 1); Loupiac (2001) (Gallus); O'Hara (2001, pp. 392–5) (ll. 74–7); Paschalis (2001) (l. 69); Manuwald (2002) (*Hymn. Hom.* 4[*Merc.*]); Marangoni (2002–3, pp. 77–90) (l. 9); Gagliardi (2003, pp. 39–60) (Gallus); Gomez Gane (2003) (l. 66 and *Hymn. Hom.* 3[*Ap.*].3–4); Tsitsiou-Chelidoni (2003) (ll. 74–7); Clauss (2004) (Callim. *Aet.*); Monella (2005, pp. 199–203) (ll. 78–81); P. Hardie (2005) (Hes. *catal.*); R. Armstrong (2006, pp. 169–86) (Pasiphae in V. and Ov. *ars*); Cairns (2006, pp. 104–45) (Gallus); Casanova (2006) (ll. 78–81); Hunter (2006, pp. 21–8) (Gallus); Privitera (2007, esp. pp. 15–26) (ll. 78–81); Kraggerud (2008, pp. 54–6) (l. 16); Kraggerud (2008, pp. 56–8) (l. 24); Kraggerud (2008, pp. 58–9) (l. 74); Saunders (2008, pp. 128–35) (cosmogony and pastoral poetry); Peirano (2009) (ll. 74–81); Rosati (2009) (Hesiod); Delvigo (2011, pp. 60–77) (ll. 31–4); Aricò (2012) (l. 26); Fernandelli (2012) (ll. 82–4 and Callimachus' *Aitia*, fr. 75 Pf.); Peirano (2012, pp. 189–97) (ll. 74–81 and the *Ciris*); Höschele (2013) (the mime and Cytheris' theatrical performance of *E.* 6); Scafoglio (2013a, pp. 194–200) (cosmology); Stok (2013) (the expropriations and the question of the *tresuiri agris diuidendis*); Fabres-Serris (2014) (ll. 31–42); Kraggerud (2014, pp. 70–2) (l. 34); Paraskeviotis (2014c) (comic

ECLOGUE 6   291

elements in the capture scene); Heerink (2015, pp. 6–8) (ll. 43–4); Kraggerud (2017b, pp. 34–43) (ll. 1–12); Kraggerud (2017b, pp. 44–6) (l. 16); Kraggerud (2017b, pp. 47–50) (l. 24); Kraggerud (2017b, pp. 51–2) (l. 34); Kraggerud (2017b, pp. 53–4) (ll. 74–81); Schafer (2017, pp. 140–3) (l. 12); Venuti (2017) (l. 5); Marchetta (2018, pp. 433–74) (prologue); Bernstein (2020) (reverse acronym in l. 69).

1–12. The entire prologue revolves around the epiphany of the god Apollo. The closest parallel is the well-known prologue of Callimachus' *Aitia*, fr. 1.22–4 Pf. = Mass. = Hard. (see 6.4–5n.). In Callimachus, Apollo's exhortation to the young, novice poet (fr. 1.21 Pf. = Mass. = Hard.) explained why he did not compose a long, 'continuous' poem on the lives of kings and heroes (6.3–5). Here, by contrast, V. has foolishly undertaken to compose an epic poem of war: according to Apollo, that genre does not suit him. The poet's behaviour, paralleled in Hellenistic literature (e.g. Bion, fr. 9.8–11 G.; cf. also [Anacr.] 23 W.), allows V. to establish the prototype of Augustan *recusatio*, i.e. a rhetorical device whereby the poet shuns a task he deems too demanding: cf. Prop. 3.3.29–30 (the god directs the poet to a 'cave' in which, among other sacred objects, he sees a terracotta image of Silenus); Hor. *carm.* 4.15.1–4; see also Hor. *sat.* 1.10.31–5; 2.1.10–15; *epist.* 2.1.250–9 (using the verb *recusare*: 259); Prop. 2.1.17–47; Ov. *ars* 2.467–510 (this time, Apollo exhorts the *praeceptor Amoris* to go back to his erotic poetry, since he has indulged in a didactic, cosmological digression à la Silenus). Besides the *Aitia* proem, important parallels include the finale of Callimachus' hymn to Apollo (Callim. *hymn.* 2[*Ap.*].105–12) and, most notably, Theocritus' *id.* 7.48, establishing the superiority of pastoral poetry (with its Hesiodic implications) over the hackneyed chatter of Homer's imitators, who 'waste their breath clamouring vainly'. A comparison between Bion's pastoral songs and Homer's war poetry (featuring the latter's 'sadness', in reference to the grim nature of war itself: cf. 6.7n.) is found at [Mosch.] *epit. Bion.* 70–85, with a careful distinction between the bucolic and the epic genre. The god's exhortation to hold back a Homeric, Iliadic flow of inspiration may seem particularly appropriate in the light of such 'ambitious' eclogues as *E.* 4 and 5: and yet, Silenus' song will keep the pastoral poet on the track he has followed so far (i.e. a type of pastoral poetry 'contaminated' with Hesiodic, naturalistic themes). The poet's *recusatio*, presupposing his modesty, is paralleled by typically Roman behaviours in social and political contexts—soon to become ritualized during the imperial age (but cf. Julius Caesar's ostentatious refusal of the royal diadem; Augustus will follow the same path); see further U. Huttner, *Recusatio Imperii. Ein politisches Ritual zwischen Ethik und Taktik*, Hildesheim-Zürich-New York 2004. But, despite every declaration of modesty, it remains to be understood that Apollo appears only to poets of some ability and worth, as Callimachus himself states in the *Hymn to Apollo*: ὡπόλλων οὐ παντὶ φαείνεται, ἀλλ' ὅτις ἐσθλός (*hymn.* 2[*Ap.*].9). The prologue, featured in all even-numbered (and narrative) eclogues, is relatively long and uttered in the poet's own voice. The

292   ECLOGUE 6

prologue of *E.* 6 has twelve lines (a sort of 'quantitative basis' used in the rest of the eclogue: cf. p. 289), and is therefore the second-longest in the *E.* (the longest being the opening of *E.* 8: thirteen lines); it can be divided into three sequences: past (6.1–5); present (6.6–9a); future, including the dedication to Varus (6.9b–12). Note that this 'second beginning' of the *E.* repeats the ring structure of the inaugural poem: here too, as in the first eclogue, the first (6.1–5) and the last sequence (6.82–6) are both of five lines (cf. 6.82–6n.; 1.1–10n.; 79–83n.).

    1 Prima. In the sense of 'at first', 'in the beginning', i.e. almost equivalent to *primum*, as opposed to a later stage (*cum canerem*: 6.4; cf. also 6.6 *nunc*): see *Aen.* 7.117–18 *ea uox audita laborum / prima tulit finem* (and 7.120 *continuo* etc.); note also *G.* 1.144 *nam primi cuneis scindebant fissile lignum* contrasted with 1.143 *tum ferri rigor* etc. (for a similar idea cf. Hor. *epist.* 1.1.1 *prima...Camena*). Since antiquity, V.'s assertion has often been interpreted as a claim to primacy: *ostendit ergo se primum post Theocritum bucolica scripsisse* (Serv. Dan.). A noteworthy exception is Philargyrius/Philagrius, who digs deeper into the literary context: '*prima' idest non quod primus Bucolica Latina hic scripserit, sed hoc ait: prima haec me uoluit idest Thalia conscribere, mox et alia facturum.* The sense of *prima* affects the entire sentence and is determined by the whole context (including 6.3–4): note also the hyperbaton, as the adj. and the noun which it modifies are placed at either end of the sentence (*Prima...Thalea*). 'At first' Thalia, V.'s Muse, did not object to pastoral poetry; then, when V. decided to write epic poems (note the first person in 6.3 *cum canerem*), things changed because of Apollo. Note also the vertical correspondence between *prima* and *nostra* (both in line-beginning position), which contributes to the structure of the sentence. At any rate, the term *prima* does gesture towards the notion of primacy, especially in connection with the following *Syracosio* (*uersu*), as well as to the idea that pastoral is an appropriately 'lowly' beginning for V.'s oeuvre. V., in other words, was quite cautious in making his 'first' choice. Thus, the 'beginner' V. (with his Thalia) did not need any divine reprimand, unlike Callimachus; V., however, would need a similar 'correction' later on. Significantly, even the Callimachean model (cf. 6.4–5n.) focuses on biographical priority: ὅτε πρώτιστον (Callim. fr. 1.21 Pf. = Mass. = Hard.) is here echoed by *prima*. A claim to absolute primacy, by contrast, is found at *G.* 3.10 *primus ego* (but cf. Lucr. 1.926–30, as well as 1.117–18, referring to Ennius; cf. Hor. *epist.* 1.19.23 *Parios ego primus iambos*). Note that Callimachus' *Aitia* began with a temporal adverb (Πολλάκι), as shown by F. Pontani, *The First Word of Callimachus' Aitia*, ZPE 128 (1999), pp. 57–9. The temporal succession expressed by *Prima* is also true for the book of the *Eclogues* as it is: the first three eclogues, that are Theocritean for style and situations, then *E.* 4 and 5, with their *paulo maiora* themes, hence now the change imposed by Apollo: *Prima*, first word of *E.* 6 and of the second part of the book, is matched by *Extremum*, first word of the last eclogue (10.1n.). **Syracosio...uersu.** The Syracusan poet's verse, in a thematic sense (rather than in a strictly metrical one), according to the unanimous

ECLOGUE 6   293

interpretation of all ancient commentators. Theocritus used various different metres, and *id.* 8 featured exchanges of elegiac couplets; cf. *E.* 10.50 *Chalcidico... uersu* (n.). The Greek form of the adj., replacing a metrically inconvenient *Syracusanus*, emphasizes the novelty of V.'s Theocritean emulation: for *Syracosius* in markedly Hellenizing contexts cf. Cic. *ac.* 2.123; *Tusc.* 5.100; Vitr. 9.8.1; note also the echo in *Catal.* 15.1 *Vate Syracosio* (i.e. Theocritus). The 'Syracusan' origin of Theocritus' Muse is highlighted in the epigram that the manuscript tradition places among the *prolegomena* to the idylls (= *Anth. Pal.* 9.434); it probably introduced an ancient edition of Theocritus' works: 'The Chian is another, but I, Theocritus, who wrote these poems, / am one of the many Syracusans [τῶν πολλῶν...Συρακοσίων], and I have taken to myself no foreign Muse'. **ludere**. In the sense of 'playing', 'jesting' (i.e. poetry, in its Hellenistic and neoteric sense, as παίγνιον or *lusus*: cf. Catull. 50.2). Since the subject is a Muse, the verb perhaps also alludes to 'dancing'; cf. 6.27–8 *in numerum Faunosque ferasque uideres / ludere*; see 6.2n. For a reworking of the whole passage, cf. *Culex* 1–3; V. himself will use the verb again in reference to his first poetic work (whose 'protagonist' is Tityrus) in the *sphragis* that concludes his *Georgics*: 4.565 *carmina qui lusi pastorum*; see *E.* 6.4n.

  2 siluas habitare. The poet's 'estate' and the Muses' gifts appear, as a metaphor for poetry, in the finale of Theocritus' *id.* 22, esp. 222 ὡς ἐμὸς οἶκος ὑπάρχει. Here, on the other hand, a specific Muse (Thalia) does not 'feel ashamed' for living in an open (yet circumscribed) space, such as the *siluae*: cf. *E.* 2.60 *habitarunt di quoque siluas*. The idea is a variation on 3.84 *Pollio amat nostram, quamuis est rustica, Musam*. **Thalea**. One of the Muses mentioned in Hes. *theog.* 77: the Greek name, Θάλεια, can be Latinized as either *Thalea* or *Thalia* (the former appears in **PRV**; the second is a popular variant reading, known to Servius; in Greek, the two forms Θάλεια and Θαλία are frequently confused). Traditionally associated with comedy, Thalia befits *lusus* and the countryside: θάλεια/θαλία means 'abundance', 'festival', 'banquet', as e.g. in Plut. *quaest. conu.* 9.14.7.746e (note the ancient title of *id.* 7, Θαλύσια; cf. *id.* 7.3). In ancient literary criticism, the origin of comedy was generally associated with rural folk, outside urban areas (note Aristotle's critical remarks at *poet.* 3.1448a35–b3). A Syracusan poet, Epicharmus, was often regarded as the inventor of comedy, in opposition to the Attic poets (cf. again Aristot. *poet.* 3.1448a30–4; see also Theocr. *epigr.* 18.1–2 G. ἅ τε φωνὰ Δώριος χὠνὴρ ὁ τὰν κωμῳδίαν / εὑρὼν Ἐπίχαρμος). V. may have been aware of the geographical affinity between comedy and pastoral poetry (as both could be traced back to Syracuse). Thalia's cheerfulness will soon be embodied in the figure of Silenus and his surroundings (6.14n.; cf. esp. 23 *ridens*; 28 *ludere*). Thalia is credited with inventing agronomy and plant science in *schol. ad* Apoll. Rhod. 3.1–5.b, p. 215 Wend.; cf. Plut. *quaest. conu.* 9.14.4.744f–745a. Playful connotations and resounding liveliness appear again in Hor. *carm.* 4.6.25 *argutae...Thaliae*, whereas V. will assign the name *Thalea* to a sea-nymph in his epic poem (*Aen.*

294 ECLOGUE 6

5.826, modelled after Hom., *Il.* 18.39). In Roman iconography, Thalia's connection with comedy and her role in (V.'s) pastoral poetry will be conflated into a single figure: cf., among the goddess' attributes, the comic mask and the *pedum*, i.e. the pastoral staff, especially in art; this is the case, for instance, in mosaics and sarcophagi depicting the Muse (*LIMC* VII.1, s.v. *Mousa, Mousai/Musae*, esp. p. 1017, no. 18; p. 1035, esp. type F; cf. also p. 1041, no. 134, etc. [J. Lancha; L. Faedo]). The name *Thalia/Thalea* is also used of a Grace and a Nereid (cf. also, significantly, a Maenad appearing on vase paintings), as well as of a nymph, daughter of Hephaestus, that was deemed to be the ancestor of the Palici, an ancient people inhabiting eastern Sicily (cf. Aeschylus' *Aetnaeae*: *TrGF*, III, esp. frr. 6–7, pp. 127–9 Radt; on the various 'Thalias', see Roscher, V, pp. 449–57). The nymph is perhaps featured in the title of Cicero's elegy, *Thalia maesta*, assuming that Heinsius' conjecture is right: Serv. *ad E.* 1.57 *Cicero in elegia quae †tal(i)amasta† inscribitur* (Cic. *carm.* fr. 3 Bläns. = Court.; cf. p. 235 Soub.). Indeed, a 'sad Thalia' would be quite an effective oxymoron. Here, the female figure appears in the context of literary playfulness (and, perhaps, dance: cf. *ludere* at 6.1n.) and bears a Greek name meaning 'cheerful', which evokes festive entertainment. Note that the proper noun *Paizousa* ('The Player') is attested at least once for an actress (*CIL* VI 366), i.e. in a theatrical context. In antiquity, the mime actress Cytheris was said to have successfully recited *E.* 6. This tradition, entirely unverifiable, may have something to do with Thalia's theatrical playfulness: *cum eam postea Cytheris meretrix cantasset in theatro, quam in fine Lycoridem uocat* (Serv. *ad E.* 6.11; see further above, pp. 286–9). For the adjective *nostra* in reference to a specific Muse, cf. Callim. *aet.* fr. 75.77 Pf. = 174.77 Mass. = 75.77 Hard. ἡμετέρην ... Καλλιόπην.

3 reges et proelia. Kings and battles are typical epic themes from Homeric times, especially frequent in encomiastic epic poetry written in praise of contemporary figures (6.6–7): cf. Hor. *ars* 73 *res gestae regumque ducumque et tristia bella.* According to ancient interpreters and biographers, who tend to magnify his achievements, V. here establishes a topical motif which we may call 'premature sketch': Servius claims that the young poet attempted to compose the *Aeneid* itself or, perhaps, a poem on the Alban kings' exploits, which he soon abandoned due to the difficulty of the subject matter; a vaguer account is given by Donatus, *uita Verg.* 65–6 Brumm. = p. 26.9–27.1 Brugn.-Stok *cum res Romanas incohasset, offensus materia ad Bucolica transiit* (other possibilities are listed by Serv. Dan., including a mythological poem under the title *Scylla* [cf. below, 6.74–7n.] and a poem *de bellis ciuilibus,* perhaps based on 6.7n.). The motif is destined to enjoy a rich afterlife in modern literature: the young Torquato Tasso, for instance, decided to cut short an early epic experiment on the liberation of Jerusalem, while John Milton abandoned his project of an epic poem on King Arthur. In the proem to the second half of the *Aeneid,* V. will state his intention to sing of (Homeric-style) wars and kings, echoing the initial *arma uirumque: dicam horrida bella, / dicam acies actosque animis in funera reges* (*Aen.* 7.41–2; cf. also 37–40; 641–4). **Cynthius.**

ECLOGUE 6   295

Mount Cynthus (whose actual elevation barely exceeds 100 m: for its 'summits' cf. *Aen.* 1.498; 4.147) is situated in the middle of Delos, the small island sacred to Apollo, who was born there. The epithet, referring to the god, is typically Callimachean: cf. *aet.* fr. 67.6 Pf. = 166.6 Mass. = 67.6 Hard.; 114.8 Pf. = 64.8 Mass. = 114.5 Hard.; *hymn.* 4[*Del.*].10; note, however, *aet.* fr. 1.22 (cf. below, 6.4–5n.), featuring the epithet 'Lycius'. As such, it is particularly appropriate here, as the poet describes the epiphany of Apollo: it will reappear, in a similarly Callimachean context, in the proem to *G.* 3 (36 *Troiae Cynthius auctor*), opening the second half of the work (as here). The epithet is used here substantively for the first time: cf. Prop. 2.34.80. In Apoll. Rhod. 1.1, Apollo played the role of poetic and 'proemial' god; cf. also *G.* 4.7, where he appears alongside *duces…et proelia* (of bees!). In this considerably Apollonian eclogue, the god is mentioned twice more, both times with his more common epithet *Phoebus* (6.11; 6.82). Note that the *schol. Bern.* (*ad E.* 6.5) equate Apollo, and his divine authority, with Augustus, who allegedly diverted V.'s attention away from a poetic project (a sort of *Aeneid*?) conceived of as a eulogy of the 'kings of the Romans' (*in honorem regum Romanorum*; cf. here *reges et proelia*).

3–4 aurem / uellit. 'Pinching' and pulling someone's ear was a codified gesture, meant to reawaken attention and stimulate memory, which popular beliefs associated with ear lobes (Plin. *nat.* 11.251). The gesture was used, for instance, in forensic practice to remind a witness of his duty to testify: cf. Plaut. *Pers.* 745–8; Hor. *sat.* 1.9.76–7; Sen. *epist.* 94.55; Plin. *nat.* 11.251 (the so-called *antestatio*); Bettini (2000, pp. 47–51). The spatial terminology used by V. in ll. 1–2 (esp. *nostra…siluas habitare Thalea*) describes the poet's generic wanderings (*cum canerem…*) as a sort of dangerous 'border violation': Apollo, the redeeming poet-shepherd-god, brings Tityrus back into his *siluae* (cf. Hor. *sat.* 1.9.78 *sic me seruauit Apollo*, echoing Hom. *Il.* 20.443 τὸν δ' ἐξήρπαξεν Ἀπόλλων; cf. Lucil. 231–2 M. = 238–9 K.). For an echo of the whole Virgilian passage, reworked in economic terms, cf. Calp. *ecl.* 4.155–6.

4–5 pastorem, Tityre, pinguis / pascere oportet ouis, deductum dicere carmen. Cf. Apollo's warning to Callimachus, when the poet set out to write 'for the very first time' (ὅτε πρώτιστον: cf. here, differently, 6.1 *prima* [n.]): Ἀπόλλων εἶπεν ὅ μοι Λύκιος· / '…ἀοιδέ, τὸ μὲν θύος ὅττι πάχιστον / θρέψαι, τὴν Μοῦσαν δ' ὠγαθὲ λεπταλέην' 'Apollo Lycius told me: "…singer, feed the victim to make it as fat as possible, but, my dear, keep the Muse slender"' (Callim. *aet.* fr. 1.22–4 Pf. = Mass. = Hard.). In Horace's *sat.* 1.10.34–5, a Roman god (Quirinus) will divert the poet's attention from his Greek poetic experiments, reproaching him harshly: *in siluam non ligna feras insanius ac si / magnas Graecorum malis implere cateruas*. In Prop. 4.1.71, the seer Horos re-establishes the Callimachean limit of elegiac poetry (*quo ruis imprudens, uage, dicere fata, Properti?*). For a new Callimachean reworking, mediated by *E.* 6, cf. Hor. *carm.* 4.15.1–4 *Phoebus uolentem proelia me loqui / uictas et urbes increpuit lyra, / ne parua Tyrrhenum per aequor / uela darem* (yet another

296   ECLOGUE 6

'border violation'—this time, as expected of Horace, a sea border). To be sure, it is quite predictable that musical and poetic deities may appear to a poet: cf. the proem to Hesiod's *Theogony* (22–5, as well as Callimachus, *aet.* fr. 2.1–2 Pf. = 4.1–2 Mass. = 2.1–2 Hard.; the goddesses also appear to Archilochus, according to a mythical tradition attested in the so-called Mnesiepes inscription). A more specific case is perhaps that of Branchus, the simple herdsman whom Apollo turned into a seer: his story was narrated in *iamb.* (?) 17 = fr. 229 Pf. Like the young *deus* of *E.* 1, Apollo is familiar with the vocabulary of livestock rearing (cf. 5.35n.). However, the unadulterated encouragement given to Tityrus in *E.* 1.45 (*pascite ut ante boues, pueri; summittite tauros*) is now significantly modified, as the addressee is a 'new' Tityrus. Note the hammering alliteration *p p p o o d d*, only excluding the proper noun (*Tityre*) and the noun *carmen* (but cf. 6.5n.). Apollo *Cynthius* now speaks like a stately Roman god, without even feeling the need to avoid such a prosaic word as *oportet* (see again 6.5n.).

4 Tityre. This typically pastoral name, often associated with humility and modesty in Theocritus (*E.* 1.1n.), ironically hints at an identification between the character and V. (after l. 2 *nostra*, the poet will say *ego* at 6.6). Ancient readers identified the Simichidas of *id.* 7 with the author, Theocritus: cf. *schol. ad id.* 7.21, pp. 84–5 Wend., as well as the pseudo-Theocritean *Syrinx* (*Anth. Pal.* 15.21.12). In *id.* 7.72–82, Tityrus is portrayed as a fairly important pastoral singer, whose song is summarized by Lycidas with a technique similar to that used by V. in *E.* 6 (see 6.31–73n.). Here, thanks to Apollo's support (note 6.9 *non iniussa cano*), Tityrus-V. will undertake to relate Silenus' song: the paradox is underscored by the adynaton at *E.* 8.55 *sit Tityrus Orpheus*. Tityrus-V. will appear as a *uates sacer* endowed with Orphic powers in Calp. *ecl.* 4.64–7. This herdsman, who was led astray for a moment and is now brought back to his senses by Apollo, seems to remind the reader of Meliboeus' goat, which loses its way in *E.* 7.7 (*uir gregis ipse caper deerrauerat*): the name *Tityrus*, after all, can be etymologized as 'ram' (not unlike Satyr/Silenus: 1.1n.). The voc. *Tityre*, which opened the first poem, reappears now—right at the beginning of the second half of the book. Thus, the biographical connection between Tityrus and V. plays a structural role in the *E.* In the *sphragis* at the end of the *G.*, the poet mentions his Tityrus again, not without a certain symmetry between his own Neapolitan *otium* and his pastoral character's rest *sub tegmine fagi* (*G.* 4.563–6).

4–5 pinguis /...ouis. The noun, highlighted by the hyperbaton, reworks and 'pastoralizes' the Callimachean model (Callim. *aet.* fr. 1.23 θύος: i.e. vaguely, 'offering'). That sheep must be 'fat', however, is originally a Homeric notion (πίονα μῆλα): see e.g. *Il.* 12.319; *Od.* 9.217; cf. also Plat. *rep.* 1.345c πιαίνειν...αὐτὸν τὰ πρόβατα, καθ᾽ ὅσον ποιμήν ἐστιν. For a reworking of the Callimachean idea (and of V.'s *pinguis*), cf. Hor. *sat.* 2.6.14–15 *pingue pecus domino facias et cetera praeter / ingenium*; note also Hor. *epist.* 2.1.267 *pingui...munere*; Ov. *met.* 11.148 *pingue sed ingenium mansit*; *Catal.* 9.64; in prose, Cic. *Arch.* 26 (cited by Sen. *suas.* 6.27);

ECLOGUE 6   297

Gell. 17.10.8. In Greek, παχύς hints at a certain 'thick-headedness' (Aristoph. *Nub.* 842 ἀμαθὴς καὶ παχύς) and, therefore, at a negative literary judgement. Here, too, Callimachus is an authority: note his critique of Antimachus' *Lyde*, which he calls παχὺ γράμμα καὶ οὐ τορόν (fr. 398 Pf.; cf. e.g. Dion. Hal. *Pomp.* 2.5; *Isocr.* 19). Quintilian recommends a slimming diet for the mind, using a pastoral image, at *inst.* 2.10.6.

5 oportet. Whereas the *deus* in *E.* 1 did not shy away from the technical term *summittite*, Apollo now uses the prosaic term *oportet*, only occurring here in *V.* (the context reworks Callimachus' poetic program, based on 'fineness'). The verb, rare in poetry, gives an impression of prosaic realism—not without bitter irony on occasion, as in Catull. 70.4 (reworking Callim. *epigr.* 25 Pf.); cf. also Lucil. 1378 M. = 1403 K. *unde habeas quaerit nemo, sed oportet habere*; Lucr. 1.778; Hor. *sat.* 2.6.52; Prop. 2.4.1; Ov. *rem.* 23. Note the emphatic alliteration: *Pingues / Pascere oPortet ouis*. **deductum dicere carmen**. Song must be 'delicate' (λεπταλέην in Callimachus), just as the poet's pipe will be *tenuis* in 6.8. Note the auditory opposition between the harsh alliteration *pastorem...pinguis pascere* and *deductum dicere carmen*, where the alliteration echoes Theocritus' sweet melodies (cf. the opening *Tityre, tu patulae*, here reworked at 6.8). The specific reading of *deductum* as metaphorically referring to spinning (cf. Servius: *translatio a lana, quae deducitur in tenuitatem*) is an overinterpretation. In the context, the opposition between *deductum...carmen* and *pinguis...ouis* must be interpreted as 'fat sheep' vs 'thin song'. A Horatian parallel (*epist.* 2.1.225 *tenui deducta poemata filo*) does not offer much help, since it seems to testify to a more specific development of the metaphor (note the explicit *filo*; cf. also Hor. *sat.* 2.1.4). Besides Horace's authority and influence, the metaphorical interpretation is also based on the fact that the image of spinning and weaving is commonly used in relation to poetry: cf. Pind. fr. 179 Maeh.; Bacchyl. 5.9–10; 19.8 (the motif, however, is Indo-European: West, *Indo-European Poetry* [quoted above, 4.37–45n.], pp. 36–8); cf. also Ov. *amor.* 1.14.7 *uel pede quod gracili deducit aranea filum* (not in a meta-poetic context). Here, in the absence of any specification (*a lanificio*) and in connection with *dicere* and *carmen*, *deductum* must refer to thinness of sound, as in Prop. 2.33.38 *deducta...uoce* (cf. also Lucil. 985 M. = 1079 K.). Macrobius, *Sat.* 6.4.12–14, went in the right direction, quoting Pomp. *Atell.* 57–60 R.[3] *uocem deducas oportet, ut uideantur mulieris / uerba....uocem reddam ego / t e n u e m et tinnulam* (note the emphasis on the quality of *tenuitas*, i.e. 'thinness'); Afran. *com.* 339–41 R.[3]; Q. Cornificius, fr. 1 Bläns. = Court. *deducta mihi uoce garrienti*. For a possible reminiscence of *V.*'s passage, cf. *Lydia* 109 *et mea submissa meditatur carmina uoce* (in the poet's absence, the girl sings his songs to the fields and the meadows with her *submissa* voice). In the pastoral genre, 'music' and 'song' must be delicate and not loud, so as to suit such a graceful instrument as the panpipes (cf. Theocritus' incipit: *id.* 1.1–3 ἁδύ τι τὸ ψιθύρισμα... / ...ἁδὺ δὲ καὶ τὺ / συρίσδες, with the *schol. ad* 1d, p. 24, 15–16 Wend. ψιθυρίζειν τὸ ἐν τοῖς ὠσί τινα λεπτὸν

298   ECLOGUE 6

ἦχον ἠχεῖν; note also *id*. 7.89; 20.28–9; [Mosch.] *epit. Bion*. 120; for the panpipes' sound, cf. Lucr. 5.1384 *dulcis …querellas* as well as Ov. *met*. 1.708 *donum tenuem similemque querenti*). This seems to be Tityrus-V.'s own interpretation of the god's oracular *deductum*: the singer actualizes it immediately by accompanying his song with the sound of a 'delicate' reed (8 *tenui…harundine*). Thus, a probably colloquial phrase (*deducere uocem*), seems to be reinvented by V. in a metapoetic context, contrasting epic poetry with the pastoral genre. V.'s rejection of epic draws on the prologue to Callimachus' *Aitia*, fr. 1.19–20 Pf. = Mass. = Hard. 'do not ask me to produce a loud-sounding song [μέγα ψοφέουσαν ἀοιδήν]: / to thunder does not belong to me, but to Zeus': note Callimachus' focus on the quality and volume of the sound. Cf. also the vocabulary of stylistic *humilitas*, presupposing an opposition between 'high' and 'low', e.g. Cic. *orat*. 20 *subtili quadam et pressa oratione limati*; Quint. *inst*. 9.4.134: *ut saepius pressa est, ita interim insurgit*; 10.1.44 *alii pressa demum et tenuia…sana et uere Attica putant*; Plin. *epist*. 1.8.5; *OLD²*, p. 1599, s.v. *pressus* 6b. The Virgilian phrase is quoted as an example of linguistic propriety (*proprie dictum*) in Quint. *inst*. 8.2.9: *id est, quo nihil inueniri possit significantius…, ut Vergilius 'deductum carmen'*: this very 'density' of meaning has puzzled many interpreters, both ancient and modern. Coupled with *carmen*, the verb *dicere* gives rise to a solemn formula: cf. *E*. 10.3 *carmina sunt dicenda*; Hor. *carm. saec*. 8 *dicere carmen*; see also *E*. 3.55n.

6 super tibi erunt. An instance of tmesis: the compound verb *superesse* is split into its components, thereby emphasizing the word placed between them (in this case, the pronoun *tibi*); cf. *Aen*. 2.567 *super unus eram* (at the beginning of the Helen episode).

7 Vare. Almost certainly P. Alfenus Varus, an important jurist who studied under Servius Sulpicius Rufus (Gell. 7.5.1). A native of Cremona, he played an important role in northern Italy's political life: he was *consul suffectus* in 39 BCE; it is possible that he is the same Varus mentioned by Catullus, 10 and 22 (also Catull. 30 may be addressed to him). According to the Virgilian biographical tradition, he protected the poet during the land redistribution process, of which Octavian had put him in charge (*MRR*, II, pp. 377 and 386); cf. *E*. 9.26n.; *Enc. Virg*. I, pp. 92–3, s.v. *Alfeno Varo* (M. Pavan; F. Della Corte); at any rate, this kind of traditional identification ought to be taken with a grain of salt, as in *Verg. Enc*. I, p. 54, s.v. *Alfenus Varus* (D. Armstrong). As in Pollio's case (cf. *E*. 4), the consulship may have provided V. with an occasion to dedicate a poem to his protector, and certainly is one of the 'merits' (6.6 *laudes*; cf. 4.26n.) to which V. refers. His mention of *tristia bella*, on the other hand, need not imply Varus' military leadership (which is not otherwise known): it is quite likely, however, that further achievements were expected of a former consul, and lieutenant of a *diui filius*, who would be a proconsul and therefore an army commander (but it is also true that, Varus being a politician not of the first rank, it was easier for Virgil to 'refuse' to sing his deeds; things are different in *E*. 4.54 and 8.7–8). Thus, the alternative identification as Quinctilius Varus is

ECLOGUE 6   299

implausible: while the latter is known as a brilliant intellectual in Maecenas' circle, he never held military or political office. If indeed Alfenus Varus is the addressee of Hor. *carm.* 1.18 (though there is no actual proof of this), then, a few years after the *E.*, Horace interestingly transposes V.'s ideas into lyric poetry. V.'s pastoral *recusatio*, which opens the Dionysian sixth eclogue, is dedicated to Varus, while Horace would address an (Alcaic) praise of vines and wine to him (*Nullam, Vare, sacra uite prius seueris arborem*). Servius is most probably wrong in asserting that Varo shared V.'s Epicurean allegiance (*sectam Epicuream, quam didicerant tam Vergilius quam Varus docente Sirone* [see below, 6.13–86n.]), even though some scholars have detected Epicurean echoes in the fragments of Varus' juridical works (D. Liebs, *Eine Karriere in Zeiten des Umbruch*, in G. M. A. Margagliotta, A. A. Robiglio, eds., *Art, Intellect, and Politics: A Diachronic Perspective*, Leiden 2013, pp. 311–66). Servius, however, might be referring to a different Varus (Quinctilius?), unless he is thinking of L. Varius Rufus, the poet friend of V. (cf. *E.* 9.35n.), and confusing the two figures. To be sure, an Epicurean inclination would not be out of place in the addressee of an eclogue so full of Lucretian reminiscences. **tristia condere bella.** The phrase derives from the conflation of two different constructions, such as *condere carmen* (cf. *E.* 10.50–1) and *dicere bella*: cf. Ov. *trist.* 2.335–6 *Caesaris acta / condere*. The adj. *tristis* is a standard epithet of war, as Servius noted (cf. also Hor. *ars* 73 [quoted above, 6.3n.]), but here it suggests that Tityrus-Virgilius is really not enthusiastic about war themes and willing to follow Apollo's suggestion. The bucolic poet hints at a value scale which appeals to (and reworks) Callimachus, thereby expressing detachment from encomiastic epic—a rather risky genre: if the poet's attempt was botched (as often happened), the result was detrimental both to the protagonists whose historical endeavours were purportedly praised and to the authors themselves (cf. the case of Choerilus of Iasus and Alexander the Great: Hor. *epist.* 2.1.232–4; *ars* 357–8). It is Homer, not Bion, who sang 'wars' and 'tears' at [Mosch.] *epit. Bion.* 81: κεῖνος [scil. Βίων] δ' οὐ πολέμους, οὐ δάκρυα, Πᾶνα δ' ἔμελπε κτλ. (cf. 6.1–12n.). Note also the opposition between *tristia bella* and the etymology of the name *Calli-machos*.

8 **agrestem tenui meditabor harundine Musam.** In this 'second proem' (or 'proem in the middle'), the pastoral book echoes and modifies its opening: *siluestrem tenui Musam meditaris auena* (*E.* 1.2). The second person *meditaris*, whose subject was the Tityrus of *E.* 1, now gives way to *nunc ego...meditabor*, where Tityrus is explicitly identified with the poet, whereas the *siluestris Musa* of 1.2n. is now replaced by an *agrestis Musa* (here, too, the formula is Lucretian: Lucr. 5.1398; see again 1.2n.). Already in Theocritus, the opening formula ἄρχετε βουκολικᾶς Μοῖσαι φίλαι, ἄρχετ' ἀοιδᾶς, repeatedly appearing in the refrain of *id.* 1 (*id.* 1.64; 1.70, etc.), was echoed and reworked in *id.* 7.49: ἀλλ' ἄγε βουκολικᾶς ταχέως ἀρχώμεθ' ἀοιδᾶς (cf. *id.* 7.36; also *E.* 6.13 *pergite Pierides* [n.]); see also Introduction, p. 20 and n. 49. Note the balanced structure of the line (cf. 2.50n.); here adjectives and nouns form a chiastic structure with noun and adjective in agreement

300   ECLOGUE 6

enclosing the line: $a^1a^2VS^2S^1$; *tenui* (as in 1.2) is emphasized through the masculine caesura.

9–12. Once again, the addressee takes centre stage. The rhetorical tone is similar to the opening of *E*. 1: the poet suggests that his Muse, humble though she may be, can still honour Varus (note the *myricae*, echoing *E*. 4, whereas *nemus* is a variation on the *siluae* of *E*. 4.3). Through this direct intervention, the poet highlights the material, 'bookish' character of the *E.*, never explicitly referred to so far (6.12n.).

9 non iniussa cano. The verb *iubeo* is often used to request poetry, even in a 'professional' sense, as e.g. in Hor. *sat*. 1.3.2–3 (but cf. Pind. *Isthm*. 8.5a αἰτέομαι). Maecenas' *haud mollia iussa* (*G*. 3.41) are well known, but for now V. only alludes to what he will explicitly say in *E*. 8.11–12 (most probably addressed to Asinius Pollio): *iussis / carmina coepta tuis* (see n. ad loc.). In sum, there seems to be an authority external to the poet asking him for poetry: cf. *E*. 3.84 *Pollio amat nostram, quamuis est rustica, Musam* (note here *agrestem...Musam*). Human authority and exhortation are now added to divine (i.e. Apollo's) orders, following a proemial pattern operating in Hes. *theog*. 33; Callim. *aet*. fr. 1.22 Pf. = Mass. = Hard.; cf. also Prop. 2.13.4; Ov. *amor*. 2.1.3; Colum. 10.226. V.'s formulation echoes the Callimachean motto ἀμάρτυρον οὐδὲν ἀείδω (fr. 612 Pf.), which V. will rework again in *Aen*. 8.49 *haud incerta cano* (in an aetiological, and eminently Callimachean, context). The negative particle *non* doubtless refers to *iniussa*, not to the verb: such a litotes is typical of courtesy formulas: 'things not unbidden' (i.e. 'solicited'). **si quis...haec quoque, si quis.** For this kind of modesty, cf. the eulogistic passage at *Aen*. 9.446 *si quid mea carmina possunt* (Euryalus and Nisus). Note the repetition of *si quis*, somewhat timidly expressing hope: cf. *Aen*. 2.756 *inde domum, si forte pedem, si forte tulisset, / me refero.*

10 captus amore. The enthusiastic reader/listener's love (cf. *E*. 3.84; 9.56; *Aen*. 2.10) is similar to the poet's passion for his subject matter: *G*. 3.285 *capti...amore*; 3.292; see also *G*. 2.476 *ingenti percussus amore*; Lucr. 1.923–5. **leget.** Priscianus, *gramm*. III. p. 246.5 K. and the codex **d** attest the reading *legat*, perhaps meant to tone down the poet's confidence, as well as to avoid the jingle *leget...canet* (both followed by caesura). But the poet's modesty is underscored by *si quis tamen...si quis* (l. 9), and the sound effect is probably intentional. For a similar issue see *E*. 4.55, where the future (*uincet*) is similarly preferable; cf. Hor. *carm*. 1.1.35 *quod si me lyricis uatibus inseres* (some manuscripts have *inseris*). **te nostrae, Vare, myricae.** Note the emphatic position of the vocative, placed between adj. and noun: Varus is, as it were, surrounded by the sylvan landscape. Cf. 8.21n.; *G*. 2.160; 3.12; Hor. *carm*. 1.17.10 *dulci, Tyndari, fistula*; 3.29.3 *cum flore, Maecenas, rosarum*; Prop. 3.9.21. The humble plant, symbolizing V.'s pastoral poetry, appears again in connection with the eulogy of an important addressee (cf. 4.2n.). In this context, marked by patronage and exchange, the possessive adj. *nostrae* emphasizes both V.'s authorship and the originality of his poetry—*nostrae...myricae* virtually amounts to saying 'the book of the *E*.'

ECLOGUE 6 301

11 te nemus omne canet. The resounding echo of a name in the woods is featured in *E.* 1.5 (the 'first' proem to the book: cf. 6.8n.). The name in question, in this case, is the addressee's: cf. also 5.64; 10.8. **Phoebo.** Phoebus is mentioned as an object of cult (here, of poetry) at 3.62 and 5.66. The epithet 'gleaming' (φοῖβος; cf. *candentis...Phoebi* at *Aen.* 8.720) can also refer to Helios/Sun, as e.g. in Hor. *carm.* 3.21.24 and Prop. 3.20.12, even though V. usually applies it to Apollo; but cf. *Aen.* 11.913 (*Phoebe* = 'moon', as in *G.* 1.431).

12 praescripsit pagina. The single papyrus page, or *charta*: a set of *paginae* (glued sheets of papyrus) forms the book roll, though *pagina* can also denote a single written column (Cic. *Att.* 5.4.4). The verb *praescripsit* refers to the initial position occupied by Varus' name, occurring three times in the prologue to the eclogue. If the poem was published separately, perhaps it was accompanied by a title, e.g. *ad Varum / Varus* or the like (i.e. properly speaking, a *praescriptum*), which may also have appeared in the original edition of V.'s *liber* (if so, not necessarily at the beginning of a new *charta*, but at the beginning of a new *pagina* 'column'). Ancient sources and manuscripts attest two different titles, *Varus* and *Silenus*: only the former, however, is supported by V.'s text. As the second half of the *E.* begins, the text itself draws attention to its 'written' form: the formulation is even more explicit than *E.* 3.85 *lectori...uestro*. Probably influenced by V., Horace concludes his fifth satire (and, therefore, the first half of his *libellus* of satires) with a reference to the materiality of the book (*sat.* 1.5.104 *longae finis chartaeque uiaeque*). For the emphatic hyperbaton *ulla* (6.11)...*pagina* cf. 10.11n.

13–86. The prologue elicits the reader's curiosity. After the poet's mention of the Muses (whom he exhorts to move on: *pergite*), 6.13–14 feature three names quite unfamiliar to the pastoral tradition. In what follows, the reader will find a narrative of the capture of Silenus (13–30) and a summary of his song (31–86), interspersed with fragments of dialogue, exclamations, and questions. The finale, set in the evening, is a typically pastoral one (6.85–6). The topics are artfully arranged: at first, they seem to follow a roughly chronological order (but cf. 6.41n.), which has led several scholars to propose transpositions. There is, however, no strong reason to alter the transmitted order: on the contrary, the manuscripts transmit a coherent text, structured around very effective transitions (6.41–63n.; 64n.). The summary of Silenus' song can be subdivided into two sections: a longer one, composed of three parts (6.31–73n.), and a shorter one, which concludes the poem (6.74–86).

13–30. After a 'personal' note in the prologue, the poet takes on his narrative role once again (as a pastoral narrator, of course, not as an epic one) by addressing the Muses and canonically requesting their support before beginning the song itself. Along with 6.43–60n., this is the longest subsection of the poem (eighteen lines in each case). The capture of a supernatural being, subsequently forced to make revelations in exchange for freedom, is a popular motif, whose Homeric prototype appears in *Od.* 4.363–572 (where Proteus is captured by Menelaus).

302 ECLOGUE 6

V. himself reworks it in the *fabula Aristaei*, which concludes the *G.* (4.315–558). At Rome, king Numa is said to have similarly captured two old, indigenous rural deities, i.e. Picus and Faunus (Ov. *fast.* 3.285–326). As for Silenus himself, a traditional narrative had it that, imprisoned by king Midas, he revealed to him the greatest good available to humans: i.e. not to be born at all or, if born, to die at once (Cic. *Tusc.* 1.114; cf. Herodot. 8.138.3; Xen. *anab.* 1.2.13; Pausan. 1.4.5; see also Ov. *met.* 11.85–103). Another version of the myth, perhaps recorded by Theopompus in his *Thaumasia*, had Silenus handed over to Midas by certain herdsmen, who captured him while he was still drunk; in this case, Silenus made revelations *de rebus naturalibus et antiquis* (Serv. Dan. *ad* 6.13; cf. esp. Aelian. *uar. hist.* 3.18; Tert. *adu. Hermog.* 25.5 [= *FGrH* 115 F 75 b; c; e Jac.]). Here, at any rate, the Homeric model prevails—not just because V. shows great familiarity with it in the *G.*: in fact, the Proteus of *Od.* 4 is endowed with pastoral features, paradoxical though they are (he is a herder of seals: see esp. *Od.* 4.411–13; cf. *G.* 4.433–6, as well as [Theocr.] *id.* 8.52), and the whole Homeric episode can be read as a complex philosophical/naturalistic allegory, according to Heracl. *all. Hom.* 64–7; *schol. Od.* 4.456; Eustath. *ad Od.* 1503, esp. 7–13 (Proteus = 'matter'; Eidothea = 'the goddess of form': cosmogony and metamorphosis will be the thematic thread of Silenus' song). The names here chosen by V. have their own philosophical 'readability' (cf. 6.13n.), and it is likely that the poet meant to evoke an atmosphere of ancient wisdom, in keeping with his own Epicurean interests and those of his friends. However, Servius' allegorical reading seems to be an overinterpretation (*ad* 6.13): *nam uult exequi sectam Epicuream, quam didicerant tam Vergilius quam Varus docente Sirone. et quasi sub persona Sileni Sironem inducit loquentem, Chromin autem et Mnasylon* [for this form of the name cf. 6.13n.] *se et Varum uult accipi* 'for he seeks to follow the Epicurean school, of which both V. and Varus were pupils, under Siro's guidance. And, in a way, Silenus is a disguise for Siro and his teachings, whereas Chromis and Mnasyllus stand for V. himself and Varus'. Note also that only Varius Rufus and Quinctilius (Varus?), not Alfenus Varus, are known to have been part—along with V.—of an Epicurean circle in Campania: cf. *Enc. Virg.* I, pp. 92b and 93b, s.v. *Alfeno Varo* (M. Pavan; F. Della Corte). It bears mentioning that king Midas can be associated with Orphism: he is said to have been initiated to the mysteries by Orpheus himself (Ov. *met.* 11.92–3; cf. Orph. T 160 Kern = 527 II Bern.). An interpretive tradition, going back (at least) to Servius, identifies Chromis and Mnasyllus with two young satyrs: it is more natural, however, to picture them as simple shepherds (*pueri*: cf. 6.14n.). Revelations like those of Silenus are generally bestowed on mortals, and Chromis' name is attested in reference to a bucolic singer (6.13n.). In Nemesianus' reworking, two young (human) herdsmen encounter the sleeping Pan: *ecl.* 3, esp. 6–8.

13 Pergite, Pierides. Yet another marker of a 'new beginning', echoing the opening refrain of *id.* 1.64, etc. (see above, 6.8n.); cf. also 94 ἄρχετε βουκολικᾶς Μοῖσαι πάλιν ἄρχετ᾿ ἀοιδᾶς 'begin, o Muses, begin again the pastoral song'. Here, the poet exhorts the Muses to 'go on', as the book itself moves forward (for

ECLOGUE 6   303

similar editorial references cf. *G.* 2.1–2 *Hactenus…/ nunc*; 3.1 *Te quoque*; 4.1 *Protinus*). The poet's invocation to the Muse will reappear, albeit somewhat delayed, in the 'second proem' or 'proem in the middle' of the *Aeneid*: *nunc age, qui reges, Erato, quae tempora* etc. (7.37; cf. also *Aen.* 7.641–2 *pandite nunc Helicona, deae, cantusque mouete / qui bello exciti reges* etc.). Note the lively opening, featuring alliteration of /p/, in keeping with the preceding *praescripsit pagina*. For the epithet, see 3.85n. **Chromis.** The first of the two audacious youngsters (6.14n.). His name appeared in *id.* 1.23–5, where, however, it referred to a singer of exotic origin: 'if you will sing / as you sang in the contest with Chromis from Libya (Λιβύαθε), / I shall give you a she-goat…'. V. here seems to allude to Theocritus' opening poem, all the while focusing on one of its 'marginal' strands: in Theocritus, Chromis will not be mentioned again (for the 'Libyan shepherds' cf. *G.* 3.339, as well as Hom. *Od.* 4.85–9). V.'s North African echo is in line with the Homeric model (Proteus is an Egyptian god), but Callimachus himself could have been characterized as 'Libyan' in origin (*Anth. Pal.* 7.42.5 ἐκ Λιβύης; in *epigr.* 22 Pf., Callimachus alludes to Daphnis' glory among the shepherds). Towards the end of *Aen.* 1, at the (newly established) Carthaginian court, the singer Iopas (who was taught by Atlas in Africa) enlivens the banquet with a didactic, naturalistic song, closely resembling Silenus' (*Aen.* 1.740–7). While Homer's Proteus and Eidothea (6.13–26n.) were philosophically etymologized in antiquity, the name *Chromis*, used by Homer in reference to a Trojan commander at *Il.* 2.858 (cf. *Aen.* 11.675: another Trojan leader), evokes the philosophical notion of χροά/χροιά, i.e. 'skin', 'surface', employed by the Pythagoreans to denote 'appearance' (Aristot. *sens.* 3.439a31), and also attested in Epicurus and his school: fr. 81, p. 126.29 Us.; Philod. *sign.* 18.7.8 (where it is closely followed by its synonym χρῶμα: 18.3). See further H. Usener, *Glossarium Epicureum*, Rome 1977, p. 728, s.v. χρόα; cf. *SVF*, I, p. 26.1, no. 91 v. Arn. (Zeno). **Mnasyllos.** The name is not attested in the pre-Virgilian pastoral tradition. Its fem. form appears in *Anth. Pal.* 7.730.1 = *HE* 2883 G.-P. (Perses). It may hint at the idea of memory (μνάομαι 'to remember'). In the Servian manuscript tradition, it appears mostly as *Mnasylos*. The name *Mnasyllus* (transmitted in this form, with some variant readings) will be assigned to an important shepherd in Calp. *ecl.* 6 (28, 46, 48, etc.). **in antro.** The place is very well suited to revelations and mysteries, especially of a Dionysian nature (Dionysus himself was raised in a cave, according to *Hymn. Hom.* 26[*Bacch.*].6). For caves in the context of Dionysian—and poetic—enthusiasm cf. esp. Hor. *carm.* 3.25.1–6. See further H. Lavagne, *Operosa antra. Recherches sur la grotte à Rome de Sylla à Hadrien*, Rome 1988; Merkelbach (1988, pp. 63–6 = 1991, pp. 76–8). In the preceding eclogue, a cave was the backdrop for an exchange of songs concerning Daphnis (5.6n.).

14 Silenum. A prominent figure in Dionysus' retinue, Silenus is renowned for his old age and venerable appearance as well as for his salacity (cf. 6.26). He is said to be Dionysus' teacher (for a euhemeristic interpretation cf. Diod. Sic. 4.4.3) and to possess an ancient, precious sort of wisdom, as is shown by the various versions of his conversation with king Midas (see 6.13–26n.) and Plato's well-known

304   ECLOGUE 6

comparison between him and Socrates (*symp.* 215a–b; 216d). Silenus' role of peda-
gogue and guardian of the young god is well attested iconographically (note esp.
the famous Louvre sculpture that portrays Silenus with the boy Dionysus in his
arms) and makes him particularly suited to interacting with *pueri* (as here).
Scientific, astronomical knowledge is attributed to the satyrs in a fragmentary
satyr drama, perhaps written in the fifth century BCE: *POxy* 1083, fr. 1.14–15.
Originally a common noun, Silenus' name is first attested as a proper noun in
Pind. frr. 156–7 Maeh.; see further *Enc. Virg.* IV, pp. 849–50, s.v. *Sileno* (R. Rocca;
F. Cairns). His appearance in a pastoral context is paralleled by Sophocles'
Ichneutae and, above all, by a Hellenistic pastoral fragment in hexameters: there, it
seems, Pan is reproached by Silenus for not having a pipe and goes on to make one
(*Pap. Vind. Rain.* 29801, on which see Bernsdorff 1999, esp. pp. 42–3). Thus, a
'didactic' role is well suited to Silenus even before *E.* 6 (where he appears to be
interested in *calami*—the Hesiodean ones: see 6.69; for Silenus' connection with
Pan's *calami*, cf. Prop. 3.3.29–30). No wonder, however, that the 'capture of Silenus'
is set against a rural, bucolic backdrop: he is probably caught by shepherds in
Theopompus' narrative (cf. above, 6.13–26n.), and by *ruricolae* in Ov. *met.* 11.91.
Silenus' presence in Augustan iconography is widely attested: for instance, the
temple of Apollo on the Palatine is decorated with antefixes perhaps depicting the
mask of the drunken Silenus (G. Carettoni, *Terrecotte 'Campana' dallo scauo del
tempio di Apollo Palatino*, in RPAA, s. III, 44, 1971–2, pp. 123–39, esp. 135–7 and
fig. 10; but cf. M. J. Strazzulla, *Il principato di Apollo*, Rome 1990, pp. 85–8). The
image of a captured Silenus is depicted on a third-century CE mosaic from Tunis
(Saint-Denis 1963, p. 35). V.'s treatment of the capture of Silenus is paralleled by
Dionysian iconography dealing with the capture and taming of wild animals.
Three ancient mosaics from Italy are especially significant: one (most probably
from Rome) is at the British Museum; another is at the National Archaeological
Museum in Naples (from Pompeii's House of the Centaur); the third, particularly
interesting, is from Antium, now at the Centrale Montemartini Museum in Rome
(first century BCE). The Antium mosaic depicts a lion tamed by wine (there is a
large empty vessel in front of it) and awaken by three Cupids, who subdue it and
prepare it to be ridden by Dionysus. The lion's neck and legs are tied; the Cupids
surround it, and two of them play musical instruments (cymbals and a rather
pastoral-looking syrinx) to facilitate the lion's awakening. For further reading, see
C. Salvetti, *I mosaici antichi pavimentali e parietali e i sectilia pavimenta di Roma
nelle collezioni capitoline*, con un'appendice di G. Bevilacqua, *Musiva et Sectilia* 6,
2009, Pisa-Rome 2013, pp. 227–30 (cf. p. 230 for the other two mosaics mentioned
above). The early date of the Antium mosaic shows that this kind of imagery was
quite widespread in V.'s time, and the subject matter of all three mosaics probably
goes back to a single Hellenistic model: a painting or, perhaps, the well-known
sculpture by Arcesilaus, depicting a lioness tamed by Cupids. This artwork was
apparently part of Varro's collection, according to Plin. *nat.* 36.41: *Arcesilaum quoque*

magnificat Varro, cuius se marmoream habuisse leaenam aligerosque ludentes cum ea Cupidines, quorum alii religatam tenerent, alii cornu cogerent bibere, alii calciarent soccis, omnes ex uno lapide. Artworks like this one must have been of interest to Asinius Pollio, who owned Arcesilaus' sculptural depiction of Centaurs and Nymphs (Plin. *nat.* 36.33 *Centauri Nymphas gerentes*). Perhaps even Varro's piece ended up in Pollio's collection. Pollio's taste for Dionysian subjects is confirmed by Pliny the Elder, who mentions Praxiteles' *Sileni* and *Maenades* (*nat.* 36.23), as well as Eutychides' *Liber Pater* (*nat.* 36.34), among the artworks displayed in Pollio's *monumenta* (i.e. the newly rebuilt *Atrium Libertatis*). In an original and humorous reinterpretation of the topos, Propertius, drunk on wine and alone on the streets of the city, happened to be tied up by a group of Cupids, who took him back to Cynthia's house, at least according to the testimony of the poet himself (Prop. 2.29a). **pueri.** The boys' connection with *Silenus* and the apostrophe of Silenus himself at 6.24 (cf. also l. 20 *timidis*) point at the difference (in nature and in strength) between the old deity and the two audacious youngsters. The mythical precedents (6.13–26n.) and the narrative construction of the episode portray them as common shepherds (hence the need for a divine helper, Aegle: see 6.20n.). Note also that the task of *cogere...ouis stabulis* (6.85n.) is obviously assigned to them. This, however, does not rule out that V. may also have kept in mind Silenus' typical iconography, frequently depicting him amidst young satyrs, i.e. his pupils and followers; cf. the well-known Pompeian fresco from Villa dei Misteri: *LIMC* VIII.1, s.v. *Sileno*, p. 1112, no. 14 (E. Simon). Gods can mingle with Virgilian shepherds (cf. esp. *E.* 10.24), and such a reading of *E.* 6 helps to understand a passage like *G.* 2.493–4 *fortunatus et ille deos qui nouit agrestis / Panaque Siluanumque senem Nymphasque sorores.* **somno...iacentem.** The phrase will be used of Proteus in *G.* 4.404, thus corroborating the Homeric reminiscence.

15–17. V.'s characterization of the old drinker features an impressive array of details, along with some amusement on the narrator's part: Silenus' mythical and cosmological revelations seem to have something to do with the time he spent with Iacchus/wine on the previous day. As Horace will put it in *epist.* 1.19.3–5, *ut male sanos / adscripsit Liber Satyris Faunisque poetas, / uina fere dulces oluerunt male Camenae.*

15 inflatum...uenas. The vasodilatory power of wine was known to the ancients, who believed that liquids (and food in general) had a direct effect on blood circulation: *G.* 3.482–3; Lucr. 4.955; Hor. *sat.* 2.3.153–4; Sen. *epist.* 122.6. The swelling (and heat) caused by wine must have seemed particularly suited to enthusiastically 'sublime' poetry. Note the so-called Greek accusative (cf. *E.* 1.54n.). **ut semper.** The parenthetical remark underscores the habitual nature of Silenus' drinking: cf. also the worn-out handle of his drinking-vessel (6.17). **Iaccho.** Silenus' Dionysian connection becomes even more explicit through this metonymic use of the ritual epithet of Bacchus, *Iacchus*, originally associated with the Eleusinian mysteries: cf. *E.* 7.61; *G.* 1.166 *mystica uannus Iacchi*; for a similar metonymy, see *E.* 5.69 *multo...Baccho* (which is the only other mention of wine in the *E.*: n. ad loc.).

306 ECLOGUE 6

16 serta. Garlands and woven wreaths (usually featuring ivy and flowers) are among the most typical attributes of Dionysus and his followers, though obviously they also suit a poet-singer. Here they take centre stage, and will play a crucial role in the whole scene: cf. 6.19 (where they are used to tether Silenus), as well as 6.22n.; 23n. Plutarch discusses various types of flowers and plants used for symposiastic wreaths in Plut. *quaest. conu.* 3.1–2.645d–649e (for instance, ivy wreaths are said to counteract drunkenness: 3.1.647a); cf. also Athen. 15.669c–686c. Symposiastic garlands are frequently featured in portraits of drunken revellers, at least since Plato, *symp.* 212d–e; the same is true of their Latin equivalent, i.e. the *comissator*: cf. Plaut. *Amph.* 999; *Men.* 463–4; 628–9; Petron. 65.7. **tantum…delapsa.** Most probably, *tantum* modifies *delapsa* rather than *iacebant*, thereby specifying the meaning of *procul*: 'at a distance, having just slipped off his head' (and therefore 'nearby'; cf. Servius: *non longius prouolutam coronam*); see also Manil. 4.632; Val. Fl. 8.289; *OLD*[2], p. 2101, s.v. *tantum*, 8c. The adv. *procul* need not imply great distance: cf. *Aen.* 10.835. Objects falling to the ground, or about to fall, are typical of literary and iconographic depictions of drunken characters: cf. the drunken Komos in Philostr. *imag.* 2, whose torch slips from his hand (τὸ ἐν τῇ δεξιᾷ λαμπάδιον ἔοικε διαφεύγειν τὴν χεῖρα); see also 6.14n. **capiti.** To be read as dat., as is most probably the case with *Aen.* 10.271. Besides metrical convenience (avoiding here a sequence of three short syllables: *căpĭtĕ*), it adds an affectionate nuance to the description of Silenus (his head, almost personified, seems to have suffered a loss). For an echo cf. Sil. 16.434–5 *delapsa corona / uictoris capiti*; but cf. (with a personal pronoun) Cic. apud *schol. Cic. Bob.*, p. 174, 9–10 St. *cornua illi…nunc esse delapsa*; see further *ThlL* V.1.414.28–32, s.v. *delabor*. Parallels are provided by e.g. Ov. *ars* 2.528 *capiti demptas…rosas*; Liv. 38.47.4 *coronam…capiti detrahunt*; Sen. *dial.* 6[*Marc.*].13.1. Others have pointed to the archaic abl. *capiti*, as in Catull. 68.124, for which cf. *ThlL* III.384.45–56.

17 et grauis…pendebat cantharus. The image is described with visual effectiveness: in the famous Borghese Vase from the *horti Sallustiani* (40–30 BCE; Louvre Museum, Borghese cols. 1808 Ma 86), a faun holds up a drunken, potbellied satyr, whose cup has just fallen from his hand; note also 6.14n. (though the cup is on the ground in the case of the captured lion). **attrita…ansa.** The consequence of habitual drinking: *frequenti scilicet potu*, as Servius observes.

18 senex. Old age is typical of both literary and iconographic portrays of Silenus (note esp. the so-called Papposilenus): cf. Plaut. *Rud.* 317–19; Ov. *ars* 1.543; *met.* 11.90; 14.639; *fast.* 1.399; 6.339; Nemes. *ecl.* 3.60. Here, in the context of poetic transmission and teaching, the term also implies a certain venerable aura (cf. below, 6.70n.). Amidst the sacred objects in Propertius' cave, Silenus is called 'father' (Prop. 3.3.29: *Sileni patris imago*). Note, however, the humorous connotations of the 'old drunkard', a traditional figure which inspired medical and scientific theories: in a treatise *On Drunkenness* (Περὶ μέθης), Aristotle had asserted that old people are more readily exposed to

ECLOGUE 6   307

intoxication (fr. 108 Rose). The topic is discussed by Plutarch in *quaest. conu.* 3.3.650a–e.

18–19 spe carminis ambo / luserat. As Silenus appears reluctant to accommodate the boys' request, the reader might notice an analogy with Tityrus-V., who needs Apollo's command to go back to the pastoral world. Tityrus' name, after all, can be etymologized as 'satyr' or 'silenus' (1.1n.). For the phrase cf. *Aen.* 1.352 *uana spe lusit amantem*; see also Lucr. 4.1101 *simulacris ludit amantis* (the simple verb *ludo* + acc., in the sense of 'mocking', is common in comedy: e.g. Plaut. *Capt.* 877). Note *ambo*, which in V. is the normal acc. form (whereas Ovid will use both *ambo* and *ambos*).

19 ipsis ex uincula sertis. The image is reworked by Ovid in *met.* 11.91–2 *uinctumque coronis / ad regem duxere Midan*. Here *ipsis* emphasizes the fact that, as ancient art confirms, these very Dionysian objects are used to tie up the old Silenus (given his status as a semi-divine figure, it is possible that only objects belonging to the same divine sphere can be used to 'act upon' him).

20 Aegle. The 'resplendent' (αἴγλη, 'splendour'): an etymological connection with light is well suited to feminine beauty, here underscored at 6.21; cf. 1.5 *formosam…Amaryllida* (n.). The name is quite common for a nymph: Aegle is the mother of the Charites and is also one of the Hesperides (cf. *E.* 6.61n.). Here, the radiance of her name makes an appearance as soon as Silenus sees her (*iamque uidenti*). In her role as divine helper, Aegle corresponds to Homer's Eidothea, the 'goddess of form' (6.13–26n.). On the importance of light in ancient myth and religion, see M. Christopoulos, E. D. Karakanta, O. Levaniouk (eds.), *Light and Darkness in Ancient Greek Myth and Religion*, Lanham 2010 (with references). Note that *addit se sociam* has an epic flavour (*Aen.* 2.339; 6.169–70; 9.149–50), which ironically contrasts with *timidis*.

21 Aegle Naiadum pulcherrima. Silenus' sexual union with a Naiad is attested by Pindar, fr. 156.2–3 Maeh. Ναΐδος ἀκοίτας / Σιληνός (Ναΐς is an alternative form of Ναϊάς). In Prop. 2.32.37–40, the Naiad is mentioned in a Dionysian context featuring Silenus; cf. Ov. *fast.* 1.405–14 (also below, 6.26n.). Note the repetition of the proper noun, appearing first at the end of a line, then at the beginning of the following one (20–1). For a Greek parallel (featuring, however, a common noun), cf. Theocr. *id.* 1.29–30. The superlative of *pulcher* is applied to a divine creature, in lieu of the more typically pastoral *formosus* (*E.* 1.5n.; but cf. 4.57n.). **iamque uidenti.** Silenus wakes up from his deep sleep and is now in full possession of his faculties; for this use of the verb, cf. 5.57n.

22 sanguineis frontem moris et tempora pingit. Silenus' forehead and temples, no longer 'protected' by the symposium wreaths, are now painted in dark red by Aegle, who uses blood-coloured mulberries for that purpose. The berries must be those produced by a variety of mulberry plant quite widespread in antiquity, i.e. *Morus nigra*: cf. Hor. *sat.* 2.4.22 quoted below; Mart. 1.72.5 (cf. Serv. Dan. ad loc.; he adds that *sanguineis* hints at Pyramus' blood: see Ov. *met.* 4.125–7; *RE* VI.A1,

308   ECLOGUE 6

col. 287, s.v. *Thisbe* [G. Türk]). The gesture is both playful and apotropaic, since Aegle paints Silenus in the colour that Roman ritual traditionally associated with divine status; this was especially true of rural deities (for Pan, cf. *E.* 10.27n.), Bacchic cults, and fertility rites or deities: cf., for instance, Priapus in Hor. *sat.* 1.8.5; Tib. 1.1.17–18; Ov. *fast.* 1.415; 6.319; in reference to Dionysus/Bacchus and his cults, cf. Pausan. 2.2.6; 7.26.11; 8.39.6; Tib. 2.1.55. In the famous parade of Ptolemy II Philadelphus, the Sileni were clothed in red or purple garments (Athen. 5.197e). The mulberries, obviously ripe and juicy, suffice to set the whole scene in summertime: cf. Hor. *sat.* 2.4.21–3 *ille salubris / aestates peraget, qui nigris prandia moris / finiet, ante grauem quae legerit arbore solem*; see also *Anth. Lat.* 395.27 R. = 391.27 Sh. B.

23 ridens. The text of P is corrected into *inridens*; but *rideo* + acc. (cf. *Aen.* 5.182) is more appropriate for the good-natured atmosphere (Silenus laughs at the trick), whereas *inrideo* implies scorn or aggressiveness (cf. *Aen.* 7.435), which would be out of place here. For the general tone cf. *E.* 3.9; note also 4.60n. **quo uincula nectitis?** Unlike Homer's Proteus, Silenus will sing even without being tethered: he sounds amused, and, this time, he will not run away. Thus, the god lets the boys understand that, if he wanted to, he could escape and make fools of them—their success is a mere illusion (6.24n.). Dionysus, after all, is a 'liberator' by nature (*Lyaeus, Liber*): when the young god is captured by Tyrrhenian pirates (*Hymn. Hom.* 7[*Bacch.*].12–14), no bond can keep him tied; Bacchic initiation rituals seem to have involved being tied to a stage machine (Liv. 39.13.13). For other testimonies concerning Dionysian bondage and liberation, esp. featuring satyrs in satyr drama, see Merkelbach (1988, pp. 103–4 = 1991, pp. 116–17). The verb itself (*soluere*) appears immediately, in the imperative (6.24); but Silenus does not seem to give the boys enough time to untie him: he immediately (6.26 *simul*) starts singing.

24 pueri. The apostrophe points at the boys' human nature: cf. above, 6.13–26n.; 14n. (fauns, in turn, will soon make an appearance: they are explicitly mentioned at 6.27). **satis est potuisse uideri.** The context, in which Silenus asks for what purpose they tied him up and begs to be freed, makes it natural to interpret the phrase as 'it is enough [i.e. 'let it suffice'] to have the appearance of having been able to do it', i.e. *uideri* is the governing verb (cf. *Aen.* 5.231 *possunt, quia posse uidentur*). This inter-pretation still stands even if *potuisse* is the governing verb: '...to have been able to appear (to have done it)'. Either way, *uideri* clearly implies the god's superiority and a veiled threat: Silenus will surely play the *pueri's* game (6.23 *dolum ridens*) and give them what they want for now, but it is best not to anger him further. On the other hand, if *potuisse* is the governing verb, an alternative reading is theoretically pos-sible but ultimately unpersuasive: 'let it suffice that I could appear to you'. This is certainly the way in which the phrase *potuisse uideri* is used in Prudentius, *apoth.* 10 *haud umquam...Deum potuisse uideri* (cf. Lucr. 1.270 *esse in rebus, nec posse uideri*). Here, however, this cannot be the intended meaning: the *pueri* can hardly be content with the sight of Silenus, since they clearly have some familiarity with him (6.18–19). What the boys are interested in is Silenus' song, which in fact takes centre stage in the poem. The expression *potuisse uideri* has puzzled many scholars, some of whom have posited rather unconvincing conjectures. Due to its prosodic form, the verb *uideri* necessarily appears in the last foot (cf. *E.* 3.65 *cupit ante uideri*; note Lucr. 1.224; 1.889, etc.), as is normally the case in hexameter poetry, even when *uideri* governs another infinitive: cf. Hor. *epist.* 2.1.87 *solus uolt scire uideri*; Sil. 7.471 *metuit dubitasse uideri*; note also Ov. *met.* 2.322 *potuit cecidisse uideri*. A sententious—almost oracular—solemnity is far from surprising in Silenus' opening speech, which, as Horace will observe (*ars* 239), must distance itself from colloquial language and comic parlance. Irony and dissimulation are typical of Silenus (hence his well-known connection with the Socratic 'mask': cf. above, 6.14n.). He straddles an ambiguous boundary between reality and fiction: his dissimulatory subtlety is ridiculed by Ovid, *fast.* 3.747–8 *audit in exesa stridorem examinis ulmo, / aspicit et ceras dissimulatque senex*. Silenus' attitude resonates with the poet in this eclogue, which is so replete with possibilities, potentialities, and projects (some of which are now actualized, while others are postponed).

25 cognoscite. 'Learn': the verb emphasizes the rational dimension, corresponding to the didactic topics of the incipient song; cf. esp. the opening cosmological discussion. Lucretius often applies the verb to the learner (for the imperative cf. Lucr. 1.921 *cognosce et clarius audi*); V. will use it, in a Lucretian context, at *G.* 2.490 (see also *E.* 4.27).

26 aliud mercedis. The sly allusion to sex befits the cunning, satyr-like personality of Silenus (*inextinctae…libidinis* in Ov. *fast.* 1.413), who appears to rule out any erotic interest in the two boys (*carmina uobis*). Dionysian cult did not normally foster homosexuality, which is—however—attested, for instance, in the case of the Italian *Bacchanalia* (see Merkelbach 1988, pp. 107–8 = 1991, pp. 119–20). Silenus is said to have had sexual intercourse with a Naiad (6.21n.), and the present line is probably the main motivation for Servius' assertion (*ad* 6.13 [see 6.13–26n.]: *quibus ideo coniungit puellam, ut ostendat plenam sectam Epicuream, quae nihil sine uoluptate uult esse perfectum*. Silenus' song will assign a very important role to female characters and, significantly, his allusive use of the term *merces* is paralleled in the language of comedy: cf. esp. χάρις in Aristoph. *Eccl.* 1048. **incipit ipse.** For the hexameter ending, cf. *Aen.* 10.5 (in a solemn context: Jupiter takes the floor in the divine council).

27–30. The bringing of nature to life is described through the appearance, in succession, of fauns (half-beasts), animals (*Faunosque ferasque*), and finally trees (even the stiff oaks wave their tops to the beat). The phenomenon is not new to the reader of V.'s *E.*; for the closest parallel, cf. 5.62–4.

27 tum uero. In poetry, the adv. *uero* belongs to the elevated register (11x in *G.*; 44x in *Aen.*); see Axelson (1945, pp. 86–7). This is the only occurrence in the *E.*, where *uerum* appears 3x (1.24; 3.2; 35); for *uero* cf. Enn. *ann.* 17 Sk. *face uero*

310   ECLOGUE 6

quod...pater orat. For the phrase *tum uero* cf. Cic. *Arat.* 436 Soub.; Catull. 64.231; Lucr. 6.1153 (besides Prop. 2.1.14). It is very frequent in the *Aen.* (e.g. 2.105 *tum uero ardemus scitari*) and in Ov. *met.*, e.g. 2.227, as well as in later epic poetry. **in numerum.** A technical phrase for rhythm, occurring 3x in Lucretius: 2.631; 4.769; 788; cf. *G.* 4.175 (the Cyclopes at work). **Faunosque ferasque.** Faunus was originally an Italic deity, probably a half-man, half-wolf creature, soon assimilated to the Greek satyrs (hence the plural). His appearance then became satyr-like, with horns and goat's feet. In his anthropomorphic form, he was remembered as one of Latium's first kings, father of the eponymous king Latinus (*Aen.* 7.48; 81–2). No wonder that the fauns are the first to react to Silenus' song, since they were identified with the ancestral voices of Italic poetry (see Ennius, *ann.* 207 Sk. *uorsibus quos olim Faunei uatesque canebant*, in relation to Saturnian metre: they now listen to hexameters; cf. Varr. *ling.* 7.36, as well as Lucr. 4.581, which V. might have in mind here; Hor. *epist.* 1.19.4). Etymologically, *Faunus* was connected to *fari*, *fatum* or φωνή (Varr. *ling.* 7.36; Serv. *ad Aen.* 7.47; 7.81; another folk etymology, perhaps more plausible, connects Faunus, a fertility god, to *faueo*). See further *Enc. Virg.* II, pp. 480–1, s.v. *Fauno* (P. Baccini Leonardi); *Enc. Or.* II, pp. 374–5, s.v. *Fauno* (F. Trisoglio); cf. also *Verg. Enc.* II, p. 476, s.v. *Faunus* (J. D. Hejduk). For the animals' dance, cf. Theocr. *id.* 6.44. Note the alliterative phrase *Faunosque ferasque*, featuring the 'epic' coordination *-que...-que*; cf. 8.22n. **uideres.** For the similar epiphany of Dionysus, depicted as leading a *chorus* of Nymphs and satyrs, cf. Hor. *carm.* 2.19.1–2: *Bacchum in remotis carmina rupibus / uidi docentem.*

28 ludere. Here, without a doubt, in the narrow sense of 'dancing' (see *OLD²*, p. 1153, s.v. 1), immediately taken up by *motare*. The dance, soon 'infecting' animals and trees, was often considered as a primeval activity, coeval with the birth of the universe: Lucian. *salt.* 7. **rigidas...cacumina quercus.** The line anticipates the motif of animated trees, which Silenus' song will develop: cf. 6.62–3n.; 71n. (where *rigidas* is taken up to emphasize the miracle). For the frequentative verb *motare*, with an explicitly joyful connotation (6.29 *gaudet*), cf. the similar *nutantem* at *E.* 4.50 (4.52 *laetentur*). For the hexameter clausula, cf. 2.3 = 9.9 *cacumina fagos* (syntactically different).

29–30. Nature's cheerful response is deemed to be superior to that prompted by two divine singers, Orpheus and Apollo (who will reappear at the end of the poem, with a ring-composition effect: 6.82). Notions and images of *E.* 4 are, once again, taken up here: besides *laetentur* (see 6.28n.), cf. *E.* 4.55–7, featuring Orpheus and Apollo (with some contextual differences).

29 Parnasia rupes. The cliff of Mount Parnassus (2457 m), the tallest mountain in Phocis, towering above Apollo's sanctuary at Delphi: thus, the phrase is almost a metonymy for Apollo, in full possession of his musical, poetic, and oracular faculties. The Castalian spring, sacred to Dionysus and the Nymphs (*G.* 3.291–3), is located in a nearby ravine, not far from the sanctuary. The local cult of Dionysus was explained, especially in Orphic circles, by the fact that, after being dismembered by the Titans,

ECLOGUE 6   311

the god was buried on Mount Parnassus by Apollo himself (Orph. fr. 35 Kern = 322 I Bern.; cf. Callim. fr. 643 Pf.; Euphor. fr. 13 Pow. = 14 v. Gron. = Light.; Philochor. *FGrH* 328 F 7 Jac., with V. Costa's commentary, *Filocoro di Atene*, vol. 1, *Testimonianze e frammenti dell'Atthis*, Rome 2007, pp. 90–5). Macrobius observes: *item Boeotii, Parnassum montem Apollini sacratum esse memorantes, simul tamen in eodem et oraculum Delphicum et speluncas Bacchicas uni deo consecratas colunt...in hoc monte Parnasso Bacchanalia alternis annis aguntur, ubi et Satyrorum, ut adfirmant, frequens cernitur coetus* (Macr. *Sat.* 1.18.3; 5). For *rupes* with a geographical epithet, cf. Catull. 61.27–8 *Thespiae / rupis*, as well as 68.53.

30 Rhodope...et Ismarus. Both places are associated with Orpheus (called *Thracius* at 4.55) and Dionysian cult; *Rhodope* is a mountain range that separates western Thrace from Macedonia. Rhodope is again connected to Orpheus at *G.* 4.461 (it is described as a remote, inhospitable place, at *E.* 8.44; *G.* 1.332; 3.351; 462; see also Theocr. *id.* 7.77), and to Dionysus in Ov. *met.* 6.589. As for *Ismarus*, it is a mountain in southern Thrace, which Propertius mentions in the context of an allusion to Orpheus (Prop. 2.13.6 [cf. below, 6.69–73n.]); note also Ov. *amor.* 3.9.21 *Ismario...Orpheo*); its Bacchic-Dionysian fame was mainly due to the presence of well-reputed vineyards, perhaps alluded to by Homer in *Od.* 9.196–8; cf. *G.* 2.37–8 *iuuat Ismara Baccho / conserere*; see also Ov. *fast.* 3.410. The more common neut. plur. form (*Ismara*), appearing in *G.* 2.37, is here eschewed in favour of a 'personifying' masc. form, almost creating a geographical couple with the fem. *Rhodope*. The connection between Orpheus and Dionysian cults is reinforced by the singer's violent death at the hands of the Maenads (*G.* 4.520–2). In the version of the myth narrated by Aeschylus in his *Bassarae* or *Bassarides*, the Bassarids (led by Dionysus) probably killed Orpheus for abandoning the Dionysian cult and embracing that of the Sun/Apollo; cf. [Erat.] *catast.* 24; *TrGF*, III, p. 138 Radt.; M. L. West, *The Orphic Poems*, Oxford 1983, pp. 12–13. **miratur.** Most manuscripts have the sing. form (note P); the plur. *mirantur*, a *lectio facilior*, is found in R and some Carolingian manuscripts. For a similar issue cf. *Aen.* 2.317 (*praecipitat* P; *-tant* M). **Orphea.** Certainly disyllabic here: cf., by contrast, *E.* 3.46.

31–73. This is the first part of the summary of Silenus' song and, much longer than the second (and last) section at 6.74–86, it contains a wide variety of topics, culminating in Gallus' initiation scene. This first section can be subdivided into three subsections: 31–42 (cosmogony and mythical prehistory); 43–60 (myths of unrequited love); 61–73 (further myths and Gallus' initiation). For the summary of a poetic song, besides Apollonius' epic model (cf. 6.31–42n.), see also Theocr. *id.* 7, where Lycidas summarizes the song that will be sung by Tityrus during the banquet in honour of Ageanax: ὁ δὲ Τίτυρος ἐγγύθεν ᾀσεῖ / ὥς ποκα τᾶς Ξενέας ἠράσσατο Δάφνις ὁ βούτας κτλ. (*id.* 7.72–3); ᾀσεῖ δ' ὥς ποκ' ἔδεκτο τὸν αἰπόλον εὐρέα λάρναξ κτλ. (*id.* 7.78); cf. below, 6.31n.; 47–60n.

31–42. Silenus' song begins with a cosmogony, here summarized in accordance with a pattern of thought that was quite widespread in antiquity: through a

312 ECLOGUE 6

gradual combination of elements, an ever more complex variety of forms and living beings is generated. Orpheus' name, which has brought the narrative frame to a close, evokes his song in the model passage of Apollonius Rhodius, which Silenus echoes on multiple occasions: ἤειδεν δ' ὡς γαῖα καὶ οὐρανὸς ἠδὲ θάλασσα, / τὸ πρὶν ἐπ' ἀλλήλοισι μιῇ συναρηρότα μορφῇ, / νείκεος ἐξ ὀλοοῖο διέκριθεν ἀμφὶς ἕκαστα· / ἠδ' ὡς ἔμπεδον αἰὲν ἐν αἰθέρι τέκμαρ ἔχουσιν / ἄστρα σεληναίης τε καὶ ἠελίοιο κέλευθοι· / οὔρεά θ' ὡς ἀνέτειλε, καὶ ὡς ποταμοὶ κελάδοντες / αὐτῇσιν Νύμφῃσι καὶ ἑρπετὰ πάντ' ἐγένοντο 'He [Orpheus] sang of how earth and heaven and sea, / once mingled together in a single form, / were separated each from other because of ruinous strife; / and of how the stars and the paths of the moon and the sun / keep their eternal laws forever; / of how the mountains rose, and of how the resounding rivers / with their Nymphs came about, and of how all living creatures were born' (*Arg.* 1.496–502; Iopas' song in *Aen.* 1.740–6 is similarly reminiscent of Apollonius). The first great 'metamorphosis', i.e. the origin of the universe, opens Ovid's epic poem (*met.* 1.5–88); cosmological interests were crucial to Hesiod's *Theogony*: cf. Callim. *aet.* fr. 2.2–3 Pf. = 4.2–3 Mass. = 2.2–3 Hard. As ancient readers observed, the notions and language here used by V. for cosmological topics are markedly Lucretian: in particular, Macrobius (*Sat.* 6.2.22–4) compares *E.* 6.31–7 with Lucr. 5.432–9; 446–8; 455 (he also compares *E.* 6.35–6 with Lucr. 5.437–8 at *Sat.* 6.4.11, and *E.* 6.33 with Lucr. 6.205–6 at *Sat.* 6.5.4). For other Lucretian parallels, cf. Lucr. 2.1052–63; 5.65–70; 416–31; 772–825 (besides scattered echoes of the anthropological doctrine contained in Lucr. 5). In the *Aeneid*, the revelation given by Faunus' oracle to Latinus (6.27n.) will also echo Lucretius: *Aen.* 7.89 *multa modis simulacra uidet uolitantia miris* (with which cf. Lucr. 1.123; see also *G.* 1.477). Note that king Midas was said to have interrogated Silenus *de rebus naturalibus et antiquis* (Serv. Dan. *ad E.* 6.13). In order to assuage Apollo's wrath, the young Hermes of *Hymn. Hom.* 4[*Merc.*].425–8 had sung a theogony starting with the beginning of time (note also *Hymn. Hom.* 4[*Merc.*].409–10, seemingly suggesting that Hermes is tied in bonds, just like Silenus). An Epicurean substratum here is shown by the fact that Silenus' cosmogony is as 'godless' as the atomists' cosmological doctrine was: cf. Introduction, p. 17 (divine intervention will play a limited role in Ovid's cosmogony, too: but cf. *met.* 1.21 *deus et melior…natura*). Note that V. omits any allusion to the Empedoclean principle of *neikos*, which Apollonius had mentioned (*Arg.* 1.498). Through *hinc* (6.41n.) V. connects cosmogony and the first appearance of life on earth with the birth of the human species and its mythical prehistory, narrated in three crucial episodes (the Flood and Pyrrha; the Golden Age; Prometheus).

31 namque canebat uti. The use of the archaic *uti* in this metrical position evokes Lucretius: cf. Lucr. 1.192; 663; 2.22, etc. Note the echo of Apollonius at the very beginning of the song: ἤειδεν δ' ὡς (see above, 6.31–40n.); but cf. also

Theocr. *id.* 7.73 ὥς ποκα; 7.78 ἀσεὶ δ᾽ ὥς (on which see above, 6.31–73n.). **magnum per inane**. The Lucretian echo is obvious: the same phrase appears several times in the first two books of *De rerum natura* (the ones strictly devoted to physics): Lucr. 1.1018 *copia ferretur magnum per inane soluta*; 1.1103; 2.65; 105; 109. Lucretius uses the phrase *per inane* very frequently; the substantive adjective can also govern another adjective (as here *magnum*): cf. Lucr. 1.509 *uacuum per inane*. But the whole motif of the 'void' is eminently Lucretian and Epicurean. In Epicurus' thought, the notion of void is crucial when it comes to distinguishing atomistic doctrines that are scientifically correct from those that are not (hence Lucretius' criticism of Empedocles and other pluralist thinkers at Lucr. 1.742–5). The point is rightly made by Servius ad loc.: *Epicurei uero...dicunt duo esse rerum principia, corpus et inane* (cf. Epic. *ad Herod.* 39).

32 semina. Like its Greek equivalent (σπέρματα), the term is common in cosmological vocabulary: Lucretius often uses the phrase *semina rerum* (e.g. 1.59), which will reappear in Ov. *met.* 1.9 *non bene iunctarum discordia semina rerum*. However, V.'s formulation, featuring a series of coordinated genitives (32–3, cf. *E.* 8.22n.), might hint at an Empedoclean notion of 'principle' rather than at Democritean atomism (for Democritus—and Epicurus—atoms do not have qualities). Lucretius himself refuted Empedocles' doctrine in 1.714–33, esp. 714–15 *et qui quattuor ex rebus posse omnia rentur / ex igni terra atque anima procrescere et imbri*; on the other hand, Lucretius considers the natural elements as large clusters of atoms (*syntheta*, according to Servius *ad E.* 6.31), which occupy an intermediate position within cosmology: cf. esp. Lucr. 5.443–8. In general, V. here seems to aim at reconciling Epicurean orthodoxy and popular cosmological beliefs: key notions of Epicureanism are introduced through common patterns of thought without their substance being altered. For the enjambed *semina* (also with *coacta*, though in reverse order), cf. Lucr. 2.1059–60 *semina rerum / coacta*. **terrarumque animaeque marisque**. The repeated *-que* emphasizes the threefold structure, to which a fourth element is added in the following line (6.33 *et...simul*). Note the Lucretian use of *anima* in the sense of 'air': Lucr. 1.715 *ex igni terra atque anima procrescere et imbri* (it also means 'breath', with obvious etymological echoes, at Lucr. 5.236 and 1230).

33 liquidi...ignis. This 'liquid fire' may seem paradoxical, especially after the sea has been mentioned. But the adj. has its original meaning of 'flowing', and therefore 'pure', 'light', 'limpid'; cf. Lucr. 6.205 *liquidi color aureus ignis*, as well as Lucr. 5.500–1 *liquidissimus aether / atque leuissimus* (cf. Servius' gloss: *puri id est aetheris*; but V. here seems to avoid precise, technical terms). **his ex omnia primis**. The text transmitted by most manuscripts is favoured by many editors and known to Serv. Dan. (cf. Macr. *Sat.* 6.2.22): *his exordia primis*, supported by numerous Lucretian occurrences of *exordia*; cf. esp. Lucr. 5.430; 471, as well as 2.333; 1062; 3.31. Yet the text of **P**, *his ex omnia primis*, is preferable as it is *difficilior* and

314 ECLOGUE 6

importantly paralleled by Lucr. 1.59–61 *semina rerum / appellare suemus et haec eadem usurpare / corpora prima, quod ex illis sunt omnia primis* (Silenus here alludes to the well-known Lucretian definition of *semina*). For the anastrophe of the preposition, cf. 6.19 *ipsis ex uincula sertis*. Note that this textual choice makes it almost necessary to print *omnis* in the following line (6.34). This, at any rate, is certainly one of the most difficult textual and interpretive issues in the *E*.

34 omnis et ipse tener mundi concreuerit orbis. As the following lines make clear, *mundi...orbis* refers to an amorphous mass, located at the centre of the universe, from which the world arose; as such, it cannot refer exclusively to the heavens, nor to a specific element. The adj. *tener* denotes the still semi-fluid state of the primeval Earth; note also that, in V., *mundus* often refers to an earthly dimension: cf. *E.* 4.9; 4.50; *G.* 1.240; 2.336; cf. Lucr. 5.780–1 *mundi nouitatem et mollia terrae / arua*. For the process of separation and aggregation of single elements, see Lucr. 5.443(437)–508, esp. 495 *terrae concreto corpore pondus*, featuring the typically Lucretian verb *concrescere* (cf. Lucr. 1.840; 1019; 4.134; 1261, etc.). The various 'beings' will not be separated from one another until 6.35–6, starting with land and sea. **omnis.** The reading *omnia*, which would complement *exordia* at 33, must be discarded in favour of *omnis*, presupposed by P's *omnisa* (then corrected into *omnia*) and approved by Sabbadini. The sterile and merely emphatic repetition *omnia / omnia* does not fit into the concise style of the summary and is ultimately unpersuasive, despite some Lucretian parallels (cf. Lucr. 6.528–9, where the repetition is consistent with Lucretius' typical argumentative style): 'as all things derive from these principles, / all things, and even the world itself etc.' Even the synaloepha in the first foot, affecting a dactylic word, is more typical of Lucretius than V. (though it occasionally occurs in V.): for *omnia et* cf. Lucr. 1.710. In sum, if V./Silenus said *ut his ex omnia primis, / omnia et ipse...orbis*, he would sound more Lucretian than Lucretius. Note also that the reading *omnia...omnis* allows for a more fluid syntax, with the intransitive verb *concreuerit* governing the sentence as a whole.

35 durare...discludere. Both these alliterating verbs must be governed by *coeperit*, whose subject is *mundi...orbis*: they are thus used transitively, as is normally the case. For *durare* cf. *G.* 1.89–91 *seu...calor ille uias et caeca relaxat / spiramenta... / seu durat magis et uenas astringit hiantis*; for *discludere* cf. Lucr. 5.443–4 (= 437–8) *diffugere inde loci partes coepere paresque / cum paribus iungi res et discludere mundum*, quoted as a parallel by Macr. *Sat.* 6.4.11 (but Lucretius' use of the verb is slightly different); see also Caes. *Gall.* 7.8.2 *mons Cebenna, qui Aruernos ab Heluiis discludit*. For the origin of the sea, cf. Lucr. 5.483–91, esp. 487 *expressus salsus de corpore sudor*. **Nerea ponto.** This sea is separated from the rest of the ocean by a solidified landmass. Thus, Silenus offers a scientific reinterpretation of the myth of Nereus, son of Pontus: cf. Hes. *theog.* 233 Νηρέα δ' ἀψευδέα καὶ ἀληθέα γείνατο Πόντος. The sea-god Nereus, father of the Nereids and endowed with prophetic powers, will often reappear after V. as a personification of the sea: cf. e.g. [Tib.] 3.7.58 *placidum per Nerea*; Ov. *her.* 9.14. The term *pontus* is older and more strictly poetic (Enn. *ann.* 217 Sk.; Catull. 36.11; Lucr. 1.271); here, however, the Hesiodic parallel, along with the proximity of *Nerea* and the extended meaning of the noun ('sea / ocean') may be enough ground for printing *Ponto* with an initial capital (which, however, may lead to some confusion with Pontus [Euxinus]; cf. 8.95). Note also *theog.* 132, where Pontus (son of Gaia, just like Uranus) predates Oceanus. For similar marine personifications, cf. 4.32 *Thetin*; 10.5 *Doris* (Nereus' wife). The device lends itself readily to exaggeration: note the parody in Pers. 1.94.

36 rerum…sumere formas. As if the world were 'clothed' in forms, objects, and living beings: cf. Ovid's reworking at *met.* 1.87–8 *sic modo quae fuerat rudis et sine imagine tellus / induit ignotas hominum conuersa figuras.* **paulatim.** For a gradual natural development (or maturation), cf. *E.* 4.28; but the adv. is common in Lucretius, e.g. 1.188–9 *omnia quando / paulatim crescunt.*

37 nouum…solem. The adj. evokes the moment in which the sun was generated and gave rise to the familiar sequence of dawns and sunsets: cf. Hor. *carm. saec.* 10–11 *aliusque et idem / nasceris.* The line need not imply that Silenus considers the birth of the sun as subsequent to that of the Earth: note, at any rate, that the newly formed lands are the ones 'astonished' at the sight of the sun; in Lucr. 5.471–7, sun and moon are generated by separation from the amorphous mass of all lands (which have not yet completely taken shape). Orphic cosmologies assigned a fundamental role to the Sun, called *Phanes*, as Macrobius observes (though not altogether aptly) in *Sat.* 1.17.34 *item Φάνητα appellant ἀπὸ τοῦ φανεῖν, et Φανέον ἐπειδὴ φαίνεται νέος, quia sol cotidie renouat sese; unde Vergilius* [G. 3.325] *'mane nouum'* (cf. also *G.* 2.332). Here, the astonishment at the newborn sun allows comparison with Orph. fr. 86.2–3 Kern = 123.2–3 Bern. (Herm. *in Plat. Phaedr.* 247c) τοὶ δ' ἄλλοι ἅπαντες / θαύμαζον καθορῶντες ἐν αἰθέρι φέγγος ἄελπτον 'all the others / were astonished, seeing an unusual radiance in the heavens' (i.e. that of *Phanes*/Sun). Also comparable (yet distinct) is the philosophical tradition that highlights nature's wondrous perfection as an argument for the existence of the gods: see Cic. *nat. deor.* 2.95 (Aristot. fr. 12 Rose); Philo, *praem.* 41–2; Sen. *dial.* 6[*Marc.*].18.2–3. As a charismatic formula, *Nouus sol* will appear on Neronian coins: M. Griffin, *Nero: The End of a Dynasty*, London 1984, p. 296, n. 46. V.'s reader will see both sun and moon reappear in the opening of the *G.*, immediately followed by Liber/Bacchus (*G.* 1.6–7). **stupeant.** Wonder and admiration are common reactions to new *inuenta* (here, in fact, a new celestial body): cf. Apoll. Rhod. 1.549–51 (the ship Argo); Catull. 64.15. The present subjunctive, appearing after *fuissent* (6.32), *concreuerit* (6.34), and *coeperit* (6.36), conveys the immediacy of the action and makes for some syntactical variation; it is followed by *cadant* (6.38), *incipiant* (6.39), and *errent* (6.40). **lucescere.** The inchoative verb evokes an early, still faltering appearance of light. Note also that the

316   ECLOGUE 6

impersonal use of the verb refers to dawn: cf. Plaut. *Amph.* 533; Catull. 14.17; *ThlL*, VII.2.1703.7–14.

38 altius atque cadant summotis nubibus imbres. The appearance of the new star is followed by the first meteorological phenomena, especially the first rainfalls. V.'s text seems to imply that the genesis of clouds is due to the sun's action upon water surfaces (and even the land), a notion active in antiquity (see esp. Lucr. 6.470–80; cf. Epic. *ad Pyth.* 99, as well as Xenoph. 11 A 46 D.-K.). As the earth keeps growing, the clouds reach increasingly higher atmospheric strata, with the result that rain falls from ever higher altitudes (*altius*). The postponement of *atque* is quite audacious (though here it is perhaps facilitated by the alliteration), and will not occur again in V.; cf. Hor. *epod.* 17.4; *sat.* 1.5.4; *ThlL* II.1049.69–1050.9. R reads *utque*, probably in an attempt to normalize the text.

39 incipiant siluae…surgere. An expected mention of the *siluae*, i.e. the properly pastoral environment, which is visualized here in its first appearance (cf. *E.* 4.3). The *siluae* played an important role in Lucretius' 'anthropology': cf. Lucr. 5.955; 962; 992; 1243, etc. **cumque.** A very rare hexameter ending, featuring a double conjunction (but cf. Lucr. 2.114).

40 ignaros…montis. The variant reading *ignotos* (P) is probably a trivialization, although worth consideration. The mountains themselves are 'unaware', just as the lands were 'astonished' at l. 37: a typically bucolic personification of nature. **errent.** The roaming movements of the first animals (*rara…animalia*), to whom the world is still unknown: after all, the *siluae* have only now come into being. The verb anticipates an important topic of the central section of Silenus' song, i.e. wandering (6.52; 58; 64): animals, like lovers, are characterized by casual and aimless motion, due to their lack of rationality.

41 hinc. The adverb makes the transition sound somewhat vague: how could Silenus pass from the origin of animals to the Flood and the myth of Pyrrha? In his summary of Orpheus' song (cf. 6.31–40n.), Apollonius Rhodius had compressed a whole cosmogony into a few lines, then moving on to the reign of Ophion and Eurynome, followed by that of Kronos (1.503–6). Note that 6.41–2 can be read as a sort of hinge between the scientific cosmology at 6.31–40 and the mythological narrative at 6.43–60. On the other hand, the rapid succession of *hinc* (6.41, denoting a logical and temporal transition) and *his adiungit* (6.43, indicating an 'addition' of new topics) gives the impression that 6.41–2 should go with what precedes rather than what follows. **Pyrrhae iactos.** The myth of Deucalion and Pyrrha is alluded to here by a reference to Pyrrha alone, almost anticipating Silenus' preference for female figures in the remainder of his song. The name *Pyrrha*, moreover, evokes πῦρ 'fire', the object of Prometheus' theft (6.42n.), thereby re-establishing a link to the theme of light after the Flood. Deucalion, son of Prometheus, and Pyrrha, daughter of Epimetheus (and Pandora), survived the Flood on account of their piety, and were subsequently assigned the task of regenerating humankind. Following the orders of Hermes

(Apollod. 1.7.2 [48]) or the goddess Themis (Serv. Dan.; cf. Ov. *met.* 1.377–83), they threw a number of stones behind them: as the stones fell on the ground, they were turned into men and women. Hence the well-known folk etymology connecting λαός 'people' with λᾶας 'stone', which V. himself presupposes in *G.* 1.62–3 and 2.340–2 (Hes. fr. 234 M.-W.; Serv. *ad G.* 1.63; cf. also Callim. fr. 496 Pf.; Lucr. 5.925–6; Ov. *met.* 1.414–15). **Saturnia regna.** Silenus' mention of 'Saturn's reign', i.e. the Golden Age, is quite surprising; the phrase is certainly in asyndeton (since it cannot be in apposition to *lapides...iactos*). We do not know how Silenus could connect one topic to the other, but the mythical Flood was traditionally placed under Zeus' reign (Pind. *Ol.* 9.52), i.e. after that of Saturn: cf. Ov. *met.* 1, esp. 113–15; 253–312; Apollod. 1.7.2 (47). No wonder that some scholars have doubted the genuineness of the text here: the obvious comparison with *E.* 4.6 (identical hexameter clausula) leads to more, rather than less, suspicion. Note that Calvus, in one of his short poems (perhaps *Io?*), must have referred to the happy age that preceded Jupiter's reign: *dicunt Iouem commutasse omnia, cum bonus a malo non discerneretur, terra omnia liberius ferente, quod Caluus canit* (*schol. Bern. ad G.* 1.125, p. 186 H.; cf. fr. 20 Bläns. = Court.; cf. *E.* 4.39n.).

42 **Caucasiaque...uolucris furtumque Promethei.** The order of events is again unusual, yet expressive: first, the terrible punishment, then the crime. In the myth (from Hesiod onwards), Prometheus is the son of the Titan Iapetus and Clymene, daughter of Oceanus; in order to favour humankind, he deceives Zeus in the division of the sacrificial ox. When Zeus, as a punishment, deprives humans of fire, Prometheus steals it from Olympus and gives it back to them by hiding it in a fennel stalk. Then, Zeus sends Pandora (Pyrrha's mother: 6.41n.), and her jar full of evils, while Prometheus is punished by having his liver perpetually devoured by an eagle, until Heracles frees him (Hes. *theog.* 521–616; cf. also *op.* 47–105). The epithet *Caucasias*, here referring to *uolucres*, aligns the text with Aeschylus' version, according to which Prometheus was indissolubly tied not to a column in an unspecified location (Hes. *theog.* 522), but to a cliff in a remote region of Scythia (*Prom.* 1–2), near the Caucasus mountains: cf. Apoll. Rhod. 2.1247–8 Καυκασίων ὀρέων...ἐρίπναι / ἠλίβατοι; it is on Caucasus that Lucian sets his *Prometheus* (23). From Hesiod onwards, there is only one bird, i.e. Zeus' eagle: *theog.* 523; Aesch. *Prom.* 1022; Apoll. Rhod. 2.1250; Apollod. 1.7.1 (45); Sen. *Herc. f.* 1207; Mart. 11.84.10 (the same applies to Promethean iconography: see *LIMC* VII.1, pp. 531–53, s.v. *Prometheus* [J.-R. Gisler]). The plural will reappear in Prop. 2.25.14 and Ov. *Ib.* 292. In *E.* 4, the return of the Golden Age is slowed down (at least for some time) by the appearance of new technologies: first seafaring and agriculture, then war (*E.* 4.31–6). Here, by contrast, the theft of fire is mentioned immediately after the *Saturnia regna*. The name *Promethei*, here in line-ending position, features synizesis in its final syllable: cf. 6.30n; 78n. For the double *-que* cf. 6.27n.; also 6.32n. For a similar inversion of the logical order, with an emphatic effect, cf. *G.* 3.60–1 *aetas... / desinit ante decem, post quattuor incipit annos.* **refert.** This is the first verb of speech

318   ECLOGUE 6

in the present tense (cf. 6.31 *canebat*): as such, it switches the focus back to the narrator, i.e. Silenus. Its position and meaning (a rather anodyne one: 'he relates') seem
to emphasize the conceptual unity of all three topics (the rebirth of humankind, the
Golden Age, Prometheus), regardless of their relative chronology.

43–60. After the transition at 6.41–2, introducing the human species through
time-honoured origin myths, and a reference to Hylas and the Argonaut expedition 6.43–4), Silenus goes on to treat a number of mythical themes, all featuring
female heroines. In the Hesiodic corpus, as it was read at least since the Hellenistic
age, the *Theogony* (a theological and cosmogonic poem) was followed by the
Catalogue of Women (or *Ehoiai*), relating the vicissitudes of mythical heroines.
This text was widely read in Rome and left a tangible mark on Latin poetry (see
P. Hardie 2005). Catalogues of 'depraved' heroines play an important role in
Roman love-elegy and in Parthenius' *Erotika Pathemata*, dedicated to Cornelius
Gallus (and perhaps in Cornelius Gallus himself?): cf. esp. Prop. 3.19; Ov. *ars*
1.283–342, as well as *met*. 10.153–4, where the speaker is Orpheus. After a series
of 'highbrow' topics, the change in subject matter may appear as an abrupt variation, as Servius noted (*ad* 6.41): according to him, the transition could be
'hedonistically' motivated by the pleasure of *fabulae*. In 6.61–3, the summary
resumes in a concise style after the narrative expansion of 6.45–60, concluded by
the direct speech at 6.55–60 (as is the case with 6.61–73n.).

43 his adiungit. Coupled with *refert*, the verb introduces a sequence of mythical, heroic events in logical and chronological terms. The pronoun *his* summarizes
the preceding section and holds it together (cf. also 6.41n.). The well-known story
of Hylas, whose unnamed protagonist is Heracles, mediates the transition from
great foundation myths (Prometheus, the Argonauts, and Prometheus' liberator)
to stories of ill-fated women and impossible loves. Silenus seems to echo the first
book of Apollonius' *Argonautica* (6.31–40n.), which features Hylas' ill-starred fate
(*Arg.* 1.1207–1325): thus, the identity of the *nautae* of 6.43 (= Argo's sailors) does
not need further clarification. **Hylan…relictum.** The boy Hylas, whom Heracles
loved and brought along to the Argonaut expedition, was abducted by the
Nymphs on account of his beauty as he went into the woods near Cios (in Mysia)
to fetch water. Besides Apollonius, Theocritus also reworked the myth in his *id*. 13,
which is entirely devoted to it. At Rome, the story was treated by Varro of Atax,
author of a poem on the Argonaut expedition (Ov. *amor*. 1.15.21–2), as well as by
Propertius, 1.20, and later by Valerius Flaccus, 3.521–97. In *G*. 3.6, the story is used
as an example of a hackneyed mythical theme; cf. *Enc. Virg*. II, p. 904, s.v. *Ila*
(D. Giordano); *Verg. Enc*. II, pp. 633–4, s.v. *Hylas* (D. Petrain); also *LIMC* V.1,
pp. 574–9, s.v. *Hylas* (J. H. Oakley); see further Pretagostini (1984, pp. 89–103); De
Vos (1997); Mauerhofer (2004). **quo fonte.** With Callimachean accuracy, Silenus
reveals the name of the spring where Hylas was abducted. Apollonius' solution
(Apoll. Rhod. 1.1222) looks like a tautology: the place is said to be called Πηγαί
(i.e. 'springs'); cf. Prop. 1.20.33 *hic erat Arganthi Pege sub uertice montis*. According

ECLOGUE 6   319

to the author of the *Orphic Argonautica*, Hylas rashly ventured into the Nymphs' cave (*Argon. Orph.* 645: σπέος).

44 ut litus 'Hyla, Hyla' omne sonaret. In all versions of the myth, it is Heracles who calls out to the boy, while the woods resound with his name; in Silenus' song, by contrast, all the sailors call out to Hylas (*clamassent*) and, correspondingly, the shore is the one said to resound. As a surprising consequence, the resonance effect is distanced from its natural bucolic context, which may even be hinted at by the name *Hylas* (suggesting, despite a difference in prosody, the Greek ὕλη, 'raw matter' or 'woods'; cf. also *Argon. Orph.*, 645 ὕλῃ ἐνιπλαγχθείς), as was perhaps noted by Valerius Flaccus, 3.596–7 *rursus Hylan et rursus Hylan per longa reclamat / auia: responsant siluae et uaga certat imago*. The threefold repetition of the name (*Hylan... Hyla, Hyla*) not only reworks the Theocritean model (*id.* 13.58 τρὶς μὲν "Υλαν ἄυσεν) but also creates a refined echo effect, described by the verbal pair *clamassent...sonaret* and phonetically rendered through the prosodic variation of the redoubled *Hyla, Hyla omne* (from long to short final syllable, as though the boy's name were fading away), underscored by the double hiatus. For a similar yet simpler case, cf. 3.79; see also Ov. *met.* 3.501; Hopkinson (1982). In a mythical variant transmitted by Anton. Liber. 26.4, the Nymphs try to prevent Heracles from finding the boy by turning him into an echo. For an accurate reworking of the myth in Roman elegy, cf. Prop. 1.20 (for the echo, note esp. Prop. 1.20.48–50 *tum sonitum rapto corpore fecit Hylas. / cui procul Alcides iterat responsa; sed illi / nomen ab extremis montibus aura refert*). In Statius, an allusion to V.'s line is ironically prepared and 'outclassed' by a fourfold repetition of the name: Stat. *silu.* 1.2.197–9 *Asteris et uati totam cantata per urbem / Asteris ante dapes, nocte Asteris, Asteris ortu / quantum non clamatus Hylas.*

45–60. As a further addition to the Hylas episode, 6.45–60 introduce the myth of Pasiphae, who had sexual intercourse with a bull. The story occupies the entire central section of the eclogue (6.45–60). Pasiphae's ill-starred fate is compared to that of Proetus' daughters, who believed themselves to be heifers, but did not engage in bestiality (6.48–51). Both stories are eminently 'pastoral' and connect the mythological section of *E.* 6 to the bucolic context of V.'s book. Here V. (or Silenus?; cf. 6.47–60n.) uses a 'miniature' version of the typically Alexandrian technique (employed in Catull. 64) of the narrative digression, or ecphrasis, whose most important paradigms were Callimachus' *Hecale* and Moschus' *Europa* (featuring love affairs and bovine metamorphoses, as well as a digression on the myth of Io [Mosch. *Eur.* 43–57]; Europa's story appeared in Hesiod, fr. 140 M.-W.). Calvus' epyllion *Io* must have been an important model for V.: see below, 6.47n.

45 fortunatam, si numquam armenta fuissent. A pathetic formula, which V. will use again at *Aen.* 4.657–8 (but note also *E.* 1.16 *si mens non laeua fuisset*); cf., by contrast, *G.* 2.458 *fortunatos nimium, sua si bona norint*. The assertion is somewhat paradoxical in the context of a pastoral book, in which *armenta* have been previously mentioned twice: *E.* 2.23 (but see n. ad loc.) and 4.22.

320 ECLOGUE 6

46 Pasiphaen. The Cretan princess, wife of Minos and mother of the Minotaur. Her story, very widespread in both literature and iconography, will be reworked by Ovid, *ars* 1.289–326; *met.* 8.131–7; cf. *Enc. Virg.* III, pp. 1005–6, s.v. *Pasifae* (E. Simon); *Verg. Enc.* II, p. 975, s.v. *Pasiphaë* (D. O. Ross); also *LIMC* VII.1, pp. 193–200, s.v. *Pasiphae* (J. K. Papadopoulos). In the main mythographical sources, her insane passion for the bull is due either to Poseidon's wrath (Apollod. 3.1.4 [9]; cf. Diod. Sic. 4.77.2) or to Aphrodite's (Hyg. *fab.* 40.1). The tale played an important role in Euripides' *Cretans*: cf. *TrGF*, V.1, pp. 502–16 Kann. (Aristophanes, *Ran.* 849–50, alludes to the 'perverted nuptials' narrated by Euripides). The name of Pasiphae, daughter of the Sun (and perhaps herself an ancient Cretan deity of light), hints at 'light for all' (*Πασιφάη*), as is further emphasized by the adj. *niuei* (*iuuenci*): cf. Fulg. *myth.* 2.7, p. 47.18–19 H. *Pasiphaen...id est quasi pasinfanon, quod nos Latine omnibus apparentem dicimus*. The epithet *πασιφαής* appears in *Hymn. Orph.* 8.14 (the Sun); 36.3 (Artemis-Moon); Maneth. *Apotelesm.* 3(2).346 (Aphrodite). An oracular deity named Pasiphae, and thus revealer of truths, was worshipped at the Thalamae sanctuary in Laconia (Pausan. 3.26.1, connecting her with Helios and identifying her with Selene; cf. Plut. *Agis* 9). Note also that the young bull is said to have belonged to the Sun's herd in the version transmitted by Philargyrius/Philagrius *ad* 6.60. The gift of 'snow-white' wool will enable Pan to entice the Moon in *G.* 3.391–3, whereas a white bull (with golden horns) is featured at *G.* 1.217–18 (i.e. the constellation). The astrological significance of the story is confirmed by the Minotaur's name, which was originally Asterius: Apollod. 3.1.4 (11). In the *Aeneid*, Pasiphae's story will appear on the doors of Apollo's temple (*Aen.* 6.23–7; cf. 6.447). Taking the shape of a young bull, Zeus abducted Europa, mother of Minos, and led her to Crete, where she gave birth to their three sons: Minos, Rhadamanthus, and Sarpedon (Apollod. 3.1.1 [2–3]; the myth of the bull, particularly in relation to female figures, plays a crucial role in Cretan cult). **niuei...iuuenci**. The whiteness of Pasiphae's bull reappears in Prop. 2.32.58 *candida forma bouis*; Ov. *ars* 1.290–2 (and in the visual arts: cf. *LIMC* VII.1, p. 196, no. 13). For another lover-bull, i.e. Europa's, cf. Ov. *met.* 2.861 *candida...ora*; 865 *latus...niueum*; see also Mosch. *Eur.* 85 (where the bull is reddish brown, but with a bright, silver ring on its forehead; cf. possibly Phryn., *TrGF* I.3, fr. 16, p. 77 Sn.); Lucian. *dial. mar.* 15.2. Victims offered to Capitoline deities, and to celestial or light deities more generally, were white in colour: Ov. *amor.* 3.13.13 *niueae...iuuencae*, as well as Iuv. 12.3 *niueam...agnam*. **solatur**. Compared to other verbs used here, but vaguer in meaning (*canere, adiungere*, vel sim.), *solatur* conveys a nuance of emotional participation, which is made explicit in the following lines. The 'creative' (i.e. poietic) action will become physically concrete in 6.62.

47–60. The summary is now interspersed with apostrophes and dialogic sections, until Pasiphae herself starts to speak: the reader is left wondering whether these are Silenus' exact words or the poet's free and pathetically amplified

ECLOGUE 6   321

interpretation (cf. *solatur*). In V.'s Theocritean model, i.e. *id.* 7 (see above, 6.31–73n.), the narrator Lycidas summarizes Tityrus' song. In Theocritus, however, the ensuing speech features a eulogy and a *makarismos* (*id.* 7.83–9 ὦ μακαριστὲ Κομᾶτα κτλ.), unlike here (6.47 *a, uirgo infelix* etc.). The mythical past, full of metamorphoses and other overlaps between young women and heifers, may have contributed to a tradition of anthropomorphic depictions of bovines: see e.g. the well-known passage of Lucr. 2.352–66 (with which cf. *E.* 8.85–9).

47 a, uirgo infelix, quae te dementia cepit! Echo and variation of a line from Calvus' *Io* (fr. 9 Bläns. = Court.): *a, uirgo infelix, herbis pasceris amaris*, as observed by Servius Dan. For the pathetic emphasis of the apostrophe cf. also Catull. 64.71 *a, misera* (Ariadne, addressed by the narrator). The allusion to Calvus presupposes an analogy between Io, turned into a heifer, and Pasiphae, which will be made explicit by Ovid, *ars* 1.323 (*Pasiphae*) *et modo se Europen fieri, modo postulat Io*. Calvus' epyllion could have referred to Pasiphae's myth, and maybe to that of the Proetides as well (*E.* 6.48n.). Calvus' half-line, echoed again at 6.52n., is here paired with a rhetorical question appearing at 2.69 *a, Corydon, Corydon, quae te dementia cepit?* (cf. *Aen.* 9.601 *quis deus Italiam, quae uos dementia adegit?*). Thus, neoteric reminiscences are intertwined with V.'s new pastoral style: in fact, the former legitimize the latter. The exclamation *a*, which occurred at 1.15, will reappear at 6.77 (*E.* 6 only has it in line-beginning position, as in Calvus). Ovid will also allude (somewhat ironically) to Calvus' line, perhaps echoing Silenus' song as well: *met.* 1.632–4 (*Io*) *frondibus arboreis et amara pascitur herba / proque toro terrae non semper gramen habenti / incubat infelix*. **uirgo.** The echoes of Calvus (here and at 6.52) help to explain the use of this term in relation to Pasiphae. The ancients attempted to justify it: cf. Serv. Dan. (ad loc.) *quidam 'uirgo' non quod uirum illo tempore non haberet, sed quia talis ei poena iam uirgini destinata sit, intellegunt*; see further *Enc. Virg.* V.1, p. 560a, s.v. *uirgo* (V. Fontanella). As a matter of fact, *uirgo* could also denote a young bride, thereby underscoring the legitimacy of her new status: cf. Hor. *carm.* 2.8.22–23; see, however, Ov. *her.* 6.133 *adultera uirgo* (Medea). In V., the less solemn *puella* is common (e.g. *E.* 6.61: the virgin Atalanta).

48 Proetides. The daughters of Proetus, king of Argolis (three in number, according to ancient mythographers, who assign them various names). In the oldest version of the myth, they were driven mad by Hera, whom they had offended, or by Dionysus, whose cult they had opposed (see Hesiod's *Catalogue*, fr. 131 M.-W.; cf. Apollod. 2.2.2 [26]). Believing themselves to be heifers, they lowed and wandered around the mountains of the Peloponnese, having become a sort of 'bovine' maenads (a fitting punishment if Dionysian impiety was at issue). The manner and consequences of their recovery are narrated in Ov. *met.* 15.322–8; cf. Diod. Sic. 4.68; Apollod. 1.9.12 (102); see further *Enc. Virg.* IV, pp. 261–2, s.v. *Pretidi* (A. M. Mesturini); Casadio (1994, pp. 51–122); Hirschberger (2004,

322   ECLOGUE 6

pp. 300–2). Note the short vowel in the nom. ending, in a markedly Hellenizing (and neoteric) context. **falsis mugitibus**. The image of these 'false' cows, with their 'false' lowing, is quite humorous—particularly in the context of a pastoral book: for similarly 'terrible voices' cf. Bacchyl. 11.56. From l. 48 onwards, M is a witness to the text.

49 at non tam. Note the series of monosyllables: such sequences often appear in line-beginning position, but this is a particularly conspicuous case; cf. *E.* 9.63, as well as 6.73n. The effect is underscored by the alliteration *at...tam... turpis...tamen*. **pecudum**. Already used at 2.8, the noun (fem. in V.'s time) vaguely refers to 'four-footed' domesticated livestock, as opposed to wild animals: cf. the folk etymology at Varr. *ling.* 5.95 *a pede pecudem appellatur*. Note the distinction in *G.* 3.243 *et genus aequoreum, pecudes pictaeque uolucres*. Here, the noun is close to *turpis* (modifying 6.50 *concubitus*, with an emphatic hyperbaton), which frequently expresses horror or revulsion inspired by the animal world: cf. *G.* 4.395 *turpis... phocas*, as well as *G.* 3.52 *forma bouis cui turpe caput* (in a positive context); Hor. *epist.* 1.2.25; for the adj. in a moral sense, cf. *Aen.* 4.194 *turpique cupidine captos*. **secuta**. This is the text of **MP**, whereas **R** and the Carolingian manuscripts have *secuta est* (as in Macr. *Sat.* 4.6.3).

50 collo timuisset. For the construction of *timeo* + dat., cf. *Aen.* 2.729 *comitique onerique timentem*. See also Hor. *carm.* 3.27.7 *ego cui timebo*, etc.; *OLD²*, p. 2140, s.v. 1b. Note how the singular form of the verb, agreeing with *ulla*, switches the focus from the general to the particular after the plural form *implerunt* (6.48), thereby emphasizing the negative force of the sentence.

51 in leui...fronte. The Proetides' 'forehead' (*humana scilicet*, as Serv. Dan. observes) is smooth because the horns that they imagine having do not exist: their *cornua* are a mere hallucination. Their fear of the plough (l. 50) is equally paradoxical, since young maidens ought to fear (or, rather, desire) the 'yoke' of marriage. V. perhaps alludes to Hesiod's version, *Catal.* fr. 133.4–5 M.-W., according to which the Proetides lost their hair as part of their punishment: the allusion is especially likely as it is placed between two half-lines of Calvus, literaly 'The Bald' (47a; 52a: for a similar trick cf. Ov. *her.* 14.109–10; S. Hinds, *Generalising about Ovid*, in *Ramus*, 16, 1987, pp. 4–31, esp. 18). For *leuis* in the sense of 'hairless', cf. *Aen.* 7.349 *leuia pectora*; Iuv. 10.199 *leue caput*.

52 a! uirgo infelix, tu nunc in montibus erras. The girl keeps wandering, looking for the roaming animal (6.58 *errabunda...uestigia*), just like the *rara animalia* at 6.40 (n.); similarly, in *E.* 8.85–9, a *bucula* will get lost because of her love for her calf. In this new reworking of Calvus' line (see 6.47n.), V.'s second half-line is even closer to the original context: Io, too, could be described as wandering in mountains (but note the semantic analogy between *errare* and 6.47 *dementia*). The lingering memory of Calvus' second half-line (*herbis pasceris amaris*) seems to resurface at 6.54 *pallentis ruminat herbas* (note the assonance *erras-herbas*), and perhaps again in *amarae* and *amaro*, which conclude 6.62 and 6.68,

ECLOGUE 6   323

respectively. The repetition of l. 47 frames the digressive address to the Proetides and introduces the resumption of the narrative (6.53 *ille*, etc.).

53 latus niueum. Another reference to whiteness (for *niueus*, 'snow-white', cf. 6.46n.), contrasted here with the darkness of the holm-oak forest (cf. *Aen.* 9.381 *ilice nigra*), as well as with the lively colours of the hyacinths on which the bull reclines; cf. Ov. *met.* 2.865. Note the so-called acc. of respect, here featuring an adj. (but the governing verb is a participle, *fultus*, with the force of a middle-voice form: cf. *Aen.* 1.658 *faciem mutatus et ora Cupido*). For the chromatic detail *niueos...artus*, cf. *Ciris* 399 (perhaps Calvus' Io was turned into a white heifer). For *latus*, in reference to a solitary bull quietly resting (on a riverbank), cf. Erucius in *Anth. Pal.* 6.255.4–5 (= *GPh* 2227–8 G.-P.) ποταμοῦ...ἐπ' ἀϊόνι / ψυχόμενον χηλάς τε καὶ ἰξύας. **molli fultus hyacintho.** Following a neoteric pattern, the fifth-foot syllable in arsis is lengthened and precedes a Greek word: cf. Catull. 64.20 *non despexit hymenaeos* and 66.11 *auctus hymenaeo*; see also *Aen.* 7.398 *canit hymenaeos*. The phenomenon will be featured again, but before a Latin word, in the (Dionysian) opening of *G.* 2.5 *grauidus autumno*. Calvus' Io may have included a reference to the uncomfortable nature of the bedding used by the metamorphosed girl, as seems to be deducible from Ov. *met.* 1.633–4 (see above, 6.47n.): if so, note the opposition to the comfortable and anthropomorphic posture adopted by the snow-white bull; for a further contrast, cf. the young, defeated bull at *G.* 3.224–34, esp. 229–31 *et inter / dura iacet pernox instrato saxa cubili / frondibus hirsutis et carice pastus acuta*. The comfort of some 'greon' bedding will be provided for the *bucula* of *E.* 8.87. For another 'soft' (*mollis*) hyacinth, cf. *G.* 4.137 (and *Aen.* 11.69; see also Hom. *Il.* 14.348–9). For its colour, red and very 'sweet' (*suaue rubens*), cf. *E.* 3.63, as well as *G.* 4.183 *ferrugineos hyacinthos* (which, however, must be 'reddish brown'). Since a boy loved by Apollo was turned into a hyacinth, the flower is well suited to an erotic context: cf. *E.* 3.63n. and 6.83n.; for a four-syllable word in line-ending position see 2.24n.

54 pallentis ruminat herbas. The grass is 'pale', i.e. light green (cf. *E.* 2.47; 3.39; 5.16). The animal obviously chooses the softest variety of grass. Note the focus on colour (now in relation to the animal's mouth), as well as the chromatic contrast between the two neighbouring adjectives (*nigra pallentis*). The lovesick bull, by contrast, neglects food in *E.* 3.100–1. The verb *ruminare* belongs to the language of animal husbandry (cf. Colum. 6.6.1) and hints at the pastoral context of V.'s book. For the same clausula cf. Ov. *amor.* 3.5.17 *reuocatas ruminat herbas* (note also *hal.* 119 *ruminat escas*). Calpurnius Siculus prefers a different 'technical' term for the same idea, *palear* (i.e. 'dewlap'): (*taurus*) *matutinas reuocat palearibus herbas* (3.17).

55–60. Soon after another (bovine) love for a bullock has been mentioned as a possibility, the heroine herself begins to speak, in keeping with a well-established poetic pattern: cf. Ariadne in Catull. 64.132–201 (note that Ariadne is Pasiphae's daughter). Apart from 6.69–73, where Linus speaks, the heroine's words provide

324 ECLOGUE 6

the only instance of direct speech in Silenus' song, even though they are not introduced by a verb of saying (contrast 69 *dixerit*; but 57 *oculis...nostris* could not be explained otherwise). Direct speech is usually avoided in didactic poetry: Aratus has only one instance (*phaen.* 123–6), whereas the G. include direct speech only in the final episode of the fourth book, when Aristaeus will talk amidst tears and moans (*G.* 4.321–32). In both this section and the following (61–73), direct speech plays an important role in concluding the section itself. The bucolic diaeresis marks the opening of the direct speech in 6.55.

55 aliquam...sequitur. Perhaps the bullock prefers another one, as happens in unhappy loves; cf. 10.23 *alium...secuta est*; but here the rival is evidently a young cow (*in magno...grege*), towards which the animal has its normal attraction (as in the painting described by Philostr. *imag.* 1.16, p. 318.32 ἱλαρὸν βλέπων ἐς τὴν βοῦν Kays.).

55–6 Nymphae, / Dictaeae Nymphae. Cf. *Aen.* 8.71 *Nymphae, Laurentes Nymphae*, as well as *G.* 4.321 *mater, Cyrene mater.*

56 Dictaeae Nymphae. i.e., the Nymphs of Mount Dicte, in Crete. According to Callimachus, *hymn.* 3[*Dian.*].189–200, the toponym originated from the ill-fated love of Minos—Pasiphae's (human) husband—for the nymph Britomartis, Artemis' hunting companion. He kept pursuing her amidst cliffs and mountains until she lost any hope of escape and threw herself into the sea, where she was saved by fishermen and their nets (δίκτυον): hence, she was called Δίκτυννα (*Dictynna*), and the mountain Δικταῖος (*Dictaeus mons*: cf. Serv. Dan. *ad Aen.* 3.171); *LIMC* III.1, pp. 391–4 (C. Boulotis). The whole myth, full of flights and pursuits, may be in the background here: in fact, Callimachus' etymology might be echoed in the 'closing' of valleys (*claudite...saltus*), as if these were nets, ready to capture the white bullock (cf. 6.58n.). The epithet 'Dictaeus', crucial to Cretan cult (the newborn Zeus is said to have been raised in a cave of Mount Dicte: note the god's epithet at *G.* 2.536; cf. also *G.* 4.152), was featured in Orpheus' song (Apoll. Rhod. 1.508–9 Ζεὺς ἔτι κοῦρος... / Δικταῖον ναίεσκεν ὑπὸ σπέος), and will reappear in *Aen.* 4.73, again in the context of valleys and pursuits (Dido is compared to a wounded hind); see further *Enc. Virg.* II, pp. 108–9, s.v. *Ditteo* (R. Rocca). In Crete, as in Rhodes, the cult of the Sun was very widespread (U. von Wilamowitz-Moellendorff, *Der Glaube der Hellenen*, I, Berlin 1931, pp. 110–13 and 253–7; E. Hall, *Inventing the Barbarian. Greek Self-Definition through Tragedy*, Oxford 1989, p. 144), and the whole island was considered as a land of age-old mysteries: cf. Eur. *Cret.* fr. 472 Kann., on which see A. T. Cozzoli, *Euripide, Cretesi, fr. 472 N.² (79 Austin)*, in A. Masaracchia (ed.), *Orpheus and Orphism*, Rome 1993, pp. 155–72. Orpheus himself is said to have been a pupil of the Idaean Dactyls (who moved to Crete from Mount Ida in Phrygia), according to Ephorus, *FGrH* 80 F 104 Jac. (Diod. Sic. 5.64.4 = Orph., T 42 Kern = 519 Bern.). **nemorum iam claudite saltus.** The exhortation is similar to a pastoral instruction: cf. *E.* 3.111 *claudite iam riuos, pueri* (for *iam* in commands, cf. also 8.61; 109; *G.* 1.45;

ECLOGUE 6   325

Aen. 2.148, etc.). The noun *saltus* generally denotes walkable woodlands (note here *nemorum*) and can even refer to a 'mountain pass': thus, these *saltus* offer the bullock ample space to roam and feed itself; cf. *G.* 3.142 *saltibus in uacuis* and 323 (see also *Aen.* 11.904 *saltus...apertos*). They could also be 'closed' for hunting purposes, as if they were large, natural nets: cf. *G.* 1.140 *magnos canibus circumdare saltus*; *Aen.* 4.121.

57 si qua forte. The phrase *si qua* expresses rather feeble hopes (cf. *Aen.* 6.882): here, *forte* adds further doubts.

58 errabunda...uestigia. The echo of Catull. 64.113 *errabunda regens tenui uestigia filo* (Theseus finds his way through the labyrinth) evokes the remainder of the story, also featuring pursuits and bull-like monsters. The line provides the only instance, in V.'s *E.*, of an adj. in -*bundus*, thereby emphasizing the Catullan reminiscence (Pianezzola 1965, pp. 138–9; cf. Lucr. 4.692, where the term opens the line, as here and in Catullus): the adj. *errabundus* does not occur again in V.'s works after the *E.* Theocritus describes the bull as naturally inclined to leave the herd and wander alone in the woods: *id.* 9.4–5; 14.43 αἰνός θην λέγεταί τις, 'ἔβα τάχα ταῦρος ἀν' ὕλαν'; 25.132; cf. also Aristot. *hist. anim.* 6.18.572b18–20; 9.3.611a2–3; *Anth. Pal.* 6.255.2–5 = *GPh* 2225–8 G.-P. (Erucius); Opp. *cyn.* 2.50–1; but note Soph. *Oed. tyr.* 477–9. The emphasis on sight (6.57 *oculis...nostris*) suggests that *uestigia* is used literally, in the sense of 'traces', 'footprints': Pasiphae asks the Nymphs to close the valleys, in the hope that she will then be able to locate the animal's traces (and, of course, the animal itself). The logic of hunting is, once again, in the background: see e.g. *E.* 2.12 *tua dum uestigia lustro*; cf., by contrast, *Aen.* 5.566–7 *uestigia primi / alba pedis* (referring to the bottom of the animal's legs). Ancient interpreters were not wrong in reading the adjective *errabunda* as hinting at the animal's 'uncertain' or 'wavering' motion, as in Homer's εἰλίπους (cf. Hom. *Il.* 6.424): '*errabunda bouis uestigia*' illud expressit quod uno uerbo Homerus ait εἰλίποδας βοῦς, hoc est flexis pedibus incedentes (Serv.; cf. *schol. Bern.* ad loc.). The 'traces' (*uestigia*) allow the roaming animal's path to be recognized (the girl herself 'wanders' after it: 52 *erras*), while the shape and nature of its footprints reveal its unmistakably bovine gait. The idea of 'roaming' reappears at 64.

60 stabula...Gortynia. Throughout antiquity, Gortyn was one of Crete's most important cities (cf. Hom. *Il.* 2.646, mentioning it and its walls, along with Cnossus) and its capital in the Roman period. A miraculous plane tree, which never lost its leaves, was said to grow in the area: it is near the tree that, according to the myth, Jupiter had intercourse with Europa (Plin. *nat.* 12.11). A reference to *Gortynia templa* is found at Catull. 64.75 (where, however, many editors accept Palladius' conjecture *tecta*; Catullus seems to have erroneously placed Minos' palace and the labyrinth there). According to Servius, Gortyna's stables harboured the Sun's herds (*Solis armenta*): thus, Gortyna is an appropriate destination for the bright-coloured, divine bullock. Callimachus calls the nymph Britomartis (Dictynna) 'Gortynis' at *hymn.* 3[*Dian.*].189.

326   ECLOGUE 6

61–73. This section introduces further myths with female protagonists, thus paving the ground for the episode of Gallus' initiation. The text is difficult and several transpositions have been proposed: e.g. 61–3 after 73, or 64–73 after 81. However, despite the great variety of topics, which is part of Silenus' 'mystery game' (how could he move from one topic to the next so quickly?), the myths are smoothly connected with one another and give an overall impression of coherence. In fact, the female figures at 61–3 mediate the transition from the 'hapless' heroines at 45–60 to the *poeta creator* (62), who reappears at 70–1. The Gallus episode, with the direct speech at 69–73, aptly brings the section to a close (for a similar mechanism cf. 5.43–60, where Pasiphae's direct speech to the Nymphs concludes the section). Note that the anaphora of *tum* (61; 62; 64) holds 6.61–3 together and introduces the story of Gallus, the 'new' Hesiod. The opening of the following section (74 *Quid loquar* etc.) makes it clear that the poet's narrative is coming to an end.

61 tum canit. The summary resumes with the verb that had opened it (6.31 *canebat*); the same transition formula will reappear at 6.64. M's incorrect reading *capit* is a typical instance of psychological error (cf. 6.59 *captum* and the whole 'hunting' scene at 6.55–60); a second hand corrected it into *canit*. **Hesperidum miratam mala puellam.** Yet another young woman, this time a proper *puella*. Female deities also reappear here (the Hesperides), along with the topic of flight and pursuit, which has just been addressed (cf. esp. l. 59 *captum*), but which now reaches a happy ending (= a 'capture'). Silenus sings of the myth of Atalanta, the princess hostile to love, who forced her suitors to participate in a running contest (she then defeated and killed them), until she fell victim to Milanion's (in the Arcadian version) or Hippomenes' deception (in the Boeotian version). During the contest, the young suitor dropped three golden apples (Aphrodite's gift to Milanion, or Cybele's gift to Hippomenes; but the two versions were soon confused with one another): she stopped to pick them up and therefore had to submit to marriage. The story, mentioned in a pastoral context by Theocritus (*id.* 3.40–2), was very popular in antiquity, also in the visual arts: see *Enc. Virg.* I, pp. 386–7, s.v. *Atalanta* (G. Arrigoni); *Virg. Enc.* I, pp. 140–1, s.v. *Atalanta* (L. Fratantuono); *LIMC* I, pp. 940–50, s.v. *Atalante* (J. Boardman). Catullus (2b) alludes to the myth, which will become an example of successful courtship in Propertius, 1.1.9– 10; in Ovid, the story of Atalanta and Hippomenes will be narrated by Orpheus: *met.* 10.560–707. By referring to the story of Atalanta, Silenus may intend to introduce the theme of metamorphosis, which characterizes the remainder of his song (except for the interlude on Cornelius Gallus): Atalanta, full of desire for her new lover, had intercourse with him in a forest sacred to Cybele, who punished the two for such a desecration by turning them into lions and yoking them to her chariot (Serv. *ad Aen.* 3.113; *Myth. Vat.* 1.39.3; cf., differently, Hyg. *fab.* 185.5–6). For *aurea mala*, though not belonging to the Hesperides, cf. *E.* 3.71; 8.52–3. **Hesperidum.** That the game-changing apples come from the Hesperides' garden is asserted in the scholia on Theocr. *id.* 3.40–2b–c, pp. 127–8 Wend.; cf. *Catal.* 9.25 *Hesperidum ni munere capta fuisset*; Prob.; *schol. Bern.*, p. 131 H.; Serv. *ad Aen.* 3.113; *Myth. Vat.* 1.39.2. However, apple trees producing golden fruit had been offered by the Earth as a gift to Zeus and Hera for their wedding (Pherecyd. *FGrH* 3 F 16 Jac.). The reference to the apples of the Hesperides, framed by the 'snow-white' bullock and the sisters of Phaethon (6.62n.), is in keeping with the solar sensibility that characterizes Silenus' song. The apples of the Hesperides, divine daughters of the Night residing in the westernmost part of the world (and mentioned by Hesiod, *theog.* 215–16), were closely connected with solar symbolism, especially since they could be read as an astral allegory (*schol. uet. ad* Hes. *theog.* 215, p. 45 Di Greg. Ἑσπερίδας. τὰς ἑσπερινὰς ὥρας λέγει, μῆλα δὲ χρυσᾶ τὰ ἄστρα). They were also featured in Orphic mythology, as is testified to by fr. 34 Kern = 306 Bern. (Clem. Alex. *protr.* 2.17.2; cf. also Hes. *theog.* 275). The Hesperides and their sacred branches will reappear in *Aen.* 4.484–5; but Aegle herself—the 'gleaming' Naiad (6.21)—is the namesake of one of them: Hes. fr. 360 M.-W. (Serv. Dan. *ad Aen.* 4.484); Apoll. Rhod. 4.1428. The girl's admiration (*miratam*) is readily explained by the divine light of the sun enlivening the apples: cf. l. 37 *stupeant lucescere solem*. A reference to the Hesperides may have been particularly appreciated by Gallus, who seems to have used the adj. *Hesperius* (coupled with *Eous*) to indicate the extreme boundaries of the world: cf. Ov. *amor.* 1.15.29–30; *ars* 3.537; Prop. 2.3.43–4; *Ciris* 352.

62 Phaethontiadas. The Sun's daughters, commonly known as the Heliades, are here named after their ill-starred brother Phaethon, struck by Zeus' thunderbolt for daring to drive the chariot of his father, the Sun, thereby endangering the whole universe: cf. [Sen.] *Herc. O.* 187; Prisc. *gramm.* II, p. 65.7–11 K. Consumed by grief, they benefited from the compassion of Zeus, who turned them into trees (poplars, or so it seems, at *Aen.* 10.190; cf. Apoll. Rhod. 4.604; Ov. *Pont.* 1.2.32; here, alders [6.63 *alnos*]). The metamorphosis is located on the banks of the river Eridanus, traditionally identified with the Po, where Phaethon is said to have fallen: cf. Ov. *met.* 2.324; but see also Pherecyd., *FGrH* 3 F 74, as well as Timaeus, *FGrH* 566 F 68 Jac. V.'s use of the adelphonymic underscores the source of the Heliades' mourning: but with some irony, since Phaethon (φαέθων) is one of the Homeric attributes of Helios/Sun (see esp. Hom. *Il.* 11.735; cf. *Aen.* 5.104–5; Val. Fl. 3.213; see also Orph. frr. 73; 238.10 Kern = 125; 541.10 Bern.). Thus, the Heliades' brother is a mortal man (Phaethon) who did not succeed in assimilating himself to his divine father (Phaethon/Helios). The story is potentially set on the banks of the river Po, in Cisalpine Gaul (or the Rhône, in Transalpine Gaul, according to Aeschylus [?], fr. *73a R. [Plin. *nat.* 37.32]; cf. Apoll. Rhod. 4.596–629). At any rate, a 'Gallic' setting for the myth seems appealing to the Mantuan poet V. as well as to Gallus, who seems to have been a native of Narbonese Gaul. Gallus himself is about to appear, though associated with another river (the Permessus), and he will be mentioned again, along with the *alnus*, in the finale of *E.* 10 (see

328 ECLOGUE 6

6.63n.). The myth of the Heliades features a strong desire for assimilation with the Sun (which elicits Zeus' wrath: note the analogy between Phaethon and Prometheus, who steals fire at 6.42): thus, the story aptly concludes the central section of the eclogue, before V.'s mention of the Muses and the *chorus* of another 'gleaming' god (Phoebus Apollo: 6.66). That the tale of Phaethon could play a role in a rational re-interpretation of *natura rerum* is shown by Lucr. 5.396–410.

62-3 circumdat... / ...erigit. Silenus' poetic action is now described in demiurgic terms, as though he were himself performing the transformation: 'excellent praise for the singer, as if he were not singing of the event, but producing it through his song', as Servius observes. The device, not devoid of some satiric potential, is used in a pastoral context by [Mosch.] *epit. Bion.* 80–4; cf. Hor. *epist.* 1.19.31; Iuv. 1.162–3 (with E. Courtney's commentary, London 1980, pp. 117–18 [2013[2], p. 97], ad loc.) and 7.151 *perimit saeuos classis numerosa tyrannos*; Lieberg (1982a). In modern narratology, this device corresponds to the notion of 'metalepsis' defined by G. Genette; cf. S. Matzner, G. Trimble (eds.), *Metalepsis. Ancient Texts, New Perspectives*, Oxford 2020. Silenus echoes the Orphic magic of poetic 'creation' (ποιεῖν), which directly affects nature: a 'gift' that Silenus shares with Hesiod (see 6.70–1n.). The reader has seen its effects on trees at 6.28; Ovid will describe the Heliades' metamorphosis, 'enveloping' the girls with bark: *met.* 2.346–66 (esp. 353 *complectitur inguina cortex*). The Heliades' forest will be among the first plants mentioned by Orpheus in Ov. *met.* 10.91. **musco...amarae / corticis.** The detail anticipates the final mention of *alni*, while *musco* evokes a somewhat damp landscape: see *G.* 3.144 *flumina, muscus ubi et uiridissima gramine ripa*; 4.18 (but cf. Lucr. 5.951 *umida saxa, super uiridi stillantia musco*). Moss, which is typically soft and comfortable, is here joined with the bark of a tree, which is of course 'bitter' (as is normally the case with forest trees: cf. Serv. Dan. *epitheton naturale*): see e.g. Plin. *nat.* 12.96 *corticem, tutum amaritudine* (where, however, the plant is cinnamon). The use of *cortex* as a fem. noun drew the attention of ancient grammarians, according to Quint. *inst.* 1.5.35; cf. Serv. ad loc.; *ThlL* IV.1069.15–40; V. elsewhere uses the masc., as e.g. at *G.* 2.74; *Aen.* 7.742; 9.743. The fem., which will end up prevailing in spoken Latin (as is shown by late imperial technical and medical literature), is first attested in Lucr. 4.50(51) *uel cortex nominitandast* (cf. also *Culex* 282; Phaedr. 2.6.12). The need to correct such a usage may have given rise to R's wrong reading, *amaro* (cf. below, 6.68 *apio...amaro*). Finally, it is likely that the bitterness of the bark is meant to emphasize the sadness of the whole story (Cornelius Gallus, an elegiac and 'plaintive' poet, is about to make an appearance: cf. 6.64n.). The Heliades' inconsolable sorrow will go on in their new, arboreal form, if it is true that their tears are turned into amber (Ov. *met.* 2.364–6).

63 alnos. The *alnus*, i.e. 'alder', typically grows in very wet soils (cf. *G.* 2.110; see also Varr., *rust.* 1.7.7; Vitr. 2.9.10), as is confirmed by Isidore's folk etymology: Isid. *orig.* 17.7.42 *alnus uocatur quod alatur amne*. The plant, therefore, suits a

ECLOGUE 6   329

'fluid' and tearful context such as the Heliades' grief. The tree, typical of the Po valley, appears three times in the *E.* (here and at 8.53; 10.74). Alder timber can be used for making canoes and other boats for use on rivers (cf. *G.* 1.136 *tunc alnos primum fluuii sensere cauatas*; 2.451 *nec non et torrentem undam leuis innatat alnus*). In Homer, Odysseus uses its Greek equivalent, i.e. κλήθρη, along with the trunks of other kinds of trees, to build his raft following Calypso's instructions: ὅθι δένδρεα μακρὰ πεφύκει, / κλήθρη τ' αἴγερός τ', ἐλάτη τ' ἦν οὐρανομήκης, / αὖα πάλαι, περίκηλα, τά οἱ πλώοιεν ἐλαφρῶς (*Od.* 5.238–40). No wonder that, after V., *alnus* becomes a fairly common poetic metonymy for 'ship': cf. Lucan. 3.520; Val. Fl. 3.536; Stat. *Theb.* 3.23. The growth of alders is very rapid during springtime (cf. *E.* 10.74, in a context where Gallus is featured prominently), but here it is instantaneous and miraculous. For Silenus' interest in the magic of trees, cf. also Hesiod's effect on *orni*, another tree that could be assimilated to the Greek κλήθρη (6.71n.).

64 errantem…Gallum. This is the first appearance of C. Cornelius Gallus in the *E.* Born into a provincial family from *Forum Iulii* (perhaps Fréjus, in *Gallia Narbonensis*) around 69–68 BCE, Gallus made a literary name for himself thanks to four books of elegiac poems dedicated to Lycoris, which earned him the title of founder of Roman love-elegy (Ov. *trist.* 4.10.53–4). A contemporary of V., he must have been an important point of comparison for the poet of the *E.*—at times a sort of *alter ego*, allowing V. to pit Gallus' *bios* against his own. He became increasingly involved in political and military activities (initially with the support of Asinius Pollio, who mentions him in a 43 BCE letter to Cicero: *fam.* 10.32.5 *Gallum Cornelium familiarem meum*; cf. also *fam.* 10.31.6) and, after Actium and the occupation of Alexandria, in which he played an important role, he was appointed *praefectus Aegypti*. However, having come into conflict with the *princeps*, perhaps due to his excessive political ambition (he seems to have accepted veneration from his subjects, in line with Egypt's theocratic mentality), Gallus was sent into exile, and his goods were confiscated. He committed suicide in 27–26 BCE. See further *Enc. Virg.* I, pp. 893–6, s.v. *Cornelio Gallo* (M. Pavan; G. D'Anna); *Virg. Enc.* II, p. 520, s.v. *Gallus* (D. O. Ross); Courtney (1993, pp. 259–70); Hollis (2007, pp. 219–52). For the stele erected by Gallus in 29 BCE to celebrate his victories along the southern border of Egypt, see Hoffmann, Minas-Nerpel, and Pfeiffer (2009): the stele cannot be considered proof of Gallus' supposed insolence towards Octavian. Given his ties of friendship with Asinius Pollio, Gallus may have helped V. during the expropriations, although no information is available outside the Virgilian biographical tradition. At any rate, Gallus' relationship with Pollio was nourished by common poetic and cultural interests (cf. again Cic. *fam.* 10.32.5). This might help to explain the crucial importance of Gallus in the *E.*, second only to that of Pollio himself. Nothing survives of Gallus' elegiac poems, aside from a few lines, almost all of which are transmitted by a papyrus found in 1978 (provided that the text is to be attributed to Gallus, as most scholars now think, ever since the *editio princeps*: Anderson,

330   ECLOGUE 6

Parsons, Nisbet 1979). Gallus' interest in Alexandrian erudition, and especially in Euphorion of Chalcis (6.72n.), must have made his elegies more like Propertius' than Tibullus' (Propertius, in fact, is an attentive reader of *E.* 6, as is shown by Prop. 2.10; 13; 3.3). The poet and scholar Parthenius of Nicaea, who helped make Alexandrian poetry popular at Rome, dedicated to Gallus his Ἐρωτικὰ Παθήματα, thereby offering a set of topics for him to focus on in both his elegies and his hexameter poetry (Parthen. *praef.* 2, p. 550 Light. 2009 = p. 308.7–8 Light. 1999 = p. 42.7–9 Mar.). Here, too, Linus prompts Gallus to compose poetry. This time, however, the genre is different from love-elegy, since Gallus is entrusted with the aetiological, Callimachean topic of the Grynean grove (which Gallus probably treated in one of his poems: cf. 6.72n.). *E.* 10 seems to imply that, at least occasionally, Gallus engaged with bucolic poetry, but his erotic and elegiac mission will be reasserted even more forcefully at the end of V.'s pastoral book (but see below, pp. 464–5). Gallus here appears after a series of unmistakably neoteric reminiscences, esp. featuring Calvus and Catullus: they will accompany him and Tibullus in Ov. *amor.* 3.9.59–66. The verb *errare*, used here at 6.40n. and 6.52n. (cf. also 6.58 *errabunda...uestigia* [n.]), denotes unsteady and perhaps pensive motion, but could also allude to a less-than-successful poetic choice, which Gallus is exhorted to rethink. In *E.* 10, by contrast, Gallus is adamant in pursuing his new endeavours (a true 'change of direction': cf. 10.50 *ibo* [n.]; 10.52 *certum est*), at least until the ensuing 'crisis' at 10.60. It is no wonder that an intellectual like Gallus can pensively 'wander' (*errantem*) amidst natural landscapes: this is also the case with Albius (most probably the elegiac poet Tibullus) in Hor. *epist.* 1.4.4 *an tacitum siluas inter reptare salubris*. Note also the (somewhat audacious) gloss in Philarg./ Philagr. I-II, p. 120 Hagen *errantem idest amantem*. Could Gallus be looking for the object of his desire (like Pasiphae at 52), or at least expressing his feelings through song (like the anxious Corydon at *E.* 2.4: *adsidue ueniebat*)? **Permessi ad flumina.** The river Permessus flows from the spring Aganippe (10.12n.) on Mount Helicon: Hesiod drew a distinction between the river, where the Muses bathe, and the summit of Mount Helicon, where they dance and sing (Hes. *theog.* 5–8), thereby perhaps pointing to a hierarchy of values (but cf. Nicand. *ther.* 12 Ἡσίοδος...παρ' ὕδασι Περμησσοῖο). The Permessus appeared in Callimachus' dream at *aet.* fr. 2a.20 (*add.* p. 103) Pf. = 3.7 Mass. = 2b.2 Hard. If a poet, such as Gallus, 'wanders' around the banks of the river Permessus, he is refraining from aiming at the summit of poetry, i.e. the peak of Mount Helicon. In fact, it is one of the Muses who will lead him there (6.65 *in montis*), where he will find, in Hesiod's wake, the entire *chorus* of Phoebus (6.66). Propertius will mention the river Permessus as an allegory for erotic poetry in the finale of 2.10: *nondum etiam Ascraeos norunt mea carmina fontes, / sed modo Permessi flumine lauit Amor* (Prop. 2.10.25–6; but cf. 2.13.4). Note, however, that Propertius identifies the 'Hesiodic springs' with Roman historical epic, modelled after Ennius. In the proem to his *Annales*, Ennius had quenched his thirst at the Hippocrene spring, thereby combining Hesiod's (and Callimachus') initiation scene with traditional war epic (*ann.* 1–10 Sk.; cf. also *uar.* 45 V.[2]; below, 6.65n.), which V. rejects in the prologue of *E.* 6 and Propertius will shun in 3.3, esp. 1–6 (cf., again, 10.12n.). Thus, Gallus' wanderings in a typically Hesiodic and Callimachean landscape may simply hint at the poet's potential interest in aetiological poetry, even though for now he is primarily devoting his time to love-elegy (as far as we know, that is). Thus, the Muse and Linus must intervene.

65 Aonas in montis. The *Aones* were an ancient population settled near Thebes (Strab. 9.2.3[401]): thus, V. is referring to Mount Helicon. The adj. form, extremely rare, and the Hellenizing acc. plur. ending suggest refined *doctrina*. For a Greek ending applied to the normal form of the adj., cf. *E.* 10.12 *Aonie Aganippe* (Gallus' eclogue). Such a use of Aonia to denote Boeotia as a whole must go back to Callimachus, *hymn.* 4[*Del.*].75; cf. also fr. 572 Pf., as well as (maybe) *aet.* fr. 2a.30 (*add.* p. 103) Pf. = 3.9 Mass. = 2b.4 Hard. (for later echoes see *G.* 3.11 quoted below; Ov. *Pont.* 4.2.47; but cf. Catull. 61.28). Ennius seems to have described himself as clambering on 'the Muses' cliffs' (*ann.* 208 Sk.): according to Lucretius, he brought his evergreen bay wreath down from Mount Helicon (Lucr. 1.118 *detulit*); cf. *G.* 3.11 *Aonio rediens deducam uertice Musas*; note also *G.* 3.291–4 (esp. 291 *me Parnasi deserta per ardua*). A mountain landscape, corresponding to Hesiod's and Callimachus' Hippocrene, is similarly presupposed by Theocr. *id.* 7.92 ἀν' ὤρεα βουκολέοντα. **ut duxerit una sororum.** In his *recusatio*, which is heavily indebted to *E.* 6, Propertius will mention a Muse's intervention after Apollo's exhortation: Calliope, in fact, lays her hand on him (Prop. 3.3.37 *me contigit una dearum*) and prompts him to continue composing love-elegies. Following a series of mythical women, a female figure here leads V.'s poet-friend Gallus by the hand.

66 adsurrexerit. A gesture of deference, especially before political authorities (Cic. *Pis.* 26; Petron. 65.4; see also Cic. *inu.* 1.48, where it denotes respect for old age); cf. *G.* 2.98. The prefix expresses direction in both the gesture itself and the accompanying shift of gaze, meant to welcome the honoured guest: cf. Hom. *Il.* 1.533–5, where the gods stand up from their chairs as soon as Zeus arrives (esp. 535 ἀντίοι ἔσταν ἅπαντες; cf. also *Il.* 15.86). Similar honours are paid to Apollo in *Hymn. Hom.* 3[*Ap.*].3–4.

67 Linus...pastor. V. seems to consider Linus a son of Apollo (*E.* 4.57). Being also connected with the cult of the Muses on Mount Helicon (Pausan. 9.29.6–9), Linus plays an important role in Phoebus' *chorus*. Moreover, his allegiance to the Hesiodic-didactic tradition (and to the Orphic one: cf. *E.* 4.56n.) qualifies him as a standard-bearer of Callimachean, aetiological poetry. Servius Dan. asked why he is described as a shepherd: note that Hesiod himself was initiated into poetry by the Muses while performing pastoral tasks (*theog.* 22–3; 26). With *pastor Silenus*, or V. (?), may allude to the Argive boy named Linus, also a son of Apollo, raised by a shepherd among lambs and eventually torn to pieces by the shepherd's dogs: the story was found in the first book of Callimachus' *Aitia* (frr. 26–31

332   ECLOGUE 6

Pf. = 28–34 Mass. = 25e–31b Hard.). The two Linuses could hardly be kept distinct, especially since both, in the various versions of the respective myths, died a miserable death (cf. 6.68n.). Note that Linus the singer played a crucial role in Theocritus' *id.* 24.105–6: as an old man (γέρων), he taught his letters to the boy Heracles. Scholars have proposed identifying Theocritus' Linus with Philitas of Cos, who tutored the young Ptolemy II Philadelphus (Hunter 1996, p. 17, n. 67). A 'Philitean' overtone would be significant for someone who exhorts the elegiac poet Gallus to compose Callimachean poetry. Philitas will also be summoned by Propertius to endorse the poet's elegiac mission through the mediation of Calliope, the Muse of epic poetry (Prop. 3.3.51–2; cf. 3.1.1–2 *Callimachi Manes et Coi sacra Philitae, / in uestrum, quaeso, me sinite ire nemus*). Propertius also considers *Inachius…Linus* as a model of 'Orphic' poetry, capable of enchanting its listeners: cf. Prop. 2.13.8 (quoted below, 6.69–73n.). In his capacity as Heracles' tutor (e.g. in Theocritus), the singer Linus was known for his elderly appearance. The iconography, in fact, shows him bearded: cf. *LIMC* VI.1, p. 290, no. 1 (with Musaeus), s.v. *Linos* (J. Boardman); IV.1, p. 833, nos. 1666–73, s.v. *Herakles* (J. Boardman).

68 floribus atque apio crinis ornatus amaro. The *apium* is most probably a type of celery: especially widespread in humid regions (see *G.* 4.121 *uirides apio ripae*; cf. Hor. *carm.* 2.7.23–4 *udo…apio*), it corresponds to the Greek σέλινον, known for being used to make the wreaths awarded to Isthmian and Nemean athletic victors (Pind. *Ol.* 13.32–4; *Nem.* 4.85–8; *Isthm.* 2.12–16; Callim. *aet.* fr. 59 Pf. = 156 Mass. = 54 Hard; cf. also Iuv. 8.226). For its use in symposia, cf. Hor. *carm.* 1.36.15–16; 2.7.23–5; 4.11.3; but see also Anacr. fr. 30.1 Gent. = *PMG* 410.1 P., and notably Theocr. *id.* 3.23. The epithet *amaro*, especially appropriate for the plant's leaves, may hint at the sorrowful connotation of the character or, rather, of both characters named Linus (cf. 6.67n.), whose name was connected either with λίνος, the ritual lament usually sung at vintage festivals (Hom. *Il.* 18.569–72; Hes. fr. 305 M.-W.), or with αἴλινος, the refrain of a traditional dirge (Pind. fr. 128c.6 Maeh.; note also [Mosch.] *Epitaph. Bion.* 1 αἴλινά μοι στοναχεῖτε, in the incipit; Ov. *amor.* 3.9.23; cf. also Herodot. 2.79). The term σέλινον can phonetically hint at Λίνος himself. Wrangling with his musical pupil Heracles, Linus was fatally struck by him with a lyre (Apollod. 2.4.9 [63]; cf. Plaut. *Bacch.* 155 *fiam, ut ego opinor, Hercules, tu autem Linus*); according to another version, he was killed by Apollo for his insolent arrogance in the musical art (Pausan. 9.29.6; but cf. 9.29.9, where the author tries to keep the two Linuses distinct). An awful death characterized Callimachus' Argive boy, too: he was torn to pieces by the dogs of his adoptive father (see 6.67n.). In an elegiac lament, Martial will have Apollo mourn Linus' death: *ipse meum fleui…Linon* (Mart. 9.86.4). The *apium/σέλινον* seems to have been used in funerary contexts (Plut. *Timol.* 26.1). Hence, a further qualification for the character who must divert Gallus' attention from the 'mournful' genre *par excellence*, i.e. elegiac poetry. The adj. *amaro* is closely anticipated by *amarae* (6.62), similarly in final position.

ECLOGUE 6   333

69–73. While the Muses gave Hesiod a bay-wood *skeptron* in *theog*. 30–1, Linus gives Gallus a shepherd's pipe (6.69n.), which Hesiod himself is said to have used to lead mountain-ashes to the valley (6.71n.). The pastoral investiture at *E*. 2.36–9 similarly featured the gift of a wind instrument (the *fistula*). Pindar was said to have taught his pupil Olympicus how to play the pipes: cf. Aristodem. *FGrH* 383 F 13. Similar initiation scenes could be the subject matter of iconographic depictions, as e.g. in the relief of Archelaus of Priene: see D. Clay, *Archilochos Heros* (quoted above, 3.85n.), esp. pp. 91–3. As these lines show Gallus the way, so Parthenius gives instructions to the future poet (i.e. Gallus) in the prologue to his *Erotika pathemata* (p. 550 Light. 2009 = p. 308.3–11 Light. 1999 = p. 42.3–13 Mar.). In *E*. 6, V. similarly offers a concise catalogue of myths to his poet-friend. The entire Virgilian scene will be reworked by Propertius in elegiac terms: *hic* [i.e. *Amor*] *me tam gracilis uetuit contemnere Musas, / iussit et Ascraeum sic habitare nemus, // non ut Pieriae quercus mea uerba sequantur, / aut possim Ismaria ducere ualle feras, // sed magis ut nostro stupefiat Cynthia uersu: / tunc ego sim Inachio notior arte Lino* (Prop. 2.13.3–8: note the reference to Linus, on which see 6.67n.). Based on these lines and *Culex* 94–7 (esp. 96 *Ascraeo…poetae*), some scholars have surmised that initiation scenes were also part of Gallus' own poetry: this is certainly possible but, due to the limited evidence available, still indemonstrable.

69 hos…calamos. The distinctive instrument of pastoral poetry replaces the epic *skeptron* of Hesiod's *Theogony*, whose initiation scene was reworked by Theocritus in *id*. 7 (and by V. in *E*. 5: cf. 5.88n.). In the story of the Argive Linus, Callimachus mentioned the rhapsodic staff, probably in relation to himself (fr. 26.5 Pf. = 30.5 Mass. = 26.5 Hard.). No wonder, at any rate, that the singer Linus shows interest in musical instruments, even though the lyre (his typical attribute) does not appear here.

70–1. Hesiod is credited with a typical (*solebat*) power to move trees, otherwise associated with Orpheus: cf. *E*. 3.46 *Orphea…siluasque sequentis* (cf. also *G*. 4.510). Orphism, in fact, had tried to appropriate the figure of Hesiod as a singer of wisdom (he is mentioned, along with Orpheus and Musaeus, in Aristoph. *Ran*. 1032–3; direct kinship was sometimes posited in antiquity: cf. below, 6.70n.). Here, the speaker is Linus, whose relationship with Orphism is well attested (6.67n.). Hesiod's 'bewitching' ability, having a tangible effect on his listeners' minds, was familiar to ancient commentators: *schol. uet. in* Hes. *op. et dies, proleg.*, p. 4.15–17 Pert. (but cf. also 6.71n.). Hesiod played a crucial role in Hellenistic poetry, and it bears mentioning that a short poem entitled *Hesiod* was attributed to Euphorion (fr. 22a-b Pow. = 23 v. Gron. = Light.). Even aetiological poets à la Callimachus (cf. below, 6.72 *origo*) regarded Hesiod's didactic poetry as an important archetype; cf. also Callimachus' epigram on Aratus: Ἡσιόδου τό τ' ἄεισμα καὶ ὁ τρόπος (*epigr*. 27.1 Pf.).

70 Ascraeo quos ante seni. The adj. *Ascraeus* refers to Hesiod, a native of Ascra, near Mount Helicon: *G*. 2.176; Prop. 2.10.25; *Culex* 96 *Ascraeo…poetae*. The

334 ECLOGUE 6

epithet *senex*, in turn, adds a connotation of stateliness as well as an allusion to an 'old' poetic source: cf. Hor. *sat.* 2.1.34; *epist.* 2.1.56; Pers. 1.124. Hesiod was said to be a descendant of Orpheus and Linus (Procl. *uita Hom.* 19–23 Sever.; *Certam. Hom. et Hes.* p. 227.46–52 All. = p. 239.47–54 Rz.[3] = Orph. TT 7; 8 Kern = 871; 873 Bern.), and Hesiod called Linus 'learned in every sort of wisdom' (Hes. fr. 306 M.-W.).

71 cantando rigidas deducere montibus ornos. For a similar 'descent' of ash trees caused by magic, cf. *Aen.* 4.491 (but see *E.* 8.69 for the verb *deducere*). For the felling of ash trees in a sacred area, albeit without Orpheus' intervention, cf. Lucan. 3.440 *procumbunt orni.* At *E.* 6.62–3, Silenus had 'clothed' Phaethon's sisters in bark and turned them into alders, and l. 28 had testified to the 'kinetic' effect of Silenus' song upon oak trees (*rigidas...quercus,* here paralleled by *rigidas...ornos,* occupying the same hexameter positions). Hesiod's pipes, endowed with Orphic powers, will now help Gallus sing of the origin of arboreal creatures (i.e. the Grynean grove). Knowledge of the origin of trees, and of their sometimes human past (or divine nature), may be what enables the singer to 'animate' them and lead them at will. According to Servius Dan., *Ornus* was the name of one of Oceanus' daughters: suffering from unrequited love for Jason, she was turned into a tree (Serv. Dan. *ad Aen.* 2.626). Hesiod himself was an authority on Oceanus' daughters: cf. *theog.* 346–66, where they are said to be three thousand in number, and the poet mentions quite a few of them by name (note also Orph. fr. 49.20–7 Kern = 387.4–10 Bern.). In a fragment of Philitas (fr. 10 Pow. = 12 Sbard. = 25 Spanoud. = 8 Light.), the alder asserts that it cannot be 'uprooted' by uncouth farmers, but only by a learned man, who knows the art of words and tales: οὔ μέ τις ἐξ ὀρέων ἀποφώλιος ἀγροιώτης / αἱρήσει κλήθρην, αἱρόμενος μακέλην, // ἀλλ' ἐπέων εἰδὼς κόσμον καὶ πολλὰ μογήσας / μύθων παντοίων οἶμον ἐπιστάμενος (among the Greek equivalents of *ornus*, ancient lexicographers mention κλήθρος/κλήθρη, normally identified with *alnus*/'alder'; cf. K. Spanoudakis' commentary, Leiden-Boston-Cologne 2002, p. 324, ad 25.2c; for the *alnus*/κλήθρη, cf. 6.63n.). In Philitas' puzzling riddle (the fragment comes from one of his Παίγνια), the tree itself comes to life and speaks: the text perhaps alludes to the power of *doctrina*, especially in the poetic sense (i.e. μῦθοι); at any rate, V. may have interpreted it in such a way. Hesiod considered the Bronze Age of men to have been born from ash trees (Hes. *op.* 145; for the Meliae, i.e. the Ash-Tree Nymphs, cf. *theog.* 187; Callim. *hymn.* 1[*Iou.*].47; 4[*Del.*].79–85; fr. 598 Pf.; Callimachus was an authority on the matter, even for writing the treatise Περὶ νυμφῶν [fr. 413 Pf.]), whereas the Arcadians were born from various species of trees (including ash trees) according to Statius, *Theb.* 4.275–81. Hesiod also narrated terrible storms, capable of tearing down majestic trees: *op.* 508–10 (oaks, pine trees, and poplars are uprooted by a huge landslide in *scut.* 374–8); V. will sing of how the Trojan ships, once forming a pine forest on Mount Ida, are turned into sea-nymphs on the shores of Latium (*Aen.* 9.77–122). Both poets 'drag down'

ECLOGUE 6   335

trees through the power of their song. **cantando.** The instrumental, here emphatically preceding the governing inf. (cf. 3.25n.), must be explained in terms of the Roman religious mentality, in which the magical force of song (*carmen*) was deemed capable of moving crops (cf. *E.* 8.99). Such an action, called *excantare*, was forbidden as early as the *XII Tables* (an action to which Prop. 3.3.49 lays claim through Calliope—the object being, however, *puellae*).

72 Grynei nemoris...origo. The Grynean grove, from the ancient city of Gryne in Asia Minor, just south of Pergamum in Mysia, where a famous Apollonian oracle was located (hence, the god's epithet *Gryneus*: cf. *Aen.* 4.345–6 *sed nunc Italiam magnam Gryneus Apollo, / Italiam Lyciae iussere capessere sortes*; see also Parthen. fr. 10 Light. = 6 Mar.). Serv. Dan. *ad Aen.* 4.345 tells us that the Amazon Gryne was raped by Apollo in the same location: a mythical event which may have interested an elegiac poet such as Gallus. According to Servius, the grove hosted the contest between Calchas and Mopsus, which Hesiod probably set in Claros (seat of another important oracle of Apollo: Hes. fr. 278 M.-W.). Servius reports that Euphorion set the episode in the Grynean grove (fr. 97 Pow. = 101 v. Gron. = 102 Light.). A papyrus fragment perhaps transmits a poem by Euphorion on the topic (*PBerol* 13873 = fr. 131 v. Gron. = 108 Light.); but cf. *SH* fr. 429, esp. p. 215 Ll.-J.-P. Servius also asserts that Euphorion inspired Gallus' Latin reworking of the episode, which presumably predated *E.* 6; see further *Enc. Virg.* II, pp. 807–8, s.v. *Grinio* (G. D'Anna); *Virg. Enc.* II, p. 580, s.v. *Grynean grove* (L. Morgan). The Grynean grove, known for its pleasantness, must have readily lent itself to be celebrated by pastoral, Hesiodic 'pipes' (above, 6.69 *calami*): *arboribus multis iucundus, gramine floribusque uariis omni tempore uestitus, abundans etiam fontibus* (Serv. Dan.; cf. Pausan. 1.21.7). V. may have alluded to the contest between the divine singers Mopsus and Calchas in *E.* 5 (cf. *E.* 5.1n.). The term *origo*, which can be read as a Latin translation of αἴτιον, clearly alludes to Hellenistic aetiological poetry (e.g. Callimachus' *Aitia*).

73 ne quis sit lucus quo se plus iactet Apollo. Aetiological success is expressed in Callimachean terms: 'but from me / Apollo will be called Delius, nor will any other / land be equally dear to a god' (*hymn.* 4[*Del.*].268–70, where Delos itself is the speaker). In the Romans' religious vocabulary, the word *lucus* has a sacral connotation, even in the context of a literary metaphor, as e.g. in Quint. *inst.* 10.1.88: *Ennium sicut sacros uetustate lucos adoremus, in quibus grandia et antiqua robora iam non tantam habent speciem quantam religionem.* Note the considerable number of monosyllables and spondees here: cf. *Enc. Virg.* III, esp. p. 571b, s.v. *monosillabo* (J. Hellegouarc'h). The unstressed indefinite pronoun must here be printed as *quis*, whereas the form *qui* is probably a learned conjecture or perhaps a haplography (**MP²R**): cf. Löfstedt (1933, p. 87, n. 3); also *E.* 1.18n.; **R** has the incorrect reading *nec* in lieu of *ne*.

74–86. The direct intervention of the poet's voice marks the beginning of the second main section of the eclogue, which is much shorter than the first (31–73)

336 ECLOGUE 6

and brings the poem to a close. Note that ll. 85–6 make for a concise epilogue, which accompanies the text back into its pastoral context (a quiet evening; the tally of the sheep). The phrase *quid loquar* expresses a sort of acceleration in the narrative, which preludes to the end of the song. At any rate, the eclogue is at this point already more than seventy lines long, while the average length of a Virgilian eclogue is around eighty-three lines (cf. Introduction, p. 22, n.56). The short epilogue also features the poet's voice: 85–6.

74–81. The rhetorical formula *quid loquar?* (6.74), appearing right after the solemn investiture scene, marks a change of pace in the summary, which now approaches its end (cf. 6.82 *omnia*, with a resumptive and conclusive force); for this particular device (*praeteritio*), see e.g. *G.* 2.118 *quid…referam*; *quid loquar ancora* in Ov. *ars* 3.169; *trist.* 2.399; Manil. 2.596; Mart. 9.3.11. Two more metamorphosis tales are added, again featuring female protagonists: Scylla and Philomela. The pathetic exclamations of 6.47 and 6.52 (*a uirgo infelix*) reappear here with some variation: cf. 6.77 *a! timidos nautas* and 6. 81 *infelix sua tecta*.

74 aut. The variant reading *ut* (**R**), which has even recently been defended by some scholars, would force the reader to wait until 6.78 to find the subordinate verb (*narrauerit*), thereby making the syntax rather laborious, due to the long relative clause *quam fama secuta est* (74–7). The reading *aut*, transmitted by most manuscripts, immediately creates a clear juxtaposition between the two myths (*aut…aut*), while allowing for a free, intuitive syntax. Given the catalogue-like style of the passage, the phrase *quid loquar* (with an accusative) is rather clear per se, and the reader can supply *ut…narrauerit* at 6.78 to complete both sense and syntax. The summary then continues, but now the primary narrator (Tityrus-V.) makes his own voice heard (*loquar*) and puts an emphasis on the complex mythical story of Scylla through the relative clause *quam fama secuta est* (6.74). Note also the resumptive *omnia* at 6.83. **Scyllam Nisi.** The formulation ('Scylla, daughter of Nisus') highlights the overlap between two originally distinct mythical figures. One is the daughter of Nisus, king of Megara: she fell in love with the young Minos as he besieged the city, and cut off the lock of hair (or the single hair: either red or variously coloured in the sources) on which her father's life depended. Once he had conquered Megara, however, Minos scorned the girl's love: while pursuing him, she was turned into a *ciris*, a seabird (κεῖρις / *tonsilla*, etymologized from κείρω 'to cut', in memory of the misdeed: Ov. *met.* 8.150–1; *Ciris* 488; *Prob. ad E.* 6.74). The cut lock of hair, which V. will mention in his reworking of the myth (*G.* 1.404–9, esp. 405 *pro purpureo poenas dat Scylla capillo*), is a distinctive feature in the iconography: see *LIMC* VII.1, p. 793, s.v. *Skylla II* (F. Canciani). In what is probably the oldest version, Scylla was bribed with a golden necklace: Aesch. *Choeph.* 613–22. The other Scylla, doubtless alluded to in 6.75–6, is the Homeric sea monster, with dog-like features, six heads, and twelve feet, dwelling on the continental side of the strait of Messina, in front of Charybdis (the monster killed six of Odysseus' companions: *Od.* 12.85–100;

12.201–59; it will reappear in *Aen.* 3.424–8). Originally a beautiful girl, daughter of Phorcys, she was turned into a monster by Circe, jealous of the sea-god Glaucus, who had fallen in love with her (Ov. *met.* 14.17–19; 28–36; an epyllion entitled *Glaucus* was composed by Catullus' friend Q. Cornificius). According to another version, Amphitrite turned her into a monster out of jealousy of Poseidon (Serv. Dan.; note also the variant whereby Poseidon himself punished her when she rejected him: Serv. Dan. *ad Aen.* 3.420); see further Roscher, IV, esp. p. 1034, s.v. *Skylla* I. Soon, however, the two Scyllas were conflated into a single figure, through a gradual process to which V. himself may allude in *E.* 6.74 (*quam fama secuta est*): in fact, the girl's transformation into a dog-like monster must have seemed appropriate for the Megarian Scylla, regarded as embodying female *libido*; cf. Prop. 3.19, esp. 21–4; also below, 6.75n. A desire to add a clear form of punishment to the story of the first Scylla may have motivated, in certain versions (including the one used by V. in *G.* 1), a reference to her father Nisus' transformation into a sea-eagle (ἁλιάετος), perpetually doomed to pursue Scylla-*ciris*. While mythographers strive to keep the two Scyllas distinct (Apollod. *epit.* 7.29; Hyg. *fab.* 198; 199), Latin authors freely juxtapose a 'pure' version concerning the Megarian Scylla (cf., again, *G.* 1.404–9; Prop. 3.19.21–8; Ov. *met.* 8.6–151) with 'contaminated' tales (cf. Prop. 4.4.39–40; Ov. *amor.* 3.12.21–2; *fast.* 4.500). An attempt at reconciling the two is found in the pseudo-Virgilian *Ciris*, where, although the distinction is emphasized, a digression concerning the Homeric Scylla is inserted into the story of the Megarian Scylla (and our passage is literally quoted: *Ciris* 54–61); see further *Enc. Virg.* IV, pp. 724–6 (P. Pinotti); *Virg. Enc.* III, p. 1136, s.vv. *Scylla and Charybdis*; *Scylla Nisi* (M. Hopman). Note that the Megarian Scylla, whom the reader encounters immediately after Gallus' Hesiodic-Callimachean initiation, may have appeared in Callimachus' *Aitia*, fr. 113 Pf. = 63 Mass. (cf. *Hec.* fr. 288 Pf. = 90 H.: see again 6.75n.; for Scylla the monster cf. Hes. fr. 262 M.-W.) as well as in Parthenius' *Metamorphoses*, fr. 24 Light. = 20 Mar. Note also that Scylla occurs twice as a sea monster in Catull. 60.2 and 64.156. According to Serv. Dan. *ad E.* 6.3, the story of Scylla was treated in V.'s juvenile poetry: *alii Scyllam eum scribere coepisse dicunt, in quo libro Nisi et Minois, regis Cretensium, bellum describebat.* This tradition clearly goes back to the *Ciris*, a poem attributed to V. (in the so-called *Appendix*), and Scylla's presence in it. The exact nature of the *Ciris* is widely discussed: imitation, forgery, or authentic work by V. or someone close to him (like Cornelius Gallus)? The most plausible hypothesis is that the poem was written after V. to 'fill a gap' left by this passage, where the subject of Scylla is alluded to then quickly brushed aside. In a similar way, Columella will compose the tenth book of his *De re rustica* on horticulture, a topic that V. did not have time to treat (*G.* 4.116–24). The author of the *Ciris* may not wish to pass off as V., but he certainly describes himself as a poet-intellectual similar to him (and similarly Epicurean), while also writing several lines identical to V.'s or at least replete with Virgilian echoes. If the author of the *Ciris* is indeed a

338   ECLOGUE 6

first-century CE imitator (which seems plausible), it is striking that he 'pretends' to belong to V.'s circle, as though he were one of those friends of V.'s with whom the poet had shared experiences, philosophical ideas, and poetic drafts (cf. V.'s reworkings of Varius Rufus' poetry at *E.* 8.88n. and 9.35n.). Thus, any parallels between *E.* 6 and the *Ciris* must be understood as later imitations based on V.'s text.

75 candida succinctam latrantibus inguina monstris. The echo of Lucr. 5.892–3 *rabidis canibus succinctas semimarinis / corporibus Scyllas* is emphasized by the contrast between the white colour of the girl's skin, typical of female beauty, and the horror of the 'barking monsters'; cf. Prop. 4.4.40 *candida…in saeuos inguina uersa canis*; Ov. *met.* 13.732 *illa feris atram canibus succingitur aluum*; [Tib.] 3.4.89. In comparison to Lucretius, note V.'s construction of *succinctus* with a 'retained' accusative, for which cf. Enn. *ann.* 519 Sk. *succincti corda machaeris.* The Homeric Scylla was pictured as a 'twofold' creature, a monster in the lower body and a gorgeous girl in the upper body; cf. *Aen.* 3.426–8 *pulchro pectore uirgo / pube tenus, postrema immani corpore pistrix / delphinum caudas utero commissa luporum*; cf. Catull. 60.2 *Scylla latrans infima inguinum parte*; [Tib.] 3.4.89 *Scyllaque uirgineam canibus succincta figuram*; Ov. *met.* 14.59–67. For this reason, too, the figure was soon interpreted as an allegory of female *libido* (cf. Heracl. *all. Hom.* 70.11), in line with the 'dog-like' implications of her name (σκύλαξ 'dog' / 'puppy'; cf. *Od.* 12.85–6; note also *Aen.* 3.432 *Scyllam et caeruleis canibus resonantia saxa*; Ov. *met.* 7.64–5); see also *Ciris* 69 *inguinis est uitium et ueneris descripta libido*. The same applies to the unfaithful Megarian girl: cf. Aesch. *Choeph.* 621 κυνόφρων; note also Callim. *Hec.* 288 Pf. = 90 H. 'Scylla, a brothel woman, bearing a truthful name, / cut the purple lock of hair [πορφυρέην ἤμησε κρέκα]'. *E.* 6.75 and the two following lines are quoted in *Ciris* 59–61, where *a! timidos* is replaced with *deprensos.*

76 Dulichias…rates. Dulichium is one of the suitor princes' kingdoms, over which Odysseus ruled before setting sail for Troy: Hom. *Od.* 1.245–6, which V. reworks in *Aen.* 3.270–1. In the catalogue of *Il.* 2.625–30, the troops of Dulichium and the Echinades islands (off the coast of Acarnania), led by Meges, appear immediately before Odysseus' army. Ancient interpreters considered Dulichium one of the Echinades (*schol. ad Il.* 2.625, p. 314 Erbse; cf. Strab. 8.2.2 [335]; 10.2.10 [453]). It is likely, therefore, that some Hellenistic source had used 'Dulichian' as a synonym of 'Odyssean'; cf. *Enc. Virg.* II, p. 152, s.v. *Dulichio* (G. Mancinetti Santamaria); *Virg. Enc.* I, p. 388, s.v. *Dulichium* (G. C. Lacki). Here, the plural adds a generalizing nuance, given that Odysseus only had one ship when he sailed through the strait of Messina (Hom. *Od.* 12.205). **uexasse.** The verb denotes a very violent action: cf. Cic. *Phil.* 11.8 *in eius corpore lacerando atque uexando…oculos pauerit suos* (note here 77 *lacerasse*); Lucr. 1.583, etc. As Probus observed, V.'s word choice cannot be criticized for being too 'mild' (*uerbum…leuis ac parui incommodi nec tam atroci casui congruens*:

ECLOGUE 6   339

Macr. *Sat.* 6.7.4; cf. also 6.7.7–11): see Serv. and Serv. Dan. ad loc.; also Gell. 2.6.1–2; 5–8. It is unclear, however, whether *uexare* can be read as an intensified form of *ueho*, to which idea Probus appeals in his refutation of V.'s detractors (perhaps the two roots are cognate, but distinct): see Ernout-Meillet, pp. 730–1, s.v. It is possible, at any rate, that the verb alludes to a folk etymology: *Scylla* < σκύλλω, which basically means 'to rip off, tear apart'. In the early Middle Ages, Beda will make this connection explicitly (perhaps following some Virgilian interpreters): *Scylla habet nomen a spoliando siue uexando nautas: spolio enim et uexo Latine, Graece dicitur skyllo* (*gramm.* VII, p. 289.9 K.). The author of the *Ciris* uses a very strong verb when introducing Scylla: *monstro saxum infestasse uoraci* (*Ciris* 57); *uexasse* then appears at *Ciris* 60; Scylla is *rapax* in Catull. 64.156. **gurgite in alto.** The reader inevitably thinks of Charybdis (*Od.* 12, esp. 242–3). While Odysseus and his companions manage to escape from the whirlpool, Scylla hides in a recess amidst the rocks and catches them (Hom. *Od.* 12.245–6).

77 timidos nautas. The sailor may be described as intrinsically 'fearful', since he faces the dangers of the sea: Hor. *carm.* 1.14.14 *timidus nauita* (cf. also *ars* 28). Here, however, V. echoes the Homeric scene, esp. *Od.* 12.224 δείσαντες ... ἑταῖροι (cf. also 203; 243). **canibus lacerasse marinis.** This half-line is replete with etymological echoes of Scylla's name: note the violent connotation of *lacerasse* (σκύλλω [see above, 6.76n.]; cf. also κείρω for κεῖρις [see 6.74n.]); *canibus* alludes to Scylla's canine nature (σκύλαξ). Only Scylla's lower body, which came into contact with the water 'polluted' by Circe, seems to have undergone the metamorphosis: Ov. *met.* 14.59–61.

78–81. The (inevitably incomplete) summary of Silenus' song is concluded by a gruesome story, set in Thrace, featuring Tereus, his wife Procne, and her sister Philomela. The old and widespread saga, which is transmitted in several different versions, is attested by both iconography and epic poetry: cf. Hom. *Od.* 19.518–23 and Hes. *op.* 568. The classic form of the story was established by Sophocles' play *Tereus*, reworked at Rome by Livius Andronicus and Accius (cf. also Aesch. *Ag.* 1140–9; Thuc. 2.29.3; Catull. 65.13–14). In the most common version, accepted and further vulgarized by Ovid (*met.* 6.424–674), Tereus—king of Thrace, married to Procne, the daughter of Pandion king of Athens—raped his sister-in-law Philomela and cut out her tongue to prevent her from revealing his crime. As soon as the truth was nonetheless uncovered, Procne took vengeance by killing her own and Tereus' son Itys (or Itylos), whose flesh she cooked for her husband. Upon becoming aware of the trick, Tereus began pursuing both his wife and his sister-in-law, but all three were turned into birds (whose exact identities are disputed among the sources). See further *Enc. Virg.* IV, pp. 291–2, s.v. *Procne* (S. Rocca); V.1, pp. 129–30, s.v. *Tereus* (F. Sallusto); *Virg. Enc.* III, p. 1000, s.v. *Philomela* (S. Wheeler); also *Enc. Or.* II, p. 473, s.v. *Procne* (R. Dimundo). Quite surprisingly, a metamorphosis is also attested in the case of Procne's son Itys, who was turned

340 ECLOGUE 6

into a species of dove, according to Serv. *ad* 6.78; cf. *Myth. Vat.* 1.4. Various versions of the myth must have coexisted in V.'s time, creating inevitable confusion as to which character plays which role (see below, 6.80–1n.). The two sisters cooperate in their revenge, and therefore tend to be interchangeable: here, however, Philomela seems more properly to play the role of *domina* (i.e. she is the evil king's wife), both because she is depicted as making food (79 *quas…dapes… pararit*) and because the house is 'hers' (81 *sua tecta*). That such a version of the myth existed in a Greek source known to V. can be hypothesized based on Eustathius, *ad Od.* 19.519 (esp. p. 215.22 Stallb. ἡ Φιλομήλα γαμεῖται Τηρεῖ τῷ Θρᾳκί). In juxtaposing the myth of Tereus and Philomela with that of Scylla (daughter of Nisus), Silenus may hint at the possible kinship between the respective families; the respective settings, at least, are very similar (Attica / Athens). A type of blood relation is alluded to in *Ciris* 201–2 (see R. O. A. M. Lyne's commentary, Cambridge 1978, p. 183, ad loc.; cf. also *Ciris* 409–10 and 469). Note also that the myths of both Philomela and the Megarian Scylla feature bird transformations. Silenus (or V.) freely reworks the story, mentioning Tereus' metamorphosis first (6.78), then the gruesome banquet (6.79), and, finally, Philomela's transformation (6.80–1). Ovid, too, sometimes starts by relating the substance of the metamorphosis, then narrates the full story: cf. *met.* 3.138–42 (Actaeon); 4.51–4 (Pyramus and Thisbe).

78 ut mutatos Terei narrauerit artus. In a very old yet less widespread version, Tereus was turned into a bird of prey, specifically a type of hawk (perhaps the sparrowhawk), as soon as he swung his sword at the two sisters (cf. κίρκος in Aesch. *Suppl.* 62; Hyg. *fab.* 45.5 *accipitrem factum dicunt*; note also Nonn. *Dionys.* 2.138–9). In the version used by Ovid, he is turned into a hoopoe (*met.* 6.671–4), as in Philocles (cf. 6.80–1n.); see further F. Bömer's commentary, Heidelberg 1976, pp. 178–9 ad *met.* 6.671, as well as G. Rosati's commentary, Milan 2009, pp. 351–2 ad *met.* 6.671–4 (for a discussion of the myth, with references, see pp. 316–22). Particularly in those versions in which Tereus is turned into a bird of prey, his body retains its menacing appearance even after the metamorphosis. Both hawks and hoopoes, of course, are known for their sharp, penetrating eyesight (the hoopoe in Greek is ἔποψ, connected to ἐπόπτης in e.g. Soph. fr. 581.1 R.). The very name of Tereus contains an etymological hint at τηρεῖν. Note the synizesis in the ending of *Terei* (Greek nom. Τηρεύς); cf. above, 6.42 *Promethei*.

79 quas…dapes, quae dona. The irony is obvious, as in *Aen.* 10.881–2; cf. Ov. *met.* 9.181; Val. Fl. 1.550–1. Gifts were customarily offered to dinner guests, who carried them home after the banquet (*dapes*): here, however, the gift is Itys' head; cf. Ov. *met.* 6.658–9 *prosiluit Ityosque caput Philomela cruentum / misit in ora patris.* Our passage will be echoed by Seneca in *Th.* 983–4 *capio fraternae dapis / donum* (where Thyestes is still unaware of his sons' murder—but not for long).

80 quo cursu. To be taken literally: Philomela (it is to her that ll. 80–1 refer, not to Tereus) tries to escape, while still in her human form. For a different case

ECLOGUE 6   341

cf. *Aen.* 6.194 *cursum…per auras*, where Aeneas addresses Venus' doves (this is, therefore, a real 'flight').

80–1 quibus ante / …sua tecta super uolitauerit alis. The phrase *quibus…alis* 'with what wings', underscored by the hyperbaton, eschews any explicit mention of the bird into which Philomela was turned, thereby enhancing the reader's curiosity. According to a tradition going back to Sophocles' *Tereus*, Procne was turned into a nightingale and Philomela into a swallow: cf. *Anth. Pal.* 9.70 = *HE* 2655–8 G.-P. (Mnasalc.); Stat. *silu.* 3.3.174–6 (but cf. 5.3.84); note also the anecdote in Aristot. *rhet.* 3.3.1406b14–19. In a version which may go back to Philocles' *Tereus* (distinguished from Sophocles' play by its subtitle: *Τηρεὺς ἢ Ἔποψ*, i.e. 'Tereus or the hoopoe'; cf. *TrGF*, I, pp. 140–2 Sn.), and which enjoyed great popularity among Latin authors, Philomela was changed into a nightingale, while Procne became a swallow (Hor. *carm.* 4.12.5–8; Ov. *ars* 2.383–4; *fast.* 2.853–6). In rationalistic terms, the swallow (with its shrill cries) was more appropriate for Philomela, whose tongue had been cut out. However, her speaking name ('lover of song') must have fostered the spread of the Philomela-nightingale version, since the nightingale, because of its melodious song, is a common metaphor for poetry and poets: cf. Bacchyl. 3.98; Eur. fr. 588.3 Kann.; see also Callim. *epigr.* 2.5 Pf. In *G.* 4.15 *manibus Procne pectus signata cruentis*, V. considers Procne a swallow (with typical spots on the chest: cf. Ov. *met.* 6.669–70, as well as *ars* 2.384), mentioning her among the birds that kill bees in order to feed their chicks (*G.* 4.17 *nidis immitibus*), whereas Philomela-nightingale appears at *G.* 4.511–15, in the concrete context of rural life (this time, the ploughman takes her chicks from the nest, thereby eliciting her lament). Here, however, V. does not explicitly tell us which version of the myth Silenus embraced, and it is possible that, as in 6.74 *quam fama secuta*, Philomela's double motion alludes to the two rival accounts (swallow or nightingale?). It is clear, at any rate, that *deserta petiuerit* must be the bird's final destination, preceded (*ante*) by one last flight around the house. Therefore, Philomela is likely a nightingale (cf. 6.81 *infelix* [n.]). Swallows and nightingales can be contrasted with each other on account of their respective nesting habits: cf. Ov. *met.* 6.668–9 (*quarum petit altera siluas, / altera tecta subit*), where the two species are not explicitly mentioned, and Petron. 131.8 ll. 6–7 *siluestris aedon / atque urbana Procne* (explicitly identified). In the famous simile of the 'black swallow', the bird scours the house of a wealthy gentleman (*Aen.* 12.473–80); for a countryside flight, however, cf. *G.* 1.377 *arguta lacus circumuolitauit hirundo*, a verbatim quotation of Varr. At. *carm.* fr. 22.4 Bläns. = 14.4 Court.; for a further parallel, cf. Ov. *met.* 2.489–90 *a quotiens, sola non ausa quiescere silua, / ante domum quondamque suis errauit in agris* (Callisto, turned into a bear).

81 infelix. Unhappiness is crucial to the myth at hand: even its final metamorphosis leaves ample room for tears and groans: besides *G.* 4.511–15 (see above, 6.80–1n.), cf. Catull. 65.13–14; Prop. 2.20.5–6; Hor. *carm.* 4.12.5–6 *Ityn flebiliter gemens / infelix auis* (none of the three authors explicitly mentions the bird

342 ECLOGUE 6

species, and perhaps intentionally so; the context, however, makes it clear that all three refer to the nightingale). The whole line is quoted in *Ciris* 51 (where *caeruleis* replaces *infelix*).

82–6. The line-beginning *omnia* (6.82) corresponds to *quid loquar* (6.74) and, after a series of questions (6.78–81), hints at an approaching conclusion. While the song echoes across the entire pastoral world (6.83–4), the last two lines draw attention to the need for night-time rest, which concerns animals, herdsmen, and poetry itself. Note the reappearance of the god from the poem's proem, Apollo, along with Tityrus-V.'s pastoral life: after a *deductum carmen*, here are the *pingues oues*. The counting and gathering of animals conclude the poem and the following eclogue will begin with the unification of two different flocks, i.e. Corydon's and Thyrsis'. The finale of *E*. 6 further proves that Mnasyllus and Chromis abide by the logic of the pastoral world. They, too, presumably have animals to take back home (above, 6.24n.). The length of this final sequence is five lines, a measure typical in the *E*. that here repeats circularly the first sequence of the eclogue, ll. 1–5 (cf. 6.1–12n.; 1.1–10n.). The true epilogue, however, is in the last two lines, which mark the end of pastoral activities (and, therefore, of pastoral song).

82 omnia, quae Phoebo quondam meditante. All the songs now sung by Silenus (6.84 *ille canit*) had once been sung by Apollo. Yet *omnia* has a generalizing effect, not limited to the last few lines of the poem, but also affecting the immediately preceding section, 6.74–81 (note that, at 73, Apollo makes an appearance as a 'character' in the initiation episode: this seems to be at odds with the idea that the god himself is the mediator or source of the narrative preceding 6.74). The story of the Megarian Scylla, alluded to at 74–7, could be of particular interest to the god, who was venerated at Megara (he was also said to have built the city walls there: *Ciris* 105–9). As was the case with Tityrus in the opening scene of the book (*E*. 1.1–5), the act of *meditari* is paralleled by a 'learning' process affecting nature in the whole pastoral world (6.83–4). While Apollo had reproached Tityrus at the beginning of the eclogue, the finale now features Apollo in his capacity as singer and musician (like Tityrus himself). The mention of *auctoritas* for its material is a feature of learned poetry, as is the case with the episode of Acontius and Cydippe in Callimachus, who reveals the source of the story (Xenomedes, a local historian of the island of Kea: *aet.* fr. 75 Pf. = 174 Mass. = 75 Hard., esp. ll. 76–7). Here, however, the source is Apollo himself, who 'teaches' the bay trees (83). The preeminence of Apollo's authoritative role can be explained with the need for an emphatic raising of the tone towards the end of the eclogue. The poet, who starts talking in the first person again (74 *loquar*), accelerates the narrative rhythm, with the result that the summary becomes even more concise and elliptical. Such accelerations and abrupt transitions are typical of epic narratives: note, for instance, the summary of Odysseus' *logoi* when the hero reconnects with Penelope (a narrative interrupted only by sleep: *Od*. 23.310–43); cf. V.'s resumptive use of *haec* to signal a narrative transition (e.g. at *Aen*. 4.195).

83 audiit Eurotas iussitque ediscere lauros. Cf. *E.* 1.5 *resonare doces...siluas* (cf. 6.11 *te nemus omne canet*); the idea that natural elements can 'learn' the content of pastoral song is here projected onto a mythical archetype (Apollo's music). Here the Eurotas itself, personified as rivers frequently are, is the one who 'listens' and commands the bay trees to learn thoroughly (*ediscere*) the song. Ancient interpreters regarded V.'s mention of Sparta's well-known river as a reference to Hyacinthus, the Spartan boy who was loved by Apollo and suffered an accidental death (cf. 3.106–7n.): *nam hunc fluuium Hyacinthi causa Apollo dicitur amasse* (Serv. Dan.; the god promises him eternal memory in Ov. *met.* 10.203–6, in a scene presumably set not far from the river Eurotas, which is mentioned at *met.* 10.169). Bay trees, too, have Apollo's love in their past, even though their anthropomorphic past is feminine: here, Eurotas' 'command' may allude to Daphne's refusal of the god's love—once turned into a *silua*, she must abide by the pastoral law of 'resonance'. For Apollo's attempt to seduce Daphne through song cf. Nonn. *Dionys.* 15.310–11 (for further, especially iconographical, testimonies see Knox 1990, pp. 190–3). Bay and hyacinth appear together as Apollo's *munera* at *E.* 3.62–3 (for the hyacinth cf. also 6.53n.). The mention of the Eurotas locates the origin of Silenus' song in the Peloponnese, motherland of bucolic poetry: according to ancient geography (Dionys. Perieg. 409–13; Strab. 6.2.9 [275]; 8.3.12 [343]; Pausan. 8.44.3–4; 54.2–3; cf. Callim. fr. 699 Pf.; Prob. *ad E.* 6.82) the Eurotas, in some points of its course, mixed with the Alphcus, the river lover of Arethusa, so representative of the Theocritean and Virgilian Arcadia (10.1n.). **lauros.** Most manuscripts have the correct reading, i.e. the second-declension acc. form (*laurus* M); V. uses both the second and the fourth declension for this noun: *lauri* (*E.* 2.54); *laurus*, acc. pl. (*Aen.* 3.91); cf. 8.13n., as well as 7.6n.

84 pulsae referunt ad sidera ualles. Cf. *E.* 5.62–3 (indicating joy); Lucr. 2.327–8 *clamoreque montes / icti reiectant uoces ad sidera mundi*; for the term *sidus* cf. 5.43n.

85 cogere...ouis stabulis numerumque referre. The return of sheep to their fold and the tally of the flock are among the shepherd's daily tasks (cf. *E.* 3.34; note also Proteus and the seals at *G.* 4.436 *numerumque recenset*; see further below, 6.86n.; cf. Nemes. *ecl.* 2.88–90; 3.66–9). This practice, typically associated with evening tiredness, naturally induces sleep. It is also a pastoral variation on the theme of 'unyoking oxen' (from the plough), which marked the end of the day (esp. in epic poetry): cf. 2.66n. Hence the epithet αὔλιος for the evening star (from αὐλή 'stable': cf. here *stabulis*), as in Apoll. Rhod. 4.1630 and Callim. *aet.* fr. 177.6 Pf. (with R. Pfeiffer's apparatus note) = 149.6 Mass. = 54c.6 Hard; cf. also *Hymn. Hom.* 5[*Ven.*].168–9. **referre.** This is the text of R and, originally, MP as well (cf. Serv. Dan.; Non. p. 608 L.), whereas the emended text of MP has *referri*, most probably a learned conjecture. The active form is the one expected here, paralleled by *cogere*, with the two balancing infinitives enclosing the line.

344 ECLOGUE 7

86 iussit et inuito processit Vesper Olympo. Eurotas' command (6.83), ordering the learning of the song, is now followed by that of Vesper, the evening star, which marks the end of the day (cf. Tityrus-V.'s opening words: 6.9 *non iniussa cano*). The heavens reluctantly (*inuito...Olympo*) see the 'approaching' evening star, which follows its daily path (for *procedere* in astronomical contexts cf. 9.47n.). The celestial bodies must have been pleased by the song, which has reached the stars (6.84 *ad sidera*), and the reader is prompted to imagine a long summer day (6.22n.). The narrative started with morning-time and an act of 'seeing' (the two boys at 6.14; Silenus at 6.21), and it is now concluded by darkness: the overall length of a whole day is exceptional for a single eclogue and implies the mass of literary material included in Silenus' song. In Homer's *Iliad* (at least, in the Alexandrian edition), the first book ends with the sun hiding below the horizon (1.605), whereas the eighth book begins with sunrise and ends with sunset (awaiting a new dawn: Hom. *Il.* 8.565). In *Il.* 8.239–40, Hera pushes the Sun down below the horizon against his will (8.240 ἀέκοντα); cf. also Callim. *hymn.* 3[*Dian.*].180–2. **Vesper Olympo.** For the line-ending, in which a Roman name is coupled with a Greek one, cf. Catull. 62.1–2, where it opens the long-awaited song and ceremony: *Vesper adest, iuuenes, consurgite; Vesper Olympo / exspectata diu uix tandem lumina tollit* (cf. also the finale of Catull. 61, echoed at *E.* 3.111n.); it will reappear verbatim at *Aen.* 1.374 (in the context of a very long narrative); 8.280. Vesper, who presides over the end of the pastoral day, is connected to the mythical herdsman Proteus through a simile at *G.* 4.433–5: *ipse, uelut stabuli custos in montibus olim, / Vesper ubi e pastu uitulos ad tecta reducit / auditisque lupos acuunt balatibus agni* etc. (cf. here 6.85n.). A fitting contrast between light and darkness concludes a poem in which solar illumination has played a crucial role. The structural importance of the eclogue is confirmed by its finale, which anticipates and alludes to the epilogue of the entire book (cf. esp. 10.77 *uenit Hesperus*). For *Olympus* as a learned synonym of 'sky' cf. *G.* 1.450; see also Ov. *fast.* 3.415; Manil. 1.178. After l. 86, R ceases to transmit the text.

Eclogue 7

[Meliboeus]

The seventh eclogue begins with the memory of the day on which Daphnis, Corydon, and Thyrsis met near a 'rustling holm-oak' (7.1–5). Based on 7.6–8, we can infer that the narrator is a shepherd, whom Daphnis then addresses: his name turns out to be Meliboeus (7.9). Having been invited to attend the contest between Corydon and Thyrsis, Meliboeus accepts, although somewhat reluctantly (he wonders who might take care of the lambs during his absence). Meliboeus then goes on to relate the poetic exchanges of the two herdsmen (7.21–68), until in the two final lines he goes back to speaking in his own voice, and asserts that Corydon won the contest, thereby establishing the herdsman's fame (7.69–70).

In *E.* 7, V. goes back to the agonistic form experimented with in *E.* 3: now, however, unlike the case of Menalcas and Damoetas, no personal motivations underlie the agon (or, at least, we do not know of any: Meliboeus cannot tell us the whole story, given that he arrives on stage when the contest has already been decreed to happen). The reader's attention is immediately drawn to poetic skill (7.5 and 16). In comparison with *E.* 3, another major difference is that Menalcas and Damoetas bear names belonging to Theocritean (or pseudo-Theocritean: cf. above, p. 147) contestants, whereas in *E.* 7 both Corydon and Thyrsis have entirely new, individual personalities. In this regard, Servius' evaluation of *E.* 7 would be better applied to *E.* 3: Serv. *ad E.* 7.1 *ecloga haec paene tota Theocriti est* 'this poem is almost entirely Theocritean'. *E.* 7 doubtless contains much Theocritean material, but V. here shows the development of his approach to reworking Theocritus. Compared to *E.* 3, this eclogue has fewer comic elements (limited to the initial dialogue between Daphnis and Meliboeus: see esp. 7.7–8n.; 8–9n.). At any rate, *E.* 7 lacks an introduction or a pre-agon in which the future contestants can taunt each other sarcastically. In sum, the theme, structure, and outcome (Corydon's victory) of this 'Theocritean' eclogue are entirely Virgilian.

Although Meliboeus repeatedly refers to the equal age of the two contestants, both of whom he calls *Arcades* (a very important epithet in the *E.*), V.'s originality is perhaps underscored by the characters' flocks (Thyrsis' sheep; Corydon's less valuable goats: cf. 7.3n.) and is certainly highlighted by the herdsmen's names. Thyrsis, which does not reappear in the rest of the book, is the name of the well-known singer of *id.* 1, whereas Corydon is one of the great characters of V.'s pastoral world, and the protagonist of *E.* 2. While the contest of *E.* 3 ended in a draw, now the shepherd Thyrsis (despite his illustrious name) is defeated by the Virgilian goatherd. Once the outcome becomes clear, the reader can go back and discover the Theocritean clues as to who the winner might be (see 7.69–70n.).

Some irony can perhaps be detected in V.'s decision to entrust Thyrsis with the (intrinsically more difficult) task of 'responding' (7.20; but cf. 7.5n.): it seems as if chronological priority were reversed between the model and his follower (i.e. between Theocritus and V.). However, the presence of Daphnis (mentioned at the beginning of the poem) not only confirms the Theocritean echo in Thyrsis' name but also hints at a remote past, preceding *id.* 1 itself, in which the 'masks' of Daphnis and Thyrsis can appear alongside each other (since Daphnis has 'not yet' disappeared, and Thyrsis has 'not yet' sung of his sorrows: cf. 7.25n.). This Daphnis is given the task of mentioning the river Mincius (7.13n.), thereby alluding to a Mantuan space, which complements the Arcadian provenance of the two contestants. The reader might wonder, on the other hand, whether Corydon has 'already' composed his long monologue for Alexis, whose memory is immortalized in *E.* 2 (but cf. *E.* 5.86). Here, too, Corydon refers to a *formosus Alexis* (7.55).

346   ECLOGUE 7

But why is Corydon the winner? Having considered the eminently Virgilian reasons for his supremacy in the *E.*, we still have to address the 'technical' factors that justify his success. In this regard, generations of interpreters have made various suggestions, but the herdsman's language does not seem to play a major role; the same is true of his metrical and stylistic technique. In Theocritus' agons, the reasons for the two victories are far from evident, especially since the 'rules' that governed questioning and, above all, answering in Theocritus' genuine poems are probably neglected in the pseudo-Theocritean *id.* 8, which V. must have read as authentic (for further discussion see *Enc. Virg.* I, pp. 133–4, s.v. *amebeo, canto* [G. Serrao]; for a general overview, see *Virg. Enc.* I, p. 69, s.v. *amoebean* [B. W. Breed]). It seems, however, unlikely that V. could allow Thyrsis to perform more poorly (or less well) than Corydon. On the other hand, V. appears to shun any excessively precise justification for Corydon's victory: the reader, in fact, only knows part of the contest (i.e. what Meliboeus remembers of it). A more fruitful line of inquiry concerns the thematic choices, and therefore the characterization, of the two protagonists. It has often been observed that Thyrsis, unlike Corydon, is characterized by a peevish, aggressive attitude from the very first exchange, in which he rejects the need for divine favour and uses harsh words for Codrus, for whom Corydon expresses veneration (perhaps Theocritus' idylls contain the kernel of Thyrsis' portrayal as a 'proud' character: see 7.5n.). In *E.* 3, the pre-agon between Menalcas and Damoetas had a similarly lively tone: the two contestants exchanged rather malignant insinuations. Despite its non-agonistic nature, *E.* 5 was also centred around the contrastive characterization of a calm, mature Menalcas and a young, exuberant Mopsus. *E.* 7, however, is the first poem in which the opposition between two different characters is clearly perceptible even in the topics and styles of their songs.

The contrast also enlivens the agon, a pastoral form previously used in the book, which V. unsurprisingly aims at modifying, partly by heightening it. While the effect certainly seems pleasant to the reader, it is a disadvantage to Thyrsis: due to his inability to control his emotions, he cannot make a dent in the stylized elegance of his opponent. In fact, Meliboeus' last words depict him in the act of 'competing in vain' (7.69 *frustra contendere*). On a few occasions, Thyrsis resembles one of the aggressive antagonists who inhabit the world of Horace's *Satires*, like e.g. Crispinus in *sat.* 1.4.13–21. We cannot rule out that, by creating an 'ambitious' herdsman, V. might be alluding to such a type of literary duellist, certainly a topical figure in late Republican literary circles. In its 'competition' against *id.* 5, *E.* 3 showed how V.'s pastoral poetics is based on principles of subtle moderation, eschewing Theocritus' heavy-handed, sometimes vulgar tones. V.'s *decorum*, however, still allows Thyrsis to express aggression in a way not dissimilar from *id.* 5 (cf. esp. 7.26n.): since he aligns himself with such a 'rejected' model, he can hardly win an agon in V.'s pastoral world. That the reader must go back to *E.* 3 in order to evaluate *E.* 7 is evident from the structural balance displayed by the two poems: in fact, although the number of lines in the individual exchanges is different (two for each character in *E.* 3; four in *E.* 7), the total number of lines devoted to the actual contest is forty-eight in both cases. Yet the two eclogues are separated from each other by a world of poetry: thus, *E.* 7 is concluded by a crushing victory (as opposed to the draw in *E.* 3). V. can now allow himself to choose a winner. Moreover, the highly original sequence of *E.* 4-5-6 has a special significance for Corydon's victory. The two contestants, in fact, clearly differ in their use of religious and cultic language, with which the reader is by now familiar (having encountered the *puer*, the deified Daphnis, and Silenus). Note, in particular, the final exchange, which the reader must perceive as crucial, if not decisive, to the outcome of the agon (despite Meliboeus' narrative trick: 7.69 *haec memini*...): here, Corydon seems to have an easy time combining Hercules, Iacchus, Venus, and Phoebus (along with their respective plants), whereas Thyrsis does not mention a single deity. In previous exchanges, Thyrsis appeared faithful to his name (7.2n.) in inclining towards Dionysiac interests: after his initial mention of the ivy (7.25n.), he invoked Priapus (7.33) and Liber himself (7.58). Corydon, on the other hand, began his song with Delia-Artemis and the 'learned' *Nymphae Libethrides*, poetic deities connected with Orpheus and Euphorion (and therefore also with Silenus and Cornelius Gallus: cf. *E.* 6): he thereby aligns himself with fundamental themes and models of V.'s *E.* and shows his ability to mediate between potentially contrasting divine models. A special guest listens to the two contestants: Daphnis, whom Menalcas linked to Phoebus as well as to Bacchus and Ceres in *E.* 5, where he elaborated on Mopsus' Dionysian portrait (cf. *E.* 5.66 and 5.79; note, here too, the allegorical misunderstanding transmitted by Servius *ad* 7.21, according to whom Daphnis in *E.* 7 is Julius Caesar: 7.1–20n.).

In Theocritus' *id.* 1, Thyrsis gave the second prize to the goatherd and the first to Pan (*id.* 1.3): but *E.* 7 appears after a poem (*E.* 4) in which such pastoral value-scales are relativized, given that V. can imagine himself defeating the god Pan (*E.* 4.58-9). In *E.* 3, Palaemon, the judge whose name hints at antiquity, could not decide on a winner. But now, besides Daphnis, the agon has another spectator, namely V.'s reader—whose judgement is informed by the very trajectory of the *E.* as a book.

In terms of structure and narrative technique, *E.* 7 conceals some very original features under its disguise of typically Theocritean dialogue. In fact, while its mimetic form is in line with all of V.'s odd-numbered eclogues, the agon is not dramatized but narrated. Meliboeus, the narrator, is the only character to appear 'on stage' and ensure the 'dramatic' effect of the poem (this is why, unlike Mynors and other editors, I consider Meliboeus as the only *persona loquens* in *E.* 7 and I have used quotation marks accordingly: see below). In the Theocritean corpus, the short singing contest between Daphnis and Menalcas in *id.* 9 (most probably spurious) was introduced by an anonymous pastoral character who, after speaking

348 ECLOGUE 7

in the first person as in a mime and using direct speech to address the contestants, is revealed to be a narrator who reports on events of the past (*id.* 9.22–30). Other singing contests in the Theocritean corpus are either directly narrated by the poet (i.e. 'Theocritus': cf. *id.* 6, with an initial address to Aratus, a friend of the poet, and *id.* 8, where the narrator remains anonymous) or fully dramatized (*id.* 5). In contrast to *id.* 9, V. decides to make it immediately evident that the whole poem is the report of a narrator, who is a direct eyewitness to the contest yet does not coincide with the author. The speaker is one pastoral character among many others, as is clear from 7.6: his name is then explicitly mentioned at 7.9. This exceptional case of a pastoral character entirely replacing the narrator could be explained with the special status of Meliboeus, who bears the name of the hapless exile in *E.* 1 (see 7.8–9n.). As in *E.* 1, here V. characterizes Meliboeus as a diligent, conscientious herdsman and farmer. As a result, the voice of this character-narrator is the only one heard by the reader (non unlike e.g. the case of Theocr. *id.* 7 or Hor. *sat.* 1.8).

The original narrative structure of *E.* 7 can be highlighted in modern editions by the use of quotation marks to delimit the contest proper ('direct speech'): Meliboeus alone, i.e. the *persona loquens*, must be introduced as a character (his name has sometimes been treated as the poem's 'title'). The contest occupies forty-eight lines (as in *E.* 3: see above, pp. 346–7) and is composed of six sections of eight lines each (i.e. two speeches of four lines each per section): 21–68. The prologue (1–20) occupies twenty lines, while the epilogue has only two (69–70).

On the eclogue: Gebauer (1861, pp. 226–54); Witte (1922, pp. 8–12); Weyman (1926–7a); Mesk (1927); U. Albini (1951); Büchner (1955, cols. 1224–8); Beyers (1962); Savage (1963); Pöschl (1964, pp. 93–154); Dahlmann (1966); Fuchs (1966); Klingner (1967, pp. 118–25); Putnam (1970, pp. 222–54); Leach (1974, pp. 196–203); Frischer (1975); Benzer (1976); Van Sickle (1978, pp. 158–78); Alpers (1979, pp. 125–7); Camilloni (1979–80); Fantazzi, Querbach (1985); Camuffo (1986); M. O. Lee (1989, pp. 48–57); Papanghelis (1997); T. K. Hubbard (1998, pp. 108–11); Binder, Effe (2001, pp. 86–9); Sullivan (2002); von Albrecht (2007, pp. 28–30); Cucchiarelli (2010; 2011); Gagliardi (2017a).

Specific issues: Kumaniecki (1926) (date); Sandbach (1933) (l. 69); Snell (1945) (Arcadia); Barigazzi (1950) (l. 25); MacKay (1961, pp. 157–8) (l. 70); Veremans (1964–5) (metre); Della Corte et al. (1965) (l. 21 and Euphorion); Van Sickle (1967) (Arcadia and editorial form); Levi (1967–8) (Arcadia); Nethercut (1968) (Thyrsis = Horace); Wülfing von Martitz (1970) (Thyrsis as a Theocritean poet); Braun (1971) (agon in *E.* 3 and 7); Bettini (1972) (l. 70); Waite (1972) (love as the crucial topic of the agon); Chausserie-Laprée (1978) (phonetic and structural symmetries); Hudson-Williams (1980, pp. 130–2) (ll. 29–36); Geymonat (1981b) (Lucilius); Bernardi Perini (1983) (Mincius in l. 13); Heyworth (1984, p. 73) (l. 70); Michelazzo (1985) (ll. 29–30); Timpanaro (1986, pp. 146–8) (ll. 65–6); Jenkyns (1989, pp. 30–4) (Arcadia); Foster (1991, pp. 109–10) (l. 36); Lindahl (1994, pp. 163–5) (Corydon's name as a structural element in the *E.*); Starr (1995) (ancient interpreters and biographical reading); Zucchelli (1995) (ll. 41–3); Egan (1996) (ll. 61–70); Touratier (1996) (ll. 1–20); Harrison (1998) (l. 70); Lightfoot (1999, p. 65) (ll. 21; 25); Manzanero Cano (2000) (ll. 27–8); Schäfer (2001) (Roman traditional contests in *E.* 3 and

7); MacDonald (2003) (Theocritus in *E.* 3 and 7); Petrovitz (2003) (allusive art); Kraggerud (2006b, pp. 38–41) (l. 5); Kraggerud (2006b, pp. 41–4) (ll. 29–32); Kraggerud (2006b, pp. 44–6) (ll. 33–6); Kraggerud (2006b, pp. 46–8) (ll. 37–44); Kraggerud (2006b, pp. 48–9) (l. 64); Canetta (2008) (l. 21); Magnelli (2010) (l. 21); Morelli (2010) (ll. 21–8); Ottaviano (2012, pp. 202–9) (ll. 45–68); Johnston, Papaioannou (2013) (Arcadia); Gioseffi (2014, pp. 189–90) (ll. 21; 32); Paraskeviotis (2014a) (ll. 69–70); Heyworth (2015, pp. 213–15) (ll. 14–17); Kraggerud (2017b, pp. 55–7) (l. 5); Kraggerud (2017b, pp. 58–60) (ll. 29–32); Kraggerud (2017b, pp. 61–2) (ll. 33–6); Kraggerud (2017b, pp. 63–5) (ll. 37–44); Kraggerud (2017b, pp. 66–71) (ll. 53–60); Kraggerud (2017b, pp. 72–3) (l. 64); Cucchiarelli (2021a, pp. 96–100) (ll. 7–8); Jolowicz (2021, p. 18 and n. 131) (l. 4 and Erucius' epigram).

1–20. The first twenty lines of the eclogue (which has seventy lines in all) are devoted to a preamble, in which Meliboeus describes the setting of the agon. After the actual contest (forty-eight lines), Meliboeus will speak again and utter two final lines. As was the case with Simichidas in Theocritus' *id.* 7, here Meliboeus' narrative voice relates the events throughout the poem (see above, p. 348). Note the allegorical interpretation transmitted by Servius *ad 7.21: et multi uolunt in hac ecloga esse allegoriam, ut Daphnis sit Caesar, Corydon Vergilius, Thyrsis uero, qui uincitur, Vergilii obtrectator, scilicet aut Bauius aut Anser aut Maeuius* (but the comparison with Daphnis in *E.* 5 ought to be based on the respective divine models: cf. above p. 347).

1–5. V.'s narrative opening draws on two Theocritean agons: 'One day Damoetas and the cowherd Daphnis gathered / their herds in a single spot [εἰς ἕνα χῶρον / τὰν ἀγέλαν … συνάγαγον], o Aratus: one of them / half-bearded, the other's chin reddish with down; they both sat near a water-spring / at noon of a summer's day, and thus they sang' (*id.* 6.1–4); 'Fair Daphnis was grazing his oxen when / Menalcas met him on the high mountains: as the story goes, he was grazing his flocks. / Both were red-haired, both boys, / both skilled in playing the pipes and singing' [ἄμφω τώγ' ἤστην πυρρότριχω, ἄμφω ἀνάβω, / ἄμφω συρίσδεν δεδαημένω, ἄμφω ἀείδεν] (*id.* 8.1–4; it is possible that, in the Theocritean collection known to V., *id.* 8 appeared in the seventh position, which would be mirrored by *E.* 7: cf. Introduction, pp. 19–20). Here, however, the narrator will turn out to be himself a character; the contestant Daphnis, on the other hand, becomes a witness and—seemingly—a referee (cf. 7.70n.). While the preceding eclogue was concluded by the evening tally of sheep, this poem is opened by a rounding up of flocks (2 *compulerantque greges*).

1 Forte. A typical narrative opening, as e.g. in Hor. *sat.* 1.9.1 *Ibam forte uia Sacra*; Stat. *silu.* 4.6.1 *Forte remittentem curas* etc. (note the initial adverb, as in V.); here, however, the narrative *ego* does not appear until 7.6. Cf. *E.* 3.50, where Palaemon unwittingly passes by Menalcas and Damoetas. **sub arguta … ilice.** The shade of a leafy tree welcomes the shepherd, as e.g. Tityrus in the initial *E.* 1.1; here Daphnis, rather than reclining, is seated (the typical pose of Theocritus' singers: *id.* 1.12), but the other 'wandering' character is called Meliboeus in both cases. Thanks to its leafy crown, the holm-oak produces an evocative rustle (*Aen.*

350   ECLOGUE 7

12.702; cf. also Hor. *epod.* 10.8). The epithet *arguta*, 'clear-sounding', well suited to musical instruments (cf. the *fistula* at 7.24) or poets themselves (Hor. *epist.* 2.2.90), is appropriate for the entrance of Daphnis: cf. *id.* 1.1–2 (the sweet sound of th pine-tree; see also Mosch. fr. 1.8 G.); *E.* 8.22 *argutumque nemus pinusque loquentis*; 10.58; cf. also *G.* 1.143 *argutae...serrae*.

2 **compulerantque greges**. Cf. 2.30; *id.* 6.2 συνάγαγον. The idea of 'gathering' or 'assembling' can be applied to both livestock and pastoral poems: cf. the well-known epigram of Artemidorus the grammarian (*Anth. Pal.* 9.205; cf. Introduction, p. 19). Correspondingly, the 'loss' of animals sometimes indicates the end of the poem itself, as e.g. in *E.* 1.74 (Meliboeus); here, by contrast, the two shepherds put together both flocks and songs. **Corydon et Thyrsis**. The two names are highlighted by the chiastic repetition at 7.2–3; l. 16 will make it clear that such a pair of names must have a striking effect on the listener. While Thyrsis' name is familiar from Theocritus' *id.* 1 (perhaps known to the ancients as *The Song of Thyrsis*: cf. also 7.5n.), Corydon's glory is entirely Virgilian: cf. 2.1n. The Dionysian overtones of Thyrsis' name (for the thyrsus cf. 5.31n.) will soon be activated by the ivy he mentions at the outset of his address to the shepherds (7.25n.). Propertius seems to allude to this eclogue by mentioning Thyrsis and Daphnis at 2.34.67–8. Note the order in which the two characters are introduced (Corydon, then Thyrsis): this structure is replicated at 7.16 and 7.20 (by contrast, the order is reversed, as in a chiasmus, at 7.3n., where more space is allotted to Corydon). This is, in fact, the order in which the two will sing their songs, and the reader will soon find out that Corydon, whom Meliboeus mentions first, is bound to come out on top (cf. also 8.1n.). **in unum**. Cf. *id.* 6.1 εἰς ἕνα χῶρον (see 7.1–5n.).

3 **Thyrsis ouis, Corydon...capellas**. The distinction between sheep and goats, here made evident by the chiastic structure in ll. 2–3 (note also the correspondence between *ouis...capellas* and *greges*), is part of a typically pastoral value-scale (in descending order: cowherd, shepherd, then goatherd; cf. *E.* 1.6n.). This is all the more evident in a context featuring Daphnis, the shepherd *par excellence*. The distinction was emphasized by Theocritus in *id.* 5, starting from the very first exchange: there, as here, the goatherd (Comatas) defeats the shepherd (Lacon). While Thyrsis owns the more valuable *ouis*, Corydon's *capellae* are the animals endowed with fertility. In contrast to the perfect balance between the two contestants at 7.4–5, now Corydon takes centre stage and a very positive connotation is associated with his goats (*distentas lacte capellas*: contrast the 'minimalist' phrasing *Thyrsis ouis*). This is a small clue as to who the winner will be (note again that, in Theocritus' *id.* 5, the winner is the goatherd), but certainly a significant one in case of a 'second reading', when the outcome is already known. Meliboeus might be expected to introduce the two contestants impartially, while obviously knowing that 'Corydon is Corydon' (cf. below, 7.70n.). **distentas lacte**. Cf. *E.* 4.21; 9.31. In *id.* 6, the summertime setting was explicit (cf. *id.* 6.4: see above, 7.1–5n.); that *E.* 7, too, is set in a fertile season (presumably spring) is suggested by various details,

ECLOGUE 7   351

such as the swollen udders (also alluding to a late time of the day: cf. also 7.15n.), the tender myrtles (7.6), the newborns and their weaning (note 7.9 *haedi*; 7.15 *depulsos a lacte...agnos*), as well as the bees' buzzing (7.13). In the agon of *E*. 3, the setting was a springtime one according to Palaemon (*E*. 3.56–7). The description of the animals, which is simply omitted in Thyrsis' case, draws attention to Corydon: Meliboeus is soon revealed to be rather scrupulous and observant when it comes to the health of livestock and plants.

4 ambo...Arcades ambo. The model of *id*. 8 (cf. below, 7.5n.) is complemented by an epigram of Erucius, in which the two herdsmen Glaucon and Corydon (note the name!) are called Ἀρκάδες ἀμφότεροι 'both Arcadians' (*Anth. Pal*. 6.96.2 = *GPh* 2201 G.-P.; note here the short ending in *Arcades*, as in Greek: cf. *E*. 6.48; see further 7.26n.). There is perhaps no way of ascertaining the relative chronology, but note a crucial difference: in the epigram, the two herdsmen are 'suitably' placed in Arcadia, as is shown by their devotion to Pan's cult on Mount Cyllene (*Anth. Pal*. 6.96.3 = *GPh* 2202 G.-P.), whereas V. does not hesitate to mention the herdsmen's Arcadian provenance alongside the river Mincius (*E*. 7.13). Similar 'mixtures' can be found in *id*. 1, where Thyrsis is called 'Aetnean' (*id*. 1.65), even though his Daphnis invokes Pan (who dwells on the Arcadian Mount Maenalus) and asks him to reach Sicily (*id*. 1.124–6). Analogously, in *E*. 2.21, Corydon boasts about his thousand she-lambs grazing on the Sicilian mountains. In V.'s collection, the only 'precedent' for this Arcadian reference is at *E*. 4.58–9, which is only a poetically vague geographical allusion, like Parnassus and Thrace at *E*. 6.29–30. From here onwards, however, Daphnis' invocation (*id*. 1) seems to be materialized: Arcadia and the Arcadians (along with Pan) start joining the pastoral world. In fact, Damon's refrain will repeatedly refer to 'Maenalian verse' (8.21n.), whereas *E*. 10 will assign a fundamental role to Arcadia and its inhabitants (*E*. 10.26; 31; 33; for Arethusa cf. 10.1n.). For Arcadia as the birthplace of pastoral poetry cf. Introduction, pp. 13–14; suffice it here to mention Polybius, 4.20.7–9, where the Arcadians are characterized by an actual familiarity with music and song, which they are said to practise from childhood. A clear echo of the Virgilian passage, except for the significant mention of Arcadia, is found at Nemes. *ecl*. 2.16–17 *ambo aeuo cantuque pares nec dispare forma*, / *ambo genas leues, intonsi crinibus ambo*; cf. also *E*. 5.1–2 *boni...ambo*, / *tu calamos inflare leuis, ego dicere uersus*. In conclusion, it is clear that the significance of *Arcas/Arcades* in the *E*. is by no means limited to a mere geographical reference, but has a strong symbolic connotation, hinting at the poetic skills typical of the Arcadian people. **aetatibus**. The plural replaces the expected singular, making the two characters appear more concrete and individualized (i.e. two 'single' youths).

5 et cantare pares et respondere parati. Through his insistence on duality and equivalence here and at 7.4 (note the alliteration *pares...parati*), V. seems to prepare his reader for a draw: instead, the contest will end with a clear victory. This reference to the characters' skills in both singing and replying (the latter being a very important art, according to Servius *ad E*. 3.28) anticipates the

352   ECLOGUE 7

amoebean structure of the contest. The first 'responder' is Thyrsis, who gets to sing the second song (and is eventually defeated). Yet in the pastoral tradition, all speeches and songs are intertwined and, ideally, 'respond' to one another. Playing the pipes and singing were featured in *id*. 8.4 ἄμφω συρίσδεν δεδαημένω, ἄμφω ἀείδεν (see 7.1–5n.). In *id*. 1, Thyrsis was credited with a good reputation as a contestant (*id*. 1.24); here, Thyrsis appears as a young poet, who is still 'growing up' (7.25n.). Note the construction with the infinitive, rather unexpected for *pares* but perfectly normal for *paratus* (cf. *Aen*. 5.108 *et certare parati*; for *paro* with an infinitive, cf. *E*. 2.72n.): yet the two adjectives are almost assimilated to each other, thanks to alliteration and paronomasia (cf. the Italian idiomatic expression 'pari e patta'); see also *E*. 5.1–2 *boni… / tu calamos inflare…ego dicere uersus* (n.); 10.32 *cantare periti*. The syntax is simplified in Nemes. *ecl*. 2.16 (see above, 7.4n.); for a similar wording, cf. Catull. 62.18 *dicere iam incipient, iam respondere decebit*.

6 mihi. Ethic dative, as in *E*. 3.100; *G*. 1.45. **dum teneras defendo a frigore myrtos.** The myrtles, still young or at least in their growing stage (*teneras*: cf. *E*. 1.8; 6.34), must be protected from spring frost; cf. Ov. *amor*. 1.15.37 *metuentem frigora myrtum*. They tend to grow on the coast, precisely because its climate is more temperate (cf. *G*. 2.112; 4.124; Ov. *amor*. 1.1.29; Mart. 4.13.6); besides, hostility to cold weather seems to befit Venus' plant. As he is absorbed in the task, Meliboeus does not realize that his boisterous bill goat has escaped. The ground surrounding young, delicate plants was customarily covered with straw in order to protect them from the cold (Plin. *nat*. 17.16): here, however, V. probably refers to a form of overhead shelter (perhaps leafy branches). Note the construction of *dum* with the present tense, used alongside a secondary tense (*deerrauerat*) in the main clause (cf., for instance, *Aen*. 1.494–7; 6.171–4). As a result, the narrative acquires a vivid immediacy (cf. the primary *aspicio… uidet*; secondary sequence reappears at ll. 14–19). Some manuscripts have *myrtus*, but the second-declension form seems preferable here; it also appears at *G*. 4.124. It may be that V. is not always consistent in his usage, as e.g. in the case of *laurus/lauri*: cf. *E*. 6.83n. Here and further on in the poem, V. emphasizes the characterization of Meliboeus as a very conscientious herdsman, who pays great attention to both livestock and plants (note the affective connotation of *teneras*): cf. 1.70 *tam culta noualia*.

7 uir gregis ipse caper. The 'husband' of the flock, i.e. almost the 'man' of the house (note the emphatic *ipse*); cf. *id*. 8.49 ὦ τράγε, τᾶν λευκᾶν αἰγῶν ἄνερ 'o billy-goat, husband of the white sheep', with a rather uncommon linguistic usage that the Theocritean scholia *ad loc*. (p. 209 Wendel) single out as 'misapplied' (καταχρηστικῶς…φησίν). Nevertheless, this way of referring to a 'male animal' is attested in technical and scientific prose: cf. Aristot. *hist. anim*. 10.637b12–15. Note also Hor. *carm*. 1.17.7 *olentis uxores mariti*; Ov. *ars* 1.522. For a technical use of *maritus* cf. *G*. 3.125; Colum. 7.6.4. The phrasing is rather emphatic, since the conscientious Meliboeus wants to stress the irrevocability of the damage that his

ECLOGUE 7   353

herd was going to suffer if deprived of its male animal. **deerrauerat**. Note the synizesis of the first two vowels; cf. Lucr. 3.861 (860) *deerrarunt*.

7–8 **atque ego Daphnin / aspicio**. It has now become clear that the speaking voice belongs to a character (rather than to the poet): his first-hand experience of the events is underscored by the enjambement. Note the hinge with *atque*, highlighting lively surprise after the narrative style of the preceding lines: cf. *Aen.* 7.29–30 *atque hic Aeneas…lucum / prospicit* (see also 10.219–20); but cf. Plautus, esp. *Mil.* 287–8 *per impluuium huc despexi in proxumum / atque ego illi aspicio osculantem Philocomasium*; *ThlL* II.1075.82–1076.5 (note the audacious *atque* of *G.* 1.203, observed by Gell. 10.29.4). Meliboeus here 'sees' Daphnis, whose name evokes veneration (note also Servius' identification of Daphnis as 'Caesar': cf. *ad E.* 7.21). Yet, unlike Menalcas (who saw Daphnis in a similar pastoral situation and addressed him first: *id.* 8.5 πρᾶτος δ᾽ ὢν ποτὶ Δάφνιν ἰδὼν ἀγόρευε Μενάλκας), Meliboeus does not talk to Daphnis. On the contrary, Daphnis addresses Meliboeus as soon as they see each other (7.8–9 'ocius' inquit / 'huc ades etc.'). In the 'code of conduct' of Rome's *urbanitas*, the younger or less venerable person should greet the other person; note Volteius Mena's apologies to Philippus (who had greeted him first: *prior*) in Hor. *epist.* 1.7.66–9: *ille Philippo / excusare laborem et mercennaria uincla / quod non mane domum uenisset, denique quod non / prouidisset eum*. Like Volteius, Meliboeus here behaves as a very busy worker who does not have any time to waste (cf. 17 *mea seria* in contrast to *illorum…ludo*). The *rusticus* Meliboeus does not appear to be particularly polite, but Daphnis knows how to engage with him.

8–13. In his speech, partly meant to reassure Meliboeus and exhort him to attend the contest, Daphnis describes the setting in which the agon will take place—a typically 'pre-agonistic' task: cf. *E.* 3.55–9; 5.4–7.

8–9 **ocius… / huc ades**. The adverb *ocius*, frequently used in comedy, belongs to the colloquial register: hence the expressive use of the comparative degree, which effectively replaces the positive (Paul. Fest. p. 193 L. *ocius et ocissime positiuum Latinum non habent*; a learned back-formation possibly explains *ociter*, attested only since Apul. *met.* 1.23.8; cf. H.-Sz., pp. 168–9). For *ocius* with a verb of motion, cf. Plaut. *Curc.* 276 *exi, inquam, ocius*; *Merc.* 930, etc.; *ThlL* IX.2.415.1–16. Already used also in archaic tragedy, the adverb is mainly employed in poetry, where it suffices to convey dialogic liveliness: cf. Hor. *sat.* 2.7.117–18 *ocius hinc te / ni rapis*, etc. (the poet addressing his slave Davus); see also, in epic poetry, *Aen.* 8.101 *ocius aduertunt proras*; 278; 555; 9.402; 10.786 (but cf. Hom. *Il.* 2.440 θᾶσσον ἐγείρομεν…Ἄρηα); Lucan. 3.150; Stat. *Ach.* 1.504, etc. (the adv. is also attested in historiography, esp. Livy and, later, Ammianus Marcellinus; it also appears in Petronius and Pliny the Elder); see further *ThlL* IX.2.414.19–25. The adverb points at the mime-like liveliness of *E.* 7, which is overall greatly reduced compared to *E.* 3 and Theocritus' quasi-comic contests. The phrase *huc ades* is typical of V.'s pastoral style: cf. *E.* 2.45n.; contrast the normal construction with a verb of motion at

354   ECLOGUE 7

E. 7.11 *huc uenient*, where the iterated adverb aims at persuasion (cf. also *E.* 7.12 *hic*). In *E.* 1, Meliboeus gave voice to the sorrow of exile using a similar expression: cf. 1.51 *hic inter flumina nota* (cf., here, 7.13 *Mincius*); 1.53 *hinc tibi* (the bees: cf., again, 7.13 *examina*); 1.56 *hinc*. Note, finally, a likely echo in Persius, 3.7–8 *ocius adsit / huc aliquis*. **o Meliboee.** Cf. *E.* 1.6 (Tityrus' first utterance). The herdsman whom Daphnis addresses is finally revealed to be a namesake of the wretched exile of *E.* 1, whose name also opened *E.* 3 (where Meliboeus is the potential owner of a flock); cf. *E.* 5.87. In opposition to the old Meliboeus' forlorn *carmina nulla canam* (*E.* 1.77), this Meliboeus is given a crucial, poetic role as sole witness—and therefore narrator—of the agon (7.69 *haec memini*). His voice, after all, is the first pastoral voice heard by the reader in *E.* 1, whereas Tityrus' name reappeared, in a prominent position, at the outset of *E.* 6: after making an appearance as Tityrus-V., the poet leaves the stage to Meliboeus in *E.* 7. The reader of the *E.* has encountered Meliboeus in *E.* 1, where he is portrayed as a hapless exile. Here, by contrast, a Meliboeus has the unparalleled honour to narrate a whole pastoral episode: the 'great' contest of Corydon and Thyrsis. **caper tibi saluus et haedi.** Daphnis' reassurance points to Meliboeus' characterization, with which the reader is familiar from *E.* 1 (note the etymology: 'he who takes care of oxen' [1.6n.]): he is a scrupulous herdsman, very attached to his animals as well as his land (cf., for instance, *E.* 1.15 *spem gregis, a! silice in nuda conixa reliquit*; see also 1.77–8). The reader only knows that the billy goat has escaped, and the reference to the kids must sound like a generalizing addition (spoken with some affectionate irony); but Meliboeus will, in fact, worry about his lambs (7.15). Goatherds were traditionally characterized as struggling with boisterous animals, typically hard to subdue (as is shown here by the esca d billy goat): cf. Colum. 7.6.9 *magister autem…acer, durus, strenuus, laboris patientissimus, alacer atque audax esse debet, ut qui per rupes, per solitudines, per uepres facile uadat.*

10 si quid cessare potes, requiesce sub umbra. A further possible echo of *E.* 1, where Meliboeus did not seem to accept Tityrus' invitation (whereas Daphnis' words will have a different fate here): *E.* 1.79 *hic* [cf. here *huc* at 7.9] *tamen hanc mecum poteras requiescere noctem*. In *E.* 1, Meliboeus could certainly not allow himself to rest under a shady beech tree like Tityrus (1.1 *sub tegmine fagi*; 1.4 *in umbra*). The act of *cessare* appears to be difficult for a character with the diligent name Meliboeus; thus, *si quid…potes* must be taken as a courtesy formula, along the lines of *si quid habes* (3.52n.).

11 ipsi…iuuenci. The young bullocks will spontaneously (*ipsi*: cf. esp. *E.* 4.21) come to drink, after grazing in the meadows (cf., similarly, the goats at *E.* 9.24). Even if we do not assume that these animals belong to Meliboeus, this mention of bovine species is well suited to his name. The speaker, moreover, is a character bearing the name of the 'divine cowherd': upon Daphnis' death, the watering of *boues ad flumina* is suspended (*E.* 5.24–5), whereas the calves of *id.* 1 join the other cattle in mourning him (*id.* 1.75). **per prata.** Thus, the path is easy to follow

ECLOGUE 7   355

and readily overseen, besides being ideal for grazing; for the supine *potum*, with alliteration, cf. *E.* 9.24n.

12 tenera...harundine. In *E.* 1.48 the Mantuan region was described as marshy, whereas here the emphasis is on the pleasant banks of Mantua's river, whose name appears (underscored by the enjambement) at the beginning of 7.13. For a similar, though weakened, effect, cf. V.'s self-quotation (full of pastoral echoes) at *G.* 3.14–15 *tardis ingens ubi flexibus errat / Mincius et tenera praetexit harundine ripas* (note also 2.414 *ripis fluuialis harundo; harundine glauca* in *Aen.* 10.205: see *E.* 7.13n.). The *harundo*, at any rate, is generally used as raw material to build pastoral flutes: hence its metonymic sense (*E.* 6.8). Note here the adjective *tenera*, which establishes a 'sympathetic' connection between Daphnis and Meliboeus (the latter, as a narrator, has just said *teneras...myrtos* at 6). The Verona fragment (**V**) transmits *E.* 7.12–37.

13 Mincius. In *E.* 1, obviously set in the confiscated lands around Mantua (even though only Rome was explicitly mentioned, unlike Mantua and Cremona, which will appear in *E.* 9), the Hyblaean bees provided a rather surprising geographical and literary reference (*E.* 1.54n.; cf. here 7.37n.). Now, immediately after Meliboeus' mention of Arcadia, the arch-Sicilian Daphnis names the river Mincius, while the bees, a symbol of poetry, reappear. Note the personification of the river, 'clothing' its banks with reeds: for another Virgilian occurrence, besides *G.* 3.15 (see 7.12n.), cf. the warlike scene at *Aen.* 10.204–6 *hinc quoque quingentos in se Mezentius armat, / quos patre Benaco uelatus harundine glauca / Mincius infesta ducebat in aequora pinu* (thus, the Mincius appears once in each of V.'s works, and always in the second half of the work). **eque sacra resonant examina quercu.** This oak is sacred—hardly a surprise, given that the oak is Jupiter's tree: cf. *G.* 3.332 *magna Iouis antiquo robore quercus* (but see also *E.* 1.17). Its cavities harbour swarms of bees which are themselves dear to Jupiter, since they nurtured him as a child: cf. *G.* 4.149–52 (but see Callim. *hymn.* 1[*Iou.*].49–51). For the resounding noise of swarms, cf. *id.* 5.46 ὧδε [cf. here 12 *hic*] καλὸν βομβεῦντι ποτὶ σμάνεσσι μέλισσαι. The tree, with its hollow cavities, seems to amplify the bees' noise or let it 'resonate': cf. *E.* 9.15 *caua...ab ilice cornix* (n.).

14 quid facerem? neque...nec. For a similarly lively and colloquial wording, cf. *E.* 1.40–1; for analogous uses of the verb, but in the present tense, cf. Hor. *sat.* 2.1.24; Prop. 3.16.5; Ov. *ars* 2.548. **Alcippen...Phyllida.** Alcippe's name, occurring only here in V., appears in Theocritus' *id.* 5.132–3: 'I do not like Alcippe, who did not kiss me the other day, / taking me by the ears, when I gave her a beautiful pigeon'. Phyllis, on the other hand, is familiar to the reader of V.'s *E.*: a beautiful yet reassuring girl, not impossible to seduce (*E.* 3.76n.; cf. 7.59; 63). By pairing the two names, Meliboeus perhaps hints at certain differences between the two girls: Alcippe is 'respectable' (she is very reserved in Theocritus, whereas V. never mentions her again) and bears a solemn name (as a suffix, -*ipp*- was typical of Greek aristocratic names, whereas *alc*- evokes ἀλκή 'strength': cf. *E.* 5.11n.), which

356 ECLOGUE 7

contrasts with the slender simplicity of *Phyllis* ('little leaf'). To be sure, Servius overinterprets the passage, albeit elegantly, by considering Alcippe and Phyllis as the respective partners of the two contestants, Thyrsis and Corydon. Yet, here and elsewhere, V. certainly evokes (with some irony) the concrete reality of the herdsmen's society: love affairs, solitude, and relationships. Once again, the characterization of Meliboeus in *E.* 7 is consistent with that of *E.* 1: there, too, Meliboeus was occasionally portrayed as a lonely observer of other herdsmen's girlfriends (such as Amaryllis: cf. *E.* 1.36–9). That someone ought to attend to the herd or other work-related duties while the herdsmen sing is obvious to most people in the pastoral world: cf. e.g. *E.* 5.12 *pascentis seruabit Tityrus haedos.*

   15 **depulsos a lacte domi…clauderet agnos.** The verb *depellere* is a technical term for 'weaning' (cf. *E.* 1.21n.). The need to gather the lambs into their fold hints at evening (7.3n.). The reading *hedos* (i.e. *haedos*) of M^1 must be rejected (M^2 corrects into *agnos*): it is probably due to a simple psychological error, given that so far Meliboeus has only been associated with goats (for line-ending *haedi* cf. 7.9; but note 7.11 *iuuenci*). Gathering groups of animals and, if necessary, bringing the lambs into the fold is one of the herdsman's chief duties (cf. also the kids at 2.30 *haedorum…gregem* [n.]). In the Cyclops' cave, while he is grazing his sheep, kids and lambs are gathered behind bars and meticulously separated by age groups: cf. *Od.* 9.219–22; the goal, besides protecting them, is weaning them in the best possible way, as is shown by the technical literature: see Varr. *rust.* 2.2.15–18; Colum. 7.3.17–19; cf. Ov. *medic.* 15 [*matrona*] *claudebat, quos filia pauerat, agnos.*

   16 **et certamen erat, Corydon cum Thyrside, magnum.** The two names reappear together, emphatically placed between the noun and the adj., which is thereby postponed and underscored. For a literal echo, cf. Calp. *ecl.* 2.9 *et magnum certamen erat sub iudice Thyrsi,* where, however, the contest is between two entirely new characters, Astacus and Idas; for a further reworking, cf. Stat. *Theb.* 6.436–7 *postremum discrimen erant* [v.l. *erat*] *Chromis asper et asper / Hippodamus* (the name Chromis is eminently Virgilian: cf. *E.* 6.13n.). Emphasized by the caesura (and by the diaeresis after the fifth foot), the news of the agon seems to spread in the form in which it could presumably circulate orally among herdsmen: 'Corydon against Thyrsis!'. A similar notion occurs in *E.* 3, a few lines before the contest starts, though in that instance it is verbalized by one of the contestants (Damoetas): *res est non parua* (3.54). For the agon as a pastoral subgenre, cf. *Enc. Virg.* I, pp. 133–4, s.v. *amebeo, canto* (G. Serrao); *Virg. Enc.* I, p. 69, s.v. *amoebean* (B. W. Breed); on the Greek historical and epigraphical evidence, see Manieri (2009).

   17 **posthabui…illorum mea seria ludo.** Meliboeus is, once again, characterized as 'serious' and hard-working. In this case, however, he considers both options yet postpones work itself (note *tamen*, referring to 7.14–16 as a whole: a subtle element of characterization, given the herdsman's general behaviour). For poetry

as *ludus*, cf. esp. *E.* 1.10 *ludere quae uellem* (Tityrus to Meliboeus); 6.1; see also Ov. *trist.* 1.8.31 *tot lusus et tot mea seria.* For a verbatim quotation, cf. Auson. *Mos.* 206-7 *sua seria ludo / posthabet: excludit ueteres noua gratia curas.* The whole preamble, and particularly its last few lines, is used by V. to kindle the reader's curiosity and expectations.

18 alternis...contendere uersibus ambo. The dual pronoun (*ambo*) marks the beginning of the actual agon, whose amoebean structure is anticipated by the repetition *alternis...alternos* (7.19); see also *E.* 3.59; but cf. *id.* 8.30-2. The verb will reappear in the penultimate line of the poem, denoting Thyrsis' competitiveness—entirely pointless by then, but seemingly unstoppable (7.69 *frustra contendere*). **igitur.** The adv. is typically used in prose and aims at colloquial mimesis. Elsewhere, V. only uses it in speeches: cf. *Aen.* 4.537 and 9.199; see Axelson (1945, p. 93).

19 alternos Musae meminisse uolebant. The reading *uolebant* (where *Musae* is the subject) is certainly the correct one: cf. *E.* 3.59 *amant alterna Camenae*, even though Servius transmits *uolebam* (where *Musae* is voc.). The act of 'remembering' is here attributed to the goddesses themselves, whose prerogatives included memory (their mother is Mnemosyne herself): cf. *Aen.* 7.645 *et meministis enim, diuae, et memorare potestis.* Needless to say, *meminisse* also refers to the singer's recalling of his song in performance: 7.69 *haec memini* (cf. *E.* 9.38; 45; 52-3; see also 8.62-3; *G.* 3.90).

20 hos...illos. Meliboeus, like V., strives to describe with great precision the amoebean principle, so that it may be clear to the listener (and the reader). Corydon will start singing in the immediately following lines (*hos*, referring to the closest object), whereas Thyrsis will reply (*referebat*) in the ensuing group of lines (*illos*, referring to the more distant object), and so on (*in ordine*); cf. *id.* 8, esp. 31-2 εἶτα δ' ἀμοιβαίαν ὑπελάμβανε Δάφνις ἀοιδάν / βουκολικάν. This line is in effect a sort of 'stage direction', allowing the text to be intelligible even without graphic markers attributing lines to each character.

21-68. The central section of the poem is occupied by the agon proper, which is forty-eight lines long (over twice the length of the remaining twenty-two lines: twenty in the introduction and two in the epilogue). Compared to V.'s other agon, i.e. *E.* 3, the number of lines per speech is now doubled (four instead of two), and therefore the same is true of each pair of speeches (eight lines rather than four). Conversely, as a result of this, the number of speeches is halved (six pairs in *E.* 7 vs twelve in *E.* 3), while the total number of lines remains the same. Throughout the contest, several topics follow one another with various effects of echo and alternation. The topics themselves are typically pastoral: deities, nature and natural elements, eros. Some scholars have cast doubt on the order transmitted by the manuscripts, and various transpositions have been proposed (see esp. 7.56-60n.). However, no argument against the transmitted text appears to be conclusive and, in general, the interpretive gain granted by a given transposition is compensated by a loss in expressiveness somewhere else. In sum, it is best to

358   ECLOGUE 7

preserve the transmitted text, which offers the following thematic succession: an initial prologue (21–8); an invocation-cum-dedication to a deity (29–36); a pair of speeches addressed to Galatea (37–44); an opposition between early summer and the winter months (45–52); a contrast between autumn and summer, with an emphasis on eros (i.e. on the presence/absence of the beloved person: 53–60); finally, a 'triumphant' conclusion featuring an overall combination of gods, natural elements (plants), and the erotic theme (7.61–8).

21–8. The first, prefatory exchange introduces the two contestants. In *E*. 3, Damoetas and Menalcas began their songs with the gods—the former appealing to Jupiter, the latter to Phoebus (3.62 *et me Phoebus amat*). Similarly, in *id*. 5, Comatas referred to the Muses' predilection for him, whereas Lacon mentioned the god of poetry himself (*id*. 5.82 καὶ γὰρ ἔμ' Ὠπόλλων φιλέει μέγα 'and Apollo loves me greatly'). Here, Corydon's song begins by invoking a specific type of Nymphs, the *Libethrides* (*E*. 7.21n.); he also mentions a model he aspires to equal, i.e. the poet Codrus (7.22). Thyrsis, by contrast, does not invoke any deity and directly addresses the Arcadian herdsmen, whom he asks for a poetic investiture; he also expresses disdain for Codrus. In *E*. 3.84–9, the two contestants (whose agon ended in a draw) agreed in praising Pollio, whereas the disagreement concerning Codrus is more than obvious here.

21 Nymphae...Libethrides. The Nymphs were described as teachers of poetry in *id*. 7.92, and thereby put on a par with the Muses (this idea puzzled ancient interpreters; V. avoids any objection in his own reworking of the passage at *E*. 9.32–3 [n.]); the two groups were not, however, explicitly equated with each other, *pace* Servius (who quotes Varro as an authority: cf. 10.10n.). By choosing a learned, Alexandrian epithet (note the short vowel in the voc. ending, as in l. 4 *Arcades*), Corydon immediately aligns himself with the poetic programme outlined by Silenus in the preceding eclogue. That the Libethrides, or Libethrian Nymphs, were associated with two distinct places was clear to ancient scholars and geographers. On the one hand, the sources testify to a Boeotian cult of the Libethrian Nymphs connected with Mount Libethrius, not far from Coronea and Mount Helicon (Pausan. 9.34.4, mentioning a spring named 'Libethrias'; hence, presumably, Servius Dan.'s note: *a fonte Boeotiae*). On the other hand, the Macedonian city of Libethra in Pieria (at the foot of Mount Olympus) was better known: that region, too, was renowned for its cult of the Muses (cf. Lycophr. *Alex.* 273–5). The two places were easily confused with each other. Strabo, for instance, posited a Thracian origin for the Boeotian cult of the Muses (9.2.25[410]; cf. also 10.3.17[471]). In general, the epithet *Libethrides* appears, along the lines of *Pi(m)pleides* (cf. Hor. *carm.* 1.26.9; Callim. *hymn.* 4[*Del.*].7), as a learned synonym of *Pierides* (cf. 3.85n., as well as 6.13). Varro numbers it among the Muses' epithets at *ling.* 7.20 *ita enim ab terrestribus locis aliis cognominatae Libethrides, Pipleides, Thespiades, Heliconides* (cf. also Maxim. Astrolog. περὶ καταρχῶν 141). Silenus'

poem, and particularly Cornelius Gallus (singer of the Grynean grove: *E.* 6.72n.; cf. 10.50n.), are potentially in the background, given that V. probably knew Euphorion's 'Libethrian virgins' (παρθενικαὶ Λιβηθρίδες): *SH* fr. 416.2, p. 205 Ll.-J.-P. (editors, however, print Maas' emendation Λιβηθρίδος 'of the Libethrian land': cf. fr. 32.2 v. Gron. = 34.2 Light.). The toponym was also linked to Orphic cult: Orph. fr. 342; TT 223d; 225; 249; 250 Kern = 771a; 870.1; 870.6; 507.1–2 Bern.). Note, finally, the Libethrian Nymphs' appearance in two anonymous Hellenistic fragments, i.e. *SH* 993.7, p. 512 Ll.-J.-P. (perhaps an investiture scene à la Hesiod) and 988.1, p. 505 Ll.-J.-P. (seemingly describing a sculpture in which Phaethon is struck by a thunderbolt; concerning the issue raised in the apparatus, p. 505, ad loc. '*hae* [scil. *Libethrides*] *quid cum Phaethonte agant non videmus*', note that, according to Pausan. 9.30.9–12, the oracle of Dionysus prophesied the demise of the city of Libethra if the Sun were to see the bones of Orpheus buried there: that event could have been triggered by the earthquakes provoked by Phaethon's fall, as e.g. in Ov. *met.* 2.210–11; 260–1; in sum, such Orphic Muses are not out of place in a description of Phaethon's vicissitudes). **noster amor.** A parenthetical apposition: Corydon's incipit features a precious gem of V.'s pastoral style, the *schema Cornelianum* (see *E.* 1.57n.). The apostrophe to the Nymphs is expected from an inhabitant of Arcadia; the same is true of hunting, mentioned in the following exchange (ll. 29–32; cf. *E.* 10.55–60).

22 meo Codro. The poet Codrus (cf. 5.11n.) is here unconditionally praised, to the point that he is compared to Phoebus. His name marks a divide among Virgilian poet-herdsmen: some praise him, like Corydon (note the affectionate use of the possessive *meo*: cf. *E.* 10.2), whereas others abuse him, like Thyrsis (as well as, it seems, Mopsus in *E.* 5.11). The character might be entirely fictional, even though ancient sources (Serv. Dan.; *schol. Veron.*, pp. 399–400 [III.2 Th.-H.] = p. 82 Basch.; cf. Lunelli 2001, p. 105) suggest that Codrus stands for a poet of V.'s time: perhaps Q. Cornificius (who was, however, dead by 42–41 BCE); modern interpreters have variously thought of Cornelius Gallus, Varius, and Messalla. It seems, on the other hand, that an elegiac fragment by Valgius Rufus (quoted in the *schol. Veron.*) presupposes the *E.*'s text, and could even testify to an ancient identification between Codrus and V. himself: *Codrusque ille canit quali tu uoce canebas / atque solet numeros dicere, Cinna, tuos* (fr. 2.1–2 Bläns. = Court.). Note that Codrus' 'rhythms' are here compared to Cinna's, known for his erudite scholarship and praised in *E.* 9.35. No wonder that the learned, Hellenistic *Libethrides* are invoked in the same context. **concedite.** The imperative is here used to express a plea. For such a courteous formula, cf. the opening of *E.* 10.1–2 (in V.'s own voice): *Extremum hunc, Arethusa, mihi concede laborem: / pauca meo Gallo* (cf., here, *meo Codro*).

22–3 (proxima Phoebi / uersibus ille facit). The incidental clause is rhythmically circumscribed by the bucolic diaeresis in 7.22 and the masculine caesura in

360 ECLOGUE 7

7.23, along with the lengthening of the second syllable of *facit* in arsis (cf. *E.* 1.38n.; 3.97n.). In this instance, the verb *facit* is equivalent to the Greek ποιεῖν, denoting poetic 'production' (as in Plat. *Phaed.* 61a–b): cf. Ter. *Eun.* 8; Cic. *Cat. Mai.* 22; for the adj. *proximus* indicating the best approximation to (divine) excellence, cf. Hor. *carm.* 1.12.19–20 (where it contrasts with *secundum* in l. 18). Note the neuter plural *proxima*, with its generalizing effect, placed between the neuter singular *carmen, quale*, and the masculine plural *uersibus*. Here, it is also metrically convenient and better suited for poetic style, less 'predictable' than prose: cf. *Aen.* 9.27–8 *Messapus primas acies, postrema coercent / Tyrrhidae iuuenes*. Being close to a god is a great source of pride: contrast the great scholar and scientist Eratosthenes, who was sarcastically nicknamed 'Beta' due to his being the 'second best' intellectual in many fields, but the first in none of them: cf. Suida, s.v.; R. Pfeiffer (1968, p. 170). Needless to say, a certain caution towards the god of poetry is quite appropriate in the context of an invocation to the Muses. **Phoebi.** Codrus is the closest poet to Phoebus in the art: therefore, he is second to the god, in accordance with the principle stated in *id.* 1.3 (i.e. submission to divine authorities). By contrast, Amyntas' attempt to outdo even Phoebus is deplored by Mopsus as an act of arrogance in *E.* 5.9; note the reading *Phoebo* (**V**).

23 si non possumus omnes. V. will echo and modify the phrase in his own voice at *E.* 8.62–3. Corydon's good manners evoke the serene and affectionate tone that characterizes the literary circles led by Pollio and Maecenas (or, at least, their representation in Augustan poetry: cf. esp. Hor. *sat.* 1.9 and 10). The reading *possimus* (M¹P¹V*cr*) perhaps derives from a grammarian's normative concerns.

24 hic arguta sacra pendebit fistula pinu. The 'pious' Corydon's renunciation of song takes the form of a votive offering. For a reworking, cf. Tib. 2.5.29–30 *pendebatque uagi pastoris in arbore uotum, / garrula siluestri fistula sacra deo* (see also Hor. *carm.* 3.26.3–4; *epist.* 1.1.4–5); but cf. Theocr. *epigr.* 2.2–3 G. [scil. Δάφνις] ἄνθετο Πανὶ τάδε, / τοὺς τρητοὺς δόνακας, etc. The motif is typically epigrammatic: cf. *Anth. Pal.* 6.1 (= *Furth. Gr. Epigr.* 604–7 P.); 6.2 (= *Furth. Gr. Epigr.* 756–9 P.); 6.4 (= *HE* 2283–90 G.-P.); 6.14 (= *HE* 168–73 G.-P.); 6.15 (= *Furth. Gr. Epigr.* 404–7 P.); 6.16 (= *GPh* 3596–601); cf. 3.12–13n. The pipes, or panpipes, are here associated with a tree which itself has a human past: Pitys (Πίτυς), the nymph unhappily loved by Pan, was turned into a pine tree (cf. Prop. 1.18.20 *Arcadio pinus amica deo*; see also Long. 1.27.2; 2.7.6; 39.3; Nonn. *Dionys.* 2.108; 42.258– 60; the similar vicissitudes of Syrinx are alluded to by Corydon in *E.* 2.32–3n.). Note also that, as the Arcadian Corydon certainly knows, the pine was (and still is) typical of Mount Maenalus in Arcadia: cf. *E.* 8.22–4; 10.14–15. Later in the agon, Thyrsis will refer to a specific, domestic variety of pine tree, apparently distinct from the mountain type (7.65n.). The custom of hanging ritual objects on tall pine trees will reappear in the Bacchic ritual of *G.* 2.388–9. Note that the adjective *arguta*, paired with the locative *hic*, creates an effect of resonance and correspondence between Corydon's incipit and its context, described by

ECLOGUE 7   361

Meliboeus at the beginning of the poem: *arguta* is also said of the *ilex* under which Daphnis is seated at 7.1. For *pendere* + abl. cf. *E.* 4.29.

25–6 Pastores… / Arcades. The parenthetical apposition that Corydon uses to begin his invocation of the Nymphs is paralleled by Thyrsis' conspicuous hyperbaton, separating the noun (*pastores*) from what would appear to be its corresponding adjective: both are thereby placed in line-beginning position and vertically juxtaposed, with the crucial insertion of the action *hedera crescentem ornate poetam* in the middle. Note the prosodic variation affecting the ending *-es*: the syllable is long in the Latin word but short in the Greek one (7.4n.).

25 hedera. The Dionysian implications of Thyrsis' name are immediately activated: he begins his song with a mention of ivy (cf. *E.* 4.19n.), which he hopes the Arcadian herdsmen will use to adorn him (after all, the thyrsus itself was typically interwoven with ivy: see 5.31n.). He is probably thinking of an ivy wreath (cf. *E.* 8.12–13; for *ornare*, see 6.68), which will explicitly be the case with the helichrysum (*baccare*) at 7.27. **crescentem.** This is the preferable reading (P), whereas *nascentem* is probably a (clarifying?) trivialization, perhaps prompted by the echo of *E.* 4.18–20, where ivy and helichrysum adorned the newborn *puer*. The verb *cresco*, originally an agricultural term ('to sprout, germinate'), is here used as a near-synonym of *nascor*: cf. *G.* 2.336; Traina (1975b); *E.* 4.49n. Thyrsis, whose lack of self-control becomes increasingly obvious, thinks of himself as a poet (cf. 7.5 and 16). He can only conceive of his future (and his present) as a continuous 'growth' which will eventually lead him to acquire the status of *uates* (7.28 *uati…futuro*). Horace will be somewhat more modest in *carm.* 3.30.7–8 *usque ego postera / crescam laude recens* (cf. *epist.* 2.2.101). In *id.* 1, Theocritus hinted at Thyrsis' progressive 'development', with excellence as a goal: καὶ τᾶς βουκολικᾶς ἐπὶ τὸ πλέον ἵκεο μοίσας (*id.* 1.20). Thyrsis himself appears quite self-confident when he introduces his own song (*id.* 1.64 Θύρσις ὅδ᾽ ὡξ Αἴτνας, καὶ Θύρσιδος ἁδέα φωνά), not without some self-praise. Despite the difference in context, Euphorion might be in the background: *Anth. Pal.* 6.279.4 = *HE* 1804 G.-P. ἀεὶ κισσὸς ἀεξόμενος (especially if J. Toup's conjecture ἀεξομένῳ is accepted: cf. fr. 1.4 Light.; see further B. A. van Groningen's commentary, Amsterdam 1977, p. 16, *ad epigr.* 1.4). For other echoes of Euphorion at the outset of this agon, cf. *E.* 7.21n.

26 inuidia rumpantur ut ilia Codro. This iambic image depicts an 'explosion' (*rumpi* is middle-passive), here emphasized by the anastrophe of *ut*: cf. Ov. *her.* 16.221[223] *rumpor et inuideo*; Prop. 1.8.27 *rumpantur iniqui*; Mart. 9.97, where the phrase *rumpitur inuidia* (*quidam*) is repeated twelve times. The noun *ilia* (the sing. *ile* is very rare) properly denotes the lower belly or groin: cf. Cels. 4.1.14…*inter coxas et pubem imo uentre posita sunt*. The abdominal region and its muscles are of course affected by efforts, hiccoughs, and contractions: cf. *G.* 3.507 *ilia singultu tendunt*; *Aen.* 9.415; Colum. 10.26 (for a reference to the effects of laughter cf. Ov. *ars* 3.285). The formula *ilia rumpere* is distinct but still comparable in terms of expressive harshness: it was used in a sexual sense in Catull. 11.20

362 ECLOGUE 7

(where groin rupture is wished upon three hundred lovers as part of the poet's invective against Lesbia). Literary circles are replete with *inuidia*: cf. esp. Callim. *aet.* fr. 1.17 Pf. = Mass. = Hard.; *hymn.* 2[*Ap.*].107 (but see Hes. *op.* 26); cf. also Hor. *carm.* 4.3.16.

27 ultra placitum laudarit. The subject is Codrus, who unwittingly praises Thyrsis, perhaps due to the presence of other herdsmen. His praise, however, might end up being exaggerated (*ultra placitum*) as a result of spite, thereby acting as a bad omen (hence *mala lingua* in 7.28). In fact, even proportionate praise could call for apotropaic gestures or formulas: note the Cyclops in *id.* 6.34–40 (who praises himself). In Latin, the term *praefiscini* (from *fascinum*) could be used for that purpose: Titin. 109–10 R.[3]; Plaut. *Rud.* 461. Here the *baccaris* wreath seems to fit the bill. Unconditional praise, typical of flatterers, has an immediate effect on someone who seeks attention and approval (see Plutarch's treatise *Quomodo adulator ab amico internoscatur*), though here, too, there is a limit: cf. Hor. *sat.* 2.5.96–8. **baccare.** In V., the term only appears here and at *E.* 4.19 (in the same position, i.e. the fifth foot), along with ivy; the identity of the plant is debated (helichrysum?), and Dionysian implications are perhaps in the background: see n. ad loc. Servius Dan's remark here, *herba est ad depellendum fascinum*, is most probably derived from the text itself. Note the effectiveness of Thyrsis' opening 'epigram': either an ivy wreath will make Codrus green with envy, or a helichrysum one will protect Thyrsis from Codrus' spite.

28 uati...futuro. The sacral term *uates* is more solemn than *poeta* (for another pairing of the two terms, cf. 9.32–4n., where they probably point, once again, to different degrees of solemnity); cf. Newman (1967, esp. pp. 18–23) and C. O. Brink's commentary, Cambridge 1971, pp. 390–1, ad Hor. *ars* 400; in V. e.g. *G.* 3.491; 4.387 (Proteus); *Aen.* 6.12 *Delius...uates*; 7.41. Note the hyperbaton, postponing the participle to the end of the line: the inevitability of Thyrsis' poetic future is thereby emphasized. **mala lingua.** The expression, soon to become a stereotypical formula (like *malus oculus*), appears in Catull. 7.12; cf. Ov. *amor.* 2.2.49; Sen. *dial.* 5[*de ira* 3].22.5; Mart. 3.80.2.

29–36. After mentioning poetic goddesses, Corydon invokes Diana/Delia, the tutelary deity of hunting, to whom the boy Micon offers the head of a wild boar and the antlers of a deer (in fact, he is ready to portray the goddess by carving a fine marble sculpture). Thyrsis, by contrast, invokes Priapus (another deity belonging to the Dionysian world: cf. *E.* 7.33–6n.). For now, his statue is carved in marble; however, if the flock prospers, the god will have a portrait in gold: Thyrsis, in fact, seems to aim at surpassing his opponent's grand gesture (cf. Serv. *ad E.* 3.28...*maius aut contrarium*). While Corydon emphasizes the 'tender' figure of the boy Micon (though cf. below, 7.29–30n.), once again Thyrsis places himself at the centre of his universe (7.35 *fecimus*) and establishes a direct (maybe all too direct) exchange relationship between the god's favour and the votive offering. Note the rhetorically loaded sequence *exspectare sat est...nunc te...at tu,* *si*...(whereas Corydon opts for a more subdued phrasing and a less explicit *si proprium hoc fuerit* [7.31n.]). Corydon's mention of Delia and, above all, of the 'little' boy Micon, seems to echo the Corydon of *E.* 2, who loved boys and hunting (cf. esp. *E.* 2.28–30). As in his invocation of the Nymphs, Corydon's images are Arcadian in nature (cf. *E.* 10.55–60). In this second exchange, V. approaches a new 'subgenre': the pastoral votive epigram on a hunting theme (cf. Theocr. *epigr.* 2 G., starring Daphnis; note also the subgenre's various attestations in *Anth. Pal.* 6, featuring Artemis and Pan as dedicatees: 6.10–16; 34–5; 37; 111; 253; 326), here coupled with the agonistic echo of *id.* 5.53–4; 58–9. When it comes to hunting, young Arcadians seem to be somewhat coarse in their interaction with deities, as V. doubtless knows from *id.* 7.106–14, and perhaps from the interpretive tradition associated with it: cf. *schol. ad id.* 7.106–8a, p. 104.9–15 Wend. (the Arcadian boys scourge their statue of Pan with sea squills if the god does not favour their hunting endeavours).

29–30. These two lines must be taken as a votive epigram accompanying the offering: note the immediacy of the votive act (hence the deictic *hoc* in 7.29). The main verb is omitted, in keeping with epigraphic style: cf. *Aen.* 3.288 *Aeneas haec de Danais uictoribus arma* as well as Daphnis' 'self-epitaph' at *E.* 5.43–4 (which includes no verbs at all). The reader is led to imagine that here, in accordance with a commonplace of ancient epigrams, Corydon is the author of the text describing Micon's offering. Some scholars have posited that these lines are uttered by Micon himself: but the text gives us no reason to think so, and this would make the adjective *paruus* less clear (29). Micon is clearly the dedicator, in line with the epigrammatic tradition, but here the 'authority' (and authorship) of Corydon is quite evident (compared to him, the boy is *paruus*): see also below, 7.31–2n. In the Hellenistic epigram tradition, the author often composes (more or less fictionally) 'on behalf of' the offerer: besides Theocr. *epigr.* 2 G. (mentioned above), where the offerer is Daphnis, cf. the hunting epigram in Rhian. *Anth. Pal.* 6.34 (= *HE* 3230–5 G.-P. = fr. 66 Pow.), featuring Polyaenos; Leonid. *Anth. Pal.* 6.35 (= *HE* 2255–60 G.-P.), featuring Teleson; note also Erucius, *Anth. Pal.* 6.96 = *GPh* 2200–6 G.-P., in which the offerers are Glaucon and Corydon ('both from Arcadia': quoted above, 7.4n.). Note the deixis (29 and 31 *hoc*), similarly featured in Thyris' epigram (33 *haec*) and typical of the ancient epigrammatic style more generally (cf. again *Aen.* 3.288; also *E.* 5.43 *hinc*).

29 Saetosi. This is the only occurrence of the term in V., who elsewhere uses the more solemn, epic epithet *saetiger* (cf. the formula *saetigerique sues*, frequently varied but always appearing, as here, in line-beginning position: cf. *Aen.* 7.17; 11.198; 12.170). The boar is a grown-up animal, and correspondingly has a full set of bristles; a wild boar's head (*caput hoc apri*) is an appropriate offering to the huntress goddess, as the unfortunate case of the hunter *hybristes* in Callimachus shows: cf. *aet.* fr. 96 Pf. = 199 Mass. = 96; 96a Hard. **Delia.** The goddess of hunting, i.e. the virgin Artemis-Diana, is here referred to by the epithet she shares with her

364 ECLOGUE 7

brother Apollo (both were born in Delos): cf. *E.* 3.66n. She protects woods, water, and mountains; note her visit to Arcadia and Pan in Callim. *hymn.* 3[*Dian.*].87–109, where she catches four stags and yokes them to her chariot. According to ancient scholars, the goddess played a crucial role in the birth of the pastoral genre (hence this 'appropriate' invocation at the beginning of an agon): cf. *schol. Theocr. proleg.*, pp. 2.21–3.2 Wend.; Introduction, p. 12 and n. 28. Alongside Apollo, she will also loom large in Augustan culture (cf. Horace's *Carmen saeculare*). Soon after 36 BCE, the *Diana Siciliensis*, who helped Octavian at Naulochus, was portrayed on coins celebrating his victory: *BMCRE*, I, p. 84, nos. 489–91, pl. 12.11–12; *RIC*², I, pp. 54–5, nos. 194–7, 204 (cf. pl. 4); Pollini (1990, esp. p. 347).

29–30 paruus / ...Micon. Here Micon, who appears as the owner of a vineyard in *E.* 3.10, is evidently a boy (Corydon's hunting companion?), as is shown by the epithet *paruus*. Both proper noun and epithet perhaps suggest μικός/μικκός (note, however, the long root vowel), a dialectal equivalent of μικρός 'little': cf. *id.* 8.64. Note also Lat. *mica* 'crumb' (with long root vowel). In V., epithets frequently clarify the etymology of proper nouns: cf. *Aen.* 3.516 *pluuias...Hyadas.*

30 ramosa...uiuacis cornua cerui. Pronged, imposing antlers, befitting an adult deer. The animal's longevity (*uiuacis*) is proverbial, at least since Hesiod (fr. 304.1–2 M.-W.; cf. Iuv. 14.251 *longa et ceruina senectus*): here, however, its 'liveliness' is emphasized (through the adj. in *-ax*: cf. Varr. *rust.* 3.14.5) and observed from the hunter's point of view. As a consequence, the prey is hard to catch, and all the more valuable (the pronged antlers prove the animal's advanced age). For a literal echo, cf. Ov. *met.* 3.194 *uiuacis cornua cerui.* Deer antlers appear, as an offering to Pan, in Erucius' epigram (cf. above, 7.4n.; see also Leonid. *Anth. Pal.* 6.110 = *HE* 2551–4 G.-P.). An epithet of Artemis/Diana was 'deer-shooting', ἐλαφηβόλος, and she was often depicted together with the animal (e.g. holding a fawn in her arms: *LIMC* II.1, pp. 664–5, esp. nos. 562–4 [L. Kahil]; catching or killing an adult deer: ibid., pp. 820–1, esp. nos. 157–60 [E. Simon]). V. hints at the custom of offering prey to Latona's daughter (*Latonia*) in *Aen.* 9.407–8 (but cf. Soph. *Ai.* 178). Correspondingly, Corydon's votive offering seems to suit the context (cf. 7.31n.), but his scruples are justified, given that only the Eretrian Artemis seems to have accepted every sacrificial offering; cf. Callim. *iamb.* 10, *argum.* The pronged antlers will reappear at *Aen.* 1.190 *cornibus arboreis.*

31–2. Following a typically epigrammatic description of the votive act, these lines focus on a negotiation with the deity to improve the outcomes of hunting. While Micon is obviously the dedicator, Corydon's 'authorship' is perfectly clear: Corydon is a hunter, companion, and protector of his young friends/lovers (hence the adjective *paruus* in reference to the boy: cf. above, 7.29–30n.); similarly, in *E.* 2.29, Corydon had invited the boy Alexis to hunt deer with him. Here, the lover lends his own voice to his beloved boy and composes an epigrammatic dedication for him (29–30), in order to obtain the greatest possible rewards from the goddess (for the boy, but also for himself: Corydon counts on the boy's gratitude).

ECLOGUE 7   365

31 si proprium hoc fuerit. Ancient interpreters connected this use of *proprius* with its meaning 'perpetual', 'eternal', as in *Aen.* 6.871 *propria haec si dona fuissent*; Hor. *sat.* 2.6.5; cf. Serv. Dan. '*proprium' sane ueteres perpetuum, stabile, firmum dicebant*; *ThlL* X.2.2107.71–2108.38. In that case, however, *hoc* would necessarily refer to the goddess' favour, either in poetry (Servius: *quod supra petierat, scilicet ut talia carmina faceret qualia Codrus effecerat*) or, more plausibly, in hunting (Albini). Yet it seems unlikely that this *hoc* should not refer to the same object denoted by *hoc* at 7.29, i.e. Micon's votive offering (a wild boar's head and the antlers of a deer). If so, *proprius* must have its sacrificial meaning of 'suitable', attested in Plaut. *Capt.* 862 *agnum adferri proprium pinguem*. The term is used in a similar sense by Augustus, in his prayer for the *Ludi saeculares* (17 BCE): cf. *Act. lud. saec. Aug.* (= *CIL* VI.4.2, p. 3241, no. 32323) 103 *bouem marem Ioui optimo maximo proprium immolauit*; cf. *ThlL* X.2.2106.24–48. It is preferable, therefore, to construe: 'If this offering is going to be appropriate'. Corydon politely presents in a hesitating manner what should, in fact, be certain (considering the value of the offering: above, 7.30n.). If his scruples prove to be unwarranted due to a pre-emptive demonstration of favour on the goddess' part (note *fuerit*, highlighting anteriority with respect to 7.32 *stabis*), then he will add the marble statue as a further offering. **leui de marmore**. For *de* + abl. expressing material, cf. Ov. *met.* 14.313 *niueo factum de marmore signum*. Note also *Perv. Ven.* 23 *facta de cruore*, almost a Romance turn of phrase. **tota**. Marble, smooth and valuable, is the statue's only material component. The sculpture will portray the goddess' entire figure, i.e. without unseen parts (of lesser value).

32 puniceo stabis suras euincta coturno. In accordance with ancient practice, the statue is painted in various colours. It is pictured as rising up (*stabis*) on high purple buskins, bound on her legs. Buskins were typically used by hunters as a means of protection against scratches, wounds, or stings: see Serv. *ad Aen.* 1.337; Prob. *ad G.* 2.8; *ThlL* IV.1086.79–1087.4. A reference to buskins is also found in a (probably) late Republican hymn to Diana, which V. perhaps knew: Laevius (?), *carm.* fr. 32.1 Bläns. = 12a Court. *sed iam purpureo suras include cothurno*. The poem presumably invoked the goddess, asking her to take an active role in the hunt. Ancient sources implausibly attributed it to Livius Andronicus: see Courtney (1993, p. 129). For a Virgilian parallel, see *Aen.* 1.337 *purpureoque alte suras uincire cothurno*, where the speaker is Venus (portrayed as a young Diana-like huntress); cf. also Val. Fl. 1.384; Nemes. *cyn.* 90; Coripp. *Iust.* 2.104. Dionysus' 'buskins' (cf. *G.* 2.8) were known for their red hue: Nonn. *Dionys.* 18.200. In order to explain V.'s use of the singular form (*coturno*), which is not particularly puzzling per se (and reduces the *sigmatismos: puniceiS StabiS SuraS*), Servius emphasizes the fact that the left buskin is interchangeable with the right one: *ideo singulari usus est numero, quia hoc genus calciamenti utrique aptum est pedi*. Note the acc. of respect, here featuring a middle participle.

33–6. In Thyrsis' words, the chaste goddess of hunting is opposed to the obscenely exuberant Priapus, who protects gardens and fertility. He is the protagonist of a

366 ECLOGUE 7

witty, erotic/votive epigram by Theocritus (4 G.); cf. also *id.* 1.81–91 (Thyrsis). In his capacity as son of Dionysus (and Aphrodite, according to a tradition attested by Diod. Sic. 4.6.1; cf. Serv. *ad G.* 4.111), Priapus was part of Dionysian retinues. Here, he receives a kind of offering typically associated by the Romans with Liber (cf. below, 7.33n.). The way in which Thyrsis explicitly outlines an exchange of favours between the god and himself (cf. Hippon. fr. 42a–b Deg. = 32 W.[2]) is especially typical of Priapean literature, usually sceptic and parodic in tone, but belongs more generally to the rhetoric of votive offerings, as in the Hellenistic epigram tradition: cf. Philipp. *Anth. Pal.* 6.231, esp. 6.7–8 εἰ δ' ὡς ἐκ πελάγους ἐρρύσαο… / κἢκ πενίης, θύσει χρυσόκερων κεμάδα (= *GPh* 2779–80 G.-P.). On Priapus as a deity, cf. *Enc. Virg.* IV, pp. 269–70, s.v. *Priapo* (S. Fasce); *Enc. Or.* II, pp. 472–3, s.v. *Priapo* (M.-P. Pieri); *Virg. Enc.* III, pp. 1037–8, s.v. *Priapus* (J. Henderson). On the god's importance in Roman poetry, see Fantham (2009, pp. 133–59). Modest offerings are a recurring theme in epigrammatic poetry, especially in the case of simple, rustic deities such as Priapus, to whom even humble vegetables can be offered: cf. *Priap.* 53.6 *quamuis pauca damus*; 86.9 *parua…munera*; *Anth. Pal.* 6.22; 89; 102; 232 (= *GPh* 3440–5; 2508–15; 2741–8; 2014–21 G.-P.). Thyrsis, by contrast, strives to outclass Corydon's gifts (cf. *marmoreum* at 35, echoing 31 *de marmore*) and goes as far as to mention gold, the most valuable metal (though cf. below, 7.36n.).

33 Sinum lactis et haec…liba. The *sinus*, or *sinum*, was a large bowl normally used for wine (note the long root vowel, distinguishing it from *sĭnus* 'curve, fold': see Varr. *ling.* 5.123; cf. also Plaut. *Curc.* 82; Valg. *carm.* fr. 5.2 Bläns. = Court.; *OLD*[2], p. 1952, s.v. *sinum* (the *schol. Veron.*, p. 400 [III.2 Th.-H.] = pp. 82–3 Basch., mention a remark by the grammarian Asper, who quotes several ancient sources: *uas uinarium…non, ut quidam, lactarium*; cf. Lunelli 2001, pp. 111–13). The *liba*, small cakes spread with honey, were featured in the *Liberalia*: cf. Ov. *fast.* 3.735–6; 761–2. Note that, in this line, ictus and word accent coincide (but cf. *E.* 1.70n.). For a similar construction with the gen., cf. *E.* 5.68 *crateras… pinguis oliui.* For the deixis (*haec*), see 7.29–30n. **quotannis.** In the *E.*, the adv. has appeared in ritual contexts, but always denoting events recurring more frequently than yearly: see *E.* 1.42 (twelve times a year), as well as 5.67 and 5.79 (where the libations seem to be rather frequent: 5.67n.). Here, by contrast, the offering clearly occurs only once a year.

34 sat. Abbreviated familiar form of *satis*: cf. 3.111n. **custos…pauperis horti.** Variously echoed in Tib. 1.1.17–20 *pomosis…ruber custos ponatur in hortis / terreat ut saeua falce Priapus aues.* // *uos quoque, felicis quondam, nunc pauperis agri / custodes, fertis munera uestra, Lares*; note also *Priap.* 1.5; 24.1; 80.9.

36 aureus esto. Cf. Hor. *sat.* 2.3.183 *aeneus ut stes*; Ov. *her.* 20.237 (239) *aurea ponetur mali felicis imago*; see also Calp. *ecl.* 2.59 *inter pampineas ponetur faginus ulmos*, where *faginus*, as here, is most probably adj., modifying 57 *hic solus* [*deus*] (Gronovius' conjecture for the transmitted *huic soli*). Generally speaking, ancient

ECLOGUE 7   367

statues of Priapus were made of wood (esp. in a modest setting such as 7.34 *pauperis horti*): cf. *Priap.* 6.1 *ligneus...Priapus*; 10.4–5; but note also Hor. *sat.* 1.8.1–3. Marble, therefore, would be more than sufficiently exceptional (7.35 *marmoreum*); but Thyrsis seems to go even further by referring to a sculpture made of gold: the use of gold in religious contexts was often stigmatized in moralizing discourse (cf. Sen. *epist.* 31.11; Iuv. 11.115–19), and here it seems somewhat hyperbolic yet appropriate for Thyrsis' character. Thyrsis, however, might simply be alluding to a gold-plated statue (vel. sim.), as e.g. in Pers. 2.55–6. For the use of *aureus* in the sense of *auro ornatus*, or *auratus*, cf. ThlL II.1490.69–1491.23. For a similar rhetoric concerning votive offerings, cf. Theocr. *epigr.* 4.15–18 G. (see above, 7.33–6n.). Note the pronoun in line-ending position at 7.35 (*at tu*: cf. 5.88n., in line-opening position), emphasizing the idea that the god will be generously compensated, provided he will show his favour to the herd: cf. 3.31n.

37–44. Corydon here mentions one of the best-known Theocritean characters, i.e. the Nereid Galatea (7.37n.). Quite unexpectedly, however, l. 40 will reveal that the speaker is not the Cyclops but Corydon himself. Thyrsis, too, seems to reply in his own voice (cf. 7.41n.), playing the role of Corydon's rival. In keeping with his characterization, he heightens the tone of the exchange (note his harsh imagery, his impatience, and his concluding command to the bullocks). Role-playing is typical of pastoral poetry, particularly when it comes to its singing contests (cf. *E.* 3.76–9). The address to Galatea (evoking the Cyclops, a figure traditionally associated with her) is eminently pastoral and Theocritean. Hence Corydon's creative twist: he addresses the sea nymph not as Polyphemus, but as himself.

37 **Nerine Galatea.** The divine patronymic (from Nereus, a marine deity: cf. 6.35n.) rules out that this Galatea is a human girl, like the Galatea mentioned at 1.30–1 (n.) or at 3.64 (*lasciua puella*); similarly, in 9.39 (*huc ades, o Galatea*), the phrase *in undis* clarifies that V. is talking about the sea nymph: Galatea is traditionally imagined (or depicted) as totally intent on her marine world (see e.g. Philostr. 2.18, esp. p. 371.6–7 Kays.). For the epithet, cf. Catull. 64.28 *tene Thetis tenuit pulcherrima Nereine?* (where *Nereine* is M. Haupt's conjecture). The Cyclops' love for Galatea was an agonistic theme of *id.* 6 (as V.'s Daphnis perhaps 'remembers', since he was the protagonist of that poem; note also *id.* 11; Bion, fr. 16 G.; [Bion], *epith. Achill. et Deid.* 1–3). In *E.* 2, i.e. the love song for Alexis, Corydon reworks the Cyclops' lament as his main Theocritean model (there, as in *E.* 7.40, Corydon 'stands in for' the Cyclops). **thymo.** Thyme was greatly appreciated by beekeepers, due to the fragrance that it lends to honey, and was also considered beneficial to the beehive: cf. *G.* 4.169; 241; 270; also [Quint.] *decl. mai.* 13.13, p. 279.12–14 Håk. (note its use as a metonymy for honey itself: cf. e.g. Mart. 5.39.3). Sicilian thyme was deemed to be excellent: Varr. *rust.* 3.16.14; Colum. 9.14.19; for Hybla, in particular, cf. *E.* 1.54n.

38 **hedera formosior alba.** A particular variety of ivy, whose leaves have a uniformly pale green colour (cf. 3.39n.), or a brighter area in the middle. According

368   ECLOGUE 7

to Pliny (Plin. *nat.* 16.147), this type of ivy was used to make poets' garlands (here, at any rate, the context is an erotic one: contrast above, 7.25). Theocritus' *id.* 11.46 features a 'black' variety of ivy. The Cyclops' address to Galatea started by emphasizing Galatea's whiteness, quite appropriate etymologically (γάλα 'milk'); Corydon here echoes it—without, however, resorting to pastoral comparisons: 'O white Galatea..., / whiter than curdled milk, softer than a lamb, / more superb than a calf, more splendid than unripe grapes' (*id.* 11.19–20; for a similar incipit, cf. Ovid's Cyclops in *met.* 13.789 *candidior folio niuei, Galatea, ligustri*). In *E.* 2, too, Corydon began his song with an etymological pun on Alexis' name (2.6n.). Note the series of comparative adjectives (37–8 *dulcior... / candidior...formosior*), which V. certainly regarded as a distinctive feature of the Theocritean source; Ovid used as many as twenty-six comparatives in his reworking (*met.* 13.789–807).

39 cum...pasti repetent praesepia tauri. The lovers' meeting is scheduled for sunset, when the animals return to their folds (*praesepia*, i.e. properly 'enclosures', originally surrounded by a fence) after grazing (or working, as in *E.* 2.66). In Theocritus' treatment of Galatea, night played an important role (*id.* 11.44). Note that the goatherd Corydon (7.3n.) opts for a reference to bulls (*tauri*), probably intended as a solemn synonym for oxen: cf. *G.* 1.45 (as well as e.g. Hor. *carm.* 3.13.11); below, 7.44n.

40 si qua tui Corydonis habet te cura. Contrast, again, the opening of *E.* 2.6 *o crudelis Alexi, nihil mea carmina curas?* For the affectionate use of the possessive adj., cf. above, 7.22 *meo Codro* (in Corydon's speech). Here, however, the pronoun *te* emphasizes erotic devotion, which the lover hopes will be reciprocal (note his urgent address to Galatea: *uenito*); cf. Prop. 2.9.46 *solus ero, quoniam non licet esse tuum*. Note the gentle caution in the speaker's tone ('if you ever think of Corydon', rather than 'if you care for Corydon'): cf., similarly in reference to states of mind, *Aen.* 4.581 *idem omnis simul ardor habet*; Ov. *met.* 7.800 *mutua cura duos et amor socialis habebat* (note also, in Greek, Eur. *Or.* 1255 φόβος ἔχει με); for states of the body, cf. Enn. *ann.* 396 Sk. *totum sudor habet corpus; Aen.* 3.147 *animalia somnus habet; ThlL* VI.3.2431.1–82. For a similar kind of inversion, cf. *E.* 2.38 *te nunc habet ista secundum* (where the *fistula* has a second owner, i.e. Corydon). **uenito.** Cf. *id.* 11.42 ἀλλ' ἀφίκευσο ποθ' ἀμέ 'come to me now!'; for an erotic invitation, cf. Prop. 2.22.43 *si es non dura, uenito*; for a deliberately non-erotic use, cf. *E.* 3.77n.

41 Immo ego. Here, in all likelihood, Thyrsis speaks for himself, as the rival of Corydon (whose name has just appeared in 7.40). Correspondingly, *immo ego* is most naturally ascribed to Corydon's opponent: otherwise, this would be Galatea's reply to Corydon. But the Nereid (cf. 7.37) cannot address the bullocks as in 7.44. To be sure, *E.* 3 displayed some exchange of roles between the two contestants: there, however, the vocatives had a disambiguating function (see *E.* 3.76–9). **Sardoniis...amarior herbis.** The adj. contradicts Corydon's *dulcior*, whereas Corydon's thyme and ivy are now replaced by disgusting plants, unpleasant to

ECLOGUE 7   369

taste or touch, or otherwise worthless. Sardinian herbs were known for their bitter taste, esp. in the case of a certain toxic plant, perhaps a variety of buttercups (*Ranunculus Sardous* or *R. sceleratus*), which causes convulsions similar to laughing grimaces: Pausan. 10.17.13 'the island is free from lethal poisons, with the exception of one plant: this terrible herb is similar to *apium* [or celery: σελίνῳ], and they say that whoever feeds on it will die laughing; this is why Homer [*Od.* 20.302] and others among his successors [cf., for instance, Plat. *rep.* 1.337a] call 'sardonic' a type of laughter which is far from beneficial' (the Homeric passage was discussed in antiquity; cf. A. Natale, *Il riso di Hephaistos. All'origine del comico nella poesia e nell'arte dei Greci*, Rome 2008, pp. 42–52). Similarities between this plant and *apium*, also testified to by Philargyrius/Philagrius and Serv. (*apiastrum*), may be confirmed by 6.68 *apio...amaro* (n.); see further *Enc. Virg.* IV, pp. 677–8, s.v. *Sardegna* (S. Runchina); *Virg. Enc.* III, p. 1119, s.v. *Sardinia* (D. A. Secci). Sardinian honey, too, appears to have been sharp in flavour: cf. Hor. *ars* 375 (with Porph. ad loc.; contrast the thyme honey from Hybla: above, 7.37n.); see also *E.* 9.30 *Cyrneas...taxos* (n.). For *amarus* used of plants, cf. 1.78 and 6.62 (as well as *E.* 6.68).

42 horridior rusco. The butcher's broom, *ruscus/ruscum* (more rarely *rustum*: Fest. p. 322 L. *rustum ex rubus*), is a bushy type of weed. In *G.* 2.413, the manuscripts oscillate between *rusci* and *rusti*; cf. also Colum. 4.31.1. The plant's 'hairy' appearance is phonetically evoked: cf. *G.* 3.315 *horrentisque rubos* (here, however, *ruscus* adds one more sibilant sound). **proiecta uilior alga**. A type of seaweed, here particularly despicable insofar as it is 'thrown out' (*proiecta*) of its natural environment; *alga* is proverbially worthless: see e.g. Hor. *sat.* 2.5.8 *et genus et uirtus, nisi cum re, uilior alga est* (the speaker is Ulysses, a 'sailor'); also *carm.* 3.17.10 *alga...inutili*; Iuv. 4.48. Note the line-ending phonetic echo *alba* 7. 38)...*alga*.

43 toto...longior anno. Yet another comparative, but very different from those used by Corydon (which have been countered by *amarior, horridior*, and *uilior*). A single day is longer than a whole year for the waiting lover. In late antiquity, Theocritus' extreme formulation of the idea gained great popularity: *id.* 12.2 οἱ δὲ ποθεῦντες ἐν ἤματι γηράσκουσιν; see *Anth. Pal.* 12.171.3-4 = *HE* 1517–18 G.-P. (Dioscor.); Iulian. *epist.* 52.374c; Auson. *epist.* 8(12).4, p. 232 Peip.; but cf. Ov. *her.* 11.29(31) *nox erat annua nobis*.

44 ite domum pasti...ite iuuenci. By addressing the bullocks, Thyrsis seems to refer to a more concrete reality (and a less stylized one) than Corydon's bulls (39). Similar commands, placed at the end of single eclogues, frame V.'s entire pastoral book (cf. *E.* 1.74; 10.77). Note, here, the incidental clause, appealing to the animals' 'modesty'. **si quis pudor**. Thyrsis is so impatient as to desire Galatea's love for the immediate future: correspondingly, the bullocks should leave their pastures and go back home, thereby showing some discretion. In fact, were they to keep grazing, their presence would be impossible for the herdsman to avoid, and he would be prevented from achieving his aim. Such references to *pudor* (here and in

370   ECLOGUE 7

similar colloquial phrases) do not necessarily imply disdain, but can certainly strengthen an exhortation. For an even more explicit formulation, cf. Prop. 1.9.33 *quare, si pudor est, quam primum errata fatere.* In the Theocritean corpus, animals sometimes witness meetings of human lovers: cf. *id.* 6.29–30; note also *E.* 3.8n.

45–52. Place descriptions are a typically agonistic, and sometimes pre-agonistic, theme: cf. *id.* 5.31–4; 45–9; *E.* 5.1–7. While Corydon evokes a summer-like landscape, drenched in sunlight (compare the scenery of *E.* 2, starring an 'ardent' Corydon), Thyrsis' reply features a wintry, domestic space, pervaded by the reassuring heat of a generous hearth (7.49). In Theocritus' *id.* 9, Daphnis and Menalcas described the contrast between summer and winter (Daphnis chose the former): *id.* 9.7–21. The polar opposites of heat and cold will reappear in the pastoral ethnography of *G.* 3.349–83. Thyrsis' wintry scene is unfamiliar to the reader of the *E.*, which generally feature spring-time or summer-time settings: see, however, *E.* 5.70 *ante focum, si frigus erit; si messis, in umbra* (where the year is bisected, as here, into a hot and a cold season); cf. also *G.* 1.299–301. Tibullus perhaps echoes ll. 49–50 in his first elegy: Tib. 1.1.6 *dum meus adsiduo luceat igne focus.*

45–8. Their theme and structure make clear that these four lines condense the two quatrains of *id.* 8.33–40: note the invocation of natural elements (with 7.45 *fontes et…herba* cf. *id.* 8.37 κρᾶναι καὶ βοτάναι, γλυκερὸν φυτόν), exhorted in the third line to take care of the animals (with 7.47 cf. *id.* 8.35 and 39); the final line and a half features an 'unexpected' occurrence (with considerable differences: 7.47–8n.). Note that *herba* and *umbra*, the two words that conclude 45–6 with some assonance, reappear in the same position at the beginning of Thyrsis' speech (57–8 *herba…umbras*), but in a diametrically opposite context.

45 Muscosi fontes. For the mention of moss, cf. Catull. 68.58 *riuus muscoso… e lapide*; Prop. 2.30.26 *rorida muscosis antra…iugis*; Hor. *epist.* 1.10.7. **somno mollior herba.** Grass is soft in Lucretius' prototypically Epicurean place of relaxation: *prostrati in gramine molli* (Lucr. 5.1392); cf. *E.* 5.46; *G.* 2.470. For bedding softer than sleep itself, cf. the agon of *id.* 5.50–1: 'Here, if you come, you will tread on lambskin and wool, / softer than sleep [εἴρια…ὕπνω μαλακώτερα]'; see also *id.* 15.125. Sleep, at any rate, is 'soft' ever since Hom. *Il.* 10.2 μαλακῷ δεδμημένοι ὕπνῳ. The whole scene is quite typically pastoral: cf. *id.* 9.9–13. Note the prevalence of spondees in the line, showing relaxed stillness.

46 rara uiridis tegit arbutus umbra. Here, shelter is not provided by a large beech tree (as in *E.* 1.1 *patula fagus*), but by a plant that generally grows in bushes or shrubs (i.e. the wild strawberry [3.82n.]): in spite of the heat, however, it still has its typical bright green hue (even though its leaves are 'sparse'); cf. *E.* 5.7.

47 solstitium pecori defendite. Compare, once again, Corydon's song for Alexis: *E.* 2.8–13 *nunc etiam pecudes umbras et frigora captant*, etc. For the dat. construction (in the sense of 'averting from') cf., with the plural, Plaut. *Most.* 899–900 *maxumam qui his iniuriam / foribus defendat*; Hor. *carm.* 1.17.2–4

ECLOGUE 7   371

Faunus…igneam / defendit aestatem capellis…meis; with the singular, Sil. 5.490–1 *defendere…morti / dedecus*. The term *solstitium*, denoting the winter solstice or (more frequently, depending on the context) the summer solstice, occurs chiefly in prose, especially in technical and agricultural texts (cf. Cat. *agr.* 41.1). It only occurs twice in V.: here and in V.'s didactic poem on farming (*G.* 1.100–1 *humida solstitia atque hiemes orate serenas, / agricolae*; here Corydon addresses springs, bushes, and grass). For the term in Augustan poetry, cf. also Hor. *epist.* 1.11.18; Ov. *trist.* 5.10.7; the adjective *solstitialis* appears in Lucr. 5.617. Here, Corydon clearly refers to the summer solstice, which signals the arrival of summer heat (47–8 *uenit aestas / torrida*). It is 'the year's longest day', with so much light that *umbra* is never enough (note 46 *rara…umbra*); cf. Plin. *nat.* 18.256 *longissimus dies totius anni* (the summer solstice is June 24 according to Pliny; June 26 in Ov. *fast.* 6.790).

47–8 uenit aestas / torrida. Quite surprisingly, unlike the author of *id.* 8, V. does not announce the arrival of Daphnis (*id.* 8.35 ἔνθῃ) or Menalcas (40 τεῖδ' ἀγάγῃ; cf. also *id.* 8.43 and 8.47), but that of torrid summer: cf. *id.* 9.12 θέρευς φρύγοντος (perhaps echoed by V.: cf. below, 7.51–2n.).

48 lento…in palmite. A shoot, relatively sinuous and flexible compared to the trunk: for this use of *lentus* in the *E.*, cf. 1.25 and esp. 3.38 *lenta…uitis*. The variant reading *laeto* (**M¹**) is a trivialization, perhaps modelled after *G.* 2.363–4 *dum se laetus ad auras / palmes agit* (cf. also 262 *laetum…uitis genus*). In this regard, Servius' annotation is not decisive, because it can presuppose both forms: *non enim dicit aestatem esse, cum adhuc turgere gemmarum palmites dicat. et bene tarde frondere uites commemorat in Venetia, quae est prouincia frigidior.* **gemmae.** In the spring season, after the winter pruning, new buds appear on the shoots or the woody vine-branches: these buds are what *gemma* refers to (*ThlL* VI.2.1753.60–1754.32); as for the vine itself, cf. *G.* 2.335 [scil. *pampinus*] *trudit gemmas*; note also Ov. *fast.* 3.238 *in tenero palmite gemma tumet* (cf. 1.152; *trist.* 3.12.13).

49 Hic focus. For another occurrence in the *E.*, cf. 5.70; the singular is also employed at *G.* 4.48. Elsewhere, V. always uses the more solemn plural, both in the *G.* and in the *Aen.* (cf. *Aen.* 12.118). The hearth frequently appears in a *laus ruris*: Hor. *epod.* 2.43 (with Porph. ad loc.: *proprie hoc rusticae uitae est focum amare*); Tib. 1.1.6, quoted above, 7.45–52n. Note Persius' irony at 1.71–2: *corbes / et focus et porci et fumosa Palilia faeno* (with W. Kissel's commentary, Heidelberg 1990, p. 203, ad loc.). A similar 'praise of fire', which enables us not to worry about the winter, appears in Theocr. *id.* 9.19–21 (cf. above, 7.45–52n.), where, however, the emphasis is on cooking and gastronomy: ἐν πυρὶ δὲ δρυΐνῳ χορία ζεῖ, ἐν πυρὶ δ' αὖαι / φαγοὶ χειμαίνοντος κτλ. (see also below, 7.51–2n.). Here, by contrast, V. insists on the idea of 'indoor space' (note *postes* 'doorposts', which presuppose a door and a house), emphasizing the visual aspect (7.50 *nigri*) and sensory stimuli in general (7.51 *frigora*). The idea of shelter, in contrast to the outside weather

372   ECLOGUE 7

(rain), appears in a fragment of Sophocles' *Tympanistae* transmitted (in a meta-phorical context) by Cicero: κἂν ὑπὸ στέγῃ πυκνῆς ἀκούειν ψακάδος εὐδούσῃ φρενί (Cic. *Att.* 2.7.4; note also Plut. *Aem.* 1.3; Stob. 4.17.12; cf. *TrGF*, IV, fr. 636, p. 459 Radt); see further Tib. 1.1.47–8. **taedae pingues.** As Servius observes, *desudantes picem*, and therefore well suited to a great, smoky fire: hence the abundance of smut (7.50 *adsidua...fuligine*) on the doorposts.

49–50 hic plurimus ignis / semper. An 'inextinguishable fire' (ἀκάματον πῦρ), made possible by abundant firewood, is part of what Theocritus' Polyphemus boasted about in his invitation to Galatea (*id.* 11.51). Here, by contrast, there is no trace of erotic innuendo.

50 adsidua postes fuligine nigri. The detail evokes the generous nature of the hearth, with no need for explicit specifications. At the same time, pastoral mod-esty is underscored. In Aesch. *Ag.* 774–5, Justice shines in 'smoky dwellings' (δυσκάπνοις δώμασιν), i.e. those of humble people: cf. Eur. *El.* 1139–40; Ov. *fast.* 5.505 *tecta...nigro deformia fumo*; Mart. 2.90.7–8 *me focus et nigros non indignantia fumos / tecta iuuant*; [Quint.] *decl. mai.* 13.4, p. 260.11–12 Håk. The ceiling surrounding the fire vent is, of course, black: note the significant folk etymology of the term μέλαθρον (used by Homer: cf. *Od.* 8.279; see *Etym. Magn.* p. 576.16 Gaisf. ἀπὸ τοῦ μελαίνεσθαι ὑπὸ τοῦ καπνοῦ); here, however, even the doorposts are blackened, since some of the smoke goes out through the door.

51–2. The whole sequence presupposes *id.* 9.20–1 'I do not worry about / win-ter any more [ἔχω δέ τοι οὐδ᾽ ὅσον ὥραν / χείματος] than a toothless man does about nuts, if he has a soft cake'; cf. also *id.* 9.12–13 'I care as much for ardent summer [τῶ δὲ θέρευς φρύγοντος ἐγὼ τόσσον μελεδαίνω], / as a lover listens to the words of his father and his mother'. The imagery used by Thyrsis in his comparisons includes the typically pastoral tropes of the wolf and the stream in spring. In sum, any gastronomical connotations are cast aside, in contrast to Theocritus' *id.* 9 (where they play a fundamental role: also above, 7.49n.).

51 hic. The reading *hinc*, transmitted by Servius Dan. (*hoc est ex hac causa*), is perhaps due to some grammarian's sophistication. For a similar anaphora of *hic*, cf. *E.* 9.40–1 (3x) and esp. 10.42–3 (4x). For a different case, see *E.* 1.51–8, where the two instances of *hinc* do not have the causal force that seems to be required here.

52 numerum. Counting the animals is one of the herdsman's typical tasks, par-ticularly as they go back to the fold for the night (cf. *E.* 6.85); but the wolf, natur-ally inclined to killing, will certainly not take heed of how many animals are in the flock, let alone of the person who scrupulously counted them (the wolf, moreover, could easily slaughter dozens of victims and eat just one of them). Cf. Otto (1890, p. 199, no. 984, s.v. *lupus*), mentioning the German saying 'der Wolf frißt auch die gezählten Schafe' (i.e. 'the wolf eats the counted and uncounted sheep'). **torrentia flumina ripas.** For the scant respect that overflowing rivers have for their banks (and whatever happens to be on them), cf. *Aen.* 10.362–3. Note, by

ECLOGUE 7   373

contrast, the anticipation of spring in Hor. *carm.* 4.7.3–4 *decrescentia ripas / flumina praetereunt.* The same participle used here describes a 'foaming' river in *G.* 2.451 *torrentem undam*; *Aen.* 2.305 (where *torrens* is substantive); 6.550 *rapidus flammis ambit torrentibus amnis* (paradoxically ambivalent: a fiery river, 'foaming' and 'burning' at the same time); 10.603, etc. Note the subtle semantic contrast with 7.51 *Boreae...frigora*; cf. 7.47–8 *aestas / torrida.*

53–60. The contestants challenge each other on a typically pastoral theme, i.e. the correspondence between human feelings and natural phenomena (for the theme in the *E.*, cf. 1.38–9). The connection between the beloved's presence and a luxuriant landscape is featured in Daphnis' agonistic song at *id.* 8.41–3: 'spring is everywhere, everywhere pastures, everywhere milk / gushing from udders, and cubs grow up, // wherever the fair Naiad goes' (for a similar procedure, applied to the beloved Milon, cf. *id.* 8.45–8; note that the order of the lines is perhaps altered in the manuscripts). Thyrsis, by contrast, describes a landscape tormented by excessive heat, which only Phyllis' arrival (and rain) will be able to refresh. V. here transfers to an erotic scene a motif normally featured in religious contexts (esp. in hymns), i.e. nature's prosperity as a reaction to divine presence (or the reverse, i.e. divine absence engendering barrenness: *E.* 5.35n.). The mention of Alexis (7.55n.) leaves no doubt that this Corydon is 'identical' to the singer of *E.* 2. For a striking similarity cf. an epigram by Meleager, who looms large in Corydon's song for Alexis (2.1n.): 'if grim eyes are fixed on me, I only see winter; / but if cheerful eyes look at me, there comes blooming spring' (*Anth. Pal.* 12.159.5–6 = *HE* 4566–7 G.-P.). Note, finally, another point of opposition between the two contestants: homosexuality vs heterosexuality (as in *E.* 3.70–3). Some scholars have considered 53–6 more fitting for Thyrsis than for Corydon from a metrical and stylistic point of view, and have therefore proposed various kinds of transposition. Overall, however, there does not seem to be any compelling reason to alter the text of the manuscripts. In particular, the mention of *formosus Alexis* (echoing Corydon's love song in 2.55n.) would make little sense if attributed to Thyrsis, whereas it is full of meaning if uttered by Corydon.

53–4 Stant... / strata iacent. A similar contrast between high and low, vertical and horizontal, appears in the triumphant finale of *id.* 7: 'Many poplars and elm trees were swaying high up / above our heads... / Everything had the scent of a rich harvest, the scent of autumn. / Pears at our feet, apples rolled abundantly alongside us' (*id.* 7.135–6; 143–5). Corydon, too, is now describing autumn. Note, in l. 53, two instances of full hiatus (one of them featuring the polysyndeton *et...et*, for which cf. 3.6n.): both, along with the spondee in the fifth foot, presuppose a rhythmically solemn, *staccato* reading; for partly similar cases cf. 2.24 and 8.44 (involving Greek words). Corydon here reworks Greek elegiac couplets (*id.* 8.41–3: see *E.* 7.53–60n.) and turns them into Latin hexameters.

53 iuniperi. Juniper grows in dense, thorny bushes, and its berries ripen in late autumn (in technical prose, the same Latin term denotes both plant and berries: cf. Scrib. Larg. 186; Plin. *nat.* 24.27). The noun has only two occurrences in

374   ECLOGUE 7

V. (both referring to the plant): here and at *E.* 10.76. **castaneae hirsutae.** The sweet chestnut tree, motionless in its stature (*stant*), still 'carries' its fruits, in spite of the season approaching its end (see below, 7.54; the ripened fruit naturally tends to fall: cf. 1.37). The term *castanea* is ambivalent, since it can denote either the plant (*G.* 2.15) or its fruit (cf. also *E.* 1.81): here, as with the juniper, V. must be thinking of the tree. For its typical 'curl', justifying the epithet *hirsuta* (here applied to the plant as a whole), cf. Pallad. *ins.* 131–2 *poma hirsuta uirentis / castaneae.* Chestnuts and apples are among the gifts that Corydon offers to Alexis in *E.* 2.51–2. This line is the third and last fifth-foot spondaic hexameter in the *E.*: cf. 5.38n. For the double hiatus, cf. 7.53–4n.

54 passim. The adv. is used to denote luxuriant plants at 4.19; cf. 7.55 *rident* (n.). **sua quaeque...poma.** When following the possessive *suus*, the pronoun *quisque* is generally attracted to its case. Thus, there is no need to accept Bentley's conjecture *quaque* (referring to *sub arbore*), supported by b²c². For a similar phenomenon, cf. Cic. *Tusc.* 4.28 *haec...procliuitas ad suum quodque genus*; *fin.* 5.46; Liv. 33.46.9; Tac. *ann.* 14.27.3.

55 rident. Cf., again, *E.* 4.20n. **formosus Alexis.** An explicit reference to the opening of *E.* 2 (*formosum...Alexin*). The image of a drought (7.56 *flumina sicca*) recalls one of the fundamental themes of *E.* 2, i.e. the erotic and meteorological 'heat' connected with the boy's absence and indifference (see *E.* 2.1 *ardebat*; 2.6–13). In *E.* 2, the song of a lonely lover, the hypothesis here formulated (*at si formosus Alexis...abeat*) is actualized; cf. also 7.56n.

56 montibus his. Yet another echo of *E.* 2 (cf. 2.5 *montibus*). **abeat.** The future *aberit* is P's reading; for the idea, cf. *id.* 8.43 and 8.47. **flumina sicca.** Corydon's speech ends with a contrastive echo of 7.52 *torrentia flumina ripas.*

57–60. After late spring (7.45–8), winter (49–52), and autumn (53–6), here comes the height of summer, which Thyrsis will now describe. Note how the opening of his speech takes up Corydon's last words (*flumina sicca*).

57 uitio...aëris. Unhealthy air was deemed responsible for diseases in humans, animals, and entire regions, according to a medical and physiological doctrine at least as old as the Hippocratic treatise *On Airs, Waters, and Places* (and later defended by the Stoics). In all likelihood, Servius' interpretation (*id est pestilentia corrupti aeris affligitur* [scilicet *ager* vel *herba*]), taking Thyrsis to allude to a plague epidemic, is influenced by texts like Lucr. 6.1093–1102, esp. 6.1097 *fit morbidus aer*; cf. Sen. *nat.* 6.27.2 *aer ipse...corruptus internorum ignium uitio*; see also *G.* 3.478 *morbo caeli*; *Aen.* 3.138 *corrupto caeli tractu.* Here, however, air is less dramatically described as 'heavy', i.e. 'adulterated' by stillness and excessively high temperatures. In fact, grass dies of thirst (*moriens sitit...herba*), whereas fire purifies soil defects in *G.* 1.88 *excoquitur uitium atque exsudat inutilis umor.* **sitit...herba.** Any type of grass, serving any purpose (cf. e.g. *E.* 3.55 *in molli consedimus herba*; Hor. *epist.* 1.14.35 *somnus in herba*). In a pastoral context, however, the term *herba* specifically denotes pasture: grazing animals love fresh, green grass (cf. *E.* 6.54). For a similarly metaphorical use of the verb *sitio*, cf. Cic. *orat.* 81, where the manuscripts oscillate between *lasciuire* and *sitire agros* (see below, 7.60n.): see *G.* 4.402 *sitiunt herbae*; cf. Cat. *agr.* 151.4; *OLD*², p. 1956, s.v. *sitio* 2a.

58 Liber. Yet another Dionysian reference in Thyrsis' words—this time, an explicit one. The god, whose prerogatives include loosening, liberating, and governing fluids, here does not foster prosperity in the arid fields (*inuidit*), since he does not let the sprouting vines cast their shade on the hills. In Statius' *Thebaid* (Book 4), a terrible drought is caused by Bacchus, who orders the Nymphs to dry up water springs (see esp. *Theb.* 4.684–96; with 4.699 *haurit sitis ignea campos* cf. here l. 57 *sitit...herba*).

59 Phyllidis aduentu. Phyllis' arrival, following the drought of 7.58, points at the botanical significance of her name (φύλλον 'leaf': cf. *E.* 3.107n.; 5.10n.; 10.41n.). Phyllis, like spring itself, lets the whole grove flourish (*nemus omne uirebit*): see e.g. Varr. *ling.* 6.9 *uer, quod tum uirere incipiunt uirgulta*; but cf. Lucr. 1.7 *aduentumque tuum* (note the hymnic style: cf. Callim. *hymn.* 3[*Dian.*].129–35). Ovid will compare the mythical Phyllis, abandoned by Demophoon, to maenads loosening their hair in Ov. *rem.* 593–4 *ibat, ut Edono referens trieterica Baccho / ire solet fusis barbara turba comis*. **nemus omne.** Elsewhere, the phrase refers to cultivated groves, as in *G.* 2.308 and 401. Here, the point of view is that of a herdsman-farmer, who worries about pasture grass and vineyards: cf. 7.57–8.

60 Iuppiter et laeto descendet plurimus imbri. The supreme god, Jupiter, 'descends' on earth with abundant, fruitful rain. In this visually powerful image, it is as if the sky itself came down to earth, burdened with a heavy load of clouds and water: see e.g. Hor. *epod.* 13.1–2 *horrida tempestas caelum contraxit et imbres / niuesque deducunt Iouem*; cf. also *G.* 1.324 *ruit arduus aether* and *Aen.* 1.129 *caeli...ruina*; for *Iuppiter* personifying the heavens cf. *G.* 1.418; 2.419. The idea that Jupiter/Zeus fertilizes the earth with his rains has a long tradition in philosophical prose (note Anaxagoras, 59 A 117 D.-K.; cf. Theophr. *hist. plant.* 3.1.4; Varr. *rust.* 1.40.1), as well as in Attic drama (cf. Eur. fr. 839 Kann.; but see Aesch. *Danaides* fr. 44 Radt). For a Homeric precedent, cf. the well-known ἱερὸς γάμος at Hom. *Il.* 14.346–51 (which was 'physiologically' allegorized in antiquity); the motif also appears in Lucr. 1.250–1 *postremo pereunt imbres, ubi eos pater aether / in gremium matris terrai praecipitauit*, as well as in the late *Perv. Ven.* 59–62. Cf. also *TrGF*, V.2, pp. 880–1 Kann.; see further Schierl, *Die Tragödien des Pacuuius* (quoted above, 2.24n.), pp. 205–7. Echoing Thyrsis' words, V. will rework the image in *G.* 2.325–6 *tum pater omnipotens fecundis imbribus Aether / coniugis in gremium laetae descendit*. Here, the epithet *laeto* resonates with its etymological background ('fat', and therefore 'fertile': hence, *laetamen*), which must have been still active in the rural language, according to Cic. *orat.* 81 (note, however, that Cicero interprets the phenomenon as a metaphorical usage): *<ea> translatione fortasse crebrior, qua frequentissime sermo omnis utitur, non modo urbanorum, sed etiam rusticorum, si quidem est eorum gemmare uites, lasciuire* [v.l. *sitire*] *agros,*

376   ECLOGUE 7

laetas esse segetes, luxuriosa frumenta (cf. *G.* 1.1 *laetas segetes*). At the same time, the adj. hints at a joyful freshness that befits the erotic context: the reader pictures Phyllis taking shelter with her lover.

61–8. The final exchange shows fundamental differences between the two contestants' use of divine language, which played an essential role in the central poems of the book and is now a reason to declare a winner (in opposition to the draw of *E.* 3). In his four lines, Corydon brings together Heracles and Iacchus (i.e. Bacchus), as well as Venus and Phoebus, along with their respective plants. Corydon's tutelary deities are all crucial to late Republican (and, later, Augustan) society and culture, and he arranges them in a harmonious order, with regular intervals and artfully crafted symmetries (7.61–2). Thyrsis, by contrast, does not mention a single god: he seems to regard the trees he names as mere components of the landscape, whereas Corydon acknowledges the mythical (human or divine) past of each plant, in accordance with a principle operating in Silenus' eclogue (cf. *E.* 6.62–3n.; 71n.). The contrast is most apparent in the case of poplars, the only species mentioned by both characters (7.66n.). In Callim. *iamb.* 4, the contrast between two different plants, i.e. olive tree and bay, pointed to the opposition between two different poetic and literary-critical styles (the respective tutelary deities, i.e. Pallas and Apollo, were also involved: Callim. fr. 194.64–72 Pf.). Although Thyrsis suffers defeat, his four lines are far from flavourless (as some scholars have thought): the repetition at 7.65 and 68 is a sign of wit rather than weariness (cf. below, 7.68n.), and aptly brings the agon to a close, at least as far as Meliboeus can remember. Note the role reversal in comparison with the previous exchange: Thyrsis now praises a boy's beauty (Lycidas), whereas Corydon extols Phyllis'. Their respective speeches adopt different rhetorical approaches: while Corydon uses a priamel structure (as in 'everyone has their preferences, but for me…'), Thyrsis operates with an encomiastic structure similar to that of Mopsus' song (*E.* 5.32–5: 'you are the most beautiful of all beautiful things'). No wonder, finally, that the last exchange features an iterative style which is typically pastoral, besides being paralleled in folk poetry: cf. *PMG* 852, p. 453 P. Note that this final pair of speeches condenses various themes and topics of the contest: natural elements, deities, and love (for both boys and girls).

61 **Populus Alcidae gratissima.** White (λευκαί) poplars were said to have been brought to Greece by Heracles (Pausan. 5.14.2), here denoted by his 'papponymic', i.e. the name of his paternal grandfather. Alcaeus was, in fact, the father of Amphitryon (note the epithet *Amphitryoniades* at *Aen.* 8.103), i.e. the hero's putative father. *Alcides* often occurs in Latin poetry, perhaps also thanks to its phonetic proximity to ἀλκή 'strength', besides the fact that the Latin nom. *Hercules* does not fit the hexameter: see e.g. *Aen.* 5.414; 6.123; 8.203; Hor. *carm.* 1.12.25; but cf. Callim. *hymn.* 3[*Dian.*].145. According to the myth, here narrated by Servius Dan., Heracles returned from the underworld and adorned his head with the leafy branches of one of the poplars that grow in the Elysian Fields: he did so in memory of Leuce, the Oceanid abducted and loved by Pluto; cf. also *G.* 2.66 and *Aen.* 8.276–7 (for the Heliades' metamorphosis see 7.66n.). After the fertilizing action of *Iuppiter* upon the fields, which brought Thyrsis'

ECLOGUE 7 377

speech to a close in 7.60, one of Jupiter's most illustrious children now appears: Heracles, too, was the 'fruit' of the god's 'descent' to earth. In Theocritus' *id.* 2.120–1, Heracles' poplar is associated with Dionysus and his fruits (i.e., in that case, apples), whereas here his vines are immediately mentioned (*uitis Iaccho*). The plant must have belonged to the folklore of V.'s homeland, if it is true that the inhabitants of Mantua's region had the custom of planting a poplar at the birth of a child (V. was said to have his own tree, too: the *arbor Vergilii*, a prodigious and much-venerated tree; cf. Don. *uita Verg.* 15–20 Brumm. = p. 19.9–20.4 Brugn.-Stok); already in Homer the poplar grows in humid and marshy soil: αἴγειρος ὥς, / ἥ ῥα τ᾽ ἐν εἰαμενῇ ἕλεος μεγάλοιο πεφύκει (*Il.* 4.482–3; in the simile for a young warrior killed); cf. the κερκίς (a variety of white poplar) in Callim. *Hec.* fr. 48.7 H. For the superlative in *-issimus*, rare in the *E.*, cf. 3.57n. **uitis Iaccho.** The vine is juxtaposed with its tutelary deity, here denoted by his ritual epithet (see 6.15n.).

62 formosae myrtus Veneri. Myrtle is dear to 'fair Venus', since it is said to have covered her naked body when she was generated out of sea foam. The plant, in fact, grows in coastal regions (7.6n.); see further *Enc. Virg.* III, p. 540, s.v. *mirto* (T. Mantero). Along with bay, with which it is paired here, myrtle is also mentioned by Corydon at *E.* 2.54–5: both plants, he says, have a distinct smell. Myrtle and bay were similarly paired together in Roman ritual practice—the former being used in *ouationes*, the latter in triumphs (Gell. 5.6.20–3; cf. also Plin. *nat.* 15.125). Venus' myrtle, presumably alluding to the *gens Iulia* (cf. 9.47n.), will adorn Octavian's temple in *G.* 1.28, where V. will imagine the ruler's future deification. **sua laurea Phoebo.** On Apollo's predilection for bay, see *E.* 3.63n. (where bay and hyacinth are referred to as *sua munera*). Yet the god's love for Daphne was an unhappy one, far from enjoying the 'fair' goddess' favour: note the epithet *innuba* applied to *laurus* in Ov. *met.* 10.92.

63 Phyllis amat corylos. Phyllis' entirely arbitrary passion for *coryli* (i.e. 'hazel-trees') has parallels in the *E.* (cf. 1.14; in 5.21 the trees are summoned by Mopsus to describe the Nymphs' grief for Daphnis). The *coryli* will reappear, along with myrtles (given the similar hardness of their wood), in *G.* 2.64–5; in *G.* 2.299, V. will forbid the coupling of hazel-trees and vines, the former being deemed harmful to the latter. Corydon, a pastoral lover, gives prominence to Phyllis' passions. As Ovid will recommend, *quicquid probat illa, probato* (Ov. *ars* 2.199). Note also that the 'invincible' *coryli* are phonetically close to the singer's name, which will soon triumphantly reappear twice: 7.70 *Corydon Corydon*. In *E.* 2.52, Corydon mentioned 'his' beloved Amaryllis' predilection for *castaneae nuces.*

64 corylos. The reading *Veneris*, which Servius Dan. attributes to the grammarian Hebrus, should probably be interpreted as a learned conjecture aiming at balancing the structure of the sentence (*myrtus* + the gen. of the deity would correspond to *laurea Phoebi*). Note also that, if *Veneris* replaces *corylos*, the whole line becomes a sort of gnomic motto, easy to memorize and quote (hence the likelihood of textual corruption?). Here, however, the verb *uincet* seems to require a direct object, which completes the sentence both logically and

378 ECLOGUE 7

phonetically (note the echo of 7.63 *corylos*). Finally, Corydon seems to display an 'Apollonian' inclination, in contrast to Thyrsis' 'Dionysian' tendencies: hence the mention of Phoebus, which is in itself sufficient to conclude Corydon's speech.

65 Fraxinus in siluis pulcherrima. Thyrsis' assertion ('the ash-tree is the most beautiful in the woods') is not paralleled elsewhere in V.'s pastoral landscape, albeit largely made up of *siluae*. In the whole book, the tree appears only here and at 7.68, whereas the *Georgics* will highlight its imposing appearance (G. 2.65–6 *ingens fraxinus*, followed by the 'Herculean' poplar) and the *Aeneid* will mention, once again, its place in the forest (*Aen.* 11.136; note 11.134 *per siluas*). For the adj. form *fraxineus*, cf. G. 2.359; *Aen.* 6.181 (always in line-initial position, like the noun). Note that the first word of the line coincides with the first dactyl: the device is not particularly rare (cf. 7.61, in Corydon's speech), but Thyrsis uses it systematically in his final quatrain (cf. also G. 3.527–31: 5x in a row). The phenomenon must have contributed to some textual confusion in ancient manuscripts, testified to by Servius Dan. (*fraxinus in siluis* trades spots with the following *populus in fluuiis*: see further 7.66n.). Readers may perceive some echoes of an Ennian 'deforestation' scene: Enn. *ann.* 175–9 Sk. (note esp. 177–8 *fraxinus frangitur atque abies consternitur alta, / pinus proceras peruortunt*, which Macrobius compares with *Aen.* 6.179–82 at *Sat.* 6.2.27): note the line-beginning *fraxinus*, as here, followed by *abies* and *pinus* (albeit in a different order). **pinus in hortis.** The garden setting and the contrast with *siluae* seem to rule out a reference to *Pinus syluestris*, a typically mountain-dwelling species (cf. *E.* 8.22n.; 10.14–15n.; note here *abies*, appearing 'on high mountains'). More probably, Thyrsis refers to the Italian stone pine (*Pinus pinea*), a species of more modest proportions (perhaps Ovid's *culta...pinus*: *ars* 3.692). Cypress trees are assigned a similar role in Theocr. *id.* 18.29–30: 'the great harvest grows, adorning the fertile fields, / and the cypress adorns the garden' (καὶ κάπῳ κυπάρισσος).

66 populus in fluuiis. The poplar is 'dearest to Hercules', according to Corydon (*E.* 7.61n.), and is now mentioned in connection with its fluvial habitat: cf. Plin. *nat.* 16.77 *non nisi in aquosis proueniunt salices, alni, populi* (G. 2.110–11 *fluminibus salices... / nascuntur*). In *Aen.* 10.190, V. refers to the fact that the Heliades were turned into poplars (traditionally located near the river Po), even though his Silenus asserts that alder trees were the result of the metamorphosis (*E.* 6.62–3). For the noun *fluuius*, cf. 5.76n. **abies in montibus altis.** In Latin literature, fir trees appear as early as Enn. *ann.* 177 Sk. quoted above (along with *fraxinus*). V. mentions them in the *Georgics* as well (G. 2.68), and several times in the *Aeneid* (cf. *Aen.* 2.16; 5.663). For the phrase *montibus altis* (also in Lucretius), cf. *E.* 1.83n.

67 saepius...reuisas. Both the adv. and the verb (a desiderative form of *uidere*) insist on the idea of repeated returns. Thyrsis has sung of Phyllis' *aduentus* in 7.59, and these final exchanges keep repeating themes and forms, constantly echoing one another. **at si me, Lycida formose.** Cf. 7.55 *at si formosus Alexis* (Corydon has 'appropriated' Phyllis: now Thyrsis echoes the praise of Alexis);

ECLOGUE 7   379

note the postponed *at* (in contrast to 7.55), which is a feature of Hellenistic and neoteric style (cf. Catull. 64.58 *immemor at iuuenis*). The result is a stark antithesis with 7.65–6, where the speaker's assertion is corroborated by the omission of the copula: now, Lycidas' presence changes everything. Note the long vowel quantity in the voc. ending *Lycida* (as in Greek; cf. *E.* 3.1 *Damoeta*). Lycidas' name, which is eminently Theocritean, appears here for the first time in V. and will occur again at 9.2n. In the *E.*, the name is associated with youth (here, Lycidas is clearly a *puer formosus*; cf. *puer* in Moeris' speech at 9.66).

68. The echo of 7.65, ending on the same note (*pinus in hortis*; cf. Thyrsis in 7.34 *horti*) is not a mere repetition, hinting at tiredness (as some scholars have thought), but provides witty overtones to the eclogue's finale. While Corydon, in his last line (7.64), overturns the meaning of 7.62 (the second line of his quatrain; note the theme and variation: *Phoebo/Phoebi*), Thyrsis now intensifies the effect of the same procedure by negating the first line of his quatrain (7.65). Should Lycidas visit him in the *siluae*, his company will be preferable to the ash tree, or to the pine tree in *horti*, whereas rivers and high mountains (less appealing landscapes from an erotic point of view) recede into the background. **cedat.** The reading *cedet* is found in **P**: it must have been influenced by *uincet*, which actually responds to *amabit*, whereas the subjunctive here aptly parallels *reuisas* and seems necessary to the overall symmetry (*amabit-uincet / reuisas-cedat*).

69–70. These two lines conclude the poem. Meliboeus now takes centre stage again and reveals who the winner is. This epilogue is the shortest one in V.'s pastoral book (along with the finale of *E.* 9—which, properly speaking, is the very last speech in the dialogue) and is exactly half the length of the epilogue of *E.* 3, the other singing contest (where Palaemon's 'verdict' occupies four lines: 3.108–11). Once the reader finds out that Corydon is the winner, several 'Theocritean' clues may retrospectively come to mind. In Theocr. *id.* 5, in fact, the first prize was awarded to the goatherd (Comatas, who placed great emphasis on his job in his very last speech), whereas the shepherd Lacon was defeated: Corydon himself is a goatherd. In *id.* 5.80, Comatas gave the first speech at the outset of the contest, as Corydon does here (note also the similarity of the respective names, featuring the same first syllable: Co-matas and Co-rydon). In sum, any readers of V. who 'place a bet' on their knowledge of Theocritus will themselves be the 'winners'.

69 Haec memini. The motif of memory, here appearing in the first person, immediately evokes the narrator (Meliboeus), whose recollection of Corydon's victory concludes the poem. The inevitably partial nature of subjective memory (the contest, we must infer, is not narrated in its entirety) subtly allows the text not to engage in any exhaustive explanation of victory and defeat. The deictic *haec*, which here plays a resumptive role, provides a distant echo of *hos...illos* [scil. *uersus*] at 7.20, thereby framing Meliboeus' summary of the singing contest. **frustra contendere.** The uselessness of competition appears in Morson's verdict at the end of *id.* 5: 'It is not fair, Lacon, for magpies to compete with a nightingale, /

380   ECLOGUE 8

nor for hoopoes to challenge swans: but you, poor dear!, like to be quarrelsome [ἐσσὶ φιλεχθής]' (136–7). The verb, which previously appeared in 7.18 at the beginning of the agon, now marks its end (in fact, Thyrsis now seems to reawaken to the contest, but in vain: cf. Callim. *iamb.* 4, fr. 194.93–5 Pf.).

70 ex illo Corydon Corydon est tempore nobis. Cf. *id.* 8.92 κῆκ τούτω πρᾶτος παρὰ ποιμέσι Δάφνις ἔγεντο 'and ever since that day Daphnis became the first among the herdsmen' (penultimate line). Based on the Greek model and the peculiarity of the transmitted text, Heyworth has proposed the conjecture *ex illo primus Corydon est tempore nobis.* Yet the text can be explained as a witty ampli-fication of the model, centred around the twofold occurrence of the name (first used literally, then antonomastically: a bit like saying, 'Cicero is Cicero'). Corydon, once an anonymous herdsman, has become the famous singer Corydon, i.e. the author of the song for Alexis, 'already' known to V.'s reader. Echoes of *E.* 2 are frequent in the poem (cf. esp. 7.55n.) and reach their climax in this final, almost explicit acknowledgement (the repetition of Corydon's name was itself a feature of *E.* 2.69, albeit in a different syntactical structure, which is deliberately reworked here: *a, Corydon, Corydon, quae te dementia cepit!*). A similar procedure, used to negate (rather than affirm) an antonomasia, is found in the finale of Callim. *epigr.* 51.4 Pf. ἃς ἄτερ οὐδ' αὐταὶ ταὶ Χάριτες Χάριτες 'without whom [i.e. Berenice] the Graces are not themselves Graces'; cf. Aristoph. *Ach.* 708. A pun based on proper nouns is a fitting way of definitively ending a contest: cf. Hor. *sat.* 1.7.33–5 (with obvious differences). Evidently, Corydon's fame is entirely Virgilian, since both Theocritus' Corydon and the etymologically related bird (κορυδός/κορυδαλλός, a sort of lark) were not renowned for excellence in singing (cf. *E.* 2.1n.), even though the κορυδός was called the first and 'oldest' among all birds (Aristoph. *Au.* 472–3); cf. *schol.* Theocr. *id.* 10.48–51g, p. 238.3–4 Wend., where the bird is called 'first' in the sense of 'earliest to rise'. In his commentary, Servius only paraphrases the general sense, without giving an etymological account of the name. Curiously, however, he thinks that V.'s use of antonomasia is a way of characterizing Meliboeus as a naive herdsman, unable to complete the expression of his thoughts (*uictor, nobilis supra omnes: quam rem quasi rusticus implere non potuit*).

Eclogue 8

[Alphesiboeus]

Like all even-numbered eclogues, the eighth eclogue begins with a proem (cf. 1.16n.), in which the poet introduces the topic, i.e. the 'singing contest' (8.3 *certantis*) between the herdsmen Damon and Alphesiboeus (8.1–5). The poet then addresses an illustrious dedicatee (8.6–13), whose glory lies in both military and poetic achievements (in all likelihood, Asinius Pollio: cf. below, p. 383 and

8.6n.), and finally outlines the framework in which Damon's song takes place (8.14–16). Damon voices the lament of a wretched, unnamed lover, whom the girl Nysa scorns in favour of Mopsus, whereupon he expresses a wish to take his own life (8.17–61). The second song, by Alphesiboeus, is introduced by an even shorter prologue (8.62–3). This time, the protagonist is a woman (herself unnamed) who, assisted by her servant Amaryllis, performs a magic ritual to force her beloved Daphnis to return from the city. She eventually succeeds, or so it seems, in her endeavour (8.64–109).

Here, V. goes back to a well-established pastoral form, i.e. a contest made up of long songs, which he has used in *E.* 5. In this case, too, the number of lines assigned to each song is precisely the same. While Mopsus and Menalcas praised the late Daphnis by uttering twenty-five lines each, here each of the two songs comprises forty-six lines (provided that l. 28a is authentic: but see n. ad loc. and 8.76n.). Note also the thematic correspondence between the two songs, albeit less evident than in *E.* 5 (there is no explicit cross-reference): here, both songs have love as their subject matter; yet the suicidal thoughts of the first song contrast with the happy ending of the second. Similarly, in *E.* 5, a funeral lament was contrasted with a deification.

After the sequential unit formed by the central poems (which are so distinctly Virgilian) and Corydon's victory in *E.* 7 (which marked the end of that sequence), *E.* 8 returns to Theocritean emulation (cf. 8.1n.). Specifically, Damon's song echoes *id.* 3, in which the anonymous goatherd lamented his unhappy love and eventually decided to take his own life (V.'s suicidal character seems to be a goatherd himself: see 8.33n.; cf. also the pseudo-Theocritean *id.* 23). However, in this new love monologue (paralleled by *E.* 2) V. subtly reworks and stylistically refines Theocritus' characterization of the naive herdsman. The theme of female magic, too, has a Theocritean precedent, *id.* 2, set in the city and, therefore, most probably excluded from the corpus of the 'properly' pastoral idylls (but cf. Introduction, pp. 19–20 and nn. 46–8). However, since Damon often echoes *id.* 1 (Daphnis) as well, V. may have aimed at creating a 'diptych' by simultaneously emulating the two Theocritean poems that feature a refrain, even though *id.* 1 and *id.* 2 presumably occupied very different positions in the Theocritean collection known to V. For the same reason, *id.* 1 and *id.* 2 must have been juxtaposed with each other in the later manuscript tradition, on which modern editions of Theocritus' text are based (note that Alphesiboeus' *carmen* ends precisely with Daphnis' return from the city, almost re-establishing pastoral 'normality' in opposition to the urban setting of *id.* 2).

To be sure, nothing proves that Alphesiboeus' Daphnis, obsessively invoked in *E.* 8, should be identified with Theocritus' pastoral hero (nothing, analogously, proves the contrary). There is no doubt, however, that such a 'resounding' name enriches *E.* 8 with echoes and suggestions. In the *Eclogue* book, the names Mopsus and Alphesiboeus only occur here and in *E.* 5, whose protagonist was the deceased,

382 ECLOGUE 8

deified Daphnis. In Menalcas' song, Alphesiboeus appeared among the enthusiastic, Dionysian revellers celebrating Daphnis (*E.* 5.73), whereas he now narrates how 'a' Daphnis, this time a city-dweller, elicited the erotic passion of an unnamed woman. As for Mopsus, in *E.* 5 he was a follower of Daphnis and declared his Bacchic affiliation, whereas now Damon's Mopsus is associated with a girl whose name is unmistakably Dionysian (8.18n.).

E. 8 must be read as the work of a poet who challenges his own pastoral invent-iveness, to the point that he describes himself somewhat ironically as tired and perhaps even inadequate (8.63n.). The poem thereby acquires greater force, enriched by several echoes from other eclogues in the book. Even an ordinarily pastoral name, such as Amaryllis, is rich in evocative resonances, considering that an Amaryllis was associated with the motif of the return from the city in *E.* 1.36–9 (8.77n.). The opposition between an unhappy character, forced to surrender, and a resourceful one, who seeks and finds supernatural help, echoes the sorrowful contrast between Tityrus and Meliboeus. Such a subtle network of correspondences appeals to a reader who is by now expert in V.'s poetic technique. The irony implicit in this game of similarities and differences lends unity to *E.* 8, which critics and scholars have often described as a desultory poem. The finale of the eclogue deceives the reader's agonistic expectations, initially fuelled by the technical verb *certare* (8.3). Unlike the preceding poem, *E.* 8 ends without a winner and, unlike in *E.* 5, there is no final 'ceremony' featuring an exchange of compliments or gifts. Not unlike the enigmatic prologue, which features a composite structure and an anonymous addressee, the poem's finale is rather indefinite and inconclusive. The poet alludes to the fact that, after *E.* 8, his pastoral-Theocritean vein will soon be dried up: magic, the only Theocritean topic hitherto missing from V.'s pastoral book, is now introduced in Alphesiboeus' song. Besides referring to his own 'tiredness', the poet also mentions the idea of 'concluding' (*desinam*: see 8.11n.). In fact, the two final eclogues (*E.* 9 and 10) will cast an eminently retrospective gaze on pastoral poetry, in both its Theocritean and its Virgilian incarnation.

In a poem full of tacit allusions and 'anonymity', the reader's cooperation is required, even in relation to the specific theme of love, which grants both unity and identity to *E.* 8. First of all, Damon's song is an original reworking of the epi-thalamium form, which is often evoked in order to be contradicted (a sort of 'anti-epithalamium'). While V. must have had Catullus in mind, it is undeniable that epithalamia were frequently blended with pastoral poetry: cf. esp. [Bion] 2 G., i.e. the *Epithalamium of Achilles and Deidamia*, as well as Theocr. *id.* 18 and Himerius' remarks in *or.* 9, esp. 9.3 and 9.5 (authors of epithalamia are quite familiar with the pastoral style: in Claud. *carm. min.* 25.36 H., Hymenaeus himself will play 'Maenalian numbers' on the *fistula*; cf. Wilson 1948). Secondly, the juxtaposition of the two songs ironically builds on *E.* 2. While Corydon's monologue there ended on a note of balance and return to normality, somewhat indebted to *id.* 11 and its 'remedy' (φάρμακον), suicidal despair is now followed by a variation on the theme of Theocritus' Φαρμακεύτριαι (*id.* 2). From the lover's point of view, the 'songs' are an alternative to despair: these, however, are magic songs, featuring the threat of more powerful herbs (provided by a mysterious character, Moeris). A distinctive feature of magic itself in *E.* 8 is a certain Theocritean liveliness, full of neoteric and Catullan echoes. Pliny, *nat.* 28.19, explicitly asserts that Catullus himself composed some 'emulation of love spells' (cf. Catull. fr. 4 Myn.). Without a doubt, *E.* 8 (along with *E.* 4) contributed to V.'s late antique and medieval fame as a 'wizard': cf. Apul. *apol.* 30.6–7 (see below, pp. 507–8).

The importance of the erotic theme (and the epithalamium), along with the various allusions to Catullus and Calvus (another neoteric poet: 8.4n.), can strengthen the argument for equating the addressee of *E.* 8 with Pollio (see 8.6n.), who was personally close to the neoteric movement and to Catullus in particular. Without explicitly naming him, V. here echoes his own *E.* 3, where Pollio made his appearance in an atmosphere of neoteric liveliness. Besides being an important Roman politician, Pollio managed to combine military triumphs with literary glory, and used the revenue from his military campaigns (*ex manubiis*) to build a great library (cf. Plin. *nat.* 7.115). At the time of the *E.*, Pollio was a renowned author of tragedies at Rome: in *E.* 8, both Damon's pathetic monologue (featuring a 'tragic' outcome: suicide) and Alphesiboeus' dramatized song may pay homage to themes and literary techniques of tragic poetry, seen through a pastoral lens. V. gives voice to an anonymous female character and describes her as a sorceress, not without some allusions to Medea (even in Damon's song: cf. 8.47n.; 48n.; 95n.) and, more generally, to the great heroines of Greek tragedy. To be sure, V. follows here the Theocritean model: but *id.* 2, clearly featuring an urban setting, does not belong to Theocritus' 'properly pastoral' poems. Hence, Alphesiboeus' pastoral song contains the only female voice in 'properly pastoral' poetry. Calpurnius Siculus and Nemesianus will only use male voices, as Theocritus did in his rustic idylls. V.'s innovation, here mediated by the narrator Alphesiboeus, is matched in the fourth book of the *Aeneid*, whose protagonist is a great tragic heroine (Dido). The idea of a female protagonist, who suffers from lovesickness because she has been abandoned (not unlike Catullus' Ariadne and, later, Dido herself), may be of interest to a tragic poet with neoteric sympathies, such as Pollio. Taken together, these clues suggest that Pollio is, in fact, the addressee of *E.* 8 beyond any reasonable doubt: Pollio, and Pollio alone, is the pillar around which triumphal bay and Dionysian ivy are woven together into one wreath.

The particular form of this eclogue, a narrative poem with a prologue, is worth deeper analysis in terms of both structure and diegesis. If 8.28a is genuine (see n. ad loc.), the poem is 110 lines long (the number resonates with Pollio's interests and action: cf. 8.6n.) and is therefore one of the longest poems in the collection,

384   ECLOGUE 8

second only to *E.* 3 (which has 111 lines, though 3.43 is probably spurious [see n. ad loc.]: its deletion would equalize the length of the two 'Pollonian' eclogues; cf. p. 150). The length of *E.* 8 is certainly noteworthy, although the refrains obviously contribute to it: if the repeated lines are subtracted from the total (again, including l. 28a), the final result is ninety lines, i.e. just over the book's average and exactly matching *E.* 5. The two songs, which occupy ll. 17–61 and ll. 64–109, form a coherent and harmonious unity: besides having the same number of lines, as mentioned above (forty-six each, very close to the forty-eight total lines of the two 'proper' contests, i.e. *E.* 3 and 7), the songs feature a variety of internal echoes and correspondences (see 8.17–61n.; 64–109n.). Note also the importance of decimal quantities: each song consists of ten stanzas and ten refrains (ten is a fundamental number in this book made of ten poems). The structural symmetry of the two songs, which makes them representative of the *E.* as a whole, is in clear contrast with the 'imperfection' of the prologue. The prologue, the longest in the book (sixteen lines), contains a dedication that does not fulfil the typical requirements of a dedicatory address (the addressee's name is never mentioned) and gives the impression of having been forcibly inserted into the prologue (see 8.1–16n.). The reader must wait until ll. 62–3 to encounter a typical component of poetic prologues, i.e. the invocation to the Muses, which functions as an 'interlude' between the two songs (see n. ad loc.). In opposition to the balanced, harmonious structure of the two main songs, the prologue stands out for its conspicuously irregular arrangement, which resembles a mosaic of heterogeneous elements.

In terms of narrative technique, the diegetic form of *E.* 8 features two overlapping layers. On the first level, the poet-narrator tells the story of how Damon and Alphesiboeus sang alternately. On the second level, Damon produces a monologue without action while Alphesiboeus comes up with a lively mime featuring two actors. However, Alphesiboeus most probably abides by the conventions of the monologic form, since the single speeches seem to be uttered by the protagonist alone, i.e. the anonymous love-smitten woman who performs the magic ritual (but cf. 8.105–8n.).

On the eclogue: Bethe (1892, pp. 590–6); Klotz (1920, pp. 151–8); Weyman (1926–7b; 1927–8); E. Pfeiffer (1933, pp. 34–47); Büchner (1955, cols. 1228–36); Otis (1963, pp. 105–20); Fantazzi (1966, pp. 179–82); Klingner (1967, pp. 134–46); Wormell (1969, pp. 10–12); Putnam (1970, pp. 255–92); Richter (1970); Leach (1974, pp. 153–8); Van Sickle (1978, pp. 178–83); Alpers (1979, pp. 132–5); Tandoi (1981); E. A. Schmidt (1987, pp. 174–7); M. O. Lee (1989, pp. 58–69); Rudd (1996, pp. 58–61); T. K. Hubbard (1998, pp. 111–17); Papanghelis (1999, pp. 50–7); Binder, Effe (2001, pp. 89–91); Lipka (2001, pp. 48–53; 76–7; 140–1); Gioseffi (2004a, pp. 39–62); von Albrecht (2007, pp. 31–4); Fabre-Serris (2008, pp. 77–82); Davis (2012, pp. 99–119); Kania (2016, pp. 128–44); Marchetta (2018, pp. 7–97; 269–392).

Specific issues: Bennett (1930) (Asinius Pollio); Lavagnini (1935) (Theocritus and Sophron); Wilkinson (1936) (ll. 53–9); Pasquali (1942, p. 186 = 1951, pp. 14–15 = 1994,

p. 278) (l. 88 and Varius' *De morte*); Andriani (1964) (ll. 17; 30); Levi (1966) (ll. 6–13); Braun (1969) (ll. 52–6; Damon's refrain); Bowersock (1971) (date); Garson (1971, pp. 200–3) (Theocritus); Levi (1971) (*addendum* to Levi, 1966); Van Sickle (1974) (l. 107); Muecke (1975, pp. 177–8) (the pastoral genre); Tupet (1976, pp. 223–83) (magic); Cupaiuolo (1977, pp. 36; 120–6) (structure); O. Skutsch (1977) (l. 76); Solodow (1977) (*E*. 8-10 and the poet's 'weariness'); Tarrant (1978) (addressee); Bowersock (1978) (answer to Tarrant, 1978); Timpanaro (1978, pp. 270–87) (l. 41); Van Sickle (1981) (addressee); Gallazzi (1982) (ll. 53–62: *P. Narm. Inv.* 66.632); La Penna (1982) (suicide of 'Damon' at dawn); Kenney (1983, pp. 44–59) (love and elegy); Mayer (1983a, pp. 21–7) (addressee); Néraudau (1983) (Asinius Pollio as a poet); Köhnken (1984) (addressee); Nussbaum (1984) (ll. 37–41); Zetzel (1984) (Servius; addressee = Augustus); Segal (1987) (Theocr. *id.* 2); Mankin (1988) (addressee); Faraone (1989) (ll. 80–1); Jenkyns (1989, pp. 28–30; cf. 1998, pp. 160–1) (Arcadia); Farrell (1991a) (addressee); Barchiesi (1994) (Horace's Canidia and magical 'reversibility'); Gigante Lanzara (1994) (ll. 52–60); Sallmann (1995) (magic); Esposito (1996, pp. 23–32) (l. 55 and Calp. *ecl.* 4); Green (1996) (addressee); Hollis (1996, pp. 26–7) (ll. 85–8); Coppola (1998) (ll. 6–10); Sallmann (1998) (Damon's song); Perutelli (2000) (l. 88); Bernardi Perini (2002) (ll. 85–9); Clauss (2002–3) (l. 7); Marangoni (2002–3) (l. 11); Danielewicz (2005, p. 324) (ll. 42–7: acrostic *inanis*); MacDonald (2005) (Theocr. *id.* 2); Katz, Volk (2006) (erotic magic); Nauta (2006) (ll. 6–13); Scafoglio (2006, pp. 73–5) (female characters); Thibodeau (2006) (addressee); Cairns (2008, pp. 63–70) (addressee); Lebek (2008) (ll. 85–9); Vox (2009) (Theocr. *id.* 6); Dzino (2011) (Asinius Pollio and the siege of Salona); Jones (2011, pp. 50–1) (ll. 5–8); Heyworth (2015, pp. 215–16) (ll. 47–50); Heyworth (2015, pp. 217–18) (ll. 80–1); Farrell (2016, pp. 400–1) (l. 66); Wasdin (2018, pp. 73–6) (epithalamium); Cucchiarelli (2019b, pp. 497; 517–18) (l. 88 and Varius' *De morte*); Gagliardi (2020) (l. 30 *Hesperus*); Guidetti (2022) (Damon's song as an 'anti-epithalamium').

1–16. This is the longest prologue to an eclogue delivered by the poet in his own voice (compare the three lines of *E*. 4–13; twelve lines in *E*. 6.1–12; eight in *E*. 10.1–8; the short preamble opening *E*. 2 is more a narrative frame than a prologue). It is concluded by three transitional lines (14–16), which introduce the setting and Damon's song. Similarly, Alphesiboeus' song is introduced by a two-line 'interlude' at 8.62–3, in which the poet addresses the Muses (not mentioned here). A further subdivision can be detected between the long syntactical structure at 8.1–5, in which the topic is outlined, and 8.6–13 addressing V.'s illustrious friend: here, the style is exclamatory, featuring a conspicuous direct question in 8.7. The structure of the passage draws the reader's attention to the 'intrusion' of 6–13 into an otherwise 'normal', eight-line prologue (1–5 + 14–16: cf. *E*. 10.1–8). Note also that the incipit proper is five lines long: five is an important number in the *E*. (cf. 1.1–10n.; Introduction, p. 24, n. 60). In this poem, structures and quantities are very significant, considering the artful symmetries between the two songs and, as a result, the conspicuous asymmetry of 6–13. In 1–5, the poet gestures towards the idea of 'enchantment', which foreshadows the content of Alphesiboeus' song (see 8.4n.), while the mention of a lynx may allude to Damon's 'Maenalian' song (8.3n.).

386   ECLOGUE 8

For a Theocritean parallel, cf. *id.* 17, i.e. the encomium of Ptolemy II, which is similarly introduced by a long proem (twelve lines); see 8.11n.

1 Pastorum Musam. A variation on the theme of Tityrus' inaugural *siluestrem... Musam* (*E.* 1.2). The echo of *E.* 1 points to a new beginning, precisely as the book moves towards a conclusion. The *E.* have already proven their originality (esp. *E.* 4 and 6) and their innovativeness in terms of agonistic form (*E.* 7): the poet now returns to his typically pastoral (and Theocritean) style. An idea of repetition is also implicit in 8.5. Note the spondaic rhythm in the first three feet of the line. **Damonis et Alphesiboei.** These names, previously unattested in the Greek pastoral tradition, are featured only in three of V.'s *E.*: Damon appears here and at *E.* 3.17; 23 (note that the third eclogue is explicitly placed under the auspices of Asinius Pollio), whereas Alphesiboeus only appears here and at *E.* 5.73 (in the nom. case and, as here, in line-ending position; for a similar case featuring a five-syllable Greek name, cf. *E.* 3.37). The names' order of appearance mirrors the order of the two songs: the same is true of the contestants in *E.* 7 (cf. 7.2n.).

2 immemor herbarum...mirata iuuenca. The amazement of this heifer, captivated by the Orphic enchantment of song, instantly activates the pastoral etymology of Alphesiboeus' name (i.e. 'he who gains oxen': 5.73n.). For the phrase *immemor herbarum* see *G.* 3.498 *immemor herbae* (the sick horse); cf. also *G.* 3.216 *nec nemorum patitur meminisse nec herbae* (love's effect on the bull); for *herba* in the context of pastures, cf. *E.* 3.55; 93; 6.59; 7.57. In the finale of *id.* 6 (a competition-laden, but scarcely 'agonistic', poem), the heifers are described as happily dancing to the music of Damon's flute and Daphnis' pipes (45 ὠρχεῦντο...πόρτιες). For music's effect on animals, cf. also *E.* 6.27 (another reference to dance: not to 'static' enchantment, as here). In *E.* 5.26, mourning (not song) impedes grazing. Alphesiboeus' song includes the mention of a 'forgetful' *bucula*: in that case, however, the emphasis is on the passage of time (88 *nec serae meminit decedere nocti*), while the forgetfulness is not caused by music (the *bucula* seeks her *iuuencus*). Note that, in l. 4, a prototype of V.'s humanized heifer (Calvus' *Io*) will soon make an appearance through a verbatim quotation (see n. ad loc.).

3 certantis. A technical term for the agon, potentially echoing the preceding poem (cf. esp. *E.* 7.16 *certamen...magnum*). Here, however, competition and its mechanisms will only be referred to one more time, i.e. at 8.62 (*responderit*). The amazement seizing nature (the heifer, the lynxes, and the rivers) pushes competition into the background. **stupefactae...lynces.** The lynx is a wild animal, here obviously enchanted by sweet song: for a Theocritean parallel see *id.* 1.71–2, where jackals, wolves, and a lion mourn Daphnis' death; cf. also *Aen.* 1.323 *maculosae...lyncis.* The animal is connected with Pan (*Hymn. Hom.* 19[*Pan.*].24) and often associated with Mount Maenalus, here repeatedly referred to (8.21n.): cf. esp. Callim. *hymn.* 3[*Dian.*].88–9 ὁ δὲ κρέα λυγκὸς ἔταμνε / Μαιναλίης ('he [i.e. Pan] was cutting the meat of a Maenalian / lynx'). V. himself will establish a link

ECLOGUE 8   387

between the lynx and Dionysian cult in G. 3.264 *lynces Bacchi*. Lynxes were said to have taken part in the Dionysian parade staged by Ptolemy II in Alexandria (see Callixeinus of Rhodes, *FGrH* 627 F 2.32 Jac. = Athen. 5.201c); cf. also Prop. 3.17.8; Ov. *met.* 3.668; 4.24–5; 15.413; Pers. 1.101; Nemes. *ecl.* 3.65 (in Eur. *Alc.* 579, the lynxes are enchanted by Apollo's music). The appearance of a Dionysian animal must have pleased the illustrious addressee, a renowned tragedian (and man of action), regardless of whether he ought to be identified with Asinius Pollio (which is very likely: see below 8.10n.). For wild animals taking part in song, cf. the Bacchic passage at *E.* 6.27–8 (*feras…uideres / ludere*: a more dynamic participation). For amazement engendered by (Orpheus') song, cf. *G.* 4.481 *quin ipsae stupuere domus atque intima Leti* (tigers are similarly tamed in G. 4.510). See further *Enc. Virg.* IV, esp. p. 1046, s.v. *stupeo* (L. Cristante).

4 mutata suos requierunt flumina cursus. The rivers, 'transformed' (in their nature), 'brought their flow to a halt': in the same way the cows turn away from the grass and the lynxes, such wild and active predators, remain stunned. The transitive (and causative) use of the verb *requiesco* presupposes Calvus' *Io*, fr. 13 Bläns. = Court. *sol quoque perpetuos meminit requiescere cursus*; see the pseudo-Virgilian *Ciris* 233 *rapidos…requiescunt flumina cursus*; cf. also Prop. 2.22.25. The syntactic peculiarity of this line is confirmed by the trivialized reading *liquere* in γ² (while γ has *linquere*). For the possibility of a syntactic calque on Greek ἀναπαύω see Lunelli (1969, pp. 79–89). Correspondingly, it is unpersuasive to read *suos…cursus* as internal acc. with *mutata* (cf. *Aen.* 1.658) and *requierunt* as intransitive, which would redundantly imply that the rivers change their flow (by slowing it down?) and then come to a halt. The rivers' return to their source appears in Euripides' adynaton at *Med.* 410–11, while halting rivers is part of Medea's magical arts in Apoll. Rhod. 3.532 καὶ ποταμοὺς ἵστησιν ἄφαρ κελαδεινὰ ῥέοντας (cf. Val. Fl. 6.443 *mutat agros fluuiumque uias*). For an unspecified 'enchantment' involving rivers, cf. Orpheus in Apoll. Rhod. 1.27 θέλξαι ἀοιδάων ἐνοπῇ ποταμῶν τε ῥέεθρα (note also Hor. *carm.* 1.12.9–10 [*Orphea*] *rapidos morantem / fluminum lapsus*; Prop. 3.2.3–4). While the lynxes' amazement befits Damon's Maenalian song (see above, 8.3n.), the effect of poetry on the rivers is better suited to Alphesiboeus' interest in magic: cf. *Aen.* 4.487–9 *haec se carminibus promittit…sistere aquam fluuiis*. As for *mutare*, note that the verb refers to the 'preternatural' aspect of metamorphosis in l. 70; cf. *E.* 6.78. V.'s allusion to Calvus' *Io* acquires particular significance if the poem's addressee is Asinius Pollio, who was both personally and intellectually close to Catullus and the neoteric circle (see 8.6n.).

5 Damonis Musam dicemus et Alphesiboei. The three key names featured in the first line (i.e. the two singers and the Muse) reappear here, at the end of the poem's opening, with the contestants framing the hexameter. They also anticipate one of the main stylistic traits of the eclogue: the use of repetition and redundancy, typical of folk poetry, particularly in its pastoral genre (cf. esp. 8.47–50n.).

388 ECLOGUE 8

6–13. These eight lines are conspicuously extraneous to the rest of the prologue: note the abrupt allocution *tu mihi*, which is then left hanging due to a new sentence in 8.7. Without this passage, the prologue would be perfectly 'normal': eight lines (1–5 + 14–16) introducing the two songs that occupy the remainder of the poem. As a result, the reader has the impression that 6–13 is a fragment, an enthusiastic yet unfinished train of thought, by means of which the poet dedicates his *carmina* (i.e. the whole pastoral collection?) to an important addressee. The passage reads almost like a remnant of what could have been a more fleshed-out dedicatory prologue (or epilogue) to the whole book: an ivy wreath (8.12–13 *hanc...hederam*), which ought to be worn by V.'s important friend. Yet this quasi-impromptu dedication ends up being limited to *E.* 8 alone and resembling a non-dedication, since the dedicatee is never explicitly named. Without a doubt, the addressee is Pollio (see 8.6n.; 8n.; 10n.; 11n.; 11–12n.): V. seems to imply that Pollio's name is so crucial to the *E.* that it does not even need to be mentioned. Perhaps, however, V. did not want to establish excessively close ties between his own work and the name of Pollio (a supporter of Mark Antony) at a time in which, after 40 BCE, any dream of peace and equilibrium among the triumvirs (i.e. Pollio's main political project) appeared ever more unrealistic.

6 tu mihi. The verb (presumably 'listen!', or the like) is never expressed, as the sentence is interrupted by the two questions at 8.7–10. The sentence is deliberately left unfinished, but the emphasis on the two initial pronouns (*tu mihi*) draws the reader's attention to an 'open debate' between the poet and the addressee. In this context, the two subordinate clauses introduced by *seu...seu* appear to be parenthetical; further clarification is then offered at 8.8 (*mihi...tua*). For the two pronouns, cf. *Aen.* 1.135 *quos ego...—sed motos praestat componere fluctus.* Here, however, the reader has the impression that the thought is somehow complete, not interrupted by an actual aposiopesis (unlike at *Aen.* 1.135), despite the syntactical discontinuity of the phrasing. The key is that the two protagonists (*tu mihi...*) are eventually reunited, as is clear from 8.7–10. As in a true aposiopesis, at any rate, a crucial detail is missing: i.e. the name of V.'s addressee. Yet the reader of V.'s pastoral book can have no doubts as to who the *tu* might be: in all likelihood, it is Asinius Pollio, previously celebrated in *E.* 3 and extolled in *E.* 4 as V.'s illustrious dedicatee. As Pollio was about to set sail for Greece and Cilicia, the neoteric poet Cinna dedicated a *Propemptikon* to him, presumably around 56 BCE: the poem became a Roman prototype of the genre, which seems to be echoed here. The clearest confirmation of Pollio's identity comes from the historical and geographical references at 8.6–7, the mention of tragic production (8.10), and other clues, such as the echo of neoteric motifs and style. Finally, if Pollio is the addressee of this poem, V. would create a symmetry between the third and the third-to-last eclogue, both dedicated to him. Both poems are the longest in the book: over one hundred lines each. More precisely, the total number of lines in *E.* 8 is 110 (assuming that 8.28a is genuine), a very significant figure for Pollio. In fact, during his consulship (40 BCE), Pollio was assigned the task of inaugurating

ECLOGUE 8 389

a new *saeculum*, i.e. 110 years, according to the counting system most commonly used in the Augustan age (cf. Hor. *carm. saec.* 21 *undenos deciens per annos*; see 4.5n.). Note that *E.* 3, too, is most probably 110 lines long (given the deletion of 3.43n.), and that in *E.* 3 the Golden Age is mentioned in relation to Pollio's political project (see 3.89n.). In sum, V. provides his readers (and Pollio himself) with several clues as to the identity of the mysterious *tu* invoked in *E.* 8. V.'s omission of the verb and his silence on the addressee's identity foreshadow another feature of the eclogue as a whole, a rather reticent poem (the protagonists of both songs remain unnamed, and...who wins the contest?). **seu magni superas iam saxa Timaui.** The Timavus is a karst river which, originating in what is now Mount Snežnik (in Slovenia), enters karst caves and resurfaces not far from the Adriatic Sea, outflowing in the gulf of Panzano (part of the gulf of Trieste) near San Giovanni di Duino (see *Enc. Virg.* V.1, pp. 177–9, s.v. *Timavo* [M. Pavan]; *Virg. Enc.* III, pp. 1270–1, s.v. *Timavus* [D. Mankin]). The river's impressive resurgence springs, commonly known today as the Mouths of the Timavus, are described by V. in *Aen.* 1.244–6 (note esp. *Aen.* 1.245 *per ora nouem uasto cum murmure montis*); cf. also *G.* 3.475 *Iapidis arua Timaui.* Its outlet faced two small islands, here referred to as *saxa*; the saline nature of the outlet (or some of its branches) must have fuelled the local belief that the river is the 'origin and mother of the sea' (Strab. 5.1.8 [214]). The cult of the Timavus river, well attested till the end of the second century BCE, further motivates the adjective *magni* (used of deities at e.g. *E.* 3.104; *G.* 3.1; *Aen.* 3.104); cf. Sil. 12.215 *sacro...Timauo.* The temporal adverb *iam* describes the unnamed addressee as passing the *saxa* in front of the Timavus river after sailing along the Illyrian coast (8.7n.): this implies that he was sailing along the coast of Illyria from south to north, evidently heading to Italy. The same itinerary leads Antenor, a fugitive from Troy, to founding *Patauium* (Padua) in *Aen.* 1.242–6: *Antenor potuit... / Illyricos penetrare sinus atque intima tutus / regna Liburnorum et fontem superare Timaui, / unde per ora nouem uasto cum murmure montis / it mare proruptum et pelago premit arua sonanti* (note the verb *superare*, as here). It cannot be ruled out that Antenor's legend may have been of interest to a tragic poet such as the eminent addressee (cf. *E.* 8.10n.). A tragedy on the *Antenoridai* was composed by Sophocles, as Strabo reports (13.608 = *TrGF*, IV, frr. 137–9, pp. 160–2 Radt), and Accius wrote a play on the same subject (*trag.* 119–26 R.[3]). In the Augustan age, the otherwise unknown poet Largus (mentioned by Ov. *Pont.* 4.16.17–18) had an interest in the topic. The Timavus river itself was commonly connected to the Trojan legend: note the epithet *Antenoreus* in Lucan. 7.194 and *Phrygius* in Claudian. 7.120; for other testimonies see *Enc. Virg.* I, pp. 191–3, s.v. *Antenore* (L. Braccesi); *Virg. Enc.* I, p. 92, s.v. *Antenor* (A. Feldherr). It is possible that Pollio himself, on his way back from Illyria, made a stop in northern Italy: at least for some time, he operated in the Cisalpine region during the expropriations (see below, 8.7n.). However, while Antenor in the *Aeneid* goes past the river's source by land to reach

390 ECLOGUE 8

the location of the future city of Padua, V.'s very important friend seems to be travelling by sea past the islets near the river's outlet. The young Tiberius will make a stop in Padua on his way to Illyria during the campaign of 21 BCE: *cum Illyricum petens iuxta Patauium adisset Geryonis oraculum*, etc. (Suet. *Tib.* 14.3). At any rate, the Timavus river was a very important landmark in the region, not least because it marked the boundary between Italy and the Illyrian people: hence the phrase *Iapydis arua Timaui* in *G.* 3.475. In sum, the Timavus river certainly deserves to be mentioned in the itinerary of a Roman general who carried out successful campaigns in the western part of the Balkan Peninsula (i.e. almost certainly Pollio: see again 8.7n.). One of the most celebrated victories against the Illyrians was that of C. Sempronius Tuditanus, who was awarded a triumph in 129 BCE and made sacred offerings (probably an altar) to the Timavus river, according to a fragmentary inscription in Saturnian verse from Aquileia (*CIL* V, p. 1031, n. 8270 = *CLE* 1859 Buech.). That campaign may have been the subjectmatter of Hostius' *Bellum Histricum*, a poem which must have given a certain literary fame to the geography and topography of Illyria (on Sempronius Tuditanus' activity in the area, cf. also Plin. *nat.* 3.129). The (future) triumphant general is awaited at Rome for the ceremony: and Rome is where the poet now is, eager for his return.

6–7 seu... / siue. The alternative between different places, introduced by *seu...siue* vel sim., is typical of invocations, paralleled in the pastoral tradition by Theocr. *id.* 1.123–4; but cf. Hom. *Il.* 16.514–16; Aesch. *Eum.* 292–8; Aristoph. *Nub.* 269–74.

7 oram Illyrici legis aequoris. The ancients normally sailed along the coast, in order to avoid the dangers of the open sea: *G.* 2.44 *primi lege litoris oram*. Here, the expected *litoris* is replaced by *aequoris*: this is perhaps because it would have been more difficult to sail very close to a coast so notoriously jagged. The poet imagines that his illustrious friend's fleet follows a more or less straight route along the 'edge' of the Illyrian Sea (at any rate, expressive inversion is typical of V.'s poetic language). Note also that the coast of Illyria was inhabited by warlike and rebellious tribes, as in Iuv. 8.117 (*uitandum est*) *Illyricum...latus*. If the addressee of *E.* 8 is indeed Pollio, however, it is hardly surprising that he followed such a route to return to Rome (instead of crossing the Adriatic Sea to reach Brundisium, as was commonly done at the time). In fact, Pollio probably wanted to make a stop and join other forces in Cisalpine Gaul, where he had been governor for some time (see 3.84n.; for Pollio's occupation of Venetia during the Perusine War, cf. Vell. 2.76.2; see also above 8.6n.). Despite the lack of direct evidence, it cannot be ruled out that he also carried out military operations against Illyrian tribes on the northern coast (cf. 8.8n.; 12–13n.). **en erit umquam.** For this type of question/exclamation, cf. 1.67 *en umquam patrios* (n.). The interjection *en* reappears at 8.9 (for a similar repetition of *en* cf. *E.* 1.71). For a similar syntactical break, see *E.* 3.40; but cf. *G.* 1.384; 4.67; 252. With such a laudatory phrase (this is not a real doubt), the poet expresses his impatience to see his important friend again, and finally have the opportunity to celebrate him: cf. *E.* 4.53–4.

8 mihi cum liceat tua dicere facta. The *mihi* left hanging in 8.6 is now reasserted and integrated with a new thought: the poet intends to celebrate his friend's achievements (*mihi…liceat*). At the time of the *E.*, Asinius Pollio was returning home from Illyria: there, in his capacity as proconsul of Macedonia and counting on Mark Antony's support, he had led important military operations, suppressing the Parthinian revolt and celebrating a triumph on 25 October 39 BCE: cf. *Fast. triumph. Capitol.* (*CIL* I².1, p. 50) 715; Cass. Di. 48.41.7; Appian. 5.75 (320); *MRR*, II, pp. 387–8. He then used his war booty to build what soon became a crucial hub of Augustan culture, the *Atrium Libertatis* with its public library (Suet. *Aug.* 29.5; Plin. *nat.* 7.115; 35.10; Isid. *orig.* 6.5.2). Others, less plausibly, favour an identification with Octavian, who actually spent time in Dalmatia several years later (in 35 BCE). On the debated issue see *Enc. Virg.* II, pp. 914–16, s.v. *Illirico* (M. Pavan), along with Tarrant (1978); Nauta (2006, pp. 312–13). The *Parthini* (or *Partheni*) were located in southern Illyria, on the hills near Epidamnus (Dyrrhachium) and Apollonia, though it is possible that Pollio also carried out military operations against coastal tribes in the northern Adriatic regions. His confiscations in Dalmatia are recorded in Flor. *epit.* 2.25, whereas Servius (*ad E.* 3.88; 4.1) talks about his conquest of Salona (near present-day Split in Croatia); cf. also Porph. ad Hor. *carm.* 2.1.15. It is quite suspicious, however, that the story is connected to the existence of a son of Pollio named *Saloninus* (Serv. *ad E.* 4.1; cf. above, p. 197). Pollio's siege of Salona is described in detail in the second chapter of Thomas Archidiaconus' *Historia Salonitana* (XII sec.), a local chronicle of dubious reliability. At any rate, in Hor. *carm.* 2.1.16, Pollio's triumph is called 'Dalmatian', with a clear geographical reference to the Illyrian region (and perhaps to the general's military operations in the rest of Illyria as well: see below, 8.12–13n.). Significantly, the same hexameter clausula appeared in the fourth eclogue, dedicated to Pollio: *spiritus et quantum sat erit tua dicere facta* (*E.* 4.54: a wish to celebrate the *puer*, which here seems to be transferred to the *puer*'s 'ambassador'). Note, in *E.* 8.8 and the following lines, the rhythmic predominance of dactyls, befitting the liveliness of both syntax and thought.

9 en erit ut. Cf. 8.7 *en erit umquam*: another repetition, as in 8.1 and 5; but here the distance is shorter. **liceat totum mihi ferre per orbem.** In contrast to Pollio's return trip home along the Adriatic coast, the poet now opens up global horizons to his friend's poetic genius.

10 sola Sophocleo tua carmina digna coturno. The phrase presupposes primacy, underscored by alliteration of /s/ and /c/: only Pollio's poetry is worthy of wearing Sophocles' buskin, i.e. the emblem of the tragic poet deemed to be the greatest of the well-known triad (cf. Aristotle's judgement in the *Poetics*; but see Aristoph. *Ran.* 76). Pollio's excellence in tragic poetry is testified to by Horace, *sat.* 1.10.42–3 (cf. also *carm.* 2.1.9–12, esp. 12 *Cecropio…coturno*, which appears to be a variation on *Sophocleo…coturno* and, therefore, confirms that Pollio is V.'s addressee: see further below, 8.12–13n.), whereas Octavian's one 'experiment' as

392 ECLOGUE 8

a tragedian was not successful (Suet. *Aug.* 85.2). If V., as has been supposed, were addressing Octavian, here he would both offend Pollio and embarrass Octavian himself. Note, finally, that the reader is familiar with Pollio's poetry from *E.* 3.86 (*noua carmina*; the mention of a bull in the same context is well suited to tragedy). V., therefore, wants to extend to the entire world a project he started in *E.* 3, i.e. the celebration of his friend's poetry. For the phrase *carmina digna* + abl., cf. Cornelius Gallus, fr. 4.1–2 Bläns. = 2.6–7 Court. *tandem fecerunt carmina Musae / quae possem domina deicere digna mea*; see also *E.* 4.3n. and 9.36n., as well as 10.2n. That Pollio had a strong interest in tragedy, which could be connected with a war scenario (as here), is confirmed by Pollio's letter to Cicero from Cordoba (Cic. *fam.* 10.32.5), in which Pollio mentions one of his own *praetextae*.

11 a te principium, tibi desinam. 'Origin' in the chronological sense, because Pollio was the first admirer of V.'s Muse, as is clarified by the following *iussis / carmina coepta tuis*. If the phrase were interpreted in an 'editorial' sense (where *principium* = *E.* 1), it would support the view that *tu* = Octavian, the young *deus* who opens the book. Cf. Theocr. *id.* 17, esp. 3–4 ἀνδρῶν δ᾽ αὖ Πτολεμαῖος ἐνὶ πρώτοισι λεγέσθω / καὶ πύματος καὶ μέσσος 'but among men let Ptolemy be named first / and at the end, and in the middle'; see Hom. *Il.* 9.96–7 ἄναξ ἀνδρῶν Ἀγάμεμνον, / ἐν σοὶ μὲν λήξω, σέο δ᾽ ἄρξομαι, 'leader of men, Agamemnon, / you will be my end, you will be my beginning' (in both passages, unlike here, the interlocutor's name is explicitly stated, even though the *Iliad* passage is far from laudatory). For a more specifically metapoetic parallel, cf. Hes. *theog.* 34 σφᾶς δ᾽ αὐτὰς πρῶτόν τε καὶ ὕστατον αἰὲν ἀείδειν (i.e. the Muses, who gave the staff to the poet). Asinius Pollio's role as a promoter of the arts is emphasized in *E.* 3.84 (and 3.88–9), as well as in Hor. *sat.* 1.10.84–8. Note also that, according to *E.* 4.11–12, Pollio's consulate marks a new beginning and a regeneration of history and of the cosmos as a whole (thus, the encomium of the grown-up *puer* takes place in the latter part of V.'s life: cf. *E.* 4.53–4). The formula *ab Ioue principium*, here evidently reworked, is importantly paralleled in a 'Pollionian' passage: *E.* 3.60n. Everything seems to confirm that Pollio is the dedicatee, and that he appreciates echoes and reworkings of Aratus (which feature prominently in *E.* 3). The idea will reappear in Hor. *epist.* 1.1.1 *prima dicte mihi, summa dicende Camena* (Maecenas). **desinam.** The reading *desinam* (P) is certainly correct (cf. Hom. *Il.* 9.97 ἄρξομαι), whereas M's *desinet*, known to ancient commentators, may have gained popularity because it eliminates the clash of *desinam* and *accipe* (without elision; here the hiatus coincides with a syntactical break and the bucolic diaeresis, as in *Culex* 245). The poet's promise to 'conclude' with the dedicatee refers to an unspecified future. At any rate, the verb *desinam* introduces the idea of an ending for the first time in the pastoral book (cf. 8.63n.).

11–12 accipe iussis / carmina coepta tuis. Maecenas' *haud mollia iussa* for the *Georgics* are well known (*G.* 3.41). For the meaning of the verb, however, cf. *E.* 6.9

ECLOGUE 8 393

non iniussa cano (n.). The early support that Asinius Pollio provided to V. is alluded to at *E.* 3.84. Based on the context, V. seems to be referring to his own pastoral poetry in general, rather than to *E.* 8 alone: if so, it is quite peculiar that this general reference appears in the third-to-last poem rather than in the first or the last one (see 8.6–13n.).

12–13 hanc… / inter uictricis hederam tibi serpere lauros. The bay leaves, symbolizing the glory of military victory (*uictricis*), are coupled with ivy, alluding to V.'s poetic offering to Pollio (note *hanc*, emphasized by the hyperbaton: see 8.6–13n.); cf. *E.* 4.19 *errantis hederas*, as well as 7.25 (in the context of poetic glory). Pollio strove to reconcile Antony with Octavian: correspondingly, the bond between two different cultural (and political) symbols captures the syncretism characterizing *E.* 4; for a political reworking of the motif, cf. Quint. *inst.* 10.1.92 (Domitian). Dionysus' plant, at any rate, must please a tragic author such as the addressee of this poem. As a matter of fact, ivy and bay can and do grow together, the former enveloping the latter (hence *hederam…serpere*). The union of these two plants symbolizes the pairing of military action and literary culture: Pollio's profile fits the bill. Note that, a few years later, he used the booty from his military victories to build a monumental library (Plin. *nat.* 7.115 *bibliotheca, quae prima in orbe ab Asinio Pollione ex manubiis publicata Romae est*). **lauros.** Charisius, *gramm.* I, p. 135.26 K. = p. 172.18 Barw. quotes the line with the fourth-declension form *laurus*; the same applies to the nom. plur. form in *Aen.* 3.91 *liminaque laurusque dei*; cf., however, *E.* 6.83 *lauros* (but *laurus* M; see n. ad loc.). The military triumph, which the bay leaves celebrate, follows closely V.'s mention of the tragic buskin (10 *Sophocleo…coturno*): the same sequence accompanies Pollio's name in Hor. *carm.* 2.1.12–16, further confirming the addressee's identity here (see above, 8.10n.).

14–16. Three 'transitional' lines introduce the poet's report of the two 'competing' songs. Note that the landscape which provides a backdrop to the unhappy lover's monologue contrasts with the setting of Corydon's monologue in *E.* 2: there, burning heat and noonday sun dominated the scene; here, by contrast, a cold dawn emerges from nocturnal darkness (8.14n.), a time not unsuited to suicide (8.20n.; 58–60n.).

14 Frigida…noctis…umbra. Cf. *E.* 2.8 *nunc etiam pecudes umbras et frigora captant.* The scene is set in fine weather, perhaps between late spring and early summer (cf. below, 8.15). Note the 'framing' positioning of adj. and noun: the line, like the sky, can 'barely' (*uix*) free itself from 'cold darkness'.

15 cum ros in tenera pecori gratissimus herba. The line will reappear verbatim in the spring-like context of *G.* 3.326 *et ros in tenera pecori gratissimus herba* (where *cum* is replaced by *et*); cf. also Varr. *rust.* 2.2.10 *cum prima luce exeunt pastum, propterea quod tunc herba ruscida* (= *roscida*) *meridianam, quae est aridior, iucunditate praestat* (referring, however, to summer). The adj. *tenera*, used of grass (8.2n.), corresponds to ἀπαλά in the sense of 'tender', 'delicate' (to chew):

394   ECLOGUE 8

cf., for instance, *id.* 8.67–8. The adj. *mollis*, on the other hand, means 'soft', 'comfortable' (to walk on, or to sit on, vel sim.), as in *E.* 3.55 *in molli consedimus herba* (see n. ad loc.; cf. *id.* 5.55). For the superlative *gratissimus*, a type rare in *E.*, cf. *E.* 7.61; see also 3.57n.

   16 incumbens tereti…oliuae. Damon is presumably leaning on the trunk of an olive tree, of round or oblong shape, free from unevenness (*tereti*, i.e. 'smooth', perhaps because the tree is still young): cf. *Aen.* 6.207 *teretis circumdare truncos* and 7.665 *tereti…mucrone.* With subtle realism, V. does not describe the singer as reclining on the grass (which is still wet, it seems, with fresh dew; contrast *E.* 3.55 [see 8.15n.]), but lets the reader imagine him standing, suggested by *incumbens.* For a similar posture, cf. perhaps Mezentius in *Aen.* 10.835 *arboris acclinis trunco* (Plin. *nat.* 8.39 *non cubantem et adclinem arbori,* referring to a species of moose, apparently incapable of bending its hocks and lying down); but cf. esp. Ov. *met.* 6.335 *incumbens arbore palmae* (Latona in labour; see F. Bömer's commentary [quoted above, 6.78n.], p. 98, ad loc.). V. probably has Theocr. *id.* 3.38 in mind: ποτὶ τὰν πίτυν ὧδ' ἀποκλινθείς (cf. also Callim. *hymn.* 4[*Del.*].209–10: once again, Latona). In V., *oliua* normally refers not just to the fruit, but the entire tree (cf. *E.* 5.16; *G.* 2.3); here, *oliuae* could be read as a synecdoche for 'olive-wood staff' (cf. *id.* 7.18–19), on which Damon would lean while singing and playing the *tibia* alternately: see Ov. *fast.* 1.177 *deus incumbens baculo, quod dextra gerebat; trist.* 4.1.11; *ThlL* VII.1.65–8. **sic coepit.** In the rarefied atmosphere of early morning, Damon begins his song, without the reader being given any further information (e.g. where is Alphesiboeus?). The use of *sic* draws the reader's attention to what follows, thereby making any conjunctions (such as *tum*) unnecessary after 8.14–15.

   17–61. Damon's song is composed of ten stanzas of variable length, each followed by a refrain line (assuming that 8.28a is genuine: cf. n. ad loc.). Unlike the case of *id.* 1 (see below, 8.21n.), the refrain does not open the herdsman's song; rather, the morning star (*Lucifer*) marks its beginning (contrast *id.* 1.64 ἄρχετε; cf., here, 8.21 *incipe*). Note also that Hesperus, astronomically identical with this star (8.17n.), will be summoned to conclude the entire book (*E.* 10.77 *uenit Hesperus, ite capellae;* but cf. *E.* 6.86). The number of lines in the single stanzas precisely matches Alphesiboeus' song, with a variation (perhaps an intentional one) in the last three stanzas (8.64–109n.). In terms of subject matter, note that the song includes three groups of three stanzas (starting with the *incipe* in the refrain, after a few introductory lines), adding up to nine stanzas (and ten refrain lines). Stanzas 2–4 (ll. 22–31) introduce the situation; then, stanzas 5–8 (ll. 32–51) develop the 'anti-epithalamium'; finally, stanzas 9–10 (ll. 52–61) reassert the lover's despair, making further use of adynata (ll. 52–6; cf. ll. 27–8): here, the protagonist's suicidal thoughts are expressed. Note that Alphesiboeus' 'reply' has a similar, albeit less evident, structure: 8.64–109n.

   17 Nascere…Lucifer. The star's etymology is activated: Lucifer 'brings' daylight along, preceding sunrise; cf. *Aen.* 2.801–2 *surgebat Lucifer… / ducebatque* diem (but see below on *ueniens age*); note also the simile featuring the young Pallas at *Aen.* 8.589–91. The Roman *Lucifer*, corresponding to the Greek Ἑωσφόρος, was identified by ancient scientists with Hesperus, the evening star (at least since Pythagoras, according to a tradition attested by Plin. *nat.* 2.37); in reality, both 'stars' are different manifestations of the planet Venus. According to a Latin literary cliché, perhaps echoing Callim. *Hec.* fr. 291 Pf. (= 113 H.), the planet appears twice in 24 hours (i.e. in the evening and in the following morning: this is in fact impossible, since Venus will set well before the sun if it appears before dawn, and vice versa): cf. Catull. 62.34–5; Cinn. fr. 6 Bläns. = Court.; *Ciris* 351–2; Hor. *carm.* 2.9.10–12. Here, on the other hand, Lucifer is kept distinct from the epithalamial Hesperus, mentioned with bitterness in 8.30n. From the lover's perspective, the new day can only bring sorrow, due to deceit and abandonment. Note the reversal of the traditional epithalamial celebration of the wedding night: here, dawn signals the beginning of a new day, and therefore the lover's separation from Nysa, whereas sunset means reunion with Mopsus. The opening of Damon's song befits the actual time of the day at which he starts singing (above, 8.14). **praeque…ueniens age.** Servius, presupposing an instance of the so-called tmesis (cf. above, 6.6n.), paraphrases *praeueniens age diem clarissimum.* Yet *prae* emphasizes the force of the verb *ago,* i.e. 'to push' (ahead), while *ueniens* expresses forward motion (thus, *Aen.* 2.802 *ducebatque diem* is a rather different image: here, Lucifer 'drags along' the day). Damon exhorts Lucifer to appear (cf., for instance, the invocation to Bacchus in *G.* 2.7), performing his duties as 'bearer of light', and remarks on the star's advanced position (*prae*): cf. Ov. *fast.* 3.877 *tres ubi Luciferos ueniens praemiserit Eos.* **diem…almum.** Note the pathetic contrast between the formulaic phrase *diem…almum* (the 'life-bringing' day; the ancients rightly connected *almus* with *alo*: Paul. Fest. p. 6 L.; *ThlL* I.1703.24–31) and the protagonist's wish for death, immediately expressed in 8.20 *extrema…hora.* For the phrase, cf. *Aen.* 5.64; *Ciris* 349; Hor. *carm.* 4.7.7–8; Manil. 3.187 *dies…alma.* For the suicidal protagonist's 'farewell to the sun', cf. Soph. *Ai.* 845–65; Callim. *epigr.* 23.1 Pf.

18 coniugis…Nysae. The noun must be read from the betrayed lover's point of view: he perceives his own love bond as a true *coniugium* (cf. the *foedus*-rhetoric in Catullus, esp. 87) and considers the girl, who has been taken away from him, as his legitimate *coniunx* (though it must have been obvious to Roman readers that, in legal terms, this bond might well have been a mere *contubernium* between enslaved people); Theocritus' goatherd had chosen the less loaded term νύμφα at Theocr. *id.* 3.9. Note the 'epithalamial' sarcasm of 8.32 *o digno coniuncta uiro* (below, also 8.29 *uxor* [n.]): see *Aen.* 3.330–1 *ereptae magno flammatus amore / coniugis* (Ov. *her.* 8.18); cf. Prop. 2.8.29 *abrepta desertus coniuge Achilles,* as well as *Aen.* 4.172 *coniugium uocat, hoc praetexit nomine culpam.* The correspondence with 8.66 is subtle yet clear: there, *coniunx* refers to Daphnis (the term occurs only on these two occasions in the *E.*). The girl's name, unattested in the

396 ECLOGUE 8

pre-Virgilian pastoral tradition, has precise Dionysian implications: *Nysa*, in fact, was the mythical place (a mountain, a plain, or perhaps a city, variously situated in India, in Arabia, or elsewhere) where Dionysus was born and raised (cf. *Hymn. Hom.* 1[*Bacch.*].8; for *Nysa* as a mountain cf. *Aen.* 6.805). Nysa, or Nyssa (Νῦσα/Νύσσα), was also the name of the nymph who nurtured the infant god (Terpand. fr. 8 B. = 6 Gost., with A. Gostoli's commentary, Rome 1990, pp. 143–6, ad loc.; Serv. Dan. *ad E.* 6.15; cf. also Nonn. *Dionys.* 29.272); the god subsequently founded the city of Nysa in her honour (Arrian. *anab.* 5.1.6); cf. below, 8.26n. As for Alexis in *E.* 2 (i.e. the other unattainable object of desire in the *E.*), the Greek name Nysa is rich in literary echoes and references which, however, are alien to the pastoral world: is this a hint that, like Corydon, this lover does not stand a chance? The very opposite is the case with Daphnis in Alphesiboeus' song: you cannot get a more pastoral name than Daphnis (even though, at least initially, he does not seem willing to come back from the city: see 8.68n.). **indigno...amore.** Cf. 10.10. In erotic contexts, *dignus* refers to the lover's 'value' and, correspondingly, to that of the love bond itself (cf. [Tib.] 3.13.10; Ov. *rem.* 275); its opposite is *indignus*, for which cf. Ov. *rem.* 15; see also [Theocr.] *id.* 23.20 ἔρωτος ἀνάξιε.

19 queror. The anonymous lover's song will be a 'lament', often echoing the themes and forms of love-elegy. Both the term and the idea are typical of Roman erotic language, at least since Catull. 64.195 *meas audite querelas*; Pichon (1966, p. 248, s.v. *queri*). V transmits ll. 19–44.

19–20 et diuos... / ...adloquor. The lover addresses the gods, who (fruitlessly) bore witness to reciprocal oaths of love exchanged between him and the girl: here V. is carefully reworking Catull. 64.188–91, as well as 64.208–9. Yet it is well known that love promises must not be taken seriously: cf. Hes. fr. 124 M.-W.; Plat. *symp.* 183b; Callim. *epigr.* 25.3–4 Pf.; Catull. 70.3–4; *Aen.* 4.520–1; see *E.* 3.73n. Note also, in the epigram tradition, Dioscorides at *Anth. Pal.* 5.52 = *HE* 1491–6 G.-P., where the beloved Arsinoe breaks a love oath and triggers a sort of anti-epithalamial *paraklausithyron*. The variant reading *adloquar* is incorrect: the syntax requires the present tense (cf. here 19 *dum queror et*), which is also used in the verbatim quotation of these lines at *Ciris* 405–6. **quamquam nil testibus illis / profeci.** The idea of an 'agreement', ratified through an oath that involves the gods, is rather common (along with legal language in general) in love poetry: cf. Catull. 109. In Apoll. Rhod. 4.88–90, for instance, Medea summons the gods as 'witnesses' (ἐπίστορας; here *testibus*) to Jason's promise; note also Prop. 3.20.15–18 (esp. 18 *testis sidereae...corona deae*). But, of course, lovers' oaths do not reach the ears of the gods: cf. *E.* 3.73n.

20 extrema...hora. For the pathetic tone, cf. Catull. 64.191 *postrema comprecer hora*. In pastoral poetry, the union of lovesickness and death can readily bring Daphnis to mind: in fact, echoes of *id.* 1 will immediately be elicited by the refrain. For the intention of suicide, implied here, 8.58–60n.

21 incipe Maenalios mecum, mea tibia, uersus. The refrain line, which will reappear ten times (including l. 28a), is first uttered by Damon after four

ECLOGUE 8   397

introductory lines. The pattern differs from *id.* 1, in which the refrain opens Thyrsis' song: ἄρχετε βουκολικᾶς, Μοῖσαι φίλαι, ἄρχετ' ἀοιδᾶς 'begin, dear Muses, begin the pastoral song' (*id.* 1.64, reworked in [Mosch.] *epitaph. Bion.* 8, etc. ἄρχετε Σικελικαί, τῶ πένθεος ἄρχετε, Μοῖσαι 'begin, Sicilian Muses, the funeral lament'; note that both V. and [Moschus] use Theocritus' rhythmic sequence _ ⌣ ⌣ _ ⌣ ⌣ _ _); see below, 8.61n. In Theocritus, the refrain was allowed to interrupt the syntactical structure of a sentence (as e.g. in *id.* 1.82 and 2.105; cf. also [Mosch.] *epitaph. Bion.* 45), whereas in both songs of V.'s *E.* 8, each stanza is a self-contained unit. While Damon here echoes Theocritus' Thyrsis, Alphesiboeus will rework the only other refrain structure appearing in Theocritus, that in *id.* 2. For this typical feature of 'folk-poetry' style, cf. Schilling (1990). Note the emotionally emphatic position of the voc., further emphasized by the alliterative /m/, which highlights the idea of 'company' (*mecum*): cf. Hor. *carm.* 1.32.2 *lusimus tecum* (addressed to the *barbiton*, but also featuring the hymnic and religious notion of 'with your favour'). **Maenalios...uersus.** In reworking the refrain of *id.* 1, Damon replaces 'pastoral' (βουκολικᾶς) with the epithet which, deriving from Mount Maenalus, distinctly identifies Arcadia and, therefore, V.'s pastoral innovation, particularly in the wake of *E.* 7 (cf. esp. 7.4 *Arcades ambo*; cf. 10.14–15n.). Mount Maenalus, at any rate, appeared in *id.* 1.124, whereas [Moschus]'s refrain featured Sicilian Muses (*epit. Bion.* 8, etc.). **tibia** The *tibia*, corresponding to the Greek *aulos*, was a reed instrument (sometimes, however, made of bone). Ennius uses the term *tibia* in the context of the Muses (*ann.* 293 Sk.), drawing a traditional connection between the sound of the instrument and the hexameter form. Note also Lucr. 5.1384–5 *inde minutatim dulcis didicere querelas, / tibia quas fundit digitis pulsata canentum* (note, as here, the emphasis on lament, albeit sweet): in Lucretius, the instrument appears in the context of primeval farmers' life. Theocritus, in turn, mentions the *aulos* at *id.* 5.7; 6.43; 10.34; cf. also *epigr.* 5.1 G. (and *id.* 20.29). The term *tibia* occurs only here in the *E.*: perhaps V. chooses the term because of its phonetic qualities, particularly considering that the refrain is repeated multiple times; but he might just be seeking variation of the two more common terms, i.e. *calami* (8.24n.) and *fistula* (8.33n.), both appearing here near each other. The herdsman is evidently alone: thus, he must be the one who plays the *aulos* (*mea tibia*), clearly alternating between instrumental performance and song: cf. 5.14n.

22 **Maenalus.** At 8.22–4, the epithet *Maenalios* is explained: Maenalus is an Arcadian mountain, where Pan dwells. The mountain possesses the crucial ability to become 'sentient', i.e. to understand and repeat songs (the woods are 'sonorous', and the pine trees can 'speak'), by virtue of a phenomenon of natural 'resonance' which appears in 1.5n. (*siluae*). Note also that the mountain witnessed Atalanta's endeavours in the Arcadian version of her myth (6.61n.): cf. *schol.* Theocr. *id.* 1.124a, p. 80.10–14 Wend. **-que...-que.** The use of a double, correlative *-que*, modelled after Homer's τε...τε, is featured in Ennius (cf. *ann.* 170; 592 Sk.). For

398 ECLOGUE 8

other occurrences in the *E.*, see 5.28; 6.27; 10.23; a threefold *-que* appears at 6.32. Note that, in all these cases (except for 10.23), the phenomenon affects the fifth foot of the hexameter, in which a short syllable is useful. In both *G.* and *Aen.*, the device reappears almost immediately (cf. *G.* 1.11 and *Aen.* 1.18). **pinusque loquentis.** The mountain pine still characterizes the slopes of Maenalus (cf. *E.* 10.14–15 *pinifer... / Maenalus*). That the mountain is capable of speaking is hardly a surprise, considering its human past (7.24n.; 10.14–15n.). Pine trees are described as 'calling out' to the absent Tityrus at 1.38. The 'sweet' sound of a pine tree opened Theocr. *id.* 1.1–2 (see 1.1n.; cf. also Mosch. fr. 1.8 G. ἁ πίτυς ᾄδει), whereas in Nemes. *ecl.* 1.30–1 the 'racket' of a *garrula pinus* will be deemed excessive. Note the variant reading *pinosque* (**P²**), also known to the *schol. Veron.*, p. 401 (III.2 Th.-H.) = p. 83 Basch. (cf. Lunelli 2002, p. 119). It seems, however, that in V. *pinus* is a fourth-declension noun (for a similarly uncertain case, cf. *G.* 2.443). For *loquor* used of trees, cf. Catull. 4.12.

23 audit amores. The term *amores* denotes both the love-affairs themselves and the songs that describe them: cf. *E.* 10.34 and 53, as well as 5.10 *Phyllidis ignes* (n.). In this *audit*, the act of listening is performed by a friend, a confidant, in contrast with e.g. Catull. 64.166 (*aurae*) *nec missas audire queunt nec reddere uoces*, or Prop. 2.33.23. According to Horace, Lucilius can confide his secrets to his books (*sat.* 2.1.30–4) and Sappho to her lyre, capable of understanding love and making it eternal: *spirat adhuc amor / uiuuntque commissi calores / Aeoliae fidibus puellae* (*carm.* 4.9.10–12).

24 Panaque, qui primus calamos non passus inertis. Corydon, V.'s first unhappy lover and monologuist, had mentioned the pastoral myth of Pan and Syrinx (2.32–3n.). Note the elegance of the idea: even in her plant form (a marsh reed), Syrinx is not allowed to rest by the god (*calamos non passus inertis*); at the same time, however, the *primus inuentor* typically does not allow nature (*natura*) to remain 'inactive' (*iners*), since he moulds it through *ars*; cf. Lucil. 452 M. = 446 K. *iners, ars in quo non erit ulla*; Maltby (1991, p. 302, s.v. *iners*). Both notion and vocabulary reappear at *G.* 1.122–4 *primusque per artem / mouit agros... / nec torpere graui passus sua regna ueterno* (Jupiter's action). The parallel in *G.* 1 is among the reasons for rejecting M's reading *primum* (contrast 2.32n.).

26 Mopso Nysa datur. Three simple words state all the reasons for the lover's anguish (the proximity of the two names is full of sorrow): Nysa is given in marriage to Mopsus. Readers who remember the Dionysian affiliation of V.'s only other Mopsus (cf. 5.29–31n.) might find it hardly surprising that he marries a Nysa (see 8.18n.). Note also that, in *E.* 5, Mopsus showed knowledge of, and ability to emulate, Theocr. *id.* 1 (this, too, makes him a natural rival to the unnamed lover, who constantly takes inspiration from *id.* 1). The name will reappear (also referring to a luckier rival) in Calp. *ecl.* 3.8–9 *Lycidan ingrata reliquit / Phyllis amatque nouum post tot mea munera Mopsum*. Note, in the opening word of this stanza and the two following ones, the alliteration of /m/: *Maenalus* (cf. the refrain:

Maenalios Mecum Mea); *Mopso; Mopse.* For *dare* in the sense of 'giving in marriage', without further specification, see *Aen.* 1.345; cf. Pacuv. *trag.* 167 R.³, as well as Liv. 42.12.3. **quid non speremus amantes?** The use of *spero* in the sense of 'expecting' (something negative) will be featured in *Aen.* 4.292; 419 (Dido).

27–8. The union of Mopsus and Nysa, which the speaker considers absurd, is equated with the actualization of two consecutive adynata. The rhetorical device is analogous to the one used by the dying Daphnis in *id.* 1.132–6: 'Now you brambles will bear violets, and so will you thorns, / and let the fair narcissus bloom on the juniper. / Let everything be changed, and the pine tree bear pears, / since Daphnis is dying; and let the deer pursue the hounds [καὶ τὰς κύνας ὤλαφος ἕλκοι] / and let owls from the mountains sing to nightingales'; but cf. below, 8.52–6n.

27 iungentur…grypes equis. In this context, following 8.26 *datur*, it seems inevitable to read *iungentur* as 'they will be united', i.e. 'they will form a couple', as in Hor. *carm.* 1.33.8 *iungentur capreae lupis*; cf. Cic. *diu.* 2.143; Ov. *ars* 3.650 and *met.* 14.762 (an active form of the verb appears at *Aen.* 1.73). Here, the adynaton is a second-order impossibility, since griffins (animals with the body of a lion and the head and wings of an eagle) were legendary creatures: *fabulosi*, according to Plin. *nat.* 10.136. Dwelling in Scythia, griffins often fought against the one-eyed Arimaspian knights and their horses: cf. esp. Aesch. *Prom.* 803–6, as well as Herodot. 3.116; 4.13.1 (battles against griffins were also widespread in ancient iconography). For the motif of unions against nature, quite frequent in adynata, see Hor. *epod.* 16.30–2 *nouaque monstra iunxerit libidine / mirus amor, iuuet ut tigris subsidere ceruis, / adulteretur et columba miluo*; Hor. *carm.* 1.33.8; *ars* 13 (but cf. Aristoph. *Pax* 1075–6). This Virgilian passage is likely to have originated the myth of hippogriffs, legendary animals widespread in medieval lore and memorably described by Ariosto in *Orlando Furioso* 4.18.2. **aeuoque sequenti.** As in the myth of the ages, the poet presents a sequence of eras, each of which is here characterized by its own monstrous novelty. Pollio, if he is the addressee of *E.* 8, must have recognized a (humorous?) reworking of the prophecy which V. previously dedicated to him (cf. *E.* 4.11 *decus hoc aeui, te consule, inibit*); see below, 8.52–6n.

28 cum canibus timidi uenient ad pocula dammae. For the prodigy, cf. *E.* 4.22 *nec magnos metuent armenta leones*, as well as the Theocritean adynaton at *id.* 1.135 [see 8.27–8n.]. V.'s striking use of *damma* as a masc. form (while the fem. is more common; cf. also *G.* 3.539 *timidi dammae ceruique fugaces*) was noted by Quint. *inst.* 9.3.6. For *pocula* in relation to the watering of animals, see Colum. 7.10.7. Here, however, there are traces of miraculous anthropomorphism, whereas the comparison between humans and animals at *G.* 3.529 (*pocula sunt fontes liquidi*) has a polemical ring to it.

28a. It is most probably preferable to follow γ, which here inserts a refrain line, symmetrical to l. 76 (which there is no reason to delete: see n. ad loc.). Thus, the 'stanzas' at 29–30 and 77–8 are the only ones composed of two lines (for a Theocritean parallel cf. *id.* 1.71–2 and 77–8). The restored sense is perfect, and the two songs, each including ten stanzas, stand out for their structural symmetry (cf.

400   ECLOGUE 8

above, pp. 383–4; see also 8.17–21n.; 64–109n.). Note, moreover, that both 'microstanzas' are formed by pairs of lines very similar to each other, in terms of rhythm and sound effects: with l. 29 *facés: tibi ducitur* cf. 8.30 *nucés: tibi deserit*; analogously, ll. 77–8 both have *necte* in line-opening position (whereas *necto* ends l. 78; note also the repeated voc. *Amarylli*). If l. 28a is genuine, the total number of lines in the poem is 110: see p. 383.

29 nouas incide faces. Pinewood torches were made specifically for the nuptial procession: cf. Catull. 61.77; 114 (121). Here, however, the adj. implies bitterness: the torches are 'new', but made for the wedding of a girl who used to be someone else's *coniunx* (8.18). The making of such torches is described in greater detail at *G.* 1.292 *ferroque faces inspicat acuto*. Here too, perhaps, the torches are only cut in their upper part, thus resembling ears of wheat. **tibi ducitur uxor.** The phrase is common in relation to weddings: the new bride is literally 'led' into her husband's house through the ceremony of *deductio*. The noun *uxor* occurs only here in V., who prefers *coniunx*; here, perhaps, the choice is prompted by the echo of Catull. 61.185 (192) *uxor in thalamo tibi est* (but cf. *uxorius* in *Aen.* 4.266). **sparge, marite, nuces.** As the bride and the groom met, it was customary to throw walnuts on the ground. Such propitiatory gestures, along with the so-called *Fescennina iocatio*, were part of apotropaic wedding customs well attested even in non-Roman and modern folklore (*nuces iuglandes…nuptialium Fescenninorum comites*, according to Plin. *nat.* 15.86). The ancients debated the interpretation of the gesture: some considered walnuts as a symbol of fertility (Plin. *nat.* 15.86), whereas others assigned greater importance to the cheerful sound that they produced when hitting the ground *en masse* (cf. Serv. Dan.). Walnuts reappear in *G.* 1.187–90, where their abundance indicates a good wheat harvest. Abandoning childhood games, which typically feature walnuts (Hor. *sat.* 2.3.171; Pers. 1.10; Sen. *dial.* 2[*const. sap.*].12.2), is often treated as a rite of passage (via marriage) towards adulthood: V.'s main model continues to be Catull. 61.121–8 (128–35), where *maritus* occurs multiple times (for the vocative cf. 61.135 [142]; 184 [191]). The epithalamial motif appears in Theocritus' *id.* 18, i.e. the *Epithalamium of Helen* (even though her marriage to Menelaus is destined for a dark future). In *E.* 8.30, the Catullan echo points again to the epithalamial genre; yet the unhappy lover's song will be, in effect, an anti-epithalamium.

30 tibi deserit Hesperus Oetam. According to Servius Dan., Hesperus had a specific cult (significantly connected to the *puer* Hymenaeus) on Mount Oeta, which marked the southern boundary of Thessaly. Note esp. the echo of Catull. 62.7 *Oetaeos ostendit Noctifer ignes*; cf. also *Culex* 203; *Ciris* 350; Stat. *silu.* 5.4.8. Here, V. mentions the Greek name of the mountain, coupled with the Latin form *Vesper* in Catull. 62.32 and 64.329 (cf. *E.* 6.86n.). The star symbolizing the epithalamial genre concludes the first set of four stanzas. Note also the 'framing' echo of 8.17, in which the planet appeared in its morning form, i.e. *Lucifer* (see n. ad loc.); for *Hesperos* in Greek poetry, cf. esp. Sapph. fr. 104 V.; Bion, fr. 11

G. (significant for its pastoral setting). For a mention of Mount Oeta in a possibly epithalamial context, cf. Parthen. *SH* fr. 666, p. 315 Ll.-J.-P. **Oetam**. Note the variant reading *Oetan*, found in V and the *schol. Veron.*, p. 402 (III.2 Th.-H.) = p. 84 Basch. (cf. Lunelli 2001, p. 127). Latin authors, however, seem to oscillate between the Hellenizing form *Oeten* (only the -η form occurs in Greek: Οἴτη), attested since Ov. *met.* 9.165; 204 (cf. Lucan. 3.178 and 7.449; Sen. *Herc. f.* 981; Stat. *Theb.* 1.119), and the Latin form ending in /a/, which is certainly the correct reading here (*Oetam* M; *Hoeta* P). The form in /a/ is also used by Livy at 36.15.10 *extremos ad orientem montes Oetam uocant* (cf. also Liv. 36.30.2; 37.5.4; Plin. *nat.* 37.141) and appears in *Culex* 203 (*procedit Vesper ab Oeta*) and *Ciris* 350.

32 o digno coniuncta uiro. Epithalamia typically highlighted the groom's virtues (cf. Catull. 62.59 *cum tali coniuge, uirgo*; 64.323–4), as well as the matching qualities of both bride and groom (Catull. 64.334–6). Here, however, the couple is a perfect match in terms of 'unworthiness'; for this kind of (anti-)epithalamial sarcasm, cf. *Aen.* 7.555–6 *talia coniugia et talis celebrent hymenaeos / egregium Veneris genus et rex ipse Latinus* (Juno, a *pronuba* goddess, addressing Allecto). The construction with *o* + participle, often found in Greek tragedy (cf. Aesch. *Pers.* 709 ὦ βροτῶν πάντων ὑπεροχὼν ὄλβον; Soph. *Ai.* 845; Eur. *Tro.* 764), is well suited to solemn or emotionally laden contexts, such as the beginning of an address: cf. *Aen.* 1.597 *o sola infandos Troiae miserata labores*; 4.31; 5.870; 6.83; note also Catull. 64.22. **dum despicis omnis**. Such contempt greatly offends the lover, who feels betrayed, disappointed, and unhappy: cf. *E.* 2.19 *despectus tibi sum*. The idea that Nysa, in her stubborn pride, despises 'everyone' (*omnes*, not just the hapless lover) may have been a sort of consolation (Serv. Dan. *quoniam ipse despicitur, putat omnes despici*); yet now the girl is being 'given away' (8.26 *datur*) to her future husband.

33 dumque tibi est odio mea fistula dumque capellae. The pastoral instrument *par excellence*, whose invention is alluded to in 8.24 (the instrument is presumably the pride of the poet-herdsman: *mea*), is abhorred by Nysa, much like the herdsman's goats. Similarly, the *fistula* and Corydon's rustic gifts, including some speckled *capreoli*, did not seem to impress Alexis in *E.* 2.36–44. This reference to young goats is the only detail that points to the lover's pastoral identity, which is shared by the anonymous goatherd of Theocr. *id.* 3 (note the mention of goats in *id.* 3.1). Further echoes will follow. That goatherds are typically unlucky lovers is explicitly stated by Priapus in *id.* 1.86–8.

34 hirsutumque supercilium promissaque barba. Both features obviously have an anti-erotic effect. They appear (respectively) in *id.* 1.30–2 'I know, beautiful girl, why you shun me: / because one long hairy eyebrow [λασία μὲν ὀφρύς] spans over / my entire forehead, from one ear to the other' (the Cyclops speaks) and *id.* 3.8–9 'from so close, perhaps, I appear to you as snub-nosed, / o nymph, and pointy-bearded [προγένειος]'. Thus, the reading *promissaque*, besides being better attested than *demissaque* (P), is supported by the Theocritean parallel (*id.* 3.9); an unkempt

402   ECLOGUE 8

and prominent beard is characteristic of the archaic Roman man: Liv. 5.41.9 *barbam...*, *ut tum omnibus promissa erat*; cf. *ThlL* X.2.1863.5–25; *OLD*[2], p. 1634, s.v. 1b. In other words, the goatherd's beard is 'pointy' and 'protruding' (which is what προγένειος means: cf. also Long. 1.16.5), in keeping with typical iconographic depictions of satyrs and Dionysus himself (cf. *LIMC* III.1, s.v. *Dionysos*, e.g. nos. 55, 80, 90, 254, 363, 365 [C. Gasparri]). The effect of the goatherd's appearance on a girl is repulsive; contrast *Aen.* 3.593, where Achaemenides' beard is more simply 'unkempt', i.e. 'hanging down' (*immissaque barba*).

35 nec curare deum credis mortalia quemquam. Like Corydon in *E.* 2.27n. and 2.65n., this unhappy lover seems to share some ideas and vocabulary with Epicureanism: Cic. *diu.* 2.104 *qui* (i.e. *Epicurus*) *negat quicquam deos nec alieni curare nec sui*; Lucr. 5.82 *deos securum agere aeuum*; Hor. *sat.* 1.5.101; but see Enn. *trag.* 271 Joc. = 317 V.[2] (cf. Aesch. *Ag.* 369–73). Here, however, Nysa herself, not her hapless lover, is the one who (mistakenly?) believes that the gods are not involved in human affairs. For such a sense of *mortalia*, cf. *Aen.* 1.462 *mentem mortalia tangunt*, as well as the 'optimistic' Ov. *met.* 13.70 *aspiciunt oculis superi mortalia iustis*; see further *ThlL* VIII.1512.52–75. The sing. form appears e.g. in Lucr. 3.800 *mortale aeterno iungere*. The charge of 'impiety' against a lover who seems not to care for divine justice (or for his own promises in front of the gods) is also featured in Alphesiboeus' song (8.103n.). As in *E.* 2.27, the Epicurean allusion appears in a context full of pastoral elements: note, in *E.* 2, the references to outward appearance (2.25–6) and *sordida rura* (2.28); here, the singer insists on the (Cyclops-like?) figure of the herdsman, whose body is certainly far from attractive (8.33–4). The resulting humorous contrast must have amused the learned readers of V.'s *E.*, who (like Varius Rufus, quoted verbatim at 8.85–8n.) share V.'s Epicurean background (see further 8.108n. for a similar Epicurean echo of *E.* 2).

37–8. A clear reworking of *id.* 11 (echoed in 8.34): 'I fell in love with you, girl, when for the first time / you came over with my mother, as you wanted to pick hyacinth flowers / on the mountain, and I showed you the way [ἐγὼ δ' ὁδὸν ἁγεμόνευον]' (*id.* 11.25–7). The mythical and divine dimension of the Cyclops, who owes to his mother (the sea-nymph Thoosa: Hom. *Od.* 1.71) the opportunity to meet Galatea, is now replaced by a scene of everyday life in a quite specific countryside landscape (37 *saepibus in nostris*: contrast Theocritus' vague 'mountain'; for the hedge, cf. *E.* 1.53). The 'mother' is now the girl's mother, in accordance with traditional customs, whereas the herdsman is still their 'guide': *dux ego uester eram* (38); note that *uester* rules out that the other woman might be the lover's mother, who surely would not need her son's guidance among 'her' hedges (*saepibus in nostris*). Finally, Theocritus' hyacinths are replaced by (*roscida*) *mala*, a common erotic symbol (cf. *E.* 1.37n.; 2.51n.). The mention of dew seems to set the scene in early morning (cf. 8.15n.) and adds overtones of youthful purity: cf. the roses-girls in *Perv. Ven.* 13–22; note also the verbal assonance with *E.* 4.30 *roscida mella*.

ECLOGUE 8 403

39 alter ab undecimo. The young goatherd was in the twelfth year of his life, i.e. he was eleven years old: note that *alter* is opposed to *undecimus*, thereby closing the sequence. Servius' interpretation is overcomplicated, but worth mentioning: *id est tertius decimus. 'alter' enim de duobus dicimus*. Note the implicit personification of *annus* as the subject of *acceperat* (whose object is *me*), in accordance with a common usage of the verb, typically in reference to space (cf. Lucr. 3.984 *domus*; Cic. *Att.* 5.14.2 *Asia*), but here referring to time: cf. G. 3.190 (where, however, *accesserit* is the correct reading); *ThlL* I, 312.45-7.

40 fragilis…ramos. The epithet adds a subtly psychological note: the boy can now reach the highest branches (which are the youngest, most 'fragile' ones), so as to snap them off: contrast the goat in Iuv. 11.67 *necdum ausus uirgas humilis mordere salicti.* **a terra.** Simply 'standing on the ground', i.e. without any further support. The reading *ab* is found in MP; but cf. G. 1.457 *a terra* (where, however, *ab terra* is transmitted by Prob. *gramm.* IV, p. 240.3 K.); generally speaking, the preposition *ab* is not used in front of the dental /t/.

41 ut uidi, ut perii, ut me malus abstulit error. The repeated *ut* expresses the simultaneous nature of the lover's feelings; the correlation is intuitively centred around the different forces of *ut*. Thus, the line must be paraphrased as follows: 'as soon as I saw you, so did I perish, so did an evil error lead me astray' (a temporal *ut* is followed by two correlative *ut*; this interpretation, however, does not rule out exclamatory emphasis, affecting the entire sentence). Such a syntactical audacity is paralleled twice in Theocritus: *id.* 2.82–3 χὠς ἴδον ὡς ἐμάνην, ὥς μοι πυρὶ θυμὸς ἰάφθη / δειλαίας 'as soon as I saw him, I immediately went insane, immediately was my heart hit by fire, / wretched that I am', and *id.* 3.41–2 ἁ δ' Ἀταλάντα / ὡς ἴδεν ὡς ἐμάνη, ὡς ἐς βαθὺν ἅλατ' ἔρωτα 'Atalanta / went insane as soon as she saw him, and immediately fell in deep love' (the two poems are the main models of *E.* 8). The hiatus at *id.* 3.42 is echoed here in *perii, ut* and emphasized by the preceding elision between *uidi* and *ut*. For another important parallel, cf. the erotic passage of Hom. *Il.* 14.294 (in the 'Deception of Zeus'): ὡς δ' ἴδεν, ὥς μιν ἔρως πυκινὰς φρένας ἀμφεκάλυψεν 'as soon as he saw her, love immediately seized his sturdy mind' (cf. also *Il.* 1.512–13; 19.16; 20.424). For similar audacity, cf. Catull. 62.45 *sic uirgo, dum intacta manet, dum cara suis est*; also Ov. *her.* 12.33 (35) *et uidi et perii* and 16.133 (135); for the immediate effects of love, cf. Plaut. *Truc.* 45 *extemplo et ipsus periit et res et fides.* The entire line is quoted verbatim at *Ciris* 430. The protagonist's *error* is a form of 'deviation', here described as particularly 'evil' (*malus*): the lover is led astray, as though he were insane; cf. *Aen.* 10.110 *errore malo…monitisque sinistris*, as well as G. 3.249 (and 3.513). The second half-line is quoted in Ov. *trist.* 2.109 *illa…die, qua me malus abstulit error*; note the forceful alliteration *me malus*, here repeated by Alphesiboeus in 8.83.

43–5. Another Theocritean reworking, this time inspired by *id.* 3.15–16: 'Now I know Love as he is: a frightful god. He was certainly suckled / by a lioness and raised in a wild wood'. The parents' savage nature is commonplace in ancient

404   ECLOGUE 8

invectives, at least since Hom. *Il.* 16.33–5 (Patroclus to Achilles): 'You are merciless: not Peleus, lord of horses, was your father, / nor Thetis your mother. The gray sea it was that generated you, / and the lofty cliffs: so hard is your heart [πέτραι τ' ἠλίβατοι, ὅτι τοι νόος ἐστὶν ἀπηνής]'; cf. Eur. *Med.* 1342–3, as well as two Catullan poems that V. perhaps echoes here, i.e. 60 and 64.154–6. The true genesis of Eros was also a mythical and cosmogonic issue, on which Hesiod expressed his view in *theog.* 116–22. According to Sappho, for instance, Eros was the son of Earth and Heaven (*schol. ad* Apoll. Rhod. 3.26b, p. 216 W. = Sapph. fr. 198 V.); cf. F. Lasserre, *La figure d'Éros dans la poésie grecque*, Paris 1946, esp. pp. 130–49. The motif is reframed in a humorous key by Meleager in *Anth. Pal.* 5.177.5–6 = *HE* 4194–5 G.-P.: οὔτε γὰρ αἰθήρ / οὐ χθών φησι τεκεῖν τὸν θρασύν, οὐ πέλαγος 'neither heaven, / nor earth, nor sea admit to having given birth to him, the savage god [i.e. Eros]'. The present passage, along with Catull. 64.154–6 and Eur. *Med.* 1342–3, will be echoed by Dido in *Aen.* 4.366–7 *duris genuit te cautibus horrens / Caucasus Hyrcanaeque admorunt ubera tigres.*

43 nunc scio quid sit Amor. Cf. *id.* 3.15 νῦν ἔγνων τὸν Ἔρωτα (see above, 8.43–5n.). For a later parallel cf. Ov. *met.* 13.762 *quid sit Amor sentit*; note also Ov. *amor.* 3.6.24. Note the short *o* in *scio*: cf. 3.103n. **duris in cautibus.** Note the reading *nudis* in P[1] (not as well attested as *duris* MP[2]V); but *Aen.* 4.366 *duris…cautibus* (see 8.43–5n.) is better explained as an intentional echo of *duris* than as the possible source of a scribal error here (*nudis > duris*), while the motif of 'hardness' appears, albeit with a different thrust, in the Homeric model: Hom. *Il.* 16.35 ἀπηνής (cf. Catull. 60.3). The connection between birth and hard stones (*duris*) is found in one of antiquity's most famous origin myths, i.e. the story of Deucalion and Pyrrha: cf. *G.* 1.62–3 *Deucalion uacuum lapides iactauit in orbem, / unde homines nati, durum genus* (2.340–1 *uirumque / terrea progenies duris caput extulit aruis*); note also Lucr. 5.925–6 *genus humanum multo fuit illud in aruis / durius, ut decuit, tellus quod dura creasset*; Ov. *met.* 1.414 *inde genus durum sumus.* For a reference to Deucalion without the adjective *durus*, see Colum. 10.66–7 *nos abruptae tum montibus altis / Deucalioneae cautes peperere* (note *cautes*: cf. *cautibus* in the present passage). In Greek, the mythical tale was corroborated by the folk etymology λαός < λᾶας, attested e.g. in Hes. fr. 234 M.-W.; Pind. *Ol.* 9.43–6; Callim. fr. 496 Pf. Such common notions are here applied to a much more specific case: Amor was born on hard stones, and is not human; cf. 8.45 *nec generis nostri…nec sanguinis.* Note also that the idea of 'naked' cliffs (*nudis in cautibus*) is less appropriate for the context, as it would introduce a rather humanizing, sympathetic point of view which would hardly suit this invective: contrast *E.* 1.15 *silice in nuda conixa* (where the goats give birth, pathetically, on 'naked' rocks; cf. 1.47 *lapis…nudus*), which could be the root of the error.

44. An 'exotic' line, accumulating remote toponyms that seem unfamiliar (even from the point of view of sound: e.g. *Tmaros*), with a hiatus between *Rhodope* and *aut*; note also the four-syllable *Garamantes* at the end (cf. *E.* 2.24n., which, however, features only Greek names). For a likely Theocritean model, cf. *id.* 7.77 *ἢ Ἄθω ἢ Ῥοδόπαν ἢ Καύκασον ἐσχατόωντα*, which V. will rework in *G.* 1.332 *aut Athon aut Rhodopen aut alta Ceraunia telo.* **Tmaros.** A mountain in Epirus (*Tmaros* or *Tomaros*), dominating the western side of the valley in which the oracle of Dodona was situated. The first (likely) attestation is in Pindar, *Pae.* 6[fr. 53f].109 Maeh., but V. must have been particularly interested in the Callimachean occurrences (*aet.* fr. 23.3 Pf. = 25.3 Mass. = 23.3 Hard.; *hymn.* 6[*Cer.*].51). The sound *Tm-*, here facilitated by the preceding *aut*, is simplified as *Maros* in MP (cf. *Aen.* 5.620 *Tmarii...Dorycli; Mari* M). The variant reading *Ismarus*, also found in the lemma of some Servian manuscripts, must be explained as an echo of *E.* 6.30, where *Rhodope* and *Ismarus* occur together. **Rhodope.** A mountain chain at the border between Thrace and Macedonia, often associated with Orphic and Dionysian cults: cf. 6.30n. **extremi Garamantes.** An African population neighbouring the Gaetuli in the eastern Sahara. The *Garamantes* were held to inhabit the southern end of the known world: hence the epithet, corresponding to the Homeric *ἔσχατοι ἀνδρῶν* (*Od.* 1.23, used of the Ethiopians [cf. *E.* 10.68n.], who are called *Garamantici* in Sol. 30.2). Recall also *id.* 7.77 *ἐσχατόωντα*; in *Aen.* 6.794–5, Augustus will be imagined as crossing that extreme boundary (as well as the Indian, i.e. eastern, one): *super et Garamantas et Indos / proferet imperium.*

45 nec generis nostri...nec sanguinis. The double synonym (*generis... sanguinis*) emphasizes total exclusion from the human species: for *sanguen* in reference to lineage, cf. *Aen.* 1.329; 6.778; 7.49. **edunt.** This Hellenizing 'historical' present is commonly used with verbs meaning 'to generate' or 'to raise', whose consequences (i.e. parenting) persist in the present: cf. *G.* 1.279 *creat; Aen.* 8.141 *generat;* 10.518 *educat* (but contrast e.g. *E.* 2.663 *obtruncat*); Prop. 4.4.54 *nutrit.* For Greek parallels, cf. Eur. *Andr.* 9 *τίκτω*; Soph. *Oed. tyr.* 437 *ἐκφύει*.

47–50. The folk-poetry style of these lines has rightly been interpreted as a marker of neoteric taste (cf. Catull. 62.20–4; see also the late antique *Perv. Ven.* 29–35 and 40–1). The undeniable redundancy (note esp. the second half-line identically repeated at ll. 48 and 50), along with the ambivalence of the term *mater*, has led some to posit a textual corruption: no emendation or deletion, however, has proved to be persuasive (l. 50 is the likeliest candidate for deletion). It is, therefore, preferable to think that V.'s Damon is here displaying his skills in the (typically pastoral) iterative style. After all, transferring a tragic theme to a pastoral context is itself part of Damon's experiment. The mimetic force of these lines is fully grasped by Sedulius Scottus, who reworks the passage in *carm. pasch.* II 6–8 (*Corp. Script. Eccl. Lat.*, X, p. 44) *heu, noxia coniunx! / noxia tu coniunx magis an draco perfidus ille? / perfidus ille draco, sed tu quoque noxia coniunx* (Eva and the Serpent): note also the prose paraphrase at *op. pasch.* II 1 (ibid., p. 197): *heu, coniunx crudelis et noxia! an ille magis draco perfidus homicida? ille draco perfidus homicida, sed tu coniunx quoque crudelis et noxia.* A certain taste for ethical debates was widespread in ancient culture, among both philosophers (from

406 ECLOGUE 8

the sophistic age onwards) and rhetoricians, but also in genres of 'popular phil-osophy' like the diatribe: this is particularly true of a well-known character such as Medea (see below, 8.48n.; also 49n.).

47 saeuus Amor docuit…matrem. This mother who kills her own children (cf. *natorum sanguine*) must be an allusion to Medea, featuring an echo of Enn. *trag.* 216 Joc. = 254 V.²: *Medea…amore saeuo saucia.* This is further confirmed by the likely emulation of Apoll. Rhod. 4.445–9 'cruel Eros, great calamity, great disgrace for mortals [σχέτλι᾿ Ἔρως, μέγα πῆμα, μέγα στύγος ἀνθρώποισιν], / you are the source of terrible discord, of sighs and lament / and, besides these, countless other evils you generate. / May you rise up and take arms, o god, against the children of my enemies, / just as you instilled loathsome madness into the Medea's mind [οἷος Μηδείη στυγερὴν φρεσὶν ἔμβαλες ἄτην; cf. here *docuit*]'; see further 8.49n. The insistence on the word *mater*, repeated four times in the stanza (i.e. once per line) but without a proper noun, must have stimulated the creativity of readers and poets, who made the *mater*'s identity explicit: cf. esp. Ov. *amor.* 2.14.29 *Colchida respersam puerorum sanguine culpant* (see 8.48n.) and *trist.* 2.387 *natorum sanguine mater* (i.e. Medea: note the verbatim quotation from V.); see also *Culex* 249–50 *impietate fera uecordem Colchida matrem, / …meditantem uulnera natis.*

48 crudelis tu quoque, mater. Once again, Medea: the goatherd expresses his view on the dreadful sorceress' direct responsibility. Thus, if the text is genuine, the ancient identification of this *mater* with *Amor*'s mother (i.e. Venus), is unper-suasive (cf., however, Hor. *carm.* 1.19.1 *mater saeua Cupidinum*; note also Daphnis scolding Cypris and Eros in Theocr. *id.* 1.100–3): see, for instance, Serv. Dan. *ad* 8.47 *alii hoc loco cum Amore matrem Venerem culpari uolunt.* Medea's guilt, which Euripides had previously problematized (cf. esp. *Med.* 1261–70; 1323–60), was also discussed in philosophical contexts, particularly by the Stoic Chrysippus: see *SVF*, II, p. 120, nos. 347; p. 255.5–12, no. 906; III, p. 124.15–19, no. 473; *nocens* is used of Medea in Ov. *her.* 12.106 (108); Sen. *Med.* 246; 280 (see also Val. Fl. 7.461; 8.425–6); note *culpant* at Ov. *amor.* 2.14.29, in the context of a 'debate' involving Procne (*amor.* 2.14.31 *utraque saeua parens: sed tristibus utraque causis,* etc.). For the example of Medea as typical of declamation schools, see e.g. Theon. *progymn.* 94, pp. 59.17–60.2 Patillon; Ps. Hermog. *progymn.* 2, p. 5 Rabe = pp. 183–4 Patillon; also Mar. Victorin. *in Cic. inu.* 1.17, p. 199.39–40; 1.28, p. 229.20–4; 1.29, p. 236.26–8 Halm; and the rhetorical exercise in *POxy* LXXVI 5093. This half-line, along with ll. 47–50, will later be reworked by Hosidius Geta in his *Medea* (esp. 444; cf. 400–1; 441–2); but see *Anth. Lat.* 13.7 R. (Procne murdering her son Itylus). V. himself echoes the line with an estranging effect in Aeneas' invocation to his divine mother, Venus: *quid natum totiens, crudelis tu quoque, falsis / ludis imaginibus?* (*Aen.* 1.407–8); note *Culex* 292 *sed tu crudelis, crudelis tu magis·Orpheu* (cf., here, 8.49 *crudelis mater magis*).

49 puer improbus. Another likely reworking of Apoll. Rhod. 4.445 σχέτλι᾿ Ἔρως (see above, 8.47n.). Both epithet and Apollonian echo reappear in *Aen.*

ECLOGUE 8   407

4.412 *improbe Amor, quid non mortalia pectora cogis?* (cf. also *G.* 1.145–6 *labor omnia uicit / improbus*, overwriting *E.* 10.69 *omnia uincit Amor*). The 'debate' on the nature, appearance, and attributes of Eros/*Amor* also belongs to the scholastic and rhetorical tradition, from the time of the Sophists (cf. Alexis, fr. 20 K.-A.) to, for example, Quint. *inst.* 2.4.26.

50. The answer repeats all the key terms featured in the preceding question: note the chiastic arrangement of the adjectives in ll. 49–50 (*crudelis…improbus… improbus…crudelis*). The final phrase *crudelis tu quoque mater* is somewhat elusive, and the line as a whole does not answer the question in 8.49 (is the mother more cruel or the son more evil?): rather, it reasserts the main idea with a strong effect of repetition.

52–6. After 8.27–8, more adynata appear here: once again, they are coupled with 'Golden Age' rhetoric. However, even the most astonishing prodigies are but fragments of chaos: not the result of the birth of a redeeming *puer*, but the consequence of an *Amor* that has been shown to be *improbus*. The echo of Daphnis' farewell in *id.* 1 is now even more apparent than at 8.27–8 (note *nunc* in l. 52, with which cf. *id.* 1.132 νῦν). Moreover, it is paired with a reworking of the *aurea aetas* of *E.* 4, which Asinius Pollio, the likely dedicatee of this poem, must have noticed (cf. also 3.89n.); see *E.* 8.27n. Note that the protagonists of these impossible prodigies are, in fact, common inhabitants of V.'s pastoral world: sheep, oaks (cf. above, 1.17 and 7.13), alders (6.63n.), tamarisks (8.54n.), and Tityrus himself.

52 ouis ultro fugiat lupus. A further, more precise echo (cf. 8.28) of *id.* 1.135 τὰς κύνας ὥλαφος ἕλκοι 'and let the deer pursue the hounds' (while Daphnis referred to hunting, the goatherd mentions sheep and wolves). In comparison to *E.* 4.22 *nec magnos metuent armenta leones*, note that here the violent relationship between predator and prey is not eliminated but reversed: *ultro* ('spontaneously', 'of its own initiative') refers to the fact that the wolf flees at the sight of sheep, without even waiting for an attack on their part.

52–3 aurea durae / mala ferant quercus. Both epithets are expressively foregrounded, and their opposition is thereby highlighted. Golden apples, which might bring the Hesperides to mind are now produced by stiff, ordinary oaks (cf. *E.* 3.71 and 6.61n.). Note V.'s variation on the theme of *E.* 4.30 *durae quercus sudabunt roscida mella*, which appears to be deliberately alluded to here (for Pollio's enjoyment?). Note the phonetic and rhythmic proximity in *mella/mala* (cf. above, 8.37 *roscida mala*). The verb *sudare* is used of *myricae* at 8.54.

53 narcisso floreat alnus. Cf. *id.* 1.113 ἁ δὲ καλὰ νάρκισσος ἐπ᾽ ἀρκεύθοισι κομάσαι 'and let the fair narcissus bloom on the juniper'. Note also Mopsus' reworking in *E.* 5.38–9 *pro purpureo narcisso / carduus et spinis surgit paliurus acutis* (on narcissus/Narcissus see 5.38n.).

54 pinguia corticibus sudent electra myricae. Tamarisks here produce amber, referred to by the Greek term ἤλεκτρον (which is also used of the similarly

408   ECLOGUE 8

coloured alloy of gold and silver). Amber, in fact, was believed to ooze in oily form (note *pinguia*) from the bark of the poplars into which the weeping Heliades had been turned: see Ov. *met.* 2.346–66, esp. 365 *de ramis electra nouis* (cf. also *E.* 6.62–3). Here, however, the miraculous process is attributed to a plant that symbolizes V.'s pastoral 'humility'. The dedicatee of *E.* 4 must have noticed this detail, since *myricae* opened that poem (*E.* 4.2), which then moved on to the Sibyl's prophecy (for *myricae* and *Saturnia regna* cf. *E.* 6.10 and 6.41, respectively). Note also *E.* 3.89 *ferat et rubus asper amomum* (see 8.52–6n.).

55 certent et cycnis ululae. Cf. *id.* 1.136 κῆξ ὀρέων τοὶ σκῶπες ἀηδόσι γαρύσαιντο 'and from the mountains the owls compete with the nightingales' (cf. *Anth. Pal.* 9.380.2), here reworked on the basis of *id.* 5.136–7 οὐ θεμιτόν...ποτ' ἀηδόνα κίσσας ἐρίσδειν, / οὐδ' ἔποπας κύκνοισι 'magpies are not allowed...to compete with nightingales, / nor hoopoes with swans'. In particular, swans were deemed to be peerless in singing melodiously (especially when about to die): cf. *E.* 9.36n. The *ulula* is a nocturnal bird, perhaps properly the *Strix aluco*, or tawny owl. The onomatopoeia suggests grief and sorrow (cf. *Aen.* 2.487–8; 11.189–90). For the construction, see 5.8 *tibi certat* (n.); V.'s syntax perhaps echoes Lucr. 3.6–7 *quid enim contendat hirundo / cycnis.* Cf. also *G.* 2.96. The *ululae* are a hapax in V., whereas the swans reappear at 7.38 and 9.29 (cf. also 9.36). **sit Tityrus Orpheus.** The text presupposes the negative reputation of Theocritus' Tityrus as a singer (even though, in *id.* 7.72–7, a herdsman named Tityrus sang of Daphnis' lovesickness, a topic obviously crucial to *id.* 1): cf. 1.1n. V.'s typical modesty is also implied: it is as if the very opening of the *E.* were not relevant here. Note also the subtle irony: *E.* 6 showed that, following an occasional epic digression, Tityrus-V.'s voice could really become that of an 'Orphic' singer, i.e. Silenus (who is, in fact, capable of surpassing Orpheus himself: *E.* 6.30; cf. also 4.55). The same applies to the *myricae*: see above, 8.54n. Calpurnius' Meliboeus will describe Tityrus-V.'s poetic stature in Orphic terms: Calp. *ecl.* 4.64–9.

56 Orpheus in siluis. The detail acquires greater significance if compared to *E.* 3.46 *Orphea...siluasque sequentis*; cf. also 5.43 *Daphnis ego in siluis.* **inter delphinas Arion.** During his sea journey from Sicily to Corinth, the musician Arion was robbed of all his possessions by crew members who realized how valuable his cargo was. Before throwing him into the sea, they allowed him to play his lyre one more time, but his melodies were so fascinating that a dolphin saved him and brought him back to the shore (Herodot. 1.23–4; Ov. *fast.* 2.79–118). For the character, perhaps originally a historical figure (a native of Lesbos, he lived in Corinth at the time of Periander's tyranny, 625–585 BCE) but soon mythologized, cf. *Enc. Virg.* I, pp. 313–14, s.v. *Arione* (C. Prato); Perutelli (2003). Note, here, the chiastic structure of the line, framed by the two proper names.

58–60. The speaker's initial reference to *extrema...hora* is here pathetically amplified: the anonymous lover appears determined to take his own life (cf. esp. 8.60n.). In *id.* 3, such a desperate desire appeared twice: *id.* 3.25–7 'I shall throw

ECLOGUE 8   409

off my clothes and leap into the waves, / where Olpis the fisherman watches for tuna: / and if I die, you will certainly be happy' (a passage here emulated by V.); *id.* 3.53–4 'I shall fall to the ground and lie there, where the wolves will devour me: / this will be for you like sweet honey down your throat' (at the end of the song). However, the monologue in *id.* 3 is a sort of serenade (note the initial verb κωμάσδω, with κῶμος and κωμαστής appearing among the ancient titles of the poem) and Theocritus' goatherd plays every single card in his deck, no matter how pathetic, to win the girl. By contrast, the unnamed lover ventriloquized by V.'s Damon has been betrayed, and his suicidal speech seems far from being a vain threat. Rather, the agitated tone of his final sentences, full of logical leaps, echoes tragic models, such as Ajax's farewell monologue preceding his suicide in Soph. *Ai.* 815–65 (according to Arctinus' *Aethiopis*, Ajax killed himself at the end of the night: *schol. ad* Pind. *Isthm.* 4.58b, III, p. 231.8 Drachm. περὶ τὸν ὄρθρον [= fr. 5, p. 71 Bernabé]). A much more extreme case will be Dido's turbulent frenzy in *Aen.* 4.590–629, similarly featuring dawn as a backdrop (*Aen.* 4.584–5).

58 omnia uel medium fiat mare. uiuite siluae. As the reader will soon find out, the lover wants to leap into the sea. The phrase sounds unexpected, but it echoes l. 56 symmetrically: let everything become sea (following Arion's dolphins), and farewell to the woods (which surrounded Orpheus). The sea naturally contrasts with the pastoral world, as in *id.* 11.45–9, which V. emulates in *E.* 9.39–43, esp. 39 *quis est nam ludus in undis?* (cf., here, 8.59 *in undas*). Now, however, V. seems to rework and deliberately misinterpret *id.* 1.134 πάντα δ' ἄναλλα (v.l. ἔναλλα) γένοιτο, as if Theocritus had used the neut. plur. of ἐνάλιος 'marine' rather than a form of ἄναλλος/ ἔναλλος 'reversed, upside down'. This lover's farewell to the *siluae* will reappear in the voice of another lover, Cornelius Gallus, in *E.* 10.63 *concedite siluae*; recall Daphnis in *id.* 1.115–18 (as well as Soph. *Ai.*, esp. 862–3). For the transformation of *rus* into sea in the context of a curse, see *Dirae* 61 *dicantur mea rura ferum mare*. In colloquial farewell formulas, *uiue/uiuite* is frequently coupled with *uale/ualete* (note the alliterative effect): cf. Catull. 11.17; Hor. *sat.* 2.5.110; *epist.* 1.6.67. **fiat.** The reading *fiat* (**MP**) is certainly preferable to the better attested *fiant*: for the sing., cf. *Dirae* 46 *cinis omnia fiat* (where *fiant* is transmitted by a minority of manuscripts); Ov. *met.* 1.292 *omnia pontus erat*. Note also that late antique and medieval scribes might have been confused by the frequency of the phrase *omnia...fiant* (vel sim.) in the Vulgate: cf. *Matth.* 5.18 and 24.34; *Marc.* 13.30; *Luc.* 21.32.

59 praeceps aërii specula de montis in undas. Properly speaking, a *specula* is a height from which the gaze can range afar: Varr. *ling.* 6.82 *specula, de quo prospicimus*. Note the likely echo of *id.* 3.26 ὥπερ τὼς θύννως σκοπιάζεται Ὄλπις ὁ γριπεύς 'where Olpis the fisherman watches for tuna' (see above, 8.58–60n.), although V. eliminates any realistic detail. Rather, the mountain is here 'airy', lost in the atmosphere (for *aerius* cf. 1.58n.); cf. *Aen.* 5.586 *e speculis* (Dido), as well as 10.454 *specula...ab alta*; for a quasi-verbatim echo of the line, cf. *Ciris* 302. Daphnis' death was mysteriously connected with water at *id.* 1.138–41 (perhaps

410   ECLOGUE 8

he drowned in a spring?). According to a different tradition, he accidentally fell off a cliff (*schol.* Theocr. *id.* 8.93a, p. 214.15–17 Wend.). Legend has it that Sappho leapt off the Leucadian cliff into the sea, committing suicide for love (Strab. 10.2.9[452]; Ov. *her.* 15.163–72; *Leucadia* was the name of Varro Atacinus' *puella*, according to Prop. 2.34.86); cf. also Prop. 2.17.13 *nunc iacere e duro corpus iuuat…saxo*. Note the postponement of the preposition *de*, which follows both the noun and the epithet *aerii* (agreeing with *montis*): for a simpler inversion, see *G.* 4.333 *thalamo sub fluminis alto*; *Aen.* 7.234; cf. Lucr. 3.1088 *tempore de mortis*. Here, the emphasis is on the two adjectives *praeceps aerii*, with a pathetic effect. The largest water surface near Mantua is Lake Benacus (today Lago di Garda), similar to sea for its waves: *fluctibus et fremitu adsurgens Benace marino* (*G.* 2.160; it is the 'father' of Mincius, its emissary, in *Aen.* 10.205–6). But it seems clear here that *undas* refers to the sea (hinted at the reader's imagination in the previous line [58 *mare*]) and this is the only reference to a marine location, and therefore extra-Mantuan, of the *Eclogues*, together with that of the other love monologue in Corydon's eclogue (2.25–6). Unlike Theocritus' goatherd (*id.* 3.9), the unhappy lover does not consider suicide by hanging, dishonourable for the Roman mentality: cf. *E.* 2.7n.

60 extremum hoc munus morientis habeto. Of the many gifts which Nysa receives from her lover (cf. Alexis and his contempt for Corydon's gifts: *E.* 2.44 *munera nostra*), his death and disappearance into the sea will be the last ones. The pathetic implication is that she will be pleased by the disappearance of such an obsessive lover: cf. *id.* 3.27 and 54 (see above, 8.58–60n.), as well as the pseudo-Theocritean *id.* 23.20–1 δῶρά τοι ἦνθον / λοίσθια ταῦτα φέρων, τὸν ἐμὸν βρόχον 'here I am, carrying my last gift for you, my noose' (the lover goes on to hang himself). In a different yet comparable context, cf. *Aen.* 4.429 *extremum hoc miserae det munus amanti*. Note, in *extremum munus*, the echo of 8.20 *extrema…hora*, with a ring-composition effect (the monologue has reached its end: cf. also *E.* 10.1n.). Due to the obvious limits of narrative diegesis, literary narrators can hardly narrate their own suicide: in general, they merely announce it (as a result, the reader is in doubt as to whether the threat is eventually carried out). This is the case, for instance, with the so-called 'epistolary novel' by Chion of Eraclea, whose narrator-protagonist foreshadows his own death in his final letter (17.2–3). For a verbatim quotation, cf. *Ciris* 267.

61 desine Maenalios, iam desine, tibia, uersus. This is the only (and final) variation on the refrain, now adapted to the finale of Damon's song. V. thereby simplifies the Theocritean model, in which the refrain appeared in three different forms, one at the beginning of the song, one at its centre, and one at its end: ἄρχετε βουκολικᾶς, Μοῖσαι φίλαι, ἄρχετ' ἀοιδᾶς 'begin, dear Muses, begin the pastoral song' (*id.* 1.64, etc.; see 8.21n.); ἄρχετε βουκολικᾶς, Μοῖσαι, πάλιν ἄρχετ' ἀοιδᾶς 'begin, dear Muses, begin the pastoral song again' (*id.* 1.94, etc.); λήγετε βουκολικᾶς, Μοῖσαι, ἴτε λήγετ' ἀοιδᾶς 'end, dear Muses, end the pastoral song' (*id.* 1.127, etc.).

ECLOGUE 8   411

62-3. The poet, who did not mention the Muses in the prologue, now summons them and declares his own inadequacy (8.63n.). This 'proem in the middle' (cf. above, p. 285) is unique to *E*. 8, which also features a rather atypical prologue (see 8.1–6n.). Similarly, at the outset of the second half of the *Aeneid*, V. addresses the Muse Erato: *Aen*. 7.37 *Nunc age, qui reges Erato*, etc. This is also a way of enlivening the poem and reactivating momentum: the eclogue has accumulated a great number of lines; note the subtle irony, as in Hor. *sat*. 1.5.53 (*Musa, uelim memores*), introducing, in the middle of the satire, the contest between Messius Cicirrus and Sarmentus. In Homer, the poet asked the Muses to help him introduce the second half of *Il*. 2, i.e. the very challenging catalogue of ships (*Il*. 2.484–93).

62 Haec Damon. The reference to Damon does not merely conclude his song, which has clearly come to an end, but also introduces a new idea: 'thus far have I managed to sing; now I need the Muses' help'. This concise way of 'closing the inverted commas' without a *uerbum dicendi* is also used by V. in his epic poem: cf. esp. *Aen*. 10.16 *Iuppiter haec paucis*. **quae responderit Alphesiboeus.** The notion of 'replying' is crucial to the agonistic form (*E*. 7.5n.): echoes of *E*. 3, 5, and 7 lead the reader to wonder what prompts a correspondence between those poems and *E*. 8. Structure certainly plays a very important role (see below, 8.64–109n.).

63 dicite, Pierides. The phrase echoes and clarifies 8.62 *uos*. The epithet *Pierides*, applied to the Muses, is only used by V. in the *E*.: cf. 3.85, where it appears alongside Asinius Pollio (see n. ad loc.). For the phrase *dicite, Pierides* at the beginning of a line, cf. [Tib.] 3.1.5; Ov. *fast*. 2.269; 6.799. For *dicite* in the context of a metapoetic proem, see e.g. Prop. 3.1.5; for the poetic use of *dico* in the sense of 'singing/reciting poems', cf. *E*. 3.55n. **non omnia possumus omnes.** Cf. *E*. 7.23 (Corydon invoking the Libethrides), as well as *G*. 2.109. The notion, a proverbial one, goes back at least to Hom. *Il*. 13.729; 23.670–1. It is perhaps significant, however, that the closest parallel is found in a satire, i.e. Lucil. 218 M. = 224 K., which Macrobius mentions in relation to this passage at *Sat*. 6.1.35. V.'s own line became proverbial, also according to Macr. *Sat*. 5.16.7; cf. Otto (1890, pp. 254–5, no. 1288); see further Tosi (2007, pp. 234–5, no. 494). Some scholars have read this line as hinting at Alphesiboeus' presumed superiority (correspondingly, he is taken to be the winner of the contest): rather, the poet here corrects his bold *dicemus* (8.5) and seems to admit his own tiredness, due to the length of the song (for memory and the Muses, cf. *E*. 7.19n.). The opening of *E*. 10, which V. will introduce as his 'last endeavour', is not far away. Note, finally, that Alphesiboeus' song is the greatest example of V.'s consistent emulation of a single Theocritean poem in the *E*. (in this case, *id*. 2).

64-109. Alphesiboeus 'replies' to Damon's song with a different Theocritean imitation, which focuses on *id*. 2. Although V., as usual, downplays Theocritus' realism, the theme of magic must be of interest to him (and perhaps well suited to the addressee, if the poem is dedicated to Pollio?) due to the considerable success that it seems to have enjoyed in neoteric circles (cf. above, p. 383). At the same

412   ECLOGUE 8

time, V. establishes a prototype that will play a crucial role in Augustan literature, in which literary stylizations of the motif will recur frequently, perhaps giving voice to the anxieties of a socially and politically troubled age (cf. esp. Horace's Canidia in the *Epodes*). From a numerical and structural point of view, Alphesiboeus' song is symmetrical with Damon's. If ll. 28a and 76 are genuine, we have a sequence of ten stanzas, the first seven of which (ll. 64–94) precisely correspond, in quantitative terms, to parallel sections in Damon's song: four lines (64–7: cf. 17–20); then three (69–71: cf. 22–4); three (73–5: cf. 26–8); two (77–8: cf. 29–30); four (80–3: cf. 32–5); five (85–9: cf. 37–41); and three (91–3: cf. 47–50). The last three stanzas replicate the last three of Damon's song in length (four, five, and three lines: ll. 47–61), but in a different order (five lines: 95–9; then three: 101–3; and finally four: 105–8). Such a structural variation, appearing near the end, could be meant to point at the differences in the conclusions of the respective songs: unlike Damon's protagonist, Alphesiboeus' sorceress achieves success (see below, 8.96n.), following the mention of a mysterious Moeris. In terms of thematic structure, Alphesiboeus' first stanza (like Damon's) is a standalone piece, functioning as a *propositio* that introduces the song (cf. 8.67 *nihil hic nisi carmina desunt*, followed by the refrain at 8.68). As a result, the bulk of the song is, once again, composed of nine stanzas and ten refrain lines. A further, triadic subdivision (analogous to Damon's) can be detected: stanzas 2–4 describe the initial preparation of the spell (8.69–79); stanzas 5–7 describe the spell itself (8.80–94; note that each stanza mentions Daphnis' name); stanzas 8–10 describe a new attempt, featuring different and, apparently, more powerful ingredients (8.95–108). On ancient magic rituals, especially the *agoge* (ἀγωγή), through which lovers aim at 'leading' the object of their desire into their home (or their bed), see Winkler (1991). For a notable example of such spells, cf. *PGM*, IV.296–466 (Engl. trans. in Betz 1992, pp. 44–7).

64–7. The opening of Theocr. *id.* 2 included objects and actions typical of magic rituals: 'Where are the bay-leaves? Bring them over, Thestylis. Where are the filters? / Adorn the cup with purple wool, / so that I may bind that terrible lover of mine' (*id.* 2.1–3). However, Theocritus' opening bay-leaves (Πᾷ μοι ταὶ δάφναι;) will not appear here until 8.82–3, in connection with Daphnis' name (note the magic value of etymology: 8.83n.). While the name of Theocritus' protagonist, Simaetha, is explicitly mentioned at *id.* 2.101 and 114, Alphesiboeus' sorceress remains unnamed (like Damon's lover); her assistant, corresponding to Theocritus' Thestylis, is named at 8.77–8. In ancient magic rituals (or, rather, their literary descriptions), sorceresses are often two in number: cf. Hor. *sat.* 1.8 (Canidia and Sagana); *epod.* 5 (Canidia and Sagana, accompanied by a less active Folia); presumably, this was also true of Sophron (see below, 8.69n.). Here, the respective roles are somewhat unclear (cf. 8.105–8n.) and we only hear the name of Amaryllis, but it seems clear from the outset that there are two 'actors', since three second-person imperatives and a first-person purpose clause appear

ECLOGUE 8   413

in the same breath (*effer...cinge...adole...ut...experiar*; cf. Theocr. *id.* 2.1–3 φέρε, Θεστυλί...στέψον...ὡς...καταδήσομαι); same pattern in the conclusion of the song: cf. 8.101n. Note that, in the *E.*, this is the only instance of a female character speaking in the first person.

64 Effer aquam. The first stage of the ritual takes place outdoors but within a space belonging to the *domus*, where 'altars' are set up. This is consistent with Roman custom: see Wissowa (1912, p. 475); cf. below, 8.92–3n.; 101n.; 107n.; 109n. The action of 'bringing' something is featured at both the beginning and the end of the song: cf. 101 *fer cineres* (note also 106 *dum ferre moror*). **molli uitta.** The fillet is 'soft', i.e. probably made of wool: cf. *id.* 2.2 (for which see 8.64–7n.); Prop. 4.6.6 *terque focum circa laneus orbis eat*. **haec altaria.** Deixis will often be used to draw the assistant's (as well as the reader's) attention to the objects that play a major role in the ritual: cf. 8.73–4; 80; 83; 91; 93; 95; 97; 102. For *altaria* (which reappears in 8.74 and 105), cf. 1.43n.; 5.66n.; here, the verb *adoleo* makes explicit their connection with combustion (8.65n.).

65 uerbenasque...pinguis. The noun *uerbenae* (also attested in the sing.: Plaut. *Truc.* 480) can denote a variety of aromatic plants, including bay, rosemary, and myrtle (but also the olive tree), whose branches, when picked in sacred places, were gathered into bundles for ritual purposes: cf. Serv. Dan. ad loc.; Serv. *ad Aen.* 12.120. Hence V.'s choice of the adj. *pinguis*, which refers to 'freshness' (the branches have recently been picked) as well as to the 'oily' and 'balm-like' nature of the plants, perfectly suited to burning (as in *E.* 7.49 *taedae pingues*). Cf., in a ritual context, Hor. *carm.* 1.19.13–14 *hic / uerbenas, pueri, ponite* (along with incense, as here); but see e.g. Ter. *Andr.* 726; for medicinal use, cf. Cels. 2.33.4. In *G.* 4.131, the term seems to denote a particular species of plant, perhaps *Verbena officinalis* (cf. Plin. *nat.* 25.105–7). **adole.** The verb *adoleo* and the idea of 'burning' often recur alongside the term *altaria* (above, 8.64n.), which usually functions as object: see, for instance, Lucr. 4.1236–7 *sanguine... / conspergunt aras adolentque altaria donis*; *Aen.* 7.71 *adolet dum altaria taedis* (cf. *Aen.* 8.285 *incensa altaria circum*, as well as *G.* 3.490 *ardent altaria fibris*); Paul. Fest. p. 5 L. *altaria sunt in quibus igne adoletur*; see further *ThlL* I.793.80–794.30. Here, by contrast, the objects of 'burning' are *uerbenae* and incense. Phonetic affinity with the verb *adolesco*, derived from *alo*, may have contributed to the ancient connection between *adoleo* and rituals of 'growth' (*augere*): Non. pp. 81–2 L. *'adolere' uerbum est proprie sacra reddentium, quod significat uotis uel supplicationibus numen auctius facere...et intellegi debet ab eo quod est adoleuit, id est creuit, et adultum, quod est auctum et aucta aetate aut aliqua causa maius solito factum, ducere proprietatem*. It is, however, a mistake to paraphrase V.'s *adole* with *adde, cumula*, as Nonius himself does (Non. p. 82 L.; contrast *Aen.* 11.50 *cumulatque altaria donis*, as well as 5.54 and 7.211); cf. *G.* 4.379 and *Aen.* 1.704; see further Ernout-Meillet, p. 29, s.v. *adoleo*; *Enc. Virg.* I, p. 29, s.v. *adoleo* (R. Rocca). **mascula tura.** This incense is 'virile', i.e. of the most valuable quality, known for its large, round

414   ECLOGUE 8

'drops' (Plin. *nat.* 12.61–2). However, given the context (a ritual of love magic), erotic overtones cannot be ruled out (cf. again Plin. *nat.* 12.61). Note that *mascula* is a partial phonetic anticipation of the keyword *magicis* (8.66n.).

66 coniugis. Here, too, the object of love is a 'spouse', as in the opening of Damon's song (8.18n.), which Alphesiboeus obviously echoes. As in Theocritus, the two seem to have previously been lovers: in Theocritus, however, their union is explicitly deemed 'irregular' (Theocr. *id.* 2.35–6). **magicis…sacris**. This seems to be the first appearance of the adjective *magicus* in Latin (its Greek equivalent, μαγικός, is of rather late coinage, too: it is first attested in the imperial age). For its widespread use in poetry, cf. *Aen.* 4.493; Prop. 2.28.35; Tib. 1.2.49; Hor. *epist.* 2.2.208; Ov. *amor.* 3.7.35; *ThlL* VIII.51, esp. 54–71. Here, *magicis* specifies the sense of the otherwise vague term *sacris*, perhaps echoing the *schol. ad* Theocr. *id.* 2.10a, p. 271 Wend. (in which ἐκ θυέων is glossed with ἐκ τῶν θυσιῶν, μαγειῶν). Note the sound effect *sanos…sacris*, along with the assonance *mascula…magicis*. **auertere**. A 'deviation', soon clarified as Daphnis' return from the city (8.68). Reversibility, a typically magical quality, will play a crucial role in Hor. *epod.* 17, Horace's palinode to Canidia (esp. *epod.* 17.4–7); cf. also *sat.* 1.8.19–20; see further Barchiesi (1994).

67 nihil hic nisi carmina desunt. Here, the term *carmina* has the archaic meaning of 'spell', 'magic words'. The refrain line (*mea carmina*), with its numerous iterations, will soon fill the void (*desunt*).

68 ducite ab urbe domum, mea carmina, ducite Daphnin. Simaetha's first refrain is in the background: ἶυγξ ἕλκε τὺ τῆνον ἐμὸν ποτὶ δῶμα τὸν ἄνδρα 'magic wheel, drag that man to my house' (*id.* 2.17, etc.; by contrast, the second refrain is not emulated here: *id.* 2.69 φράζεό μευ τὸν ἔρωθ' ὅθεν ἵκετο, πότνια Σελάνα 'consider, venerable Moon, where my love came from'). In comparison to Theocritus' poem, V. adds the beloved's name and the topographic detail *ab urbe*, which hints at one of the *E.*'s fundamental oppositions, i.e. that between city and countryside. While *id.* 2 was set in a city, here the *urbs* is an alien dimension which takes the beloved away from his usual abode in the countryside: the same was true of *E.* 1, and potentially of *E.* 9 as well (Corydon's beloved boy in *E.*2, Alexis, was also *urbanus*; cf. Theocritus' Delphis, described as a foreigner in *id.* 2.29 [see below, 8.80n.]). Note the alliteration *ducite…domum…ducite Daphnin*, affecting the three key elements of the line, i.e. the verb, the acc. (of motion towards), and the direct object. The refrain and its alliterative qualities are clearly meant to perform a magical function: for the repeated imperative, typical of folk poetry, recall the refrain in Catull. 64.327 *currite ducentes subtegmina, currite, fusi* (cf. *E.* 4.46–7n.). As in Damon's song, the refrain will only be varied once, in its final occurrence (8.109n.). **Daphnin**. Daphnis' name, paronomastically close to Theocritus' Delphis (*id.* 2.77: both, moreover, are linked with Apollo), inevitably brings to mind the great pastoral singer. While it is of course impossible to equate the two Daphnis (which, however, appeared obvious to Serv. Dan. ad loc.), such

ECLOGUE 8   415

an important name can only be full of echoes and allusions (it seems that, even in everyday life, anyone bearing the name *Daphnis* was easily exposed to irony: cf. the case of Lutatius Daphnis, whom Gaius Melissus nicknamed 'Pan's love', according to Suet. *gramm.* 3.5). *E.* 5 has clearly shown that Daphnis is a concrete component of V.'s pastoral world (in that poem he was celebrated by a certain Alphesiboeus, among others). According to an ancient tradition, recorded by Ov. *met.* 4.276–8 (note the epithet *Idaeus* in *met.* 4.277, probably connecting Daphnis with Mount Ida in the Troas), Daphnis was loved by a nymph who, on seeing her love unrequited, grew angry and turned him into a stone (as it were, through a magic spell). Recall also *id.* 1.82–5 'wretched Daphnis, why do you waste away? Your girl / hurries along on foot around every spring, every grove, /.../ looking for you'; V.'s Daphnis, however, eventually seems to surrender: a wiser choice.

69–71. Note the insistence with which the term *carmen* is repeated in these lines (cf. also the frequentative verb *canto* in 8.71), following its appearance in the refrain. The unnamed sorceress strives to fill the 'lack' of songs observed in 8.67. For another list of magic virtues (i.e. a magic 'aretalogy'), cf. *Aen.* 4.487–91.

69 carmina uel caelo possunt deducere lunam. For this traditional ability of magic practitioners, originally associated with Thessalian sorceresses (and later with Medea), see Aristoph. *Nub.* 749–52; Plat. *Gorg.* 513a; Hor. *epod.* 5.45–6 and 17.77–8; Prop. 1.1.19 *deductae...fallacia lunae*; Tib. 1.8.21 *cantus et e curru Lunam deducere temptat* (note the threefold repetition of *cantus* in Tib. 1.8.19–21, modelled on V.); Ov. *amor.* 2.1.23 *carmina sanguineae deducunt cornua lunae*; Lucan. 6.499–506; Petron. 129.10 *praecipue in hac ciuitate, in qua mulieres etiam lunam deducunt* (note the emphatic *etiam*, corresponding to V.'s *uel*: 'also', 'even') and 134.12 ll. 8–9; cf. also *Aen.* 4.489 *uertere sidera retro*. Recall the (possible) title of Sophron's mime which Theocritus is said to have emulated in *id.* 2: Γυναῖκες αἳ τὰν θεὸν φαντὶ ἐξελᾶν, i.e. 'Women who claim to drive out the goddess' (Athen. 11.480b).

70 carminibus Circe socios mutauit Ulixi. Circe is the Homeric archetype of the sorceress: she appeared, along with Medea (and the less renowned Perimede), in *id.* 2.15–16; cf. above, 8.48n. In the *Odyssey*, however, Homer does not emphasize her 'songs', but rather her 'drugs' and the 'touch' of her rod, which she uses to turn Odysseus' companions into pigs: cf. *Od.* 10.236 and 238. Circe's erotic connotations were obvious to Homer's audience and highlighted by allegorical and philosophical interpretations of the myth, reading the companions' metamorphosis as a symbol of man's degradation in the grip of bodily pleasure: cf. Diogenes the Cynic, quoted in Di. Chrys. 8.21–2, and esp. Heracl. *all. Hom.* 72; Athen. 1.10e–f; Plut. *coniug. praec.* 5.139a; cf. also Cic. *diu. in Caec.* 57; Hor. *epist.* 1.2.23–31; see further Tochtermann (1992); Bettini, Franco (2010, pp. 90–120). In spite of her dreadful powers, the mythical sorceress seems to be unlucky in love: after being abandoned by Odysseus (*Od.* 10.483–9), she is also rejected by Glaucus (Ov. *met.* 14.37–50). **Vlixi.** Archaic gen. form (like *Achilli*), probably

416   ECLOGUE 8

derived from an originary *Ulixei* (cf. *Achillei*), featuring the ending *-i* typical of roots in *-os/-us*, perhaps on the basis of a hybrid nom. **Ulixeus* (cf. **Achilleus*). The gen. *Ulixi* is common in V., always appearing in line-ending position: see e.g. *Aen.* 2.7; 90; but cf. Liv. Andr. fr. 30 Bläns. (= 16 Mor.). The form is still used by Ovid (*met.* 14.671), but falls out of use towards the end of the first century CE. Note the Virgilian echo in Petron. 134.12 ll. 12–13 *Phoebeia Circe / carminibus magicis socios mutauit Ulixes* (where, however, ll. 11–16 have been suspected of interpolation). This normalized form also appears on a Pompeian graffito (found on the Building of Eumachia, a sort of 'new Circe': cf. Gigante 1979, p. 167; Ferraro 1982, pp. 11–12).

71 **frigidus in pratis cantando rumpitur anguis.** The Marsi, an ancient population inhabiting central Abruzzo, were credited with the ability to make snakes 'explode' by singing magical litanies: cf. Lucil. 575–6 M. = 576–7 K. *ut Marsus colubras / disrumpit cantu* and Pompon. fr. 118 R.[3] *mirum ni haec Marsa est, in colubras callet cantiunculam* (the tradition is still alive in local folklore of Abruzzo); see also Ov. *met.* 7.203 (Medea) *uipereas rumpo uerbis et carmine fauces* (cf. *amor.* 2.1.25), as well as Hor. *epod.* 17.29; cf. Tupet (1986, pp. 2617–26). V.'s reference to the Marsi's practice appears right after the Homeric Circe, whose geographical connection with Cape Circeo made her relevant to the origins of Italy's pre-Roman populations (the Marsi, in fact, were traced back to a son of Circe and Odysseus: Plin. *nat.* 7.15). Snakes are among the most typical dangers in the pastoral world: note here the adj. *frigidus*, hinting at the animal's cold blood (and venom), as in *E.* 3.93 ('Pollio's' poem). The line-framing *frigidus…anguis* might be meant iconically to represent the legth of the snake: for a similar effect at the end of a sentence (though in a syntactically more complex context), see *G.* 2.154 *squameus…anguis*; cf. also *G.* 1.244 *maximus…Anguis* (the constellation), as well as *Aen.* 2.379 and 8.300. The phrase *in pratis* makes the explosion visually conspicuous, against a green backdrop of grass. For a similar yet stronger chromatic effect, cf. *E.* 4.43, as well as 7.11n. For the instrumental gerund (*cantando*), see *E.* 6.71n.; also 9.56 *causando*.

73–4 **terna…triplici… / …terque.** Each of the three bands is 'woven' in three different colours, i.e. made of three different threads, adding up to nine. This explains the distributive *terna*, taken up by 8.77 *ternos*. The number three, here multiplied by itself, plays a crucial role in folklore, esp. in magic and ritual: note *id.* 2.43 'three times I offer libations, and three times…I say'; cf., in Dido's ritual, *Aen.* 4.510–11 (where the number three is mentioned three times); note also *Aen.* 6.506; Tib. 1.2.56 (on odd numbers see 8.75n.). The stanza itself is composed of three lines (8.73–5), in which the number three is mentioned three times; note also that nine stanzas are properly involved in the sorceress' *carmen*. This passage, full of magic, is quite heavy on alliteration (esp. /t/). For a later reworking, cf. *Ciris* 371–3.

73 **tibi.** In accordance with magic ritual, the woman addresses a symbolic substitute for her lover, i.e. a small portrait or statuette (8.75 *effigiem*). **primum.**

ECLOGUE 8   417

The ritual will proceed by increasingly challenging degrees: this is the first level. **triplici…colore**. Perhaps white, red, and black—the three colours typically associated with Hecate and triple deities in general (*E.* 8.75n.); cf. Apul. *met.* 11.3.5 (Isis' garment, with the addition of a yellow crocus). See further Abt (1908), p. 105 (on white and black in ancient magic rituals).

74 **licia circumdo**. These 'bands', wrapped around the portrait, symbolize the binding power of magic: note the enjambement between ll. 73–4, which 'visualizes' the gesture (*terna… / licia circumdo*). The same goes for the protagonist's movement around the altar, equally emphasized by enjambement at ll. 74–5 *haec altaria circum / effigiem duco*.

75 **effigiem**. For the use of images, typically statuettes, in erotic magic, cf. *Aen.* 4.508; Hor. *sat.* 1.8.30. **numero deus impare gaudet**. The vague noun is perhaps meant to avoid naming a specific underworld deity (a typically superstitious pre-caution). As Servius noted, the deity here alluded to might be Hecate herself, who appeared (along with Selene) in the opening of *id.* 2.10–16: note the voc. δαῖμον in *id.* 2.11; for *deus* used of female deities cf. *Aen.* 2.632. No wonder that Hecate rejoices in odd numbers: being a triple deity (Hecate/Proserpina, Selene, Diana), she was venerated at three-way crossroads (cf. *Aen.* 4.609 *nocturnisque Hecate triuiis ululata per urbes*, as well as *id.* 2.36 ἁ θεὸς ἐν τριόδοισι); see further *Enc. Virg.* II, pp. 160–3, s.v. *Ecate* (I. Chirassi Colombo); *Virg. Enc.* I, pp. 355–6, s.v. *Diana* (J. D. Hejduk). Predilection for the numbers three and nine also appears in a symposiastic context at Hor. *carm.* 3.19.11–17 (cf. esp. 13 *qui Musas amat imparis*), probably reminiscent of this passage. In fact, this is a *mystica lex*, according to Auson. *carm.* 336 (*Griphus ternarii numeri*), I, p. 200 Peip. Odd numbers, deemed to be indivisible, played an important role in ancient customs and rituals (sometimes surviving to this day). A few lines below, another deity will be explicitly mentioned: the less disquieting Venus (8.78). For the formulation, cf. *E.* 3.59 *amant alterna Camenae*.

76. This line should not be deleted, as Perret proposed: it is unanimously attested by the manuscript tradition, and there is no reason to suppose that it might have been interpolated here (esp. without the symmetrical 8.28a, only restored in γ [see n. ad loc.]). If 8.76 is genuine, the total number of refrain lines is ten, just as in Theocritus (considering only the first version of the refrain: *id.* 2.17 [see above, 8.68n.]; cf. the last occurrence of the line at *id.* 2.63).

77–8. The three colours reappear, along with the respective threads (8.73–4), which are now tied in three distinct knots: here, as in 8.73–4, the repetition is threefold (*necte…necte…necto*), and further underscored by the position of each verb (beginning of 8.77; beginning and end of 8.78). Note the hammering alliteration (cf. *nodis*, as well as *tribus…ternos*; *Veneris…uincula*).

77 **Amarylli**. This female name frequently appears in V.'s pastoral poetry (as in Theocritus'): here, it hints at the poem's rustic setting. Note, however, that *Amaryllis* is also the name of the girl wooed by the goatherd in *id.* 3 (which

418   ECLOGUE 8

Damon emulates), and that her namesake in *E.* 1 knows what it means to long for an absent lover who has left for the city: *mirabar quid maesta deos, Amarylli, uocares…Tityrus hinc aberat* (1.36–8).

78 modo. For *modo* used to strengthen an imperative (here following the voc.), cf. 4.8 *tu modo* (n.). '**Veneris' dic 'uincula necto'**. The symbolic meaning of *licia* is made explicit. The woman intends to bind her beloved to her using Venus' 'bands': note both alliteration and assonance in *Veneris…uincula* (*uincio* is connected with the goddess' name and role by Varro in *ling.* 5.61–2). At any rate, the idea of 'fetters' and 'bonds' is common in magic rituals, particularly when it comes to binding magic: for an equivalent term in Greek, cf. κατάδεσις/κατάδεσμος. The entire formulation presupposes *id.* 2.21 'scatter the grain, and say at the same time [ἅμα καὶ λέγε ταῦτα]: "I am scattering Delphis' bones"'.

80–3. The analogical principle governing sympathetic magic now involves fire and the beloved's name. These four lines seem to establish a magical link between the ritual and the beloved person, who will be the object of a full-blown 'attack' from 8.85 onwards. With the exception of the refrain lines, Daphnis' name is mentioned for the first time here: cf. *id.* 2.23–6 'Delphis tormented me, and now I burn bay-leaves / for Delphis [Δέλφις ἔμ' ἀνίασεν· ἐγὼ δ' ἐπὶ Δέλφιδι δάφναν / αἴθω]; as these leaves crackle loud, / immediately catching fire, and we do not even see their ashes, / so may Delphis' flesh waste in the flame'. Here, however, the etymology of the beloved's name is also activated: see below, 8.83n.

80 limus ut hic durescit, et haec ut cera liquescit. As the fire is kindled on the altar, *limus* ('mud', 'clay') is cooked and hardened, while wax melts. There is no need to think of two distinct statuettes (note Serv. Dan. ad loc.: *se de limo facit, Daphnidem de cera*), in addition to the portrait mentioned at 8.75; rather, these are further magical ingredients fetched for the ritual (unlike the case of Hor. *sat.* 1.8.30). Through his reference to clay, Alphesiboeus seems to add complexity to the model of *id.* 2.28–9 ὡς τοῦτον τὸν κηρὸν ἐγὼ σὺν δαίμονι τάκω, / ὡς τάκοιθ' ὑπ' ἔρωτος ὁ Μύνδιος αὐτίκα Δέλφις 'as I melt this wax with the goddess' assistance, / so may Delphis of Myndus [a Dorian city in Caria] immediately melt with desire'; fire, flame of love, and wax statuette (of Eros himself) recur together in *Anacreontea* 11. Here, however, the main point seems to be the 'sympathetic' effect of fire, whose twofold action can both harden and soften things magically. In the same way, Daphnis is the object of love's action, which can either 'harden' him (as appears to be the case) or 'soften' him (as the woman hopes). The ultimate consequence of this 'hardening' process, i.e. rejection, is not ideal for either the beloved or the woman herself (who, in such a case, could not be reunited with her *coniunx*: cf. 8.66). Analogical doubling is emphasized by the parallel, rhyming construction of the two *cola*, evoking the rhythm of ancient ritual *carmina*: cf. *terra pestem teneto, salus hic maneto* (quoted in Varr. *rust.* 1.2.27); Cat. *agr.* 160; note also the coincidence between ictus and accent (but see *E.* 1.70n.). Note, finally, that both verbal forms have an inchoative suffix: the regular cadence contributes to the chanting tone.

ECLOGUE 8   419

81 uno eodemque. Unity is strengthened by prosody: note the elision with synizesis (*eodem* is disyllabic, as in Lucr. 2.663; 6.961; 1040); cf. *Aen.* 12.847 *uno eodemque tulit partu*, as well as 10.487 *una eademque uia*; see further *Enc. Virg.* IV, p. 879b, s.v. *sinizèsi* (S. Timpanaro); for *unus idemque* cf. Lucr. 2.919 (918) *una eademque*. **sic nostro Daphnis amore.** Like, hopefully, Delphis in *id.* 2 (see 8.80n.), Theocritus' Daphnis was said to 'melt' for love (note, here, 8.80 *ut cera liquescit*): *id.* 1.66 Δάφνις ἐτάκετο (cf. *id.* 1.82, as well as 7.76). The poet's language here implies commonly used descriptions of love as fire (cf. *E.* 2.1n.). For the connection between Daphnis, fire, and wax see also the Byzantine scholion commenting on *id.* 1 in the ms. Vaticanus 913 (H in C. Wendel's edition: cf. pp. xx–xxi): p. 11b.25–6 Dueb. = p. 66.12–14 Ahr. τήκεσθαι τὸ κατ' ὀλίγον ὑπορρεῖν τῷ πυρὶ δαπανώμενον, οἷον ἐπὶ κηροῦ 'melting in the sense of liquefying little by little under the consuming effect of fire, as in the case of wax' (note the mention of fire, as here: *uno eodemque igni*); see 8.83n. For an interpretation of the context and the significance of this line within the ritual as a whole, cf. above, 8.80n.

82 sparge molam. Cf. *id.* 2.18 ἄλφιτά τοι πρᾶτον πυρὶ τάκεται 'first of all, barley flour is consumed by fire'; *id.* 2.33 νῦν θυσῶ τὰ πίτυρα 'now I shall burn the bran'. Properly speaking, *mola* is the mill used to crush and pulverize wheat and other cereals. By metonymy, the term comes to denote—as here—the result of such a procedure, i.e. 'flour' (sometimes mixed with salt: *mola salsa*), commonly used in religious rituals, particularly sacrifices (hence, *immolare*: cf. *Aen.* 4.517 *mola manibusque piis altaria iuxta*). For its use in wedding ceremonies, see Serv. Dan. *ad G.* 1.31; for its specifically magical (or, at any rate, superstitious) use, cf. Tib. 1.5.14; Mart. 7.54.5; Drac. *Romul.* 10.195. **et fragilis incende bitumine lauros.** Bitumen has a well-known incendiary effect, sometimes used metaphorically, as in Hor. *epod.* 5.81–2 *amore sic meo flagres uti / bitumen atris ignibus*. Note the phonetic qualities of the epithet *fragilis*, making the crackling flames perceptible (bay-leaves are 'fragile' because they are thin and rigid): cf. Lucr. 6.112 *fragilis <sonitus> chartarum*. Burning bay leaves tend to produce loud sounds: cf. Lucr. 6.154–5 (on a wildfire) *nec res ulla magis quam Phoebi Delphica laurus / terribili sonitu flamma crepitante crematur* (note also *crepitet* in Tib. 2.5.81 quoted below). The auditory aspect of combustion, which the sorceress hopes will be intense and complete, was deemed to be an important clue to the success of the ritual: cf. *id.* 2.24–6 (see above, 8.80–3n.), as well as Tib. 2.5.81–3 *succensa sacris crepitet bene laurea flammis, / omine quo felix et sacer annus erit. // laurus ubi bona signa dedit, gaudete coloni* (for the extinction of fire as an ill-boding sign, cf. Prop. 2.28.36). In 8.105–6, the sudden appearance of a flame will foreshadow the beloved's arrival. Along with Daphnis' name (8.80–3n.), his namesake plant (bay) appears here for the first time in Alphesiboeus' song: it was featured in the opening of *id.* 2.1 πᾷ μοι ταὶ δάφναι. Here, as in 6.83n., M reads *laurus*; cf. above, 8.13n.

83 me malus. For the same alliterative conjunction, cf. 8.41: the phrase has a thematic value in both songs, which focus on troubled love. **ego hanc in Daphnide**

420   ECLOGUE 8

laurum. The etymological connection between the name Daphnis and bay (δάφνη), perhaps also perceptible in 8.81–2, is here evident (even though the sorceress does not explicitly comment on it); cf. similarly 8.107 *Hylax in limine latrat*. A comparable association is suggested by a Theocritean line that V. echoes here: *id*. 2.23 ἐγὼ δ' ἐπὶ Δέλφιδι δάφναν (for *laurus*/δάφνη as the Delphic plant *par excellence* cf. Lucr. 6.154). Note also the linked consecutive line-endings *lauros*/*laurum*/*Daphnin* (8.82–4). The use of *in* + abl. of the person, corresponding to Theocritus' ἐπὶ Δέλφιδι, can also be explained as a pun on certain phrases common in erotic contexts, such as Ter. *Eun*. 567 *in hac commotu' sum*; cf. ThlL VII.1.781.24–37; in connection with the idea of 'burning' (for love), cf. esp. Hor. *epod*. 11.4 *in pueris aut in puellis urere*; Ov. *met*. 7.21–2 *in hospite…ureris*. Thus, 'if wicked Daphnis burns me (*me…urit*), I burn…these bay-leaves for him'.

   85–9. The stanza opening the second half of the *carmen* is, thus far, the longest (five lines; cf. 8.95–9); it is entirely devoted to a complex simile. In the corresponding stanza, Damon's unnamed lover had remembered the time when he fell in love (8.37–41). Note, however, precise echoes in both thematic and verbal terms (8.88n.). V. here chooses a typically pastoral image, thereby 'correcting' the Theocritean model, which featured mares (non-pastoral animals) and mentioned an eminently urban space, i.e. the gymnasium: *id*. 2.48–51 'this plant [the thorn-apple] drives all / fillies and swift mares insane on the mountains. / So may I see Delphis, too, and may he enter this house / like a madman, coming out of the wrestling-school, his body covered in shiny oil'. Note also, in 8.88, a literal quotation of an analogous earlier simile, Varius' *De morte*, fr. 4 Bläns. = Court.: *ceu canis umbrosam lustrans Gortynia uallem / si ueteris potuit ceruae comprendere lustra, / saeuit in absentem et circum uestigia latrans / aethera per nitidum tenues sectatur odores; / non amnes illam medii, non ardua tardant, / perdita nec serae meminit decedere nocti* (Macrobius observed the allusion in *Sat*. 6.2.20, which transmits the fragment). V.'s reference to this Epicurean poet is unsurprisingly coupled with an echo of a well-known Lucretian passage, i.e. Lucr. 2.355–66 (a cow desperately looking for her calf; cf. Ov. *fast*. 4.459–60). Note that the author of this song is an Alphesiboeus (i.e. 'one who gains oxen'), and that the reader knows how the competition between the two herdsmen enchanted a *iuuenca* in 8.2 (herself *immemor*, i.e. of *herbae*: cf. here *nec meminit* in 8.88).

   85 talis amor Daphnin qualis. For a simile comparable in structure, cf. *E*. 5.45–6 *tale tuum carmen nobis… / quale sopor*, etc. (in Daphnis' poem). The verb will appear only in 8.89 with the repetition of *talis amor*; an analogous procedure is used in 8.1 and 5. **iuuencum**. Maternal love: the sought-after one is a young bullock, as in Lucr. 2.352 (*uitulus*); cf. Lucr. 2.360 *desiderio perfixa iuuenci*. Erotic attraction can be ruled out: in bovine behaviour, female animals hardly need to 'pursue' a male (note the exceptional case, mentioned in *E*. 6, of the *puella* Pasiphae, who was the object of divine punishment: cf. 6.46n.).

86 per nemora atque altos quaerendo bucula lucos. The heifer's moans, resounding in the woods, are phonetically evoked by the assonance of dark vowels in *bucula lucos* (cf. also 8.87 *riuum uiridi procumbit in ulua*; note the hyperbaton *altos...lucos*, visualizing the distance). For a more obvious case, cf. Lucr. 2.358–9 *completque querelis / ...nemus*, which V. reworks in *Aen.* 8.215–16. The diminutive *bucula*, an eminently 'pastoral' word, reappears only twice in V., and both times in the G. (1.375 and 4.11). Wandering is typical of herds, but here the *bucula*'s movements hint at great anxiety, analogous to a lover's feeling: cf. Corydon in *E.* 2.4 and 15, as well as Pasiphae chasing the white bull in *E.* 6.52.

87 propter aquae riuum. Right before a verbatim quotation of Varius (8.88n.), here is a further echo of Lucr. 2.29–30 = 5.1392–3 *prostrati in gramine molli / propter aquae riuum*. But the Lucretian (i.e. Epicurean) archetype of pastoral life is here reversed. In fact, V.'s emphasis is on an utter inability to benefit from nature's generosity (water, fresh air, and soft grass): contrast *E.* 6.54 and 59. **uiridi procumbit in ulua.** Bending its front legs, the animal leans forward: the image is vivid and realistic, just like the detail *uiridi...ulua* (the green grass of a marsh, probably evoking landscapes familiar to the poet, such as the banks of the river Mincius). Cf. *Aen.* 6.416 *glauca...in ulua*; Cat. *agr.* 37.2 *circum salicta herbam altam uluamque*, also featuring willow trees. Note the alliteration, linking *propter* (the first word in this line) to the verb *procumbit*; cf. also *perdita* in the following line.

88 perdita, nec serae meminit decedere nocti. A literal quotation of Varius' *De morte*, fr. 4.6 Bläns. = Court. *perdita nec serae meminit decedere nocti* (cf. above, 8.85–9n.). Despite the obvious similarities (both poets focus on female animals: a heifer and a bitch), there is a great difference between the two passages: one animal is urged on by the instinct of hunting (the bitch pursuing the deer), the other by maternal affection (the heifer with the calf). For the clausula *serae...decedere nocti*, cf. G. 3.467. Varius, in turn, may be echoing a Homeric passage such as *Il.* 8.502 πειθώμεθα νυκτὶ μελαίνῃ. V. will allude to Varius' *De morte* again in his two later works, and Varius himself will soon make an appearance in the *E.* (see 9.35n.). Note also, in Calvus' line echoed by V. at 8.4 (*sol quoque...meminit*), the idea of a lover's impaired perception of time, implied by the comparison with the sun's path; cf. Hor. *carm.* 2.9.10–12 *nec tibi Vespero / surgente decedunt amores / nec rapidum fugiente solem.* **perdita.** In Varius' poem, the adj. is affected by inversion, since it refers to what follows (*perdita nec serae meminit decedere nocti*; Hollis 2007, p. 237, ad loc., would otherwise be right in being suspicious of the transmitted text: his objections must, at any rate, be kept in mind), whereas here the adj. either depends on the preceding *procumbit* or is, more probably, used incidentally and emphatically. Cf. *E.* 2.58–9 *floribus Austrum / perditus et liquidis immisi fontibus apros* (as well as *Aen.* 4.561–2). See also G. 3.446–67 *aut medio procumbere campo / pascentem et serae solam decedere nocti*, where *pascentem* (positionally corresponding to *perdita*) is governed by *procumbere campo*. The image is a variation on a Theocritean theme (*id.* 2.49

μαίνονται), all the while echoing Damon's *perii* (8.41). The adj. *perditus*, along with its adverbial form, belongs to the erotic vocabulary: cf. Catull. 45.3; 64.70; 104.3; see further *ThlL* X.1.1275.31–46.

89 mederi. Cf. *medicina furoris* at *E.* 10.60, i.e. Theocritus' φάρμακον (*id.* 11.17). In both cases, however, love is hard to heal.

91–3. According to a stereotype of magical thinking, the spellbinding of the beloved can be produced through objects belonging to him or her (and therefore functioning as a ritual substitute), as in *id.* 2.53–4 'this fringe [κράσπεδον] Delphis has lost from his cloak, / and this I now pluck in pieces and throw into the devouring fire'; but cf. also, for instance, Lucian. *dial. mer.* 4.4–5.

91 has…exuuias. The term *exuuiae* (lit. 'spoils') is vaguer than Theocritus' 'fringe', and can encompass clothing, jewellery, and various other objects (including hair, etc.). Dido will place Aeneas' weapons and *exuuiae*, along with the 'marital' bed, on the pyre set up in the palace (*Aen.* 4.494–8; 507); cf. Apul. *met.* 3.18.4 *qua nidor suarum ducebat exuuiarum*, as well as Lucian. *dial. mer.* 4.4. **perfidus ille.** 'Perfidious', i.e. contrary to *fides* or 'traitor'. Daphnis (we suppose) has betrayed the woman's love. The adj. belongs to the vocabulary of love-elegy and erotic poetry in general (cf., for instance, Catull. 64.174; Prop. 1.11.16; Tib. 1.8.63; Ov. *amor.* 3.3.10), and will be used by Dido in *Aen.* 4.421 (*perfidus ille*, referring to Aeneas; cf. also *Aen.* 4.305 and 366). Here, however, the term is also connected with juridical language and procedures: pledges, debts, and subsequent 'obligations' (8.92n.).

92 pignora. 'Pledges' of love, which the sorceress now sends down to the Earth (8.93 *tibi mando*), in order to bind (8.93 *debent*) the 'insolvent' Daphnis. The Earth is summoned to collect the debt, forcing Daphnis to cross the threshold of the woman's house (or, worse, swallowing him into the underworld: cf. *id.* 2.160 [see 8.95–9n.]).

92–3 quae nunc ego limine in ipso, / Terra, tibi mando. Through the woman's words, Alphesiboeus makes her gestures visible: such a mimetic technique seems to hint at drama and stage directions. The sorceress approaches the threshold and buries objects belonging to Daphnis near it; then, in 8.101, she orders Amaryllis to carry 'out' the ashes produced by the fire. Note, in *tibi*, the archaic prosody (the second vowel is long), for which cf. 5.79n. The personification of Earth (*tibi*), venerated in its divine form somewhat interchangeably as *Tellus* or *Terra*, aims at corroborating the ritual. Aeneas will address *Tellus* in the context of the solemn ritual at *Aen.* 7.136–7 *primam…deorum / Tellurem* (cf. 4.166 *prima . . . Tellus*). *Terra* is referred to as the Giants' mother (like the Greek goddess Gaia) in *G.* 1.278–9. **limine in ipso.** It is to her threshold that the woman wants to attract Daphnis. The threshold, a liminal space between the inside and the outside (of a house, a public building, or a whole city), plays a very important role in popular beliefs and superstitions, and correspondingly also in ancient magic rituals (cf. *id.* 2.60, mentioning Delphis' door). No wonder that, in erotic contexts, the threshold is emotionally associated with the beloved's arrival: cf. again *id.* 2.104, as well as

Catull. 68.70–2 *mea se molli candida diua pede // intulit et trito fulgentem in limine plantam /…constituit*; Prop. 1.18.12. The detail will reappear, crucially, in 8.107 *Hylax in limine latrat*.

95–9. Towards the end of *id.* 2, Theocritus' Simaetha similarly threatened dangerously to intensify her magical action, addressing the Moon: 'if he keeps / vexing me, he will knock on the door of Hades, by the Moirai; / such terrible poisons I stored in this basket, I tell you: / an Assyrian stranger, my Lady, taught them to me' (*id.* 2.159–62). For a different geographical reference, also evoking the East, cf. below, 8.95n. (Pontus).

95 has herbas. Another instance of deixis, following *has…exuuias* (8.91; cf. 8.64n.): 'these herbs', which the woman is obviously showing to Amaryllis, will keep playing a menacing role at the centre of the scene (cf. 8.97 and 102), until the final, decisive stanza. **Ponto…lecta uenena.** The Pontic region, on the southern coast of the Black Sea, was known for various poisons produced there, including aconite, the most lethal of them all: Theophr. *hist. plant.* 9.16.4; Strab. 12.3.7 (543); Plin. *nat.* 27.4; cf. also *G.* 2.152 (it seems, however, that at least one variety of aconite could grow in Italy, too: see Dioscor. *mat. met.* 4.77). A renowned king of Pontus was Mithridates the Great, whose fame is closely connected with poisons and antidotes obtained from plants (cf. Ov. *met.* 15.755–6 *Mithridateisque tumentem / nominibus Pontum*; Plin. *nat.* 25.5–6; 62; 127; Iuv. 6.661). Colchis, Medea's homeland, is also on the Black Sea: the sorceress, featured in *id.* 2 along with Circe (cf. above, 8.70n.), is alluded to yet not explicitly mentioned by Alphesiboeus here; cf. Cic. *Manil.* 22 *ex eodem Ponto Medea illa quondam profugisse dicitur*, as well as Ov. *met.* 7.406–7; Iuv. 14.114.

96 Moeris. This is the first instance of a name (apparently unfamiliar to the pastoral tradition) which plays an important role both here and in *E.* 9. In this poem, Moeris knows terrible poisons; he can also turn himself into a wolf and displace crops. The name's exotic overtones are due to an ancient Egyptian king called Moeris (Herodot. 2.13.1); etymologically, however, the name can be linked to μοῖρα 'fate' and the Μοῖραι, the goddesses invoked by Simaetha (*id.* 2.160 quoted above, 8.95–9n.); see further *Enc. Virg.* III, pp. 491–3, s.v. *Meri* (F. Michelazzo); *Virg. Enc.* II, p. 836, s.v. *Moeris* (J. Van Sickle). As for *E.* 9, it will show that even the bearer of such a name can safely survive the proscriptions (9.1n.), but only thanks to lucky chance (and the correct interpretation of an omen). The appearance of Moeris, and the celebration of his powers, mark Alphesiboeus' choice to abandon any precise numerical correspondence between his song and Damon's: could it be that the simple mention of Moeris' name unleashes a peerless force, like that of fate itself?

97–9. These lines describe three magical procedures, testified to by the narrator's direct experience: eye-witness testimony is a typical component of 'fable-like' narratives (cf. Hor. *sat.* 1.8.23; but see below, 8.99n.). For the emphatic word-order *ego saepe… /…saepe… /…uidi*, cf. *G.* 1.316–18; see further La Penna (1987).

424 ECLOGUE 8

97 saepe lupum fieri et se condere siluis. The first prodigy attributed to Moeris is particularly fitting for the pastoral context: turning himself into a wolf, he hides in the woods (similarly, in *E.* 6.80–1, Philomela's metamorphosis was associated with her escape to desolate places). For the main Latin treatments of the werewolf (or *uersipellis*, i.e. 'skin-changer'), cf. Ov. *met.* 1.209–39, esp. 232–3 *nactusque silentia ruris / exululat*; Petron. 62 (esp. 7 *ululare coepit et in siluas fugit*); Plin. *nat.* 8.80–3; see further Tupet (1986, pp. 2647–52). The wolf is among the oldest components of the Romans' collective imagination, as is confirmed by the archaic figures called *Luperci*, whose rituals were traced back to Evander, the Palatine hill, and the Arcadian Pan called *Lycaeus*: cf. *Aen.* 8.343–4; see further *Enc. Virg.* III, pp. 284–6, s.v. *Luperci* (U. Bianchi). Even though the magical herbs are of foreign origin, their effects (including this transformation) are typical of Roman superstition.

98 saepe animas imis excire sepulcris. Shades are here summoned from the deepest graves, without, however, disturbing their mortal remains. Such a procedure, sometimes called *psychomantia* (Cic. *diu.* 1.132), is part of necromancy: see *Aen.* 4.490; but cf. also Hom. *Od.* 10.516–37 (as well as e.g. Laius' appearance in Sen. *Oed.* 530–658, esp. 577–86, emphasizing chthonic 'depth': cf. here *imis… sepulcris*). The ritual could have a macabre aspect if direct contact with the corpse or parts of it was involved, as in Lucan. 6.507–872 (cf. Hor. *sat.* 1.8.22).

99 satas alio…traducere messis. The third, and final, portent is the so-called *translatio frugum*, considered as a serious offence in the *Twelve Tables*: cf. *tab.* 8.8a–b Warm. (Plin. *nat.* 28.17–18; Serv.); see also Tib. 1.8.19; Ov. *rem.* 255. The underlying belief was that, through obsessive chanting, someone could transfer crops from one field to another (Tupet 1986, pp. 2610–17). The participle *satas* underscores the fact that the seeds have been sown by others, and perhaps refers to the actual workings of the spell: the 'transfer' seems to take place at the moment of germination, i.e. when the seeds are still underground (the woman claims to have seen Moeris in action; she does not claim, however, to have seen the effects of the last two spells).

101 fer cineres…foras. A new command, echoing the opening of Alphesiboeus' song: 8.64 *effer aquam*. Amaryllis is now asked to carry 'out' (i.e. outside of the house) the ashes. This action brings the scene and the song to a close (cf. also 106 *dum ferre moror*). In her address to Amaryllis (here mentioned again), the protagonist uses the first person (8.102 *ego*) to express her intention to strike Daphnis fatally (8.103 *agrediar*): the distinction between second and first person (*fer…Amarylli / ego…adgrediar*), as at the beginning of the song, reaffirms the presence of two characters on the scene (cf. 8.64–7n.).

101–2 riuoque fluenti / transque caput iace, nec respexeris. The procedure is meant to conclude the ritual and make it irrevocable: cf. the instructions that Tiresias gives to Alcmene in *id.* 24.93–6 'Early tomorrow morning, let a housemaid collect the ashes from the fire [i.e. the remains of the two snakes strangled by Heracles in his crib], / and throw them all into the river, so that they may be carried away [if we read φέρεσθαι, as V. seems to do; however, φέρουσα has good chances to be the correct reading: cf. Gow 1952, II, p. 430 ad *id.* 24.94] / towards the rugged rocks, beyond the boundaries, and let her come back / without turning around [ἂψ δὲ νέεσθω / ἄστρεπτος]. The idea of throwing something 'behind one's back' (*trans...caput*), for which cf. Ov. *met.* 1.383 (Deucalion and Pyrrha), plays an important role in both ancient and modern folklore. The prohibition on 'looking back' (cf. ἄστρεπτος), frequent in rituals involving chthonic forces, is meant to protect the person performing the ritual without neutralizing its effects. Cf. Aesch. *Ch.* 99; Apoll. Rhod. 3.1039; *PGM*, I, p. 68, no. 4.45 ἄπιθι ἀνεπιστρεπτί (where the ritual involves the river Nile, or one of its branches: cf. esp. 4.40–5); Ov. *fast.* 5.439; see also Hom. *Od.* 5.349–50; Eur. *Andr.* 293–4. Whereas Theocritus' Daphnis (*id.* 1.140–1) disappeared in a mysterious (or metaphorical?) whirlpool, V.'s Daphnis will soon reappear and be reunited with the woman who loves him. The ashes themselves will suddenly catch fire (8.105–6) and avoid a 'second death' by water. The mention of baneful herbs at 8.95–9 conveys the impression that the final ritual alone achieves the goal of bringing Daphnis back. For the dat. of motion *riuo...fluenti* (governed by *iacio*), cf. *Aen.* 10.683 (*sese*) *fluctibus an iaciat mediis* (note, however, the reflexive pron.) and 9.712 *ponto iaciunt*; see also Ov. *met.* 3.127 *iecit humo* [v.l. *humi*]...*arma.* For a reworking of V.'s passage, cf. Val. Fl. 3.442–3. In prose, cf. Colum. 2.17.5 *semina subiacenti solo iecerit.*

103 **nihil ille deos, nil carmina curat** Daphnis has no concern for the gods (cf. Nysa in 8.19–20) or the *carmina* (= the magical ones, but also poetry): this explains the woman's resort to baneful herbs. Note the prosodic variation *nihil/nil*, as in *E.* 2.6–7 *nihil mea carmina curas? / nil nostri miserere?* Here, the tension accumulated during the ritual reaches its climax: the threat is a serious one and may have fatal consequences for the careless beloved. Hence the emphasis on his 'impiety'. However, after the last iteration of the refrain (begging the *carmina* to bring Daphnis back), a surprise is introduced at 8.105 and the action takes a new course (as the final line confirms: 8.109 *ab urbe uenit...Daphnis*).

105–8. The servant, Amaryllis, is often taken to be the speaker in 8.105–6 (Serv. Dan. ad loc.: '*aspice*' *hoc ab alia dici debet*). Surprisingly enough, her voice would be heard here for the first and last time and the absence of any clear signal of direct speech makes it difficult to understand where Amaryllis' speech would stop (hence some believe Amaryllis concludes her speech not at 106 but at 107). The main argument in support of this hypothesis is that *dum ferre moror* (8.106) seems inappropriate in the mouth of the sorceress, who has ordered her assistant to 'carry out' the ashes (8.101 *fer cineres, Amarylli, foras*). It seems preferable to assign ll. 105–7 to the protagonist, and therefore to consider the entire final speech (8.105–8) as a single monologue. As a result, the action referred to in 8.106 (*dum ferre moror*) is distinct from *fer cineres...foras* (8.101), which, coming five lines

426   ECLOGUE 8

earlier, must belong to the previous stanza: the refrain's main function is precisely to separate the various stages of the ritual. After giving an order to Amaryllis, the protagonist must now gather the ashes and hand them over to her: the ashes are obviously still on the altar, where a sudden flame appears (8.105). The verb *moror* (8.106) expresses hesitation, which would be pointless on the servant's part but is wholly understandable in the case of the protagonist, who hesitates before performing a potentially fatal action (8.103 *adgrediar*). Then, all of a sudden, *aspice* suggests that the protagonist interrupts the procedure: she does not gather the ashes or give them to the servant, who certainly will not be able to put the woman's order (8.101) into practice. The final exclamation of surprise is directed at Amaryllis but also at the protagonist herself: her words take on a more intimate feel, as if she were addressing herself (note 8.108 *credimus?* etc.). Here, the Theocritean model continues to lurk in the background: in *id.* 2, a similar change in the sorceress' communication style can be observed. After urging Thestylis to mix herbs on the threshold of her unfaithful lover (*id.* 2.59–62), Simaetha remains alone (*id.* 2.64 μώνα ἐοῖσα) and evokes the various stages of her passion in a long monologue. V. reworks Theocritus by blurring the picture: that the servant has not yet carried out the order remains unclear until 8.106, when the ashes are still on the altar. In conclusion, there is no need to assume an exception to the monologic rule, imagining that the finale of *E.* 8 contains a dialogue that is not even clearly marked out from its context. As Thestylis in Theocritus' *id.* 2, the servant of *E.* 8 does not utter a single line (in Theocritus' *id.* 15, the slave Eunoa is similarly mute, whereas Praxinoa addresses her multiple times: see *id.* 15.27–33), and Alphesiboeus' song abides by the formal conventions of the monologue (uttered by a nameless character), thereby mirroring Damon's monologue. Thus, besides the various thematic and structural symmetries between the two songs of *E.* 8, a mimetic and narrative similarity can also be detected. For the idea that the outcome of a magic ritual can suddenly and unexpectedly change before the performer's eyes (8.105 *aspice*; 107 *nescio quid certe est*), cf. Canidia's speech in Hor. *epod.* 5.61–2 *quid accidit? cur dira barbarae minus / uenena Medeae ualent?* (note the absence of any words uttered by Sagana or Folia).

105–6. The *altaria* (8.64n.) take centre stage again: a flame is suddenly rekindled on them, crackling (*tremulis...flammis*). The event is interpreted as a good omen (8.106 *bonum sit*; cf. above, 8.82n.). See *G.* 4.384–6; Ov. *her.* 12.112 (114); *met.* 10.278–9; *Pont.* 4.9.53–4; but cf. above, also the 'perverted ritual' at Soph. *Ant.* 1005–11, as well as the anecdote in Plut. *Cic.* 20.1, to which Servius alludes here (*ad* 105), referring to a poem by Cicero himself (in all likelihood the *De consulatu suo*): *sicut Cicero in suo testatur poemate* (cf. Cic. *carm.* fr. 5 Bläns.). For a different, more dramatic portent cf. the flames that envelop Lavinia's hair as she approaches the ritual altar (*Aen.* 7.71–7; the eponymous *laurus sacra* appears right afterwards).

106 sponte sua...cinis ipse. Further emphasis is placed on the ashes 'themselves', to which the reader's attention was drawn in 8.101 (note *ipse* in sentence-ending position). It is now revealed that the ashes are still on the altar:

ECLOGUE 8   427

thus, the threat at 8.101–3 was never actualized. This 'spontaneous' rekindling of the ashes bodes well: note, after the plur. form in 8.101, the use of the sing. with *ipse*. The flame anticipates the arrival of Daphnis 'himself'. **bonum sit**. A common propitiatory formula, here appearing in a very brief form. For more extended versions of it, frequently used in Latin literature, cf. *quod bonum atque fortunatum sit mihi* (Plaut. *Cas.* 382; note also *Cas.* 402) or, in an epigraphic context, e.g. *CIL* VI.4.2, p. 3279, no. 32367.56 *faustum felix fortunatum salutare sit* (cf. Cic. *diu.* 1.102; Liv. 3.54.8; Messall. *or.* fr. in Suet. *Aug.* 58.2 [*ORF*, p. 533 Malc.³]; Suet. *Cal.* 15.3). The analogous phrase *hoc bene sit* appears in Pers. 4.30; cf. Plaut. *Merc.* 327 *bene sit tibi*; Pers. 735; but see Aesch. *Ag.* 217 εὖ γὰρ εἴη.

107 nescio quid certe sit. The same line-opening phrase appears in Catull. 80.5; *nescio quid certe est*; cf. also Pers. 5.51. Note the *sermocinatio*-like style: as in a theatrical monologue (or a sort of 'a parte'), the protagonist seems to address herself or 'think aloud', even though Amaryllis is still around (see above, 8.105–8n.). **et Hylax in limine latrat**. In the crucial space of the threshold (cf. 8.92 *limine in ipso* [n.]), the dog suddenly starts barking (*latrat*): the event is underscored by the Greek name *Hylax*, which is a 'speaking name', as is frequently the case with domestic animals (cf. ὑλακτεῖν 'to bark'; the same applies to *Hylactor* in Ov. *met.* 3.224). The dog's attitude is, presumably, far from hostile (the beloved must have been known to the house's animals: cf. 3.67n.); contrast Hor. *epod.* 6.1–4 (and *sat.* 2.6.114–15). In Theocr. *id.* 2.35, the dogs' bark reveals Hecate's arrival. The manuscript tradition is unanimous in reading the more familiar mythological name *Hylas*, showing that the transmitted text of V. was far from flawless at least since late antiquity. *Hylax*, appearing in the Humanistic editions since 1475, is most probably a conjecture.

108 credimus? Note V.'s use of the indicative, even though a deliberative subjunctive would not have been out of place: as a result, the text acquires a tone of colloquial immediacy. Cf. *Aen.* 4.534–5 *en, quid ago? rursusne procos inrisa priores / experiar…?* (note the variation *ago…experiar*) as well as *Aen.* 10.675. **an, qui amant, ipsi sibi somnia fingunt?** Lovers' imagination is proverbial, including 'daydreams': cf. Ter. *Andr.* 971–2 *num illic somniat / ea quae uigilans uoluit?*; Publil. *sent.* A 16 *amans quod suspicatur uigilans somniat* (more generally Caes. *Gall.* 3.18.6 *libenter homines id quod uolunt credunt*). A similar yet distinct type of dream is the erotic dream, with its manifold manifestations: Hom. *Od.* 20.87–90; Lucr. 4.1030–6; Hor. *sat.* 1.5.82–5 and *carm.* 4.1.37–40; Ov. *her.* 19.59–66 and *met.* 9.468–71. The phrase *fingere somnia* appears in Lucr. 1.104–5 and Lucil. 487–8 M. = 493–4 K.; cf. also *Aen.* 8.42 *ne uana putes haec fingere somnum* (perhaps hinting at Epicurean rationalism, which will, however, immediately be proved wrong by the events). Were it not for the final, decisive refrain line, this would be the last line uttered by the sorceress, thereby concluding Alphesiboeus' song (and the entire poem) on the uncertain boundary between dream and reality (cf. the ending of Aeneas' katabasis in *Aen.* 6.893–9, featuring the mysterious 'twofold

428   ECLOGUE 9

gates' of Sleep). The 'rationalistic', quasi-Epicurean doubt that concludes *E.* 8 might itself be a final note of humour, meant to amuse the philosophically savvy readers of the *E.* (cf. above, 8.35n.). Similarly, *E.* 2 ended on an Epicurean note: Corydon had successfully implemented Epicurus' strategies against erotic madness (2.29–73). Note, in *qui amant*, the hiatus in thesis and the shortened vowel in the monosyllable *qui*: cf. 2.65n. (featuring, however, a Greek name). For a similar phenomenon affecting disyllabic words, see 3.79n.

109 parcite, ab urbe uenit, iam parcite carmina, Daphnis. The refrain line is only varied in its last occurrence, as in Damon's song. However, unlike the case of 8.61 (*desine*), a happy surprise is added here. Note the repeated imperative, which separates the subject (*Daphnis*) from its verb: cf., differently, *E.* 3.93–4. Colloquial liveliness is also produced by the use of *iam* with the imperative, very frequent in the language of comedy (cf. *ThlL* X.1.337.72–338.3). A different word-order (*iam carmina parcite*) appears in M, presumably influenced by the other refrain lines, in which *carmina* occupies the fourth foot, followed by the imperative (*mea carmina ducite*): thus, P's word-order (*iam parcite carmina*) is a *lectio difficilior*, and corresponds better to Damon's last half-line (*iam desine, tibia, uersus*). Note also that the obsessively alliterative chant *ducite...domum...ducite Daphnin*, with which the reader is familiar, is finally resolved, with a conclusive emphasis on a different imperative (*parcite...parcite*, featuring different sound effects as well). The poem is concluded by Daphnis' return from the city (*ab urbe*), while Moeris seems to head to the city (*in urbem?*) at the beginning of the following eclogue (*E.* 9.1n.).

Eclogue 9

[Moeris]

The ninth eclogue begins with Lycidas asking Moeris where he is going (to the city?). Moeris replies by lamenting his sorrowful fate: because of the expropriations, he now has no choice but to bring goat-kids to the new owner of his land as a gift (9.6n.). Lycidas' surprise, due to his assumption that the singer Menalcas had saved their place from the confiscations, prompts Moeris to narrate that both he and Menalcas had run the risk of losing not just their land, but their lives (9.16). The first two exchanges (adding up to four speeches: 9.1–16) introduce the situation. Lycidas, then, takes the floor again, drawing attention to the fundamental theme of the poem, i.e. song (previously hinted at in 9.11–12). Taking a cue from Lycidas, who quotes three of Menalcas' lines (9.23–5), Moeris replies by quoting three more lines (9.27–9). However, when Lycidas exhorts his companion to spend more time singing, Moeris recites with some difficulty a mere five lines on the topic of the Cyclops in love (9.39–43). In order to deflect Lycidas' further exhortation, Moeris cites his old age as an excuse: Menalcas himself will fulfil any need for song (9.51–5). Lycidas keeps insisting, to no avail (even though his final speech is the longest one in the whole dialogue: 9.56–65): the two will only be able to sing together once Menalcas arrives (9.67).

The eclogue begins *in medias res*, plunging directly into the pastoral scene: note the lively mimetic and dialogic style, centred around the two characters, who name each other in the first two lines. This mimetic immediacy, however, aims at conveying a sense of loss and defeat, as well as the need to limit any hope to a minimum. Moeris, in particular, shows his inability to remember, sing, and transmit song: as a consequence, despite Lycidas' insistence, the exchange of songs between two herdsmen (a typically pastoral situation) fails to be actualized.

This sense of incapacity is further amplified in comparison to an obvious Theocritean model: *id*. 7. This well-known idyll, also known as *Thalysia*, was similarly set on a road. The narrator, Simichidas, told the story of how, travelling together with Eucritus and Amyntas, he encountered Lycidas the goatherd, on the road leading from the city to the countryside. The event soon became an occasion for cheerfully exchanging songs, and later gifts as well. In *E*. 9, Lycidas tries several times (both in the opening and in the rest of the dialogue) to replicate the role which his namesake played in Theocritus' poem, i.e. that of a stimulus, an 'occasion' (see 9.1n.; 32–6n.; 56–65n.). However, the herdsman he has encountered is not Simichidas, known for his cheerful personality and his readiness to sing (cf. esp. *id*. 7.35–8), but Moeris, old, tired, and unhappy, since he is not going to a country festival (such as the *Thalysia*), but to the city, as it seems, in order to pay his humiliating tribute. Theocritus' *id*. 7, with its harmonious relationship between city and countryside (culminating in a feast), is now proven to be an impossible dream in both *E*. 1 and *E*. 9 (cf. 1.79–83n.).

In the preceding poem, *E*. 8, Alphesiboeus' song and its obsessive refrain line (*ducite ab urbe domum*, etc.) drew attention to the city, a place often presented as incompatible with the pastoral world and described as imposing, redeeming, and threatening at once in *E*. 1 (apart from marginal echoes in *E*. 2, the first poem of the book has not, so far, been evoked by V.). In *E*. 8.109, Daphnis was exhorted to come back from the city, and this is precisely what he did in the final refrain line. In *E*. 8, the unnamed lover's spell ended up by achieving success, soon after the mention of a mysterious and otherwise unfamiliar Moeris (see 8.96n.). Yet even the powers attributed to the Moeris of *E*. 8 would not allow his namesake in *E*. 9 to escape the confiscations (at best, his ability to interpret the crows' cries has saved his life: cf. 9.15). In Alphesiboeus' song, magic appeared as a cure for unhappy love and abandonment, two of the greatest sorrows afflicting pastoral characters. Now, however, the violent forces of war and abuse jeopardize the very existence of the pastoral world, and *carmina* are helpless against them.

In *E*. 9, Moeris is travelling on a road that leads to the city, in a direction opposite to that of Theocritus' protagonists in *id*. 7 and Daphnis in *E*. 8. The poet does not mention Lycidas' reasons for being on the road, but Moeris' sorrowful reply evokes *E*. 1 and the expropriations: a phenomenon which, it seems, the entire

430   ECLOGUE 9

bucolic book has not succeeded in obliterating. Thus, the confiscations reappear now, towards the end of the collection. Their inexorability is further emphasized by a subtly symmetrical structure, centred around *E.* 5 (see Introduction, p. 22). Note that *E.* 6 corresponds to *E.* 4 in terms of topic and form (both being quite exceptional), *E.* 7 is an amoebean just like *E.* 3, and *E.* 8 focuses on love monologues like *E.* 2. Now, in *E.* 9, Moeris partially shares the fate of the wandering Meliboeus who appeared in *E.* 1. Moeris' fate, in other words, is written in the structural correspondences of V.'s pastoral book.

E. 5, which functions as an axis of symmetry in the collection and has just been evoked in *E.* 8, also features echoes and original reworkings of *id.* 7. Note that the careful balance of *E.* 5, particularly concerning the quotations and their exchanges, is taken up in *E.* 9. Here, a pair of three-line quotations (23–5 and 27–9) are followed by a pair of five-line quotations (39–43 and 46–50; but cf. 9.44–50n.): similarly, in *E.* 5, Mopsus and Menalcas exchange two songs of the same length (= twenty-five lines; the same is true also of Damon and Alphesiboeus in *E.* 8: see above, pp. 383–4). However, Menalcas' name, which in *E.* 5 denotes a 'grown-up' pastoral singer, is now the name of a great poet, renowned in the herdsmen's community, but nevertheless remaining off stage. The other characters await his arrival, and he seems to owe his life to a miracle. Despite his (all too weak?) attempts, Moeris alone cannot replace him. The contrast between old age and youth, previously thematized in *E.* 5, now overlaps with a contrast between Lycidas' future (9.35n.) and a past to which Moeris belongs and which Moeris himself is no longer capable of evoking. This is due to the confiscations which, as in *E.* 1, have interrupted the continuity of pastoral time. Embodying a sort of young Tityrus, Lycidas is the only one who can safely keep being a pure pastoral character.

Across the ages, V.'s readers have observed the correspondence between *E.* 1 and 9, rich in echoes and allusions, which can readily be detected (cf. esp. 9.15n.; 50n.; above, p. 61; Introduction, pp. 6–8). Besides the most obvious thematic link between the two poems (i.e. land confiscations), several structural and narrative analogies can be detected. Note, for instance, the encounter of the two herdsmen, one of whom is travelling; the quest for background information; finally, some small but significant details, such as the goat-kids (abandoned in *E.* 1 and gifted to the new landowner here in *E.* 9: in both poems, the animals are effectively 'lost' from the herdsman's point of view; see 9.6n.). Without a doubt, V. aims at a 'synchronic' effect on his readership: the two poems, in their variety of tones and situations, form a unified framework enclosing the pastoral volume. As a consequence, vexed questions of chronological priority, concerning which of the two eclogues was composed first, can safely be ignored. Since *E.* 1 functions as a proem to the whole collection, it is set at the moment when the book is published (at any rate, it is more plausible to think of *E.* 1 as later). Like the first eclogue, *E.* 9 merely alludes to the historical figure of V., without making room for a full-blown allegory. Theocritus' choice to set *id.* 7 (*Thalysia*) in Cos, where at some point he probably lived, entailed an obvious biographical reference, and Hellenistic readers did not fail to identify Simichidas with the poet himself. Yet it would be pointless to try, as ancient grammarians and Virgilian interpreters did, to reconstruct a coherent sequence of events alluded to in *E.* 1 and 9. Rather, it was most probably the narrative contained in the two poems (Tityrus is saved, but Menalcas is a victim of the expropriations) that gave rise to an ancient tradition according to which V. was exposed to a twofold danger (cf. Serv. Dan. *ad E.* 9.1; Serv. *praef. E.* p. 3.3–14 [III.1 Th.-H.]): the poet initially managed to keep his lands, but later ran the risk of losing them along with his life (cf. 9.50n.). The poet's deliberate vagueness concerning the details of the narrative (e.g. is Moeris Menalcas' friend or a slave?), as well as the numerous difficulties associated with any attempt to make sense of names and situations, must not discourage the modern interpreter from seriously engaging with the ancient biographical tradition, which might contain some factual, historical data.

While *E.* 9 escapes from any biographical 'fable', the poem certainly conveys a clear notion of V.'s views on poetry and its role in history. The connection between *E.* 9 and *E.* 8 (based on the figure of Moeris) shows the helplessness of *carmina* (magical though they might be) in the face of 'the shafts of Mars' (9.12). It is hardly accidental that the four quotations featured in *E.* 9 contaminate 'purely' pastoral forms with an encomiastic style: such a 'mixture' is typical of the *E.* as a whole. In fact, the first quotation is addressed to Tityrus, featuring typically pastoral commands (9.23–5), while the second (9.27–9) is a eulogy of Varus, echoing the prologue to *E.* 6; the remaining two quotations mention the lovesick Cyclops (9.39–43) and the *sidus Iulium* (9.46–50), i.e. the celestial form of the deified Julius Caesar.

This series of poetic excerpts is concluded by an echo of *E.* 1. In 9.50, the exhortation to 'graft pear trees', based on well-grounded hopes for posterity, tragically evokes the words that Meliboeus addressed to himself in *E.* 1.73. It is fair to ask which of the two lines V. composed first: as observed, it is likely that *E.* 9 is older than *E.* 1, and the poetic quotations included in it might predate the poem as a whole by a few years. The significance of such intratextual symmetries, at any rate, ought to be obvious to V.'s reader. Without a young, redeeming *deus* in the city (be it Rome or the more modest Mantua, or perhaps Cremona), it is hard to nurture solid hopes for a serene future: it would be vain, in the face of a violent, 'foreign' soldier, to look to Caesar's star itself.

The Tityrus-Meliboeus diptych in *E.* 1, representing the dichotomy of survivors and victims, is replicated in the symmetry of *E.* 1 and *E.* 9 (i.e. the opening and the quasi-finale of the book, respectively). Due to its position, *E.* 1 plays the role of a 'proem' and introduces the pastoral collection by situating it within the contemporary context: one herdsman is exiled, while the other can stay—so the *E.* begin on a note of hope. *E.* 9, the second-to-last poem in the collection, guides the reader's comprehension of the text as the book is about to end (note that *E.* 10

432   ECLOGUE 9

is a sort of standlone piece). To be sure, Lycidas was clearly left unscathed by the expropriations, but here the emphasis is on the victims, Menalcas and Moeris, who almost lost their lives. A further thematic analogy links the two eclogues together: at the outset of the book, the herdsmen ran the risk of seeing their songs 'annihilated' (which is what had happened to Meliboeus: *E.* 1.77 *carmina nulla canam*); in the ninth eclogue, when the book is coming to an end, great emphasis is placed on the fragmentation of poetry and music. While the herdsmen's songs are scattered into fragments, memory does not help and the protagonists have to wait indefinitely for Menalcas to return. The eclogue is dominated by this kind of 'centrifugal' motion, in stark contrast to the 'gathering' (of both animals and songs) which is more typical of a pastoral book (cf. the well-known epigram by Artemidorus of Tarsus, *Anth. Pal.* 9.205; see Introduction, p. 19). In *E.* 10, V. will again gather his *capellae* and bring all his poems together, with the help of Gallus-Daphnis (used as a foil).

Like all the odd-numbered eclogues, *E.* 9 has a dialogic form. The poem's opening is very lively, especially thanks to Lycidas' initial one-liner (9.1n.). The mimetic style of *E.* 9 is characterized by a close connection between words and actions: the characters are walking along their way, perhaps slowing down to sing at times, but always in motion (cf. 9.59–60n.). Yet the action never really gets off the ground, and the songs remain fragmentary (no more than five lines each), thereby creating an effect of confusion and vague expectation. This is confirmed by the length of the poem: *E.* 9, with its sixty-seven lines, is one of the shortest poems in the collection (second only to *E.* 4, which has sixty-three lines). Its brevity is particularly conspicuous due to the poem's proximity to *E.* 8, the longest in the book. *E.* 9 is similar to *E.* 1 in its unbroken continuity: not unlike *E.* 1, *E.* 9 features a single situation and can be divided into three sections: first, sixteen lines introducing the situation (1–16); then, thirty-nine central lines containing four poetic fragments (the first two, consisting of three lines each, are certainly attributed to Menalcas, while the author of the second two, of five lines each, is not mentioned: 17–55); finally, twelve lines concluding the poem (56–67). As is normal in the *E.*, the two protagonists each get the same number of speeches (i.e. six per character): there is, however, a slight yet perceptible disproportion between the number of lines uttered by the insisting Lycidas (38) and those assigned to the reluctant Moeris (29).

On the eclogue: Bethe (1892); Leo (1903); Jachmann (1922, pp. 113–15); Waltz (1927); Weyman (1930); Pease (1931); Oppermann (1932); Arnaldi (1943, pp. 230–43); Büchner (1955, cols. 1236–41); Hanslik (1955); Wagenvoort (1956b); Vretska (1962); Segal (1965); Klingner (1967, pp. 148–58); De Michelis (1968); Traina (1968b); G. Williams (1968, pp. 316–27); Putnam (1970, pp. 293–341); E. A. Schmidt (1972a); Berg (1974, pp. 132–42); Gawantka (1975); Van Sickle (1978, pp. 183–7); Alpers (1979, pp. 136–54); Ronconi (1981); M. O. Lee (1989, pp. 70–6); Hardy (1990); Horsfall (1995c, pp. 237–9); P. Hardie (1998, pp. 17–18); Henderson (1998a); T. K. Hubbard (1998, pp. 117–27); Lipka (2001, pp. 54–6,

ECLOGUE 9   433

141–3); Perkell (2001b); Rupprecht (2004); von Albrecht (2007, pp. 34–6); A. Powell (2008, pp. 197–202); Davis (2012, pp. 41–61); Kania (2016, pp. 52–9, 67–70).

Specific issues: Bayet (1928) (the expropriations); Johnston (1931) (ll. 53–4); Bondurant (1935) (l. 50); J. Martin (1946) (the expropriations); C. Becker (1955, pp. 316–19) (the power of poetry and *E.* 8); Cipolla (1962) (V.'s 'anti-Augustanism'); Paratore (1962) (l. 45); Tugwell (1963) (ll. 59–60); Wellesley (1966) (V.'s country); Wilkinson (1966) (the expropriations); Robertson (1966–7) (biographical allegory); Steinmetz (1968, pp. 121–2) (characterization and dramatic technique); Neumeister (1975) (Theocr. *id.* 7); Winterbottom (1976) (the expropriations); Buchheit (1977a) (l. 13 and Plin. *epist.* 9.25.3); Solodow (1977) (*E.* 8–10 and the poet's 'weariness'); Brugnoli (1979) (l. 36); Veyne (1980) (the expropriations); Brenk (1981) (l. 60); Tracy (1982) (ll. 59–61); G. Zanker (1985) (ll. 11–13); Boyle (1986, pp. 15–35) (poetry and power); D'Anna (1987b) (ll. 32–6); Glei (1991, pp. 49–52) (war); Baudy (1993, pp. 311–18) (Daphnis in *E.* 5 and 9); Merli (1997) (l. 52); Levi (1998, pp. 65–7); A. Becker (1999) (poetry's existential force); Calzolari (1999) (Andes and the expropriations); Luther (2002, pp. 35–56) (historical context); Korenjak (2003) (Virgilian biography); Pellegrino (2003) (ll. 1–36); Dion (2006, pp. 86–94) (ll. 46–9); Loupiac (2006) (ll. 27–9; 46–50); Osgood (2006, pp. 108–201) (the expropriations); Grishin (2008) (acrostic at ll. 34–8); Meban (2009) (survival and social memory); Breed (2012) (l. 6 and the *Dirae*); Ottaviano (2012, pp. 209–15) (ll. 37–55); Peirano (2012, p. 17) (l. 6 and the *Dirae*); Pandey (2013, pp. 423–5) (ll. 46–50); Stok (2013) (the expropriations and the question of the *tresuiri agris diuidendis*); Adkin (2015) (the acrostic at ll. 34–8 and ll. 39–43); Pandey (2018) (ll. 46–50); Cucchiarelli (2019a, pp. 265–6) (l. 26); Cucchiarelli (2019b, pp. 512–16) (the land confiscations in Varius Rufus' *De morte*).

1–16. The dramatized action reads smoothly and continuously throughout the eclogue as a whole. In the poem's opening, the two characters introduce themselves and the situation to the reader (two speeches per character). The theme of the land confiscations takes centre stage, after having been in the background of the collection since the end of *E.* 1.

1 Quo te, Moeri, pedes? an quo uia ducit, in urbem? Cf. the goatherd Lycidas in Theocr. *id.* 7.21: 'Simichidas, where do you footslog at noonday? [πᾶ...πόδας ἕλκεις;]'. Lycidas is also the name of V.'s herdsman, as the reader immediately finds out (9.2n.). In the opening of *id.* 7, however, Simichidas is immediately said to walk away 'from the city' (*id.* 7.2 ἐκ πόλιος), whereas the opposite is true here (*in urbem*). Note the brachylogy in *Quo te...pedes*: the verb (e.g. *ducunt* or *ferunt*) is understood, even though it can readily be inferred from *ducit*; cf. Hor. *epod.* 16.21 *ire pedes quocumque ferent*; *carm.* 3.11.49; Plin. *epist.* 7.5.1 *ipsi me, ut uerissime dicitur, pedes ducunt.* For a Greek parallel for the question, besides *id.* 7.21 (cf. also *id.* 13.70 and 14.42), see Hom. *Il.* 18.148. Choosing a road as the setting of a narrative or a dialogue is typical of mimes and of Plato, esp. *Phaedr.* 227a–b and *symp.* 173b; it then becomes a feature of Roman satire, as e.g. in Hor. *sat.* 2.4.1 *unde et quo, Catius?* (cf. also *sat.* 1.9); for echoes in Latin novels, cf. Petron. 117.11–124.2; Apul. *met.* 1.2–21. The detail *in urbem* contrasts with the ending of the preceding eclogue (*E.* 8.109 *ab urbe uenit*), while Moeris' name also evokes *E.* 8

434   ECLOGUE 9

(cf. below, 9.15n.; 54n.; on the name, unfamiliar to the pastoral tradition, see 8.96n.). For the opening question, with the omission of a verb in the first line, cf. *E.* 3.1–2 *Dic mihi, Damoeta, cuium pecus?* etc. (the third eclogue is also a mimetic poem): there, however, Damoetas immediately offered a (negative) answer, unlike the Moeris of *E.* 9. The phrase *quo uia ducit* will reappear with minor variations in *Aen.* 1.401. The city is presumably Mantua, as in *E.* 1.20, rather than Cremona; cf. below, 9.27n.; 28n. Lycidas' one-liner seems to call for a similarly short reply (cf. below, 3.1–2n.): yet Moeris needs five lines to explain the unprecedented, sorrowful situation. The echoes of Theocritus have a contrastive effect: in *id.* 7, Lycidas' colloquial opening took place in a festive, joyful context; here, the reader is tricked into thinking that the same is true of *E.* 9, whereas the very opposite proves to be the case.

2 O Lycida. V. only uses the name twice: here and at 7.67 *Lycida formose*, where it denotes a beloved boy (both occurrences are in the voc., with a long *ā*, as in Greek: see 3.1n.; cf. below, 9.12). This Lycidas, too, must be quite young, as can be inferred from the contrast with the elderly Moeris: in 9.66 (the second-to-last line in *E.* 9), Lycidas will be called *puer*. V.'s choice of the name confirms his allusion to *id.* 7, which the reader might have already detected: in Theocritus, Lycidas utters the words echoed here in the incipit (cf. *id.* 7.13; 27; also 9.1n.). Theocritus' Lycidas is an enigmatic figure: a singer-goatherd (*id.* 7.13 αἰπόλος) who couples great humility with an aura of sacred solemnity (in fact, some scholars equate him with a deity: perhaps Apollo, or a combination of Apollo and Pan). By contrast, the 'professional' role of V.'s Lycidas is never explicitly mentioned, even though he will eventually seem ready to carry Moeris' burden, i.e. the goats (9.62–5). Note that the etymology of *Lycidas* may suggest a wolf (λύκος): Moeris will say that 'the wolves saw him first' (9.54n.). The interjection *o* expresses forceful emotion: cf. esp. *E.* 1.6 *o Meliboee.* **uiui peruenimus.** The adj. emphasizes Moeris' misfortune: it would have been preferable to die, rather than reach such a point of despair. Note, in *peruenimus*, the emphatic value of the prefix. For a similar use of both verb and construction (but with a very different meaning), cf. Varr. *rust.* 2.9.9 (*canes*) *illuc peruenerint…ut…in dominum adferant dentes*; see further *ThlL* X.1.1855.29–42, as well as *OLD²*, p. 1501, s.v. 10. For similar uses of *uiuus*, see Cic. *Att.* 10.8.8 *id spero uiuis nobis fore*; but cf. also Ter. *Hec.* 62 *numquam illa uiua ducturum uxorem domum*; Liv. 4.1.6; the adj. appears in a very negative context (as here) in Ter. *Eun.* 73 *uiuos uidensque pereo*; cf. Cic. *Sest.* 59; *OLD²*, p. 2296, s.v. 1d. As 9.16 shows, the phrase is not merely proverbial: Moeris' life was actually in danger. His brief narrative sketch anticipates a running theme of the poem, i.e. the passage of time, which will prove to be crucial to the characterization of the elderly herdsman (cf. esp. 9.51–4).

2–3 aduena nostri /…ut possessor agelli. Moeris immediately refers to the expropriations, known to the reader from *E.* 1: here, too, the new landowner is a military veteran, inevitably a 'foreigner'; cf. *E.* 1.70–1 *impius…miles… / barbarus* (cf. Hor. *sat.* 2.2.128 *nouus incola*). Note the sarcastic etymological contrast between *peruenimus* and *aduena*, placed next to each other (for the disparaging use of the noun, cf. *Aen.* 4.591; 12.261). The new owner, perhaps embittered by difficulties tied to land distribution (cf. Cass. Di. 48.8), arrogantly lays claim to his 'possession': Cicero (*leg. agr.* 2.69; 98) calls Sulla's similarly incoming veterans *Sullani possessores*; the term frequently occurs in the context of social conflict (cf. Cic. *Quinct.* 30; *off.* 2.78, etc.; see further *ThlL* X.2.102.40–103.34). The new landowners sometimes chose to take up residence elsewhere (here, perhaps, the new *possessor* resides in the city to which the road leads?), while sometimes they actually occupied the land. At any rate, they could decide to keep the former owners and their slaves there as labourers (for historical testimonies cf. Keppie 1983, pp. 125–7; Osgood 2006, p. 219). This may well be the fate of Menalcas and his loyal Moeris, though here Moeris (like the poet) prefers to insist on the more tragic outcomes of the expropriations: i.e. those cases in which the new landowners 'expel' the old ones (which is what happened to Meliboeus, exiled in *E.* 1; see below, also 9.4n.). Note the hyperbaton *nostri...agelli*, facilitated by the line-ending placing of both terms, which are thereby emphasized. **agelli.** The diminutive of *ager*, clearly having an affective value ('my little estate'), occurs only here in V. It immediately sets the tone of the poem: a sorrowful one. The term often reappears in Horace, who uses it to refer to his Sabine *angulus* (cf. Hor. *epist.* 1.14.1) and always places it at the end of the hexameter (as is normally the case, since the word has a bacchiac rhythm; note, however, Iuv. 6.57); see further *Enc. Or.* II, esp. p. 816b, s.v. *diminutivi* (A. Traina). The two parenthetical clauses at 9.3 and 6 also belong to colloquial style. As in *E.* 1, the herdsmen here narrate their painful vicissitudes in an unadorned, everyday language, thereby eliciting sympathy on the reader's part.

3 (**quod numquam ueriti sumus**). Without a doubt, *quod* is the correct reading: *quo* (found in the *recentiores*) is an easy mistake after *peruenimus*. The entire phrase must be parenthetical: otherwise, the syntax would appear quite convoluted (what to make of *aduena nostri?*).

4 '**haec mea sunt; ueteres migrate coloni**'. Note the deictic (and brutal) force of the gesture implicit in *haec*. The phrasing echoes standard legal formulas used for claiming a property right (*rei uindicatio*), which explicitly referred to *ius*: e.g. *meum esse ex iure Quiritium* (A. Berger, *Encyclopedic Dictionary of Roman Law*, Philadelphia 1953, p. 582a, s.v. *meum*). Here, by contrast, the context and the tone clearly point to abuse of power. All dwellers must now leave the land, which has a new owner. It was technically possible for both the previous landowners and their slaves to remain as labourers (cf. above, 9.2–3n.); yet Moeris' words make it clear that these *coloni* are exiled, like Meliboeus in *E.* 1 (cf. esp. 1.64–6; contrast Tityrus' fate in 1.46 *ergo tua rura manebunt*). For an echo of this passage, cf. [Quint.] *decl. mai.* 13.2, p. 267.1–2 Håk. (see *E.* 1.68n.); another likely echo is found in a *carmen populare* concerning the *Domus Aurea*, transmitted by Suet. *Ner.* 39.2 (*uers. pop.* 14c Courtney = p. 164 Büchn.): *Roma domus fiet: Veios migrate Quirites, / si non et Veios occupat ista domus.* **coloni.** The term, in its legal and technical sense,

436   ECLOGUE 9

denotes farmers settled on land which they do not own: thus, they are themselves *aduenae* (note, however, *ueteres*) and must pay a tribute to the actual *possessores*: Aug. *civ.* 10.1, p. 402.25–6 Domb.-K. *appellantur coloni...propter agriculturam sub dominio possessorum*; Isid. *orig.* 9.4.36. These lines seem to imply that Moeris is not a landowner; Menalcas, by contrast, may have been the actual owner of his land and pasture, which underwent confiscation (see below, 9.10n.): perhaps Lycidas is one of his slaves? At any rate, *nostri...agelli* (2–3) must probably be considered, at least from Moeris' point of view, as a mere expression of affection (see n. ad loc.).

5 nunc uicti, tristes. Note the asyndeton and the line-opening series of long syllables, here expressing sadness. **fors omnia uersat.** Cf. *E.* 1.11–12 *totis... / turbatur agris* (here, in lieu of an impersonal verb, an abstract noun is used as the syntactical subject). The notion of *fors* is analogous, albeit far from identical, to the Greek μοῖρα, which Moeris carries in his name (see 8.96n.). However, while the Moeris of 8.99 was capable of *translatio frugum*, this Moeris runs the risk of being himself 'transferred' away from his fields and, it seems, from his homeland. The traditional idea of fortune's reversals, symbolized by the *rota fortunae*, was often referred to in the age of the civil wars: note, for instance, Nep. *Att.* 10.1–3: *conuersa subito fortuna est...tanta uarietas his temporibus fuit fortunae, ut modo hi modo illi in summo essent aut fastigio aut periculo* (about the case of Atticus after the second triumvirate). For the language of *fortuna* in the context of the land confiscations, cf. Hor. *sat.* 2.2.126–8 *saeuiat atque nouos moueat Fortuna tumultus: / quantum hinc imminuet? quanto aut ego parcius aut uos, / o pueri, nituistis ut huc nouus incola uenit?*

6 hos illi...mittimus haedos. Another deictic, this time sorrowfully referring to the young goats that Moeris is carrying on his shoulders, or perhaps in a basket: cf. 9.62 *hic haedos depone.* What might look like normal custom (cf. *E.* 1.20–1) is, in fact, a marker of painful servitude. It is now clear beyond any doubt that Moeris is not among those farmers who were forced to leave their fields. In the finale of *E.* 1 (1.74–8), it became clear that the goats were being led to their new owner (1.12n.), while the newborn twin goats, normally a boon for the herd, had to be abandoned by Meliboeus. Here, by contrast, the goat-kids (probably two, as in *E.* 1) are gifted to the new owner, but similarly taken away from the herd. (**quod nec uertat bene**). Note the archaic *nec*, common in Plautus: e.g. *Bacch.* 119 *tu dis nec recte dicis*; *Most.* 240. It derives from *ne* + *ce* (cf., in Greek, οὐκ from οὐ), and must therefore not be confused with the abbreviated form *nec = neque* (on which cf. *E.* 2.34). The distinction, presumably clear to the ancient grammarians (cf. Fest. p. 158 L.: *nec = non* in archaic Latin), was inevitably subject to confusion: see Cat. *agr.* 141.4 *si quid tibi...neque satisfactum est* (in an archaic prayer); cf. also *neque opinantibus* for *nec* [= *non*] *opinantibus* in *Bell. Alex.* 63.5. For a similar use of *nec* in a parenthesis, see *Ciris* 239 *quod nec sinat* [*sinit* codd.] *Adrastea*; cf. also Plin. *epist.* 2.2.3. The correct reading is surely *uertat bene* (in M), featuring an inversion of the standard use of the phrase: for an early parallel, cf. Ter. *Ad.* 191 *minis uiginti* *tu illam emisti (quae res tibi uortat male).* The reading *bene uertat*, known to Donatus, *ad* Ter. *Phorm.* 678 and Servius (here and *ad Aen.* 4.647), must have gained popularity early on in the manuscript tradition. As in the case of *fors* (cf. above, 9.5n.), the maledictory phrase is noteworthy in the mouth of a character whose name evokes a fearsome wizard. Note the linguistic and phonetic echo *uersat-uertat*, which has polemical implications: since fortune 'overturns' all things, the speaker hopes that (at least) something might 'turn against' the new landlord (i.e. 'may it not turn out well'). The parenthetical clause contains the kernel of what would later become the *Dirae*, i.e. the 'curses', against the new landowners (one of the texts included into the *Appendix Vergiliana*). A similar hint is found in *E.* 1.69, where Meliboeus makes it clear that the fields will scarcely bear fruit under the new landowner (see n. ad loc.).

7–10. Lycidas' surprise testifies to the belief (widespread among V.'s herdsmen) that Menalcas had managed, 'thanks to his songs', to keep possession of 'all' his goods. However, the optimism implicit in the instrumental abl. *carminibus* (9.10) will soon be cast into doubt, and ultimately deprived of meaning by Moeris' reply (9.11–13). Menalcas' land possessions appear here to be quite extended: with a gentle slope, they encompass both hills and rivers (though the text is somewhat vague, and the reader is free to surmise that the area in question also encompasses other landowners' possessions). The biographical tradition has it that V.'s farm could offer enough land to sixty veterans (Prob. *praef. E.* p. 328.1 H.): this is probably a biographical overinterpretation of these lines in *E.* 9. Tityrus' possessions seemed much more modest in *E.* 1.46–50: cf. esp. 1.47–8n.; by contrast, Menalcas' land (which is more valuable) gets confiscated: see below, 9.9n.; 10n.

7 Certe equidem. The particle *equidem* is rather common (37x in V.) and generally emphasizes the speaker's subjectivity ('as for me', 'as far as I know', vel sim.), occasionally with a hint of embarrassment. It only occurs twice in the *E.*: here and at 1.11, where Meliboeus reacts to the information that Tityrus gives him (the situation is obviously analogous: note that, in both poems, *equidem* appears in the opening of the third speech). Similar redundancies are typical of colloquial language, as is clear from Latin comedy: cf. Plaut. *Mil.* 433; *Pers.* 209; but see also Lucr. 3.1078 (which, however, editors emend to *certa quidem...finis*); Apul. *met.* 8.10.2 *istud equidem certe.* **se subducere.** In the sense of 'decreasing' in height (rather than 'increasing'), as Servius noted (cf. *Aen.* 3.565). Lycidas here offers an accurate description of Menalcas' possessions, dividing them into three parts: the place in which the 'hills begin to subside' (*se subducere...incipiunt*), their gradual receding (9.8 *mollique iugum demittere cliuo*), and the valley rich in water and old beech trees (9.9). Lycidas' reference to hills has prompted some attempts for an identification of the place (perhaps near Valeggio on the Mincius river?): but cf. 9.10n. Note the use of the reflexive pronoun (emphasized by alliteration *se subducere*), which implies a kind of personification, as e.g. in Enn. *ann.* 382–3 Sk. *gloria maxima sese / nobis ostentat* and Ov. *trist.* 2.170 *uictoria...se praestet.* Here,

438 ECLOGUE 9

the personification probably has emotional overtones of affection: the herdsmen perceive these hills as family members of sorts.

8 molli…cliuo. See *G.* 3.292; for *mollis* used of 'gentle' slopes cf. Liv. 27.18.15 *donec mollioris adscensus uiam inueniret.*

9 usque ad aquam. Presumably a river, such as the Mincius, or perhaps a lake, or a marsh? (cf. below, 9.57n.). The phrase *usque ad* is commonly used in Roman land-surveying texts to denote the boundaries of a field (cf., for instance, Hyg. *grom.* p. 75.16–17 Thul.; also *CIL* V, p. 886, no. 7749.7 *usque ad riuom*). Tityrus' modest possessions, it seems, were mostly flat and occupied by marshes (*E.* 1.47–8): apparently, only those lands that were under *aqua* ended up safe from confiscation (9.10n.). **ueteres, iam fracta cacumina, fagos.** Beech trees are a staple of V.'s pastoral landscape: cf. the opening of the book, *E.* 1.1 (in line-ending position, as here). In this case, they appear in a cluster: for a precise parallel, featuring a parenthetical apposition or *schema Cornelianum* (1.57n.), cf. 2.3 *densas, umbrosa cacumina, fagos* (n.). It was near some old beech trees that the young Menalcas had played a trick on Daphnis (*E.* 3.12 *ad ueteres fagos*). In *E.* 9, however, Menalcas is a grown-up herdsman, whereas the old beeches are (now) but 'broken treetops'. Without clearly identifying the two characters with each other, V. suggests to the 'expert' reader a deep network of temporal layers, echoes, and allusions. The mention of *fagi* is full of nostalgia: the trees are now damaged, and therefore incapable of performing their pastoral function (i.e. providing *umbra*: cf. 1.1 *sub tegmine fagi*; 4 *in umbra*). The beech trees, symbolizing an old, traditionally pastoral landscape, will reappear in Calp. *ecl.* 7.5 *ueteres fagos noua quam spectacula mauis.* The incorrect yet widespread reading *ueteris…fagi* (in P) is most likely the result of a trivial error, probably triggered by an echo of 1.1: cf. Quint. *inst.* 8.6.46, as well as (perhaps) Pers. 5.59 *fregerit articulos, ueteris ramalia fagi.* The old, broken treetops create an atmosphere of familiarity: the landscape is certainly known to herdsmen who were born and raised there, but completely unfamiliar to an *aduena* soldier.

10 omnia carminibus uestrum seruasse Menalcan. Menalcas' name is one of the most important ones in V.'s pastoral world. This character's namesakes include two boys in *E.* 2.15 and 3.13, as well as a mature singer in *E.* 5.4 (*tu maior… Menalca*); following *E.* 9, the name will make its last appearance at *E.* 10.20. Through Menalcas' name, therefore, V.'s pastoral book seems to outline a chronological trajectory (see above, 9.9n.). Here, V. might allude to specific locations near Mantua (note especially the broken treetops at 9.9), but ancient and modern attempts to identify Menalcas with the poet (or even to read Lycidas' words as a description of the poet's lands) are, of course, fanciful. Note the affectionate nuance of the possessive adj.: other, similar instances will follow (cf. 9.12; 16; 22), evoking a local sense of belonging typical of the herdsmen's community, which is now threatened by history. The language at 27–9 seems to imply that Menalcas tried to use his poetry (*carminibus*) to win the favour of someone like Varus (9.26n.), who certainly had the power to decide whose land would be expropriated in the Mantuan territory. Note that the resumptive *omnia* points to Menalcas' extended land possessions (*E.* 9.7–10n.). According to Servius Dan. ad loc., Alfenus Varus granted the Mantuans very little land, and mostly marshes: hence the protest of a certain Cornelius (possibly Cornelius Gallus: cf. Manzoni 1995, pp. 23–4; A. Balbo, *I frammenti degli oratori romani dell'età augustea e tiberiana*, I, Alessandria 2007², pp. 2–9 [frg. 1]; on Gallus' assistance to V. during the confiscation, cf. Donat. *uita Verg.* 66–70 Brumm. = p. 27.1–5 Brugn.-Stok). Alfenus Varus' hostility is also emphasized by the *schol. Bern. ad E.* 8.6, p. 145 H., though all these testimonies may solely be based on V.'s text.

11 Audieras, et fama fuit. Note the colloquial brevity: *audieras* takes up *audieram* (9.7), while *et* is almost equivalent to *nam* (in accordance with everyday usage). Alliteration completes the picture.

11–12 sed carmina tantum / nostra ualent. An immediate echo of *carminibus* (9.10), contrasting with Lycidas' naivety (he seems to believe that songs can actually succeed in preserving the singer's land from expropriation).

12 tela inter Martia. In V.'s *E.*, the god of war appears only here (adjectivally) and at 10.44 *insanus amor duri me Martis in armis* (contrast *E.* 1.70, simply referring to a *miles*); for the phrase cf. Sil. 4.505 *donata, tela inter Martia luce.* Using 'Mars' shafts' is, in fact, a successful way to impose one's will. Servius quotes Cic. *Mil.* 11 *silent enim leges inter arma*, on which see Otto (1890, p. 192, no. 946); Tosi (2007, p. 552, no. 1223). In this light, Cicero's own *cedant arma togae* (*carm.* fr. 11 Bläns. = 12 Court.) seems paradoxical. The idea that (civil) wars hinder intellectual activity is outlined by Cicero (in relation to oratory) at *Brut.* 324 *perterritum armis hoc studium… nostrum conticuit subito et obmutuit.* For a singer killed in battle (by Turnus), cf. Cretheus at *Aen.* 9.774–7: poetry was obviously unable to help him (note esp. *Aen.* 9.775–6 *Musarum comitem, cui carmina semper / et citharae cordi numerosque intendere neruis*).

13 Chaonias dicunt aquila ueniente columbas. Note the 'enclosing' word-order, almost a linguistic picture of the predator penetrating *into the midst* of the doves. The epithet 'Chaonian', which V. (*Aen.* 3.334–5) will trace back to the Trojan hero Chaon, here alludes to the well-known oracle of Zeus at Dodona: in that sanctuary, particular importance was assigned not only to oak trees but also to sacred doves. A dove, in fact, was said to have requested its foundation, speaking in a human voice (Herodot. 2.55); cf. Parke (1967, pp. 34–45). Doves are dear to Zeus in Hom. *Od.* 12.62–3. Properly speaking, Chaonia, situated on the coast of northern Epirus, is distinct from Thesprotia (inland and farther south), where Dodona was (the sanctuary then fell under Molossian rule: see Strab. 7.7.11[328]). The epithet is used of Zeus and his oracle in Euphor. fr. 48 Pow. = 52 Gron. = 51.3 Light. Ζηνὸς Χαονίοιο προμάντιες; cf. *G.* 2.67 *Chaoniique patris glandes.* For the opposition between doves and eagles, cf. Ov. *ars* 1.117; *met.* 1.506; Mart. 10.65.12. A more common contrast is that between doves and hawks or sparrowhawks, for which cf. Hom. *Il.* 15.237–8; 21.493–5; see also *Aen.*

440 ECLOGUE 9

11.721–4, as well as Lucr. 3.751–2 and Hor. *carm.* 1.37.17–18 (the phrase, at any rate, is proverbial: note V.'s *dicunt*). Note also the fable of the hawk and the nightingale (the latter, a singing bird, being a symbol of poetry), which is featured in Hesiod even before Aesop (Hesiod is the inventor of fable as a genre, according to Quint. *inst.* 5.11.19): cf. Hes. *op.* 207–8 δαιμονίη, τί λέληκας; ἔχει νύ σε πολλὸν ἀρείων· / τῇ δ' εἶς ᾗ σ' ἂν ἐγώ περ ἄγω καὶ ἀοιδὸν ἐοῦσαν 'O wretched one, why do you wail? You are in the hands of someone much stronger than you: / you will go wherever I carry you, even though you can sing' (the predator addressing its prey). For the sudden appearance of the eagle, which terrifies the other birds (note, here, *ueniente*), cf. Alc. (?) fr. 27 Bgk.[4] = inc. auct. 10 V.; Bacchyl. 5.16–23; Hor. *carm.* 4.4.1–12 (for various other birds of prey cf. Hom. *Il.* 16.582–3; 17.460; *Od.* 22.302–6; Soph. *Ai.* 169–71). The eagle is a regal bird, closely associated with Zeus himself; yet it is also one of the most distinctive symbols of the Roman army, since it appeared on the legions' standards (cf. Tac. *ann.* 2.17.2 *Romanas aues, propria legionum numina*; *ThlL* II.371.74–372.68; cf. Plin. *epist.* 9.25.3) and played an important role in the ritual used to found new colonies: cf. Cic. *Phil.* 2.102 (note that, in connection to the veterans' colonies, the eagle appears on Octavian's coins after the Perusine War: *RRC*, I, pp. 529–30, nos. 525.2–4). It bears mentioning that the oracle of Dodona, which the Aetolians attacked in 219 BCE, was pillaged by L. Aemilius Paulus' troops in 167 BCE: the oracle itself, therefore, experienced the strength of the (Roman) *tela Martia*. For the eagle in an augural context, cf. *Aen.* 1.390–400 and 12.247–56 (eagles attacking swans, in both occurrences); as for the doves, fearful Trojan women will be compared to them in *Aen.* 2.516 (during the capture of the city; for Venus' doves cf. *Aen.* 6.190). References to terms and events connected with divination seem appropriate for a character like Moeris (see above, *E.* 9.5n.; 6n.), and anticipate the appearance of a new bird omen, involving a crow (9.15).

14 me. It is clear that Moeris played a crucial role in helping himself and Menalcas escape from danger. **nouas incidere lites.** Cf. *E.* 3.11 *uitis incidere…nouellas*, as well as 8.29 and 10.53. Both verb and phrase befit the language of a rustic herdsman, accustomed to cutting back the new growth of plants and trees (see *ThlL* VII.1.907.5–20); but cf. also Cic. *ad Q. fr.* 3.1.11 *poema…quod institueram, incidi*; Hor. *epist.* 1.14.36 *incidere ludum*; Liv. 32.37.5.

15 ante sinistra caua…ab ilice cornix. In *E.* 1.16–17, Meliboeus made a fatal mistake in ignoring the omen implicit in the oak trees struck by lightning. Moeris, by contrast, knows how to interpret the crow's song, here amplified by a hollow cavity in the trunk of a holm-oak. This kind of sagacity suggests some affinities between this Moeris and his namesake in *E.* 8. For the crow (κορώνη in Greek) as a prophetic bird, cf. Callim. *Hec.* fr. 260.50 Pf. = 74.9 H. In Ov. *met.* 2.550, a crow will say: *ne sperne meae praesagia linguae*. In Roman religious thought, the left-hand side is generally propitious: Varr. *ling.* 7.97 *quae sinistra sunt bona auspicia existimantur* (by contrast, it is deemed unfavourable by the Greeks: cf. Ov. *her.* 2.115). A crow appearing on the left-hand side is a noteworthy omen in Plaut.

ECLOGUE 9   441

Asin. 260–1; Cic. *diu.* 1.85; cf. also Hor. *carm.* 3.27.15–16 *laeuus…picus, /…uaga cornix* (in the technical language of augury, both *coruus* and *cornix* were called *oscines*, i.e. birds whose divinatory value lies in their cry, not in their flight: see Fest. 214 L.; cf. Cic. *fam.* 6.6.7). According to Serv. Dan. ad loc., *ante sinistra* must be read as one word (*antesinistra indiuise legendum*). However, the term *antesinister* is entirely unparalleled, and is probably an invention of Latin grammarians. V.'s text may phonetically hint at the 'resonance' of the bird's cry thanks to the bird's position on a treetop (cf. *E.* 7.13) and the hollow (*caua*) trunk of the tree itself.

16 tuus hic Moeris. The possessive adj. (with its affectionate force: cf. 10 *uestrum…Menalcan*) and the demonstrative elicit Lycidas' emotional participation: cf. Cic. *rep.* 6.16 *auus hic tuus*; Hor. *epist.* 2.1.18 *tuus hic populus* (but see Ter. *Heaut.* 875; *Eun.* 344). In this case, however, *hic* refers to the speaker, as in Plaut. *Amph.* 615 *geminus Sosia hic factust tibi* (note, as here, the proper noun); cf. also *Aen.* 1.98 *animam hanc*; see further *ThlL* VI.3.2703.38–81.

17–55. The central section of the eclogue contains quotations of four poetic fragments, either directly ascribed to Menalcas (the first two, of three lines each: 9.23–5; 27–9) or without explicit attribution (the last two, of five lines each: 9.39–43; 46–50). This part of the eclogue has an 'agonistic' potential, or at least it could result in an exchange of songs, as Lycidas would like it to; but Moeris hesitates and the poems remain fragmentary.

17 Heu, cadit in quemquam tantum scelus? Note the rhetorical question: hence the use of *quisquam*, which denotes a person who actually exists (but should not have been there): cf. Hor. *sat.* 2.2.103; Cic. *Tusc.* 1.6. The phrase must refer to the new landowner, who almost became a murderer (note *scelus*; *quisquam*, therefore, is not the victim): cf. Cic. *off.* 3.81 *cadit…in uirum bonum mentiri?*; Curt. 7.4.11 *in te superbia non cadit.* The use of *cado* with *in* + acc. is quite frequent in Cicero: cf. also e.g. *fin.* 3.29; *ThlL* III.30.62–84. For the interjection *heu*, cf. *E.* 3.100n.

17–18 heu, tua nobis / paene simul tecum solacia rapta, Menalca! Lycidas echoes Moeris' last words (*nec uiueret ipse Menalcas*), abruptly addressing the absent Menalcas himself (*tua…tecum…Menalca*): it is to him that *tibi* refers in 9.21, as is confirmed by *canebat* in 9.26. Thus, the immense wrong (*tantum scelus*) would have been to lose, along with the great pastoral singer, the solace (*solacia*) provided by his presence and his songs. The apostrophe, typical of funeral lament, reasserts the fact that the catastrophe was close at hand (*paene*); see below, 9.19n.; 19–20n. For the solace offered by poetry, cf. 6.46n. **heu tua nobis.** For the clausula, which contributes to the poem's nostalgic atmosphere, cf. 3.23n.

19 quis caneret Nymphas? It is typical for a pastoral singer to evoke and sing of the Nymphs, as in *E.* 7.21. Here, however, Lycidas echoes the mournful tone of *E.* 5.20–1 (the weeping Nymphs). Due to the risk run by Menalcas, who almost died, the herdsmen came close to needing a funeral lament, featuring a typical series of plaintive questions (*quis caneret…? quis humum…?*), as in [Mosch.] *epit. Bion.* 51–2 τίς ποτὶ σᾷ σύριγγι μελίξεται, ὦ τριπόθητε; / τίς δ' ἐπὶ σοῖς καλάμοις θήσει

442   ECLOGUE 9

στόμα; 'Who will play on your panpipe, o much desired man? / Who will put his lips on the pipes of your flute?' (Bion, like V.'s Menalcas, is described as irreplaceable); cf. also Long. 1.14.3–4.

19–20. A verbal reminiscence of *E.* 5.40 *spargite humum foliis, inducite fontibus umbras*: note, here, the flowers scattered on the ground (*humum florentibus herbis / spargeret*) and the springs covered in shade (*uiridi fontis induceret umbra*). Now the echo of *E.* 5 and its mournful tone becomes explicit. The verbs, however, now refer directly to the singer (*spargeret…induceret*), projecting onto him the 'poietic' and Orphic abilities that the reader knows from *E.* 6.62. Recall Menalcas' own words in *E.* 5.51: *Daphninque tuum tollemus ad astra*.

21 uel quae sublegi tacitus tibi carmina nuper. In silence (*tacitus*), so as not to be conspicuous, Lycidas managed (respectfully and deferentially) to 'gather up' (i.e. memorize) some lines sung by Menalcas as he was going to meet Amaryllis. For *nuper* in the context of poetic composition, cf. *E.* 5.13. For the use of *uel* with a relative pronoun, cf. *E.* 3.50 *uel qui uenit ecce Palaemon*; Nonius (p. 523 L.) attests the variant reading *nam quae*.

22 delicias…nostras. 'Our' delight or beloved, i.e. that of both Lycidas and the other herdsmen: almost = 'our dear Amaryllis'; but cf. below, 9.23–5n.

23–5. These three lines, remarkable for their mimetic liveliness, are written in an eminently pastoral and Theocritean style: we recall Menalcas' 'authorship' of *E.* 3, as well as 5.87. As ancient readers observed (cf. esp. Gell. 9.9.7–11), these lines effectively translate Theocr. *id.* 3.3–5 'Tityrus, my dear friend, graze the goats, / and lead them to the spring, Tityrus, and make sure that the billy-goat, / that tawny Libyan one, does not butt you'. Right before uttering these lines, Theocritus' unnamed goatherd expresses his erotic intentions towards Amaryllis, not unlike V.'s Menalcas (cf. above, 9.22n.). Perhaps this maliciously confirms that Amaryllis is not dear to one herdsman alone (recall that, in *E.* 1, Tityrus himself had a liaison with an Amaryllis). We remember that Amaryllis' name resounded in the *siluae* at the outset of the bucolic book: thus, the girl belongs to V.'s entire pastoral world. Here, typically pastoral elements characterize the style of Menalcas' song: note the parenthetical clauses (9.23 and 25), which break the flow of a polysyndeton, and the repetition of both proper nouns and verbs (*Tityre…Tityre*; *pasce…pastas*; *age…agendum*).

23 dum redeo (breuis est uia). Menalcas has, in fact, left (9.22) without completing the song, at least as far as Lycidas knows. Perhaps Amaryllis will hear the remainder of it, as in *id.* 3. The use of *dum* + indicative in the sense of 'until', 'as long as', is a colloquial idiom: cf. *G.* 3.296 (where it adds colour to the didactic poet's first-person speech); see also Ter. *Eun.* 206 *exspectabo dum uenit*; Cic. *Att.* 10.3 *opperior dum ista cognosco*; Plin. *epist.* 1.5.15.

24 et potum pastas. Note the alliteration (*pasce* appears in the fifth foot of the preceding line); cf., with non-consecutive alliteration, *E.* 7.11 *potum uenient per prata iuuenci*. For the grazing-watering sequence, cf. Varr. *rust.* 2.2.12 *pascunt* *diem totum ac meridiano tempore semel agere potum satis habent*: note the active supine, as here in *potum...age*. This is an archaic and colloquial usage, typical of technical prose and generally accompanied by a verb of motion. In the whole passage, in fact, Menalcas seems to imitate the severe, archaizing diction of the technical *de re rustica* language (see below on the gerund construction). For a similar case of active supine in V., cf. *Aen.* 9.241 (particularly noteworthy due to the lack of a verb of motion; but see Serv. Dan. ad loc.). The first quotation from Menalcas' poetry conveys the image of a herdsman who takes great care of his animals, sings in a Theocritean style, and ranks rather high in the pastoral hierarchy (he gives orders to Tityrus): in sum, this Menalcas is not very different from the Meliboeus of *E.* 1 and, like Meliboeus, he is a victim of the expropriations. **inter agendum**. This gerund construction, rare in Classical Latin, sounds archaic and solemn (here, it also takes up *age*), as Serv. ad loc. observed: among the parallels quoted by Servius, note Ennius' *inter ponendum* (fr. inc. 2 V.²); cf. *G.* 3.206 *ante domandum*. Note the wordplay based on repeated verbal forms: *pasce...pastas... age...inter agendum*.

25 occursare capro (cornu ferit ille) caueto. The billy goat is often capable of rash initiatives: cf. *E.* 7.7. The apostrophe to Tityrus, as in Theocr. *id.* 3, might have a specific significance: his name, in fact, can be etymologized as 'ram' (cf. *E.* 1.1n.). Note the frequentative form *occursare*, rich in expressive force and typical of a 'humble' stylistic register: cf. Plaut. *Truc.* 282 (but see also Lucr. 5.718); see further *ThlL* IX.2.403. For the use of *caueo* + inf., frequent in poetry, cf. also Cic. *Att.* 3.17.3 (in an everyday-language context). Note the hammering alliteration of /c/ and the insistence on the sound /r/, i.e. the *littera canina*: danger is looming.

26 Immo haec. Further echoes of *E.* 5: cf. esp. 5.13 (see above, 9.19–20n.). **quae Varo necdum perfecta canebat**. The line clearly introduces the encomiastic theme, which is now added to the typically pastoral style of the preceding quotation. Note the repetition of the name (reappearing as a voc. at the outset of 9.27) and the cautious phrase *necdum perfecta*: the form *necdum*, a compound of the emphatic negative *nec* (9.6n.), is more expressive than *nondum*; further pathetic amplification is to follow (cf. esp. 9.28n.). In the proem to *E.* 6, Tityrus-V. had promised Varus to sing his praises: cf. 6.7n. for the addressee's identity (in all likelihood, Alfenus Varus). Varus' close connection with V. himself might explain the incorrect reading *canebam* (found in P, but emended by P²). V., for his part, devoted (at least) one eclogue to Varus. The concrete possibility of losing Menalcas, a firstclass poet, activates the emotional potential of the unfinished: artworks that have not undergone final revision can be, for that very reason, more intriguing and moving than wholly finished products. Note the imperfect *canebat*, which here hints at incompleteness and can be compared to formulaic phrases like *Apelles faciebat* (in reference to artworks); cf. Pliny's remarks at Plin. *nat.* praef. 26–7 (on which see further Papini 2017; on *opus imperfectum* in general, see Papini 2019). Here, at any rate, V. adds a subtle display of respect and caution towards Varus:

444   ECLOGUE 9

the reader is left wondering whether he actually received these poems (i.e. if Menalcas managed to send them to him), so perhaps this is why Varus was unable to intervene in Menalcas' favour and thereby replicate the miracle of Tityrus' *deus* (*E.* 1).

27 superet modo Mantua nobis. It becomes clear that the praise of Varus is, in fact, conditional upon the survival of Mantua (and its region). V. subtly reworks the encomiastic stereotype which inextricably connects an individual's glory with the immortality of cities or places: cf. Hor. *carm.* 3.30.8–9 *dum Capitolium / scandet cum tacita uirgine pontifex* (but see Posidipp. quoted by Athen. 13.596c, esp. ll. 7–8 = *HE* 3148–9 G.-P. = 122.7–8 Aust.-Bast.). Note that V. can situate his celebratory power in Mantua (rather than in Rome), as in *G.* 3.12–18 (concerning Caesar Octavian: cf. *E.* 8.6n.). The intransitive use of *superare* (= 'to survive') is typical of V., who elsewhere applies it to people (in a sense, however, Mantua is personified here): see, for instance, *Aen.* 2.597; 3.339 (with Serv. ad loc.: *noue dictum … et caret exemplo, ut pauca in Vergilio*); cf. also Lucr. 1.790 *immutabile … quiddam superare necessest*; Liv. 29.24.11. For the turn of phrase, cf. *G.* 3.10 *modo uita supersit*—which, however, does not feature expressive alliteration (note here *modo Mantua*). According to a biographical tradition, recorded by Serv. Dan. *ad* 9.10, the Mantuans regained ownership of their lands thanks to V. himself: it cannot be ruled out that the poet actually managed to obtain at least some concessions. This passage appears to be a snippet of the song thanks to which, according to pastoral tradition, Menalcas was able to hold on to his land possessions (see above, 9.10n.).

28 Mantua uae miserae nimium uicina Cremonae. Note the sorrowful emphasis, featuring a line-opening epanalepsis: cf. Catull. 64.132–3 *perfide, ab aris, / perfide* and 64.186–7 *omnia muta, / omnia* (as well as 64.259–60; 321–2; 403–4); see also *Aen.* 2.405–6 *lumina frustra, / lumina* (Cassandra is captured). Note the 'framing' placement of the two toponyms. According to a tradition recorded by Serv. Dan. *ad E.* 9.7 and 10, the magistrate Octavius Musa, in charge of the expropriations, was active in the Mantuan region, after completing his task in Cremona: his work was then continued by Alfenus Varus, who granted Mantua nothing but a small strip of marshy land (hence the forceful oratorical reaction of a Cornelius, perhaps Cornelius Gallus: cf. above, 9.10n.). The proximity of Mantua is, above all, a geographical one (about 60 km); perhaps, however, the city was blamed for its neutrality in the aftermath of Philippi: see *Enc. Virg.* III, p. 353a, s.v. *Mantova*; I, p. 925a, s.v. *Cremona* (P. Tozzi); *Virg. Enc.* II, pp. 785–6, s.v. *Mantua* (W. Briggs); I, p. 310, s.v. *Cremona* (J. D. Morgan). The whole passage is echoed by Silius Italicus, who reworks it as an encomium of V. himself: Sil. 8.592–4. Servius ad loc. asserts that Cremona sided with Brutus and Cassius, though there is no external evidence for this. What is certain is that, as Ps.-Probus observes, Cremona was targeted for its well-known wealth, and the neighbouring Mantua had to make up for the losses suffered by Cremona, in keeping with the common practice of land confiscations (on which see Sic. Flacc. *grom.* p. 124.9–12 and p. 128.19–24 Thul.; note also Agenn. *grom.*, p. 40.1–3 Thul., possibly based on Frontinus). The connection between the two cities is also featured in the biographical tradition, according to which V. lived in Cremona up until his coming of age, when he moved to Mantua; cf. Don. *uita Verg.* 20–1 Brumm. = p. 20.5–6 Brugn.-Stok; note also *Catal.* 8.6.

29 cantantes sublime ferent ad sidera cycni. In *E.* 5, Menalcas declared his intention to carry Daphnis 'up to the stars' through the power of poetry: *tollemus ad astra; / Daphnin ad astra feremus* (51–2). Menalcas here seems to promise a glorious catasterism to a (not-so-glorious) Roman magistrate, provided that Mantua is saved. In *E.* 1, after all, Tityrus called Octavian a young 'god' upon being saved from the confiscations. Stars and political power will soon reappear in 9.46–50 (the *astrum* of Caesar, a descendant of Venus); for the term *sidus*, cf. 5.43n. **cycni.** The swan (κύκνος in Greek), a symbol of poetry by virtue of its close connection with Apollo, is here featured as a means of divinization. It seems that Varus, whose Apollonian privilege is referred to in *E.* 6.11–12, might even take the god's place here, given that Apollo himself was often pictured as travelling on a chariot pulled by swans, going from Delphi to the land of the Hyperboreans (cf. Alcaeus' hymn to Apollo, at least according to Himerius, *orat.* 48.10–11: see fr. 307c V.; cf. also Aelian. *nat. anim.* 11.1; Hor. *carm.* 2.20.15–16; Mart. Cap. 9.927; Isid. *orig.* 12.7.19). In ancient iconography, Apollo is frequently depicted as flying on a swan (cf. *LIMC* II.1, p. 227, nos. 343–4 [W. Lambrinudakis et al.]); swans will reappear on the reliefs of the *Ara Pacis*, i.e. both the decorative frieze (where swans are coupled with acanthus leaves) and the so-called portrait of the goddess *Tellus* (perhaps the *Pax Augusta*), which features one of two *Aurae* flying on a swan. In the opening of Callimachus' *Hymn to Apollo*, the swan's song signals the presence of the god (5 ὁ δὲ κύκνος ἐν ἠέρι καλὸν ἀείδει); cf. also *hymn.* 4.[*Del.*].249 κύκνοι...μέλποντες (where the text is uncertain). Horace asserts that, thanks to his poetic success, he himself will be able to fly: not on the back of a swan, but through his actual metamorphosis into a swan (which is not explicitly named: Hor. *carm.* 2.20.10 *album mutor in alitem*). In V., the bird's connection with Mantua is obvious, both because swans were actually part of Mantua's typical landscape (cf. *G.* 2.198–9 *et qualem infelix amisit Mantua campum / pascentem niueos herboso flumine cycnos*, evoking the expropriations and the present passage) and because of the myth of Cycnus, the Ligurian king who, while singing of his beloved Phaethon's unhappy fate (he fell from the heavens into the river Eridanus), was turned into a swan and reached the stars: cf. *Aen.* 10.193...*linquentem terras et sidera uoce sequentem* (with *et sidera* cf. *ad sidera* here). See also Phanocles, fr. 6 Pow.; Pausan. 1.30.3; Ov. *met.* 2.367–80 (where, however, Cycnus carefully avoids the cruel sky and prefers to dwell in waters: 377–80); Claudian. 28.168–77 H. For the geographical location of the myth of Phaethon and Cycnus (on the banks of the river Po), cf. *E.* 6.62n.; for the swans of the river Po, see also Lucian. *electr.* 4–5; Serv. *ad Aen.* 11.457; see further *Enc. Virg.* I, p. 779, s.v. *Cicno* (E. Salomone

446   ECLOGUE 9

Gaggero), with references; Bader (1998); also *Virg. Enc.* I, p. 327, s.v. *Cycnus* (R. Katz). Note the irony implicit in the fact that the poem, an 'incomplete' one (9.26 *necdum perfecta*) and perhaps doomed to perpetual imperfection, ran the risk of actually being Menalcas' 'swan song' (for the swan as a symbol of poetry, cf. below, 9.36n.). The adverbial use of *sublime*, originally a substantive adjective, is quite common: cf., for instance, Lucr. 4.133 *sublime feruntur*; note also G. 3.108; for its use with the verb *uolo*, see *Aen.* 10.664 *sublime uolans* (and Lucr. 6.97).

30–1 Sic... / sic. The correlation, here underscored by the line-opening anaphora, will reappear at the beginning of the following eclogue: *E.* 10.4–6 *sic... / incipe* (cf., here, *incipe* in 9.32); see 10.4n. Note the choice of typically pastoral images (bees; the cows' milk), quite appropriate for a herdsman who escaped from such terrible dangers: hence, the implicit wish to return to full pastoral prosperity.

30 Cyrneas...taxos. The adj. derives from Kyrnos, the Greek name for Corsica, renowned in antiquity for its bitter honey (like Sardinia, at least according to Hor. *ars* 375 with Porph. ad loc.; cf. *E.* 7.41n.): *melle Corsico, quod asperrimum habetur* (Plin. *nat.* 30.28). The cause of this bitterness was thought to lie in either the numerous local box trees (Plin. *nat.* 16.71; cf. Theophr. *hist. plant.* 3.15.5) or wild hemlock (Ov. *amor.* 1.12.9–10). Yew-trees, on the other hand, are not attested elsewhere as growing in Corsica, since they were deemed to be harmful to bee-keeping (cf. G. 4.47, echoed by Nemes. *ecl.* 1.76–7; for a vaguer statement, cf. G. 2.257 *taxique nocentes*). Servius' note, *taxus uenerata arbor est, quae abundat in Corsica*, may well be based solely on V.'s text. According to Serv. Dan. ad loc., the name Kyrnos derives from that of Heracles' son; cf. Herodot. 1.167.3–4 (and 1.165.1); Sen. (?) *epigr.* 2. (236 R.). The toponym is rare and elsewhere unparalleled in V.: this might explain the incorrect reading *Grynaeas* (or *Gryneas*) in P and some Carolingian manuscripts; *Cyrneas*, known to Servius, appears in M[1]. Note the phonetic affinity between the two Greek terms, *Cyrneas* and *cycni* (9.29), very close to each other; cf. also *cytiso* in 9.31.

31 cytiso pastae distendant ubera uaccae. Udders full of milk appeared in *E.* 4.21–2 (goats, not cows); cf. *E.* 7.3. For clover as particularly well suited to livestock grazing, cf. 1.78n.

32–6. A precise echo of *id.* 7, highlighted by its central position in the eclogue: 'I, too, am a resounding mouth of the Muses, and everyone says / that I am an excellent poet [ἀοιδὸν ἄριστον]: but I am not a gullible one, / no, by Zeus: in my opinion, I could not yet beat the valiant / Sicelidas from Samos, nor Philitas, / in a singing contest: I would be competing with them as a frog among crickets' (*id.* 7.37–41). In Theocritus, Simichidas addresses these words to Lycidas: now it is V.'s Lycidas who adapts them to a new poetic context (9.35n.; 37–8n.).

32 incipe. A formulaic way of introducing pastoral song: cf. *E.* 3.58; 5.10; 12; 8.12 (refrain); 10.6. **si quid habes.** The phrase is used as an exhortation to sing in 3.52n.; cf. also 5.10–11 (also featuring *incipe*). While the two preceding quotations can safely be ascribed to Menalcas, here the text is much more elusive: the compliments and wishes at 9.30–2, the formula *si quid habes*, and Moeris' words in 9.37–8 might suggest that Moeris himself is the author here, or at least that Moeris is prompted to utter songs so that Lycidas can poetically respond to them (hence *et me...poetam*), regardless of Menalcas and 'his' poetry. Yet Serv. Dan. ad loc. had a different opinion (followed by many modern readers): *non dixit tuum, sed Menalcae*; cf. also below, 9.55. Note, at any rate, that this eclogue stresses (even more explicitly than others) the idea that pastoral poetry is the common patrimony of all herdsmen, who must cherish and transmit it: Moeris is very close to Menalcas, who shares poems and songs with him. **et me fecere poetam.** The traditional idea is that poetry is a gift of the Muses (*Pierides* in 9.33), and the poet is correspondingly their 'product': cf. *E.* 10.70 *haec sat erit, diuae, uestrum cecinisse poetam*. Here V. is reworking Theocr. *id.* 7.92 Νύμφαι κῆμὲ δίδαξαν, though without equating the Nymphs with the Muses (which had puzzled Theocritean interpreters in earlier antiquity: e.g. *schol. ad 92*, p. 102 Wend. ἐχρῆν γὰρ εἰπεῖν 'αἱ Μοῦσαι'). That equation, however, operates *de facto* in *E.* 7.21. Note that the text may also activate the etymology of *poeta*/ποιητής (*facio* ≈ ποιέω); the term is one notch below *uatem* (9.34).

33 Pierides. Cf. 3.85n.

34 uatem. While *poeta* (9.32) emphasizes technical skill (i.e. 'composing' poetry), the term *uates* adds solemn, sacral overtones corresponding to Theocritus' ἀοιδός (*id.* 7.38: see above, 9.32–6n.). This crescendo triggers Lycidas' modesty (*sed non ego credulus illis*). For a similar juxtaposition of the two terms, in the context of the *pastores*' evaluation, cf. *E.* 7.25–8. For the acrostic *undis* (9.34–8), cf. below, 9.39n. **credulus.** A simplification of Theocritus' ταχυπειθής (lit. 'quick to believe'): *id.* 7.38. There seems to be some irony here, especially since Theocritus' Lycidas was an authoritative and somewhat mysterious figure, possibly a semi-deity. Here, by contrast, V.'s Lycidas repeats the words of Theocritus' Simichidas, a much more modest literary incarnation of the poet himself. Note that Simichidas spoke 'deliberately' (*id.* 7.42 ἐπίταδες) and received compliments and a 'poetic investiture' from Lycidas: Moeris' behaviour is quite different (cf. 9.37–8n.).

35 adhuc. A small but significant hint at Lycidas' youth (with an echo of Theocr. *id.* 7.39 οὐ γάρ πω): like Thyrsis in *E.* 7.25–8, Lycidas has plenty of time to hope for future poetic glory. From now on, the contrast between Lycidas (with his youthful enthusiasm and desire for song) and Moeris, an old and weary herdsman, will become ever more evident, culminating in the final exclamation (almost a reproach) at 9.66: *desine plura puer*. The reader, however, cannot find out if Lycidas will, in fact, have a future as a poet: V. himself will soon come to his 'last effort' (*E.* 10.1). The temporal scope of the *E.* has nearly reached its end. **Vario.** L. Varius Rufus, one of the first and foremost members of Maecenas' circle and a close friend of V.'s, with whom he shared his Epicurean apprenticeship. Both figures, along with Plotius Tucca, are honoured by Horace in *sat.* 1.5.40–2 *Plotius et Varius Sinuessae Vergiliusque / occurrunt, animae qualis neque candidiores / terra tulit neque quis me*

448   ECLOGUE 9

sit deuinctior alter (the two poets, in fact, had introduced Horace to Maecenas: *sat.* 1.6.54–5). Varius, mainly known for his epic, encomiastic poetry (apparently focusing on contemporary history: cf. Hor. *sat.* 1.10.43–4; *carm.* 1.6.1–4; *ars* 53–5), acquired even greater fame as a tragedian: his *Thyestes* was performed during the celebrations for Octavian's victory at Actium (in 29 or 28 BCE). Finally, according to a rather unanimous biographical tradition, Augustus entrusted him (and Tucca) with the task of publishing the posthumous edition of V.'s *Aeneid.* See further *Enc. Virg.* V.1, pp. 441–3, s.v. *Varius* (P. V. Cova); Courtney (1993, pp. 271–5); Cova (1996); Hollis (1996; 2007, pp. 253–81); *Virg. Enc.* III, pp. 1325–6, s.v. *Varius* (D. Armstrong); Cucchiarelli (2019b). While Lycidas here declares his inadequacy in comparison to Varius, the preceding eclogue featured Alphesiboeus' literal echo of Varius' poem *De morte* (8.85–9n.). Here, V.'s explicit praise of Varius in the context of the expropriations may have political overtones, given that Varius openly took sides with Octavian. Varius' *De morte* (fr. 1 Bläns. = Court.) includes a harsh attack on Antony, criticizing his unscrupulous confiscation measures (see p. 61; cf. also 1.71–2n.). It should be noted, additionally, that the poet Anser, perhaps contemptuously alluded to in 9.36 (yet this leaves room for many doubts: see below, n. ad loc.), had apparently Antonian sympathies. V. will echo Varius' *De morte* again in the finale of *G.* 2 (esp. 2.506) and at *Aen.* 6.621–2. Note how alliteration (*Vario uideor*) highlights the proper noun, which sounds similar to *Varo* (9.26), but is all the more separated from it. No wonder, however, that the reading *Varo* is attested here (M; cf. also Serv. Dan. ad loc.; Servius' *Vario* is found in P). **Cinna.** C. Helvius Cinna, of Transpadane origin (perhaps born in Brescia in the early first century BCE), was a contemporary and friend of Catullus (cf. Catull. 95), and composed neoteric poetry, particularly lyric poems and epigrams. He was also the author of a *Propemptikon* for Asinius Pollio (seemingly dating from 56 BCE). His fame is closely connected with an epyllion, the *Zmyrna*, known for its arcane and refined erudition: he was said to have worked on it for nine years. One of Cinna's distinctive stylistic traits (*Eous* for *Lucifer*) will be echoed by V. in *G.* 1.288 (Serv. Dan. ad loc.). This Cinna is probably the same Helvius Cinna who, during Julius Caesar's funeral, was lynched by the enraged mob, who mistook him for L. Cornelius Cinna, one of Caesar's murderers (whereas the poet was, in fact, one of the dictator's friends and associates). Cinna's importance in the history of Latin poetry is tied particularly to his interest in Parthenius and Euphorion: see Courtney (1993, pp. 212–14); Hollis (2007, pp. 11–48). Barring arbitrary taste, V.'s mention of Cinna in this passage could be motivated by a possible friendship of Cinna with Asinius Pollio, whose literary predilections are often analogous to V.'s own. Perhaps a reminiscence of Cinna's tragic death (due to mere homonymy) would be appropriate in this context, since the two singers, Menalcas and Moeris, have seen their lives unjustly endangered. Note also Cinna's Transpadane provenance and his Caesarian allegiance: both traits facilitate his appearance (along with Varius) in the speech of a 'Mantuan' singer like Lycidas. The two poets, Cinna and Varius, are a

ECLOGUE 9   449

generation apart: such a discrepancy seems to echo Theocritus' *id.* 7, in which a contemporary poet, Sicelidas (= Asclepiades) was mentioned alongside an older one, Philitas, who belonged to the first generation of Alexandrian poets (*id.* 7.40: see above, 9.32–6n.).

36 digna. For the use of *dignus* + abl., in the context of poetic song, cf. *E.* 8.10n. For the alliterative connection between the adj. and *dicere* (9.35), cf. Cornelius Gallus, fr. 4.1–2 Bläns. = 2.6–7 Court. *carmina... / quae possem domina deicere digna mea.* **argutos inter strepere anser olores.** Theocritus' frog and crickets (*id.* 7.41 βάτραχος δὲ ποτ' ἀκρίδας ὥς τις ἐρίσδω) are now replaced by V.'s goose and swans: the image, with its poetic and ornithological implications, echoes *id.* 5.136–7 (magpies and nightingales; hoopoes and swans). In *id.* 7, right after the passage quoted above, Lycidas polemically refers to the 'Muses' birds', who vainly make a racket in front of Homer (*id.* 7.47–8 καὶ Μοῖσαν ὄρνιθες ὅσοι ποτὶ Χῖον ἀοιδόν / ἀντία κοκκύζοντες ἐτώσια μοχθίζοντι); cf. also Pind. *Ol.* 2.87–8 (the eagle and the squawking crows); but see 8.55 *certent et cycnis ululae* (n.). Ancient readers of V. identified this *anser* with an otherwise unknown poet named *Anser*, who celebrated Antony's achievements, as is evident from Servius' note ad loc.: *alludit ad Anserem quendam, Antonii poetam, qui eius laudes scribebat: quem ob hoc per transitum carpsit* (criticizing an Antonian poet would seem appropriate right after the mention of the anti-Antonian Varius [see 9.35n.]). These stories, however, are most probably the result of the usual imaginative constructions accumulated on the margins of V.'s text, which make it very difficult to reconstruct any historical data. At any rate, a somewhat uncomplimentary allusion to an Antonian man named Anser is found in Cic. *Phil.* 13.11; for a rather critical approach cf. *Enc. Virg.* I, p. 188, s.v. *Anser* (G. Brugnoli); a less sceptical view is presented in *Virg. Enc.* I, p. 91, s.v. *Anser* (J. T. Katz). Note, however, that a poet named Anser seems to have been known to Ovid, who associates him with Cinna: *Cinna quoque hic comes est, Cinnaque procacior Anser* (Ov. *trist.* 2.435), whereas Propertius' personification (a reworking of V.'s passage) is certainly full of allusions and irony: *nec minor hic...canorus / anseris indocto carmine cessit olor* (Prop. 2.34.83–4). The opposition between geese and swans, pertaining to the quality of the respective songs, is particularly noteworthy, given the obvious similarities between the two species, which are sometimes coupled together: Lucil. 268 M. = 269 K.; Plin. *nat.* 10.63; Ov. *met.* 2.539. Note that there is no trace of competition here: the goose is simply said to 'spoil' the swans' harmonies through its cry. The adj. *argutus* may also refer to natural sounds, provided that they are somehow semantically loaded: cf. *E.* 7.1; 8.22. **olores.** The swan's Latin name is here preferred to the Greek term *cycni*, used at 9.29 (in a similar position: i.e. at the end of a line and of a speech; cf. also *cycnis* at 8.55). Cinna and Varius, after all, are Roman poets. For the swan as a 'king' of the musical art (whence its analogy to the poet), cf. Eur. *Her.* 691–4; *I. T.* 1104–5; Lucr. 3.6–7; 4.181–2; Hor. *carm.* 2.20.1–3; 10–12. Horace himself calls Pindar a 'swan', using the Greek term: *carm.* 4.2.25

450   ECLOGUE 9

Dircaeum…cycnum (cf. *Anth. Pal.* 2.382–3 [Christod.]; 7.30.1 = *HE* 276 G.-P. [Antip. Sid., referring to Anacreon]). The swan's sweetest song, according to a well-known legend, is the last he sings: cf. Plat. *Phaed.* 84e–85b; see also Aesch. *Ag.* 1444–6; Cic. *Tusc.* 1.71. On the relevant terminology, see further Sauvage (1975, pp. 228–42); Capponi (1979, pp. 215–16).

37–8. Theocritus' seventh idyll, closely reworked here (above, 9.32–6n.), continued with a true celebration of poetry, centred around the figure of Lycidas: the latter responded to Simichidas' modesty by complimenting him and giving him his staff (*id.* 7.43–4). Nothing of the sort happens here, despite the explicit mention of Lycidas' name (37): the action moves along quickly, without compliments or celebrations. In Theocritus, Lycidas responded positively to Simichidas' exhortation (*id.* 7.35–6): 'see, my dear friend, if you like / this little song that I composed on the mountain not long ago' (*id.* 7.50–1). Lycidas' modesty ('little song') was accompanied, in reality, by a not so short song (thirty-eight lines: *id.* 7.52–89); here, instead, poetry is hindered by Moeris' mnemonic difficulties. What follows is a very short, five-line piece on the 'standard' topic of Galatea and love. Like his Theocritean predecessor, however, Moeris appears to refer to a poem of his own, as seems to be confirmed by 38 *neque est ignobile carmen* (at any rate, the poetic fragment at 39–43 and 46–50 cannot be directly attributed to Menalcas; more generally, pastoral songs are part of a common patrimony). This is the first appearance of the theme of memory, which will play a major role in the remainder of the eclogue: as a narrative stratagem, insufficient ability to recollect the past is featured in the finale of Plato's *Symposium* (233c–d; but cf. *E.* 8.63n.). Note the rather free use of syntax, which evokes spoken language (but *carmen* must not necessarily be the direct object of *uoluto*). Horace will represent himself as silently meditating at the time of poetic composition: cf. Hor. *sat.* 1.6.123 (note, here, 9.37: *tacitus* and *mecum ipse uoluto*).

37 mecum ipse uoluto. Here, for the first time, V. uses the frequentative form of *uoluo*, to refer to intense meditation: along with *corde*, the verb will compose a Virgilian epic formula: *Aen.* 1.10 *talia flammato secum dea corde uolutans*; 4.533 *secum…corde uolutat* (interior monologue); 6.185 *suo tristi cum corde uolutat*; cf. also *Aen.* 6.157–8; 10.159–60; 12.843. V. might be echoing an archaic poetic usage (Ennius?), as seems to be confirmed by Lucilius' epic parody: Lucil. 1017 M. = 1101 K. *haec tu me insimulas? nonne ante in corde uolutas…*(the sentence must have continued by mentioning the object of such reflection); cf. Laev. *carm.* fr. 3 Bläns. = Court. *meminens…corde volutat* (here 38 *si ualeam meminisse*). The phrase recalls Homer's φρεσὶ μερμηρίζειν (e.g. *Od.* 1.427).

39–43. A precise reworking of *id.* 11.42–9, focusing on one of the most typically Theocritean subjects, i.e. Galatea and the Cyclops (echoed on multiple occasions in the *E.*): 'Come to me now, and you shall lack nothing: / let the grey sea roll against the shores. / More sweetly, in my cave, will you pass the night with me. / There grows the bay tree, and the swaying cypresses, / along with dark ivy and sweet-clustered grapes; / there is fresh water, which deep-wooded Aetna / sends down for me from

ECLOGUE 9 451

its white snow, a divine nectar. / Who would, in place of these things, choose the sea and the waves?'. The Theocritean echo makes this eclogue far from *ignobile*: regardless of Moeris' obvious modesty, the poem is actually quite easy to 'know'; yet the singer's memory is challenged. The main model is contaminated with at least two echoes of *id*. 7 (cf. below, 9.41n.; 42n.), but variations on the theme of Galatea also appear in a fragment of Bion (16 G.) and in [Mosch.] *epit. Bion*. 58–63. Moeris' fragment is short, but its length is standard in the E. (i.e. five lines: cf. Introduction, p. 24, n. 60): note that the next and last fragment is also five lines long (46–50).

39 huc ades. The phrase, here reasserted in the concluding 9.43, previously appeared in 2.45n. (note the significant consonance with Corydon's eclogue, modelled after *id*. 11 and the topos of the Cyclops in love); cf. also 7.9n. **o Galatea**. In the E., even when the name is borne by human girls or common pastoral lovers, an echo of its Theocritean past seems unavoidable (cf. E. 1.30n.; 3.64n.). Here, without a doubt, the poet refers to the sea-nymph Galatea, as *undis* immediately clarifies (cf. also below, 9.41 *antro*). For an even more explicit apostrophe, cf. E. 7.37 *Nerine Galatea*. Note the musicality of the name (preceding the feminine caesura), featuring assonance of /e/ sounds (here in arsis: *ades…est*). The idea of wooing Galatea by the sea, and never losing hope of being next to her, is found in Bion, fr. 16.3–4 G. (λισσόμενος Γαλάτειαν ἀπηνέα· τὰς δὲ γλυκείας / ἐλπίδας ὑστατίω μέχρι γήραος οὐκ ἀπολειψῶ): Bion's Cyclops seems to be much more hopeful and optimistic than Theocritus'. By contrast, in [Mosch.] *epit. Bion*. 58–63, Galatea leaves the sea in despair after the death of Bion, whose songs she preferred to the Cyclops' (see below). **quis est nam ludus in undis?** The question, which Theocritus employed to conclude a rhetorical structure at *id*. 11.49 (see above, 9.39–43n.), appears here at the beginning of the apostrophe. But cf. also *id*. 11.60–2: 'Now indeed, beloved girl, here and now will I learn to swim, /… / so that I may see why it is so dear to you to dwell in the deep [τί ποχ' ἀδὺ κατοικεῖν τὸν βυθὸν ὕμμιν]'. Galatea leaves the sea and grazes the herds of the late Bion in [Mosch.] *epit. Bion*. 61–3 ἀ καλὰ Γαλάτεια…/…λασαμένα τῶ κύματος ἐν ψαμάθοισιν / ἔζετ' ἐρημαίαισι, βόας δ' ἔτι σεῖο νομεύει. The term *ludus* may contain a malicious allusion to erotic pleasures (Serv. Dan. glosses *uoluptas*): cf. Plaut. *Bacch*. 116; see also e.g. Catull. 61.203 (210). The Nymphs, after all, are innately connected with the act of 'playing' (παίζειν), at least since Hom. *Od*. 6.105–6. Perhaps it is not accidental that the word *undis* is anticipated in the acrostic at 9.34–8 (indeed, its occurrence seems to confirm that the acrostic is authorial). **quis est nam**. As two distinct morphemes, *quis* and *nam* appear (in this order) at Plaut. *Aul*. 136 *quis ea est nam optuma?*; *Bacch*. 1121; *Merc*. 967, etc.; cf., by contrast, G. 4.445–6 *nam quis te…nostras / iussit adire domos?* (with Serv. ad loc.); *Aen*. 2.373. Most Virgilian occurrences of the phrase (and all its instances in the E., except for this one) feature *nam* in the first position (but cf. *namque* at E. 1.14n.); for *nam* in the second position, cf. G. 4.16; *Aen*. 1.444; 4.421; for *nam* in the third position (only twice), see *Aen*. 9.803; 12.206 (cf. also Hor. *carm*. 1.18.3).

40–1 hic…hic…/…hic. Note the recurrence of deictic terms, framing the two line-initial uses of *huc* (9.39 and 43). The first *hic* also appears in line-opening position, whereas the other two are placed in rhythmically less conspicuous positions. Such deictic insistence is typical of the pre-agonistic stage, during which the contestants debate on the location of the agon: cf. e.g. *id.* 5.31–4; 45–6.

40 uer purpureum. Spring, in all its blooming colours (cf. here 40–1 *uarios… flores*), is here. The most conspicuous colour is bright purple-red: the adj. *purpureum* hints at brilliance (cf. λευκὸν γάρ in Theocr. *id.* 18.27); see *G.* 2.319 and 4.54 *purpureosque…flores*; *E.* 5.38 *purpureo narcisso*; André (1949, esp. p. 98).

41 fundit humus flores. For V.'s use of this verb in relation to plant luxuriance, cf. *E.* 4.20. **candida populus.** The poplar, here 'looming' over the cave as a protective and sheltering force, appeared (along with the elm tree) in the shady grove of *id.* 7.8 αἴγειροι πτελέαι τε εὔσκιον ἄλσος ὕφαινον. The species here referred to is *Populus alba* (the white poplar, for which cf. Hor. *carm.* 2.3.9 *alba…populus*), but the epithet *candidus*, insisting on brightness, suggests an upright, luminous column, almost marking the boundary between the 'purple-red' spring at 9.40–1 and the relaxing shades (*umbracula*) at 9.42. The detail is meant to lure (Theocritus') Galatea, whose name evokes the whiteness of milk (*id.* 11.19–20 ὦ λευκὰ Γαλάτεια… / λευκοτέρα πακτᾶς): see *E.* 7.37–8 *Nerine Galatea… / candidior cycnis, hedera formosior alba* (with which cf. 2.6n.). Theocritus' Cyclops similarly mentioned white objects to entice the beloved: cf. *id.* 11.48 and esp. 11.56. **antro.** An echo of the Cyclops' cave (*id.* 11.46); cf. also *E.* 5.6n.

42 imminet et. For the idea expressed by the verb, cf. Hor. *carm.* 3.13.14–15 *cauis impositam ilicem / saxis*; for a more precise parallel, Sen. *Herc. f.* 689–90 *horrent opaca fronde nigrantes comae / taxo imminente*, etc. (describing the underworld: *locus horridus*). **lentae texunt umbracula uites.** The vine, framing and sheltering (like an arbour) the entrance of the cave, alludes to the poetic prototype of the *locus amoenus*, namely Calypso's cave (Hom. *Od.* 5.68–9), which V. previously reworked in *E.* 5.6–7. By contrast, Theocritus' Cyclops merely mentions 'sweet-clustered grapes' (*id.* 11.46 ἄμπελος ἁ γλυκύκαρπος). For the phrase *lentae…uites*, cf. *E.* 3.38; 10.40. For *texunt*, cf. *id.* 7.8 ὕφαινον (Heinsius' emendation; see *E.* 9.41n.). **umbracula.** The term evokes that 'shady' atmosphere which is so distinctive of V.'s pastoral book, from its opening to its conclusion. Here, however, V. builds upon technical language: cf. Varr. *rust.* 1.51.2 (as well as Colum. 3.19.3).

43 huc ades. A concluding ring-compositional echo of 9.39. **insani feriant sine litora fluctus.** Cf. *id.* 11.43 τὰν γλαυκὰν δὲ θάλασσαν ἔα ποτὶ χέρσον ὀρεχθεῖν 'let the grey sea roll against the shores': to Theocritus' sea-waves V. adds the epithet 'foolish' (*insani*), just as it would be foolish for someone to brave the storm. A commonplace of moralizing literature holds that only senseless audacity leads people to grapple with the dangers of seafaring (cf. *E.* 4.32n.). Here, the idea of nature's 'fury' also plays an important role: cf. Mosch. fr. 1.5 G.; Catull. 25.13; Hor. *carm.* 3.4.30 *insanientem…Bosphorum*; 7.6; Prop. 3.7.6; Tib. 2.4.9; Sen. *nat.* 6.17.1;

see also *G*. 1.481 *insano...uertice* (of the overflowing Po). V., moreover, hints at the traditional (and Theocritean) characterization of the Cyclops as 'naïve': from the sea-nymph Galatea's point of view, it might indeed be 'foolish' to dwell on dry land. The sea is ultimately alien to the pastoral world and its symbolism, which is mostly made of land-based and reassuring images: cf. *E*. 10.5n. The construction *sine* + subj. is a relic of archaic parataxis, here with a strongly emphatic effect.

44–50. Presumably a single speech uttered by Lycidas (as in **Mγ**), in precise symmetry with Moeris' (two introductory lines, followed by a five-line fragment of poetry). In 9.23–9, Lycidas chose a 'purely' pastoral topic, while Moeris' quotation was encomiastic in nature; here, the roles are reversed. Note the perfect balance between pastoral (i.e. Theocritean) style and Roman eulogistic rhetoric: the two are equally distributed between the characters. However, the transmitted text ascribes 9.46–50 to Moeris (which, it seems, is the way Serv. Dan. read the passage). If the manuscript tradition were correct, Moeris would seamlessly continue the melancholic remarks he makes at 9.51–4. The attribution of 9.46–50 to Moeris has been buttressed by interpreters with Lycidas' difficulty in recollecting poetic memories (9.45 *si uerba tenerem*: note *tenebam* in **P**[1], corrected by **P**[2]; see further n. ad loc.). Nevertheless, Lycidas' words are analogous to Moeris' (cf. 9.38 *si ualeam meminisse*) and, being younger than Moeris, he might politely intend to encourage his older friend by showing that he, too, has to jog his memory. Otherwise, it would be quite unclear how Moeris would know to which poem Lycidas refers, since he claims to have overheard it in rather uncertain circumstances (9.44 *pura solum sub nocte canentem*). In 9.21–5, Lycidas displayed his ability to 'record' Menalcas' songs, part of which he went on to quote: with 9.21 *uel quae sublegi tacitus tibi carmina nuper...?* cf. 9.44 *quid, quae te pura...?*; note also *ista* in Moeris' words (on which see 9.55n.). Lycidas' imperfect subj., *tenerem* diverging from Moeris' *ualeam*, is thus motivated both by attraction (note *audieram...memini* in l. 45) and, above all, by the fact that the lines quoted by Lycidas are simply an excerpt, presumably the opening, of a poem. Moreover, in the three preceding cases, the poetic quotations conclude the speeches of each character (cf. 9.25; 29; 43). Finally, Moeris' remarks on the drawbacks of old age (9.51) are best understood as the beginning of his speech, not preceded by any poetic quotation (hence Lycidas' reaction in 9.56: *causando*, etc.).

44–5. According to Lycidas, the poet performed this song under a clear night sky, which made for great audibility. Under that starry sky, Moeris celebrated the appearance of Caesar's star. Note the correspondence between the poem's content and the time at which it was sung, as in Damon's case (*E*. 8.17n.).

44 pura...sub nocte. Cf. Arat. *phaen.* 323 καθαρῇ ἐπὶ [v.l. ἐνὶ] νυκτί, concerning astronomical observation (note Cicero's Latin version *nocte serena*: *Arat*. 104 Soub.). Note also the idea of the poet's 'vigil', which appeared in Callimachus' well-known epigram in praise of Aratus himself: *epigr*. 27.4 Pf., reworked in Latin by Cinna, fr. 13 Bläns. = Court.; note also Lucr. 1.142 *noctes uigilare serenas*

454 ECLOGUE 9

(following Aratus and perhaps Cicero). Night-time is normally a period of rest in the pastoral world: this also applies to poetry and song, which typically end at sunset (cf. the finale of *E.* 6; Giacomo Leopardi's *Canto notturno di un pastore errante dell'Asia* is not properly 'pastoral' after all). Here, however, the circumstances are exceptional, due to the appearance of a new star.

45 numeros memini, si uerba tenerem. Properly speaking, *numeri* refers to 'rhythms'—those of both the singer's hexameters and the musical accompaniment (for a less explicit distinction between poetry and music, cf. *E.* 5.14–15). There is some irony in the idea that a humble herdsman has trouble remembering words so openly political and celebratory. Note the desiderative nuance (*si uerba tenerem*: 'if only I had hold of the words'), here underscored by the implicit apodosis ('I would flawlessly perform the song', vel sim.; cf. above, 9.44–50n.). For the optative *si* used absolutely (though with a present subjunctive), cf. *Aen.* 6.187 (*o si* in 11.415; the sole *o* is found at *E.* 2.28). This is likely a feature of everyday speech, here used to express regret: cf. Petron. 8.1 *si scires…quae mihi acciderunt.*

46–50. In this fragment, Daphnis' name is connected to the beneficial effect of Caesar's star on nature (see below, 9.47n.: *sidus Iulium*). Here, V. seems to hark back to the central theme of *E.* 5, in which Daphnis was closely connected with celestial bodies and agricultural prosperity. In fact, *E.* 5 is now playfully reworked in a series of various echoes: Daphnis is now (or so it seems) the name of an ordinary herdsman, who happens to be the namesake of that deified pastoral hero (note the proximity here of Daphnis and Caesar, which highlights their differences). Nothing assures us that the author of these lines is Menalcas, who nonetheless bears the same name as the poet who celebrated Daphnis in *E.* 5 (alternatively, the author might be Moeris, i.e. Menalcas' friend and follower). Nowhere in the *E.* does a Virgilian character more explicitly take sides with the Caesarian party than here. After praising the anti-Antonian poet Varius (9.35n.), Lycidas now quotes one of Moeris' (or Menalcas'?) most unmistakably political songs. In these lines, which purport to be drafts or sketches, V. touches upon themes and notions crucial to his next poem, the *Georgics* (cf. below, 9.48–9n.).

46 antiquos signorum suspicis ortus. In 9.48–50, it will become clear that Daphnis' gaze is that of a farmer, interested in observing the skies and looking for signs useful for agriculture, as in *G.* 1 (cf. esp. 1.205 and 257); but already in a Homeric similitude the shepherd is happy to see in a serene night the stars and the moon, a sign of good weather (*Il.* 8.555–9). Note the enallage, transferring the epithet *antiquos* from *signorum* to *ortus* and thereby emphasizing the *new* appearance (*ortus*) of Caesar's comet.

47 Dionaei processit Caesaris astrum. Caesar's star, which 'moved forward' in the sky: *procedere* is here used in its technical, astronomical sense, indicating the rise, or the appearance, of a heavenly body or phenomenon. Cf. Cic. *Arat.* 391 Soub. (but see Enn. *ann.* 348 Sk.), as well as *E.* 6.86 *inuito processit Vesper Olympo.* In July 44 BCE, i.e. four months after the murder of Julius Caesar (and while

ECLOGUE 9 455

Octavian was celebrating the *ludi uictoriae Caesaris*, established in 46 BCE as *ludi Veneris Genetricis*), a comet appeared in the northern sky, and many Romans began to consider it as a sign that Caesar had entered the gods' world; as early as 43 BCE, divine honours were paid to the late dictator, and in July 42 his birthday was celebrated with religious solemnity, while the month of his birth (*Quintilis*) was renamed *Iulius*: cf. Plin. *nat.* 2.93–4; Suet. *Iul.* 88; Cass. Di. 45.7.1–2; Serv. (here and *ad Aen.* 8.681); also Mark Antony was from the very beginning a supporter of the cult of *Divus Iulius*, so much so that he took on the priesthood of it (to please Octavian, according to Plut. *Ant.* 33.1). Caesar's comet (the *sidus Iulium*) soon became one of the most common emblems of the principate, crucial to the iconography of *Divus Iulius* and widely featured in the visual arts (esp. on coins and public monuments, as well as on jewels and other objects of everyday use): note Weinstock (1971, esp. pp. 370–84); *RRC*, II, p. 744; Ramsey, Lewis Licht (1997); see now also Pandey (2018). For poetic mentions of the *sidus Iulium*, cf. *Aen.* 8.681 *patrium...sidus*; Hor. *carm.* 1.12.47 *Iulium sidus*; Prop. 4.6.59 *Idalio...ab astro*; Ov. *met.* 15.840–51. Comets were traditionally believed to portend collective catastrophes or natural disasters: cf. Sen. *nat.* 7 (esp. 28), and Plin. *nat.* 2.91–4; also e.g. Iuv. 6.407–12. The appearance of the *sidus Iulium* and the imperial rhetorical tradition ushered in a much more positive conception of the phenomenon. Significantly, the Augustan poets attribute negative connotations only to the Greek term *cometa/cometes* (e.g. *G.* 1.488 and Tib. 2.5.71 quoted below); Seneca will later write about a comet appeared in 60 CE: *hunc* [scil. *cometen*] *qui sub Nerone Caesare apparuit et cometis detraxit infamiam* (*nat.* 7.17.2). Thus, V.'s choice of a different Greek word, *astrum*, seems intentional (cf. *E.* 5.51–2n.): the context is obviously reassuring. By contrast, in the finale of *G.* 1 V. will use the technical term *cometae*, in the plural (i.e. several comets: not the *sidus Iulium*), to refer to the disquieting portents that followed Julius Caesar's death: *nec diri totiens arsere cometae* (*G.* 1.488; cf. Plut. *Iul.* 69.4–5). Equally disquieting is the only other occurrence of *cometes* in V.: i.e. in the simile at *Aen.* 10.272–3 (*non secus ac liquida si quando nocte cometae / sanguinei lugubre rubent*); cf. also Tib. 2.5.71 *belli mala signa cometen*, etc. Note that, in the Neronian age, Calpurnius will probably refer to the *cometes* of 54 CE yet emphasizing (perhaps contrastively?) its reassuring powers: *placida radiantem luce cometen* (Calp. *ecl.* 1.78; cf. also Sen. *nat.* 7.17.2, quoted above). It may not be accidental that Suetonius (*Iul.* 88) Latinizes the Greek term κομήτης as *stella crinita*. **Dionaei...Caesaris.** The epithet derives from the goddess Dione, daughter of Tethys and Oceanus: her union with Zeus generated Aphrodite/Venus (who is called *Dionaea mater* in *Aen.* 3.19). Her cult was particularly fervent in Dodona (cf. 9.13 *Chaonias*, in Moeris' speech), and her name clearly connects her with δῖος 'bright, luminous' (cf. Ζεύς / Διός). While Homer keeps Dione distinct from her daughter Aphrodite (cf. *Il.* 5.370–2), Hellenistic and Roman literature tends to conflate the two figures: cf. Theocr. *id.* 7.116; Catull. 56.6; Hor. *carm.* 2.1.39; Ov. *amor.* 1.14.33. Hence V.'s use of the epithet, which provides a good

456 ECLOGUE 9

alternative to *Venerius*, a metrically unwieldy and potentially pejorative term (for instance, it is used of Verres in Cic. *Verr.* 2.2.24). That Julius Caesar is associated with the goddess who founded the *gens Iulia* (namely *Venus Genetrix*, whose cult was fostered by Caesar himself: Weinstock 1971, pp. 80–3) is perhaps significant in an eclogue which assigns great importance to the dangers of war and *tela Martia* (12): the reader recalls that the reassuring picture of Mars comfortably lying in Venus' arms opened Lucretius' Epicurean poem.

48–9. The new star is endowed with the ability to enliven nature, which is typical of charismatic kingship (cf. *E.* 4.37–45n.), and which previously in the *E.* appeared (with the very opposite effect) in 5.36–9n., where Daphnis' death engendered grief and misery in the countryside: but cf. 5.58–9 for the *alacris uoluptas* that pervades woods and fields as soon as Daphnis is deified in the sky (n. ad loc.). Towards the end of Menalcas' song, the cult of the deified Daphnis was coherently associated with that of Bacchus and Ceres (*E.* 5.79–80): note, here, *segetes* (9.48) and *uua* (9.49). V.'s next work now seems to be outlined: *G.* 1.1–3 will ask the question of what gladdens the growing corn and what star (*quo sidere*) ought to protect ploughing and viticulture; note also the apostrophe at *G.* 1.5–7, in which Liber and Ceres are associated with the Sun and the Moon (the subject matter of *G.* 1–2 revolves around cereals and viticulture); but cf. *E.* 10.76n. Cereals and exuberant vines are similarly paired together at *E.* 4.28–9. The portrayal of a benevolent god/sovereign, particularly attentive to agriculture, is also found in the opening of the *Georgics* itself, where V. predicts the divinization of the *diui filius* Caesar Octavian (possibly in the role of *auctor frugum*: *G.* 1.27).

48 astrum quo…et quo. Rhetorical emphasis, created by the epanalepsis of *astrum* (cf. the clausula of 9.47) and the rigidly coordinated *quo…et quo* (abl. of efficient cause), distinguishes Caesar's star from ordinary comets, generally considered as a sign of meteorological perturbations (Plin. *nat.* 2.91) or other disasters (cf., again, *G.* 1.488; also above, 9.47n.). **segetes.** The term *seges*, which ancient (false?) etymologies typically traced back to *sero* and *semen* (cf. Varr. *ling.* 5.37; see Maltby 1991, p. 556, s.v.), has two earlier occurrences in the *E.*, at 1.71 (in the words of the exiled Meliboeus) and 5.33 (in the encomium of Daphnis) before its central role in the *Georgics* (fifteen instances there; only six in the *Aeneid*).

49 duceret…colorem. Cf. Ov. *met.* 3.484–5 *solet uua… / ducere purpureum…colorem*; Lucan. 6.828; see also Sen. *nat.* 1.5.6; Curt. 10.3.4.

50 insere, Daphni, piros: carpent tua poma nepotes. Some reassurance seems to come from comparing this with *E.* 1.73 *insere nunc, Meliboee, piros, pone ordine uitis*, where the exhortation to graft pear trees was bitterly ironic, given the certitude of the expropriation (cf. *E.* 1.72 *his nos conseuimus agros*). As Servius observes, Daphnis' work relies upon a stable, righteous order (cf. also Serv. Dan. ad loc.): thus, his fruits will not be wasted. It is almost as if V. here 'recants' what he had said in *E.* 1.73 (Serv.: *ac si diceret, nihil est quod possis timere: nam illud respicit, quod supra inuidiose ait*). As a result, Daphnis' descendants will be able to benefit from their ancestor's work, in line with a commonplace of Roman morality (cf. Caecilius Statius' well-known dictum, for which see 1.73n.; the pear tree, as a matter of fact, is very long-lived). Here, unlike in e.g. Cic. *Cat. Mai.* 24–5, there is no trace of any optimistic outlook on work and old age (both being compensated by generational continuity): in fact, as Moeris immediately remarks, 'everything, even memory, is taken away by old age' (9.51). According to Palladius 9.6, pear trees were generally grafted in August: however, if the ground is damp, the procedure can occur in July and still bear fruit of good quality (Pallad. 8.3.1); this seems to be the case in the Mantuan area, where to this day the countryside is particularly well suited for growing pear tress. And it was in July (44 BCE) that Caesar's star appeared in the sky: above, 9.47n.

51 Omnia fert aetas, animum quoque. The notion (a traditional one) is expressively formulated in an epigram attributed to Plato: *Anth. Pal.* 9.51 = *Furth. Gr. Epigr.* 628–9, p. 174 P. (αἰὼν πάντα φέρει, etc.); cf. Hor. *ars* 175–6 *multa ferunt anni uenientes commoda secum, / multa recedentes adimunt.* To be sure, the *animus* (or θυμός) should be the last thing to grow old, according to a dictum attributed to Alcaeus (fr. 442 V.): hence Moeris' emphasis, i.e. 'everything is taken away by old age—even (eventually) the *animus*'. Old age should, by nature, be loquacious (Cic. *Cat. Mai.* 55): this, however, does not seem to be the case with Moeris; the stereotypical *senex* in Hor. *ars* 173 is *querulus.* **fert.** Here used as equivalent (*simplex pro composito*) to *aufert*, with great subtlety: cf. 5.34n. **animum.** To be understood as the seat of intellectual faculties, especially memory: cf. *Aen.* 2.12; 3.250 = 10.104; 12.439; see further Negri (1984, esp. p. 146), as well as *Enc. Virg.* I, pp. 176–7, s.v. *animus* (M. Isnardi Parente). Note also the additional sense of 'desire', 'enthusiasm'.

51–2 saepe ego longos / cantando puerum memini me condere soles. As a child, Moeris was wont to spend long summer days singing (for Lycidas' young age, cf. below, 9.66). V. here reworks a well-known and similarly nostalgic epigram by Callimachus: 'Someone told me, Heraclitus, that you were dead, and pushed me / to tears: I remembered how many times we both // let the sun set with our chats [...ἐμνήσθην δ' ὁσάκις ἀμφότεροι // ἥλιον ἐν λέσχῃ κατεδύσαμεν]' (*epigr.* 2.1–3 Pf.), echoing the audacious image of 'letting the sun set' (contrast the normal use of the verb in e.g. *G.* 1.438 *sol se...condet in undas*; *condo* also has the common meaning of 'putting away': cf. Hor. *carm.* 4.5.29 *condit quisque diem collibus in suis*), which will be simplified by Persius in 5.41 *tecum etenim longos memini consumere soles* (cf. Ov. *trist* 5.13.27–8 *solebamus consumere longa loquendo / tempora*, as well as Hor. *carm.* 2.7.6–7, varied in *epist.* 1.5.11 *aestiuam sermone benigno tendere noctem*). For further echoes and reminiscences of Callimachus' epigram, cf. Dion. Chrys. 10.21; Aelian. *nat. anim.* 6.58; Aristaenet. *epist.* 1.24, p. 56, l. 21 Maz.; Mus. *Her. et Leand.* 287–8. Note the expressive hyperbaton *longos /...soles* (both in line-ending position). Here, *soles* is an iterative plural, as in Catull. 8.3; cf. also Hor. *carm.* 4.5.8. For sunset marking the limit of song, cf. *E.* 6.85–6. Note the instrumental gerund *cantando* (3.25n.), and

458   ECLOGUE 9

what the freedman Plocamus complains in Petron. 64.3 *quadrigae meae decucurrerunt... cum essem adulescentulus, cantando paene tisicus factus sum*.

53 oblita mihi...carmina. The participle of *obliuiscor* can be used in a passive sense: cf. Prop. 1.19.6 *oblito...amore*; Val. Fl. 1.792; 2.389 (see also Plaut. *Mil.* 1359, with the gerundive); *ThlL* IX.2.111.79–112.19. Land-confiscations are not suitable for *carmina*; cf. *E.* 1.77 *carmina nulla canam*.

54 lupi Moerim uidere priores. According to a widespread popular superstition, a human could be made mute by a wolf, if the latter sees him first: cf. Plin. *nat.* 8.80; also Plat. *rep.* 1.336d. In *id.* 14.22–6, Theocritus playfully exploits the ambiguity implicit in the beloved's name, i.e. *Lykos* ('Wolf'). Here, too, Moeris' interlocutor (Lycidas) bears a name related to wolves (9.2n.). In *E.* 8, Moeris was credited with the ability to turn himself into a wolf and hide in the woods (8.97), while this Moeris is forced to (poetic) silence by wolves. The Greek form *Moerin* (found here in P) is a rather isolated reading, possibly influenced by the analogy with *Daphnin* and *Alexin*; the manuscript tradition almost unanimously transmits *Moerim* at both 9.53 and 8.98.

55 ista satis referet. The phrase is most intelligible if *ista* refers to the lines uttered by Moeris' interlocutor (Lycidas: cf. above, 9.44–50n.). Rather than qualifying *saepe*, as Serv. Dan. seems to believe, *satis* modifies the verb, with colloquial liveliness (cf. Sen. *contr.* 10.4.10 *hic satis rettulit*). Menalcas will bring the songs back, thereby fulfilling Lycidas' craving. Note the swift dactylic rhythm here, seemingly indicating that the issue has been resolved. But Lycidas will insist one more time, using spondaic rhythm (9.56n.). For *sed tamen* in line-opening position (here with the goal of settling the question), cf. *E.* 1.18n.

56–67. The third and final section of the poem signals the resolution of the matter at hand, with a clear imbalance between the speeches uttered by the two protagonists. In his final speech, in which Lycidas tries again to spur Moeris to sing, his affectionate insistence is made apparent by the number of lines he utters (ten): this is, in fact, the longest speech in the eclogue (contrast 9.17–25 = nine lines). Once again, V. echoes *id.* 7 (cf. below, 9.59–60n.; 64n.), as well as the opening of *E.* 5 (cf. 9.60–2n.). Yet those models can no longer be actualized: certainly not in this poem. Moeris' reply is only two lines long (66–7).

56 Causando nostros in longum ducis amores. Lycidas subtly echoes the words just uttered by Moeris, although *cantando* (9.52) is here replaced by *causando*, emphatically placed in initial position, so as to express the young man's impatience; as for the *longos...soles* of the past (9.51–2), Lycidas replaces them with Moeris' long hesitation (cf. *in longum ducis*) and defeatist attitude. Note the slow, spondaic rhythm (featuring only one dactyl, in the fifth foot): for similar sequences, cf. *E.* 1.72; 76; 78; 3.31; 5.37–8; here, moreover, Lycidas' spondees expressively contrast with Moeris' dactyls (9.55). For *amor* as a desire for song and poetry, cf. *E.* 6.10n.; differently, 8.23 and 10.54. The phrase as a whole, and especially the gerund, seem to echo Lucr. 1.398 *quamuis causando multa moreris*.

ECLOGUE 9   459

57 omne...stratum silet aequor. Nature is silent, as though it were waiting for the herdsmen's song to re-establish the normal 'resonance' of the pastoral world. For a similarly quiet situation (described in a similar language), see nature's reaction to Jupiter's words in *Aen.* 10.101–3 *eo dicente deum domus alta silescit | et tremefacta solo tellus, silet arduus aether, | tum Zephiri posuere, premit placida aequora pontus.* For silence in pastoral poetry, cf. Calp. *ecl.* 2.15–20; 4.97–101; 108. The noun *aequor* is rather vague, since it can refer to any kind of flat surface (note its frequent coupling with a gen., such as *caeli, ponti, campi*, etc.); cf. for instance, in reference to earth, *G.* 2.541; note also *Aen.* 11.599 and *E.* 1.59n. Thus, we cannot assume that *omne...aequor* must here refer to water surfaces: V. might also be talking about plains or lakes, or even lagoons and marshes (though certainly not the sea, given that the general context is the area around Mantua). For *aequor* 'sea' used with *sterno*, cf. *Aen.* 5.820–1 *tumidumque |...sternitur aequor aquis* (note the disambiguating abl.); Ov. *her.* 7.49 *strataque aequaliter unda*; cf. Theocr. *id.* 2.38 σιγῇ μὲν πόντος, σιγῶνται δ' ἀῆται. Literally, therefore, V.'s *omne...aequor* means 'every even surface'. Note the alliteration, uniting the two verbal forms: the sound /s/ often hints at stillness (cf. esp. *E.* 1.55n.).

58 uentosi ceciderunt murmuris aurae. An innovative construction, compared to the standard *uenti* (gen.) *murmurantis aurae* (nom.); at any rate, the noun *aura* frequently takes an epexegetic gen., even in metaphorical contexts: cf. *Aen.* 7.646 *famae...aura*, as well as Cic. *Mur.* 35 *parua...aura rumoris* (as quoted in Quint. *inst.* 8.6.49); *Sest.* 101 *honoris aura.* For the gen. used of winds (but featuring a proper noun), cf. *G.* 2.330 *Zephyri...tepentibus auris.* For this particular use of the verb, cf. *G.* 1.354 *caderent Austri* (but see Varr. *Men.* 471 Buech. = Astb.[2] [= 467 Cèb.]); Ov. *met.* 8.2; Stat. *Ach.* 1.694; Liv. 29.27.10; 36.43.11, etc.; see further *ThlL* III.27.43–54. Note also *Aen.* 7.27–8 *uenti posuere omnisque repente resedit | flatus; Aen.* 10.103 quoted above, 9.57n. Such a sudden 'ceasing' of the winds, in the 'humble' context of countryside life, might bring to mind imminent rainfall: Lycidas, true to his efforts to persuade Moeris, will soon take this into account.

59–60. A precise echo of *id.* 7.10–11: κοὔπω τὰν μεσάταν ὁδὸν ἄνυμες, οὐδὲ τὸ σᾶμα / ἁμῖν τὸ Βρασίλα κατεφαίνετο 'we had not yet travelled half of the road, nor had we seen / Brasilas' grave', etc. Lycidas perhaps hopes that, as in Theocritus' *Thalysia*, the mention of a grave will mark the beginning of a song: here, instead, it marks its conclusion. Theocritus also referred to a funerary monument (that of the eponymous hero Arcas) in *id.* 1.125–6. In the *Aeneid*, Ceres' 'mound' and temple signal a key turn in the narrative: passing next to them, Aeneas realizes that Creusa is no longer following him (*Aen.* 2.742 *tumulum antiquae Cereris sedemque sacratam*); for the Homeric grave, see also below, 9.60n. Since the beginning of the eclogue (9.1 *quo te...pedes? an, quo uia ducit...?*), the reader has been under the impression that the two protagonists continue walking along the road throughout the poem—perhaps with some breaks or slowdowns

460   ECLOGUE 9

depending on the pace of conversation and song. The reader's impression is now confirmed: cf. 60 *incipit apparere*).

59 hinc adeo. When reinforcing a demonstrative (vel sim.), *adeo* often appears in the second position: cf. *E.* 4.11n., as well as 1.12.

60 Bianoris. According to Servius, the hero is to be identified with Ocnus, the legendary founder of Mantua, son of the river-god Tiber and the prophetess Manto (*Aen.* 10.198–200). This information, however, is suspiciously unparalleled, and it is scarcely plausible to think that V. here refers to such a specific place in the Mantuan region (assuming that it actually existed); but see *Enc. Virg.* I, pp. 504–5, s.v. *Bianore* (P. Tozzi); III, pp. 815–16, s.v. *Ocno* (G. Garbugino); also *Virg. Enc.* I, p. 184, s.v. *Bianor* (S. Harrison). V. is perhaps influenced by an epigram by Diotimus, which he might have known through Meleager's *Garland*: 'Birth pangs—why? What is the use of having children? / May they not be generated by parents who will have to see them dead! / Bianor's mother made his grave, as he was still a boy [ἠιθέῳ γὰρ σῆμα Βιάνορι χεύατο μήτηρ]. / Her son should have done this for her' (*Anth. Pal.* 7.261 = *HE* 1735–8 G.-P.). At any rate, the name sounds typically heroic: a Trojan hero named Bienor (or Bianor) appeared in the *Iliad*, where he was killed by Agamemnon (*Il.* 11.92 ἕλε δ' ἄνδρα Βιήνορα, ποιμένα λαῶν; but note Aristarchus' reading Βιάνορα: *schol.* A, III, p. 142 Erbse). Bianor's grave has to be imagined as a conspicuous landmark within its surroundings, evoking a heroic past that had left tangible traces in the Italian (and Mantuan) territory: revitaliz-ing and immortalizing that noble past is a task for an epic bard, not for a 'humble' pastoral poet. In the *Aeneid*, V. will mention the Trojan Aeolus' grave in Latium (*Aen.* 12.547 *solo Laurente sepulcrum*). In Homer, monumental graves are tied to the very identity of epic poetry as a genre: such monuments are analogous to song itself when it comes to glory and fame (cf. esp. *Il.* 7.84–91). Hector's burial and grave concludes the *Iliad*: cf. Hom. *Il.* 24.801 χεύαντες δὲ τὸ σῆμα and 24.804 ὣς οἵ γ' ἀμφίεπον τάφον Ἕκτορος ἱπποδάμοιο (the last line of the poem). In the finale of *E.* 9, so rich in references to poets, poems, and poetic potentialities (with an explicit mention of the epic poet Varius Rufus), right before the final eclogue devoted to Cornelius Gallus, the literary echoes of Bianor's grave evoke the epic genre, while the pastoral characters walk by it unaware of its hidden meaning. V.'s mention of Bianor is also crucial to the ninth eclogue's plot: unlike the new land-owners, who are 'foreigners' (9.2 *aduenae*), the herdsmen, or *ueteres coloni* (9.4), possess a deeply rooted knowledge of the territory and its 'monuments', some of which possibly go back to a foundational, Homeric past.

60–2. The place is appropriate for singing. Note the exhortation and the deictic gesture (*hic*), as in *E.* 5.3. Here, however, Lycidas' wish will not be fulfilled, in spite of the threefold repetition (featuring arsis in the first and the last *hic*).

60–1 densas / agricolae stringunt frondes. A reference to *frondatio*, i.e. the pruning of excessive foliage (cf. *densas*), potentially to be used as fodder: cf. 1.56n.; 2.70n. According to Colum. 11.2.55, the procedure was performed either before

ECLOGUE 9   461

dawn or, as here, at sunset (cf. below, 9.63 *nox*). The shrinking *umbra* (a distinctively pastoral notion: cf. *E.* 1.1 and esp. 2.3 *densas, umbrosa cacumina, fagos*) might be a further allusion to the imminent conclusion of the *E.*, as well as to the beginning of a new work devoted to the *agricolae* themselves (cf. 10.76n.), in which both *frondatio* and the verb *stringo* will reappear together: note *G.* 2.368 *tum stringe comas* (for *stringo* in this technical sense, cf. Hor. *epist.* 1.14.28; for the vaguer sense of 'plucking' or 'cutting', cf. Cat. *agr.* 65.1; Varr. *rust.* 1.55.1).

62 haedos depone. The reference to goats, which echoes and clarifies 9.6, is another sign of imminent closure: yet the situation is not resolved through a break in the walk and the beginning of song, as Lycidas had hoped. **tamen ueniemus in urbem.** The travellers' final destination (= the city) is reasserted, in opposition to the preceding eclogue (note its very last line: *E.* 8.109 *ab urbe uenit*); see below, 9.67n. For the emphatic *tamen* (placed at the beginning of a new sentence or colon), cf. 10.31n.; but see, for instance, Plaut. *Pseud.* 1314 *negabas daturum esse te mihi: tamen das* (where, however, the text is uncertain); Cic. *diu. in Caec.* 21 (with hammering anaphora); *Marcell.* 4; *OLD²*, p. 2098, s.v. 1a.

63 aut si nox. For the three initial monosyllables, cf. *E.* 6.49. **pluuiam ne colligat.** For the 'gathering' of liquids (esp. rain), see Cic. *nat. deor.* 2.59; 101; *top.* 38 (as well as Lucr. 4.1065); cf. also *G.* 1.114 (and 3.327); see further *ThlL* III.1608.73–1609.60. Perhaps echoing V., Quintilian (*inst.* 10.1.109) translates an unknown passage of Pindar: *non enim pluuias, ut ait Pindarus, aquas colligit* (= fr. 274 Maeh.). The possibility of rain is somehow foreshadowed by the 'ceasing' of the winds (above, 9.58n.).

64 usque…eamus. For *usque* modifying a verb and expressing continued action, see *Aen.* 6.487 *iuuat usque morari*; cf. Plaut. *Epid.* 305 *usque opperiar*; Hor. *sat.* 1.9.15 *usque tenebo*, as well as *epist.* 1.10.24 *tamen usque recurret*; *OLD²*, pp. 2325–6, s.v. 5. **laedet.** The future tense is preferable (*laedet* P; *laedit* M; *laedat* f), especially since it is supported by the Theocritean model: ὥτερος ἄλλον ὀνασεῖ 'the one will benefit the other' (*id.* 7.36; cf. above, 9.56–65n.). Note also the future nuance implicit in *licet usque…eamus*, which could hardly be reconciled with a vague, gnomic statement. The implication seems to be that a long walk becomes easier through conversation (and, a fortiori, song): cf. *Aen.* 8. 309 *uario…uiam sermone leuabat*.

65 ego hoc te fasce leuabo. A final gesture (with deixis): Lycidas declares his readiness to take the burden off Moeris' shoulders, thereby making it easier for him to sing. Here, *fasce* could refer to any type of basket, perhaps used to carry the kids (9.6 *hos…haedos*) which Moeris will offer to the new landlord: cf. *Moret.* 79 Kenn. *uenalis umero fasces portabat in urbem*. The sing. *fascis* often implies a very heavy burden: *G.* 3.347 *iniusto sub fasce* and 4.204, as well as Petron. 117.11. Note also the pronoun *ego*, expressing Lycidas' keen eagerness. However, despite Lycidas' efforts, his offer will be declined (as in *E.* 1, when Tityrus' kind and hospitable offer did not seem to be enough to stop Meliboeus), and the two herdsmen will keep walking.

66 Desine plura, puer. Cf. *E.* 5.19 *sed tu desine plura, puer*: in Menalcas' words, however, the protagonists' arrival at the cave marked the beginning of song, whereas

462   ECLOGUE 9

here the phrase signals their final cessation. Moeris and Lycidas wait for Menalcas to arrive (contrast *incipe* in 9.32). In *E.* 6, Chromis and Mnasyllus were two 'boys' desirous of poetry, and often disappointed (by the elderly Silenus): cf. *E.* 6.14; 18–19. Note also the contrastive echo of the finale of *E.* 4: *incipe parue puer* (4.62; both are penultimate lines in the respective eclogues). After all, *E.* 4 and *E.* 9 are the shortest poems in the book (and the second-to-last ones in the respective halves of the collection: *E.* 1–5 vs 6–10). *E.* 4, however, marks the beginning of a new era seen through the eyes of a child, whereas here the boy must be patient and accept to wait. **puer.** Note that the second syllable (in arsis, before caesura) is prosodically long, despite being followed by a vowel (contrast *E.* 5.19). This is best explained as a further emphatic device: differences in age imply differences in hierarchy, as in *E.* 5.4 *tu maior; tibi me est aequum parere, Menalca*. Instances like 10.69n. (*amor*) and *Aen.* 11.469 (*pater*) feature morphological archaisms that might legitimate, by extension, a case like the present one. See also *E.* 1.38; 3.97; 7.23. The inferior reading *puer nunc quod nunc*, transmitted by a large number of manuscripts, is probably meant to normalize the prosody. **et quod nunc instat agamus.** In *E.*, a hard-working Meliboeus did not hesitate to neglect his duties and listen to the amoebean songs of Thyrsis and Corydon (*E.* 7.17). Here, by contrast, Moeris resembles the travelling Meliboeus of *E.* 1, who bade farewell to Tityrus and poetry at once (*E.* 1.77 *carmina nulla canam*: cf., here, 9.67 *carmina…canemus*). As in the finale of *E.* 2, work duties divert attention away from concerns and anxieties.

67 cum uenerit ipse. The pronoun *ipse* implies great respect for Menalcas, the real protagonist of the poem. The finale of *E.* 8, alluded to in 9.62 (see n. ad loc.), is evoked one last time: the end of *carmina*, once caused by Daphnis' return, here corresponds to the arrival of Menalcas himself, a necessary precondition for good poetry (*carmina…canemus*). In a sense, this is also a 'new beginning', the last of its kind in the *E.*: note the conclusive *surgamus* and *uenit Hesperus* in 10.75 and 10.77. The reader recalls that *E.* 5 was concluded by Menalcas, the herdsman who knows all sorts of songs (such as those of *E.* 2 and 3) and is capable of praising the deified Daphnis. Now, in order to listen to the remainder of a 'Caesarian' song (addressed to a lesser Daphnis), the herdsmen must wait for Menalcas' reappearance. A Menalcas will, in fact, arrive in the next poem (cf. *E.* 10.20n.): yet he will by no means resemble the absent protagonist of *E.* 9. **canemus.** This verbal form is the last word of the eclogue, with the corresponding noun *carmina* framing the line (note also *carmina* in the last line of the preceding *E.* 8, where the noun functioned as a keyword in the refrain). The future tense could be interpreted as programmatic, not unlike *G.* 3.1: *te quoque magna Pales, et te memorande canemus*, etc. (note also Ov. *ars* 1.33). Here, however, it reads rather like a vague 'postponement' to an unspecified date: the sort of thing one says to children to appease them. Horace will also use the term as the last word of *Odes* 4 (and, therefore, of his entire lyric corpus), in an all-too-optimistic context of future songs:… *Troiamque et Anchisen et almae / progeniem Veneris canemus* (Hor. *carm.* 4.15.31–2).

Eclogue 10

[Gallus]

Like all even-numbered eclogues, the tenth and last poem has a narrative character and begins with a prologue uttered by the poet in his own voice. It announces the main theme of the poem: V. asks the nymph Arethusa (10.1n.) to inspire him to compose just a few more lines, devoted to Cornelius Gallus and his unhappy love for Lycoris (10.1–8). The following section (10.9–30) describes Gallus' sorrowful yearning. Little solace is provided to him by natural elements, including both plants and animals (10.13–18), or by pastoral characters, such as Menalcas (10.20), and even divine figures: Apollo, Silvanus, Pan (10.21–30). Gallus himself then begins to speak: in a lively monologue (10.31–69), he expresses his desire to become part of the pastoral world, inviting his distant beloved, Lycoris, to join him (10.42–9). But another reverie, full of life in the woods, including hunts, arrows, forests, and cliffs, is suddenly interrupted by the realization that it is impossible to find a cure for love: hence Gallus' farewell to the woods (10.63), featuring a well-known motto (10.69 *omnia uincit Amor*). In the epilogue (10.70–7), the poet's voice is heard again: he declares that he has sung long enough (10.70) and, following a final expression of affection for Gallus (10.72), he bids farewell to his audience. Night is falling, and it is now time for the goats to return home: in other words, for the poem and the book to come to an end. A few, simple verbs describe an intersection of linear motions: *surgamus*; *uenit*; *ite*. This is a sign of calm, after so much unrest and anxiety: Arethusa herself, the protagonist of the poem's prologue, is a very mobile nymph (even though the poet who addresses her is serenely 'sitting': 10.71).

The first word, *extremum*, calls the reader's attention to the editorial aspect of the book, which has now come to an end: this is also an exhortation (in the wake of *E.* 7–9) to take a retrospective glance at the collection as a whole. Correspondingly, it becomes clear that *E.* 10 recapitulates motifs and literary forms that pervaded the entire book and now reappear together to conclude it. In fact, Gallus' lovesickness echoes a Theocritean model, *id.* 1, which has been evoked multiple times in the *E.*, though never through direct emulation (as here): *E.* 5 narrated Daphnis' death, as well as the ensuing grief and deification, whereas *E.* 1 featured even more distant echoes of *id.* 1 (such as Meliboeus' farewell to the pastoral world, 'almost like' Daphnis'). Along with Theocritus' Daphnis, a wholly Virgilian figure is reworked, i.e. Corydon: in *E.* 2, the unrequited lover of Alexis was entrusted with the task of opening the core section of the pastoral book. Gallus' monologue contains dense allusions to Corydon's, particularly centred around the idea that love is incurable: another Theocritean model, the Cyclops of *id.* 11, comes to the fore (as in *E.* 2). In comparison to *E.* 2, however, note the additional description of an eminently Arcadian landscape: the book has now trespassed across the threshold of *E.* 7, in which Corydon's name was explicitly associated with Arcadian provenance (*E.* 7.4). At any rate, the purely literary themes of Daphnis and Corydon do not

464   ECLOGUE 10

prevent *E.* 10 from referring to contemporary events. The preceding poem, *E.* 9, ended on a note of anxiety and uncertainty, due to the sudden incursion of *tela Martia* (9.12) into the pastoral world: centre stage is now taken by a poet who declares himself to be held back by Mars' weapons (10.44) and pictures his beloved girl in cold, distant lands, where she went in order to follow a new lover, similarly engaged in military operations (10.23 and 46–9). Plants and pastoral deities such as Pan and Apollo sympathize with Gallus' grief. He addresses the Arcadians, and Mount Maenalus itself is moved by his words. The reader must, however, picture Lycoris' passionate lover in the role (and perhaps in the garments) of a Roman general.

The eclogue begins with an invocation to Arethusa and an evocation of the Doric and Sicilian origins of pastoral poetry (10.4–5), so as to recapitulate the main geographical (and literary) coordinates of the genre. Yet even Gallus' Arcadia is located in a literary dimension, activated by poetic imagination. V. has accustomed his readers to 'Arcadian' herdsmen who, along with Daphnis, compete poetically on the banks of the Mincius river. Now the poet Gallus, who wandered between Permessus and Helicon in *E.* 6, represents himself as an Arcadian singer while, in the extra-poetic world, he is at war (no need, therefore, to change *me* into *te* at 10.44n.). Through its complex combination of contemporary history, urban erotic adventures, poetry, and politics, *E.* 10 reflects the literary personality of its distinguished addressee in a deliberately nervous, agitated way. If, indeed, it was Cornelius Gallus who took sides with the Mantuan landowners (including V.) during the expropriations (cf. 9.28n.), it would be all the more significant for such an affectionate homage to follow *E.* 9 (and its ultimately fruitless praises of Varus). At any rate, the juxtaposition of the two poems at the end of the book effectively highlights the painful events which surround V. and his poetry. The juxtaposition is underscored by the herdsmen's awaiting of Menalcas in *E.* 9: now, in fact, a Menalcas mysteriously arrives (10.20n.).

Note, finally, a further intratextual echo: that of *E.* 6, in which Gallus appeared as a character in Silenus' song. In *E.* 10, however, Gallus bears little resemblance to the poet to whom Linus assigned the task of singing the aetiology of the Grynean grove (6.69–73). Rather, in expressing his contradictory feelings, Gallus declares (albeit briefly) his intention to 'remodulate' his previous *carmina*, using the Theocritean pipes (for the debated interpretation of 10.50–1, see nn. ad loc.). Thus, in the transition from *E.* 6 to *E.* 10, V.'s Gallus tests a difficult combination of genres, blending didactic poetry (in the wake of Hesiod and Callimachus) with the lover's alienated subjectivity, which will become typical of Roman love-elegy. This kind of 'experimental' poetry, which must have characterized Gallus' actual output, had a deep impact on later Latin poetry, as is shown, for instance, by Prop. 2.13 (which some critics read as two separate poems; cf. also Prop. 3.5). According to Servius, V.'s Gallus here reworks his own elegies (cf. 10.46–9n.; but see 50n.). Thus, from Gallus' (and V.'s) point of view, *E.* 10 is a precious opportunity to combine pastoral poetry with love-elegy, thereby observing their mutual analogies and differences.

The contrast between V. and the elegiac poet Cornelius Gallus allows V. to take shelter in the objective forms of narrative poetry, thereby bringing the pastoral book to a close. Yet Gallus himself, despite his elegiac restlessness, cannot escape from V.'s pastoral world: Corydon has previously experienced the emotional turmoil of love, and Gallus' farewell to the woods is preceded not only by Theocritus' Daphnis but by the herdsman of *E.* 8 as well. In asserting the inexorability of *Amor* (10.69), Gallus ultimately reworks a motif established by Pan himself, who is the pastoral and Arcadian god *par excellence* (10.28–30). Perhaps the tale of Orpheus in the finale of the *G.* evokes the figure of V.'s friend Gallus, who fell out of favour with the *princeps* and committed suicide (in *met.* 10, Ovid seems to be aware of the connection: when Ovid's Orpheus descends into the underworld, he displays many similarities with V.'s Gallus and repeats some of Gallus' keywords: below, 10.53n.; 69n.). But now, while Gallus laments his unhappy love, the pastoral poet does not hesitate to strike the pose of a Theocritean character, surrounded by goats and working on a finely interwoven basket. Theocritus' Cyclops had similarly managed to escape from lovesickness and folly: 'whither have your senses flown? / Should you go weave baskets and cut young shoots / to feed your lambs, perhaps you would regain your senses to a greater degree' (*id.* 11.72–4; for the 'young shoots' cf. below, 10.7n.).

The very juxtaposition between the lover's obsession and the practical necessities of countryside labour at the end of the poem foreshadows the values of a new, georgic work. An important Theocritean parallel is the opposition, in *id.* 10, between love song and (agricultural) work song: cf. below, 10.75n. (in the Theocritean edition used by V., both *id.* 10 and *id.* 11 may have occupied a position similar to *E.* 10: i.e. they may have concluded a series of ten 'purely' pastoral idylls: cf. Introduction, pp. 19–20). In the wake of the great Hellenistic poets (esp. Callimachus), V. perhaps wanted the epilogue of his pastoral book to anticipate his next poetic endeavour: an 'editorial' connection.

E. 10 is often interpreted (with some good reasons) as a sort of 'afterthought' which adds a eulogy of Gallus to a book that has already reached completion at the end of *E.* 9. In reality, however, *E.* 10 is perfectly integrated within the bucolic *liber* as a whole (of which it is the *extremus labor*), and is closely tied to the rest of the book through several structural and thematic links. Besides occasionally echoing *E.* 1, *E.* 10 closes the circle by placing emphasis on the figure of Gallus, who was prominently featured in *E.* 6. Thus, *E.* 6 and 10 perfectly 'frame' the beginning and the end of the second half of the book. Being a man of letters, the poet Gallus was certainly not deaf to this kind of editorial subtlety (even though nothing substantial survives of his own work). A fragment of Suetonius seems to hint at Gallus' interest in the material aspects of literature: a certain type of papyrus leaf, whose preparation was commissioned by Gallus, apparently took its

466   ECLOGUE 10

name from Gallus himself (Suet. p. 132 Reiff.: *Corneliana a Cornelio Gallo prae-fecto Aegypti primum confecta*). Through its diegetic form, *E.* 10 completes the overall structure of the book, which began with a dramatic eclogue and must now end (based on the principle of alternation) with a narrative one: while V. was not allowed to speak in the first person in *E.* 1, the poet's voice can now be heard in the conclusion. From a structural point of view, the poem can be divided into three parts (the first and the third having the same number of lines and echoing each other): a proem (1–8); a central section (9–69), with Gallus as protagonist, which can be subdivided into two segments (introduction and arrival of the main characters at 9–30; Gallus' monologue at 31–69); an epilogue (70–7).

On the eclogue: F. Skutsch (1901, pp. 2–27); Jahn (1902); Leo (1902, pp. 14–22); F. Skutsch (1906, pp. 155–90); Pohlenz (1930); Weyman (1931); E. Pfeiffer (1933, pp. 47–55); Büchner (1955, cols. 1241–7); Steidle (1962, pp. 320–34); C. Hardie (1966–7); Klingner (1967, pp. 160–74); G. Williams (1968, pp. 233–9); Posch (1969, pp. 54–85); Putnam (1970, pp. 342–94); Grillo (1971, pp. 46–52, 61–70); Berg (1974, pp. 186–90); Leach (1974, pp. 158–70); Boyle (1975, pp. 196–9); Coleman (1975, pp. 148–50); Ross (1975, pp. 85–106); Cupaiuolo (1977, pp. 126–35); Van Sickle (1978, pp. 188–205); Alpers (1979, pp. 222–40); Conte (1980a); Cupaiuolo (1981); Van Sickle (1986, pp. 157–85); Di Stefano (1989); M. O. Lee (1989, pp. 96–100); Perkell (1996); Rudd (1996, pp. 70–3); Rumpf (1996); Martindale (1997b, pp. 113–15); P. Hardie (1998, pp. 13–14); T. K. Hubbard (1998, pp. 127–39); Papanghelis (1999, pp. 50–9); Lipka (2001, pp. 56–60 and 102–7); Perkell (2001a, pp. 33–8); Breed (2006a, pp. 117–35); von Albrecht (2007, pp. 36–8); Fabre-Serris (2008, pp. 47–94); Davis (2012, pp. 141–61); Gagliardi (2014b); Heerink (2015, pp. 92–100); Seider (2016); Marchetta (2018, pp. 99–268).

Specific issues: Jacoby (1905, pp. 67–81) (Gallus); Hubaux (1930, pp. 87–100) (Gallus); Wendel (1934) (l. 18); Snell (1945) (Arcadia); Bréguet (1948) (Gallus); Bardon (1949) (Gallus); Stégen (1953) (Gallus); Tescari (1953) (l. 69); Cova (1955) (ll. 75–6); Hubaux (1957) (Parthenius; Gallus; Propertius); Winniczuk (1959–60) (Gallus); Alfonsi (1961) (*E.* 2); Coleman (1962) (Gallus and the finale of *G.* 4); Estevez (1962) (song and the unity of *E.* 10); Drijepondt (1963) (Gallus); Kidd (1964) (emulation); Della Corte et al. (1965) (l. 50 and Euphorion); Van Sickle (1967) (Arcadia and editorial form); Dyer (1969) (ll. 73–4); D'Anna (1971) (ll. 44–5); Chausserie-Laprée (1974) (V.'s poetics of resonance); Gaisser (1977) (Tib. 2.3); Grondona (1977) (Tibullus; Propertius); Kelley (1977) ('quotation'/emulation of Gallus); Pasoli (1977) (Gallus; Prop. 1.8); Solodow (1977) (*E.* 8–10 and the poet's 'weari-ness'); Van Sickle (1977a) (Gallus); Zetzel (1977) (Gallus and elegy); Anderson, Parsons, Nisbet (1979) (the 'new' Gallus); Monteleone (1979a, pp. 46–51) (Prop. 1.20 and Gallus); Yardley (1980) ('quotation'/emulation of Gallus); Barchiesi (1981) (the 'new' Gallus); D'Anna (1981) (Gallus; Propertius); Keppie (1981) (the expropriations); Puccioni (1981) (the 'new' Gallus); Kennedy (1982, pp. 385–7) (Gallus and *Culex*); Hinds (1983) (ll. 2–3 and the 'new' Gallus); Kennedy (1983) (ll. 75–7); Kenney (1983, pp. 45–57) (love and elegy); Viljamaa (1983) (Gallus); Newman (1984) (the 'new' Gallus); Protomártir Vaquero (1984) (style); Caballero de Del Sastre (1986) (love); Rosen, Farrell (1986) (ll. 52–61); Kennedy (1987) (Gallus and Arcadia); G. Williams (1987) (Theocr. *id.* 7); Whitaker (1988) (Gallus' 'pastoral' elegies?); Jenkyns (1989, pp. 34–6; cf. 1998, pp. 165–7) (Arcadia); Arkins

(1990) (ll. 4–6); Chwalek (1990) (elegy); Courtney (1990, p. 107) (Gallus); M. J. Edwards (1990) (ll. 50–1; Hesiod and Gallus); Koster (1990) (Gallus' death); A. Michel (1990) (Gallus); Álvarez Hernández (1991) (Gallus); Dehon (1991) (Gallus); Glei (1991, pp. 243–7) (war); Álvarez Hernández (1992–3) (Gallus); Courtney (1993, pp. 268–70) (Gallus); O'Hara (1993) (*medicina amoris*); Fabre-Serris (1995) (Prop. 1.20 and Gallus); Langslow (1995) (ll. 75–7); Manzoni (1995) (Gallus); Kyriakou (1996) (*E.* 6); Wimmel (1996–7) (ll. 65–6); Paschalis (1997) (l. 1); Theodorakopoulos (1997) (ll. 65–7); Maurer (1998) (l. 59); Lightfoot (1999, pp. 59–76) (Euphorion and Gallus); Traina (1999a) (love); Cucchiarelli (2000) (Ov. *met.* 10); Geymonat (2000) (the mountains); Maleuvre (2000, pp. 357–92) (*laudes Galli*); Loupiac (2001) (Gallus and Orpheus); Luther (2002, pp. 57–65) (historical context); Otranto (2002) (l. 67); Torlone (2002) (Daphnis and Gallus); Gagliardi (2003, pp. 15–38) (ll. 75–7); Van Sickle (2003) (elegy); Geymonat (2004) (l. 77); Bauzá (2006) (*eros* and *thanatos*); Cairns (2006, pp. 104–45) (Gallus); Gagliardi (2007, pp. 463–7) (ll. 75–7); Harrison (2007, pp. 59–74) (elegy and pastoral poetry); Marchetta (2007) (ll. 75–7); Cucchiarelli (2008) (ll. 75–7); Gagliardi (2011) (ll. 73–4); Keith (2011) (Lycoris/Volumnia/Cytheris); Gagliardi (2013) (relationship with *E.* 1); Höschele (2013, pp. 52–4) (ll. 2–3); Johnston, Papaioannou (2013) (Arcadia); Quartarone (2013) (ll. 75–6); Gagliardi (2014a) (ll. 53–4, 74); Gagliardi (2014c) (ll. 46–9); Gagliardi (2014d) (Bion, *epit. Adon.*; [Mosch.] *epit. Bion.*); Gagliardi (2014e) (Arcadia); Gagliardi (2015) (l. 18); Kraggerud (2017b, pp. 74–9) (l. 44); Marchetta (2018, pp. 475–91) (epilogue); Gagliardi (2017b) (l. 22).

1–8. As in every narrative eclogue, the poet utters the prologue in his own voice. This time, however, the prologue introduces the idea that this is the last poem in the book (10.1n.). According to the poet, the collection must include a composition devoted to Gallus and, to that end, he asks the nymph Arethusa for help. Arethusa is a key figure in the Syracusan (i.e. Theocritean) world of pastoral poetry. As for the poet, he is ready to follow the nymph and sing along with her. He depicts himself in his usual pastoral context: i.e. while his goats are grazing (10.7n.). Resonance, a crucial feature of V.'s pastoral soundscapes, is taken care of by the *siluae* (10.8n.). The prologue combines and recapitulates some fundamental notions of V.'s pastoral book and frames the poem alongside the epilogue (70–7). The correspondence between prologue and epilogue is both structural and numerical: they each count eight lines.

1 Extremum hunc…mihi concede laborem. An unmistakable reference to the editorial position of the poem, at the end of the book: thus, the tenth eclogue is the poet's 'last' labour, and the book itself here legitimates a sequential reading of the *E.* (entailing relative notions of 'before' and 'after'); the first word of *E.* 10, *Extremum*, matches the first word of *E.* 6, *Prima*, from which the second part of the book was opened (6.1n.); note the further emphasis provided by the line-enclosing hyperbaton *extremum…laborem* (cf. also 10.2–3n.: *pauca… / carmina*); in a context of end (of life as much as of song) cf. 8.60n.; also *G.* 2.417 *iam canit effectos extremus uinitor antes*. Historical chronology, on the other hand, cannot be deduced from this: we cannot know whether *E.* 10 was, in fact, the *last* eclogue composed by the poet. The term *labor* (which also denotes poetic work at *G.* 2.39

468   ECLOGUE 10

inceptum...laborem) harks back to Alexandrian aesthetics, based on painstaking polishing and literary 'toil' (πόνος): cf. Theocr. *id.* 7.51; Phil. fr. 10.3–4 Pow. = 12.3–4 Sbard. = 25.3–4 Spanoud. = 8.3–4 Light.; see also Catull. 1.7 and Hor. *sat.* 1.4.12. Contrast 10.64, describing Gallus' suffering: here, the noun also hints at actual 'fatigue' and, therefore, at the poet's inability to keep composing, which he declared in 8.63n. (note that, in *E.* 9, Moeris similarly experiences difficulties in continuing to sing: cf. 9.67 *carmina tum melius...canemus*); see also below, 10.2 *pauca.* The verb *concedere* appears in Corydon's invocation to the *Libethrides*, similar deities (cf. 7.22n.). **Arethusa.** The nymph was venerated at the Syracusan spring of the same name, to which the dying Daphnis bade farewell in the finale of *id.* 1.117. Legend has it that, as the nymph was bathing in the river Alpheus, the river-god vainly attempted to rape her. In order to escape from him, the nymph turned herself into a spring, and Alpheus pursued her even under the sea, until they both resurfaced on the small island of Ortygia, site of the oldest nucleus of Syracuse (*schol.* Theocr. *id.* 1.117, pp. 67–8 Wend.; Pind. *Nem.* 1.1–7, where the spring is summoned to inspire poetry; Mosch. fr. 3 G.; Strab. 6.2.4 [270–1]; Pausan. 5.7.2; 8.54.3; also *Anth. Pal.* 9.362; 683). The myth is echoed in *Aen.* 3.694–6, in which Arethusa receives the homage of Aeneas and his companions; cf. also *G.* 4.344; 351; Ov. *met.* 5.572–642; Sen. *dial.* 6[*Marc.*].17.3; Lucan. 3.176–7; Plin. *nat.* 31.55; Stat. *silu.* 1.2.203–8; 3.68–9. Considered as a distinctive symbol of Syracuse, the nymph's profile was commonly featured on Syracusan coins: see further *LIMC* II.1, pp. 582–4, s.v. *Arethousa* (H. A. Cahn). As an emblem of Theocritean pastoral poetry (cf. [Mosch.] *epit. Bion.* 10 νάμασι τοῖς Σικελοῖς...τᾶς Ἀρεθοίσας; 77–8; see below, 10.5n.), Arethusa draws the reader's attention to *id.* 1, which will be a major model for the poem as a whole. Her path from the Peloponnese (the river Alpheus flows through Arcadia and Elis) to Syracuse seems to personify a Sicilian-Arcadian connection which will soon become apparent (cf. 10.31; 33; 55; 57), and which is typical of V.'s *E.*: cf. 4.1 *Sicelides Musae*; 6.1 *Syracosio...uersu.* Arethusa's tale is a story of love and escape, full of analogies with the story of Gallus and Lycoris (note also that the mention of a water deity is quite appropriate for an 'inspired' poet like Gallus, who wandered around the Permessus in *E.* 6.64). The name *Arethusa* was, however, frequently used to designate springs: Homer, for instance, mentions one in Ithaca (Hom. *Od.* 13.408). A fragment of the Argive poet Telesilla asserts that Artemis was the one who escaped from the river-god Alpheus (*PMG* 717, p. 372 P.). Here Arethusa plays the role of an inspiring Muse, in keeping with the Theocritean equation Nymphs = Muses (Theocr. *id.* 7.92), which V. has implicitly espoused at *E.* 7.21n. The geographical reference to the Sicilian sea and Arethusa is quite significant in an eclogue full of geo-literary coordinates, within which the poets can freely move thanks to the liberty of their poetic imagination (not without interpretive complexities as a below, result: cf. below, 10.44n.).

2–3 pauca... / carmina. The poet's request is a minimal one (*pauca*). Once again, Alexandrian literary values such as brevity and refinement are in the background (cf. above, 10.1n.), and V.'s book as a whole should not reach excessive length, in line with Callimachus' well-known doctrine (Callim. *aet.* fr. 1.9–10 Pf. = Mass. = Hard.; cf. 465 Pf.). The nymph Arethusa is not fond of hesitation, perhaps due to her flight or to etymological suggestions (θοός 'swift', 'agile'; cf. also the nymph Θόωσα): she will be called *uelox* in *G.* 4.344. Note the hyperbaton, as in 10.1: here the distance between adjective and noun is even greater, since *carmina* appears at the beginning of the following line, with a further emphatic effect (cf. Lucr. 1.933–4 = 4.9–10 *lucida... / carmina*, where the distance is shorter; Catull. 64.382–3 *felicia... / carmina*). **meo Gallo.** Certainly dat. of advantage, with the usual affectionate use of the possessive adj.: Gallus is the dedicatee of the poet's last labour, inspired by the nymph (note *mihi*). However, V.'s turn of phrase points to an important role played by Gallus: soon, indeed, he will begin to speak. On the life and work of Cornelius Gallus see *E.* 6.64n. **quae legat ipsa Lycoris.** The phrase expresses a fundamental feature of elegiac poetry, i.e. the idea that the beloved girl is also the poet's intended reader (hence, the idea of poetry itself as a means of courting), as was presumably evident in Gallus' own love-elegies. The names of Gallus and Lycoris are closely tied to each other in the later poetic tradition: cf. notably Ov. *amor.* 1.15.30 *et sua cum Gallo nota Lycoris erit*; *ars* 3.537; Prop. 2.34.91–2. Here V. might allude to words or notions typical of Gallus' own work (e.g. the idea that poetry must be worthy of the beloved): cf. Gall. fr. 4.1–2 Bläns. = 2.6–7 Court. (a papyrus fragment which, in all likelihood, must be ascribed to Gallus' elegiac collection): *tandem fecerunt carmina Musae / quae possem domina deicere digna mea* (cf. Ov. *met.* 5.344–5 *utinam modo dicere possim / carmina digna dea!*). **Lycoris.** According to Servius (*ad* 10.1), the girl is to be identified with the mime actress Cytheris, later called Volumnia upon becoming a freedwoman of P. Volumnius Eutrapelus, a close friend of Mark Antony (the identification appears to be confirmed by the metrical equivalence of real name and poetic pseudonym *Lycoris/Cytheris*, a conventional feature of Roman love poetry). In 49 BCE, she became the mistress of Antony himself, who carried her on his open litter according to Cic. *Att.* 10.10.5; 16.5; *Phil.* 2.58. As late as 44 BCE, Cicero malignantly calls Antony *hic autem noster Cytherius*, i.e. devout to Venus in general and to Cytheris in particular (Cic. *Att.* 15.22); see further *Enc. Virg.* III, s.v. *Licoride* (M. Bonaria); *Virg. Enc.* II, p. 770, s.v. *Lycoris* (D. O. Ross). However, Gallus' rival (10.23) cannot be equated with Antony given the time that had passed. Cytheris plays a considerable role in the famous (and improbable) anecdote concerning the 'meeting' of V. and Cicero (Serv. *ad E.* 6.11: see pp. 288–9). In spite of the etymological echoes of *Lycoris* (which are far from reassuring: λύκος 'wolf'), it cannot be ruled out that the pseudonym chosen by Gallus for the girl has Apollonian implications, as will be the case with Propertius' *Cynthia* and Tibullus' *Delia*: Apollo was called *Lycius*, as in Callim. *aet.* fr. 1.22 Pf. = Mass. = Hard. (cf. Prop. 3.1.38), the interpretation of which was debated in antiquity (cf. G. Massimilla's commentary, Pisa 1996, p. 218, *ad loc.*),

470   ECLOGUE 10

and which V. himself will rework in *Aen.* 4.345–6 *sed nunc Italiam magnam Gryneus Apollo, / Italiam Lyciae iussere capessere sortes* (cf. also *Aen.* 4.377 with Serv. Dan. ad loc.; for the Apollonian epithet *Gryneus*, see 6.72n.). Moreover, *Lycoreia* (Λυκώρεια) was the name of a place on Mount Parnassus, which gave rise to several epithets of the god, such as *Lycoreus*: cf. Callim. *hymn.* 2[*Ap.*].19; Euphor. fr. 80.3 Pow. = 85.3 v. Gron. = 116.3 Light. (*Lykoreios* in Apoll. Rhod. 4.1490); see further *RE*, XIII.2, cols. 2382–5, s.vv. *Lykoreia* I (F. Bölte); *Lykoreus* (R. Ganszyiniec).

4–5. A likely reminiscence of Mosch. fr. 3.4–6 G. (Alpheus pursuing Arethusa): καὶ βαθὺς ἐμβαίνει τοῖς κύμασι τὰν δὲ θάλασσαν / νέρθεν ὑποτροχάει, κοὐ μίγνυται ὕδασιν ὕδωρ, / ἁ δ' οὐκ οἶδε θάλασσα διερχομένῳ ποταμοῖο 'he enters deep into the waves, flowing beneath / the sea, and his water is not mixed with waters, / and the sea knows nothing of the river that passes through it'. On Moschus in V., especially in relation to these lines, see *Enc. Virg.* III, pp. 606–7, s.v. *Mosco* (A. Perutelli).

4 sic tibi. The wish is conditional upon fulfilment of the request that follows: for a similar use of *sic* in the *E.*, see 9.30n.; cf. Hor. *carm.* 1.3.1–8 *sic te diua potens*, etc. with R. G. M. Nisbet and M. Hubbard's commentary, Oxford 1970, p. 45 ad 1.3.1. The future *subterlabere* is addressed to the nymph Arethusa, who still has not crossed the sea, at least in the poet's imagination: her action is, in fact, infinitely repeated. Note the unusual rhythm of the line, which begins with three short words (monosyllable-disyllable-monosyllable) followed by the pentasyllable *subterlabere* in the third, fourth, and fifth foot. For a similar structure, cf. *Aen.* 3.528 *di maris et terrae tempestatumque potentes* (in a rather similar context).

5 Doris amara suam non intermisceat undam. According to a mythical tradition, Doris was one of Oceanus' daughters, wife of Nereus and mother of the Nereids: cf. Hes. *theog.* 240–2; Apollod. 1.2.2 (8); Ov. *met.* 2.269 and 13.742. Here, similarly to *E.* 4.32 *Thetim* (n.), the name is used metonymically as synonymous with the Sicilian sea, taking up 10.4 *fluctus...Sicanos*, but imparting an ethnic and linguistic twist to it, since the Greek colonization of Sicily (including Syracuse itself) was largely due to Doric populations. The spring called Arethusa in Syracuse today is infiltrated by sea water, which makes it salty (contrast Sen. *dial.* 6[*Marc.*].17.3). At any rate, a Doric 'mixture' (*suam non intermisceat undam*) is perhaps inevitable for a nymph who oversees Theocritean pastoral poetry, or Δωρὶς ἀοιδά ('Doric poetry'), as it is defined in [Mosch.] *epit. Bion.* 12; cf. *also* 1 Δώριον ὕδωρ (the 'Doric water', a key element of pastoral poetry, appears in the very first line of the epitaph; note 18 Δώριος Ὀρφεύς). Theocritus had allowed himself some irony regarding his own Doric dialect, in a mime significantly set in the cosmopolitan city of Alexandria, *The Syracusan Women*: 'We speak the language of the Peloponnese: / Dorians, I believe, are allowed to speak Doric [Δωρίσδειν δ' ἔξεστι, δοκῶ, τοῖς Δωριέεσσι]' (*id.* 15.92–3: Praxinoa addresses a man who makes fun of the two women and their accent). Used in conjunction with *tellus*, the adj. *Doris* denotes Sicily in Sen. *Herc. f.* 81; it appears as a synonym of 'sea' in Ov. *fast.* 4.678; Stat. *Theb.* 9.370-1 *amaram Dorida*; see further *ThlL, onom.* III.241.48–55 (e.g. Suet. *Tib.* 56, where the adj. denotes the Dorian dialect; cf. also Diom. *gramm.* I, p. 440.5 K.). That 'bitterness' is a typical quality of sea water is confirmed by a folk etymology recorded in Isid. *orig.* 13.14.1 *proprie autem mare appellatum eo quod aquae eius amarae sint*: by contrast, the pastoral value that needs to be safeguarded here is Theocritus' 'sweetness', appearing at the outset of *id.* 1.1 (note also V.'s reference to the purity of water, a typically Callimachean image: Callim. *hymn.* 2[*Ap.*].111–12). Here, at any rate, the focus is on a graceful female figure, whose mention prompts the pastoral poet to consider the sea as an alien, negative element: for a similar dynamics, cf. *E.* 9.43 *insani feriant sine litora fluctus* (addressing Galatea). The issue of linguistic purity is later raised by Horace at the very end of his satiric *libellus* (note the use of *intermiscere*): *patriis intermiscere petita / uerba foris* (Hor. *sat.* 1.10.29–30).

6 incipe. The verb is typically used to exhort someone to sing: cf. *E.* 9.32n. It is common for poets to 'ask' the Muse for song: generally speaking, the poet of the *E.* often talks about collaboration with the Muses (4.1 *Sicelides Musae...canamus*; 6.13 *pergite Pierides*). And yet, starting in 8.63, he hints at his tiredness: now he asks Arethusa to grant him the *extremus labor* by beginning the new song herself. **sollicitos...amores.** Cf. *id.* 1.19 τὰ Δάφνιδος ἄλγεα, announcing the idyll's main theme. The plural can be used to refer to a single love story or a single beloved: cf. Catull. 45.1; Prop. 4.4.37. Note the insistence on the noun in 10.34 and 53–4 (53 *meos...amores* [n.]): it is possible that *Amores* was the title of Gallus' elegiac collection (which Ovid would then echo); see Serv. *ad* 10.1 *et amorum suorum de Cytheride scripsit libros quattuor* (for this kind of title, cf. Phanocles' Ἔρωτες ἢ Καλοί—where, however, the emphasis is on homosexual love). The adj. *sollicitus* belongs to erotic vocabulary (cf. Catull. 66.24; Pichon 1966, p. 265, s.v. *sollicitus*). Here, however, the whole phrase suggests a proverbial dictum: see, for instance, Publil. *sent.* A 34 *amor otiosae causa est sollicitudinis* and Cic. *Att.* 2.24.1 *non ignoro quam sit amor omnis sollicitus atque anxius*; cf. esp. Ov. *her.* 18.196 *solliciti...amoris* and *rem.* 557 *sollicitos...amores*; note also Hor. *sat.* 2.3.252–3 and Petron. 137.7. The line-ending *amores* is in assonance with *amara* (10.5): cf. *E.* 3.109–10.

7 dum tenera attondent simae uirgulta capellae. The poet immediately establishes his traditional role as pastoral singer, then reasserted in the epilogue (but cf. 10.16–17n.). Note also the temporal clause with *dum* (which sets the pastoral stage here and at 10.71), another marker of symmetry between prologue and epilogue. For analogous concerns see Meliboeus' words in the prologue to *E.* 7, esp. 9–17. The adj. *simae*, as in *id.* 8.50 σιμαί...ἔριφοι, may hint at the lascivious nature of the *capellae*. A snub nose was regarded as a marker of sexual exuberance in both animals (cf. Plin. *nat.* 8.202 on billy goats) and humans, as can be inferred from ancient physiognomical treatises (*Script. physiogn. Graec. et Lat.*, I, p. 228.19–20; II, p. 203.16–18 Foerst.). The detail is echoed in Ov. *ars* 2.486 *sustinet inmundum sima capella marem*; cf. Liv. Andr. *trag.* 5 R.[3] *lasciuum Nerei simum*

472 ECLOGUE 10

pecus (on the 'wanton' nature of dolphins see Gell. 6.8.1). The term is used of human figures in *id.* 3.8 and Nemes. *ecl.* 3.34 (Silenus). A malicious, albeit vague, hint at lasciviousness would be consistent with the typical characterizations of goats in pastoral poetry, besides softening the pathetic tone of the opening: cf. 2.64 *lasciua capella* (n.), as well as *E.* 3.8 (he-goats testifying to human eros). While the poet sings Gallus' erotic adventures, the goats keep grazing (cf. *E.* 5.12): they will eventually reach satiety in 10.77, which concludes the eclogue and the entire book. Note the reference to tender shoots (*siluestria... / uirgulta* in *G.* 2.2–3), which points to the meticulousness of V. as a 'herdsman': recall *id.* 11.73–4 καὶ θάλλον ἀμάσας / ταῖς ἄρνεσσι φέροις 'and you could pluck shoots / to feed the lambs'; cf. Nemes. *ecl.* 1.6–7 *incipe, dum salices haedi, dum gramina uaccae / detondent.* Right before a vindication of the dignity of *oues* (one ought not be 'ashamed' of them: 10.16–17), the poet zooms in on the snub-nosed goats: we get a close-up of the animals as they graze on tender grass (10.7–8).

8 non canimus surdis, respondent omnia siluae. This 'final proem' reasserts the woods' ability to 'resonate' (pathetic fallacy), with which the reader is familiar from *E.* 1.5 (n.), and which is now actualized by the phonetic insistence on /o/ in arsis (*nON...respONdent OMnia*). For the opposite idea, i.e. the portrayal of nature as deaf (here *surdis*) to human grief, cf. Callim. fr. inc. sed. 714.3–4 Pf. ἦ ὅτε κωφαῖς / ἄλγεα μαψαύραις ἔσχατον ἐξερύγῃ 'or finally when he laments / his sorrow to the deaf gusts of wind'; Catull. 64.164 *sed quid ego ignaris nequiquam conqueror auris*, etc.? (in *E.* 2, the *siluae* do not seem to be very sympathetic to Corydon: see 2.5n.); for a probable reminiscence, cf. Ov. *met.* 11.52–3 *flebile lingua / murmurat exanimis, respondent flebile ripae.* For a litotes with similar force, cf. 6.9 *non iniussa cano* (n.). The meaning is here expressed with even more colloquial liveliness, thanks to the proverbial phrase *surdo canere*: cf. Prop. 4.8.47 *cantabant surdo*; Ov. *amor.* 3.7.61; Liv. 40.8.10. For a similar Greek phrase see Aristaenet. *epist.* 1.28, p. 64.21 Maz. (note the widespread Latin variant *surdo narrare fabulam*: cf. Ter. *Heaut.* 222; Hor. *epist.* 2.1.199–200; Otto 1890, p. 335, no. 1715; Tosi 2007, p. 208, no. 448).

9–69. The central section of the eclogue (sixty-one lines) develops and concludes the narrative. It can be divided into two parts. The first (9–30) is rather lively and includes the first appearance of various characters who visit Gallus and ask him about the cause of his passion (21). Two of them, Apollo and Pan, utter separate speeches (22–3 and 28–30). The second part (31–69) includes Gallus' monologue, which is characterized by 'theatrical' gestures, second thoughts, and emotional turbulence.

9–30. In these twenty-two lines, V. introduces the situation, closely following Theocritus' *id.* 1. Unlike Daphnis, whose vicissitudes are located in Eastern Sicily (between Mount Etna and the rivers Anapo and Acis: Theocr. *id.* 1.68–9), Gallus is now in Arcadia, under a deserted cliff (10.14–15). V. is both condensing and rationalizing Theocritus' text (in *id.* 1.64–100, the introductory segment of

Thyrsis' song counted thirty-seven lines, or twenty-eight, if the nine refrain lines are excluded: contrast V.'s twenty-two lines). In Theocritus, after the address to the Nymphs (*id.* 1.66–9), several animals are depicted as mourning (wolves, lions, and domestic animals such as cows), then a god (Hermes) intervenes, followed by various herdsmen (cowherds, shepherds, and goatherds) and two more gods (Priapus and Aphrodite: *id.* 1.77–98). V. brings order into Theocritus' deliberately lively and casual arrangement by separating three well-defined categories: natural elements (10.13–18), human beings (herdsmen: 10.19–21), and deities (Apollo, Silvanus, Pan: 10.21–30). The first category is further subdivided into plants and rocks on the one hand (13–15) and animals on the other, with much less variety than in *id.* 1, since V. only mentions sheep (10.16–18). Throughout this section, Gallus clearly remains silent, like Daphnis, even though V. does not say this explicitly (see instead Theocr. *id.* 1.92). Gallus' eventual 'reply' is devoid of any dialogic elements, which stood out in the opening of Daphnis' speech (a huffish reply to Aphrodite): cf. below, 10.31–69n.

9–12. In Theocritus' first idyll, Thyrsis' song began in a similar way (following a brief self-introduction): 'Where were you when Daphnis was melting? O Nymphs, where were you? / Perhaps down through the beautiful valleys of Peneus, or those of Pindus? [ἢ κατὰ Πηνειῶ καλὰ τέμπεα, ἢ κατὰ Πίνδω;] / For certainly you did not inhabit the mighty stream of the river Anapus, / nor Aetna's rocky peak, nor the sacred water of Acis' (*id.* 1.66–9). The enumeration of a deity's potential places of abode is typical of religious invocations: the speaker thereby strives to direct the request correctly. Cf., for instance, Hom. *Il.* 16.514–15; Aesch. *Eum.* 292–8; see esp. Eur. *Bacch.* 553–64 (exhorting Dionysus to come).

10 Naides. Marine deities, akin to Arethusa (the Latin form is either *Nais* or *Naias*, as in Greek, depending on the metrical circumstances: cf. *E.* 2.46 and 6.21). Much like Theocritus' Nymphs, the Naides here are assimilated to the Muses and at the same time kept distinct from them, insofar as they are the Muses' pastoral counterpart: cf. 7.21 *Nymphae…Libethrides* (n.), as well as *id.* 7.92. Daphnis is said to have married a Nais in *id.* 8.93 (cf. *E.* 5.20n.). In *id.* 1, Thyrsis speculated that the Nymphs might be in some faraway place, rather than in their typical Sicilian dwelling. Now, by contrast, V. rules out that they might be on Mount Parnassus, or Mount Pindus, or at the spring Aganippe, at the base of Mount Helicon in Boeotia (that Gallus was welcome on Mount Helicon is asserted in *E.* 6: cf. below, 10.12n.). A friendly, familiar deity is expected never to desert his or her devotees: cf. Callim. *aet.* fr. 1.37–8 Pf. = Mass. = Hard. In 10.21, Apollo will actually rescue Gallus. Note the ending of *Naides*, featuring the usual short /e/ (as in Greek). **indigno…amore peribat.** Theocritus' euphemistic reference to Daphnis' 'wasting' (which points to actual death) is here replaced with metaphorical per- ishing, i.e. lovesickness: cf. Prop. 1.4.12 and 6.27; Ov. *rem.* 21. Deities, such as the Naides, tend to stay away from dying humans (Eur. *Hipp.* 1437–8; cf. also *Alc.* 22–6; Men. *Asp.* 97–8). Other gods, however, will soon arrive (10.21–30). For the

474 ECLOGUE 10

phrase *indigno...amore*, cf. *E.* 8.18n. Here, the main source of unhappiness is the object of love (Lycoris, who apparently does not 'deserve' it: *indigno...amore*), though its subject, Gallus himself, is partly responsible for his own fate, too (cf. Daphnis δύσερως in Theocr. *id.* 1.85: see 10.22n.). The agreement of most ancient manuscripts (M²PR) with some of the Carolingian ones makes the reading *peribat* preferable to *periret* (M¹): cf. Theocr. *id.* 1.66 ἐτάκετο. Following 10.9, R starts transmitting the text again (after a long gap beginning at *E.* 7.1). Here the elegiac Gallus appears as a desperate lover, whom nothing and no one can console, but he was a very capable man of action and it must not have been a coincidence that it was he, a skilled orator and love poet, who had the delicate task of dealing with Cleopatra, after Antony's death, keeping her from committing suicide and gaining time by talking at length with her (Plut. *Ant.* 79.1 ἐμήκυνε τὸν λόγον).

11 Parnasi...iuga. Theocritus' choice of the river Peneus contrasts with V.'s predilection for Mount Parnassus, the well-known Phocian mountain which hosted the sanctuary of Delphi, sacred to Apollo and the Muses, and previously referred to in *E.* 6.29 (note that *E.* 6, too, featured Gallus as a prominent character: cf. below, 10.12n.). Nevertheless, the names of both Peneus and Parnassus start with a /P/, thereby alliterating with *Pindi.* **Pindi.** A mountain range between Thessaly and Epirus, where the river Peneus originates: cf. Pind. *Pyth.* 9.15–17. In V.'s formulation, *iuga* (vel sim.) is understood: for a similar phenomenon see Theocr. *id.* 1.67 (τέμπεα; but cf. Ahrens' conjecture Πίνδον). Note the emphatic hyperbaton affecting negative conjunctions: *neque...iuga...neque... / ulla*; for a similar case, featuring even greater distance between *ulla* and the noun, cf. *E.* 6.11–12 (also emphatic).

12 moram fecere. Cf. *Aen.* 3.473 *fieret uento mora ne qua ferenti* (with the dat., as here: 10.11 *uobis*). The phrase is an idiom: Plaut. *Epid.* 691 *tibi moram facis*; *Most.* 75; see further *ThlL* VIII.1470.28–35. **Aonie Aganippe.** A spring at the foot of Mount Helicon, situated near the well-known grove of the Muses (Pausan. 9.29.5): not to be confused with the spring Hippocrene, which was apparently located at a much higher altitude, and played a fairly important role in Callimachus' dream at *aet.* fr. 2a.20–4 (*add.* p. 103) Pf. = fr. 3.6 Mass. = 2b, 1 Hard. (the two are conflated together in Ov. *fast.* 5.7 *Aganippidos Hippocrenes*); *Enc. Virg.* I, pp. 50–1, s.v. *Aganippe* (P. Fedeli); *Virg. Enc.* I, pp. 36–7, s.v. *Aganippe* (L. Fratantuono). Closely associated with the river Permessus (see also Claud. *carm. min.* 30.8 H.; Serv. Dan.; *schol. uet. ad* Iuv. 7.6, p. 120 Wessn.), the spring Aganippe hints at a poetic geography familiar to Gallus: cf. *E.* 6.64n.; *E.* 6 is also echoed by the epithet *Aonius.* Thus, such sacred places are now asked not to hinder valuable, potentially crucial divine intervention (such as that of the Muse in *E.* 6.65). Note the hiatus between the two Greek words, intensifying the Hellenizing effect of the phrase: the phenomenon was featured in Corydon's words *Actaeo Aracyntho* at *E.* 2.24 (similarly including a four-syllable word in line-ending position), and was almost certainly congenial to Cornelius Gallus' own taste. A hiatus between Latin words will closely follow (see below 10.13n.).

ECLOGUE 10   475

The adj. here appears in its most common form (*Aonius*; cf. *G.* 3.11; Prop. 1.2.28), but with a Greek ending (cf. the mention of Aganippe in Catull. 61.28–30, perhaps echoed by V.); contrast *E.* 6.65 *Aonas in montis* (n.). The incorrect reading *Aoniae* (MP) is readily prompted by *fecere*, but presupposes the irrational plural *Aganippae* (cf., however, Prob. *gramm.* IV.258.10 K. *Aoniae Aganippe*). Servius annotated (concerning both noun and epithet): *nominatiui sunt singulares.*

13–15. Cf. *id.* 1.71–2 'For him the jackals and the wolves wept, / even the lion mourned his death in the dense woods' (note V.'s close reworking of Theocritus: see above, 10.9–12n.). Sylvan beasts are now replaced by plants enlivened, as usual, by an Orphic and pastoral miracle. V. here seems to avoid any mention of weeping animals (cf. below, 10.16–18n.), echoing *id.* 7.73–5: 'how Daphnis the cowherd once fell in love with Senea, / and how the mountain grieved for him, and how the oaks / that grow on the banks of the river Himera sang his dirge'. Cf. Bion, *epit. Adon.* 18–19; 31–9; [Mosch.] *epit. Bion.* 1–7. At any rate, *id.* 1.71–2 is also reworked in *E.* 5.27 (the lions' tears: see n. ad loc.). Note that the threefold *etiam* at 10.13–14 mirrors the strong effect of repetition in Theocritus' *id.* 7.66–83 (where the hammering anaphora is further emphasized by the refrain: ἄρχετε...ἄρχετε). Similarly, repeated words are accumulated in the following lines: note esp. the structurally crucial repetition at 10.16 *stant et...*; 10.19 *uenit et* (n.)...; 10.24 *uenit et* (n.).

13 lauri. Bay, a symbol of poetic glory (and, at Rome, of military fame as well), here opens a series of grieving natural elements: quite appropriately so, given that Gallus (a poet) is the protagonist; note also the Apollonian and poetic geography just referred to (10.11–12). Moreover, the plant has a human past as Daphne, a girl vainly wooed by the god, not unlike Lycoris and Arethusa (cf. *E.* 3.62–3). Note the hiatus *lauri etiam*, paralleled in *E.* 3.63 *lauri et*, closely following the Greek hiatus at l. 12. **etiam fleuere myricae.** A 'humble' shrub, typical of V.'s pastoral world (see 4.2n.). The verb *fleuere* (cf. also 10.15) seems to activate the plant's possible Greek etymology (μύρομαι 'to drip', 'to weep'), which the ancients connected with a girl named *Myrice* (?), turned into tamarisks according to a myth only attested in Hesychius: εἶδος δένδρου, ὀνομασθὲν ἀπὸ τοῦ μύρεσθαι τὴν εἰς αὐτὸ μεταβαλοῦσαν κατὰ τοὺς μύθους (s.v. μυρίκη). **etiam.** Note R's incorrect reading *illum*: the repeated word must be *etiam*, which thus creates a threefold anaphora. Contrast the Theocritean model, which perhaps gave origin to the textual corruption: *id.* 1.71–2 (τῆνον...τῆνον.../...τῆνον). Perhaps ancient scribes, too, worried about the hiatus between *lauri* and *etiam*.

14–15. Following the mention of Mediterranean plants such as bay and tamarisks, the landscape becomes freezing and mountainous (note *gelidi...Lycaei* in 10.15). Along with Maenalus, Mount Lycaeus appeared in *id.* 1 as Pan's typical dwelling, which the god was exhorted to abandon in order to rescue Daphnis. Theocritus' invocation to the Arcadian god (*id.* 1.123–6) is amplified by V., whose *E.* 10 is set in Arcadia: Pan himself will soon make an appearance (10.26–30). Perhaps playing on homonymy, Propertius 1.20 addresses a friend named Gallus (presumably not the protagonist of *E.* 10) and exhorts him to look after the poet's beloved boy, so that the poet himself will not have to wander around deserted places, as Hercules did when Hylas was abducted by the Nymphs (cf. esp. Prop. 1.20.13 *duros montes et frigida saxa*).

14–15 pinifer... / Maenalus. The conspicuous hyperbaton affects noun and epithet (both symmetrically placed in line-initial position), thereby greatly emphasizing the adj., while the noun almost appears as the solution to a riddle (though not an obscure one, if the reader recalls *E.* 8.22–3; cf. also *Aen.* 4.248–9 *Atlantis... / piniferum caput*; 10.708 *Vesulus...pinifer*). As the phrase *sola sub rupe* confirms (cf. below, 10.14n.), the landscape continues to be a wild, mountainous one: no wonder that the pine-tree grove on Mount Ida, mentioned at *Aen.* 9.85, is sacred to Cybele (mountains are particularly dear to her: cf. *Hymn. Hom.* 14[*Cybel.*].5; Eur. *Hipp.* 144; *schol.* Pind. *Pyth.* 3.139b, II, p. 81 Drach.). Like bay, pine trees have a human past, featuring a girl vainly wooed by a god (in this case, Pan himself: see *E.* 7.24n.). It is clear from *E.* 8.22–3 (*pinusque loquentis / semper habet, semper pastorum ille audit amores*) that pine trees can speak, and that Mount Maenalus is wont to listen to herdsmen's love stories. In the case of Ovid's Orpheus, the poet's reference to the human past of a tree is explicit (Cyparissus = cypress): Ov. *met.* 10.106–42.

14 sola sub rupe iacentem. Cf. Catull. 64.154 *quaenam te genuit sola sub rupe leaena*, etc.; for the cliff cf. *E.* 1.76 (the landscape, however, is even more rugged here), as well as *G.* 4.508–9 (as a backdrop to Orpheus' sorrows). The adj. emphasizes Gallus' solitude in all senses, including the erotic one: the poet has been abandoned by Lycoris, as the reader will soon discover in Apollo's words (10.22–3); cf. also 2.4 *solus* (n.). The verb here has a dark, ominous connotation, quite unlike the case of 10.40 (or that of *E.* 1.1: Tityrus' *recubans*): cf. Bion, *epit. Adon.* 7 κεῖται... ἐν ὤρεσι. The idea of 'lying down' in sad solitude (esp. on a bed) recurs often in Roman elegy: cf. Prop. 2.21.6 *tu, nimium credula, sola iaces*.

15 gelidi...saxa Lycaei. Mount Lykaion is situated in Arcadia, west of the Megalopolis plain, near the river Alpheus. Besides its connection with an age-old cult of Zeus (Pind. *Ol.* 9.96), Lykaion is known for witnessing Pan's birth, according to Pind. fr. 100 Maeh.; cf. *id.* 1.123, as well as *G.* 1.16; see also *G.* 3.1–2 and 314; *Enc. Virg.* III, pp. 210–11, s.v. *Liceo* (A. Casanova). For the wolves associated with the mountain (apparently in Varro), cf. Maltby (1991, pp. 353–4, s.v. *Lycaeus*). The mountain is here called 'freezing' and, in 10.22–3, Lycoris will wander in its snowy, inhospitable landscape (note the etymological connection *Lycaeus / Lycoris*). **fleuerunt.** Variation on the theme of 10.13 *fleuere*. These tears appear somewhat paradoxical, being produced by an icy mountain (unless V. alludes to melting snow). For the verb in the sense of 'dripping' cf. Lucr. 1.348–9 *in saxis ac speluncis permanat aquarum / liquidus umor et uberibus flent omnia guttis*; cf. also *G.* 4.461; Ov. *met.* 11.46 (Orpheus in both cases).

16–18. Another close reworking of Theocritus: 'At his feet, many cows, many bulls, / many heifers and calves were mourning' (*id.* 1.74–5). Here, however, other

ECLOGUE 10   477

animals are summoned to represent typically pastoral fauna: V.'s sheep replace Theocritus' cattle (Daphnis, after all, was a cowherd); cf. below, 10.16n. Moreover, there is no trace of the lament and weeping that Theocritus attributed to wild animals as well (*id.* 1.71-2; cf. also Eryphanis' song in Athen. 14.619d ἀλλὰ καὶ τῶν θηρῶν τοὺς ἀνημερωτάτους συνδακρῦσαι τῷ πάθει; *PMG* 850, p. 452 P.). Achilles' horses were renowned for their lament—a Homeric invention, notoriously difficult to imitate (Hom. *Il.* 17.427; cf. *Il.* 23.279-84).

16 stant et oues circum. Gallus' sheep, in a steadfast posture (*stant*), surround him as a sign of respect for his grief: the lament of Theocritus' animals is here replaced by a more sober, but no less empathetic attitude.

16-17 nostri nec paenitet illas, / nec te paeniteat pecoris. The repeated verb, with polyptoton, emphasizes a hierarchy of values which is typically pastoral: Gallus should not be ashamed of the flock, just as the flock is not ashamed of V.; cf. 2.34 *nec te paeniteat calamo triuisse labello* (both passages highlighting 'regret' for an action or situation currently happening or already happened). While V. modestly admits to the humble nature of the pastoral genre (it is the sheep who should not feel 'ashamed'), he simultaneously appears quite self-confident as he approaches the end of his work, and explicitly exhorts his friend to adjust his expectations (contrast *E.* 4.2-3). Note also that, somewhat ironically, V. replaces Daphnis' cattle with (less valuable) sheep: the pastoral hierarchy, opposing cowherds to goatherds, was asserted in *id.* 1.86 (note also *id.* 1.80: cf. below, 10.19-21n.); see *E.* 1.6n.; Introduction, p. 9 and n. 19. While Gallus is associated with *oues*, V. assigns the even humbler *capellae* to himself (10.7 and 10.77).

17 diuine poeta. For the clausula, and especially the adjective, cf. *E.* 5.45n. (referring to Mopsus, who has just sung his lament for the death of Daphnis). The epithet alone appears in 6.67 *diuino carmine pastor* (i.e. Linus, leading Gallus to receive a solemn poetic investiture).

18 formosus…Adonis. The youth whom Aphrodite loved: the 'beautiful' boy *par excellence*, whose premature death filled the goddess with sorrow (he was killed by a boar that a jealous Ares sent against him). Adonis appeared in *id.* 1, as part of a series of unhappy love stories for which Daphnis reproached Aphrodite (cf. *id.* 1.109-10 ὡραῖος χὠδωνις, etc.), whereas in *id.* 3 the tale was used as an example in defence of pastoral life (cf. *id.* 3.46-8 'and did not Adonis, as he grazed his sheep on the mountains, / drive the fair Cytherea to such frenzy that / even in death she did not pull him away from her breast?'; see also *id.* 20.35-6). For a similar argument concerning Proteus, cf. *id.* 8.51-2. Theocritus also mentions Adonis (and his death) in *id.* 15.102-5; cf. Bion, *epit. Adon.*, which significantly reworks *id.* 1 (e.g. in the introductory refrain: καλὸς Ἄδωνις at *epit. Adon.* 1; 2; 5). In order to praise his *siluae*, Corydon similarly used a mythical example (the tale of Paris), refined and more convincing in the eyes of the *formosus* Alexis (*E.* 2.60-1). For the epithet in relation to a proper noun with initial *A-*, cf. 4.57 *formosus Apollo*; see also *E.* 2.1; 5.87; 7.55, as well as *E.* 1.5 *formosam…Amaryllida.*

478   ECLOGUE 10

On Adonis, a divine figure of Eastern origin, connected with the cult of Aphrodite-Astarte, see further *LIMC* I.1, pp. 222–9, s.v. *Adonis* (B. Servais-Soyez), and esp. p. 226 for depictions of Adonis as a hunter.

19–30. As in *id.* 1, a description of the animals' empathy is followed by the arrival of various human and divine figures. Here, however, there is a clear distinction between (human) herdsmen and gods, whereas Hermes was the 'very first' to arrive in Theocr. *id.* 1.77.

19–21. Cf. *id.* 1.80–1 'then the cowherds came along, and the shepherds, and the goatherds, / and all kept asking what he was suffering from' (in V., too, human rescuers ask a brief question: a direct one, however, unlike that of *id.* 1.81). Theocritus' pastoral hierarchy (cowherds, then shepherds, then goatherds) is now reworked in terms of even greater humility: V.'s *upilio* is followed by swineherds, who never appear elsewhere (either in the *E.* or in Theocritus: see below, 10.19n.).

19 upilio. The term, also transmitted in the alternative form *opilio* (P²; *upilio* MR; Serv.), is found only here in classical Latin poetry and belongs to the vocabulary of rural folk: it must have originally meant 'shepherd', given the likely etymological connection to *ouis*, but it could also be used of goatherds (cf. Apul. *met.* 8.19.1 *senex...quem circum capellae pascentes opilionem esse profecto clamabant*). Note the term's assonance with a Greek equivalent such as ὠπόλος (= ὁ αἰπόλος, cf. *id.* 1.80 ὠπόλοι [see above, 10.19–21n.]); as Servius' annotation suggests, the first syllable of *opilio* (lengthened here) was short by nature: see *ThlL* IX.2.707.25–33. After a defence of the humble sheep (10.16–17), the poet now uses a humble term to refer to the shepherd. Note that *uenit et* echoes 10.16 *stant et* and resumes the description after the quasi-parenthetical observations at 10.16–18; cf. also 10.24 *uenit et* (n.). **tardi...subulci.** Pig farming was an important component of Italic life in the countryside (cf. *G.* 2.72; 520), though no other trace of *sues* or *subulci* appears in V.'s bucolic world (the same is true of Theocritus); cf., however, Plat. *Theaet.* 174d ἕνα τῶν νομέων, οἷον συβώτην ἢ ποιμένα ἤ τινα βουκόλον. Thus, there is no compelling reason to accept the easy conjecture *bubulci* (despite its attractions: see e.g. La Cerda ad loc.), even though the epithet *tardus* is commonly applied to oxen (Tib. 1.1.30 *tardos...boues*; Prop. 2.33.24; 3.5.35). In fact, ploughing, a typical task of *bubulci* (Colum. 2.2.25; 6.2.8), was a slow, exhausting process: cf. *G.* 1.163 *tarda...plaustra*; 2.206 *plura domum tardis decedere plaustra iuuencis* (the same is true of the ploughman's celestial counterpart, i.e. Bootes: Catull. 66.67; Ov. *met.* 2.176–7; cf. also *fast.* 3.405). The reading *subulci* is known to the entire manuscript tradition, as well as to the grammarians (cf. Ter. Maur. 1191; Serv. *gramm.* IV, p. 459.18 K.), whereas *bubulci* is not supported by Apul. *flor.* 3.3 *Vergilianus upilio seu busequa*, whose context does not concern *E.* 10. By contrast, the sudden appearance of swineherds is quite appropriate in the context of a rustic term (*upilio*) and befits V.'s humble tone more generally: the poet's intention is perhaps to 'salvage' these forgotten pastoral figures, neglected by Theocritus (hence *tardi*, as though they had been 'left behind'?). In the *Aeneid*, pigs will be mentioned in passages whose Homeric counterpart features no trace of them: e.g. the sacrifice at *Aen.* 11.197–9 (but cf. Enn. *ann.* 96 Sk.). Homer's *Odyssey*, in keeping with its colour, humbler, and more realistic in comparison to the *Iliad*, gives a prominent role to a swineherd (Eumaeus, called ὑφορβός or συβώτης), whose portrayal was particularly appreciated in antiquity due to the poet's masterful rendering of such a humble character within an epic narrative: cf. Dion. Hal. *comp.* 3.7–12 Aujac-Lebel (the term συφορβός, for which cf. *Od.* 14.504, is probably mentioned at in Philod. *poemat.* 1 fr. 159). Acorns, i.e. the most common food of pigs (G. 2.520 *glande sues laeti redeunt*), are about to be mentioned (at 10.20).

20 uuidus hiberna...de glande Menalcas. Note the line-framing word-order. Menalcas is 'wet', presumably because he has been gathering acorns. The scene is set in winter, as is clear from the epithet *hiberna* (cf. 10.23): thus, Menalcas' acorns must be wet due to rain, snow, or dew (cf. G. 1.305). While acorns are part of the typical food of primitive humankind (G. 1.148), V. must here refer to animal fodder, particularly useful during the winter months: acorns can obviously be given to pigs (as in G. 2.72 and 2.520), but also to oxen, as in Cat. *agr.* 54 (who recommends storing them in water). Along with oak trees, Menalcas appeared in the pastoral song of the legendary poet Eriphanis, who had fallen in love with Menalcas himself (*PMG* 850, p. 452 P.; cf. Athen. 14.619d): μακραὶ δρύες, ὦ Μέναλκα. According to an ancient tradition, which V. perhaps alludes to in *E.* 5.52, Menalcas was Daphnis' lover (and, correspondingly, an ideal figure for *E.* 10). **uuidus.** This is P's reading (*huuidus*), whereas *umidus* (**R**) is a trivialization. For a similar case cf. G. 1.418 *Iuppiter uuidus Austris* (**M**; *umidus* in the rest of the manuscript transmission). The adj. *uuidus* means 'soaked', almost in a passive sense (*madidus*), which is appropriate for a human being (cf. Hor. *carm.* 2.19.18; 4.5.39), whereas the meaning of *umidus* is 'moist', 'liquid', often in an active sense (i.e. soaking other things): cf. G. 1.462 *quid cogitet umidus Auster*. **uenit... Menalcas.** A character named Menalcas now appears, following an eclogue centred around his absence and his imminent arrival (cf. *E.* 9.67 *cum uenerit ipse, canemus*); on this character cf. esp. 3.13n.; 9.10n.

21 'unde amor iste' rogant 'tibi'? Besides *id.* 1.81 [cf. above, 10.19–21n.], cf. also *id.* 1.77–8 'Daphnis, / who is destroying you? For whom do you burn with love?' (Hermes' affectionate question: see below, 10.22n.). Gallus does not reply to this or any of the following questions, though this is never explicitly stated by V. (contrast Theocritus' Daphnis at *id.* 1.92: τὼς δ' οὐδὲν ποτελέξαθ' ὁ βουκόλος). Gallus will eventually burst into an emotional fit at 10.31, without his words having any actual relation to his visitors' questions (10.31–69n.).

21–30. In *id.* 1, Daphnis was visited by several gods (in order of appearance): Hermes, Priapus, and Aphrodite (*id.* 1.77–99), while herdsmen were mentioned at *id.* 1.80–1 (cf. above, 10.19–21n.). Here, by contrast, three human figures, whose arrival is marked by the verb *uenio* (19–20), are followed by three deities: Apollo, Silvanus, and Pan, also featuring forms of *uenio* (21; 24; 26). In [Mosch.]

480 ECLOGUE 10

epit. Bion. 26–31, the deceased Bion is mourned by Apollo and numerous other forest deities. As Servius observed (*ad* 10.26), all three gods have experience as unrequited or tragically unhappy lovers (cf. below, 10.21n.; 24n.; 26n.), and can therefore sympathize with Gallus. Furthermore, the arrival of Pan and Apollo is anticipated by the mention of bay (= Daphne: 10.13n.) and the Maenalian pine trees (10.14–15n.). In Theocritus, by contrast, Daphnis was the one who reminded Aphrodite of her past love affairs: *id.* 1.105–10.

21 uenit Apollo. Cf. *id.* 1.81 ἦνθ' ὁ Πρίηπος (at line-end, as here). The god of poetry, also known for his pastoral past, had abandoned the countryside upon Daphnis' death (*E.* 5.35n.), and now comes back to offer solace to Gallus, who ought to be dear to him (cf. *E.* 6.73). Apollo is also a god of deliverance (ἀλεξίκακος; cf. Hor. *sat.* 1.9.78; see Hom. *Il.* 20.443, as well as 16.523–9; cf. *E.* 6.3–4n.), often providing warnings and instructions to the poet, as in the prologue to *E.* 6. Yet Gallus will not disavow his commitment to love poetry. On the god's unhappy love stories (Daphne and Hyacinthus) cf. above, 10.13n. and 3.63n.

22 Galle, quid insanis? The question asked by Theocritus' Hermes, who seemed not to know who the object of Daphnis' love was (*id.* 1.77–8), is now replaced by the omniscient Apollo's exhortation (cf. Serv.: *cum alii interrogent…Apollo diuinat*), which echoes Priapus' words (minus his somewhat coarse tone) in *id.* 1.81–5: 'Priapus arrived / and said: "wretched Daphnis, why do you waste away? The girl / wanders on foot around every spring and every grove /…/ looking for you: ah, you are so clueless in love matters, you do not know what to do! [δύσερως…ἄγαν καὶ ἀμήχανος]"' (in V., by contrast, Lycoris is on the run with another lover). Erotic 'insanity' is a typical feature of elegiac love and poets: cf. Prop. 2.14.18; 34.25; 3.17.3; Tib. 2.6.18; Ov. *ars* 1.372; 2.563; *her.* 12.193 (195); but note, for instance, Eur. *Iph. Aul.* 1264–5 μέμηνε…Ἀφροδίτη; cf. below, 10.44n., as well as 38 and 60. The equation between *amor* and *furor* is a typically Virgilian notion: see e.g. *Aen.* 4.101. Note the colloquial use of *quid* = *cur* in a direct question: cf. Ter. *Eun.* 304 *quid tu's tristis?*; see further H.-Sz., p. 458. **tua cura Lycoris.** The appositional use of *cura* could go back to Cornelius Gallus himself; but cf. *E.* 1.57 *raucae, tua cura, palumbes*, as well as *G.* 4.345 and *Aen.* 1.678. As with *insanire*, the term is common in elegiac poetry, perhaps due in part to Gallus' influence: cf. Prop. 1.1.36; 8.1; 2.34.9; Tib. 2.3.31; Ov. *amor.* 1.3.16; *her.* 16.96; Stat. *silu.* 4.4.20–1 *tua cura potissima, Gallus, / nec non noster amor* (a Gallus from the Flavian age, with probable allusion to V.'s Gallus); see further *ThlL* IV.1475.42–60. The same is true of *furor* (10.38n.). Note the phonetic wordplay <u>cura</u> Ly<u>coris</u>, perhaps echoing the Theocritean model: ἁ δέ τυ κώρα (*id.* 1.82): hence the interlinguistic allusion *cura*/κούρη = κώρα/Lycoris. On the notion of *cura*, which can have legal connotations, see *E.* 1.32n. If Arethusa is the speaker, or at least the inspirer of the poet's song (6 *incipe*), she will remember some of the wording used here in her address to Cyrene at *G.* 4.354–5: *ipse tibi, tua maxima cura, / tristis Aristaeus Penei genitoris ad undam*, etc.

ECLOGUE 10 481

23 perque niues alium perque horrida castra secuta est. Both landscape and scene are in clear contrast with *id*. 1.82–4: the girl follows another man amidst military encampments located in snowy regions (note *horrida castra*: the camp is 'bristling', i.e. full of weapons and pointed stakes). Leaving for a military campaign was an obvious reason to give up a love relationship: see e.g. Tib. 2.6.9 *castra peto, ualeatque Venus ualeantque puellae*; note also Propertius' reworking of *E*. 10 (and Gallus?) in Prop. 4.3.43–8, where the *puella*'s name is, significantly, Arethusa (cf. esp. Prop. 4.3.45 *Romanis utinam patuissent castra puellis*). It could, however, happen that the *puella* would follow her lover to faraway, inhospitable lands, as seems to be the case with Cynthia in Prop. 1.8, evidently emulating *E*. 10 (note the allusion to V.'s name in Prop. 1.8.10: *et sit iners tardis nauita Vergiliis*); see Moore (2010); as a matter of fact, mistresses and courtesans used to follow soldiers at war (e.g. Plut. *Ant*. 67.6 αἱ συνήθεις γυναῖκες). The familiar opposition between a soldier's life and a lover's, despite the obvious analogies (both are a form of *seruitium*), led Roman elegiac poets to develop a rhetoric of *militia amoris*, explicitly theorized by Ovid, esp. in *amor*. 1.9.1 *militat omnis amans et habet sua castra Cupido*; cf. Prop. 2.7.15–16. In *E*. 10.44, Gallus will reveal that he, too, is held back by an 'insane' love for Mars' weapons (see n. ad loc.). In erotic and elegiac vocabulary, *alius* commonly denotes the 'other' man, i.e. the poet's rival (but the fem. form is also used: cf. Prop. 1.12.19; 2.14.21); for *sequor* in this context cf. *E*. 6.55 *aliquam...sequitur*. All considered, it is quite unlikely that Gallus' rival is Mark Antony (*pace* Servius), since Lycoris' association with him, attested as early as 49 BCE, predates *E*. 10 by many years (see above, 10.2n.): Lycoris' new lover might be a subordinate of Agrippa, who led a military expedition in Transalpine Gaul and crossed the Rhine in 38 BCE; see *RE*, 9.A.1, col. 1234, s.v. *M. Vipsanius Agrippa* (R. Hanslik). Note that, in the *E*., this is the only instance of *-que...-que* not occurring in the fifth foot (see 8.22n.); cf. also below, 10.65–6 (a slightly different case).

24 agresti capitis Siluanus honore. Silvanus, Italic god of *siluae*, archaic protector of herds and rural activities in general, will reappear in *G*. 1.20, holding a cypress-sapling in his hand to honour the memory of his beloved Cyparissus (cf. Ov. *met*. 10.106–42): like his kindred deity Pan, soon mentioned in 10.26n., Silvanus highlights the transition between the finale of V.'s *E*. and the beginning of his next poem, the *G*. (he only reappears at *G*. 2.494 and *Aen*. 8.600). For further reading see *Enc. Virg*. IV, pp. 853–4, s.v. *Silvano* (F. Trisoglio), as well as Dorcey (1992); on the iconography of the god, similar to that of other rustic deities, see *LIMC* 7.1, pp. 763–73, s.v. *Silvanus* (A. M. Nagy). Silvanus was also deemed to be a protector of boundaries, or *tutor finium* (Hor. *epod*. 2.22); cf. *Grom*. p. 302.13 Lach. [*Siluanus*] *primus in terram lapidem finalem posuit*. Here, to be sure, Lycoris can be viewed as 'trespassing' across (Rome's) boundaries. All of the figures mentioned in this passage seem to say something (21–2 *omnes... rogant...Apollo...inquit*), with the sole exception of Silvanus, the archaic god of Roman religion, who remains silent: Pan (his Greek, pastoral counterpart) will be

482   ECLOGUE 10

much more loquacious. For *honos* used of sylvan beauty cf. *G.* 2.404 *siluis Aquilo decussit honorem*; Hor. *epod.* 11.6. Note, at the outset of 10.24, the second-to-last occurrence of a postponed conjunction, which separates the various stages of the action (10.16 *stant et*; 10.19 *uenit et*; 10.24 *uenit et*) based on a repetition pattern also used by Theocritus. The last occurrence of this formula will finally introduce Gallus' speech at 10.31 (*tristis at*), featuring an adversative conjunction.

25 florentis ferulas et grandia lilia quassans. The plant known as giant fennel (*Ferula communis*) produces rather large flowers, featuring umbrella-shaped clusters and long stalks, which Silvanus presumably holds in his hand, shaking them as he walks. It is less plausible, though often asserted, that he carries the plants on his head, wearing them in a garland woven together with lilies: the god, in fact, is usually depicted as wearing a simple crown made of pine-tree leaves, while his hands are full of branches, flowers, and fruit (see *LIMC* [quoted above, 10.24n.], esp. pp. 763–6; cf. *G.* 1.20). Note also that *Ferula communis* is far from well suited for garlands, especially since the poet here refers to the plant as a whole, including the stalk (*florentis* would otherwise be superfluous: cf. *E.* 9.19 *florentibus herbis*; 1.78; *G.* 3.126; the lilies, too, are described as large: *grandia*); cf. *Aen.* 5.854–5 *ramum...quassat*, as well as *Aen.* 9.521–2. For a comparable yet distinct passage, cf. Lucr. 4.586–7 *cum Pan / pinea semiferi capitis uelamina quassans* (note *capiti*, an explicit specification). Pan, whom V. will soon mention in 10.26, is quite similar to Silvanus: both are characterized by a strong dynamism, typical of sylvan deities.

26 Pan deus Arcadiae. Following the Italic interlude centred around Silvanus, it is now the turn of Pan, 'god of Arcadia': for the same line-initial phrase, see *G.* 3.392 (incipit in Pindar's 'hymn to Pan': Ὦ Πάν, Ἀρκαδίας μεδέων [fr. 95.1 Sn.-M.]); cf. also *E.* 4.58–9. Thus, Apollo and Pan join forces to provide solace for Gallus, just as bay and Maenalian pines (along with V.'s *myricae*) sympathized with him at 10.13–15 (see 10.13n.; 14–15n.). For Pan's unhappy love for Pitys, cf. 7.42n. In Theocritus, Pan did not appear in person, but was invoked by Daphnis, who begged him to leave Arcadia (Theocr. *id.* 1.123–6). Here, by contrast, Gallus is in Arcadia, and yet V. feels the need to emphasize the presence of the pastoral deity par excellence (note the autoptic formula below). **quem uidimus ipsi.** A marker of autopsy (cf. *E.* 8.99, as well as 10.42), which the poet uses to establish his presence on the scene. V. himself, who plays the role of an industrious poet-herdsman in both the prologue and the epilogue, now asserts that he was present at the scene in Arcadia and saw the god with his own eyes. This is a clear indication that the whole eclogue is governed by the absolute freedom of poetic imagination: no wonder, in this regard, that Gallus suddenly reveals that he is 'held back' by military obligations (10.44n.). The appearance of Pan could elicit terror or, well, 'panic', as in [Eur.]? *Rhes.* 36–7, and that of Apollo was no less challenging: cf. Callim. *hymn.* 2[*Ap.*].9–11 (in *E.* 6.20, too, Chromis and Mnasyllus are *timidi* in front of Silenus as soon as they seize him). Note esp. the Dionysian scene described by Horace at *carm.* 2.19.1–4, esp. 1–2 *Bacchum in remotis carmina rupibus / uidi docentem, credite posteri.* Such 'visions', or, at any rate, imaginative illusions, are deemed to be typical of literature (esp. of poetry) and are shared by V. and Gallus (cf. below, 10.58n.; see also Hor. *carm.* 2.1.21 *audire magnos iam uideor duces*). In Theocr. *id.* 1, despite Daphnis' invocation, Pan did not make an appearance (cf. *id.* 1.123–30): Daphnis' wish is now fulfilled—yet, as we shall see, in vain. This explains the emphasis placed on Pan by the autoptic formula, which solely refers to the goat-footed divine ruler of Arcadia: V. surpasses Theocritus by placing Pan himself on the stage. At any rate, the countryside dwellers that inhabit the pastoral world (including, of course, the poet) 'know' the rural gods quite well: especially Pan and Silvanus, as V. says in *G.* 2.493–4 *fortunatus et ille deos qui nouit agrestis, / Panaque Siluanumque senem Nymphasque sorores.*

27 sanguineis ebuli bacis minioque rubentem. The red colour is typically associated with gods and divine status. This line insists on it by mentioning both *ebulum* ('danewort'), a herbaceous plant similar to elderberry (cf. Colum. 10.10 *rutilas…ebuli bacas; Enc. Virg.* II, p. 157, s.v. *ebbio* [G. Maggiulli]), and *minium* ('minium' or 'cinnabar'), a mineral pigment used in Rome to paint statues of gods (esp. of Jupiter) and the bodies of military generals during triumphs (cf. Plin. *nat.* 33.111–22, esp. 111–12). Compare the rustic follower of Bacchus in Tib. 2.1.55 *minio suffusus…rubenti*; red is also the colour of the rural god Priapus: Tib. 1.1.17–18; Ov. *fast.* 1.415; 6.333. Here, the chromatic detail and the poet's *uidimus ipsi* attenuate Pan's divine force, making his figure more approachable to humans: cf. *E.* 6.22 *sanguineis frontem moris*, etc. (n. ad loc.; note, as here, the line-beginning *sanguineis*). Like the mulberries at 6.22, these *ebulum* berries can be used as a humble, rustic type of dying agent, whereas the *minium* is considered to be more noble and qualified (and therefore appropriate for the appearance of a god crucial to pastoral poetry).

28–30. In his speech, Pan highlights *Amor*'s cruelty, which played a crucial role in *id.* 1, esp. in the dialogue between Daphnis and Aphrodite: 'did you not swear, Daphnis, that you would bind Love, / and have you not been bound by fierce Love yourself?' (*id.* 1.97–8; cf. also 92–3 'he saw / his bitter love [πικρὸν ἔρωτα] through to the end'). The god is qualified to speak on the topic, due to both his personal experience and his Arcadian dwelling (cf. *E.* 8.22–4). Note, finally, that Love's cruelty was featured in Damon's 'Maenalian song' (*E.* 8.47–50).

28 ecquis erit modus? A precise echo of *E.* 2.68 *quis enim modus adsit amori?* (n.); but cf. also Plaut. *Merc.* 652 *quis modus tibi exilio tandem eueniet?* (where exile is a direct consequence of love: see 10.31–69n.). Love's insatiable nature ought to lead lovers to seek moderation. However, this quotation of Corydon's eclogue (an intratextual model for *E.* 10) has a contrastive effect, since Gallus will prove to be an inconsolable lover (10.60–9n.). Note also *Aen.* 4.98 *sed quis erit modus…?* (Juno; the context does not concern love).

29–30. The three images that Pan associates with Love 'never satiated with tears' all belong to the rural world, thereby confirming the god's Arcadian and

484 ECLOGUE 10

pastoral identity. In the last eclogue, V. employs a characterization technique typical of the book as a whole: cf. *E.* 1.19–25 (although Theocritus' Priapus is a much
more conspicuous case: *id.* 1.86–8). The result is a fourfold structure, conveying a
sense of completeness (cf. 1.59–63n.): for similar quadripartite structures in this
eclogue, see below, 10.42–3; 65–8.

29 nec gramina riuis. Even though grass is never satiated with water, the
reader recalls Palaemon's words: *claudite iam riuos, pueri, sat prata biberunt* (*E.*
3.111). Pastoral wisdom knows the need for moderation; cf. below, 10.30n.

30 nec cytiso saturantur apes. For cytisus (a fodder-plant) as dear to bees,
cf. Plin. *nat.* 13.131 (as well as [Democr.] 68.300.8, p. 215.6 D.-K.); Colum. 5.12.1;
see also *E.* 1.78n.; 2.64; 9.31. Note that Pan could be regarded as the protector of
beekeeping, as is known from Greek epigrams: cf. *Anth. Pal.* 9.226.6 = *GPh* 3477
(Zonas Sard.), as well as *Anth. Pl.* 189 = *HE* 2783–6 G.-P. (Nicias [?]). **nec fronde
capellae.** Even this eclogue, and thus the entire book, must end—and it will be
concluded by satiated goats: *E.* 10.77n. (cf. also 7n.; 29n.).

31–69. Gallus' thirty-nine-line discourse is the single longest speech in the
book, if we exclude singing performances like *E.* 8 and Corydon's song in *E.* 2,
which is effectively a monologue. V. pays homage to his friend even from a quantitative point of view, given the exceptional space allotted to Gallus (which is possibly greater than the space allotted to Daphnis by Theocritus, i.e. forty-four lines
from *id.* 1.99 to 142, but thirty-three lines if the eleven refrain lines are not
counted). In contrast to the Theocritean model, V. eliminates any dialogic and
communicative elements. In Theocritus, Daphnis overcame his initial silence (*id.*
1.92) and reacted with resentment to Aphrodite's speech (100–13) before being
absorbed by his own thoughts. Here, Gallus might be expected to reply (at least)
to Apollo, who is the last to address him: instead, Gallus follows his own train of
thought. After addressing the Arcadians, he focuses on his own obsessions and
erotic fantasies. V. perhaps wants to avoid giving the impression that Gallus is
truly part of the pastoral context, or has become a pastoral character himself: the
fiction might otherwise appear too far-fetched, or even disrespectful towards
Gallus. As a result, *E.* 10 is a standalone piece of sorts, almost a 'cameo appearance' of Gallus, who stays true to his own literary voice and identity (as it seems,
he even reworks themes and wordings of his own elegies: cf. below, 10.46–9n.).
More conspicuously than in *E.* 2, V. here employs the technique of the tragic
monologue (particularly that of the 'deliberative' type, in which the protagonist
meditates on possible courses of action): cf. notably Eur. *Med.* 364–409. V. will
use the technique again in Dido's long monologue at *Aen.* 4.590–658. Another
tragic model of considerable importance is Phaedra's delirious speech, in which
she pictures herself following Hippolytus on his hunting trips: Eur. *Hipp.* 208–49;
see below, 10.42–3n.; 50n. Note also, in comedy, the monologue of the young
lover Moschion in Menander, *Sam.* 623–32: 'If things were fine with the girl / and
I did not have all these obstacles—the oath, my desire, / time, custom: I am a

ECLOGUE 10   485

slave to these things—, / I would not have been accused again, in my presence, / of such a misdeed. But who cares: / I will leave the city for a distant land, I would rather / be in Bactria or Caria, at war over there. / And yet, dearest Plangon, because of you I now / will not do anything heroic: it is impossible, nor does Eros / allow me to do it, as he now controls my mind [οὐ γὰρ ἔξεστ' οὐδ' ἐᾷ / ὁ τῆς ἐμῆς νῦν κύριος γνώμης Ἔρως]' (no wonder that comedy and love-elegy have much in common: Lycoris/Cytheris the actress was presumably aware of this). Similarly, in Plautus' *Mercator*, the young Charinus decides to go into exile so as to run away from his unhappy love (Plaut. *Merc.* 643–8), even though his friend Eutychus raises some reasonable objections (649–57): cf. esp. 652–4 *quis modus tibi exsilio tandem eueniet, qui finis fugae? / quae patria aut domus tibi stabilis esse poterit? dic mihi. / cedo, si hac urbe abis, amorem te hic relicturum putas?* (by contrast, the remedy seems to work for Theocritus' Simos, who enrolls in the army and sails away from unrequited love: Theocr. *id.* 14.52–6 [esp. 52 φάρμακον...ἀμηχανέοντος ἔρωτος]). In spite of V.'s defence of the pastoral world, addressed to Gallus in 10. 16–17 (esp. 17 *nec te paeniteat pecoris*), Gallus does not seem seriously to consider engaging in any pastoral activity (with the sole exception of his regrets at 10.35–6); for him, hunting is a form of sport (10.55–60). Perhaps he would have had little success as a herdsman, due to his obsessive erotic passion: cf. the young Idas in Nemes. *ecl.* 2.27–34.

31 tristis at ille. The adj. refers to both Gallus' sad fate (as in *E.* 9.5) and the pathetic, at times aggressive, way in which he expresses his thoughts (cf. *E.* 2.14 and 6.7, as well as *Aen.* 2.115). In *id.* 1, Daphnis initially remained silent in the face of Priapus and the herdsmen's attempts to comfort him (*id.* 1.92), but then replied with resentment to Aphrodite's provocative speech (*id.* 1.100–13). For the postponed *at*, a Hellenistic and Catullan element that perfectly suits Gallus' style (and significantly introduces his speech), cf. *E.* 7.67n. Here, the postponed conjunction echoes and concludes a repetition pattern featuring the postponed *et*: see above, 10.19n.; 24n.; and also 13–15n. **tamen cantabitis**. The abrupt opening of Gallus' speech opposes the eternal dimension of song (note the intensifying, frequentative force of the verb) to the sorrowful present circumstances—for which poetry seems to offer some 'compensation': the vocative *Arcades* suits Pan very well, but is also appropriate for Silvanus and Menalcas (and Gallus' words here give an impression of generality). Servius rightly observed that *tamen* is the first of Gallus' words (rather than being V.'s last): this is a colloquial word-order; cf. Hor. *epist.* 1.6.42–3 '*qui possum tot?' ait; 'tamen et quaeram et quot habebo / mittam*' and *E.* 9.62n.

32 montibus haec uestris. The dat. is hardly surprising after 10.15: the Arcadian mountains truly 'listen' to poetry and song. Compare *E.* 8.22–4, as well as 2.5 *montibus et siluis studio iactabat inani*. The reading *nostris* (P[1]) can readily be explained as a psychological error.

32–3 soli cantare periti / Arcades. Probably a nominal-style sentence, featuring *Arcades* (10.33) as a subject and just omitting the verb. Yet this second *Arcades* may

486 ECLOGUE 10

also be read as an appositional voc., referring to the first *Arcades* (10.31). For the adj. + infinitive, a syntactical Hellenism, cf. *E.* 5.1n.; see also 7.4–5 *Arcades ambo, / et cantare pares et respondere parati* (n.; as his speech begins, Gallus displays great familiarity with the agon of *E.* 7). For *peritus* + infinitive cf. Pers. 2.34; Tac. *Agr.* 8.1.

33 tum quam molliter ossa quiescant. The poet's 'death' is presented as a future and seemingly natural event. However, as in 10.10 (*peribat*), Daphnis' cruel fate is in the background. Imagining one's own death is typical of love-elegy (cf. Prop. 1.19; 2.13.17–58; Tib. 1.3), the metre of which, the elegiac couplet, was considered as intrinsically 'sad' and 'lamenting' (cf. Hor. *ars* 75–6). Note that the funerary formula *ossa quiescant* is modified by the adv. *molliter*, which seems appropriate for a poet of 'soft' (or 'languid') songs, such as love-elegies: cf. Prop. 1.7.19; 2.1.2; Ov. *trist.* 2.349; *Pont.* 3.4.85. Compare the whole phrase with another funerary formula, *sit tibi terra leuis* (quoted verbatim in Mart. 9.29.11). Here, V. perhaps echoes Gallus' own poetry, as seems to be suggested by the line-ending *molliter ossa cubent* found at Ov. *amor.* 1.8.108; *her.* 7.162 (164); *trist.* 3.3.76. V.'s line will often be imitated in epitaphs: cf. e.g. *CLE* 773.1 Buech.

34 uestra meos…si fistula dicat amores. The *fistula* is the pastoral instrument *par excellence*, invented by Pan, one of Gallus' divine rescuers, who has just talked to him (cf. *E.* 2.32–3 and 8.24, as well as 2.37 and 3.22). Pastoral music is again coupled with Gallus' poetry at 10.50–1. The phrase *meos…amores* perhaps alludes to the title of Gallus' elegiac collection dedicated to Lycoris (see above, 10.6n.).

35–43. After fantasizing about his own death, and an Arcadian future in which his figure has become pure memory and an object of song, Gallus now loses himself in an entirely unrealistic reverie (*utinam…fuissem*) concerning a serene life in the pastoral world, full of love and rest. This is what Corydon did in *E.* 2.28–55; here, however, Gallus immediately returns to the obsessive thought of his beloved Lycoris, whom he imagines for a moment as accompanying him to those pleasant places (10.42–3). Gallus' nostalgic tone evokes the reveries of *id.* 7, esp. 63–70 and 86–90. In Roman love poetry (esp. elegy), the city is the space for love affairs, whereas simple life in the countryside (*rus*) is sometimes longed for as a dream, which never appears completely actualizable: cf. Prop. 2.19; Tib. 1.1.1–50; 1.5.21–36; 2.3.

36 custos gregis. This is how Daphnis defined himself in his own epitaph at *E.* 5.44 (*formosi pecoris custos*); cf. also 3.5. **maturae uinitor uuae.** This reference to viticulture concludes a series of Arcadian 'skills'. Note the pleonastic construction (*uinitor uuae*) and the allusion to convivial drinking (the grapes are ripe and ready to be pressed). No wonder that, in 10.37, erotic pleasures make an appearance. Farming tasks are mentioned in the *E.* since the very beginning (note Tityrus' *rura* at 1.46 and *frondator* at 1.56), and they now appear at the end of the book. Here they are mentioned in the context of Gallus' Arcadian dream; note also 10.76n. V.'s next work, the *Georgics*, will entirely be devoted to farming itself (see 10.70–7n.).

37 Phyllis...Amyntas. Both characters are representative of V.'s notion of pastoral beauty (both feminine and masculine). In fact, they appeared together in *E*. 3 (esp. 3.74 and 3.76); for Phyllis alone, cf. *E*. 5.10 and 7.59. In *E*. 2, Corydon had mentioned Amyntas' name to make Alexis jealous or, at least, to attract his attention (*E*. 2.35; 39; cf. also 5.8). Thus, Gallus shows his great familiarity with the soon-to-be-completed pastoral book of his friend V. (confirming that he is a sort of 'ideal reader' of the *E*.) For the construction *siue...siue*, cf. *E*. 5.5–6 and 8.6–7. Note that, here and in the following line, Amyntas appears in line-ending position. The same is true of *amores* at 10.53–4: this kind of repetition is typical of the pastoral style, though perhaps it was also featured in Gallus' elegies?

38 seu quicumque furor. Cf. Hor. *sat*. 2.3.325 *mille puellarum, puerorum mille furores* (Damasippus' reproach to the poet); note also *E*. 10.22n.; for the idea that there can always be 'another new love', cf. Theocr. *id*. 7.105...εἴτ᾽ ἔστ᾽ ἆρα Φιλῖνος ὁ μαλθακὸς εἴτε τις ἄλλος. Despite his fascination with the pastoral world, Gallus cannot help using the typically elegiac vocabulary of erotic madness (cf. *E*. 2.69 *dementia*). One of Theocritus' rare references to Arcadia (in an urban mime) includes a mention of the so-called *hippomanes*, capable of engendering erotic frenzy in both animals and humans: ἱππομανὲς φυτόν ἐστι παρ᾽ Ἀρκάσι κτλ. (Theocr. *id*. 2.48–51). Thus, amorous folly is apparently endemic in Arcadia. **si fuscus Amyntas.** Cf. *E*. 2.16 *niger* (referring to the *puer* Menalcas). For the repetition of *Amyntas* at the end of the line cf. 9.37n.

39 et nigrae uiolae sunt et uaccinia nigra. Gallus' language now resembles that of a pastoral poet: he employs a typically rustic analogy (cf. above, 10.29–30n.), known to the reader from Corydon's eclogue (*E*. 2.18 *alba ligustra cadunt, uaccinia nigra leguntur*: note the phrase *uaccinia nigra*, here used in a different syntactical construction). Unlike Corydon, Gallus echoes Theocritus in mentioning violets, while the idea of 'choice' (*leguntur* / λέγονται) is now brushed aside: cf. *id*. 10.28–9 καὶ τὸ ἴον μέλαν ἐστὶ καὶ ἁ γραπτὰ ὑάκινθος, / ἀλλ᾽ ἔμπας ἐν τοῖς στεφάνοις τὰ πρᾶτα λέγονται 'violets, too, are black, and so is the hyacinth, with its inscribed letters, / and yet they are the first to be gathered in garlands' (note the coordination καὶ...καὶ, here taken up by *et...et*). Cf. also Asclep. *Anth. Pal*. 5.210.3–4 = HE 830–1 G.-P. = 5.3–4 Sens; Philod. *epigr*. 5.1 Gig. = 17.1 Sid. (*Anth. Pal*. 5.121.1 = GPh 3206 G.-P.); Long. 1.16.4. An emphasis on dark skin-colour (in relation to a woman) seems to have been featured in Domitius Marsus, as can be inferred from Mart. 7.28.7–8 *et Maecenati, Maro cum cantaret Alexin, / nota tamen Marsi fusca Melaenis erat*. Here, therefore, Gallus may make his contribution (as Corydon previously did) to a half-serious debate on the subject (cf. Lucr. 4.1160, as well as Ov. *ars* 2.643–4; *her*. 15.35–6). In *Aen*. 11.69 *seu mollis uiolae seu languentis hyacinthi*, the Latin word *uaccinium* will be replaced by its probable (and nobler) Greek equivalent i.e. the hyacinth (see further 2.18n. for a discussion of the plant's identity).

40 inter salices lenta sub uite. The mention of willow-trees evokes a typically north Italic, and therefore eminently Virgilian, landscape (cf. *E*. 1.54; 78; see also

488   ECLOGUE 10

3.65; 83; 5.16), presumably familiar to Gallus as well. For the custom of placing vines against willows, cf. Colum. 5.7.1, where it is presented as typically Celtic (and somewhat disadvantageous); other uses of willow-trees are mentioned at *E.* 3.83; *G.* 2.434; Plin. *nat.* 16.174–7. For the vine arbour, cf. Hor. *carm.* 1.38.7–8; *Culex* 74–5; Nemes. *ecl.* 4.46–8 (as well as *E.* 5.7n.). The image is common in Dionysian iconography: cf. *LIMC* III.1, p. 457, no. 373, s.v. *Dionysos* (C. Gasparri); for the phrase *lenta…uite,* cf. *E.* 3.38; 9.42, while the adjective refers to *salix* in *E.* 3.83 and 5.16 (the two plants are rather similar in terms of 'pliability'). **iaceret.** This is the most commonly transmitted reading (note P^2R), whereas MP^1 have *iaceres.* The second person sing. would entail a direct address to the beloved, strongly contrasting with the other verbs used in this context (all in the third-person sing.); cf. also Theocr. *id.* 7.89 κατεκέκλισο (in a passage that V. might have had in mind: esp. *id.* 7.88–9). However, despite the incoherence of Gallus' thought and syntax, *iaceret* is preferable.

41 serta…Phyllis legeret. The girl bears a 'botanical' name (Φυλλίς, derived from φύλλον 'leaf', 'branch'): no wonder that she gathers and weaves garlands (see *E.* 3.107n.; 7.59n.). In the myth, moreover, Phyllis was turned into a tree (cf. 5.10n.), according to the version recorded by Serv. *ad E.* 5.10 (see also Hyg. *fab.* 59.3); cf. Ov. *rem.* 606. Phyllis' name will reappear twice in Horace: *carm.* 2.4.14 and 4.11.3. See further *Enc. Or.* I, pp. 734–7, s.v. *Fillide* (F. Citti).

42–3. The pleasant features of the place are underscored by the deictic adv. *hic,* repeated four times (both the first and the last occurrence coinciding with the ictus). This kind of anaphora is typical of the pastoral style, to which Gallus is adapting his poetry: see e.g. Theocr. *id.* 11.45–8 (but cf. Callim. *aet.* fr. 27 Pf. = 28 Mass. = 25e Hard.); note also *E.* 9.40–1n. (the implicit invitation, however, cannot be accepted: 9.60–2n.). The voc. *Lycori* is placed in the middle of the anaphoric sequence, which thereby 'embraces' it (cf. 6.10n.). For the image, cf. Eur. *Hipp.* 208–11 (Phaedra's delirious speech). For the fourfold structure, and its aura of completeness, cf. above, 10.29–30n.

42 mollia prata. A somewhat idealized, and typically pastoral, landscape (cf. its echo at *Lydia* [*Dirae*] 119, in the context of a broader reworking of *E.* 10); note also *G.* 2.384 *mollibus in pratis*; Ov. *ars* 1.279; Stat. *silu.* 2.1.107. In an elegiac and metapoetic context, Propertius writes *mollia sunt paruis prata terenda rotis* (Prop. 3.3.18; I am indebted to Luciano Landolfi for this point). Note the 'soft' nature of the pastoral paradise (cf. 10.33 *molliter*), soon contrasting with the harshness of Mars (10.44) and the cold river Rhine (10.47).

43 ipso…consumerer aeuo. Cf. Lucr. 5.1431 (*hominum genus*) *semper et <in> curis consumit inanibus aeuum.* Here, however, V. gives a new twist to the construction by using a passive form of the verb.

44 nunc insanus amor duri me Martis in armis. Erotic madness is inherent to elegiac poetry (cf. above, 10.22n.); here, however, the emphasis is on Gallus' 'insane' passion for the 'fierce Mars', who keeps the poet busy with weapons and

ECLOGUE 10   489

battles (contrast 10.42 *mollia prata*). Thus, *duri Martis* is an objective gen. governed by *amor* (not a possessive gen. governed by *in armis*): cf. *Aen.* 7.550 *insani Martis amore* (and 7.461 *saeuit amor ferri et scelerata insania belli*; note also 9.760 *caedis…insana cupido*); Stat. *Theb.* 4.260 (also 3.598 *Mauortis amore*); Val. Fl. 6.156; Hos. Get. *Med.* 285; for *amor* in a non-erotic sense, cf. *E.* 6.10. It is hard to tell which military operations Gallus is referring to, and it cannot be ruled out that he is here reworking his own poetry. At any rate, the events that Gallus has in mind here must not be too far in the past: perhaps the Eastern campaign led by Antony in 38 BCE, in which Gallus may have taken part. Yet he could also refer to naval battles against Sextus Pompey's pirates (who could easily be called *hostes*: cf. 10.45). The use of *amor* is somewhat surprising, but the paradox is certainly deliberate: Gallus' passion is absurd from the point of view of Roman love-elegy, and therefore *insanus*. An authoritative god such as Apollo calls Gallus 'insane' due to his lovesickness (10.22 *quid insanis?*), but for the elegiac Gallus it is 'insane' to love anything other than Lycoris, even if the Roman *uir*'s most important task, i.e. war, is at stake. Various obstacles had prevented Theocritus' Daphnis from freely devoting himself to love (note δύσερως in Theocr. *id.* 1.85: see above, 10.22n.), but here the theme is adapted to suit Rome's traditional *mos maiorum* ethics (and this is V.'s homage to Gallus' duties as a politician and military commander). The personal pronoun *me* has raised reasonable doubts, since the martial environment seems to contradict 14–15, where Gallus languishes alone under an Arcadian cliff. Hence the considerable success of C. A. Heumann's correction *te*, which causes *insanus amor* to be read as an 'insane love' for Gallus' rival (i.e. 'insane' from Gallus' point of view), even though *duri…Martis* must necessarily refer to *in armis* (i.e. 'now an insane love keeps you among the weapons of fierce Mars', etc.; note the forceful verb *detinet*). The transmitted text is supported by the difficulty of justifying a *te* > *me* corruption and the fact that *me* suits its context perfectly: note the opposition between 10.44 (*nunc*) and 10.42-3, as well as the contrast between 10.44 *me* and 10.46 *tu* (with the ensuing exclamation, expressing incredulity: see n. ad loc.). It seems odd to imagine Lycoris 'among the weapons' of her beloved *miles* (cf. 10.23): is she wearing armour herself? Is she facing the enemy troops and their arrows at 10.45? To be sure, Lycoris was not the kind of woman who could be depicted in a warlike situation without any fear of ridicule, even if Gallus' elegiac hyperbole is accounted for. At most, as far as we know, the mime actress Cytheris/Volumnia was carried in a litter along with Antony (cf. 10.2-3n.; note *horrida castra* next to *niues* at 10.23: encampments, not battlefields). On occasion, ancient literary women take part in a battle and face the enemy: note, for instance, Scylla in Ov. *met.* 8.38-9 *impetus est illi, liceat modo, ferre per agmen / uirgineos hostile gradus.* This, however, is generally represented as an unlikely possibility (cf. also Prop. 4.3 esp. 45, for which see 10.23n.). Thus, Abascanthus' wife Priscilla is ready to follow her husband to the dangerous North, and Statius praises her in a careful reworking of *E.* 10: *tecum gelidas comes illa per arctos / Sarmaticasque hiemes Histrumque et*

490 ECLOGUE 10

pallida Rheni / frigora, tecum omnes animo durata per aestus / et, si castra darent, u e l l e t gestare pharetras, / u e l l e t Amazonia latus intercludere pelta (Stat. *silu.* 5.1.127–31). Nothing is resolved by the conjecture *inermem* in lieu of *in armis* (P has *inermis*, corrected by P^2), which forces *duri…Martis* to refer to *amor*, with some bizarre results (Lycoris' love for fierce Mars would urge her to go unarmed into battle and face the enemy arrows). The correct reading, i.e. the transmitted *me*, implies that the entire preceding scene is to be interpreted as a poetic reverie, and that Arcadia is but an idealized landscape, in which the poet can take shelter even while he is serving in the army (be it in Italy or elsewhere). In other words, the poet's own 'reality', which he experiences through his poetry (i.e. the only kind of reality that matters in the *E.*), features a lovesick Gallus in Arcadia—almost a new Daphnis. Then, however, the poet returns to his senses and traumatically regains contact with the 'empirical' reality of war: hence the adversative force of *nunc* (cf., in a comparable context, Tib. 1.10.13 *nunc ad bella trahor*; note also Prop. 2.14.16; *OLD*^{2}, p. 1327, s.v. *nunc* 11). Through Gallus' voice, V. emphasizes a fundamental aspect of the relationship between poetry and empirical existence: no reader could seriously think that Gallus 'actually' languishes at the foot of a cliff in Arcadia any more than he 'actually' wanders around Mount Helicon along with a Muse in *E.* 6.64–73. Similarly, in *E.* 3, the poet's allegiance to a certain literary taste (i.e. Pollio's) is codified in terms of physical displacement (3.88 *ueniat quo te quoque gaudet*); cf. also, before V., Lucr. 4.1–2 = 1.926–7: *auia Pieridum peragro loca nullius ante / trita solo. iuuat integros accedere fontis*. In *E.* 10, the poet's idea of 'reality' is summarized at 10.26, where the autoptic formula implies true suspension of disbelief (*uidimus ipsi*, with the god Pan as the direct object) while situating V. himself in an Arcadian landscape (see 10.26n.). Gallus will once again represent himself as moving at 10.50 (*ibo*), so as to highlight his own allegiance (or his 'return'?) to Sicilian pastoral poetry. He will then bid farewell to the woods, but in terms that clarify how they were a fantasy: it is in fact the woods that have to 'go' (10.63 *ipsae rursus concedite siluae* [n.]). In the whole eclogue, the perception of space, time, and reality appears to be highly relative: hence, Gallus concludes that any displacement, even to the most remote regions of the world (10.64–9), is nothing in the face of *Amor*'s force.

45 tela inter media. Cf. 9.12 *tela inter Martia* (remember, here, *Martis* at 10.44). Note the intensive use of *medius*, 'right in the middle': Gallus says it again, also in reference to himself, at 10.65 (*frigoribus mediis*: this is a further argument in favour of *me* in 10.44). For the phrase in the same metrical position, referring to the heroic *puer Ascanius*, cf. *Aen.* 10.237 *tela inter media atque horrentis Marte Latinos* (featuring Mars yet again).

46–9. After focusing on himself (10.44–5), Gallus focuses on Lycoris again; now he seems to face the reality of her escape (recall Apollo's revelation at 10.23). In his note on 10.46, Servius asserts: *hi autem omnes uersus Galli sunt de ipsius translati carminibus* 'all these lines are drawn from Gallus' own poems' (presumably his elegies for Lycoris). In all likelihood, Servius refers to 10.46–9, which

ECLOGUE 10   491

forms a coherent unity, before the semantic transition marked by *ibo* at 50; *translati* must probably be taken not in the sense of literal quotation, but in that of reworking. Note the intensely pathetic rhythm, emphasized by the repeated exclamations and the insistent assonance on /a/: *tu procul A pAtriA... / AlpinAs, A!... / A!... / A!...AsperA plAntAs.* For a more moderate use of this technique, cf. *E.* 1.14–15 (Meliboeus); Catull. 64.135 (Ariadne abandoned by Theseus); see also *Aen.* 4.279–84. Perhaps from here on V. also evokes the pentameter rhythm of (Gallus'?) love-elegy: cf. esp. 10.48n., as well as 10.69n. In 10.50–1, Gallus himself says that he wants to adapt his previous compositions to the pastoral context (there, however, he need not solely refer to elegies: see 10.50n.). For a variation on the theme, cf. Tib. 2.6.1 *castra Macer sequitur: tenero quid fiet Amori?*

46 nec sit mihi credere tantum. A parenthetical exclamation, introduced by *nec* (= *neque*: cf. *E.* 2.34; contrast 9.6). For *tantum* used as a noun, cf. *Aen.* 1.231 *in te committere tantum* (in line-ending position, as here). This emphatic outburst only makes sense if Gallus addresses Lycoris here at 10.46 (*tu*) but not at 10.44 (and *tu*, by contrast, would sound repetitive after *te* in 10.44). If it is hard to picture her in a snowy landscape, it is even more implausible to find a *puella* in the midst of a battlefield (see 10.44n.). Correspondingly, it would be quite bizarre if then Gallus were only worried about the cold (in particular, the ice on the ground): a concern that seems appropriate only for 10.23.

47 Alpinas, a! dura niues et frigora Rheni. An echo of 10.23 (confirming the truth of what Apollo said). Adjectives referring to 'hardness' are now used in relation to Lycoris (note *dura...frigora*: icy and difficult to bear; 49 *glacies aspera*), in opposition to the 'softness' of love and pastoral life (10.42n.; cf. also 10.49 *teneras... plantas*). For a similar opposition between elegiac lament and military commitment (the latter being an object of celebration), cf. Hor. *carm.* 2.9.17–20 *desine mollium / tandem querellarum et potius noua / cantemus Augusti tropaea / Caesaris et rigidum Niphaten.*

48 me sine sola uides. From Gallus' point of view, the 'lonely' one is Lycoris herself, even though (as the reader knows) she is following another lover (while Gallus is, in fact, alone: cf. 10.14n.). Note the anastrophe *me sine* (in lieu of *sine me*), typical of poetic language and here facilitated by alliteration (*sine sola*); cf. Ov. *her.* 8.80 *sine me, me sine, mater, abis?*, as well as *G.* 3.42 *te sine*; *Aen.* 12.883; Calp. *ecl.* 3.51; Stat. *Theb.* 4.202; Val. Fl. 5.44. The sharply punctuated first half-line is in effect a half-pentameter (by Gallus?).

48–9. For the lover's concern that the beloved might injure his or her feet or legs, cf. Prop. 1.8.5–8; [Tib.] 3.9.10 and esp. Ov. *met.* 1.508–9 (Apollo pursuing Daphne); see also Nonn. *Dionys.* 16.91–3. For a reworking of this passage (and perhaps of an elegy by Gallus?), cf. Prop. 1.8.7–8 *tu pedibus teneris positas fulcire pruinas, / tu potes insolitas, Cynthia, ferre niues?*

50 ibo. The verb is taken up in 10.59: (*iam uideor*) *ire*, similarly in line-beginning position. With this line and the following hunting scenes cf. Phaedra's

492 ECLOGUE 10

words in Eur. *Hipp.* 215–22: 'take me to the mountain: I shall go [εἶμι] into the woods / and among the pine trees, where the hounds race / in pursuit of wild beasts, etc.'; such an abrupt change in direction (with a clear destination: 52 *certum est*) seems to contrast with Gallus' wandering in *E.* 6.64. Yet this 'pastoral' will soon end up as an utter failure (10.60–9n.). **Chalcidico...uersu.** Gallus' 'Chalcidian verse' must refer to some of his own compositions, modelled after Euphorion of Chalcis (in Euboea), the poet and scholar whom Antiochus the Great employed as a librarian (third century BCE). Cicero singled him out as a crucial model for the *poetae noui*, whom he called *cantores Euphorionis* (Cic. *Tusc.* 3.45); see further *Enc. Virg.* II, pp. 421–2, s.v. *Euforione* (A. Barigazzi); *Virg. Enc.* I, p. 459, s.v. *Euphorion* (D. O. Ross). This interpretation, supported by Quint. *inst.* 10.156 and Serv. ad loc., is confirmed by the fact that Euphorion's poetry was evoked in the investiture scene at *E.* 6.72 *Grynei nemoris...origo* (n.). Here, echoing *E.* 6, Gallus considers 'playing' on the Sicilian pipes his short poem devoted to the Grynean grove, and perhaps similar compositions as well (cf. *E.* 6.69 *hos...calamos*). The point seems to be that Gallus wants to adapt his learned, refined poetry to suit the pastoral genre. Echoing his neoteric predecessors, Gallus declares his admiration for Hellenistic literature, and Euphorion in particular. In this context, *uersus* would refer to the thematic and stylistic aspects of Gallus' poetry, not just metre (cf. 6.1 *Syracosio...uersu* [n.], as well as 8.21). Perhaps the ancients' understandable desire to connect Gallus' fame primarily with his elegiac production (hence, 'I shall play on the Sicilian flute my love-elegies' ≈ 10.34) led Virgilian scholiasts to assert without evidence that Euphorion himself composed elegies: *Euphorion elegiarum scriptor Chalcidensis fuit, cuius in scribendo secutus colorem uidetur Cornelius Gallus* (Prob.). The ingenious hypothesis whereby *Chalcidico* alludes to Theocles of Chalcis, much less widely known than Euphorion, is unpersuasive. According to an ancient tradition, Theocles was not only the founder of Naxos in Sicily but also the inventor of the elegiac couplet: *Etym. Magn.* s.v. ἐλεγαίνειν, p. 327, esp. 7–10 Gaisf. τὸ ἐλεγεῖον μέτρον ἀπὸ τούτου κληθῆναι τινὲς νομίζουσιν, ὅτι Θεοκλῆς Νάξιος ἢ Ἐρετριεὺς πρῶτος αὐτὸ ἀνεφθέγξατο μανείς (cf. *RE*, V.2, cols. 2260–1, s.v. *Elegie* [O. Crusius]). At any rate, V.'s formulation does not necessarily imply that Gallus wants to 'rewrite' his poems: elsewhere, words and music are described as distinct entities (cf. *E.* 5.2; 9.45), and here music alone is said to change. Finally, that elegiac couplets can be used for topics similar to that of *E.* 6 is shown by Callimachus' *Aitia* and some papyrus fragments on metamorphosis, perhaps coming from Parthenius' *Metamorphoses* (?): *POxy* 4711 (LXIX, London 2005, esp. p. 47 [W. B. Henry]). In theory, it cannot be ruled out that Gallus' poems 'à la Euphorion' were written in elegiac couplets, regardless of whether Euphorion himself used that metre or not. In the preface to the *Erotika Pathemata*, addressed to Gallus, Parthenius declares his desire to offer him a useful compendium for use in both hexameter poetry and love-elegy (εἰς ἔπη καὶ ἐλεγείας: Parthen. p. 550 Light. 2009 = p. 308.7 Light. 1999 = p. 42.8 Mar.).

ECLOGUE 10   493

Having lost so many crucial sources (including, in particular, the virtual entirety of Gallus' poetry), we can hardly reach a conclusive solution. At any rate, Gallus is now striving to rethink *even* his elegiac production in pastoral terms: this is especially true of 10.46–9n. The point here is the transition from Euphorion's erudite, Hellenistic poetry to the 'harmonies' of the Sicilian herdsman.

51 pastoris Siculi modulabor auena. From the point of view of the poet Gallus, it seems natural to equate the 'Sicilian herdsman' with Theocritus (cf. *E.* 6.1), though a reference to Daphnis cannot be ruled out: after all, he is the prototype of the Sicilian poet-herdsman, as well as being the protagonist of *id.* 1, after which Gallus' words and gestures are modelled. Gallus is now entrusted with a task that he previously assigned to the Arcadian herdsmen (10.31–2). The verb *modulor*, as at *E.* 5.14, presupposes the existence of a poetic text to be 'set to music'; cf. also Hor. *epist.* 2.2.143 *uerba sequi fidibus modulanda Latinis*.

52 in siluis inter spelaea ferarum. The woods, a distinctive space of V.'s pastoral world (cf. *E.* 1.5; 4.3), are here coupled with caves inhabited by wild beasts. Both anticipate the theme of hunting (10.55–60). The term *spelaeum* is a learned, Hellenizing word (σπήλαιον), as Servius remarked. It will reappear in *Ciris* 467 and, much later, in Claudian, 26.345 H. (obviously emulating V.). The more common term is *spelunca*, also derived from Greek (σπῆλυγξ), but of earlier origin.

53 malle pati. The idea of 'preferring to suffer', common in Greek, is first attested here in Latin: cf. Liv. 3.2.4 *pati hostilia malle*; Sen. *dial.* 12[*Helu.*].16.7; Mart. 9.92.10; [Quint.] *decl. mai.* 4.10, p. 71.11; 19.8, p. 379.20 Håk.; see also Ov. *met.* 10.25 *posse pati uolui* (where Ovid's Orpheus is greatly indebted to both *E.* 10 and *G.* 4: cf. 10.69n.).

53–4 teneris…meos incidere amores / arboribus. The act of carving the beloved's name on the bark of a tree goes back to one of the prototypes of elegiac poetry: the description of Acontius' melancholic solitude in Callim. *aet.* fr. 73 Pf. = 172 Mass. = 73 Hard. 'cut such letters in the bark of trees, / so as to say "Cydippe is fair"' (the Callimachean intertext can also be detected in Corydon's eclogue: see *E.* 2.1n.; 2.3n.; but cf., at the very beginning of the book, 1.5n.). The motif then reappears in Hellenistic epigrams: cf. Glaucon in *Anth. Pal.* 9.341 = *HE* 1819–24 G.-P.; anon. *Anth. Pal.* 12.130 = *HE* 3762–7 G.-P.; but see also Theocr. *id.* 18.47–8. Through V. (and Gallus?), the motif then enters Roman elegy: cf. Prop. 1.18.19–22 *uos eritis testes, si quos habet arbor amores / fagus et Arcadio pinus amica deo. // a quotiens teneras resonant mea uerba sub umbras, / scribitur et uestris Cynthia corticibus!* (note the mention of *fagus*, a symbol of the *E.*, and of *pinus*, whose human counterpart was loved by the Arcadian god Pan); Ov. *her.* 5.21–30; Flor. *carm.* 6 Di Giov. = *Anth. Lat.* 248 R. = 241 Sh. B. For the bark of a tree used to write a (rather long) text, cf. 5.13–14. Note the framing hyperbaton *teneris…arboribus*, suggesting that the young trees are the 'hosts' of the words carved on them: *tener* is quite frequent in the *E.* and hints at the 'tender' youth of animals and plants (cf. 10.7 *tenera…uirgulta* and 1.8 *tener…agnus*). It is obviously easy to write on a young tree's bark (*E.* 5.13 *uiridi…cortice fagi*). Yet *tener* also denotes erotic softness,

494   ECLOGUE 10

especially in reference to love poetry and poets: cf. Catull. 35.1 *poetae tenero*; Ov. *ars* 3.333 *teneri...carmen...Properti* (followed by a mention of Gallus). Both trees and *amores* grow together at 10.54 (see below). If *Amores* was indeed the title of Gallus' elegiac collection (see 10.54n.), here *meos...a/Amores* (or MEOS AMORES in ancient capital letters) may amount to a self-citation.

54 crescent illae, crescetis, amores. The repeated verb underscores the connection between trees and love stories (the term *amores*, appearing at the end of 10.53 and 54, perhaps alludes to the title of Gallus' elegiac collection: cf. above, 10.6n.; 34n.; 53n.). For the repetition of a given word at the end of two consecutive lines, see 10.37n. At 10.53, both Gallus' 'loves' and the young trees are associated with their future 'growth', which can also concern poetic glory (7.25n.). A tree's growth, at any rate, is a frequent metaphor for any type of development: cf. Hor. *carm.* 1.12.45 *crescit...uelut arbor* (see Hom. *Il.* 18.56–7; for a metaphorical use in relation to virtue/ἀρετά, cf. Pind. *Nem.* 8.40–2; see further 10.74n.). The text suggests that Gallus' 'inscription' only features the beloved girl's name, perhaps as part of a short sentence (as in Callimachus: see 10.53–4n.). The same is true of later reworkings such as Prop. 1.18.22; Ov. *her.* 5.23 *et quantum trunci, tantum mea nomina crescunt*; Flor. *carm.* 6.2 Di Giov. = *Anth. Lat.* 248.2 R. = 241.2 Sh. B. *notaui nomen ardoris mei*. The need for communication is inherent to poets, especially elegiac ones: cf. 10.2 *sed quae legat ipsa Lycoris*; see also [Theocr.] *id.* 23.46–8.

55–7. After abandoning his reveries of a 'soft' pastoral life, which ended up leading him back towards Lycoris (10.35–43n.), Gallus describes another typically Arcadian scene: hunting (cf. the Arcadian Corydon at *E.* 7.29–32, as well as the lover Corydon in *E.* 2.29; see also Theocr. *id.* 5.106–7). Hunting was traditionally opposed to erotic passion, particularly since Artemis herself was a virgin: cf. Eur. *Hipp.* 10–19; Lycophronid. fr. 2.3 (*PMG* 844, p. 446 P.: perhaps dedicated to Artemis or Pan); see also Mnasalc. *Anth. Pal.* 9.324 = *HE* 2663–6 G.-P. (where Aphrodite contrasts with the herdsman's 'sylvan Muse'). It is for this reason that, in Roman elegy, hunting often appears as an alternative to love: cf. Prop. 2.19.17–29 (obviously echoing *E.* 10); [Tib.] 3.9.5; 19–22; Ov. *rem.* 199–206; see also *Perv. Ven.* 37–41. Here, however, 10.60–9 will show that Gallus cannot become a true lover of hunting, as Corydon was. For other hunting scenes in V., cf. *G.* 3.40–5; 409–13; *Aen.* 1.184–94; 4.129–59; 7.479–99.

55 interea. The adv. refers to the rather long amount of time that the young trees (10.54) need to grow. **mixtis...Nymphis.** Artemis/Diana herself can be a hunting companion. The Nymphs escort her as a retinue (see Hom. *Od.* 6.105; cf. *Aen.* 1.499–500); see further *E.* 3.66n. **Maenala.** For the Arcadian location cf. above, 10.15 and 7.21n. The plural, metrically convenient, reappears at *G.* 1.17.

56 acris...apros. Cf. Hor. *epod.* 2.31–2 *aut trudit acris hinc et hinc multa cane / apros in obstantis plagas*. Boars were fierce, as is readily shown by the mythical example of Adonis (above, 10.18n.). This type of hunting suits Homeric warriors (cf. Hom. *Od.* 19.439–54, on Odysseus' wound), as its technique is somewhat similar to that of epic duels: cf. Hom. *Il.* 11.292–5; 414–20; 13.470–7; 17.281–5. A more cautious attitude is shown by Propertius (perhaps in an effort to keep some distance from V.'s Gallus): 2.19.21–2 *non tamen ut uastos ausim temptare leones / aut celer agrestis comminus ire sues.* Both boar-hunting and deer-hunting generated great noise and chaos (due to nets, weapons, etc.): cf., below, 10.57, as well as *G.* 3.411–13. Gallus' hunting fantasy could not be more remote from the pastoral idyll (featuring Lycoris) with which his speech began: 42 *hic gelidi fontes, hic mollia prata* (cf. Corydon at 2.59 *liquidis immisi fontibus apros*).

56–7 non me ulla uetabunt / frigora. The cold, which Gallus mentioned at 10.48 (hoping that it will not harm his beloved), is no longer a concern to him.

57 Parthenios canibus circumdare saltus. Mount Parthenius marks the southeastern boundary of Arcadia. In antiquity, it was known for its forests and, above all, for providing the backdrop to the myth of Atalanta (the unattainable girl: cf. *E.* 6.61). A dark parallel is Prop. 1.1.11 (*Milanion*) *nam modo Partheniis amens errabat in antris* (perhaps also recalling Gallus). The mountain occurs only here in V., and perhaps evokes a 'chaste' or 'virginal' landscape ($\pi\alpha\rho\theta\acute{\epsilon}\nu os$). Servius etymologizes the name as *a uirginibus, quae illic uenari consueuerant*, whereas Servius Dan. proposes other explanations: e.g. *quod ibi uirginitas Callistonis delibata sit* (more probably, the name is connected to the 'virgin' Atalanta herself, originally a local deity: see *Enc. Virg.* III, p. 987a, s.v. *Partenio* [A. Fo]). Note, at any rate, that the poet who wrote this line is *Vergilius/Virgilius*, also known as *Parthenias*, residing in *Parthenope*, and future author of a narrative concerning, *inter alia*, the death of the warrior *Parthenius* (*Aen.* 10.748: Parthenius is killed by Rapo, i.e. 'The Abductor'). Finally, the Greek poet Parthenius of Nicaea was a friend of Gallus and is said to have initiated him into the study of Hellenistic poetry (esp. Euphorion). For the second half-line, cf. *G.* 1.140. Note also the assonance with *Partho* at 10.59.

58 per rupes...lucosque sonantis. Gallus now pictures himself running around cliffs and forests amidst the noise of hunting (cf. *G.* 3.43–5), a firm contrast with 10.14 where he was motionless at the foot of a solitary cliff. For the line-ending phrase *lucosque sonantis*, cf. *G.* 4.364. **uideor.** Poetic imagination is a gift that Gallus and V. have in common: cf. esp. 10.26n.

59–60 Partho torquere Cydonia cornu / spicula. The Parthians were renowned for their archery skills: cf. *G.* 3.31; 4.313–14. The same is true of the Cretans, here referred to by the epithet *Cydonius* (cf. Hor. *carm.* 4.9.17–18 *Cydoneo / ...arcu*: Cydonia was a Cretan city; see *ThlL, onom.* II.786.8–15): cf. *G.* 3.345 *Cressamque pharetram* and *Aen.* 5.306–7 *Cnosia.../ spicula*, as well as Hom. *Il.* 23.850–83 (the Cretan Merion); Pind. *Pyth.* 5.41; Callim. *epigr.* 37 Pf. (also *hymn.* 3[*Dian.*].81 $K\upsilon\delta\acute{o}\nu\iota o\nu...\tau\acute{o}\xi o\nu$); Hor. *carm.* 1.15.17. Both Parthian and Cydonian archers will reappear towards the end of the *Aeneid*, 12.857–8, along with their *telum immedicabile* (858). V.'s playful use of erudite epithets is emphasized by enjambement: in

496 ECLOGUE 10

other words, if the bow is Parthian, the arrows can only be from Crete. Note also, in this context of resonance (58 *lucosque sonantis*), the echo *Parthenios* (57) ≈ *Partho. torquere*. The verb describes the tension of the bowshot, thereby hinting at the torsion of both bow and bowman: cf. *Aen.* 11.773 *spicula torquebat Lycio Gortynia cornu*, as well as 9.606 *spicula tendere cornu*. **cornu.** This is the first Latin occurrence of the metonymy *cornu* = 'bow' (*arcus*), metrically useful and destined to enjoy great success in Roman poetry: cf. *Aen.* 7.497; 9.606; *Ciris* 299; Ov. *met.* 1.455; Stat. *Theb.* 3.588; *ThlL* IV.969.13–35 (note that Pandarus' bow is made of horn in Hom. *Il.* 4.105–11; cf. *Od.* 21.395, where κέρας is used similarly; see *LSJ* s.v. III.1).

60–9. Gallus suddenly realizes that he cannot escape from his passion, either by taking shelter in the woods or by reaching the most remote lands at the edges of the Earth. Similarly, at the very end of *E.* 2, Corydon suddenly came back to his senses, contradicting what he had just said. Yet the herdsman Corydon went back to his rural, pastoral duties (*E.* 2.69–73), whereas Gallus now surrenders to Love. The *modus*, which Pan hoped would help Gallus (10.28) as it helped Corydon (cf. *E.* 2.68), now appears to be unattainable. Rather, V. himself will play the role of a herdsman, thereby bringing the book to a close.

60 tamquam haec sit nostri medicina furoris. The train of thought is suddenly interrupted, and Gallus contradicts the dreams and reveries that filled the preceding lines (esp. 10.58 *iam mihi...uideor*). The notion of *medicina* (*amoris*), and perhaps the term itself, may have occurred in Gallus' own poetry, possibly echoed by Prop. 1.5.27–8 *non ego tum potero solacia ferre roganti, / cum mihi nulla mei sit medicina mali*; cf. 2.1.57–8 *omnis humanos sanat medicina dolores: / solus amor morbi non amat artificem*. At any rate, the question of a 'cure for love' (or φάρμακον) played an important role in Theocr. *id.* 11 (esp. 1–4; 13–18), echoed in *E.* 2.73n.; note also *id.* 14.52 τὸ φάρμακον...ἀμηχανέοντος ἔρωτος. For a similar use of the verb *medeor*, cf. *E.* 8.89. From Gallus' point of view, *furor* seems to be inherent to love, regardless of any particular object of love such as Lycoris: cf. 10.38. Note the change in tone, underscored by the use of *tamquam*, which only occurs here in V. and is generally rare in poetry: see Axelson (1945, pp. 88–9). The reading *sint* (**M**) must have arisen from a misunderstanding of *haec*, as if the demonstrative adj. referred to *spicula* (or to 10.58–9 as a whole) rather than modifying *medicina*. Wherever the lover may physically happen to be, and whatever he may try to focus his imagination on, *Amor* absorbs his entire mind and leads it towards itself (i.e. towards the beloved): cf., for instance, Plaut. *Asin.* 156–8; *Cist.* 211–12.

61 aut deus ille malis hominum mitescere discat. The notion is directly connected to Pan's statement at 10.28–30 (on *Amor*). Here, *malis* is most probably instrumental abl. (human suffering does not move the god: cf. Acc. *trag.* 683–4 R.[3] *nullum est...cor tam ferum / quod non...mitescat malo*; Sil. 6.380 *uestro... mitescere fletu*; *ThlL* VIII.1145.38–48). For both notion and phrasing, cf. *G.* 4.470 *nescia...humanis precibus mansuescere corda* (referring to the underworld gods);

ECLOGUE 10   497

for love's cruelty, cf. 8.47 *saeuus Amor* (n.). In opposition to *haec...medicina*, the emphatic *ille* ('that' well-known god) highlights the impossibility of *mitescere*: cf. 10.64 *illum*; note also, in a different context, *Aen.* 5.391 *ubi nunc nobis deus ille*.

62 iam...rursus. Now, following the visionary energy of 10.50–60 (note, in particular, the repetition of the verb *ire* at 10.50 and 59), Gallus suddenly changes direction, using the adv. *rursus* (literally 'backwards', from *re-uersus*: cf. Don. *ad* Ter. *Ad.* 71). The term reappears at 10.63, ordering the *siluae* to go back where they came from. **Hamadryades.** The forest-dwelling Nymphs (or, literally, dwelling 'together with the oaks') symbolize the pastoral world, both divine and mortal, which Gallus renounces. Note that the *siluae* are immediately mentioned at 10.63. According to Servius, the *Hamadryades* were distinct from the *Dryades*, since the former's destiny was closely tied to oak-trees (cf. *schol. ad* Apoll. Rhod. 2.476–83a, p. 166.5 Wend. διὰ τὸ ἅμα ταῖς δρυσὶ γεννᾶθαι; see also Ov. *met.* 8.770–3). Whether or not Servius is right, the name clearly emphasizes the symbiotic relationship between the two (feminine) entities: cf. *E.* 5.59 *Dryadasque puellas*; *G.* 3.40 *Dryadum siluas*. The *Hamadryades* may well have been featured in Gallus' own work, along with other sylvan deities: this hypothesis is supported by *Culex* 94–5 *o pecudes, o Panes et o gratissima tempe / fontis Hamadryadum*, etc.; cf. also Prop. 2.32.37.

62–3 nec carmina nobis / ipsa placent. Song itself, by contrast, was the 'remedy' used by the Cyclops to cure his lovesickness: cf. *id.* 11.17–18; Nemes. *ecl.* 2.14–15 and 4.19. The negative is strengthened by *ipsa* (cf. *Aen.* 4.601–2 *non socios, non ipsum absumere ferro / Ascanium*), which in turn is taken up by *ipsae...siluae*.

63 concedite siluae. Gallus bids farewell to the woods in a rather straightforward manner, as if the *siluae* were animate beings: cf. Plaut. *Amph.* 984 *concedite atque apscedite omnes, de uia decedite*; see *ThlL* IV.7.75–8.54 (note the comitative preverb: cf. 10.62 *Hamadryades*). Contrast the suicidal singer in *E.* 8.58 (*uiuite siluae*), who bade farewell to the woods shortly before jumping into the sea (but cf. Daphnis in *id.* 1.115–18, esp. 117 χαῖρ' Ἀρέθοισα). This is a subtle yet perceptible sign that the setting of this eclogue is an eminently imaginary one. While 10.9–27 outlined the convergence of pastoral figures towards Gallus, and 10.35–60 described Gallus' fascination with the Arcadian *siluae*, now the dream is shattered. Whereas Orpheus had the ability to let the *siluae* follow him (*E.* 3.46), Gallus now sends them away, since they are but a product of his imagination. Contrast [Tib.] 3.9.15 *tunc mihi, tunc placeant siluae*. It should also be remembered that in *ecl.* 6.69–73 Gallus seems to have acquired some power over the trees, because he received from Linus the *calami* with which Hesiod brought down the ash trees (*orni*) from the mountains and which he had to use to sing the Grynean grove.

64 non illum nostri possunt mutare labores. Blind to any type of *labor*, Love cannot be vanquished by anything or anyone. We recall Pan's words at 10.28: *Amor non talia curat* (see below, 10.69n.). For *mutare* used of a person, in the sense of 'changing' behaviour vel sim., cf. *Aen.* 5.679 and 12.240; but see Cic. *Scaur.* 45

498 ECLOGUE 10

(*d*), p. 20.10–11 Olech. *quem purpura regalis non commouit, eum Sardorum mas-
truca mutauit?* (*mutarit* Courtney); cf. Prop. 1.12.11; *OLD²*, pp. 1265–6, s.v.

65–8. The icy landscape shown at 10.23 and 10.47–8 now reappears along with
intense heat (10.67–8). The same opposition was featured in *E.* 1, as Meliboeus set
out to abandon the pastoral world (*E.* 1.64–6 *Afros…Scythiam…Britannos*). Here,
however, the image points to the fact that no location change (not even an imaginary one) can mitigate the god's power. *Amor* does not have any consideration for
labores (10.64), since he has long seized hold of the poet's mind. A moralizing
commonplace of ancient diatribe holds that no journey can distract the mind
from its anxieties: cf. Lucr. 3.1060–75; Hor. *epist.* 1.11.27 *caelum, non animum
mutant qui trans mare currunt*; Sen. *epist.* 28.1 (thus, according to the Cynics, it is
preferable to give up on any intention to travel: Diog. Laert. 6.29). Gallus' last
words (before the final, sententious l. 69) echo a Theocritean passage: 'may you be
on the Edonian mountains in the midst of winter, / facing the river Hebrus, close
to the Bear, / and in summertime may you graze your herd in the remote lands of
the Aethiopians, / at the foot of the Blemyan cliff, where the Nile is nowhere to be
seen' (*id.* 7.111–14: Simichidas' wish to Pan is a pastoral adynaton, a sort of transhumance in reverse, to be actualized should the god refuse to fulfil the herdsman's
prayer). These lines, along with 64, form a fourfold structure (signposted by *non…
nec…-que…nec*) which conveys a sense of definiteness and irrevocability, as in
1.59–63n. Gallus bids farewell to his audience (and to the *E.*) by mentioning the
prospect of a trip to the most remote areas of the world: a similar idea was featured in Meliboeus' farewell at the beginning of the book.

65 frigoribus mediis. Note the intensive use of *medius*: 'right in the middle'.
Gallus has used it at 45 *tela inter media* in reference to himself (which constitutes
an argument in favour of *me* at 10.44, given that 'egocentric' repetitions are typical
of his monologue: see 10.44n.). For other occurrences in V., cf. *G.* 3.486 *saepe in
honore deum medio stans hostia ad aram*; *Aen.* 1.242; 2.665; 7.296; note also
Catull. 64.149. For a similar use of *medius,* but in reference to heath, and without
any particular emphasis, cf. *G.* 3.154 *mediis feruoribus.* **Hebrumque bibamus.** A
reference to Thrace and its proverbially cold climate: the Hebrus, now the Marica
(in Bulgaria, and further east forming the border between Greece and Turkey), is
the region's main river, previously mentioned at *id.* 7.112 (cf. 10.65–8n.); see
Philipp. *Anth. Pal.* 9.56.1 = *GPh* 2879 G.-P.; Hor. *carm.* 3.25.10; *epist.* 1.3.3. Thrace
is also the setting of Orpheus' death in *G.* 4, where the river Hebrus is said to
carry his severed head (*G.* 4.524 *gurgite…medio portans Oeagrius Hebrus*). V. will
mention the river one last time in the finale of the *Aeneid* (12.331–2): *qualis apud
gelidi cum flumina concitus Hebri / sanguineus Mauors,* etc. For the idea of 'drinking from a river' in the sense of 'inhabiting a region', cf. *E.* 1.62n.

66 Sithoniasque niues. The epithet refers to the Sithonians, a Thracian population inhabiting the middle peninsula of Chalcidice (therefore called Sithonia:
Herodot. 7.122). According to Pliny, *nat.* 4.41, they were among Orpheus'

ECLOGUE 10   499

ancestors; cf. also Lycophr. *Alex.* 1357. Thus, the Sithonians are somewhat similar to the Edonians mentioned in Theocr. *id.* 7.111 (on the southern coast of Thrace, near the mouth of the Strymon river). The implicit allusion to Chalcidice, however, may also hint at Chalcis in Euboea (cf. Strab. 7, fr. 11 [Epit. Vat.]; see l. 50 *Chalcidico...uersu* [n.]). Significantly, the epithet Sithonius is paralleled in Euphorion himself: fr. 58.2 Pow. = 63.2 v. Gron. = 98.2 Light.; cf. Parthen. fr. 33.3 Light. = 29.3 Mar.; note also Hor. *carm.* 3.26.10. **hiemis...aquosae.** For this 'watery winter' (here, *hiems* ≠ 'storm'), cf. *id.* 7.11 χείματι μέσσῳ. In other words: 'in the midst of winter', naturally full of rain and snow, Gallus imagines himself opting for the Sithonian land. Cf. *Aen.* 9.670–1 *cum Iuppiter horridus Austris / torquet aquosam hiemem et caelo caua nubila rumpit.*

67 cum moriens alta liber aret in ulmo. Summer, which l. 68 describes in astronomical terms, is here visualized through the withering of the inner bark (the *liber*, naturally damp: cf. *G.* 2.77 *udo...libro*) on the top of an elm tree, in other words, the part most exposed to summer heat; *alta* here points to height, as in *G.* 2.389 *ex alta...pinu.* The considerable dimensions of the tree (if left to their own devices, elm trees can grow taller than 20–30 metres: note *aeria* in *E.* 1.58 quoted below) seem to rule out that V. is referring to the 'arboretum' variety of elm trees, commonly used to support vines. As a result, we must reject Conington's ingenious conjecture *Liber* (i.e. Liber/Bacchus = the vine would be described as *moriens*). Note the adjective *alta*, which does not appear in a passage like Manil. 3.262 *Liber grauida descendit plenus ab ulmo.* On the need for treating the *liber* with caution, especially while cutting or grafting, see Cat. *agr.* 40.2 and 45.1–2. In this case, therefore, the damage is irreversible and deadly to the tree (cf. *moriens*). Elm trees, known for being quite large, were called 'aerial' in Tityrus' locus amoenus: *nec gemere aeria cessabit turtur ab ulmo* (*E.* 1.58n.): note the contrastive echo of the first eclogue (that 'aerial' elm tree, which once hosted the turtledove and its song, is now withering away). Similarly, 10.9 *ueteres, iam fracta cacumina, fagos* is a sad echo of 2.2 *densas, umbrosa cacumina, fagos.* While Gallus had imagined young, green trees at 10.53–4, he is now in front of a huge tree killed by the heat. For the two verbs in a similar context, cf. *E.* 7.57 *aret ager, uitio moriens sitit aëris herba.*

68 Aethiopum uersemus ouis. A variation on Theocritus' paradoxical theme at *id.* 7.113–14 (see above, 10.65–8n.). Now, however, ownership of flocks is attributed to the Aethiopians themselves, whose land is certainly not renowned as a prosperous livestock-rearing region (cf. Claud. 24.336–7 H. *armentaque longe / uastant Aethiopum* [where the subject is *leones*]). Inhabiting the desert near the southernmost part of Egypt, the Aethiopians were etymologically associated with heat (cf. αἴθω 'to burn'): cf. Manil. 4.758–9 *ardent Aethiopes Cancro, cui plurimus ignis: / hoc color ipse docet*; Hyg. *astr.* 1.8.3 *qui autem proximi sunt aestiuo circulo, eos Aethiopas et perusto corpore esse*; Isid. *orig.* 14.5.14. For the Aethiopians as the most remote of all human populations, cf. Hom. *Od.* 1.23 (in *Il.* 1.423 and 23.205 their land is said to border on the ocean); see also *Aen.* 4.480–1, as well as *E.* 8.44

500   ECLOGUE 10

extremi Garamantes (n.); see further *Enc. Virg.* II, pp. 404–6, s.v. *Etiopi* (V. La Bua). **uersemus**. The verb, which has been suspected of textual corruption (some, for instance, prefer the emendation *seruemus*), points to a particularly laborious task that is typical of animal husbandry, i.e. the herdsman's action of leading the herd into a different direction. Note, for comparison, Prop. 3.5.35 *uersare boues et plaustra* (where the ploughman is Bootes). The term, therefore, seems to contribute to the general force of these lines, hinting at vain effort (cf. above, 10.64 *labores*, as well as 66n.). The whole passage is V.'s reworking of Theocritus' absurd transhumance (see above, 10.65–8n.; note τετραμμένος in *id.* 7.112, which is notoriously difficult to interpret: albeit used in a different context, it might have prompted V. to write *uersemus*). On the hardy nature of African (Libyan) herdsmen, cf. *G.* 3.339–48. **sub sidere Cancri**. 'Under the star of Cancer': in other words, the month after the summer solstice (which is itself an important marker of astronomical revolutions: *uersare*?). Here, following a reference to the Aethiopians, the reader's mind might wander towards the tropic of Cancer, named after the constellation: cf. German. 459–81; Manil. 4.758.

69 omnia uincit Amor: et nos cedamus Amori. Towards the end of *E.* 2, Corydon exclaimed: *me tamen urit amor: quis enim modus adsit amori?* (2.68). Gallus, in the last line he utters (note the numerical similarity to Corydon's song), declares his surrender. The statement is also similar to Corydon's in terms of bipartite structure and rhythm (note the masculine caesura and the polyptoton, affecting the same parts of the hexameter). Besides implicitly answering Corydon's question, Gallus also responds to Pan's words: 10.28 *ecquis erit modus?* (in fact, Gallus ends up accepting a truth that the god had immediately presented to him, namely that Love is never satiated with tears: see above, 10.28–30 and 61n.). Thus, the lover's *labores* (10.64) are inevitably fruitless. For the vocabulary of struggle and victory (with a similar wording), cf. *G.* 1.145–6 *labor omnia uicit / improbus* (for *improbus* used of *Amor*, cf. *E.* 8.49–50; note, however, the difference between the farmer's *labor* and Gallus'); see also *G.* 3.244 *amor omnibus idem*. It bears observing that *omnia uincit Amor* is a perfect half-pentameter, in which the caesura facilitates the prosody (the /o/ in *Amor* is long, which is etymologically correct: cf. *Aen.* 11.323): the lengthening in arsis can be read as an emphatic expression, further underscored here by a caesura, in both syntax and meaning (cf. 9.66n.). The dictum, destined to become famous, is echoed by Orpheus in Ov. *met.* 10.26 *uicit Amor*, as well as 10.29 *uos quoque iunxit Amor* (note the similar, pentametric rhythm); see also *amor.* 3.2.46; *her.* 9.26; Tib. 1.4.40 *obsequio plurima uincet amor*; *Ciris* 437 *omnia uicit Amor: quid enim non uinceret ille?* (also 427 *scelus omnia uicit*); Prop. 1.9.28 *nec…cedat Amor* (cf. 1.14.8). The proverbial nature of the assertion is confirmed by Macr. *Sat.* 5.16.7; see further Otto (1890, p. 17, no. 74); Tosi (2007, pp. 639–40, no. 1412). Menander's Moschion abandoned his 'manly' pursuits (war in his case, not hunting) due to the veto of his 'master' Eros: Men. *Sam.* 630–2 [see above, 10.31–69n.]. **uincit**. The transmitted reading *uincit* (note

ECLOGUE 10   501

P) is also attested in Macr. *Sat*. 5.16.7 and 5.14.5; note, however, *uincet* in **M** and *uicit* in **R**.

70–7. These last eight lines, symmetrically corresponding to the eight-line prologue, function as the epilogue of both *E*. 10 and the *E*. as a whole. The notion of 'fullness' or 'satiety', expressed both at the beginning (10.70) and at the end (10.77) of the passage, refers to the limit by which the poet himself must abide. This is not, however, a simple 'afterthought' added to the rest of *E*. 10, since the idea of 'just measure' is deeply opposed to Gallus' 'immoderate' passion. V. depicts himself as an industrious herdsman, attending to his task (10.71n.). He thereby takes shelter in the world of narrative (i.e. objective) poetry, which contrasts rather sharply with Gallus' self-centred subjectivity. To his friend, however, V. addresses affectionate words, using the term *amor* one last time (10.73), along with an image of arboreal growth (cf. 10.54). V. perhaps wants to actualize, as far as possible, at least one of Gallus' pastoral reveries. The last three lines (10.75–7) seal the pastoral book and prepare V.'s transition towards the *Georgics* (see n. ad loc.).

70 Haec sat erit. For the phrase as a marker of conclusion, cf. *E*. 3.111 *sat prata biberunt*; note also *E*. 4.54 and 7.34. The prescriptive future allows the poet-herdsman to impose limits on poetry itself, as well as on the goats' grazing at 10.77 (note *saturae*, which has the same root as *sat/satis*). **diuae**. Cf. below, 10.72n. **uestrum...poetam**. The poet 'belongs' to the Pierides: cf. 9.32n. V. perhaps intentionally applies the Greek term to himself. Contrast the more solemn noun *uates*, often appearing in the *E*. (see 5.45n.; in 10.17, Gallus is a 'divine' *poeta*).

71 dum sedet et gracili fiscellam texit hibisco. At the end of such a lively poem as *E*. 10, the poet reveals that, while he was singing (10.70 *cecinisse*), he kept weaving a basket. The temporal clause with *dum* outlines the pastoral landscape, as in 10.7 *dum tenera attondent simae uirgulta capellae* (note the symmetry between prologue and epilogue). Tending to a useful task had diverted Corydon's attention from his obsessive passion for Alexis in *E*. 2.71–2 (note that *hibiscus* only occurs here and in Corydon's poem: 2.30). No wonder, however, that the 'new' Corydon is V., not Gallus (esp. considering 10.60–9). For the image of weaving baskets, cf. *G*. 1.266 (*facilis rubea texatur fiscina uirga*), in a passage concerning the tasks of a farmer forced by inclement weather to stay indoors: the new poem on farming is about to begin (cf. below, 10.75–7n.). For the *fiscella* as a tool used in cheese-making, see Tib. 2.3.15; Colum. 7.8.3. In his description of the cups at the outset of *id*. 1, Theocritus mentioned a boy absorbed by the task of weaving (πλέκειν) rushes together in order to make a little cage for crickets, perhaps an allegory of the pastoral poetry: *id*. 1.52–4 (whereas Europa's basket at Mosch. *Eur*. 37–43, a work of Hephaestus, was made of gold). A woven garland functions as a metaphorical substitute of the poetic collection (even in its 'title') in Meleager, who presents his στέφανος as his poetic work in both his well-known introductory epigram and in the epigram that most probably concluded the anthology: cf. *Anth. Pal*. 4.1.1–3 (note also 4.1.5 ἐμπλέξας; 4.1.9 πλέξας; 4.1.58 ἡδυεπὴς στέφανος

502 ECLOGUE 10

in the last line); *Anth. Pal.* 12.257.6 συμπλέξαι μουσοπόλον στέφανον (= respectively, *HE* 3926–8 [3930; 3934; 3983]; 4727 G.-P.). Here, metapoetic overtones were detected by Servius, especially in V.'s choice of the epithet *gracili* (Serv. ad loc.: *allegoricos autem significat se composuisse hunc libellum tenuissimo stilo*), symmetrical to *E.* 1.2 *tenui…auena*. Both passages are echoed in the first line of the pseudo-Virgilian pre-proem to the *Aeneid*: *ille ego qui quondam gracili modulatus auena*. Note also that the verb *texere* is commonly used of literary texts, or 'textures': cf. Cic. *fam.* 9.21.1. The basket is a symbolic placeholder for the book itself, since the latter, too, is made of patiently interwoven themes and forms (as the reader, by now, knows well). Tityrus' *fiscella* (= the end of V.'s *E.*) will be the starting point of Nemesianus' first eclogue, at the beginning of the day: *dum fiscella tibi fluuiali, Tityre, iunco / texitur* (*ecl.* 1.1–2; 8 *primi…clementia solis*; cf. 10.7n.). In Theocritus' *id.* 11, the model of V.'s *E.* 2, the Cyclops starts 'weaving baskets' to distract himself from his passion for Galatea: αἴ κ᾽ ἐνθὼν ταλάρως τε πλέκοις (*id.* 11.73). If *id.* 11 was the last of ten consecutive idylls in the Theocritean edition used by V. (see Introduction, pp. 19–20), then *E.* 10.71 (the seventh-to-last line in the *E.*) would be an important echo of the seventh-to-last line in the Cyclops' monologue (the ninth-to-last line counting the two concluding lines: Theocr. *id.* 11.80–1).

72 Pierides. An unambiguous reference to the Muses (contrast above, 10.10n.). The epithet, used as an attribute to the substantive adj. *diuae* (10.70; cf. *Aen.* 7.645), is emphasized by its postponement. For the term, cf. *E.* 3.85n. **uos haec facietis maxima Gallo.** For the notion, cf. Theocr. *id.* 10.24–5: 'Pierian Muses, sing with me the sinuous / maiden: whatever you touch, o goddesses, you make beautiful [ὧν γὰρ χ᾽ ἅψησθε, θεαί, καλὰ πάντα ποεῖτε]'. The adj. will reappear in the context of future fame (but with a more specific force) at *Aen.* 8.271–2 *aram…quae maxima semper / dicetur nobis et erit quae maxima semper*. The Muses' 'poietic' intervention is also featured in a fragment of Gallus' own work (see *E.* 9.2–3n.): *tandem fecerunt carmina Musae* (4.1 Bläns. = 2.6 Court.); note also Euphor. fr. 118 Pow. = 122 v. Gron. = 120 Light. Μοῦσαι ἐποιήσαντο; cf. *E.* 9.32–3 *et me fecere poetam / Pierides*.

72–3 Gallo, / Gallo. Note the repetition elegantly distributed over two lines: V. wants to mention his friend one more time before concluding. But repeated names are a typically pastoral feature, here highlighting the end of the Arcadian-elegiac interlude (cf. 10.75–7n.).

73–4. Even though the poem's coda has already begun, V. addresses some final, affectionate words to his friend. Perhaps Gallus' *amores* will not grow together with the young Arcadian trees (10.54n.), but V.'s *amor* for his friend certainly *crescit*, like a young alder tree in spring (10.74). In a context of closure such as this passage, the phrase *uere nouo* hints at future novelties and possibilities: the *E.* are coming to an end, but the poet perceives new energies foreshadowing future poems. Note that, after the general proem, the *Georgics* enter their subject in the

ECLOGUE 10   503

same words (*G.* 1.43 *uere nouo, gelidus canis cum montibus umor* etc.). On the idea that the finale of the *E.* gestures towards V.'s next poem cf. 10.75–7n.

73 in horas. The variant reading *in hora* (**P**) would imply that the tree's growth can be observed during a single hour. The correct reading *in horas* is readily explained as an intensification of the more common *in dies* (thus: 'from hour to hour'); cf. Catull. 38.3 *et magis magis in dies et horas.*

74 se subicit. For the phrase, in the sense of 'soaring high', cf. *G.* 2.19 (as well as 4.385); for a slightly different formulation, cf. *E.* 9.7 *se subducere colles.* The young tree (*uiridis*) is in the prime of its verdancy, during springtime (*uere nouo*: cf. *G.* 2.323–45; also 1.43 quoted above, 10.73–4). The thematic interests of the future georgic poet start to become clear: cf. also 10.76n. **alnus.** Alders have been mentioned at 6.63 *proceras erigit alnos* (n.), where their imposing height is a result of the poetic metamorphosis of the *Phaethontiades* at the hands of Silenus. The comparison between *amor* and alders (73–4 *tantum...quantum*) suits Gallus, who received Hesiod's pipe at *E.* 6.69–71 (a 'magical' instrument used to lead ash trees down a mountain: cf. 6.71 *rigidas deducere montibus ornos*), even though at 10.54 he merely uses the vague term *arboribus* to refer to the trees' growth. V., for his part, speaks like a true connoisseur who knows the growth patterns of each plant species very well. The *alnus*, typical of humid and marshy landscapes, adds a local, familiar touch to the last eclogue (cf. 6.63n.; note also the geographical location of Phaethon on the banks of the Po river in some versions of the myth: 6.62n.). Furthermore, the alder sounds familiar in a finale on Gallus: in *E.* 6, the *alni* and Gallus are mentioned in the same breath (6.63 and 6.64, respectively).

75–7. Following *haec sat erit* (10.70), another verb signalling conclusion (10.75 *surgamus*) clarifies that this is, in fact, the end. In its coda, the pastoral book goes back to the 'shadowy' dimension which had inaugurated it, and which was previously featured in the finale of *E.* 1 (cf. 1.83, as well as 2.67; 6.86; see below, 10.75–6n.). However, while the initial *fagus* protectively welcomed Tityrus, now the juniper's shadow is burdensome (*grauis*), prompting the singer to leave. The epilogue not only corresponds to that of the *G.*, which alludes to the first line of the *E.*, thereby strengthening the continuity between V.'s two 'rural' works; it also introduces by contrast the opening of the *G.* themselves (see 10.73–4n.; 10.74n.; 10.76n.; 77n.; cf. also 1.74n.). Through this kind of 'editorial' connection, the finale of a poetic work looks forward to the next poem. For a precedent, cf. Callimachus' *Aitia* (see 10.75n.); note also the farewell speech in *Catal.* 5, generally considered to be authentic (though without absolute certainty; cf. 10.77n.). Here, a further marker of conclusion is the accumulation of typically pastoral traits of style such as repetitions and incidental phrases used colloquially (10.77). Finally, as in a meditative murmur, these lines display a 'fade-out' effect. Various tasks of everyday life in the countryside (fear of illness; late evening; a flock to be brought back) are mingled with fragments of rural wisdom. The reader perceives an unusual sense of chorality: different voices merge together and begin

504   ECLOGUE 10

to fade away. The goats return home (10.77 *domum*), and the *E.* come to an end
on a note of serenity (in contrast to Gallus' trips to distant and inhospitable
lands: cf. 10.46–9; 65–9). Note the contrastive echo of *E.* 1, which ended with the
'exile' of Meliboeus and his animals, handed over to a new owner (cf. 10.77n.).

75 surgamus. The poet now stands up (cf. 71 *dum sedet*) and points to the way
home. He will obviously follow the flock, now ready to go (10.77n.). Verbs of
motion are common in V.'s epilogues (cf. *E.* 9.67; see e.g. Hor. *sat.* 1.10.92; 2.1.86;
epist. 2.2.215–16; note also *epod.* 17.81). Note, however, the important parallel with
the finale of Callimachus' *Aitia*, which the author probably envisioned as marking
a transition towards the *Iambi*: αὐτὰρ ἐγὼ Μουσέων πεζὸν ἔπειμι νομόν 'but I am
going to the walking pasture of the Muses' (fr. 112.9 Pf. = 215.9 Mass. = 112.9
Hard.); cf. also Ov. *amor.* 3.15.18. The idea of 'satiety', introduced in 10.70 (cf.
10.72 *haec*), suggests that it is time for the poet to move on to something new and
different: thus, *surgamus* implies the beginning of an ascent from the *humiles
myricae* (*E.* 4.2) to something higher. Similarly, Gallus reached new literary
heights at 6.65 (*Aonas in montis*). Both poet and reader are now 'full' like the
goats, and it is right for them to stand up and go (recall the well-known Lucr.
3.938 *cur non ut plenus uitae conuiua recedis?*). **solet esse grauis cantantibus
umbra.** The poet's predilection for the sun recalls the statement made by the har-
vester Milon towards the end of Theocr. *id.* 10, in which he contrasted himself
with Buceus and his unhappy love: ταῦτα χρὴ μόχθεντας ἐν ἁλίῳ ἄνδρας ἀείδειν
'this [= a work song, transmitting agricultural precepts] is what men must sing
who toil in the sun' (*id.* 10.56); for the georgic implication, cf. below, 10.76n.

75–6 umbra, / ...umbra...umbrae. The word, a key pastoral term, is repeated
three times (with epanalepsis) and placed in three conspicuous metrical positions: at the end of 10.75 and 76, as well as at the end of the first half-line in 10.76.
Cf. *E.* 1.83 *maioresque cadunt altis de montibus umbrae*; 2.67 *et sol crescentis decedens duplicat umbras.* Note also the final line of the *Aeneid* (12.952): V.'s epic
poem ends with a mention of the *umbrae* (of the underworld) towards which
Turnus descends: *uitaque cum gemitu fugit indignata sub umbras.*

76 iuniperi grauis umbra. This is a final echo of Lucretius' Epicurean teachings: cf. Lucr. 6.783–5 *arboribus primum certis grauis umbra tributa / usque adeo,
capitis faciant ut saepe dolores, / si quis eas subter iacuit prostratus in herbis* (the
notion is all the more helpful to those who follow the ideal lifestyle described in
Lucr. 2.29–30). The ancients believed that the shadow of certain trees could harm
people and plants. Such popular beliefs occasionally made their way into ancient
science and survived in farming communities up to the modern age. The popular
view is sometimes confirmed by science, as is the case with walnut trees, which
actually 'protect' themselves from other plants by producing a toxin called
juglone: cf. Plin. *nat.* 17.89 *quaedam umbrarum proprietas: iuglandum grauis et
noxia, etiam capiti humano omnibusque iuxta satis.* No further evidence suggests
that similar powers were also ascribed to the juniper, in Latin *iuniperus*, which

ECLOGUE 10   505

corresponds to the Greek ἄρκευθος or κέδρος (the latter, properly speaking, is known as prickly cedar or prickly juniper, i.e. *Iuniperus Oxycedrus*). The only mentions of this plant species in V. are found here and at *E*. 7.53. For ἄρκευθος cf. esp. Theocr. *id*. 1.133 ἁ δὲ καλὰ νάρκισσος ἐπ᾽ ἀρκεύθοισι κομάσαι; 5.97. As for κέδρος, its scented branches burn in Calypso's fireplace (*Od*. 5.59–60); see further Theophr. *hist. plant*. 3.12.3 (note παρόμοιον δὲ τῇ ἀρκεύθῳ). The juniper's shadow is, of course, quite dense, and the ancients described the plant as 'warm' (cf. Theophr. *caus. plant*. 1.21.6; Diosc. 1.75; Galen. 11.836–7 Kühn; see also Plin. *nat*. 24.54). Its medicinal powers, known to ancient science and popular wisdom, might explain V.'s idea that an incorrect use of the plant (including its shadow) can prove harmful. If eaten in excessive quantities, juniper berries can cause headaches according to Oribas. *cols. med*. 1.46.2 τὴν κεφαλὴν θερμαίνουσι καὶ ὀδυνῶσιν (note, generally, Lucr. 6.784 *capitis faciant ut saepe dolores* and, specifically on walnut trees, Plin. *nat*. 17.89 *etiam capiti humano*, both quoted above). For the use of junipers as a remedy or deterrent against snakes (whose blood is naturally 'cold'), cf. Nic. *ther*. 584; cf., again, Plin. *nat*. 24.54 (as well as Apoll. Rhod. 4.156). Note the 'softening' effect of the feminine caesura, here used along with both hephthemimeral and trithemimeral. **nocent et frugibus umbrae**. The quality of shadows is of interest to Theocritean shepherds (cf. *id*. 5.48–9), but here the epilogue marks an 'editorial' transition, explicitly foreshadowing the Hesiodic concerns of the (imminent) georgic singer. The *G*., in fact, will begin with the question of 'what gladdens the crops' (*quid faciat laetas segetes*: note how *faciat* emphasizes action and the Hesiodic ἔργον/*labor*). The new poem will immediately mention the 'most luminous stars in the universe' (the sun and the moon), sharply contrasting with *umbrae* (*G*. 1.5–6 *clarissima mundi lumina*; cf. also *G*. 1.1 *quo sidere*). The notion highlighted at *E*. 10.76 will itself appear in *G*. 1.121 (*umbra nocet*); cf. also *G*. 1.157 *falce premes umbras* (contrast *Aen*. 1.441: *lucus...laetissimus umbrae*). The disadvantages of *umbra* are ultimately a georgic problem: cf. *G*. 1.191–2; 2.410–11 (as herdsmen know, it is not a good sign when animals seek shelter in the shade too often: *G*. 3.464–9). After echoing V.'s treatment of eros in the *E*. and the Hamadryades of *E*. 10, Propertius reworks V.'s transition from the pastoral domain to georgic questions (i.e. what do plants benefit from?): *tu canis Ascraei ueteris praecepta poetae, / quo seges in campo, quo uiret uua iugo* (Prop. 2.34.77–8).

77 **ite domum saturae, uenit Hesperus, ite capellae**. The goats, which 10.7 described as grazing on soft grass, are now full and ready to go home: cf. *E*. 7.44 *ite domum pasti, si quis pudor, ite iuuenci*. Here, Meliboeus' melancholic words are echoed one last time, though it is obviously a contrastive echo (note the emphasis on *domum*): *ite meae, felix quondam pecus, ite capellae* (1.74n.); the book's opening farewell now brings it to a close. The repeated verb (*ite*), here and in the two occurrences quoted above, emphasizes the mimetic aspects of V.'s pastoral style: the lively imperative is typical of everyday speech, and V. will use it again at

506 ECLOGUE 10

Aen. 9.116–17; cf., for instance, Plaut. *Cas.* 834; *Truc.* 551; note also Prop. 4.9.16–17 *ite boues, // Herculis ite boues, nostrae labor ultime clauae* (an interesting reworking of *E.* 10); [Tib.] 3.6.7; Ov. *met.* 3.562; Calp. *ecl.* 2.55; Petron. 115.14; Stat. *Theb.* 6.809. Particularly interesting is the use of the repeated *ite* in *Catal.* 5 (often considered authentic), where it has the familiar function of signalling the transition from one phase to the next: *ite hinc…ite, rhetorum ampullae* (1)…*nos ad beatos uela mittimus portus* (8); and again *ite hinc, Camenae…ite* (11). In *Catal.* 5, the poet (perhaps a young V.?) highlights his own experience of a transition between rhetoric and poetry to Epicurean philosophy, with clear implications for his literary output (note the final invocation to the *Camenae*: he asks them to come back and visit him every now and then, *Catal.* 5.14). **saturae.** The notion of satiety, i.e. what puts an end to something because we have enough of it (note that *satur* is etymologically connected to *sat/satis* 'enough'), suits the poem's conclusion very well; cf. 3.111 *claudite iam riuos, pueri; sat prata biberunt* (the last line of V.'s third eclogue). The satiety principle can be applied to life itself, as in Lucr. 3.960 *satur ac plenus possis discedere rerum*, or to poetry and literature in general (cf. Varr. *Men.* 144 Buech. = Astb.[2] [= 131 Cèb.] *saturis auribus scolica dape*; note also Mart. 11.108.1–2 *tam longo possis satur esse libello, / lector*, opening the last epigram in the book). The poet, concerned with the goats' satiety, abides by the orders of Apollo, who in *E.* 6.4–5 exhorted Tityrus to keep his flock 'fat'. By gathering his flock, however, V. might also allude to the conclusion of the pastoral book: cf. Artemidorus of Tarsus in *Anth. Pal.* 9.205 (see Introduction p. 19). The god Pan, an authority on pastoral matters, observes the goats' insatiability at 10.30 *nec cytiso saturantur apes nec fronde capellae*, but here the poet-herdsman has enough jurisdiction to establish that the *capellae* (and the readers) have already had sufficient food, in both the literal and the metaphorical sense (grass and poetry: cf. 10.70n.). In any event, it is getting late. **uenit Hesperus.** The evening star, as in the finale of *E.* 6, signals the end of the day, of grazing, and of singing (cf. 6.86 *Vesper* [n.], as well as Nemes. *ecl.* 2.90 *Hesperus*). Here, however, Hesperus is almost personified, and its arrival underscores the idea of motion expressed by the repeated *ite* (contrast, in *E.* 6.86, the astronomical term *processit*; note also the proverbial phrase *quid Vesper serus uehat* in *G.* 1.461). The conclusion of the preceding poem (*E.* 9.67 *cum uenerit ipse*) is also echoed. Note the bucolic diaeresis, underscoring the pastoral nature of this final line; see 1.7n.; Introduction, p. 29. In the Homeric poems, the arrival of the night often signals the end of both action and song (as in *Il.* 1): here, the evening star marks the final line of the *E.* The *Georgics* will begin with a question concerning stars (*G.* 1.1 *quo sidere*). **capellae.** The goats, a symbol of the *E.* from the very beginning (*E.* 1.12; 74; 77), appear now at the end of the book.

Bibliography

Bibliographical resources, editions and commentaries, and translations are listed in chronological order under, respectively, §§1, 2, and 3 (in the introduction and in the commentary, they are normally referred to by the author's name alone). Articles, various contributions, and books (including editions of, and commentaries on, single eclogues) are cited by author and year and listed in alphabetical order under §4. Reference works are cited in abbreviated form, by author and without publication date (e.g. H.-Sz.), and listed also under §4. Within the volume, the publications not directly pertaining to V.'s *Eclogues* are cited with essential bibliographical details, while subsequent references, if any, are abbreviated and cross-referred to the first mention. Abbreviations used for journals, periodicals, and reference works conform generally to the *Année Philologique* standards.

1. Bibliographical Resources

Briggs W. W., *A Bibliography of Virgil's Eclogues (1927–1977)*, in *ANRW*, II.31.2, Berlin-New York 1981, pp. 1267–1357 (both parts of vol. II.31 are entirely dedicated to Virgilian issues).

De Nonno M., De Paolis P., Di Giovine C., *Bibliografia della letteratura latina*, in G. Cavallo, P. Fedeli, A. Giardina (eds.), *Lo spazio letterario di Roma antica*, Rome 1991, vol. V, pp. 336–62.

Virgilian bibliographies of varying scope and quality can readily be accessed through a number of websites; note also the bibliographical lists periodically published by the journal *Vergilius*. Two indispensable reference works, to be consulted on any topic, are the *Enciclopedia Virgiliana*, edited by F. Della Corte (Rome 1984–91; esp. s.v. *Bucoliche* [vol. I, pp. 540–83]) and *The Virgil Encyclopedia*, edited by R. F. Thomas and J. M. Ziolkowski (Chichester-Malden MA, 2013). Both works are referred to in both the *Introduction* and the *Commentary* as *Enc. Virg.* and *Virg. Enc.* respectively. V.'s reception, a widely studied subject, would deserve a separate treatment. The reception of V.'s works is closely tied to the late antique and medieval portrayal of the poet as a 'wizard' and a 'prophet', which has been examined in Comparetti (1872). On the *E.* and V.'s fundamental role in the Western tradition of pastoral poetry, see Curtius (1948, p. 195 = 1953, p. 190 = 1992, p. 214); for a useful, recent overview cf. *Virg. Enc.* I, pp. 401–3, s.v. *Eclogues, reception of* (P. Alpers). On V.'s medieval and modern reception, with a focus on the *E.* and the 'pastoral' genre, see esp. Gercke (1921), followed by a number of later contributions: Poggioli (1975); Halperin (1983, pp. 1–72); La Penna (1983); Lerner (1984); Cardwell, Hamilton (1986); Patterson (1987); Kallendorf (1990, p. 97); Ziolkowski (1993); Alpers (1996); Martindale (1997); Gifford (1999); Connolly (2001); Fo (2002, pp. 191–9); Heaney (2003); Lindheim (2005); Anagnostou-Laoutides (2006–7); Harrison (2008); Sirignano (2009); Wallace (2010); Wilson-Okamura (2010); Bernardi Perini (2012a); (2012b); Heaney (2013); Fo (2015); Houghton, Sgarbi (2018); Fernandelli (2019); Houghton (2019); see also Hollander (1993), a work specifically devoted to V.'s reception in Dante's *Divine Comedy*, featuring useful quotations from the sources and extensive bibliographical references (though the *E.*, it seems, are much less

508 BIBLIOGRAPHY

crucial to Dante than the *Georgics* and the *Aeneid*; see, however, my note on *E.* 1.27; further Combs-Schilling 2015 on Dante's *Eclogues*); for helpful studies of the *E.*'s reception, see Freyburger-Galland (2013) and others in *AAntHung*, 53, 1–2 (2013) (note also the *Introduction* by Johnston, Papaioannou 2013). On Virgilian reception more generally, besides the aforementioned Kallendorf (1990), see also Kallendorf (2012, 2015, and 2020): a series of studies that subtly combines the material aspect of transmission with the broader context of literary reception at large.

2. Editions and Commentaries

De La Cerda J. L., *P. Virgilii Maronis Bucolica et Georgica Argumentis Explicationibus, Notis illustrata*, Lugduni 1619 (Madrid 1608).

Heyne C. G., *Publius Virgilius Maro illustratus*, vol. I, Leipzig 1767 (4th ed. revised by G. P. E. Wagner, Leipzig 1830).

Martyn J., *The Bucolics of Vergil*, Oxford 1820[4].

Voss J. H., *Publius Vergilius Maro. Ländliche Gedichte*, Altona 1830[2] (1797[1]).

Ribbeck O., *P. Vergili Maronis Opera*, vol. I.2, *Bucolica et Georgica*, Leipzig 1859; 1894[2] (with *Prolegomena critica ad P. Vergili Maronis opera maiora*, Leipzig 1866).

Forbiger A., *P. Vergili Maronis Opera*, vol. I, *Bucolica et Georgica*, Leipzig 1872[4] (1836[1]).

Klouček W., *P. Vergili Maronis Opera*, I–II, Lipsiae 1886.

Stampini E., *Le Bucoliche di Virgilio*, vol. I, *Ecloghe 1–5*, Turin 1889 (1947).

Conington J., Nettleship H., *P. Vergili Maronis Opera*, vol. I, *Eclogues and Georgics*, London 1898[5] (1872[3]; Conington 1858[1]).

Page T. E., *P. Vergilii Maronis Bucolica et Georgica*, London 1898[1] (1965).

Albini G., *P. Virgilio Marone. I carmi bucolici*, Bologna 1898–9[1]; 1937[3].

Güthling O., *P. Vergili Maronis: Bucolica et Georgica*, Leipzig 1904.

Plessis F., *Virgile. Oeuvres*, Paris 1913.

Hosius K., *P. Vergili Maronis Bucolica: cum auctoribus et imitatoribus in usum scholarum*, Bonn 1915.

Ladewig T., Schaper C., Deuticke P., Jahn P., *Vergils Gedichte*, vol. I, *Bukolika und Georgika*, Berlin 1915[9].

Fairclough H. R., *Virgil 1: Eclogues, Georgics, Aeneid I–VI*, Cambridge MA, 1916; 1932[2] (revised by G. P. Goold, 1999).

Sabbadini R., *P. Vergili Maronis Opera*, vol. I, *Bucolica et Georgica*, Rome 1930; 1937[2] (revised by L. Castiglioni, Turin 1944).

Tovar A., *Virgilio. Eglogas*, Madrid 1936.

De Saint-Denis E., *Virgile. Bucoliques*, Paris 1942 (1967[2]).

Stégen G., *Commentaire sur cinq Bucoliques de Virgile (3, 6, 8, 9, 10)*, Namur 1957.

Holtorf H., *P. Vergilius Maro: Die größeren Gedichte*, vol. I, *Einleitung. Bucolica*, Freiburg-Munich 1959.

Perret J., *Les Bucoliques*, Paris 1961; 1978[3].

Della Corte F., *Virgilio. Le Bucoliche*, Milan 1967[12] (= Genoa 1985, with Italian translation; 1939[1]).

Mynors R. A. B., *Vergili Opera*, Oxford 1969 (reprinted with corrections 1972).

La Penna A., Grassi C., *Virgilio. Le opere. Antologia*, Florence 1971 (commentary on *E.* 1; 4; 8; 9).

Geymonat M., *P. Vergili Maronis Opera*, Turin 1973 (Rome 2008[2]).

Coleman R., *Vergil. Eclogues*, Cambridge 1977.

Coleiro E., *An Introduction to Vergil's Bucolics with a Critical Edition of the Text*, Amsterdam 1979.

Williams R. D., *Virgil. The Eclogues & Georgics*, New York 1979.
Day Lewis C., *Virgil. The Eclogues and Georgics*, Oxford 1983.
Götte J. und M., *Vergil: Landleben. Bucolica, Georgica, Catalepton*, Munich 1987[5] (including the *Vitae Vergilianae*, edited by K. Bayer; J. Götte: 1949[1]).
Clausen W. V., *A Commentary on Virgil, Eclogues*, Oxford 1994.
Traina A., *Virgilio. L'utopia e la storia. Il libro XII dell'Eneide e antologia delle opere*, Turin 1997 (2004[3]; anastatic reprint, with Afterword: Bologna 2017) (commentary on *E.* 1; 4; 9).
Gioseffi M., *P. Virgilio Marone. Bucoliche*, Milan 1998 (2005[2]).
Van Sickle J., *Virgil's Book of Bucolics, the Ten Eclogues Translated into English Verse: Framed by Cues for Reading Aloud and Clues for Threading Texts and Themes*, Baltimore 2011.
Cucchiarelli A., *Publio Virgilio Marone, Le Bucoliche*, translation by A. Traina, Rome 2012.
Ottaviano S., in *P. Vergilius Maro, Bucolica*, edidit et apparatu critico instruxit S. Ottaviano, *Georgica*, edidit et apparatu critico instruxit G. B. Conte, Berlin-Boston 2013.
Casanova-Robin H., *Virgile, Bucoliques*, Paris 2014 (text edited by E. de Saint-Denis, translation by A. Videau).
Holzberg N., *Vergil: Bucolica, Georgica/Hirtengedichte, Landwirtschaft*, Berlin-Boston 2016.
Paduano G., *Virgilio, Tutte le Opere, Bucoliche-Georgiche-Eneide-Appendix*, Milan 2016.

3. Translations

H. R. Fairclough, Cambridge MA 1916; G. Albini, Bologna 1926 (= 1960); E. de Saint-Denis, Paris 1942; 1956[3] (1978 with notes); C. Carena, Turin 1970; L. Canali, Milan 1978; G. Lee, Liverpool 1980; M. Geymonat, Milan 1981; J. und M. Götte, Munich 1987[5]; A. da Silva, Lisboa 1993 (all V.); P. Valéry, Turin 1993[2] (first publ. 1941); D. Ferry, New York 1999; R. Carvalho, Belo Horizonte 2005 (including the translation by O. Mendes, Paris 1858); G. Bernardi Perini, Mantua 2006; J. Van Sickle, Baltimore 2011; N. Holzberg, Berlin-Boston 2016; G. Paduano, Milan 2016.

4. Scholarly contributions and reference works

Abbe E. (1965), *The Plants of Virgil's Georgics*, Ithaca NY.
Ableitinger-Grünberger D. (1971), *Der junge Horaz und die Politik: Studien zur 7. und 16. Epode*, Heidelberg.
Abt A. (1908), *Die Apologie des Apuleius von Madaura und die antike Zauberei*, Giessen (= Berlin 1967).
Acuña M. L. (1998), *La égloga IV y el fin de milenio*, in *Noein*, 3, pp. 61–71.
Adams J. N. (1982), *The Latin Sexual Vocabulary*, London.
Adkin N. (2015), *Quis est nam ludus in undis? (Virgil, Eclogue IX 39–43)*, in *ACD*, 51, pp. 43–58.
Alberte E. (1991), *El tratamiento del amor en la Egloga I de Virgilio*, in *Fortunatae*, 2, pp. 225–9.
Albini U. (1951), *L'ecloga VII di Virgilio*, in *Maia*, 4, pp. 161–6.
Albrecht M. von (1977), *Römische Poesie. Texte und Interpretationen*, Heidelberg.
Albrecht M. von (2007), *Vergil—Bucolica—Georgica—Aeneis. Eine Einführung*, Heidelberg, 2nd ed. (1st ed. 2006; Italian trans. by A. Setaioli, *Virgilio. Un'introduzione. Bucoliche, Georgiche, Eneide*, Milan 2012).
Alföldi A. (1930), *Der Neue Weltherrscher der vierten Ekloge Vergils*, in *Hermes*, 65, pp. 369–84.

Alföldi A. (1975), *Redeunt Saturnia regna, IV: Apollo und die Sibylle in der Epoche der Bürgerkriege*, in *Chiron*, 5, pp. 165–92.

Alfonsi L. (1942), *Il mito di Sileno e la VI Egloga di Virgilio*, in *A&R*, s. III, 10, pp. 93–9.

Alfonsi L. (1960), *Codro Euforioneo*, in *Aegyptus*, 40, pp. 315–17.

Alfonsi L. (1961), *Dalla II alla X Ecloga*, in *Aevum*, 35, pp. 193–8.

Alfonsi L. (1966), *A proposito di Ecl. II, 61–2*, in *Aevum*, 40, p. 548.

Alfonsi L. (1982), *Virgilio e Calvo, il neoteros romano*, in *PP*, 203, pp. 108–13.

Alpers P. J. (1979), *The Singer of the Eclogues. A Study of Virgilian Pastoral with a New Translation of the Eclogues*, Berkeley-Los Angeles-London.

Alpers P. J. (1990), *Theocritean Bucolic and Virgilian Pastoral*, in *Arethusa*, 23, pp. 19–47.

Alpers P. J. (1996), *What Is Pastoral?*, Chicago.

Altevogt H. (1956), *Die erste Ekloge Vergils im Unterricht*, in *AU*, 9, pp. 5–23.

Álvarez Hernández A. (1991), *Los amores de Galo en la Arcadia de Virgilio*, in *AFC*, 12, pp. 5–22.

Álvarez Hernández A. (1992–3), *Virgilio e Gallo nell'ultima egloga del libro bucolico*, in *AFLB*, 35–6, pp. 169–99.

Anagnostou-Laoutides E. (2006–7), *Ancient Ritual and the Search for Arcadia: From Vergil to Poussin*, in *Transcultural Studies*, 2–3, pp. 19–53.

Anderson G. (1993), *The Origins of Daphnis: Virgil's Eclogues and the Ancient Near East*, in *PVS*, 21, pp. 65–79.

Anderson J. K. (1984), *Virgil, Eclogue 3, 92–3. An Enquiry*, in *CW*, 77, p. 303.

Anderson R. D., Parsons P. J., Nisbet R. G. M. (1979), *Elegiacs by Gallus from Qaṣr Ibrîm*, in *JRS*, 69, pp. 125–55.

André J. (1949), *Étude sur les termes de couleur dans la langue latine*, Paris.

André J. (1956), *Lexique des termes de botanique en latin*, Paris.

André J. (1966), *L'otium dans la vie morale et intellectuelle romaine, des origines à l'époque augustéenne*, Paris.

André J. (1985), *Les noms de plantes dans la Rome antique*, Paris.

Andriani B. (1964), *Divagazioni astronomiche sull'egloga VIII di Virgilio*, in *RAAN*, 39, pp. 213–23.

Andrisano A. M., Fabbri P. (2009), *La favola di Orfeo. Letteratura, immagine, performance*, Ferrara.

Antoine F. (1882), *De casuum syntaxi Vergiliana*, Paris.

Apostol R. (2015), *Urbanus es, Corydon: Ecocritiquing Town and Country in Eclogue 2*, in *Vergilius*, 61, pp. 3–28.

Aricò G. (2012), *Huic aliud mercedis erit (Verg. ecl. 6, 26)*, in M. Passalacqua, M. De Nonno, A. M. Morelli (eds.), with the collaboration of C. Giammona, *Venuste noster. Scritti offerti a Leopoldo Gamberale*, Hildesheim-Zürich-New York, pp. 136–47.

Arkins B. (1990), *A Note on Virgil, Eclogues 10.4–6*, in *LCM*, 15, p. 66.

Armstrong D., Fish J., Johnston P. A., Skinner M. B. (eds.) (2004), *Vergil, Philodemus and the Augustans*, Austin.

Armstrong R. (2006), *Cretan Women: Pasiphae, Ariadne, and Phaedra in Latin Poetry*, Oxford.

Armstrong R. (2019), *Vergil's Green Thoughts. Plants, Humans, and the Divine*, Oxford.

Arnaldi F. (1943), *Studi virgiliani*, Naples.

Arnold B. (1995), *The Literary Experience of Vergil's Fourth Eclogue*, in *CJ*, 90, pp. 143–60.

Austin R. G. (1927), *Virgil and the Sibyl*, in *CQ*, 21, pp. 100–5.

Axelson B. (1945), *Unpoetische Wörter: Ein Beitrag zur Kenntnis der lateinischen Dichtersprache*, Lund.

Aymard J. (1955), *Aut Ararim Parthus bibet aut Germania Tigrim (Buc. 1.62)*, in *Latomus*, 14, pp. 120–2.

Bader F. (1998), *Apollon, l'ambre et le chant du cygne*, in L. Agostiniani et al. (eds.), *Do-ra-qe pe-re. Studi in memoria di A. Quattordio Moreschini*, Pisa-Rome, pp. 47–74.

Baier T. (2003), *Vergils dichterische Selbstbestimmung in der sechsten Ekloge*, in *Pan*, 21, pp. 165–76.

Baldwin B. (1969), *Vergil, Eclogue IV.61: A Reply*, in *CJ*, 64, p. 280.

Baldwin B. (1991), *Eclogue 6: The Simple Explanation*, in *SO*, 66, pp. 97–107.

Baraz Y. (2019), *Certare alterno carmine: The Rise and Fall of Bucolic Competition*, in C. Damon, C. Pieper (eds.), *Eris vs. Aemulatio. Valuing Competition in Classical Antiquity*, Leiden-Boston, pp. 78–97.

Barchiesi A. (1981), *Notizie sul 'Nuovo Gallo'*, in *A&R*, n.s. 26, pp. 153–66.

Barchiesi A. (1994), *Ultime difficoltà nella carriera di un poeta giambico: l'epodo XVII*, in *Atti dei Convegni di Venosa, Napoli e Roma*, Venosa 1994, pp. 205–20.

Barchiesi A. (2006), *Music for Monsters: Ovid's Metamorphoses, Bucolic Evolution, and Bucolic Criticism*, in Fantuzzi, Papanghelis (2006), pp. 403–25.

Barchiesi A. (2019), *Virgilian Narrative: Ecphrasis*, in F. Mac Góráin, C. Martindale (eds.), *The Cambridge Companion to Virgil*, Cambridge, 2nd ed., pp. 413–24 (1st ed. 1997).

Bardon H. (1949), *Les élégies de Cornélius Gallus*, in *Latomus*, 8, pp. 217–28.

Barigazzi A. (1950), *Ad Verg. ecl. VII, 25 et Euphor. 140 P. (A.P. VI, 279)*, in *SIFC*, 24, pp. 29–31.

Barigazzi A. (1952), *Nuovi frammenti di Euforione, I*, in *SIFC*, 26, pp. 149–68.

Barigazzi A. (1975), *Per l'interpretazione dell'Id. 5 di Teocrito e dell'Ecl. 3 di Virgilio*, in *AC*, 44, pp. 54–78.

Bartoli A. (1900), *La lingua e la metrica di Virgilio*, Pistoia.

Barwick K. (1944), *Zur Interpretation und Chronologie der 4. Ecloge des Vergil und der 16. und 7. Epode des Horaz*, in *Philologus*, 96, pp. 28–67.

Bastianini G. M. (1982), *Repertor Vergilianus*, Naples.

Batstone W. (1990), *How Virgil's Pastoral Makes a Difference*, in *Arethusa*, 23, pp. 5–17.

Baudy G. J. (1993), *Hirtenmythos und Hirtenlied. Zu den rituellen Aspekten der bukolischen Dichtung*, in *Poetica*, 25, pp. 282–318.

Baumbach M. (2001), *Dichterwettstreit als Liebeswerbung in Vergils 5. Ekloge*, in *Philologus*, 145, pp. 108–20.

Bauzá H. F. (1983), *Una nueva consideración del tiempo y de la cultura: a propósito de un passaje virgiliano, Buc. IV 22–25*, in *Revista Bíblica*, 45, pp. 197–202.

Bauzá H. F. (1984), *Il paesaggio simbolico delle Bucoliche*, in E. Paratore et al. (eds.), *Atti del Convegno mondiale scientifico di studi su Virgilio*, Milan, vol. I, pp. 195–204.

Bauzá H. F. (1987), *La natura del canto di Sileno*, in *Sileno*, 13, pp. 21–31.

Bauzá H. F. (2006), *Eros y Thanatos en la Arcadia: reflexiones en torno a la Bucólica X*, in C. Santini, L. Zurli, L. Cardinali (eds.), *Concentus ex dissonis. Scritti in onore di Aldo Setaioli*, 2 vols., Naples, vol. I, pp. 77–83.

Bayet J. (1928), *Virgile et les triumviri 'agris dividundis'*, in *REL*, 6, pp. 271–99.

Beaujeu J. (1982), *L'enfant sans nom de la IVᵉ Bucolique*, in *REL*, 60, pp. 186–215.

Becker A. (1999), *Poetry as Equipment for Living: A Gradual Reading of Vergil's Ninth Eclogue*, in *ClassicsIreland*, 6, pp. 1–22.

Becker C. (1955), *Vergils Eklogenbuch*, in *Hermes*, 83, pp. 314–49.

Becker M. (2003), *Iam nova progenies caelo demittitur alto*, in *Hermes*, 131, pp. 456–63.

Beghini G. (2020), *Il latino colloquiale nell'Eneide. Approfondimenti sull'arte poetica di Virgilio*, Bologna.

Benario H. W. (1954), *Ecl. III.60*, in *CW*, 47, p. 199.

Benko S. (1980), *Virgil's Fourth Eclogue in Christian Interpretation*, in *ANRW*, II.31.1, Berlin-New York, pp. 646–705.

512   BIBLIOGRAPHY

Bennet H. (1930), *Vergil and Pollio*, in *AJPh*, 51, pp. 325–42.

Benzer G. (1976), *Einige Ansätze strukturalistischen Interpretierens in der klassischen Philologie. Mit Beiträgen zu Vergil, ecl. VII; Horaz, iamb. II und C. 1.9; Tibull I, 6*, diss. Innsbruck.

Berg W. (1965), *Daphnis and Prometheus*, in *TAPhA*, 96, pp. 11–23.

Berg W. (1974), *Early Virgil*, London.

Beringer L. (1932), *Die Kultworte bei Vergil*, diss. Erlangen.

Bernabé A., Casadesús F. (eds.) (2008), *Orfeo y la tradición órfica*, 2 vols., Madrid.

Bernardi Perini G. (1983), *Il Mincio in Arcadia*, in *Nel bimillenario della morte di Virgilio*, Mantua, pp. 51–72 (= Bernardi Perini 2001, pp. 207–23).

Bernardi Perini G. (1999-2000), *Virgilio, il Cristo, la Sibilla: sulla lettura 'messianica' della quarta egloga*, in *AAPat*, 112, pp. 115–24.

Bernardi Perini G. (2001), *Il Mincio in Arcadia. Scritti di filologia e letteratura latina*, Bologna.

Bernardi Perini G. (2002), *La bucula disperata (Verg. ecl. 8, 85–89)*, in *Paideia*, 57, pp. 24–33.

Bernardi Perini G. (2012a), *Virgilianesimo di Seamus Heaney*, in *Liburna*, 5, pp. 53–63.

Bernardi Perini G. (2012b), *'My hedge-schoolmaster Virgil'. Dall''egloga messianica' alla Bann Valley Eclogue*, in M. Passalacqua, M. De Nonno, A. M. Morelli (eds.), with the collaboration of C. Giammona, *Venuste noster. Scritti offerti a Leopoldo Gamberale*, Hildesheim-Zürich-New York, pp. 697–709.

Bernays L. (2006), *Zur Priorität der 4. Ekloge Vergils gegenüber der Epode 16 des Horaz*, in *MH*, 63, pp. 19–22.

Bernays L. (2008), *Eine vergessene Konjektur zu Vergils Vierter Ekloge*, in *RhM*, 151, pp. 110–11.

Bernsdorff H. (1999), *Das Fragmentum Bucolicum Vindobonense (P. Vindob. Rainer 29801)*, Göttingen.

Bernstein F. M. (2020), *Patronage, Poetic Lineage, and Wordplay: A New Dedicatory Acronym in Vergil's Sixth Eclogue*, in *Antichthon*, 54, pp. 32–53.

Bethe E. (1892), *Vergilstudien II. Zur ersten, neunten und achten Ecloge*, in *RhM*, 47, pp. 577–96.

Bettini M. (1972), *Corydon, Corydon*, in *SCO*, 21, pp. 261–76.

Bettini M. (1988), *Turno e la rondine nera*, in *QUCC*, 59, pp. 7–24 (= Bettini 2000, pp. 125–43).

Bettini M. (2000), *Le orecchie di Hermes. Studi di antropologia e letterature classiche*, Turin.

Bettini M., Franco C. (2010), *Il mito di Circe*, Turin.

Betz H. D. (1992), *The Greek Magical Papyri in Translation*, Chicago-London, 2nd ed. (1st ed. 1986).

Beyers E. E. (1962), *Vergil, Eclogue VII, a Theory of Poetry*, in *AClass*, 5, pp. 38–47.

Bieler L. (1935-6), *ΘΕΙΟΣ ΑΝΗΡ: Das Bild des 'göttlichen Menschen' in Spätantike und Frühchristentum*, 2 vols., Vienna.

Binder G. (1983), *Lied der Parzen zur Geburt Octavians. Vergils vierte Ekloge*, in *Gymnasium*, 90, pp. 102–22.

Binder G. (1995), *Grenzüberschreitungen: Von Rom nach Arkadien, vom Mythos zur Geschichte*, in *Lampas*, 28, pp. 82–101.

Binder G. (2000), *Amor omnibus idem: Liebeswahn als Konstante in Vergils Dichtung*, in B. Effe, R. F. Glei (eds.), *Genie und Wahnsinn. Konzepte psychischer 'Normalität' und 'Abnormität' im Altertum*, Trier, pp. 123–48.

Binder G., Effe B. (2001), *Antike Hirtendichtung. Eine Einführung*, Düsseldorf-Zürich, 2nd ed.

Bing P. (2016), *Epicurus and the iuvenis at Virgil's Eclogue 1.42*, in *CQ*, n.s. 66, pp. 172–9.

Birt T. (1918), *Vergil Bucol. 4, 62: qui non risere parentes*, in *BPhW*, 38, cols. 186–92.

BMCRE = Coins of the Roman Empire in the British Museum, London 1975.

Boll F. (1923), *Sulla quarta ecloga di Virgilio*, in *Memorie della R. Accademia delle Scienze di Bologna. Classe di Scienze morali*, s. II, vols. 5–7 (= *Die vierte Ekloge des Virgil*, in F. B., *Kleine Schriften zur Sternkunde des Altertums*, Leipzig 1950, pp. 332–56).

Bollack M. (1967), *Le retour de Saturne (une étude de la IVe Églogue)*, in *REL*, 45, pp. 304–24.

Bollók J. (1996–7), *Die Kosmologie als Schlüssel zum Verständnis der VI. Ekloge Vergils*, in *AAntHung*, 37, pp. 225–333.

Bömer F. (1949–50), *Tityrus und sein Gott*, in *WJA*, 4, pp. 60–70.

Bömer F. (1952), *Über die Himmelserscheinung nach dem Tode Caesars*, in *BJ*, 152, pp. 27–40.

Bömer F. (1953), *Der akkusativus pluralis auf -is, -eis, und -es bei Vergil*, in *Emerita*, 21, pp. 182–234.

Bömer F. (1954), *Der akkusativus pluralis auf -is, -eis, und -es bei Vergil*, in *Emerita*, 22, pp. 175–210.

Bömer F. (1957), *Beiträge zum Verständnis der augusteischen Dichtersprache*, in *Gymnasium*, 64, pp. 1–21.

Bonanno M. G. (1990), *L'allusione necessaria. Ricerche intertestuali sulla poesia greca e latina*, Rome.

Bondurant A. L. (1935), *A Long-Lived Pear Tree*, in *CW*, 28, p. 96.

Boneschanscher E. J. (1982), *Procne's Absence Again*, in *CQ*, n.s. 32, pp. 148–51.

Borca F. (1998), *Il paesaggio nilotico nelle letterature greca e latina*, in *MD*, 41, pp. 185–205.

Borgeaud P. (1978), *Recherches sur le dieu Pan*, Geneva (English trans. by K. Atlass, J. Redfield, *The Cult of Pan in Ancient Greece*, Chicago 1988).

Boucher J.-P. (1966), *Caius Cornélius Gallus*, Paris.

Bowersock G. W. (1971), *A Date in the Eighth Eclogue*, in *HSPh*, 75, pp. 73–80.

Bowersock G. W. (1978), *The Addressee of Virgil's Eighth Eclogue: A Response*, in *HSPh*, 82, pp. 201–2.

Bowie E. L. (1985), *Theocritus' Seventh Idyll, Philetas and Longus*, in *CQ*, n.s. 35, pp. 67–91.

Boyd B. W. (1983), *Cydonea mala: Vergilian Word-Play and Allusion*, in *HSPh*, 87, pp. 169–74.

Boyle A. J. (1975), *A Reading of Virgil's Eclogues*, in *Ramus*, 4, pp. 187–203 (cf. Boyle 1986, pp. 15–35).

Boyle A. J. (1986), *The Chaonian Dove. Studies in the Eclogues, Georgics, and Aeneid of Virgil*, Leiden.

Braccesi L. (2012), *Giulia, la figlia di Augusto*, Bari.

Braun L. (1969), *Adynata and versus intercalaris im Lied Damons (Vergil, Ecl. 8)*, in *Philologus*, 113, pp. 292–7.

Braun L. (1971), *Der Sängerstreit der Hirten in Vergils dritter und siebenter Ekloge*, in *Gymnasium*, 78, pp. 400–6.

Braund S. (1997), *Virgil and the Cosmos: Religious and Philosophical Ideas*, in Martindale (1997a), pp. 204–21.

Breed B. W. (2000a), *Imitations of Originality: Theocritus and Lucretius at the Start of the Eclogues*, in *Vergilius*, 46, pp. 3–20.

Breed B. W. (2000b), *Silenus and the imago vocis in Eclogue 6*, in *HSPh*, 100, pp. 327–39.

Breed B. W. (2006a), *Pastoral Inscriptions: Reading and Writing Virgil's Eclogues*, London.

Breed B. W. (2006b), *Time and Textuality in the Book of the Eclogues*, in Fantuzzi, Papanghelis (2006), pp. 333–67.

514 BIBLIOGRAPHY

Breed B. W. (2012), *The Pseudo-Vergilian Dirae and the Earliest Responses to Vergilian Pastoral*, in *Trends in Classics*, 4, pp. 3–28.

Bréguet E. (1948), *Les Élégies de Gallus d'après la Xe Bucolique de Virgile*, in *REL*, 26, pp. 204–14.

Brenk F. E. (1980), *The Twofold Gleam. Vergil's Golden Age and the Beginning of Empire*, in *Thought*, 55, pp. 81–97.

Brenk F. E. (1981), *War and the Shepherd. The Tomb of Bianor in Vergil's Ninth Eclogue*, in *AJPh*, 102, pp. 427–30.

Brisson J.-P. (1992), *Rome et l'âge d'or. De Catulle à Ovide, vie et mort d'un mythe*, Paris.

Brown E. L. (1963), *Numeri Vergiliani: Studies in Eclogues and Georgics*, Brussels.

Brown E. L. (1978), *Damoetas' Riddle. Euclid's Theorem I,32*, in *Vergilius*, 24, pp. 25–31.

Brugnoli G. (1979), *Anseres de Falerno depellantur*, in *Linguistica e Letteratura*, 4, pp. 345–68 (= G. B., *Studi di filologia e letteratura latina*, ed. by S. Conte, F. Stok, Pisa 2004, pp. 59–83).

Buchheit V. (1977a), *Catull, Vergil, Martial und Stella in Plinius Epist. 9, 25*, in *SO*, 52, pp. 83–7.

Buchheit V. (1977b), *Der Dichter als Mystagoge (Vergil, ecl. 5)*, in *Atti del Convegno virgiliano sul bimillenario delle Georgiche*, Naples, pp. 203–19.

Buchheit V. (1984), *Wunder der Dichtung (Vergil, ecl. 3, 88 f)*, in *WJA*, N. F. 10, pp. 73–6.

Buchheit V. (1986), *Frühling in den Eklogen. Vergil und Lukrez*, in *RhM*, 129, pp. 123–41.

Buchheit V. (1990), *Der frühe Vergil und Oktavian*, in *SO*, 65, pp. 53–62.

Büchner K. (1955), *P. Vergilius Maro, der Dichter der Römer*, in *RE*, VIIIA1, cols. 1021–1264; A2, cols. 1265–1493 (= Büchner 1956).

Büchner K. (1956), *P. Vergilius Maro: Der Dichter der Römer*, Stuttgart.

Buisel M. D. (1986), *Sobre la identidad del puer de la IV Egloga*, in *Actas del VII Simpósio nacional de estudios clásicos 1982*, Buenos Aires, pp. 93–105.

Buisel M. D. (1999), *Discurso mítico y discurso histórico en la IV Egloga de Virgilio*, in *Auster*, 4, pp. 41–62.

Burckhardt F. (1971), *Zur doppelten Enallage*, in *Gymnasium*, 78, pp. 407–21.

Caballero De Del Sastre E. (1986), *El insanus amor en la Egloga X de Virgilio*, in *AFC*, 11, pp. 45–54.

Cairns F. (1999), *Virgil Eclogue 1.1–2: A Literary Programme?*, in *HSPh*, 99, pp. 189–93.

Cairns F. (2006), *Sextus Propertius the Augustan Elegist*, Cambridge.

Cairns F. (2008), *C. Asinius Pollio and the Eclogues*, in *PCPhS*, 54, pp. 49–79.

Callataÿ G. de (1996), *The Knot of the Heavens*, in *JWI*, 59, pp. 1–13.

Calzolari M. (1999), *Andes e le confische del 41–40 a.C. nel Mantovano: il contributo della ricerca topografica alla biografia di Virgilio*, in *AVM*, 67, pp. 35–92.

Cameron A. (1995), *Callimachus and His Critics*, Princeton.

Camilloni M. T. (1979–80), *Una lettura di Virg., Ecl. VII*, in *Sileno*, 5–6, pp. 303–14.

Campbell A. Y. (1958–9), *Vergiliana. Ecl. 4, 62–3; Aen. II.645–646; VIII.65 and 74–75*, in *PCPhS*, 180, pp. 5–6.

Campbell J. S. (1982), *Damoetas's Riddle: A Literary Solution*, in *CJ*, 78, pp. 122–6.

Camuffo M. A. (1986), *Una propuesta de análisis de texto: la Egloga VII de Virgilio*, in *Actas del VII Simpósio nacional de estudios clásicos 1982*, Buenos Aires, pp. 133–42.

Cancik H. (1986), *Delicias Domini. Ein Kulturgeschichtlicher Versuch zu Vergil, Ekloge II*, in U. J. Stache, W. Maaz, F. Wagner (eds.), *Kontinuität und Wandel: Lateinische Poesie von Naevius bis Baudelaire. Franco Munari zum 65. Geburtstag*, Hildesheim, pp. 15–34.

Canetta I. (2008), *Muse e ninfe nella settima ecloga di Virgilio*, in *Eikasmós*, 19, pp. 209–24.

Capponi F. (1979), *Ornithologia Latina*, Genoa.

Carcopino J. (1930), *Virgile et le mystère de la IVe Églogue*, Paris.

(1986), *Virgil in a Cultural Tradition. Essays to Celebrate*

Bucoliques de Virgile, Paris.

...to di Dioniso in Argolide, Rome.

...ela da rondine a usignolo, in C. Santini, L. Zurli, L. Cardinali
...is. Studi A. Setaioli, Naples, pp. 165–78.

*Jeux d'encadrement dans les Bucoliques: éléments de poétique
...nes (pour une esthétique du couplet)*, in *Euphrosyne*, n.s. 35,

...incipit della Chioma callimachea in Virgilio, in *RFIC*, 101, pp. 329–32.
...9–7), Echi lucreziani nelle Ecloghe virgiliane, in *RSC*, 14, pp. 313–42; 15,
..., 176–216.

... E. (1971), *Sull'età dell'oro in Lucrezio e Virgilio*, in *Studi di storiografia antica in
memoria di Leonardo Ferrero*, Turin, pp. 99–114.

Cazzaniga I. (1960), *Colori Nicandrei in Virgilio*, in *SIFC*, 32, pp. 18–37.

Ceccarelli L. (2008), *Contributi per la storia dell'esametro latino*, 2 vols., Rome.

Chausserie-Laprée J.-P. (1974), *Échos et résonances au début de la dixième Bucolique*, in
P. Gros, J.-P. Morel (eds.), *Mélanges de philosophie, de littérature et d'histoire ancienne
offerts à Pierre Boyancé*, Rome, pp. 173–80.

Chausserie-Laprée J.-P. (1978), *Les 'constructions' de la septième Bucolique*, in J. Collart et al.
(eds.), *Varron, grammaire antique et stylistique latine*, Paris, pp. 353–64.

Chwalek B. (1990), *Elegische Interpretationen zu Vergils zehnter Ekloge*, in *Gymnasium*, 97,
pp. 304–20.

Cichorius C. (1922), *Römische Studien*, Leipzig.

CIL = *Corpus Inscriptionum Latinarum*.

Cipolla G. (1962), *Political Audacity and Esotericism in the Ninth Eclogue*, in *AClass*, 5,
pp. 48–57.

Citroni M. (1995), *Poesia e lettori in Roma antica. Forme della comunicazione letteraria*,
Rome-Bari.

Citroni M. (2001), *Affermazioni di priorità e coscienza di progresso artistico nei poeti latini*,
in E. A. Schmidt (ed.), *L'histoire littéraire immanente dans la poésie latine, Entretiens de
la Fondation Hardt*, 47, Vandoeuvres-Geneva, pp. 267–314.

Clarke M. L. (1972–73), *Three Notes on Virgil*, in *PVS*, 12, pp. 48–50.

Clausen W. (1964), *Callimachus and Latin Poetry*, in *GRBS*, 5, pp. 181–96.

Clausen W. (1972), *On the Date of the First Eclogue*, in *HSPh*, 76, pp. 201–6.

Clausen W. (1976), *Cynthius*, in *AJPh*, 97, pp. 245–7.

Clausen W. (1977), *Cynthius: An Addendum*, in *AJPh*, 98, p. 362.

Clausen W. (1982), *Theocritus and Virgil*, in E. J. Kenney (ed.), *The Cambridge History of
Classical Literature*, vol. II, *Latin Literature*, Cambridge, pp. 301–19.

Clausen W. (1990), *Virgil's Messianic Eclogue*, in J. Kugel (ed.), *Poetry and Prophecy. The
Beginnings of a Literary Tradition*, Ithaca NY, pp. 65–74.

Clauss J. J. (1997), *An Acrostic in Vergil (Eclogues I 5–8): The Chance That Mimics Choice?*,
in *Aevum(ant.)*, 10, pp. 267–87.

Clauss J. J. (2002–3), *Large and Illyrical Waters in Vergil's Eighth 'Eclogue'*, in *Hermathena*,
173–4, pp. 165–73.

Clauss J. J. (2004), *Vergil's Sixth Eclogue: The Aetia in Rome*, in M. A. Harder, R. F. Regtuit,
G. C. Walker (eds.), *Callimachus II*, Leuven 2004, pp. 71–93.

Clay D. (2004), *Vergil's Farewell to Education (Catalepton 5) and Epicurus' Letter to
Pythocles*, in Armstrong, Fish, Johnston, Skinner (2004), pp. 25–36.

516 BIBLIOGRAPHY

Clay J. S. (1974), *Damoetas' Riddle and the Structure of* 118, pp. 59–64.

Clay J. S. (2009), *Vergil Eclogue 4.28: Where's the Miracle?,*

CLE = *Carmina Latina Epigraphica.*

Colafrancesco P. (2001), *Iconografia e iconologia del dio Pan* 23, pp. 27–51.

Coleiro E. (1979), *L'Epodo XVI di Orazio e la Quarta Egloga prima?,* in φιλίας χάριν. *Miscellanea di studi classici in onore* vol. II, pp. 515–27.

Coleiro E. (1981), *Verg. Buc. 3, 109–110. Una nuova interpretazione,* in *Letterature Problemi e metodo. Studi in onore di E. Paratore,* 4 vols., Bologna, vol. I, pp. 435–9.

Coleman R. (1962), *Gallus, the Bucolics, and the Ending of the Fourth Georgic,* in *AJPh,* 83, pp. 55–71.

Coleman R. (1966), *Tityrus and Meliboeus,* in *G&R,* 13, pp. 79–97.

Coleman R. (1975), *Vergil's Pastoral Modes,* in *Ramus,* 4, pp. 140–62.

Combs-Schilling J. (2015), *Tityrus in Limbo: Figures of the Author in Dante's Eclogues,* in *Dante Studies,* 133, pp. 1–26.

Comparetti D. (1872), *Virgilio nel Medioevo,* 2 vols., Livorno (2nd ed. Florence 1896; 3rd ed. by G. Pasquali, Florence 1937–41; English trans. by E. F. M. Benecke, *Vergil in the Middle Ages,* Princeton 1997).

Connolly J. (2001), *Picture Arcadia: The Politics of Representation in Vergil's Eclogues,* in *Vergilius,* 47, pp. 89–116.

Conte G. B. (1980a), *Il genere e i suoi confini. Interpretazione della decima egloga,* in G. B. C., *Il genere e i suoi confini. Cinque studi sulla poesia di Virgilio,* Turin, pp. 11–43 (= Conte 1984, pp. 13–53 = Conte 1986, pp. 100–29 = Volk 2008, pp. 216–44).

Conte G. B. (1980b), *Proemi al mezzo,* in G. B. C., *Il genere e i suoi confini. Cinque studi sulla poesia di Virgilio,* Turin, pp. 122–36 (= Conte 1984, pp. 122–33 = *Proems in the Middle,* in F. Dunn, T. Cole, eds., *Beginnings in Classical Literature,* Cambridge 1992, pp. 147–160).

Conte G. B. (1984), *Virgilio. Il genere e i suoi confini,* Milan, 2nd ed.

Conte G. B. (1986), *The Rhetoric of Imitation. Genre and Poetic Memory in Virgil and Other Latin Poets,* Ithaca NY.

Conte G. B. (2002), *Virgilio. L'epica del sentimento,* Turin.

Conte G. B. (2007), *The Poetry of Pathos. Studies in Virgilian Epic,* Oxford.

Conte G. B. (2016), *Marginalia. Note critiche all'edizione teubneriana di Virgilio,* Pisa (= *Critical Notes on Virgil. Editing the Teubner Text of the 'Georgics' and the 'Aeneid',* Berlin-Boston 2016).

Conte G. B. (2020), *Parerga virgiliani. Critica del testo e dello stile,* Pisa.

Coppola A. (1998), *Asinio Pollione poeta. Nota a Verg. ecl. 8, 6–10,* in *RFIC,* 126, pp. 170–4.

Coronati L. (1984), *Osservazioni sulla traduzione greca della IV ecloga di Virgilio,* in *CCC,* 5, pp. 71–84.

Corssen P. (1925), *Die vierte Ekloge Virgils,* in *Philologus,* 81, pp. 26–71.

Cottino G. B. (1906), *La flessione dei nomi greci in Virgilio,* Turin.

Courcelle P. (1957), *Les exégèses chrétiennes de la quatrième églogue,* in *REA,* 59, pp. 294–319.

Courtney E. (1981), *The Formation of the Text of Vergil,* in *BICS,* 28, pp. 13–29.

Courtney E. (1990), *Vergil's Sixth Eclogue,* in *QUCC,* 63, pp. 99–112.

Courtney E. (1993), *The Fragmentary Latin Poets,* Oxford.

Courtney E. (2002-3), *The Formation of the Text of Vergil—Again,* in *BICS,* 46, 189–94.

Courtney E. (2004), *The 'Greek' Accusative,* in *CJ,* 99, pp. 425–31.

Courtney E. (2009), *Four Suggestions on Vergil*, in WJA, N. F. 33, pp. 81–3.

Cova P. V. (1955), *Proposta di interpretazione di tre passi delle Bucoliche*, Pavia.

Cova P. V. (1976), *Otium e libertas in Virgilio*, in RCCM, 18, pp. 275–83.

Cova P. V. (1996), *Il poeta Vario tra neoteroi e augustei*, in Athenaeum, 84, pp. 562–73.

Cremona V. (1977), *Distrazioni critiche e unità poetica della prima bucolica*, in Atti del Convegno virgiliano sul bimillenario delle Georgiche, Naples, pp. 287–308.

Cremonesi E. (1958), *Rapporti tra le origini della poesia bucolica e della poesia comica nella tradizione peripatetica*, in Dioniso, 21, pp. 109–21.

Cucchiarelli A. (2000), *'Fabula Galli' (Ov. met. 10, 25–9)*, in MD, 44, pp. 211–15.

Cucchiarelli A. (2008), *Epiloghi ed inizi da Callimaco a Virgilio (Ait. fr. 112 Pf.; georg. 4, 559–566; ecl. 10, 75–77)*, in P. Arduini, S. Audano, A. Borghini, A. Cavarzere, G. Mazzoli, G. Paduano, A. Russo (eds.), *Studi offerti ad Alessandro Perutelli*, 2 vols., Rome, vol. I, pp. 363–80.

Cucchiarelli A. (2010), *Ivy and Laurel: Divine Models in Virgil's Bucolics*, in HSPh, 106, pp. 155–78.

Cucchiarelli A. (2011), *Virgilio e l'invenzione dell'età augustea (Modelli divini e linguaggio politico dalle Bucoliche alle Georgiche)*, in Lexis, 29, pp. 229–74.

Cucchiarelli A. (2019a), *Monumenti più forti del fuoco. Incompiuto, immortalità e potere nella poesia augustea*, in ScAnt 25, pp. 261–76.

Cucchiarelli A. (2019b), *Varia historia ovvero 'come vendere la Città' (Vario Rufo tra politica e poesia da Virgilio a Lucano)*, in BSL, 49, pp. 495–539.

Cucchiarelli A. (2021a), *Cortesie da pastori. Pragmatica della comunicazione nelle ecloghe 3, 5 e 7 di Virgilio*, in ScAnt 27, pp. 87–102.

Cucchiarelli A. (2021b), *Un punto di svolta: le Bucoliche di Virgilio*, in L. Galasso (ed.), *La letteratura latina in età ellenistica*, Rome 2021, pp. 191–215.

Cupaiuolo F. (1977), *Trama poetica delle Bucoliche di Virgilio*, Naples.

Cupaiuolo F. (1981), *La decima ecloga di Virgilio, un problema sempre aperto*, in C&S, 20, pp. 50–9.

Cupaiuolo F. (1996), *Sull'alessandrinismo delle strutture formali dell'ecloga VI di Virgilio*, in BSL, 26, pp. 482–503.

Curchin L. (1988), *Vergil's 'Messiah': A New Governor of Spain?*, in AHB, 2.6, pp. 143–4.

Currie H. Macl. (1976), *The Third Eclogue and the Roman Comic Spirit*, in Mnemosyne, s. IV, 29, pp. 411–20.

Currie H. Macl. (1978), *Virgil, Eclogue 6, 13 ff. and the Numa-Egeria Legend*, in LCM, 3, pp. 289–91.

Curtius E. R. (1948), *Europäische Literatur und lateinisches Mittelalter*, Bern (English trans. by W. R. Trask, *European Literature and the Latin Middle Ages*, New York 1953; Italian trans. by A. Luzzatto, M. Candela, ed. by R. Antonelli, *Letteratura europea e Medio Evo latino*, Florence 1992).

Cutolo P. (1992), *Per il callimachismo di Virgilio nella IV ecloga*, in E. Flores et al. (eds.), *Miscellanea di studi in onore di Armando Salvatore*, Naples, pp. 35–43.

Dahlmann H. (1966), *Zu Vergils siebentem Hirtengedicht*, in Hermes, 94, pp. 218–32 (= H. D., *Kleine Schriften*, Hildesheim-New York 1970, pp. 166–80).

Dainotti P. (2015), *Word Order and Expressiveness in the Aeneid*, Berlin-Boston.

Dangel J. (1999), *Formosam doces Amaryllida siluas: écritures métriques et métamorphoses poétiques*, in J. Luque Moreno, P. R. Díaz y Díaz (eds.), *Estudios de métrica latina*, vol. I.2, Granada, pp. 257–80.

Danielewicz J. (2005), *Further Hellenistic Acrostics: Aratus and Others*, in Mnemosyne, s. IV, 58, pp. 321–34.

D'Anna G. (1965), *Alcune osservazioni sull'Antiopa di Pacuvio*, in Athenaeum, 43, pp. 81–94.

D'Anna G. (1971), *Verg. Ecl. X. 44–45*, in *RCCM*, 13, pp. 48–61 (= D'Anna 1995, pp. 33–46).

D'Anna G. (1981), *Cornelio Gallo, Virgilio e Properzio*, in *Athenaeum*, 59, pp. 284–98 (= D'Anna 1995, pp. 47–65).

D'Anna G. (1985), *Rileggendo l'inizio della sesta Bucolica di Virgilio*, in M. Renard, P. Laurens (eds.), *Hommages à Henry Bardon*, Brussels, pp. 1–9 (= D'Anna 1995, pp. 11–20).

D'Anna G. (1987a), *L'amour selon Virgile*, in *LEC*, 55, pp. 151–61 (= *La concezione dell'amore in Virgilio*, in D'Anna 1995, pp. 21–31).

D'Anna G. (1987b), *Virg. Ecl. 9, 32–36 e Prop. 2, 34, 83–84*, in S. Boldrini et al. (eds.), *Filologia e forme letterarie. Studi offerti a Francesco Della Corte*, 5 vols., Urbino, vol. II, pp. 427–38 (= D'Anna 1995, pp. 103–14).

D'Anna G. (1995), *Studi su Virgilio*, Rome, 2nd ed.

Daremberg-Saglio = C. Daremberg, E. Saglio, *Dictionnaire des Antiquités grecques et romaines*, Paris 1877–1919.

Davis G. (2004), *Consolation in the Bucolic Mode: The Epicurean Cadence of Vergil's First Eclogue*, in Armstrong, Fish, Johnston, Skinner (2004), pp. 63–74 (cf. Davis 2012, pp. 17–39).

Davis G. (2011), *The Epicurean Critique of amor insanus in Vergil's Sixth Eclogue*, in *Vergilius*, 57, pp. 35–54 (cf. Davis 2012, pp. 121–4).

Davis G. (2012), *Parthenope: The Interplay of Ideas in Vergilian Bucolic*, Leiden-Boston.

De Cazanove O. (1986), *Le thiase et son double. Images, statuts, fonctions du cortège divin de Dionysos en Italie centrale*, in O. De Cazanove et al., *L'association dionysiaque dans les sociétés anciennes*, Rome, pp. 177–97.

Degl'Innocenti Pierini R. (2008), *Il parto dell'orsa. Studi su Virgilio, Ovidio e Seneca*, Bologna.

Dehon P.-J. (1991), *Le cadre des plaintes de Gallus (Virg., B., X, 9–69)*, in *Latomus*, 50, pp. 364–70.

Della Corte F. (1981), *La quarta egloga di Virgilio*, in *C&S*, 20, n. 80, pp. 37–49 (= Della Corte 1985b, pp. 17–29).

Della Corte F. (1982), *La proanafonesi della IV egloga*, in *Maia*, 34, pp. 3–11 (= Della Corte 1985b, pp. 7–16).

Della Corte F. (1983–4), *Da Proteo a Sileno e da Sileno a Proteo*, in *Sandalion*, 6–7, pp. 165–78 (= Della Corte 1985b, pp. 51–64).

Della Corte F. (1985a), *La toga calda di Titiro*, in M. Renard, P. Laurens (eds.), *Hommages à Henry Bardon*, Brussels, pp. 74–6 (= Della Corte 1985b, pp. 257–9).

Della Corte F. (1985b), *Opuscula IX*, Genoa.

Della Corte F. (1991), *Il faggio di Titiro*, in *Vichiana*, s. III, 2, pp. 123–43 (= Della Corte 2000, pp. 47–67).

Della Corte F. (2000), *Opuscula XIV*, Genoa.

Della Corte F. et al. (1965), *Euforione e i poeti latini*, in *Maia*, 17, pp. 158–76.

Delvigo M. L. (2011), *Servio e la poesia della scienza*, Pisa-Rome 2011.

Deman A. (1956), *La condition sociale de Tityre*, in *Latomus*, 15, p. 373.

De Michelis E. (1968), *L'Egloga di Meri*, in *StudRom*, 16, pp. 269–79.

De Nigris Mores S. (1972), *Sugli aggettivi latini in -ax*, in *Acme*, 25, pp. 263–313.

De Nonno M. (2012), *Cui non risere parentes*, in M. Passalacqua, M. De Nonno, A. M. Morelli (eds.), with the collaboration of C. Giammona, *Venuste noster. Scritti offerti a Leopoldo Gamberale*, Hildesheim-Zürich-New York, pp. 149–60.

Deremetz A. (1987), *Le carmen deductum ou le fil du poème. À propos de Virgile*, in *Latomus*, 46, pp. 762–77.

Deremetz A. (1995), *Le miroir des Muses: poétiques de la réflexivité à Rome*, Villeneuve d'Ascq.

Der neue Pauly = H. Cancik, H. Schneider (eds.), *Der neue Pauly. Enzyklopädie der Antike*, Stuttgart 1996–2003.

Deschamps L. (1980a), *Qui sont les Faunes dans la sixième Bucolique?*, in *Orphea voce*, pp. 109–28.

Deschamps L. (1980b), *Quomodo Varronis De lingua Latina libri ad P. Virgili Maronis locum quemdam interpretandum pertineant*, in *VL*, 79, pp. 17–24.

Desport M. (1952), *L'incantation virgilienne*, Bordeaux.

De Vos M. (1997), *Dionysus, Hylas e Isis sui monti di Roma. Tre monumenti con decorazione parietale in Roma antica (Palatino, Quirinale, Oppio)*, Rome.

Dick B. F. (1970), *Vergil's Pastoral Poetic: A Reading of the First Eclogue*, in *AJPh*, 91, pp. 277–93.

Diehl E. (1930), *Pompeianische Wandinschriften und Verwandtes*, Berlin, 2nd ed.

Di Lorenzo E. (1988), *Strutture allitterative nelle ecloghe di Virgilio e nei bucolici latini minori*, Naples.

Dion J. (1993), *Les passions dans l'oeuvre de Virgile. Poétique et philosophie*, Nancy.

Dion J. (2006), *Les étoiles dans les Bucoliques: astronomie et politique*, in *REL*, 84, pp. 82–102.

Dionisotti C. (2007), *Ecce*, in *BICS*, 50, pp. 75–91.

Di Stefano A. (1989), *Lessemi e mitologemi nella egloga 10 di Virgilio*, in *AAPel*, 65, pp. 165–84.

Dix T. K. (1995), *Vergil in the Grynean Grove: Two Riddles in the Third Eclogue*, in *CPh*, 90, pp. 256–62.

Dobbin R. F. (1995), *Julius Caesar in Jupiter's Prophecy, Aeneid, Book 1*, in *ClAnt*, 14, pp. 5–40.

Dognini C. (1996–97), *Virgilio e la memoria di Cesare*, in *InvLuc*, 18–19, pp. 139–51.

Doig G. (1968), *Vergil's Art and the Greek Language*, in *CJ*, 64, pp. 1–6.

Domenicucci P. (1989), *I 'Capretti' di Virgilio. Note sul catasterismo di Giulio Cesare*, in M. A. Cervellera, D. Liuzzi (eds.), *L'astronomia a Roma nell'età augustea*, Lecce, pp. 91–106.

Dönt E. (1981), *Zur Deutung von Vergils fünfter Ekloge*, in *WJA*, N. F. 7, pp. 135–7.

Döpp S. (1995), *MHΛΟΝ ΚΥΔΩΝΙΟΝ (Malum Cydonium): Quitte oder Apfel?*, in *Hermes*, 123, pp. 341–5.

Dorcey P. F. (1992), *The Cult of Silvanus. A Study in Roman Folk Religion*, Leiden-New York-Cologne.

Dostálová R. (1997), *Qui non risere parenti*, in *LF*, 120, pp. 217–24.

Dover K. J. (1971), *Theocritus. Select Poems*, London.

Drijepondt H. L. F. (1963), *La Xᵉ Églogue de Virgile, un avertissement bienveillant à Gallus*, in *AClass*, 6, pp. 149–50.

Du Bois P. (1988), *Sowing the Body: Psychoanalysis and Ancient Representations of Women*, Chicago-London 1988 (Italian trans. by M. Tartara, *Il corpo come metafora. Rappresentazioni della donna nelle Grecia antica*, Rome-Bari 1990).

Dubrocard M. (1990), *Des Bucoliques à l'Énéide: quelques remarques sur l'évolution du vocabulaire caractéristique de Virgile*, in J. Granarolo, M. Biraud (eds.), *Hommage à René Braun*, 2 vols., Nice-Paris, vol. I, pp. 261–80.

Dubuisson M. (1987), *La chevrette de Mélibée (Virgile, Bucoliques I, 15)*, in *Kentron*, 3, pp. 93–6.

Duckworth G. E. (1958), *The Cradle of Flowers (Ecl. IV.23)*, in *TAPhA*, 89, pp. 1–8.

Duckworth G. E. (1962), *Structural Patterns and Proportions in Vergil's Aeneid*, Ann Arbor.

Duckworth G. E. (1969), *Vergil and Classical Hexameter Poetry: A Study in Metrical Variety*, Ann Arbor.

Dufallo B. (2013), *The Captor's Image: Greek Culture in Roman Ecphrasis*, Oxford.

520   BIBLIOGRAPHY

Dupont F. (2004), *Comment devenir à Rome un poète bucolique? Corydon, Tityre, Virgile et Pollion*, in C. Calame, R. Chartier (eds.), *Identités d'auteur dans l'Antiquité et la tradition européenne*, Grenoble, pp. 171–89.

DuQuesnay I. M. Le M. (1976–7), *Virgil's Fifth Eclogue*, in *PVS*, 16, pp. 18–41.

DuQuesnay I. M. Le M. (1977), *Vergil's Fourth Eclogue*, in F. Cairns (ed.), *Papers of the Liverpool Latin Seminar*, Liverpool, pp. 25–99.

DuQuesnay I. M. Le M. (1979), *From Polyphemus to Corydon*, in D. West, T. Woodman (eds.), *Creative Imitation and Latin Literature*, Cambridge, pp. 35–69 and 206–21.

DuQuesnay I. M. Le M. (1981), *Vergil's First Eclogue*, in F. Cairns (ed.), *Papers of the Liverpool Latin Seminar*, vol. III, Liverpool, pp. 29–182.

Dyer R. R. (1969), *Vergil Eclogue 10. 73–74 and the Suckering Habit of the White Alder*, in *CPh*, 64, pp. 233–4.

Dyson S. L. (2003), *The Roman Countryside*, London.

Dzino D. (2011), *Asinius Pollio in Dalmatia: What Happened in Salona 39 BC?*, in *Klio*, 93, pp. 158–66.

Ebbeler J. (2010), *Linus as a Figure for Pastoral Poetics in Vergil's Eclogues*, in *Helios*, 37, pp. 187–205.

Echave-Sustaeta J. de (1980), *Virgilio desde dentro. La égloga V*, in *AFFB*, 6, pp. 115–34.

Eckerman C. (2016), *Freedom and Slavery in Vergil's Eclogue 1*, in *WS*, 129, pp. 257–80.

Edwards C. (1996), *Writing Rome: Textual Approaches to the City*, Cambridge.

Edwards M. J. (1990), *Chalcidico versu*, in *AC*, 59, pp. 203–8.

Effe B. (1977), *Die Genese einer literarischen Gattung: die Bukolik*, Konstanz.

Egan R. B. (1980), *Satis est potuisse videri*, in *CW*, 73, pp. 379–83.

Egan R. B. (1996), *Corydon's Winning Words in Eclogue 7*, in *Phoenix*, 50, pp. 233–9.

Eisenhut W. (1961), *Deducere carmen. Ein Beitrag zum Problem der literarischen Beziehungen zwischen Horaz und Properz*, in G. Radke (ed.), *Gedenkschrift für G. Rohde*, Tübingen, pp. 91–104 (= W. E., ed., *Properz*, Darmstadt 1975, pp. 247–63).

Elder J. P. (1961), *Non iniussa cano: Virgil's Sixth Eclogue*, in *HSPh*, 65, pp. 109–25.

Enc. Or. = *Enciclopedia Oraziana*, edited by S. Mariotti, 3 vols., Rome 1996–8.

Enc. Virg. = *Enciclopedia Virgiliana*, edited by F. Della Corte, 5 vols., Rome 1984–91.

Engels D., Nicolaye C. (eds.) (2008), *Ille operum custos. Kulturgeschichtliche Beiträge zur antiken Bienensymbolik und ihrer Rezeption*, Hildesheim-Zürich-New York.

Ernout A. (1949), *Les adjectifs latins en -osus et en -ulentus*, Paris.

Ernout A. (1963), *Facere vitula*, in *RPh*, 37, pp. 183–5.

Ernout A. (1970), *Composés avec in- 'privatif' dans Virgile*, in *RPh*, 44, pp. 185–202.

Ernout-Meillet = A. Ernout, A. Meillet, *Dictionnaire étymologique de la langue latine*, quatrième tirage augmenté d'additions et de corrections nouvelles par J. André, Paris 1959.

Esposito P. (1996), *Per la storia della ricezione di Virgilio bucolico: l'ecloga IV di Calpurnio Siculo*, in *Orpheus*, n.s. 17, pp. 13–34.

Estevez V. A. (1962), *Pastoral Disillusionment. Ecloga X*, in *CB*, 38, pp. 70–1.

Evenhuis J. B. (1955), *De Vergilii ecloga sexta commentatio*, diss. Groningen.

Faber R. (1995), *Vergil, Eclogue 3.37, Theocritus 1 and Hellenistic Ecphrasis*, in *AJPh*, 116, pp. 411–17.

Faber R. (2000), *The Literary Metaphor of the Chisel (tornus) in Eclogue 3.38*, in *Hermes*, 128, pp. 375–9.

Fabia P. (1931), *Decem menses (Virgile, Églogue IV, 61)*, in *REL*, 33, pp. 33–40.

Fabre-Serris J. (1995), *Jeux de modèles dans l'alexandrisme romain: les hommages à Gallus dans la Bucolique X et l'Élégie I, 20 de Properce et ses échos ovidiens*, in *REL*, 73, pp. 124–37.

Fabre-Serris J. (1998), *Du...si numquam fallit imago de la deuxième Bucolique au...sensi nec mea me fallit imago du livre III des Métamorphoses*, in C. Auvray-Assayas (ed.), *Images romaines*, Paris, pp. 221–33.

Fabre-Serris J. (2008), *Rome, l'Arcadie et la mer des Argonautes. Essai sur la naissance d'une mythologie des origines en Occident*, Villeneuve d'Asq.

Fabre-Serris J. (2009), *Figures romaines de Dionysos à la fin du Ier siècle av. J.-C.*, in R. Duits, F. Quiviger (eds.), *Images of the Pagan Gods. Papers of a Conference in Memory of Jean Seznec*, London-Turin, pp. 281–96.

Fabre-Serris J. (2014), *La réception d'Empédocle dans la poésie latine: Virgile (Buc. 6), Lucrèce, Gallus et les poètes élégiaques*, in *Dictynna*, 11 (published online).

Fantazzi C. (1966), *Virgilian Pastoral and Roman Love Poetry*, in *AJPh*, 87, pp. 171–91.

Fantazzi C. (1974), *Golden Age in Arcadia*, in *Latomus*, 33, pp. 280–305.

Fantazzi C., Querbach C. W. (1985), *Sound and Substance. A Reading of Virgil's Seventh Eclogue*, in *Phoenix*, 39, pp. 355–67.

Fantham E. (2009), *Latin Poets & Italian Gods*, Toronto.

Fantuzzi M. (2006), *Theocritus' Constructive Interpreters and the Creation of a Bucolic Reader*, in Fantuzzi, Papanghelis (2006), pp. 235–62.

Fantuzzi M. (2008), *Teocrito e l'invenzione di una tradizione letteraria bucolica*, in D. Auger, J. Peigney (eds.), Φιλευριπίδης—*Phileuripidès. Mélanges offerts à François Jouan*, Paris, pp. 569–88.

Fantuzzi M., Papanghelis T. (eds.) (2006), *Brill's Companion to Greek and Latin Pastoral*, Leiden-Boston.

Faraone C. A. (1989), *Clay Hardens and Wax Melts: Magical Role-Reversal in Vergil's Eighth Eclogue*, in *CPh*, 84, pp. 294–300.

Faraone C. A. (2006), *Magic, Medicine and Eros in the Prologue to Theocritus' Id. 11*, in Fantuzzi, Papanghelis (2006), pp. 75–90.

Farrell J. (1991a), *Asinius Pollio in Vergil, Eclogue 8*, in *CPh*, 86, pp. 204–11.

Farrell J. (1991b), *Vergil's Georgics and the Traditions of Ancient Epic: The Art of Allusion in Literary History*, New York-Oxford.

Farrell J. (1992), *Literary Allusion and Cultural Poetics in Vergil's Third Eclogue*, in *Vergilius*, 38, pp. 64–71.

Farrell J. (2016), *Ancient Commentaries on Theocritus' Idylls and Virgil's Eclogues*, in C. S. Kraus, C. Stray (eds.), *Classical Commentaries: Explorations in a Scholarly Genre*, Oxford, pp. 397–418.

Fedeli P. (1972), *Sulla prima bucolica di Virgilio*, in *GIF*, n.s. 3, pp. 273–300.

Feldman L. H. (1953), *Asinius Pollio and His Jewish Interests*, in *TAPhA*, 84, pp. 73–80.

Fernandelli M. (2008), *Coridone e il fuoco d'amore*, in *Pallas*, 78, pp. 279–308.

Fernandelli M. (2009), *Poeta divinus. Nota a Virgilio, Ecloghe 6, 64–73*, in *Eos*, 96, pp. 251–77.

Fernandelli M. (2012), *Xenomede, Callimaco e le voci dell'Ecloga 6*, in M. F., *Via Latina. Studi su Virgilio e sulla sua fortuna*, Trieste, pp. 4–10 (updated reprint of the article first published in L. Casarsa, F. Bottari, L. Cristante, M. Fernandelli, eds., *Dignum laude virum. Studi di filologia classica e musica offerti a Franco Serpa*, Trieste 2011, pp. 47–56).

Fernandelli M. (2019), *Poesia bucolica e memoria dell'Odissea: Teocrito, Virgilio, Seamus Heaney*, in *Lingue Antiche e Moderne*, 8, pp. 225–58.

Ferrarino P. (1940), *Et rapidum cretae veniemus Oaxen: Verg. Buc. 1, 65*, in *Rendiconto delle Sessioni della R. Accademia dell'Istituto di Bologna, Classe di Scienze morali*, s. IV, 3, pp. 138–53 (= Ferrarino 1986b, pp. 118–28).

Ferrarino P. (1986a), *Qui non risere parentes. La chiusa della IV Bucolica e l'esegesi dell'egloga*, in *MusPat*, 4, pp. 9–23 (= Ferrarino 1986b, pp. 418–31).

522 BIBLIOGRAPHY

Ferrarino P. (1986b), *Scritti scelti*, Florence.

Ferraro S. (1982), *La presenza di Virgilio nei graffiti pompeiani*, Naples.

FGrH = *Die Fragmente der griechischen Historiker.*

Firpo G. (2005), *Ancora sui decem menses di Verg. Ecl. 4, 61*, in *Aevum*, 79, pp. 41–8.

Fisher R. S. (1982), *Conon and the Poet. A Solution to Eclogue, III, 40–2*, in *Latomus*, 41, pp. 803–14.

Flintoff E. (1973), *Eclogue IV.8–10*, in *CR*, n.s. 23, pp. 10–11.

Flintoff E. (1974), *The Setting of Virgil's Eclogues*, in *Latomus*, 33, 1974, pp. 814–46.

Flintoff E. (1975-6), *Characterisation in Virgil's Eclogues*, in *PVS*, 15, pp. 16–26.

Florio R. (1989), *Los antípodas de la Bucólica VI*, in *Emerita*, 57, pp. 239–62.

Fo, A. (2002), *Virgilio nei poeti e nel racconto (dal secondo Novecento italiano)*, in F. Roscetti (ed.), with the collaboration of L. Lanzetta and L. Cantatore, *Il classico nella Roma contemporanea: Mito, modelli, memoria*, Rome, pp. 181–239.

Fo, A. (2015), *Utopie pastorali e drammi della storia: Virgilio, Miklós Radnóti, Seamus Heaney*, in *I quaderni del Ramo d'Oro* online, 7, pp. 78–117.

Foster J. (1991), *Three Passages in Virgil*, in *SO*, 56, pp. 109–13.

Francese C. (1999), *Parthenius Grammaticus*, in *Mnemosyne*, s. IV, 52, pp. 63–71.

Frank T. (1916), *Magnum Jovis incrementum, Ciris 398, and Verg. Ec. IV. 49*, in *CPh*, 11, pp. 334–6.

Frank T. (1920), *Cornificius as Daphnis?*, in *CR*, 34, pp. 49–51.

Fredricksmeyer E. A. (1966), *Octavian and the Unity of the First Eclogue*, in *Hermes*, 94, pp. 208–18.

Freund S. (2000), *Vergil im frühen Christentum. Untersuchungen zu den Vergilzitaten bei Tertullian, Minucius Felix, Novatian, Cyprian und Arnobius*, Paderborn-Munich-Vienna-Zürich.

Freyburger-Galland, M.-L. (2013), *The Humanist Reception of Vergil's Bucolics*, in *AAntHung*, 53, pp. 301–10.

Freyer L. (1981), *The Riddles of Vergil's Third Eclogue*, in *Akroterion*, 26, pp. 46–51.

Frischer B. D. (1975), *At tu aureus esto. Eine Interpretation von Vergils 7. Ekloge*, Bonn.

Fuchs H. (1966), *Zum Wettgesang der Hirten in Vergils siebenter Ekloge*, in *MH*, 23, pp. 218–23.

Funaioli G. (1930), *Esegesi virgiliana antica. Prolegomeni alla edizione del commento di Giunio Filargirio e di Tito Gallo*, Milan.

Furth. Gr. Epigr. = D. L. Page, *Further Greek Epigrams*, Cambridge 1981.

Gagé J. (1955), *Apollon Romain. Essai sur le culte d'Apollon et le développement du ritus Graecus à Rome des origines à Auguste*, Paris.

Gagliardi P. (2003), *Gravis cantantibus umbra. Studi su Virgilio e Cornelio Gallo*, Bologna.

Gagliardi P. (2007), *Le umbrae nei finali virgiliani*, in *Maia*, 59, pp. 461–74.

Gagliardi P. (2011), *Ecl. 10, 73–74: Virgilio, Gallo e la crisi della poesia bucolica*, in *Hermes*, 139, pp. 21–41.

Gagliardi P. (2013), *L'ecl. 1 e l'ecl. 10 di Virgilio: considerazioni su un rapporto complesso*, in *Philologus*, 157, pp. 94–110.

Gagliardi P. (2014a), *Alberi e amore nell'ecl. 10 di Virgilio*, in *Lexis*, 32, pp. 302–14.

Gagliardi, P. (2014b), *Commento alla decima ecloga di Virgilio*, Hildesheim-Zurich-New York.

Gagliardi P. (2014c), *Il propemptikón Lycoridis nell'ecl. 10 di Virgilio*, in *Latomus*, 73, pp. 106–25.

Gagliardi P. (2014d), *L'ecl. 10 di Virgilio e la poesia bucolica post-teocritea*, in *REL*, 92, pp. 123–36.

Gagliardi P. (2014e), *Virgilio e l'Arcadia nell'ecl. 10*, in *Eirene*, 50, pp. 130–46.

Gagliardi P. (2015), *Adone nella poesia di Gallo?*, in *REA*, 117, pp. 65–75.

Gagliardi P. (2016), *Non ego Daphnim iudice te metuam. Riflessioni su Virg. ecl. 2,19–27*, in *RhM*, 159, pp. 392–408.

Gagliardi P. (2017a), *Ecloga haec paene tota Theocriti est: riflessioni sull'Ecloga 7 di Virgilio*, in *Emerita*, 87, pp. 83–98.

Gagliardi P. (2017b), *Tua cura, Lycoris: lessico erotico e schema Cornelianum da Virgilio agli elegiaci nel segno di Gallo*, in *WS*, 130, pp. 183–200.

Gagliardi P. (2019), *Uno schema particolare e l'architettura del liber bucolico virgiliano*, in *Commentaria Classica*, 6, pp. 167–91.

Gagliardi P. (2020), *Hesperus nelle Bucoliche di Virgilio*, in *Myrtia*, 35, pp. 249–73.

Gagliardi P. (2021), *Il tema dell'eco nelle Bucoliche virgiliane*, in *Pan*, 10, pp. 53–68.

Gaisser J. H. (1977), *Tibullus 2.3 and Vergil's Tenth Eclogue*, in *TAPhA*, 107, pp. 131–46.

Galinsky K. (1965), *Vergil's Second Eclogue: Its Theme and Relation to the Eclogue Book*, in *C&M*, 26, pp. 161–91.

Galinsky K. (1996), *Augustan Culture*, Princeton.

Galinsky K. (2006), *Vergil's Uses of libertas: Texts and Contexts*, in *Vergilius*, 52, pp. 3–19.

Gall D. (1999), *Zur Technik von Anspielung und Zitat in der römischen Dichtung. Vergil, Gallus und die Ciris*, Munich.

Gallavotti C. (1966), *Le coppe istoriate di Teocrito e Virgilio*, in *PP*, 21, pp. 421–36.

Gallazzi C. (1982), *P.Narm.Inv. 66.632. Vergilius, Ecloga VIII 53–62*, in *ZPE*, 48, pp. 75–8.

Garson R. W. (1971), *Theocritean Elements in Virgil's Eclogues*, in *CQ*, n.s. 21, pp. 188–203.

Gatz B. (1967), *Weltalter, goldene Zeit und sinnverwandte Vorstellungen*, Hildesheim.

Gawantka W. (1975), *Zu Vergils neunter Ekloge*, in J. Cobet, R. Leimbach, A. B. Neschke-Hentschke (eds.), *Dialogos. Für Harald Patzer zum 65. Geburtstag*, Wiesbaden, pp. 163–76.

Gebauer G. A. (1861), *De poetarum Graecorum bucolicorum inprimis Theocriti carminibus in Eclogis a Vergilio expressis libri duo*, Lipsiae.

Gercke A. (1921), *Auch ich war in Arkadien geboren*, in *NJB*, 47, pp. 313–17.

Geymonat M. (1964), *Due frammenti virgiliani ritrovati in Egitto*, in *Helikon*, 4, pp. 343–7.

Geymonat M. (1978–9), *Verg. Buc. II 24*, in *MCr*, 13–14, pp. 375–6.

Geymonat M. (1981a), *Lettura della seconda bucolica*, in Gigante (1981b), pp. 107–27.

Geymonat M. (1981b), *Tirsi critico di Lucilio nella settima egloga virgiliana*, in *Orpheus*, n.s. 2, pp. 366–70.

Geymonat M. (1982), *Ancora sul titolo delle Bucoliche*, in *BICS*, 29, pp. 17–18.

Geymonat M. (1987), *Some Textual Problems in Virgil*, in *MPhL*, 8, pp. 45–61.

Geymonat M. (1995), *The Transmission of Virgil's Works in Antiquity and the Middle Ages*, in Horsfall (1995a), pp. 293–312.

Geymonat M. (2000), *Immagini letterarie e reali del paesaggio di montagna in Virgilio*, in *Philologus*, 144, pp. 81–9.

Geymonat M. (2004), *Capellae and the End of the Eclogues*, in *HSPh*, 102, pp. 315–18.

Geymonat M. (2005), *Poesia e scienza in Virgilio: dalla III egloga al VI libro dell'Eneide*, in G. Reggi (ed.), *Letteratura e riflessione filosofica*, Lugano, pp. 165–78.

Giardina A. (1997), *L'Italia romana. Storie di un'identità incompiuta*, Rome-Bari.

Gifford, T. (1999), *Pastoral*, London-New York.

Gigante M. (1979), *Civiltà delle forme letterarie nell'antica Pompei*, Naples.

Gigante M. (1981a), *Lettura della prima bucolica*, in Gigante (1981b), pp. 17–104.

Gigante M. (ed.) (1981b), *Lecturae Vergilianae*, vol. I, *Le Bucoliche*, Naples.

Gigante M. (ed.) (1990), *Virgilio e gli Augustei*, Naples.

Gigante M. (2001), *Virgilio all'ombra del Vesuvio*, in *BCPE (Cron. Erc.)*, 31, pp. 5–26.

Gigante M. (2004), *Vergil in the Shadow of Vesuvius*, in Armstrong, Fish, Johnston, Skinner (2004), pp. 85–99.

Gigante M., Capasso M. (1989), *Il ritorno di Virgilio a Ercolano*, in *SIFC*, s. III, 7, pp. 3–6.

Gigante Lanzara V. (1994), *Verg. ecl. VIII 52–60*, in *MCr*, 29, pp. 241–3.

Gimm R. (1910), *De Vergilii stilo bucolico quaestiones selectae*, diss. Leipzig.

Giordano Rampioni A., Traina A. (1994), *Musica e poesia nelle Bucoliche: una esperienza, una proposta*, in *Aufidus*, 24, pp. 152–8.

Gioseffi M. (2004a), *Due punti di snodo in Virgilio (Il canto di Damone—Il banchetto di Didone)*, in M. Gioseffi (ed.), *Il dilettoso monte. Raccolta di saggi di filologia e tradizione classica*, Milan, pp. 39–78.

Gioseffi M. (2004b), *Pseudo-Probo ad Verg. Buc. 2.48: Narciso e i suoi pittori*, in V. de Angelis (ed.), *Sviluppi recenti nell'antichistica. Nuovi contributi*, Milan, pp. 81–108.

Gioseffi M. (2014), *A Very Long Engagement. Some Remarks on the Relationship between Marginalia and Commentaries in the Virgil Tradition*, in F. Montana, A. Porro (eds.), *The Birth of Scholiography: From Types to Texts*, Berlin-New York, pp. 176–91.

Gioseffi M. (2020), *Coridone mitomane e poeta*, in G. Polara (a cura di), *Omne tulit punctum qui miscuit utile dulci. Studi in onore di Arturo De Vivo*, Naples, I, pp. 443–58.

Gioseffi M. (2021), *Huc ades! Una nota al lessico di Virgilio*, in M. Manca, M. Venuti (eds.), *Paulo maiora canamus. Raccolta di studi per Paolo Mastandrea*, Venezia, pp. 21–32.

Glei R. F. (1991), *Der Vater der Dinge: Interpretationen zur poetischen, literarischen und kulturellen Dimension des Krieges bei Vergil*, Trier (2nd ed. 1997).

Gomez Gane Y. (2003), *An ratio inter Vergilii ecl. 6, 66 et Hymnum Hom. ad Ap. 3–4 intercedat*, in *Latinitas*, 51, pp. 144–7.

Gomez Gane Y. (2004), *Virgilio, ecl. 3, 26 e CLE 250: uincta o iuncta?*, in *Syll. Epigr. Barcin.*, 5, pp. 81–91.

Gómez Pallarès J. (2001), *Sobre Virg. Buc. 4.18–25, puer nascens, y la tradición de la écfrasis en Roma*, in *Emerita*, 69, pp. 93–114.

Goold G. P. (1986), *A Skullcracker in Virgil*, in I. Vaslef, H. Buschhausen (eds.), *Classica et Mediaevalia. Studies in Honor of Joseph Szövérffy*, Leiden, pp. 67–76.

Gotoff H. C. (1967), *On the Fourth Eclogue of Virgil*, in *Philologus*, 111, pp. 66–79.

Gow A. S. F. (1932), *Diminutives in Augustan Poetry*, in *CQ*, 26, pp. 150–7.

Gow A. S. F. (1952), *Theocritus*, 2 vols., Cambridge, 2nd ed.

Gowers E. (2005), *Virgil's Sibyl and the 'Many Mouths' Cliché (Aen. 6, 625–627)*, in *CQ*, n.s. 55, pp. 170–82.

GPh = A. S. F. Gow, D. L. Page, *The Garland of Philip*, 2 vols., Cambridge 1968.

Graf F. (1986), Βουκόλοι, in *ZPE*, 62, pp. 43–4.

Grant M. (2004), *Continuity in Pastoral: Plants and Food in Virgil*, in *PVS*, 25, pp. 125–34.

Gratwick A. S. (1973), *Corydon and His Prospects*, in *CR*, n.s. 23, p. 10.

Green R. P. H. (1996), *Octavian and Vergil's Eclogues*, in *Euphrosyne*, n.s. 24, pp. 225–36.

Gries G. Graf von (2008), *Genus et forma. Randbemerkungen zu Vergils IV. Ekloge*, in V. M. Strocka, R. von Haehling, S. Freund, M. Vielberg (eds.), *Vergil und das antike Epos. Festschrift H. J. Tschiedel*, Stuttgart, pp. 179–203.

Grillo A. (1971), *Poetica e critica letteraria nelle Bucoliche di Virgilio*, Naples.

Grimal P. (1948), *La Ve Églogue et les origines du culte impérial*, in *REL*, 26, pp. 50–2.

Grimal P. (1949), *La Ve Églogue et le culte de César*, in *Mélanges d'archéologie et d'histoire offerts à Charles Picard à l'occasion de son 65e anniversaire*, Paris, pp. 406–19.

Grimal P. (1987), *Les promesses de la deuxième Églogue*, in A. Bonanno, H. C. R. Vella (eds.), *Laurea corona. Studies in Honour of Edward Coleiro*, Amsterdam, pp. 78–83.

Grishin A. A. (2008), *Ludus in undis: An Acrostic in Eclogue 9*, in *HSPh*, 104, pp. 237–40.

Grondona M. (1977), *Gli epigrammi di Tibullo e il congedo delle elegie (su Properzio e Virgilio)*, in *Latomus*, 36, pp. 28–9.

Grüber J. (1968), *Marginalien zu Vergils vierter Ekloge*, in *Lemmata. Donum natalicium W. Ehlers*, Munich, pp. 58–65.

Guadagno C. (2007), *Riflessioni su Verg. ecl. 4, 60–63*, in *Vichiana*, s. IV, 9, pp. 41–53.

Guerrini R. (1973), *Vos coryli testes. Struttura e canto nella V egloga di Virgilio*, in *RAL*, 28, pp. 683–94.

Guidetti F. (2022), *For Whom Hesperus Shines: An Astronomical Allusion in Roman Epithalamic Poetry*, in *JRS*, 112, pp. 39–56.

Guidorizzi G., Melotti M. (eds.) (2005), *Orfeo e le sue metamorfosi. Mito, arte, poesia*, Rome.

Gummere J. F. (1934), *The Neuter Plural in Vergil*, Philadelphia.

Gurval R. A. (1995), *Actium and Augustus. The Politics and Emotions of Civil War*, Ann Arbor.

Guthrie W. K. C. (1952), *Orpheus and Greek Religion. A Study of the Orphic Movement*, London (1st ed. 1935).

Gutzwiller K. J. (1996a), *The Evidence for Theocritean Poetry Books*, in M. A. Harder, R. F. Regtuit, G. C. Wakker (eds.), *Theocritus*, Groningen, pp. 119–48.

Gutzwiller K. J. (1996b), *Vergil and the Date of the Theocritean Epigram Book*, in *Philologus*, 140, pp. 92–9.

H.-Sz. = J. B. Hofmann, A. Szantyr, *Lateinische Syntax und Stilistik*, Munich 1965 (Italian ed. of the *Stilistik* by A. Traina, *Stilistica latina*, trans. by C. Neri, updated by R. Oniga, with revisions and index by B. Pieri, Bologna 2002).

Hahn E. A. (1944), *The Characters in the Eclogues*, in *TAPhA*, 75, pp. 196–241.

Hahn I. (1983), *Die augusteischen Interpretationen des sidus Iulium*, in *ACD*, 19, pp. 57–66.

Hakamies R. (1951), *Étude sur l'origine et l'évolution du diminutif latin et sa survie dans les langues romanes*, Helsinki.

Halperin D. M. (1983), *Before Pastoral: Theocritus and the Ancient Tradition of Bucolic Poetry*, New Haven-London.

Hamblin F. R. (1928), *The Development of Allegory in the Classical Pastoral*, diss. Chicago.

Hanslik R. (1955), *Nachlese zu Vergils Eclogen I und IX*, in *WS*, 68, pp. 5–19.

Hanssen J. S. T. (1942), *Remarks on Euphony-Cacophony and the Language of Vergil*, in *SO*, 22, pp. 80–106.

Hanssen J. S. T. (1951), *Latin Diminutives. A Semantic Study*, Årbok.

Hardie C. (1956-7), *Eclogue VI as a Prelude to the Georgics*, in *PCPhS*, 170, pp. 12–14.

Hardie C. (1966-7), *The Tenth Eclogue*, in *PVS*, 6, pp. 1–11.

Hardie C. (1975), *Octavian and Eclogue I*, in B. Levick (ed.), *The Ancient Historian and His Materials. Essays in Honour of C. E. Stevens*, Westmead-Farnborough-Hants, pp. 109–22 (= *Der iuvenis der Ersten Ekloge*, in *AU*, 24, 1981, pp. 17–28).

Hardie P. (1996), *Virgil: A Paradoxical Poet?*, in F. Cairns, M. Heath (eds.), *Papers of the Leeds International Latin Seminar*, vol. IX, Leeds, pp. 103–21.

Hardie P. (1998), *Virgil*, Oxford.

Hardie P. (2005), *The Hesiodic Catalogue of Women and Latin Poetry*, in R. Hunter (ed.), *The Hesiodic Catalogue of Women. Constructions and Reconstructions*, Cambridge, pp. 287–98.

Hardie P. (2006), *Cultural and Historical Narratives in Virgil's Eclogues and Lucretius*, in Fantuzzi, Papanghelis (2006), pp. 275–300.

Hardie P. (2009), *Lucretian Receptions. History, The Sublime, Knowledge*, Cambridge.

Hardy R. B. (1990), *Vergil's Epitaph for Pastoral: Remembering and Forgetting in Eclogue 9*, in *SyllClass*, 2, pp. 29–38.

Harrison S. J. (1998), *The Lark Ascending: Corydon, Corydon (Vergil, Ecl. 7, 70)*, in *CQ*, n.s. 48, pp. 310–11.

Harrison S. J. (2007), *Generic Enrichment in Vergil & Horace*, Oxford.

526 BIBLIOGRAPHY

Harrison S. J. (2008), *Virgilian Contexts*, in L. Hardwick, C. Stray (eds.), *A Companion to Classical Receptions*, Malden MA, pp. 113–26.

Harrison S. J. (2021), *Prophetic, Poetic and Political Ambiguity in Vergil Eclogue 4*, in M. Vöhler, T. Fuhrer, S. Frangoulidis (eds.), *Strategies of Ambiguity in Ancient Literature*, Berlin-Boston, pp. 273–84.

Hatzikosta S. (1987), *Non-existent Rivers and Geographical Adynata. Verg. Ecl. 1.64–66 (65–67)*, in *MPhL*, 8, pp. 121–33.

Havet L. (1914a), *Notes critiques sur les Bucoliques de Virgile*, in *RPh*, 38, pp. 81–92.

Havet L. (1914b), *Virgile, Bucoliques 3, 100*, in *RPh*, 38, pp. 165–8.

HE = A. S. F. Gow, D. L. Page, *Hellenistic Epigrams*, 2 vols., Cambridge 1965.

Heaney S. (2003), *Eclogues in extremis: On the Staying Power of Pastoral*, in *PRIA*, 103C, pp. 1–12 (= Volk 2008, pp. 245–60).

Heaney S. (2013), *Virgilio nella Bann Valley*, edited by G. Bernardi Perini, C. Prezzavento, Mantua.

Heerink M. (2015), *Echoing Hylas: A Study in Hellenistic and Roman Metapoetics*, Madison WI-London 2015.

Hejduk J. D. (2020), *The God of Rome: Jupiter in Augustan Poetry*, Oxford.

Helck H. (1932a), *Incondita iactare. Ein Beitrag zur Erklärung der 2. Ekloge Vergils*, in *PhW*, 52, pp. 963–72.

Helck H. (1932b), *Vergils 2. Ekloge*, in *PhW*, 52, pp. 1553–8.

Henderson J. (1998a), *Virgil, Eclogue 9: Valleydiction*, in *PVS*, 23, pp. 149–76.

Henderson J. (1998b), *Virgil's Third Eclogue: How Do You Keep an Idiot in Suspense?*, in *CQ*, n.s. 48, pp. 213–28 (= Henderson 1999c, pp. 145–69 = Volk 2008, pp. 125–54).

Henderson J. (1999c), *Writing Down Rome. Satire, Comedy, and Other Offences in Latin Poetry*, Oxford.

Hendry M. (1995), *When Goats Look Askance. An Animal-Husbandry Joke in Virgil (Ecl. 3.8–9)*, in *LCM*, 20, pp. 51–2.

Herescu N. I. (1946), *Au dossier des decem menses (Virg. Ecl. IV, 61)*, in *RPh*, 20, pp. 12–21.

Herescu N. I. (1955), *Les decem menses et les calculs chronologiques des Romains*, in *REL*, 33, pp. 152–65.

Herescu N. I. (1957), *Le souvenir d'une berceuse dans la IVᵉ Églogue de Virgile*, in *Orpheus*, 4, pp. 125–30.

Herrmann L. (1930), *Les masques et les visages dans les Bucoliques de Virgile*, Brussels.

Herrmann L. (1946), *Paulatim flavescet campus*, in *LEC*, 14, p. 64.

Herrmann L. (1964), *Non iniussa cano. Virgile, Bucoliques VI, 8*, in *Latomus*, 23, pp. 77–80.

Heurgon J. (1967), *Tityre, Alfenus Varus et la Iᵉ Églogue de Virgile*, in *CT*, 15 (*Mélanges d'archéologie et d'histoire offerts à Charles Saumagne*), pp. 39–54.

Heuzé P. (1985), *L'image du corps dans l'oeuvre de Virgile*, Rome.

Heuzé P. (2006), *Esthétique du précis et du flou dans les Bucoliques*, in *REL*, 84, pp. 103–11.

Heyworth S. J. (1984), *Two conjectures (Horace, Carm. 1.12.33–40; Vergil, Ecl. 7.70)*, in *PCPhS*, 30, pp. 72–3.

Heyworth S. J. (2007), *Pastoral*, in S. J. Harrison (ed.), *A Companion to Latin Literature*, Malden MA-Oxford, pp. 148–58.

Heyworth S. J. (2015), *Notes on the Text and Interpretation of Vergil's Eclogues and Georgics*, in H.-C. Günther (ed.), *Virgilian Studies. A Miscellany Dedicated to the Memory of Mario Geymonat*, Nordhausen, pp. 195–249.

Highet G. (1974), *Performances of Vergil's Bucolics*, in *Vergilius*, 20, pp. 24–5.

Hinds S. (1983), *Carmina digna. Gallus P Qaṣr Ibrîm 6–7 Metamorphosed*, in F. Cairns (ed.), *Papers of the Liverpool Latin Seminar*, vol. IV, Liverpool, pp. 43–54.

Hinds S. (1998), *Allusion and Intertext. Dynamics of Appropriation in Roman Poetry*, Cambridge.

Hirschberger M. (2004), *Gynaikōn Katalogos und Megalai Ēhoiai. Ein Kommentar zu den Fragmenten zweier hesiodeischer Epen*, Leipzig.

Hoffmann F., Minas-Nerpel M., Pfeiffer S. (2009), *Die dreisprachige Stele des C. Cornelius Gallus. Übersetzung und Kommentar*, Berlin-New York.

Hofmann H. (1985), *Ein Aratpapyrus bei Vergil*, in *Hermes*, 113, pp. 468–80.

Hofmann J. B. (1951), *Lateinische Umgangssprache*, Heidelberg, 3rd ed. (Italian trans. by L. Ricottilli, *La lingua d'uso latina*, Bologna 2003, 3rd ed.).

Hollander R. (1993), *Le opere di Virgilio nella Commedia di Dante*, in A. A. Iannucci (ed.), *Dante e la 'bella scola' della poesia. Autorità e sfida poetica*, Ravenna, pp. 247–343.

Hollis A. S. (1996), *Virgil's Friend Varius Rufus*, in *PVS*, 22, pp. 19–33.

Hollis A. S. (2007), *Fragments of Roman Poetry c. 60 BC–AD 20*, Oxford.

Holzberg N. (2006), *Vergil: der Dichter und sein Werk*, Munich.

Hommel H. (1950), *Vergils 'messianisches' Gedicht*, in *Theologia Viatorum*, 2, pp. 182–212 (= Oppermann 1963, pp. 368–425).

Hoogma R. P. (1959), *Der Einfluss Vergils auf die Carmina Latina Epigraphica*, Amsterdam.

Hopkinson N. (1982), *Juxtaposed Prosodic Variants in Greek and Latin Poetry*, in *Glotta*, 60, pp. 162–7.

Horsfall N. (1981), *Some Problems of Titulature in Roman Literary History*, in *BICS*, 28, pp. 103–14.

Horsfall N. (1990), *Virgil and the Illusory Footnote*, in F. Cairns, M. Heath (eds.), *Papers of the Leeds International Latin Seminar*, vol. VI, Leeds, pp. 49–63.

Horsfall N. (1991), *Virgil, Parthenius and the Art of Mythological Reference*, in *Vergilius*, 37, pp. 31–6.

Horsfall N. (ed.) (1995a), *A Companion to the Study of Virgil*, Leiden-New York-Cologne.

Horsfall N. (1995b), *Virgil: His Life and Times*, in Horsfall (1995a), pp. 1–25.

Horsfall N. (1995c), *Style, Language and Metre*, in Horsfall (1995a), pp. 217–48.

Horsfall N. (1995d), *Virgil's Impact at Rome: The Non-literary Evidence*, in Horsfall (1995a), pp. 249–55.

Höschele R. (2013), *From Ecloga the Mime to Vergil's Eclogues as Mimes: ein Gedankenspiel*, in *Vergilius*, 59, pp. 37–60.

Houghton, L. B. T. (2019), *Virgil's Fourth Eclogue in the Renaissance* (Cambridge).

Houghton, L. B. T., Sgarbi, M. (eds.) (2018), *Virgil and Renaissance Culture*, Tempe AZ.

Housman A. E. (1900), *Elucidation of Latin Poets [II]: Virgil buc. IV 24*, in *CR*, 14, pp. 257–9 (= J. Diggle, F. R. D. Goodyear, eds., *The Classical Papers of A. E. Housman*, vol. II, Cambridge 1972, pp. 519–22).

Hubaux J. (1927), *Le réalisme dans les Bucoliques de Virgile*, Liège.

Hubaux J. (1930), *Les thèmes bucoliques dans la poésie latine*, Brussels.

Hubaux J. (1957), *Parthenius. Gallus. Virgile. Properce*, in *Atti dell'Accademia Properziana del Subasio*, s. V, 5, pp. 31–8.

Hubaux J., Leroy M. (1934), *Vulgo nascetur amomum*, in *AIPhO*, 2 (*Mélanges J. Bidez*), pp. 505–29.

Hubbard M. (1975), *The Capture of Silenus*, in *PCPhS*, 21, pp. 53–62.

Hubbard T. K. (1995a), *Allusive Artistry and Vergil's Revisionary Program: ecl. 1–3*, in *MD*, 34, pp. 37–67 (= Volk 2008, pp. 79–109; cf. Hubbard 1998, pp. 48–75).

Hubbard T. K. (1995b), *Intertextual Hermeneutics in Vergil's Fourth and Fifth Eclogues*, in *CJ*, 91, pp. 11–23 (cf. Hubbard 1998, pp. 77–99).

Hubbard T. K. (1998), *The Pipes of Pan: Intertextuality and Literary Filiation in the Pastoral Tradition from Theocritus to Milton*, Ann Arbor.

Hudson-Williams A. (1980), *Some Passages in Virgil's Eclogues*, in *CQ*, n.s. 30, pp. 124–32.

Hunter R. L. (1996), *Theocritus and the Archaeology of Greek Poetry*, Cambridge.

528 BIBLIOGRAPHY

Hunter R. L. (1999), *Theocritus: A Selection (Idylls 1, 3, 4, 6, 7, 11 and 13)*, Cambridge.

Hunter R. L. (2001), *Virgil and Theocritus: A Note on the Reception of the Encomium to Ptolemy Philadelphus*, in *SemRom*, 4, pp. 159–63 (= R. L. H., *On Coming After*, vol. I, *Hellenistic Poetry and Its Reception*, Berlin-New York 2008, pp. 378–83).

Hunter R. L. (2006), *The Shadow of Callimachus. Studies in the Reception of Hellenistic Poetry at Rome*, Cambridge.

Huxley H. H. (1969), *Vergil's Defective Meter?*, in *CJ*, 64, p. 280.

Huyck J. (1987), *Vergil's Phaethontiades*, in *HSPh*, 91, pp. 217–22.

ILS = Inscriptiones Latinae Selectae.

Irwin M. E. (1989), *Colourful Sheep in the Golden Age: Vergil, Eclogues 4, 42–5*, in *EMC*, 33, pp. 23–37.

Jachmann G. (1922), *Die dichterische Technik in Vergils Bukolika*, in *NJB*, 49, pp. 110–19 (= G. J., *Ausgewählte Schriften*, Königstein 1981, pp. 303–22).

Jachmann G. (1923), *Vergils sechste Ekloge*, in *Hermes*, 58, pp. 288–304.

Jachmann G. (1952a), *Die vierte Ekloge Vergils*, in *ASNSP*, s. II, 21, pp. 13–62.

Jachmann G. (1952b), *L'Arcadia come paesaggio bucolico*, in *Maia*, 5, pp. 161–74.

Jackson Knight W. F. (1944), *Roman Vergil*, London (2nd ed. 1966, with two appendices on V.'s language).

Jacobson H. (1982), *A Philosophical Topos at Vergil, Eclogues 6, 37–8*, in *LCM*, 7, p. 42.

Jacoby F. (1905), *Zur Entstehung der römischen Elegie*, in *RhM*, 60, pp. 38–105.

Jahn P. (1902), *Aus Vergils Frühzeit*, in *Hermes*, 37, pp. 161–72.

Janko R. (2000), *Philodemus, On Poems*, Oxford.

Jeanmaire H. (1930), *Le messianisme de Virgile*, Paris.

Jeanmaire H. (1939), *La Sibylle et le retour de l'âge d'or*, Paris.

Jenkyns R. (1989), *Virgil and Arcadia*, in *JRS*, 79, pp. 26–39.

Jenkyns R. (1998), *Virgil's Experience*, Oxford.

Johnston M. (1931), *Vergil, Ecl. IX.53–4*, in *CW*, 24, p. 103.

Johnston, P. A., Papaioannou, S. (2013), *Introduction: Idyllic Landscapes in Antiquity: The Golden Age, Arcadia, and the locus amoenus, AAntHung*, 53, pp. 133–44.

Jolowicz D. (2021), *Latin Poetry in the Ancient Greek Novels*, Oxford.

Jones F. (2011), *Virgil's Garden. The Nature of Bucolic Space*, London.

de Jonge, C. C. (2019), *Dionysius and Horace: Composition in Augustan Rome*, in R. L. Hunter, C. C. de Jonge (eds.), *Dionysius of Halicarnassus and Augustan Rome: Rhetoric, Criticism and Historiography*, Cambridge-New York, pp. 242–66.

Jouteur I. (2007), *La bucolique III de Virgile ou Le spectacle d'une transfiguration*, in *Euphrosyne*, n.s. 35, pp. 63–82.

K.-S. = R. Kühner, C. Stegmann, *Ausführliche Grammatik der lateinischen Sprache*, Teil 2, *Satzlehre*, 2 vols., Hannover 1914².

Kalinka E. (1943), *Qui = cui*, in *Glotta*, 30, pp. 222–3.

Kallendorf C. (1990), *Nachleben*, in *Vergilius*, 36, pp. 82–100.

Kallendorf C. (2012), *A Bibliography of the Early Printed Editions of Virgil, 1469–1850*, New Castle.

Kallendorf C. (2015), *The Protean Virgil. Material Form and the Reception of the Classics*, Oxford.

Kallendorf C. (2020), *Printing Virgil: the Transformation of the Classics in the Renaissance*, Leiden.

Kania R. (2012), *Orpheus and the Reinvention of Bucolic Poetry*, in *AJPh*, 133, pp. 657–85.

Kania R. (2016), *Virgil's Eclogues and the Art of Fiction. A Study of the Poetic Imagination*, Cambridge.

Karanika A. (2006), *Agonistic Poetics in Virgil's Third Eclogue*, in Skoie, Bjørnstad Velázquez (2006), pp. 107–14.

BIBLIOGRAPHY 529

Kaster R. A. (1983), *The Echo of a Chaste Obscenity, Verg. E. VI.26 and Symm. Ep. VI.22.1*, in *AJPh*, 104, pp. 395–7.

Katz J. T. (2008), *Vergil Translates Aratus: Phaenomena 1–2 and Georgics 1.1–2*, in *MD*, 60, pp. 105–23.

Katz J. T., Volk K. (2006), *Erotic Hardening and Softening in Vergil's Eighth Eclogue*, in *CQ*, n.s. 56, pp. 169–74.

Kayachev B. (2017), *He-Who-Must-Not-Be-Named: Aratus in Virgil's Third Eclogue*, in *HSPh*, 109, pp. 339–52.

Keith A. (2011), *Lycoris Galli/Volumnia Cytheris: a Greek Courtesan in Rome*, in *EuGeStA*, 1, pp. 23–53.

Keith A. (2018), *Pascite boves, summittite tauros: Cattle and Oxen in the Virgilian Corpus*, in S. Harrison, S. Frangoulidis, T. D. Papanghelis (eds.), *Intratextuality and Latin Literature*, Berlin-Boston, pp. 99–129.

Kelley S. T. (1977), *The Gallus Quotation in Vergil's Tenth Eclogue*, in *Vergilius*, 23, pp. 17–20.

Kellum B. A. (1990), *The City Adorned: Programmatic Display at the Aedes Concordiae Augustae*, in Raaflaub, Toher (1990), pp. 276–96.

Kennedy D. F. (1982), *Gallus and the Culex*, in *CQ*, n.s. 32, pp. 385–7.

Kennedy D. F. (1983), *Shades of Meaning. Virgil, Ecl. 10.75–77*, in *LCM*, 8, p. 124.

Kennedy D. F. (1987), *Arcades ambo: Virgil, Gallus and Arcadia*, in *Hermathena*, 143, pp. 47–59.

Kenney E. J. (1983), *Virgil and the Elegiac Sensibility*, in *ICS*, 8, pp. 49–52.

Keppie L. (1981), *Vergil, the Confiscations, and Caesar's Tenth Legion*, in *CQ*, n.s. 31, pp. 367–70.

Keppie L. (1983), *Colonisation and Veteran Settlement in Italy 47–14 B.C.*, London.

Kidd D. A. (1964), *Imitation in the Tenth Eclogue*, in *BICS*, 11, pp. 54–64.

Kinzler D. (1968), *Vergil, Eclogue IV, 61*, in *CJ*, 64, pp. 130–1.

Klingner F. (1927), *Virgils erste Ekloge*, in *Hermes*, 62, pp. 129–53 (= *Das erste Hirtengedicht Vergils*, in F. K., *Römische Geisteswelt*, Stuttgart 1965, 5th ed., pp. 312–26).

Klingner F. (1967), *Virgil. Bucolica, Georgica, Aeneis*, Zürich.

Klotz A. (1920), *Beiträge zum Verständnis von Vergils Hirtengedichten*, in *NJA*, 45, pp. 145–58.

Knaack G. (1883), *Analecta*, in *Hermes*, 18, pp. 28–33.

Knox P. E. (1985), *Wine, Water, and Callimachean Polemics*, in *HSPh*, 89, pp. 107–19.

Knox P. E. (1986), *Adjectives in -osus and Latin Poetic Diction*, in *Glotta*, 64, pp. 90–101.

Knox P. E. (1990), *In Pursuit of Daphne*, in *TAPhA*, 120, pp. 183–202.

Köhnken A. (1984), *Sola...tua carmina (Vergil, Ecl. 8, 9 f)*, in *WJA*, N. F. 10, pp. 77–90.

Kollman E. D. (1975), *A Study of Proper Names in Vergil's Eclogues*, in *CW*, 69, pp. 97–112.

Korenjak M. (2003), *Tityri sub persona: Der antike Biographismus und die bukolische Tradition*, in *A&A*, 49, pp. 58–79.

Korzeniowski G. S. (1999), *The Clausula-Type 'et mihi Damon' and the Chronology of Virgil's Eclogues*, in *Sileno*, 25, pp. 115–36.

Koster S. (1990), *Cum Gallus amore peribat: der Tod des praefectus Aegypti im Spiegel der 10. Ecloge*, in C. Boerker, M. Donderer (eds.), *Das antike Rom und der Osten: Festschrift für K. Parlasca*, Erlangen, pp. 103–23.

Kovacs D. (2011), *Virgil, Eclogue 4.53–4: Enough of What?*, in *CQ*, n.s. 61, pp. 314–15.

Kovacs D., Omrani B. (2012), *Virgil, Eclogues 4.28*, in *CQ*, n.s. 62, pp. 866–8.

Köves-Zulauf T. (1990), *Römische Geburtsriten*, Munich.

Kowara M. J. (1995), *Elisions in Virgil's Fifth Eclogue*, in *Vergilius*, 41, pp. 61–2.

Kraggerud E. (1989), *Three Problematic Passages in Vergil (Ecl. 4, 8; Georg. 4, 453–456; Aen. 1, 1–7)*, in *SO*, 64, pp. 110–24 (pp. 110–12; cf. Kraggerud 2017b, pp. 16–18 and 81–2).

530 BIBLIOGRAPHY

Kraggerud E. (1990), *Further Problems in Vergil (Ecl. 4, 4; G. 2, 508f.; Aen. 4, 126; 12, 648; 790; 835)*, in *SO*, 65, pp. 63–77.

Kraggerud E. (1996), *Against the Consensus: Some Problems of Text and Interpretation in Vergil*, in *SO*, 71, pp. 102–14.

Kraggerud E. (2005), *Verg. ecl. 10, 44: A Pivotal Line*, in *Eranos*, 103, pp. 35–7 (cf. Kraggerud 2017b, pp. 74–9 and 94).

Kraggerud E. (2006a), *Numitorius' Parody of Vergil, Ecl. 3. 1-2*, in *SO*, 81, pp. 85–7.

Kraggerud E. (2006b), *Textual and Exegetical Issues in Vergil's Fifth and Seventh 'Eclogues'*, in *SO*, 81, pp. 29–57 (cf. Kraggerud 2017b, pp. 23–5 and 82–3; 26–7 and 81–2; 28–9 and 83–4; 30–3 and 84–5; 55–7 and 88–90; 58–60 and 90–1; 61–2 and 91; 63–5 and 91; 72–3 and 93).

Kraggerud E. (2007), *Two Cases of Emendanda in the Eclogues*, in *SO*, 82, pp. 87–9 (cf. Kraggerud 2017b, pp. 13 and 80–1; 14–15 and 81).

Kraggerud E. (2008), *In usum editorum: On some Readings and Conjectures in Vergil*, in *SO*, 83, pp. 52–67 (pp. 53–9; cf. Kraggerud 2017b, pp. 21–2 and 82; 44–6 and 87; 47–50 and 87–8; 53–4 and 88).

Kraggerud E. (2014), *Unfounded Consensus: On Vergil Ecl. 6. 34; G. 1. 36; A. 1. 458*, in *SO*, 88, pp. 70–9 (pp. 70–2; cf. Kraggerud 2017b, pp. 51–2 and 88).

Kraggerud E. (2017a), *Some New Vergilian Loci and Second Thoughts on Old Ones*, in *SO*, 91, pp. 93–117 (pp. 93–105; cf. Kraggerud 2020, pp. 265–71; 272–7).

Kraggerud E. (2017b), *Vergiliana. Critical Studies on the Texts of Publius Vergilius Maro*, London (including a revised version of the author's textual-critical and interpretive notes on the *E.* appeared between 1989 and 2008).

Kraggerud E. (2020), *Critica. Textual Issues in Horace, Ennius, Vergil and Other Authors*, London-New York.

Kraus W. (1981), *Vergils vierte Ekloge: Ein kritisches Hypomnema*, in *ANRW*, II.31.1, Berlin-New York, pp. 604–45.

Krenkel W. (1958-9), *Zu Vergil, Ecl. III, 104–105 und seinem Erklärer Asconius Pedianus*, in *Wissenschaftliche Zeitschrift der Universität Rostock*, 8, pp. 27–32 (= J. Irmscher, K. Kumaniecki, eds., *Römische Literatur der augusteischen Zeit*, Berlin 1960, pp. 36–8).

Kronenberg L. (2016), *Epicurean Pastoral: Daphnis as an Allegory for Lucretius in Vergil's Eclogues*, in *Vergilius*, 62, pp. 25–56.

Kropp A. (1998), *Die vierte Ekloge und der Archetyp von der Geburt des Kindes*, in *AU*, 41, pp. 65–81.

Kumaniecki C. F. (1926), *Quo ordine Vergilii eclogae conscriptae sint*, in *Eos*, 29, pp. 69–79.

Kurfess A. (1955), *Vergils 4. Ekloge und christliche Sibyllen*, in *Gymnasium*, 62, pp. 110–12.

Kyriakou P. (1996), *Pergite Pierides: Aemulatio in Vergil's Ecl. 6 and 10*, in *QUCC*, 81, pp. 147–57.

Ladewig T. (1870), *De Vergilio, verborum novatore*, Neu-Strelitz.

Lagrange M.-J. (1931), *À propos du messianisme de la IVe églogue de Virgile*, in *RBi*, 40, pp. 613–14.

Landolfi L. (1996), *Il volo di Dike (da Arato a Giovenale)*, Bologna.

Landolfi L. (2020), *Pan deus Arcadiae (Verg. ecl. 10, 26): l'EYPHMA, l'AITION (tra Virgilio bucolico e Ovidio epico)*, in *RhM*, N. F. 9, pp. 31–52.

Langholf V. (1990), *Vergil-Allegorese in den Bucolica des Calpurnius Siculus*, in *RhM*, 133, pp. 350–70.

Langlois P. (1961), *Les formations en -bundus: index et commentaire*, in *REL*, 39, pp. 117–34.

Langslow D. R. (1995), *A Punning Reminiscence of Vergil, Ecl. 10, 75-7 in Horace Epist. 1.5.28-9*, in *CQ*, n.s. 45, pp. 256–60.

BIBLIOGRAPHY 531

Lanternari D. (1989), *L'aspetto neo-pitagorico della IV Ecloga di Virgilio*, in *SMSR*, 55, pp. 213–21.

La Penna A. (1962), *Esiodo nella cultura e nella poesia di Virgilio*, in *Hésiode et son influence, Entretiens de la Fondation Hardt*, 7, Vandoeuvres-Geneva, pp. 213–52.

La Penna A. (1963a), *La seconda ecloga e la poesia bucolica di Virgilio*, in *Maia*, 15, pp. 484–92.

La Penna A. (1963b), *Orazio e l'ideologia del principato*, Turin.

La Penna A. (1981a), *Lettura della terza bucolica*, in Gigante (1981b), pp. 131–9.

La Penna A. (1981b), *Manilio, Virgilio e... Bavio*, in *Maia*, 33, pp. 215–16.

La Penna A. (1982), *Albe tragiche (da Virgilio a Leopardi)*, in *Belfagor*, 37, pp. 27–40 (= La Penna 1991, pp. 321–36).

La Penna A. (1983a), *Il canto, il lavoro, il potere*, introduction to Virgilio, *Le Georgiche*, translation and notes by L. Canali, Milan, pp. 5–112 (pp. 5–70 = introduction to Virgilio, *Bucoliche*, translation and notes by L. Canali, Milan 1986, pp. i–lxvi = La Penna 2005, pp. 3–61).

La Penna A. (1983b), *Le scelte di Sannazaro in Arcadia*, in V. Pöschl (ed.), *2000 Jahre Vergil. Ein Symposion*, Wiesbaden, pp. 87–108 (= La Penna 1991, pp. 169–92).

La Penna A. (1987), *Vidi: per la storia di una formula poetica*, in A. Bonanno, H. C. R. Vella (eds.), *Laurea corona. Studies in Honour of Edward Coleiro*, Amsterdam, pp. 99–119.

La Penna A. (1989), *'... cum flore, Maecenas, rosarum...' Su una collocazione artistica del vocativo in poesia latina*, in *Mnemosynum. Studi in onore di Alfredo Ghiselli*, Bologna, pp. 335–53.

La Penna A. (1991), *Tersite censurato e altri studi di letteratura fra antico e moderno*, Pisa.

La Penna A. (1997), *Fallit imago: una polemica di Manilio contro Virgilio e Lucrezio (Nota a Manilio IV 306)*, in *Maia*, 49, pp. 107–8.

La Penna A. (2005), *L'impossibile giustificazione della storia. Un'interpretazione di Virgilio*, Rome-Bari.

La Rocca E. (2008), *Lo spazio negato. La pittura di paesaggio nella cultura artistica greca e romana*, Milan.

Larson J. (2001), *Greek Nymphs. Myth, Cult, Lore*, Oxford.

Lavagnini B. (1935), *Virgilio, Teocrito e Sofrone*, in *AC*, 4, pp. 153–5.

Leach E. W. (1966), *Nature and Art in Vergil's Second Eclogue*, in *AJPh*, 87, pp. 427–45.

Leach E. W. (1968), *The Unity of Eclogue VI*, in *Latomus*, 27, pp. 13–32.

Leach E. W. (1971), *Eclogue IV: Symbolism and Sources*, in *Arethusa*, 4, pp. 167–84.

Leach E. W. (1974), *Vergil's Eclogues. Landscapes of Experience*, Ithaca NY-London.

Leach E. W. (1988), *The Rhetoric of Space. Literary and Artistic Representations of Landscape in Republican and Augustan Rome*, Princeton.

Lebek W. D. (2008), *Das Gleichnis des Varius Rufus, De morte frg. 4 (ceu canis umbrosam usw.) und das erste Gleichnis Vergils, Ekloge 8, 85–89 (Talis amor Daphnim usw.)*, in V. M. Strocka, R. von Haehling, S. Freund, M. Vielberg (eds.), *Vergil und das antike Epos. Festschrift H. J. Tschiedel*, Stuttgart, pp. 205–20.

Leclercq R. (1996), *Le divin loisir: Essai sur les 'Bucoliques' de Virgile*, Brussels.

Lecrompe R. (1970), *Virgile, Bucoliques: Index verborum, relevés statistiques*, Hildesheim.

Lee G. (1977), *A Reading of Virgil's Fifth Eclogue*, in *PCPhS*, n.s. 23, pp. 62–70.

Lee G. (1981), *Imitation and the Poetry of Virgil*, in *G&R*, 28, pp. 10–22.

Lee M. O. (1984), *Virgil: The Eclogues*, New York.

Lee M. O. (1989), *Death and Rebirth in Virgil's Arcadia*, Albany.

Lefèvre E. (2000), *Catulls Parzenlied und Vergils vierte Ekloge*, in *Philologus*, 144, pp. 62–80.

Leigh M. (2016), *Vergil's Second Eclogue and the Class Struggle*, in *CPh*, 111, pp. 406–33.

Lembach K. (1970), *Die Pflanzen bei Theokrit*, Heidelberg.

532   BIBLIOGRAPHY

Lentini G. (1997), *Un'imitazione teocritea nel terzo libro delle Georgiche*, in *MD*, 38, pp. 179–83.

Leo F. (1902), *Vergil und die Ciris*, in *Hermes*, 37, pp. 14–55 (= Leo 1960, vol. II, pp. 29–70).

Leo F. (1903), *Vergils erste und neunte Ekloge*, in *Hermes*, 38, pp. 1–18 (= Leo 1960, vol. II, pp. 11–28).

Leo F. (1960), *Ausgewählte kleine Schriften*, 2 vols., Rome.

Lerner L. (1984), *The Eclogues and the Pastoral Tradition*, in C. Martindale (ed.), *Virgil and His Influence: Bimillennial Studies*, Bristol, pp. 193–213.

Leumann M. (1977), *Lateinische Laut- und Formenlehre*, Munich, 2nd ed.

Levi P. (1966), *The Dedication to Pollio in Virgil's Eighth Eclogue*, in *Hermes*, 94, pp. 73–9.

Levi P. (1967–8), *Arcadia*, in *PVS*, 7, pp. 1–11.

Levi P. (1971), *Zu Vergils achter Ekloge*, in *Hermes*, 99, p. 126.

Levi P. (1998), *Vergil: His Life and Times*, London.

Lieberg G. (1977), *L'armonia delle sfere in Virgilio? Osservazioni sull'epilogo della sesta ecloga*, in *Atti del Convegno virgiliano sul bimillenario delle Georgiche*, Naples, pp. 405–20 (= *L'harmonie des sphères chez Virgile? Remarques sur l'épilogue de la sixième Églogue*, in *BAGB*, 37, 1978, pp. 343–58).

Lieberg G. (1982a), *Poeta creator. Studien zu einer Figur der antiken Dichtung*, Amsterdam.

Lieberg G. (1982b), *Virgile et l'idée de poète créateur dans l'antiquité*, in *Latomus*, 41, pp. 255–84.

Liegle J. (1943), *Die Tityruskloge*, in *Hermes*, 78, pp. 209–31.

Lightfoot J. L. (1999), *Parthenius of Nicaea*, Oxford.

LIMC = Lexicon Iconographicum Mythologiae Classicae, Zürich-Munich 1981–99.

Lindahl S. (1994), *Die Anordnung in den Hirtengedichten Vergils*, in *C&M*, 45, pp. 161–78.

Lindheim N. (2005), *The Virgilian Pastoral Tradition*, Pittsburgh, PA.

Ling R. (1991), *Roman Painting*, Cambridge.

Lipka M. (2001), *Language in Vergil's Eclogues*, Berlin-New York.

Lipka M. (2002), *Notes on fagus in Vergil's Eclogues*, in *Philologus*, 146, pp. 133–8.

Löfstedt E. (1933), *Syntactica*, vol. II, Lund (= Malmö 1956).

Lohmann A. (1915), *De Graecismorum usu Vergiliano quaestiones selectae*, Münster.

Loupiac A. (2001), *Orphée-Gallus, figure de l'évolution morale et poétique de Virgile des Bucoliques à l'Énéide*, in *REL*, 79, pp. 93–103.

Loupiac A. (2003), *Notula vergiliana: les coupes d'Alcimédon (Buc. III, 34–47), emblèmes des interrogations de Virgile?*, in *BAGB*, pp. 130–5.

Loupiac A. (2006), *Notula vergiliana. 2, Les métamorphoses d'un 'adynaton': sur quelques vers des Bucoliques I et IX*, in *BAGB*, pp. 142–7.

Lovejoy A. O., Boas G. (1935), *Primitivism and Related Ideas in Antiquity*, Baltimore (= Baltimore-London 1997).

LTUR = E. M. Steinby (ed.), *Lexicon Topographicum Urbis Romae*, 6 vols., Rome 1993–2000.

Lucarini C. M. (2007), *L'origine della poesia bucolica in Grecia*, in *GIF*, 59, pp. 213–44.

Luiselli B. (1967), *Studi sulla poesia bucolica*, Cagliari.

Lunelli A. (1969), *Aerius. Storia di una parola poetica (Varia neoterica)*, Rome.

Lunelli A. (ed.) (1980), *La lingua poetica latina*, Bologna (3rd ed. 1988).

Lunelli A. (2001), *Scholiorum in Vergilium Veronensium Reliquiae: Notizie degli scavi, edizione provvisoria. I: In Bucolica*, in *Maia*, 53, pp. 63–131.

Luther A. (2002), *Historische Studien zu den Bucolica Vergils*, Vienna.

Lyne R. O. A. M. (1978), *Ciris. A Poem Attributed to Vergil*, Cambridge.

Maass E. (1929), *Stimichon*, in *RhM*, 78, pp. 218–19.

Macdonald J. S. (2003), *Dueling Contests: Theocritus and Vergil's Third and Seventh 'Eclogues'*, in C. Deroux (ed.), *Studies in Latin Literature and Roman History*, vol. XI, Brussels, pp. 199-207.

Macdonald J. S. (2005), *Structure and Allusion in Idyll 2 and Eclogue 8*, in *Vergilius*, 51, pp. 12-31.

Mackay L. A. (1961), *On Two Eclogues of Virgil*, in *Phoenix*, 15, pp. 156-8.

Mackay L. A. (1971), *Meliboeus exul*, in *Vergilius*, 17, pp. 2-3.

Maggiulli G. (1995), *Incipiant cum primum surgere: mondo vegetale e nomenclatura della flora di Virgilio*, Rome.

Magnelli E. (2010), *Libetridi in Euforione, Virgilio e altrove*, in *MD*, 65, pp. 167-75.

Maia De Carvalho P. (1966), *À propos de Virg. Buc. II, 30 (haedorum gregem viridi compellere hibisco). Une réplique horatienne à l'idéal bucolique*, in *REA*, 68, pp. 278-81.

Malaspina E. (1986), *Il Tuscum iurgium nell'amebeo virgiliano (Ecl. 3.104-107)*, in *RCCM*, 28, pp. 7-15.

Maleuvre J.-Y. (2000), *Violence et ironie dans les Bucoliques de Virgile*, Paris.

Malosti S. (1967), *Uno stilema virgiliano: l'ablativo di estensione*, in A. Traina (ed.), *Studi sulla lingua poetica latina*, Rome, pp. 19-101.

Maltby R. (1991), *A Lexicon of Ancient Latin Etymologies*, Leeds.

Manieri A. (2009), *Agoni poetico-musicali nella Grecia antica*, vol. I, *Beozia*, Pisa-Rome.

Mankin D. (1988), *The Addressee of Virgil's Eighth Eclogue: A Reconsideration*, in *Hermes*, 116, pp. 63-76.

Mannsperger D. (1973), *Apollo gegen Dionysos. Numismatische Beiträge zu Octavians Rolle als Vindex Libertatis*, in *Gymnasium*, 80, pp. 381-404.

Manuwald G. (2002), *Das Singen des kleinen Hermes und des Silen. Zum homerischen Hermeshymnos und zu Vergils Sechster Ekloge*, in *RhM*, 145, pp. 150-74.

Manzanero Cano F. (2000), *Baccare frontem cingite: eco de una práctica mágica en Virg., Buc. VII 27-28*, in *CFC(L)*, 19, pp. 53-7.

Manzoni G. E. (1995), *Foroiuliensis poeta. Vita e poesia di Cornelio Gallo*, Milan.

Marangoni C. (2002-3), *Tua, Maecenas, haud mollia iussa. Materiali e appunti per la storia di un topos proemiale*, in *Incontri Triestini di Filologia Classica*, 2, pp. 77-90.

Marchesi C. (1961), *Pastorale virgiliana*, in *Helicon*, 1, pp. 19-27.

Marchetta A. (1994a), *Due studi sulle Bucoliche di Virgilio. I. L'incipit bucolico di Virgilio: ecl. 2,1. II. La semantica di formosus*, Rome.

Marchetta A. (1994b), *Valenza ideologico-letteraria dell'interiezione 'a' in Virgilio*, in *RCCM*, 36, pp. 317-41.

Marchetta A. (2007), *Luce e ombra nei finali di Catullo, Lucrezio, Virgilio*, in *StudRom*, 55, pp. 3-77.

Marchetta A. (2018), *Rileggendo le Bucoliche di Virgilio*, Rome.

Marcone A. (2010), *Un 'dio presente': osservazioni sulle premesse ellenistiche del culto imperiale romano*, in S. Bussi, D. Foraboschi (eds.), *Roma e l'eredità ellenistica*, Pisa-Rome, pp. 205-10.

Marinčič M. (2001), *Der Weltaltermythos in Catulls Peleus-Epos (C. 64), der 'Kleine Herakles' (Theocr. Id. 24) und der römische 'Messianismus' Vergils*, in *Hermes*, 129, pp. 484-504.

Marinčič M. (2002), *Roman Archaeology in Vergil's Arcadia (Vergil Eclogue 4; Aeneid 8; Livy 1.7)*, in D. S. Levene, D. P. Nelis (eds.), *Clio and the Poets: Augustan Poetry and the Traditions of Ancient Historiography*, Leiden, pp. 143-61.

Marino S. (2006), *'Qualis apes aestate nova...': Bienen als Symbol, Metapher, Vergleich und Gleichnis bei Vergil*, in *AU*, 49, pp. 22-9.

534 BIBLIOGRAPHY

Mariotti S. (1952), *Livio Andronico e la traduzione artistica*, Urbino (2nd ed. 1986).

Mariotti S. (1963), *Intorno a Domizio Marso*, in *Miscellanea di studi alessandrini in memoria di Augusto Rostagni*, Turin, pp. 588–614 (= S. M., *Scritti di filologia classica*, Rome 2000, pp. 91–118).

Marouzeau J. (1931), *Répétitions et hantises verbales chez Virgile*, in *REL*, 9, pp. 237–57.

Marouzeau J. (1946), *Traité de stylistique latine*, Paris (2nd ed.).

Martin J. (1946), *Vergil und die Landanweisungen*, in *WJA*, 1, pp. 98–107.

Martin R. H. (1943), *The Golden Age and the κύκλος γενέσεων (Cyclical Theory) in Greek and Latin Literature*, in *G&R*, 12, pp. 62–71.

Martindale C. (ed.) (1997a), *The Cambridge Companion to Virgil*, Cambridge.

Martindale C. (1997b), *Green Politics: The Eclogues*, in Martindale (1997a), pp. 117–24.

Martínez Astorino P. (2006), *Dafnis en la bucólica V de Virgilio: la alusión compleja y los límites de la identidad*, in *Auster*, 10–11, pp. 89–100.

Marx F. (1898), *Virgils vierte Ekloge*, in *NJB*, 1, pp. 105–28.

Massimilla G. (1996), *Callimaco, Aitia, Libri primo e secondo*, Pisa.

Massimilla G. (2010), *Callimaco, Aitia, Libri terzo e quarto*, Pisa-Rome.

Mauerhofer K. (2004), *Der Hylas-Mythos in der antiken Literatur*, Munich-Leipzig.

Maurach G. (2008), *Über das Hirtengespräch in Vergils ecl. 3*, in *Philologus*, 152, pp. 230–45.

Maurer K. (1998), *Gallus' Parthian Bow*, in *Latomus*, 57, pp. 578–88.

Maury P. (1944), *Le secret de Virgile et l'architecture des 'Bucoliques'*, in *Lettres d'Humanité*, 3, pp. 71–147.

Mayer R. (1983a), *Missing Persons in the Eclogues*, in *BICS*, 30, pp. 17–30.

Mayer R. (1983b), *The Civil Status of Corydon*, in *CQ*, n.s. 33, pp. 298–300.

Mayer R. (1999), *Grecism*, in J. N. Adams, R. Mayer (eds.) (1999), *Aspects of the Language of Latin Poetry*, Oxford, pp. 157–82.

Mayer R. (2007), *Impressions of Rome*, in *G&R*, s. II, 54, pp. 156–77.

Mayor J. B., Fowler W. W., Conway R. S. (1907), *Virgil's Messianic Eclogue: Its Meaning, Occasion, and Sources*, London.

McKay K. J. (1972), *Frustration of Anticipation in Vergil, Ecl. VI?*, in *Antichthon*, 6, pp. 53–9.

Meban D. (2009), *Virgil's Eclogues and Social Memory*, in *AJPh*, 130, pp. 99–130.

Merkelbach R. (1956), *ΒΟΥΚΟΛΙΑΣΤΑΙ. Der Wettgesang der Hirten*, in *RhM*, 99, pp. 97–122.

Merkelbach R. (1988), *Die Hirten des Dionysos. Die Dionysos-Mysterien der römischen Kaiserzeit und der bukolische Roman des Longus*, Stuttgart. (Italian trans. by E. Minguzzi, *I misteri di Dioniso: il dionisismo in età imperiale e il romanzo pastorale di Longo*, Genoa 1991).

Merlan P. (1963), *Zum Schluss von Vergils vierter Ekloge*, in *MH*, 20, p. 21.

Merli E. (1997), *ἥλιον ἐν λέσχῃ κατεδύσαμεν: sulla tradizione latina di un motivo callimacheo*, in *Maia*, 49, pp. 385–90.

Merone E. (1961), *L'allitterazione nelle Bucoliche di Virgilio*, in *Aevum*, 35, pp. 199–219.

Mesk J. (1927), *Der Schiedsspruch in der siebenten Ekloge Vergils*, in *Philologus*, 83, pp. 453–8.

Mette H. J. (1973), *Vergil, Bucol. 4. Ein Beispiel 'generischer' Interpretation*, in *RhM*, 116, pp. 71–8.

Meulder M. (1996), *Virgile n'a-t-il pas écrit la IVe Bucolique à la fin de 39 av. J.-C.?*, in *Latomus*, 55, pp. 815–28.

Michel A. (1989), *Catulle dans les Bucoliques de Virgile: histoire, philosophie, poétique*, in *REL*, 67, pp. 140–8.

Michel A. (1990), *Virgile et Gallus*, in Gigante (1990), pp. 55–68.

Michel J. (1955), *Une allusion à la Paix de Brindes dans la première Bucolique (v. 59–66)?*, in *Latomus*, 14, pp. 446–53.

Michelazzo F. (1985), *Il virgiliano parvus Micon (Buc. 7. 29–30)*, in *Prometheus*, 11, pp. 218–22.

Miller J. F. (2009), *Apollo, Augustus, and the Poets*, Cambridge.

Mizera S. M. (1982), *Lucretian Elements in Menalcas' song, Eclogue 5*, in *Hermes*, 110, pp. 367–71.

Moch K. E. (2017), *Certamen magnum: Competition and Song Exchange in Vergil's Eclogues*, in *Vergilius* 63, pp. 63–91.

Monella P. (2005), *Procne e Filomela: dal mito al simbolo letterario*, Bologna.

Monteil P. (1964), *Beau et laid en latin. Étude de vocabulaire*, Paris.

Monteleone C. (1979a), *Cornelio Gallo tra Ila e le Driadi (Virgilio, Properzio e una controversia letteraria)*, in *Latomus*, 38, pp. 28–53.

Monteleone C. (1979b), *Esegesi ovidiana dell'egloga seconda di Virgilio*, in *RhM*, 122, pp. 88–90.

Monteleone C. (1982–3), *Sul testo dell'ecloga quarta di Virgilio*, in *QuadFoggia*, 2–3, pp. 33–74.

Monteleone C. (1994), *Palaemon. L'Ecloga III di Virgilio: lusus intertestuale ed esegesi*, Naples.

Moore R. (2010), *Roman Women in the Castra: Who's in Charge Here?*, in C. Deroux (ed.), *Studies in Latin Literature and Roman History*, vol. XV, Brussels, pp. 49–78.

Moore-Blunt J. (1977), *Eclogue 2: Virgil's Utilisation of Theocritean Motifs*, in *Eranos*, 75, pp. 23–42.

Morelli A. M. (2010), *Come cominciare (e perdere) il canto amebeo: Verg. ecl. 7, 21–28*, in *MD*, 65, pp. 147–65.

Morelli A. M., Tandoi V. (1984), *Un probabile omaggio a Cornelio Gallo nella seconda egloga*, in V. Tandoi (ed.), *Disiecti membra poetae*, Foggia, vol. I, pp. 101–16.

Moretti G. (1996), *Cydonia mala (per l'interpretazione di Aen. 10, 324–325, con una nota su Theocr. 5, 94–95)*, in *QUCC*, 81, pp. 159–69.

Morgan L. (1992), *'Quantum sat erit': Epic, Acne and the Fourth Eclogue*, in *LCM*, 17, pp. 76–9.

Moya Del Baño F. (1993), *La sonrisa del 'puer' en Virgilio (E. 4, 62). Apostillas a la interpretación de J. L. de la Cerda*, in *Helmantica*, 44, pp. 235–50.

Moya Del Baño F. (1996), *Nota a Ver., E. 4, 32: Thetim o la sutil evocación de las palabras*, in *Myrtia*, 11, pp. 135–7.

MRR = T. R. S. Broughton, *The Magistrates of the Roman Republic*, 2 vols., Cleveland 1951–2.

Muecke F. (1975), *Virgil and the Genre of Pastoral*, in *AUMLA*, 44, pp. 169–80.

Musso O. (1968), *Nota a Verg. Ecl. V. 14*, in *Aevum*, 42, p. 477.

Najock D. (2004), *Statistischer Schlüssel zum Vokabular in Vergils Eklogen*, Hildesheim.

Naumann H. (1981), *Das Geheimnis der vierten Ekloge*, in *AU*, 24, pp. 29–47.

Nauta R. R. (2006), *Panegyric in Virgil's Bucolics*, in Fantuzzi, Papanghelis (2006), pp. 301–32.

Negri A. M. (1984), *Gli psiconimi in Virgilio*, Rome.

Néraudau J.-P. (1983), *Asinius Pollion et la poésie*, in *ANRW*, II.30.3, Berlin-New York, pp. 1732–50.

Nethercut W. R. (1967), *Trees and Identity in Aeneid VIII and Bucolic II*, in *Vergilius*, 13, pp. 16–27.

Nethercut W. R. (1968), *Vergil and Horace in Bucolic 7*, in *CW*, 62, pp. 93–8.

Nethercut W. R. (1970), *Menalcas' Answer: The Hyacinth in Bucolic 3.106–7*, in *CJ*, 65, pp. 248–54.

Nethercut W. R. (1979), *The Cradle of Flowers in B. 4, 23*, in *Vergilius*, 25, pp. 32–5.

Neuegebauer O. (1963), *Decem tulerunt fastidia menses*, in *AJPh*, 84, pp. 64–5.

Neumeister C. (1975), *Vergils IX. Ekloge im Vergleich zu Theokrits 7. Idyll*, in J. Cobet, R. Leimbach, A. B. Neschke-Hentschke (eds.), *Dialogos. Für Harald Patzer zum 65. Geburtstag*, Wiesbaden, pp. 177–85.

Newman J. K. (1967), *The Concept of Vates in Augustan Poetry*, Brussels.

Newman J. K. (1984), *The New Gallus and the Origins of Latin Love Elegy*, in *ICS*, 9, pp. 19–29.

Nicastri L. (1989), *La quarta ecloga di Virgilio e la profezia dell'Emmanuele*, in *Vichiana*, 18, pp. 221–71.

Nielsen R. M. (1972), *Virgil: Eclogue 1*, in *Latomus*, 31, pp. 154–60.

Nilsson N. O. (1955), *Ad Verg. Ecl. V.15*, in *Eranos*, 53, pp. 199–200.

Nisbet R. G. M. (1978), *Virgil's Fourth Eclogue: Easterners and Westerners*, in *BICS*, 25, pp. 59–78 (= Nisbet 1995, pp. 47–75 = Volk 2008, pp. 155–88).

Nisbet R. G. M. (1991), *The Style of Virgil's Eclogues*, in *PVS*, 20, pp. 1–13 (= Nisbet 1995, pp. 325–37 = Volk 2008, pp. 48–63).

Nisbet R. G. M. (1993), *Adolescens Puer (Virgil, Eclogues 4.28–30)*, in H. D. Jocelyn, H. Hurt (eds.), *Tria Lustra: Essays and Notes Presented to John Pinsent*, Liverpool, pp. 265–7 (= Nisbet 1995, pp. 381–5).

Nisbet R. G. M. (1995), *Collected Papers on Latin Literature*, Oxford.

Norden E. (1924), *Die Geburt des Kindes. Geschichte einer religiösen Idee*, Leipzig.

Notopoulos J. A. (1967), *Silenus the Scientist*, in *CJ*, 62, pp. 308–9.

Nováková J. (1964), *Umbra. Ein Beitrag zur dichterischen Semantik*, Berlin.

Nussbaum G. (1984), *Vergilian Artistry: A Note on Eclogues 8, 37–41*, in *LCM*, 9, pp. 94–5.

Nussbaum G. (1990), *The Ending of Eclogue I*, in *LCM*, 15, pp. 139–41.

OCD = The Oxford Classical Dictionary, Oxford 1996, 3rd ed. (rev. 3rd ed. 2003).

O'Hara J. J. (1993), *Medicine for the Madness of Dido and Gallus: Tentative Suggestions on Aeneid 4*, in *Vergilius*, 39, pp. 12–24.

O'Hara J. J. (1996), *True Names. Vergil and the Alexandrian Tradition of Etymological Wordplay*, Ann Arbor (2nd ed. 2017).

O'Hara J. J. (2001), *Callimachean Influence on Vergilian Etymological Wordplay*, in *CJ*, 96, pp. 369–400.

Ohly K. (1928), *Stichometrische Untersuchungen*, Leipzig.

Oksanish J. M. (2017), *Amant Alterna Camenae: Vergil's Third Eclogue at the Dawn of Roman Literary History*, in *TAPhA*, pp. 101–33.

OLD² = Oxford Latin Dictionary, Oxford 2012, 2nd ed. (reprinted with corrections, 2016; 1st ed. 1968–82).

Opelt I. (1976), *I vezzeggiativi del linguaggio virgiliano e dell'Appendix*, in *A&R*, n.s. 21, pp. 169–79.

Oppermann H. (1932), *Vergil und Oktavian. Zur Deutung der ersten und neunten Ekloge*, in *Hermes*, 67, pp. 197–219.

Oppermann H. (ed.) (1963), *Wege zu Vergil: Drei Jahrzehnte Begegnungen in Dichtung und Wissenschaft*, Darmstadt.

Osgood J. (2006), *Caesar's Legacy: Civil War and the Emergence of the Roman Empire*, Cambridge.

Otis B. (1963), *Virgil. A Study in Civilized Poetry*, Oxford.

Otranto R. (2002), *Le parole dei libri. Isidoro, Etym. VI,13 e Virgilio, Ecl. X, 67*, in *QS*, 56, pp. 191–8.

Ott W. (1974), *Rückläufiger Wortindex zu Vergil: Bucolica, Georgica, Aeneis*, Tübingen.

Ott W. (1978), *Metrische Analysen zu Vergil, Bucolica*, Tübingen.

Ottaviano S. (2010), *Nota a Verg. ecl. 3,79*, in *MD*, 65, pp. 137–46.

Ottaviano S. (2011), *Due nuove proposte per il testo delle Bucoliche (ecl. 3, 102; 5, 30)*, in *MD*, 67, pp. 203–13.

Ottaviano S. (2012), *Ars et ratio. Problemi di struttura e proporzione nelle Bucoliche (ecl. 7, 45–68; 9, 37–55)*, in *MD*, 69, pp. 199–216.

Ottaviano S. (2013), *Virgil, Eclogue 4.53–4: A Quantum of Spiritus is Not Enough*, in *CQ*, n.s. 63, pp. 897–9.

Ottaviano S. (2016), *A Singular Smile: Note on Virgil, Eclogue 4. 62–63 with an Appendix on Syntax*, in *Hermes*, 144, pp. 497–511.

Otto A. (1890), *Die Sprichwörter und sprichwörtlichen Redensarten der Römer*, Leipzig.

Pagés G. H. (1986), *Rusticidad e cortesanía en la primera égloga virgiliana*, in *Actas del VII Simpósio nacional de estudios clásicos 1982*, Buenos Aires, pp. 345–9.

Pandey N. B. (2013), *Caesar's Comet, the Julian Star, and the Invention of Augustus*, in *TAPhA*, 143, pp. 405–49.

Pandey N. B. (2018), *The Poetics of Power in Augustan Rome. Latin Poetic Responses to Early Imperial Iconography*, Cambridge.

Papanghelis T. D. (1997), *Winning on Points: About the Singing-Match in Virgil's Seventh Eclogue*, in C. Deroux (ed.), *Studies in Latin Literature and Roman History*, vol. VIII, Brussels, pp. 144–57.

Papanghelis T. D. (1999), *Eros Pastoral and Profane: On Love in Virgil's Eclogues*, in S. Braund, R. Mayer (eds.), *Amor: Roma. Love and Latin Literature. Eleven Essays (and One Poem) presented to E. J. Kenney*, Cambridge, pp. 44–59.

Papanghelis T. D. (2006), *Friends, Foes, Frames and Fragments: Textuality in Virgil's Eclogues*, in Fantuzzi, Papanghelis (2006), pp. 369–402.

Papini M. (2017), *Firmare un'opera come fosse l'ultima: l'imperfetto e l'incompiuto in Plinio il Vecchio*, in *BCAR*, 108, pp. 39–54.

Papini M. (2019), *L'incompiuto nel mondo antico tra archeologia e letteratura: un'introduzione*, *ScAnt*, 25, pp. ix–xxvi.

Paraskeviotis G. C. (2014a), *Eclogue 7, 69–70: Vergil's Victory over Theocritus*, in *RCCM*, 56, pp. 265–71.

Paraskeviotis G. C. (2014b), *The Mythological Exemplum in Vergil's 'Eclogues'*, in *Hermes*, 142, pp. 418–30.

Paraskeviotis G. C. (2014c), *Verg. ecl. 6, 13–30. Mimic Humour in Silenus' Scene*, in *Arctos*, 48, pp. 279–83.

Paraskeviotis G. C. (2016), *The Echo in Vergilian Pastoral*, in *Ant. Class.*, 85, pp. 45–64.

Paratore E. (1962), *Spicilegio polemico, V: ad Verg. Buc. IX, 45*, in *RCCM*, 4, pp. 88–92.

Paratore E. (1964), *Struttura, ideologia e poesia nell'ecloga VI di Virgilio*, in M. Renard, R. Schilling (eds.), *Hommages à Jean Bayet*, Brussels, pp. 509–37.

Parke H. W. (1967), *The Oracles of Zeus*, Oxford.

Parke H. W. (1988), *Sibyls and Sibylline Prophecy in Classical Antiquity*, London-New York.

Parker H. N. (1992), *Fish in Trees and Tie-Dyed Sheep: A Function of the Surreal in Roman Poetry*, in *Arethusa*, 25, pp. 293–323.

Paschalis M. (1990), *Aliquot…videns mirabor aristas?: On the Interpretation of Virgil, E. 1.69*, in *LCM*, 15, pp. 57–8.

Paschalis M. (1993), *Two Implicit Myths in Virgil's Sixth Eclogue*, in *Vergilius*, 39, pp. 25–9.

Paschalis M. (1995), *Virgil's Sixth Eclogue and the Lament for Bion*, in *AJPh*, 116, pp. 617–21.

Paschalis M. (1997), *Virgil's Arethusa (Ecl. 10.1) and the Bucolic Tradition*, in J.-T. A. Papademetriou (ed.), *Acts of the First Panhellenic and International Conference on Ancient Greek Literature (23–26 May 1994)*, Athens, pp. 713–26.

Paschalis M. (2001), *'Semina ignis': The Interplay of Science and Myth in the Song of Silenus*, in *AJPh*, 122, pp. 201–22.

Paschalis M. (2007), *Pastoral Palimpsests: Essays in the Reception of Theocritus and Virgil*, Heraklion.

Pascucci G. (1981), *Lettura della quarta bucolica*, in Gigante (1981b), pp. 171–97 (= G. P., *Scritti scelti*, Florence 1983, vol. II, pp. 873–99).

Pasini G. F. (1991), *Grammatica del chiasmo in Virgilio*, Bologna.

538 BIBLIOGRAPHY

Pasoli E. (1977), *Gli Amores di Cornelio Gallo nell'ecloga X di Virgilio e nell'elegia I, 8 di Properzio; riconsiderazione del problema*, in *RCCM*, 19, pp. 585–96.

Pasqualetti O. (1978-9), *Cenni sull'orditura tematica della prima ecloga virgiliana*, in *Euphrosyne*, n.s. 9, pp. 179–85.

Pasquali G. (1942), *Arte allusiva*, in *L'Italia che scrive*, 25, pp. 185–7 (= *Pagine stravaganti quarte e supreme*, Venezia 1951, pp. 11–20 = *Pagine stravaganti*, edited by C. F. Russo, Florence 1994, II, pp. 275–82).

Patterson A. (1987), *Pastoral and Ideology: Virgil to Valéry*, Berkeley.

Pease A. S. (1931), *A Note on Vergil, Eclogues I and IX*, in *CJ*, 26, pp. 538–40.

Peirano I. (2009), *Mutati artus: Scylla, Philomela and the End of Silenus' Song in Virgil Eclogue 6*, in *CQ*, n.s. 59, pp. 154–62.

Peirano I. (2012), *The Rhetoric of the Roman Fake. Latin Pseudepigrapha in Context*, Cambridge.

Pellegrino C. (2003), *Verg. Buc. 9, 1–36: una poetica interprete dei nuovi tempi*, in F. Benedetti, S. Grandolini (eds.), *Studi di filologia e tradizione greca in memoria di A. Colonna*, Perugia, pp. 619–31.

Pelling C. B. R. (1996), *The Triumviral Period*, in *The Cambridge Ancient History*, vol. X, *The Augustan Empire, 43 B.C.-A.D. 69*, Cambridge, pp. 1–69.

Perkell C. (1990), *On Eclogue 1.79–83*, in *TAPhA*, 120, pp. 171–81 (= Volk 2008, pp. 110–24).

Perkell C. (1996), *The 'Dying Gallus' and the Design of Eclogue 10*, in *CPh*, 91, pp. 128–40.

Perkell C. (2001a), *Pastoral Value in Vergil: Some Instances*, in S. Spence (ed.), *Poets and Critics Read Vergil*, New Haven-London, pp. 26–43.

Perkell C. (2001b), *Vergil Reading His Twentieth-Century Readers: A Study of Eclogue 9*, in *Vergilius*, 47, pp. 64–88.

Perkell C. (2002), *The Golden Age and Its Contradictions in the Poetry of Vergil*, in *Vergilius*, 48, pp. 3–39.

Perotti P. A. (2004), *'Quem fugis?' (Verg. Ecl. 2, 60; Aen. 5, 742; 6, 466)*, in *Orpheus*, n.s. 25, pp. 13–21.

Perret J. (1971), *Sileni theologia (à propos de Buc. 6)*, in H. Bardon, R. Verdière (eds.), *Vergiliana. Recherches sur Virgile*, Leiden, pp. 294–311.

Perret J. (1982), *Daphnis pâtre et héros. Perspectives pour un âge d'or*, in *REL*, 60, pp. 216–33.

Perret J. (1983), *L'exaltation de Daphnis*, in *Hommages à J. Cousin*, Paris, pp. 123–32.

Perrot J. (1961), *Les dérivés en -men et -mentum*, Paris.

Perutelli A. (1976), *Natura selvatica e genere bucolico*, in *ASNS*, s. III, 6.3, pp. 763–98.

Perutelli A. (1995), *Bucolics*, in Horsfall (1995a), pp. 27–62.

Perutelli A. (2000), *Varius, fr. 4 Courtney = Blänsdorf e Verg. ecl. 8, 88*, in *MD*, 45, pp. 137–45.

Perutelli A. (2003), *Tante voci per Arione*, in *MD*, 51, pp. 9–63.

Petersmann G. (1977), *Zum Wettstreit der Hirten in Vergils III. Ekloge*, in *Hermes*, 105, pp. 202–28.

Petrini M. (1995), *The Child and the Hero: Coming of Age in Catullus and Vergil*, Ann Arbor.

Petrovitz W. (2003), *Towards a Grammar of Allusion: A Cross-Linguistic Study of Vergil's Seventh Bucolic*, in *CW*, 96, pp. 259–70.

Pfeiffer E. (1933), *Virgils Bukolika: Untersuchungen zum Formproblem*, Stuttgart.

Pfeiffer R. (1928), *Ein neues Altersgedicht des Kallimachos*, in *Hermes*, 63, pp. 302–41.

Pfeiffer R. (1949), *Callimachus*, vol. I, *Fragmenta*, Oxford.

Pfeiffer R. (1968), *History of Classical Scholarship*, Oxford.

PGM = K. Preisendanz, *Papyri Graecae magicae. Die griechischen Zauberpapyri*, Stuttgart 1973-4, 2nd ed.

BIBLIOGRAPHY   539

Phillimore J. S. (1916), *Some Cruces in Virgil Re-considered*, in *CR*, 30, pp. 146–52.

Pianezzola E. (1965), *Gli aggettivi verbali in -bundus*, Florence.

Pianezzola E. (1979), *Forma narrativa e funzione paradigmatica di un mito. L'età dell'oro latina*, in G. D'Anna (ed.), *Studi di poesia latina in onore di A. Traglia*, 2 vols., Rome, vol. II, pp. 573–92.

Pichon R. (1966), *Index verborum amatoriorum*, Hildesheim (= *De sermone amatorio apud Latinos elegiarum scriptores*, Paris 1902).

Picone G. (1978), *O Meliboee, deus nobis haec otia fecit*, in *Pan*, 6, pp. 105–14.

Picone G. (1989), *Il viaggio e il malinteso: strutture spazio-temporali nella prima ecloga di Virgilio*, in *Pan*, 9, pp. 29–41.

Picone G. (1993), *L'esilio e l'Arcadia. Rappresentazioni dello spazio e del tempo nella poesia di Virgilio*, in B. Amata (ed.), *Cultura e lingue classiche*, vol. III, Rome, pp. 291–307.

Pietzcker C. (1965), *Die Landschaft in Vergils Bukolika*, diss. Freiburg.

Plowden G. F. C. (1995), *Fallax herba veneni: What Twice Was Thought*, in *LCM*, 20, p. 21.

PMG = D. L. Page, *Poetae Melici Graeci*, Oxford 1962.

Poggioli R. (1975), *The Oaten Flute: Essays on Pastoral Poetry and the Pastoral Ideal*, Cambridge MA.

Pohlenz M. (1930), *Das Schlussgedicht der Bucolica*, in *Studi virgiliani, pubblicati in occasione delle celebrazioni bimillenarie dalla R. Accademia Virgiliana di Mantova*, Mantua, pp. 205–26.

Pollini J. (1990), *Man or God: Divine Assimilation and Imitation in the Late Republic and Early Principate*, in Raaflaub, Toher (1990), pp. 334–63.

Polt C. (2016), *A Catullan/Apollonian 'Window Reference' at Vergil Eclogue 4.31–36*, in *Hermes*, 144, pp. 118–22.

Posch S. (1969), *Beobachtungen zur Theokritnachwirkung bei Vergil*, Innsbruck.

Pöschl V. (1964), *Die Hirtendichtung Virgils*, Heidelberg.

Potter D. S. (1990), *Prophecy and History in the Crisis of the Roman Empire: A Historical Commentary on the Thirteenth Sibylline Oracle*, Oxford.

Powell A. (2008), *Virgil the Partisan. A Study in the Re-integration of Classics*, Swansea.

Powell B. P. (1976), *Thrust and Counter-Thrust in Eclogue 3*, in *ICS*, 1, pp. 113–21.

Pretagostini R. (1984), *Ricerche sulla poesia alessandrina. Teocrito, Callimaco, Sotade*, Rome.

Prioux É. (2005), *Deux jeux de mots sur le nom d'Aratos: note sur Virgile, B. III, 42 et Aratos, Phaen. 2*, in *RPh*, 79, pp. 309–17.

Privitera T. (2007), *Terei puellae: metamorfosi latine*, Pisa.

Protomártir Vaquero S. M. (1984), *Virgilio, Bucólica 10. Estudio estilístico*, in *Helmantica*, 35, pp. 197–208.

Puccioni G. (1981), *Nota al 2° frammento di Cornelio Gallo*, in *CCC*, 2, pp. 311–13.

Pulbrook M. (1987a), *Vergil's Fourth Eclogue and the Rebirth of Rome*, in Pulbrook (1987c), pp. 37–49.

Pulbrook M. (1987b), *Octavian and Vergil's Fifth Eclogue*, in Pulbrook (1987c), pp. 214–34.

Pulbrook M. (1987c), *Studies in Greek and Latin Authors*, Maynooth.

Putnam M. C. J. (1965), *The Riddle of Damoetas (Virgil, Ecl. 3, 104–5)*, in *Mnemosyne*, s. IV, 18, pp. 150–4.

Putnam M. C. J. (1970), *Virgil's Pastoral Art: Studies in the Eclogues*, Princeton.

Putnam M. C. J. (1975), *Virgil's First Eclogue: Poetics of Enclosure*, in *Ramus*, 4, pp. 163–86.

Putnam M. C. J. (1995), *Pastoral Satire*, review of K. Freudenburg, *The Walking Muse: Horace on the Theory of Satire*, Princeton 1993, in *Arion*, 3, pp. 303–16.

Quartarone L. N. (2013), *Shifting Shadows on the Landscape: Reading umbrae in Vergil and other Poets*, in *AAntHung*, 53, pp. 245–59.

540 BIBLIOGRAPHY

Raaflaub K. A., Toher M. (eds.) (1990), *Between Republic and Empire. Interpretations of Augustus and His Principate*, Berkeley-Los Angeles-Oxford.

Radke A. E. (1973), *Zu Vergil, Ecl. III, 109–10*, in *RhM*, 116, pp. 143–9.

Radke G. (1956), *Aurea funis*, in *Gymnasium*, 63, pp. 82–6.

Ramorino Martini L. (1986), *Influssi lucreziani nelle Bucoliche di Virgilio*, in *CCC*, 7, pp. 297–331.

Ramsey J., Lewis Licht A. (1997), *The Comet of 44 BC and Caesar's Funeral Games*, Atlanta.

RE = Real-Encyclopädie der classischen Altertumswissenschaft.

Reed J. D. (1997), *Bion of Smyrna*, Cambridge.

Reitzenstein R. (1893), *Epigramm und Skolion: Ein Beitrag zur Geschichte der alexandrinischen Dichtung*, Giessen.

Reynolds L. D. (1983), *Virgil*, in L. D. R. (ed.), *Texts and Transmission. A Survey of the Latin Classics*, Oxford, pp. 433–6.

RIC = H. Mattingly et al., The Roman Imperial Coinage, 10 vols., London 1923–94.

Richter A. (1970), *Virgile. La huitième bucolique*, Paris.

Roberts J. T. (1983), *Carmina nulla canam: Rhetoric and Poetic in Virgil's First Eclogue*, in *CW*, 76, pp. 193–9.

Robertson F. (1966–7), *Allegorical Interpretations of Virgil*, in *PVS*, 6, pp. 34–45.

Roche P. (2014), *Meleager's Grasshopper (12 G-P = AP 7.195) and Tityrus' Bees (Verg. Ecl. 1.53-55)*, in *Mnemosyne*, 67, pp. 450–3.

Rochette B. (1998), *Cara deum suboles, magnum Iovis incrementum (Virg. B. 4, 49)*, in *Latomus*, 57, pp. 417–19.

Rodríguez Adrados J.-V. (1998), *Diez meses y una sonrisa (Verg. Ecl. IV 60–63)*, in J. L. Vidal, J. Alvar Ezquerra (eds.), *IX congreso español de estudios clásicos: Madrid, 27 al 30 de septiembre de 1995*, vol. V, *Literatura latina*, Madrid, pp. 165–8.

Rohde G. (1925), *De Vergili eclogarum forma et indole*, Berlin (= Rohde 1963, pp. 11–70).

Rohde G. (1963), *Studien und Interpretationen zur antiken Literatur, Religion und Geschichte*, Berlin.

Roiron F. X. M. Y. (1908), *Étude sur l'imagination auditive de Virgile*, Paris.

Ronconi A. (1981), *Lettura della nona bucolica*, in Gigante (1981b), pp. 319–45.

Rosati G. (2009), *The Latin Reception of Hesiod*, in F. Montanari, A. Rengakos, C. Tsagalis (eds.), *Brill's Companion to Hesiod*, Leiden, pp. 343–408.

Roscher = W. H. Roscher (ed.), *Ausführliches Lexicon der griechischen und römischen Mythologie*, Leipzig 1884–1937 (= Hildesheim-New York 1977–8).

Rose H. J. (1942), *The Eclogues of Vergil*, Berkeley-Los Angeles.

Rosen R. M., Farrell J. (1986), *Acontius, Milanion, and Gallus: Vergil, Ecl. 10, 52–61*, in *TAPhA*, 116, pp. 241–54.

Rosenmeyer T. G. (1969), *The Green Cabinet: Theocritus and the European Pastoral Lyric*, Berkeley.

Roskam G. (2007), *'Live Unnoticed' (λάθε βιώσας). On the Vicissitudes of an Epicurean Doctrine*, Leiden-Boston.

Ross D. O. (1975), *Backgrounds to Augustan Poetry: Gallus, Elegy and Rome*, Cambridge.

Rossi L. E. (1971), *Mondo pastorale e poesia bucolica di maniera: l'Idillio ottavo del Corpus teocriteo*, in *SIFC*, 43, pp. 5–25.

Rostagni A. (1960), *Virgilio, Valgio e... Codro. Chi era costui?*, in *Studi in onore di Luigi Castiglioni*, 2 vols., Florence, vol. II, pp. 807–33.

RRC = M. H. Crawford, Roman Republican Coinage, 2 vols., Cambridge 1974.

BIBLIOGRAPHY 541

Rudd N. (1976), *Architecture: Theories about Virgil's Eclogues*, in N. R., *Lines of Enquiry. Studies in Latin Poetry*, Cambridge, pp. 119–44 (= P. Hardie, ed., *Virgil: Critical Assessments of Classical Authors*, I, London-New York 1999, pp. 91–115).

Rudd N. (1996), *Virgil's Contribution to Pastoral*, in *PVS*, 22, pp. 53–77.

Ruiz Arzalluz I. (1995), *Augusto, Nerón y el 'puer' de la cuarta égloga*, in *Aevum*, 69, pp. 115–45.

Ruiz de Elvira A. (1994), *Qui non risere parentes*, in *Emerita*, 62, pp. 295–6.

Rumpf L. (1996), *Extremus Labor: Vergils 10. Ekloge und die Poetik der Bucolica*, Göttingen.

Rumpf L. (1999), *Bukolische Nomina bei Vergil und Theokrit: Zur poetischen Technik des Eklogenbuchs*, in *RhM*, 142, pp. 157–75 (English trans. in Volk 2008, pp. 64–78).

Rundin J. (2003), *The Epicurean Morality of Vergil's Bucolics*, in *CW*, 92, pp. 159–76.

Rupprecht K. (2004), *Warten auf Menalcas: Der Weg des Vergessens in Vergils neunter Ekloge*, in *A&A*, 50, pp. 36–61.

Rutherford R. B. (1989), *Virgil's Poetic Ambitions in Eclogue 6*, in *G&R*, 36, pp. 42–50.

Ryberg I. S. (1958), *Vergil's Golden Age*, in *TAPhA*, 89, pp. 112–31.

Saint-Denis E. de (1963), *Le chant de Silène à la lumière d'une découverte récente*, in *RPh*, 37, pp. 23–40.

Saint-Denis E. de (1976), *Encore l'architecture des 'Bucoliques' virgiliennes*, in *RPh*, 50, pp. 7–21.

Sallmann K. (1995), *Poesie und Magie: Vergils 8. Ekloge*, in *ZAnt*, 45, pp. 287–302.

Sallmann K. (1998), *Wer singt Damons Lied? Noch einmal zu Vergils 8. Ekloge*, in A. E. Radke (ed.), *Candide iudex: Beiträge zur augusteischen Dichtung. Festschrift für W. Wimmel*, Stuttgart, pp. 275–81.

Salvatore A. (1981), *Lettura della quinta bucolica*, in Gigante (1981b), pp. 201–23.

Sandbach F. H. (1933), *Victum frustra contendere Thyrsin*, in *CR*, 47, pp. 216–18.

Sargeaunt J. (1920), *The Trees, Shrubs and Plants of Virgil*, Oxford.

Saunders T. (2008), *Bucolic Ecology. Virgil's Eclogues and the Environmental Literary Tradition*, London.

Sauron G. (2004), *La peinture pompéienne et la poésie augustéenne*, in *REL*, 82, pp. 144–66.

Sauvage A. (1975), *Étude de thèmes animaliers dans la poésie latine*, Brussels.

Savage J. J. (1953–4), *The Riddle in Virgil's Third Eclogue*, in *CW*, 47, pp. 81–3.

Savage J. J. (1956), *Apollo-Hercules: Two Themes in the Fourth Eclogue*, in *Vergilian Digest*, 2, pp. 5–10.

Savage J. J. (1958), *The Art of the Third Eclogue of Virgil (55–111)*, in *TAPhA*, 89, pp. 142–58.

Savage J. J. (1960), *The Art of the Second Eclogue of Virgil*, in *TAPhA*, 91, pp. 353–75.

Savage J. J. (1963), *The Art of the Seventh Eclogue of Virgil*, in *TAPhA*, 94, pp. 248–67.

Savage J. J. (1965), *Vergil and the Pleiades*, in *Vergilius*, 11, pp. 1–5.

Scafoglio G. (2006), *Le figure femminili nelle Bucoliche di Virgilio*, in *Euphrosyne*, n.s. 34, pp. 65–76.

Scafoglio G. (2013a), *From Tamarisks to Stars: Cosmic Inspiration in Vergil's Eclogues*, in *AAntHung*, 53, pp. 185–209.

Scafoglio G. (2013b), *Since the Child Smiles: A Note on Virg. Ecl. 4.62–3*, in *CJ*, 109, pp. 73–87.

Schäfer A. (2001), *Vergils Eklogen 3 und 7 in der Tradition der lateinischen Streitdichtung*, Frankfurt am Main-New York.

Schafer J. K. (2017), *Authorial Pagination in the Eclogues and Georgics*, in *TAPhA*, 147, pp. 135–78.

542 BIBLIOGRAPHY

Schauroth E. G. (1949–50), *A Virgilian Riddle and Its Source*, in *CW*, 43, pp. 8–10.

Schiesaro A. (1997), *The Boundaries of Knowledge in Virgil's Georgics*, in T. Habinek, A. Schiesaro (eds.), *The Roman Cultural Revolution*, Cambridge, pp. 63–89.

Schilling R. (1990), *Le refrain dans la poésie latine*, in M. von Albrecht, W. Schubert (eds.), *Musik und Dichtung. Neue Forschungsbeiträge, V. Pöschl zum 80. Geburtstag gewidmet*, Frankfurt am Main-Bern-New York-Paris, pp. 117–31.

Schindel U. (1969), *Meliboeus redux*, in *Hermes*, 97, pp. 472–89.

Schmidt E. A. (1968), *Paliurus. Zu Vergil, Ecl. V, 38 f.*, in *Hermes*, 96, pp. 637–8.

Schmidt E. A. (1969), *Hirtenhierarchie in der antiken Bukolik?*, in *Philologus*, 113, pp. 183–200.

Schmidt E. A. (1972a), *Poesia e politica nella nona egloga di Virgilio*, in *Maia*, 24, pp. 99–119.

Schmidt E. A. (1972b), *Poetische Reflexion. Vergils Bukolik*, Munich.

Schmidt E. A. (1974), *Zur Chronologie der Eklogen Vergils*, Heidelberg.

Schmidt E. A. (1975), *Arkadien: Abendland und Antike*, in *A&A*, 21, pp. 36–57 (= E. A. Schmidt 1987, pp. 239–64; English trans. in Volk 2008, pp. 16–47).

Schmidt E. A. (1982), *Bukolik und Utopie. Zur Frage nach dem Utopischen in der antiken Hirtenpoesie*, in W. Voßkamp (ed.), *Utopieforschung. Interdisziplinäre Studien zur neuzeitlichen Utopie*, 2 vols., Stuttgart, vol. II, pp. 21–36 (= E. A. Schmidt 1987, pp. 13–28).

Schmidt E. A. (1984), *La più antica egloga di Virgilio*, in *Atti del Convegno mondiale scientifico di studi su Virgilio*, 2 vols., Milan, vol. I, pp. 66–75.

Schmidt E. A. (1987), *Bukolische Leidenschaft oder Über antike Hirtenpoesie*, Frankfurt am Main.

Schmidt E. A. (1998), *Freedom and Ownership: A Contribution to the Discussion of Virgil's First Eclogue*, in F. Cairns, M. Heath (eds.), *Papers of the Leeds International Latin Seminar*, vol. X, Leeds, pp. 185–201.

Schmidt V. (1972), *Virgile et l'apogée de la louange de Cynthie (Properce II 3, 23–32)*, in *Mnemosyne*, s. IV, 25, pp. 402–7.

Schmidt V. (1977), *Redeunt Saturnia regna. Studien zu Vergils vierter Ecloga*, Groningen.

Schmitzer U. (2008), *Wann kam Tityrus nach Rom? Ein Versuch der Annäherung an Vergils Eklogen*, in V. M. Strocka, R. von Haehling, S. Freund, M. Vielberg (eds.), *Vergil und das antike Epos. Festschrift H. J. Tschiedel*, Stuttgart, pp. 149–77.

Schoepsdau K. (1974), *Motive der Liebesdichtung in Vergils dritter Ekloge*, in *Hermes*, 102, pp. 268–300.

Schönbeck G. (1962), *Der locus amoenus von Homer bis Horaz*, diss. Heidelberg.

Schröder B.-J. (1999), *Titel und Text. Zur Entwicklung lateinischer Gedichtüberschriften, mit Untersuchungen zu lateinischen Buchtiteln, Inhaltsverzeichnissen und anderen Gliederungsmitteln*, Berlin-New York.

Schultz C. E. (2003), *Latet anguis in herba: A Reading of Vergil's Third Eclogue*, in *AJPh*, 124, pp. 199–224.

Segal C. P. (1965), *Tamen cantabitis, Arcades: Exile and Arcadia in Eclogues One and Nine*, in *Arion*, 4, pp. 237–66 (= Segal 1981, pp. 271–300).

Segal C. P. (1967), *Vergil's 'Caelatum Opus': An Interpretation of the Third Eclogue*, in *AJPh*, 88, pp. 279–308 (= Segal 1981, pp. 235–64).

Segal C. P. (1969), *Vergil's Sixth Eclogue and the Problem of Evil*, in *TAPhA*, 100, pp. 407–35 (= Segal 1981, pp. 301–29).

Segal C. P. (1971), *Two Fauns and a Naiad? (Virgil, Ecl. 6, 13–26)*, in *AJPh*, 92, pp. 56–61 (= Segal 1981, pp. 330–5).

Segal C. P. (1976), *Caves, Pan, and Silenus. Theocritus' Pastoral Epigrams and Virgil's Sixth Eclogue*, in *ZAnt*, 26, pp. 53–6 (= Segal 1981, pp. 336–9).

BIBLIOGRAPHY 543

Segal C. P. (1977), *Pastoral Realism and the Golden Age: Correspondence and Contrast between Virgil's Third and Fourth Eclogues*, in *Philologus*, 121, pp. 158–63 (= Segal 1981, pp. 265–70).

Segal C. P. (1981), *Poetry and Myth in Ancient Pastoral*, Princeton.

Segal C. P. (1987), *Alphesiboeus' Song and Simaetha's Magic: Virgil's Eighth Eclogue and Theocritus' Second Idyll*, in *GB*, 14, pp. 167–85.

Segura Ramos B. (1974), *El adjectivo en -bilis/-e en Virgilio y en las 'Metamorphosis' de Ovidio: consideraciones métrico-semánticas*, in *Durius*, 2, pp. 89–94.

Seibert J. (1972), *Alexander der Grosse*, Darmstadt.

Seider A. M. (2016), *Genre, Gallus, and Goats: Expanding the Limits of Pastoral in Eclogues 6 and 10*, in *Vergilius*, 62, pp. 3–23.

Seng H. (1999), *Vergils Eklogenbuch: Aufbau, Chronologie und Zahlenverhältnisse*, Hildesheim.

Serbat G. (1989), *Le datif dans les Bucoliques de Virgile*, in *Minerva*, 3, pp. 213–29.

Seretti E. (2020), *L'emulo di Pan: una nota a Verg. ecl. 2, 32–33*, in *RaRe*, 15, pp. 53–62.

Settis S. (2002), *Le pareti ingannevoli. La villa di Livia e la pittura di giardino*, Milan.

Simon E. (1962), *Dionysischer Sarkophag in Princeton*, in *MDAI(R)*, 69, pp. 136–58.

Simonetti Abbolito G. (1987), *Effetti fonici virgiliani*, in *Orpheus*, n.s. 8, pp. 235–63.

Sinko T. (1930), *De Virgilii rebus bacchicis*, Cracow.

Sirignano, G. (2009), *L'esametro di Dante e la tradizione bucolica latina*, in *Annali dell'Istituto Universitario Suor Orsola Benincasa*, 2, pp. 851–81.

Skanland V. (1967), *Litus: The Mirror of the Sea. Vergil, Ecl. 2, 25*, in *SO*, 42, pp. 93–101.

Skoie M. (2006), *City and Countryside in Vergil's Eclogues*, in R. M. Rosen, I. Sluiter (eds.), *City, Countryside, and the Spatial Organization of Value in Classical Antiquity*, Leiden-Boston, pp. 297–325.

Skoie M., Bjørnstad Velázquez S. (eds.) (2006), *Pastoral and the Humanities: Arcadia Re-inscribed*, Exeter.

Skutsch F. (1901), *Aus Vergils Frühzeit*, Leipzig.

Skutsch F. (1906), *Gallus und Vergil*, Leipzig.

Skutsch O. (1956), *Zu Vergils Eklogen*, in *RhM*, 99, pp. 193–201.

Skutsch O. (1969), *Symmetry and Sense in the Eclogues*, in *HSPh*, 73, pp. 153–69.

Skutsch O. (1970), *The Original Form of the Second Eclogue*, in *HSPh*, 74, pp. 95–9.

Skutsch O. (1971), *The Singing Matches in Virgil and Theocritus and the Design of Virgil's Book of Eclogues*, in *BICS*, 18, pp. 26–9.

Skutsch O. (1977), *A propos de la huitième églogue*, in *RPh*, 51, p. 366.

Skutsch O. (1980), *Numbers in Virgil's Bucolics*, in *BICS*, 27, pp. 95–6.

Slater D. A. (1912), *Was the Fourth Eclogue Written to Celebrate the Marriage of Octavia to Mark Antony? A Literary Parallel*, in *CR*, 26, pp. 114–19.

Smith P. L. (1965), *Lentus in umbra. A Symbolic Pattern in Virgil's Eclogues*, in *Phoenix*, 19, pp. 298–304.

Smith P. L. (1970), *Vergil's Avena and the Pipes of Pastoral Poetry*, in *TAPhA*, 101, pp. 497–510.

Snell B. (1938), *Die 16. Epode von Horaz und Vergils 4. Ekloge*, in *Hermes*, 73, pp. 237–42.

Snell B. (1945), *Arkadien: Die Entdeckung einer geistigen Landschaft*, in *A&A*, 1, pp. 26–41 (= Snell 1946, pp. 233–58).

Snell B. (1946), *Die Entdeckung des Geistes: Studien zur Entstehung des europäischen Denkens bei den Griechen*, Hamburg (English trans. by T. G. Rosenmeyer, *The Discovery of the Mind. The Greek Origins of European Thought*, Oxford 1953; Italian trans. by V. Degli Alberti, A. Solmi Marietti, *La cultura greca e le origini del pensiero europeo*, Turin 1963).

Snijder H. (2010), *The Cosmology of Octavian's Divine Birth in Vergil's Fourth Eclogue*, in C. Deroux (ed.), *Studies in Latin Literature and Roman History*, vol. XV, Brussels, pp. 178–95.

Solodow J. B. (1977), *Poeta Impotens: The Last Three Eclogues*, in *Latomus*, 36, pp. 757–71.

Solodow J. B. (1986), *Raucae, tua cura, palumbes: Study of a Poetic Word Order*, in *HSPh*, 90, pp. 129–53.

Soubiran J. (1966), *L'élision dans la poésie latine*, Paris.

Spoerri W. (1969), *L'épicurisme et la cosmogonie du Silène*, in *Actes du VIIIe Congrès de l'Association Guillaume Budé, 1968*, Paris, pp. 447–56.

Spoerri W. (1970a), *Zur Kosmogonie in Vergils 6. Ekloge*, in *MH*, 27, pp. 144–63.

Spoerri W. (1970b), *Antike Vergilerklärer und die Silenoskosmogonie*, in *MH*, 27, pp. 265–72.

Springer C. (1983), *Aratus and the Cups of Menalcas. A Note on Eclogue 3.42*, in *CJ*, 79, pp. 131–4.

Stachon M. (2017), *Über die Dichter Bavius und Mevius*, in *Gymnasium*, 124, pp. 303–19.

Starr R. J. (1995), *Vergil's Seventh Eclogue and Its Readers: Biographical Allegory as an Interpretative Strategy in Antiquity and Late Antiquity*, in *CPh*, 90, pp. 129–38.

Steenkamp J. (2011), *The Structure of Vergil's Eclogues*, in *AClass* 54, pp. 101–24.

Stégen G. (1953), *La composition de la dixième Bucolique de Virgile*, in *Latomus*, 12, pp. 70–6.

Steidle W. (1962), *Zwei Vergilprobleme. 1. Die Götter in Georgica I. 5b–23. 2. Zum Verständnis der 10. Ecloge*, in R. Muth (ed.), *Serta Philologica Aenipontana*, Innsbruck, pp. 311–34.

Steinmetz P. (1968), *Eclogen Vergils als dramatische Dichtungen*, in *A&A*, 14, pp. 115–25.

Stewart Z. (1959), *The Song of Silenus*, in *HSPh*, 64, pp. 179–205.

Stöckinger M. (2016), *Vergils Gaben. Materialität, Reziprozität und Poetik in den Eklogen und der Aeneis*, Heidelberg.

Stok F. (2013), *Triumviri agris dividendis. Una leggenda virgiliana*, in *Argos*, 36, pp. 9–27.

Stok F. (2014), *Esegesi antiche della sesta egloga*, in C. Longobardi, C. Nicolas, M. Squillante (eds.), *Scholae discimus. Pratiques scolaires dans l'Antiquité tardive et le Haut Moyen Âge*, Lyon, pp. 151–76.

Stok F. (2018), *Was Phylargyrius a Christian?*, in *GIF*, 70, pp. 233–47.

Stroh W. (1993), *Horaz und Vergil in ihren prophetischen Gedichten*, in *Gymnasium*, 100, pp. 289–322.

Stroppini G. (1993), *Amour et dualité dans les Bucoliques de Virgile*, Paris.

Stroppini G. (1997), *Amour, dialogue et unité dans l'oeuvre de Virgile: Bucoliques, Géorgiques, Énéide I–IV*, in *LEC*, 65, pp. 97–115.

Stuart D. R. (1921), *On Vergil Eclogue IV.60–63*, in *CPh*, 16, pp. 209–30.

Sudhaus S. (1901), *Jahrhundertfeier in Rom und messianische Weissagungen*, in *RhM*, 56, pp. 37–54.

Suerbaum W. (2005), *Von Arkadien nach Rom: Bukolisches in der 'Aeneis' Vergils*, in *Philologus*, 149, pp. 278–96.

Sullivan M. B. C. (2002), *Et eris mihi magnus Apollo: Divine and Earthly Competition in Vergil's Seventh Eclogue*, in *Vergilius*, 48, pp. 40–54.

SH = H. Loyd-Jones, P. Parsons, *Supplementum Hellenisticum*, Berlin-New York 1983.

Sutton D. F. (1974), *Father Silenus: Actor or Coryphaeus?*, in *CQ*, n.s. 24, pp. 19–23.

SVF = I. von Arnim, *Stoicorum Veterum Fragmenta*, 4 vols., Lipsiae 1903–24.

Syme R. (1939), *The Roman Revolution*, Oxford.

Tandoi V. (1981), *Lettura dell'ottava bucolica*, in Gigante (1981b), pp. 265–317.

Tarn W. W. (1932), *Alexander Helios and the Golden Age*, in *JRS*, 22, pp. 135–60.

Tarrant R. J. (1978), *The Addressee of Virgil's Eighth Eclogue*, in *HSPh*, 82, pp. 197–9.

Tarrant R. J. (1997), *Poetry and Power: Virgil's Poetry in Contemporary Context*, in Martindale (1997a), pp. 169–87.

BIBLIOGRAPHY   545

Tartari Chersoni M. (2008), *Motivi aristofaneschi nelle Bucoliche 'romane' di Virgilio?*, in *GIF*, 60, pp. 91–103.

Tescari O. (1953), *Amor omnibus idem. Nota virgiliana*, in *StudRom*, 1, pp. 121–3.

Theodorakopoulos E. (1997), *Closure: The Book of Vergil*, in Martindale (1997a), pp. 155–65.

Thibodeau P. (2006), *The Addressee of Vergil's Eighth Eclogue*, in *CQ*, n.s. 56, pp. 618–23.

Thill A. (1979), *Alter ab illo. Recherches sur l'imitation dans la poésie personnelle à l'époque augustéenne*, Paris.

Thill A. (1983), *L'epyllion de Pasiphae (Virg., Buc. VI, 45–60)*, in *Hommages à Jean Cousin*, Paris, pp. 145–57.

ThlL = Thesaurus linguae Latinae.

Thomas J. (2000), *L'otium dans les Bucoliques: temps suspendu et temps de l'éclair*, in *Euphrosyne*, n.s. 28, pp. 213–20.

Thomas P. (1928), *Note sur le vers 79 de la première Bucolique de Virgile*, in *RPh*, 7, pp. 138–40.

Thomas R. F. (1979), *Theocritus, Calvus, and Eclogue 6*, in *CPh*, 74, pp. 337–9.

Thomas R. F. (1981), *Cinna, Calvus, and the Ciris*, in *CQ*, n.s. 31, pp. 371–4.

Thomas R. F. (1983a), *Callimachus, the Victoria Berenices, and Roman Poetry*, in *CQ*, n.s. 33, 1983, pp. 92–113 (= Thomas 1999, pp. 68–100).

Thomas R. F. (1983b), *Virgil's Ecphrastic Centerpieces*, in *HSPh*, 87, pp. 175–84.

Thomas R. F. (1986), *From recusatio to Commitment: The Evolution of the Vergilian Programme*, in F. Cairns, M. Heath (eds.), *Papers of the Leeds International Latin Seminar*, vol. V, Leeds, pp. 61–73 (= Thomas 1999, pp. 101–13).

Thomas R. F. (1998), *Voice, Poetics and Virgil's Sixth Eclogue*, in J. Jasanoff, H. C. Melchert, L. Olivier (eds.), *Mír Curad: Studies in Honor of Calvert Watkins*, Innsbruck, pp. 669–76 (= Thomas 1999, pp. 288–96).

Thomas R. F. (1999), *Reading Virgil and His Texts: Studies in Intertextuality*, Ann Arbor.

Thome G. (2000), *Vergil als alexandrinischer Dichter*, in *Philologus*, 144, pp. 90–115.

Thornton A. H. F. (1969), *A Roman View of the Universe in the First Century B.C.*, in *Prudentia*, 1, pp. 2–13.

Thornton B. (1988), *A Note on Vergil, Eclogue 4.42–45*, in *AJPh*, 109, 226–8.

Thummer E. (1983), *Vergilius ludens. Erwägungen zur vierten Ekloge*, in P. Handel, W. Meid (eds.), *Festschrift für Roberth Muth*, Innsbruck, pp. 531–40.

Timpanaro S. (1978), *Ut vidi, ut perii*, in S. T., *Contributi di filologia e di storia della lingua latina*, Rome, pp. 219–87.

Timpanaro S. (1986), *Per la storia della filologia virgiliana antica*, Rome.

Timpanaro S. (1991), *De ciri, tonsillis, tolibus, tonsis et de quibusdam aliis rebus*, in *MD*, 26, pp. 103–73 (= *Nuovi contributi di filologia e storia della lingua latina*, Bologna 1994, pp. 87–164).

Timpanaro S. (2001), *Virgilianisti antichi e tradizione indiretta*, Florence.

Tochtermann S. (1992), *Der allegorisch gedeutete Kirke-Mythos*, Frankfurt am Main.

Torlone Z. M. (2002), *From Daphnis to Gallus: The Metamorphosis of the Genre in the Eclogues*, in *NECJ*, 29, pp. 204–21.

Tosi R. (2007), *Dizionario delle sentenze latine e greche*, Milan (1st ed. 1991).

Touratier C. (1996), *Les temps dans un récit (Virgile, Ecloga 7.1–20)*, in R. Risselada, J. R. de Jong, A. M. Bolkestein (eds.), *On Latin: Linguistic and Literary Studies in Honour of Harm Pinkster*, Amsterdam, pp. 163–72.

Tracy S. V. (1982), *Sepulcrum Bianoris. Vergil Eclogues 9, 59–61*, in *CPh*, 77, pp. 328–30.

Tracy S. V. (1990), *Theocritean Bucolic and Virgilian Pastoral: Commentary on Alpers*, in *Arethusa*, 23, pp. 49–57.

Tracy S. V. (2003), *Palaemon's Indecision*, in P. Thibodeau, H. Haskell (eds.), *Being There Together: Essays in Honor of Michael C. J. Putnam on the Occasion of His Seventieth Birthday*, Afton, pp. 66–77.

Traina A. (1965), *Si numquam fallit imago. Riflessioni sulle Bucoliche e l'epicureismo*, in *A&R*, n.s. 10, pp. 72–8 (= Traina 1975c, pp. 163–74 = Traina 1986, pp. 163–74 and 400; English trans. in P. Hardie, ed., *Virgil: Critical Assessments of Classical Authors*, I, London-New York 1999, pp. 84-90).

Traina A. (1968a), *La chiusa della prima egloga virgiliana (vv. 82–83)*, in *Lingua e Stile*, 3, pp. 45–53 (= Traina 1975c, pp. 175–88 = Traina 1986, pp. 175–88 and 400–1).

Traina A. (1968b), *La struttura della IX ecloga*, in *Lingua e Stile*, 3, pp. 54–7 (= Traina 1975c, pp. 189–95 = 1986, pp. 189–95 and 401).

Traina A. (1975a), *Convexo nutantem pondere mundum (Verg. Ecl. 4, 50). Cosmologia e poesia*, in *Scritti in onore di Carlo Diano*, Bologna, pp. 435–47 (= Traina 1975c, pp. 197–218 = Traina 1986, pp. 197–218 and 401).

Traina A. (1975b), *Magnum Iovis incrementum (ecl. 4, 49)*, in *Scritti in onore di Carlo Diano*, Bologna, pp. 449–53 (= Traina 1975c, pp. 219–26 = Traina 1986, pp. 219–26 and 402).

Traina A. (1975c), *Poeti latini (e neolatini). Note e saggi filologici*, Bologna (2nd ed. 1986).

Traina A. (1991), *Soror alma (Verg. Aen. 10, 439)*, in *Maia*, 43, pp. 3–7 (= Traina 1994b, pp. 45–52).

Traina A. (1994a), *Musica e poesia nelle Bucoliche di Virgilio*, in *Aufidus*, 24, pp. 152–8 (= Traina 1998, pp. 69–76).

Traina A. (1994b), *Poeti latini (e neolatini). Note e saggi filologici*, vol. IV, Bologna.

Traina A. (1995), *Un probabile verso di Ennio e l'apposizione parentetica*, in *MD*, 34, pp. 187–93 (= Traina 1998, pp. 11–17).

Traina A. (1998), *Poeti latini (e neolatini). Note e saggi filologici*, vol. V, Bologna.

Traina A. (1999a), *Amor omnibus idem. Contributi esegetici a Virgilio, Georg. 3, 209–283*, in *BSL*, 29, pp. 441–58 (= Traina 2003, pp. 39–62).

Traina A. (1999b), *Forma e suono. Da Plauto a Pascoli*, Bologna, 2nd ed. (1st ed. 1977).

Traina A. (2003), *La lyra e la libra*, Bologna.

Traina A. (2008), *Un esperimento di traduzione: i vv. 1–18 della prima egloga virgiliana*, in *Aufidus*, 22, pp. 33–41.

Traina A., Bini M. (1986), *Supplementum Morelianum*, Bologna.

Trappes-Lomax J. (2004), *Hiatus in Vergil and in Horace's Odes*, in *PCPhS*, 50, pp. 141–58.

TrGF = B. Snell, S. Radt, R. Kannicht, *Tragicorum Graecorum Fragmenta*, 5 vols., Göttingen 1971–2009.

Tsitsiou-Chelidoni C. (2003), *Nomen omen: Scylla's Eloquent Name and Ovid's Reply (Met. 8, 6–151)*, in *MD*, 50, pp. 195–203.

Tugwell S. (1963), *Virgil, Eclogue IX. 59–60*, in *CR*, n.s. 13, pp. 132–3.

Tupet A.-M. (1976), *La magie dans la poésie latine*, vol. I, *Des origines à la fin du règne d'Auguste*, Paris (2nd ed. 2009).

Tupet A.-M. (1986), *Rites magiques dans l'Antiquité romaine*, in *ANRW*, II.16.3, Berlin-New York, pp. 2591–675.

Turcan R. (1977), *César et Dionysos*, in *Hommage à la mémoire de Jérôme Carcopino*, Paris, pp. 317–25.

Uden J. (2004), *Constantine and Stanley Fish: Re-reading Christian Interpretations of Eclogue 4*, in *Classicum*, 20, 1, pp. 10–16.

Ursini F. (2021), *Una poetica della dissimulazione. Verità e finzione nelle Metamorfosi e nelle altre opere ovidiane*, Pisa-Rome.

Uruschadse A. (1985), *Vergils vierte Ekloge*, in *Klio*, 67, pp. 205–9.

Vaccaro A. J. (1966), *Adjetivación atributiva en las Églogas*, in *REC*, 10, pp. 7–23.

Van der Waerden B. L. (1952), *Das Grosse Jahr und die ewige Wiederkehr*, in *Hermes*, 80, pp. 129–55.

Van Groningen B. A. (1958), *Quelques problèmes de la poésie bucolique grecque*, in *Mnemosyne*, s. IV, 11, pp. 293–317.

Van Groningen B. A. (1977), *Euphorion*, Amsterdam.

Van Sickle J. B. (1967), *The Unity of the Eclogues: Arcadian Forest, Theocritean Trees*, in *TAPhA*, 98, pp. 491–508.

Van Sickle J. B. (1974), *The Origin of the Reading Hylax in Vergil, Ecl. 8, 107*, in *RFIC*, 102, pp. 311–13.

Van Sickle J. B. (1975), *Epic and Bucolic (Theocritus, Id. VII; Virgil, E. I)*, in *QUCC*, 19, pp. 45–72.

Van Sickle J. B. (1977a), *Et Gallus cantavit: A Review Article*, in *CJ*, 72, pp. 327–33 (review of Ross 1975).

Van Sickle J. B. (1977b), *Virgil's 6th Eclogue and the Poetics of Middle Style*, in *LCM*, 2, pp. 107–8.

Van Sickle J. B. (1978), *The Design of Virgil's Bucolics*, Rome (2nd ed. London 2004).

Van Sickle J. B. (1981), *Commentaria in Maronem Commenticia: A Case History of Bucolics Misread*, in *Arethusa*, 14, pp. 17–34.

Van Sickle J. B. (1983), *Order in Callimachus and Vergil*, in *Actes du VIIᵉ Congrès de la Fédération Internationale des Associations d'Études Classiques*, vol. I, Budapest, pp. 289–92.

Van Sickle J. B. (1984), *How Do We Read Ancient Texts? Codes and Critics in Virgil, Eclogue One*, in *MD*, 13, pp. 107–28.

Van Sickle J. B. (1986), *Poesia e potere. Il mito Virgilio*, Rome-Bari.

Van Sickle J. B. (1987), *'Shepherd Slave': Civil Status and Bucolic Conceit in Virgil, Eclogue 2*, in *QUCC*, 56, pp. 127–9.

Van Sickle J. B. (1992), *A Reading of Virgil's Messianic Eclogue*, New York-London.

Van Sickle J. B. (2000), *Virgil vs. Cicero, Lucretius, Theocritus, Plato, and Homer: Two Programmatic Plots in the First 'Bucolic'*, in *Vergilius*, 46, pp. 21–58.

Van Sickle J. B. (2003), *Quali codici d'amore nella X egloga?: il poeta elegiaco contestualizzato nel Bucolicon liber di Virgilio*, in *Giornate filologiche F. Della Corte*, vol. III, Genoa, pp. 31–62.

Van Sickle J. B. (2004), *Virgil Bucolics 1.1–2 and Interpretive Tradition: A Latin (Roman) Program for a Greek Genre*, in *CPh*, 99, pp. 336–53.

Vazquez B. (1952), *A Vergilian Parallel in Callimachus*, in *Aegyptus*, 32 (*Raccolta di scritti in onore di Girolamo Vitelli*, III), pp. 253–6.

Venuti, M. (2017), *Deductum dicere carmen: Nota a Verg. ecl. 6, 5*, in *Paideia*, 72, pp. 683–99.

Verdière R. (1971), *Notes de lecture*, in H. Bardon, R. Verdière (eds.), *Vergiliana. Recherches sur Virgile*, Leiden, pp. 378–9.

Veremans J. (1964–5), *La métrique en fonction de la compréhension des textes latins (Virgile, VIIᵉ Bucolique)*, in *JE*, 37, pp. 35–57.

Veremans J. (1969), *Éléments symboliques dans la IIIᵉ Bucolique de Virgile. Essai d'interprétation*, Brussels.

Veyne P. (1980), *L'histoire agraire et la biographie de Virgile dans les Bucoliques I et IX*, in *RPh*, 54, pp. 233–57.

Viarre S. (1990), *Les commentaires antiques de la 6ᵉ Bucolique de Virgile*, in *AC*, 59, pp. 98–112.

Viarre S. (2007), *À propos de la sixième Bucolique, inspiration et devenir*, in C. Filoche (ed.), *L'intertexte virgilien et sa réception: écriture, récriture, et réflexivité chez Virgile et Rutilius Namatianus*, Dijon, pp. 7–18.

Viljamaa T. (1983), *Gallus 'Soldier' or 'Shepherd'?*, in *Arctos*, 17, pp. 119–22.

548 BIBLIOGRAPHY

Villaseñor Cuspinara P. (2001), *Carmen seculare de Horacio y Écloga IV de Virgilio: el ritmo del tiempo*, in *Nova Tellus*, 19, pp. 155–72.

Virg. Enc. = *The Virgil Encyclopedia*, edited by R. F. Thomas, J. M. Ziolkowski, 3 vols., Chichester-Malden MA, 2013.

Volk K. (ed.) (2008), *Oxford Readings in Classical Studies: Vergil's Eclogues*, Oxford.

Vox O. (2009), *La maschera di Dafni. L'Idillio VI di Teocrito e l'Ecloga VIII di Virgilio*, in G. Laudizi, O. Vox (eds.), *Satura Rudina. Studi in onore di P. L. Leone*, Lecce, pp. 305–30.

Vretska K. (1962), *Vergils neunte Ekloge*, in *AU*, 6.2, pp. 231–46.

Wagenvoort H. (1956a), *Virgil's Fourth Eclogue and the Sidus Iulium*, in Wagenvoort (1956c, pp. 1–29; first publ. 1929).

Wagenvoort H. (1956b), *Virgil's Eclogues I and IX*, in Wagenvoort (1956c, pp. 233–73; first publ. 1953).

Wagenvoort H. (1956c), *Studies in Roman Literature, Culture and Religion*, Leiden.

Wagenvoort H. (1962), *Indo-European Paradise Motifs in Virgil's 4th Eclogue*, in *Mnemosyne*, s. IV, 15, pp. 133–45.

Waite S. V. F. (1972), *The Contest in Virgil's Seventh Eclogue*, in *CPh*, 67, pp. 121–3.

Wallace A. (2010), *Virgil's Schoolboys: The Poetics of Pedagogy in Renaissance England*, Oxford.

Wallace-Hadrill A. (1982), *The Golden Age and Sin in Augustan Ideology*, in *P&P*, 95, pp. 19–36 (= R. Osborne, ed., *Studies in Ancient Greek and Roman Society*, Cambridge 2004, pp. 159–76).

Waltz A. (1927), *La I^e et la IXe Bucoliques*, in *RBPH*, 6, pp. 31–58.

Wasdin K. (2018), *Eros at Dusk: Ancient Wedding and Love Poetry*, Oxford.

Weber W. (1925), *Der Prophet und sein Gott. Eine Studie zur vierten Ekloge Vergils*, Leipzig.

Weinreich O. (1932), *Zu Vergils vierter Ekloge, Rhianos und Nonnos*, in *Hermes*, 67, pp. 359–63 (= O. W., *Ausgewählte Schriften*, Amsterdam 1973, vol. II, pp. 402–6).

Weinstock S. (1971), *Divus Iulius*, Oxford.

Welch K. (2012), *Magnus Pius. Sextus Pompeius and the Transformation of the Roman Republic*, Swansea.

Wellesley K. (1966), *Virgil's Home*, in *WS*, 79, pp. 330–50.

Wendel C. (1901), *De nominibus bucolicis*, Leipzig.

Wendel C. (1934), *Probus ad Verg. Buc. X.18*, in *Hermes*, 69, p. 345.

Westendorp Boerma R. E. H. (1958), *Vergil's Debt to Catullus*, in *AClass*, 1, pp. 51–63.

Weyman C. (1917a), *Similia zu Vergils Hirtengedichten. I. Ekloge*, in *Wochenschrift für klass. Philol.*, 34, cols. 137–41.

Weyman C. (1917b), *Similia zu Vergils Hirtengedichten (Fortsetzung)*, in *Wochenschrift für klass. Philol.*, 34, cols. 209–14.

Weyman C. (1917c), *Similia zu Vergils Hirtengedichten (Fortsetzung und Schluß). II. Ekloge*, in *Wochenschrift für klass. Philol.*, 34, cols. 232–40.

Weyman C. (1917d), *Similia zu Vergils Hirtengedichten (Fortsetzung). III. Ekloge*, in *Wochenschrift für klass. Philol.*, 34, cols. 865–75.

Weyman C. (1918a), *Similia zu Vergils Hirtengedichten. IV. Ekloge*, in *Wochenschrift für klass. Philol.*, 35, cols. 187–91.

Weyman C. (1918b), *Similia zu Vergils Hirtengedichten. IV. Ekloge (Fortsetzung)*, in *Wochenschrift für klass. Philol.*, 35, cols. 211–16.

Weyman C. (1918c), *Similia zu Vergils Hirtengedichten (Fortsetzung). V. Ekloge*, in *Wochenschrift für klass. Philol.*, 35, cols. 519–24.

Weyman C. (1920–1), *Similia zu Vergils Hirtengedichten. Sechste Ekloge, I*, in *WS*, 42, pp. 169–73.

Weyman C. (1922–3), *Similia zu Vergils Hirtengedichten. Sechste Ekloge, II*, in *WS*, 43, pp. 98–100.

Weyman C. (1924–5), *Similia zu Vergils Hirtengedichten. Sechste Ekloge, III*, in *WS*, 44, pp. 114–17.

Weyman C. (1926–7a), *Similia zu Vergils Hirtengedichten. Siebente Ekloge, IV*, in *WS*, 45, pp. 122–6.

Weyman C. (1926–7b), *Similia zu Vergils Hirtengedichten. Achte Ekloge, V*, in *WS*, 45, pp. 248–51.

Weyman C. (1927–8), *Similia zu Vergils Hirtengedichten. Ekloge VIII (VI)*, in *WS*, 46, pp. 101–2.

Weyman C. (1930), *Similia zu Vergils Hirtengedichten. Ekloge IX (VII)*, in *WS*, 48, pp. 212–17.

Weyman C. (1931), *Similia zu Vergils Hirtengedichten. Ekloge X (VIII)*, in *WS*, 49, pp. 142–8.

Whitaker R. (1988), *Did Gallus Write 'Pastoral' Elegies?*, in *CQ*, n.s. 38, pp. 454–8.

White H. (2006), *Textual Problems in Horace and Virgil*, in *Veleia*, 23, pp. 379–89.

White K. D. (1970), *Roman Farming*, London.

Whittaker H. (2007), *Virgil's Fourth Eclogue and the Eleusinian Mysteries*, in *SO*, 82, pp. 65–86.

Wieland H. (1966), *Iubeto (zu Verg. Ecl. 5, 15)*, in *MH*, 23, pp. 212–15.

Wifstrand Schiebe M. (1981), *Das ideale Dasein bei Tibull und die Goldzeitkonzeption Vergils*, Uppsala.

Wigodsky M. (1972), *Vergil and Early Latin Poetry*, Wiesbaden.

Wigtil D. N. (1981), *Toward a Date for the Greek Fourth Eclogue*, in *CJ*, 76, pp. 336–41.

Wilamowitz-Moellendorff U. von (1906), *Die Textgeschichte der griechischen Bukoliker*, Berlin.

Wili W. (1930), *Vergil*, Munich.

Wilkinson L. P. (1936), *Eclogue VIII, 53–9*, in *CR*, 50, pp. 120–1.

Wilkinson L. P. (1966), *Virgil and the Evictions*, in *Hermes*, 94, pp. 320–4.

Williams G. (1968), *Tradition and Originality in Roman Poetry*, Oxford.

Williams G. (1974), *A Version of Pastoral, Virg. Ecl. 4*, in T. Woodman, D. West (eds.), *Quality and Pleasure in Latin Poetry*, London, pp. 31–46.

Williams G. (1978), *Change and Decline. Roman Literature in the Early Empire*, Berkeley.

Williams G. (1980), *Figures of Thought in Roman Poetry*, New Haven-London.

Williams G. (1987), *A Look at Theocritus Idyll 7 through Virgil's Eyes*, in *Hermathena*, 143, pp. 107–20.

Williams R. D. (1976), *Virgil, Eclogues 4, 60–63*, in *CPh*, 71, pp. 119–21.

Wills J. (1993), *Virgil's cuium*, in *Vergilius*, 39, pp. 3–11.

Wills J. (1996), *Repetition in Latin Poetry*, Oxford.

Wilson E. F. (1948), *Pastoral and Epithalamium in Latin Literature*, in *Speculum*, 23, pp. 35–57.

Wilson-Okamura D. S. (2010), *Virgil in the Renaissance*, Cambridge.

Wimmel W. (1953), *Über das Verhältnis der 4. Ecloge zur 16. Epode*, in *Hermes*, 81, pp. 317–44.

Wimmel W. (1960), *Kallimachos in Rom*, Wiesbaden.

Wimmel W. (1961), *Vergils Eclogen und die Vorbilder der 16. Epode des Horaz*, in *Hermes*, 89, pp. 208–26.

Wimmel W. (1983), *Der Augusteer Lucius Varius Rufus*, in *ANRW*, II.30.3, Berlin-New York, pp. 1562–621.

Wimmel W. (1996–97), *Gallus und Thrakien bei Vergil und Horaz (zu Horaz c. 3, 25)*, in *WJA*, N. F. 21, pp. 229–37.

Wimmel W. (1998), *Vergils Tityrus und der perusinische Konflikt. Zum Verständnis der 1. Ecloge*, in RhM, 141, pp. 348–61.

Winkler J. J. (1991), *The Constraints of Eros*, in C. A. Faraone, D. Obbink (eds.), *Magika Hiera. Ancient Greek Magic and Religion*, New York-Oxford, pp. 214–43.

Winniczuk L. (1959–60), *Cornelius Gallus. Poet and Statesman*, in Eos, 50, pp. 127–45.

Winterbottom M. (1976), *Virgil and the Confiscations*, in G&R, 23, pp. 55–9 (= I. McAuslan, P. Walcot, eds., *Virgil*, Oxford 1990, pp. 65–8).

Wissowa G. (1902), *Monatliche Geburtstagsfeier*, in Hermes, 37, pp. 157–9.

Wissowa G. (1912), *Religion und Kultus der Römer*, Munich, 2nd ed.

Witek F. (2006), *Vergils Landschaften. Versuch einer Typologie literarischer Landschaft*, Hildesheim.

Witte K. (1922), *Der Bukoliker Vergil*, Stuttgart.

Wlosok A. (1974), *Cumaeum carmen (Verg. Ecl. 4,4): Sibyllenorakel oder Hesiodgedicht?*, in *Forma futuri. Studi in onore del cardinale Michele Pellegrino*, Turin, pp. 693–711.

Wlosok A. (1983), *Zwei Beispiele früchristlicher Vergilrezeption. Polemik (Lact. div. inst. 5, 10) und Usurpation (Or. Const. 19–21)*, in V. Pöschl (ed.), *2000 Jahre Vergil. Ein Symposion*, Wiesbaden, pp. 63–86.

Wojaczek G. (1969), *Daphnis. Untersuchungen zur griechischen Bukolik*, Meisenheim am Glan.

Woodman A. J. (1991), *Virgil, Eclogue 6.39–40 and Lucretius*, in LCM, 16, p. 92.

Woodman A. J. (1997), *The Position of Gallus in Eclogue 6*, in CQ, n.s. 47, pp. 593–7.

Woodman A. J. (2010), *Virgil, Eclogues 4.28–9*, in CQ, n.s. 60, pp. 257–8.

Wormell D. E. W. (1960), *The Riddles in Virgil's Third Eclogue*, in CQ, n.s. 10, pp. 29–32.

Wormell D. E. W. (1969), *The Originality of the Eclogues: sic parvis componere magna solebam*, in D. R. Dudley (ed.), *Virgil. Studies in Latin Literature and Its Influence*, London, pp. 1–26.

Wright J. R. G. (1983), *Virgil's Pastoral Programme: Theocritus, Callimachus and Eclogue 1*, in PCPhS, n.s. 29, pp. 107–60.

Wülfing von Martitz P. (1970), *Zum Wettgesang der Hirten in der siebenten Ekloge Vergils*, in Hermes, 98, pp. 380–2.

Yardley J. C. (1980), *Gallus in Eclogue 10. Quotation or Adaptation*, in Vergilius, 26, pp. 48–51.

Zanker A. T. (2016), *Vergil's Sheep and Simonides, PMG 576*, in Mnemosyne, 69, pp. 301–6.

Zanker G. (1985), *A Hesiodic Reminiscence in Virgil, E. 9.11–13*, in CQ, n.s. 35, p. 235.

Zanker P. (1987), *Augustus und die Macht der Bilder*, Munich (English trans. by A. Shapiro, *The Power of Images in the Age of Augustus*, Ann Arbor 1988; Italian trans. by F. Cuniberto, *Augusto e il potere delle immagini*, Turin 1989).

Zetzel J. E. G. (1977), *Gallus, Elegy and Ross*, in CPh, 72, pp. 249–60.

Zetzel J. E. G. (1981), *Latin Textual Criticism in Antiquity*, New York.

Zetzel J. E. G. (1984), *Servius and Triumviral History in the Eclogues*, in CPh, 79, pp. 139–42.

Zetzel J. E. G. (2018), *Critics, Compilers, and Commentators: An Introduction to Roman Philology, 200 BCE–800 CE*, Oxford.

Ziolkowski J. M., Putnam M. C. J. (eds.) (2008), *The Virgilian Tradition: The First Fifteen Hundred Years*, New Haven-London.

Ziolkowski T. (1993), *Virgil and the Moderns*, Princeton.

Zucchelli B. (1995), *Il giuramento di Tirsi (Verg. ecl. 7, 41–43)*, in Paideia, 50, pp. 355–66.

Index of Proper Names

All references are to the Latin text of the *E*.

Achilles 4.36
Actaeus 2.24
Adonis 10.18
Aegle 6.20, 21
Aegon 3.2, 5.72
Aethiopes 10.68
Afri 1.64
Aganippe 10.12
Alcides 7.61
Alcimedon 3.37, 44
Alcippe 7.14
Alcon 5.11
Alexis 2.1, 6, 19, 56, 65, 73, 5.86, 7.55
Alphesiboeus 5.73, 8.1, 5, 62
Alpinus 10.47
Amaryllis 1.5, 30, 36, 2.14, 52, 3.81, 8.77, 78, 101, 9.22
Amor 8.43, 47, 10.28, 29, 69
Amphion 2.24
Amyntas 2.35, 39, 3.66, 74, 83, 5.8, 15, 18, 10.37, 38, 41
Antigenes 5.89
Aon 6.65
Aonius 10.12
Apollo 3.104, 4.10, 57, 5.35, 6.73, 10.21 (cf. also Cynthius, Phoebus)
Aracynthus 2.24
Arar 1.62
Arcades 7.4, 26, 10.31, 33
Arcadia 4.58, 59, 10.26
Arethusa 10.1
Argo 4.34
Arion 8.56
Ariusius 5.71
Armenius 5.29
Ascraeus 6.70
Assyrius 4.25
Auster 2.58, 5.82

Bacchus 5.30, 69, 79 (cf. also Iacchus, Liber)
Bavius 3.90
Bianor 9.60
Boreas 7.51
Britanni 1.66

Caesar (C. Iulius) 9.47
Calliopea 4.57
Camenae 3.59
Cancer 10.68
Caucasius 6.42
Ceres 5.79
Chalcidicus 10.50
Chaonius 9.13
Chromis 6.13
Cinna 9.35
Circe 8.70
Codrus 5.11, 7.22, 26
Conon 3.40
Corydon 2.1, 56, 65, 69, 5.86, 7.2, 3, 16, 20, 40, 70
Cremona 9.28
Cumaeus 4.4
Cydonius 10.59
Cynthius 6.3
Cyrneus 9.30

Damoetas 2.37, 39, 3.1, 58, 5.72
Damon 3.17, 23, 8.1, 5, 16, 62
Daphnis 2.26, 3.12, 5.20, 25, 27, 29, 30, 41, 43, 51, 52, 57, 61, 66, 7.1, 7, 8.68, 72, 76, 79, 81, 83, 84, 85, 90, 93, 94, 100, 102, 104, 109, 9.46, 50
Dardanius 2.61
Delia 3.67, 7.29
Dictaeus 6.56
Dionaeus 9.47
Dircaeus 2.24
Doris 10.5
Dryades 5.59
Dulichius 6.76

Eurotas 6.83

Fauni 6.27

Galatea 1.30, 31, 3.64, 72, 7.37, 9.39
Gallus (C. Cornelius) 6.64, 10.2, 3, 6, 10, 22, 72, 73
Garamantes 8.44

552 INDEX OF PROPER NAMES

Germania 1.62
Gortynius 6.60
Gryneus 6.72

Hamadryades 10.62
Hebrus 10.65
Hesperides 6.61
Hesperus 8.30, 10.77
Hybla 7.37
Hyblaeus 1.54
Hylas 6.43, 44
Hylax 8.107

Iacchus 6.15, 7.61
Illyricus 8.7
Iollas 2.57, 3.76, 79
Ismarus 6.30
Iuppiter 3.60, 4.49, 7.60

Liber 7.58
Libethrides 7.21
Linus 4.56, 57, 6.67
Lucifer 8.17
Lucina 4.10
Lycaeus 10.15
Lycidas 7.67, 9.2, 12, 37
Lycisca 3.18
Lycoris 10.2, 22, 42
Lyctius 5.72

Maenala 10.55
Maenalius 8.21, 25, 28a, 31, 36, 42, 46, 51, 57, 61
Maenalus 8.22, 10.15
Maevius 3.90
Mantua 9.27, 28
Mars 10.44
Martius 9.12
Meliboeus 1.6, 19, 42, 73, 3.1, 5.87, 7.9
Menalcas 2.15, 3.13, 58, 5.4, 64, 90, 9.10, 16, 18, 55, 10.20
Micon 3.10, 7.30
Mincius 7.13
Mnasyllos 6.13
Moeris 8.96, 98, 9.1, 16, 53, 54, 61
Mopsus, 5.1, 10, 8.26, 29
Musa 1.2, 3.84, 6.8, 8.1, 5
Musae 3.60, 4.1, 6.69, 7.19

Naiades 6.21, Nais 2.46, 10.10
Neaera 3.3
Nereus 6.35
Nerine 7.37
Nisus 6.74

Nymphae 2.46, 3.9, 5.20, 21, 75, 6.55, 56, 7.21, 9.19, 10.55
Nysa 8.18, 26

Oaxes 1.65
Oeta 8.30
Olympus 5.56, 6.86
Orpheus 3.46, 4.55, 57, 6.30, 8.55, 56

Palaemon 3.50, 53
Pales 5.35
Pallas 2.61
Pan 2.31, 32, 33, 4.58, 59, 5.59, 8.24, 10.26
Parcae 4.47
Paris 2.61
Parnasius 6.29
Parnasus 10.11
Parthenius 10.57
Parthus 1.62, 10.59
Pasiphae 6.46
Permessus 6.64
Phaethontiades 6.62
Philomela 6.79
Phoebus 3.62, 5.9, 66, 6.11, 29, 66, 82, 7.22, 62, 64
Phyllis 3.76, 78, 107, 5.10, 7.14, 59, 63, 10.37, 41
Pierides 3.85, 6.13, 8.63, 9.33, 10.72
Pindus 10.11
Poenus 5.27
Pollio (C. Asinius) 3.84, 86, 88, 4.12
Pontus 8.95, 96
Priapus 7.33
Proetides 6.48
Prometheus 6.42
Pyrrha 6.41

Rhenus 10.47
Rhodope 6.30, 8.44
Roma 1.19, 26

Sardonius 7.41
Saturnius 4.6, 6.41
Satyri 5.73
Scylla 6.74
Scythia 1.65
Sicanus 10.4
Sicelides (Musae) 4.1
Siculus 2.21, 10.51
Silenus 6.14
Silvanus 10.24
Sithonius 10.66
Sophocleus 8.10
Stimichon 5.55
Syracosius 6.1

INDEX OF PROPER NAMES 553

Tereus 6.78
Terra 8.93
Thalea 6.2
Thestylis 2.10, 43
Thetis 4.32
Thracius 4.55
Thyrsis 7.2, 3, 16, 20, 69
Tigris 1.62
Timavus 8.6
Tiphys 4.34
Tityrus 1.1, 4, 13, 18, 38, 3.20, 96, 5.12, 6.4, 8.55, 9.23, 24

Tmaros 8.44
Troia 4.36

Ulixes 8.70

Varius 9.35
Varus 6.7, 10, 12, 9.26, 27
Venus 3.68, 7.62, 8.78
Vesper 6.86
Virgo 4.6

Zephyrus 5.5

Index of Latin Words

The index is selective. All references are to page numbers.

a! 76, 146, 321, 491
adeo 214
adoleo 413
aequipero 272
aërius 96
aetas 206–7, 212, 457
agellus 435
ager 175, 435
agricola 460–1
aliquot 102 and n.*
altaria 88, 276–7, 413
animus 457
antrum 107, 303
apium 332, 369
ardeo 117
arista 103, 223
armentum 128
astrum 272, 455
atque 260–1, 316, 353
auena 66–7, 268

barbarus 104
bonum sit 427

cacumen 120
calamus 64, 66, 135, 156–7, 304, 398
calathus 138
candidus 125–6, 274, 452
cano 108, 248–9, 294, 300, 441, 472
capella 74–5, 79, 106, 195, 471–2, 484, 506
caput 306
carmen 107–8, 207, 297–8
casa 132
certo (certamen) 163, 237, 252, 382, 386
cicuta 135–6
cornu 495–6
cortex 328
cresco 361, 494
cuius, -a, -um 26, 152
cupressus 80
cura 83
cytisus 108

da = dic 77
deductus 297–8

deliciae 119
demens (dementia) 142, 145–6, 321
denique 122
dignus 206, 273, 396, 449 (cf. *indignus*)
dulcis 68
dum (+ indicative) 352, 442

ecce 138, 276
errabundus 325
et 80, 84, 192
excipio 158

facio 138, 182
fagus (faginus) 65–6, 119–20, 156, 164–5, 438, 503
formosus 27 n. 68, 69, 117, 130, 236 (cf. *informis*)
fretum 97

gemellus 75
grauis 92

haedus 436, 461
hedera 166, 217, 361, 367–8
heu 189
hibiscus 132–3
hordeum 268
huc ades 138, 353, 451

inconditus 116, 120
incrementum 232–3
indignus 396 (cf. *dignus*)
infelix 153, 268, 321–2, 341–2
informis 130 (cf. *formosus*)
ingemo 263
iubeo 256–7, 300
iuniperus 373–4, 504
iuuencus/iuuenca 144, 186–7, 320, 354, 369–70, 386, 420, 442, 478

labor 467, 500, 505
labrusca 251
lasciuus 143, 179
laurus 141, 178, 343, 393, 420, 475
laus 222
lentus 68, 79–80, 184, 257, 265, 371, 452, 487–8

INDEX OF LATIN WORDS 555

libertas 80–1
linquo 68
ludo 73, 293

magis 74
magister 153
maneo 90–1
meditor 67
medius 490, 498
miles 104
modo 211–12
mola 419
myricae 205–6, 300, 407–8, 475

nam 451
namque 75
nec 436
neque 190–1
niger 125–6, 487
numerus 310, 343
nuto 233–4

oliua 394
oportet 297
oro 137
otium 72, 275

peculium 83–4
pinus 85, 228, 378, 398
poculum 163–4, 277, 399
poeta 271, 362, 447, 501
post 101–2
posthac 106, 173
primus (*primum*) 88, 134–5, 212,
  292, 398
proprius 365
puer 88–9, 113, 122, 157, 197, 199, 211,
  273, 462

quadripes 261–2
quandoquidem 174
-que…-que 263, 275, 309, 317, 397–8
qui sit 77
quin age 173
quisquam 441

rapidus 100, 123
ratis 226
recubo 65
requiesco 387
respicio 81
rideo 218, 240–1, 308
rus 11, 90, 132, 141, 185
rusticus 141, 185

sat 196
senex 90, 306, 334
serpens 188, 220, 416
sidus 270
silua 66, 196, 204–6, 263, 293, 316, 378, 409,
  472, 493, 497
simus 471–2
solstitium 370–1
stultus 78
suauis 139, 178
suboles 232
subulcus 478–9
summitto 89
supero 444

tamen 81, 461, 485
tegmen 65
telum 439–40, 456, 464, 490
tener 140, 174, 314, 393–4, 471–2, 493–4
tenuis 66–7
tibi 281
tibia 66, 347
tugurium 101

uaccinium 126, 139, 487
uates 271, 362, 447, 501
uerbenae 413
uiburnum 79–80
uictima 84
uirgo 321
uitula 162–3, 182
umbra 22 n. 55, 68, 110, 117, 144, 250, 269–70,
  354, 370, 393, 452, 504–5
uoluptas 275, 456
usque 461
ut 403

General Index

The index is selective. All references are to page numbers.

Accius 227, 262, 339, 389, 496
accusative of respect ('Greek' accusative)
   27 n. 69, 94, 194, 323, 365
Achilles 164, 192, 199, 222, 226, 227, 231, 404, 477
acrostic 63, 447, 451
adynaton 96–7, 103, 262, 280, 296, 387, 399, 498
Aelian 13 n. 29, 64, 124, 259, 261, 302, 445, 457
Aeneis 10, 14, 17 n. 41, 18, 22 n. 55, 24, 27 n. 68,
   28 n. 73, 29 n. 76, 30, 31, 69, 74, 81, 88, 111,
   114, 124, 127, 139, 140, 145, 146, 164, 167,
   174, 194, 211, 221, 227, 275, 281, 294, 295,
   303, 310, 312, 320, 371, 378, 383, 389, 411,
   448, 456, 459, 460, 478, 495, 498, 502, 504
   Aen. 1: 17 n. 41, 74, 77, 86, 90, 91, 92, 93, 94,
      96, 97, 98, 99, 100, 104, 121, 140, 142, 146,
      153, 154, 165, 169, 170, 190, 211, 216, 234,
      251, 263, 270, 276, 281, 282, 295, 303, 307,
      312, 344, 365, 375, 386, 388, 389, 401, 402,
      406, 434, 440, 450, 491
   Aen. 2: 76, 88, 93, 94, 95, 97, 99, 122, 138, 145,
      154, 165, 171, 181, 190, 191, 210, 212, 214,
      222, 231, 233, 239, 261, 266, 298, 300, 322,
      394, 440, 444, 459
   Aen. 3: 77, 86, 96, 98, 111, 112, 125, 130, 158,
      160, 163, 180, 190, 191, 205, 207, 231, 236,
      261, 337, 338, 363, 374, 393, 395, 402, 439,
      444, 468
   Aen. 4: 68, 75, 82, 98, 115, 145, 153, 169, 180,
      195, 205, 211, 229, 232, 234, 252, 268, 295,
      319, 322, 324, 327, 334, 335, 368, 387, 395,
      404, 406–7, 409, 410, 415, 416, 417, 419,
      421, 422, 424, 427, 450, 470, 476, 483, 484
   Aen. 5: 75, 85, 97, 131, 142, 155, 162, 164, 172,
      185, 194, 226, 240, 276, 293–4, 308, 325, 352,
      409, 459, 495
   Aen. 6: 16 n. 37, 78, 79, 80, 81, 84, 88, 90, 92,
      95, 97, 104, 105, 121, 130, 137, 138, 142,
      154, 158, 163, 166, 167, 168, 180, 181, 190,
      197, 200, 205, 207, 210, 211, 213, 227, 233,
      234, 259, 263, 264, 269, 270, 320, 341, 362,
      365, 378, 394, 405, 427, 440, 448, 450
   Aen. 7: 14 n. 34, 75, 85, 88, 93, 98, 111, 124,
      137, 138, 142, 163, 165, 174, 177, 209, 223,
      224, 228, 229, 231, 232, 251, 262, 265, 292,

      294, 303, 310, 312, 322, 323, 353, 357, 394,
      401, 411, 413, 422, 426, 459, 489, 502
   Aen. 8: 14 and n. 34, 107, 165, 167, 208, 210,
      213, 222, 232, 240, 274, 300, 301, 324, 344,
      376, 395, 427, 455, 461, 502
   Aen. 9: 77, 79, 82, 86, 124, 125–6, 154, 160,
      164, 187, 192, 221, 233, 269, 276, 300, 321,
      334, 360, 364, 425, 439, 499, 506
   Aen. 10: 65, 68, 75, 76, 79, 85, 108, 140, 155, 165,
      174, 190, 223, 226, 227, 248, 252, 253, 256,
      262, 275, 306, 309, 327, 340, 355, 378, 403,
      409, 425, 427, 445, 455, 459, 460, 490, 495
   Aen. 11: 78, 118, 126, 139, 141, 163, 174, 262,
      265, 269, 301, 303, 378, 487, 496
   Aen. 12: 68, 74, 85, 104, 122, 144, 160, 173,
      221, 228, 248, 249, 269, 276, 282, 289, 341,
      349–50, 440, 460, 491, 498, 504
Aeschylus 170, 274, 294, 311, 317, 327, 336, 338,
   339, 340, 372, 375, 390, 399, 401, 402, 425,
   427, 450, 473
agon (*certamen*, contest, agonistic form) 147–9,
   161, 162–3, 175–6, 191–2, 250, 344–8, 353,
   356, 357, 373, 379–80, 382, 386, 411
   (*see also* amoebean)
agriculture 4, 9, 10, 26, 27 n. 68, 60, 91, 92, 93, 95,
   103–6, 111, 112, 115, 120, 123, 145, 155, 171,
   199, 201, 209, 216, 221, 223, 228, 232, 244,
   258, 265–6, 268, 269, 279–80, 281, 293, 317,
   361, 371, 436, 454, 456, 465, 481, 503–4, 505
   (see also *Georgics*, 'technical' language)
Ajax 192, 193–4
Alcaeus 9, 206, 278, 440, 445, 457
Alcimedon 65, 149, 151, 164, 165, 168, 171,
   216–17, 254, 286
Alexander the Great xi, 100, 199–200, 215, 221,
   227, 245, 264, 299
Alexandria x, xi, 7 and n. 13, 15, 202, 244, 329,
   387, 470
Alexis 111–12, 116, 117, 118–19, 122, 124,
   125–6, 127, 146, 345, 368, 370, 373, 374,
   378, 380, 396, 401, 414, 463, 477, 487, 501
allegoresis/allegory
   biographical or historico-political
      interpretation (of the *E.*) xi, 6 n. 12, 7 and

nn. 13–15, 90, 113, 136, 148, 181–2, 189, 244–5, 258–9, 264, 265, 272, 273, 288, 302, 330, 347, 349, 430, 502 (*see also* biography)
philosophical interpretation (of Homer and Hesiod) 219, 302, 327, 338, 375, 415
alliteration 27 and n. 71, 63, 75, 79, 82, 94, 119, 134, 136, 144, 152, 164, 172, 175, 183, 234, 239, 270, 272, 279, 296, 297, 303, 310, 314, 316, 322, 351–2, 355, 391, 397, 398–9, 403, 409, 414, 416, 419, 421, 428, 437, 439, 442, 443, 444, 448, 449, 459, 474, 491
Amaryllis 64, 65, 68, 70, 82, 83, 125, 139, 180, 183, 184, 356, 381, 382, 417–18, 423, 424, 425–6, 427, 442
amoebean 14, 175, 176, 243, 346, 352, 356, 357, 430, 462 (*see also* agon)
Amphion 128–9
Amyntas 135, 136, 137, 179, 180, 181, 182, 194, 252, 253, 256, 487
anaphora *see* repetition
anastrophe 110, 314, 361, 491
'animated' nature *see* pathetic fallacy
Antipater of Sidon 260
Antipater of Thessalonica 164, 167
Antonius (M.) *see* Mark Antony
antrum see cave
Aphrodite *see* Venus
Apollo (Phoebus) xi, 17, 20 n. 49, 64, 65, 73, 88, 95, 142, 156, 176, 178, 179, 180, 192, 193, 200, 201, 203, 206, 207, 208, 212, 213, 217, 218, 236, 242, 244–5, 246, 248, 253, 266–7, 274, 279, 284–5, 286, 287, 288–9, 291, 292, 295–6, 297, 301, 304, 310–11, 328, 331, 332, 335, 342, 343, 347, 360, 364, 376, 377, 378, 414, 445, 469–70, 472, 473, 474, 475, 476, 480, 484, 489, 490, 491, 506
Apollodorus (Mythographus) 129, 134, 193–4, 236, 254, 265, 317, 320, 321, 332, 337, 470
Apollonius Rhodius 110, 138, 144, 166, 180, 225, 226–7, 236, 248, 254, 286, 293, 295, 311, 312, 315, 316, 317, 318, 324, 327, 343, 387, 396, 404, 406, 425, 470, 497, 505
aposiopesis 154, 388
Appendix Vergiliana see single works (e.g. *Ciris, Culex*, etc.)
Appian 3 n. 2, 4 nn. 5–7, 5 n. 8, 87, 96, 99, 105, 199, 223, 227, 268, 391
Apuleius 94, 103, 118, 131, 191, 267, 284, 353, 383, 417, 422, 433, 437, 478
Aracynthus 29, 129, 474
Aratus 167–8, 176, 177, 193, 201, 208–9, 212, 215, 216, 223, 225, 242, 324, 333, 348, 349, 392, 453–4

Arcadia (Arcadian, *Arcas*) 8 and n. 17, 9 n. 18, 13–15, 17–18, 61, 78, 85, 117, 127, 132, 165, 228, 234, 236–7, 326, 334, 343, 345, 351, 355, 358, 360, 361, 363–4, 397, 424, 463–4, 465, 468, 472, 475, 476, 482, 485–6, 487, 489, 490, 493, 494, 497, 502
Archilochus 96, 97, 186, 296, 333
Arethusa 15, 21 n. 52, 343, 351, 359, 463, 464, 467, 468, 469, 470, 473, 475, 480, 481
Ariosto, Ludovico 399
Aristophanes 82, 96, 101, 105, 130, 179, 196, 297, 309, 320, 333, 380, 390, 391, 399, 415
Aristotle 9 n. 22, 21, 144, 158, 161, 210, 224, 232, 233, 281, 293, 303, 306, 315, 325, 341, 352, 391
Artemidorus of Daldi 76, 79
Artemidorus of Tharsus 19, 350, 432, 506
arts (visual arts, iconography) xi, 10, 11 and n. 27, 13 n. 30, 80, 92, 95, 107, 110, 128–9, 130, 138, 149, 170, 200, 218, 264, 265, 294, 304–5, 306, 320, 324, 326, 332, 333, 343, 359, 364, 367, 402, 445, 455, 481, 488
Asclepiades 449, 487
Atalanta 155, 285, 321, 326, 397, 403, 495
Athena *see* Minerva
Augustus *see* Octavian
Avienus 216, 240

Bacchus *see* Dionysos
Bacchylides 220, 297, 322, 341, 440
Bavius 148, 184, 187, 268 (*see also* Maevius, parody)
bay 123, 139, 140, 141, 178, 257, 259, 342, 343, 376, 377, 383, 393, 412, 413, 418, 419, 420, 475, 476, 480, 482
bee (honey) 8, 93, 94, 100, 139, 187, 223, 224–5, 280–1, 355, 367, 446, 484
biography (of V.) 6–8, 24, 61, 78, 81, 113, 114, 125, 189, 202, 238, 244, 259, 270, 284, 288–9, 294, 296, 349, 377, 383, 430–1, 438, 443, 444–5, 448, 495, 507–8 (*see also* allegoresis/allegory)
Bion (and [Bion]) 69, 111, 135, 175, 180, 205, 261, 283, 291, 367, 382, 400, 442, 451, 475, 476, 477
book (*libellus/liber*, collection of poems, volume, editorial effects) ix–x, 3–4, 16 n. 40, 18–25, 63, 66, 67, 110, 113, 117, 144, 145, 147, 167, 186, 196, 201, 206, 246, 252, 284, 285–6, 292, 296, 299, 300, 301, 302–3, 344, 346, 347, 369, 376, 382, 386, 388, 429–30, 431–2, 438, 463, 465–6, 467, 484, 501, 503, 505–6
(*see also* chronology)

558 GENERAL INDEX

botanical terminology *see* agriculture, 'technical' language
bucolic poetry (origin of) 12–13, 71, 116–17, 120, 147–8, 161, 364

Caecilius Statius 106, 457
Caelius (?) 192
Caesar (C. Iulius), Julius Caesar, Divus Iulius x, xi, 4, 5, 59, 61, 76, 80, 87, 88, 103, 105, 184, 185, 198, 207, 229, 232, 239, 244–6, 251, 258–9, 262, 265, 272, 273, 274, 276, 281, 288, 291, 347, 431, 445, 448, 453, 454–5, 456
Caesar Octavianus *see* Octavian
caesura 30, 67, 69, 73, 85, 105, 122, 127, 141, 154, 189, 213, 215, 227, 232, 236, 272, 300, 356, 359, 451, 462, 500, 505
Callimachus (Callimachean) 66, 67, 73, 82, 113, 244, 256, 279, 286, 287, 288, 296–7, 298, 299, 300, 303, 330–2, 333, 335, 464, 465, 469, 504
  aet.: 66, 68, 79, 88, 113, 119, 143, 144, 146, 154, 157, 167, 168, 186, 203, 212, 235, 244, 254, 256, 272, 281, 283, 286, 291, 292, 294, 295–6, 298, 300, 312, 330–1, 333, 335, 337, 342, 343, 362, 363, 405, 469, 473, 474, 488, 492, 493, 503, 504
  epigr.: 66, 68, 111–12, 120, 143, 145, 157, 168, 181, 245, 260, 297, 303, 333, 341, 380, 395, 396, 453, 457, 495
  Hec.: 129, 319, 338, 377, 395, 440
  hymn.: 12 n. 28, 14, 75, 94, 98, 100, 105, 121, 142, 179, 187, 203, 212, 213, 216, 217, 218, 222, 232, 267, 279, 291, 324, 325, 331, 334, 335, 344, 355, 358, 364, 375, 376, 386, 394, 405, 445, 470, 471, 482, 495
  iamb.: 143, 188, 213, 217, 244, 257, 272, 280, 296, 364, 376, 380
Calpurnius Siculus 7 n. 12, 16 n. 38, 19 n. 46, 63, 65, 66, 67, 71, 85, 98, 101, 102 n.*, 106, 109, 110, 117–18, 127, 128, 130, 132–3, 136, 140, 141, 155, 156, 159, 160, 161, 165, 166, 172, 177, 178, 182, 196, 209, 213, 234, 249, 250, 254, 256, 259, 261, 262, 267, 270, 273, 276, 295, 296, 303, 323, 356, 366, 383, 398, 408, 438, 455, 459, 491, 505–6
Calvus (C. Licinius) 228, 287, 317, 319, 321, 322, 330, 333, 383, 386, 387, 421
Cassius Dio 3 n. 2, 4 nn. 6–7, 5 n. 8, 59, 84, 87, 104, 198, 199, 211, 223, 233, 259, 268, 391, 435, 455
Catalepton 8 n. 17, 16, 63, 70, 176, 271, 293, 296, 327, 445, 503, 506
Cato the Elder 8 n. 17, 75, 76, 87, 155, 165, 182, 208, 222, 257, 266, 268, 275, 371, 375, 418, 421, 436, 461, 479, 499
Cato the Younger 81

Catullus 11, 12 n. 27, 25, 26, 30 n. 77, 68, 69, 70, 73, 74, 75, 83, 91, 92, 94, 95, 96, 100, 106, 108, 120, 121, 122, 125, 127, 135, 138, 146, 148, 157–8, 163, 166–7, 168, 174, 175, 178, 181, 184, 185, 186, 191, 196, 201, 206, 209, 212, 216, 220, 225, 226, 227, 228, 230, 231, 233, 238, 241, 242, 244, 263, 265, 271, 272, 273, 287, 297, 298, 306, 311, 315, 319, 321, 323, 325, 326, 330, 337, 338, 339, 344, 352, 361, 362, 367, 370, 379, 382, 383, 387, 395, 396, 398, 400, 401, 403, 404, 405, 414, 423, 427, 444, 448, 469, 471, 472, 475, 476, 485, 491, 494, 503
cave (grotto, *antrum*) 107, 109, 141, 243, 249, 250–1, 252, 255, 265, 287, 291, 303, 306, 319, 324, 356, 450, 452, 493
Ceres 223, 224, 244, 264, 281, 347, 456, 459
certamen see agon
characterization (bucolic characters, ethopoeia, ethos, rural/rustic simplicity) ix, 8, 9–10, 11, 16, 19, 21, 23, 25–6, 28, 60, 63, 64, 67, 70–1, 77–8, 91, 101–2, 104, 111–12, 114, 117, 120, 126, 129, 132, 135, 141, 148, 152, 163, 174, 183, 185, 187, 188, 195, 196, 243, 246, 247–8, 265, 282, 284, 296, 305, 306, 346, 347, 348, 352, 353, 354, 356, 367, 371, 380, 381, 382, 429, 430, 434, 437, 438, 440, 442, 443, 453, 463, 464, 465, 478–9, 484, 487, 496, 503
charismatic power *see* gods
chronology (composition and chronology of the *E.*) 3–4, 24–5, 61, 81, 93, 113, 147–8, 200–1, 345, 430–1, 438, 467 (*see also* book)
cicada 66, 123, 124, 189, 280–1
Cicero 5 n. 9, 26 n. 64, 60–1, 65, 71, 74, 76, 78, 79, 80, 81, 83, 86, 87, 90, 95, 100, 105, 106, 109, 125, 126, 152, 157, 164, 167, 172, 173, 176, 177, 185, 186, 190, 192, 197, 199, 211, 217, 222, 228, 232, 248, 249, 268, 272, 279, 288, 293, 294, 298, 301, 306, 329, 338, 372, 374, 375, 380, 392, 402, 423, 426, 434, 435, 439, 440, 441, 449, 454, 461, 469, 471, 492, 497–8
Cinna (C. Helvius) 144, 168, 359, 388, 448, 449, 453
Circe 337, 339, 415, 416, 423
Ciris 129, 174, 231, 323, 327, 336, 337–8, 339, 340, 342, 387, 395, 396, 400, 401, 403, 409, 410, 416, 436, 493, 496, 500
city-countryside 8, 16, 61, 112–13, 115, 414, 429, 486
clausula-type '*et mihi Damon*' 30, 131, 159–60, 441
CLE (*Carmina Latina Epigraphica*) 160, 266, 390, 486
Cleopatra 198, 200, 202, 474

GENERAL INDEX 559

closure (epilogue, finale) 22 n. 55, 25 n. 62, 27, 65, 71, 97, 110, 114, 121, 125, 143, 144, 145, 169, 176, 187, 196, 203, 215–16, 217, 230, 235, 237–8, 240, 242, 281, 285, 301, 327, 330, 336, 342, 344, 348, 357, 373, 379, 382, 388, 426, 431, 436, 454, 460, 461, 462, 463, 465, 467, 471, 481, 482, 498, 501–6
codices *see* manuscripts
Codrus 254–5, 346, 358, 359, 362, 365
collection of poems *see* book
colloquial language 11, 25–8, 69, 74, 77, 78, 79, 80, 85, 101, 106, 126, 138, 148, 151–2, 153, 159, 160, 163, 172, 173, 188, 189, 205, 212, 235, 236, 239, 252, 255, 256, 298, 309, 353, 355, 357, 370, 409, 427, 428, 434, 435, 437, 439, 442, 443, 458, 472, 480, 485, 503 (*see also* comedy)
Columella 18 n. 44, 78–9, 84, 92, 95, 96, 108, 126, 129, 132, 133, 137, 138, 139, 146, 159, 182, 189, 193, 224, 225, 226, 269, 281, 300, 323, 337, 352, 354, 356, 361, 367, 369, 399, 404, 425, 452, 460, 478, 483, 484, 488, 501
comedy (comic, humour, irony) 10 n. 23, 11 and n. 27, 26 and n. 64, 71, 80, 83, 85, 86, 101, 112, 114, 120, 127, 130, 143, 145, 149, 151–2, 153, 154, 157, 167, 172, 177, 182, 187, 189, 195, 206, 214, 252, 293–4, 307, 309, 328, 345, 353, 356, 428, 437, 454, 484–5 (*see also* colloquial language)
confiscations (expropriations) x, 3–4, 6, 9, 22, 27, 59–60, 61, 74, 76, 81, 83, 84, 85, 86, 90, 92, 99, 101, 104, 105, 115, 184, 189, 196, 201, 231, 329, 355, 389, 391, 428, 429, 430, 433, 434–5, 436, 437, 438, 439, 444, 445, 448, 456, 458, 464
Conon 166, 167, 168
contest *see* agon
Copa 101, 124, 138
Cornificius (Q.) 137, 173, 244, 254, 268, 297, 337, 359
Corydon xi, 9 nn. 18 and 20, 11, 16 n. 38, 19, 24, 27, 68, 70, 78, 85, 101, 111, 115, 116–19, 145, 146, 151, 152, 156, 160, 173, 177, 179, 182, 194, 243, 246, 248, 252, 254, 271, 283, 287, 321, 330, 342, 344–6, 349, 350, 351, 380, 393, 396, 398, 401, 402, 410, 411, 414, 421, 428, 451, 463, 465, 468, 472, 474, 477, 484, 486, 487, 494, 496, 500, 501
cosmogony (cosmology) 17, 233–4, 237, 274, 286, 291, 302, 305, 309, 311–12, 313, 316, 318, 404
countryside *see* city-countryside
Culex 124, 166, 180, 189, 254, 293, 328, 333, 392, 400–1, 406, 488, 497
Cyclops *see* Poliphemus

dactyl (dactylic rhythm) 29 and nn. 74–5, 65, 73, 160, 185, 261, 264, 272, 314, 378, 391, 458
Damoetas 23 n. 59, 111, 131, 136, 147, 148, 156, 157, 169, 170, 173, 177, 180, 181, 243, 278, 283, 345, 346, 434
Dante (Alighieri) 81
Daphne 141, 178, 343, 377, 475, 480
Daphnis ix, xi, 7, 9 n. 18, 11, 14, 19, 20, 22, 60, 61, 64, 90, 96, 106, 113, 114, 131, 133, 135, 136, 147, 155, 156, 157, 159, 162, 179, 180, 195, 237, 242–5, 246, 248, 249, 250, 251, 255, 259–60, 262, 264, 267, 286, 303, 344, 345, 347, 349–50, 351, 355, 361, 363, 367, 370, 373, 377, 380, 381–2, 386, 395, 396, 399, 407, 408, 409, 412, 414–15, 418, 419, 420, 425, 429, 432, 438, 454, 456, 463, 468, 472, 473–4, 475, 479, 480, 483, 485, 489, 493, 497
deictic, deixis 85, 162, 190, 250, 363, 366, 379, 413, 423, 435, 436, 452, 460, 461, 488
Delia (girl?) 179–80
Delia (goddess) *see* Diana
diaeresis (bucolic diaeresis) 29, 68, 72, 74, 151, 172, 243, 256, 324, 359, 392, 506
dialogue (dialogic) 21, 23, 25, 26, 28, 61, 63, 73, 80, 89, 147, 149–50, 151, 195, 246, 248, 251–2, 258, 353, 426, 429, 432, 433, 473 (*see also* mimesis)
Diana (Artemis, Delia, Lucina) 12 and n. 28, 79, 132, 142, 161, 179–80, 201, 212–13, 275, 320, 347, 362–3, 363–4, 365, 417, 468, 494
Dicaearchus 15 n. 37, 210, 224
dictum *see* proverb
didactic poetry 17, 164, 166, 221, 228, 248, 250, 284, 286, 288, 291, 303, 304, 309, 324, 331, 333, 371, 442, 464
diminutive 26, 28, 74, 75, 137, 421, 435 (*see also* hypocoristic)
Dio Cassius *see* Cassius Dio
Diodorus Siculus 13 n. 29, 15 n. 35, 131, 180, 210, 236, 259, 264, 265, 303, 320, 321, 366
Dione *see* Venus
Dionysius of Halicarnassus 10 n. 23, 14 and n. 34, 16 n. 37, 28 n. 73, 210, 297
Dionysus (Bacchus, Liber) xi, 17, 165–6, 186, 199–200, 215, 217, 220, 223, 224, 231, 238, 241, 243, 244–245, 246, 251, 258, 263–4, 274, 276, 278, 279, 281, 282, 287, 299, 303–5, 307, 308, 309, 310–11, 315, 319, 321, 323, 347, 350, 359, 360, 361, 362, 365, 366, 375, 376, 377, 378, 382, 383, 387, 393, 396, 398, 402, 405, 456, 473, 482–3, 488, 499
Diotimus 460
Dirae 61, 90, 91, 93, 103, 105, 108, 186, 409, 437

560 GENERAL INDEX

divine child see *puer*
divine models, divinity *see* gods
Divus Iulius *see* Caesar (C. Iulius)
Domitius Marsus 136, 187, 487

eagle 317, 439, 440
ecloga (history of the term) 18–19
ecphrasis 24, 150, 151, 164, 166, 170, 251, 319
editorial effects *see* book
'editorial' link 25 n. 62, 465, 501–6
elegy (love-elegy, elegiac) 8 n. 17, 16, 86, 95, 96,
    104, 112–13, 117, 118, 120, 131, 141, 142,
    143, 144, 149, 175, 208, 217, 235, 255, 256,
    270, 271, 294, 295, 318, 319, 328, 329, 330,
    331, 332, 335, 359, 370, 373, 396, 422, 464–5,
    469, 471, 474, 476, 480, 481, 485, 486, 488,
    489, 491, 492, 493, 494, 502 (*see also* love)
elision (synaloepha) 30 and n. 78, 75, 160, 185,
    243, 256, 263, 314, 392, 403, 419
enjambement 30 and n. 77, 134, 136, 156, 174,
    215, 218, 226, 229, 259, 261, 313, 353, 355,
    417, 495
Ennius 27, 65, 68, 76, 77, 80, 94, 95, 100, 105,
    118–19, 128, 154, 155, 178, 179, 210, 214,
    218, 225, 226, 227, 233, 234, 260, 261, 262,
    272, 292, 309, 310, 315, 330–1, 338, 368, 378,
    397, 402, 406, 437, 443, 450, 454, 479
epic poetry (epic style, *epos*) 8, 12 n. 27, 17 n. 41,
    26, 27, 77, 78, 112, 154, 165, 172, 177, 207,
    221, 222, 232, 234, 235, 260, 262, 282, 284,
    286, 289, 291, 292, 294, 298, 299, 301, 307,
    310, 311, 312, 330–1, 332, 333, 339, 342,
    343, 353, 363, 408, 411, 448, 450, 460, 479,
    495, 504
Epicurus (Epicureanism) xi, 12, 16, 17, 18, 60,
    61, 65, 66, 69, 71–2, 73, 82, 87, 109, 110,
    114, 117, 119, 131, 143, 145, 146, 174, 195,
    211, 228, 245–6, 274, 275, 276, 281, 287,
    288, 299, 302, 303, 309, 312, 313, 337, 370,
    402, 420, 421, 427, 428, 447, 456, 504, 506
epigram (epigrammatic) 8 n. 17, 13 n. 31, 66, 73,
    94, 109, 112, 117, 118, 122, 123, 124, 136,
    138, 145, 156, 164, 167, 168, 185, 187, 194,
    245, 260, 266, 293, 333, 350, 351, 360, 362,
    363, 364, 366, 373, 396, 432, 448, 453, 457,
    460, 484, 493, 501, 506
epilogue *see* closure
epitaph 259, 270, 280, 363, 470, 486
epithalamium (wedding ceremonies) 138, 175,
    196, 238, 241, 242, 327, 382, 383, 394, 395,
    396, 400–1, 419
Eriphanis 116, 157, 479
eros *see* love
Erucius 13 n. 31, 323, 325, 351, 363, 364
ethopoeia, ethos *see* characterization

etymology (etymological wordplay, folk
    etymology, paraetymology) 64, 70, 71, 72,
    86, 88, 101, 107, 117, 118, 119, 122, 126,
    127, 130, 135, 137, 165, 167, 176, 221, 227,
    231, 236, 251, 253, 254, 270, 275, 277, 284,
    296, 299, 303, 307, 310, 313, 317, 322, 324,
    328, 336, 339, 340, 354, 364, 368, 372, 375,
    380, 386, 394, 404, 412, 418, 420, 423, 434,
    443, 447, 456, 469, 471, 475, 476, 478, 495,
    499, 500, 506 (*see also* names)
Eudoxus 167, 168, 193
Euhemerus (euhemeristic) 210, 303
Euphorion 135, 178, 182, 191, 193, 209, 248,
    311, 330, 333, 335, 347, 359, 361, 439, 448,
    470, 492–3, 495, 499, 502
Euripides 80, 102, 107, 111, 119, 121, 128, 170, 179,
    194, 217, 220, 226, 229, 231, 240, 265, 276, 320,
    324, 341, 368, 372, 375, 387, 401, 404, 405, 406,
    425, 449, 473, 480, 482, 484, 488, 492, 494
exile ix, 4 and n. 7, 59, 60, 68, 71, 74, 76, 89, 90,
    92, 97, 99, 101, 102, 107, 110, 184, 222, 329,
    348, 354, 431, 435, 456, 483, 485, 504
expropriations *see* confiscations

facetum see *molle atque facetum*
"farewell speech" 67, 503
farming *see* 'technical' language
Faunus 256, 302, 310, 312
finale *see* closure
Florus 5, 199, 223, 391, 493, 494
folk etymology *see* etymology
frondatio 95, 145, 146, 460–1
fruit (as a gift of love) 84, 140, 181, 327

Galatea 70, 71, 82–3, 109, 111, 112, 118, 120, 121,
    122, 126, 128, 131–2, 136, 153, 179, 180, 181,
    184, 274, 358, 367, 368, 369, 372, 402, 450,
    451, 452, 471, 502
Gallus (C. Cornelius) 5 n. 9, 6 n. 10, 13, 15 n. 36,
    20, 22, 25 n. 63, 27, 61, 67, 95, 112, 119, 120,
    126, 131, 135, 143, 145, 154, 179, 180, 184–5,
    193, 244, 245, 246, 248, 255, 262, 285, 287,
    288, 311, 318, 327, 329–30, 332, 333, 335, 337,
    347, 359, 392, 409, 432, 439, 444, 449, 460,
    463, 464–5, 466, 469, 473, 475, 480, 484, 486,
    487, 489, 492–3, 494, 495, 496, 500, 502, 503
garland 25 n. 62, 126, 138, 140, 269, 306, 368,
    482, 487, 488
Georgics 7, 17, 18, 22 n. 55, 25 n. 62, 27 n. 68, 30,
    59, 63, 65, 66, 69, 71, 74, 75, 80, 91, 92, 104,
    106, 111, 114, 128, 153, 160, 164, 166, 167,
    170, 171, 215, 221, 228, 232, 234, 259, 268,
    288, 293, 296, 302, 315, 324, 378, 392, 421,
    454, 456, 465, 486, 501, 503–6
    (*see also* agriculture, 'technical' language)

G. 1: 17 and n. 41, 69, 70, 79, 86, 92, 95, 97, 98, 104, 109, 112, 123, 128, 129, 132, 134, 135, 145, 146, 153, 161, 163, 166, 167, 168, 184, 187, 196, 208, 214, 215, 217, 218, 223, 226, 228, 232, 233, 234, 248, 258, 259, 262, 268, 269, 274, 275, 278, 281, 292, 305, 314, 315, 317, 325, 329, 336, 337, 341, 350, 353, 371, 375, 376, 377, 390, 398, 400, 404, 405, 407, 416, 422, 448, 454, 455, 456, 459, 476, 479, 481, 501, 502, 505, 506

G. 2: 65, 66, 68, 69, 74, 75, 84, 87, 90, 92, 94, 95, 97, 99, 101, 102 n.*, 105, 106, 108, 120, 124, 134, 139, 146, 153, 155, 160, 165, 169, 175, 178, 208, 209, 214, 220, 221, 224, 228, 252, 257, 265, 266, 300, 303, 305, 311, 315, 319, 323, 360, 361, 365, 371, 373, 375, 377, 378, 390, 395, 398, 404, 410, 416, 439, 445, 446, 452, 459, 461, 467, 472, 478, 479, 481, 482, 483, 488, 499, 503

G. 3: 66, 69, 76, 78, 79, 84, 87, 92, 93, 102 and n.*, 122, 124, 130, 142, 154, 159, 162, 167, 169, 178, 184, 189, 190, 211, 212, 234, 235, 251, 261, 266, 267, 271, 275, 292, 295, 300, 303, 305, 310, 315, 317, 318, 320, 322, 323, 325, 328, 331, 352, 355, 361, 369, 370, 374, 378, 386, 389, 390, 393, 399, 403, 413, 421, 438, 443, 444, 461, 462, 474, 476, 482, 495, 497, 498, 500, 505

G. 4: 7, 11, 17 n. 41, 65, 71, 72, 73, 79, 84, 92, 93, 95, 96, 111, 123, 131, 139, 143, 144, 145, 153, 155, 165, 169, 170, 173, 224, 249, 260, 261, 264, 269, 280, 281, 286, 295, 296, 302, 305, 310, 311, 322, 323, 324, 332, 337, 341, 343, 344, 355, 367, 375, 387, 410, 413, 426, 451, 452, 476, 480, 496, 498

Germanicus 86, 168, 209, 216, 281, 500

gods (divinity, divine models, charismatic power) x–xi, 17, 71–2, 73, 86, 98, 133, 178, 199–201, 213, 215, 227–8, 241–2, 244, 264, 266, 267, 274, 287, 347, 349, 376, 455, 456, 483

Golden Age (myth of the ages) 187, 196, 201, 202, 207, 209–10, 212, 215, 216, 218, 223, 224, 227, 256, 275, 312, 317, 318, 389, 399, 407

golden line (*versus aureus*) 139, 224, 251

graffiti (from Pompei) 127, 141, 152, 416

Grecisms *see* Hellenisms

'Greek' accusative *see* accusative of respect

grotto *see* cave

Helios (Sun, sun-myths) 202, 213, 274, 287, 301, 307, 311, 320, 324, 325, 327 (*see also* Orpheus, Apollo)

Hellenisms (Hellenistic style and language, Grecisms) 25–8, 30–1, 88, 126, 129, 138, 152, 154, 165, 192, 207, 215, 217, 221, 223, 234, 248, 252, 264, 269, 271, 272, 293, 322, 331, 333, 351, 361, 373, 379, 386, 387, 401, 407–8, 434, 445, 446, 473, 474, 475, 480, 486, 493, 501 (*see also* accusative of respect, etymology, names)

Hercules (Heracles) xi, 14 n. 34, 86, 165, 172, 199, 200, 215, 220, 221, 222, 227, 231, 232, 236, 241–2, 284, 317, 318, 319, 332, 347, 376, 377, 378, 425, 446, 476

Hermesianax 168, 272

Herod ('the Great') 202, 214

Herodas 151

Herodotus 14, 79, 96, 100, 302, 332, 399, 408, 423, 439, 446, 498

Hesiod (Hesiodic) 17, 73, 88, 89, 112, 124, 147, 164, 167, 185–6, 191, 196, 201, 207, 208, 209, 210, 212, 215, 224, 226, 231, 233, 235, 236, 242, 283, 284, 285, 286, 287, 291, 296, 304, 312, 314–15, 317, 318, 319, 321, 322, 326, 327, 329, 330, 331, 333, 334, 335, 337, 359, 364, 404, 440, 464, 497, 503, 505

hexameter 12 n. 27, 23, 29–30, 63, 65, 67, 73, 77, 82, 85, 88, 92, 95, 122, 140, 155, 159, 165, 174, 175, 187, 207, 208, 232, 233, 234, 235, 256, 268, 272, 279, 283, 309, 310, 316, 317, 330, 334, 373, 374, 376, 387, 391, 397, 398, 435, 454, 492, 500

hiatus 30 and n. 79, 129, 140–1, 143, 154, 178, 183, 319, 373, 374, 392, 403, 404, 428, 474, 475

Homer (Homeric) 8, 10 n. 23, 28 n. 73, 66, 98, 102–3, 107, 109, 111–12, 142, 143, 162, 164, 176, 183, 191, 222, 234, 251, 266, 270, 282, 283, 285, 286, 296, 299, 301, 302, 303, 325, 327, 344, 397, 449, 450, 460, 479, 494, 506 (*see also* Homeric Hymns)

Il.: 66, 87, 88, 98, 109, 142, 144, 154, 164, 165, 176, 177, 178, 192, 194, 206, 211, 216, 218, 222, 225, 234, 237, 242, 253, 254, 262, 266, 267, 270, 278, 279, 282, 283, 288, 291, 294, 295, 303, 325, 327, 329, 331, 332, 338, 344, 353, 370, 375, 377, 390, 392, 403, 404, 411, 415, 421, 433, 439, 454, 455, 460, 477, 480, 494, 495, 499, 506

Od.: 8, 10 n. 23, 28 n. 73, 70, 71, 79, 90, 93, 100, 102–3, 107, 111, 128, 133, 136, 143, 153, 180, 215, 216, 225, 228, 230, 241, 251, 253, 270, 286, 288, 301, 302, 303, 311, 329, 336–7, 338, 339, 369, 405, 415, 424, 425, 439, 450, 451, 452, 468, 479, 494, 495, 496, 499

562 GENERAL INDEX

Homeric Hymns (*Hymn. Hom.*) 88, 93, 134,
142, 147, 154, 162, 165, 275, 276, 303, 308,
312, 331, 343, 386, 396, 476
honey *see* bee
Horace 3 n. 1, 4 n. 6, 11, 16 and nn. 38–9, 23,
24 n. 61, 77, 103, 114, 115, 118, 123, 127,
149, 176, 182, 185, 201, 205, 207, 213, 240,
295, 296, 297, 299, 301, 346, 391, 435, 445,
450, 462, 471
  ars: 132, 170, 183, 185, 239, 240, 271, 294, 299,
  309, 339, 362, 369, 446, 457, 486
  carm. 1: 68, 73, 90, 93, 96, 100, 107, 123, 131,
  132, 178, 214, 232, 259, 278, 283, 299, 300,
  339, 352, 360, 370–1, 387, 397, 399, 406,
  413, 440, 455, 470, 494
  carm. 2: 98, 127, 143, 185, 222, 249, 310, 332,
  391, 393, 421, 445, 452, 457, 483, 488, 491
  carm. 3: 16, 86, 95, 110, 139, 176, 180, 185,
  220, 225, 236, 250, 254, 264, 322, 361, 369,
  391, 417, 441, 444, 452
  carm. 4: 72, 73, 77, 86, 87, 94, 106, 117, 125,
  179, 182, 201, 210, 216, 235, 257, 276, 282,
  293, 295, 341, 373, 398, 440, 449–50, 457,
  462, 488, 495
  carm. saec.: 174, 201, 207, 208, 212, 213, 231,
  298, 315, 364, 389
  epist. 1: 16, 118, 126, 163, 185, 239, 257, 292,
  305, 330, 353, 392, 435, 440, 457, 461,
  485, 498
  epist. 2: 16 n. 38, 67, 74, 148, 155, 296, 297,
  299, 309, 361, 441, 493
  epod.: 4 n. 7, 73, 90, 93, 96, 103, 104, 106, 107,
  109, 115, 123–4, 135, 144, 162, 173, 187,
  188, 200, 206, 218, 219, 220, 224, 227, 228,
  280, 371, 375, 399, 412, 414, 415, 419, 420,
  426, 427, 433, 494
  sat. 1: 3 n. 1, 11 n. 27, 16 n. 39, 24 n. 61, 73,
  77, 90, 96, 108, 114–15, 148, 149, 153, 176,
  185, 201, 205, 211, 218, 228, 295, 300, 301,
  346, 348, 349, 380, 391, 402, 411, 412, 447,
  448, 450, 471
  sat. 2: 4 n. 6, 61, 77, 86, 109, 137, 151, 190,
  272, 296, 297, 308, 353, 362, 366, 369, 398,
  400, 427, 433, 434, 436, 441, 487
Hosidius Geta 183, 406
humour *see* comedy
hunting 10, 12 n. 28, 115, 116, 117, 119, 124,
132, 133, 156–7, 158, 179, 180, 181, 212,
275, 324, 325, 326, 359, 362, 363, 364, 365,
407, 421, 484, 485, 491, 493, 494, 495, 500
Hyacinth 178, 193–4, 343, 480
Hybla (Hyblaean) 8, 89, 93, 94, 355, 367, 369
hymn (hymnic style, invocation, prayer) 12, 72,
73, 86, 134, 138, 176, 212, 214, 263, 273,
276, 358, 359, 360, 361, 362, 363, 364, 365,

373, 375, 384, 390, 397, 464, 468, 473, 475
(*see also* Homeric Hymns)
hyperbaton 27, 29, 74, 101, 156, 163, 170, 212,
261, 292, 296, 301, 322, 341, 361, 362, 393,
421, 435, 457, 467, 469, 474, 476, 493
hypocoristic 29, 137 (*see also* diminutive)

iconography *see* arts
ictus 104, 160, 272, 280, 366, 418, 488
indirect tradition (*see also* transmission of the
text, manuscripts) 31, 134, 160, 165, 239–40
infinitive 27, 76–7, 137, 146, 248, 271, 309, 343,
352, 486
inscription (carving words in the bark of a tree)
65, 255–6, 270, 493–4
investiture (poetic initiation) 59, 73, 285, 311,
326, 331, 333, 336, 342, 358, 359, 447,
477, 492
invocation *see* hymn
irony *see* comedy
iteration *see* repetition
ivy 163, 165, 166, 170, 171, 216, 217, 265, 306,
347, 350, 361, 362, 367, 368, 383, 388, 393

Julius Caesar *see* Caesar (C. Iulius)
Jupiter (Iuppiter, Zeus) 7 n. 13, 14, 66, 71, 86, 88,
128, 176, 177, 178, 185, 187, 192, 210, 213,
215, 220, 225, 226, 231, 232, 233, 241, 242,
253, 266, 281, 283, 309, 317, 320, 324, 325,
327, 331, 355, 358, 375, 398, 439, 440, 455,
459, 476, 483
Juvenal 14 n. 32, 68, 81, 90, 95, 109, 110, 143,
146, 158, 159, 161, 173, 209, 230, 240, 320,
322, 328, 364, 367, 390, 403, 423, 455

Laevius 267, 365, 450
landscape xi, 5, 9 n. 18, 10 n. 24, 15 and n. 35,
21 n. 52, 66, 75, 76, 80, 85, 91, 92, 93, 100,
107, 108, 110, 114, 117, 119, 120, 126, 142,
156, 159, 206, 223, 262, 269, 271, 276, 300,
328, 330, 331, 370, 373, 376, 378, 379, 393,
402, 421, 438, 445, 463, 475, 476, 481, 487,
488, 490, 491, 495, 498, 501, 503
(*see also* arts)
laurel *see* bay
lengthening in arsis 30, 85, 189, 323, 360,
462, 500
Leonidas (of Tarentum) 139, 363, 364
Leopardi, Giacomo 454
libellus/liber see book
Libethrides (Nymphs) 205, 347, 358–9, 411,
468, 473
Linus 222, 235–6, 237, 289, 331–4, 464, 477, 497
Livius (T.) 4 n. 6, 14 and n. 34, 16 n. 37, 76, 85,
99, 101, 120, 121, 132, 148, 190, 239, 262,

G. 1: 17 and n. 41, 69, 70, 79, 86, 92, 95, 97, 98, 104, 109, 112, 123, 128, 129, 132, 134, 135, 145, 146, 153, 161, 163, 166, 167, 168, 184, 187, 196, 208, 214, 215, 217, 218, 223, 226, 228, 232, 233, 234, 248, 258, 259, 262, 268, 269, 274, 275, 278, 281, 292, 305, 314, 315, 317, 325, 329, 336, 337, 341, 350, 353, 371, 375, 376, 377, 390, 398, 400, 404, 405, 407, 416, 422, 448, 454, 455, 456, 459, 476, 479, 481, 501, 502, 505, 506

G. 2: 65, 66, 68, 69, 74, 75, 84, 87, 90, 92, 94, 95, 97, 99, 101, 102 n.*, 105, 106, 108, 120, 124, 134, 139, 146, 153, 155, 160, 165, 169, 175, 178, 208, 209, 214, 220, 221, 224, 228, 252, 257, 265, 266, 300, 303, 305, 311, 315, 319, 323, 360, 361, 365, 371, 373, 375, 377, 378, 390, 395, 398, 404, 410, 416, 439, 445, 446, 452, 459, 461, 467, 472, 478, 479, 481, 482, 483, 488, 499, 503

G. 3: 66, 69, 76, 78, 79, 84, 87, 92, 93, 102 and n.*, 122, 124, 130, 142, 154, 159, 162, 167, 169, 178, 184, 189, 190, 211, 212, 234, 235, 251, 261, 266, 267, 271, 275, 292, 295, 300, 303, 305, 310, 315, 317, 318, 320, 322, 323, 325, 328, 331, 352, 355, 361, 369, 370, 374, 378, 386, 389, 390, 393, 399, 403, 413, 421, 438, 443, 444, 461, 462, 474, 476, 482, 495, 497, 498, 500, 505

G. 4: 7, 11, 17 n. 41, 65, 71, 72, 73, 79, 84, 92, 93, 95, 96, 111, 123, 131, 139, 143, 144, 145, 153, 155, 165, 169, 170, 173, 224, 249, 260, 261, 264, 269, 280, 281, 286, 295, 296, 302, 305, 310, 311, 322, 323, 324, 332, 337, 341, 343, 344, 355, 367, 375, 387, 410, 413, 426, 451, 452, 476, 480, 496, 498

Germanicus 86, 168, 209, 216, 281, 500

gods (divinity, divine models, charismatic power) x–xi, 17, 71–2, 73, 86, 98, 133, 178, 199–201, 213, 215, 227–8, 241–2, 244, 264, 266, 267, 274, 287, 347, 349, 376, 455, 456, 483

Golden Age (myth of the ages) 187, 196, 201, 202, 207, 209–10, 212, 215, 216, 218, 223, 224, 227, 256, 275, 312, 317, 318, 389, 399, 407

golden line (*versus aureus*) 139, 224, 251

graffiti (from Pompei) 127, 141, 152, 416

Grecisms *see* Hellenisms

'Greek' accusative *see* accusative of respect

grotto *see* cave

Helios (Sun, sun-myths) 202, 213, 274, 287, 301, 307, 311, 320, 324, 325, 327 (*see also* Orpheus, Apollo)

Hellenisms (Hellenistic style and language, Grecisms) 25–8, 30–1, 88, 126, 129, 138, 152, 154, 165, 192, 207, 215, 217, 221, 223, 234, 248, 252, 264, 269, 271, 272, 293, 322, 331, 333, 351, 361, 373, 379, 386, 387, 401, 407–8, 434, 445, 446, 473, 474, 475, 480, 486, 493, 501 (*see also* accusative of respect, etymology, names)

Hercules (Heracles) xi, 14 n. 34, 86, 165, 172, 199, 200, 215, 220, 221, 222, 227, 231, 232, 236, 241–2, 284, 317, 318, 319, 332, 347, 376, 377, 378, 425, 446, 476

Hermesianax 168, 272

Herod ('the Great') 202, 214

Herodas 151

Herodotus 14, 79, 96, 100, 302, 332, 399, 408, 423, 439, 446, 498

Hesiod (Hesiodic) 17, 73, 88, 89, 112, 124, 147, 164, 167, 185–6, 191, 196, 201, 207, 208, 209, 210, 212, 215, 224, 226, 231, 233, 235, 236, 242, 283, 284, 285, 286, 287, 291, 296, 304, 312, 314–15, 317, 318, 319, 321, 322, 326, 327, 329, 330, 331, 333, 334, 335, 337, 359, 364, 404, 440, 464, 497, 503, 505

hexameter 12 n. 27, 23, 29–30, 63, 65, 67, 73, 77, 82, 85, 88, 92, 95, 122, 140, 155, 159, 165, 174, 175, 187, 207, 208, 232, 233, 234, 235, 256, 268, 272, 279, 283, 309, 310, 316, 317, 330, 334, 373, 374, 376, 387, 391, 397, 398, 435, 454, 492, 500

hiatus 30 and n. 79, 129, 140–1, 143, 154, 178, 183, 319, 373, 374, 392, 403, 404, 428, 474, 475

Homer (Homeric) 8, 10 n. 23, 28 n. 73, 66, 98, 102–3, 107, 109, 111–12, 142, 143, 162, 164, 176, 183, 191, 222, 234, 251, 266, 270, 282, 283, 285, 286, 296, 299, 301, 302, 303, 325, 327, 344, 397, 449, 450, 460, 479, 494, 506 (*see also* Homeric Hymns)

Il.: 66, 87, 88, 98, 109, 142, 144, 154, 164, 165, 176, 177, 178, 192, 194, 206, 211, 216, 218, 222, 225, 234, 237, 242, 253, 254, 262, 266, 267, 270, 278, 279, 282, 283, 288, 291, 294, 295, 303, 325, 327, 329, 331, 332, 338, 344, 353, 370, 375, 377, 390, 392, 403, 404, 411, 415, 421, 433, 439, 454, 455, 460, 477, 480, 494, 495, 499, 506

Od.: 8, 10 n. 23, 28 n. 73, 70, 71, 79, 90, 93, 100, 102–3, 107, 111, 128, 133, 136, 143, 153, 180, 215, 216, 225, 228, 230, 241, 251, 253, 270, 286, 288, 301, 302, 303, 311, 329, 336–7, 338, 339, 369, 405, 415, 424, 425, 439, 450, 451, 452, 468, 479, 494, 495, 496, 499

562 GENERAL INDEX

Homeric Hymns (*Hymn. Hom.*) 88, 93, 134, 142, 147, 154, 162, 165, 275, 276, 303, 308, 312, 331, 343, 386, 396, 476
honey *see* bee
Horace 3 n. 1, 4 n. 6, 11, 16 and nn. 38–9, 23, 24 n. 61, 77, 103, 114, 115, 118, 123, 127, 149, 176, 182, 185, 201, 205, 207, 213, 240, 295, 296, 297, 301, 346, 391, 435, 445, 450, 462, 471
   ars: 132, 170, 183, 185, 239, 240, 271, 294, 299, 309, 339, 362, 369, 446, 457, 486
   carm. 1: 68, 73, 90, 93, 96, 100, 107, 123, 131, 132, 178, 214, 232, 259, 278, 283, 299, 300, 339, 352, 360, 370–1, 387, 397, 399, 406, 413, 440, 455, 470, 494
   carm. 2: 98, 127, 143, 185, 222, 249, 310, 332, 391, 393, 421, 445, 452, 457, 483, 488, 491
   carm. 3: 16, 86, 95, 110, 139, 176, 180, 185, 220, 225, 236, 250, 254, 264, 322, 361, 369, 391, 417, 441, 444, 452
   carm. 4: 72, 73, 77, 86, 87, 94, 106, 117, 125, 179, 182, 201, 210, 216, 235, 257, 276, 282, 293, 295, 341, 373, 398, 440, 449–50, 457, 462, 488, 495
   carm. saec.: 174, 201, 207, 208, 212, 213, 231, 298, 315, 364, 389
   epist. 1: 16, 118, 126, 163, 185, 239, 257, 292, 305, 330, 353, 392, 435, 440, 457, 461, 485, 498
   epist. 2: 16 n. 38, 67, 74, 148, 155, 296, 297, 299, 309, 361, 441, 493
   epod.: 4 n. 7, 73, 90, 93, 96, 103, 104, 106, 107, 109, 115, 123–4, 135, 144, 162, 173, 187, 188, 200, 206, 218, 219, 220, 224, 227, 228, 280, 371, 375, 399, 412, 414, 415, 419, 420, 426, 427, 433, 494
   sat. 1: 3 n. 1, 11 n. 27, 16 n. 39, 24 n. 61, 73, 77, 90, 96, 108, 114–15, 148, 149, 153, 176, 185, 201, 205, 211, 218, 228, 295, 300, 301, 346, 348, 349, 380, 391, 402, 411, 412, 447, 448, 450, 471
   sat. 2: 4 n. 6, 61, 77, 86, 109, 137, 151, 190, 272, 296, 297, 308, 353, 362, 366, 369, 398, 400, 427, 433, 434, 436, 441, 487
Hosidius Geta 183, 406
humour *see* comedy
hunting 10, 12 n. 28, 115, 116, 117, 119, 124, 132, 133, 156–7, 158, 179, 180, 181, 212, 275, 324, 325, 326, 359, 362, 363, 364, 365, 407, 421, 484, 485, 491, 493, 494, 495, 500
Hyacinth 178, 193–4, 343, 480
Hybla (Hyblaean) 8, 89, 93, 94, 355, 367, 369
hymn (hymnic style, invocation, prayer) 12, 72, 73, 86, 134, 138, 176, 212, 214, 263, 273, 276, 358, 359, 360, 361, 362, 363, 364, 365,

373, 375, 384, 390, 397, 464, 468, 473, 475 (*see also* Homeric Hymns)
hyperbaton 27, 29, 74, 101, 156, 163, 170, 212, 261, 292, 296, 301, 322, 341, 361, 362, 393, 421, 435, 457, 467, 469, 474, 476, 493
hypocoristic 29, 137 (*see also* diminutive)

iconography *see* arts
ictus 104, 160, 272, 280, 366, 418, 488
indirect tradition (*see also* transmission of the text, manuscripts) 31, 134, 160, 165, 239–40
infinitive 27, 76–7, 137, 146, 248, 271, 309, 343, 352, 486
inscription (carving words in the bark of a tree) 65, 255–6, 270, 493–4
investiture (poetic initiation) 59, 73, 285, 311, 326, 331, 333, 336, 342, 358, 359, 447, 477, 492
invocation *see* hymn
irony *see* comedy
iteration *see* repetition
ivy 163, 165, 166, 170, 171, 216, 217, 265, 306, 347, 350, 361, 362, 367, 368, 383, 388, 393

Julius Caesar *see* Caesar (C. Iulius)
Jupiter (Iuppiter, Zeus) 7 n. 13, 14, 66, 71, 86, 88, 128, 176, 177, 178, 185, 187, 192, 210, 213, 215, 220, 225, 226, 231, 232, 233, 241, 242, 253, 266, 281, 283, 309, 317, 320, 324, 325, 327, 331, 355, 358, 375, 398, 439, 440, 455, 459, 476, 483
Juvenal 14 n. 32, 68, 81, 90, 95, 109, 110, 143, 146, 158, 159, 161, 173, 209, 230, 240, 320, 322, 328, 364, 367, 390, 403, 423, 455

Laevius 267, 365, 450
landscape xi, 5, 9 n. 18, 10 n. 24, 15 and n. 35, 21 n. 52, 66, 75, 76, 80, 85, 91, 92, 93, 100, 107, 108, 110, 114, 117, 119, 120, 126, 142, 156, 159, 206, 223, 262, 269, 271, 276, 300, 328, 330, 331, 370, 373, 376, 378, 379, 393, 402, 421, 438, 445, 463, 475, 476, 481, 487, 488, 490, 491, 495, 498, 501, 503 (*see also* arts)
laurel *see* bay
lengthening in arsis 30, 85, 189, 323, 360, 462, 500
Leonidas (of Tarentum) 139, 363, 364
Leopardi, Giacomo 454
libellus/liber see book
Libethrides (Nymphs) 205, 347, 358–9, 411, 468, 473
Linus 222, 235–6, 237, 289, 331–4, 464, 477, 497
Livius (T.) 4 n. 6, 14 and n. 34, 16 n. 37, 76, 85, 99, 101, 120, 121, 132, 148, 190, 239, 262,

264, 265, 281, 306, 374, 399, 401, 402, 427, 438, 493

Livius Andronicus 143, 176, 339, 365, 416, 471

Longus 65, 66, 68–9, 95, 126, 133, 134, 135, 136, 237, 264, 360, 402, 442, 487

love (*amor/Amor*, eros) 13, 68, 70, 80, 82, 111–12, 114, 115, 123, 124, 141, 145, 146, 176, 179, 182, 189, 253, 343, 373, 381, 382, 383, 395, 396, 400, 404, 406, 412, 422, 427, 463, 464, 465, 471, 479, 480, 481, 486, 488–9, 494, 496, 500, 505
(*see also* elegy, *medicina amoris*)

Lucanus 72–3, 77, 97, 130, 207, 214, 277, 329, 334, 353, 389, 415, 424, 456, 468

Lucianus 14 n. 32, 128, 130, 188, 233, 242, 282, 310, 320, 422, 445

Lucilius 24 n. 61, 77, 103 n.*, 119, 126, 295, 297, 398, 411, 416, 427, 449, 450

Lucina 206, 212–13, 238

Lucretius 14 n. 33, 16 n. 40, 17, 65, 66, 69, 70, 71, 72, 73, 74, 82, 92, 93, 97, 100, 110–11, 114, 120, 128, 131, 134, 135, 136, 139, 143, 145, 146, 154, 156, 167, 173, 174, 189, 211, 224, 225, 228, 229, 232, 233, 234, 240, 245–6, 256, 263, 265, 271, 274, 275, 276, 281, 282, 287, 288, 292, 298, 299, 307, 308, 309, 310, 312–16, 321, 325, 328, 331, 338, 343, 353, 370, 374, 375, 378, 397, 402, 404, 408, 410, 413, 419, 420, 421, 427, 444, 453, 456, 458, 469, 476, 482, 488, 490, 498, 504, 505, 506

lustratio 279–80

Lutatius Catulus 118

Lycidas 23 n. 59, 64, 65, 178, 182, 239, 243, 283, 376, 379, 429, 432, 433, 434, 441, 442, 450, 459

Lycophron 227, 358, 499

Lydia [*Dirae*] 67, 488

Maecenas 4, 6, 16 n. 39, 85, 87, 115, 118, 149, 182, 201, 299, 300, 360, 392, 447

Maevius 148, 184, 187–8, 268 (*see also* Bavius, parody)

magic 17, 114, 123, 170, 191, 202, 272, 328, 329, 334, 335, 381, 382, 383, 387, 411–12, 414, 415, 429, 431, 503

makarismos 65, 90, 91, 93, 105, 272, 321

Manilius 123, 131, 233, 234, 238, 254, 306, 336, 344, 395, 499, 500

Mantua (Mantuan) x, 3, 7, 8–9, 11, 12, 15, 21 n. 52, 78, 79, 92, 93, 94, 110, 130, 159, 189, 192, 248, 251, 270, 327, 345, 355, 377, 410, 431, 434, 438–9, 444–5, 448, 457, 459, 460, 464

manuscripts, manuscript tradition, textual transmission (of V.) 18–19, 30–1, 69, 77,

122, 131, 134, 152, 160, 165, 190–1, 207, 217–18, 222, 234, 235, 239, 249, 251, 256, 258, 262, 263, 269, 281, 293, 300, 301, 303, 308, 311, 313, 314, 316, 322, 326, 328, 335, 336, 343, 344, 352, 355, 356, 357, 360, 369, 371, 373, 374, 378, 379, 387, 392, 393, 398, 401, 403, 404, 405, 409, 417, 419, 427, 428, 436–7, 438, 441, 443, 446, 448, 453, 458, 461, 462, 474, 475, 478, 479, 485, 488, 496, 500, 501, 503 (*see also* transmission of the text, indirect tradition)

Mark Antony x, 4 and n. 6, 5 and n. 8, 6 n. 10, 17 n. 42, 59, 61, 86, 87, 99, 104, 105, 184, 197–9, 200, 202, 210, 216, 218, 222, 241, 246, 388, 391, 393, 448, 449, 455, 469, 474, 481, 489

Martial 7 n. 12, 72, 109, 117, 118, 123, 126, 132, 137, 141, 187, 190, 221, 226, 230, 317, 332, 352, 361, 372, 419, 486, 487, 493, 506

Medea 138, 321, 383, 387, 396, 406, 415, 416, 423, 426

medicina amoris (φάρμακον) 112, 114, 119, 121, 144, 383, 422, 485, 496 (*see also* elegy, love)

Meleager 25 n. 62, 66, 94, 117, 118, 124, 138, 144, 178, 179, 185, 260, 266, 269, 373, 404, 460, 501–2

Meliboeus ix, 4, 7, 11, 12, 13, 19 n. 45, 20, 21 nn. 51 and 53, 23 n. 59, 24 n. 60, 27, 35, 59, 60, 61, 63, 67, 70–1, 80, 85, 89–90, 93, 99, 104, 105, 106, 107, 145, 149, 152, 242, 345, 347, 348, 353, 354, 356, 357, 379, 380, 430, 431, 443, 498, 505

Menalcas ix, xi, 7 and n. 12, 13 n. 29, 23 and n. 59, 26 n. 66, 64, 116–17, 125, 136, 147, 149, 150, 155, 156, 157, 159, 160, 169, 171, 173, 175, 179–80, 182, 183, 237, 243, 244–5, 250, 271, 282, 284, 345, 346, 430, 431, 436, 437, 438, 479

Menander 80, 154, 274, 473, 484, 500

Menander Rhetor 67, 70

Mercury (Hermes) xi, 109, 128, 129, 134, 147, 238, 242, 259, 260, 261, 266, 312, 316, 473, 478, 479, 480

messianism (Messiah) 201–2, 211, 219, 220

metalepsis 328, 334 (*see also* magic, Orpheus, pathetic fallacy, resonance)

Milton, John 294

mimesis (mimetic, dialogic-mimetic form) 8–12, 21–2, 24 n. 60, 25 and n. 64, 29, 61, 78, 149, 151, 155, 166, 174, 188, 191, 195, 246, 249, 251–2, 258, 347, 357, 405, 422, 426, 429, 432, 434, 442, 505
(*see also* dialogue)

Mincius 9 n. 18, 21 n. 52, 92, 93, 345, 351, 354, 355, 410, 421, 437, 438, 464

564 GENERAL INDEX

Minerva (Pallas, Athena) 110, 135, 142, 180, 217, 257, 376, 395

Moeris 7, 19, 21 n. 51, 23 n. 59, 75, 78, 178, 235, 258, 379, 383, 412, 423, 424, 428, 429–30, 431, 433–4, 436, 440, 441, 453, 454, 458

molle atque facetum 11 and n. 27, 114–15, 185

monosyllable 30, 77, 134, 143, 159, 322, 335, 428, 461, 470

Mopsus xi, 23 and n. 59, 243, 245, 248, 251, 252, 253, 261, 265, 271, 272, 282, 284, 346, 381, 382, 398–9, 430

Moretum 84, 123, 132, 461

Moschus (and [Moschus]) 9 n. 18, 65, 66, 69, 120, 139, 142, 164, 170, 205, 237, 261, 262, 283, 291, 298, 299, 319, 320, 328, 332, 350, 397, 398, 441, 451, 452, 468, 470, 475, 479, 501

motto *see* proverb

Naevius 68, 171, 262

names (bucolic names, etymology of proper names) 64, 70, 71, 117–19, 122, 125, 130, 131, 135, 136, 137, 165, 167, 172, 182, 227, 236, 253, 254, 275, 284, 296, 299, 303, 307, 310, 324, 339, 340, 350, 354, 355–6, 364, 368, 380, 386, 394, 412, 417–18, 420, 423, 434, 443, 464, 465, 472, 476, 495, 499

Nemesianus 10 n. 23, 65, 66, 71, 80, 96, 108, 124, 127, 156, 178, 189, 217, 240, 241, 249, 256, 281, 287, 302, 306, 343, 351, 352, 365, 383, 387, 398, 446, 472, 485, 488, 497, 502, 506

Nepos (Cornelius) 25, 68, 104, 272, 281, 436

Nicander 182, 188, 193, 206, 269, 288, 330

Nigidius Figulus 200, 209, 210, 213

Nonnus 134, 215, 217, 220, 279, 340, 343, 360, 365, 396, 491

Numitorius 18, 26 n. 67, 152 (*see also* parody)

obtrectatores see parody

Octavia 198, 199, 200, 213, 241

Octavian (Augustus) x–xi, 3 n. 3, 4–6, 17 nn. 41–2, 59–60, 65, 71, 73, 76, 86–7, 89, 96, 99, 104, 148, 167, 173, 181, 184, 197–9, 200, 201, 208, 211, 215, 216, 218, 227, 232, 241, 242, 266, 298, 329, 364, 377, 391–2, 393, 440, 444, 445, 448, 455, 456

order *see* structure

Orpheus (Orphism, Orphic) 64, 69, 129, 143, 144, 149, 170–1, 209, 210, 217, 219, 234, 235–6, 237, 260, 264, 272, 284, 285, 286–7, 288, 296, 302, 310–11, 312, 315, 316, 318, 324, 326, 327, 328, 331, 332, 333, 334, 347, 359, 386, 387, 405, 408, 409, 442, 465, 475, 476, 493, 497, 498, 500

Ovid 14, 18 n. 44, 21 n. 54, 30, 60–1, 67, 68, 70, 76, 79, 86, 94, 95, 97, 101, 107, 108, 109, 112, 113, 122, 126, 127, 130, 134, 137, 139, 141, 145, 146, 158, 160, 164–5, 170, 177, 179, 183, 186, 192, 193, 205, 208, 209, 212, 223, 224, 225, 226, 233, 245, 249, 253–4, 256, 260, 265, 269, 274, 288, 291, 296, 297, 298, 299, 306, 307, 309, 311, 312, 313, 315, 320, 321, 322, 326, 328, 338, 339, 340, 341, 352, 356, 357, 361, 364, 365, 368, 371, 372, 375, 377, 378, 394, 395, 402, 403, 404, 408, 409, 415, 416, 423, 424, 425, 437, 439, 440, 445, 449, 456, 457, 459, 465, 469, 470, 471, 472, 476, 481, 489, 491, 493, 494, 500

Pacuvius 68, 128, 129, 272, 375, 399

Padus *see* Po

Palaemon 7 n. 14, 23 n. 59, 148, 149, 161, 162, 172, 173, 174, 175–6, 194–5, 196, 249, 250, 347, 349, 351, 379, 484

Pales 244, 266–7, 462

Pallas *see* Minerva

Pan 14 and n. 33, 78, 85, 93, 94, 99, 122, 124, 133, 134–5, 144, 156, 179, 217, 236–7, 263, 266, 275, 276, 287, 302, 304, 308, 320, 347, 351, 360, 363, 364, 386, 397, 398, 415, 424, 434, 463, 464, 465, 472, 473, 475, 476, 479, 480, 481, 482, 483–4, 485, 486, 490, 493, 494, 496, 497, 498, 500, 506

paraetymology *see* etymology

parataxis 234, 256, 453

parenthesis 27, 95, 101, 134, 141, 154, 157, 188, 190, 191, 201, 305, 388, 435, 436, 437, 442, 478, 491

parenthetical apposition (*schema Cornelianum*) 27, 95, 116, 119, 153, 359, 361, 438

Paris 72, 113, 118–19, 142, 477

parody (esp. Virgilian parodies, *obtrectatores*, *Vergiliomastiges*) 18, 26 n. 67, 63, 68, 95, 128, 143, 145, 152, 268, 315, 349, 366, 450

paronomasia 195, 352, 414

Parthenius of Nicaea 129, 131, 259, 260, 288, 318, 330, 333, 335, 337, 401, 448, 492, 495, 499

Pasiphae 286, 289, 319, 320, 321, 323, 324, 325, 326, 330, 420, 421

pathetic fallacy ('animated' nature) 10 n. 23, 69, 85, 121, 263, 276, 286, 310, 328, 334, 335, 373, 397, 472, 475, 476 (*see also* resonance)

perfect (*-ere/-erunt*) 155, 239

Persius 81, 122, 191, 217, 228, 315, 334, 354, 367, 371, 387, 400, 427, 438, 457, 486

Pervigilium Veneris 132, 175, 275, 365, 375, 402, 405, 494

Petronius 88, 121, 129, 167, 173, 192, 260, 306, 331, 341, 353, 415, 416, 424, 433, 454, 458, 461, 471, 505

Phaethon 327–8, 334, 359, 445, 503

Phanocles 119, 445, 471

Philargyrius/Philagrius 7 n. 12, 102, 109, 118, 120, 187, 192, 193, 209, 248, 251, 259, 292, 320, 369

Philitas 65, 69, 133, 283, 332, 334, 446, 449

Philocles 130, 340, 341

Philodemus 16 n. 39, 109, 110, 114, 228, 303, 479, 487

Philomela 336, 339–41, 424

Philoxenus 82, 111, 118

Phyllis 125, 141, 179, 180, 182–3, 194, 253–4, 355–6, 373, 375, 376, 377, 378, 487, 488

Pindar 94, 177, 186, 215, 220, 232, 241, 242, 257, 279, 282, 283, 297, 300, 304, 307, 317, 332, 333, 404, 405, 409, 449–50, 461, 468, 474, 476, 482, 494, 495

Plato 18, 21, 66, 69–70, 118, 122, 124, 143, 151, 158, 210, 226, 232, 233, 248, 249, 258, 279, 281, 282, 288, 296, 303–4, 306, 315, 360, 369, 396, 415, 433, 450, 457, 458, 478

Plautus 26, 69, 73, 77, 81, 83, 86, 96, 97, 100, 101, 119, 126, 136, 138, 142, 144, 148, 153, 157, 163, 172, 173, 174, 181, 182, 189, 191, 195, 212, 214, 226, 232, 236, 240, 241, 248, 252, 255, 257, 266, 274, 276, 295, 306, 307, 316, 332, 353, 362, 365, 370, 403, 427, 436, 437, 441, 451, 461, 483, 485, 496, 497, 506 (*see also* comedy)

Pliny the Elder 10 and n. 24, 12 n. 27, 14 and n. 32, 66, 75, 92, 95, 100, 104, 108, 129, 132, 134, 137, 139, 140, 149, 155, 158, 161, 165, 166, 168, 170, 187, 188, 191, 193, 205, 213, 218, 224, 229, 230, 238, 251, 257, 264, 268, 269, 278, 281, 287, 295, 304–5, 325, 327, 328, 352, 353, 368, 371, 373, 377, 378, 383, 390, 391, 393, 394, 395, 399, 400, 401, 413, 414, 416, 423, 424, 443, 446, 449, 455, 456, 458, 468, 471, 483, 484, 488, 498, 504, 505

Pliny the Younger 19 n. 45, 122, 186, 252, 298, 433, 436, 440, 442

Po (Padus) 11, 93, 327, 328, 378, 445, 503

politeness (*urbanitas*) 148, 173, 353, 453

Pollio (C. Asinius) xi, 3, 5–6, 7, 8, 11, 12, 17 n. 42, 21 n. 51, 25 n. 63, 80, 85, 113–14, 118, 129, 148, 149, 150, 158, 162, 164, 166, 167, 169 n.*, 172, 175, 176, 177, 184–5, 186–7, 188, 196–9, 201, 202, 204, 206, 211, 214, 216, 217, 221, 222, 224–5, 232, 259, 279, 287, 298, 300, 305, 329, 358, 360, 380,

383, 386, 387, 388–9, 390, 391–2, 393, 399, 407, 411, 416, 448, 490

Polybius 14, 237, 278–9, 351

Polyphemus (Cyclops) 8, 10 n. 23, 19, 20, 82, 107, 109, 111–12, 113, 120, 121–2, 127, 128, 130, 131, 136, 137, 138, 139, 141, 144–5, 179, 182, 282, 356, 362, 367, 368, 372, 401, 402, 428, 431, 450–1, 452, 463, 465, 497, 502

Posidippus 280, 444

prayer *see* hymn

'premature sketch' 294

Priamel 376

Priapea 92, 101, 154, 159, 366–7

Priapus 124, 133, 149, 156, 165, 249, 261, 266, 308, 347, 362, 365–7, 401, 473, 479, 480, 483, 484, 485

Procne 260, 339, 341, 406

proem (proemial function, prologue) 6 n. 10, 17, 20 n. 49, 21, 22, 59, 67, 73, 115, 116, 118, 167, 168, 176, 196, 202, 203, 205, 206, 222, 246, 281, 284–5, 288, 289, 291–2, 294, 295, 296, 298, 299, 300, 301, 303, 330–1, 333, 342, 348, 358, 380, 381, 382, 383, 384, 385, 386, 388, 411, 430, 431, 443, 463, 466, 467, 471, 472, 480, 482, 501, 502

Propertius 61, 67, 68, 75, 77, 81, 83, 86, 87, 90, 94, 95, 96, 97, 99, 101, 104, 105, 107, 113, 115, 117, 119, 124, 129, 141, 142, 143, 144, 159, 179, 181, 191, 207, 212, 217, 229, 235, 239, 241, 253, 270, 271, 274, 291, 295, 297, 306, 307, 311, 318, 319, 320, 326, 330, 331, 332, 333, 338, 350, 360, 361, 368, 370, 387, 395, 396, 405, 410, 413, 414, 415, 419, 449, 455, 464, 469, 472, 473, 475–6, 478, 480, 481, 486, 488, 490, 491, 493, 494, 495, 496, 497, 498, 500, 505, 506

proverb (dictum, motto) 79, 99, 100, 105, 114, 124, 141, 143, 145, 153, 155, 163, 188, 268, 300, 364, 369, 377, 411, 427, 434, 440, 457, 463, 471, 472, 498, 500, 506

Ptolemies (Ptolemaic) x, 7 and n. 13, 87, 166, 168, 199, 213, 215, 244, 308, 332, 386, 387, 392

Publilius Syrus 427, 471

puer (divine child) 196, 202, 210–11, 212, 216, 217, 232, 236, 238, 267, 347

quadrisyllable (in line-ending position) 129, 233, 323, 404, 474

Quintilianus (and [Quintilianus]) 5 n. 9, 7 n. 12, 10 n. 23, 11 n. 27, 16 and n. 38, 18 n. 44, 70, 74, 88, 101, 108, 120, 154, 165, 177, 192, 239, 240–1, 262, 268, 277, 281, 282, 297, 298, 328, 335, 367, 372, 393, 399, 407, 435, 438, 440, 459, 461, 492, 493

566 GENERAL INDEX

reception (of the *E.*) 507–8 (*see also* Ariosto, Dante, Leopardi, Milton, Sannazaro, Tasso)
recusatio 286, 288, 291, 299, 331
refrain 20 n. 47, 107, 128, 169, 230, 270, 299, 302, 330, 332, 351, 381, 384, 394, 396–7, 398–9, 410, 412, 414, 415, 417, 418, 425, 427, 428, 429, 446, 462, 473, 475, 477, 484
repetition (anaphora, iteration) ix, 27 and n. 70, 28, 63, 67, 71, 72, 77, 79, 82, 93, 106, 118, 121, 122, 134, 136, 142, 152, 160, 169, 170, 171, 173, 175, 206, 207, 209, 214, 220, 230, 234, 235, 236, 237, 239, 250, 252, 253, 263, 265, 272, 280, 281, 300, 307, 314, 319, 323, 326, 350, 357, 372, 376, 379, 380, 386, 387, 390, 391, 405, 407, 414, 415, 417, 420, 425, 442, 443, 446, 457, 460, 461, 475, 482, 485, 487, 488, 494, 497, 498, 502, 503
resonance ix, 14 n. 34, 68–9, 121, 256, 319, 343, 360, 373, 382, 397, 441, 459, 467, 472
  (*see also* pathetic fallacy)
riddle 148, 168, 176, 178, 183, 188, 191–2, 193, 194, 334, 476
Rome x–xi, 6, 7, 8, 9 n. 18, 15, 21 n. 52, 59, 60, 77–8, 79, 86, 87, 142, 148, 149, 185, 193, 199, 214, 218, 222, 267–8, 390, 431, 444
rural, rustic simplicity *see* ethopoeia

saeculum (*Ludi saeculares*) 201, 207–8, 212, 365, 388
Sannazaro, Jacopo 13
Sappho 112, 139, 145, 178, 194, 398, 400, 404, 410
Saturnus (*Saturnia regna*, Kronos) 206, 208–10, 215, 228, 286, 316, 317, 408
schema Cornelianum see parenthetical apposition
Scylla 285, 294, 336–8, 339, 340, 342, 489
Seneca (and [Seneca]) 61, 72, 77, 81, 91, 100, 102, 120, 125, 126, 129, 130, 132, 158, 165, 180, 186, 208, 210, 225, 226, 265, 267, 284, 295, 305, 306, 315, 317, 327, 340, 362, 367, 374, 400, 401, 406, 424, 446, 452, 455, 456, 468, 470, 493, 498
Seneca the Elder 185, 186, 190–1, 296, 458
Serv. (Serv. Dan.) xi, 3 n. 4, 6 n. 12, 7 and nn. 12–13, 10 n. 23, 11 n. 26, 16 n. 39, 18 n. 44, 19 and n. 46, 20, 21, 25 n. 64, 31, 64, 67, 68, 70, 72, 74, 77, 81, 84, 86, 92, 93, 97, 104, 118, 122, 124, 126, 128, 130, 139, 140, 143, 154, 158, 160, 161, 170, 171, 177, 180, 181, 182, 183, 189, 190, 193, 194, 197, 200, 201, 205, 208, 213, 214, 218, 221, 222, 230, 232, 238, 239, 244, 251, 254, 256, 258–9, 260, 265, 266, 267, 268, 269, 272, 273–4, 277, 287, 288, 292, 294, 297, 299, 302, 306, 309, 310, 313, 321, 325, 335, 343, 345, 349, 362, 365, 372, 374, 377, 380, 395, 400, 403, 406, 418,

419, 426, 437, 443, 444, 446, 447, 449, 455, 456, 460, 464, 469, 471, 480, 481, 485, 490–1, 495, 497, 502
Sextus Pompey x, 4 and n. 7, 5, 15 n. 35, 59, 86, 90, 99, 104, 127, 198–9, 223, 225, 268, 489
Sibyl (Sibylline Oracles) 187, 196, 202, 203, 206–7, 208, 210, 211, 213, 214, 220, 227, 230, 408
Sicily (Sicilian) 4–5, 7, 8, 9 n. 18, 15, 21 n. 52, 59, 66, 71, 89, 90, 93, 94, 111, 113, 127, 129, 130, 199, 202, 205, 207, 259–60, 262–3, 294, 351, 355, 364, 367, 397, 464, 468, 470, 472, 473, 490, 492, 493
sidus Iulium 208, 244, 267, 273, 431, 454–5
Silenus 17, 69, 166, 167, 171, 210, 241, 246, 251, 278, 283, 285–6, 287, 288, 289, 291, 293, 296, 301, 302, 303–4, 305, 306, 312, 347, 358–9, 376, 378, 408, 462, 464, 472, 482, 503
Silius Italicus 125, 156, 205, 207, 212, 226, 249, 261, 264, 306, 309, 371, 389, 439, 444, 496
Silvanus 80, 463, 473, 479, 481–2, 483
Simichidas 7 and n. 13, 20 n. 49, 243–4, 283, 296, 349, 429, 431, 433, 446, 447, 450, 498
simplex pro composito 68, 132, 266, 457
Siro 16 and n. 39, 288, 299, 302
slavery (slaves, servile status) 4 and n. 7, 9 n. 20, 15 n. 35, 64, 71, 81, 83–4, 85–6, 88, 90, 99, 113, 117, 118, 127, 143, 153, 158, 353, 395, 426, 431, 435, 436
Solon 124, 186, 226
Sophocles 80, 94, 186, 194, 226, 228, 266, 304, 325, 339, 340, 341, 364, 372, 389, 391, 395, 401, 405, 409, 426, 440
Sophron 21, 26 n. 64, 123, 412, 415
spondee (spondaic) 29, 77, 216, 231, 233, 257, 259, 261, 269, 335, 370, 373, 374, 386, 458
Statius 19 n. 45, 79, 125, 129, 144, 173, 194, 209, 221, 240, 241, 263, 319, 329, 334, 341, 349, 353, 356, 375, 400, 401, 459, 468, 471, 480, 488, 489–90, 491, 496, 505
structure (order) 19–25, 61, 115, 145, 149–50, 175, 176, 202–3, 206, 216, 230, 243–4, 246–7, 258–9, 273, 280, 289, 346–8, 380–1, 383–4, 385, 394, 399–400, 411, 412, 429, 430, 432, 466, 467, 472, 501, 503, 504, 505 (*see also* book)
sublime 274, 282, 305
Sun *see* Helios
superlative (*-issimus*) 175, 307, 377, 394
synaloepha (*see* elision)
synizesis 189, 317, 340, 353, 419
Syracuse (Syracusan) x, 7 and n. 13, 8, 9 n. 18, 12, 21, 26 n. 64, 94, 96, 118, 172, 193, 244, 263, 285, 292–3, 467, 468, 470
Syrinx 94, 133, 134, 360, 398

GENERAL INDEX 567

Tasso, Torquato 294
'technical' language (botanical, agricultural, and
pastoral terminology, farming) 9 and n. 21,
26 and n. 68, 78, 84, 89, 101, 104, 106, 137,
155, 178, 184, 226, 232, 268, 280, 297, 323,
328, 352, 356, 371, 373–4, 438, 443, 452,
460–1 (*see also* agriculture, *Georgics*, Cato
the Elder, Columella, Varro Reatinus)
Terence 77, 81, 85, 145, 148, 151, 154, 172, 173,
174, 212, 236, 241, 253, 274, 360, 413, 420,
427, 434, 436–7, 441, 442, 472, 480, 497
(*see also* comedy)
Tereus 339–41
Terpander 396
textual transmission *see* transmission of the text
Theocritus (and [Theocritus], Theocritean
corpus) ix, x, 4, 7, 8–10, 12, 13, 14, 15,
19–20, 23, 24, 60, 61, 64, 71–2, 111, 112, 147,
148, 149, 172, 191, 265, 292–3, 345, 346, 381,
382, 453
   epigr.: 73, 80, 122, 124, 126, 133, 141, 156,
178, 264, 274, 293, 360, 363, 367, 397
   id. 1: ix, 14, 22, 63, 65, 66, 67, 68, 69, 72, 73,
75, 85, 90, 94, 96, 106, 107, 122, 127, 149,
154, 161, 163, 165, 166, 168, 169, 170,
205, 206, 236–7, 242–3, 245, 246, 249,
250, 253, 255, 259, 260, 261, 262–3, 266,
267, 268, 269, 270, 271, 272, 279, 281,
282, 297, 299, 302–3, 307, 345, 347,
349–50, 351, 352, 354, 360, 361, 366, 381,
386, 390, 394, 396–7, 398, 399, 401, 406,
407, 408, 409–10, 415, 419, 425, 459, 463,
468, 471, 472–3, 474, 475, 476–7, 478,
479–81, 482, 483, 484, 485, 489, 493, 497,
501, 505
   id. 2: 10 n. 23, 14 n. 33, 27, 84, 123, 180, 191,
209, 377, 381, 383, 397, 403, 411, 412–13,
414–15, 416, 417, 418, 419, 420, 421–3, 426,
427, 459, 487
   id. 3: 64, 65, 70, 82, 84, 107, 111, 120, 121,
122, 137, 142, 145, 159, 181, 183, 255, 279,
326, 327, 332, 381, 394, 395, 401, 403, 404,
408–9, 410, 417–18, 442, 443, 472, 477
   id. 4: 7 and n. 13, 68, 70, 117, 133, 136, 147,
151, 152, 153, 154, 184, 188, 189, 191,
261, 281
   id. 5: 23, 67, 83, 84, 108, 110, 117, 123, 127,
131, 132, 147, 148, 154, 155, 156, 157, 160,
161, 162, 164, 165, 168, 172, 173, 174, 175,
176, 177, 178, 179, 181, 183, 187, 189, 195,
234, 250, 258, 268, 277, 346, 348, 350, 355,
358, 363, 370, 379–80, 394, 397, 408, 449,
452, 494, 505
   id. 6: 82, 84, 111, 120, 130, 131, 136, 147, 156,
157, 159, 162, 168, 175, 179, 182, 278,

282–3, 310, 348, 349, 350, 362, 367, 370,
386, 397
   id. 7: x, 7 and n. 13, 8, 16, 20 and n. 49, 63, 64,
65, 93, 96, 99, 104, 107, 109, 117, 123, 124,
135, 139, 146, 168, 177–8, 205, 232, 239,
243–4, 255, 258, 263, 271, 275, 278, 279,
283, 284, 285, 291, 293, 296, 298, 299, 311,
313, 321, 331, 333, 348, 349, 358, 363, 373,
394, 405, 408, 429, 430–1, 433, 434, 446,
447, 449, 450, 451, 452, 455, 458, 459, 461,
468, 473, 475, 486, 487, 488, 498, 499, 500
   id. 8: 9 n. 19, 19, 20 nn. 48–50, 78, 94, 95, 107,
127, 132, 135, 142, 156, 157, 160, 161, 162,
163, 164, 169, 172, 175, 183–4, 186, 195, 243,
248, 250, 260, 266, 267, 271, 293, 302, 346,
348, 349, 351, 352, 353, 357, 364, 370, 371,
373, 374, 380, 394, 471, 473, 477
   id. 9: 10, 63–4, 66, 73, 78, 89, 147, 175, 238,
272, 283, 325, 347–8, 370, 371, 372
   id. 10: 78, 89, 95, 108, 112, 123, 126, 142–3,
145, 186, 269, 380, 397, 465, 487, 502, 504
   id. 11: 80, 82, 107, 109, 111, 112, 113, 120,
121, 122, 123, 127, 128, 132, 133, 137, 138,
139, 141, 144–5, 146, 218, 282, 367, 368,
372, 383, 402, 409, 422, 450–1, 452, 463,
465, 472, 488, 496, 497, 502
   id. 12: 111, 119, 212, 369
   id. 13: 20 n. 50, 226–7, 318, 319, 433
   id. 14: 80, 82, 88, 325, 433, 458, 485, 496
   id. 15: x, 7 n. 13, 72, 96, 172, 188, 244, 370,
426, 470, 477
   id. 16: x, 7, 20 n. 50, 72, 104, 124, 144, 199,
227–8, 263
   id. 17: x, 72, 87, 166–7, 176, 177, 199, 213,
215, 216, 228, 233, 241, 274, 284, 386, 392
   id. 18: 66, 79, 80, 255, 266, 378, 382, 400,
452, 493
   id. 20: 20 n. 50, 67, 82, 111, 135, 141, 397, 477
   id. 22: 14, 66, 80, 293
   id. 23: 111, 116, 121–2, 138, 381, 396, 410, 494
   id. 24: 20 n. 50, 199, 219, 220, 221, 222, 235,
236, 237, 241, 242, 269, 332, 424–5
   id. 25: 84, 144, 156
   id. 26: 276
   id. 27: 69
   id. 30: 144
Theophrastus 220, 224, 268, 269, 281, 375, 423,
446, 505
Theopompus 227, 302, 304
Thestylis 123, 137, 139, 412, 426
Thyrsis xi, 23, 63, 70, 106, 107, 113, 161, 169,
236, 242–3, 246, 253, 254, 263, 271, 274,
342, 345, 346, 347, 350, 351, 352, 356, 357,
358, 359, 361, 366, 367, 373, 375, 376, 397,
447, 473

568 GENERAL INDEX

Tibullus (and [Tibullus]) 61, 67, 73, 76, 81, 86, 87, 106, 109, 110, 113, 123, 132, 136, 138, 141, 142, 148, 153, 155, 164, 166, 180, 181, 189, 207, 208, 210, 216, 218, 220, 224, 225, 229, 261, 270, 308, 315, 330, 338, 360, 366, 370, 371, 372, 396, 411, 414, 415, 416, 419, 424, 452, 455, 469, 478, 480, 481, 483, 490, 491, 494, 497, 500, 501, 506

Timaeus 259, 327

title (of the book, of the single eclogues) 18–19, 63, 259, 301, 348

Tityrus ix, x–xi, 6 n. 11, 7–8, 10, 11, 16 n. 40, 19, 20 n. 49, 23 n. 59, 59–61, 63–5, 69, 70, 71, 72, 73, 77, 82, 83–4, 85, 90–1, 108, 159, 245, 255, 273, 276, 284, 285, 293, 295–6, 299, 311, 321, 336, 342, 344, 408, 431, 506

transmission of the text 30–1 (*see also* manuscripts, indirect tradition)

Troia (Trojan) 14, 77, 125, 226, 227, 303, 334, 389, 439, 440, 460

'unyoking of oxen' (βουλυτός) 144, 343

urbanitas see politeness

Valerius Flaccus 77, 97, 129, 165, 173, 207, 248, 254, 306, 318, 319, 327, 329, 340, 365, 387, 406, 425, 458, 489, 491

Valgius Rufus 132, 359, 366

Varius Rufus 4 n. 6, 6 n. 10, 12 n. 27, 16 and n. 39, 61, 105, 114, 145, 246, 299, 302, 338, 359, 402, 420, 421, 447–9, 454, 460

Varro Atacinus 232, 233–4, 318, 341

Varro Reatinus 8 n. 17, 14 n. 32, 15 n. 37, 19 n. 45, 66, 69, 76, 77, 78, 79, 81, 83, 84, 86, 89, 95, 97, 101, 104, 108, 119, 120, 122, 126–7, 137, 142, 143, 153, 155, 162, 166, 176, 210, 222, 223, 224, 226, 231, 267, 270, 280, 304–5, 310, 322, 328, 356, 358, 364, 366, 367, 375, 393, 409, 418, 434, 440, 442, 452, 456, 459, 461, 476, 506

Varus (Alfenus) 184, 205, 222, 235, 284–5, 298–9, 300, 301, 302, 431, 438–9, 443–4, 445, 464

Venus (Aphrodite, Dione) xi, 17, 95, 98, 132, 142, 143, 145, 180, 181, 194, 242, 244, 245, 259, 261, 266, 267, 272, 274, 276, 320, 326, 341, 347, 352, 365, 366, 376, 377, 395, 406, 417–18, 440, 445, 455–6, 469, 473, 477–8, 479, 480, 481, 484, 485, 494

Vergiliomastiges see parody

visual arts *see* arts

vocative 27, 77, 121, 183, 240–1, 300, 368, 400, 485, 488

volume *see* book

wedding ceremonies *see* epithalamium

wolf 107, 142–3, 158, 310, 372, 386, 407, 423, 424, 434, 458, 469, 473, 476

Zethus 128

Zeus *see* Jupiter

The manufacturer's authorised representative in the EU for product safety is
Oxford University Press España S.A. of el Parque Empresarial San Fernando de
Henares, Avenida de Castilla, 2 – 28830 Madrid (www.oup.es/en or product.
safety@oup.com). OUP España S.A. also acts as importer into Spain of products
made by the manufacturer.

www.ingramcontent.com/pod-product-compliance
Lightning Source LLC
Chambersburg PA
CBHW061836200325
23816CB00003BA/242